Transportation Economics

Transportation Economics

Theory and Practice

A CASE STUDY APPROACH

PATRICK S. McCARTHY
Georgia Institute of Technology

BLACKWELL
Publishers

First published 2001

2 4 6 8 10 9 7 5 3 1

Blackwell Publishers Inc.
350 Main Street
Malden, Massachusetts 02148
USA

Blackwell Publishers Ltd
108 Cowley Road
Oxford OX4 1JF
UK

Library of Congress Cataloging-in-Publication Data

McCarthy, Patrick S.
Transportation economics: theory and practice: a case study approach / Patrick S. McCarthy.
p. cm.
Includes bibliographical references and index.
ISBN 0-631-22180-8 (hbk.: alk. paper) — ISBN 0-631-22181-6 (pbk.: alk. paper)
1. Transportation—Case studies. I. Title.

HE151.M418 2000
388—dc21

00-030524

British Library Cataloguing in Publication Data
A CIP catalogue record for this book is available from the British Library.

Typeset in 10/12 Photina
by Graphicraft Limited, Hong Kong
Printed in Great Britain by TJ International, Padstow, Cornwall

This book is printed on acid-free paper.

To Patricia

CONTENTS

PREFACE

Transportation is a topic of interest to economists, civil engineers, urban planners, policymakers and administrators, managers, and marketers. Interest in transportation issues by such a diverse group implies that the focus of a textbook on transportation will clearly depend upon the author's objective. This book is no exception, and the focus here will be on the role that economics plays in shaping the way in which goods and people overcome the friction of space. A primary objective of this textbook is to examine transportation markets and analyze how standard economic tools provide important insights on the allocation of society's scarce resources to transportation activities, as well as to explore the role that government policy plays in affecting the allocation of resources.

Transportation is a derived demand, derived from a desire to consume some good or service at a location that differs from where the good or service is produced. It is also true that, for many, the *study* of transportation is a derived demand, derived from an interest in a related activity. Land use, industrial organization, public economics, government regulation, and trade are subject areas in economics that typically form a subset of courses in an economics curriculum. Intracity transportation issues are examined in urban economics courses; a subset of intercity transportation markets is discussed in courses on industrial organization; and some transportation markets are examined in courses on regulation and public economics, in order to illustrate the effects of government intervention in markets. Agricultural economists are interested in transportation for its implications in shipping agricultural products and, more generally, international economists study the effect of transportation costs on the international movement of goods. Although an analysis of the general role of transportation in each of these areas is sensible, given the nontransport focus of the course, it is inefficient if one's interest in transportation markets reflects a direct rather than a derived demand. This text examines the economics of transportation markets, what determines the transportation decisions of travelers and shippers as well as the production decisions of transportation suppliers, whether government intervention in transportation markets is economically justified, and how these interventions affect the allocation of resources in transportation.

In any course on transportation, one immediately realizes that there are numerous ways to transport people and goods. Passenger and freight travel can occur by air, rail, bus, private automobile, water, and pipeline. Many texts on transportation devote separate chapters to the separate modes, identifying unique aspects and similarities of each modal market with that of its competitors. Because of its emphasis on economics and the allocation of resources, the approach in this text is to develop the economic constructs relevant to transportation markets and then illustrate these principles with detailed applications from one or more of the transportation markets. A common thread throughout the text is that an understanding of transportation markets requires a solid grounding in economics principles, combined with instructive empirical applications of the principle.

The progression of economic topics in this text is generally similar to that found in many microeconomics textbooks: consumer demand theory (chapters 3 and 4) followed by the theory of production and cost (chapters 5 and 6), and market structures (chapters 7 and 8). Chapter 9 examines principles of investment and chapter 10 focuses upon public-sector pricing and investment. Chapters 11–13 discuss topics of particular relevance to transportation, congestion (chapter 11), transportation and land use (chapter 12), and the public health implications of transportation (chapter 13). In each chapter, I have developed the theoretical material so that students from disciplines outside of economics and with little previous training in economics should have no difficulty keeping pace. For those students who have taken intermediate microeconomics, some of the material, particularly in chapters 3, 5, 6, 7, and 8, will be familiar. However, in my experience students appreciate the review. And few students, if any, have seen a detailed development and application of empirical models derived from theoretical constructs.

Each chapter is an integrated blend of economic theory and application. However, a unique feature of this approach, which differentiates it from other applied economics texts, is the detailed analysis of econometric results from the transportation literature. Similar to many applied economics textbooks, this text develops economic models in order to provide students with important cause-and-effect linkages between variables of interest. Rarely, however, do textbooks provide students with more than a passing acquaintance of how these economic models are empirically tested and used to generate policy implications. This text includes numerous econometric case studies that illustrate the economic principles developed. For each of these case studies, testable economic hypotheses are identified and discussed, econometric results are summarized and analyzed for their consistency with economic theory, and the study's implications for public policy are examined. This approach provides students with insights on both the theoretical and applied foundations of transportation economics. I have also included homework questions that test a student's knowledge of the theory, as well as one's ability to interpret empirical models and use these models to draw implications for transportation policy.

Because of the textbook's emphasis upon econometric case studies, chapter 2 is a review of basic linear regression analysis. In using econometric case studies, I have found that students can generally master a good working knowledge of hypothesis testing and *t*-statistics within a week or two. This enables them to understand and analyze the empirical applications in the text with little problem.

The case studies included in the chapters were chosen with a number of objectives in mind. First, it is important that the selected case illustrates an economic principle that has been discussed. This reinforces the theory-and-practice approach of the text. Second, as much as possible, the case studies are representative of research in the area. I have tried to select cases that cover the major transport modes, including highway (automobile, public transit, and motor carrier), airline, and rail modes, with some attention devoted to water carriage. And third, the empirical models represent applications of the statistical techniques reviewed in chapter 2 or those techniques on discrete choice and cost function analysis developed in chapters 4 and 5.

Although there are no international transportation case studies, I do not believe that the absence of such cases is a major limitation, since the same economic principles that govern domestic transportation also apply to international transport problems. I decided to concentrate on domestic transportation cases because economic regulation of transportation markets in the USA, and their subsequent deregulation, spawned a wealth of interesting and insightful economics analyses.

Recognizing that only a limited number of cases can be included, I have also provided a set of general references at the end of each chapter, as well as specific references in a given area that are modal specific. This affords readers the opportunity to explore additional interesting work – both domestic and international – on the subject.

In addition to providing students with specific information on institutional aspects of the transportation industry, the evolution of transportation policy and its effects on transport markets, a broad pedagogical goal of this text is to provide students with a solid working knowledge of economics that includes an understanding of: (1) basic economic principles and models; (2) how these constructs are used to explain existing market structures and activities, and to predict the impact that changes in public policy would have upon these markets; and (3) the role of empirical analysis and statistics in testing a theory's predictions and generating quantitative estimates of public policy effects.

In keeping with an empirical focus of the text, the Appendix contains URL addresses to numerous Internet transportation resources. These references include transportation departments within and outside the US government, university transportation centers, mode-specific sources, and Internet references by topic area. Also included is a list of international URLs. Although this list is by no means exhaustive, these references will point the interested student to an ever-expanding set of related links. Further, Blackwell Publishers will maintain a web page for this text, located at http://www.blackwellpublishers.co.uk/mccarthy. Periodically, additional case studies on a spectrum of domestic and international transportation topics will be posted at this site in order to keep students abreast of recent developments in the field and their implications for public policy.

This book has been "in progress" over the past five years, during which time (and even longer) I was affiliated with the Department of Economics at Purdue University. I will always be grateful for the teaching and research support that the department and the Krannert Graduate School of Management at Purdue provided during the course of writing this book. I am also grateful to all transportation researchers, without whose collective efforts this book would not have been possible. And I am especially indebted to the numerous reviewers who spent considerable time and effort commenting on the book's structure, topics, and case studies. Although all remaining errors rest with me, their comments and suggestions have substantively improved the text.

Patrick S. McCarthy

1

An Overview of Transportation Activities in the United States

INTRODUCTION

Transportation economics is an applied area of economics that is concerned with the efficient use of society's scarce resources for the movement of people and goods from an origin to a destination. As you might imagine, the scope of transportation activities is enormous, since issues related to the transport of *any* good or person, by *any* means, for *any* origin–destination pair, and at *any* time is an appropriate subject of analysis for a transport economist. Because so many of our daily and annual activities entail, in one form or another, our own personal travel or the shipment of goods that we desire to consume, transportation-related activities play a large role in our nation's total annual production of goods and services. The purpose of this chapter is to provide a brief look at the extent and scope of transportation-related activities in the US economy. This overview will examine the total impact of transportation on the US economy, both in relation to the nation's output of goods and services, as well as its impact upon employment and the consumption of energy. In addition, the chapter will characterize the amount of transportation that annually occurs. That is, how much is the nation "on the move," how many goods are annually shipped from one place to another, and how have these movements changed over the years?

Necessarily, the nation must provide the needed physical capital in the way of roads, rail trackage, airports and runways, ports, and other infrastructure in order to facilitate the movement of people and goods across space. We will also examine the amount and quality of our nation's transportation infrastructure. Over the years, the nation has invested significant resources to transportation infrastructure in order to further the nation's mobility. How extensive are these networks and are they keeping up with the transport demands of the public? Further, how well is the nation's transportation network meeting the performance needs of shippers and travelers? Are users receiving safe and reliable service or is the system providing deteriorating services? Although not intended to answer all of these questions, this chapter will provide you with a useful description of the nation's existing transportation network and how it has changed during the past few decades.

TRANSPORTATION AND THE ECONOMY

THE IMPORTANCE OF TRANSPORTATION TO THE ECONOMY

Table 1.1 summarizes transportation expenditures in constant 1992 dollars (that is, adjusting for the effects of inflation) over the 35-year period from 1960 to 1995. Total expenditures on transportation have risen by 133% from $464.9 billion in 1960 to $1,084.6 billion in 1995. Similar rises are seen separately for passenger and freight transport expenditures. The passenger transportation bill rose by 160% between 1960 and 1995, whereas the freight bill has risen by just less than 100%. During this same time period, the economy as a whole was growing. In 1992 dollars, gross domestic product (GDP) was $2,263 billion in 1960 and rose to $6,724 billion in 1995, expanding more quickly than transportation.[1] The last row of table 1.1 gives transportation expenditures as a proportion of the nation's GDP. Between 1960 and 1980, expenditures on transportation were 20.5% of gross domestic product. More recently, the economy's real expenditures on transportation have accounted for a smaller proportion of gross domestic product, 17.1% in 1990 and 16.1% in 1995. Not only do these figures indicate that transportation-related activities are an important component of the nation's economy, but they also suggest that the economy has become more efficient in moving people and freight.

For both passenger and freight, the largest component of transportation expenditures is for highways. In 1992 dollars, total highway expenditures rose from $377.1 billion in 1960 to $905.8 billion in 1995. As a proportion of GDP, highway expenditures accounted for 16.7% in 1960 and 13.5% in 1995, indicating that the decrease in transportation expenditures as a proportion of GDP between 1960 and 1995 is primarily due to a decrease in highway expenditures.

Not surprisingly, the technological advances in air travel have led to spectacular increases in transport expenditures on air transport over the 35-year period. In 1960, real passenger and freight expenditures on air transport were $15 billion and $1.5 billion respectively. By 1995, passenger expenditures increased to $76 billion, reflecting an 11.6% *annual* increase. With 1995 expenditures of $17.5 billion, air freight grew at an even faster pace, averaging an annual increase of 30.5% between 1960 and 1995. Primarily reflecting a shift from rail to

Table 1.1 Transportation expenditures (billions of 1992 dollars)

	1960	1970	1980	1990	1995[a]
Total Passenger Transportation Bill	260.0	375.0	560.6	673.3	674.9
Total Freight Transportation Bill	205.4	275.6	354.3	374.7	409.6
Total National Transportation Bill	464.9	650.6	914.5	1,047.9	1,084.6
Transportation Bill as a percentage of gross domestic product	20.5	19.1	19.8	17.1	16.1

[a] 1995 figures are preliminary.
Source: US Department of Transportation, Bureau of Transportation Statistics, *1997 National Transportation Statistics*, Washington DC, table 2-6; Bureau of Economic Analysis

truck, real expenditures on rail freight, on the other hand, have actually fallen. Between 1960 and 1995, real freight expenditures on rail fell from $38.8 billion to $31.9 billion, an average annual decrease of 0.5%; during the same period, real expenditures on intercity truck freight rose from $77.2 to $203.8 billion.

TRANSPORTATION EMPLOYMENT

Table 1.2 provides information on the number of individuals employed in transportation. In the table, the transportation sector includes air, local and interurban passenger transit, liquid and natural gas pipeline, railroad, transportation services, trucking and warehousing, and water. This sector of the economy accounted for 3.8% of US civilian employment in 1960 and fell to 3.3% in 1995. If we include those employed in manufacturing transportation equipment, such as motor vehicles, aircraft, railroads, and ships, the percent of the labor force working in transportation rises to 6.5% in 1960 and 4.8% in 1995. Related industries primarily reflect activities associated with motor vehicles, including automobile repair and services, gasoline service stations, and highway construction and maintenance. When adding in these workers as well as government employees, transportation in 1960 accounted for one out of every ten jobs. But, consistent with the decline in transportation expenditures between 1960 and 1995, the percentage of workers in transportation-related industries in 1995 fell to 8%, part of which may be due to higher levels of productivity in the transportation industry. Between 1959 and 1994, the average annual growth in labor productivity for all businesses was 2.0%. Average annual labor productivity growth in air transportation over the same period was 4.6%. Similarly, with growth rates of 3.8%, 5.9%, and 2.8%, labor productivity in petroleum pipelines, railroads, and trucking outpaced that for the economy as a whole.

Table 1.2 Employment in transportation and related industries (thousands)

	1960	1970	1980	1990	1995
Transport sector	2,471.3	2,694.3	3,175	3,731.8	4,098
Equipment manufacturing	1,772.9	1,949	1,995.3	2,073.3	1,864.8
Related industries	2,027.2	2,652.4	2,961.7	3,671.5	3,929
Government employment	532	711	670.8	673.3	101
Total transportation employment	6,803.4	8,006.7	8,802.8	10,149.9	9,993
US civilian employment	65,347	78,780	99,879	119,081	124,716
Transportation in US employment (%)	10.4	10.2	8.8	8.5	8.0

Source: US Department of Transportation, Bureau of Transportation Statistics, *1997 National Transportation Statistics*, Washington DC, table 2-18

TRANSPORTATION AND ENERGY CONSUMPTION

In addition to its impact upon the economy and employment, transportation is a major user of energy. Table 1.3 contrasts the energy consumption of the United States as a whole with the transportation sector. Here we see that transportation accounts for around 25% of total

Table 1.3 US energy consumption in the transport sector (quadrillion BTU)

Year	Transport Sector	Total Energy Consumption	Percentage of Total Energy Consumption
1960	10.6	43.8	24.2
1970	16.09	66.43	24.2
1980	19.69	75.96	25.9
1990	22.617	84.17	26.9
1995[a]	24.063	90.62	26.6

[a] 1995 figures are preliminary.
Source: US Department of Transportation, Bureau of Transportation Statistics, *1997 National Transportation Statistics*, Washington DC, table 4-2

Table 1.4 Energy intensiveness by mode[a]

Year	Certificated Air Carriers (BTU per passenger–mile)	Passenger Car (BTU per passenger–mile)	Combination Truck (BTU per passenger–mile)	Class I Railroads (BTU per revenue freight ton–mile)
1960	8,483	3,978	n/a	839
1970	9,781	4,624	29,008	643
1980	6,009	4,491	25,655	589
1990	4,855	3,938	25,143	418
1995	4,290	3,013	23,621	370

[a] The reported number for Air Carriers relates to domestic operations. A similar decrease has occurred for international operations. For Combination Truck, the numbers represent vehicle–miles as well as passenger–miles, since the driver is the only occupant of a combination truck.
Source: US Department of Transportation, Bureau of Transportation Statistics, *1997 National Transportation Statistics*, Washington DC, tables 4-17, 4-18, 4-19, 4-21

US energy consumption – and the trend is rising. In 1960, 24.2% of the energy consumed went to transportation-related activities. By 1995, this increased to 26.6%, the bulk of which is in the consumption of fossil fuels, and specifically petroleum. In 1960, for example, 1.628 billion barrels of oil, equivalent to 10.1 quadrillion BTUs, were consumed in the United States.[2] In 1995, petroleum consumption in transportation increased to 4.263 billion barrels of oil, or 23.2 quadrillion BTUs. As a proportion of all petroleum products consumed in the USA, transportation's share has steadily increased. In 1960, transportation-related activities consumed 52.4% of all petroleum products. In 1995, transportation's share was 66%.

Where is the petroleum going? – mostly to fuel motor vehicle travel. In 1995, motor vehicle travel consumed 143.3 trillion gallons of fuel, 68.3 trillion of which fueled automobiles. Another 3.4 trillion gallons moved Class I railroads, and 17.3 billion gallons fueled domestic and international operations among US air carriers.

Although transportation is a huge consumer of fuels, there have been dramatic technological improvements in energy efficiency. Table 1.4 reports the energy intensiveness for air carriers, motor vehicles, and rails. In each case, we see that there has been an improvement in the amount of energy expended per unit of travel. After an initial increase between 1960 and 1970, airlines have enjoyed a significant improvement in energy consumption per passenger–mile. Between 1960 and 1995, BTU per passenger–mile fell by 49%. Rails have also experienced a large reduction in the use of energy, decreasing by 55.8% over the 35-year period. Improved roads, motor vehicle downsizing, and technological advances in motor vehicle travel have resulted in increasing fuel efficiency per passenger–mile. For passenger cars, energy intensiveness fell by 24.2%; for combination trucks, there was an 18.5% reduction between 1970 and 1995.[3]

PASSENGER AND FREIGHT MOVEMENTS IN THE UNITED STATES

Tables 1.5 through 1.7 report the level of passenger, vehicle, and freight movements in the USA between 1960 and 1995. In order to capture the amount as well as the extent of travel, transport economists calculate passenger–miles, vehicle–miles, and ton–miles, respectively. A *passenger–mile* is the movement of one passenger one mile; a *vehicle–mile* is the movement of one vehicle one mile; and a *ton–mile* is the shipment of one ton of freight one mile.[4]

In terms of overall quantity of travel, we see in table 1.5 that highway travel is extensive. Accounting for nearly 1.5 trillion miles in 1960, passenger–miles have grown to over 4 trillion in 1995, a 170% increase for the period. Although, in 1995, airline passenger–miles were only a tenth of highway passenger–miles, there has been more than a tenfold increase in air passenger–miles in the 35-year period, rising from 31.1 billion to 403.2 billion. On the other hand, transit has been relatively stagnant, with transit passenger–miles increasing by less than 1% between 1980 and 1995. Rail fared considerably worse. With 17.1 billion passenger–miles in 1960, by 1995, rail accounted for only 5.1 billion passenger–miles, a 70% drop over the period. Overall, excluding transit, total passenger–miles between 1960 and 1995 rose by nearly 200%.

From table 1.6, we see a similar increase in vehicle–miles traveled between 1960 and 1995, although the extent of the growth is larger. The significant rise of the airline sector is again apparent. In 1960, certificated aircraft accumulated a total 860 million vehicle–miles. This jumped to 2.1 billion by 1970 and by 1995, air carrier vehicle–miles totaled 4.6 billion, a

Table 1.5 Passenger–miles (billions)

Year	Air Carrier, Certificated, Domestic	Highway	Transit	Rail
1960	31.1	1,498.2	n/a	17.1
1970	108.4	2,116.9	n/a	6.2
1980	204.4	2,630.4	39.9	4.5
1990	345.9	3,271.3	41.1	6.1
1995	403.2	4,052.6	41.8[a]	5.1

[a] Data for transit are preliminary estimates for 1994. 1995 data are not available.

Source: US Department of Transportation, Bureau of Transportation Statistics, *1997 National Transportation Statistics*, Washington DC, table 1-7

Table 1.6 Vehicle–miles (millions)

Year	Air Carrier, Certificated, Domestic	Highway	Transit	Class I Rail Freight Car–Miles	Amtrak Car–Miles
1960	0.86	762.1	n/a	28.2	2.2
1970	2.068	1,111.8	n/a	29.9	0.69
1980	2.523	1,530.3	2.3	29.3	0.23
1990	3.963	2,148.2	3.2	26.2	0.30
1995	4.618	2,427.8	3.6	30.4[a]	0.29

[a] Data for transit are estimates for 1994. 1995 data are not available.
Source: US Department of Transportation, Bureau of Transportation Statistics, *1997 National Transportation Statistics*, Washington DC, table 1-8

Table 1.7 Billion ton–miles of freight (revenue share)[a]

Year	Air Carriers, Domestic	Intercity Truck	Class I Rail	Domestic Water Transport	Oil Pipeline
1960	0.55 (0.005)	285.0 (0.670)	572.3 (0.298)	413.3 (n/a)	233.0 (0.028)
1970	2.2 (0.010)	412.0 (0.709)	764.8 (0.221)	596.2 (0.036)	431.0 (0.024)
1980	4.5 (0.014)	555.0 (0.697)	919.0 (0.184)	921.8 (0.050)	588.2 (0.055)
1990	9.1 (0.026)	735.0 (0.788)	1,034.0 (0.121)	833.5 (0.028)	584.1 (0.037)
1995	12.5 (0.033)	921.0 (0.807)	1,305.7 (0.110)	807.6 (0.026)	599.0 (0.029)

[a] Revenue shares are based upon ton–mile data reported in this table and revenue per ton-mile in 1992 dollars. Data for 1995 are preliminary.
Source: US Department of Transportation, Bureau of Transportation Statistics, *1997 National Transportation Statistics*, Washington DC, table 1-9

435% increase, more than twice the increase in highway vehicle miles at 218%. Interestingly, although transit passenger–miles increased by less than 1% between 1980 and 1995, we see in table 1.6 that vehicle–miles traveled increased considerably more, just over 56%, suggesting that public transit service networks expanded over the 35-year period. And, consistent with the 70% fall in rail passenger–miles, rail car–miles servicing passengers fell from 2.2 billion vehicle miles in 1960 to 290 million in 1995, an 86% decrease. Rail car–miles for freight shipments, however, increased by 78% during this period.

Table 1.7 summarizes the rise in freight ton–miles and changes in modal revenue shares between 1960 and 1995. Although a small proportion of total ton–miles shipped, air freight is continuing to increase at a high rate. After a large spurt in the 1960s, air freight averaged a strong annual ton–mile increase of 18.7% between 1970 and 1995, by which year air freight's revenue share grew from 0.5% to 3.3%. Freight movements on intercity trucks increased by 223% over the 35-year period, representing a healthy 6.3% annual increase, followed by pipeline, rail, and water ton–miles, which annually increased by 4.4%, 3.6%, and 2.7% respectively. Note also the ton–mile and revenue share changes in intercity truck and rail over the period. Not only has the ton–mile growth of intercity truck freight outpaced that of rail, but we also see that truck revenue shares have grown while rail revenue shares have fallen from 29.8% in 1960 to 11.0% in 1995, suggesting that rail is shipping fewer high-value goods and more low-value goods.[5]

Underlying the increases in passenger–miles, vehicle–miles, and freight ton–miles in the past three decades, the nation's population increased 45.5%, from 180.6 million to 263.4 million. In addition, real per capita income (1992 dollars) rose from $7,926 to $17,460, an average annual increase of 3.4%. Increases in population and income increase the demand for passenger travel and the nation's output. The impact of rising incomes on motor vehicle travel, for example, can be seen through the number of registered vehicles. The total number of registered vehicles increased 170%, from 74.5 million to 205.3 million, 136.1 million of which were automobiles and motorcycles. In addition to the number of vehicles, the number of automobiles and motorcycles per licensed driver rose from 0.713 to 0.739 between 1960 and 1995.

TRANSPORTATION NETWORKS AND PERFORMANCE

Increases in the amount of travel, whether measured by passenger (vehicle)–miles traveled or ton–miles shipped, have generally more than kept pace with the economy's overall growth. Complementing this growth in passenger and commodity transport, we can also examine how the quantity and quality of the nation's transport infrastructure have changed. This includes investment in roads, rails, airports, waterways, and pipeline networks, as well as other capital that are necessary for the movement of commodities and people.

TRANSPORTATION INFRASTRUCTURE

Table 1.8 summarizes the changes in the physical extent of the transportation system in the United States over the past 30 years. In 1994, there were just under 2 million miles of ground transport infrastructure devoted to the movement of goods and people – and more than half of these network miles were for the transportation of gas. US infrastructure has not increased

Table 1.8 The physical extent of the US transportation system (miles)[a]

Year	Airway	Highways	Class I Rail	Inland Waterway	Oil Pipeline	Gas Pipeline
1960	293,003	265,477	207,334	25,253	190,944	630,900
1965	268,275	268,898	199,798	25,380	210,867	767,500
1970	291,122	271,517	196,479	25,543	218,671	913,300
1975	313,178	265,905	191,520	25,543	225,889	979,300
1980	341,283	300,456	164,822	25,543	218,393	1,051,774
1985	373,891	301,006	145,764	25,777	213,605	1,118,875
1990	388,000	305,347	119,758	25,777	208,752	1,206,774
1994	394,000	342,834	109,332	25,777	200,500	1,260,997

[a] The figures reported are for intercity mileage.

Source: US Department of Transportation, Bureau of Transportation Statistics, *1997 National Transportation Statistics*, Washington DC, table 1-1

Table 1.9 Government transportation revenues and expenditures by mode

Year	Highway	Air	Transit	Water	Pipeline	Rail[a]
Revenues (billions of 1987 dollars)						
1982	32.859	2.809	4.147	1.733	0	n/a
1986	41.389	7.199	6.035	1.788	0	n/a
1990	44.356	9.025	6.389	2.348	0.009	n/a
1994	47.835	10.264	7.039	2.492	0.015	n/a
Expenditures (billions of 1987 dollars)						
1982	43.413	7.126	13.645	5.248	0.011	2.585
1986	52.544	8.952	15.562	5.552	0.008	0.931
1990	55.514	11.230	17.024	4.504	0.023	0.487
1994	58.687	14.016	19.146	5.067	0.028	0.652

[a] There are no government revenues for rail.
Source: US Department of Transportation, Bureau of Transportation Statistics, *Federal, State, and Local Transportation Financial Statistics: Fiscal Years 1982–94*, Washington DC, table 1

uniformly over the past 30 years. There has been a 29% increase in highway mileage between 1960 and 1994, whereas Class I rail mileage decreased significantly, falling by nearly 50% from 207,334 in 1960 to 109,332 in 1994. Miles of inland waterways increased slightly between 1960 and 1990, but have since remained constant.

The infrastructure changes observed in table 1.8 illustrate an important economic point, that scarce resources ultimately move to their best and highest-valued uses. Although we may want to have all cities connected by rail, air, and highway, our limited resources preclude this possibility. We must decide how best to use our limited resources, and the figures in table 1.8 suggest that society's best use of its scarce resources required increased investments in air and highway infrastructure and decreased investments in rail infrastructure.

Table 1.9 reports government revenues received and government expenditure outlays associated with the nation's transportation system. Transportation revenues include user charges, taxes, or transport fees that are spent on transportation activities.[6] Transportation costs, on the other hand, include all costs incurred by federal, state, and local governments for providing transportation infrastructure, equipment, and operating services.

As a proportion of total expenditures, highway users have consistently paid a high proportion of costs. In 1982, for example, highway users paid 75.5% of costs, increasing to 81.5% in 1994. The largest sources of revenue for highways are the federal Highway Trust Fund and state motor fuel taxes. Revenues also come from vehicle and operator license taxes as well as toll revenues. In addition to state and local collections, transit receives revenues from the Highway Trust Fund. Also, these revenues have consistently covered less than 50% of transit expenditures, accounting for 30% of expenditures in 1982 and rising to 36% of expenditures in 1994.[7]

Whereas air users only contributed 39% to expenditures in 1982, by 1994 revenues from the Airway and Airport Trust Fund, as well as state and local airport charges, accounted for nearly 73% of expenditures. Water revenues showed the largest increase, rising from 32% of expenditures to 50% of expenditures in 1994.

In constant 1987 dollars, total government capital expenditures (that is, expenditures which improve productive capacity), on transportation have consistently been in the 45–48% range. However, there has been considerable variation in these expenditures by mode. Between 1982 and 1994, airport and airway capital expenditures increased from 39% of total air expenditures to 50.9%. Highway capital shares remained steady in the 53–55% range. And transit capital expenditures fell from 27.8% of total transit expenditures in 1982 to a low of 23.8% in 1988, but rebounded by 1992 to 28.9%. For the rail mode, the capital share fell significantly from 26.8% of total rail expenditures in 1982 to 10.9% in 1989. By 1992, however, capital expenditures accounted for 42.1% of the total. The increase reflected the effect of falling total expenditures upon rail (as seen in table 1.9) combined with increasing capital expenditures as part of the Amtrak Northeast Corridor Improvement Program.

THE CONDITION OF THE NATION'S INFRASTRUCTURE

The ability of the nation's transport system to meet the needs of travelers and shippers not only reflects the quantity of transport infrastructure and capital equipment – that is, the number of airports and ports, highway mileage, miles of track, and so forth – but also the quality of services provided by these capital.

Table 1.10 reports the physical condition of our nation's road network and its system of commercial airport runways, as defined by the percentage of the system that is in poor condition and in need of immediate attention. In each category we see an overall improvement. In 1986, 7% of the nation's runways was in poor condition. This declined to 3% by 1993. Similarly, the quality of our nation's urban and rural roads has improved. The nation's interstate system is in better condition than noninterstate roads and there was an overall improvement in the quality of all roads between 1993 and 1995. In 1990, between 8.3% and 10.6% of urban and rural roads provided substandard service. But, over the next 5 years, there were significant improvements in the serviceability of the nation's interstate system. Only 1.8% of interstate roads were found to be in poor condition. The improvements on noninterstate rural roads did not match those on the interstate highways. 8.3% of all rural roads were in poor condition in 1990, followed by a minor deterioration in 1993, and then a relatively large improvement. By 1995, only 5.5% of all rural roads were in poor condition. There was also a significant improvement in the percentage of urban interstate roads in need of immediate repair. In fact, one out of every ten miles of urban roads was in poor condition. This significantly

Table 1.10 The percentage of the nation's runways and highways in poor condition

Year	Commercial Airport Runways (%)	Rural Interstate Roads (%)	All Rural Roads (%)	Urban Interstate Roads (%)	All Urban Roads (%)
1986	7	n/a	n/a	n/a	n/a
1990	5	8.7	8.3	8.6	10.6
1993	3	7.5	8.4	10.7	10.6
1995	n/a	1.8	5.5	1.8	8.5

Source: US Department of Transportation, Bureau of Transportation Statistics, *1997 National Transportation Statistics*, Washington DC, tables 1-31, 1-32

improved for urban interstate roads by 1995. However, for noninterstate roads there has been little change.

The numbers in table 1.10 reflect an underlying increase in infrastructure spending by the government. The annual growth rate in total infrastructure investment for 1993–4 was 10.6%, which outpaced the 7.4% annual growth rate between 1984 and 1994. Highways received the bulk of these monies, 76.3%; air transportation received 10.8%.

Although the figures in table 1.10 indicate that fewer rural and urban roads are in need of immediate repair, the table also indicates that there has also been a reduction in the proportion of roads that are in very good condition. Between 1990 and 1995, for example, the proportion of urban roads in very good condition declined from 40.4% to 16.9%; a similar reduction from 35.8% to 18.6% was observed on rural roads. Both interstate and noninterstate roads experienced reductions in the proportion of the highest-quality roads.

THE PERFORMANCE OF THE TRANSPORTATION SYSTEM

A transportation network's physical condition provides a measure of the system's condition and its ability to provide users with safe and reliable transport. More specifically, how well does the system perform? Can users expect their transportation needs to be reliably and safely met?

With respect to delays experienced by users, few indicators exist of how well the system is performing. For 50 urban areas, the Texas Transportation Institute calculated the number of daily person–hours of delay on the area's roads.[8] As seen in the table below, total person–hours of delay nearly doubled between 1982 and 1993, from 7.2 million to 14.1 million person–hours:

	1982	1986	1990	1992	1993
Person–hours of delay for 50 urban areas (000s)	7,260	10,334	12,581	13,572	14,150

In addition, estimates of volume : capacity ratios (that is, traffic flow per vehicle hour divided by maximum flow per vehicle hour) on urban roads are higher today than in the past. Analysts estimate that highway systems begin to experience recurring congestion when the volume : capacity ratio reaches 80%. In 1994, 68% of urban interstate highways experienced a volume : capacity ratio during peak period travel greater than or equal to 80%, considerably higher than the 52% figure in 1980.

Congestion on rails is hard to measure, but one indicator that is oftentimes cited is freight train–miles per mile of track owned. Between 1960 and 1995, this measure increased from 1,200 to 2,500, suggesting that some deterioration in transport reliability may have occurred over the period.

In the airline industry, the government has recently begun to collect data giving air carrier on-time performance, defined as the number of times air carriers arrive more than 15 minutes late.[9] Overall, 80% of airline flight operations on the largest carriers were on time in 1988; this increased slightly to 81.5% in 1994 and then fell back to 78.6% in 1995. The total number of delayed operations in 1987 was 356,000, which declined to 248,000 in 1994, a

Table 1.11 Accident rates by mode, 1960–1995[a]

Year	US Air Carriers (per 100 million aircraft–miles)	Motor Vehicle (per 100 million VMT)	Rail (per 100 million train–miles)	Waterborne Transport (number)	Recreational Boating (per 100,000 boats)	Pipeline (per 1,000 miles of pipeline)
1960	7.96	n/a	n/a	n/a	109.5	n/a
1970	2.01	n/a	965.2	2,582	51.4	6.5
1980	0.51	n/a	1,143.4	4,624	64.1	1.1
1990	0.48	302	472.9	3,613	58.3	0.86
1995	0.62	273	367.1	4,196	74.2	1.2

[a] A level of exposure was not available for Waterborne Transport. 1995 figures for US Air Carriers, Waterborne Transport, and Recreational Boating are preliminary.
Source: US Department of Transportation, Bureau of Transportation Statistics, *1997 National Transportation Statistics*, Washington DC, tables 3-4, 3-11, 3-25, 3-26, 3-28, p. 244

30% decrease. How costly are delays to carriers and passengers? In constant 1994 dollars, the total delay cost was $8.4 billion in 1988, rising to $9.5 billion in 1995. The bulk of the increase during this period was due to increasing delay costs to passengers.

System-wide on-time performance on Amtrak is currently a bit lower than that for air carriers. After rising from 69% in 1980 to 81% in 1985, Amtrak on-time performance during the 1990s hovered in the mid-70% range.

We have seen in tables 1.5 and 1.6 that, in 1995, the transportation network accumulated 4.5 billion passenger–miles and 2.4 billion vehicle–miles. With this amount of exposure, there will be accidents. Another measure of how well the transportation system performs is safety. Table 1.11 reports accident rates by mode. In terms of percentage improvement, the safety record for US air carriers has improved significantly. Experiencing 7.9 accidents per 100 million aircraft–miles in 1960, this has fallen 92% to 0.62 accidents per 100 million aircraft–miles in 1995. The total number of air carrier fatalities in 1995 was 229, 52 of which were associated with on-demand air taxis.

Accident information for motor vehicle travel is not readily available, although there is some indication in table 1.11 that the highway system has become safer. The number of accidents per 100 million vehicle–miles has fallen by 9% between 1990 and 1995. More relevant to highway safety, however, is the fatality rate. Annually, motor vehicle travel accounts for tens of thousands of fatalities. In 1960, there were 36,399 fatalities. This rose to 51,091 in 1980 and has since fallen back to 40,716 in 1994, with a slight increase in 1995 to 41,798. Normalizing by exposure, the number of persons killed per 100 million vehicle–miles traveled was 5.1 in 1960, and this has steadily fallen to a 1.7 level throughout most of the 1990s, representing an overall decrease of 66%. However, there are differences in the fatality rate by type of road and by type of vehicle. The fatality rate on urban roads in 1995 was 1.20, less than half the 2.57 rate on rural roads. If one focuses only upon interstate highways, the rates are even lower. The fatality rates on rural and urban interstate highways were 1.20 and 0.63, respectively, in 1995. Passenger cars experienced a 1.5 overall fatality rate in 1995, compared with 1.4 for light trucks and 0.4 for large trucks in the same year. The least safe highway mode is the motorcycle, with a 1995 fatality rate of 22.7.

Table 1.12 National emissions of pollutants by highway vehicles (million short tons)

Year	Carbon Monoxide	Nitrogen Oxides	Volatile Organic Compounds	Particulate Matter	Sulfur Dioxide	Lead[a]
1960	58.3	4.4	10.4	0.55	0.11	n/a
1970	88.0	7.4	13.0	0.44	0.41	172.0
1980	78.0	8.6	9.0	0.40	0.52	1.7
1990	62.9	7.5	6.8	0.36	0.57	1.5
1995	58.6	7.6	6.1	0.30	0.30	1.4

[a] The numbers for lead correspond to thousands of short tons (2,000 pounds).
Source: US Department of Transportation, Bureau of Transportation Statistics, *1997 National Transportation Statistics*, Washington DC, tables 4-32 to 4-37. Numbers for 1990 and 1995 are preliminary

Between 1970 and 1995, the accident rate in the rail sector decreased by more than half, falling from 965.2 to 367.1. These accidents exclude highway – rail grade crossings and accounted for 785 fatalities in 1970. There was a significant decrease in fatalities by 1975, and since that period the number of fatalities has generally been in the high 500s to low 600s range. In 1995, 567 persons lost their lives in rail accidents.

Waterborne transport and recreational boating have also improved their safety records. In 1970, there were 178 waterborne transport fatalities associated with 2,582 accidents. Although, in 1995, the number of accidents increased to 4,196, the number of fatalities fell to 46. As for recreational boating, there has been a four-fold increase in the number of "numbered" boats between 1960 and 1995, from 2.5 million to 11.7 million. The accident rate has fallen by about 25% over this period, but the fatality rate has experienced a much larger improvement, falling from 32.8 fatalities per 100,000 numbered boats to 7.1 in 1995. The actual number of fatalities in 1960 was 819, rose to over 1,100 from 1965 through 1985, and has since fallen to the 800–900 range. In 1995, 836 persons were killed in recreational boating.

The transport of oil and gas in pipelines generally result in few pipeline-related accidents, but even these have fallen over the years, down from 1,428 incidents and 30 fatalities in 1970 to just 349 incidents and 21 fatalities in 1995. Combined with the increased number of pipeline–miles, this has led to a decrease in the number of accidents per 1,000 miles of pipeline from 6.5 in 1970 to 1.2 in 1995.

Relative to the quantity of travel that annually occurs, the nation's transportation system provides users with a relatively safe environment. However, 43,549 individuals lost their lives in transportation crashes in 1995, the vast majority of which were on the nation's highways, indicating that much additional work remains if the nation's transportation network is to improve its performance on this margin.

A final performance measure of the nation's transportation network is the extent to which transportation activities despoil the environment, primarily through air and water pollution. Table 1.12 provides information on the amount of emitted pollutants that contribute to air pollution. In the table, we see that, after increasing from 58.3 to 88 million tons in 1970, there has been a steady decline so that the 1995 level has returned to the 1960 level, despite the significant increase in the number of vehicles and vehicle–miles traveled. Volatile organic compounds and emissions of particulate matter have steadily decreased over the 30-year period, while there has been some increase in nitrogen oxide and sulfur dioxide emissions. Lead emissions have significantly fallen since development of nonleaded gasoline.

These improvements are the result of a series of federal emission standards that have become increasingly restrictive. For example, between 1980 and 1995, allowable passenger car emissions of carbon monoxide have been reduced from 7.0 grams per mile to 3.4 grams per mile; allowable nitrogen oxides for gasoline fueled vehicles from 2.0 to 0.4 grams per mile; and particulates from 0.60 (in 1985) to 0.08 grams per mile. Similar decreases in allowable standards have been applied to light duty and heavy duty trucks.

Although other transport modes contribute to air pollution, motor vehicle travel is the most important source of these environmental damages, accounting, in 1995, for 95% of carbon monoxide emissions, 83.4% of nitrogen oxides, 89% of volatile organic compounds, 67% of fuel-related particulate matter, 50% of sulfur dioxides, and 88% of lead emissions. In addition, transportation-based emissions for each of these pollutants account for a sizable portion of total emissions, with the exception of sulfur dioxide.

TRANSPORTATION ISSUES FOR THE MILLENNIUM

The past sections have characterized the nation's physical transportation system, its performance, and the importance of transportation to the economy. Throughout the 20th century, an expanding and migrating population, economic growth, technological advances, and changes in the regulatory environment had significant impacts upon intercity and intracity mobility. These same factors will continue to be important as we enter the new millennium. However, just as the shape and performance of our present transportation system is a reflection of past decisions, current decisions will have important implications on how the nation's transportation system evolves. The US Department of Transportation (USDOT), in its most recent vision statement for the 21st century, defines its mission as one of "ensuring a fast, safe, efficient, accessible and convenient transportation system" that provides for the nation's national security interests and enhances social welfare today and on into the future. Within this vision statement are four strategic goals for the nation's transportation system:

- *Safety*. The department seeks to promote public health and safety by eliminating transportation-related fatalities, nonfatal injuries, and property damage.
- *Mobility*. The fundamental purpose of any transportation system is mobility of people and goods. The task for the government is to ensure that the transportation system is accessible to all travelers and shippers, incorporates the latest information technology, is integrated across alternative modes, and is operationally efficient.
- *Economic growth and trade*. Providing an efficient and flexible transportation system not only increases mobility but also enhances the competitiveness of domestic firms, which spurs regional as well as national economic growth. Moreover, an efficient transportation system also requires an appropriate market environment that is free of unnecessary economic regulations.
- *The human and natural environment*. Because transportation systems intrude upon communities and the environment, government transportation policy seeks to sustain communities and protect the environment from activities associated with transportation.

Economic analysis provides policy-makers with important insights on the effects that changes in the nation's demographics, production and information technology, and the economic environment will have upon each of these interrelated objectives. In developing a fast and efficient transportation system, it is important to understand how economic growth affects the demand for alternative transportation modes, what impact these effects have upon the environment and safety, whether it is necessary for the government to intervene in the market and, if so, in what form. Similarly, information technology competes with and complements existing transportation alternatives. To what extent do these technologies affect the cost of a firm's doing business, and do these new technologies have a significant impact upon the location decisions of firms and households?

An important problem for governments in achieving an efficient transportation system is knowing when economic regulations are appropriate. In the early part of the 20th century, economic regulations imposed on the trucking, airline, and rail industries may have been economically justified. Over time, however, these regulations produced a considerable drag on the efficient provision of transportation to society, leading policy-makers to deregulate the sectors. But we now see a number of mergers occurring in various transportation sectors. Are these mergers appropriate from an economic perspective or does this imply the need for re-regulation? Or consider congested highways. These markets consistently characterize an economically inefficient transportation network. What strategies or regulatory policies could the government implement to increase both the mobility and the efficiency of the system?

Underlying each of the objectives identified above is the physical transportation system itself. How much transportation capacity should the nation build and maintain – and, once built, how can we most efficiently use the capacity?

In the coming chapters, we will see how economic theory provides a framework for qualitatively analyzing a large variety of transportation issues, and forms a basis for statistical models that provide the necessary quantitative information required by policy-makers who strive to develop fast, safe, and efficient transportation systems for the movement of people and freight.

Included among the important transportation topics that we consider in detail are the following.

Transportation demand

- Transportation as a derived demand that generates interspatial flows of goods and people.
- Consumer demands for intraurban travel, including automobile, rapid transit, and bus trips.
- Choice of transportation mode in one of the most important transportation decisions, the trip to work.
- Consumer demands for interurban travel, including airline, automobile, motor bus, and rail.
- Choice of the mode that shippers use to move freight.

Transportation supply

- Cost characteristics of transportation firms, including truckload and less-than-truckload motor carriers, airline carriers, rail carriers, and public transit systems.

- The extent to which firms experience economies of scale, economies of capacity utilization, and economies of traffic density.
- Firm demands for productive inputs and the substitutability among inputs in the production of transportation.
- Investment and the impact that additional capital has upon transportation firm costs.

Market structure

- Market structure in the motor carrier, air, rail, and bus sectors, and the impact upon the efficient provision of transportation in the presence of economic regulation.
- Market concentration in transportation and economic rents.
- Mergers and their impacts upon resource allocation in transportation.
- How firms faced with economic deregulation strategically act to protect and enhance their wealth.
- Price discrimination in transportation.
- The effects of price controls in transportation markets on resource allocation.

Public-sector issues

- Applications of first-best pricing and investment in rails, roads, and urban transit.
- Applications of second-best pricing in urban transit and airline sectors.
- Optimal pricing and investment in the presence of congestion.
- The efficiency and distribution effects of congestion pricing.

Transportation and land use in urban areas

- Residential and firm demands for land in monocentric and multicentric urban areas.
- The role of transportation costs and transportation improvements upon metropolitan land use and urban development.
- Firm location decisions in an urban area.
- Telecommuting and urban development.

Public health concerns

- The level of safety provided by alternative transportation modes.
- Consumer demands for safety.
- Safety regulation and risk compensation effects.
- Fuel efficiency standards and their impact upon highway safety.
- Motor vehicle fatalities, average speed, and speed variation.
- Firm profitability and safety investment.
- The health effects from motor vehicle pollution.

NOTES

1 Gross domestic product (GDP) is the total amount of final goods and services produced annually by the economy. In contrast to table 1.1, which gives annual expenditures on transportation-related activities as a proportion of gross domestic product, one could ask what proportion of gross domestic product is for transportation-related output. In 1992 dollars, this proportion has remained relatively steady at 10%. In 1991, 10.5% of GDP was for transportation; in 1995, this slightly rose to 11%.

2 A BTU (British thermal unit) is the quantity of heat required to increase the temperature of a pound of water 1 degree Fahrenheit.

3 Not all of the improvement in energy intensiveness is solely attributable to improved fuel efficiency. Changes in an airline's load factor (that is, the ratio of passengers carried to the number of seats available), motor vehicle occupancy, and the quantity of freight and distance shipped will also influence a mode's energy intensiveness.

4 Although common output measures, passenger–miles, vehicle–miles, and ton–miles are nevertheless ambiguous. For example, knowing that output is 1,000 passenger–miles does not tell how the output was produced; that is, whether one person traveled 1,000 miles, 200 persons traveled 5 miles, or some other combination of miles and passengers whose product is 1,000.

5 In 1992 dollars, rail revenue per ton–mile decreased from 5.2 to 2.3 cents per ton–mile between 1960 and 1995; intercity truck revenue per ton–mile rose slightly from 23.3 to 24.2 during the same period.

6 Neither revenues generated from transportation sources but not used for transportation nor revenues from nontransportation sources but used for transportation are counted in the transportation revenues reported in table 1.9.

7 Because the definition of transportation costs is more inclusive than is the definition for transportation revenues, annual revenues typically fall short of annual costs.

8 A person–hour of delay is defined as one person being delayed 1 hour.

9 As you might expect, weather is the primary cause for delay, accounting for 75% of all delays in 1994, up from 67% in 1988.

2

The Statistical Analysis of Economic Relations

INTRODUCTION

In order to understand the individual transportation decisions of passengers and firms, and the implications that these decisions have for the allocation of society's scarce resources to transportation, an important component of a transportation economics course is model-building. How can we best explain the transportation choices of consumers and shippers? What factors are most important in a passenger's decision to travel by one mode or another? What role does travel time and reliability play in a freight shipper's decision to use one carrier over another? What determines whether a firm uses relatively more capital or more labor in the production of transport services? How do changes in the price of inputs or outputs influence a firm's activities? And what role do technological advances have upon transport firm activities?

In addition, governments have a significant presence in the transportation sector. How do government regulatory policies affect a carrier's provision and a shipper's cost of transportation? How well did we predict the economic effects of transportation deregulatory legislation, such as occurred in the latter part of the 1970s and the early 1980s, on the structure of the transportation sector? Did society expect to reap net benefits from such a change? And in the post-deregulatory period, did the predicted economic effects occur, and is society better off than in the pre-deregulatory period?

ECONOMIC MODELS OF BEHAVIOR

Economic models of the consumer, the firm, and the market for transportation are an essential ingredient to answering these questions. An economic model of individual or market behavior is a simplified description of behavior which purports to identify primary cause-and-effect relationships between economic variables. Economic models have three important characteristics. First, economic models are *explanatory* in that they identify those economic forces which are most relevant to a decision-maker's consumption or supply behavior. In their ability to explain economic behavior, economic models are causal. Changes in one or more of the determining factors induce decision-makers to alter their consumption or supply decisions.

As a corollary to their explanatory role, economic models that successfully capture the important determinants of a decision-maker's behavior are also *predictive*. A well formulated economic model will predict the way in which a particular determinant affects behavior if it is changed. It is seen in the following chapter, for example, that the price of an airline trip is an important determinant of the number of airline trips taken. Economic theory tells us that an increase in trip price, holding all else constant, is expected to decrease the number of trips taken. This is simply the law of demand, and it embodies both the explanatory and predictive role that economic theory plays. A model's ability to accurately forecast the effects of changes in its determining variables is an important attribute by which good models are distinguished from bad.

Second, economic models are *representative* and are intended to characterize important determinants of the "average" behavior under investigation. By definition, a model is a simplification of reality that reduces the phenomenon being analyzed to its essential elements. All irrelevant factors are eliminated. But what constitutes "average" behavior? That depends upon the purposes of the model. Some models are more detailed than others, but each may be an accurate depiction of reality for the model's purposes. For example, students taking a first course in economics will use graphs to study the operation of markets. Although a graphical approach is "accurate" for the purposes of teaching economics to principles' students, it is not accurate for the purposes of teaching graduate economics students. For these students, a more detailed approach to economics is "accurate." To take another example, consider the transportation costs that a New York garment firm faces for shipping dresses. Depending upon the firm's objectives, different levels of detail (that is, alternative models of cost) will be relevant. If the firm is concerned about its annual cost allocations to transportation, then the overall percentage of total costs going to transportation will be sufficient. However, if the firm is trying to decide which carrier to use, then it will want more detailed information on prices, number of pick-ups, delivery times, and so forth, for each of the possible carriers.

There are obvious trade-offs as one moves from simpler to more detailed models of economic behavior. Models that stress the primary determinants of behavior to the exclusion of specific details have widespread applicability. More complicated models, on the other hand, may do a better job of explaining and predicting behavior. However, for the user's purposes, a more complicated model may not be worth the gain achieved if the cost of obtaining the additional information is exorbitantly high. Moreover, a more detailed model's applicability to many different decision-makers and varied circumstances will be limited.

In the theory of the firm, for instance, many of the insights that we obtain will not depend upon whether the firm in question transports wheat or coal or vegetables. Indeed, it won't even depend upon the firm being in the transportation business. The theory is sufficiently general to identify the major determinants of firm behavior. However, firms engaged in transportation are distinct from nontransport firms in that time plays a more important role. Freight shippers oftentimes base transport decisions not simply upon the price charged but also upon the time involved in transporting the good. Similarly, passengers have an opportunity cost of their time, and will consider the amount of travel time as well as out-of-pocket cost when choosing between public and private travel modes. Thus, when modeling shipper or traveler transportation decisions, it will be important to recognize the role that travel time plays.

A third characteristic of an economic model is that it provides *qualitative* insights on the effects that changes in one's economic environment have upon behavior. All else held constant, the law of demand tells us that, faced with an increase in the per-mile price of shipping a ton of apples, shippers will decrease the quantity of apples shipped; that is, shippers move up the market demand curve. The inverse relationship between per-mile price and the quantity of apples shipped is a qualitative result that provides the *direction* of change but *not* the *amount* of change. As another example, consider the effect of an increase in the gasoline tax. Our theory of markets tells us that this will lead to an increase in the equilibrium price of gasoline and a reduction in the equilibrium quantity sold, all else held constant. Again, these are qualitative results, because they provide no information on the amount by which the consumption of gasoline falls when the gasoline price increases.

To summarize, models of economic behavior are useful in the formulation of transportation policy because they identify the important causal linkages between economic variables among a group of decision-makers. And because economic models are explanatory, they are also predictive. But their predictive power is limited in the sense that they yield qualitative rather than quantitative predictions from changes in the economic environment.

ECONOMETRIC MODELS OF ECONOMIC BEHAVIOR

Data! Get your fresh data! This is the hallmark of the information age in which we currently live. Technological innovations in communications, computer, and related industries have substantially expanded the ease with which information is collected, processed, and distributed. The recent development of the World Wide Web and the information highway provides users with instant access to detailed information and databases in all corners of the world. We are bombarded daily with data purporting to inform, convince, improve, or otherwise shape our lives. We are also in constant search for new information for our own individual purposes. What airline offers the best price for my upcoming trip? Which express delivery service can guarantee delivery in the shortest time? Which make and model of new car offers the best occupant protection in side impact collisions? In traveling from Washington DC to Philadelphia, how much time is saved if I travel by air rather than railroad?

Necessarily, the increased consumer demands for higher-quality–lower-priced products have implications for firm information demands. Transportation firms that can more quickly identify new customers, exploit new data about their customer base, find new sources of less expensive inputs, and improve production techniques will, at least for a time, have a competitive edge over their rivals. And although their objectives are different, governmental bodies at all levels have large appetites for new information. State and federal governments play a significant role in the allocation of our nation's resources to the transportation sector, and part of that process requires the most recent data available. Indeed, our nation's appetite for data is easily reflected by the annual expenditures of the federal government on household and firm surveys, as well as by the number of market research companies, whose sole purpose is to collect, process, and sell data to interested firms.

However, the vast existing stock of information, as well as the continuing investment in new information, poses its own problems. Suppose that Speedy Airways decided to accumulate all possible information that had any bearing on its ability to provide air service to its customer base at the lowest possible price. In all likelihood, Speedy would be allocating some of its scarce resources to data-gathering activities, resources which could have been better utilized elsewhere in the company – for example, more ticket agents, baggage handlers, aircraft maintenance, and pilot training. But even if a firm does accumulate this mass of information, it must decide which data are relevant for its purposes and it must identify the quantitative relationship among these relevant factors.

Economic theory solves one but not both of these problems. By directing one's attention to those relatively few factors which are most important to economic decision-making, economic theory enables the decision-maker to limit the scope of the information required to make informed decisions. But we saw above that economic theory only yields qualitative predictions, which are oftentimes inadequate for meeting the needs of consumers, firms, and governments. After all, theory may tell us that a rise in input prices, all else constant, raises a firm's cost. But it is of the utmost importance to the firm if the marginal cost of production rises by 1% or 100%. Similarly, economic theory may indicate that unpriced congestion leads to an inefficient allocation of resources to trip making. But the size of the congestion cost as well as the cost of implementing an appropriate pricing scheme will influence society's optimal response to unpriced congestion.

An Econometric Model of Airline Demand

An *econometric model* is a statistical specification of an economic model that enables the analyst to quantify the economic relationships identified in the theoretical framework. To illustrate the relationship between an economic and an econometric model, consider the following economic model of the demand (discussed in detail in chapters 3 and 4) for airline passenger miles:

$$\text{Miles} = f(\text{Price per Mile, Per Capita Income}; e, \beta_1, \ldots, \beta_K) \tag{2.1}$$

Equation (2.1) states that the number of passenger miles "is a function" (this is the meaning of the notation $f(\cdot)$) of Price per Mile and Per Capita Income. According to equation (2.1), the direction of causality flows *from* price and income *to* the number of miles traveled. Accordingly, we shall hypothesize the following *causal* relationships between the economic variables:

(i) All else constant, an increase in the price per passenger mile will reduce the number of miles flown. That is, ΔMiles/ΔPrice per Mile < 0.

(ii) All else constant, an increase in Per Capita Income increases the demand for airline travel. That is,

$$\Delta\text{Miles}/\Delta\text{Per Capita Income} > 0 \tag{2.2}$$

In addition to price and income, Miles in (2.1) is seen to depend upon a variable e. Although price and per capita income may be the most important determinants of the number of miles flown, it would be surprising if these two variables were the only determinants of airline travel demands. There are likely to be a variety of other (omitted) factors, such as prices of alternative means of travel, number of travelers, preferences for air travel, distance to the nearest airport, and so forth, that will also influence an individual's demand. Including e in the demand model reflects the net influence that all other factors not *explicitly* considered have on individual demands.

Last, passenger demand for airline travel is seen to depend upon K unknown parameters β_1 through β_K, which summarize the mathematical relationship between Miles, Price per Mile, and Per Capita Income.

A particularly convenient specification of the demand model in (2.1) is to assume that Miles is *linearly related* to price and income. This leads to the following expression:

$$\begin{aligned}\text{Miles} &= f(\text{Price per Mile, Per Capita Income}) \\ &= \beta_1 + \beta_2\text{Price Per Mile} + \beta_3\text{Per Capita Income} + \varepsilon \qquad (2.3)\end{aligned}$$

In equation (2.3) it is seen that K equals three, reflecting the three parameters β_i ($i = 1, 2, 3$). β_1 is the intercept that identifies the average number of miles traveled when Price per Mile and Per Capita Income equal zero. β_i ($i = 2, 3$) gives the marginal effect of an increase in price and per capita income, respectively, on Miles. From hypotheses (i) and (ii), $\beta_2 < 0$ and $\beta_3 > 0$. Combined with a linear specification, hypotheses (i) and (ii) imply that a unit increase in Price per Mile will lead to β_2 fewer traveled miles, and a unit increase in Per Capita Income is expected to produce β_3 additional miles taken. Note also that the linear specification in (2.3) may only approximate the true mathematical relationship between Miles, Price per Mile, and Per Capita Income. As a result, the term ε is included in (2.3) not only to reflect the omitted variables, e, in the demand model but also to capture any approximation error associated with a linear functional form.

The economic model in (2.3) is transformed into a *statistical* specification – that is, an econometric model of individual demand for airline travel – by assuming that the error term ε is random, with a known probability distribution. The most common assumption for the error term is that it follows a normal (bell-shaped) distribution with mean zero and constant variance. In econometrics jargon, Miles is now referred to as the "dependent" or "left-hand side" variable; that is, the variable to be explained by the model. Price per Mile and Per Capita Income, on the other hand, are the "independent" or "explanatory" or "right-hand side" variables; that is, variables that are used to explain the behavior of the dependent variable. And ε is an "error term" that captures the influence of all other factors affecting the number of miles traveled. Data is available for Miles, Price per Mile, and Per Capita Income.

As we have already seen, the error term ε is assumed to be unobservable, but the assumption that it is randomly distributed with a normal distribution enables the analyst to make *statistical inferences* about the unknown parameters, β_i ($i = 1, 2, 3$). In other words, it will be possible to obtain numerical estimates of the three parameters, β_1, β_2, and β_3, and test hypotheses about them from a sample of data. The following sections briefly describe this methodology.

LEAST-SQUARES REGRESSION

Solving equation (2.3) for the error term yields the following expression:

$$\begin{aligned}\varepsilon &= \text{Miles} - \beta_1 - \beta_2\text{Price per Mile} - \beta_3\text{Per Capita Income} \\ &= \text{Miles} - \widehat{\text{Miles}} \\ &= \text{residual} \qquad (2.4)\end{aligned}$$

where $\widehat{\text{Miles}}$ is the predicted value of Miles, so that the residual is simply the difference between the observed miles traveled, given Price per Mile and Per Capita Income, and the predicted number of passenger miles traveled. If our sample consists of n observations, then for each observation in the sample there will be an associated error, ε_i ($i = 1, \ldots, n$).

Is there a generally accepted criterion for obtaining estimates of the parameters β_i ($i = 1, 2, 3$)? One criterion that could be used is to find those values of β_i ($i = 1, 2, 3$) such that the sum

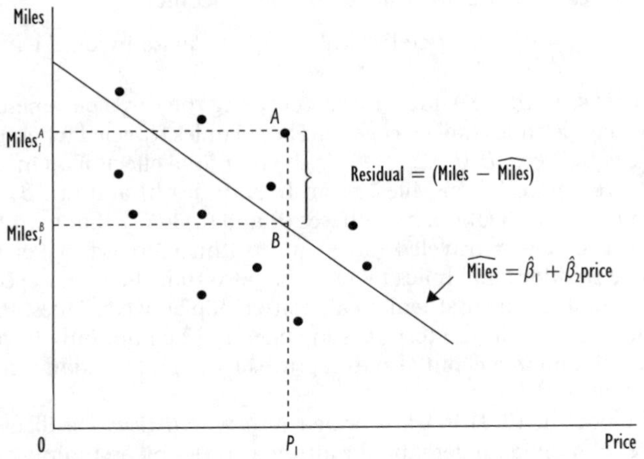

Figure 2.1 Linear regression of Miles on Price.

of the residuals for the entire sample, $\sum_{i=1}^{n} \varepsilon_i$, is as small as possible. However, this criterion for estimating the β_is would be inappropriate, since the model could produce large positive errors that are offset by large negative errors so that, on average, the total error would be small. Even though the model would do a poor job of fitting the data, its small total error would indicate a good model fit.

Alternatively, suppose that we square the error term and solve for the β_is that minimize the *sum of squared residuals*, $\sum_{i=1}^{n} \varepsilon_i^2$ (also known as the sum of squared errors). Squaring the residuals has two effects. First, it eliminates the sign on the error term, so that positive and negative errors are treated the same. And, second, it more than proportionately increases the penalty associated with larger errors. This method of obtaining parameter estimates by minimizing the sum of squared errors is referred to as the *method of least squares*. The least-squares *estimator* is the formula that is used to produce the least-squares *estimate*.[1]

Figure 2.1 illustrates this method when trip price is the only explanatory variable and there are 12 observations. In this case, the estimated regression equation is given by

$$\widehat{\text{Miles}} = \hat{\beta}_1 + \hat{\beta}_2 \text{Price Per Mile} \tag{2.5}$$

and the residual for observation i is $\varepsilon_i = (\text{Miles}_i - \widehat{\text{Miles}_i})$. At point A in the figure, Miles_i^A is the observed number of passenger miles demanded when Price Per Mile is P_1. The predicted number of miles from the regression equation is Miles_i^B, denoted by point B. The error or residual is the vertical difference between Miles_i^A and Miles_i^B, as shown by the line segment AB. Squaring AB gives the squared error for this observation. And the least-squares estimates of β_1 and β_2 are those values, denoted by $\hat{\beta}_1$ and $\hat{\beta}_2$ in equation (2.5), that minimize the sum of the squared errors over all of the sample observations.

Returning to our original equation which includes per capita income and price, let the estimated regression equation be given by

$$\widehat{\text{Miles}} = \hat{\beta}_1^1 + \hat{\beta}_2^1 \text{Price per Mile} + \hat{\beta}_3^1 \text{Per Capita Income} \tag{2.6}$$

where $\hat{\beta}_i^1$ ($i = 1, 2, 3$) is the least-squares estimate of β_i, $\hat{\beta}_2^1 < 0$, and $\hat{\beta}_3^1 > 0$. For the moment, ignore the superscript 1. All else held constant, $\hat{\beta}_1^1$ is the marginal effect of an increase in price on quantity of passenger miles demanded, which reflects a movement up the demand curve for airline travel. $\hat{\beta}_2^1$ gives the marginal effect on demand from an increase in per capita income, all else held constant, and denotes the extent to which an increase in per capita income shifts the demand curve rightward.

It is important to keep in mind that the estimates of β_i ($i = 1, 2, 3$) were obtained from a *sample* of observations. Suppose that we obtain a second sample of observations and run another least-squares regression of Miles on Price per Mile and Per Capita Income. This leads to another set of estimates, $\hat{\beta}_i^2$ ($i = 1, 2, 3$), where the superscript 2 indicates that these estimates were obtained from a second sample. Thus, in the previous paragraph the superscript 1 denotes the set of coefficient estimates obtained from the first sample. If we obtain a third, fourth, fifth, and on out to a total of S different samples of travelers, we will get a different set of least-squares estimates, $\hat{\beta}_i^s$, for each sample s ($s = 1, \ldots, S$). And each of these sets of numbers will contain estimates of the *true but unknown* parameter β_i ($i = 1, 2, 3$). An important result is that the S estimates for each of the unknown parameters β_i, $\hat{\beta}_i^s$ ($s = 1, \ldots, S$), form a probability distribution that is characterized by a mean and a variance.

The fact that least-squares parameter estimates come from a probability distribution means that we can explore whether least-squares estimators have other desirable properties in addition to their minimizing the sum of squared residuals. It turns out that they do. First, least-squares estimators are *unbiased*. This means that if we were to collect S different samples, and obtain S different sets of estimates, $\hat{\beta}_i^s$ ($i = 1, \ldots, S$), of the parameters, then the average of these estimates would equal the true parameter if S were large enough. In other words,

$$\frac{1}{S}\sum_{s=1}^{S}\hat{\beta}_i^s = \beta_i, \qquad i = 1, 2, 3 \tag{2.7}$$

A second property of least-squares estimators is *consistency*. This simply means that parameter estimates based upon larger samples will provide closer approximations to the true values in comparison with parameter estimates based upon smaller samples. Intuitively, if we have a large number of sample observations, we can be more confident that our estimated parameter is close to its true value.

A third desirable property that least-squares parameter estimators possess is *efficiency*. Recall that the variance of a probability distribution gives the dispersion of the variable around its mean. If the distribution has a small variance, then most of the values of the random variable are relatively close to the mean; that is, there is less dispersion around the mean. Conversely, a large variance says that the values of the variable are more dispersed around the mean. Efficiency relates to a parameter estimator's variance and is used to choose between different estimators. If, for example, we have two estimators, both of which are unbiased estimators of the parameter, then we would select the estimator with the smallest variance because it would on average be closer to the true value. An important result in econometrics is that least-squares estimators are *most efficient*; that is, among the set of unbiased linear estimators, least-squares estimators have minimum variance.[2]

Figures 2.2 and 2.3 illustrate the concepts of consistency and efficiency, respectively, for an unknown parameter β. In figure 2.2, $\hat{\beta}$ is assumed to be a consistent estimator of β, which implies that, as the sample size increases, the sampling distribution becomes more "peaked."

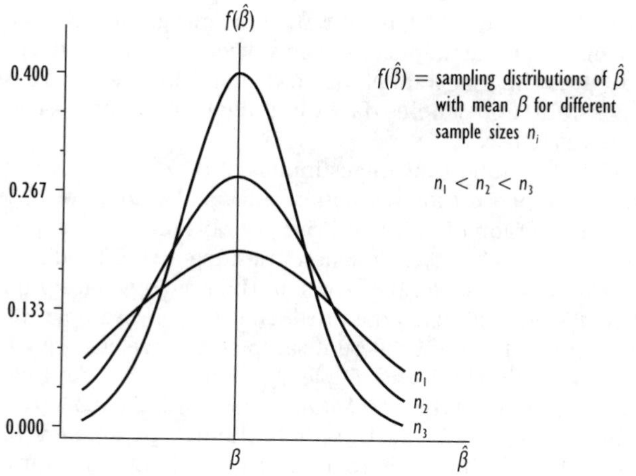

Figure 2.2 A consistent estimator.

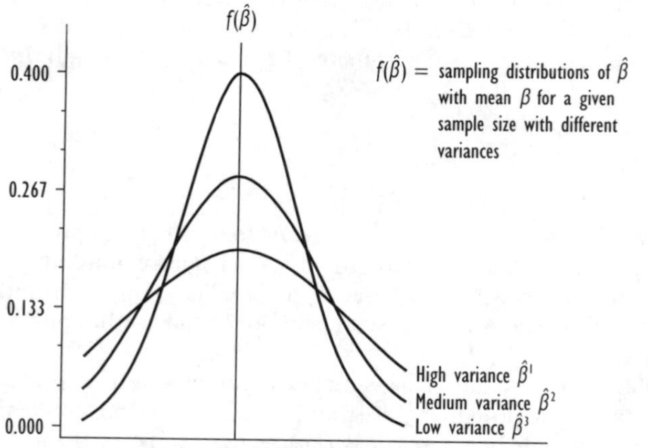

Figure 2.3 An efficient estimator.

That is, the dispersion of the sampling distribution around the mean is becoming smaller and the estimates, on average, more precise as the sample size increases.

Figure 2.3 depicts three sampling distributions associated with three different unbiased estimators of β, $\hat{\beta}^1$, $\hat{\beta}^2$, and $\hat{\beta}^3$. $\hat{\beta}^1$ is associated with the "flattest" distribution, $\hat{\beta}^2$ with the moderately steeped sampling distribution, and $\hat{\beta}^3$ with the "steepest" sampling distribution. The sample variance is greatest for $\hat{\beta}^1$ and least for $\hat{\beta}^3$. Because of its smaller variance, $\hat{\beta}^3$ is relatively more efficient and, given that each estimator is unbiased, would be the preferred estimator of β.

In practice, an analyst only obtains one sample and uses this sample to obtain least-squares estimates of the true but unknown parameters β_i ($i = 1, 2, 3$). The fact that these are least-squares estimates implies that they are unbiased, consistent, and efficient – properties which improve our confidence in the parameter estimates.

As a final point, parameter estimates based upon sample information are random variables that come from a probability distribution. This means that it is possible to make additional statements, in the form of confidence intervals and statistical tests, that increases our information on the values of the true (but unknown) parameters. These issues are described below.

Estimating the Demand for Airline Travel

From our discussion above, the demand for passenger–miles is a function of two variables, Price per Mile and Per Capita Income. And this led to two hypotheses regarding the causal relationship between the variables:

1 All else constant, an increase in Price per Mile is expected to reduce the quantity of passenger miles demanded.
2 All else constant, an increase in Per Capita Income is expected to increase the demand for airline travel.

Although, theoretically, a causal relationship between these variables is expected, the two hypotheses need to be statistically tested.

Consider figure 2.4, which depicts annual airline data for the period 1970–88. Price per Mile, which is measured by Revenue per Passenger–Mile (cents), and Per Capita Income (thousands)

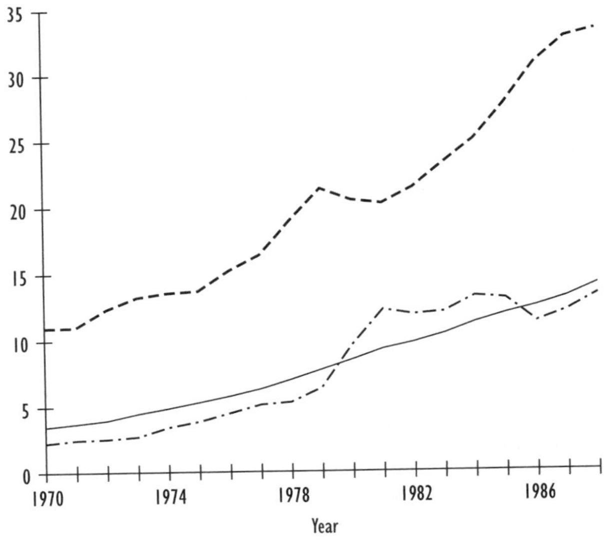

Figure 2.4 Time Series Airline Data, 1970–86. - - - - -, Passenger–Miles (tens of billions); — - —, Revenue per Passenger–Mile (cents, 1982–4 dollars); ——, Per Capita Income (in thousands of 1982–4 dollars).

are both expressed in constant (or inflation adjusted) 1982–4 dollars. For the entire 19-year period, the overall trend of Passenger–Miles, Revenue per Passenger–Mile, and Per Capita Income is positive. Passenger–Miles, in particular, exhibits a significant increase from 109.5 billion in 1970 to 334 billion in 1988. There was a lull in passenger–miles flown during the 1979–1981 period, but after 1981 passenger–miles rose at a faster pace. In contrast, the rise in Per Capita Income has been moderate and steady over the period. Prices rose at a rate similar to that of Per Capita Income between 1970 and 1979, increased dramatically between 1979 and 1981, and then remained relatively constant, except for a dip around 1985. The large increase in prices during the 1979–81 period most likely reflects a 60% inflation-adjusted increase in fuel prices.

We also see the dampening effect that this had on passenger–miles flown. As prices rose during this two-year period, passenger–miles reversed its upward trend.

In addition to the sharp rise in fuel prices, the airline industry was deregulated in 1978, which was expected to infuse the industry with a strong rush of competitive air that would be beneficial to the flying public. Figure 2.4 appears to bear this out. Once the industry adjusted to the increased fuel prices, prices have either remained constant or slightly fallen. At the same time, passenger–miles flown have risen sharply, and only tapered off in the late 1980s as fares began to rise.

Based upon this annual data, an econometric model of the demand for airline passenger–miles, given in equation (2.3), was estimated. For this model, Miles is passenger–miles, in billions; Price per Mile is measured by cents per passenger–mile, in 1982–4 dollars; and Per Capita Income is measured in thousands of 1982–4 dollars. The least-squares regression results are reported below:[3]

$$\begin{aligned}\widehat{\text{Miles}} &= \hat{\beta}_1 + \hat{\beta}_2\text{Price per Mile} + \hat{\beta}_3\text{Per Capita Income}\\ &= 15.7 - 8.7\text{Price per Mile} + 0.031\text{Per Capita Income} \qquad (2.8)\end{aligned}$$

According to the estimation results in equation (2.8), a 1 cent increase in the price of an airline passenger–mile, holding Per Capita Income constant, reduces the number of passenger–miles demanded by 8.7 billion miles per year. Similarly, a $1,000 increase in Per Capita Income, holding Price per Mile constant, increases the demand for passenger–miles by 0.031 billion or 31 million miles. From the previous section, these estimates are unbiased, consistent, and efficient. Note also that these results conform to our initial hypotheses that the coefficient of price is negative and the coefficient of income is positive.

CONFIDENCE INTERVALS

Notwithstanding that our estimated results are consistent with the hypotheses identified in (2.2), each estimated coefficient is a random variable that has an associated probability distribution. As a result, it may be that the parameter estimate we obtained in the regression model is quite "far" from the true value of the parameter. A standard method that is used for determining how close each coefficient estimate is to the true parameter value is to construct a *confidence interval* around our estimate.

In order to construct a confidence interval, we exploit our earlier assumption that the error term ε (equation (2.3)) in our econometric model for airline demand follows a normal distribution which implies that the least-squares parameter estimate $\hat{\beta}_i$ of β_i is also normally

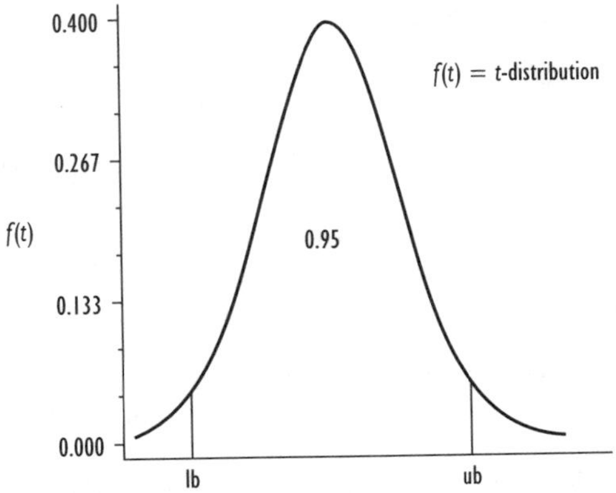

Figure 2.5 The t-distribution.

distributed with mean β_i and constant variance $\sigma^2_{\hat{\beta}_i}$; that is, $\hat{\beta}_i \sim N(\beta_i, \sigma^2_{\hat{\beta}_i})$. If we knew the true sample variance of the parameter estimate, $\sigma^2_{\hat{\beta}_i}$, our confidence interval could then be based upon the statistic, $(\hat{\beta}_i - \beta_i)/\sigma_{\hat{\beta}_i}$, which has a standard normal distribution N(0,1).[4] Unfortunately, the true sample variance of the parameter estimate, $\sigma^2_{\hat{\beta}_i}$, is rarely if ever known, so that we must estimate $\sigma^2_{\hat{\beta}_i}$ from our sample data. Denoting the estimated sample variance of $\hat{\beta}_i$ by $s^2_{\hat{\beta}_i}$, it can be shown that the statistic, $(\hat{\beta}_i - \beta_i)/s_{\hat{\beta}_i}$, has a t-distribution with degrees of freedom equal to the sample size minus the number of parameters estimated.[5] $s_{\hat{\beta}_i}$ is the square root of the estimated sample variance and is referred to as the *standard error of the estimate*. Figure 2.5 depicts a typical t-distribution, which is seen to resemble the shape of a normal distribution. As the sample size increases, a t-distribution more closely approximates a normal distribution. Notice the two areas in the tails of the distribution. If we want to construct a 95% confidence interval, then we want to identify lower (lb) and upper (ub) bound numbers for the true parameter value such that the area under the curve and between these two numbers equals 0.95. Since the t-distribution is symmetric, the area to the right of ub is 0.025 and the area to the left of lb is 0.025. Alternatively, if we wanted to construct a 99% confidence interval, we would want lower and upper bound numbers around the true parameter such that the area between these bounds equals 0.99. In this case, the two tails would each have areas equal to 0.005 (the sum of which equals 0.01). In general, if we want to construct an α% confidence interval, then we determine lower and upper boundaries around the true parameter value such that the area in each of the tails equals $[(1-p)/2]$%. For the t-distribution, let $t_{p,\text{d.f.}}$ be the value of the t-distribution with degrees of freedom (d.f.) and p% in the tails of the distribution. $t_{0.05,8}$, for example, is the value of the t-distribution with eight degrees of freedom and 5% of the area in the tails of the distribution. A table for t-distribution values would indicate that $t_{0.05,8}$ is 2.306, which says that values greater than 2.306 or less than −2.306 comprise 5% of the area in the tails of this curve.[6]

Suppose in our airline demand model (equation (2.8)), that we want to construct a 95% confidence interval around the true values of the parameters of price and per capita income, β_2 and β_3, respectively. Since we know that the ratio $(\hat{\beta}_i - \beta_i)/s_{\hat{\beta}_i}$ $(i = 2, 3)$ has a t-distribution with 16 degrees of freedom (sample size of 19 minus three, the number of estimated parameters), we can construct a 95% confidence interval from the following expression:

$$P\left(-2.120 < \frac{\hat{\beta}_i - \beta_i}{s_{\hat{\beta}_i}} < 2.120\right) = 0.95$$

$$\Rightarrow \quad P(-2.120 \cdot s_{\hat{\beta}_i} < \hat{\beta}_i - \beta_i < 2.120 \cdot s_{\hat{\beta}_i}) = 0.95$$

$$\Rightarrow \quad P(\hat{\beta}_i - 2.120 \cdot s_{\hat{\beta}_i} < \beta_i < \hat{\beta}_i + 2.120 \cdot s_{\hat{\beta}_i}) = 0.95 \qquad (2.9)$$

where 2.120 is the value of the *t*-distribution with 16 degrees of freedom that corresponds to 2.5% of the area associated with each tail of the distribution, that is, $t_{0.025,16} = 2.120$. Thus, the 95% confidence interval for β_i can be equivalently expressed as $(\hat{\beta}_i - t_{0.025,16} \cdot s_{\hat{\beta}_i}, \hat{\beta}_i + t_{0.025,16} \cdot s_{\hat{\beta}_i})$.

Equation (2.10) reproduces the estimated model in equation (2.8), but also reports the standard error of each estimate below the coefficient estimate of the explanatory variable:

$$\widehat{\text{Miles}} = 15.7 - \underset{(1.0)}{8.7}\,\text{Price per Mile} + \underset{(0.0013)}{0.031}\,\text{Per Capita Income} \qquad (2.10)$$

As seen in equation (2.10), the standard error of the estimate for Price per Mile is 1.0 and the standard error of the estimate for Per Capita Income is 0.0013. Based upon this information, and recalling that $t_{0.025,18}$ equals 2.120, the 95% confidence interval for each coefficient is given in the table below:

	Confidence Intervals for Airline Demand Coefficient Estimates
Price per Mile	(−10.80, −6.60)
Per Capita Income	(0.0284, 0.0337)

Thus, with 95% confidence, the true value of the marginal effect of price and income, respectively, on the demand for passenger–miles will be found for this sample in the intervals above.

Hypothesis Tests

A major objective of many empirical studies is to test hypotheses regarding the relationship between the dependent and independent variables. In our airline demand model, for example, Price per Mile and Per Capita Income were hypothesized to affect the demand for passenger–miles.

The methodology for hypothesis testing first requires that we identify two hypotheses, a *null hypothesis* (H_0) and an *alternative hypothesis* (H_A). The null hypothesis defines the *hypothesized* value of the true parameter, denoted by β_0, versus the alternative hypothesis that the true parameter does not equal this value. Note that the hypothesized value β_0 is a known value defined by the analyst. In the airline model, for example, if we believe that Per Capita Income is an important determinant of passenger–miles flown, then our two hypotheses would be

$$H_0\colon \beta_2 = 0$$

$$H_A\colon \beta_2 \neq 0 \qquad (2.11)$$

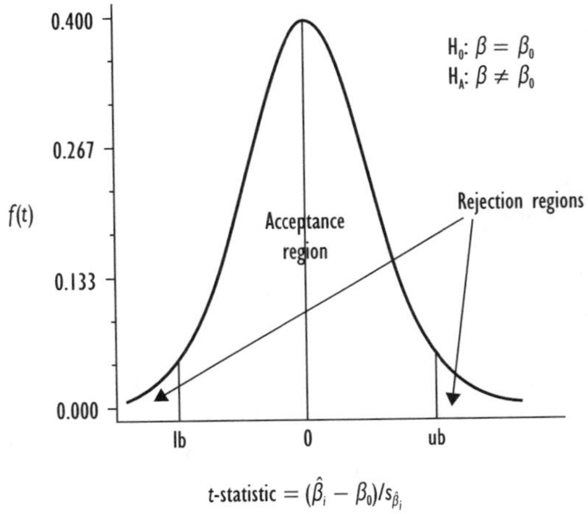

Figure 2.6 Hypothesis tests.

In this case, the hypothesized value of the true parameter, β_0, is zero. By hypothesizing that $\beta_2 = 0$ in the null hypothesis, we are essentially positing that Per Capita Income is *not* an important determinant of miles flown. The alternative hypothesis, on the other hand, states that income's coefficient is not equal to zero, which is equivalent to saying that income *is* an important determinant of miles flown. Notice also that the alternative hypothesis does not specify *how* income affects miles flown. That is, the alternative hypothesis does not indicate whether income has a positive or a negative effect on miles flown – it simply states that income has an effect. Because the alternative hypothesis allows income's effect to be positive or negative, the test of the null hypothesis is said to be a *two-tail test*.

Once we have identified the null and alternative hypotheses, the next step is to identify the statistic on which the test will be based, and the associated distribution of this statistic *under the null hypothesis*; that is, if the null hypothesis is true. Our test statistic is the familiar statistic $(\hat{\beta}_i - \beta_i)/s_{\hat{\beta}_i}$, which we have already seen to have a *t*-distribution with degrees of freedom equal to the difference between the number of observations and the number of estimated parameters. In general, this statistic cannot be calculated, since β_i is the true but *unknown* parameter. However, *under the null hypothesis that β_i equals β_0*, this statistic becomes $(\hat{\beta}_i - \beta_0)/s_{\hat{\beta}_i}$, which is a *known* number. Thus, by testing the null hypothesis that the true but unknown parameter β_i is actually equal to β_0, we are testing whether our calculated coefficient estimate, $\hat{\beta}_i$, is sufficiently far from β_0 relative to its standard error so as to reject the null hypothesis and accept the alternative hypothesis. Figure 2.6 graphically depicts this test.

The final step in carrying out a hypothesis test is to identify a decision rule for testing the null hypothesis. There are three possible outcomes to a hypothesis test:

1 Reject a false hypothesis or accept a true hypothesis.
2 Reject a true hypothesis (Type 1 error).
3 Accept a false hypothesis (Type 2 error).

In case 1, we have made the correct decision. We reject the null hypothesis if $\beta_i \neq \beta_0$; alternatively, we cannot reject the null if $\beta_i = \beta_0$. Cases 2 and 3, however, correspond to mistakes, and we would like to reduce as much as possible the probability of making either type of mistake. Unfortunately, for a given sample, it is not possible to simultaneously reduce the probability of a Type 1 or Type 2 error. When we reduce the probability of making a Type 1 error, we increase the probability of making a Type 2 error. Conversely, reducing the probability of a Type 2 error increases the probability of making a Type 1 error.

To clarify the trade-off between Type 1 and Type 2 errors, suppose that our decision rule is to *never reject* the null hypothesis. In this case, the probability of making a Type 1 error will be zero. Since in no case do we reject the null hypothesis, we will never reject a null hypothesis that is true. On the other hand, there will be *some* null hypotheses that are indeed false, so that the probability of a Type 2 error is greater than zero but less than one.

Alternatively, in an effort to reduce the probability of a Type 2 error, suppose that we alter our decision rule to *always reject* the null hypothesis. This decision rule reduces the probability of a Type 2 error to zero since, by rejecting every null hypothesis, we will never be accepting a null hypothesis that is actually false. But what does this decision rule do to the probability of a Type 1 error? The probability of a Type 1 error increases, since there will now be some true null hypotheses that are rejected. Thus, relative to our first decision rule, an attempt to reduce the probability of a Type 2 error resulted in increasing the probability of a Type 1 error.

Since it is not possible to simultaneously reduce the probability of making Type 1 and Type 2 errors, the standard procedure is to define a decision rule that sets the probability of a Type 1 error at some maximum acceptable value, called the *significance level*, and then choose an estimator that reduces the probability of a Type 2 error as much as possible. In most cases, the significance level is set at either 0.05 or 0.01, which says that the probability of rejecting a null hypothesis that is actually true is 5% or 1%, respectively.[7]

To summarize the hypothesis testing procedure, suppose that we have the following hypotheses:

$$H_0\colon \beta_i = \beta_0$$
$$H_A\colon \beta_i \neq \beta_0$$

Based upon a *t*-distributed test statistic and assuming a 5% significance level, then under the null hypothesis, we can make the following probability statement:

$$\Pr\left(-t_{0.025,\text{d.f.}} < \frac{\hat{\beta}_i - \beta_0}{s_{\hat{\beta}_i}} < t_{0.025,\text{d.f.}}\right) = 0.95$$

$$\Rightarrow \quad P(-t_{0.025,\text{d.f.}} \cdot s_{\hat{\beta}_i} < \hat{\beta}_i - \beta_0 < t_{0.025,\text{d.f.}} \cdot s_{\hat{\beta}_i}) = 0.95$$

$$\Rightarrow \quad P(\hat{\beta}_i - t_{0.025,\text{d.f.}} \cdot s_{\hat{\beta}_i} < \beta_0 < \hat{\beta}_i + t_{0.025,\text{d.f.}} \cdot s_{\hat{\beta}_i}) = 0.95 \qquad (2.12)$$

$t_{0.025,\text{d.f.}}$ is the *critical t-value* which defines the boundaries for rejecting the null hypothesis when the significance level is 5%. If the value of the test statistic, $(\hat{\beta}_i - \beta_i)/s_{\hat{\beta}_i}$, is either greater than $t_{0.025,\text{d.f.}}$ or is less than $-t_{0.025,\text{d.f.}}$, we reject the null hypothesis and accept the alternative hypothesis that $\beta_i \neq \beta_0$. An alternative way of seeing this result is to note that equation (2.12) constitutes the *acceptance region*. It identifies those values of the estimated parameter $\hat{\beta}_i$ that are not far enough from the hypothesized value of the true parameter for the null hypothesis to be rejected.

Notice also the similarity between equations (2.9) and (2.12). Equation (2.9) gives the confidence interval for the *unknown true parameter*. It defines a range of values for the actual population parameter. Equation (2.12) gives a range of values for an estimated parameter *under the null hypothesis*, that is, assuming that the true population parameter has the value specified in the null hypothesis.

In practice, the absolute value of the test statistic is compared with the absolute value of the critical t-value, and the null hypothesis is either rejected or not rejected depending upon this comparison. For the above case,

$$\text{if } \left|\frac{\hat{\beta}_i - \beta_0}{s_{\hat{\beta}_i}}\right| > |t_{0.025,\text{d.f.}}|, \text{ then we can reject the null hypothesis}$$

$$\text{if } \left|\frac{\hat{\beta}_i - \beta_0}{s_{\hat{\beta}_i}}\right| < |t_{0.025,\text{d.f.}}|, \text{ then we cannot reject the null hypothesis} \qquad (2.13)$$

To illustrate the procedure for hypothesis testing, consider again our airline demand model and suppose that we want to test the null hypothesis that Per Capita Income has no effect upon the demand for travel. Our null and alternative hypotheses were given in (2.11) and are reproduced below:

$$\text{H}_0\text{: } \beta_2 = 0$$
$$\text{H}_A\text{: } \beta_2 \neq 0$$

Our test statistic is $(\hat{\beta}_2 - \beta_0)/s_{\hat{\beta}_2}$ which, under the null hypothesis, becomes $\hat{\beta}_2/s_{\hat{\beta}_2} = 0.031/0.0013 = 23.85$. Recalling that this test statistic has a t-distribution with 16 degrees of freedom and assuming a 5% level of significance, the *critical t-value* is 2.120. Since 23.85 is larger than 2.120, the coefficient of income is *significantly different from zero*, and we reject the null hypothesis that Per Capita Income has no effect on airline travel demand and accept the alternative hypothesis that it is an important determinant of demand. If we wish to test the null hypothesis at a 1% significance level, the only change to this procedure will be the number that represents our critical t-value, which is 2.921 for a 1% significance level. Necessarily, the critical t-value is larger, since it represents a stronger test of the null hypothesis, but the result remains the same, since 2.921 remains well below the calculated test statistic of 23.85.

Since the alternative hypothesis in the above test was accepted for sufficiently large positive or large negative values of the estimated parameter, the test was termed a two-tail test. In many cases, the alternative hypothesis identifies the sign of the coefficient. In the airline demand equation, for example, we could have specified the null and alternative hypotheses as:

$$\text{H}_0\text{: } \beta_2 = 0$$
$$\text{H}_A\text{: } \beta_2 > 0 \qquad (2.14)$$

As before, the null hypothesis is that Per Capita Income is not important in explaining airline travel demand. The alternative hypothesis, however, now specifies that Per Capita Income is an important factor and identifies the direction of the effect that increases in income have upon airline travel.[8] Since the alternative hypothesis specifies the sign of the coefficient, $\beta_2 > 0$, our test is only based on one tail of the distribution and is appropriately termed a *one-tail test*. If a positive sign is specified in the alternative hypothesis, as in this case, the upper tail of the *t*-distribution is relevant. If the effect is hypothesized to be negative, the lower tail would be relevant.

To test the one-tail hypothesis on Per Capita Income given in equation (2.14), the only change in our testing procedure relative to a two-tail test is the number that represents the critical *t*-value. For a 5% level of significance, the critical value is $t_{0.05,16} = 1.746$. Thus, our decision rule is

$$\text{if } \frac{\hat{\beta}_2 - \beta_0}{s_{\hat{\beta}_2}} = \frac{\hat{\beta}_2}{s_{\hat{\beta}_2}} > t_{0.05,16} = 1.746, \text{ then we can reject the null hypothesis}$$

$$\text{if } \frac{\hat{\beta}_2 - \beta_0}{s_{\hat{\beta}_2}} = \frac{\hat{\beta}_2}{s_{\hat{\beta}_2}} < t_{0.05,16} = 1.746, \text{ then we cannot reject the null hypothesis} \tag{2.15}$$

Based upon the regression results reported in equation (2.10), the test statistic is still 23.85, so that we would reject the null hypothesis in favor of the alternative hypothesis. This should not be surprising, since a one-tail test at a 5% level of significance is a *weaker* test than a two-tail test at a 5% level of significance. The critical value for the one-tail test is *smaller* than for the two-tail test. Since we previously rejected the null hypothesis on a two-tail test, we must reject the null hypothesis using a one-tail test.

Testing the airline demand model for consistency with the law of demand provides a further example of a one-tail test. According to the law of demand, there is an inverse relationship between price and quantity demanded. Thus, our hypotheses are:

$$\mathrm{H_0}: \beta_1 = 0$$

$$\mathrm{H_A}: \beta_1 < 0 \tag{2.16}$$

Based upon a 5% level of significance, our critical *t*-value is again 1.746. Our test statistic is different, however, since it's based upon the parameter and standard error estimates for Price per Mile rather than Per Capita Income. Under the null hypothesis, we have the following decision rule:

$$\text{if } \frac{\hat{\beta}_1 - \beta_0}{s_{\hat{\beta}_1}} = \frac{\hat{\beta}_1}{s_{\hat{\beta}_1}} < -t_{0.05,16} = -1.746, \text{ then we can reject the null hypothesis}$$

$$\text{if } \frac{\hat{\beta}_1 - \beta_0}{s_{\hat{\beta}_1}} = \frac{\hat{\beta}_1}{s_{\hat{\beta}_1}} > -t_{0.05,16} = -1.746, \text{ then we cannot reject the null hypothesis} \tag{2.17}$$

Since $\hat{\beta}_1/s_{\hat{\beta}_1}$ equals -8.7, which is less than -1.746, we reject the null hypothesis and conclude that the estimation results are consistent with the law of demand. Notice, in this case, that the decision rule is based upon a negative value. This is because the alternative hypothesis specifies that the price has a negative effect upon the quantity of airline travel demanded, so that the statistical test is based upon the lower tail of the *t*-distribution.

Table 2.1 Hypothesis test decision rules: test statistic, $t^* = (\hat{\beta}_i - \beta_0)/s_{\hat{\beta}_i}$

	H_A	Critical *t*-Value	Decision Rule to Reject H_o
One-Tail Test			
5% level of significance			
area in upper tail: 5%	$\beta > \beta_0$	1.645	$t^* > 1.645$
area in lower tail: 5%	$\beta < \beta_0$	–1.645	$t^* < -1.645$
1% level of significance			
area in upper tail: 1%	$\beta > \beta_0$	2.326	$t^* > 2.326$
area in lower tail: 1%	$\beta < \beta_0$	–2.326	$t^* < -2.326$
Two-Tail Test			
5% level of significance			
area in each tail: 2.5%	$\beta \neq \beta_0$	$\|1.96\|$	$\|t^*\| > \|1.96\|$
1% level of significance			
area in each tail: 0.5%	$\beta \neq \beta_0$	$\|2.576\|$	$\|t^*\| > \|2.576\|$

For large sample sizes (greater than 120 observations) and based upon standard levels of significance, table 2.1 summarizes critical *t*-values and the associated decision rules for testing the null hypothesis that $\beta_i = \beta_0$ against one-sided and two-sided alternative hypotheses. Note that in order to test the most common null hypothesis, that the true parameter is zero, $\beta_0 = 0$, we replace β_0 with zero in the test statistic (column 1) and in the specification of the alternative hypotheses (column 2). The critical *t*-values and decision rules for rejecting the null hypothesis remain the same.

GOODNESS OF FIT AND R^2

In addition to examining whether our estimated model is consistent with the implications of economic theory, it is of interest to know how well the econometric model fits the data in general. In other words, do variations in the explanatory variables do a good job of explaining variations in the dependent variable? A commonly reported measure of a model's *goodness of fit* is an R^2 statistic. This statistic gives the proportion of variation in the dependent variable that is due to all of the explanatory variables in the model. An R^2 equal to 0.75, for example, says that the model's explanatory variables explain 75% of the variation in the dependent variable. At the extremes, the model's explanatory variables could explain none or all of the variation in the dependent variable, implying that R^2 would equal zero in the former case and one in the latter.[9]

CROSS-SECTION VERSUS TIME SERIES DATA

Data obtained for econometric analyses are of two types: cross-section data and time series data. Cross-section data reflect observations on individuals, households, firms, countries, or some other unit of analysis *at a given point in time*. Thus, for example, the average number of automobiles per household, by state, in 1990 is a cross-section data set. An analysis of revenue ton–miles shipped by Class I motor carriers in 1992 represents a cross-section data set. On the other hand, the airline travel demand model estimated previously represents a time series data set, because each observation corresponds to a *different time period*. As a general rule, R^2 statistics for time series data will be larger than a corresponding goodness-of-fit measure based upon cross-section information. The reason is that the dependent variable, as well as the explanatory variables, tend to move together over time. This suggests that one should be careful not to blindly jump to the conclusion that a time series model with a high R^2 is necessarily better than an analogously specified model based upon cross-section data.

MODEL SPECIFICATION

An important reason for differences in R^2 between two models is *model specification*; that is, what variables are included in the econometric model. Has the model been misspecified by excluding relevant variables either inadvertently or due to the unavailability of data? A model that includes all relevant explanatory variables will have a higher R^2 than a model that excludes one or more of these variables. Two examples of specification issues that are important in the analysis of transportation problems are the use of time trends and dummy variables.

A *time trend* is a variable that is included in time series models to capture the influence of factors that are correlated with time but are excluded from the model because they are either not quantifiable or the data are unavailable. The numeric value of the time trend simply equals the observation number. In the airline demand model analyzed above, price and income were identified as two important determinants of demand. A richer specification might also include frequency departure, the distance to the nearest airport, and the prices of alternative modes of travel. Notwithstanding the absence of these factors in the estimated model, their net effect could be empirically captured by introducing a time trend in the model. In this case, the time trend would have a value of 1 for 1970, 2 for 1971, 3 for 1972, . . . , and 19 for 1988.

A time trend is also used to reflect technological change. Over time, there have been considerable technological gains in the transportation sector, such as flexible manufacturing techniques, containerization in rail and ocean liner shipping, high-speed rail, and intelligent vehicle highway systems. Although technological progress is generally not measurable, we know that such improvements increase a firm's productivity, all else held constant. Thus, in regression models that estimate firm production and cost functions, a time trend is often included among the set of explanatory variables, in order to pick up any shifts in these functions due to technological progress.

A *dummy variable* is a variable that either has a value of 0 or a value of 1. During the late 1970s and on into the early 1980s, Congress passed significant pieces of legislation that deregulated the transportation industry. To a greater or lesser degree, every major public mode of transport was deregulated, including airline, motor carrier, bus, rail, and ocean liner.[10] In each case, an important empirical issue is whether the deregulatory legislation altered the structure of the industry. For example, prior to the Airline Deregulation Act (ADA) of 1978, the airline industry was heavily regulated by the federal government. Before 1978, potential entrants had to demonstrate that their services were required to satisfy an existing demand that was not being met by existing carriers. Between 1978 and 1981, as the industry moved toward open access, this requirement was weakened such that entering firms simply had to show that their services were consistent with existing demands for air travel. In 1982 and subsequent years, all "fit, willing, and able" carriers were permitted entry into the industry. An additional feature of the legislation affected pricing. Prior to 1978 ADA, competition among airlines was based upon in-flight services, departure frequency, and type of equipment. Price competition was limited until 1983, when fares were completely deregulated. With an objective toward making this segment of the industry more competitive and efficient, the 1978 ADA substantially eased restrictions on entry and price competition. Did the legislation have its desired effect? This is a question that can only be answered empirically; that is, by looking at the data and determining whether there were significant differences in entry, price competition, and demand before and after the 1978 ADA. In other words, did the 1978 ADA lead to a *structural change* in the industry? In a regression framework, this is answered by including a dummy variable in the regression equation to represent the hypothesized structural shift. A *dummy variable* for the onset of airline deregulation is a variable that takes a value of zero in the pre-deregulatory period and a value of one in the post-deregulatory period.

Consider our airline demand model, which consists of 19 observations representing the period 1970–88. A test of the hypothesis that airline deregulation altered the structure of airline travel demands can be tested by estimating the following regression model:

$$\begin{aligned}\text{Miles} &= \beta_1 + \beta_2\text{Price per Mile} + \beta_3\text{Per Capita Income}\\ &\quad + \beta_4\text{Deregulation} + \varepsilon \end{aligned} \tag{2.18}$$

where Deregulation = 0 for the years 1970–7 and = 1 for the years 1978–88. The underlying null hypothesis is that deregulation had no effect upon miles traveled versus the alternative hypothesis that it did affect demand. Since the effect can be either positive or negative, this constitutes a two-tailed test of the null hypothesis. Can we identify how deregulation affects our regression line? Yes. Suppose that the null hypothesis is true and that deregulation has no effect on travel demand. Then the coefficient of the variable "Deregulation" is not significantly different from zero and the estimated model is

$$\widehat{\text{Miles}} = \hat{\beta}_1 + \hat{\beta}_2\text{Price per Mile} + \hat{\beta}_3\text{Per Capita Income} \tag{2.19}$$

which is identical to the original model estimated in equation (2.8). On the other hand, if the null hypothesis is false and deregulation actually affected travel demand, then the coefficient of "Deregulation" is not zero and the estimated model is:

$$\begin{aligned}\widehat{\text{Miles}} &= \hat{\beta}_1 + \hat{\beta}_2\text{Price per Mile} + \hat{\beta}_3\text{Per Capita Income} + \hat{\beta}_4(1)\\ &= (\hat{\beta}_1 + \hat{\beta}_4) + \hat{\beta}_2\text{Price per Mile} + \hat{\beta}_3\text{Per Capita Income}\\ &= \hat{\beta}_1' + \hat{\beta}_2\text{Price per Mile} + \hat{\beta}_3\text{Per Capita Income}\end{aligned} \tag{2.20}$$

where $\hat{\beta}_1' = \hat{\beta}_1 + \hat{\beta}_4$. As seen in equation (2.20), the effect of deregulation is to shift the regression line by $\hat{\beta}_4$ passenger miles. All else constant, if $\hat{\beta}_4$ is positive, then deregulation structurally shifted the regression line upward; if negative, then deregulation led to a downward shift in airline travel demand.

Figure 2.7 depicts the effect of deregulation on the demand for airline passenger–miles, where it is assumed in the figure that the structural effect was positive.

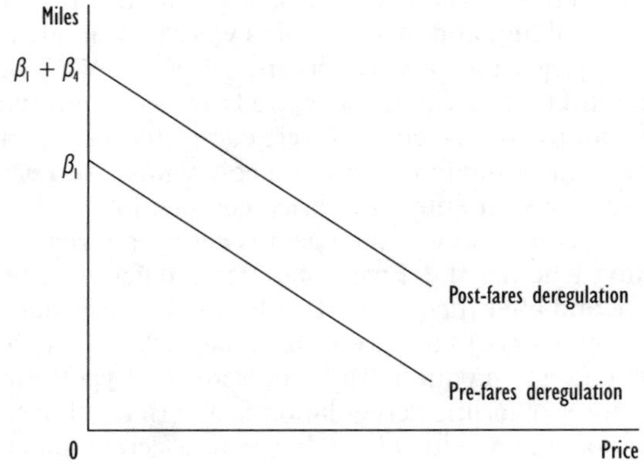

Figure 2.7 The effect of a structural shift on a linear regression line.

FUNCTIONAL FORM

A third reason for differences in R^2 is the model's *functional form,* which reflects the mathematical specification of the regression equation. In the basic model of airline travel demand that we have been using, a *linear* functional form was adopted. Although this may appear to be restrictive, in fact it is quite flexible. What is required in regression analysis is that the regression model be *linear-in-parameters.* What is not required in regression analysis is that the model be linear in the explanatory variables.

To illustrate the difference between linear-in-parameters and linear-in-variables, consider the basic airline demand model that we have been using:

$$\text{Miles} = \beta_1 + \beta_2\text{Price per Mile} + \beta_3\text{Per Capita Income} + \varepsilon \tag{2.21}$$

As expressed, this model is both linear-in-parameters and linear-in-variables. But let's suppose that we know that the demand for air travel is not linearly related to price or income. Does this mean that we cannot estimate the demand for air travel? No. Consider a second model with two explanatory variables, z_1 and z_2, which is expressed as

$$\text{Miles} = \alpha + \alpha_1 z_1 + \alpha_2 z_2 + \varepsilon \tag{2.22}$$

where z_1 is defined as the "logarithm of Price per Mile" and z_2 is defined as the "logarithm of Per Capita Income." Although our new demand model is linear-in-parameters and also linear in the explanatory variables z_i ($i = 1, 2$), it *is not* linear in price, nor in per capita income. Substituting in for these variables, the model in equation (2.22) can be expressed as

$$\text{Miles} = \alpha + \alpha_1[\log(\text{Price per Mile})] + \alpha_2[\log(\text{Per Capita Income})] + \varepsilon \tag{2.23}$$

The model in equation (2.23) is linear in the unknown coefficients but nonlinear in price and per capita income. Since we could define z_1 and z_2 in equation (2.22) any way we wanted, regression analysis accommodates a wide variety of functional forms. As long as the resulting model continues to be linear-in-parameters, linear regression can be used to estimate the parameters.[11]

In economics, four functional forms that are often used in empirical analyses are the linear, log–linear, linear–log, and double log (or "log–log") models, each of which is expressed below for our airline demand model:

$$
\begin{aligned}
&\text{linear} && \text{Miles} = \beta_1 + \beta_2(\text{Price per Mile}) + \beta_3(\text{Per Capita Income}) + \varepsilon \\
&\text{log–linear} && \log(\text{Miles}) = \beta + \beta_1(\text{Price per Mile}) + \beta_2(\text{Per Capita Income}) + \varepsilon \\
&\text{linear–log} && \text{Miles} = \beta + \beta_1[\log(\text{Price per Mile})] + \beta_2[\log(\text{Per Capita Income})] + \varepsilon \\
&\text{double-log} && \log(\text{Miles}) = \beta + \beta_1[\log(\text{Price per Mile})] + \beta_2[\log(\text{Per Capita Income})] + \varepsilon
\end{aligned}
\tag{2.24}
$$

The *linear* model specifies both the dependent and independent variables in linear form. In the *log–linear* model, the dependent variable is in logarithms and the explanatory variables are in linear form. Conversely, the *linear–log* model specifies the dependent variable linearly and the explanatory variables in logarithmic form. Finally, in the *double-log* model, all variables are specified logarithmically.

Why do we consider alternative functional forms? It is because we are ultimately trying to find an empirical model that best explains the data we observe. And although economic theory gives us the qualitative relationship between variables, it is silent on the quantitative relationship. Since many different functional forms are consistent with the qualitative predictions from economic theory, it is important to try alternative functional forms in order to determine which empirical model does the best job in explaining observed behavior. How do we know which functional form to select? This is the role of our goodness-of-fit criterion, R^2. The higher R^2 is, the better a given functional form fits the data. A related rationale for using a nonlinear functional form is the interpretation of the coefficients. For the price variable in each of the four models in equation (2.24), table 2.2 interprets the marginal effect of an increase in the variable and its interpretation.

Table 2.2 Marginal effect for alternative empirical specifications

Model	Marginal Effect[a]	Interpretation
Linear	$\frac{\Delta\text{Miles}}{\Delta\text{Price}} = \beta_2$	Change in the number of passenger miles from a unit increase in Price per Mile
Log–linear	$\frac{\Delta\log(\text{Miles})}{\Delta\text{Price}} = \frac{\Delta\text{Miles/Miles}}{\Delta\text{Price}} = \beta_2$	Percentage increase in passenger miles from a unit increase in Price per Mile
Linear–log	$\frac{\Delta\text{Miles}}{\Delta\log(\text{Price})} = \frac{\Delta\text{Miles}}{\Delta\text{Price/Price}} = \beta_2$	Change in the number of passenger miles due to a 1% increase in Price per Mile
Double-log	$\frac{\Delta\log(\text{Miles})}{\Delta\log(\text{Price})} = \frac{\Delta\text{Miles/Miles}}{\Delta\text{Price/Price}} = \beta_2$	Percentage change in the number of passenger miles due to a 1% increase in Price per Mile

[a] Price is Price per Mile.

Table 2.3 Elasticity measure for alternative empirical specifications

Model	Elasticity[a]
Linear	$\frac{\Delta \text{Miles}/\text{Miles}}{\Delta \text{Price}/\text{Price}} = \beta_2\left(\frac{\text{Price}}{\text{Miles}}\right)$
Log–linear	$\frac{\Delta \text{Miles}/\text{Miles}}{\Delta \text{Price}/\text{Price}} = \beta_2(\text{Price})$
Linear–log	$\frac{\Delta \text{Miles}/\text{Miles}}{\Delta \text{Price}/\text{Price}} = \beta_2\left(\frac{1}{\text{Miles}}\right)$
Double-log	$\frac{\Delta \text{Miles}/\text{Miles}}{\Delta \text{Price}/\text{Price}} = \beta_2$

[a] Price is Price per Mile.

As we have already seen, the interpretation of the price coefficient in the linear model is simply the change in the quantity of passenger–miles demanded when there is a unit increase in price. In the log–linear model, however, the unit increase in price results in a *percentage change* in miles. For the linear–log model, β_2 is the change in miles demanded resulting from a *1% increase* in price. Finally, the double-log model gives the percentage change in miles demanded resulting from a 1% increase in price.

As seen in the table, a unit change in a logarithmically specified variable is a percentage change, a quantity which is often of greater interest to the analyst. And when both the dependent variable and the explanatory variable have a logarithmic specification, the coefficient is an *elasticity*, defined as the percentage change in the dependent variable resulting from a 1% change in an explanatory variable. Economists frequently use elasticities to characterize the sensitivity of a dependent variable due to changes in explanatory variables, because elasticities are dimensionless; that is, they are pure numbers that do not depend upon the units in which the variables are measured. Hence, if one is interested in estimating demand elasticities, the simplest functional form is the double-log model, since the coefficient estimates are identically elasticity estimates.[12]

To conclude this section, table 2.3 indicates how the elasticities are calculated for each of the four models in table 2.2. Only for the double-log model are no other calculations necessary once the model is estimated.

The Airline Demand Model Revisited

In this section, we present linear, log–linear, linear–log, and double-log estimation results for our airline demand model. In each of these models, a time trend is also included in order to capture the effects of any systematic changes in travel demand due to economic and other factors that have not been included in the econometric model. As discussed above, a major development in the airline industry during this period was the Airline Deregulation Act of 1978. In order to test whether this led to a structural shift in demand, a dummy variable

Table 2.4 Estimation results for alternative empirical specifications[a]

Model 1 – linear model

$$\text{Miles} = 13.17 - \underset{(-10.4)}{9.74}\text{Price per Mile} + \underset{(10.9)}{0.034}\text{Per Capita Income} - \underset{(-1.1)}{2.06}\text{Time} + \underset{(2.9)}{13.95}\text{Deregulation}$$

$R^2 = 0.9963$

Model 2 – log–linear

$$\log(\text{Miles}) = 4.56 - \underset{(-6.23)}{0.032}\text{Price per Mile} + \underset{(2.31)}{0.000039}\text{Per Capita Income} - \underset{(-5.33)}{0.054}\text{Time} + \underset{(4.68)}{0.124}\text{Deregulation}$$

$R^2 = 0.9957$

Model 3 – linear–log

$$\text{Miles} = 2{,}941 - \underset{(-9.35)}{115.8}\log(\text{Price per Mile}) + \underset{(2.56)}{386.3}\log(\text{Per Capita Income}) - \underset{(-5.88)}{39.1}\log(\text{Time}) - \underset{(-0.19)}{1.42}\text{Deregulation}$$

$R^2 = 0.9923$

Model 4 – double-log

$$\log(\text{Miles}) = 6.06 - \underset{(-8.67)}{0.40}\log(\text{Price per Mile}) + \underset{(17.9)}{1.36}\log(\text{Per Capita Income}) - \underset{(-1.76)}{0.043}\log(\text{Time}) + \underset{(2.46)}{0.070}\text{Deregulation}$$

$R^2 = 0.9958$

[a] t-statistics are in parentheses below each explanatory variable's coefficient.
Source: Author's calculations

"Deregulation" is included. Deregulation has a value of zero for the years 1970–7 and a value of one for 1978–88. Table 2.4 presents the estimation results for each of these models. The goodness-of-fit statistic R^2 is over 0.99 for each model, indicating that the included variables do a good job in explaining the variation in the dependent variables. Which model is best? That depends on how one defines "best." Between Models 1 and 3, which have the same dependent variable, the R^2 for the linear model is highest, indicating the best fit.[13] Between Models 2 and 4, which also have the same dependent variable, the values of R^2 are virtually identical. On the basis of R^2, then, it is difficult to choose between Models 2 and 4.

Are each of the models consistent with the underlying hypotheses regarding the effect of Price per Mile and Per Capita Income on demand? Yes. In each model, both variables have their hypothesized signs and, based upon the t-statistics reported below the coefficients, are significantly different from zero.

Are the results consistent with respect to our expectations regarding the effect of deregulation? Recall that deregulation made entry into the industry easier and enabled carriers to engage in more price competition. Economic theory suggests that greater access to a market and enhanced price competition will shift the market demand curve to the right. Thus, one would expect that airline deregulation, all else constant, would increase passenger miles traveled. The results presented in table 2.4 are generally consistent with this. Deregulation

Table 2.5 Estimated elasticity measures for alternative specifications

Model	Elasticity with Respect to: Price per Mile	Per Capita Income
1 Linear	−0.38	1.37
2 Log–linear	−0.25	0.32
3 Linear–log	−0.58	1.92
4 Double-log	−0.40	1.36

Source: Author's calculations

has a *positive* effect upon demand in three out of the four cases. The exception is the linear–log model, where deregulation has a *negative* sign; however, since its *t*-statistic is well below the critical value at a 5% level of significance, the coefficient for deregulation is not statistically different from zero. Thus, in Model 3, deregulation is found to have no impact on the demand for air travel. What's the truth? Unfortunately, answers are never crystal clear. However, combining the fact that Model 3 has a (slightly) lower R^2 with the finding that the deregulatory effect is contrary to that predicted from economic theory, one would conclude that Models 1, 2, or 4 are more accurate descriptions of airline demands than Model 3. Is there any other information that can help us discriminate between the remaining three models? Consider table 2.5, which reports the elasticities associated with each of the models. Again, there are some interesting differences here. The two models that best fit the data, Models 1 and 4, have Price per Mile and Per Capita Income elasticity estimates that are nearly identical. Relative to Models 1 and 4, the log–linear model produces a smaller price elasticity and a significantly lower income elasticity. Model 3, on the other hand, has elasticity measures more closely aligned to Models 1 and 4. In that Model 2's elasticity estimate for income is significantly different from that produced with alternative functional forms, one should be suspicious of these results unless further evidence to the contrary is available.

Thus, based upon a model's overall fit of the data, its consistency with the predictions of economic theory, and its overall conformability to results obtained from alternative functional forms, the estimation results in table 2.4 suggest that either the linear model, Model 1, or the double-log model, Model 4, best depicts passenger demands for air travel in this example. As a final point, if the analyst were ultimately interested in price and income elasticities, Model 4 would be selected since no further data manipulation is required once the model is estimated. The estimated parameters, β_2 and β_3, are point estimates for price and income elasticity, respectively.

CHAPTER HIGHLIGHTS

- An economic model identifies the most important factors that explain the behavior of some underlying economic variable of interest. Economic models are explanatory, generally characterize average behavior, and identify the qualitative relationships between variables.

- An econometric model is a statistical model that enables one to quantify the causal relationships identified in an economic model. Econometric models are used to make statistical inferences on the importance of "explanatory variables" in explaining the variation in the "dependent" variable.
- A common method for estimating parameters in an econometric model is the method of least squares. The "least-squares estimates" are estimates of an empirical model's parameters obtained by minimizing the sum of squared errors from a sample of observations. Least-squares estimators are unbiased, consistent, and efficient.
- Hypothesis tests are used to statistically determine whether variation in an explanatory variable explains at least part of the variation in a dependent variable. All hypothesis tests involve a null hypothesis, which identifies an hypothesized true value of the parameter, and an alternative hypothesis. If the alternative hypothesis specifies a two-sided effect (positive or negative), the hypothesis test is two-tailed; if the alternative hypothesis specifies a one-sided effect, the hypothesis test is one-tailed.
- In regression models, *t*-statistics are used to test hypotheses on the statistical significance of the explanatory variables. In large samples (more than 120 degrees of freedom), if the calculated *t*-statistic under the null hypothesis was greater than 1.960 (2.576) in absolute value, then we would reject the null hypothesis at a 0.05 (0.01) level of significance. On a one-tail test, we would reject the null hypothesis at a 0.05 (0.01) level of significance if the calculated *t*-statistic was greater than 1.645 (2.326) in absolute value.
- A regression model's goodness of fit gives the proportion of variation in the dependent variable which is "explained" by explanatory variables included in the empirical model.
- Cross-section and time series data are common forms of sample information used to estimate empirical models. Cross-section data provide information on observations units at a point in time. Time series data provide information on an observation unit over a period of time.
- Common statistical specifications for estimating empirical models and testing hypotheses on economic relationships include the linear model, the log–linear model, the linear–log model, and the double-log model.

Review questions

1. What is an economic model and, ideally, what characteristics would we like our economic models to satisfy?
2. Suppose that we have a simple economic model that shipper demands for transportation services depend upon the transportation rate charged.
   (a) Identify the cause and effect relationship in this model.
   (b) Why is this model a qualitative model of shipper demands?
   (c) How would you transform this economic model into an econometric model of shipper demands?
   (d) In your econometric model, how would you test the hypothesis that demand depends upon transportation rate charged?

3. You are concerned about the damage that automobile pollution is causing our nation's environment and are interested in the effect that gasoline prices have upon gasoline consumption.
   (a) Specify your economic model as well as your econometric model of gasoline consumption. In your econometric model, what are the unknown parameters and what is the interpretation of each parameter?
   (b) What hypothesis will you test in your econometric model of gasoline consumption? Would this be a one-tail or two-tail test, and why?

4. What do we mean when we say that we want our economic models to be representative? The table below identifies two groups of individuals. The "population" is the group on which we would like to get information, and the "sample" is the group from whom we collect information and make inferences about the population. For each pair of groups, identify whether the sample would be representative of the population.

Population	Sample
Vacation travelers	Households with incomes > \$50,000
Airline operations	Airlines currently offering service
Public transit firms	Bus companies in Indiana
Work trips	Automobile owners
Freight shippers	Agricultural producers
Air travelers	Travelers at Chicago's O'Hare Airport

5. Consider the following econometric model of T individual bus demands:

$$(\text{Bus Trips})_t = \alpha + \beta(\text{Fare})_t + \gamma(\text{Income})_t + \varepsilon_t$$

where $(\text{Fare})_t$ is the fare (in dollars) per bus trip paid by individual t and $(\text{Income})_t$ (in dollars) is individual t's income.
   (a) What sign would you expect β and γ, respectively, to have, and why?
   (b) From the econometric model, what impact will a 50 cent increase in bus fare have upon ridership? What impact will a \$1 increase in income have upon bus ridership? What about a \$1,000 increase in household income?
   (c) The method of least squares estimates α, β, and γ by minimizing the sum of squared errors, $\sum_t \varepsilon_t^2$. Why is this method preferred to an alternative procedure that would estimate α, β, and γ by minimizing the sum of errors, $\sum_t \varepsilon_t$?
   (d) From a statistical viewpoint, what desirable properties do linear regression estimates have?

6. For a policy-maker, one objective of econometric models is to forecast the values of economic variables. Suppose, for example, that the head of the Department of Transportation wants to predict the rail petroleum consumption next year. To do so, she looks at petroleum consumption over the past 20 years, takes the average, and uses the average as an estimate of next year's consumption.

(a) Why is this estimate likely to be an incorrect estimate of next year's petroleum consumption?

(b) Show that estimating next year's consumption by the average consumption over the past 20 years is comparable to the following regression model:

$$\text{Rail Petroleum Consumption} = \alpha + \varepsilon_t, \qquad t = 1, \ldots, 20$$

where α is estimated by the method of least squares. (Hint: see footnote 1 in this chapter.) According to this model, what impact will a \$1 increase in the price of oil have upon rail petroleum consumption?

(c) On the advice of her economic staff, the policy-maker revises her model to include the price of oil:

$$\text{Rail Petroleum Consumption} = \alpha + \beta(\text{Price of Oil}) + \varepsilon_t, \qquad t = 1, \ldots, 20$$

In this case, what would be the policy head's prediction of next year's consumption of oil by railroads? And what effect will a \$1 increase in the price of oil have upon rail petroleum consumption?

7. You work for an airline and are trying to determine the effect that fuel prices and distance traveled have upon airline fares. You estimate the following model using regression analysis:

$$\log(\text{fare}) = \underset{(1.3)}{-4.5} + \underset{(0.15)}{0.36} \log(\text{fuel price}) + \underset{(0.03)}{0.68} \log(\text{distance}), \qquad R^2 = 0.90$$

where the numbers in parentheses are the standard errors. The model was estimated on a cross-section of 100 routes flown by a major airline.

(a) What is the economic model underlying the relationship between airline fares, fuel prices, and distance traveled? What are the qualitative hypotheses associated with this model?

(b) Are the econometric results presented above consistent with the qualitative economic hypotheses?

(c) Derive a 95% confidence interval for the true values of the coefficients of the two explanatory variables. What does this interval tell you?

(d) According to the estimated equation, what effect will a 1% increase in fuel prices have upon airline fares? In the early 1980s, fuel prices increased by 60%. Based upon the above equation, what effect would this have upon airline fares?

(e) Suppose that the average length of trip on a major airline is 1,000 miles, whereas the average trip length on a smaller regional airline is 400 miles. According to the above equation, what effect would this difference in trip length have upon airline fares?

8. You are interested in the effect that increased speed limits have had upon intercity freight carriage by truck. To that end, you estimate the following econometric model on time series data from 1976 to 1991. From 1976 to 1986, the speed limit on rural interstates was 55 mph. In 1987, the federal government passed legislation that allowed individual states to raise the speed limits to 65 mph:

$$(\text{Truck Carriage})_t = \alpha + \beta_1(\text{GDP})_t + \beta_2(\text{Speed Limit})_t + \varepsilon_t \qquad t = 1976, \ldots, 1991$$

where Truck Rate is the truck shipping cost per ton–mile, Rail Rate is the railroad shipping price per ton–mile, and GDP is gross domestic product. Speed Limit is a dummy variable that equals 0 for the years 1976–86 and equals 1 for the years 1987–91.

(a) What is the expected sign on β_1? Would you use a one-tail or two-tail test to test this hypothesis?

(b) From the above equation, identify the percentage effect that a 5% increase in GDP would have upon truck shipments. That is, what is the elasticity of Truck Freight Carriage with respect to GDP? Alternatively, what effect would a 5% increase in GDP have upon the absolute amount of ton–miles shipped?

(c) What do you think the effect of higher speed limits on truck shipments would be? That is, do you expect β_2 to be positive, negative, or uncertain? Graphically depict the regression line during the period 1976–86 and then show how the increased speed limit would affect the regression line.

9. For small-package transportation firms, there is a seasonal increase in the demand for their services during the holiday season. Consider the following quarterly time series model of firm revenues for small-package transportation firms:

$$\log(\text{Revenues})_t = \alpha + \beta_1\text{Time} + \beta_2(\text{Fourth Quarter})_t + \varepsilon_t, \qquad t = 1, \ldots, T$$

where the variable Time takes on the value 1 for $t = 1$, 2 for $t = 2$, and so on. Fourth Quarter is a dummy variable that equals one for the fourth quarter of the year (October–December) and is included to capture the holiday seasonal effect. During the first three quarters, Fourth Quarter equals zero.

(a) What is the interpretation of β_1?

(b) What is the interpretation of β_2, and would you expect β_2 to be greater than or less than zero? Assuming that $\beta_1 > 0$, graph the relationship between the dependent variable and Time for the months of January through September. What does this relationship look like during the fourth quarter of the year?

10. You operate an inland water transport service and hypothesize that your average costs per cargo ton–mile of operation (*AVCOST*) depend upon the average length of haul (*AVH*) and route density (*DEN*). You estimate the following equation using a cross-section of 38 observations of water transport firms:

$$AVCOST = \underset{(0.01)}{0.04} - \underset{(0.042)}{0.15}AVH - \underset{(0.235)}{0.80}DEN, \qquad R^2 = 0.85$$

where *AVCOST* = average costs = total costs divided by cargo ton–miles; *AVH* = average length of haul = cargo ton–miles divided by tons carried; and *DEN* = route density = cargo ton–miles divided by route mileage. Numbers in parentheses are standard errors.

(a) How well do the two explanatory variables explain average costs?

(b) Interpret the coefficients.

(c) Calculate a 99% confidence region for the true marginal effect of density on average cost.

(d) Assuming that the average cost per ton–mile is 18 cents and average length of haul is 300 miles, what is the elasticity of average cost with respect to average length of haul?

APPENDIX: PERCENTAGE POINTS OF THE *t*-DISTRIBUTION[a]

Degrees of Freedom	One Tail = 0.25 Two Tails = 0.5	0.1 0.2	0.05 0.1	0.025 0.05	0.01 0.02	0.005 0.01	0.0025 0.005
1	1.000	3.078	6.314	12.706	31.821	63.656	127.321
2	0.816	1.886	2.920	4.303	6.965	9.925	14.089
3	0.765	1.638	2.353	3.182	4.541	5.841	7.453
4	0.741	1.533	2.132	2.776	3.747	4.604	5.598
5	0.727	1.476	2.015	2.571	3.365	4.032	4.773
6	0.718	1.440	1.943	2.447	3.143	3.707	4.317
7	0.711	1.415	1.895	2.365	2.998	3.499	4.029
8	0.706	1.397	1.860	2.306	2.896	3.355	3.833
9	0.703	1.383	1.833	2.262	2.821	3.250	3.690
10	0.700	1.372	1.812	2.228	2.764	3.169	3.581
11	0.697	1.363	1.796	2.201	2.718	3.106	3.497
12	0.695	1.356	1.782	2.179	2.681	3.055	3.428
13	0.694	1.350	1.771	2.160	2.650	3.012	3.372
14	0.692	1.345	1.761	2.145	2.624	2.977	3.326
15	0.691	1.341	1.753	2.131	2.602	2.947	3.286
16	0.690	1.337	1.746	2.120	2.583	2.921	3.252
17	0.689	1.333	1.740	2.110	2.567	2.898	3.222
18	0.688	1.330	1.734	2.101	2.552	2.878	3.197
19	0.688	1.328	1.729	2.093	2.539	2.861	3.174
20	0.687	1.325	1.725	2.086	2.528	2.845	3.153
21	0.686	1.323	1.721	2.080	2.518	2.831	3.135
22	0.686	1.321	1.717	2.074	2.508	2.819	3.119
23	0.685	1.319	1.714	2.069	2.500	2.807	3.104
24	0.685	1.318	1.711	2.064	2.492	2.797	3.091
25	0.684	1.316	1.708	2.060	2.485	2.787	3.078
26	0.684	1.315	1.706	2.056	2.479	2.779	3.067
27	0.684	1.314	1.703	2.052	2.473	2.771	3.057
28	0.683	1.313	1.701	2.048	2.467	2.763	3.047
29	0.683	1.311	1.699	2.045	2.462	2.756	3.038
30	0.683	1.310	1.697	2.042	2.457	2.750	3.030
40	0.681	1.303	1.684	2.021	2.423	2.704	2.971
60	0.679	1.296	1.671	2.000	2.390	2.660	2.915
120	0.677	1.289	1.658	1.980	2.358	2.617	2.860
∞	0.674	1.282	1.645	1.960	2.326	2.576	2.807

[a] *Source*: Calculated using Excel® function TINV.
Examples: For 20 degrees of freedom and a one-tail test, $P(t > 1.725) = 0.05$;
for 20 degrees of freedom and a two-tail test, $P(-1.725 < t < 1.725) = 0.10$.

NOTES

1 To clarify the difference between estimator and estimate, suppose that I want to use a sample of observations to estimate the population mean μ based upon the method of least squares. If I have a sample of n observations, x_i ($i = 1, \ldots, n$), then each x_i can be expressed as $x_i = \mu + \varepsilon_i$, where ε_i is an error term. Minimizing the sum of squared errors implies that we choose the estimate $\hat{\mu}$ to minimize $\Sigma_{i=1}^{n}(x_i - \hat{\mu})^2$. It can be shown that the resulting least-squares *estimator* for μ, $\hat{\mu}$, is simply the sample mean. That is, $\hat{\mu} = \bar{x} = (1/n)\Sigma_{i=1}^{n}x_i$. This is the *formula* used to obtain an estimate of the unknown parameter μ. If, from our sample of information, we calculate the sample mean to be 6.7, this value is the least-squares *estimate* of the population mean.

2 Many estimators of a parameter, including the least-squares estimator, can be expressed as a linear function of the dependent variable. The efficiency property says that, among the set of all estimators of a parameter that can be written as a linear function of the dependent variable and are unbiased, the least-squares estimator has the lowest variance.

3 Data for the regression was obtained from the *1990 Economic Report of the President* and ENO Transportation Foundation (1990).

4 $N(\mu,\sigma^2)$ is commonly used to denote a random variable that is normally distributed with mean μ and variance σ^2. If μ is 0 and σ^2 is 1, then the random variable is said to have a standard normal distribution and is denoted by $N(0,1)$.

5 See any standard statistics or econometrics text; for example, Ramanathan (1998).

6 The appendix to this chapter provides a table of t-values associated with different degrees of freedom and levels of significance.

7 For any given significance level, the probability of making a Type 2 error can be reduced by increasing the size of the sample.

8 Since the alternative hypothesis is that an increase in Per Capita Income increases airline travel, airline travel is hypothesized to be a *normal good*; that is, a good whose consumption increases with income.

9 These results assume that the equation contains an intercept term, such as β_1, in equation (2.3). Also, if Y_t is the observed dependent variable and $\hat{Y}_t$ is the value of Y_t predicted from the equation, it can be shown that R, the square root of R^2, is the correlation between Y_t and $\hat{Y}_t$.

10 The effects of these deregulatory actions will be considered in chapter 8.

11 As an example of a transformation that would not satisfy this requirement, define z_1 and z_2 as $z_1 = (\text{Price per Mile})^\delta$ and $z_2 = (\text{Per Capita Income})^\lambda$, which, when substituted into (2.22), give:

$$\text{Miles} = \alpha + \alpha_1(\text{Price per Mile})^\delta + \alpha_2(\text{Per Capita Income})^\lambda + \varepsilon$$

which is not linear in δ and λ.

12 Thus, for the double-log model in table 2.2, β_2 is simply the *own-price elasticity* of demand.

13 It is not appropriate to compare R^2 for different models if the dependent variables are defined differently. In table 2.4, it is valid to compare the R^2 for Model 1 with that of Model 3, and the R^2 for Model 2 with that of Model 4, since the dependent variable for each is defined identically.

REFERENCES AND RELATED READINGS

ENO Transportation Foundation Inc. 1990: *Transportation in America*, 8th edn.

Gujarati, D. N. 1995: *Basic Econometrics*, 3rd edn. New York: McGraw-Hill.

Hill, R. C., Griffiths, W. E., and Judge, G. G. 1997: *Undergraduate Econometrics*. New York: John Wiley.

Maddala, G. S. 1992: *Introduction to Econometrics*, 2nd edn. Englewood Cliffs, New Jersey: Prentice-Hall.

Ramanathan, R. 1998: *Introductory Econometrics with Applications*, 4th edn. Fort Worth, Texas: The Dryden Press.

Studenmund, A. H. 1997: *Using Econometrics: A Practical Guide*, 3rd Edn. Reading, Mass.: Addison-Wesley.

3

Transportation Demand – The Divisible Goods Case

INTRODUCTION

Consider a world in which there are two goods, transportation (T) and all other consumption (x). Assume that both goods are desirable and perfectly divisible; that is, each good can be consumed in any unit, or fraction thereof. Annual ton–miles of freight shipped, the number of public transit passengers per week, household gasoline consumption per month, annual railroad coal shipments, and monthly throughput in a pipeline are examples of transportation goods that are divisible. On the other hand, many goods in transportation are nondivisible or discrete. For example, a firm that is considering the purchase of a new truck for its expanding operations may have only two choices available, a two-axle, four-wheel truck or a truck tractor with a 48 ft semitrailer. In this case, the truck purchased is the transportation good which is clearly not divisible. The firm cannot purchase any size of truck that it desires, but is constrained to either the two-axle, four-wheel truck or the truck tractor with a semitrailer. The truck chosen in this example represents an "either–or" choice and is referred to as a discrete commodity.

Because many important decisions and goods in transportation – reflecting household and firm travel modes, private versus public carriage, size of household or firm vehicle fleet, trip destinations, and time of travel – represent a choice of one alternative over a limited number of competing alternatives, transportation demand theory will be separately developed for the divisible and the discrete good cases. This chapter develops the standard theory of consumer behavior for divisible commodities, extends the analysis to market demands for transportation, and concludes with a discussion on the transition from the theoretical development of market demands to the empirical estimation of market demands for forecasting and policy analysis.

Building upon the material in this chapter, chapter 4 develops a theory of transportation demand for transportation goods and services that are discrete. Similarities as well as differences in the theoretical development and the empirical estimation of discrete transportation demands will be highlighted.

ASSUMPTIONS UNDERLYING A THEORY OF CONSUMER DEMANDS

Assuming that transportation and all other consumption are desirable commodities, we denote by (T,x) a commodity bundle that contains T units of transportation and x units of all other goods. For example, Bill is given commodity bundle A, defined as (10,20), which provides Bill with ten units of transportation and 20 units of all other goods. This bundle would give Bill some level of economic welfare. If this commodity bundle is compared with a second commodity bundle B, which included 15 transportation units while holding all other goods constant at 20, Bill's level of economic welfare would increase, since he would receive more T without having to give up any units of x. Similarly, increasing the amount of all other goods to 22 while holding transportation at ten units increases Bill's level of welfare. By the same procedure, one could demonstrate that commodity bundle (10,8) decreases Bill's level of economic welfare, as do commodity bundles (8,20) and (8,8).

Consider a third commodity bundle C, which is defined as $(T,x) = (15,8)$. In this case, Bill receives 15 units of transportation and eight units of all other goods. Is Bill better off with commodity bundle A or commodity bundle C? From the information given, we can't tell. Although Bill has more transportation, he also has less of all other goods. Whether Bill prefers commodity bundle A to C (that is, whether A yields a higher level of economic welfare than C) or is indifferent between them (A provides Bill with the same level of economic welfare as C) depends, in general, upon Bill's underlying preferences for the two goods. If Bill is a traveling man who enjoys scenic drives, attending a variety of cultural and sporting events, and visits to nearby cities, he would prefer commodity bundle C to A; alternatively, if Bill were agoraphobic (he had a fear of going outdoors), he would place very little value upon travel (or those goods and services whose consumption requires travel) and would prefer commodity bundle A.

In order to develop a model of consumer behavior, it is necessary to impose three assumptions upon an individual's preferences for commodity bundles.[1] First, consumer preferences are assumed to be *complete*, which says that one's preferences are sufficiently well defined to enable a consumer to rank different commodity bundles. If Denise's preferences are complete then, faced with commodity bundles A and B, she will be able to say whether she prefers A to B, B to A, or whether she is indifferent between A and B.[2]

Second, consumer preferences are assumed to be *transitive*. Suppose that a consumer is faced with three commodity bundles, A, B, and C. If this consumer prefers commodity bundle A to commodity bundle B and commodity bundle B to commodity bundle C, then transitivity implies that the consumer prefers commodity bundle A to commodity bundle C. Thus, transitivity imposes consistency or rationality on a consumer's preference structure.

Third, consumer preferences are *nonsatiable*, which states that no consumption bundle will ever completely satiate an individual, since we can always define a preferred consumption bundle with more of at least one good and no less of any other good. Given any two commodity bundles, A and B, if commodity bundle A contains one more unit of at least one good and no less of any other good in comparison with bundle B, then the individual prefers consumption bundle A. We previously saw that Bill preferred commodity bundle B = (15,20) to commodity bundle A = (10,20) because B had more of T and no less of x. Had ten units of transportation completely satiated Bill, then Bill would not have preferred commodity bundle B to A.

These three assumptions are sufficient to derive an ordinal index of one's preferences, called a *utility function*, which can be expressed as[3]

$$U = U(T,x;\phi) \tag{3.1}$$

Equation (3.1) states that an individual's economic welfare depends upon the amounts of T and x that an individual consumes. Suppose that the utility of consumption bundle A is 100 and the utility for consumption bundle B is 95. Then the individual *prefers* commodity bundle A to commodity bundle B. Alternatively, we can say that bundle A yields a higher level of economic welfare than bundle B. On the other hand, if the utility associated with A equals the utility associated with B, then the individual is *indifferent* between the two consumption bundles; that is, A and B yield equal levels of economic welfare.

It is also seen in (3.1) that a consumer's economic welfare depends upon a parameter, ϕ, which reflects an individual's underlying preferences for the goods. The presence of ϕ in the utility function implies that two consumers may have the same amounts of T and x and yet not receive the same level of utility. This is because the two individuals may have different preferences for the two goods. Consider commodity bundle C = (50,10), which includes a high level of transportation relative to all other goods, and D = (10,50), which includes a high level of all other goods relative to transportation. If ϕ_1 reflects the preferences of individual 1 who values transportation highly and ϕ_2 denotes the preferences of consumer 2 who values all other goods highly, then

$$U(50,10;\phi_1) > U(10,50;\phi_1)$$
$$U(50,10;\phi_2) < U(10,50;\phi_2)$$

INDIFFERENCE CURVES

If we hold utility constant at some level, then equation (3.1) also defines consumer indifference curves. An *indifference curve* is a locus of points along which each commodity bundle gives the consumer exactly the same level of utility. Figure 3.1 depicts three such indifference curves. The assumption that both T and x are divisible ensures that every commodity bundle (that is, combination of T and x) will lie on some indifference curve; completeness ensures that the consumer can rank each bundle; transitivity implies that the curves will be parallel; and

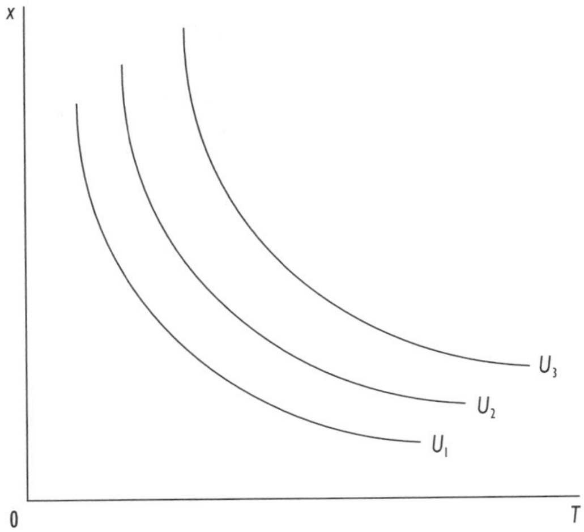

Figure 3.1 Indifference curves for x and T.

nonsatiability guarantees that indifference curves which lie further to the right will be associated with higher levels of utility. If U_i ($i = 1, 2, 3$) is the utility associated with curve i, then $U_1 < U_2 < U_3$ in figure 3.1.

Note also that the indifference curves in figure 3.1 are drawn convex to the origin. Convexity reflects the behavioral assumption that the more of a good a consumer has the less of other goods the consumer is *willing* to forego to obtain an additional unit of the good. The value (in terms of foregone x) to a consumer from a unit increase in T, holding utility constant, is the *marginal rate of commodity substitution* (*MRCS*).

To derive the *MRCS*, note that total utility can change only if the level of T or the level of x changes. Define Δ to be "change in." Then a change in total utility can be expressed as

$$\begin{aligned}\Delta U &= \frac{\Delta U}{\Delta t}\Delta T + \frac{\Delta U}{\Delta x}\Delta x \\ &= MU_t \Delta T + MU_x \Delta x \qquad (3.2)\end{aligned}$$

where MU_i is the marginal utility of good i ($i = T,x$). The total change in utility equals the change in transportation T times the marginal utility of T plus the change in x times the marginal utility of x. If, moreover, we hold utility constant, then $\Delta U = 0$ and (3.2) can be expressed as

$$\begin{aligned}-\frac{\Delta x}{\Delta T} = \frac{MU_T}{MU_x} &= \text{marginal rate of commodity substitution} \\ &= \text{marginal value of } T \text{ (in terms of foregone } x\text{)} \qquad (3.3)\end{aligned}$$

As seen in (3.3), an alternative interpretation of *MRCS* is the marginal value or marginal benefit, expressed as a ratio of marginal utilities, of an additional unit of transportation.

Consider figure 3.2 and assume that John is currently consuming ten units of T and 20 units of x per week. Suppose, in addition, that ten units of T and 20 units of x provide John with the same level of utility as 15 units of T and 15 units of x. Based upon this information, John's preferences are such that he is willing to give up five units of x to get an additional five units of T, holding utility constant. In other words, John's marginal value of one more unit of transportation is

$$-\frac{\Delta x}{\Delta T} = \frac{5}{5} = 1 \qquad (3.4)$$

In figure 3.2, this is seen as a movement from point H to point I. Now suppose that John is consuming 15 units each of T and x and he now moves to point J. In this case, John is willing to give up three units of x to get five more units of T, which implies that his marginal value of T falls to

$$-\frac{\Delta x}{\Delta T} = \frac{3}{5} = 0.6 \qquad (3.5)$$

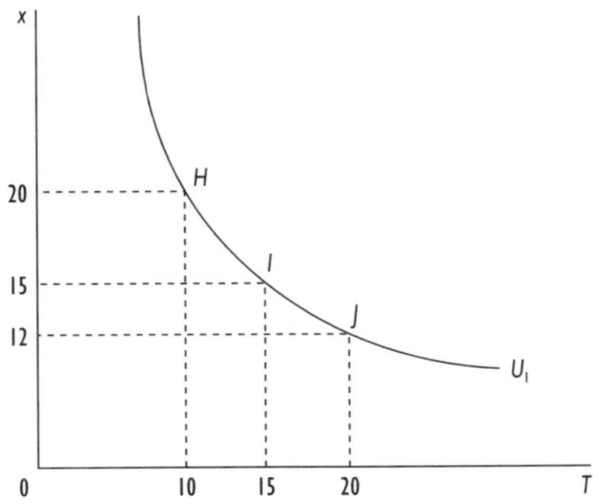

Figure 3.2 The decreasing marginal rate of commodity substitution.

The more transportation John consumes, the smaller the amount of all other goods x he is willing to give up to get an additional unit of T. In other words, additional units of T become *less valuable* the more T John consumes.[4]

BUDGET CONSTRAINT

In addition to its effect upon one's level of economic welfare, an increase in T has another effect. It reduces the availability of resources that can be spent on x. This can be seen from an individual's resource or *budget constraint*:

$$Y = p_T T + p_x x \tag{3.6}$$

Y is the level of income per period, p_T is the per unit price of the transportation good, and p_x is the per unit price of all other goods. Equation (3.6) states that an individual's income per period is the sum of his expenditures on each of the commodities. Figure 3.3 depicts the consumer's budget constraint, where the shaded area corresponds to those combinations of T and x that the consumer *can* afford. Commodity bundles to the right of the budget line are not available to the consumer, given the economic environment. Equation (3.7) gives the budget constraint in slope–intercept form:

$$x = -\frac{p_T}{p_x}T + \frac{Y}{p_x} \tag{3.7}$$

where p_T/p_x, the relative price of T, is the negative slope of the budget line and reflects the opportunity cost of T; that is, the amount of x the consumer *must* sacrifice in order to increase his consumption of T by one unit. Y/p_x is the intercept on the y-axis and represents the purchasing power of income in terms of x. Correspondingly, the intercept on the x-axis is Y/p_T and denotes the purchasing power of income in terms of T.

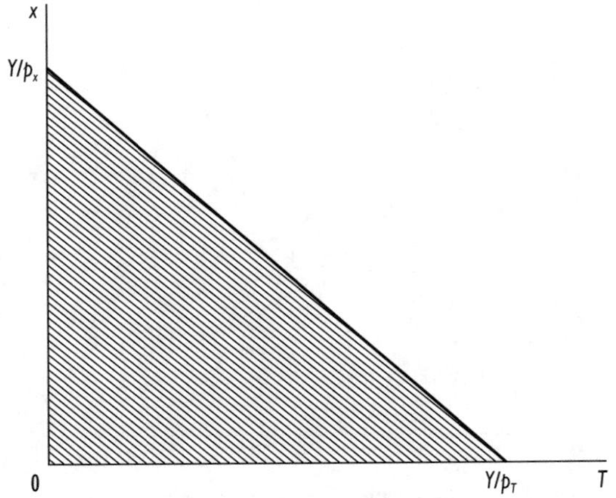

Figure 3.3 The opportunity set over x and T.

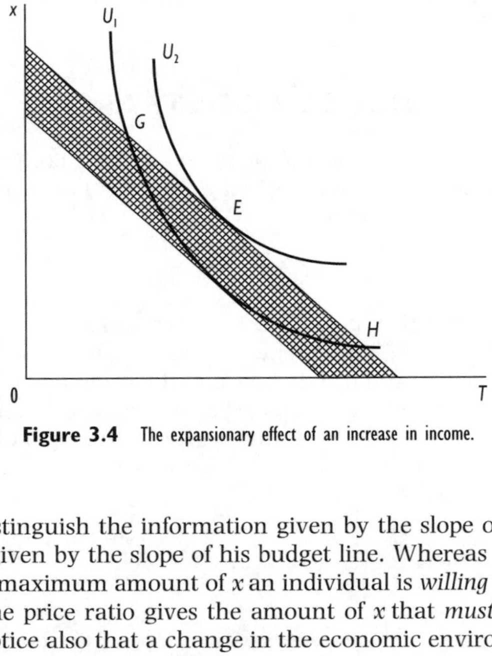

Figure 3.4 The expansionary effect of an increase in income.

It is important to distinguish the information given by the slope of a consumer's indifference curve from that given by the slope of his budget line. Whereas the slope of an indifference curve reflects the maximum amount of x an individual is *willing* to sacrifice to obtain an additional unit of T, the price ratio gives the amount of x that *must* be sacrificed to get an additional unit of T. Notice also that a change in the economic environment will alter the set of commodity bundles that are affordable to the individual. All else constant, increasing a consumer's income per period of time leads to a rightward *parallel* shift in the budget line and expands his choice set. Figure 3.4 illustrates the expansionary effect of increasing consumer income, where the shaded area depicts the set of additional commodity bundles that are now

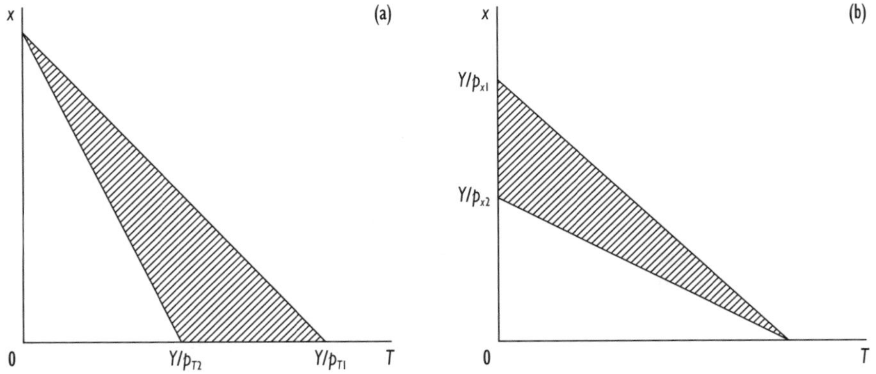

Figure 3.5 The impact on the opportunity set from an increase in the price of (a) T and (b) x.

affordable as a result of the higher income (ignore the indifference curves for the present). Similarly, changes in the price of T or x, all else constant, alter a consumer's choice set. Consider, for example, improvements in transportation technology which lead to lower transportation prices. As seen in figure 3.5(a), this has the effect of pivoting the budget line counterclockwise on the y-axis intercept and shifting the x-axis intercept further to the right. The net result increases the consumer's purchasing power, since more commodity bundles are now affordable by the reduction in transport costs. Figure 3.5(b) illustrates the contractionary effect on a consumer's budget set from an increase in the price of all other goods. In both of these figures, the shaded area depicts the change in purchasing power subsequent to a change in price.

CONSUMER EQUILIBRIUM

A consumer's objective is to select that commodity bundle which maximizes his or her level of economic welfare subject to the constraint on his or her economic resources. The consumer solves this constrained utility maximization problem by consuming levels of T and x such that the slope of the budget line equals the slope of the indifference curve. In other words, the equilibrium condition for the consumer is

$$MRCS = p_T/p_x$$
$$\Rightarrow \text{marginal value of } T = \text{opportunity cost of } T \tag{3.8}$$

A utility-maximizing individual will consume T and x such that the rate at which he or she *is willing* to sacrifice x for another unit of T (that is, $MRCS$) equals the rate at which he or she *must* give up x (in the marketplace) to obtain one more unit of T (that is, the price ratio).

Graphically, the solution is depicted in figure 3.4 as point E, the tangency point between indifference curve 2 and the budget line. All points to the right of the budget line correspond to higher levels of economic welfare that are not attainable with the current budget. On the other hand, there are various combinations of T and x, between points G and H, on indifference curve U_2 that the consumer could purchase. Each of these, however, yields less utility than points on indifference curve U_2.

DEMAND FUNCTIONS

If we consider the consumer's equilibrium depicted in figure 3.4, we see that the optimal consumption bundle depends upon two sets of information: the *economic environment* as defined by the consumer's income Y and the prices of the two goods, p_T and p_x; and the *consumer's tastes and preferences*, denoted by ϕ, which characterize his or her utility function. In general, the solution to a consumer's constrained utility-maximization problem is a set of demand functions that depend upon the prices of goods, individual income, and one's preference structure:

$$\begin{aligned} T^* &= T(p_T, p_x, Y; \phi) \\ x^* &= x(p_T, p_x, Y; \phi) \end{aligned} \tag{3.9}$$

where the asterisks refer to the optimal levels of consumption. Each of these equations simply says that the optimal demand depends, in some way, upon commodity prices, income, and preferences.

EFFECT OF INCOME ON OPTIMAL CONSUMPTION

Recall that an increase in income, holding constant the prices of T and x, expands a consumer's purchasing power by a parallel shift of the budget line to the right. Seeking to maximize utility, a consumer experiencing an increase in income will move to a point on the new budget line which is again just tangent to one of his indifference curves. As depicted in figure 3.6, and given indifference curves U_1 and U_2, the increase in income shifts the budget line from AB to

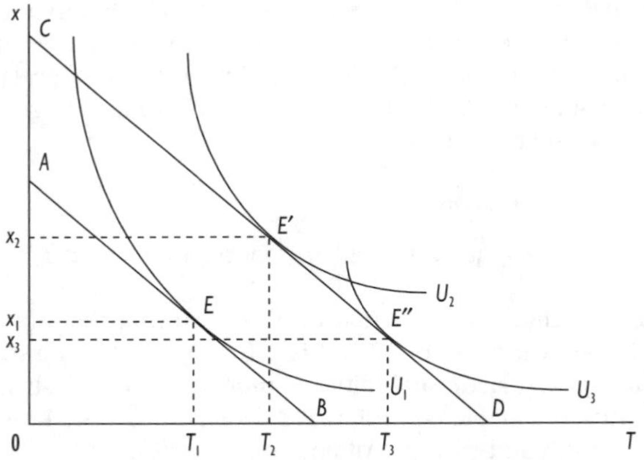

Figure 3.6 The effect of an increase in income on consumption.

CD and the consumer moves from point *E* to point *E′*. Consistent with an expanding set of consumption opportunities afforded by the increase in income, the consumer's level of economic welfare increases. Also, as drawn, the optimal consumption of *T* increases from T_1 to T_2, and the optimal consumption of *x* increases from x_1 to x_2. In this case, both *x* and *T* are referred to as *normal* goods, since an increase in income leads to an increase in the consumption of each good. Alternatively, an *inferior* good is a good whose consumption decreases when there is an increase in income. In figure 3.6, this is illustrated as a move from *E* to point *E″*, which would occur if the higher indifference curve were U_3 instead of U_2. In this case, *T* is a normal good but *x* is an inferior good, since the increase in income causes the consumer to increase his or her consumption of transportation (T_1 to T_3) but lower the consumption of all other goods (x_1 to x_3). It is important to note here that U_2 and U_3 represent *alternative* indifference curve locations resulting from an increase in income. They could not both depict indifference curves for the same individual, since the two curves intersect – and we have previously seen that transitive preferences lead to indifference curves that are parallel.

Demand Curves and Consumption at the Intensive Margin

Holding p_x and *Y* constant, suppose that the price of transportation falls. Then the right-hand side of equation (3.8), p_T/p_x, falls – which implies that the *MRCS* of an additional unit of *T* is greater than the price ratio. In other words, the marginal value that a consumer places upon an additional unit of transportation is now greater than the marginal cost of obtaining one more unit of transportation. In that a consumer's objective is to maximize economic welfare, the reduction in the price of *T* induces the consumer to increase the quantity of *T* purchased.[5] Thus, holding p_x and *Y* constant, we obtain a predicted negative relationship, depicted in figure 3.7, between the quantity of transportation consumed and its price. A decrease in the price of transportation, all else constant, increases the quantity of transportation consumed. Conversely, an increase in p_T reduces the quantity of *T* consumed, all else held constant.

Similarly, if we were to hold p_T and *Y* constant in the demand function for *x*, we would also obtain a downward-sloping demand curve for all other goods, *x*. It is important to understand

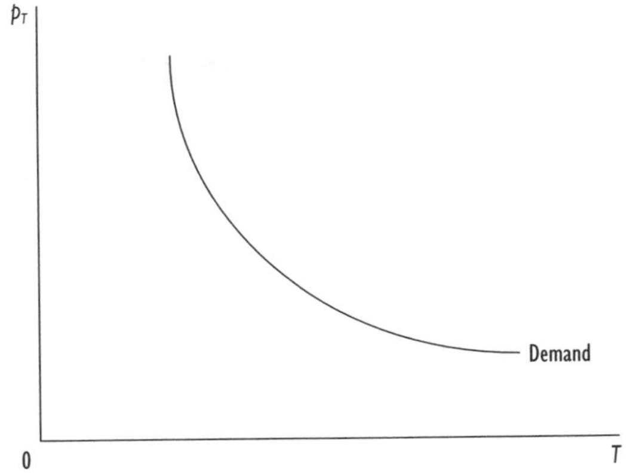

Figure 3.7 The demand curve for *T*.

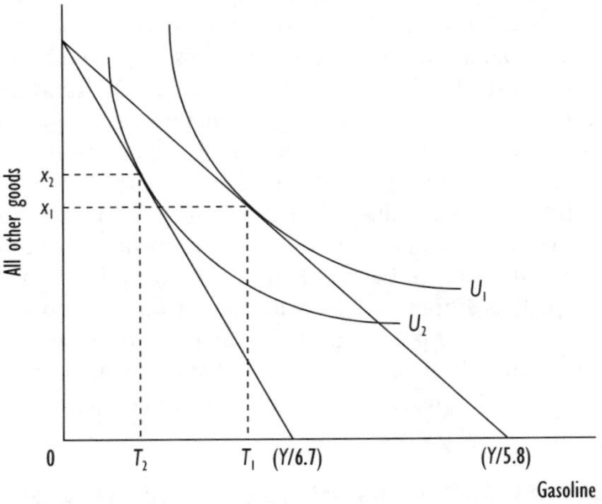

Figure 3.8 The effect of an increase in the price of gasoline on consumption.

that a change in price *does not* induce the consumer to completely forego consumption but, rather, alters the quantity of the good consumed. Consumption, in this case, is said to occur at the *intensive margin*. For a divisible good that is consumed in positive amounts, consumers react to a change in the good's price by continuing to consume the good but altering the quantity consumed.

For example, between 1986 and 1991, the real per-mile cost of motor vehicle gasoline and oil (in 1982–4 dollars) rose from 5.8 to 6.7 cents (US Bureau of the Census, 1993). Depicted in figure 3.8, where T represents gasoline and x all other goods, the real price rise induces car owners to reduce their consumption of gasoline (from T_1 to T_2), use their automobiles less frequently, and increase their consumption of all other goods (from x_1 to x_2). The price rise does not, however, cause consumers to completely abandon the use of their cars and reduce their consumption of gasoline to zero.

MARKET DEMAND FOR TRANSPORTATION

The market demand for transportation is the amount of transportation demanded by all consumers at each price. Recall that the individual demand function for transportation (from equation (3.9)) was expressed as

$$T^* = T(p_T, p_x, Y; \phi)$$

Suppose that there are N consumers in the population. Then the market demand for transportation, D_T, is simply the horizontal summation of individual demands:

$$D_T(p_T, p_x, Y_1, \ldots, Y_N; \phi_1, \ldots, \phi_N) = \sum_{i=1}^{N} T(p_T, p_x, Y_i; \phi_i) \tag{3.10}$$

Similar to individual consumer demands, the market demand for T depends upon the price of transportation and the price of all other goods. However, whereas individual demand is a function of one's income, market demand is a function of *each* consumer's income, which implies that the distribution of income influences the market demand for T. In most empirical studies of market demand, only a measure of aggregate income (which is the sum of individual consumer incomes) is included in the model, because data on the distribution of income is often unavailable. However, if we assume that, for each consumer, an increase in income has the same *marginal effect* upon consumption, then the distribution of income will not affect market demand, and the market demand function becomes

$$D_T = D_T(p_T, p_x, Y^a; \phi_1, \ldots, \phi_N)$$

where Y^a is aggregate income.[6] Finally, and similar to the analysis at the individual level, holding the price of all other goods and aggregate income constant (indicated by a bar ($^-$) over the relevant term) gives the market demand for transportation as a function of its price. The market demand for transportation becomes

$$D_T(p_T) = D_T(p_T, \bar{p}_x, \bar{Y}^a; \phi_1, \ldots, \phi_N) \tag{3.11}$$

which leads to the familiar downward-sloping market demand curve for transportation, depicted in figure 3.9(a).[7]

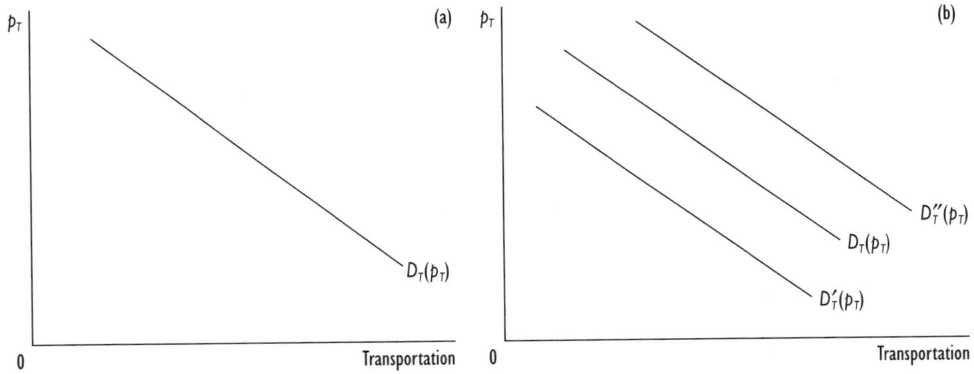

Figure 3.9 Change in quantity demanded versus change in demand.

Increase in Demand from $D_T(p_T)$ to $D''_T(p_T)$ Due to:	Decrease in Demand from $D_T(p_T)$ to $D'_T(p_T)$ Due to:
Increase in income	Decrease in income
Increase in population	Decrease in population
Decrease in price of complements	Increase in price of complements
Increase in price of substitutes	Decrease in price of substitutes
Decrease in taxes on T	Increase in taxes on T
Increase in preferences for T	Decrease in preferences for T

CHANGES IN MARKET DEMAND

From equation (3.10), the location of the demand curve for transportation depends upon the price of all other goods, aggregate income, the number of consumers, and preferences of consumers. Also, the prices of many commodities, including transportation services, include one or more taxes. A change in any or all of these factors will alter the *location* of the demand curve. For example, suppose that a population boom increases the number of transportation consumers from N to N', where $N' > N$. Since the summation in (3.10) is now over a larger number of individuals, the market demand curve for transportation shifts to the right (all else held constant). Similarly, if transportation is a normal good, an increase in income shifts the market demand for transportation to the right, all else constant; alternatively, if T is an inferior good, an increase in income would shift the market demand for transportation to the left.

Suppose that an increase in the price of all other goods *increases* the demand for transportation. In this case, transportation and all other goods are said to be *substitutes in consumption* and the increase in p_x shifts the market demand curve for transportation to the right. Alternatively, assume there are three commodities: automobile trips, gasoline, and all other goods. If an increase in the price of gasoline *decreases* the consumption of automobile trips, then gasoline and automobile trips are said to be *complements in consumption*. In this case, an increase in the price of gasoline shifts the market demand curve for automobile trips to the left.[8]

Finally, a change in preferences toward transportation, all else constant, shifts the market demand for T to the right, whereas a change in preferences toward all other goods shifts the market demand for T to the left. The effects of these changes on the market demand for transportation are illustrated in figure 3.9(b).

DEMAND FOR TRANSPORTATION – ESTIMATION

INDIVIDUAL DEMAND FOR TRANSPORTATION – IDENTICAL CONSUMERS

Although the divisibility of a good is unimportant in defining demand, it turns out to be very important when we collect data and try to empirically identify the demand for transportation. Let's examine how we would go about estimating demand in the continuous consumption good case. For this, we'll make the following simplifying assumptions:

- all individuals are identical with regard to their preferences
- all individuals receive the same income Y
- all individuals face the same level of prices for T and x
- individuals have identical socioeconomic characteristics
- T and x are divisible goods

Figure 3.10 characterizes the equilibrium consumption of each good for the "typical" consumer. Given that all individuals are identical in all respects, our model predicts that each individual consumes T^* units of T and x^* units of x. In actuality, the model is not able to

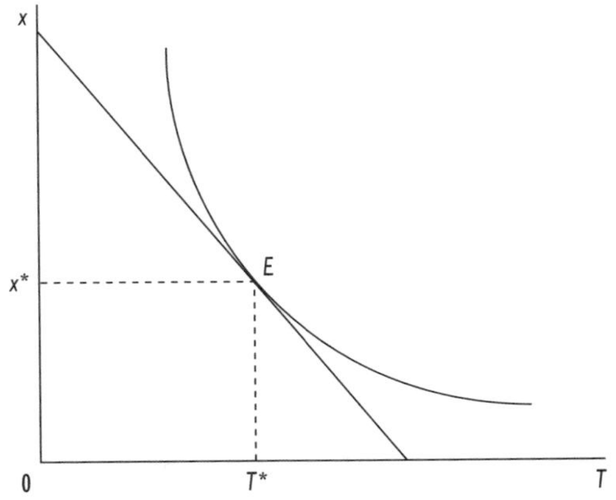

Figure 3.10 Equilibrium consumption for the typical consumer.

precisely predict individual consumption levels. There are observation errors which represent differences between observed and predicted consumption. In general, observation errors arise from three sources: measurement error, optimization error, and varying tastes.

Measurement error reflects the fact that the model does not attempt to identify all factors that influence one's travel behavior, but only the most important determinants. If, for example, cost per mile is the most important variable determining the number of miles traveled per week, predicted mileage will differ from observed mileage when events occur that are not explicitly included in the model, such as additional trips to the grocery store when unexpected guests arrive. Measurement error also includes difficulties that an analyst may encounter in accurately measuring the relevant variables. This may be due to incorrect coding of data, incorrect reporting of data by a respondent, or faulty transmission of the data from one medium (book) to another (a computer file).

Optimization error, on the other hand, reflects mistakes, due for example to incomplete information, that individuals make in their consumption decisions. For example, recognizing that a trip to Chicago to watch the Chicago Bears play the Minnesota Vikings will cost $20.00 and take 2 hours, an individual makes the trip. Halfway to Chicago the driver encounters severe rainstorms, which add 2 hours to his trip time. Had the driver been aware of the impending inclement weather, he would have canceled the trip. *Ex post*, the trip would not have been made. *Ex ante*, however, the individual's decision was rational because the expected benefits of the trip, based upon the available information, exceeded the trip's expected costs. In this example, optimization errors are only errors *ex post*.

Even in the presence of full information, however, individuals may make mistakes. An example of *ex ante* optimization error occurs in the field of highway safety. Because the probability of a highway fatality is so low, on the order of 2.5 fatalities per 100 million vehicle–miles traveled or a probability of 0.000000025 per mile, individuals may systematically underestimate the risk effects of alternative actions. For example, recognizing that the probability of a fatality is so low, an individual decides against wearing a seat belt because he or she considers the marginal life-saving effect to be virtually nil. Alternatively, everyone

Table 3.1 Hypothetical travel for a population of five consumers

Individual	Weekly Miles Predicted	Weekly Miles Traveled	Error	Percentage Error
1	100	115	15	15
2	100	91	−9	−9
3	100	107	7	7
4	100	94	−6	−6
5	100	93	−7	−7

recognizes the potential life-stilling effect of drinking and driving. Yet, although one may know that the probability of a highway fatality would double, to 0.00000005 per mile, after two drinks, the absolute probability level is so small as to be ignored.

Last, taste variation reflects different preferences among consumers for the underlying commodities. If consumers in the population have widely different preferences for the goods, then observed demands will dramatically differ from predicted demands. The common procedure in empirical analyses is to assume that differences in preferences introduce at most minor variations between observed and predicted demands. This is a reasonable assumption for two reasons. First, if individuals are homogenous with respect to income and socioeconomic characteristics, it is reasonable to assume that they will have similar, if not identical, preferences. Variations between observed and predicted demands will be small relative to differences caused by observation or measurement errors. Second, since we are oftentimes interested in consumer sensitivity to changes in the economic environment, differences in preferences are likely to play a small role in explaining consumer responses to changes in prices or income because consumption occurs at the intensive margin. Changes in the economic environment, through their effects on incomes or price ratios, lead to marginal – that is, relatively small – changes in consumption. Individuals respond by consuming a bit more or a bit less of the good. Observed variations in consumption, then, are assumed to reflect observed variations in the economic environment rather than unobserved differences in consumers' preferences.

In order to incorporate the difference between observed and predicted demands, we specify *observed consumer demands* for T and x as

$$T^{o} = T(p_T,p_x,Y;\phi) + \varepsilon_t = T^* + \varepsilon_T$$
$$x^{o} = x(p_T,p_x,Y;\phi) + \varepsilon_x = x^* + \varepsilon_x \qquad (3.12)$$

where the superscript o denotes "observed" and ε_i $(i = T,x)$ is an error term. If we maintain the assumption that consumers have identical tastes and further assume that observed demands are distributed *randomly* about their predicted (optimal) values, then the sole cause of observation errors are measurement/optimization errors.[9]

In general, our empirical model is expected to characterize average consumer behavior. Consider the data in table 3.1. Predicted and observed weekly travel information on five individuals is listed. Given our assumptions that all individuals face the same economic environment and have identical preferences, each traveler is *predicted* to travel 100 miles per week.

However, the *observed* amount of travel for each of the five individuals differs from that predicted. Individual 1 travels 15 miles more than that predicted, whereas individual 2 travels 5 miles less. There are three important features to note from the data in table 3.1. First, as a proportion of total miles traveled, the errors are relatively small, ranging from a low of –6% to a high of 15%. This implies that the underlying model has identified the most important determinants of weekly travel. Second, the errors are both positive and negative, which indicates that the model is not consistently over- or under-predicting travel behavior. Third, and most important, the total error for the group of five travelers is zero. From the weekly miles actually traveled, the average mileage is 100, which equals the predicted mileage. This is what is meant by saying that the errors are random about their predicted values. For this group of travelers, the positive errors offset the negative errors, so that the average miles traveled equal the predicted miles.

DEMAND FOR TRANSPORTATION – NONIDENTICAL CONSUMERS

It was assumed above that all consumers were identical with respect to incomes received, prices faced, socioeconomic characteristics, and preferences for the commodities. In reality, when data are collected, incomes, the price of transportation, and socioeconomic characteristics all vary by consumer.[10] This has two implications. First, the predicted value of T, T^*, for each consumer differs, because each individual faces a different economic environment and (potentially) has different preferences for transportation. Second, it is expressly this difference across observations that permits the analyst to estimate consumers' sensitivities to changes in the economic environment and, to a limited degree, identify preference differences across consumers.

To see this, assume that transportation consumption data are collected from a group of N individuals and that the demand for transportation given in (3.12) is a linear function of p_T, p_x, Y, and socioeconomic characteristic S_i:

$$T_i^o = t(p_{Ti}, p_{xi}, Y_i; \phi_i) + \varepsilon_{ti} = \beta_0 + \beta_1 p_{Ti} + \beta_2 p_{xi} + \beta_3 Y_i + \beta_4 S_i + \varepsilon_i, \qquad i = 1, \ldots, N \quad (3.13)$$

where T_i^o is the observed amount of travel for individual i, p_{Ti} is the price of travel for individual i, p_{xi} is the price of all other goods for individual i, Y_i is consumer i's income, S_i is a socioeconomic characteristic (for example, age of consumer, size of consumer's household) for individual i, and ε_{ti} is consumer i's error term. Although socioeconomic characteristics (other than income) were not explicitly included in T's demand function, $t(p_T, p_x, Y; \phi)$, these are generally correlated with one's unobserved preferences for goods, ϕ. Thus, differences in socioeconomic and demographic characteristics *among* consumers are assumed to capture substantive differences in preferences which consumers have for their consumption commodities. β_i ($i = 1, \ldots, 4$) are parameters to be estimated that will enable the analyst to *quantitatively* characterize average transportation demand for this group of individuals.

To summarize, if observation errors are random and substantive differences in tastes are reflected by socioeconomic characteristics, then the standard theory of consumer behavior provides a good description of consumption activities, and all deviations between observed and predicted demands are due to random measurement/optimization errors.

MARKET DEMAND FOR TRANSPORTATION

At the aggregate level, variations in market demand are mirror images of variations that occur at the individual level. As the price of transportation increases, each individual consumes a little less transportation, which results in a small decrease in the market demand for travel. Since individuals are consuming at the intensive margin, variations in market demands are also occurring at the intensive margin. Moreover, since the market demand for a good depends upon the distribution of underlying preferences ϕ_i $(i = 1, \ldots, N)$ across consumers, we assume, as in the individual case, that any important differences will be captured by socioeconomic and demographic variables. Thus, when analyzing market demands for continuous goods, it is reasonable to assume that observation errors are primarily the result of measurement/optimization errors.

In the following sections, we will illustrate these concepts and issues by analyzing the demands that consumers have for three important travel decisions: automobile use, urban transit use, and intercity airline travel.

CASE STUDY – THE DEMAND FOR GASOLINE, REGULATION, AND AUTOMOBILE TRAVEL

However one measures mobility, motor vehicle travel in privately owned vehicles is the predominant mode for intracity and intercity travel in the United States. 94% of all motor vehicle trips in 1990 were taken in private transportation, 2.2% on public transportation modes, and 3.8% by all other means. In 1991, automobile passenger miles totaled 1,623 billion, representing 80.7% of total intercity travel, and the motoring public consumed 1.75 billion barrels of petroleum, accounting for 45.7% of all petroleum consumption.[11]

Given the dominance of motor vehicle travel in the USA, are consumers sensitive to changes in its price? In the 1993 national budget discussions, there was considerable interest in raising the gasoline tax, both for its effect on deficit reduction and for its potential in reducing urban congestion and pollution through its impact upon automobile travel. Part of the input that goes into any policy discussion of increased gasoline taxes is the likely effects of raising the tax on the demand for gasoline. Holding all else constant, an increase in the federal gasoline tax is expected to reduce the quantity of gasoline consumed. But by how much? Is the demand for gasoline price elastic or price inelastic?

A related question concerns governmental policy that alters the manner in which gasoline is allocated. During the 1970s, the USA suffered through two energy crises, the first occurring in late 1973 and early 1974 when OPEC restricted exports due to the Arab–Israeli war. The Iranian revolution in 1979 produced a second crisis, as Iran's output fell to virtually zero in 1980. Of particular interest is the fact that during the early part of the 1970s, President Nixon imposed economy-wide price controls in an effort to control inflation. Although most of these controls were gone by the mid-1970s, price controls on oil were still in effect. This raises an important question. Because price controls prevent the monetary price of gasoline from rising, what impact did the price controls have on the opportunity cost of gasoline when the 1973–4 oil crisis hit?

To answer this, the demand for gasoline must be estimated. In a study on monthly gasoline demands and automobile travel in California, Lee (1980) assumed the market demand for gasoline in California, G_t, to be

$$G_t = f(\text{Real Gas Price, Real Personal Income, Population, Season, Gasoline Crisis}) \tag{3.14}$$

G_t is the average daily demand for gasoline in month t, and is hypothesized to depend on the real price of gasoline (Real Gas Price), real income (Real Personal Income), the number of persons in the state (Population), the time of year (Season) which reflects seasonal variations in demand, and the gasoline crisis.

A brief digression on real versus nominal prices

Because our data is a time series, it is important to notice in (3.14) that demand is assumed to depend upon "real" gasoline price and "real" income. This is to be contrasted with price and income, which are expressed in "nominal" terms. Whereas nominal prices are prices that are quoted in current dollars, real prices are quoted in "constant" or "inflation-adjusted" dollars. Why is it important to use real prices and income in time series analyses? The reason is that our consumption decisions depend upon our level of purchasing power and the *relative* prices of goods. If a 10% increase in one's income is accompanied by a 10% increase in all prices, one's purchasing power over goods and services *has not changed*. Similarly, if the prices of all goods increase by 10%, relative prices have not changed and a person's consumption of different goods will not change.

Suppose that the price of gasoline was $1.10 per gallon in 1993 and $1.155 per gallon in 1994, which implies that the price of gasoline increased by 5% between the two years. Does this represent a 5% increase in the real price of gasoline – that is, the price of gasoline *relative to the price of all other goods*? It does not if there was a general rise in all prices between 1993 and 1994. If price-level inflation in the economy was 3% between 1993 and 1994, then the real price of gasoline, expressed in constant or inflation-adjusted 1993 prices, did not rise by 5% but by a much lower 1.9%.

To see this, suppose that we arbitrarily define a price index for all goods in the economy and set this index to 100 in 1993.[12] With a 3% inflation rate, the value of this price index in 1994 would be 103 (100×1.03). In order to convert the 1994 nominal gasoline price to a 1993 constant or inflation-adjusted price, we calculate the following product:

$$\text{1994 real gas price} = (\text{1994 nominal gas price})\ \frac{\text{1993 price index}}{\text{1994 price index}}$$

$$= \$1.155\left(\frac{100}{103}\right) = \$1.121$$

which represents a $(1.121 - 1.10)/1.10 = 1.9\%$ real increase in the price of gasoline. Economic theory predicts that, all else constant, the 1.9% rise in the real price of gasoline will reduce the quantity demanded. Alternatively, if the inflation rate between 1993 and 1994 was 5%, then from the above formula, the 1994 real gas price would be 1.155 (100/105) = $1.10. As expected, there is no change in the real price of gasoline in 1994 and, all else constant, we would expect to see no change in the quantity of gasoline demanded.

For time series analyses, it is important that all prices and income be converted to constant or real dollars in order to measure the actual change in relative prices or purchasing power that has occurred over time.

The demand for gasoline in California

In order to quantitatively estimate California's market demand for gasoline, Lee expressed observed average daily demands per month, G_t^o (thousands of gallons), as a linear function of the Real Gas Price (1967 dollars per gallon) in month t, Real Personal Income (billions of 1967 dollars) in month t, population (millions) in month t, 11 seasonal variables S_{ti} which reflect the month during which travel occurred, five gasoline crisis variables, and an error term.[13] Specifically,

$$G_t^o = \beta_0 + \beta_1(\text{Real Gas Price})_t + \beta_2(\text{Real Income})_t + \beta_3(\text{Population})_t + \sum_{i=1}^{11} \psi_i S_{ti} + \tau_1 \text{DEC73} + \tau_2 \text{JAN74} + \tau_3 \text{FEB74} + \tau_4 \text{MAR74} + \tau_5 \text{APR74} + \varepsilon_t \quad (3.15)$$

where ε_t is a random error term for month t. The relevant hypotheses for this equation are given below.

The five gasoline-crisis variables are dummy variables for each of the months, December 1973 through April 1974, during which the crisis was expected to affect gasoline consumption. For example, DEC73 = 1 if the observation is December 1973; otherwise, it has a value of zero. Similarly, APR74 = 1 if the observation occurred in April 1974 and zero otherwise. The other three gasoline-crisis variables have analogous interpretations. If each of the gasoline-crisis variables is zero, then the observation is for a nongasoline-crisis month.

Hypotheses

HYPOTHESIS 1 According to the law of demand, an increase in the opportunity cost of gasoline decreases the quantity of gasoline demanded, all else constant. The opportunity cost (*OPC*) of gasoline is made up of two costs – the real retail price of gasoline (*RPG*) and the time cost of queuing up for purchasing the gas (*QC*):

$$\text{Opportunity Costs} = \text{Real Gas Price} + \text{Queuing Costs}$$

In the absence of gasoline rationing, we can assume that queuing costs are negligible, implying that $QC = 0$ and the opportunity cost of gasoline is simply the real price paid at the pump. By the law of demand, then, β_1 is expected to be negative.

HYPOTHESIS 2 In late 1973 and early 1974, the combined effect of a reduced supply of Mideast oil and US price controls on the retail price of gasoline resulted in significant queues at gasoline stations. Through its effect upon the time costs of purchasing gasoline, the gasoline crisis raised the opportunity cost of gasoline to consumers. Thus, assuming that gasoline rationing significantly increased queuing costs from December 1973 through April 1974, it is expected that τ_i $(i = 1, \ldots, 5) < 0$. Our second hypothesis is that each of the gasoline-crisis variables reduces the consumption of gasoline, all else held constant.

HYPOTHESIS 3 Further insights on the crisis-induced queuing costs can be obtained from equation (3.15). The effect of an increase in the real price of gasoline during a noncrisis month is β_1. In contrast, the effect of an increase in the price of gasoline during a crisis month, December 1973 for example, is

$$\beta_1(\text{Real Gas Price})_{\text{DEC73}} + \beta_1(\text{Queuing Costs})_{\text{DEC73}}$$

where an increase in *RPG* is assumed to have the same marginal effect on quantity demanded as an increase in *QC*. Although we do not have information on queuing costs, Lee hypothesized that ration-induced queuing did occur in December 1973 which, by raising time costs, increased the opportunity cost of gasoline and reduced the quantity demanded. From this information, it is thus possible to estimate the effect on queuing costs due to the gasoline crisis in December 1973. In particular, the effect on gasoline demands due to the crisis can be expressed as the product of two effects – the impact of the crisis on queuing costs multiplied by the effect of an increase in queuing costs on gasoline demands:

$$\frac{\Delta G_t}{\Delta \text{Crisis}} = \frac{\Delta G_t}{\Delta QC} \frac{\Delta QC}{\Delta \text{Crisis}}$$

which implies

$$\tau_1 = \beta_1 \frac{\Delta QC}{\Delta \text{Crisis}}$$

Rearranging this last equation gives

$$\frac{\Delta QC}{\Delta \text{Crisis}} = \frac{\tau_1}{\beta_1} = \text{estimated gasoline crisis queuing cost effect per gallon for December 1973} \quad (3.16)$$

In other words, the estimated queuing cost associated with each month of the crisis is given by the ratio of two estimated parameters from the regression equation, τ_i/β_1 ($i = 1, \ldots, 5$). Since, from the law of demand, β_1 and τ_i ($i = 1, \ldots, 5$) are expected to be negative, their ratio is expected to be positive. Our third hypothesis, which follows as a corollary to hypotheses 1 and 2, is that the estimated effect of the gasoline crisis on the opportunity cost of gasoline is positive.

HYPOTHESIS 4 If gasoline is a normal good, an increase in real income, all else constant, is expected to increase the consumption of gasoline. That is, the demand curve for gasoline will shift to the right. This hypothesis is equivalent to the statement that $\beta_2 > 0$.

HYPOTHESIS 5 Since the market demand for gasoline is the summation of individual consumer demands, an increase in population is expected, all else constant, to shift the demand curve for gasoline to the right, which is equivalent to the statement that $\beta_3 > 0$.

Estimation results

The parameters of this model, β_i ($i = 0, \ldots, 3$), ψ_i ($i = 1, \ldots, 11$), and τ_i ($i = 1, \ldots, 5$) were estimated on monthly data from January 1970 through December 1975, a total of 72 observations. Table 3.2 summarizes the estimation results for this model.

First, notice from the reported R^2 in table 3.2 that the model fits the data well. 92% of the variation in gasoline demand is explained by the variables included in the model. In addition, the *t*-statistics for each of the variables except APR74 are significantly different from zero. This indicates that, excepting APR74, each of the variables in table 3.2 is an important determinant of gasoline demands in California during the five-year period.

Table 3.2 The demand for gasoline, 1970–5

Dependent variable – average daily consumption of gasoline per month ('000s)

Explanatory Variable	Coefficient Estimate	*t*-statistic
Constant	−25,193.1	−3.38
Real Gasoline Price ($)	−18,552.8	−5.34
Real Income (billion $)	277.3	6.29
Population (millions)	1,567.9	2.92
DEC73	−1,801.5	−2.84
JAN74	−1,629.7	−2.57
FEB74	−2,313.1	−3.60
MAR74	−2,524.1	−3.88
APR74	162.7	0.25

$R^2 = 0.92$

Source: Lee (1980), table 2, p. 40. Lee did not report the coefficient estimates for the seasonal dummy variables

The demand curve for gasoline

The demand curve for gasoline is a relationship between the consumption of gasoline and the real retail price of gasoline, holding all else constant. The coefficient for Real Gasoline Price is −18,552.8, which gives us both qualitative and quantitative information. First, the sign of the estimated coefficient is negative, which is consistent with our underlying theory of consumer behavior as embodied in the law of demand and hypothesis 1. An increase in the real price, all else constant, reduces quantity demanded. Moreover, since the *t*-statistic for price is well above 2 (in absolute value), we can be confident that, in a statistical sense, the estimated coefficient is not equal to zero. Alternatively, we can use the results presented in table 3.2 to construct a 95% confidence interval for β. Recalling that the *t*-statistic is the coefficient estimate divided by the standard error of the estimate, we have $s_{\hat{\beta}} = (-18{,}552.8/-5.34) = 3{,}474.3$. With this information, the 95% confidence interval for β is (−25,852.3, −11,253.3).[14] As you can see, the estimated value for β_1 falls comfortably in this interval, which again assures us that β is significantly different from zero.

Quantitatively, the value of the coefficient tells us the change in thousands of gallons demanded per day when the monthly real price of gasoline increases $1. For California motorists, a $1 increase in the real price of gasoline decreases the average daily quantity of gasoline demanded by over 18 million gallons, less than one day's average consumption of gasoline. In addition to the effect of an increase in the real retail price of gasoline on quantity demanded, we argued above in hypothesis 2 that, by raising the time cost of purchasing gasoline, the gasoline crisis increased the opportunity cost of gasoline. As a result, the quantity demanded would be expected to fall. Are the results consistent with this hypothesis? From table 3.2, the answer is yes. In four of the five months representing the gasoline crisis, the estimated coefficient is both negative and significantly different from zero. Because of the increased time costs brought on by the gasoline crisis, average daily consumption of gasoline fell 1.8 million gallons in December 1973, 1.6 million in January 1974, 2.3 million in February 1974, and 2.5 million in March 1974. The crisis was not an important factor in April 1974. Although its coefficient estimate is positive, the *t*-statistic is well below 1.0, indicating that we cannot reject the null hypothesis that this coefficient is equal to zero. Thus, the April results imply that the queues were becoming shorter and that the crisis was ending.

Given that average daily consumption was approximately 25 million gallons, the results indicate that in March 1974, the gasoline crisis resulted in a 10% reduction in gasoline consumption.

Change in the demand for gasoline

Whereas the demand curve gives a relationship between quantity demanded and price, a movement along the demand curve, changes in nonprice determinants of demand shift the location of the demand curve.

Hypothesis 4 postulated that gasoline is a normal good, whose consumption increases with an increase in real income. The results in table 3.2 confirm the hypothesis. A 1 billion dollar increase in real personal income leads to a 277,000 gallon increase in average daily gasoline consumption. In order words, the per day demand curve for gasoline shifts rightward by 277,000 gallons. Similarly, a 1 million person increase in population shifts the demand curve rightward, increasing average daily consumption over 1.567 million gallons. Another way of interpreting this result is that an additional person increases daily demand by a bit more than one and a half gallons per day, which certainly seems plausible.

Price and income elasticities

The price elasticity of the demand for gasoline consumption gives the percentage change in quantity demanded resulting from a 1% increase in the real price of gasoline, and is defined as

$$\frac{\Delta G/G}{\Delta RPG/RPG} = \frac{\Delta G}{\Delta RPG}\frac{RPG}{G} = \beta_1\frac{RPG}{G}$$

for the linear model. Replacing β_1 with 18,552.8 from table 3.2 and *RPG* and *G* with their respective sample means, $\overline{RPG}$ and $\overline{G}$, Lee calculated the gasoline price elasticity of demand to be –0.216. A 1% increase in the real retail price of gasoline decreases the average daily consumption of gasoline by 0.216%. Alternatively, a 10% increase in the real retail price decreases the quantity demanded by 2.16%. Also, since $-1 < -0.216 < 0$, the demand for gasoline is price inelastic, which implies that an increase in the price of gasoline will increase consumer expenditures upon gasoline.[15]

Because the data are a monthly time series covering a five-year period, the price elasticity of demand measures the *short-run* response to changing prices. Over a longer period of time, people have a greater opportunity to adjust to higher prices by purchasing more fuel-efficient vehicles, taking trips that require less fuel inputs, and so forth. As predicted by economic theory, *long-run* measures of the gasoline price elasticity of demand are considerably higher and have been estimated to lie in the –0.8 range.

Employing a similar procedure, the income elasticity of the demand for gasoline was calculated to be 0.876. Gasoline is a normal good and a 10% increase in real personal income increases the consumption of gasoline by 8.76%.

Queuing cost premia

What was the order of magnitude of the queuing costs associated with the gasoline crisis? From equation (3.16), an estimate of the queuing prices for each month of the crisis (December 1973 through April 1974) can be obtained by dividing the month's coefficient, τ_i ($i = 1, \ldots, 5$) by β_1. Table 3.3 reports these estimates, all of which are positive and consistent with hypothesis 3. The queuing costs represent a significant portion of the total opportunity cost of gasoline during the crisis and were highest during the peak of the crisis in February–March 1974. Between December 1973 and March 1974, estimated queuing costs made up 30–37% of the monetary price of gasoline.

Table 3.3 Monetary and time prices of gasoline (cents, 1967 dollars)[a]

	December 1973	January 1974	February 1974	March 1974	April 1974[b]
Monetary price	31.3	32.4	32.6	35.7	36.7
Time price	9.7	8.8	12.5	13.4	–
Opportunity cost	41.0	41.2	45.1	49.1	36.7

[a] The monetary prices reported represent the average real price of gasoline for the respective month.
[b] A time price for April 1974 was not calculated because the price shock coefficient for this month was not significantly different from zero.
Source: Lee (1980), table 4, p. 41

The demand for trips

In addition to estimating the demand for gasoline, Lee also estimated the demand for trips, TT, defined as the average number of daily trips during a month. Table 3.4 presents these estimation results, which are seen to mirror the results in table 3.2.

The R^2 statistic indicates that the explanatory variables explain 97% of the variation in the average daily demand for trips. In addition, with respect to the real retail gasoline price, real personal income, and population, the signs on the coefficients are consistent with that predicted from economic theory, and the values of the *t*-statistics for these variables provide strong evidence that these coefficients are, in a statistical sense, significantly different from zero.

The coefficient for the real retail price of gasoline indicates that, all else constant, a $1 increase in the real price will produce 370 million fewer trips demanded. On the other hand, a 1 billion dollar increase in real personal income will create over 4.5 million additional daily trips and a 1 million person increase in the population will add 65.6 million trips to average daily traffic.

The price and income elasticities with respect to the demand for trips were calculated in the same manner as discussed above and were found to be very close to those calculated for gasoline demands. In particular, a 1% increase in the real retail price of gasoline decreases the quantity of trips demanded by 0.236%; and a 1% increase in real personal income was found to increase the demand for trips by 0.792%.

It is also seen in table 3.4 that the gasoline crisis had an impact on the number of trips taken that is similar to its impact on the demand for gasoline. In table 3.2, all but one of the gasoline-crisis variables were significantly different from zero, indicating that the gasoline crisis imposed significant costs on gasoline consumers. In table 3.4, however, the *t*-statistics for DEC73, JAN74, and APR74 could not reject the null hypothesis that the estimated coefficients for these variables were not different from zero.[16] Strong gasoline-crisis effects were obtained in the months of February and March 1974. The costs imposed on consumers from the rationing program led to 51,000 fewer trips in February and 87,000 fewer trips in March. Finally, and consistent with the results in table 3.2, the *t*-statistic associated with the coefficient for APR74 was very small, which suggests that the crisis ended in April 1974.

Table 3.4 The demand for automobile trips, 1970–5

Dependent variable – average daily trips during each month ('000s)

Explanatory Variable	Coefficient Estimate	*t*-statistic
Constant	−1,211,080	−7.51
Real Gasoline Price ($)	−370,235	−4.93
Real Income (billion $)	4,578.8	4.80
Population (millions)	65,660.1	5.66
DEC73	−20,744.1	−1.51
JAN74	−20,841.2	−1.52
FEB74	−51,063.3	−3.68
MAR74	−87,070.6	−6.19
APR74	−6,221.3	−0.44
$R^2 = 0.97$		

Source: Lee (1980), table 2, p. 40. Although estimated, Lee did not report the coefficient estimates for the seasonal dummy variables

Why would the gasoline crisis have a larger effect upon the demand for gasoline than the demand for trips? Consider a typical commuter who travels 20 round-trip miles per day in her work trip. Assume that public transit is not available and, moreover, that her only weekday trips are those to work. In the short run, a dramatic increase in the price of gasoline will have no effect upon her daily commuting trips, since she must get to work. In this extreme case, the price elasticity of the demand for trips is zero! Is this also true for her demand for gasoline? No. Even in the very short run, there are gasoline-saving options for this commuter. She can reduce the amount of time she lets her car idle to warm up, drive at lower speeds, take alternative routes that require less fuel, and carpool to work with other colleagues.

In general, then, we would expect her demand for trips to be less responsive to gasoline price increases than her demand for gasoline because, in the short run, there are more substitution opportunities for reducing fuel than for reducing the number of trips.

The 1993 gasoline tax increase

Returning to the question posed at the beginning of this section, what was the likely impact of President Clinton's increase in the gasoline tax. According to the 1993 Deficit Reduction Bill, passed in late 1993, the federal gasoline tax increased by 4.3 cents per gallon. With an average per gallon price equal to $1.06, this represents an approximate 4% increase in the 1993 real price of gasoline. The above results found that gasoline has a price elasticity of demand equal to −0.216 and that the elasticity of the demand for trips with respect to the price of gasoline equaled −0.236. Assuming that these elasticities are representative of the market for gasoline and automobile trips, the 4% hike in the real price of gasoline due to the increase in the federal gasoline tax can be expected to have reduced the quantity of gasoline demanded by 0.86% and average daily trips by 0.94%. At the national level, this translates into a 1.74 million gallon daily reduction in the demand for gasoline and 5.68 million fewer automobile trips per day.

Comments

It might be noted that a potential deficiency of the models reported in tables 3.2 and 3.4 is the lack of information on relevant alternatives. Economic theory tells us that the demand for any commodity, including gasoline and automobile trips, depends not only upon its own price but also upon the price(s) of close substitutes and alternatives. Is this important? – possibly, but not necessarily. In both the demand for gasoline and the demand for automobile trips, the price included in the equations was the real price of gasoline, which reflects the monetary price of gasoline divided by the consumer price index. Since there are relatively few close substitutes or complements to gasoline, and given that movements in the consumer price index reflect movements in the prices of all commodities, including those that are close substitutes or complements, excluding their prices will likely not have a major effect on the estimation results for gasoline. Although, by a similar argument, movements in the consumer price index also reflect changes in the prices of nonautomobile trips, excluding the prices of these alternatives prevents one from estimating cross-price elasticities. In other words, from the results presented in table 3.4, it is not possible to identify the effect that increases in the cost of bus, airline, or rail travel have upon the demand for automobile trips. As will be seen in the following sections, as well as in the next chapter, travel on one mode is sensitive to the prices charged on alternative modes.

CASE STUDY – THE DEMAND FOR URBAN RAIL RAPID TRANSIT

The previous section analyzed the demand for gasoline, identified the quantitative effects of gasoline rationing upon price and output, and used these results to predict the impact that the recent 4.3 cent increase in the federal gasoline tax would have upon the consumption of gasoline and consumer tripmaking activities. Since the focus was specifically upon automobile travel, it was not possible to identify whether the proposed increase would have any effect upon urban transit trips.

In this section, we examine the demand for heavy rail urban transit. Heavy rail public transit systems are high-speed electric railways that carry high traffic volumes on multi-car trains, and have separate rights of way, sophisticated signaling systems, and rapid acceleration capabilities. Table 3.5 identifies existing fixed rail systems in the USA and their 1991 passenger loads: we can see that heavy rail plays a major role in urban mass transit. There are currently heavy transit systems in 11 of our nation's largest cities and their market share ranges from a low of 9.6% in Cleveland to a high of 61.3% in New York.[17] In 1991, heavy transit was responsible for 2.16 billion trips, 25% of all public transit trips, and 10.5 billion passenger–miles. An advantage of high-speed rail over conventional bus systems is the more competitive line haul speeds and greater comfort. At the same time, by their very nature, heavy rail systems are fixed in place and, accordingly, less able to accommodate changing business and residential land-use patterns. In addition, high-speed rail systems are capital intensive, costing anywhere from 1.3 billion dollars for Miami's system to 7.9 billion dollars for Washington DC's system (Winston and Shirley, 1998). All systems require capital grants and each system as a whole operates with an operating deficit. In 1991, passenger revenues on heavy fixed rail systems covered 44% of operating costs.

Table 3.6 summarizes recent trends in heavy rail use: we can see that system demand has hovered around 26% of total passenger–miles, although in the latter part of the 1980s there

Table 3.5 Heavy rail transit systems, 1991

Largest City Associated with Fixed Rail System	Heavy Rail Trips (millions)	Percentage of All Public Transit Trips in City
New York	1,385.8	61.3
Washington DC	188.3	51.2
Boston	172.2	54.3
Chicago	147.6	22.9
Philadelphia[a]	85.3	24.8
San Francisco	76.1	31.8
Atlanta	67.1	46.9
Miami	13.9	18.7
Baltimore	12.8	12.0
Philadelphia[b]	11.4	n/a
Cleveland	6.4	9.6
Total	2,166.9	25.1

[a] Operated by the Southeastern Pennsylvania Transportation Authority.
[b] Operated by the Port Authority Transit Corporation (PATCO) of Pennsylvania and New Jersey.
Source: American Public Transit Association 1992: *1992 Transit Fact Book*. Washington DC (Table 34, pp. 69–70)

Table 3.6 Trends in heavy rail transit ridership, 1980–90

Year	Heavy Rail Passenger–Miles (millions)	Public Transit Total Passenger Miles (millions)	Heavy Rail as a Percentage of Total Miles
1980	10,558	39,854	26.5
1982	10,049	37,124	27.1
1984	10,111	39,424	25.6
1986	10,649	40,204	26.5
1988	11,300	40,580	27.8
1990	11,475	41,143	27.9

Source: American Public Transit Association 1992: *1992 Transit Fact Book*. Washington DC (Table 38, p. 78)

has been some gain in heavy transit ridership. The people-moving capabilities of heavy rail systems emphasize the role that these systems play in alleviating congestion in our nation's major urban centers and reducing motor vehicle emissions and air pollution. But before we can develop urban transit policies to induce travelers on to heavy rail systems, we must identify what factors determine a traveler's decision to use a heavy rail system.

Doi and Allen (1986) analyzed the demand for rapid rail transit trips in Philadelphia for a particular rapid rail link between southern New Jersey and downtown Philadelphia. As seen in table 3.5, this rapid transit system is a relatively small system that served 11.4 million passengers in 1991. Part of this system is the Lindenwold high-speed line, a 14.2 mile link between southern New Jersey suburbs in Camden County and the downtown central business district in Philadelphia. At the time of the study, transit services were provided for 24 hours a day, 7 days a week, with an average daily ridership of 38,000–40,000. For this particular link, bus services are not a relevant alternative, but automobile travel is. Limited access expressways and arterial highways connect the suburbs to downtown Philadelphia through a system of bridges that cross the Delaware river.

The demand for the Lindenwold high-speed rail line was expressed as a linear function of its own price, prices associated with the primary alternative mode, and seasonal variables. In particular,

$$\begin{aligned} RR_t^o = {} & \beta_0 + \beta_1(\text{Real Transit Fare}) \\ & + \beta_2(\text{Real Gas Price})_t \\ & + \beta_3(\text{Real Bridge Toll})_t \\ & + \tau_1(\text{Summer Months}) + \tau_2(\text{October}) \\ & + \tau_3(\text{Closure}) + \varepsilon_t \end{aligned} \quad (3.17)$$

where RR_t^o is observed rapid rail transit ridership in month t. Real Transit Fare (dollars) is the price of an average trip on the line and the two variables Real Gasoline Price (dollars per gallon) and Real Bridge Toll (dollars per crossing) correspond to the price along this route by the most relevant alternative to the high-speed line, the automobile. Summer Months is a dummy variable which equals one for the months of May through September, zero otherwise, and is included in order to capture a seasonal downturn in high-speed rail ridership due to school and family vacations. Also, various sports and cultural events, combined with an absence of national holidays, produce a seasonal increase in ridership during October. This is captured with the dummy variable October, which equals one for the month of October and zero otherwise. Last, in January 1984, one of the rapid rail transit stations closed for reconstruction, which had the effect of diverting some rapid rail customers to alternative modes of travel. To capture this effect, the dummy variable Closure was included and is equal to zero for the months prior to January 1984 and one for subsequent months.

Hypotheses

Similar to the analysis on the demand for automobile travel, the demand equation identified in equation (3.17) embodies a number of fundamental hypotheses:

HYPOTHESIS 1 $\beta_1 < 0$. This reflects the law of demand that, all else constant, an increase in the relative price of rapid rail transit trips will decrease the quantity of rapid rail trips taken.

HYPOTHESIS 2 $\beta_2 > 0$, $\beta_3 > 0$. These two hypotheses reflect the assumed *substitute* relationship between rapid rail transit trips and automobile trips. All else constant, an increase in the price of automobile travel increases the demand for rapid rail transit trips. That is, the demand curve for rapid rail shifts to the right. In this analysis, the real price of gasoline as well as real toll bridge costs are included as separate variables, because the two variables are measured in different units. The price of gasoline is measured in dollars per gallon, whereas the toll cost is measured in dollars per trip.

HYPOTHESIS 3 $\tau_3 < 0$. This hypothesis reflects the impact that closing a rapid rail transit station has upon the opportunity cost of the rapid rail transit trip. For those passengers accessing the transit line at a given station, closure of the station raises the relative cost of rapid transit and, correspondingly, lowers the relative cost of alternative modes of travel. All else constant, it is expected that the coefficient for Closure will be negative.

Estimation results

Table 3.7 reports the estimation results that identify the demand for Lindenwold rapid rail trips. The model's R^2 statistic and the individual variable *t*-statistics indicate that the model does a good job in identifying the demand for Lindenwold rapid rail transit trips. 78% of the variation in rapid rail trips is explained by the model. And, based upon the *t*-statistics, all of the regression coefficients are significantly different from zero at the 0.05 level.

Table 3.7 The demand for Lindenwold rapid rail urban transit trips, 1978–84

Dependent Variable – monthly rapid rail ridership

Explanatory Variable	Coefficient Estimate	*t*-statistic
Constant	818,900	–
Real Transit Fare	−383,499	−5.63
Real Gas Price	234,048	4.36
Real Bridge Toll	928,064	4.16
Summer Months	−52,815	−10.88
October	40,273	4.59
Closure	−20,783	−2.04
$R^2 = 0.78$		

Source: Reprinted from Doi and Allen (1986), with permission from Elsevier Science. The *t*-statistic for the constant term was not reported

The demand curve for rapid rail trip

Consistent with the law of demand, an increase in the price of rapid rail transit trips is seen in table 3.7 to decrease the quantity of rapid rail transit trips demanded. A \$1 increase in the rapid rail transit fare causes consumers to move up the demand curve and demand 383,499 fewer trips per month, all else constant.

Change in the demand for rapid rail transit trips

Automobile trips from Camden suburbs to downtown Philadelphia were hypothesized to be substitutes for rapid rail trips between the two destinations. If true, then an increase in the cost of making the trip on the substitute mode would increase the demand for rapid rail transit trips; that is, the demand for rapid rail trips would shift to the right. From table 3.7, the estimated coefficients associated with Real Gas Price and Real Bridge Toll are consistent with the stated hypotheses. A dollar increase in the per gallon price of gasoline produces a rightward shift in the demand curve for rail transit, increasing monthly transit trips by 234,048. And a \$1 increase in the bridge toll is seen in table 3.7 to increase transit trips, but the effect is nearly quadruple that associated with a \$1 increase in the gallon price of gasoline. This difference reflects the larger impact upon per trip automobile costs from a \$1 increase in bridge tolls relative to a \$1 increase in the price of gasoline.

Closure and opportunity costs

Closing a rapid rail transit station was also expected to decrease the demand for rapid transit trips by raising the opportunity cost of the trip to station users. Consistent with this, the coefficient estimate of Closure in table 3.7 is −20,783, which represents the monthly loss in rapid transit patronage subsequent to the station's closing.

Similar to assessing the effect of gasoline rationing upon queuing costs, it is possible to estimate the impact that the station closure had upon opportunity costs. Consider the following relationship:

$$\frac{\Delta RR_t}{\Delta \text{Closure}} = \frac{\Delta RR_t}{\Delta \text{Opportunity Cost}} \frac{\Delta \text{Opportunity Cost}}{\Delta \text{Closure}}$$

which identifies Closure's effect on transit trips to be the product of its effect on the opportunity cost of a trip multiplied by the marginal effect of an increase in opportunity cost on transit trips. Substituting τ_3 for the first term and β_1 for the second term gives

$$\tau_3 = \beta_1 \frac{\Delta \text{Opportunity Cost}}{\Delta \text{Closure}}$$

which implies that (ΔOpportunity Cost)/(ΔClosure) = τ_3/β_1 = opportunity cost per trip. The ratio of τ_3 to β_1 gives the estimated increase in the opportunity cost of rapid rail transit due to the closure of the rapid rail transit station. From the results in table 3.7, the estimated increase in rapid rail cost is (−20,783/−383,499) = 0.054 dollars. That is, closure of the rapid rail station imposed an additional 5.4 cents on the opportunity cost of rapid rail travel.

Own- and cross-price elasticities

Based upon the linear specification and coefficient estimates presented in table 3.7, the own-price elasticity of the demand for rapid rail transit trips on the Lindenwold line is

$$\frac{\Delta RR/RR}{\Delta \text{Fare}/\text{Fare}} = \beta_1 \frac{\text{Fare}}{RR}$$

where Fare and RR are replaced by their sample averages and β_1 is the estimated coefficient reported in table 3.7. The own-price elasticity was estimated as −0.233, signifying that a 1% increase in real transit fares, all else constant, decreases monthly ridership by −0.233%. Also, since the estimated elasticity is less than one in absolute value, the demand for rapid transit trips on this line is price inelastic, implying that an increase in fares would increase revenues for the transit authority.

The cross-price elasticity of demand for rapid rail trips with respect to the price of gasoline is defined as

$$\frac{\Delta RR/RR}{\Delta \text{Real Gas Price}/\text{Real Gas Price}} = \beta_2 \frac{\text{Real Gas Price}}{RR}$$

Substituting β_2 = 234,048 from table 3.7 and using the sample averages to replace Real Gas Price and RR respectively, the cross-price elasticity is 0.113. A 10% increase in the real retail price of gasoline will increase rapid rail transit ridership by 1.13%. Similarly, the cross-price elasticity of demand with respect to bridge tolls was found to be 0.167, indicating that a 10% increase in bridge tolls would produce a slightly larger increase in transit ridership, 1.67%.

The 1993 gasoline tax increase revisited

As a final point, we can once again return to the predicted effects of the 4.3 cent rise in the federal gasoline tax. The analysis above found that the rapid rail transit elasticity with respect to the price of gasoline was 0.113. In order to get some idea of the effect of the tax increase on ridership, assume that 0.113 is representative of the cross-price elasticity of all rapid rail trips in Philadelphia. Since the increased federal tax represents an approximate 4% increase in the price of gasoline, this implies that the estimated effect on rapid rail from the increased tax is a (4)(0.113) = 0.452% increase in ridership. Based upon 1992 ridership in Philadelphia of 11.4 million persons, this translates into a modest increase of 51,528 persons. For rapid rail transit systems nationwide, which served 2.167 billion persons, a 4% increase in the price of gasoline combined with a 0.113 cross-price elasticity would produce 9.79 million additional riders.

CASE STUDY – THE DEMAND FOR SHORT-HAUL AIR SERVICE

As noted previously, four-fifths of all intercity passenger–miles occur by automobile. Notwithstanding this high percentage, however, the proportion of intercity travel by air has steadily increased over the past 30 years. Table 3.8 summarizes US intercity travel, by mode, between 1965 and 1990. Rail has remained relatively steady since 1970, but increased between 1985 and 1990; intercity bus travel, on the other hand, decreased slightly, while automobile travel fell from 89.2% in 1965 to 80.2% in 1990. Offsetting this decrease has been more than a five-fold increase in air travel, from 53.7 billion in 1970 to 345.9 billion passenger–miles in 1990.

The late 1970s and 1980s saw the passage of significant deregulatory legislation in the

Table 3.8 Intercity domestic travel: billions of passenger–miles (%)

	Private Carrier		Public Carrier		
Year	Automobile[a]	Air[b]	Air	Rail[c]	Bus[d]
1965	817.7 (89.2)	4.4 (0.5)	53.7 (5.9)	17.6 (1.9)	23.8 (2.6)
1970	1,026.0 (86.9)	9.1 (0.8)	109.5 (9.3)	10.9 (0.9)	25.3 (2.1)
1975	1,170.5 (86.4)	11.4 (0.8)	136.9 (10.1)	10.1 (0.7)	25.4 (1.9)
1980	1,210.3 (82.5)	14.7 (1.0)	204.4 (13.9)	11.0 (0.7)	27.4 (1.9)
1985	1,310.3 (80.1)	12.3 (0.8)	277.8 (17.0)	11.3 (0.7)	23.8 (1.4)
1990	1,597.5 (80.2)	13.0 (0.6)	345.9 (17.4)	13.2 (0.7)	23.0 (1.1)

[a] Includes small trucks for travel purposes.
[b] General aviation, including air taxi and small air commuter.
[c] Includes long-haul intercity and short-haul commutation but not urban rail transit.
[d] Excludes urban bus transit.
Source: ENO Transportation Foundation 1993: *Transportation in America*, 11th edn

transportation industry. For intercity passenger travel, the Airline Deregulation Act of 1978 relaxed entry requirements and allowed fare competition. By 1982, all carriers fit, willing, and able were allowed entry, and by 1983 all restrictions on fares eliminated.

One result forthcoming from deregulation in the airline industry was hub-and-spoke operations, whereby passengers traveling from a variety of origins are routed through an intermediate city (the hub). To take a simple example, suppose Polly travels from origin O (a spoke) to destination D (another spoke) once a month. Prior to the hub-and-spoke system, the airline routed Polly via a direct flight from O to D. After implementing the hub-and-spoke system, however, the airline now routes Polly through hub H in order to consolidate her trip with travelers arriving at the hub from other destinations and who have D as the same final destination. The hub-and-spoke system has two effects. First, consolidating trips at the hub lowers airline costs. But there is also some loss in revenue. Direct flights from O to D that are now routed through the hub increase the time costs – and hence the opportunity costs – of the trip, which causes Polly to reduce the quantity of trips demanded, for example from one trip per month to one trip every 6 weeks. On balance, the hub-and-spoke system makes economic sense for the airline if the savings in costs from consolidation more than offset the loss in revenue from a decrease in flights demanded.

Responding to the rise of hub-and-spoke systems, profit-seeking airline entrepreneurs have sought ways to identify new market niches for providing profitable service. One such niche is the short-haul commuter market linking nonhub smaller communities to the nearest larger hub city, which provides regularly scheduled airline services to other destinations. These commuter markets typically involve trips with one-way ranges between 100 and 300 miles, and for which highway travel (generally by car or limousine service) is the primary competitor. Although many such niches may exist, the airline must determine whether there is sufficient demand for profitable service.

Pickrell (1984) investigated this problem and specified the market demand function for short-haul commuter trips between a smaller nonhub community and the nearest airline hub city as

$$\begin{aligned}\ln(\text{Trips})_t^{\text{o}} = \beta_0 &+ \beta_1 \ln(\text{Fare})_t + \beta_2 \ln(\text{Flytime})_t \\ &+ \beta_3 \ln(\text{Freq})_t + \beta_4 \ln(\text{Seats}) \\ &+ \beta_5 \ln(\text{Enplanements}) \\ &+ \beta_6 \ln(\text{Drvcost}) + \beta_7 \ln(\text{Drvtime}) \\ &+ \beta_8 \ln(\text{Population}) + \beta_9 \text{Cert} + \varepsilon_{ti}\end{aligned} \quad (3.18)$$

Trips is the number of one-way trips from the smaller nonhub city to the larger hub city. Fare is the published air fare for a trip, Flytime is the scheduled flying time, Freq is the number of weekly departures from the origin to the destination city, Seats is the average seating capacity per departure, Enplanements is the total number of passenger enplanements at the hub city, Drvcost is the estimated out-of-pocket expenses if the trip were made by automobile, Drvtime is the estimated travel time of the trip by automobile, Population is the population in the community from which the trips originate, and Cert is a dummy variable that equals one if the route is serviced by a Civil Aeronautics Board (CAB) certificated airline and zero otherwise.

In contrast to the examples for automobile travel and rapid rail transit trips, all of the variables in (3.18), except for the constant term and the dummy variable Cert, are specified in *logarithmic* form. As we saw in chapter 2, this in no way alters the interpretation of (3.18) as a market demand function for short-haul commuter trips. However, it does assume that the determinants of short-haul air travel interact multiplicatively in forming demands and that elasticities of demand are constant. This latter point becomes immediately clear once we recall that the parameter estimates in a double-log model *are* elasticities.[18]

Hypotheses

HYPOTHESIS 1 We have previously seen that there are two primary components in the opportunity cost of travel: out-of-pocket costs and time costs. For air travel, there are two major determinants of time costs. First, there are time costs associated with "on-board" flying time; that is, the time that a traveler spends on the airplane traveling from an origin to a destination. Second, there are schedule-related time costs, which reflect the delays inherent in an airline's departure frequency. The fewer scheduled departures per week, the greater, on average, will be the delay time and associated time costs. In the above model, Flytime and Freq represent these two time-related components. Since increases in airline fares and time-related costs raise the opportunity cost of air travel, by the law of demand, it is expected that $\beta_1 < 0$, $\beta_2 < 0$, and $\beta_3 < 0$.

The variable Seats might also measure some delay cost, since smaller aircraft with less seating capacity, all else constant, reduce the likelihood of obtaining a seat for any given departure. Also, since larger aircraft are generally more comfortable, Seats may reflect a consumer's preferences for a comfortable trip. The reduced delay effect and greater comfort associated with larger aircraft imply that $\beta_4 > 0$.

HYPOTHESIS 2 A higher number of enplanements at the destination city reflects a greater level of economic activity as well as improved opportunities for connecting flights, which enhance the hub city's attractiveness to consumers. Thus, it is expected that Enplanements will shift the market demand for trips to the right. This implies that, all else constant, $\beta_5 > 0$ and indicates the extent to which the demand curve shifts rightward from an increase in destination city enplanements.

In addition, flying on a CAB-certificated airline increases the probability of an *on-line* connection (that is, maintaining the same carrier on the next leg of the trip) rather than an *interline* connection (that is, switching carriers). Assuming that Cert reflects the underlying preferences of commuters for on-line connections, it is expected that $\beta_9 > 0$. That is, holding all else constant, using a certificated carrier will shift the demand curve rightward.

HYPOTHESIS 3 According to market demand theory, one of the factors affecting market demand is the number of consumers. Since cities with larger populations are expected to have more consumers of short-haul air travel, increases in population are expected to shift the demand for short-haul air trips rightward, all else constant. Thus, the coefficient for Population, β_8, is expected to have a positive sign.

HYPOTHESIS 4 Rather than traveling to the larger hub city by commuter air service, an individual could make the trip by some other mode. For the markets studied in this analysis, the primary alternative to air travel is the automobile.[19] In order to account for the presence of this competing alternative, Drvcost and Drvtime are included to reflect the opportunity cost of an automobile trip. Increases in automobile out-of-pocket costs or automobile travel time in making a trip from the nonhub community to the larger hub city are expected, all else held constant, to shift the market demand curve for air commuter trips to the right. As automobile travel becomes more costly, either in terms of monetary or time costs, the demand curve for air travel is expected to shift rightward, which is equivalent to the hypothesis that $\beta_6 > 0$ and $\beta_7 > 0$.

Estimation results

Data for this analysis consists of a sample of 135 routes from small nonhub cities to larger hub cities in the third quarter of 1980. For this sample of routes, the number of monthly one-way trips from the departing city ranged between 100 and 650. Average population in the sample of cities was 33,000. Table 3.9 summarizes the estimation results that identify the demand function for short-haul commuter travel.

The R^2 statistic in table 3.9 indicates that the explanatory variables in this model explain 42% of the variation in short-haul commuter demands.[20] Qualitatively, all of the coefficient estimates, with the exception of Drvcost, have their expected signs. Drvcost has an unexpected negative sign; however, its associated *t*-statistic is −0.30, which says that we cannot reject the null hypothesis that this coefficient is equal to zero.

Table 3.9 The demand for short-haul commuter air service, 1980

Dependent Variable – logarithm of the number of one-way air passenger trips

Explanatory Variable	Coefficient Estimate	*t*-statistic[a]
Constant	−0.487	–
ln(Fare)	−1.08	−2.45
ln(Flytime)	−1.85	−4.24
ln(Freq)	0.58	4.10
ln(Seats)	0.32	1.14
ln(Enplanements)	0.36	2.80
ln(Drvcost)	−0.0003	−0.30
ln(Drvtime)	1.86	3.44
ln(Population)	0.109	0.66
Cert	0.61	1.76

$R^2 = 0.42$

[a] The *t*-statistic for the constant term was not reported. The parameter estimates reported here were obtained from a simultaneously estimated model of supply and demand. The supply function specified departures to be a function of the number of passenger trips and plane capacity.

Source: Pickrell, D. 1991: The regulation and deregulation of US airlines. In Button, K. (ed.), *Airline Deregulation: International Experiences*. David Fulton (Table 2.2, p. 26)

The demand curve for short-haul trips

The estimated coefficients and associated *t*-statistics for opportunity cost related variables, Fare, Flytime, and Freq, have their expected signs and are significantly different from zero at a 0.05 level. Increasing scheduled fares, flight times, and flight delays (from reduced scheduled frequencies), all else constant, each raises the opportunity cost of the flight and reduces the quantity of trips demanded. Size of aircraft, as reflected in Seats, however, has no statistically significant impact upon the quantity of trips demanded.

Size versus frequency – What course to pursue?

An interesting implication of the results for Freq and Seats in table 3.9 relates to air carriers' decisions regarding the frequency of service and size of aircraft. Should an air carrier provide fewer departures per week and use larger aircraft, or increase weekly departure frequency but use smaller aircraft? Holding all else constant, *including frequency of service*, the results in table 3.9 tell us that a 10% increase in the size of aircraft (that is, Seats) increases travel demand by 3.2%, which suggests that an airline could gain customers if it provided more seats. However, it would be incorrect to draw this conclusion. The *t*-statistic for this variable is 1.14, which tells us that the standard error of the estimate is sufficiently large that we cannot reject the null hypothesis that an increase in aircraft size has no effect upon short-haul travel demands. One must remember that a coefficient estimate that may be absolutely far from zero may not be *statistically* different from zero. Before one decides whether a variable is statistically important, it is necessary to examine the *t*-statistic.[21]

In contrast to size of plane, increasing the frequency of departures – holding all else constant, including size of aircraft – *will* increase the quantity of trips demanded. Does this have management policy implications for short-haul carriers? Yes. A policy to use smaller aircraft but schedule more frequent departures per week will produce more passenger trips for the airlines than an alternative policy that employs larger aircraft less frequently. This was observed in the early years after airline deregulation. Meyer and Oster (1981) present evidence that, early into deregulation, two-thirds of the nonhub cities that lost trunk and local carrier airline services experienced more frequent departures to the nearest medium or large hub from commuter carriers. On average, the flight frequency for these smaller commuter aircraft more than doubled in these cities.

Change in the demand for short-haul airline trips

All else constant, it is expected that an increase in the opportunity cost of substitute modes will shift the demand curve for airline trips to the right. From table 3.9, the coefficient for driving cost is *negative* but not significantly different from zero, whereas the coefficient for driving time is positive *and* significantly different from zero. This indicates that an increase automobile travel time is consistent with a rightward shift in demand for air travel. Although one might conclude from the results in table 3.9 that out-of-pocket costs are not an important influence on air travel, this may be an incorrect inference. In the study, driving cost is measured as the simple product of highway distance and per-mile cost, which excludes an important component of automobile costs – airport parking. By excluding parking costs, the model reduces the influence that variations in automobile costs have upon the demand for air travel.

It is also interesting to note that, in absolute value, the coefficient for driving time is virtually identical to the coefficient for flying time, which not only implies that travel time, whether by air or automobile, is an important determinant of demand, but also that market demand is equally sensitive to changes in travel time. For example, the sample average driving time to a larger hub city was 5 hours. If this were reduced to 4.5 hours (a 10% decrease in automobile travel time), the results in table 3.9 imply that there would be an 18% leftward shift in the demand for air trips. Alternatively, there would also occur an 18% decrease in the quantity of airline trips demanded if airline travel time increased by 10%, all else constant. Note that the decrease in automobile travel time reflects a *shift* in the demand curve, whereas an increase in airline travel time reflects a decrease in *quantity demanded*; that is, a move along the demand curve.

The coefficient for population in this model is not significantly different from zero, indicating that increases in population have little effect upon the demand for commuter air trips. Economic theory tells us that the market demand for a good is the summation of individual demands. Empirically, population is oftentimes a good indicator of the underlying number of consumers in the market. The result in table 3.9 that Population has no effect on the demand for short-haul commuter trips suggests that, in the short-haul market, a community's population is not a good indicator of the underlying factors that lead to increases in travel-generating activities. Since many short-haul trips are business-related, the level of employment activity may be a better measure of the underlying demand for short-haul airline commuter trips.

On the other hand, the number of enplanements at the larger hub city does lead to significantly higher commuter trips to the hub. A 10% increase in enplanements at the hub city's airport translates into a 3.6% increase in the demand for commuter trips in any one market to that hub. Alternatively, suppose that identical air services from a given community are available to two equally distant larger hub cities, A and B. If hub city A has 10% more passenger enplanements, then the demand for commuter trips from the community to hub A is expected to be 3.6% higher than the demand for trips to hub city B.

Do CAB-certificated air carriers increase the demand for commuter trips? Yes. The coefficient for Cert is 0.61, which tells us that certification increases the demand for commuter air service 0.61%. As previously mentioned, this most likely reflects commuter preferences for on-line connections, although it may also be capturing other factors, including the greater public awareness of certificated carriers as well as the perception that these carriers are safer.

The demand for commuter service and elasticity measures

A major advantage to specifying both the dependent and independent variables in logarithmic form is that the estimated coefficients are estimates of the corresponding elasticities. With respect to own-price elasticity measures (where price here refers to the monetary and time components of opportunity cost), commuters are most sensitive to flying time, somewhat sensitive to air fare, and least sensitive to departure frequency. A 10% increase in flying time reduces the quantity of trips demanded by 18.5%, whereas a 10% increase in air fare reduces the quantity demanded by 10.8%. Also, since the price elasticity of demand for commuter trips is a bit higher than unity, air carrier revenues on these routes will not be very sensitive to changes in air fares.

Last, the estimated elasticity of demand with respect to departure frequency is 0.58, which suggests that a 20% increase in departure frequency (and associated reductions in travel delays) produces an 11.6% increase in trip demands.

As discussed above, consumers are also relatively sensitive to automobile travel time. The cross-elasticity of the demand for airline commuter trips with respect to automobile travel time is 1.86. This has interesting implications with respect to the increasing congestion that is occurring in the nation's urban areas. If an airline hub's urban area experiences increasing congestion that results in higher automobile travel times, the effect will benefit commuter air carriers. From the results in table 3.9, a 5% increase in automobile travel time to the larger hub cities would produce a 9.3% increase in the demand for commuter air travel, all else held constant. Short-haul commuter air carriers are the beneficiaries of increasing urban congestion.

Comments

Although the model presented in table 3.9 identified important determinants of market demand, only 42% of the variation in demand was explained. As mentioned in note 21, part of the explanation for this is that the analysis is based upon cross-section data.

However, it is also important to correctly identify and measure the included explanatory variables in any empirical representation of a theoretical market demand model. The money cost of traveling from a smaller community to a larger hub city by automobile was included to reflect the cost of an alternative mode of travel. Yet, the cost of driving did not include parking costs, which can be a considerable proportion of total trip cost. Because the variable Drvcost did not appropriately reflect the full monetary price of an automobile trip, two important consequences follow. First, the theoretical link between automobile costs and the demand for commuter air trips was not confirmed in the statistical analysis. This is why the coefficient for Drvcost was not significantly different from zero. Second, by weakening the statistical relationship between automobile trip costs and the demand for short-haul trips, a smaller amount of the variation in market demand was explained.

An additional explanation for a lower R^2 value relates to the population variable. Market demand for any good is the summation of individual demands. And, in many cases, population is a good proxy for the number of consumers. The higher the number of people in a community, the more commuters there will be. The results in table 3.9, however, suggest that, in the market for 100–300 mile commuter trips, Population may not be an adequate measure of the underlying aggregate demand for commuter trips. An alternative measure more closely correlated with the business activities of communities may have better captured the extent of community demand.

CHAPTER HIGHLIGHTS

- A consumer's utility function describes the level of economic welfare that the consumer receives from alternative bundles of commodities. The utility function also depends upon the consumer's preferences, which are assumed to be complete, transitive, and nonsatiable.
- An indifference curve is a locus of points that reflects alternative commodity bundles which provide a consumer with equal amounts of economic welfare. Typically, a consumer's set of indifference curves are convex to the origin, indicating that the more a consumer has of one good the fewer other goods he or she is willing to give up to obtain an additional unit of the good. This reflects the principle of diminishing marginal rate of commodity substitution.

- If a consumer optimally allocates his or her limited resources among competing goods, then for each pair of commodities consumed, the marginal rate of commodity substitution equals the commodity's relative price. In equilibrium, a consumer's demand for each commodity depends upon relative prices, income, and preferences. Changes in the economic environment cause individuals to alter their consumption of goods at the intensive margin.
- The market demand for transportation is the horizontal summation of individual demands for transportation. A change in the price of transportation leads to a change in the quantity of transportation demanded. A change in any other determinant of transportation leads to a change in demand.
- Goods that are consumed together are complements in consumption. A rise in the price of one good decreases the market demand for the other good. Goods that compete with one another in consumption are substitutes. A rise in the price of a substitute good increases the market demand for the other good. A good whose consumption increases (decreases) with increases in income is a normal (inferior) good.
- For continuous or divisible transportation commodities, observed transportation demands are approximated by a linear-in-parameters empirical model. Ideally, the explanatory variables of the model include the price of the transportation good, the prices of related goods, and income. Socioeconomic characteristics are included in the empirical model in order to capture preference differences among demanders. Differences between observed transportation demands and predicted demands reflect consumer optimization or measurement errors.
- Because transportation trips involve the movement of people or goods over space, the opportunity cost of transportation includes both a monetary cost and a time cost. Increases in each component of cost is expected to reduce the quantity of transportation demanded. Case studies for energy and automobile trip demands in California, urban transit trips in Philadelphia, and short-haul commuter airline trips are consistent with these expectations.
- Empirical models of transportation demands not only identify relevant determinants of demand but also provide estimates on the magnitude of the effects that changes in the economic environment will have upon demands. This information facilitates improved public and private decision-making in the transportation sector.

Review questions

1. What is the difference between the demand for a divisible good and the demand for a discrete good? Which of the following are discrete transportation commodities and which are divisible?
   (a) The work-trip mode of travel.
   (b) The number of airline trips to the east coast.

(c) The number of automobiles that a household owns.
(d) Passenger–miles flown.
(e) A vacation traveler's decision to rent a car.
(f) The number of miles driven in a rental car.
(g) The choice of vehicle to own.

2. Suppose that an individual consumes transportation (T) and all other goods (G). Assume that the price of G is p_g, the price of transportation is p_t, and Y is income.

(a) If this consumer spends all of her income on transportation, how much could she buy? How much G could she buy if all of her income were spent on G? How would you answer this question if her income per period were \$250, $p_g = \$1$, and $p_t = \$3.00$?
(b) Depict the consumer's equilibrium consumption of G and T and identify the equilibrium condition.
(c) With the use of indifference curves and budget lines, demonstrate that an increase in the price of transportation will reduce the household's consumption of transportation. Can we predict what will happen to a consumer's level of economic welfare?
(d) Suppose that transportation is an inferior good. Graphically demonstrate the effect on G and T from an increase in per period incomes.

3. (a) Suppose that Bob enjoys both railroad trips and automobile scenic trips. If Bob's indifference curves for railroad and auto trips are convex to the origin, what does this say about Bob's preferences for each type of trip? Graphically depict Bob's equilibrium.
(b) Alternatively, suppose that Bob's indifference curves are concave to the origin. What does this say about Bob's preferences for rail and auto trips? In this case, what will be Bob's equilibrium consumption for railroad and automobile trips?

4. According to demand theory, the market demand curve for transportation is downward-sloping.

(a) In deriving the market demand curve for transportation, what assumptions are we making?
(b) You are a transportation economist for Amtrak and you are asked to estimate the price elasticity of demand for Amtrak services. Describe in some detail what steps you would follow to obtain the price elasticity of demand.
(c) Suppose that your analysis found that the price elasticity of demand for Amtrak services was −0.78. What impact would a 10% increase in price have upon the quantity of Amtrak services demanded? Do you know whether Amtrak revenues would rise or fall?

5. The following table gives nominal average passenger airline and intercity bus fares between 1980 and 1990. The last column gives the consumer price index for the same period:

Year	Airline Fare	Intercity Bus Fare	CPI (1990 = 100)
1980	84.55	10.57	75
1981	95.42	10.3	81.7
1982	92.08	10.9	84.6
1983	92.17	10.66	85.7
1984	97.1	11.09	87.4
1985	92.53	11.02	87.9
1986	84.99	12.35	85.8
1987	88.95	12.28	87.6
1988	96.67	17.15	89.9
1989	103.65	18.62	94.9
1990	107.86	20.18	100

(a) What is the difference between nominal prices and real (constant) prices?
(b) Set up another table that uses the information in the above table to calculate real air carrier and intercity bus fares in 1990 dollars. Comment on the differences between the nominal and real series.
(c) Between 1980 and 1990, what has happened to the relative price of air fares; that is, the real price of air fares relative to the real price of intercity bus?
(d) Assuming no change in income, use indifference curves and budget lines to identify the expected effect of the change in the relative price of air travel between 1980 and 1990 on airline and intercity bus consumption demands.

6. The following table gives real per capita income and per capita automobile passenger–miles between 1980 and 1989:

Year	Real Per Capita Income (1982–4 = 100)	Passenger–Miles Per Capita
1980	9,722	8,832
1981	9,769	8,771
1982	9,725	8,860
1983	9,930	8,916
1984	10,419	8,934
1985	10,625	9,006
1986	10,905	9,103
1987	10,946	9,285
1988	11,368	9,589
1989	11,531	9,639

(a) Holding all else constant, use budget lines and indifference curves to depict the effect that an increase in Real Per Capita Income will have upon Passenger–Miles Per Capita traveled between 1980 and 1989. Theoretically, would you expect passenger–miles traveled to be a normal good?

(b) Based upon the data in the table, the following regression model was estimated:

$$\text{Auto Passenger–Miles Per Capita} = \underset{(7.89)}{4{,}653.8} + \underset{(7.54)}{0.4231}\text{Real Per Capita Income}$$

where the numbers in parentheses are the *t*-statistics. The two-tail critical *t*-value for a model with eight degrees of freedom and a significance level of 0.01 is 3.35.

(i) Are the regression results consistent with your theoretical expectations?

(ii) What quantitative effect will a $1,000 increase in income have upon Automobile Passenger–Miles Per Capita?

(iii) The table below provides the sample means of the independent and dependent variables:

Variable	Sample Mean
Automobile Passenger–Miles Per Capita	10,494
Real Per Capita Income	9,094

Use this data to determine the effect that a 5% increase in Real Per Capita Income will have upon the demand for passenger–miles traveled.

(c) According to the empirical model estimated above, only Real Per Capita Income affects the demand for passenger–miles. Yet demand theory tells us that the price of travel is also an important determinant of automobile travel. If, as economic theory predicts, increases in the price of travel reduce the quantity of miles demanded, would you expect the estimated coefficient of income to be biased (that is, not equal its expected value) if the price of auto travel were not included in the equation? Consider two cases:

(i) there is no correlation between price and income over time;

(ii) because price and income both increase over time, they are positively correlated.

In each of these cases, can you predict the direction of the bias; that is, do you think the exclusion of price would increase or decrease the estimated coefficient of income?

(d) What other variables might be relevant determinants of the demand for automobile passenger travel?

7. Suppose that you have a sample of identical travelers – that is, consumers whose incomes are identical, prices of travel and all other goods that are identical, and preferences for travel and all other goods that are identical. Why do the observed travel demands of consumers generally differ from that predicted by economic theory? Does this imply that our economic theory is not very useful? Explain your answer.

8. Evaluate the following statement: "When transportation markets are functioning well, the opportunity cost of transportation will primarily reflect monetary costs. To the extent that time costs are present, they will be small."

9. Recall table 3.2, which reported the estimation results of an empirical model of the average daily consumption of gasoline per month in California during the period 1970–1975.

(a) Two significant by-products of automobile use are air pollution and traffic congestion. In order to reduce the extent of each, suppose that the federal government raises the gasoline tax by $.25. From table 3.2, what effect will this have on gasoline consumption in California? Use budget lines and indifference curves to demonstrate the effect of the tax on consumer welfare.

(b) Wanting to increase the price of gasoline *but not reduce economic welfare*, suppose that, in addition to the $0.25 cent tax on gasoline, the government also provides consumers with an income tax rebate amounting to $16.7 billion dollars.

(i) According to the empirical model, what would be the effect of the gasoline tax and income tax policies?

(ii) According to economic theory, would the gasoline tax rise combined with the welfare-offsetting income tax rebate produce any reduction in the demand for gasoline?

(iii) Given your analysis in parts (i) and (ii), is it possible to implement a policy that is consistent with the goals of environmentalists and yet not reduce the economic welfare of consumers?

10. Public transportation is oftentimes argued to be an inferior good.

(a) Identify why this might be so.

(b) Is public transportation an inferior good at all levels of income? If so, why; and if not, why not?

11. Consistent with the results reported in tables 3.2 and 3.4, various studies indicate that the price elasticity of demand for automobile usage lies above −0.5 (that is, below 0.5 in absolute value). What does this say about the potential success of policies designed to reduce urban congestion by monetary disincentives?

12. Hilton (1980) reports the following empirical demand model that Amtrak, the nation's passenger rail service, used in forecasting service changes. The model is based upon a sample of 71 observations of annual ridership changes on 39 routes served between 1974–5 and 1975–6:

$$R\% = -0.38 + \underset{(51.2)}{1.109F\%} + \underset{(4.58)}{0.319E} + \underset{(1.80)}{0.073T\%} + \underset{(2.10)}{4.964P\%} - \underset{(-5.73)}{18.325ED}$$

$$R^2 = 0.978$$

where $R\%$ is the annual percentage change in ridership on a route; $F\%$ is the annual percentage change in frequency [(train mile days)/(route miles)] · 365 on a route; E is the absolute change in the percentage of train days having new equipment; $T\%$ is the annual percentage change of Amtrak on-time performance on a route; $P\%$ is the annual percentage change of population in states along the routes; and *ED* is a dummy variable that equals one for recovery from energy shortage and zero otherwise.

(a) Interpret the results and discuss whether they are consistent with your expectations.
(b) When Amtrak was first formed, its proponents forecasted a demand for service that fell far short of that realized. Part of the reason for this was Amtrak's inability to attract bus passengers, due to a generally lower service frequency. Are the results in the table consistent with this?
(c) Since its inception, Amtrak has dropped a variety of luxury services. Is this behavior consistent with the above empirical model? (Hint: assume that newer equipment is also more luxurious.)
(d) Graphically identify the effect that an energy shortage has on ridership.
(e) Although the model explains over 97% of the variation in ridership changes, why might the coefficient estimates be biased? (Hint: what important economic variable is missing from the empirical model?)

13. Consider the following observations: (1) between 1978 and 1988 real per capita income increased by 25%; (2) during the same time span there was a decrease in the average number of hours spent working; (3) there was an increase in the number of single households and households with unrelated members. Why might you expect each of these factors to increase the demand for air travel?

14. (a) In 1991, public transportation received \$9.79 billion dollars in operating subsidies from federal, state, and local government. Use budget lines and indifference curves to identify the economic welfare and public transit consumption effects of the subsidy.
(b) The price elasticity of transit demand has been estimated in the range of −0.2 to −0.4. Suppose that the transit authority seeks to increase demand through a 10% reduction in fares. What impact will this have on transit demand, and what impact do you think it would have on the operating subsidies?

15. One would expect that the demand for automobile ownership in metropolitan areas would be influenced by population density. Holding all else constant, the more dense the area, the more public transit will be provided. Also, the denser the area, the more traffic congestion will be present.

(a) Assuming that the public transit fare remains constant, explain why an increased supply of public transit in denser areas would reduce the opportunity cost of public transit.
(b) Assuming no change in the per-mile monetary cost of automobile travel, explain why increased congestion will increase the opportunity cost of automobile travel.
(c) Based upon 65 large US central cities in 1970, Kain (1983) assumed that the demand for automobiles depended upon median household income and population density. He obtained the following linear regression results:

$$\text{Autos per Household} = \underset{(6.1)}{0.224} + \underset{(6.1)}{0.069}\text{Median Income} - \underset{(-13.9)}{0.013}\text{Population Density}$$

$$R^2 = 0.77$$

where Median Income is in thousands of dollars and Population is in thousands of persons per square mile. t-statistics are in parentheses.

(i) Are these results consistent with expectations?

(ii) What effect will a $1,000 increase in median family income have upon automobile ownership? From these results, what differences in automobile ownership would you expect to see between a household earning $50,000 per year and one earning $20,000 per year?

(iii) Assume that Median Income is $25,000. According to Kain's model, how many automobiles will a typical household own if it resides in a low-density area characterized by 50 persons per square mile? Compare this with a high-density city that has 100 persons per square mile.

(iv) Throughout the 20th century, we saw population movements away from rural areas and into urban areas. At the same time, household median income rose steadily. Using Kain's empirical model, what can you say about the net effect of these changes on automobile ownership? From the above results, which has the greater effect – a $1,000 increase in median income or a 1,000-person increase in population density?

NOTES

1 There are two additional technical restrictions, reflexivity and continuity. According to reflexivity, if two commodity bundles are identical in all respects, then an individual is indifferent between them. By continuity, if commodity bundle A is preferred to commodity bundle B and commodity bundle C is "close" to commodity bundle B, then commodity bundle A will also be preferred to commodity bundle C.

2 One manifestation of indifference is that a consumer would be willing to let someone else make the choice for her.

3 An ordinal index reflects the rankings of commodity bundles rather than the extent to which one bundle is preferred to another bundle. For example, suppose that commodity bundle A has a utility index of 100 and commodity bundle B an index of 50. Since the utility index is ordinal, we can only state that commodity bundle A is preferred to B. We cannot say that A is twice as preferred to B. Note that we would arrive at exactly the same ranking if bundle A had a utility of 60 (or any other utility level, as long as it was greater than 50) instead of 100.

4 Alternatively, one could focus upon the marginal utilities that define the *MRCS*. If the marginal value that individuals place on increasing amounts of a good falls, then the movement from I to J increases the consumption of transportation, thereby decreasing its marginal utility, and decreases the consumption of all other goods, which increases its marginal utility. A falling MU of T combined with a rising MU of x implies that their ratio falls; that is, the *MRCS* decreases with a move from I to J.

5 A discerning student will recognize from our discussion of budget constraints that a decrease in p_T expands a consumer's choice set and purchasing power of income. A decrease in the price of transportation thus leads to two consumption effects for T: a *substitution effect* and an *income effect*. The substitution effect reflects an increase in the consumption of T (and the decrease in the consumption of all other goods) as the consumer substitutes toward the relatively cheaper good and away from the relatively more expensive good, holding his or her level of utility constant. The income effect reflects the impact on the consumption of transportation (and all other goods) due to the increased purchasing power generated by the decrease in p_T. According to the law of demand, an individual's demand curve will always be downward-sloping – a decrease in the relative price of a good increases quantity demanded of the good, all else constant. The law of demand rules outs the possibility of inferior goods whose income effect is so large as to more than offset the substitution effect of a price change.

6 To see this, consider the following linear specification of individual demand for T which, for simplicity, is hypothesized to depend only upon individual income, $T_i = a + b_i Y_i$. Market demand is obtained by summing each side of this equation over the N consumers of the good. $D_T = \Sigma_{i=1}^{N} T_i = \Sigma_{i=1}^{N} a_i + \Sigma_{i=1}^{N} b_i Y_i = a + b\Sigma_{i=1}^{N} Y_i$, where a is equal to $\Sigma_{i=1}^{N} a_i$ and $b_i = b$ for all consumers. Thus, market demand can be written as $D_T = a + bY^{a}$, where Y^{a} is aggregate income.

7 $T(p_t)$ will be downward-sloping since, by the law of demand, each individual consumer's demand curve is downward-sloping. More formally, from (3.10), $\Delta T/\Delta p_T = (\Sigma_{i=1}^{N} \Delta T(p_T, p_x, Y_i; \phi_i)/\Delta p_T)$. Since, by the law of demand, an increase in the relative price of transportation decreases the quantity demanded for each consumer, it follows that the quantity demanded of transportation for the market will also decrease. In figure 3.9, these are drawn as linear curves for convenience.

8 More generally, two goods, x_i and x_j, are substitutes in consumption if $\Delta x_i/\Delta p_j > 0$ and complements in consumption if $\Delta x_i/\Delta p_j < 0$.

9 Ideally, we also want small observation errors. Large errors, even if random, imply that the model does a poorer job of explaining observed behavior and may lead to poorer policy predictions.

10 Although the discussion is in terms of a cross-section of consumers, it is equally true for data collected over time. With time series data, each of the observed economic factors (income, prices) is different in each time period, and socioeconomic characteristics are included to reflect changing preferences over time. With cross-section data, as noted, the observed economic data (income, prices) differ across consumers and socioeconomic characteristics capture differences in preferences across consumers.

11 Motor Vehicle Manufacturers Association, *Facts and Figures: 1992*. Other means primarily include bicycle, walk, school bus, and moped.

12 This is the basis for the widely quoted Consumer Price Index (*CPI*) measure of inflation. The *CPI* measures price increases for a fixed basket of goods defined by the Department of Commerce. The *CPI* is currently converted to constant 1982–4 dollars. In November 1993, the *CPI* was 145.8, which means that the basket of goods that cost $100 in 1982–4 currently costs $145.80.

13 The 11 seasonal variables correspond to the first 11 months in the year and take on a value of zero or one. For example, $S_{t1} = 1$ if the monthly observation is January; if not, $S_{t1} = 0$. Similarly, $S_{t2} = 1$ if the monthly observation is February; if not, $S_{t2} = 0$. And in general, S_{ti} $(i = 1, \ldots, 11) = 1$ if the observation is month i; otherwise, S_{ti} $(i = 1, \ldots, 11) = 0$. Although there are 12 months in the year, there are only 11 seasonal variables in the model. This is because the estimating equation (3.15) includes a constant term that reflects consumption in the 12th month, December. To see this, assume that the observation is December consumption of gasoline. Then each of the 11 seasonal variables will have a zero value and the constant term β_0 is the intercept. But since the observation is December consumption, β_0 is the intercept for December consumption. If, on the other hand, the observation is January consumption, then $S_{t1} = 1$ and S_{ti} $(i = 2, \ldots, 11) = 0$. The intercept for January consumption is $\beta_0 + \psi_1$. In general, each of the 11 seasonal variables reflects the increase $(\psi_i > 0)$ or decrease $(\psi_i < 0)$ in gasoline consumption relative to December's consumption, all else held constant. Variables that take on a value of zero or one are referred to as *dummy* variables. If

the regression equation includes a constant term then, at most, the number of dummy variables included equals the number of categories minus one. In the above case, since there are 12 months in the year, at most 11 (= 12 – 1) seasonal dummy variables can be included. For a more complete discussion of dummy variables, refer to chapter 2 (p. 34).

14 Equation (2.9) in chapter 2 gives the expression for confidence intervals in regression models.

15 The change in total expenditures upon a good depends upon the good's price elasticity of demand. If the good is price elastic, an increase in price leads to a fall in expenditures, because the price increase leads to a greater proportional effect upon quantity demanded. If the good is price inelastic, however, a price increase raises total expenditures on the good, because the price rise leads to a less than proportional effect on quantity demanded. Last, if a good has a unitary elasticity, then a price rise has no effect upon total expenditures. In this case, the proportional increase is price is just matched by a proportional decrease in quantity demanded. Chapter 7 contains a fuller discussion of this relationship.

16 The null hypothesis that the coefficients equal to zero could not be rejected at the standard 0.05 level of significance. If one were to adopt a 0.1 level of significance, the null hypothesis could be rejected for December 1973 and January 1974. This suggests that, although not as strong as the results in table 3.1, the gasoline crisis was having some impact upon average daily trip-making in the early months of the crisis.

17 There are actually 13 heavy transit systems in the USA, in 11 cities. The New York area operates two heavy transit systems and Los Angeles' fixed rail system recently began operations.

18 If you are unsure why this is true, see the section on functional form in chapter 2 to review elasticity formulas for alternative model specifications. To see that demands in a double-log model are formed by multiplicatively interacting the variables, consider the following model: $y = Ax_1^\alpha x_2^\beta$. Here we see that x_1 and x_2 interact multiplicatively to determine y. Taking the logarithms of both sides gives the double-log model: $\ln(y) = \ln A + \alpha \ln(x_1) + \beta \ln(x_2)$.

19 In some communities rail service or (more likely) limousine shuttle services may be available. For this analysis, these alternative modes were less important substitutes than automobile trips.

20 A low R^2 for this model is not necessarily indicative of a poor model. Recall from chapter 2 that, since variables tend to move together, regression models based upon time series data will typically have higher values of R^2 in comparison with regression models based upon a cross-section of observations at a given point in time.

21 A related concern, but one which is mentioned less frequently, is that a variable may be *economically* insignificant even though it is *statistically* significant. For example, suppose that a $10 increase in income leads to a 0.00001 increase in the demand for air travel. The t-statistic is 3.0. Although statistically significant, the effect is so small that its implication for the allocation of resources is negligible. In this case, the variable is said to be economically insignificant. For an interesting discussion of this subject, see McCloskey (1985).

REFERENCES AND RELATED READINGS

General references

Colander, D. C. 1995: *Economics*, 2nd edn. Chicago: Richard D. Irwin.
McCloskey, D. N. 1985: *The Applied Theory of Price*, 2nd edn. New York: Macmillan.
Nicholson, W. 1998: *Microeconomic Theory*, 7th edn. Fort Worth, Texas: The Dryden Press.
Stiglitz, J. E. 1997: *Principles of Microeconomics*, 2nd edn. New York: W. W. Norton.
US Bureau of the Census 1993: *Statistical Abstract of the United States: 1993*, 113th edn. Washington DC.
Varian, H. R. 1987: *Intermediate Microeconomics: A Modern Approach*. New York: W. W. Norton.

Transportation references

General

Boyer, K. D. 1998: *Principles of Transportation Economics*. Reading, Mass.: Addison-Wesley.
Button, K. J. 1993: *Transport Economics*, 2nd edn. Brookfield, Vermont: Edward Elgar.
Goodwin, P. B. 1992: A review of new demand elasticities with special reference to short and long run effects of price changes. *Journal of Transport Economics and Policy*, XXVI, 155–69.
Oi, W. Y. and Shuldiner, P. W. 1962: *An Analysis of Urban Travel Demands*. Evanston, Ill.: Northwestern University Press.
Oum, T. H., Waters, W. G. I., and Yong, J.-S. 1992: Concepts of price elasticities of transport demand and recent empirical estimates. *Journal of Transport Economics and Policy*, XXVI, 139–54.
Oum, T. H., Dodgsen, J. S., Hensher, D. A., Morrisen, S. A., Nash, C. A., Small, K. A., and Waters, W. G. II (eds.) 1995: *Transport Economics: Selected Readings*. Seoul, Korea: The Korea Research Foundation for the 21st Century.
Quandt, R. E. (ed.) 1970: *The Demand for Travel: Theory and Measurement*. Lexington, Mass.: Heath Lexington Books.
Stubbs, P. C., Tyson, W. J., and Dalvi, M. Q. 1980: *Transport Economics*. London: George Allen and Unwin.
Winston, C. and Shirley, C. 1998: *Alternate Route*. Washington DC: Brookings Institution Press.

Airline demands

Alperovich, G. and Machnes, Y. 1994: The role of wealth in the demand for international air travel. *Journal of Transport Economics and Policy*, 28, 163–73.
Cigliano, J. M. 1980: Price and income elasticities for airline travel: the North Atlantic market. *Business Economics*, 15, 17–21.
De Vany, A. 1974: The revealed value of time in air travel. *The Review of Economics and Statistics*, LVI, 77–82.
Goetz, A. R. 1992: Air passenger transportation and growth in the US urban system, 1950–1987. *Growth and Change*, 23, 217–38.
Meyer, J. and Oster, C. 1981: *Airline Deregulation: The Early Experience*. Boston, Mass.: Auburn House.
Pickrell, D. H. 1984: The demand for short-haul air service. In J. R. Meyer, and C. V. Oster (eds.), *Deregulation and the New Airline Entrepreneurs*. Cambridge, Mass.: The MIT Press, pp. 29–49.
Raphael, D. E. and Starry, C. 1996: The future of business air travel. *Transportation Research Record*, 1506: 1–7.
Verleger, P. K. J. 1972: Models of the demand for air transportation. *The Bell Journal of Economics and Management Science*, 3, 437–57.

Motor vehicle related demands

Abdelwahab, W. and Sargious, M. 1992: Modelling the demand for freight transport. *Journal of Transport Economics and Policy*, XXVI, 49–70.
Archibald, R. and Gillingham, R. 1980: An analysis of the short-run consumer demand for gasoline using household survey data. *The Review of Economics and Statistics*, LXII, 622–8.
Deaton, A. 1985: The demand for personal travel in developing countries: an empirical analysis. *Transportation Research Record*, 1037, 59–66.
Dahl, C. A. 1983: An analysis of short-run consumer demand for gasoline using household survey data: a comment. *The Review of Economics and Statistics*, LXV, 532–4.
Frech, H. E. III and William, C. L. 1987: The welfare cost of rationing-by-queuing across markets and estimates from the US gasoline crises. *The Quarterly Journal of Economics*, 101, 97–108.

Kain, J. F. 1983: Impacts of higher petroleum prices on transportation patterns and urban development. In T. E. Keeler (ed.), *Research in Transportation Economics*, vol. 1. Greenwich, Conn.: JAI Press, pp. 1–26.

Lee, W. C. 1980: Demand for travel and the gasoline crisis. *Transportation Research Record*, 764, 38–42.

Pindyck, R. S. 1979: *The Structure of World Energy Demand*. Cambridge, Mass.: The MIT Press.

Public transit demands

Berechman, J. 1993: *Public Transit Economics and Deregulation*. Amsterdam: Elsevier Science.

Cervero, R. 1990: Transit pricing research. *Transportation*, 17, 117–39.

Doi, M. and Allen, W. B. 1986: A time series analysis of monthly ridership for an urban rail rapid transit system. *Transportation*, 13, 257–69.

Gomez-Ibanez, J. A. 1985: A dark side of light rail? The experience of three new transit systems. *Journal of American Planning Association*, 51, 1–32.

Hau, T. D. 1988: The demand for public transport in Hong Kong. Paper presented at the 63rd Annual Conference of the Western Economic Association International, Los Angeles, California, July.

Jones, D. 1985: *Urban Transit Policy: An Economic and Political History*. Englewood Cliffs, New Jersey: Prentice-Hall.

Kemp, M. A. 1973: Some evidence of transit demand elasticities. *Transportation*, 2, 25–52.

Voith, R. 1987: Commuter rail ridership: the long and the short haul. *Business Review*, 7, 13–23.

Voith, R. 1991: The long-run of demand for commuter rail transportation. *Journal of Urban Economics*, 30, 360–72.

Webster, F. V. and Bly, P. H. 1982: The demand for public transport. Part II. Supply and demand factors of public transport. *Transport Reviews*, 2, 23–46.

Rail demands

Babcock, M. W. and German, H. W. 1989: Changing determinants of truck–rail market shares. *Logistics and Transportation Review*, 25, 251–71.

Hilton, G. W. 1980: *Amtrak: The National Railroad Passenger Corporation*. Washington DC: The American Enterprise Institute.

4

Transportation Demand – The Discrete Good Case

INTRODUCTION

Although many transportation decisions, such as vehicle–miles traveled, passengers carried, rate of transport use, and ton–miles shipped, are continuous or divisible, there are other transportation choices that are inherently lumpy or discrete. My decision to purchase a car, which transportation mode I take to work, which carrier to use for shipping goods, when to travel, and by what route are all decisions that reflect an "either–or" choice. I either purchase a car or I don't. If I take the bus to work, I cannot simultaneously take a car. In planning my vacation to Florida, do I travel by plane, train, automobile, or some combination of modes? For that matter, do I take the vacation in season or during the off-season?

The last chapter developed the theory of individual and market consumption demands for continuous goods. In that chapter, we saw that when the good demanded is continuous, changes in the economic environment occur at the intensive margin. Individuals consume a little more or a little less of the good when prices or incomes change. And since market demand is simply the horizontal summation of individual demands, changes in market demands also occur at the intensive margin. If the good is discrete, however, it is not possible to consume at the intensive margin. Given the option of taking a bus or an automobile to work each morning, suppose that Tom initially decides to take the bus. The transit authority then announces that, as of next Monday, bus fares will increase by 10%. How will Tom react to this fare increase? Since the choice of bus mode is discrete, it is not possible for him to respond to the fare increase by consuming a little less of the bus mode. Either he takes the bus or he takes his car. If Tom does alter his consumption of bus travel, he will do so by consuming no bus travel and switching to an alternative transportation mode which, in this case, is his automobile. As seen in this example, when the good is discrete, consumers respond to changes in their economic environments by switching from one alternative to another, a demand response which is said to occur at the *extensive margin*.

In this chapter, we extend the theory of consumption to explicitly consider goods which have an "either–or" character. Although we continue to assume that individual consumers seek to maximize their economic welfare subject to resource constraints, the "either–or" nature of the consumption good has implications for the way that we model individual and market demands, how changes in the economic environment affect demands, and how we specify our demand estimating equations.[1]

INDIVIDUAL DEMAND FUNCTIONS

In this section, we apply the standard theory of consumer behavior to characterize individual choices when the good is discrete. To do this, consider our individual from the previous chapter who has two goods available, a transportation good, T, and a composite good that represents all other consumption, x. In this case, however, assume that T represents transportation mode to work where there are two modal alternatives, bus and automobile. Define

$$\begin{aligned} T_{\mathrm{a}} &= 1 \quad \text{if automobile is taken} \\ &= 0 \quad \text{if bus is taken} \end{aligned}$$

and

$$\begin{aligned} T_{\mathrm{b}} &= 1 \quad \text{if bus is taken} \\ &= 0 \quad \text{if automobile is taken} \end{aligned}$$

Given one's preferences, ϕ, the consumer desires to maximize the following utility function:

$$U = U(T_{\mathrm{a}}, T_{\mathrm{b}}, x; \phi)$$

subject to one's budget constraint, which can now be expressed as

$$Y = p_{T\mathrm{a}} T_{\mathrm{a}} + p_{T\mathrm{b}} T_{\mathrm{b}} + p_x x$$

where p_{Ti} ($i = \mathrm{a,b}$) is the per trip cost on an automobile and bus, respectively, and p_x is the per unit price of all other goods. Similar to the standard model of consumer behavior, the demand functions for T_i ($i = \mathrm{a,b}$) and x depend upon the economic environment and an individual's underlying preferences for each of the goods. In particular,

$$\begin{aligned} T_{\mathrm{a}}^* &= T_{\mathrm{a}}(p_{T\mathrm{a}}, p_{T\mathrm{b}}, p_x, Y; \phi) \\ T_{\mathrm{b}}^* &= T_{\mathrm{b}}(p_{T\mathrm{a}}, p_{T\mathrm{b}}, p_x, Y; \phi) \\ x^* &= x(p_{T\mathrm{a}}, p_{T\mathrm{b}}, p_x, Y; \phi) \end{aligned} \tag{4.1}$$

where it is recognized that T_{a}^* and T_{b}^* are mutually exclusive – that is, they cannot be consumed jointly – and will take on values of either zero or one. If this consumer takes an automobile to work, then $T_{\mathrm{a}}^* = 1$ and $T_{\mathrm{b}}^* = 0$. Alternatively, if the consumer's work trip mode is bus, then $T_{\mathrm{b}}^* = 1$ and $T_{\mathrm{a}}^* = 0$.

CONSUMPTION AT THE EXTENSIVE MARGIN

A significant difference between the divisible and discrete choice problem relates to an individual's response to changes in the economic environment. In the discrete good case, consumers faced with an altered economic environment *switch* from one good to another. When switching occurs, the individual is consuming at the extensive margin. The altered economic environment does not induce an individual to consume a little more or a little less of a good; rather, consumption shifts from one good to another.

Does it matter whether individuals consume goods at the intensive or extensive margin? – at the individual decision-making level, no. But it does have implications for how we develop our model of market demands.

DISCRETE ALTERNATIVES AND THE INDIRECT UTILITY FUNCTION

When a consumer faces a discrete good T, with two mutually exclusive alternatives (a and b) and a divisible good x, then, subject to a budget constraint, the utility-maximizing demands for these goods are given in equation (4.1). Suppose that we substitute these demand functions into the individual's original utility function, $U(T_a,T_b,x;\phi)$. This yields

$$\begin{aligned} U(T_a^*,T_b^*,x^*;\phi) &= U(T_a(p_{Ta},p_{Tb},p_x,Y;\phi),T_b(p_{Ta},p_{Tb},p_x,Y;\phi),x(p_{Ta},p_{Tb},p_x,Y;\phi);\phi) \\ &= \hat{U}(p_{Ta},p_{Tb},p_x,Y;\phi) \end{aligned} \tag{4.2}$$

Whereas $U(T_a,T_b,x;\phi)$ is called a *direct* utility function, which a consumer maximizes subject to a budget constraint, $\hat{U}(p_{Ta},p_{Tb},p_x,Y;\phi)$ is called an *indirect utility function*, which gives the maximum utility that a consumer can achieve *for a particular economic environment* as defined by one's income and the existing level of prices. It is important to note that the indirect utility function is expressed in terms of prices, income, and preferences, whereas the direct utility function is a function of consumption quantities and preferences. The reason for this is that the indirect utility function is obtained *after* an individual has maximized his utility subject to his budgetary constraint. Since the optimal quantities of T_a, T_b, and x given in (4.1) are functions of prices, income, and preferences, the indirect utility function also depends upon prices, income, and preferences.

THE EFFECT OF CHANGES IN PRICES, INCOME, AND PREFERENCES ON INDIRECT UTILITY

For any given economic environment summarized by a consumer's income and the prices of transportation (T_a and T_b) and all other consumption (x), the maximum utility he can obtain is given by his indirect utility function. Can we determine how the indirect utility function is related to prices and income? Yes.

Suppose that the price of good x, nontransportation consumption, increases. By the law of demand, an increase in p_x reduces the optimal consumption of x, x^*. But since consumers prefer more to less (recall our preference assumptions from the last chapter), a decrease in x^* decreases an individual's level of utility. In other words, in the new economic environment characterized by a higher price of x, the maximum utility that an individual can achieve is lower.[2]

By similar reasoning, an increase in income, all else constant, increases the set of consumption bundles available to a consumer. A utility-maximizing consumer will distribute the increased purchasing power across the available commodities, with the net effect that he achieves a higher level of utility. As a result, the maximum utility that a consumer can obtain increases when consumer income rises.

Thus, we have the general result that an increase in any price, all else held fixed, reduces the maximum utility, $\hat{U}$, that an individual obtains. An increase in income, on the other hand, raises the maximum achievable utility when all else is held constant.

Indirect Utility and Optimal Choice

The importance of the indirect utility function derives from its usefulness in characterizing a consumer's transportation choice when the transportation good is discrete. Continuing to assume that "a" refers to automobile and "b" to bus, we know that an individual will take his car to work if the *budget-constrained* maximum utility received from an automobile commute is greater than the *budget-constrained* maximum utility from a bus commute. Let $\hat{U}_i(p_{Ti},p_x,Y;\phi)$ be the *conditional indirect utility function* for choice i (i = a,b). Since this indirect utility is conditioned upon a particular choice i, only the price of that alternative, p_{Ti}, is included as an argument in the function. If the conditional indirect utility for the automobile mode is greater than that of the bus mode, then the consumer will take an automobile to work. Specifically, an auto is selected for the work trip if

$$\hat{U}_{\mathrm{a}}(p_{T\mathrm{a}},p_x,Y;\phi) > \hat{U}_{\mathrm{b}}(p_{T\mathrm{b}},p_x,Y;\phi)$$

Alternatively, a bus will be chosen if the indirect utility from a bus commute is greater than the indirect utility from an auto commute:

$$\hat{U}_{\mathrm{b}}(p_{T\mathrm{b}},p_x,Y;\phi) > \hat{U}_{\mathrm{a}}(p_{T\mathrm{a}},p_x,Y;\phi)$$

It is now easy to see the advantages of the conditional indirect utility function. When there is a finite set of alternatives from which the consumer can select, we need only compare the indirect utilities for the alternatives in order to determine the chosen alternative; that is, the alternative that affords the consumer the maximum level of economic welfare, given the existing set of prices and income.

Market Demand for Discrete Transportation Goods

Similar to the divisible good case, for transportation choices that are discrete, aggregate or market demand is the horizontal summation of individual demands. For example, table 4.1 reports the number and proportion of workers who commuted to work in 1995 by private vehicle or some form of mass transit. Holding all else constant, 6.03 million commuters, representing 5.3% of the commuter travel market, demanded public transit at an average transit fare price of $0.70. Alternatively, 107.3 million commuters, representing 94.7% of the market, demanded automobile travel, given a 1995 per-mile cost of operating a vehicle equal to about 20 cents.[3] In each case, the aggregate demand for the mode represents a point on the market demand curve for that mode. Using the proportion of commuters on each mode as the measure of market demand, figure 4.1 graphs two possible market demand curves. All else constant, an increase in fare price decreases the proportion of public transit trips demanded

Table 4.1 Work-trip commuters, 1995

	Number of Commuters	Proportion of Commuters
Private vehicle	107,318,000	94.7
Mass transit	6,031,000	5.3

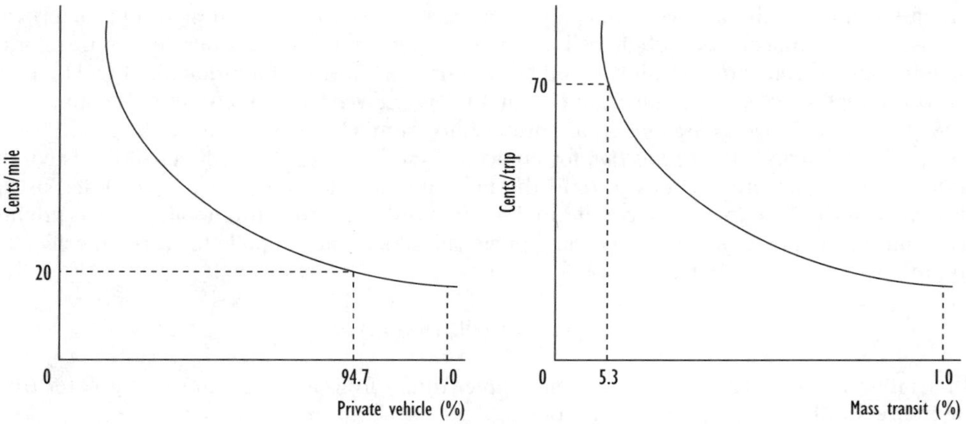

Figure 4.1 Market demands for auto and mass transit work trips.

and increases (that is, shifts rightward) the demand for automobile trips. Similarly, an increase in the per-mile cost of owning and operating an automobile is expected to decrease the proportion of automobile trips demanded but increase the demand for transit trips.

MARKET DEMAND AND CONSUMPTION AT THE EXTENSIVE MARGIN

To develop a market demand model for work trip mode choice, suppose that we adopt the same assumptions in the discrete good case as given in chapter 3 for the continuous good model. The only difference is that the transportation good T is discrete rather than continuous. In addition, we continue to assume that the transportation good corresponds to an individual's choice of automobile or bus for the work trip.

Since all individuals are identical in all respects, economic theory predicts that *each* individual selects the *same* mode in the trip to work. But this implies that the market demand for one of the modes will be zero. The problem with this prediction is that there will be *significant observation errors* which, given identical preferences, can only be due to errors of measurement or optimization.

To get a clearer understanding of this, we return to table 4.1, where 94.7% of work trips were in private vehicles and 5.3% on mass transit. If our model predicts that each individual uses a private vehicle for his work trip then, given identical preferences, measurement/optimization error is sufficiently serious to incorrectly predict one alternative in a large proportion of cases. Indeed, if the model predicted bus as the optimal choice, there would have been over 67 million incorrect predictions, all due to measurement/optimization error! Clearly, something is wrong.

Recall that in the continuous good case, variations in market demand occurred at the intensive margin, which means that each individual consumed a bit more or a bit less when economic circumstances changed. In this case, the assumption that each consumer had identical preferences was plausible. However, in the discrete good case, variations in market demand occur at the extensive margin. As the price of an automobile trip increases, fewer consumers take an automobile and more take the bus. Since changes in the economic environment cause individuals to shift from one mode to another (car to bus or bus to car), the assumption that all consumers have identical preferences is implausible, since it implies that all observation errors are due to measurement/optimization errors. Thus, for the discrete good case, we need to explicitly incorporate variations in taste across the population.

We are now in a position to specify a general market demand model when the transportation choices are discrete goods. To do so, we initially adopt the following assumptions, which allow for different preferences across consumers for the discrete good:

- individuals have different preferences for the transportation alternatives
- all individuals in the sample have identical incomes
- all individuals face the same level of prices
- individuals have identical socioeconomic characteristics
- T is discrete, with two possible alternatives, $x_{T\mathrm{a}}$ and $x_{T\mathrm{b}}$
- x is divisible

RANDOM UTILITY MODEL OF TRANSPORTATION CHOICE

Assume that each individual's indirect utility function for the automobile and bus alternatives is given by

$$\begin{aligned}\hat{U}_{\mathrm{a}} &= Y - p_x + V_{\mathrm{a}}(p_{T\mathrm{a}},Y;\phi) + \varepsilon_{\mathrm{a}}\\ \hat{U}_{\mathrm{b}} &= Y - p_x + V_{\mathrm{b}}(p_{T\mathrm{b}},Y;\phi) + \varepsilon_{\mathrm{b}}\end{aligned} \tag{4.3}$$

where V_i (i = a,b) is an observable empirical function and $(Y - p_x + V_i)$ (i = a,b) is that portion of a consumer's conditional indirect utility which is *observable and common* across all individuals in the population. It reflects "representative" or average tastes in the population. ε_i (i = a,b), on the other hand, is *unobservable and individual specific*, which reflects unobserved attributes of the alternatives as well as unobserved individual differences in preferences for the transportation alternatives.[4] Also note that, consistent with our earlier discussion, the conditional indirect utility for "a" does not depend upon the price of "b," and conditional indirect utility for "b" is not a function of alternative "a"'s price. It will be seen below, however, that the choice of alternative *will* depend upon both prices.

Consider the implication of an unobserved ε_i (i = a,b). We could have two individuals, Andrew and Rob, who face the same price of x, p_x, and have identical *observed* indirect utilities for the automobile choice, $V_{\mathrm{a}}(p_{T\mathrm{a}},Y;\phi)$. Yet Andrew could have a strong preference for auto travel which would give him a large positive ε_a, so that he would commute to work in an automobile. Rob, on the other hand, would select bus because he has a preference for public transit, which would give him a large negative value for ε_a. In general, identical observed portions of indirect utility do not imply identical *total* indirect utility levels and thus do not *necessarily* imply identical choice behavior.

Since each consumer's utility depends upon an unobserved individual specific term, ε_i (i = a,b), which is assumed to *randomly* vary from one individual to another, indirect utility also varies randomly from one individual to another. This implies that differences between observed and predicted choices reflect *unobservable taste variations* in the population. The fact that we cannot observe ε_i (i = a,b) for any individual implies that his choice cannot be predicted with certainty, but only probabilistically. Thus, for an individual randomly selected from the population, the probability that he chooses an automobile (alternative "a") in his trip to work is equal to the probability that the indirect utility associated with the automobile alternative exceeds the indirect utility associated with a bus trip:

$$\begin{aligned} P_a &= \Pr(\hat{U}_a(p_{Ta},p_x,Y;\phi) > \hat{U}_b(p_{Tb},p_x,Y;\phi)) \\ \Rightarrow P_a &= \Pr(p_x + V_a(p_{Ta},Y;\phi) + \varepsilon_a > p_x + V_b(p_{Tb},Y;\phi) + \varepsilon_b) \\ &= \Pr(\varepsilon_b - \varepsilon_a < V_a(p_{Ta},Y;\phi) - V_b(p_{Tb},Y;\phi)) \end{aligned} \tag{4.4}$$

where in the second line we have substituted the values for $\hat{U}_a$ and $\hat{U}_b$ from (4.3). Because the indirect utility of alternative "a" is not known with certainty to be greater than the indirect utility of alternative "b" for a randomly drawn individual, the model defined by equation (4.4) is referred to as a *random utility model*, and forms the basis for many empirical studies that analyze discrete transportation choices of firms, governments, and individual consumers.

PROBABILISTIC CHOICE MODELS

A distribution function gives the probability that a random variable takes on a value which is less than or equal to a given value x. If X is a random variable, the distribution function of X evaluated at point x is

$$F(x) = \Pr(X \leq x) \tag{4.5}$$

which is the probability that X is less than or equal to a specific value x. Since the distribution function is a probability, its value lies between zero and one.

Applying these concepts to our random utility model of transportation choice, we have already seen that the unobserved terms ε_a and ε_b for the automobile and bus modes are not identical for each consumer, but vary randomly across consumers. It follows, therefore, that the difference between ε_a and ε_b, $(\varepsilon_b - \varepsilon_a)$, also varies randomly in a population of consumers. In addition, we assumed that $V_a(p_{Ta},Y;\phi)$ and $V_b(p_{Tb},Y;\phi)$ were observable components of indirect utility for automobile and bus travel, respectively, which implies that their difference, $V_a - V_b$, is also observable.

Replacing the random variable X with $\varepsilon_b - \varepsilon_a$ and x with $V_a - V_b$ in equation (4.5) yields the random utility model derived in equation (4.4). In other words, the probability function in equation (4.4) is a cumulative distribution function and the random utility model represents a *probability model of transportation choice*. Specifically,

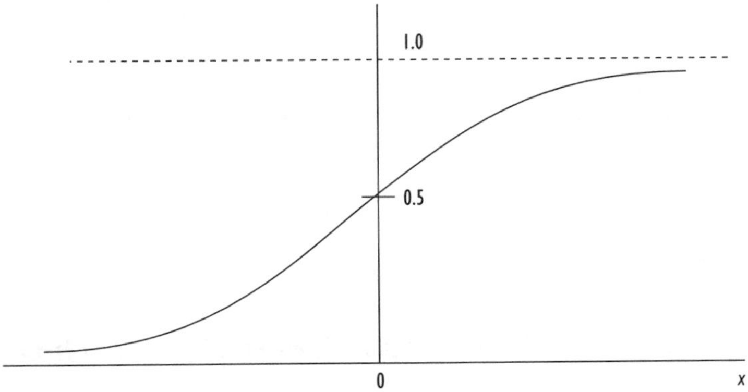

Figure 4.2 The cumulative logistic curve.

$$\begin{aligned} P_a &= \Pr(\varepsilon_b - \varepsilon_a < V_a(p_{Ta}, Y;\phi) - V_b(p_{Tb}, Y;\phi)) \\ &= F(V_a(p_{Ta}, Y;\phi) - V_b(p_{Tb}, Y;\phi)) \end{aligned} \tag{4.6}$$

where F is a distribution function.

What is the form of the distribution function F in (4.6)? Although there are many such statistical functions from which to choose, the distribution function which has been found to be most useful in transportation analysis is a *logistic* distribution function.[5] The logistic distribution function for random variable X is

$$F(x) = \Pr(X \leqslant x) = \frac{1}{1 + e^{-x}} \tag{4.7}$$

Notice that $F(x)$ lies between zero and one. As x approaches $-\infty$, e^{-x} approaches infinity, so that $F(x)$ approaches zero. Alternatively, as x approaches $+\infty$, e^{-x} goes to zero and $F(x)$ approaches one. If $x = 0$, then $F(x) = \frac{1}{2}$. Figure 4.2 depicts the logistic curve (4.7), which is seen to have an "S" shape that is common to many continuous distribution functions. Adopting the logistic distribution function for our random utility probability model, replace x in (4.6) with the observed difference in indirect utilities, $(V_a(p_{Ta}, Y;\phi) - V_b(p_{Tb}, Y;\phi))$. This defines the probability of taking an automobile to be

$$P_a = F(V_a(p_{Ta}, Y;\phi) - V_b(p_{Tb}, Y;\phi)) = \frac{1}{1 + e^{-(V_a - V_b)}} \tag{4.8}$$

$$= \frac{e^{V_a}}{e^{V_a} + e^{V_b}} \tag{4.8'}$$

where

$$V_i = V_i(p_{Ti}, Y;\phi), \qquad i = a,b$$

The probabilistic choice model in (4.8) or (4.8′) is referred to as a *binary logit* model of transportation choice. It is a binary model because only two choices are available to the trip-maker, and it is a logit model because the model is based upon a logistic distribution function.

Since the probability of taking an automobile plus the probability of taking a bus must add up to one, $P_b = 1 - P_a$, which can be easily shown to be equivalent to

$$P_b = \frac{e^{V_b}}{e^{V_a} + e^{V_b}} \tag{4.9}$$

for the binary logit model.[6]

TRANSPORTATION CHOICE DEMAND – ESTIMATION

In order to estimate our binary logit model of transportation choice, we need to identify the observable parts of a consumer's indirect utility function. Assume that the observed portion of an individual's utility is a linear-in-parameters function of price and income. This gives

$$\begin{aligned} V_a &= \beta_1 p_{Ta} + \beta_2 Y \\ V_b &= \beta_1 p_{Tb} + \beta_3 Y \end{aligned} \tag{4.10}$$

where β_i $(i = 1, 2, 3)$ are parameters. In this formulation, the marginal effect of an increase in bus fare (β_1) on bus indirect utility *is identical* to the marginal effect of an increase in the price of an automobile commuter trip (β_1) on automobile indirect utility. Income, on the other hand, is assumed to have a different marginal impact on bus choice than on automobile choice.

If the marginal effect of a variable, such as price in (4.10), is assumed to have the same impact on the indirect utility of each alternative, then the variable is referred to as a *generic* variable. If, on the other hand, the marginal effect of a variable, such as income in (4.10), depends upon the alternative (β_2 for auto and β_3 for bus), then the variable is referred to as an *alternative specific variable*; that is, a variable whose marginal effect is specific to a given alternative. Inserting V_a and V_b from (4.10) into (4.8′), the probability of choosing an automobile is

$$\begin{aligned} P_a &= \frac{\exp(\beta_1 p_{Ta} + \beta_2 Y)}{\exp(\beta_1 p_{Ta} + \beta_2 Y) + \exp(\beta_1 p_{Tb} + \beta_3 Y)} \\ &= \frac{\exp(\beta_1 p_{Ta}) \exp(\beta_2 Y)}{\exp(\beta_1 p_{Ta}) \exp(\beta_2 Y) + \exp(\beta_1 p_{Tb}) \exp(\beta_3 Y)} \\ &= \frac{1}{\exp(\beta_1 p_{Ta} - \beta_1 p_{Ta}) \exp(\beta_2 Y - \beta_2 Y) + \exp(\beta_1 p_{Tb} - \beta_1 p_{Ta}) \exp(\beta_3 Y - \beta_2 Y)} \\ &= \frac{1}{1 + \exp(\beta_1 (p_{Tb} - p_{Ta}) + (\beta_3 - \beta_2) Y)} \qquad (4.11) \\ &= \frac{1}{1 + \exp(-\beta_1 (p_{Ta} - p_{Tb}) - \bar{\beta} Y)} \qquad (4.11') \end{aligned}$$

where e^x is written as $\exp(x)$, and β_1 and $\bar{\beta}$ are parameters to be estimated from the data.

It is important to note that $\bar{\beta}$ (= $\beta_2 - \beta_3$) gives the impact of an increase in income on automobile choice *relative to* its impact on choosing a bus for the work trip. Although income was assumed to affect the indirect utility of both alternatives, only the *difference* between the two marginal effects can be identified. From equation (4.11′), if the two marginal effects of income were identical – that is, $\beta_2 = \beta_3$ – then $\bar{\beta}$ would equal zero and income would have no effect on the probability of choice.

Why can we only identify the *relative* effect of income on the choice probability? The reason is that income takes on exactly the same value in the observable part of the indirect utility for both automobile and bus choices. Since there is no variation in income across the available modes, it is not possible to obtain separate estimates of β_2 and β_3. Only their difference, $\bar{\beta}$, is estimable.

A DIGRESSION ON NORMALIZING ALTERNATIVES

Because $\bar{\beta}$ in equation (4.11′) gives the marginal impact of income on automobile choice *relative to* its impact on bus choice, the bus alternative is said to be a *normalizing* alternative. Instead of normalizing with respect to the bus alternative, suppose that we identified automobile as the normalizing alternative. Would this affect the results? No. In this case, income would enter the indirect utility of the bus alternative, but would be absent from the conditional indirect utility for the automobile alternative, as seen in (4.10′):

$$V_a = \beta_1 p_{Ta}$$

$$V_b = \beta_1 p_{Tb} + \bar{\bar{\beta}} Y \tag{4.10′}$$

What does this imply regarding the difference $V_a - V_b$? It yields exactly the same result as when the bus was the normalizing alternative, since $V_a - V_b = \beta_1(p_{Ta} - p_{Tb}) - \bar{\bar{\beta}}Y$, where $\bar{\bar{\beta}} = \beta_3 - \beta_2$. This implies that $-\bar{\bar{\beta}} = \beta_2 - \beta_3 = \bar{\beta}$ from above, and the interpretation of $\bar{\bar{\beta}}$ is the marginal effect of an increase in income on choice of bus *relative to* its effect on the choice of automobile, which is consistent with the interpretation of $\bar{\beta}$ as the marginal effect of an increase in income on choice of automobile *relative to* its effect on bus choice. Thus, equations (4.10) and (4.10′) tell us that our choice of normalizing alternative is arbitrary and will have no impact upon the estimated demand for bus and automobile choices. However, the choice of normalizing alternative *does* affect the interpretation of Y's coefficient. To sum up:

1 If Y is included in the indirect utility of the automobile, then bus is the normalizing alternative and Y's coefficient gives the marginal effect from a \$1 increase in income on auto choice relative to its effect on bus choice.
2 If Y is included in the indirect utility of bus, then automobile is the normalizing alternative and Y's coefficient gives the marginal effect from a \$1 increase in income on bus choice relative to its effect on automobile choice.
3 Points 1 and 2 are relevant for *any* variable that has the same value for each alternative. This includes, for example, demographic and other socioeconomic characteristics, such as

a consumer's age or gender. When an alternative specific variable has the same value in the indirect utility function of each alternative, only the relative effect of the variable can be identified. Although the alternative that is chosen to be the normalizing alternative will not affect the probability of choosing any alternative, it will affect the interpretation of the variable's coefficient;

4 One last point on normalizing alternatives is that if the conditional indirect utility function contains more than one alternative specific variable, such as income and driver age, it is not necessary that each variable have the same normalizing alternative. For example, in equation (4.10′), income could enter the conditional indirect utility for bus, so that automobile is the normalizing alternative with respect to income. At the same time, the variable "driver age" could enter the conditional indirect utility of the automobile mode, which means that bus is the normalizing alternative. In this latter case, the coefficient gives the marginal effect of an increase in driver age upon automobile mode choice relative to its impact upon bus mode choice.

THE DEMAND CURVE FOR AUTOMOBILE AND BUS CHOICE

Holding constant the price of bus travel, p_{Tb}, and income in equation (4.11) gives a relationship between the probability of choosing an automobile and the price of an automobile trip. The impact of an increase in the price of an automobile trip, p_{Ta}, on auto choice probability can be shown to equal

$$\frac{\Delta P_a}{\Delta p_{Ta}} = P_a(1 - P_a)\beta_1 < 0, \qquad \text{for } \beta_1 < 0 \tag{4.12}$$

Since we have already seen that, all else constant, an increase in price reduces indirect utility, we know that $\beta_1 < 0$. Combined with the fact that the probability of taking an automobile must lie between zero and one, this gives us an inverse relationship between price of auto travel and the probability of auto travel, consistent with the law of demand.

By exactly the same reasoning, the probability of choosing a bus is $1 - P_a$ which, all else constant, yields an inverse relationship between bus choice probability and bus fare. An increase in bus fare decreases the probability of choosing the bus and is expressed as

$$\frac{\Delta P_b}{\Delta p_{Tb}} = P_b(1 - P_b)\beta_1 < 0, \qquad \text{for } \beta_1 < 0 \tag{4.13}$$

CHANGE IN THE DEMAND FOR AUTOMOBILE AND BUS CHOICE

For the binary logit model, the demand curve for automobile travel shifts to the right in response to an increase in bus fares. Specifically, the marginal effect on the choice of one mode when the price of the other mode increases is given by

$$\frac{\Delta P_a}{\Delta p_{Tb}} = -P_a P_b \beta_1 > 0, \qquad \text{for automobile choice} \tag{4.14a}$$

$$\frac{\Delta P_b}{\Delta p_{Ta}} = -P_b P_a \beta_1 > 0, \qquad \text{for bus choice} \tag{4.14b}$$

These effects are symmetric for a given β_1 and are unambiguously positive as long as the marginal effect of an increase in a mode's price decreases its indirect utility; that is, $\beta_1 < 0$. Since automobile and bus choices are substitutes, an increase in the price of an automobile trip shifts the demand curve for bus travel to the right, all else held constant. Similarly, if bus fares increase, the demand curve for auto trips shifts to the right.

To further illustrate these relationships, consider the total effect of an increase in the price of an automobile trip. From equations (4.12) and (4.14b) we have

$$\frac{\Delta P_a}{\Delta p_{Ta}} + \frac{\Delta P_b}{\Delta p_{Ta}} = P_a(1 - P_a)\beta_1 - P_b P_a \beta_1 = (P_a P_b - P_b P_a)\beta_1 = 0$$

since $P_a + P_b = 1$. If an increase in the price of automobile travel decreases the probability of taking an automobile, the probability of taking the bus must correspondingly increase. An analogous result would occur if we were to analyze the effect on automobile and bus choices from an increase in the price of bus travel.

How does an increase in income affect transportation mode choice? The marginal effects of an increase in income on the probability of taking an automobile and bus, respectively, are

$$\frac{\Delta P_a}{\Delta Y} = P_a(1 - P_a)(\bar{\beta}) = P_a P_b(\bar{\beta})$$

$$\frac{\Delta P_b}{\Delta Y} = -P_b(1 - P_b)(\bar{\beta}) = -P_b P_a(\bar{\beta}) \tag{4.15}$$

Because the choice probabilities must sum to one, the effect of an increase in income on the probability of automobile choice is equal in value and *opposite* in sign to its effect on probability of bus travel. If the marginal effect of an increase in income raises the indirect utility of auto more than that of bus ($\beta_2 > \beta_3$), which implies that $\beta_2 - \beta_3 = \bar{\beta} > 0$, then the increase in income raises the probability of making the trip by automobile (by shifting the demand curve for automobile choice to the right) and correspondingly lowers the probability of making the trip by bus (by shifting the demand curve for bus choice to the left). Alternatively, if $\beta_3 > \beta_2$ then an increase in income reduces the probability of making the trip by automobile and raises the probability of a bus trip, all else held constant.

If the demand for automobile travel is a normal good and the demand for public transit is an inferior good, then we would expect an increase in income to increase the probability of choosing an automobile and decrease the probability of taking a bus, all else held constant. For the above model, this implies that the estimated value of $\bar{\beta} = \beta_2 - \beta_3$ would be positive.

OWN- AND CROSS-PRICE ELASTICITIES

Having identified the marginal effect that an increase in the price of bus or automobile travel has upon choice, it is straightforward to identify the own- and cross-price elasticities. For automobile choice, the own- and cross-price elasticities are given by

$$\begin{aligned} E^{P_a}_{p_{Ta}} &= \frac{\Delta P_a}{\Delta p_{Ta}} \frac{p_{Ta}}{P_a} = P_a(1 - P_a)\beta_1 \frac{p_{Ta}}{P_a} = (1 - P_a)\beta_1 p_{Ta} \\ E^{P_a}_{p_{Tb}} &= \frac{\Delta P_a}{\Delta p_{Tb}} \frac{p_{Tb}}{P_a} = -P_a P_b \beta_1 \frac{p_{Tb}}{P_a} = -P_b \beta_1 p_{Tb} \end{aligned} \tag{4.16}$$

Equation (4.16) gives the percentage change in the probability of taking an automobile due to a 1% increase in the price of automobile travel and the price of bus travel, respectively. The own- and cross-price elasticities for bus choice have similar forms and can be shown to equal

$$\begin{aligned} E^{P_b}_{p_{Tb}} &= (1 - P_b)\beta_1 p_{Tb} \\ E^{P_b}_{p_{Ta}} &= -P_a \beta_1 p_{Ta} \end{aligned} \tag{4.17}$$

respectively. We can also characterize the total effect of an increase in the price of auto travel on automobile and bus demands, respectively, in terms of a weighted sum of elasticities, where the weights are the probabilities of choice. In particular,

$$\begin{aligned} P_a E^{P_a}_{p_{Ta}} + P_b E^{P_b}_{p_{Ta}} &= P_a(1 - P_a)\beta_1 p_{Ta} - P_b P_a \beta_1 p_{Ta} \\ &= P_a P_b \beta_1 p_{Ta} - P_b P_a \beta_1 p_{Ta} \\ &= 0 \end{aligned}$$

The weighted sum of elasticities is zero and again reflects the fact that an increase in the choice probability of one alternative must be balanced by a decrease in the choice probability of the other alternative in order to maintain the constraint that the probabilities sum to one.

INCOME ELASTICITIES OF DEMAND

Based upon the marginal income effects given in (4.15), the income elasticity of the demand for automobile and bus travel is

$$\begin{aligned} E^{P_a}_{Y} &= \frac{\Delta P_a}{\Delta Y} \frac{Y}{P_a} = P_a(1 - P_a)(\bar{\beta}) \frac{Y}{P_a} = (1 - P_a)\bar{\beta} Y \\ E^{P_b}_{Y} &= \frac{\Delta P_b}{\Delta Y} \frac{Y}{P_b} = -P_b P_a (\bar{\beta}) \frac{Y}{P_b} = -P_a \bar{\beta} Y \end{aligned} \tag{4.18}$$

As with own- and cross-price elasticities, the sum of income elasticities, respectively weighted by the choice probabilities, equals zero, as shown below:

$$\begin{aligned} P_a E_Y^{P_a} + P_b E_Y^{P_b} &= P_a(1 - P_a)\bar{\beta}Y - P_b P_a \bar{\beta}Y \\ &= P_a P_b \bar{\beta}Y - P_b P_a \bar{\beta}Y \\ &= 0 \end{aligned}$$

VALUE-OF-TIME ESTIMATES

Up to this point, we have assumed that the only economic constraint facing an individual is a monetary constraint. Yet it is well known that one of the major considerations of one's transportation choice is travel time which, similar to income, is a scarce resource. A more realistic specification of an individual's indirect utility is to include the time associated with a trip on each mode. To do so, let t_a be the time of travel when an automobile is used and t_b the time of travel when a bus is used. Define an individual's indirect utility for automobile and bus modes, respectively, to be

$$V_a = \beta_1 p_{Ta} + \beta_2 Y + \kappa t_a \tag{4.19}$$

$$V_b = \beta_1 p_{Tb} + \beta_3 Y + \kappa t_b \tag{4.20}$$

where the price of each mode is measured in cents per trip, travel time is measured in minutes per trip, and κ is a parameter that gives the marginal effect on indirect utility from an increase in travel time. According to equations (4.19) and (4.20), the marginal effect of an increase in automobile time has the same impact on automobile indirect utility (given in (4.19)) as its effect on the bus indirect utility (given in (4.20)).

An important implication of including travel time and travel cost in indirect utility is that we can now identify a utility-preserving *trade-off* between travel time and travel cost. In particular, holding utility and household income constant, suppose that the price of a trip and the time of the trip change in such a way so as to leave utility unchanged. From (4.19) and (4.20), we obtain

$$\begin{aligned} 0 = \Delta V = \beta_1 \Delta p_{Ta} + \kappa \Delta t_a &\Rightarrow -(\Delta p_{Ta}/\Delta t_a) = \kappa/\beta_1 \\ 0 = \Delta V = \beta_1 \Delta p_{Tb} + \kappa \Delta t_b &\Rightarrow -(\Delta p_{Tb}/\Delta t_b) = \kappa/\beta_1 \end{aligned} \tag{4.21}$$

Both equations in (4.21) give identical information. If one were to ask the question, "How much would you be willing to pay in order to reduce your travel time by 1 minute, holding utility constant?," your answer would be κ/β_1 cents. In other words, κ/β_1 is the number of cents that you would have to be paid if your travel time increased by 1 minute, holding all else constant, including your level of economic welfare. Alternatively, you would be willing to pay $-\kappa/\beta_1$ cents in order to save one minute of utility-preserving travel time.

Finally, based upon the more general expressions for indirect utility given in equations (4.19) and (4.20), the binary logit model for the probability of choosing an automobile is written as

$$\begin{aligned} P_a &= \frac{\exp(\beta_1 p_{Ta} + \beta_2 Y + \kappa t_a)}{\exp(\beta_1 p_{Ta} + \beta_2 Y + \kappa t_a) + \exp(\beta_1 p_{Tb} + \beta_3 Y + \kappa t_b)} \\ &= \frac{1}{1 + \exp(\beta_1 (p_{Tb} - p_{Ta}) + \kappa(t_b - t_a) + \bar{\beta}Y)} \end{aligned} \tag{4.22}$$

where β_1, κ, and $\bar{\beta}$ are parameters to be estimated. β_1 and $\bar{\beta}$ have the same interpretations as before, κ gives the effect on indirect utility from an increase in travel time, and κ/β_1 reflects the value that trip-makers place on their travel time.

CASE STUDY – A BINARY LOGIT MODEL OF URBAN TRANSPORTATION MODE CHOICE

In order to fix the ideas developed in the previous sections, let's examine a typical study of work-trip mode choice in which two alternative modes are available, automobile and public transit. Because of their frequency, daily volume, and implications for highway and public transit investment, as well as their congestion, safety and environmental effects, work trips singularly form the most important component of intracity travel. Table 4.2 reports 1990 automobile and public transit modal splits and average travel times for different regions of the country.

For the country as a whole, 94.6% of all work trips are by automobile, while only 5.4% are by some form of public transportation. From the table, most regions in the country are either close to or below the average with the exception of the Middle Atlantic area. Included in this area are New York, New Jersey, and Pennsylvania, with work-trip public transit use equal to 25.5%, 9.0%, and 6.6% respectively. Representing 25% of annual public transit trips, New York's Metropolitan Transportation Authority is three times as large as the next largest transit system. Although table 4.2 suggests that public transit is little used for work trips, there are exceptions. In addition to the 16.1% use in the Middle Atlantic region, 37.7% of the workers in the District of Columbia, 10.3% of Illinois workers (primarily in the Chicago area), and 7.6% of workers in Hawaii use public transit.

Who characterizes public transit work-trip travelers? In 1983, 3.4% were male, 6.0% female, and 10.7% resided within a central city. Not unexpectedly, the percentage of work trips on public transit fell from 6.9% for households with annual incomes below $10,000 to 3.1% for households with incomes in excess of $40,000.

Because of their importance, work-trip modal choice decisions are extensively studied. In one of the earlier analyses of work-trip transportation demands, Domencich and McFadden (1975) estimated a binary logit model for automobile and public transit based upon a sample of 115 commuter trips. The analysis focused upon a suburban and downtown corridor in the

Table 4.2 Work-trip modal split and average travel time, 1990

Region of Country	Automobile Work Trip	Public Transit Work Trip	Average Travel Time to Work
New England	94.7	5.3	21.5
Middle Atlantic	83.9	16.1	25.7
East North Central	95.6	4.4	20.7
West North Central	98.0	2.0	18.4
South Atlantic	96.5	3.5	22.5
East South Central	98.8	1.2	21.1
West South Central	98.0	2.0	21.6
Mountain	97.8	2.2	19.7
Pacific	95.0	5.0	23.8

Source: Department of Commerce, *1993 Statistical Abstract of the United States*

Pittsburgh metropolitan area and, of the 115 trip-makers, 54% commuted by automobile and 46% by public transportation. For each of the commuters, the *observable* indirect utilities for automobile and public transit, respectively, were

$$\begin{aligned} V_a = {} & \beta_0 + \kappa_1(\text{Time}_a) + \beta_1(\text{Cost}_a) \\ & + \beta_2(\text{Autos/Worker}) + \beta_3(\text{Race}) \\ & + \beta_4(\text{White Collar}) \\ V_b = {} & \kappa_1(\text{Time}_{pt}) + \kappa_2(\text{Walk Time}) + \beta_1(\text{Cost}_{pt}) \end{aligned} \tag{4.23}$$

where Time_a is the work-trip travel time for auto trip (minutes); Cost_a is the parking charges plus vehicle operating costs per trip (cents); Autos/Worker is the number of automobiles in the household divided by the number of workers in the household; Race = 0 if white, 1 if non-white; White Collar = 0 if blue-collar job, 1 if white-collar job;[7] Time_{pt} is the public transit line-haul time plus wait and transfer time (minutes); Cost_{pt} is the public transit fare (cents); Walk Time is the walk time to and from the public transit station (minutes); and β_i ($i = 0, \ldots, 4$) and κ_i ($i = 1, 2$) are parameters to be estimated.[8] There are a number of clarifying points that we can make regarding this work-trip model of transportation mode choice:

1 Time and cost are *generic* variables, since the marginal effect of travel time and travel cost on indirect utility is assumed to be the same for the automobile and public transit modes, respectively. This is seen in (4.23) by noting that the coefficient of Time_a and Time_{pt} is κ_1 and the coefficient of Cost_a and Cost_{pt} is β_1. Observed indirect utility for public transit includes one other generic variable, Walk Time, in addition to public transit travel time and travel cost. In general, the amount of time required to access a given mode is an important determinant of mode choice and should be included in the indirect utility of each alternative. For automobile choice, however, walking time to access one's car is sufficiently small (almost zero from one's house to the garage) that the variable can be reasonably excluded from the indirect utility of the automobile. Thus, the interpretation of κ_1 is the marginal effect of an increase in transit walk time on public transit indirect utility.

2 Observed indirect utility for the automobile includes three *alternative specific variables*: Automobiles/Worker, Race, and White Collar. They are called alternative specific variables, because each is associated with a specific alternative, automobile choice in this model. Also, since each of these variables takes on the same value regardless of which transportation mode is chosen for the work trip, there must be a normalizing alternative. For this model, bus is the normalizing alternative. β_2, β_3, and β_4 give the marginal effect of each variable *relative to* the bus alternative, respectively.

3 β_0 is the coefficient of a constant term, commonly referred to as an *alternative specific constant*, that is associated with the automobile alternative. β_0 measures the relative "preference" of a reference group for the alternative whose indirect utility the constant term enters.

To see this, suppose that we want to identify the transportation mode choice for a white, blue-collar worker who faces identical travel times and costs for each mode, whose transit walking time is negligible, and who owns no automobiles.[9] In this case, the reference group is white, blue-collar workers with no automobiles and zero access time to public transit. For a commuter in this group, the difference between the indirect utility of bus and automobile is

$$\begin{aligned} V_a - V_b &= \beta_0 + \kappa_1(\text{Time}_a - \text{Time}_b) \\ &\quad + \beta_1(\text{Cost}_a - \text{Cost}_b) \\ &\quad + \beta_2(\text{Autos/Worker}) + \beta_3(\text{Race}) \\ &\quad + \beta_4(\text{White Collar}) \\ &\quad - \kappa_2(\text{Walk Time}) \\ &= \beta_0 + \kappa_1(0) + \beta_1(0) + \beta_2(0) + \beta_3(0) \\ &\quad + \beta_4(0) - \kappa_2(0) \\ &= \beta_0 \end{aligned} \tag{4.24}$$

For this reference group, β_0 is the difference between the indirect utility of automobile choice and bus choice and reflects an "automobile preference" parameter. If $\beta_0 > 0$, then the probability P_a of choosing the auto mode is greater than one-half. This is seen by substituting $V_a - V_b$ above into equation (4.8), which gives P_a $[1/(1 + e^{-\beta_0})]$. For $\beta_0 > 0$, $e^{-\beta_0} < 1$ and $P_a > \frac{1}{2}$. If $\beta_0 < 0$, $e^{-\beta_0} > 1$ and $P_a < \frac{1}{2}$. If $\beta_0 = 0$, then $P_a = \frac{1}{2}$ and a commuter in this reference group has an equal preference for bus and automobile modes.

How would one assess the preference for automobile commutes for another reference group; say, non-white, blue-collar workers? In this case, the variable Race equals 1, so that $P_a = [1/(1 + e^{-\beta_0-\beta_3})]$. A commuter in this new reference group would have a preference for an automobile commute if $P_a > \frac{1}{2}$, which is true as long as $\beta_0 + \beta_3 > 0$, since $e^{-\beta_0-\beta_3} < 1$.

Hypotheses

For the work-trip mode choice model in equation (4.23), the following hypotheses identify the expected effects of the explanatory variables:

HYPOTHESIS 1 By the law of demand, there is an inverse relationship between opportunity cost and quantity demanded where, in this model, quantity demanded is the probability of taking a given mode in the journey to work. Since the variables Time and Cost are components of a traveler's opportunity cost, it is expected that an increase in the bus trip time will decrease the probability of taking a bus and an increase in automobile trip time will decrease the probability of taking an automobile. Similarly, it is expected that an increase in the automobile (bus) trip cost will decrease the probability of taking an automobile (bus), all else held constant. For public transit, an additional component of opportunity cost is Walk Time. It is expected that an increase in this variable will also decrease the probability of taking a bus. In terms of the model's parameters, then, we expect $\kappa_1 < 0$, $\beta_1 < 0$, and $\kappa_2 < 0$.

HYPOTHESIS 2 An increase in Auto/Worker is expected to increase the probability of an automobile work trip. That is, $\beta_2 > 0$. There are two reasons for this. First, economic theory tells us that income plays an important role in consumption decisions. Although the lack of data prevented income from being explicitly included as an explanatory variable, there is strong evidence that income and automobile ownership are positively correlated. In the model, Autos/Worker acts as a *proxy* for household income, so that empirically this variable captures (at least part of) the effect of household income on a trip-maker's mode choice decision. Second, a household member's use of an automobile is constrained by the number of automobiles available. Given household demands for auto travel, therefore, an increase in Autos/Worker, all else constant, relaxes this constraint, which increases the probability of automobile use.

HYPOTHESIS 3 Similar to our development of regression models in the continuous goods case, socioeconomic characteristics such as Race and White Collar are included to reflect differences in preferences among consumers for automobile travel. *A priori*, however, we have no basis for expecting these variables to have a positive or negative effect.

Estimation results

Table 4.3 presents estimation results for the Pittsburgh study on work-trip modal demands. Table 4.3(a) highlights the indirect utility formulation of the model by identifying which variables enter the indirect utility of automobile and public transit choices respectively. Table 4.3(b), on the other hand, presents the same results in a tabular format that is oftentimes used to

Table 4.3 The binary logit model of transportation choice

(a)

	β_0	k_1	β_1	β_2	β_3	β_4	k_2
Automobile Utility	1	Time_a	Cost_a	Autos per Worker	1 if nonwhite	1 if white-collar job	0
Public Transit Utility	0	Time_{pt}	Cost_{pt}	0	0	0	Walk Time
Coefficient Estimate (*t*-statistic)	−3.82 (−7.48)	−0.0382 (−1.51)	−0.0256 (−4.45)	4.94 (4.62)	−2.91 (−2.12)	−2.36 (−2.02)	−0.158 (−3.30)

(b) Modes: auto, public transit

Variable	Coefficient Estimate	*t*-statistic
Constant (auto)	−3.82	−7.48
Time (all modes)	−0.0382	−1.51
Cost (all modes)	−0.0256	−4.45
Autos/Worker (auto)	4.94	4.62
Race (auto)	−2.91	−2.12
White-Collar (auto)	−2.36	−2.02
Walk Time (public transit)	−0.158	−3.30

Source: Domencich and McFadden (1975), p. 159

present statistical results. Table 4.3(b), for example, is very similar to the presentation of the regression results in chapter 3. Although, throughout this chapter, we adopt the format given in table 4.3(b) to present discrete choice statistical results, it is useful at this point to use both formats in order to ensure that we fully understand how the indirect utilities are defined.

The parenthetical information provided in column 1 of table 4.3(b) identifies those variables that enter automobile and public transit indirect utility functions, respectively. The constant term in table 4.3(b) is expressed as "Constant (auto)", which says that a constant term enters the indirect utility of the automobile choice but not that of public transit. To take another example, the variable "Time (all modes)" in table 4.3(b) tells us two things. First, Time is in the indirect utility of each mode, automobile and bus. Second, an increase in travel time has the same marginal effect on the indirect utility of automobile and as it does on bus. To fix these ideas, convince yourself that each variable identified in table 4.3(b) is consistent with the indirect utility model in table 4.3(a).

What do the parameter estimates tell us? In this model, the variable Constant is specific to the automobile, which indicates that public transit is the normalizing alternative. Thus, the negative sign on the constant term says that, holding constant travel time and cost on each mode, Pittsburgh commuters in the reference group – white, blue-collar workers, who own no automobiles, and face negligible access time to public transit – have a preference for taking public transit in their work trips. Notice also that the coefficients for Race and White Collar are negative. These coefficients reinforce the constant term and imply that reference groups comprised of nonwhite, blue-collar workers as well as white-collar workers also have a preference for public transit. In other words, the results in table 4.3(b) indicate that in work-trip situations where public transit is equally as fast and costs the same as an automobile trip, and getting to a bus stop takes little time, all commuters in carless households prefer public transit to automobile choice. When no cars are available to a household, this undoubtedly reflects the inconvenience of scheduling rides with other persons.

Consistent with hypothesis 2, the positive sign and large *t*-statistic on Autos/Worker gives the expected result that a larger stock of automobiles in the household, all else constant, increases the probability of taking an automobile. In that Autos/Worker captures the effect of income on transportation mode choice, this result also indicates that automobile work trips are normal goods – an increase in income increases the probability of an auto trip.

Race is a variable that equals zero for white and one for nonwhite commuters. The negative sign on the estimated coefficient of Race tells us that, all else constant, nonwhites have a higher demand for public transit than do white commuters. Similarly, the negative coefficient on White Collar, which has a value of one for a white-collar worker and zero otherwise, says that white-collar workers have a higher demand for public transit, all held constant.

Consistent with the law of demand, as specified in hypothesis 1, the coefficients for Time, Cost, and Walk Time are negative. An increase in access time or in-vehicle time on a given mode decreases the probability of the mode's choice; similarly, the more expensive a mode's trip becomes, all else constant, the less likely will that mode be chosen for the work trip.

The demand curve for automobile and public transit modes

An important characteristic of the transportation model for discrete alternatives is that it yields modal demands for *each* alternative. If we hold all variables constant except the price of auto travel, for example, the relationship between P_a, the probability of taking an automobile, and price yields a demand curve for the auto mode. Similarly, we derive a demand curve for public transit when all variables except public transit fares are held constant and we relate P_b to transit fares. Are the results presented in table 4.3 consistent with the basic precepts of consumer demand theory? Yes.

First, the estimated coefficient for Cost is negative. Since this variable enters the indirect utility of the auto and public transit alternatives, the negative sign on cost gives us the expected inverse relationship between modal demands and price. All else constant, an increase in the cost of an automobile trip to work reduces P_a, the probability of taking an automobile to work. Similarly, an increase in the price of a public transit trip reduces the probability of taking public transit, P_b, to work. Moreover, at −4.45, the *t*-statistic for Cost strongly rejects the null hypothesis that the coefficient equals zero. Cost is an important determinant of work-trip modal demands.[10]

Second, recall from the last chapter that travel time is a component of the opportunity cost of travel. Since an increase in travel time on a mode increases the opportunity cost of taking that mode, we expect the coefficient of Time to be negative. Table 4.3 confirms these expectations. The coefficient estimate of Time is negative, which implies that higher automobile and bus travel times, respectively, decrease the probability of taking an automobile or bus in the journey to work. Note, however, that Time's *t*-statistic of −1.51 rejects the null hypothesis that the coefficient is equal to zero at a 0.10 level of significance (on a one-tail test) but not at the more standard 0.05 level of significance. Thus, our confidence in this variable is somewhat weaker than that for Cost.

Third, an additional factor in the opportunity cost of bus travel is the time it takes to walk to a bus stop. An increase in Walk Time means that the bus stop is further away and, all else constant, is expected to reduce the probability of taking a bus in the work trip. The negative coefficient for Walk Time in table 4.3 verifies this. And at −3.30, the *t*-statistic strongly rejects the null hypothesis that Walk Time is not an important factor in the opportunity cost of bus travel.

Change in the demand for automobile and public transit

The demand curve for each mode is a relationship between the probability of taking that mode and the mode's opportunity cost, as reflected by mode price and mode travel time. All other factors which are expected to influence a commuter's choice of mode shift the location of the demand curve either to the right or to the left.

To illustrate, consider the effect of an increase in automobile cost on choosing bus for the work trip. Equations (4.12) and (4.14b), reproduced below, give the effect of an increase in auto cost on automobile and bus choice, respectively:

$$\frac{\Delta P_a}{\Delta p_{Ta}} = P_a(1 - P_a)\beta_1 < 0 \qquad (4.12)$$

$$\frac{\Delta P_b}{\Delta p_{Ta}} = -P_b P_a \beta_1 > 0 \qquad (4.14b)$$

Substituting the observed modal shares for P_a and P_b and the estimated value of β_1 from table 4.3(b) (or table 4.3(a)), we get the predicted impact of a 1 cent increase in the price of auto travel on modal choice demands:

$$\frac{\Delta P_a}{\Delta p_{Ta}} = 0.54(0.46)(-0.0256) = -0.0064$$

$$\frac{\Delta P_b}{\Delta p_{Ta}} = -0.46(0.54)(-0.0256) = 0.0064 \qquad (4.25)$$

Equation (4.25) tells us that the effect of a 1 cent increase in automobile cost for the trip to work reduces the probability of taking an automobile by 0.64 percentage points, from 54% to 53.36% and increases the probability of taking a bus from 46% to 46.64%. Figure 4.3 illustrates the effect on the respective demand curves from a 1 cent increase in the price of an automobile work trip.

What effect does a 1 cent increase in bus cost have upon bus and automobile choice probabilities? Since an increase in cost has the same effect on the indirect utility of bus as upon auto, we obtain exactly the same effect on the choice probabilities as given by equation (4.25). In particular,

$$\frac{\Delta P_b}{\Delta p_{Tb}} = 0.54(0.46)(-0.0256) = -0.0064$$

$$\frac{\Delta P_a}{\Delta p_{Tb}} = -0.46(0.54)(-0.0256) = 0.0064 \qquad (4.26)$$

In this case, the 1 cent increase in bus fare involves a movement along the bus probability (demand) curve and shifts the auto probability curve to the right.

Table 4.4 summarizes the probability effects of unit changes in those variables that are most likely affected through transportation policy: travel time and travel cost. As we saw above, a 1 cent increase in travel cost alters the choice probability by 0.64%. This implies that a 10 cent increase would alter the choice probability by 6.4%, which may seem high. However, data for this study was collected in 1967, and a 10 cent cost increase in 1967 was equivalent to 43 cent increase in 1993.

We also see that walk time is considerably more onerous than in-vehicle travel time. A 1 minute increase in walk time to a bus stop reduces by 3.9% the probability of choosing the bus for one's work trip. By comparison, a one minute increase in in-vehicle time lowers the probability of mode choice by only 0.95%.

Table 4.5 presents automobile and bus choice elasticities, calculated from equations (4.16), (4.17), and (4.18), associated with travel cost, travel time, and bus access walk time. Consistent

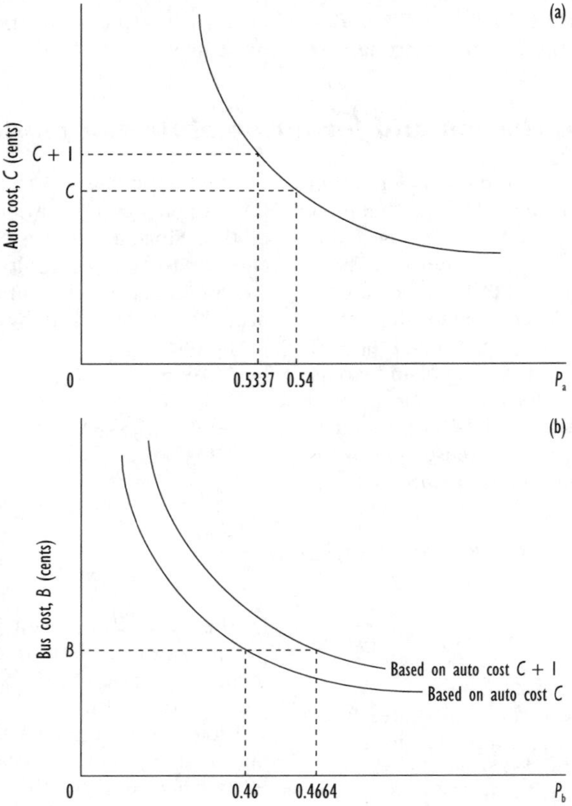

Figure 4.3 The effect on automobile and bus demands from a 1 cent increase in auto trip cost.

Table 4.4 The percentage point change in choice probabilities from alternative policies

	Percentage Point Change in	
Policy Change[a]	P_a	P_b
1 cent increase in auto cost	−0.64	+0.64
1 cent increase in bus cost	+0.64	−0.64
1 minute increase in auto time	−0.95	+0.95
1 minute increase in bus time	+0.95	−0.95
1 minute increase in walk time	+3.9	−3.9

[a] Each policy change is based on the assumption that $P_a = 54\%$ and $P_b = 46\%$.

Table 4.5 Automobile choice elasticities

Elasticity with Respect to	Automobile Choice	Bus Choice
Automobile Cost[a]	−0.59	+0.69
Bus Cost	+0.59	−0.69
Automobile Time[b]	−0.53	−0.62
Bus Time[b]	+0.53	+0.62
Walk Time[c]	+1.09	−1.28

[a] Elasticity evaluated for a current travel cost equal to \$0.50, $P_a = 0.54$, and $P_b = 0.46$.
[b] Elasticity evaluated for a current travel time equal to 30 minutes, $P_a = 0.54$, and $P_b = 0.46$.
[c] Elasticity evaluated for a current walk access time equal to 15 minutes, $P_a = 0.54$, and $P_b = 0.46$.

with the probability effects reported in table 4.4, the elasticity measures in table 4.5 indicate that workers are most sensitive to bus access walk time in comparison with cost and in-vehicle travel time. A 1% increase in walk time decreases the probability of taking a bus by 1.28%, while increasing the demand for auto choice by 1.09%.

Modal demands and the value of time

An important insight from the estimated mode choice model is obtained by comparing the coefficients for Time and Walk Time. The latter coefficient estimate is more than four times as large as the coefficient estimate for Time. This suggests that commuters in this sample find access time to a public transit facility to be much more onerous than the time spent at the station or in the vehicle. The relative burden of transit walking time can be highlighted by evaluating the value that commuters place upon transit walking time in comparison with the value attached to time spent at the station or in the vehicle. Recall from equation (4.21) that the value of time can be estimated by taking the ratio of the coefficient of the time variable to that of the cost variable. Based upon the estimation results presented in table 4.3, value-of-time estimates for travel time and walking time are as follows:

$$\text{Value of Travel Time} = \frac{-0.0382}{-0.0256}$$
$$= 1.49 \text{ cents/minute}$$
$$= \$0.89/\text{hour}$$

$$\text{Value of Walk Time} = \frac{-0.0382}{-0.0256}$$
$$= 6.17 \text{ cents/minute}$$
$$= \$3.70/\text{hour}$$

To put this in perspective, the estimated average full-time wage for the sample was \$2.85 (\$12.25 in 1993 prices). Thus, for both automobile and public transit travel time (which includes wait and transfer time for public transit) the estimated value of time was a bit less than one-third of the wage rate, whereas the estimated value of public transit walking time is nearly 30% *greater* than the wage rate. At the margin, the value that a consumer places on a 1 minute increase in in-vehicle time is more than offset by the value placed upon a 1 minute reduction in walk access time.

The differing values of time have implications for the design of transportation facilities. For example, bus systems that place a high priority on in-vehicle travel time will have fewer bus stops in order to achieve higher speeds. This may be an incorrect strategy, however, given the much higher value that transit riders place upon walk access time. A preferred strategy would entail a larger network of bus stops, in order to reduce the average distance of a bus stop from any user.

THE MULTINOMIAL LOGIT MODEL OF TRANSPORTATION CHOICE

In the previous sections, a consumer was assumed to have two options available, automobile and bus. However, in many transportation problems, more than two available alternatives actually exist. Many cities, for example, have fixed rail transit systems, light rail transit, and demand responsive services for one's work trip. In addition, the automobile mode may encompass distinct private automobile alternatives, which include driving oneself to work, riding with someone else, and carpooling.

How does the presence of more than two alternatives alter our transportation demand model? – fortunately, very little. Suppose that there are $J > 2$ alternatives. The probability that a consumer selects alternative i ($i = 1, \ldots, J$) equals the probability that the conditional indirect utility associated with alternative i, $\hat{U}_i$, is greater than the indirect utility associated with all other alternatives. That is,

$$\begin{aligned} P_i &= \Pr(\hat{U}_i > \hat{U}_j) \\ &= \Pr(V_i + \varepsilon_i > V_j + \varepsilon_j) \\ &= \Pr(\varepsilon_j - \varepsilon_i < V_i - V_j), \qquad i = 1, \ldots, J;\ i \neq j \end{aligned} \tag{4.27}$$

where V_j ($j = 1, \ldots, J$) is the observed indirect utility associated with alternative j and ε_j ($j = 1, \ldots, J$) is the unobserved random term associated with alternative j. Assuming that the differences in error terms ($\varepsilon_j - \varepsilon_i$) have a logistic distribution, the probability of selecting alternative i is

$$P_i = \frac{e^{V_i}}{e^{V_1} + e^{V_2} + \ldots + e^{V_J}} = \frac{e^{V_i}}{\sum_{j=1}^{J} e^{V_j}}, \qquad i = 1, \ldots, J \tag{4.28}$$

which is identical in form to the binary logit model in equation (4.8), except that there are more terms in the denominator to reflect the larger number of available alternatives. The transportation demand model in equation (4.28) is referred to as a *multinomial logit* model of transportation choice.

Assume, as we have done in the binary logit model, that the indirect utility associated with alternative j ($j = 1, \ldots, J$) is a linear function of the price of alternative j, travel time on alternative j, and consumer income. Then

$$\begin{aligned} V_1 &= \delta p_{T1} + \kappa t_1 + \beta_1 Y \\ V_2 &= \delta p_{T2} + \kappa t_2 + \beta_2 Y \\ V_3 &= \delta p_{T3} + \kappa t_3 + \beta_3 Y \\ &\vdots \\ V_J &= \delta p_{TJ} + \kappa t_J + \beta_J Y \end{aligned} \tag{4.29}$$

which, when substituted into equation (4.28), gives

$$P_i = \frac{\exp(\delta p_{Ti} + \kappa t_i + \beta_i Y)}{\sum_{j=1}^{J} \exp(\delta p_{Tj} + \kappa t_j + \beta_j Y)} = \frac{\exp(\delta p_{Ti} + \kappa t_i + \bar{\beta}_i Y)}{\sum_{j=1}^{J} \exp(\delta p_{Tj} + \kappa t_j + \bar{\beta}_j Y)}, \qquad i = 1, \ldots, J \tag{4.30}$$

where $\bar{\beta}_j = \beta_j - \beta_J$ and gives the marginal effect of an increase in income on alternative j *relative to* its effect on alternative J.[11] Since an identical value of income enters the indirect utility of each alternative, not all of the β_js ($j = 1, \ldots, J$) can be estimated. If we define alternative J as the normalizing alternative, then only $J - 1$ parameters $\bar{\beta}_j = (\beta_j - \beta_J)$ ($j = 1, \ldots, J - 1$) are estimable.

In general, when there are J alternatives available and a variable enters the indirect utility of each alternative with exactly the same value, then, as in the binary logit case, a normalizing alternative must be defined. At most, $J - 1$ parameters associated with this variable can be estimated.

Also, if the indirect utility expressions for the J alternatives included alternative specific constants, γ_{i0} ($i = 1, \ldots, J$), then at most $J - 1$ of these can be estimated and their interpretation will be relative to normalizing alternative. Continuing to assume that the last alternative, J, is the normalizing alternative, then the $J - 1$ parameters, $\bar{\gamma}_{i0} = \gamma_i - \gamma_J$ ($i = 1, \ldots, J - 1$) can be estimated. Similar to the binary model, each of these $J - 1$ parameters has the interpretation, "reference group preference for choice i relative to the normalizing alternative, holding all else constant."

Last, the own- and cross-elasticities for alternative i in the multinomial logit model with respect to generic variable x_k ($k = 1, \ldots, J$) are

$$\begin{aligned} E_{x_i}^{P_i} &= (1 - P_i)\beta x_i && \text{"own-" elasticity}, \quad i = 1, \ldots, J \\ E_{x_j}^{P_i} &= -P_j \beta x_j && \text{"cross-" elasticity}, \quad i,j = 1, \ldots, J;\ i \neq j \end{aligned} \tag{4.31}$$

which are straightforward generalizations of equations (4.16) and (4.17) in the two alternative cases. Here β refers to the coefficient of a generic variable x_i, and would equal δ if x_i represented price as in equation (4.30); if x_i was travel time, then β in (4.31) would be replaced by κ, the coefficient of travel time in equation (4.30). Given that alternative J is the normalizing alternative, the choice elasticities with respect to alternative specific variable z are as follows:

$$\begin{aligned} E_z^{P_i} &= \bar{\beta}_i z - \left(\sum_{j=1}^{J-1} \bar{\beta}_j P_j \right) z && \text{for nonnormalized alternatives}, \ i = 1, \ldots, J - 1 \\ E_z^{P_J} &= -\left(\sum_{j=1}^{J-1} \bar{\beta}_j P_j \right) z && \text{for normalized alternative } J \end{aligned} \tag{4.32}$$

In the sections that follow, three travel demand models are analyzed in order to highlight some important aspects of consumer travel demands: household intercity travel for nonbusiness-related activities; the demand for automobiles; and forecasting the market of a new transportation alternative. In our last example of discrete choice decision-making, we will focus upon a shipper's choice of a freight transport carrier. Although shipping activities fall more logically within the scope of firm behavior, which is discussed in chapters 5 and 6, a shipper's demand for alternative transport carriers is formally equivalent to a consumer's demand for work-trip mode choice. Similar to consumers, shippers make their modal choices based upon a mode's shipping times, shipping cost, and reliability of service.

In each of the examples, the demand model is presented, estimation results are reported and interpreted, and implications for transportation policy are identified.

CASE STUDY – INTERCITY DEMAND FOR TRAVEL

As shown in table 4.6, there has been a significant shift toward air travel in intercity modal choices during the past 30 years. In 1960, 90.4% of all passenger–miles was by automobile and 4.4% by air. In the ensuing years, automobile, rail, and bus have seen a steady loss in their share of the travel market, falling to 80.2%, 1.1%, and 0.7% in 1990 respectively, to airline travel which increased nearly fourfold over the same period to 18.0%. However, notwithstanding these significant gains, table 4.6 also indicates that the private automobile is still the primary mode of travel, accounting for four-fifths of all passenger–miles in 1990.

What explains the continued dominance of the automobile for intercity trips? Given the relatively high price of airline tickets, why don't more travelers take bus or rail in their intercity trips? And do all intercity travelers value their time the same, or can we identify a relationship between value of time and mode taken? In order to answer these questions, we shall analyze an intercity travel demand model for leisure-related trips.

Intercity trips basically occur for one of two reasons: vacation, or nonbusiness-related, and business-related. Similar to other consumption activities, intercity travel demands represent the outcomes from a constrained utility-maximization problem. Business-related intercity trips, however, are not generally the result of the traveler's constrained utility-maximizing behavior. These trips result from firm decisions to minimize transportation costs associated with day-to-day business activities.

Since we're interested in those factors that determine a consumer's intercity travel demands, the following analysis focuses upon vacation or nonbusiness-related trips, to the exclusion of business trips.

Table 4.6 US intercity travel, 1960–90: billions of passenger–miles (%)

Year	Automobile	Airline	Bus	Rail
1960	706.1 (90.4)	34.0 (4.4)	19.3 (2.5)	21.6 (2.8)
1965	817.7 (89.2)	58.1 (6.4)	23.8 (2.6)	17.6 (1.9)
1970	1,026.0 (86.9)	118.6 (10.1)	25.3 (2.1)	10.9 (0.9)
1975	1,170.7 (86.4)	148.3 (10.9)	25.4 (1.9)	10.1 (0.7)
1980	1,210.3 (82.5)	2,194.1 (14.9)	27.4 (1.8)	11.0 (0.7)
1985	1,310.3 (80.1)	290.1 (17.8)	23.8 (1.4)	11.3 (0.6)
1990	1,597.5 (80.2)	358.9 (18.0)	23.0 (1.1)	13.2 (0.7)

Source: ENO Transportation Foundation 1993: *Transportation in America*, 11th edn

Specification of indirect utility

In 1977, the Bureau of the Census conducted a nationwide travel survey of the US population. Based upon a subsample of 3,623 vacation travelers from this survey, Morrison and Winston (1985) estimated a multinomial logit intercity travel demand model for single-destination trips (excluding package tours) that originated and ended in a Metropolitan Statistical Area. For this sample of travelers, 69.3% vacationers traveled by automobile, 24.8% by air, and 2–3% by bus and rail respectively.

A leisure traveler's indirect utility for intercity travel is assumed to depend upon five basic determinants:

- a mode's round-trip cost
- the round-trip travel time
- the average time between scheduled departures
- the number of people traveling together
- household income

A primary feature of this model's specification is that *all* travel time and travel cost variables enter the model as *alternative specific* variables; that is, variables whose effects are specific to a given mode. There is no presumption that the marginal effect on a traveler's indirect utility from an increase in travel time (or travel cost) on one mode is identical to its marginal effect on another mode. And to the extent that there are observed differences in the marginal effects, not only does the model present a more accurate picture of vacation traveler behavior, but it will yield improved elasticity estimates and values of time. The hypotheses associated with the included variables are as follows:

HYPOTHESIS 1 In accordance with the law of demand, it is expected that each of the travel cost and travel time variables, including scheduled time between departures, will have a negative sign. An increase in opportunity cost lowers the probability of choice, all else constant.

HYPOTHESIS 2 According to labor–leisure choice theories of labor supply, an individual's opportunity cost of time is related to one's wage rate. This implies that the marginal effect on indirect utility from an increase in travel time will be greater for higher-income households than for lower-income households.

HYPOTHESIS 3 Because the marginal cost of an extra traveler in an automobile trip is very low in comparison with bus, rail, and air modes, it is expected that, all else constant, an increase in the total number of household travelers making the trip together will increase the demand for an automobile intercity trip. In addition, the presence of small children will influence a household's choice of mode. For short trips, the flexibility of automobile travel will likely increase its demand when small children are present; however, for longer automobile trips this flexibility is offset by the inconvenience and discomfort to each traveler, including the small children. For longer automobile trips, therefore, the presence of small children is expected to reduce the demand for an auto trip and increase the demand for trips on a public conveyance.

A priori, there is no reason to expect the mode preference parameters, denoted by the constant terms, to favor one or the other of the modes. Hence, no hypothesis for the signs on these parameters is identified.

Estimation results

From the estimation results presented in table 4.7, several general conclusions can be drawn with regard to vacation travelers' demands for intercity travel.

1 *Automobile travel.* Auto-based vacation trips depend more upon the number and age of travelers than upon the mode's service characteristics. Consistent with hypothesis 3,

Table 4.7 Vacation demand for intercity travel

Variables	Coefficient Estimate	*t*-statistic
Cost-related characteristics		
Round-trip cost, in dollars (auto)	−0.0064	−1.22
Round-trip cost, in dollars (bus)	−0.0031	−1.27
Round-trip cost, in dollars (rail)	−0.0031	−1.57
Round-trip cost, in dollars (air)	−0.0028	−1.97
Time-related characteristics		
Round-trip time, in minutes (auto)	−0.00013	−0.85
Round-trip time, in minutes, for household with income < \$20,000 (bus)	−0.00038	−2.60
Round-trip time, in minutes, for household with income ⩾ \$20,000 (bus)	−0.0016	−1.57
Round-trip time, in minutes, for household with income < \$20,000 (rail)	−0.00037	−1.58
Round-trip time, in minutes, for household with income ⩾ \$20,000 (rail)	−0.00099	−2.69
Round-trip time, in minutes (air)	−0.0014	−1.16
Average time between scheduled departures, in minutes, for household with income < \$20,000 (bus)	−0.0019	−2.27
Average time between scheduled departures, in minutes, for household with income ⩾ \$20,000 (bus)	−0.0039	−1.01
Average time between scheduled departures, in minutes (rail)	−0.00058	−0.39
Average time between scheduled departures, in minutes (air)	−0.00021	−1.83
Socioeconomic characteristics		
Number of travelers (auto)	0.622	4.61
Number of travelers less than 4 years of age and trip distance less than 400 miles (auto)	1.33	1.29
Number of travelers less than 4 years of age and trip distance greater than 400 miles (auto)	−0.67	−2.82
Mode preference constant terms		
Constant term (bus)	−1.18	−3.68
Constant term (rail)	−0.75	−2.52
Constant term (air)	−0.38	−0.81

Source: Morrison and Winston (1985), table 1, p. 220. The model also included a rental car variable which was found to have no effect upon intercity modal demands

a larger number of travelers significantly raises the probability of taking an automobile, all else constant. However, holding the number of travelers constant, for vacation trips greater than 400 miles, the more of those traveling who are young children, the less likely it is that an automobile will be used. In both of these cases, the variables have their hypothesized signs and are significantly different from zero. The presence of small children also increases the demand for short-distance automobile trips, although with a *t*-statistic equal to 1.29 we cannot reject the null hypothesis that this coefficient is zero at a 0.05 level of significance. On the other hand, a long-distance trip has a negative and statistically significant effect upon automobile choice (the t-statistic is −2.82). The importance of the size of the traveling party is reinforced by noting that the coefficient for automobile travel time has the lowest value among the modes, whereas the coefficient for travel cost is more than twice as large as any of the other modes.

2 *Public conveyance travel.* Generally, the estimation results support hypothesis 2. For rail and air, the round-trip travel cost is an important determinant of a traveler's decision to use this mode. Round-trip travel time is also important to a traveler's choice of public conveyance, although not to one's choice of an air trip (with a t-statistic for the round-trip time by air equal to −1.16, we cannot reject the null hypothesis that the coefficient is zero). The results in table 4.7 also confirm hypothesis 3. Relative to lower-income households, the marginal (disutility) effect of increased travel time for higher-income households is over four times greater for bus (−0.0016 versus −0.00038) and 2.6 times greater for rail (−0.00099 versus −0.00037). The average time between departures is also seen to be important to one's decision to use air and bus (particularly for lower-income households), but is less relevant to the choice of rail.

3 *Modal preferences.* The constant terms for bus, rail, and air (where automobile is the normalizing alternative) indicate that, all else constant, there is an equal preference for selecting an automobile or plane for the vacation trip (the t-statistic for the air travel constant term is −0.81), but consumers have a definite preference for automobile (and air) relative to bus and rail modes, and a preference for rail to bus (the coefficient for a rail trip (−0.75) is greater than that for bus (−1.18)). The relative preference for an auto-based trip most likely reflects the convenience and flexibility of the automobile in comparison with public conveyance modes, as well as the effect of other variables, such as the condition of station terminals, that are not included in the model. For example, the bus mode coefficient for the constant term is three times as large (in absolute value) than that for air travel and 60% larger than rail, which reflects a strong dislike for intercity bus trips relative to each of the other modes. This is consistent with common public perceptions regarding the inconvenience and discomfort of bus travel, as well as the relatively small and sparse bus stations in comparison with rail stations and airports.

The demand curves for intercity travel

Consistent with expectations and with the law of demand, the coefficient estimates for each of the travel time and travel cost variables are negative, giving us an inverse relationship between opportunity cost and choice probability. In addition, the results in table 4.7 indicate that the marginal disutility of cost is nearly identical for the common carrier modes (bus, rail, and air), whereas cost plays a smaller, and somewhat less significant, role in the demand for automobile travel.

Changes in intercity modal demands

Characteristic of the multinomial logit model of transportation demand is that each alternative is a substitute for the other alternatives. Thus, an increase in the cost of travel on one mode, holding all else constant, not only decreases the probability of taking that mode but increases the probability of choosing each of the other modes. For example, if the cost of air travel increases, all else constant, the demand curves for auto, bus, and rail shift rightward. Similarly, an increase in round-trip air travel time not only lowers the probability of traveling by air, a movement up its demand curve, but also produces a rightward shift in the demand curves for auto, bus, and rail.

The positive sign on the number of travelers and on the number of children less than 4 years old for short-distance trips indicates that an increase in each of these variables shifts the demand curve for auto (bus, rail, and air) to the right (left), the largest shift occurring from an increase in the total number of travelers. A one-person increase in the number of travelers increases the probability of taking an automobile by 13 percentage points, from 69.3% to 82.5%. Correspondingly, the probability of taking a public conveyance (air, bus, or rail) falls to 17.5%, a reduction of 13 percentage points.[12] And the negative sign on the number of children less than 4 years old for longer trips has exactly the opposite effect. The more young children on long trips, all else constant, including the number of travelers, the more the demand curve for the auto shifts to the left and the demands for bus, rail, and air shift to the right.

Selected choice elasticities

To see the implications of some of these demand shifts, table 4.8 reports the own-cost, own-time, and schedule delay elasticities for each of the modes. The elasticities with respect to travel cost and travel time represent changes in the opportunity cost of travel and thus movements along a demand curve. With the exception of auto cost, time and cost elasticities for automobile and air modes are generally small. This result is not surprising, however, given the relatively large share of vacation travel, 94.1%, that these two modes capture. A 1% change in a mode's time or cost will not produce a large percentage change in a mode's share if that mode already has a large market share. In contrast, bus and rail modes have the potential for significant gains in market share from improvements in service characteristics, particularly those related to round-trip travel time and schedule-related delays. For example, bus's time elasticity tells us that a 1% reduction in round-trip travel time will produce a 2% increase in market share. In addition, a 1% decrease in intercity bus or rail schedule delays increases that mode's demand by 1.2%. A further interesting result is that vacation travelers have an elastic demand for intercity rail, indicating that a fare reduction would actually increase expenditures on rail intercity trips.

Table 4.8 Service elasticity measures for intercity modal demands

	Elasticity with Respect to		
Mode	Cost	Travel Time	Time Between Departures
Auto	−0.955	−0.393	–
Bus	−0.694	−2.11	−1.23
Rail	−1.20	−1.58	−1.27
Air	−0.378	−0.434	−0.047

Source: Morrison and Winston (1985), table 3, p. 226

Value-of-time estimates

The estimates in table 4.7 were used to calculate the values that vacation travelers place upon their time. Table 4.9 summarizes these results both in absolute terms ($ per hour) and as a fraction of the wage rate. For bus and rail modes, values of time are also given for higher- and lower-income households, since separate parameter estimates were obtained for these groups.

As we have previously seen, values of time are empirically derived from demand models by dividing the relevant time coefficient by its cost coefficient counterpart. Recall, in the urban transit examples, that we examined the mode choice of a *single* traveler – a commuter going to work – so that the ratio of coefficients reflected the value that this individual traveler placed upon his or her travel time. In the present example, the value of time reflects the value that the vacationing *household* places upon saving 1 minute of travel time. In order to convert this to a *per-person* value of time, it is necessary to divide by the average number of travelers taking the mode. For example, 1.91 travelers, on average, traveled when the automobile was the selected intercity mode. The value of time estimate for automobile travel is calculated as the ratio of the estimated time coefficient to the estimated cost coefficient, multiplying by 60 (which converts the time units from minutes to hours) and dividing this ratio by 1.91; that is, $((-0.00013/-0.0064) * 60/1.91) = \$.63$. This procedure was used to obtain each of the numbers in table 4.9.

Depending upon mode and service characteristic, the value of time varies considerably. An important reason for this is that the value of time reflects both the opportunity cost, in terms of income foregone, of time spent in a given activity – travel to one's vacation destination in this case – as well as the utility or disutility of the time spent traveling. Suppose, for example, that a two-worker family with two small children residing in Los Angeles decides to take a 5 day vacation in San Francisco. The family determines that, overall, it will be better if the trip is made by car. Assuming that the trip to San Francisco is an 8 hour drive, 2 days are spent driving and 3 days vacationing in San Francisco. The opportunity cost of the travel time spent reaching San Francisco corresponds to the foregone wages that each worker could have made during those 2 days.

In addition to foregone wages, the time spent in the car for the 8 hour drive to San Francisco could be pleasant or onerous, depending upon the family's preferences for driving. If the small children continually fight during the trip, the car is old and unreliable, and neither parent enjoys driving, then the value of time for the trip

Table 4.9 Vacation traveler value-of-time ($/hour) estimates, per person

Mode		Value of Travel Time (% of wage)	Value of Time Between Departures (% of wage)
Auto	All households	0.63 (6)	–
Bus	Households with incomes < $20,000	4.33 (79)	21.67 (394)
	Households with incomes ⩾ $20,000	14.03 (87)	33.87 (210)
Rail	Households with incomes < $20,000	4.37 (79)	5.98 (58)
	Households with incomes ⩾ $20,000	8.80 (54)	5.98 (58)
Air	All households	15.37 (149)	2.32 (23)

Source: Morrison and Winston (1985), table 2, p. 224

to and from San Francisco will be greater than the foregone wages associated with the two driving days. On the other hand, if the automobile is reliable and spacious, the children enjoy playing road games, and one of the reasons for taking the car was the scenery along the chosen route and the possibility of short sightseeing stops, then the value of time will be less than the lost wages during the outbound and return drive from San Francisco. In this case, the family receives utility from the time spent traveling, which offsets to some degree the opportunity cost due to lost wages.

Consistent with the findings of other studies, the values of travel time in table 4.9 for bus, rail, and air vary between 50% and 150% of the wage rate. The value of time for automobile travel, on the other hand, is estimated at only 6% of the wage rate, which most likely reflects the utility that automobile travelers receive from sightseeing and other recreational experiences enjoyed during the trip. In contrast, vacationers choosing to travel by air reveal a preference for a high-speed mode, implying a high opportunity cost of time. This is borne out in table 4.9 where, at 150% of the wage rate, air travelers are seen to have the highest estimated values of travel time. Despite the large difference in the value of time for automobile and air, since air travel is so much faster than automobile for trip distances of 200 miles or more, the value of total time spent for the trip may still be less by air.

Although the value of bus travel time, as a fraction of the wage rate, falls comfortably in the 50–150% range, the value of time between departures is considerably higher, from 200% to 390% of the wage rate, for bus travel. This provides some interesting insights into those aspects of a bus trip that travelers find particularly burdensome. Relative to auto, rail, and air, bus travel is generally viewed less favorably by the traveling population. However, the results of table 4.9 imply that this is *not* due to exceptionally large disutilities associated with the time spent on the bus. The value of travel time represents 80–90% of the wage rate, consistent with other common carriers. Rather, the unfavorable perception of bus travel results from utility-decreasing aspects of a bus trip that are unrelated to the actual time spent on the bus.

Individuals traveling on a common carrier typically experience some amount of schedule delay. The schedule delay can arise for two reasons:

- *Frequency delay*. This represents the time between a carrier's departure and the traveler's optimal time of departure. The greater the number of departures, all else constant, the lower will be a traveler's frequency delay.
- *Capacity delay*. This reflects the inability to travel at the desired departure time because all seats are occupied. The capacity delay is the amount of time that a traveler must wait before the next available departure. Holding all else constant, including departure frequency, increases in vehicle capacity reduce capacity delays. Alternatively, reductions in capacity delays occur with increases in departure frequency, holding capacity and all else constant.

In that schedule delays oftentimes entail waiting at a mode's terminal facility, the high value of time associated with bus scheduling delays not only reflects the value of time spent waiting (some of which may occur at one's home) but the traveling public's belief that waiting at a bus terminal is not an enjoyable experience.

Also consistent with this interpretation, air travelers value lost time due to schedule delays the least. This reflects the high frequency of departing flights (thereby reducing frequency and capacity delays) as well as the generally pleasant surroundings that airports provide when travelers experience scheduling delays.

For the rail mode, the value of scheduling time is twice that of air travel, but is still well below that associated with bus travel. At existing levels of rail travel, relatively few departures are required to accommodate demand, and capacity can easily be expanded or contracted with unexpected changes in ridership. Thus, the bulk of scheduling delay for rail is apt to reflect frequency rather than capacity delays which, when combined with the fact that rail terminals provide fewer amenities than air terminals, implies that the value of time between rail departures reflects delays from infrequent departures and some disutility from the less amenable railway stations.

Policy implications

The USA is seriously considering the viability of high-speed ground transportation (HSGT) systems and, specifically, high-speed rail systems. According to the Transportation Research Board, these systems are capable of reaching top speeds in the 200–250 mph range and operating speeds in the 130–190 mph range, depending upon the technology (Transportation Research Board, 1991). Given an estimated capital cost of $16–30 million per mile, these systems must have a large ridership to be economically viable. Two features of our intercity travel model have implications for HSGT systems. First, all else constant, increasing the number of passengers for relatively short distance vacations increases demand for automobile use. Second, as reflected by the higher values that air travelers place on travel time in comparison with rail travelers, speed is more important to air travelers, presumably due to the longer distances that must be traveled within a fixed vacation period. Combined with the high capital costs, these two features suggest that HSGT rail systems will be viable in dense population centers, and for trips that are in the medium travel range, 200–400 miles. For very short trips, HSGT trip and terminal costs will exceed auto costs; and for longer trips, the 500+ mph airplane speed favors airline travel. Candidate corridors in the USA that appear to satisfy the requirements for a viable HSGT system include the Northeast Corridor from Boston to Washington DC and the Philadelphia–Pittsburgh Corridor in the east, the Minneapolis–Chicago–Detroit Corridor in the midwest, Dallas–Fort Worth in the southwest, and San Francisco–Los Angeles in the west.

CASE STUDY – HOUSEHOLD DEMAND FOR VEHICLE OWNERSHIP

Table 4.10 provides household vehicle ownership patterns between 1969 and 1983, by number of adults in the household and by household income. During this time, household vehicle ownership has continued to grow for all household sizes. Whereas over 50% of one adult households owned no vehicle in 1969, by 1983 this was down to 34%. Those owning one and two vehicles, however, increased by 15% and 5.6% respectively. Similarly, for two-adult households there was a dramatic 28% drop in the one-vehicle category and a 20% rise in owning two vehicles. Further, two adult households owning three or more vehicles rose from 1.2% in 1969 to 15.3% in 1983. This rightward shifting of categories also held for three-adult households, which experienced a decrease in the proportions with no, one, or two vehicles, but a 216% increase in the proportion having three or more vehicles. Overall, for all households, the proportion owning none or one vehicle declined during this period, while the proportion with two or more vehicles rose, with households owning three or more vehicles exhibiting the largest increase, at 316%.

One of the primary reasons for the increasing trends of automobile ownership is household income. For 1983, table 4.11 provides a glimpse of the effect that increased household incomes have upon automobile ownership. For any income category, the proportion of households with large vehicle fleets decreases, reflecting the relatively high capital costs of vehicle ownership. Moving across rows, we see a general "inverted-U" shape relationship between income and ownership. For example, the proportion of households owning one vehicle initially rises to 46.2%, followed by a subsequent decline to 12.2% for the highest-income households. The reason for the decline is that at higher incomes households shift from owning one vehicle to owning two (or more) vehicles. A similar pattern characterizes two-vehicle households, although the decline doesn't occur until income reaches $40,000. Although three- and four-vehicle households exhibit a steady rise in ownership, if the data included higher-income categories, one would expect to see an eventual decline as households shift to the next highest ownership level. Although table 4.11 illustrates

Table 4.10 Vehicle ownership by number of adults in households

	Number of Vehicles (%)			
Number of Adults	0	1	2	3 or More
One-adult households				
1969	56.2	42.3	1.5	–
1977	39.2	53.2	5.7	1.9
1983	34.0	57.1	7.1	1.8
Two-adult households				
1969	12.4	57.3	29.1	1.2
1977	7.5	33.1	48.2	11.2
1983	5.8	29.2	49.7	15.3
Three-adult households				
1969	8.2	32.2	42.6	17.0
1977	5.9	15.9	34.4	43.8
1983	5.6	13.5	27.1	53.8
All households				
1969	20.6	48.4	26.4	4.6
1977	15.3	34.7	34.4	15.6
1983	13.5	33.7	33.5	19.3

Source: US Department of Transportation, Federal Highway Administration, *1983–84 Nationwide Transportation Study*

Table 4.11 Vehicle ownership by household income, 1983

Number of Vehicles	< \$10,000 (%)	\$10,000–\$19,999 (%)	\$20,000–\$29,999 (%)	\$30,000–\$39,999 (%)	> \$40,000 (%)
0	39.5	8.8	2.3	1.5	1.1
1	42.8	46.2	30.4	17.7	12.2
2	13.6	31.6	44.8	49.7	43.8
3	3.1	10.2	15.2	20.5	25.5
≥4	1.0	3.2	7.3	10.6	17.4

Source: US Department of Transportation, Federal Highway Administration, *1983–84 Nationwide Transportation Study*

an increasing effect of household income on vehicle ownership, there are other factors besides household income that affect the level of ownership, including the availability of competing travel modes and socioeconomic characteristics. Thus, if we want to isolate the impact that income exerts upon ownership levels and investigate the sensitivity of households to income changes, we must control for these other determining factors.

Indirect utility for vehicle ownership

As part of an extensive study on automobile ownership and use, Train (1986) estimated a demand model for a household's size of vehicle fleet. Based upon socioeconomic and vehicle ownership and utilization data obtained from a 1978 national survey of households, Train expressed a household's indirect utilities for vehicle ownership levels to be:

$$V_0 = 0$$

$$\begin{aligned}V_1 = \alpha_0 &+ \alpha_1 \log(\text{Household Income})\\ &+ \alpha_2(\text{\# Workers}) + \alpha_3 \log(\text{Household Size})\\ &+ \alpha_4(\text{Transit Trips per Capita})\\ &+ \gamma(\text{Average Utility from Vehicle Type Choice})\end{aligned}$$

$$\begin{aligned}V_2 = \beta_0 &+ \beta_1 \log(\text{Household Income})\\ &+ \beta_2(\text{\# Workers}) + \beta_3 \log(\text{Household Size})\\ &+ \beta_4(\text{Transit Trips per Capita})\\ &+ \gamma(\text{Average Utility from Vehicle Type Choice})\end{aligned} \tag{4.33}$$

where V_i $(i = 0, 1, 2)$ is the indirect utility associated with owning no vehicles, owning one vehicle, and owning two vehicles. This model has several interesting features.

First, the demand model is unique because the indirect utility of the normalized alternative is zero. This occurs for two reasons. One, with the exception of Average Utility from Vehicle Type Choice, all variables are alternative specific. This implies that a normalized alternative must be defined which, in this model, is zero ownership. Also, the coefficients for each of the alternative specific variables in the indirect utility for ownership level 1 are not equal to their counterparts in the indirect utility for ownership level 2. For example, the coefficient for "# Workers" is α_2 in V_1's indirect utility and β_2 in V_2's indirect utility. Since "# Workers" is an alternative specific variable, α_2 gives the marginal effect of an increase in the number of workers on the indirect utility of owning one vehicle relative to owning no vehicles. β_2 gives the marginal effect on the indirect utility of owning two vehicles relative to owning no vehicles. Similar interpretations hold for the coefficients of the other alternative specific variables.

The second reason that $V_0 = 0$ is that Average Utility from Vehicle Type Choice is identically zero for nonownership households. As discussed in greater detail below, Average Utility from Vehicle Type Choice is a generic variable that represents the benefit a household receives from owning one or more vehicles. By definition, if a household owns no vehicles, it receives no benefit and the value of Average Utility from Vehicle Type Choice is zero.[13]

The model's specification in (4.33) is also of interest because income and household size enter in logarithmic form. To see the implication of this, assume that observed indirect utility for owning one vehicle is solely a function of the logarithm of income:

$$\hat{U}_1 = \alpha \log(\text{income})$$

Then, the marginal (indirect) utility from an increase in income is

$$\frac{\Delta \hat{U}_1}{\Delta \text{income}} = \frac{\alpha}{\text{income}} \tag{4.34}$$

If, as is expected, automobile ownership is a *normal* good, then $\alpha > 0$ and the marginal (indirect) utility of income is positive. But note that, for higher levels of income, the denominator in (4.34) increases, which *reduces* its effect on the (indirect) utility of owning one vehicle. Hence, specifying income in logarithmic form not only hypothesizes that an increase in income increases the demand for ownership but it also hypothesizes that, with further income increases, the demand for ownership increases *at a decreasing rate*. Similarly, since the number of members in a household is in logarithmic form, the model hypothesizes that increases in household size will increase vehicle ownership at a decreasing rate.

Third, a household's level of ownership decision is complicated by the fact that, to some degree, the level of ownership depends upon the type(s) of vehicle(s) owned. Consider a four-person household, consisting of two adults and two young children, that currently owns one vehicle. Will the type of vehicle (for example, a pick-up truck, sports car, sedan, and so forth) currently owned have any impact upon the household's decision to purchase another car and become a two-vehicle household? – in general, yes.

If the household currently owns a two-door sports car, it is likely that the household will purchase a second larger car in order to satisfy a variety of trip needs (for example, family outings, carpools, and weekly grocery store shopping trips) that are difficult to meet with the limited passenger and carriage capacity of a sports car. Alternatively, if it owns a large four-door sedan, then the household would be less likely to purchase a second car. Thus, for this single-vehicle household, the closer the attributes of its current vehicle match the household's needs, the less likely will the household be to alter its level of ownership, holding all else constant.

More generally, the more a household's vehicle fleet is expected to meet its travel and capacity needs, the less likely will the household alter its level of ownership. Conversely, the greater the difference between the existing fleet's attributes and household needs, the more likely it is that the household will alter its level of ownership.

Average Utility from Vehicle Type Choice is a variable that captures this interrelationship between a household's level of ownership and the type(s) of vehicle(s) in its existing fleet. For households with one vehicle, this variable gives average utility that the household can expect from the set of available vehicle types (for example, Toyota Camry, Oldsmobile Cutlass, and so forth). Similarly, for two-vehicle households, the variable gives the average utility the household can expect from the set of *vehicle pairs* (for example, the sets (Toyota Camry, Chevrolet Chevette), (Oldsmobile Cutlass, Mazda 323), and so forth) available to the household. For a given level of ownership, improvements in the expected match between fleet attributes and household needs increase the average utility of a household's vehicle type choice which, all else constant, increases the probability of that ownership level.[14]

Hypotheses

The empirical model in equation (4.33) is used to test the following hypotheses regarding household ownership demands:

Hypothesis 1 All else constant, an increase in household income increases the demand for automobile ownership; that is, $\alpha_1 > 0$ and $\beta_1 > 0$.

Hypothesis 2 All else constant, the greater the supply of public transportation, the lower is the opportunity cost of using public transportation and the lower is the demand for automobile ownership. Increased transit availability is measured by the annual number of per capita transit trips in the household's residential area. It is expected that $\alpha_4 < 0$ and $\beta_4 < 0$.

Hypothesis 3 Increases in the demand for automobile travel are expected to increase the level of ownership, all else constant. In this model, the demands for automobile travel are reflected by the number of workers as well as the total number of members in the household. This implies that $\alpha_2 > 0$, $\alpha_3 > 0$, $\beta_2 > 0$, and $\beta_3 > 0$.

Hypothesis 4 The more closely a current household's vehicle fleet matches its needs, the greater is the probability of owning that number of vehicles. Thus, the coefficient of Average Utility from Vehicle Type Choice, γ, is expected to be positive.

Estimation results

The estimation results presented in table 4.12 indicate that the hypothesized model does a good job of explaining vehicle ownership. All variables have their expected sign and, except for household size, the *t*-statistics are very high, indicating that we can be confident, in a statistical sense, that the coefficients are not equal to zero. What do the results tell us?

1 Confirming hypothesis 1, the signs on both income variables are positive and the coefficient estimate for the second income variable (Logarithm of Household Income (2)) is greater than that of the first income variable (Logarithm of Household Income (1)). Recalling that the normalizing alternative is no vehicle ownership, the positive signs and the relative magnitudes of these coefficients give us the following interpretations:

   (i) An increase in income increases the probability of owning one vehicle relative to no vehicles, increases the probability of owning two vehicles relative to no vehicles, and increases the probability of owning two vehicles *relative to* owning one vehicle.

   (ii) An increase in income has a smaller effect on the relative probability of owning a given number of vehicles the higher is household income. This result is specifically due to the logarithmic formulation of income, as discussed above.

2 What is the quantitative effect of an increase in income on choice probabilities? Since income is measured in logarithms, a unit increase in this variable reflects a 1% increase in household annual income. Given initial choice probabilities $P_0 = 0.135$, $P_1 = 0.337$, and $P_2 = 0.528$, we use equation (4.32) to calculate income elasticities of demand, where $\bar{\beta}_1 = \alpha_1 - 0 = 1.05$, $\bar{\beta}_2 = \beta_1 - 0 = 1.57$, and $z = 1$. Table 4.13 reports the income elasticities of demand for this model. No ownership and single vehicle ownership are inferior goods, since a 1% increase in income reduces no vehicle ownership 1.18% and single vehicle ownership by 0.133%. Multiple ownership, on the other hand, is a normal

Table 4.12 Household demand for vehicle ownership[a]

Explanatory Variable	Coefficient Estimate	*t*-statistic
Logarithm of Household Income (1)	1.05	3.69
Logarithm of Household Income (2)	1.57	3.52
Number of Workers in Household (1)	1.08	3.78
Number of Workers in Household (2)	1.50	4.78
Logarithm of Number of Household Members (1)	0.181	0.43
Logarithm of Number of Household Members (2)	0.197	0.39
Annual Number of Transit Trips per capita in household's area of residence (1)	−0.0009	−1.82
Annual Number of Transit Trips per capita in household's area of residence (2)	−0.0021	3.42
Average Utility from Vehicle Type Choice (1, 2)	0.635	7.14
Constant term (1)	−1.79	−2.97
Constant term (2)	−4.95	−5.19

[a] Ownership levels: 0 = no vehicles; 1 = one vehicle; 2 = two vehicles.
Source: Train (1986), table 8.1, p. 146

Table 4.13 Effects on vehicle demands from income increases[a]

Demand for	Income Elasticity	Effect of 1% Increase in Income on the Percentage Point Vehicle Demands
No vehicles	−1.18	−0.159
One vehicle	−0.133	−0.045
Two vehicles	0.387	0.204

[a] Evaluations based upon initial demands given by $P_0 = 0.135$, $P_1 = 0.337$, and $P_2 = 0.528$.

good. A 1% increase in income raises the demand for multiple ownership by 0.387%. If we multiply each income elasticity of demand by its respective choice probability P_i ($i = 0, 1, 2$), we obtain the absolute change in choice probability due to a 1% increase in annual household income. From table 4.13, a 1% increase in annual household income reduces the demand for no vehicle ownership by 0.159 percentage points, from 13.5% to 13.34%, and reduces the demand for one vehicle ownership by 0.045 percentage points. Conversely, there is an offsetting increase in the demand for multiple vehicle ownership of 0.204 percentage points. Thus, all else constant, an increase in income shifts the demand curves for no and one vehicle ownership levels to the left and shifts the demand curve for two vehicle ownership level to the right. Also, the leftward shift of the single vehicle ownership curve is less than that of the no vehicle ownership curve, consistent with the finding that the demand for owning one vehicle *rises* relative to the demand for no vehicles. Figure 4.4 depicts these changes in the demand curves.

3 Consistent with hypothesis 2, the presence of substitutes negatively affects the demand for automobile ownership. The demand for single and multiple vehicle ownership, relative to having no vehicles, decreases with an increase in the number of public transit trips. This tells us that transportation planners and other policy-makers who implement policies that successfully attract public transit riders will reduce household incentives to own a vehicle. Are these incentives large? Again, we need to investigate the *quantitative* effect of an increase in public transit ridership. Table 4.14 reports the vehicle ownership demand elasticity with respect to a 1% increase in transit trips per capita, as well as the percentage point change in choice probability from a 1% increase in public transit ridership. Although the ridership coefficients are numerically small, table 4.14 tells us that, quantitatively, these effects are not negligible. A 1% increase in transit ridership, all else constant, increases no ownership and single ownership demands by 5% and 1.8% respectively. Similarly, multiple vehicle demands decrease by 2.4%. This suggests that moderate increases in residential area ridership, brought about, for example, by improvements in public transit service levels, could have an important effect upon vehicle ownership demands, all else held constant. Multiplying the elasticities by the respective choice probabilities again enables us to identify the change in vehicle ownership demands from a 1% increase in annual per capita ridership. The largest effect from a 1% increase in transit ridership is a 1.28 percentage point fall, from 52.8% to 51.6%, in the demand for two vehicles. The decrease in multiple vehicle ownership is equally apportioned between no- and one-vehicle ownership levels, increasing each by 0.6 percentage points.

4 Hypothesis 3 is partially confirmed. Households with more workers increase the demand for vehicles, but an increase in the number of household members does not. This suggests that the underlying source of

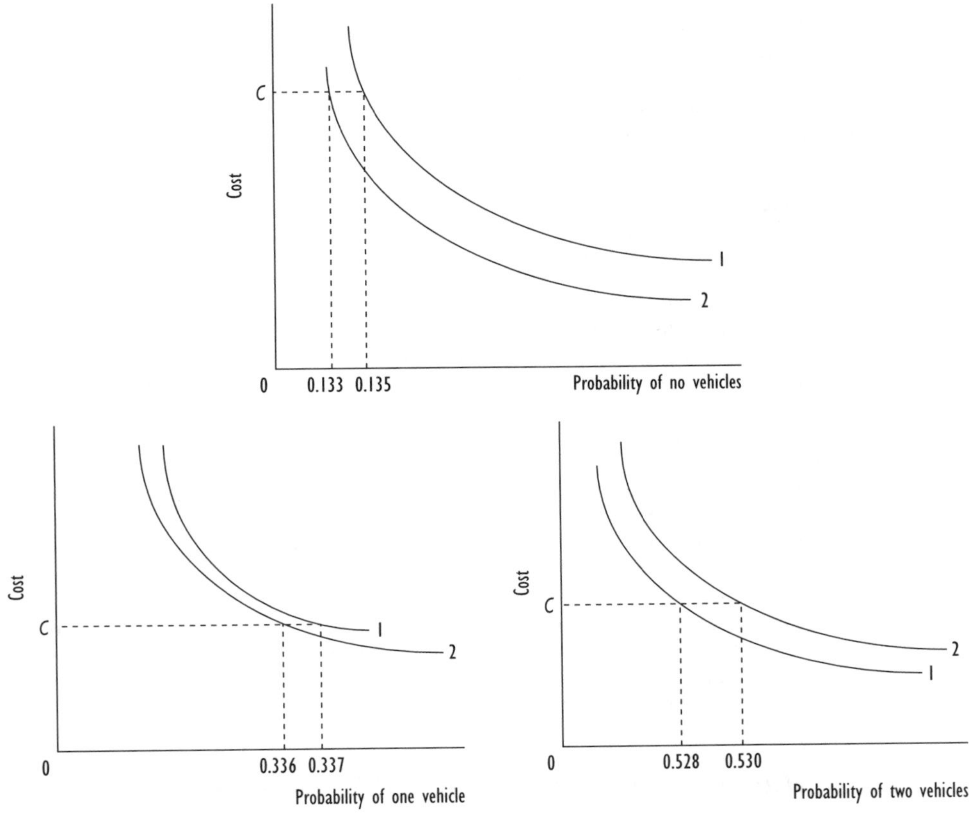

Figure 4.4 The effect of income on automobile ownership levels.

Table 4.14 Effects on increase in per capita transit trips on vehicle demands[a]

Demand for	Per Capita Transit Trips Elasticity (%)	Effect of 1% Increase in Annual Transit Trips on the Percentage Point Vehicle Demands[b]
No vehicles	5.0	0.67
One vehicle	1.81	0.61
Two vehicles	−2.44	−1.28

[a] Evaluations based upon an 35.4 average annual household number of public transit trips per capita in the area and initial vehicle demands given by $P_0 = 0.135$, $P_1 = 0.337$, and $P_2 = 0.528$.
[b] Calculated using equation (4.32), where $\bar{\beta}_1 = -0.0009$, $\bar{\beta}_2 = -0.0021$, and z is the annual number of transit trips in the respondent's residential area.

vehicle ownership is the work trip rather than size of household *per se*.

5 The positive sign for the variable Average Utility from Vehicle Type Choice confirms the importance of "attribute matching" that was identified in hypothesis 4. All else constant, the demand for a given level of ownership increases the greater the extent to which the expected attributes of a household's current vehicle fleet meets its expected travel, carriage, fuel economy, and other vehicle-related needs.

CASE STUDY – THE INTRODUCTION OF A NEW ALTERNATIVE

Up to this point, we have analyzed discrete choice problems in which a consumer must select one from some finite number of alternatives that are available. Whether the discrete commodity is sold by a private transportation firm or a public transit authority is immaterial. All that matters is that a consumer must select one from several available options.

Consider a related question. A transportation firm currently offers consumers two options for shipping a small package from Los Angeles to Indianapolis: overnight service at a high price or slow service that guarantees delivery in five working days but at a much lower price. In an attempt to increase its market share, the firm decides to introduce a new service that guarantees delivery in three working days at an intermediate price. The problem the firm faces is that providing the new service requires the firm to purchase some additional equipment and hire additional labor. The firm is certainly willing to take the chance on the new service if the expected demand for the service is sufficiently high. Moreover, although the firm will generate some new delivery business for the new service, it is also likely that the new service will cut into its existing overnight and slow delivery services. Can the firm get any idea, before its invests in additional capital and labor, what its expected demand will be? It turns out that forecasting the market share of a new and currently unavailable alternative is reasonably straightforward when the multinomial logit model characterizes consumers' transportation demands.

Multinomial logit predictions of the demand for new alternatives

To understand how an alternative which is not yet available can be predicted, recall equations (4.27) and (4.28), which summarize the multinomial logit model:

$$P_i = \Pr(\varepsilon_j - \varepsilon_i < V_i - V_j), \qquad i \neq j$$
$$= \frac{\exp(\delta p_{Ti} + \kappa t_i)}{\sum_{j=1}^{J} \exp(\delta p_{Tj} + \kappa t_j)}, \qquad i = 1, \ldots, J$$

where we have assumed that the observed indirect utility associated with alternative k ($k = 1, \ldots, J$) depends only upon an alternative's price and time:

$$V_k = \delta p_{Tk} + \kappa t_k$$

Suppose that we obtain some data on existing users and obtain estimates of the model's parameters, α and κ. Assume further that a new alternative is being developed and we want to determine the *expected* market share of this new alternative, $J + 1$. We know that the indirect utility associated with the new alternative will be

$$V_{J+1} = \hat{\delta} p_{T(J+1)} + \hat{\kappa} t_{J+1}$$

where $\hat{\delta}$ and $\hat{\kappa}$ are the estimated values for δ and κ. If a multinomial logit model continues to characterize transportation demands after the new alternative has been introduced, then the market share of that alternative will be

$$\frac{\exp(\hat{\delta}p_{T(J+1)} + \hat{\kappa}t_{J+1})}{\sum_{j=1}^{J+1}\exp(\hat{\delta}p_{Tj} + \hat{\kappa}t_j)} \quad (4.35)$$

Thus, once we have price and time estimates on the new alternative, we can predict its market share (as well as the altered market shares of the existing alternatives).

Work-trip modal choice in the San Francisco Bay Area

Within the past 25 years, several high-speed fixed rail transit systems have been built. The first of these newer systems was BART, the Bay Area Rapid Transit system, in San Francisco. Construction on the system began in the 1960s and the system began operations in 1972, with full operation in 1974. Early on, a major concern of policy-makers was financing. Would BART generate sufficient revenues to pay for the system? Because BART preceded federal aid, fare revenues, property taxes, and sales taxes were expected to pay for the operating and capital costs of the system.[15] Fare revenues, in turn, depended upon ridership, and since this was the first rapid transit system built in the USA in years, transportation policy-makers had little experience of forecasting the demand for a new alternative.

In an early study analyzing the expected market share of BART, McFadden (1974) estimated a binary logit model of work-trip choices in the San Francisco Bay Area and used that model to predict BART's market share. In his model, McFadden assumed that the demand for work-trip mode was a function of travel time, travel cost, and income. For the public transit alternative, travel time was subdivided into its individual components, which included walking time to access the bus, initial wait time at the bus stop, on-vehicle time, and waiting time involved in transfers from one bus to another.

In general, McFadden's results were consistent with our theory of consumer behavior. An increase in in-vehicle travel time and travel cost for a given mode reduced the probability of using that mode for the work trip. Also, as expected, an increase in bus walk time, bus wait time, and bus transfer wait time, all else constant, reduced the probability of taking a bus to work. Family income had a positive sign, as expected, indicating that the automobile mode was a normal good and bus travel was an inferior good.

Predicting the use of BART

The importance of this work for our present purposes is that McFadden used the model to predict the market share of a completely new alternative, BART. Combining the model's parameter estimates with engineering forecasts of BART's service characteristics, McFadden forecast the impact of BART on existing modal demands. Table 4.15 reports the market shares

Table 4.15 Original and forecast market shares of auto, bus, and BART

	Car (A) (%)	Bus (B) (%)	BART (C) (%)	Total Transit (D = A + B + C) (%)	BART Given Total Transit (C/D) (%)
Pre-BART	75.1	24.9	–	24.9	–
Post-BART	66.0	19.9	14.1	34.0	41.5

Source: Reprinted from McFadden (1974), with permission from Elsevier Science

for automobile and bus in the absence of BART and the predicted shares upon BART's introduction.

Prior to BART, the modal split between automobile and bus commute trips was 75.1% and 24.9% respectively. Since BART is a substitute for both automobile and bus trips, the model predicted that an operational BART system would capture 14.1% of work-trip commutes, 9.1% of which are from automobile trips and 5% from former bus travelers. Overall, public transit patronage increases from 24.9% to 34%, almost half of which would be trips on the high-speed BART system.

How good was McFadden's forecast of BART ridership? At the time of the study, BART was operating in San Francisco's East and West Bays, but the transbay line – which links the West Bay to the East Bay – was not operative. In October 1973, actual BART patronage averaged 9,672 commute round trips. Based upon his model of work-trip mode choice, McFadden forecast 9,658 daily round-trip commutes. Although these figures are not explicitly comparable (they included, for example, peak nonwork trips and excluded nonpeak work trips), they do highlight the important role that logit models can play in forecasting the demand for new alternatives.

CASE STUDY – THE DEMAND FOR FREIGHT TRANSPORT CARRIERS

Each of the previous examples examined an aspect of consumption demands for a discrete good. In this section, we shift our focus from the consumer to the firm and explore a shipper's demand for alternative transport carriers. Although this is not a consumer behavior problem, the example is examined in this chapter for two reasons. First, similar to the development of consumer demands for discrete alternatives, much of the research on a shipper's choice of transport carrier has been couched in a utility framework. Second, a shipper's transport carrier decision is statistically equivalent to a consumer's transportation mode choice problem.

A model of shipper transportation choice

In one of the earlier studies of shipper modal demands, Levin (1978) developed and estimated a shipper's choice of transport mode in the manufactured goods sector. Transport carriers available to the shipper are truck, rail boxcar, and piggyback, a mixed truck–rail mode. Trucks normally pick up and deliver the shipment and may provide some line-haul transport. However, rail provides the major portion of the line-haul trip by loading truck-trailers or containers on to rail flatcars. Levin postulates that a shipper's choice of carrier depends upon three sets of factors:

1 The attributes of the mode – these include such factors as transport rate, travel time, reliability and flexibility of service, and loss and damage experience.
2 The attributes of the shipment – the size of the shipment and its perishability or fragility, as well as any other special handling requirements that are likely to influence a shipper's choice of carrier.
3 The attributes of the shipper – these may reflect special considerations such as the shipper's location and accessibility to a particular mode, past experiences with alternative carriers, or future expectations about carrier availability or shipping needs.

Although recognizing the importance of modal, shipment, and shipper attributes to a shipper's mode choice decision, data limitations led to a more simplified empirical specification that included transport rate, travel time, and reliability (measured by the standard deviation of travel time).

Let a shipper's conditional indirect utility for each of the transport alternatives be given as

$$\begin{aligned}
V_{\text{truck}} &= \beta_1(\text{Truck Rate}) \\
&\quad + \beta_2(\text{Value})(\text{Truck Transport Time}) \\
&\quad + \beta_3(\text{Value})(\text{Truck Reliability}) \\
V_{\text{rail}} &= \gamma_2 + \beta_1(\text{Rail Rate}) \\
&\quad + \beta_2(\text{Value})(\text{Rail Transport Time}) \\
&\quad + \beta_3(\text{Value})(\text{Rail Reliability}) \\
V_{\text{piggyback}} &= \gamma_3 + \beta_1(\text{Piggyback Rate}) \\
&\quad + \beta_2(\text{Value})(\text{Piggyback Transport Time}) \\
&\quad + \beta_3(\text{Value})(\text{Piggyback Reliability})
\end{aligned} \tag{4.36}$$

There are a number of features in the expressions for indirect utility that are worth mentioning. First, since there is no constant term in the indirect utility for truck, this is the normalizing alternative. Also, given a lack of available data on many modal, shipment, and shipper alternatives, the net effects of these variables will be captured in the constant terms. Holding transit time and reliability constant, γ_2 and γ_3, respectively, represent the effect of the unmeasured attributes on the demand for rail and piggyback relative to the truck mode. Second, since the second and third explanatory variables have the same coefficient, β_2 and β_3 respectively, these are generic variables. Of greater interest, however, is the fact that each variable is the product of two other variables, a specification which gives an inventory cost interpretation to the variable. Suppose that a firm ships \$100,000 worth of goods by truck from Los Angeles to San Francisco and assume that the trip takes 1 day. Then the firm incurs an *in-transit inventory cost* of $(100{,}000)(1)r$, where r is a time rate of discount.[16] If either the value of the shipment or the transit time increases, then the shipper's inventory cost rises. Similarly, if the rate of time discount rises, so too does the in-transit inventory cost.

In general, in-transit inventory cost is the product of a shipment's value, transit time, and a relevant rate of time discount. Yet, from equation (4.36) we see that transit time and a shipment's value are included in each of the indirect utilities, but the rate of time discount is absent. Its absence is not all that surprising, since it would be difficult, if not impossible, to obtain information on a shipper's discount rate. However, similar to our derivation of the value of time in consumer demand models, it will be possible to infer a discount rate from the estimation results. To see this, consider the following question. For what discount rate r will a \$1 increase in in-transit inventory costs have the same impact upon indirect utility as a \$1 increase in the transport rate? The effect upon indirect utility from a \$1 increase in the transport rate and inventory costs, respectively, is

$$\frac{\Delta V}{\Delta \text{Truck Rate}} = \beta_1$$

$$\frac{\Delta V}{\Delta(\text{Value})(\text{Transit Time})(r)} = \beta_1 \tag{4.37}$$

But from the model in (4.36), we know that

$$\frac{\Delta V}{\Delta(\text{Value})(\text{Transit Time})} = \beta_2 \tag{4.38}$$

Equations (4.37) and (4.38) imply that $\beta_2 = r(\beta_1)$. Thus, once we have estimates for β_1 and β_2, we can estimate the time rate of discount by taking the ratio β_2/β_1.

Third, the reliability variable in equation (4.36) is defined in terms of the standard deviation of transit times. Consider a shipper that is deciding between two modes. Both have mean transit times equal to 8 days but mode 1's transit time varies between 7 and 9 days, whereas mode 2's transit time varies between 5 and 11 days. All else constant, mode 1 is chosen since the shipper, as well as the carrier, will be more confident in the arrival date. This variable is also multiplied by the shipment's value, in order to reflect additional inventory cost due to unreliable service.

Hypotheses

Given the variable interpretations above, the empirical model in equation (4.36) embodies three basic hypotheses:

HYPOTHESIS 1 By the law of demand, a shipper's modal choice is expected to be inversely related to the mode's transport rate. All else constant, an increase in Transport Rate on a given carrier is expected to decrease the demand for that carrier, which is equivalent to the statement that $\beta_1 < 0$.

HYPOTHESIS 2 Increases in a shipper's in-transit inventory costs are expected to reduce the demand for that mode, all else held constant. If there are in-transit inventory costs due to normal or average shipment transit time, then $\beta_2 < 0$. Alternatively, if inventory costs are due to unreliable services, as indicated by the standard deviation of transit time, then $\beta_3 < 0$.

HYPOTHESIS 3 Our third hypothesis relates to the constant terms. Since data limitations prevented a richer empirical specification of the model, the constant terms reflect numerous unmeasured attributes associated with each of the modes. In comparison with rail modes, trucking has a number of advantages. There is generally a shorter waiting period before a shipper's shipment is picked up, trucks have more flexibility in customizing their services to the needs of the shippers, and trucking generally involves fewer losses and less damage. For these reasons, a reasonable working hypothesis is that $\gamma_2 < 0$ and $\gamma_3 < 0$. That is, all else constant, unmeasured attributes of trucking are more highly valued than the unmeasured attributes of rail or piggybacking.

Estimation results

Primary data for this analysis came from the 1972 Census of Transportation and table 4.16 reports the market shares of each mode by distance shipped. Not surprisingly, truck is a dominant mode for shipments traveling less than 300 miles. However, it is interesting to note that even for distances less than 100 miles, rail still garnered over a 20% market share. For distances

Table 4.16 Market shares for 42 manufactured commodities, 1972 (%)

Distance Shipped (miles)	Truck	Rail	Piggyback
0–99	78.5	21.3	0.2
100–199	70.3	28.6	1.1
200–299	60.6	37.0	2.4
300–499	51.2	44.2	4.6
500–999	39.4	51.3	9.3
1,000–1,499	35.5	56.4	8.1
1,500 or more	26.9	62.8	10.3

Source: Levin (1978), table 1, p. 27

Table 4.17 Shipper transport mode choice

Explanatory Variable[a]	Coefficient Estimate	t-statistic
Transport Rate (1, 2, 3)	−0.0087	−8.70
(Value) (Transit Time) (1, 2, 3)	−0.0066	−1.78
(Value) (Reliability) (1, 2, 3)	0.0082	1.02
Rail Constant Term	−0.650	−4.19
Piggyback Constant Term	−2.78	−16.6

[a] Modal alternatives: 1 = Truck; 2 = rail boxcar; 3 = piggyback.
Source: Levin (1978), table 7, p. 33

of 1,000 miles or more, rail is the dominant mode. The share of piggybacking steadily increases but at its maximum only accounts for 10% of manufactured goods shipped.

Table 4.17 summarizes the estimation results, which are generally consistent with our stated hypotheses. All else constant, an increase in transport rates of a given mode decreases a shipper's demand for that carrier. Similarly, an increase in mean transit time, by increasing in-transit inventory costs, also decreases a shipper's modal demand. Since transit reliability is defined in terms of a carrier's transit time standard deviation, an increase in this variable is equivalent to a decrease in reliability. From table 4.16, however, we see that the coefficient of this variable has a *positive* sign, indicating that an increase in transit time standard deviation *increases* the mode's demand. Although inconsistent with our underlying hypothesis, a look at the t-statistic indicates that we cannot reject the null hypothesis that $\beta_3 = 0$.

Examining the constant terms in table 4.16 confirms our suspicions regarding the unmeasured attributes of each of the modes. γ_2 and γ_3 are both negative, indicating that, all else constant, shippers in this sample valued the unmeasured attributes of truck carriers more highly than those of the other two carriers. In addition, the fact that $\gamma_2 < \gamma_3$ tells us that shippers prefer the unmeasured attributes of the rail boxcar mode relative to those of the piggyback mode.

What does the model imply about the time rate of discount? Recalling that β_2/β_1 provides an estimate of r, this gives us $0.0066/0.0087 = 0.76$. In other words, shippers have a 76% time rate of discount. In comparison with standard measures of the opportunity cost of capital, this is an exceedingly high estimate. Whether it is unreasonably high is uncertain. It must be remembered that the time rate of discount is not simply measuring the interest cost of tying up funds in an inventory. Additional time-related costs that generally differ by commodity are also included. For example, reducing transit time delays for goods that are perishable (agricultural commodities) or seasonal in nature (Christmas trees and decorations) would be valued highly and add to the interest cost on the funds tied up. Similarly, maintaining quick and reliable service in order to develop a loyal customer base also implies a higher discount rate.

As a last point, Levin examined the sensitivities of shipper demands to a change in transport rates and transit times. He estimated the price elasticity of demand to be in the range of (−0.35, −0.25). That is, a 10% increase in a mode's transport rate would reduce a shipper's demand for the mode in the range of 2.5–3.5%. A similar 10% increase in mean transit time was calculated to reduce modal demand on the order of 3–7%. These results are consistent with other evidence that shippers are generally more concerned with speed of service than with price.

CHAPTER HIGHLIGHTS

- Discrete transportation demands, such as choice of travel mode to work, are of an "either–or" nature and it is not possible to consume both simultaneously. Analysis of discrete choice commodities entails comparing the indirect utility of one alternative with the indirect utility of other available alternatives. A consumer's indirect utility function gives the highest possible level of economic welfare for a given economic environment. A consumer's indirect utility function is positively related to a rise in income and negatively relative to a rise in prices.
- Among a set of discrete transportation choices, a consumer maximizes economic welfare by choosing the transportation alternative with the highest level of conditional indirect utility. For these alternatives, changes in the economic environment occur at the extensive margin as consumers switch from one alternative to another.
- Because only part of a consumer's indirect utility function is observable, a consumer's choice of a discrete transportation alternative occurs with some probability. The probabilistic model that characterizes welfare-maximizing choices among a set of discrete transportation alternatives is referred to as the random utility model. Random utility models of transportation choice characterize the demands for each of the alternatives available to the decision-maker. In random utility models, observation errors primarily reflect taste differences among the population rather than measurement or optimization errors.
- When two transportation choices are available, a very common empirical model is the binary logit random utility model. When more than two alternatives are available, the binary logit model easily generalizes to a multinomial logit model. In addition to characterizing existing demands, logit models of transportation choice are used to forecast the market share of new alternatives. In discrete choice models, generic variables are those whose marginal impact upon indirect utility is common across the available alternatives; an alternative specific variable is one whose marginal impact upon indirect utility is specific to a particular transportation alternative.
- Because travel time and travel cost typically characterize transportation choices, empirical random utility models provide a convenient method for estimating the value that consumers place upon their travel time. The value corresponds to the estimated coefficient of the travel time variable divided by the estimated coefficient of the travel cost variable.
- In random utility models of transportation choice, all available alternatives are substitutes in consumption. An increase in the opportunity cost of a given alternative reduces the probability of selecting that alternative, but shifts the probability demand curves of the other alternatives to the right.
- Consistent with other studies, an analysis of transportation mode choice in the trip to work indicates that workers are sensitive to a mode's travel time and travel cost. In addition, workers' mode choices are more sensitive to out-of-vehicle time than in-vehicle time. Workers' choices were twice as sensitive to an increase in walk time relative to travel time. Also consistent with other studies, workers in

this analysis valued out-of-vehicle time much more highly than in-vehicle travel time.

- In a case study of intercity modal choice for nonbusiness-related trips, modal choices were sensitive to a mode's transportation cost. In addition, an increase in travel time on a public conveyance had a much greater disutility effect on rail and bus relative to air travel; and, holding all else constant, travelers prefer to travel by air or auto relative to making a trip by bus or rail. Among the modes, the choice of rail mode was most elastic to a change in cost and the choice of bus mode was most elastic to a change in travel time. As a percentage of their wage rate, air travelers place the greatest value on their travel time, but bus travelers place the highest value on the time between departures (in part due to the disutility of time spent at bus stations).
- Over the past 30 years, there has been a significant increase in automobile ownership, due to a general increase in the standard of living. After controlling for household size, the availability of public transit, and the number of workers, a case study of automobile ownership in the USA confirms that household ownership is strongly influenced by household income. An increase in household income is expected to decrease nonownership and single vehicle ownership to the benefit of multiple vehicle ownership. But, importantly for public transit policy, vehicle ownership is sensitive to the availability of public transit. The demands for nonownership, single vehicle ownership, and multi-vehicle ownership were elastic with respect to the availability of public transit.
- Consistent with expectations, a case study of carrier choice by freight shippers found that an increase in the transport rate charged or a decrease in a carrier's service reliability reduced the probability of a shipper selecting that carrier. But shippers were more sensitive to reliability than to the rate charged. In addition, shippers were found to be sensitive to the inventory transit cost. Further, among the three carrier modes studied – truck, rail, and piggyback – shippers preferred truck carriers, all else constant, which reflects the greater flexibility of truck carriage to the two other modes.

Review questions

1. In 1990, there were 1.77 vehicles per household in the United States. In addition, households drove each vehicle an average of 8,531 miles annually.

(a) Is vehicle ownership a discrete good or a divisible good? Suppose that the average purchase price of vehicles increases. Briefly explain the expected effect of the price rise on vehicle ownership, and comment on whether this occurs at the intensive or extensive margin.

(b) Are annual vehicle–miles traveled a discrete good or a divisible good? What effect will an increase in household annual income have upon annual miles traveled? Does this reflect consumption at the intensive margin or the extensive margin?

2. Helen is faced with the choice of either taking a train or an airplane to visit her mother in Seattle. Assume that Helen's utility function is $U(T,A,x;\phi)$, where T represents the trip by train, A represents the trip by air, x is all other consumption, and ϕ reflects Helen's consumption preferences.

(a) Assuming that the choice of mode for the Seattle trip is a discrete good, what are the possible values that T and A can take? Briefly comment on whether it is possible for Helen to simultaneously consume T and A.

(b) What is Helen's budget constraint if she takes the train to Seattle? What is her budget constraint if she goes to Seattle by air?

(c) Given that she makes the trip by air, identify the determinants of Helen's conditional indirect utility function. If Helen made the trip by train, would her conditional indirect utility function depend on the same determinants?

(d) Suppose that Helen decides to take the train to Seattle. Assuming that Helen is a utility-maximizing consumer, what can you conclude regarding the relationship between the conditional indirect utility of traveling by train and the conditional indirect utility of traveling by air?

3. Suppose that Tom has three possible modes for his daily journey to work: automobile (A), bus (B), and rapid transit (RT). Tom's utility function for work-trip modal choice and all other consumption x is $U(A,B,RT,x;\phi)$, where the modal choices are mutually exclusive and ϕ gives Tom's consumption preferences. Tom faces the following budget constraint:

$$Y = p_a A + p_b B + p_c C + p_x x$$

where Y is Tom's income per period, p_a is the price of A, p_b is the price of B, p_{rt} is the price of RT, and p_x is the price of x.

(a) Briefly explain why Tom's utility function depends upon the consumption levels of each commodity, whereas his indirect utility function depends upon the economic environment; that is, the prices of each commodity and his income.

(b) Suppose that you know that Tom takes rapid transit to work. You also know that if rapid transit were not available, Tom would drive to work. Use this information and the conditional indirect utility function for each mode to characterize Tom's modal choice decisions.

4. In 1983, 87.4% of household trips to work was by private motor vehicle, 4.6% by public transit, and 8.0% by other modes of travel (for example, bicycle or walk). For private transportation, the average length of work trip (one way) was 8.5 miles, with an average commute time equal to 20 minutes. The operating cost per mile for private transportation was 8.36 cents. For public transit, the average commute time was 46.1 minutes per one-way trip, with an average fare equal to 60 cents. For other work-trip modes, the average one-way trip length was 5.6 miles, with an average trip time equal to 30 minutes.

(a) For each of the three modes, what is the monetary cost per trip?

(b) Assuming an average hourly wage rate equal to $10.00, what is the total cost per work trip on each mode?

(c) Given the work-trip prices in (b) and the modal percentages, graph representative demand curves for each of the three modes.

5. (a) In specifying a typical consumer's conditional indirect utility for a given transportation alternative, explain the difference between the *observed and common* portion of utility and that which is *unobserved and individual specific*.
(b) Given that individual travelers know with certainty whether the conditional indirect utility of one mode is greater than the conditional indirect utility of all other available modes, why is it necessary to develop a *random utility model* (RUM) of transportation choice? What role does unobservable taste variations play in the development of the RUM?
(c) What is the relationship between a random utility model of transportation choice and a cumulative probability distribution function?

6. Wanting to vacation in Los Angeles, Mike, who lives in Kansas City, can take direct flights on either of two airlines. Let the conditional indirect utility for airlines A and B, respectively, be

$$\hat{U}_A = Y - p_x + \alpha p_A + \gamma t_A + \beta_1 Y + \varepsilon_A$$
$$\hat{U}_B = Y - p_x + \alpha p_B + \gamma t_B + \beta_2 Y + \varepsilon_B$$

where Y is income, p_x is the price of all other goods, p_A is the price on airline A, p_B is the price on airline B, t_A and t_B are the travel times on airlines A and B respectively. ε_A and ε_B represent unobserved taste variations. α, γ, β_1, and β_2 are parameters.
(a) Mike's conditional indirect utility for airline A does not depend upon either the price or the travel time on airline B. Similarly, his conditional indirect utility for airline B does not depend upon the price or travel time on airline A. If Mike decides to fly on airline A, does this decision imply that the price and travel time on airline B had no effect on Mike's choice of airline A?
(b) If $\beta_1 = \beta_2$, does Mike's conditional indirect utility depend upon his income? Would his choice of airline depend upon income? If so, why; and if not, why not?
(c) Consider the following three sets of conditional indirect utilities for the two airlines:

(1)
$$\hat{U}_A = Y - p_x + \alpha p_A + \gamma t_A + \varepsilon_A$$
$$\hat{U}_B = Y - p_x + \alpha p_B + \gamma t_B + \beta_B Y + \varepsilon_B$$

(2)
$$\hat{U}_A = Y - p_x + \alpha p_A + \gamma t_A + \beta_A Y + \varepsilon_A$$
$$\hat{U}_B = Y - p_x + \alpha p_B + \gamma t_B + \varepsilon_B$$

(3)
$$\hat{U}_A = Y - p_x + \alpha p_A + \gamma t_A + \beta_1 Y + \varepsilon_A$$
$$\hat{U}_B = Y - p_x + \alpha p_B + \gamma t_B + \beta_2 Y + \varepsilon_B$$

By subtracting the conditional indirect utility for airline B from the conditional indirect utility for airline A, demonstrate that the indirect utility difference is the same for each. What is the relationship between β_1, β_2, β_A, and β_B?

7. Norman has to decide between purchasing a pickup truck (PU) or a sport utility (SU) vehicle. His conditional indirect utility for each type of vehicle is

$$\hat{U}_{\text{Pickup}} = Y - p_x + \alpha p_{\text{PU}} + \beta_1 Y + \varepsilon_{\text{A}}$$
$$\hat{U}_{\text{Sport Utility}} = Y - p_x + \alpha p_{\text{SU}} + \beta_2 Y + \varepsilon_{\text{B}}$$

where Y is income, p_x is the price of all other goods, p_{PU} is the price of the pickup truck, and p_{SU} is the price of the sport utility. ε_{A} and ε_{B} represent unobserved taste variations for each of the vehicle types. α, β_1, and β_2 are parameters.

(a) Based upon the above conditional indirect utilities, make the appropriate assumptions necessary to derive a binary logit model of vehicle type choice. What is the probability that Norman will purchase a pickup truck? What is the probability that he will purchase a sport utility vehicle?

(b) Evaluate the following statement: "Suppose Norman is considering the purchase of a pickup truck with an *equally priced* sport utility vehicle. If income has the same marginal effect upon Norman's conditional indirect utility of pickup trucks as it has on sport utility vehicles, then Norman has an equal probability choosing either vehicle."

(c) What is the difference between a *generic* variable and an *alternative specific* variable? In the above model, is vehicle price a generic or alternative specific variable? How about income?

8. In 1988, there were 91.3 million households in the United States. 31.1 million households owned one vehicle, 33.3 households owned two vehicles, and 14.9 million households owned three or more vehicles.

(a) In 1988, what was the probability that a household, selected at random, would own two vehicles?

(b) What was the probability that a randomly selected household in 1988 would own no vehicles?

(c) In what way can automobile ownership be described as a discrete variable? Based upon this, set up a multinomial logit empirical model of automobile ownership. What is the interpretation of the dependent variable? What do you think the primary determinants of automobile ownership would be?

(d) What effect would you expect an increase in income to have upon owning one vehicle relative to owning no vehicles? Would you expect an increase in income to increase the likelihood that a household owns three or more vehicles relative to owning no vehicles? And would you expect an increase in income to increase the likelihood that a household owns three or more vehicles relative to owning two vehicles?

9. Suppose, in a binary logit model, that the "own-" and "cross-" price elasticities of demand for mode "a" are −0.34 and +0.15 respectively. Interpret these numbers.

(a) What is the effect on the demand for mode "a" of a 15% increase in its price? Does this represent a change in demand or a change in quantity demanded?

(b) What is the effect on the demand for mode "a" when the price of mode "b" increases by 15%? Does this represent a change in demand or a change in quantity demanded?

10. Assume that three transportation alternatives are available: airline, rail, and automobile. Holding all else constant, and assuming a multinomial logit model of transportation mode choice, what will be the effect upon airline, rail, and automobile demands from a small increase in air fares? Demonstrate that the sum of these effects equals zero. Does this make sense? If so, why; and if not, why not?

11. Similar to the study reported in table 4.4, most studies of modal choice find that the value of in-vehicle travel time is less than the value that travelers place upon waiting time.

(a) What do these results tell us about the marginal disutility of in-vehicle travel time in comparison with the marginal disutility of out-of-vehicle travel time?

(b) Discuss why the value-of-time estimates derived from discrete choice models are oftentimes interpreted as marginal rates of substitution.

(c) Suppose that you're an economist for a commuter railroad system. The manager of the agency is considering either of two policies: adding additional stops, with the expected result of reducing on-line speeds but also reducing the headway (that is, the average time between trains); or removing some stops, which would increase on-line speeds but also entail longer headways. Overall, both policies are predicted to have the same effect on total travel time for the average consumer. Discuss how you would use information on riders' values of time in your policy recommendation.

12. Train (1980) developed and estimated an empirical demand model, based upon a sample of 635 individuals living in the San Francisco Bay Area, for automobile ownership. His model included four alternatives:

1 Own no automobiles (1).
2 Own one automobile (2).
3 Own two automobiles (3).
4 Own three or more automobiles (4).

and a portion of his multinomial logit model estimation results are presented in table 4.18. The numbers in parentheses reflect the alternative(s) associated with the variable. In answering the following questions, be sure to pay attention to coefficient estimates and the t-statistics.

(a) From the reported results, is an increase in the cost of automobile ownership as a proportion of income consistent with the law of demand? What does this imply about the expected level of ownership among lower-income households? What about higher-income households?

(b) In this part, we want to analyze the effect of an increase in household income on automobile ownership.

(i) Relative to owning no automobiles, what is the estimated marginal indirect utility effect of an increase in household income for households that own three automobiles?

(ii) Relative to owning no automobiles, what is the effect on indirect utility of an increase in household income for households that own four automobiles?

Table 4.18 The multinomial logit model of automobile ownership

Variable	Coefficient Estimate	*t*-statistic
Constant for one automobile (2)	−2.10	−1.36
Constant for two automobiles (3)	−12.1	−6.05
Constant for three or more automobiles (4)	−23.6	−8.42
Annual auto cost divided by household income (1–4)	−2.26	−2.23
Number persons in household (2)	0.573	2.90
Number persons in household (3)	1.76	7.21
Number persons in household (4)	2.89	10.1
Percentage of household members with driver's licenses (2)	4.24	4.68
Percentage of household members with driver's licenses (3)	9.77	8.45
Percentage of household members with driver's licenses (4)	16.9	10.8
Accessibility to nonwork destinations by transit (1)	0.270	0.884
Accessibility to nonwork destinations by auto or transit (2)	0.664	1.59
Accessibility to nonwork destinations by auto or transit (3)	0.745	1.73
Accessibility to nonwork destinations by auto or transit (4)	1.04	2.16
Home location in or near CBD (2)	−0.829	−1.76
Home location in or near CBD (3)	−1.30	−3.52
Home location in or near CBD (4)	−1.34	−2.12
Household income (2)	0.0000905	1.84
Household income (3)	0.000197	3.76
Household income (4)	0.000183	2.92

Source: Train (1980), table II, p. 364

(iii) Given your responses for (i) and (ii), what does this imply regarding the indirect marginal utility effect of an increase in household income for three-automobile households relative to four-automobile households? Or, alternatively, what is the effect on the demand for owning three cars relative to the demand for owning four cars when the household experiences an increase in income?

(c) What do the reported estimation results say about the relationship between household size and the demand for automobile ownership?

(d) Use the reported estimation results to evaluate whether households living in the suburbs are more likely to own automobiles. If so, are they also more likely to own a larger number of automobiles?

(e) A primary substitute for the automobile is public transportation. Do the results support the conclusion that public transit availability will significantly affect the demand for automobile ownership?

(f) Do the results identify a relationship between automobile ownership and the number of drivers in a household?

(g) Compare and contrast these results on the demand for automobile ownership with that of Train (1986) that is summarized in the text.

13. McFadden (1976) estimated a multinomial logit model of work-trip mode choice for the San Francisco Bay Area. A portion of his results are given in table 4.19. The work-trip modes available to the 771 commuters sampled were:

1 Automobile alone.
2 Bus with walk access.
3 Bus with automobile access.
4 Carpool.

The numbers in parentheses are the mode(s) associated with each variable.

(a) Evaluate the effects of increases in modal cost and travel times on the demand for modes. Be sure to pay attention to the mode or modes associated with each variable when interpreting the results. Are these effects consistent with your expectations?

Table 4.19 Work-trip mode choice in San Francisco Bay Area

Explanatory Variable	Coefficient Estimate	*t*-statistic
Mode cost (cents)/Post-tax wage (cents per minute) (1–4)	−0.0284	−4.31
Auto in-vehicle time (minutes) (1, 3, 4)	−0.0644	−5.65
Walk time (minutes) (2, 3)	−0.0259	−2.94
Transfer wait time (minutes) (2, 3)	−0.0689	−5.28
Number of transfers (2, 3)	−0.105	−0.77
Headway of first bus (minutes) (2, 3)	−0.0318	−3.18
Number drivers in household (1)	1.02	4.81
Number drivers in household (3)	0.990	3.29
Number drivers in household (4)	0.872	4.25
Head of household dummy variable (1)	0.627	3.37
Employment density at work location (1)	−0.00160	−2.27
Home near or in CBD (1)	−0.502	−4.18
Autos per driver (1)	5.00	9.65
Autos per driver (3)	2.33	2.74
Autos per driver (4)	2.38	5.28
Auto alone constant (1)	−5.26	−5.93
Bus with auto access constant (3)	−5.49	−5.33
Carpool constant (4)	−3.84	−6.36

Source: McFadden (1976), table 3, p. 38

(b) Relative to taking the bus with walk access, what effect on modal demand occurs when there is an increase in the number of drivers in the household? Whereas the number of licensed drivers reflects the demand for automobile use, the number of available automobiles reflects the supply. Do the results indicate that an increasing supply increases the use of automobiles in the work trip? Suppose that the number of autos in the household increases. What effect will this have upon the demand for bus with auto access relative to the demand for carpool as a work-trip mode?

(c) Based upon the reported results, who is more likely to use the automobile in the work trip, a female head of household or a male nonhead of household?

(d) What will be the effect on a worker's work-trip mode choice who lives near downtown and works in a high-density employment area? Which of the two effects is stronger?

14. Consider the following indirect utility function

$$U = a\text{cost} + b\text{time}$$

where cost is dollars and time is hours.

(a) What is the interpretation of b/a? Let w be the wage rate in dollars per hour. What is the interpretation of (b/a)/w? Now consider the following indirect utility function:

$$U = \alpha(\text{cost}/w) + \beta\text{time}$$

What is the interpretation of β/α? What is the relationship between β/α and $(b/a)/w$?

(b) Consider the work-trip modal choice model in question 13. As a proportion of the wage rate, calculate the value of time associated with automobile in-vehicle time, transit in-vehicle time, walk time, and transfer wait time. Is out-of-vehicle travel time more onerous to commuters than in-vehicle travel time? Does this seem reasonable?

(c) What is the total value of out-of-vehicle time associated with bus travel?

15. Harriet is a lumber analyst for a consulting firm. As part of her responsibilities, she must keep apprized of those factors that influence shipper demands. Recently, she developed and estimated a binomial logit model of shipper carrier demands.

(a) Theoretically, Harriet reasoned that a shipper's carrier demand would depend upon shipment cost, service quality, as measured by average transit time and average variability of transit time, and mode accessibility.

(i) Briefly identify the expected effect that each of these factors would have upon the mode's demand, all else constant.

(ii) Harriet reasoned that a shipper's carrier demand would depend upon mean transit time and mean variability in transit time, because an increase in each of these would lead to higher interest and storage costs for the shipper. Do you agree with Harriet's reasoning? If so, why; and if not, why not?

(b) For the lumber industry, the two primary modes that Harriet considered were (1) private carriage (that is, the company shipped its own goods) and (2) rail. The explanatory variables in Harriet's model were:

Shipment Size, in units of 10,000 pounds
Commodity Value, in units of $/pound
Freight Charges, in units of $10,000 per unit shipped
Mean Transit Time, in days
Standard Deviation of Transit Time, in days
Distance from a Rail Siding, in miles

Harriet's results are given in table 4.20.

Table 4.20 The shipping mode choice for Harriet

Explanatory Variable	Coefficient Estimate	*t*-statistic
Shipment Size (2)	2.5	2.8
Commodity Value (2)	7.51	4.32
Freight Charges (1, 2)	−14.14	−8.40
Mean Transit Time (1, 2)	−6.43	−4.12
Standard Deviation of Transit Time (1, 2)	−3.48	−1.73
Distance from a Rail Siding (2)	−11.21	−4.83

Number of observations = 120

(i) Are the results consistent with Harriet's theoretical reasoning? Does service quality affect shipper modal demands? Suppose that the variability of transit time for private carriage increased. Qualitatively, how would this effect the demand for private carriage, and the demand for rail?
(ii) From the reported results, would you expect larger shipments to go by rail or private carriage? How about higher-valued shipments (for example, furniture versus bulk lumber)?
(iii) From the reported results, does distance to a rail siding matter to a shipper?
(iv) How much would a typical shipper be willing to pay to save one day of transit time? How much would a shipper be willing to pay to reduce transit time variability by one standard deviation?

NOTES

1 Much of the material in this chapter is due to the pioneering work of Daniel McFadden, who has contributed extensively to the development and application of discrete choice theory in economic analysis.

2 More formally, $\Delta\hat{U}(p_{Ta},p_{Tb},p_x,Y;\phi)/\Delta p_x = (\Delta U/\Delta x^*)(\Delta x^*/\Delta p_x)$. By the law of demand, $\Delta x^*/\Delta p_x < 0$ and from our preference axiom that more is preferred to less, $\Delta U/\Delta x^* > 0$, which implies that the product is less than zero.

3 These data came from APTANet, the American Public Transit Association's website on the Internet. The associated URL is http://www.apta.com/stats.

4 In empirical analyses, the error term may also reflect unobserved attributes of the alternatives. However, we are assuming here that the only relevant attribute is price.

5 Another common distribution function is the normal distribution. When only two choices are possible, the normal distribution function leads to a model that gives virtually identical results to models based upon the logistic distribution function. The logistic distribution is easier to use when more than two alternatives are available.

6 There is a subtle but important difference in the development of continuous and discrete choice demand functions. Whereas our derivation of demand functions in the continuous good case says nothing about how the model is empirically specified, in the discrete choice model, the demand function for each alternative, P_a and P_b in this case, *imposes* a logit empirical specification.

7 Domencich and McFadden (1975) originally called this variable Blue Collar. For this discussion, the variable was renamed White Collar for ease of interpretation and to be consistent with the convention that a dummy variable name be identified with the category associated with a value of 1 for the variable.

8 In their original paper, the cost variables were defined as dollars. In order to simplify our discussion of the results, the automobile and public transit cost is defined *in cents*, which is equivalent to multiplying the cost variables in the original paper by 100 (that is, \$1 = 100 (1) cents). The only effect of this is to scale the estimated parameter by 1/100. As reported in table 4.4, the coefficient of Cost is −0.0256. In the original paper, this parameter was −2.56.

9 Note that a commuter who owns no automobiles could still travel by car if she rides to work with a co-worker or a friend that works in the same area.

10 For this problem, the number of observations is 115, so that the t-tests are based upon 108 degrees of freedom. The critical values for the t-tests will be a bit higher than those summarized in table 2.1, which are based upon "large" samples, defined as more than 120 observations.

11 Multiplying the numerator and denominator of the expression after the first equal sign in equation (4.30) by $\exp(-\beta_J Y)$ and defining $\bar{\beta}_k$ as $\beta_k - \beta_J$ gives the term after the second equals sign.

12 The changes in choice probabilities are based upon the formulation in equation (4.12) and the existing market share for automobile. Since the variable "number of travelers" (T) is only alternative specific to the automobile alternative, we can directly apply equation (4.12). Specifically, $\Delta P_a/\Delta T = P_a(1 - P_a)0.622 = (0.693)(0.307)(0.622) = 0.132$.

13 Rather than defining $V_0 = 0$, as in equation (4.33), Train could have equivalently specified the indirect utility for zero ownership to be $V_0 = \gamma$ (Average Utility from Vehicle Type Choice) which equals $\gamma(0)$ for the no-ownership alternative.

14 Since the results in table 4.12 are based upon a sample of data, a curious student might well ask the question, "How does one measure the average utility of a household's vehicle(s)?" Consider a household with one vehicle. Note that the household's demand for the type of vehicle to own could be modeled in a discrete choice context, since the household buys one type of vehicle (for example, Toyota Camry, Dodge Pickup, etc.) from a set of available alternatives. If, in an automobile market with T different types of vehicles, a multinomial logit model describes the probability of a household purchasing vehicle type t ($t = 1, \ldots, T$), then

$$P_t = \exp(V_t)/\Sigma \exp(V_j) \qquad (1)$$

Moreover, the following important result can be shown. The *expected* or *average utility* associated with a household's vehicle type decision can be *empirically measured* by the logarithm of the term in the denominator of (1). To obtain his estimate of average utility, then, Train first estimated a multinomial logit model of vehicle type choice for one- and two-vehicle households. For each of these models, the logarithm of the summation term in the denominator was his estimate of average utility from consumers' vehicle type choices.

15 The federal government provided funds to complete the final segments of the system and purchase rolling stock. Webber (1976) provides an excellent analysis of the BART experience.

16 The time rate of discount in this analysis is the shadow price of time, and reflects the discount rate that equates the market share effect from a 1$ increase in freight rates with that of a $1 increase in inventory costs.

REFERENCES AND RELATED READINGS

General references on discrete choice

Ben-Akiva, M. and Lerman, S. R. 1985: *Discrete Choice Analysis.* Cambridge, Mass.: The MIT Press.

Cramer, J. S. 1991: *The Logit Model.* London: Edward Arnold.

Domencich, T. A. and McFadden, D. 1975: *Urban Travel Demand: A Behavioral Analysis.* Amsterdam: North-Holland.

Horowitz, J. L., Koppelman, F. S., and Lerman, S. R. 1993: *A Self-Instructing Course in Disaggregate Mode Choice Modeling.* Final Report. University Research and Training Program. Urban Mass Transportation Administration. DOT-T-93-18.

Maddala, G. S. 1983: *Limited-Dependent and Qualitative Variables in Econometrics.* Cambridge: Cambridge University Press.

McFadden, D. 1973: Conditional logit analysis of qualitative choice behavior. In Zarembka, P. (ed.), *Frontiers in Econometrics.* New York: Academic Press, chapter 4, pp. 105–42.

Oum, T. H., Dodgson, J. S., Hensher, D. A., Morrison, S. A., Nash, C. A., Small, K. A., and Waters, W. G. II (eds.) 1995: *Transport Economics: Selected Readings.* Seoul, Korea: The Korea Research Foundation for the 21st Century.

Quandt, R. E. 1970: *The Demand for Travel: Theory and Measurement.* Lexington, Mass.: Heath Lexington Books.

Richards, M. G. and Ben-Akiva, M. E. 1975: *A Disaggregate Travel Demand Model.* Lexington, Mass.: Lexington Books.

Train, K. 1986: *Qualitative Choice Analysis.* Cambridge, Mass.: The MIT Press.

Transportation references

Automobile choice

Beggs, S., Cardell, S., and Hausman, J. 1981: Assessing the potential demand for electric cars. *Journal of Econometrics*, 16, 1–19.

Hensher, D. A. 1985: Empirical vehicle choice and usage models in the household sector: a review. *International Journal of Transport Economics*, 12, 231–59.

Lave, C. A. and Bradley, J. 1980: Market share of imported cars: a model of geographic and demographic determinants. *Transportation Research*, 14, 379–87.

Lave, C. A. and Train, K. 1979: A disaggregate model of auto-type choice. *Transportation Research A*, 13, 1–9.

Mannering, F. and Mahmassani, H. 1985: Consumer valuation of foreign and domestic vehicle attributes: econometric analysis and implications for auto demand. *Transportation Research B*, 19, 243–51.

Mannering, F. and Winston, C. 1991: Brand loyalty and the decline of American automobile firms. In M. N. Bailey and C. Winston (eds.), *Brookings Papers on Economic Activity: Microeconomics 1991.* Washington, DC: The Brookings Institution, pp. 67–114.

Manski, C. F. and Sherman, L. 1980: An empirical analysis of household choice among motor vehicles. *Transportation Research A*, 14, 349–66.

McCarthy, P. 1996: Market price and income elasticities of new vehicle demands. *Review of Economics and Statistics*, LXXVIII, 543–7.

McCarthy, P. and Tay, R. 1998: A nested logit model of vehicle fuel efficiency and make–model choice. *Transportation Research E*, 34, 39–51.

Train, K. 1980: A structured logit model of auto ownership and mode choice. *Review of Economic Studies*, XLVII, 357–70.

Intercity choice of mode

Alamdari, F. E. and Black, I. G. 1992: Passengers' choice of airline under competition: the use of the logit model. *Transport Reviews*, 12, 153–70.

Grayson, A. 1982: Disaggregate model of mode choice in intercity travel. *Transportation Research Record*, 835, 36–42.

Kraft, J. and Kraft, A. 1976: Mode choice characteristics as determinants of interurban transport demand. *Transportation Research B*, 10, 31–5.

Morrison, S. A. and Winston, C. 1985: An econometric analysis of the demand for intercity passenger transportation. In T. E. Keeler (ed.), *Research in Transportation*, vol. 2. Greenwich, Conn.: JAI Press, pp. 213–37.

Stopher, P. R. and Prashker, J. N. 1976: Intercity passenger forecasting: the use of current travel forecasting procedures. *Transportation Research Forum Proceedings*, pp. 67–75.

Transportation Research Board, National Research Council, Department of Transportation 1991: *In Pursuit of Speed: New Options for Intercity Passenger Transport*. Special Report 223. Washington, DC.

Urban choice of travel mode

Gomez-Ibanez, J. A. and Fauth, G. R. 1980: Using demand elasticities from disaggregate mode choice models. *Transportation*, 9, 105–25.

McFadden, D. 1974: The measurement of urban travel demand. *Journal of Public Economics*, 3, 303–28.

McFadden, D. 1976: The theory and practice of disaggregate demand forecasting for various modes of urban transportation. The Urban Travel Demand Forecasting Project, Working Paper No. 7623, November.

Meyer, J. R. and Gomez-Ibanez, J. A. 1981: *Auto, Transit, and Cities*. Cambridge, Mass.: Harvard University Press.

Train, K. 1978: A validation test of a disaggregate mode choice model. *Transportation Research B*, 12, 167–74.

Train, K. and McFadden, D. 1978: The goods/leisure tradeoff and disaggregate work trip mode choice models. *Transportation Research B*, 12, 349–53.

Webber, M. M. 1976: *The BART Experience – What Have We Learned?* Monograph No. 26. University of California, Berkeley, October.

Air and freight

Levin, R. C. 1978: Allocation in surface freight transportation: Does rate regulation matter? *Bell Journal of Economics*, 9, 18–45.

Hersch, P. L. and McDougall, G. S. 1993: The demand for corporate jets: a discrete choice analysis. *Applied Economics*, 25, 661–6.

Pitfield, D. E. 1993: Predicting air-transport demand. *Environment and Planning*, 25, 459–66.

Wilson, F. R., Bisson, B. G., and Kobia, K. B. 1986: Factors that determine mode choice in the transportation of general freight. *Transportation Research Record*, 1061, 26–31.

Winston, C. 1983: The demand for freight transportation: models and applications. *Transportation Research A*, 17, 419–27.

5

Firm Production and Cost in Transportation – The Long Run

INTRODUCTION

In chapters 3 and 4, we considered the demand side of the market for transportation goods and services. In those chapters, we developed a theory of transportation demand for the individual consumer which not only identified the underlying determinants of demand but also yielded hypotheses on the effects that changes in these determinants would have upon demand. Horizontal summation of individual consumer demands yielded a market demand for transportation. We then investigated the assumptions that were necessary to estimate a market demand function and provided numerous examples of recent transportation demand studies. Although the assumptions differed depending upon whether the transportation good was continuous or discrete, the procedure was essentially the same.

We follow a similar strategy in developing the supply side of the market for transportation. In this chapter, we develop the basic constructs which make up the theory of long-run firm production and cost in a competitive environment, which is to say that: (1) all firms have identical cost structures and the same set of technology available; (2) all firms produce a homogeneous transportation service; and (3) no firm produces a large enough amount of T to have any appreciable effect on market price. Importantly, we demonstrate that the theory of production is a theory of cost once input prices are introduced, a result which has important empirical implications. If we can empirically identify a firm's long-run cost function, then it also possible to say something about its underlying production function.

Once the relevant concepts are introduced and developed, we identify the assumptions required to empirically estimate these relationships and provide several case studies to illustrate the basic ideas.

THE LONG RUN – ALL INPUTS VARIABLE

Although there exist numerous transportation activities differentiated by mode, type of cargo, scope of operations, and labor of varying quality, we shall make the simplifying assumption that all transportation firms produce their respective outputs with two homogeneous inputs, capital (K) and labor (L). By varying the use of one or both inputs, a firm is able to alter its rate of output. If the firm has the option of changing output levels by altering its use of K and L, then both inputs are said to be variable and the firm is operating in the *long run*. Alternatively, a firm is said to be in the *short run* if one of the inputs is fixed. For example, if capital is the fixed input, the only way a firm could alter its rate of output is by varying the amount of labor that it uses.

We focus in this chapter upon a firm's long-run production activities and its associated costs. In the next chapter, we will analyze a firm's production and cost behavior for the short run when one or more inputs are assumed to be fixed.

Production Function and Productivity Curves

Given the state of technology, a firm's ability to transform K and L into some output, T, is summarized in the following production function:

$$T = f(K,L;\gamma) \tag{5.1}$$

where it is assumed that K and L are perfectly divisible inputs and γ is a parameter that reflects the current state of technology. The production function represents all technically efficient output levels. That is, it is not possible to increase output without increasing at least one of the inputs; equivalently, it is not possible to produce a given output level with any fewer inputs.

From the production function, it is possible to derive total, marginal, and average product curves. A *total product curve* for labor expresses the relationship between total output and labor, holding all else constant. Similarly, a *marginal product curve* for labor identifies the increase in total output resulting from a unit increase in labor, $\Delta T/\Delta L$, holding the other input and the state of technology constant. And an *average product curve* for labor is simply total output divided by labor, T/L. Figure 5.1 depicts a typical total product of labor TP_L curve and its associated marginal product MP_L and average product AP_L curves. The graph identifies certain relationships that will always hold for productivity curves. First, L_m is the amount of labor for which the total product of labor is greatest. Any further increase in labor beyond L_m reduces the total product of labor, which implies that the marginal product of labor is negative. Thus, the amount of labor at which TP_L is highest corresponds to the same amount of labor at which the MP_L intersects the x-axis. Second, up to labor input L_1, each additional unit of labor produces increasing amounts of output (that is, MP_L is rising) whereas after L_1 additional labor hiring increases output by smaller increments (that is, MP_L is falling and ultimately becomes negative). L_1 is the amount of labor at which the total product curve exhibits "*diminishing marginal returns*"; that is, the point at which the MP_L is at its highest point.[1] The point of diminishing returns reflects an empirical law that when some input is held constant (capital in this case), there will always come a point at which the contribution to output from further increases in the variable input (labor) begins to fall.

For example, for each of its flights, American Airlines requires capital (the plane) and labor inputs (personnel to fly and provide in-flight services). For any given size plane, the marginal product of the first labor inputs (pilot, co-pilot, navigator, and stewards) are high and increasing. But suppose that American decides to upgrade its coach customer services by maintaining an in-flight personnel passenger ratio comparable to that offered in first class. One can easily imagine the effect on overall labor productivity as stewards and stewardesses are trying to maneuver through the narrow aisle ways.

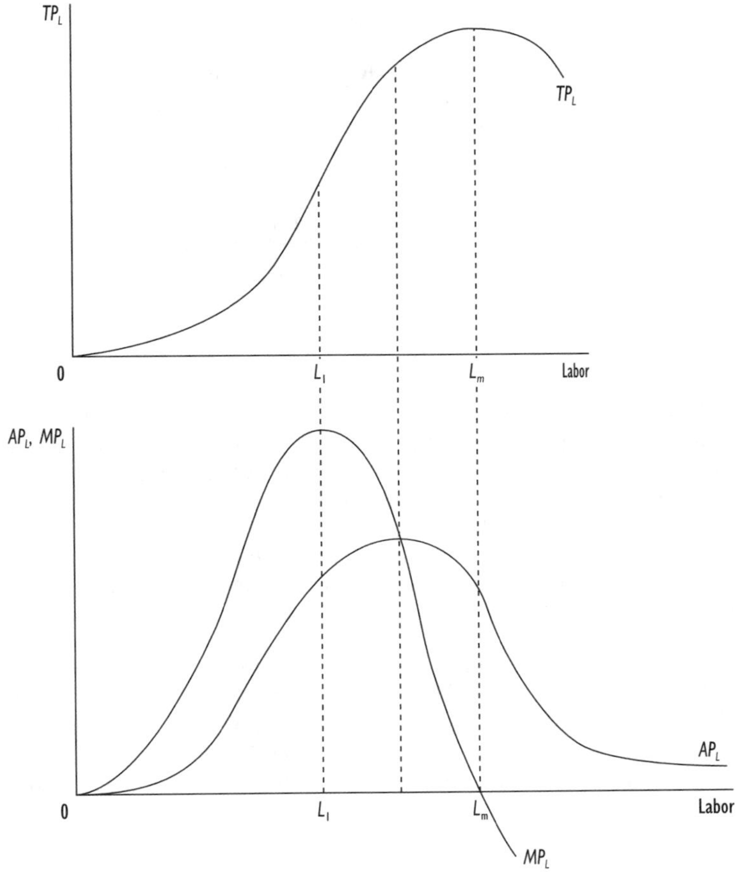

Figure 5.1 Productivity curves.

In contrast to the MP_L curve, which becomes negative after input level L_m, the average product of labor is always positive and reaches a maximum between L_1 and L_m.[2] To the left of L_1, the average product of labor must be rising, since the MP_L is increasing. And to the right of L_m, the average product of labor must be falling, since MP_L is negative. Hence, the maximum must occur between these two points. By similar reasoning, the MP_L can be shown to intersect (from above) the maximum point on the AP_L (convince yourself of this).

This discussion assumed that capital was held fixed at some level. Although this may seem reasonable, since discussions of productivity in the transportation industry oftentimes center around the productivity of labor, it is important to realize that all of the foregoing results are applicable if the fixed input is labor. Holding labor constant at some level yields a total product of capital curve from which we could derive average and marginal product of capital curves. Further, if capital and labor are *complements in production*, then increasing the level at which one input is held fixed will increase the marginal product of the other input.

ISOQUANTS

Suppose that a transportation firm wants to ship 100 ton–miles of freight.[3] It can accomplish this with alternative production processes. For example, the firm could use a labor-intensive method with 30 small trucks and 30 drivers, a moderately labor-intensive method employing five medium-sized trucks and five drivers, or a capital-intensive method using one double-trailer truck and one driver. These, and many other combinations of K and L capable of shipping the 30 ton–miles of freight, represent points on an *isoquant* curve. An isoquant is defined for any production function by all combinations of K and L that yield a specified level of output. For example, if T represents ton–miles in equation (5.1), then an isoquant for 100 ton–miles of freight would be

$$100 = f(K,L;\gamma) \tag{5.2}$$

Figure 5.2 depicts three representative isoquants corresponding to three possible output levels, 100, 200, and 300 ton–miles. The shape of an isoquant characterizes a firm's input substitution possibilities. Consider points A, B, C, and D in figure 5.2. In moving from point A to point B, the firm can substitute one laborer for five units of capital and still produce the same level of output. However, as the firm moves along the isoquant, its labor–capital substitution possibilities become less favorable. If, for example, the firm is at point C, it can only replace one unit of capital with an additional laborer. In the typical case, isoquants are convex to the origin and the degree of convexity reflects the ease of input substitutability. Isoquants that are more "angular" present the firm with fewer options for substitutability, whereas "flatter" isoquants characterize much richer substitution possibilities.[4] A measure of isoquant convexity and input substitutability is given by the *marginal rate of technical substitution* (*MRTS*). The marginal rate of technical substitution is the rate, given the state of technology, at which a firm is able to substitute L for K to efficiently produce a specific level of output. When isoquants are convex to the origin, the MRTS *declines* with increasing use of a given input. As a

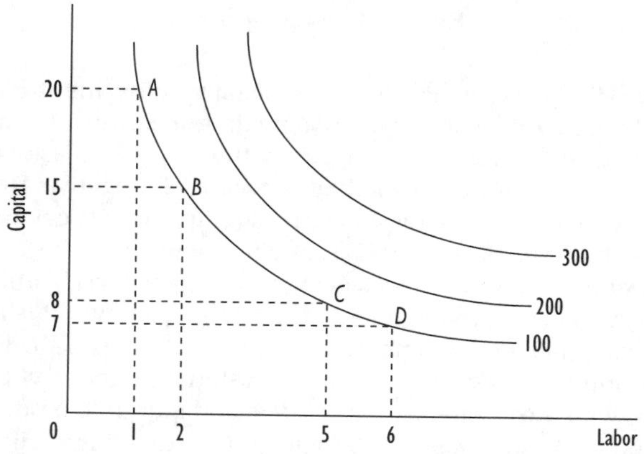

Figure 5.2 Isoquant curves.

firm uses more labor, for example, to produce a specific output level, its ability to substitute additional labor for capital diminishes.

To see this, we can express a total change in T, ΔT, as

$$\Delta T = MP_L \Delta L + MP_K \Delta K \tag{5.3}$$

as a weighted sum of the total change in each input, where the weight MP_i ($i = L,K$) is the marginal product of input i. If labor increases by 1 and capital increases by 2, then the increase in total output is 11 if the marginal products of labor and capital are 3 and 5, respectively. Assuming that $\Delta T = 0$ – that is, we are on a particular isoquant – then, from equation (5.3),

$$\begin{aligned} & 0 = MP_L \Delta L + MP_K \Delta K \\ \Rightarrow \quad & -\frac{\Delta K}{\Delta L} = \frac{MP_L}{MP_K} \\ & = \text{marginal rate of technical substitution} \end{aligned} \tag{5.4}$$

Equation (5.4) tells us that the *MRTS* is the ratio of marginal products. Also, since T is held constant, the *MRTS* is the slope, in absolute value, of an isoquant curve so that a declining *MRTS* is equivalent to an isoquant curve that is convex to the origin.

ELASTICITY OF SUBSTITUTION

Since the *MRTS* is the ratio of marginal products, its value depends upon the units in which capital and labor are measured. Suppose that labor and capital are both measured in units of 100 (that is, a one-unit increase in labor represents hiring 100 laborers) and one unit of labor substitutes for five units of capital. Thus, $MRTS = 5$ implies that 100 units of labor substitute for 500 units of capital. Alternatively, if labor is measured in units of 100 but capital is measured in units of 1,000, then $MRTS = \frac{1}{2}$ also implies that 100 units of labor can be substituted for 500 units of capital (one unit of L for $\frac{1}{2}$ units of K). In order to avoid ambiguities that arise solely from the units in which the inputs are measured, we use a dimensionless measure of input substitutability called the *elasticity of substitution.*

As a firm moves down its convex isoquant, the marginal rate of technical substitution falls, which reflects the increasing difficulty of substituting labor for capital. This is seen in figure 5.2 as a move from point A to points B, C, and D.

Note also that points on an isoquant reflect a firm's capital : labor (K/L) ratio. At point A in figure 5.2, for example, the capital : labor ratio is 20. If the firm is at point D, the K/L is 7/6. Thus, as the firm depicted in figure 5.2 slides down its isoquant from point A to points B, C, and D, not only is its *MRTS* falling but the K/L ratio is falling as well. The elasticity of substitution, σ_{KL}, reflects the proportional fall in the capital : labor ratio *relative to* a proportional fall in the *MRTS*. Suppose that the isoquant is nearly "L-shaped," which reflects few possibilities for input substitution. In this case, a dramatic shift in the *MRTS* results in relatively little change in the K/L ratio, which implies limited input substitutability. Conversely, if the isoquant is relatively flat, then a small change in the *MRTS* results in a large change in the K/L ratio. More rigorously, the elasticity of substitution is defined as

$$\sigma_{KL} = \frac{\%\Delta(K/L)}{\%\Delta(MRTS)}$$

and interpreted as the percentage change in the capital : labor ratio that results from a 1% increase in the marginal rate of technical substitution. σ_{KL} is a pure number that does not depend upon units of measurement.

RETURNS TO SCALE

The elasticity of substitution characterizes a firm's input use as it slides up or down a given isoquant. As the *MRTS* changes, a firm's capital : labor ratio changes. Alternatively, suppose that we pick a given point on an isoquant – that is, a given capital : labor ratio – and draw a ray from the origin through this point. If we then move along this ray, we are interested in how a firm's output changes as the firm *proportionately* changes its use of capital and labor. Suppose, for example, a firm increases its use of each input by 10%. If this leads to a 10% increase in output, then the firm is said to be operating under *constant returns to scale*. If output increases by less than 10%, the firm is operating under *decreasing returns to scale* and if output increases by more than 10% the firm is operating under *decreasing returns to scale*. Under fairly general specifications of the production function, it can be shown that

$$sT = MP_L L + MP_K K, \qquad s > 0 \tag{5.5}$$

where s is a returns-to-scale parameter.[5] For $s = 1$, the firm is operating under constant returns to scale; $s > 1$ implies that the firm is operating under increasing returns to scale; and if $s < 1$, the firm is experiencing decreasing returns to scale.[6] Dividing each side of equation (5.5) by T yields

$$\begin{aligned} s &= MP_L(L/T) + MP_K(K/T) \\ &= MP_L/AP_L + MP_K/AP_K \end{aligned} \tag{5.6}$$

where AP_i $(i = K,L)$ is the average product of input i. But the ratio of an input's marginal to its average product can be written as $(\Delta T/T)/(\Delta i/i)$ $(i = K,L)$, which is the *elasticity of output* with respect to input i, $E_{T,i}$. Thus, it is possible to express equation (5.6) as

$$s = E_{T,L} + E_{T,K} \tag{5.7}$$

that is, the returns to scale in production is simply the summation of individual output elasticities with respect to labor and capital, respectively.[7]

LONG-RUN COST CURVES

We have seen that a typical isoquant curve represents alternative production processes for producing some output level T_1. A firm can produce T_1 using labor-intensive (low capital : labor ratio) or capital-intensive (high capital : labor ratio) production techniques. What determines whether our transport firm uses labor- or capital-intensive methods to ship its goods?

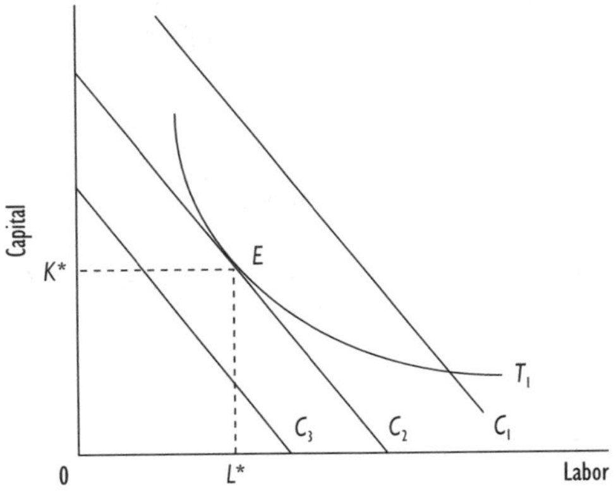

Figure 5.3 Optimal use of inputs.

The answer lies in the relative costs of inputs. Although it may be technically feasible to use labor-intensive methods to ship wheat to the Western market, the relative cost of labor may be sufficiently high that such methods are economically inefficient. If we let w and r represent the input prices for labor and capital respectively, the total cost, C, of using L and K can be expressed as

$$C = wL + rK \tag{5.8}$$

It is important to recognize that the costs defined in equation (5.8) are a firm's *opportunity* costs of production. The opportunity costs are economic costs that are *avoidable* or *escapable* if the activity is not undertaken. For example, suppose that a trucking firm hires ten laborers, paid weekly, and leases five trucks. The length of the lease for each truck is 1 year. Depending upon the time period, we can identify various opportunity costs of transport. If the time period is a day, then all costs are *fixed*. No costs can be avoided even if the firm shuts down for the day. On the other hand, if the time period is a week, and labor contracts are by the day, then labor costs are avoidable but truck leasing costs are not. In this case, the relevant opportunity costs are the labor costs while the leasing costs are irrelevant to current output decisions. If the time period is a year or more, then all costs are escapable and constitute the relevant opportunity costs of doing business. Thus, when analyzing a firm's output decisions, one must be careful to identify the relevant economic costs.

In this chapter, we are assuming that there are no fixed costs. All costs are opportunity costs. w and r reflect the per period opportunity cost of labor and capital, respectively. Just as a firm's production summarizes technically efficient combinations of K and L, its cost curves summarize economically (that is, least cost) efficient uses of K and L. To derive a firm's cost curves, suppose that our firm desires to produce T_1 units of output at the lowest possible cost. Referring to figure 5.3, a firm seeks to reach the lowest cost line consistent with isoquant T_1.[8] Although the firm could produce T_1 for cost C_1, it can reduce its costs by moving to C_2. No points on C_3, however, enable the firm to produce T_1 units. Cost line 2, therefore, minimizes the firm's costs in producing T_1 and the optimal quantities of K and L at equilibrium, given by the tangency point E, are cost-minimizing input levels. These optimal input demands for K

and L depend upon the economic environment, summarized by input prices w and r, the output level T_1, and the state of technology γ, which affects a firm's production possibilities.[9] That is,

$$K = k(T;w,r,\gamma)$$
$$L = l(T;w,r,\gamma) \tag{5.9}$$

which have been written in terms of T rather than T_1, since output can be any arbitrary level. If we substitute these demand functions into the firm's original cost function, given by equation (5.8), we obtain

$$\begin{aligned} C &= wk(T;w,r,\gamma) + rl(T;w,r,\gamma) \\ &= C(T;w,r,\gamma) \end{aligned} \tag{5.10}$$

$C(T;w,r,\gamma)$ is the *minimum cost* necessary to produce any arbitrary level of output T. Moreover, since cost is conditioned on the existing economic and technological environment, any change in the per unit input prices or any improvements in technology will alter a firm's total production costs at all levels of output.

Since total costs depend upon T, w, r, and γ, it also follows that a firm's marginal and average costs also depend upon T, w, r, and γ:

$$MC(T;w,r,\gamma) = \frac{\Delta C(T;w,r,\gamma)}{\Delta T} = \text{marginal cost of production} \tag{5.11}$$

and

$$AC(T;w,r,\gamma) = \frac{C(T;w,r,\gamma)}{T} = \text{average cost of production} \tag{5.12}$$

where marginal cost is the change in total cost due to a unit increase in output and average cost is total cost divided by output. Figure 5.4 illustrates a typical total cost curve and its associated marginal and average cost curves. As output rises from zero, total cost increases, but at a decreasing rate. This reflects the initial stage of production in which a firm is enjoying increasing returns to scale. Since input prices remain constant, proportional increases in inputs induce greater than proportional increases in outputs, which results in less than proportional cost increases. This is also reflected in the downward-sloping portion of the average cost curve. Once returns to scale are exhausted, which occurs after points C and C' in figure 5.4, proportional increases in inputs are not matched by proportional output increases, which causes total cost to rise more quickly. Accordingly, average costs begin to rise. Point C' is the minimum point on the average cost curve, referred to as the *minimum efficient scale*, at which point the firm is operating under constant returns to scale.

If a firm's average cost curve is downward-sloping, then marginal cost lies *below* average cost. Production of an additional unit must add less to cost than the average of the previous units produced. But this is equivalent to saying that marginal cost is less than average cost. Similarly, if average cost is increasing, producing an additional unit must add more to cost

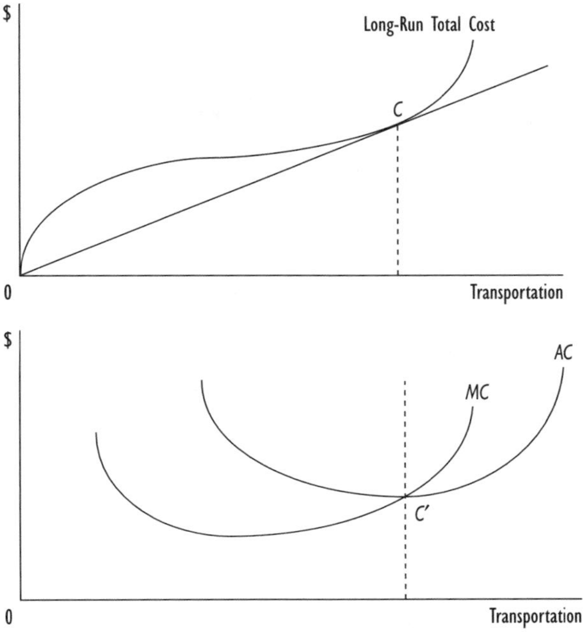

Figure 5.4 Total, average, and marginal cost curves.

than the average of the previous units produced. That is, marginal cost must be *above* average cost. Thus, if a firm faces a "U-shaped" average cost curve, the marginal cost curve intersects from below the average cost curve at its minimum point.

RETURNS TO SCALE AND LONG-RUN COSTS

Equation (5.11) tells us that marginal cost is the change in total cost resulting from a one unit increase in output, $\Delta C/\Delta T$. Additional insight into the meaning of marginal cost can be obtained by recalling the cost-minimization problem depicted in figure 5.4. Equilibrium occurs at the point of tangency between isoquant T_1 and cost line C_2. Since at the point of tangency the slopes of the two curves must be equal, it must be true that the marginal rate of technical substitution equals the input price ratio at point E:

$$MRTS = \frac{w}{r} \quad \Rightarrow \quad \frac{MP_L}{MP_K} = \frac{w}{r} \quad \Rightarrow \quad \frac{w}{MP_L} = \frac{r}{MP_K} \tag{5.13}$$

Recalling that MP_L is $\Delta T/\Delta L$, then w/MP_L is simply $w(\Delta L/\Delta T)$, which is the price of labor times the amount of labor needed to increase output by one unit. Similarly, r/MP_K is the per unit cost of capital times the amount of capital needed to produce an additional unit of T. This implies that

$$\frac{r}{MP_K} = \frac{w}{MP_L} = MC \tag{5.13'}$$

where MC is the marginal cost of producing one more unit of T. Thus, in equilibrium, marginal cost must be equalized across all inputs, *whether this is done through an increase in labor, an increase in capital, or some combination.*

Furthermore, from our discussion of production functions, we saw that a firm's returns to scale s could be expressed as

$$s = \frac{MP_L}{AP_L} + \frac{MP_K}{AP_K}$$

where the firm operates under increasing returns to scale if $s > 1$, constant returns to scale if $s = 1$, and decreasing returns to scale if $s < 1$. Assuming that firms are input price-takers, our expression for scale economies can be equivalently written as

$$\begin{aligned}
s &= \frac{MP_L}{AP_L}\frac{w}{w} + \frac{MP_K}{AP_K}\frac{r}{r} \\
&= \frac{MP_L}{w}\frac{wL}{T} + \frac{MP_K}{r}\frac{rK}{T} \\
&= \frac{1}{MC}\left(\frac{wL + rK}{T}\right) \qquad \left(\text{since } \frac{MP_L}{w} = \frac{MP_K}{r} \text{ in equilibrium}\right) \\
&= \frac{AC}{MC} = \frac{1}{E_{C,T}}
\end{aligned} \tag{5.14}$$

where $E_{C,T}$ is the elasticity of total cost with respect to output, defined as

$$E_{C,T} = \frac{\Delta C}{\Delta T}\frac{T}{C}$$

Equation (5.14) tells us that, for constant input prices, there is an *inverse* relationship between production returns to scale, s, and the elasticity of total cost with respect to output. For example, if $s > 1$, returns to scale are increasing and $E_{C,T} < 1$.[10] Table 5.1 summarizes this relationship. From an empirical standpoint, the relationship between returns to scale and

Table 5.1 The relationship between economies of scale and cost elasticity

Returns to Scale	Value of s	Value of $E_{C,T}$
Increasing	> 1	< 1
Constant	$= 1$	$= 1$
Decreasing	< 1	> 1

production cost elasticity is important because it reveals that an analysis of firm costs provides economically relevant information on a firm's production technology without having to separately estimate a firm's production function.

INPUT DEMANDS AND SHEPHARD'S LEMMA

Given input prices, w and r, equation (5.10) gives the cost function as the minimum cost necessary to produce output level T. Importantly, this cost function was obtained by substituting the optimal levels of capital and labor, $k(T;w,r,\gamma)$ and $l(T;w,r,\gamma)$, into the cost equation; that is,

$$C(T;w,r,\gamma) = wk(T;w,r,\gamma) + rl(T;w,r,\gamma) \tag{5.15}$$

An important result in cost analysis, known as Shephard's lemma, is that a change in the cost function resulting from a one unit increase in an input's price gives the conditional *optimal* demand for the input. More formally,

$$\frac{\Delta C(T;w,r,\gamma)}{\Delta w} = l(T;w,r,\gamma) = \text{conditional optimal demand for labor}$$

$$\frac{\Delta C(T;w,r,\gamma)}{\Delta r} = k(T;w,r,\gamma) = \text{conditional optimal demand for capital} \tag{5.16}$$

These are *conditional* optimal demands because they depend upon – that is, are conditioned upon – the level of output T.

Shephard's lemma follows directly from the definition of the cost function as the minimum cost of producing some level of output. Since the minimum cost only occurs when inputs are used optimally, an increase in an input's price, all else constant, will have the effect of increasing costs by the optimal amount of the input used. For example, suppose that the optimal amount of labor, $l(T;w,r,\gamma)$ in equation (5.16), is ten employees and the wage rate per laborer increases by $\Delta w = \$1$. This has the effect of increasing total costs by $\Delta C = (10)\$1 = \$10$ dollars. Thus, the change in total costs resulting from a \$1 increase in the employee wage rate, $\Delta C/\Delta w = (\$10/(\$1/\text{laborer})) = 10$ laborers, the optimal amount of labor used.

A further result occurs if we express equation (5.16) in terms of input price elasticities of demand. Multiplying the first equation in (5.16) by w/C and the second equation by r/C gives

$$E_{C,w} = \frac{w}{C(T;w,r,\gamma)} \frac{\Delta C(T;w,r,\gamma)}{\Delta w} = \frac{wl(T;w,r,\gamma)}{C(T;w,r,\gamma)}$$

$$= \text{conditional optimal } \textit{share} \text{ of labor expenditures in total costs}$$

$$E_{C,r} = \frac{r}{C(T;w,r,\gamma)} \frac{\Delta C(T;w,r,\gamma)}{\Delta r} = \frac{rk(T;w,r,\gamma)}{C(T;w,r,\gamma)}$$

$$= \text{conditional optimal } \textit{share} \text{ of capital expenditures in total costs} \tag{5.16'}$$

where $E_{C,w}$ and $E_{C,r}$ are the elasticity of total costs with respect to the wage rate and the rental price of capital, respectively. Thus, Shephard's lemma gives us the further general result that the (conditional) optimal share of an input in total costs equals the elasticity of total production cost with respect to the input's price.

We will see below that these results are of particular importance when we empirically estimate a firm's cost functions.

ELASTICITY OF SUBSTITUTION AND LONG-RUN COSTS

A final result with respect to cost functions relates to a firm's ability to substitute one input for another in the production process. Graphically, we have seen that the ease with which a firm substitutes labor for capital is depicted by the curvature of a firm's isoquant. An isoquant with very little curvature implies that labor and capital are *easily* substitutable, whereas an isoquant that is very angular reflects *few* possibilities for substitution.

We have also seen that the elasticity of substitution between capital and labor gives the percentage effect on the capital : labor ratio from a 1% increase in the marginal rate of technical substitution:

$$\sigma_{KL} = \frac{\%\Delta(K/L)}{\%\Delta(MRTS)}$$

But equation (5.13) says that, in equilibrium, the marginal rate of technical substitution equals the input price ratio. Thus, the elasticity of substitution between capital and labor, σ_{KL}, can be expressed as

$$\sigma_{KL} = \frac{\%\Delta(K/L)}{\%\Delta(w/r)} \tag{5.17}$$

which gives the percentage change in the capital : labor ratio resulting from a 1% increase in the relative price of labor. Since long-run costs reflect a firm's underlying production technology, information on the elasticity of substitution can be obtained from the cost function. Although the explicit derivation of substitution elasticities is beyond the scope of this book, their estimated values will be reported and discussed in the sections below.[11]

ALTERNATIVE MEASURES OF COST ELASTICITIES IN TRANSPORTATION[12]

Table 5.1 identified an inverse relationship between returns to scale and the cost elasticity for a two-input production function. Because transportation systems are characterized by capital stock as well as a network of routes, there exist different cost elasticity measures depending upon how the model is specified. Berechman (1993) identifies the following cost elasticities for transportation systems.[13]

Economies of scale As noted in the previous section, the standard measure for scale economies is the inverse of the cost elasticity. This is an appropriate measure of economies of scale for a transport firm where route structures are either absent or play a minor role in the production of transportation services. For example, network considerations are not generally relevant for owner–operators in the motor carrier industry that contract with a specific shipper to transport a specialized good from origin A to destination B. Assuming that route structure is not relevant, let ε_o denote returns to scale. If all inputs are variable, this is a long-run concept.

Economies of capital stock utilization Assume that a firm's output depends upon noncapital and capital stock inputs, capital stock is held fixed, and route structure is not relevant. Then our cost elasticity is a measure of the returns to capital stock utilization. If a 1% increase in output increases costs by 1% (greater than 1%, less than 1%), the firm is operating under constant (decreasing, increasing) returns to utilization. This will be denoted by $\varepsilon_{o|\mathrm{k}}$ and is necessarily a short-run concept, since capital stock is held fixed.

Economies of traffic density and generalized economies of scale Assume that the network size or route structure is important to the provision of transportation services. If all inputs are variable but network size is fixed, there will be increasing returns to traffic density if a 1% increase in output (for example, ton–miles or passenger–miles) produces a less than 1% increase in the cost of production. Alternatively, if a 1% increase in output leads to a 1% (greater than 1%) increase in total costs, the firm is operating under constant (decreasing) returns to density. In general, economies of traffic density is a short-run concept, since it holds the route structure constant. Let $\varepsilon_{o|\mathrm{nw}}$ represent economies of traffic density.

Alternatively, if all inputs are variable, a generalized economies of scale measure, $\varepsilon_{o,\mathrm{nw}}$, reflects a proportional increase in output and network size. All else constant, if $\varepsilon_{o,\mathrm{nw}}$ equals (less than, greater than) one, then a 1% increase in both output and network size (that is, route structure) increase costs by 1% (less than, more than), and the firm is operating under generalized constant (increasing, decreasing) returns to scale. This is a long-run concept.

Finally, if route structure is important but capital is held fixed, it is possible to define a short-run measure for generalized economies of capital stock utilization, $\varepsilon_{o,\mathrm{nw}|\mathrm{k}}$, which reflects the impact upon short-run costs due to a proportional increase in output and network size.

THE LONG-RUN MARKET SUPPLY FUNCTION

In the long run, all inputs are variable, so that the relevant expression for a firm's long-run profits π_{L} is:

$$\pi_{\mathrm{L}} = pT - LTC(T;w,r,\gamma) \tag{5.18}$$

where p is the price per unit of transportation T. The profits are simply the difference between total revenue and long-run total costs.

For a firm operating in the long run, we can ask two questions about its behavior. First, is there a price below which the firm will not operate in the long run? Yes! In the long run, a firm produces positive amounts of output as long as it can recover all of its opportunity costs of production; that is, as long as the price is at least as great as the long-run average cost:

$$\pi_L = pT - LTC(T;w,r,\gamma) \geqslant 0$$
$$\Rightarrow \; p \geqslant \frac{LTC(T;w,r,\gamma)}{T} = LAC(T;w,r,\gamma) \tag{5.19}$$

Second, what is the effect on long-run profits if output increases by one unit? In the long run, a unit increase in T raises marginal revenues by p, the price of T. A unit increase in T, however, also affects costs. *Long-run marginal cost* is the change in long run costs due to a unit increase in T. Because, in the long run, a firm is able to optimally adjust all of its inputs, long-run marginal cost gives the firm's lowest opportunity cost of producing an additional unit of T with existing technology.

The net effect of an increase in T on long-run profits is

$$\frac{\Delta\pi_L}{\Delta T} = p - \frac{\Delta LTC(T;w,r,\gamma)}{\Delta T} = p - LMC(T;w,r,\gamma) \tag{5.20}$$

Facing a given price p, in the long run the firm will continue to sell units as long as the price is at least as great as long-run marginal cost. Thus, the *long-run profit-maximizing condition* is

$$p = LMC(T;w,r,\gamma) \tag{5.21}$$

The optimal level of T in the long run, obtained by solving equation (5.13) for T, gives the firm's *long-run supply function*:

$$\begin{aligned} T^* &= T^{lr}(p;w,r,\gamma), \qquad && p \geqslant LAC(T;w,r,\gamma) \\ &= 0, && p < LAC(T;w,r,\gamma) \end{aligned} \tag{5.22}$$

which is coincident with its long-run marginal cost curve as long as price is at least as large as long-run average cost.

Notice that the underlying principle for economic operation in the long run requires that a firm receive sufficient revenues to cover its (variable) costs. If, however, price falls below average (variable) cost, the firm ceases to produce.

If we hold input prices and technology constant, we obtain a relationship between the optimal level of transportation T^* and price:

$$\begin{aligned} T^*(p) &= T^{lr}(p;\overline{w},\overline{r},\gamma), \qquad && p \geqslant LAC(T;\overline{w},\overline{r},\gamma) \\ &= 0, && p < LAC(T;\overline{w},\overline{r},\gamma) \end{aligned} \tag{5.23}$$

Assuming that there are F firms in the industry and summing over each of these firms gives the long-run market supply function:

$$S_T^{lr}(p;w,r,\gamma) = \sum_{f=1}^{F} T_f^{lr}(p;w,r,\gamma) \tag{5.24}$$

Since, holding input prices and the state of technology constant, the long-run marginal cost curve for each firm is upward-sloping, the long-run market supply curve will also have a positive slope; that is, $\Delta S^{\text{lr}}_T/\Delta T > 0$. And movements along the long-run market supply curve represent changes in quantity supplied; changes in input prices or technology shift the location of the curve and represent changes in supply.

Changes in Long-Run Market Supply

Figure 5.5(a) depicts the positive relationship between the market supply of transportation and price, holding all other influences upon supply constant. Movements along the supply curve reflect *changes in quantity supplied* when the price of transportation changes. Alternatively, a change in any of the other factors that determine market supply shifts the supply curve and reflects a *change in supply*, depicted in figure 5.5(b). For example, the Motor Carrier Act of 1980 significantly eased entry requirements and led to a large growth in the number of motor carriers offering transportation services. Holding all else constant, the increase in carriers shifts the supply curve rightward since, at any given price, there is now a larger number of transportation firms that are providing services.

Similarly, if the per unit price of labor or capital falls, then each firm faces a lower opportunity cost of production. All else constant, the supply curve moves to the right (or, equivalently, shifts downward). Subsidies have a similar effect upon market supply. The National Mass Transportation Assistance Act of 1974 authorized federal operating subsidies for urban public transit. The effect of these subsidies lowered the opportunity cost (to public transportation producers), which shifted the supply curve to the right.

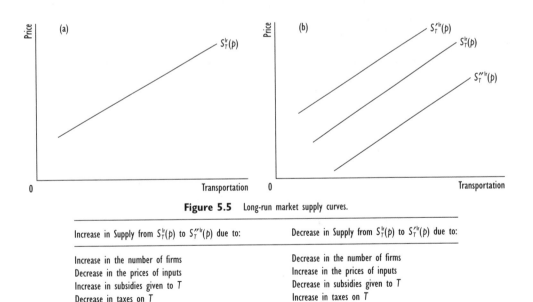

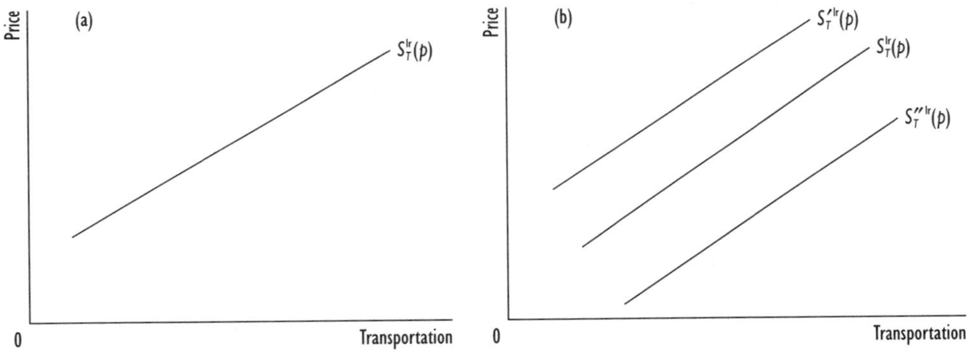

Figure 5.5 Long-run market supply curves.

Increase in Supply from $S^{\text{lr}}_T(p)$ to $S''^{\text{lr}}_T(p)$ due to:	Decrease in Supply from $S^{\text{lr}}_T(p)$ to $S'^{\text{lr}}_T(p)$ due to:
Increase in the number of firms	Decrease in the number of firms
Decrease in the prices of inputs	Increase in the prices of inputs
Increase in subsidies given to T	Decrease in subsidies given to T
Decrease in taxes on T	Increase in taxes on T
Improvements in technology Y	

The continuing technological improvements in all transport sectors – intelligent vehicle highway systems, more efficient aircraft engines, containerization, truck-on-flat-car, and the information highway – shift market supply curves rightward by enabling producers to provide more and higher-quality transport services at existing prices, all else constant.

ESTIMATING LONG-RUN COST FUNCTIONS

When faced with a given set of input prices and the state of technology, the cost function $C(T;w,r,\gamma)$ gives the long-run minimum total cost of producing some output level T. All else constant, an increase in T increases total cost, whereas a decrease in T decreases production cost. Graphically, figure 5.6 depicts the relationship between changes in T and changes in long-run total cost.

With an objective toward estimating a firm's long-run total cost function, the following simplifying assumptions are adopted (Intriligator, 1978):

- all firms in the industry face the same production technology
- all firms in the industry produce their planned outputs and seek to minimize costs at these outputs
- all firms in the industry face the same input prices for capital and labor
- all firms in the industry face the same output price for T
- T, L, and K are divisible goods

Given these assumptions, each firm is predicted to produce the same amount of T and, accordingly, would be situated at the same spot on its long-run total cost curve. In figure 5.6, (T^*,C^*) is the predicted output–cost combination for each of the firms in the industry. In reality, however, predicted costs C^* are likely to differ from observed costs due to measurement error, optimization error, or differences in the available technology.

In particular, assume that there are F firms in the industry and define costs as

$$C^o = C(T^*;w,r,\gamma) + \varepsilon_n = C^* + \varepsilon_n, \qquad n = 1, \ldots, F$$

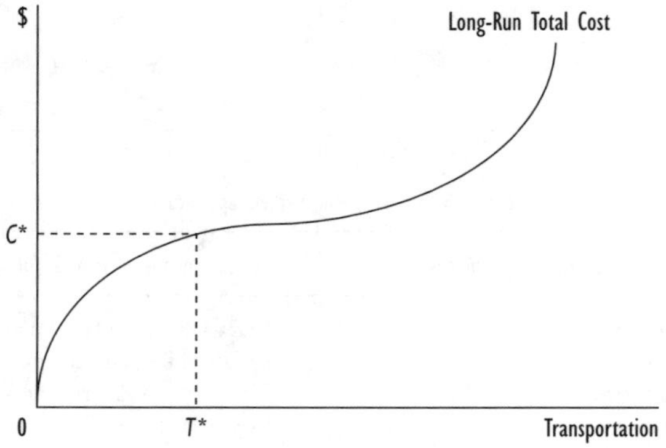

Figure 5.6 Predicted cost–output combination.

where C^o is the observed long-run total costs and ε is a random error term for firm n. Random differences between observed and predicted long-run total costs are generally due to optimization or measurement errors. Optimization errors occur because planned output does not equal actual output, or because output turns out to be nonoptimal *ex post*. Errors in measurement correspond to difficulties experienced in accurately measuring output, input prices, and technology.

If all firms produce the same level of output and are identical in all other respects, then it is unlikely that differences between predicted and observed costs would reflect differences in technology. Competition ensures that each firm have the latest technology available. However, the result that all firms produce the same level of output ignores the dynamic nature of an industry. At any point in time, an industry is a reflection of individual entrepreneurial decisions to enter or exit the industry, or to alter the scale of operations. Successful firms seek to expand their operations into other markets, while others may be reducing the size of their operations. This implies that data on a cross-section of firms at any point in time will *not* be made up of identically sized firms, but *will include* different-sized firms whose output–cost combinations correspond to alternative points along the long-run total cost curve. Thus, although firms in the industry may have the same *set* of technological options available and face the same economic environment, differences between predicted and observed output levels also reflect the use of alternative technologies due to interfirm differences in the scale of operations.

Two Examples of Production Technologies and Associated Cost Functions

Up to this point, we have derived a cost-minimizing cost function $C(T^*;w,r,\gamma)$ that identifies those factors expected to be important determinants of a firm's total costs. We have also seen that observed costs are likely to differ from predicted costs due to optimization error, measurement error, or interfirm differences in scale of operation. But how do we empirically specify a firm's cost function that is consistent with our assumptions on underlying production technology? For three different production technologies, we will examine the empirical cost function associated with the technology.

Leontif (fixed proportions) cost functions

Consider the following production function:

$$T = \min\left(\frac{L}{a},\frac{K}{b}\right), \qquad a, b > 0 \tag{5.25}$$

where a is the amount of labor required to produce one unit of output and b is the amount of capital required to produce one unit of output. A key implication of this production function is that it leads to "right angled" isoquants, depicted in figure 5.7. At the "kink" E, the amount of labor and capital required to produce T_1 units of output are aT_1 and bT_1, respectively. The slope of the ray $0R$ is the ratio of input requirements, b/a. If the firm moves along the horizontal portion of the isoquant, labor costs and total costs increase with no corresponding increase in

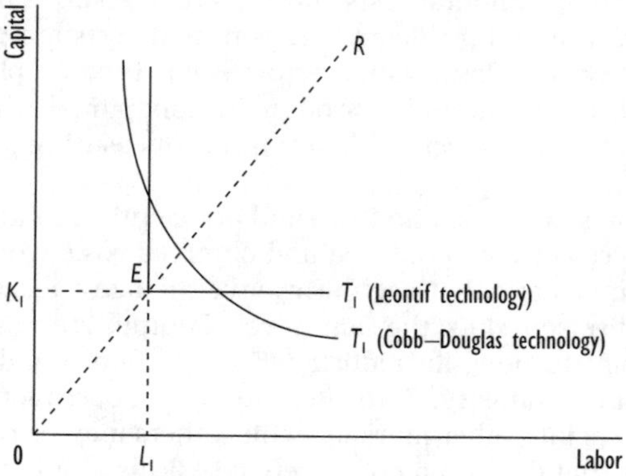

Figure 5.7 Leontif and Cobb–Douglas isoquants.

output. Similarly, if the firm increases capital without a corresponding increase in labor – that is, it moves along the vertical portion of its isoquant – capital costs and total costs increase with no increase in output. Thus, the kink at point E is optimal because at this point the firm minimizes the total cost of producing output level T_1.

The Leontif production technology given in equation (5.25) has two important properties. First, if both inputs increase proportionately, output increases in the same proportion. That is, the production function exhibits constant returns to scale. Second, there are no possibilities for input substitution. Isoquants are "right angled" and it is not possible to produce T_1 by employing more labor than L_1 and reducing capital below K_1. Similarly, it is not possible to produce T_1 output by increasing capital beyond K_1 but using fewer laborers than L_1. The property that input substitution is impossible implies that the elasticity of substitution σ_{KL} is 0.

What does the cost function for this technology look like? If the firm produces T_1 units of output, it would optimally require aT_1 units of labor and bT_1 units of capital, respectively. Given input prices w and r, the cost function for the Leontif technology is

$$C(T_1;w,r,\gamma) = w(aT_1) + r(bT_1)$$

which suggests the general regression equation

$$C(T;w,r,\gamma) = \alpha_0 + \alpha_1 x_1 + \alpha_2 x_2 + \varepsilon \tag{5.26}$$

where the explanatory variables x_1 and x_2 are wT and rT, respectively, α_0 is a constant term, α_1 is a, α_2 is b, and ε is a normally distributed error term.

Cobb–Douglas cost functions

An alternative production technology that has been extensively used in empirical analyses is the Cobb–Douglas production function:

$$T = AL^aK^b, \qquad a, b > 0 \tag{5.27}$$

where A is a constant and a and b are parameters. This technology has isoquants that are convex to the origin, depicted in figure 5.7. Cobb–Douglas production technology is more general than Leontif technology, because it allows for nonconstant returns to scale as well as for input substitutability. Recall that returns to scale s are given by the expression

$$s = \frac{MP_L}{AP_L} + \frac{MP_K}{AP_K}$$

which, for the Cobb–Douglas production function, equals the sum of the parameters $a + b$. In addition, the elasticity of substitution σ_{KL} can be shown to equal one, which, from (5.17), tells us that a 1% increase in the relative price of labor leads to a 1% rise in the capital : labor ratio. Solving for the optimal input demands and substituting into the cost equation leads to the following cost function for the Cobb–Douglas technology:

$$C(T;w,r,\gamma) = A'w^{a/(a+b)}r^{b/(a+b)}T^{1/(a+b)}$$

where A' is a constant term that is consistent with cost-minimizing behavior.[14] Taking logarithms of both sides of this equation and adding an error term produces the following empirical regression equation:

$$\ln C(T;w,r,\gamma) = \alpha_0 + \alpha_1 \ln T + \alpha_2 \ln w + \alpha_3 \ln r + \varepsilon \tag{5.28}$$

where $\alpha_0 = \ln A'$, α_1 is the inverse of production returns to scale $a + b$, $\alpha_2 = (a/(a + b))$, $\alpha_3 = (b/(a + b))$, and ε is a normally distributed error term.

Flexible Cost Functions

Although the Leontif and Cobb–Douglas production technologies in the two above examples lead to econometrically straightforward regression equations for total costs, these specifications are limited because of the theoretical restrictions that they place upon factor substitutability. Leontif production functions are most restrictive, because they not only preclude any substitution between capital and labor but also assume constant returns to scale. Cobb–Douglas production functions, although less restrictive because they allow for nonconstant returns to scale and input substitutability, are still limited because they assume that the elasticity of substitution between inputs is always one; that is, a 1% increase in the relative price of labor will always result in a 1% increase in the capital : labor ratio.

Since Leontif and Cobb–Douglas total cost functions inherently constrain the production possibilities of firms, transportation analysts in the past 15 or so years have almost exclusively relied upon "flexible" empirical cost functions to analyze the cost and production characteristics of transportation firms. These total cost functions are "flexible" because they are consistent with firm cost-minimizing behavior but do not restrict, *a priori*, a firm's production technology. In particular, there are no inherent restrictions upon a firm's scale economies, nor its substitutability between inputs.

Table 5.2 Translog cost function regression model: interpretation of first-order coefficients at the mean

Regressor	Coefficient	Interpretation
Constant term	α_0	Logarithm of total cost at the sample mean
$(\ln T - \ln \bar{T})$	α_1	Elasticity of total cost with respect to output T at the sample mean
$(\ln w - \ln \bar{w})$	α_2	Share of labor in total costs, evaluated at the sample mean
$(\ln r - \ln \bar{r})$	α_3	Share of capital in total costs, evaluated at the sample mean
$(\ln \gamma - \ln \bar{\gamma})$	α_4	Percentage change in total cost from a 1% change in technology, evaluated at the sample mean

The most popular specification of a "flexible" cost function is a "translog" cost function, derived in the appendix to this chapter. A simplified version is reproduced below:

$$\ln C(T;w,r,\gamma) = \alpha_0 + \alpha_1(\ln T - \ln \bar{T}) + \alpha_2(\ln w - \ln \bar{w}) + \alpha_3(\ln r - \ln \bar{r}) \\ + \alpha_4(\ln \gamma - \ln \bar{\gamma}) + \text{"second-order and interaction terms"} + \varepsilon \tag{5.29}$$

The α_is ($i = 0, 1, 2, 3, 4$) are referred to as "first-order coefficients." "Second-order and interaction terms" correspond to the coefficients of squared explanatory variables (for example, $(\ln T - \ln \bar{T})^2$) and the product of explanatory variables (for example, $(\ln T - \ln \bar{T})(\ln w - \ln \bar{w})$). For our purposes, the "first-order coefficients" α_i ($i = 0, 1, 2, 3, 4$) contain the most relevant economic information. Table 5.2 gives the economic interpretations for each of the first-order coefficients, *when T, w, r, and γ are evaluated at their sample mean values.*

For example, at the sample mean, the following relationships hold: $\ln T = \ln \bar{T}$, $\ln w = \ln \bar{w}$, $\ln r = \ln \bar{r}$, and $\ln \gamma = \ln \bar{\gamma}$. These restrictions imply that all terms in equation (5.29) disappear except for the constant term α_0 and the error term ε. Assuming that the error term has a mean value equal to zero, then $\ln C(\bar{T};\bar{w},\bar{r},\bar{\gamma}) = \alpha_0$; that is, the logarithm of total costs at the sample mean equals the constant term. And this implies that an estimate of total costs *at the mean* is $\exp(\alpha_0)$.

We saw in chapter 2 that $\Delta \ln x/\Delta \ln y$ is the elasticity of x with respect to y. From equation (5.29), if we calculate $\Delta \ln C(T;w,r,\gamma)/\Delta \ln T$ and evaluate the result at the sample mean, we obtain α_1, the elasticity of cost with respect to output. But, from table 5.1, the cost elasticity with respect to output provides information on returns to scale. Thus, depending upon whether α_1 is greater than, less than, or equal to one, at the sample mean, a firm will be operating under decreasing, increasing, or constant returns to scale respectively.

By a similar procedure, α_2 is $\Delta \ln C(T;w,r,\gamma)/\Delta \ln w$, the elasticity of total cost with respect to the wage rate evaluated at the sample mean. But for cost-minimizing firms, Shephard's lemma, as expressed in equation (5.16′), tells us that the wage elasticity of total cost is the (conditional) optimal share of labor in total costs. Thus, α_2 gives the optimal share of labor in total production cost at the sample mean. Likewise, α_3 gives the optimal share of capital in total production costs when evaluated at the mean.

α_4 reflects the impact of technological changes on costs and, similar to the interpretations of α_1, α_2, and α_3, gives the percentage change in total costs resulting from a 1% change in technology at the sample mean. But how does one measure technology?

In reality, there is no one simple measure of technology or technological changes, and empirical cost functions generally use *proxies* to capture the effects of technology. In transportation analyses, two types of variables are used to capture the effects of technology. First, a transportation firm's *operating characteristics* are included in the empirical model in order to reflect the technological conditions facing a firm. The rationale for including these variables is that carriers' outputs are typically heterogeneous. Consider two motor carrier firms, each of which ships 10,000 ton–miles. The first firm makes five trips to transport 10 tons of goods 1,000 miles, whereas the second firm incurs 200 trips in transporting 100 tons 100 miles. The average lengths of haul (total ton–miles divided by total tons) are 1,000 and 100, respectively, for the two firms. The average shipment sizes (total tons divided by total shipments) are 2 tons and $\frac{1}{2}$ ton, respectively. Although, as measured by ton–miles, each firm ships the same quantity, one would expect costs to differ because of the differences in firms' average lengths of haul and average shipment sizes. Hence, differences in the operating characteristics among transportation firms reflect differences in the technological conditions facing the firm.

The second type of variable included in empirical models to capture technology and technological improvement is a time variable.[15] This variable is assumed to represent a "pure productivity effect" which captures changes in firm productivity that are *not* due to all other factors included in the model. In other words, it's a residual effect after accounting for the other influences on total production costs. For example, consider the following cost function:

$$C(T;w,r,o,t)$$

where technology γ has been replaced with an operating characteristic, o, and a time trend, t. Variable o reflects the technological conditions facing the firm due to output heterogeneity and t gives a pure productivity effect. In this expression, if, after controlling for T, w, r, and o, total costs fall over time, this decrease in total production costs is interpreted as a technological effect that is not explained by the other variables in the model and, accordingly, is attributed to a "pure productivity" effect. Substitution of the operating characteristic o and time trend t for the technology parameter γ leads to the following translog cost function:

$$\begin{aligned} \ln C(T;w,r,o,t) = {} & \alpha_0 + \alpha_1(\ln T - \ln \bar{T}) + \alpha_2(\ln w - \ln \bar{w}) + \alpha_3(\ln r - \ln \bar{r}) \\ & + \alpha_5(\ln o - \ln \bar{o}) + \alpha_6(\ln t - \ln \bar{t}) \\ & + \text{"second-order and interaction terms"} + \varepsilon \end{aligned} \tag{5.30}$$

Table 5.3 provides the economic interpretation for the two new coefficients, α_5 and α_6, in the model.

In the following sections, we use empirical flexible cost functions to examine the underlying technology and associated long-run costs for three important sectors in the transportation industry: motor carriers, railroads, and airlines. In each case, we summarize the salient characteristics of the sector, identify a flexible cost model that characterizes the sector's long-run total costs, present estimation results, and discuss policy implications.

Table 5.3 Translog cost function regression model: interpretation of technology-related first-order coefficients

Regressor	Coefficient	Interpretation
$(\ln o - \ln \bar{o})$	α_5	Elasticity of total cost with respect to operating characteristic o at sample mean
$(\ln t - \ln \bar{t})$	α_6	Productivity growth rate per period of time (e.g., per year) at the sample mean

INTERCITY FREIGHT MOVEMENTS IN THE UNITED STATES

Table 5.4 summarizes ton–miles of intercity freight shipped by mode during the past 50 years. In the early part of the century, railroad movement was by far the dominant mode for intercity freight shipments. Even as late as 1929, 74.9% of intercity freight traffic moved by railroad. Motor carriers hauled 3.3% of the total, pipelines 4.4%, and water 17.4% (MacAvoy and Snow, 1977, pp. 50–1). Air freight was virtually nonexistent at the time. As intercity freight movements increased over time, we see in table 5.4 that, with the exception of water transport, whose share of traffic remained virtually constant at 15–16%, modal shares changed dramatically. Between 1940 and 1990, the total share of motor carrier freight increased from 10% to 25.7%. And within the group of motor carriers, non-Interstate Commerce Commission (ICC) traffic more than doubled its market share, while the share of ICC truck traffic tripled. Between 1940 and 1980, pipeline traffic grew by 148% and remained at this level in 1990. Although airline freight traffic was responsible for less than 1% of the total freight market during this period, it has similarly experienced a large growth rate. However, table 5.4 clearly reveals that during the past half-century rail traffic has been the big loser in transporting intercity freight, falling from 61.3% of the market in 1940 to 37.4% in 1990. This represents an average annual loss of just under 0.5%.

Table 5.4 Ton–miles (billions) of intercity freight transported during the past 50 years: the numbers in parentheses are modal shares

Year	ICC Truck	Non-ICC Truck	Rail	Air	Water	Pipeline
1940	21 (3.4)	41 (6.6)	379 (61.3)	0.02 (0)	118 (19.1)	59 (9.5)
1950	66 (6.2)	107 (10.1)	597 (56.2)	0.3 (0.03)	164 (15.4)	129 (12.1)
1960	104 (7.9)	181 (13.8)	579 (44.1)	0.9 (0.07)	220 (16.7)	229 (17.4)
1970	167 (8.6)	245 (12.6)	771 (39.8)	3.3 (0.17)	319 (16.5)	431 (22.3)
1975	200 (9.7)	254 (12.3)	759 (36.7)	3.7 (0.18)	352 (16.6)	507 (24.5)
1980	242 (9.7)	313 (12.6)	932 (37.5)	4.8 (0.19)	407 (16.4)	588 (23.6)
1985	250 (10.2)	360 (14.6)	895 (36.4)	6.7 (0.27)	382 (15.5)	564 (22.9)
1990	311 (10.9)	424 (14.8)	1,071 (37.4)	10.4 (0.36)	464 (16.2)	584 (20.4)

Source: ENO Transportation Foundation (1993)

The significant increase in motor carrier share and decrease in rail share during the past half-century represents a major modal redistribution, and implies that the bulk of traffic lost by the railroads during the period was diverted to motor carriers. This raises a number of important questions. One, do the various transportation sectors – motor carrier, rail, air, water, and pipeline – operate under different production technologies as characterized by returns to scale, substitution elasticities, and factor demand elasticities? Two, were the observed shifts in carrier traffic the direct result of technological changes that occurred in these industries during the past 50 years? Three, until the mid-1970s, each of these sectors was subject to stringent economic regulations by the federal government. What role did economic regulation play, and can we identify the likely effects of policy aimed at deregulating the transportation industries? In the following sections, we will try to provide some answers to these questions.

MOTOR CARRIER COSTS AND PRODUCTION TECHNOLOGY UNDER REGULATION

Economic regulation in the intercity transportation sector began in 1887, when Congress passed the Interstate Commerce Act in order to regulate railroad rate-setting activities. Among its provisions, the Act required that railroad shipping rates not discriminate among shippers on the basis of a shipper's location, size, or length of haul. The Act also created the ICC in order to insure that the railroads were meeting the Act's provisions. To further reduce discriminatory pricing practices, the Act required railroads to file their rates with the ICC, where they would be publicly accessible to any shipper. Although subjecting themselves to regulation, the railroads supported rate regulation because it eliminated crippling rate wars among the railroads and enabled them to maintain higher rates in their more competitive markets.

With the development of truck carriage in the early 1900s, railroads were subjected to increased competitive pressures from the emerging motor carrier industry. Competitive pressures intensified until 1935 when, supported by railroad interests, state regulatory commissions, and the ICC, Congress passed the Motor Carrier Act (MCA), which brought motor carriers under ICC control and regulated virtually every economic aspect of the motor carrier industry. The major provisions of the 1935 MCA included (Sampson et al., 1990):

1 *Carrier classification.* The Act defined five classes of motor carrier operators. *Common carriers* are for-hire carriers that serve the general pubic at reasonable rates and without discrimination. *Contract carriers* do not serve the general public, but operate under contract and special arrangements with a limited number of shippers. *Private carriers* own the goods that they transport and are not in the primary business of transporting goods. *Brokers* are firms that facilitate exchanges between shippers and carriers but do not transport any goods themselves. Finally, *exempt carriers* are carriers that are not subject to the economic provisions of the law. As of 1938, these included carriers of agricultural commodities and newspapers, vehicles owned and operated by railroads, water carriers, surface freight forwarders (pick-up and delivery), and vehicles used to transport persons and freight incidental to air travel.
2 *Entry controls.* According to the original Act, the burden of proof for common carrier entry was on the entering firm rather than the existing carrier. In particular, the common carrier needed to demonstrate that it was "fit, willing, and able to perform the proposed service,"

and that the service was required by present and future public convenience and necessity, which could only be done by showing that the proposed service was not being offered or satisfied by existing carriers. Contract carriers had a similar "fit, willing, and able" requirement, combined with a "consistent with the public interest" requirement. Operating certificates specified the route served, type of service rendered, frequency, and commodity description. Dual operation as common carrier and contract carrier over the same route or in the same territory was prohibited.

3 *Rate controls.* Similar to railroads, fares must be just and reasonable, published and observed. Fare changes required sufficient lead time. The ICC could prescribe a maximum, a minimum, or the actual rate if an existing rate was deemed unreasonable or illegal. Shippers in "similar circumstances and conditions" were to be treated the same – that is, carriers could not charge discriminatory rates.

4 *Other provisions.* Consolidations, mergers, and acquisitions had to be approved by the ICC unless they involved 20 or fewer vehicles. And, excepting small motor carriers, issuance of securities needed ICC approval. The ICC was also given the right to inspect motor carrier books and accounts.

Although a number of additional transportation bills were passed in the ensuing years, none of these substantively altered the economic restrictions placed upon the motor carrier industry in the 1935 legislation. For example, in 1942 Congress passed the Freight Forwarder Act, which extended economic regulation to *surface freight forwarders* that arrange for the transportation of small shipments. Typically, freight forwarders pick up and consolidate small shipments into larger loads, contract with motor carriers or railroads for the long-haul portion of the trip, and, at the destination, break down and deliver the shipments to the respective consignees. Thus, a freight forwarder acts as carrier to the original shipper and consignee of the shipment, but plays the role of shipper for the long-haul segment of the trip. In addition to the Freight Forwarder Act, Congress passed in 1948 the Reed–Bulwinkle Act, which allowed common carrier rate bureaus to set joint rates without fear of antitrust violations, and the Transportation Act of 1958, which limited the expansion of agricultural exemptions and banned private carriers from transporting for-hire goods.[16]

Over time, evidence began to accumulate that these constraints upon the motor carrier industry were having a significant impact upon motor carrier productivity and the efficient allocation of resources in the transport sector.[17] A consensus for deregulation culminated in the late 1970s and early 1980s with passage of several pieces of deregulatory legislation. For the motor carrier industry, administrative deregulation by the ICC began as early as 1978 and was codified in the 1980 Motor Carrier Act. With an overall objective to increase competition in the industry, the 1980 MCA relaxed entry requirements, expanded rate flexibility, eased route and carriage restrictions, and allowed for-hire services by private fleets.

We focus here on the structure of costs and underlying technology that characterized motor carrier activities *during the period of economic regulation.* We saw above that the 1935 Motor Carrier Act defined five classes of motor carrier operators. For our purposes, we are most interested in common carriers, since it is these operators that primarily fell under ICC jurisdiction.[18] For purposes of studying underlying technologies and costs, common carriers can be subdivided into *special commodity carriers* and *general freight* carriers. Many firms in the special commodity carrier category have operating authority to carry a specific commodity (for example, household goods, heavy machinery, motor vehicles, or hazardous materials). Alternatively, other firms in the "special commodities" subgroup have several operating authorities to carry a variety of goods to different destinations. Although these latter firms may carry general freight, a common characteristic is that the shipments are sufficiently large to meet the minimum requirements for a truckload shipment. These special commodity carriers are generally referred to as *truckload (TL) carriers*. Because truckload carriers pick up a shipment at an origin and deliver the same shipment to a given destination, they often make use of *owner–operators*; that is, individuals who own their own tractor–trailers. Although not possessing their own operating authorities, owner–operators offer their equipment and driving services to common carrier companies that possess such authority. Typically, owner–operators meet the excess demands of common carriers as well as the demands of surface freight forwarders that do not own their own equipment.

General freight commodity carriers, on the other hand, serve shippers whose shipments do not meet the minimum truckload requirement. These carriers are generally referred to as *less-than-truckload (LTL) carriers*. Since the typical shipment of an LTL carrier is small, LTL carriers must first bundle the separate loads into a truckload shipment, and then transport the goods to a destination point, at which the shipment is then unbundled in order to distribute the separate shipments to their final destinations. Because of its consolidation and break-bulking activities, LTL carriers find it economically advantageous to invest in a network of terminal facilities. In contrast, TL carriers have no need for terminal facilities, since they are transporting a single-truckload shipment.[19]

The transportation activities that differentiate TL from LTL carriers suggest that the underlying technologies and costs associated with TL firms differ from those of LTL firms. Empirically, this implies that it is appropriate to estimate separate cost functions for TL and LTL firms. In the following sections, we examine in some detail two analyses of motor carrier cost and technology in a *regulated* environment. The first study focuses upon the TL sector, while the second study looks at the LTL sector.

CASE STUDY – REGULATED TRUCKLOAD CARRIERS

In a recent analysis of freight regulation, McMullen and Stanley (1988) estimated a translog flexible cost function for specialized commodity (TL) motor carriers. In abbreviated form, their empirical cost function is

$$\begin{aligned}\ln C(T;p,o) = {} & \alpha_0 + \alpha_1(\ln T - \ln \bar{T}) \\ & + \alpha_2(\ln p_l - \ln \bar{p}_l) \\ & + \alpha_3(\ln p_k - \ln \bar{p}_k) \\ & + \alpha_4(\ln p_f - \ln \bar{p}_f) \\ & + \alpha_5(\ln p_{pt} - \ln \bar{p}_{pt}) \\ & + \alpha_6(\ln o_{ald} - \ln \bar{o}_{ald}) \\ & + \alpha_7((\ln o_{alh} - \ln \bar{o}_{alh}) \\ & + \alpha_8(\ln o_{ins} - \ln \bar{o}_{ins}) \\ & + \text{“second-order and interaction terms”} \\ & + \varepsilon \qquad (5.31)\end{aligned}$$

There are a number of clarifying comments on this empirical specification that are worth noting. First, for purposes of simplification, we have written the cost function on the left-hand side of equation (5.31) as $C(T;p,o)$. p is shorthand for the prices of inputs used in producing motor carrier services. Similarly, o is shorthand for a list of operating characteristics that capture differences in technologies across firms. On the right-hand side of equation (5.31), we see that there are four inputs, represented by their respective per unit prices p_l, p_k, p_f, and p_{pt}.[20] The subscripts l, k, f, and pt stand for labor, capital, fuel, and purchased transportation, respectively. Also, the right-hand side of equation (5.31) identifies three operating characteristics, o_{ald}, o_{alh}, and o_{ins}, where the subscripts refer to Average Load Per Vehicle, Average Length of Haul, and Insurance Cost Per Ton–Mile. Thus, for the TL motor carrier sector, long-run costs are hypothesized to depend upon output, the prices of four inputs, and technology, which is captured by three operating characteristics.

Second, total cost $C(T;p,o)$ for this study is measured in thousands of dollars and output T is measured in ton–miles. Average Load Per Vehicle, o_{ald}, is defined as total ton–miles divided by total vehicle miles. Average Length of Haul, o_{alh}, is defined as total ton–miles divided by total tons, and Insurance Cost Per Ton–Mile, o_{ald}, is defined as total insurance expenditures divided by total ton–miles.

Third, the parameters α_0 through α_8 are "first-order coefficients" that will characterize firm behavior *at the sample mean.*

Hypotheses

The following hypotheses on the production technology and costs associated with the truckload motor carrier sector will be tested:

HYPOTHESIS 1 The truckload sector operates under constant returns to scale. We have seen in an earlier section that the coefficient of the output variable, α_1, in a translog flexible cost model represents the elasticity of long-run total costs with respect to output. Thus, our hypothesis that the TL sector operates under constant returns to scale is equivalent to the null hypothesis that $\alpha_1 = 1$. The alternative hypothesis is that $\alpha_1 \neq 1$.

Why would we expect the TL sector to have constant returns to scale? This sector comprises a relatively large number of small firms in which owner–operators play a large role. Also, because capital requirements are relatively small, there is ease of entry and exit.[21] Further, although output for a motor carrier is heterogeneous, once interfirm differences are accounted for by the operating characteristics, the freight service provided in transporting a particular commodity between a given origin–destination pair is homogeneous. Thus, the TL sector appears to approximate the basic requirements of a competitive industry – a large number of small firms providing a homogeneous service with relatively easy entry/exit – which implies that an incumbent firm operates at the minimum point on its long-run average cost curve, its minimum efficient scale. This point characterizes constant returns to scale.

A further comment is that the nature of transport services provided suggests that route structure is not important to firms in this sector. As defined, then, the empirical model in equation (5.31) implicitly assumes that there are no economies of network size.

HYPOTHESIS 2 An increase in the price of any input increases, all else constant, long-run total costs. Thus, we expect that $\alpha_2 > 0$, $\alpha_3 > 0$, $\alpha_4 > 0$, and $\alpha_5 > 0$. A further result that follows from Shephard's lemma is that the coefficient of an input price in the translog model represents the share of that input in total costs. Not only do we expect each of the input prices to be positive, but we also expect the sum of these coefficients to equal one; that is, $\sum_{i=2}^{5}\alpha_i = 1$.

HYPOTHESIS 3 The empirical model identified in equation (5.31) includes three operating characteristics, Average Load Per Vehicle, Average Length of Haul, and Insurance Cost Per Ton–Mile. Each of these characteristics is intended to reflect differences in the underlying production technology and costs resulting from differences across firms in the types of commodities carried. Since this study focuses exclusively upon truckload firms, higher loads per vehicle can only occur if firms utilize more of their capacity by reducing the number of empty backhauls. Thus, Average Load per Vehicle reflects increased capacity utilization, which is expected to reduce costs, all else constant.

Related to this, TL firms that have longer lengths of haul experience economies of distance. For each shipment there will be pick-up and delivery costs that are independent of distance traveled, which implies that the per-mile cost of these charges decrease with distance traveled.

Thus, holding all else constant (including ton–miles), firms having longer hauls are expected to have lower costs. The coefficient for Average Length of Haul is expected to be negative.

Last, the characteristics of the goods shipped have implications for the costs associated with transporting these items. High-value commodities, perishable goods, and fragile shipments require more labor-intensive handling activities, which raise costs. Although the differential costs associated with transporting such items are not known, Insurance Cost Per Ton–Mile acts as a proxy for such costs. Higher insurance expenditures per mile are expected to reflect the shipment of more expensive goods and commodities that require special handling. All else constant, an increase in insurance expenditures per ton–mile is expected to increase total costs.

Based upon these hypotheses, it is expected that $\alpha_6 < 0$, $\alpha_7 < 0$, and $\alpha_8 > 0$.

Estimation results

Data for this analysis were based upon a sample of truckload motor carrier firms operating in 1977. Table 5.5 presents the first-order coefficients for each of the explanatory variables in equation (5.31). Also, for simplification, the information under the column "regressors" in table 5.5 is presented by identifying the relevant economic variable rather than the explicit explanatory variable from equation (5.31). For example, rather than specifying the output-related regressor as "$(\ln T - \ln \bar{T})$" in the first column of table 5.5, we use the economically more intuitive shorthand expression "Output". In order to avoid confusion, however, we also give the empirical regression model at the bottom of table 5.5.

As seen from the R^2 statistic in table 5.5, the empirical cost model for TL carriers fits the data well. 99% of the variation in total costs is explained by the explanatory variables in the equation. However, do the results make sense? Let's analyze table 5.5 to see whether the results confirm or contradict the hypotheses outlined above.

1 If truckload motor carrier firms providing specialized services approximate a competitive industry, as suggested in the first hypothesis, then we would expect to observe constant returns to scale, which is equivalent to α_1 having a value of one. From table 5.5, we see that our estimate of α_1 is 0.721, considerably below one, which says that, at the sample mean and holding all else constant, a 1% increase in output leads to a 0.721% increase in long-run total costs. At the sample mean, firms are operating under *increasing* rather than constant returns to scale. An equivalent way to say this is that firms at the sample mean are on the *downward* portion of the average total cost curve, to the *left* of the minimum point.

Is this result statistically significant? Remember that the *t*-statistic reported in table 5.5 tests the null hypothesis that the coefficient equals zero, so that the 4.6 value of the *t*-statistic tells us that we can reject this null hypothesis. However, in testing for increasing returns to scale, we are interested in whether our estimated coefficient equals one or is less than one. That is, we have a one-tail test, where our null and alternative hypotheses are

$$H_0: \alpha_1 = 1$$

$$H_A: \alpha_1 < 1$$

The relevant *t*-statistic is given by the ratio $(\hat{\alpha}_1 - 1)/s_{\hat{\alpha}_1}$, where $\hat{\alpha}_1$ is our coefficient estimate of α_1 and $s_{\hat{\alpha}_1}$ is the standard error of the estimate. Subtracting 1 from $\hat{\alpha}_1$ and dividing by $s_{\hat{\alpha}_1}$ gives the value −1.78, our *t*-statistic for testing the null hypothesis of constant returns to scale, which rejects the null hypothesis at a 0.05 level of significance.[22] Thus, the results in table 5.5 are *inconsistent* with the hypothesis that motor carrier firms in the specialized commodity TL

Table 5.5 Translog cost function regression model for carriers of specialized commodities, 1977: first-order coefficients at the sample mean

Regressor[a]	Coefficient Estimate (t-statistics)	Interpretation
Constant term	8.32 (46.1)	Logarithm of total cost at the sample mean
Output	0.721 (4.6)	Elasticity of total cost with respect to output T at the sample mean
Price of Labor	0.387 (9.8)	Share of labor in total costs, evaluated at the sample mean
Price of Capital	0.308 (12.5)	Share of capital in total costs, evaluated at the sample mean
Price of Fuel	0.127 (6.7)	Share of fuel in total costs, evaluated at the sample mean
Price of Purchased Transportation	0.178 (2.7)	Share of purchased transportation in total costs, evaluated at the sample mean
Average Load Per Vehicle	−0.674 (−3.6)	Elasticity of total cost with respect to average load, at the sample mean
Average Length of Haul	−0.093 (−0.77)	Elasticity of total cost with respect to average length of haul, at the sample mean
Insurance Cost Per Ton–Mile	0.076 (0.35)	Elasticity of total cost with respect to per ton–mile insurance costs, at the sample mean

$R^2 = 0.99$
Number of observations = 81

[a] The estimated translog cost function has the following form:

$$\ln C(T;p,o) = \alpha_0 + \alpha_1(\ln T - \ln \bar{T}) + \sum_{i=2}^{5}\alpha_i(\ln p_i - \ln \bar{p}_i) + \sum_{i=6}^{8}\alpha_i(\ln o_i - \ln \bar{o}_i)$$

$$+ \text{“second-order and interaction terms”} + \varepsilon$$

Source: McMullen and Stanley (1988), table II, p. 306

sector operate under constant returns to scale. Rather, the results are consistent with increasing returns to scale.

The implication of increasing returns to scale is that firms that transport specialized commodities can reduce their long-run costs by operating on a larger scale. An interesting question revolves around the *source* of the increasing returns to scale. In particular, are the observed returns to scale technology-based? Friedlaender and Spady (1981) also found evidence of increasing returns to scale, and suggest that these scale economies are not due to technology in the industry but are the result of the economic regulation under which these firms must operate. In the regulated environment, carriers of specialized goods were less restricted in their geographical area of operation than in the commodities that they were allowed to carry. Firms with one operating license to carry a specific commodity would likely have numerous empty backhauls. However, if the firm were able to obtain operating licenses to carry several different commodities, the firm could lower its costs by reducing the number of empty backhauls. In such a regulatory environment, a large firm with operating licenses to carry a number of different specialized commodities could exploit economies of network size; that is, the firm could lower unit costs by expanding its operating authority to multiple specialized commodities. This contrasts with the maintained hypothesis that economies of network size are zero.

2 Consistent with hypothesis 2, each of the price coefficients in table 5.5 is positive and, based upon *t*-statistics, we reject the null hypothesis that each coefficient equals zero. For the translog flexible cost function, Shephard's lemma implies that the input price coefficients are the shares of each input in total costs, implying that the coefficients lie between zero and one and that they sum to one. This is confirmed in table 5.5. Each coefficient is less than one and the sum is $0.387 + 0.308 + 0.127 + 0.178 = 1$. At the sample mean, labor is responsible for 38.7% of total costs, capital for 30.8%, fuel for 12.7%, and purchased transportation for 17.8%. The 17% share of costs attributed to purchased transportation is consistent with our description of the specialized commodity truckload sector as a segment in the industry with a strong reliance on purchased transportation in the form of owner–operators.

3 The results for firm operating characteristics are mixed. All else constant, we expect increases in the Average Load Per Vehicle to reflect better use of capital and, accordingly, lower costs. This is confirmed in table 5.5, where a 10% increase in average vehicle load reduces total costs by 6.7% at the sample mean. On the other hand, Average Length of Haul has the correct sign but a low *t*-statistic (−0.77), indicating that we cannot reject the null hypothesis that the coefficient equals zero. There are two possible reasons for this finding. First, if firms in the sample were relatively homogeneous with respect to distance traveled, this variable would exhibit little variation and we would expect to see an insignificant coefficient. Alternatively, the finding that Average Length of Haul has no effect upon long-run total costs may be due to route restrictions placed upon firms during regulation. These restrictions generally led to inefficient use of capacity and increased fuel consumption that could offset any benefits a firm received from transporting a given shipment further. If this interpretation is true, it would also imply that that the effect of the route restrictions during regulation imposed higher costs on shipments over longer distances than on those over short distances.[23] Unfortunately, without further information, it is not known which of these interpretations is valid.[24]

Higher insurance expenditures were hypothesized to reflect the increased handling of high-value, fragile, and perishable goods, which is expected to translate into higher costs. The positive coefficient on the insurance variable confirms this. However, its low *t*-statistic also tells us that we cannot reject the null hypothesis that the variable has no effect upon long-run total costs. Insurance Cost Per Ton–Mile was expected to reflect differences in long-run costs between firms due to differences in the specialized commodity carried. Acceptance of the null hypothesis that insurance expenditures are not an important determinant of long-run total costs suggests either that large interfirm cost differences due to the type(s) of good(s) transported do not exist or that Insurance Cost Per Ton–Mile is simply a poor proxy for interfirm cost differences. Without further testing, it is not possible to determine which is the true state of the world.

Factor demand and substitution elasticities

Based upon the flexible empirical cost function in equation (5.31), table 5.6 reports own-input price elasticities and elasticities of substitution between each of the four inputs. With the exception of purchased transportation, the factor demand elasticities are price inelastic. For labor, capital, and fuel, a 1% increase in the input's price, all else constant, reduces the quantity of the factor demanded by 0.56%, 0.68%, and 0.58%, respectively. Firms are more sensitive to purchased transportation, however. A 1% increase in price reduces the quantity of purchased transportation demanded by 1.9%.

Table 5.6 also reports the elasticities of substitution between each pair of inputs. Both the magnitude and the sign of these numbers are of interest. A negative sign indicates that the two inputs are *complements*, whereas a positive sign represents a *substitute* relationship between the inputs. Consider, for example, the elasticity of substitution between labor and capital, which has a value of 0.59. This tells us that a 1% increase in the relative price of labor leads to a 0.59% increase in the capital : labor ratio (holding the other two inputs constant), which indicates that the two inputs are substitutes in the production of specialized commodity motor carrier services. Since the sign of each substitution elasticity in table 5.6 is positive, a similar substitute relationship exists between the other input pairs.[25]

Because specialized commodity carriers make liberal use of owner–operators, we also expect to see a high rate of substitution between purchased transportation – which reflects owner–operator services – and a firm's use of its other inputs. This expectation is borne out in table 5.6. A 1% increase in the relative cost of a carrier's own capital, all else constant, leads to a 2.19% increase in the purchased transportation : capital ratio at the sample mean. A similar relationship holds between purchased transportation–labor and purchased transportation–fuel input pairs, where the elasticities of substitution are 2.30 and 2.78, respectively. The purchased transportation substitution possibilities identified here are also consistent with the high factor demand elasticity for purchased transportation that we identified above.

Table 5.6 Own factor demand elasticities and elasticities of substitution at the sample mean: specialized commodity truckload carriers

	Labor	Capital	Fuel	Purchased Transportation
Own-Price Elasticity	−0.566	−0.682	−0.582	−1.92
Elasticity of Substitution[a]				
Labor	–	0.590	0.177	2.30
Capital	0.590	–	0.514	2.19
Fuel	0.177	0.514	–	2.78
Purchased Transportation	2.30	2.19	2.78	–

[a] Note that the estimated elasticities of substitution are symmetric. The elasticity of substitution of labor for capital, for example, is the same as that of capital for labor.
Source: McMullen and Stanley (1988), table IV, p. 310

Discussion

There are several additional points we can make regarding the results for regulated motor carriers with authority to carry specialized commodities. First, for a specialized commodity carrier operating at the sample mean, what are its long-run total costs? Recall that long-run total costs can be estimated by taking the exponential of the constant term. At the sample mean, in 1977, a typical firm providing specialized commodity transport services to its shippers incurred annual long-run total costs equaling exp(8.32) = $4.1 million dollars. Separately, McMullen and Stanley have estimated that a firm operating at the sample mean incurs a per ton–mile cost of $0.34 (1977 dollars).

Second, as previously noted, the returns-to-scale results were unexpected given the perceived competitive nature of this segment of the motor carrier industry. If, as hypothesized, the increasing returns to scale were due to regulatory constraints placed upon these carriers rather than from the available technology, then an implication is that economic deregulation would eliminate the source of the increasing returns, so that in a deregulated environment firms will operate under constant returns to scale. Indeed, in the same analysis, McMullen and Stanley (1988) estimate a separate model for the specialized commodity truckload sector based upon cost and operating information for 1983, after motor carrier deregulation. Consistent with Friedlaender and Spady's hypothesis that increasing returns resulted from regulatory constraints rather than technology, McMullen and Stanley found that the sector operated under constant returns to scale.[26]

Third, the results in tables 5.5 and 5.6 support the use of a flexible empirical cost function rather than more restricted cost functions based upon Leontif and Cobb–Douglas technology. Leontif technology assumes no import substitutability, whereas Cobb–Douglas technology assumes an elasticity of substitution everywhere equal to one. The results reported in table 5.6 indicate that the elasticities of substitution are neither equal to zero or one nor, in general, equal for alternative input pairs.

Last, it is again important to recognize the distinction between movements along a curve versus changes in the location of a curve. The relationship between output and long-run total cost, all else held constant, reflects a *movement along* the long-run total cost curve. Alternatively, changes in any of the other variables in the empirical cost equation, again holding all else constant, reflects a change *in the location of the curve*. For example, at the sample mean, a 10% increase in output moves the firm *along a given* cost curve 7.2%; alternatively, a 10% increase in the price of labor *shifts the entire* cost curve upward by 3.8%.

CASE STUDY – REGULATED GENERAL FREIGHT CARRIERS

The results presented for the TL sector characterize specialized commodity motor carrier firms as operating under increasing returns to scale, and whose underlying technology enables firms to substitute between their owned inputs and purchased transportation. Would we expect to see similar cost and technological characteristics for general freight carriers? – No, since general freight carriers service less-than-truckload shippers which requires a network of origin and destination terminals for consolidation and break-bulking activities. Thus, the null and alternative hypotheses we want to consider here are as follows:

H_0: LTL and TL motor carriers have identical cost struc tures and production technologies

H_A: LTL and TL motor carriers have different cost structures and production technologies

In a separate study, Ying (1990b) estimated a flexible cost function for a group of 412 Class I and II common carriers of general freight operating during 1975.[27] This section comparatively analyzes the similarities and differences between the two sectors.

Table 5.7 presents Ying's estimation results for the LTL sector. The empirical cost function on which these results are based is identical to that expressed in equation (5.31), except that two additional operating characteristics are included to characterize the LTL sector: Average Shipment Size and Percent of LTL Traffic. Whereas Average Load in the truckload sector reflects the average size of load per vehicle, Average Shipment Size in the LTL reflects the average size of a shipment that the carrier receives, and is defined as total tons shipped divided by the number of shipments. All else constant, a truck transporting a small number of large shipments requires less consolidating and break-bulking activities than one transporting a large number of small shipments. Thus, increases in Average Shipment Size are expected to decrease long-run total costs, all else held constant.

Although this study focuses on LTL motor carriers, most LTL firms also have operating certificates for TL traffic. Thus, it is important to distinguish LTL firms whose operations are predominantly LTL traffic from firms whose operations have a higher proportion of TL traffic. If a carrier's customer base involves a higher percentage of LTL traffic, its handling costs are expected to be greater in comparison with another carrier that moves a smaller proportion of LTL traffic, all else held constant. Thus, increases in Percent of LTL Traffic are expected to increase long run total costs. Comparing tables 5.5 and 5.7, there are some similarities and a number of interesting differences between the operations of specialized carriers and general freight carriers. These comparisons relate to economies of scale, input use, operating characteristics, and firm sensitivity to changes in the relative price of inputs. Each of these is briefly discussed.

Economies of scale and network size

In contrast to specialized commodity carriers, firms in the LTL sector operate under *constant* returns to scale. From table 5.7, a 1% increase in output, all else constant, leads to a 1.025% increase in total costs at the sample mean. This result tells us that, at the sample mean, an LTL firm is operating under *slight* decreasing returns to scale, just to the right of the minimum point on its long-run average cost curve. But is it sufficiently close to the minimum point to characterize the firm as operating under constant returns to scale? Yes.

To see why, we use the ratio $(\hat{\alpha}_1 - 1)/s_{\hat{\alpha}_1}$ to test the null hypothesis that $\alpha_1 = 1$ against the alternative hypothesis that $\alpha_1 > 1$. This is a one-tail test and the calculated *t*-statistic is 0.64, which is statistically *insignificant* at the 0.01 level.[28] In other words, we *cannot reject* the hypothesis that, at the sample mean, an LTL firm operates under constant returns to scale.

One might be somewhat surprised to find constant returns to scale in the LTL sector, given the finding that TL carriers operated under increasing returns to scale. Why wouldn't we find a similar result for LTL carriers? The reason may likely be found by examining the differences in the underlying technology and the effect of economic regulation in each sector.

To prosper in the LTL sector – in a regulated or deregulated environment – a firm needs a network of facilities for consolidating and break-bulking its shipments. The underlying structure of the LTL sector provides a *technology-based* incentive for a firm to expand its scale of operation through a network of terminals. Based upon motor carrier network economies, we would expect to find increasing returns to scale. Yet, after we control for differences in technology across firms, the results presented in table 5.7 cannot reject constant returns to scale. But we're looking at the wrong coefficient!

Although the empirical model does not include a separate variable for an LTL's firm's route structure, it does include "% of LTL Traffic,"

Table 5.7 Translog cost function regression model for carriers of general freight first-order coefficients at the sample mean[a]

Regressor	Coefficient Estimate (t-statistic)	Interpretation
Constant term	0.556 (6.62)	Logarithm of total cost at the sample mean
Output	1.025 (25.6)	Elasticity of total cost with respect to output T at the sample mean
Price of Labor	0.624[b] (–)	Share of labor in total costs, evaluated at the sample mean
Price of Capital	0.244 (34.9)	Share of capital in total costs, evaluated at the sample mean
Price of Fuel	0.040 (21.3)	Share of fuel in total costs, evaluated at the sample mean
Price of Purchased Transportation	0.092 (6.1)	Share of purchased transportation in total costs, evaluated at the sample mean
Average Load Per Vehicle	−0.282 (−2.4)	Elasticity of total cost with respect to average load, at the sample mean
Average Length of Haul	−0.407 (−5.8)	Elasticity of total cost with respect to average length of haul, at the sample mean
Average Shipment Size	−0.114 (−1.3)	Elasticity of total cost with respect to average shipment size, at the sample mean
Percentage of LTL Traffic	0.254 (2.1)	Elasticity of total cost with respect to percentage of LTL traffic, at the sample mean
Insurance Cost Per Ton–Mile	0.121 (1.7)	Elasticity of total cost with respect to per ton–mile insurance cost, at the sample mean

$R^2 = 0.95$
Number of observations = 412

[a] The estimated translog cost function has the following form:

$$\ln C(T;p,o) = \alpha_0 + \alpha_1(\ln T - \ln \bar{T}) + \sum_{i=2}^{5}\alpha_i(\ln p_i - \ln \bar{p}_i) + \sum_{i=6}^{10}\alpha_i(\ln o_i - \ln \bar{o}_i)$$
$$+ \text{“second-order and interaction terms”} + \varepsilon$$

[b] The coefficient for labor was derived from the constraint that input coefficients sum to 1. The t-statistic was not reported.

Source: Reprinted from Ying (1990b), Appendix, p. 1006, with the permission of the Southern Economic Association

which serves as a proxy for an LTL firm's network. The higher the proportion of LTL traffic, the greater its network is likely to be and, all else constant, the greater will be the potential for economies of network size, ε_{or}. From table 5.7, we see that the coefficient for this variable is 0.254, which indicates strong economies of network size. A 10% increase in the percent of LTL traffic leads to a 2.5% increase in costs.

Further, Ying estimates that, in 1975, the minimum efficient scale for an LTL firm was around 215 million ton–miles, in an industry where general freight carriers accumulated over 85 billion ton–miles. Combined with the empirical finding of constant returns to scale, holding network size constant, this suggests that the LTL sector was quite competitive in 1975, which allowed the typical LTL firm to reach its minimum efficient scale.

This raises the same question as in the TL sector: "What will be the impact of deregulation upon LTL motor carrier firms?" Given the strong economies of network size suggested by these results, regulatory-based returns to scale may have complemented technological economies during the time period. Will the LTL segment continue to exhibit constant returns to scale, or will there be an underlying structural change? Interestingly, the bulk of evidence both before and after deregulation indicate that the LTL sector continued to operate under constant returns to scale, which suggests that the LTL sector is essentially competitive. But there is evidence to the contrary. Between 1977 and 1984, for example, the number of LTL firms decreased from 552 to 274 and the revenue share of the largest LTL firms has grown from 37.6% to 68.5% (Emerson et al., 1993). Increased concentration is evidence of increasing rather than constant returns to scale. A possible reason for these contradictory results is that prior studies have not controlled for quality. When controlling for quality differences among LTL firms, Liu (1993) finds evidence of increasing rather than constant returns to scale, indicating that larger firms have a cost advantage over smaller firms.

Input use

A comparison of table 5.5 with table 5.7 reveals other interesting differences in the two sectors. For the TL sector, labor and capital made up 38% and 30% of total costs, respectively. Purchased transportation comprised 17% and fuel accounted for 12% of total costs. In the LTL sector, labor has a much larger impact upon total costs, accounting for 62% of the total, while the share of costs due to purchased transportation falls from 17.8% to 9.2%. As a proportion of total costs, fuel costs fall from 12.7% in the TL sector to 4% in the LTL sector and capital's presence in the LTL sector is 6.4% lower than in the TL sector.

These differences directly reflect the technology differences between the two sectors. LTL firms need terminal structures to consolidate and distribute less-than-truckload shipments. This implies more handling, which raises the share of labor in total costs relative to the shares of fuel and capital. In addition, the larger role played by freight handling activities reduces the importance and, accordingly, the reliance that LTL firms place upon purchased transportation. Thus, these costs are also a smaller portion of total firm outlays.

Operating characteristics

Qualitatively, the effect of operating characteristics on LTL firm total costs are similar to those for TL firms. At the sample mean, increases in the Average Load Per Vehicle and Average Length of Haul both decrease total costs, all else constant. Similarly, an increase in Insurance Cost Per Ton–Mile increases total costs in the LTL sector, as expected. However, the *quantitative* effect of these characteristics varies between the two sectors.

It was previously argued that, in the TL sector, Average Length of Haul did not affect total costs because of route restrictions. Although the LTL sector was also subject to route restrictions, the results in table 5.7 suggest that the more extensive networks in the LTL sector more than offset the effect of route restrictions on costs. All else constant, a 1% increase in Average Length of Haul significantly reduces total costs by 0.407% at the sample mean.

Also in contrast to the TL sector, Insurance Costs per Ton–Mile significantly increases long-run total costs in the LTL sector. In that the mix of commodities in the LTL general freight sector is considerably more varied than in the TL specialized commodity sector, Insurance Cost Per Ton–Mile in the LTL sector is likely to be a better proxy for capturing interfirm cost differences, such as higher handling costs for high-valued commodities, associated with the mix of commodities carried.

Last, and again consistent with expectations, Average Shipment Size decreases long-run total costs in the LTL sector. However, with a t-statistic equal to −1.3, we cannot reject the null hypothesis that Average Shipment Size has no effect on costs at a 0.05 level of significance.

Elasticities measures

Table 5.8 reports the factor demand elasticities and elasticities of substitution for the LTL motor carrier sector. Relative to the TL sector, we again see some similarities and differences. The own-price elasticities are generally similar in the two motor carrier segments, although the own-price elasticity for purchased transportation is considerably lower in the LTL sector. This is not unexpected, given the smaller reliance in the LTL sector upon purchased transportation.

Also, as in the TL sector, each of the inputs is a substitute for every other input in the production of LTL transportation, as indicated by the positive signs on the respective elasticities of substitution. But, *with the exception* of purchased transportation, the technology underlying LTL firms allows for greater substitution possibilities between inputs. In the TL sector, the elasticity of substitution between labor and fuel was 0.177, whereas its value in the LTL sector is 0.947. Similarly, in the TL sector, the elasticity of substitution between capital and labor was 0.59. In the LTL sector, it's 0.968 and reflects the greater technological opportunities for substituting capital for labor. For instance, LTL firms could undertake its terminal activities

Table 5.8 Own factor demand elasticities and elasticities of substitution at the sample mean: general freight carriers

	Labor	Capital	Fuel	Purchased Transportation
Own-Price Elasticity	−0.372	−0.762	−0.724	−0.973
Elasticity of Substitution[a]				
Labor	–	0.968	0.766	0.947
Capital	0.968	–	0.762	1.44
Fuel	0.766	0.762	–	0.856
Purchased Transportation	0.947	1.44	0.856	–

[a] Note that the estimated elasticities of substitution are symmetric. The elasticity of substitution of labor for capital, for example, is the same as that of capital for labor.
Source: Ying (1990b), table II, p. 1002

with a small labor-intensive facility or a larger automated building.

In the TL sector, however, the elasticity of substitution between purchased transportation and every other input is uniformly *higher* than in the LTL sector. This again reflects the larger role that purchased transportation plays in the TL sector.

Final comments

We argued at the beginning of this section that the TL and LTL sectors in the motor carrier industry faced different technologies and, therefore, should be analyzed separately. The information that we have reported in tables 5.5–5.8 confirm that this was indeed the case *during regulation*. The results that we have examined reveal the following differences between the two motor carrier sectors:

1 At the sample mean, the truckload sector operated under increasing returns to scale, whereas the LTL sector, given the percentage of LTL traffic, operated under constant returns to scale, all else constant.
2 On average, capital, fuel, and purchased transportation were more important in the production of TL than LTL transportation services. On the other hand, labor played a more important role in providing LTL transportation services.
3 For both sectors, all inputs were substitutes in production. However, the demand for purchased transportation was more elastic in the TL sector and there were more substitution possibilities between purchased transportation and other inputs in the TL sector. In the LTL sector labor, capital, and fuel were more easily substitutable.
4 technological differences reflected by firm operating characteristics differed between the two sectors. At the sample mean, Average Length of Haul had little effect upon long-run total costs in the TL sector, but significantly decreased costs in the LTL sector. Similarly, Insurance Cost Per Ton–Mile seemed to better differentiate interfirm variations in output carried in the LTL sector than in the TL sector.

CASE STUDY – AIRLINE COST AND PRODUCTION UNDER REGULATION

Over the past 50 years, airline travel has been one of the fastest growing transport carriers of both passengers and freight. Absolutely, air carriers make up less than 1% of total freight ton–miles shipped per year. Yet between 1940 and 1989, the percentage increase has steadily grown at an average annual rate of 10%, from 0.02 billion ton–miles in 1940 to 10.4 billion ton–miles in 1990. This compares with 3.6%, 6.3%, and 5.6% increases in rail, trucking, and water carriers, respectively. During this period, only the 18.6% annual increase in pipeline shipments exceeded the growth rate in air freight.

In contrast to its small presence in freight shipments, the vast bulk of intercity travel in the airline industry is in the movement of people. Here again, air carriers have experienced rapid growth. In comparison with intercity auto, rail, and bus, which experienced annual passenger–mile growth rates of 4.2%, –2.1%, and 0.6%, respectively, intercity air travel grew at an average annual rate of 31.8% between 1960 and 1990 (ENO Transportation Foundation, 1992).

From the beginning of government involvement in the airline industry, an explicit aim was to foster the industry's growth. In the early 1920s, failing attempts by private airline operators to provide profitable passenger and air freight service led to passage of the 1926 Air Mail Act. By contracting with private air carriers to provide airmail delivery services, thereby transferring the responsibility of airmail carriage from army planes to private carriers, the government subsidized private air carrier operations and actively promoted the industry's growth. Mail contracts were used to expand the nation's route system, as well as to encourage passenger service. An indication of the Act's immediate success is the fact that, between 1926 and 1930, the number of private air carriers increased nearly fourfold (from 13 to 38 operators) and revenue passenger–miles (RPM) increased from 1.3 to 85.1 million.[29]

While the 1926 Act made the US Post Office responsible for allotting airmail contracts among private carriers, the ICC was given authority to set airmail rates. This led to some financial problems for the airlines during the 1930s when the ICC, acting in accordance with the Act's objective to expand nationwide air transport services, induced carriers to accept airmail rates below cost by tying these rates to new route allocations.

In 1938, Congress passed the Civil Aeronautics Act (CAA), a major piece of legislation that addressed the ailing financial health of the industry, as well as a number of other issues related to the growing passenger demands for air travel. The CAA created the Civil Aeronautics Authority, renamed the Civil Aeronautics Board (CAB) in 1940, in order to encourage the provision of efficient, economical, and safe air transportation at reasonable fares. The main provisions of the CAA dealt with market access, route restrictions, rate-setting, and subsidization.

Control of entry/exit

Similar to the Motor Carrier Act of 1935, the 1938 CAA strictly controlled entry into and exit from the market. At the time of passage, 16 *trunk carriers* were "grandfathered" into the industry. That is, carriers that provided intercity air services in 1938 were granted operating authority by the CAB to continue this service on the same routes. The burden of proof for entry into a market by a new airline was upon the entering firm, which had to demonstrate that a need existed and that it could efficiently, economically, and safely meet the need. But, with little or no experience, this proved to be so difficult that, between 1938 and deregulation in the mid-1970s, the CAB did not grant any new carrier's application for a major route.

Exit from the industry was as difficult as entry, because air carriers were mandated to provide "adequate service" to those cities and communities for which they had operating authority. Because exit from a particular market meant that the market would no longer be adequately served, the CAB was reluctant to allow a carrier to exit. Over time, firms found that mergers were the quickest way to effectuate both entry into new markets as well as exits from unprofitable markets. Of the 16 trunk lines granted authority, 11 remained at the beginning of 1970.

Route restrictions

The 1938 CAA grandfathered in both existing carriers and existing routes of carriers. Although the CAB never granted operating authority over a major route to a new entrant, it did at times grant existing carriers operating authority into new markets; that is, along a new route. These decisions were not generally based upon the carrier's ability to provide economical service but, rather, upon financial considerations. If granting authority would hinder the financial condition of another existing carrier, the CAB would deny the application. Alternatively, the application would be approved if the CAB judged that granting authority would stabilize the industry by equalizing profitability across firms. By granting route authority, the CAB could also specify the extent to which nonstop service was provided. For example, by authorizing a carrier to fly a route from city A to city C through city B, it effectively prevented the carrier from operating a nonstop service from city A to city C.

Rate restrictions

Airline carriers were required by the CAA to set rates that were just, reasonable, and nondiscriminatory. Rate discrimination occurs when two groups of consumers face different prices even though there is no difference in the cost of providing the service. Rates were deemed to be too high if they led to inordinately high rates of return on investment and unjustly low if they affected the financial health of a competing carrier. The CAB also considered adequate and safe service to the public, financial health of the industry, and differences in types of aircraft when evaluating the propriety of existing rates.

In the event that unreasonable rates were identified, the CAA gave the CAB authority to set the legal rate or specify the maximum or minimum rate to be charged.

Subsidization

The 1938 CAA maintained the practice of subsidizing air carriers through the payment of mail rates that was initiated in 1926 with the Air Mail Act. These subsidies were expected to quicken the development of a national air transportation system, as well as to maintain stable growth in the air transport industry.

Between 1938 and the mid-1970s, when the Airline Deregulation Act was passed, there were few major pieces of legislation that affected the industry. In 1958, Congress passed the Federal Aviation Act, which transferred air safety responsibilities from the CAB to a newly formed agency, the Federal Aviation Agency. The agency was renamed the Federal Aviation Administration in 1966 and brought under the auspices of the newly created Department of Transportation.

Although the CAB severely restricted entry and exit into the major trunkline routes, it experimented in the 1940s and early 1950s with entry into "feeder" markets, giving temporary operating authority to a group of *local carriers* to provide subsidized short-haul service from smaller communities to the larger markets served by the trunk carriers. In 1955, temporary operating permits for 13 local carriers became permanent. Initially, the local carriers were not to compete with trunk carriers. Over time, however, the CAB awarded local carriers some operating authority that overlapped with the more profitable trunkline routes in order to stem the growing level of subsidies paid to local carriers. As a result, in the period after permanent certification, local carriers evolved into a group of larger regional carriers that competed with trunk carriers in these areas.

Table 5.9 summarizes the various air carriers that provided domestic service in 1970. Trunk carriers accounted for nearly 90% of the total and local services provided another 6.1%. Also, in 1952, aircraft with maximum gross take-off weights of 12,500 pounds or less were exempt from economic regulation.[30] Air carriers operating these small planes are identified in table 5.9 as commuter carriers. In 1970, 174 carriers provided commuter services and accounted for less than 1% of revenue ton–miles.

Specification of costs for regulated air carriers

The development of our nation's air transport system evolved by 1970 into a two-tier system. Short-haul local/regional carriers that were primarily serving smaller communities fed traffic into the larger markets served by trunk line carriers. Because of differences in the number and sizes of markets, the size of aircraft used, average *stage length* (the average distance between take-off and landings), and average *loads* (the ratio of seat–miles sold to available

Table 5.9 Domestic providers of air transport services, 1970

Carrier Type	Number of Carriers	Revenue Ton–Miles[a] (millions)	Percentage of Total
Trunk	11	12,288.7	88.1
Local	9	851.5	6.1
All Cargo	2	301.5	2.2
Commuter	179	47.1	0.3
Other[b]	22	458.1	3.3

[a] A revenue ton–mile is one ton of revenue traffic (passenger and cargo) transported one mile.
[b] Other includes 13 supplemental carriers (providing nonscheduled charter service domestically), two carriers operating within Hawaii, four carriers within Alaska, and three helicopter services.
Source: Douglas and Miller (1974), table A-2, p. 193

seat–miles), local carriers may face different cost structures, and hence technologies, than trunk carriers. Consistent with this is the belief that the trunk carriers operate under constant returns to scale, whereas the local carriers operate under increasing returns to scale.[31] If true, the implication is that the much larger size of operations that characterizes trunk carriers gives them a competitive advantage over local carriers – or, equivalently, local carriers will be able to reduce unit costs if allowed to increase their scale of operations.

Caves, Christiansen, and Tretheway (1984) estimated a general model of total airline costs based upon trunk and local carriers operating from 1970 through 1981, a total of 208 observations.[32] The empirical cost model is a flexible translog model, which includes translog transformations of the following variables:[33]

- Output – this is defined as an index of four different services: scheduled service revenue passenger–miles, chartered service revenue passenger–miles, revenue ton–miles of mail, and revenue ton–miles of other freight. To avoid confusion, we shall simply refer to the index as Revenue Output–Miles.
- Prices of inputs – the inputs include Labor, Fuel, and Capital.
- Operating characteristics – these include Average Stage Length and Average Load.
- Network characteristics – Average Number of Points Served.

Hypotheses

There are a number of hypotheses related to the underlying cost and production function that we can test with this empirical long-run airline total cost function:

HYPOTHESIS 1 Air carriers operate under constant returns to scale. We have previously seen that when networks are an important characteristic of the operating environment, a generalized concept of returns to scale includes an expanding network. In this study of the airline market, one of the operating characteristics included in the empirical model is Average Number of Points Served, which reflects the extent of an air carrier's market; that is, the size of its network. The more points served, the wider is its distribution network and, all else constant, the larger is its Revenue Output–Miles. An implication is that if we are concerned with returns to scale, we want to obtain the impact of a 1% increase in all inputs, holding the prices of inputs, Average Stage Length, and Average Load constant, on a general measure of output which includes Revenue Output–Miles *and* the Average Number of Points Served. Suppose, for example, that an air carrier increases output by offering flights at an airport that it had not previously served. If the additional services cause no change in stage length, load factor, or output per point served, then the cost elasticity is $1/\varepsilon_{o,\text{nw}}$, where $\varepsilon_{o,\text{nw}}$ is a generalized measure of economies of scale. If costs increase in greater (less, equal) proportion to the change in output, the cost elasticity is greater than (less than, equal to) one and $\varepsilon_{o,\text{nw}}$ is less than (greater than, equal to) one. Thus, our null hypothesis that air carriers operate under constant returns to scale is equivalent to the hypothesis that $1/\varepsilon_{o,\text{nw}} = 1$.

HYPOTHESIS 2 A related hypothesis is that there exist increasing returns to traffic density where the size of the carrier's network is held fixed. If a carrier operates under increasing returns to traffic density, $\varepsilon_{o|\text{nw}} < 1$. That is, a 1% increase in Revenue Output–Miles, holding constant stage length, load factor, prices of inputs, *and the number of points served*, leads to an increase in long-run total costs by less than 1%.

HYPOTHESIS 3 Assuming that air carriers attempt to minimize the cost of production, the coefficients of the input prices will be positive and, consistent with Shephard's lemma, the coefficients represent input shares.

HYPOTHESIS 4 With respect to the operating characteristics, it is expected that increases in Average Stage Length and Average Load, all else constant, will decrease long-run total costs. Average Stage Length reflects economies with respect to trip distance as well as aircraft size. To illustrate the distance-related economies, consider Long Haul Airlines, whose only market is the route between city A and city B. It flies 1 million passenger–miles per year by transporting 100 persons 1,000 miles ten times a year. Short Haul Airlines also outputs 1 million passenger–miles per year and serves city-pair (C, D). The average load factor on each is identical. But Short Haul Airlines outputs 1 million passenger–miles by transporting 100 persons 200 miles 50 times a year. Because Short Haul Airlines makes more trips, it incurs higher ground costs. In addition, airlines experience "stacking" costs, which are unrelated to distance traveled, when an aircraft is put into a holding pattern prior to landing. Since Short Haul Airlines makes more trips, it will incur higher holding pattern costs.

In addition to economies of distance, there are also economies associated with aircraft size. The longer the trip, the greater is the incentive to use larger aircraft that have lower operating costs per mile traveled. Thus, all else constant, the null hypothesis is that an increase in Average Stage Length has no effect on long-run total costs versus the alternative hypothesis that it decreases long-run costs.

Similarly, the null hypothesis with respect to Average Load is that an increase in this characteristic will have no effect on long-run costs versus the alternative hypothesis that it will decrease long-run costs. Average Load represents the efficiency with which existing capacity is utilized. Higher Average Loads represent efficiencies of capacity utilization associated with ground-related activities such as ticketing, baggage handling, use of airplane slots, and so forth. Thus, all else constant, we expect an increase in Average Load to decrease long-run total costs.

Estimation results

Table 5.10 reports the estimated "first-order coefficients" for the translog empirical cost model. Relating these results to the underlying hypotheses, we can draw the following conclusions:

1 The null hypothesis that air carriers operate under generalized constant returns to scale cannot be rejected at the 0.05 level. From table 5.9 we see that the estimated co-

Table 5.10 Translog cost function regression model for air carriers: first-order coefficients at the sample mean[a]

Regressor	Coefficient Estimate (*t*-statistic)	Interpretation
Constant	13.243 (294.3)	Logarithm of long-run total cost, evaluated at the sample mean
Revenue Output–Miles	0.804 (23.6)	Elasticity of total cost with respect to output *T* at the sample mean
Average Number of Points Served	0.132 (4.2)	Elasticity of total cost with respect to average number of points served, at the sample mean
Price of Labor	0.356 (178.0)	Share of labor in total costs, evaluated at the sample mean
Price of Capital	0.478 (239.0)	Share of capital in total costs, evaluated at the sample mean
Price of Fuel	0.166 (166.0)	Share of fuel in total costs, evaluated at the sample mean
Average Stage Length	−0.148 (−2.7)	Share of purchased transportation in total costs, evaluated at the sample mean
Average Load Factor	−0.264 (−3.8)	Elasticity of total cost with respect to average load, at the sample mean
Number of observations = 208		

[a] The authors did not report the R^2 for this study. The estimated translog cost function has the following form:

$$\ln C(T;p,o) = \alpha_0 + \alpha_1(\ln T - \ln \bar{T}) + \sum_{i=2}^{5}\alpha_i(\ln p_i - \ln \bar{p}_i) + \sum_{i=6}^{10}\alpha_i(\ln o_i - \ln \bar{o}_i)$$
$$+ \text{"second-order and interaction terms"} + \text{"time dummy effects"}$$
$$+ \text{"firm dummy effects"} + \varepsilon$$

Source: Caves et al. (1984), table A1, p. 484

efficients for Revenue Output–Miles and Average Number of Points Served variables, respectively, are 0.804 and 0.132. Adding these together and taking the reciprocal gives us a generalized economies of scale parameter, at the sample mean, equal to $\hat{\varepsilon}_{o,\text{nw}} = 1.07$. Is this sufficiently close to one to accept the null hypothesis that the sum equals one? Yes. To see why, consider the ratio $(\hat{\alpha} - 1)/s_{\hat{\alpha}}$, where $\hat{\alpha} = \hat{\varepsilon}_{o,\text{nw}}$ and $s_{\hat{\alpha}} = s_{\hat{\varepsilon}_{o,\text{nw}}}$. This tests the null hypothesis that $\hat{\alpha} = 1$. Substituting for $\hat{\varepsilon}_{o,\text{nw}}$ and $s_{\hat{\alpha}}$ gives $(1.07 - 1)/0.05 = -1.40$.[34] Thus, when evaluated at the sample mean, we cannot reject the null hypothesis of constant returns to scale at a 0.05 level of significance. Given Average

Stage Length, Average Load, and the prices of inputs, this result tells us that a 1% increase in both Revenue Output–Miles and the Average Number of Points Served increases total costs by 1%. But recalling that the cost elasticity is the inverse of returns to scale, we can equivalently say that, holding Average Stage Length, Average Load, and input prices constant, a 1% increase in all inputs produces a 1% increase in generalized output: that is, a 1% increase in Revenue Output–Miles and in the Average Number of Points Served.

2 We also hypothesized that air carriers would operate under increasing returns to traffic density, all else held constant. Again looking at the results in table 5.9, we see that the coefficient for Revenue Output–Miles is 0.804, which is significantly different from zero at the 0.01 level. And, consistent with hypothesis 2, the coefficient is significantly different from one at the 0.01 level (the t-statistic is $(\hat{\varepsilon}_{o|\text{nw}} - 1)/s_{\hat{\varepsilon}_{o|\text{nw}}} = (0.804 - 1)/0.034 = -5.76$).[35] A 1% increase in output leads to a less than 1% increase in total costs at the sample mean, holding constant Average Stage Length, Average Load, the prices of inputs, and the Average Number of Points Served. Recognizing the inverse relationship between the elasticity of cost with respect to output and economies of density, this is equivalent to saying that a 1% increase in inputs, holding operating characteristics and network size constant, increases Revenue Output–Miles by 1.2% (that is, 1/0.804).

3 If firms engage in cost-minimizing behavior, we expect the input prices to have positive coefficients and, from Shephard's lemma, to sum to one. These expectations are met by the results given in table 5.9. For the air carriers operating during the 1970s, 35.6% of total costs were spent on labor, 47.8% on capital, and 16.6% on fuel. Not surprisingly, air carriers are relatively capital-intensive.

4 We also reject the null hypotheses that Average Stage Length and Average Load do not affect long-run total costs. Holding other factors constant, a 1% increase in Average Stage Length reduces long-run costs by 0.148% at the sample mean. Long-run costs are nearly twice as sensitive to Average Load, where a 1% increase in this variable reduces long-run costs by 0.264% at the sample mean.

Factor demand elasticities and elasticities of substitution

Table 5.11 summarizes air carrier sensitivities to changes in factor prices as well as the substitution possibilities among inputs. Each of the factor demand elasticities has the correct negat-

Table 5.11 Own factor demand elasticities and elasticities of substitution at the sample mean: air carriers operating during the period 1970–81

	Labor	Capital	Fuel
Own-Price Elasticity	−0.17	−0.21	−0.01
Elasticity of Substitution[a]			
Labor	–	0.46	−0.29
Capital	0.46	–	0.24
Fuel	−0.29	0.24	–

[a] Note that the estimated elasticities of substitution are symmetric. The elasticity of substitution of labor for capital, for example, is the same as that of capital for labor.

Source: Caves et al. (1984), table 5, p. 479

ive sign and is relatively small, which indicates an inelastic demand. All else constant, a 10% increase in fuel prices, for example, leads to a small 0.01% fall in the demand for fuel at the sample mean.

Although some substitution possibilities exist, the substitution elasticities are not very large. Capital is a substitute for both labor and fuel, indicated by the positive signs, whereas labor and fuel are complements. If all else is held constant, a 1% increase in the relative price of labor decreases the fuel : labor ratio by 0.29% at the sample mean.

Trunks versus local carriers under regulation

It is important to understand that the results reported in tables 5.10 and 5.11 are based upon carriers operating *during the 1970s*. But this period was a period of change. Between 1970 and 1976, air carriers were economically regulated by the CAB, as discussed earlier in this section. The Airline Deregulation Act was enacted in 1978, which effectively deregulated the airline industry. Thus, when we identify the estimation results as characterizing the sample mean, the sample mean in this case represents an averaging over air carriers that operated during a regulated and a deregulated period. This is important because we have concluded that, at the sample mean, air carriers were characterized by generalized constant returns to scale but increasing returns to traffic density.

Were air carriers during the regulated part of the 1970s characterized by constant returns to scale and increasing returns to traffic density? For the year 1970, when the CAB still regulated trunk and local carriers, table 5.12 differentiates trunk carriers from local carriers by average operating characteristics, returns to scale, and returns to traffic density. Looking first at the networks of the two carriers, we see that the Average Number of Points Served is nearly equal. Trunks, on average, served four fewer points than did the local carriers. With regard to operating characteristics, Average Load is similar, but the trunk carriers have a 20% higher average load than do the locals, at 52% versus 42.7%. The largest difference, however, is seen in the Average Stage Length. Local carriers, on average, have a stage length equal to 152 miles, whereas the Average Stage Length for the trunk carriers is 639 miles. Despite these differences, particularly with respect to stage length, we see that each carrier effectively operates under generalized constant returns. The returns-to-scale estimate for the trunk carriers is 1.025, versus 1.101 for the local carriers. Thus, differences

Table 5.12 Generalized returns to scale and returns to traffic density for trunk and local carriers: evaluated at the sample mean, 1970

	Trunk Carriers	Local Carriers
Returns to Scale[a]	1.025	1.101
Returns to Density	1.253	1.295
Operating Characteristics		
Average Number of Points Served	61.2	65.2
Average Stage Length	639	152
Average Load Factor	0.520	0.427

[a] For both trunk and local carriers, the null hypothesis of generalized constant returns to scale could not be rejected at the 0.05 level.

Source: Caves et al. (1984), table 4, p. 478

in stage length did not give the trunk carriers a competitive advantage during regulation.

If we examine the economies of traffic density we see that, for both carriers, operations were characterized by significant returns to traffic density. Holding Average Stage Length, Average Load, input prices, and network size (that is, Average Number of Points Served) constant, a 1% increase all inputs leads to a 1.25% and 1.29% increase in Revenue Output–Miles for trunk and local carriers, respectively.

Policy implications

Is it possible for the smaller local carriers to compete with the much larger trunk carriers? At the respective sample means, Caves et al. (1984) calculated the unit costs of local carriers to be 44% higher than those of trunk carriers. Is this due to differences in the sizes of the two carriers? – no, since the results in table 5.9 indicate that both trunk and local carriers operate under *generalized constant returns to scale*. Rather, the difference in costs between the two carriers is largely attributed to two factors:

1 Density of service for a given size network – most of the difference in costs between the two carriers reflects the extent to which a given network is used. In 1976, trunk carriers in the estimation sample produced 15.01 million revenue passenger–miles and served 66 points. This translates into 227,400 revenue passenger–miles per point served. Although local carriers served a similar number of points, 59, in 1976, their total output was 1.52 million revenue passenger–miles, which implies a traffic density per point served equal to 25,700, ten times less than for trunk carriers. Thus, it is not the size of the carrier *per se* – that is, the quantity of revenue output–miles produced – but rather the heavier use of the network that gives trunk carriers an important cost advantage.

2 Stage length – a second reason why trunk carriers have a cost advantage over local carriers is stage length. In 1976, trunk carriers in the estimation sample had an average stage length of 685 miles, compared with 197 miles for the local carrier. The longer the trip, the more an airline can exploit economies of distance and, all else constant, the greater will be their cost advantage over competitors.

Do differences in other operating characteristics or input prices give a significant cost advantage to trunk carriers? Generally, no. Differences in factor load were found to give trunk carriers a 2% advantage and differences in the number of points served were found to benefit local carriers by less than 1%. Similarly, the net effect of differences in the prices that trunk and local carriers paid inputs gave local carriers a 6% cost advantage.

How then could a local carrier compete? The implication from these results is that local carriers want to exploit economies of traffic density and economies of distance. Competing with larger trunk carriers by simply increasing revenue output–miles and number of points served *without significant* increases in network density and stage length will not remove the cost advantage of large trunk carriers. Similarly, locals cannot rely on input price differences or increases in load factors to erase the cost advantage of trunk carriers. Only significant increases in network utilization and stage lengths will move the local carrier closer to production cost parity. Of course, during regulation with fixed routes, it would be difficult for local carriers to increase stage length. Moreover, there was little need to worry about competing with the trunks, since local carriers were in distinct markets. However, these issues became more important after 1978 when the industry was deregulated. Chapter 8 discusses airline companies' strategic responses to deregulation.

CHAPTER HIGHLIGHTS

- Given the existing technology, a firm's production function is the maximum amount of output that a firm can produce from a given quantity of inputs. If all inputs to the firm are variable, the firm is in the long run; if some inputs are fixed, the firm is in the short run.
- The elasticity of substitution, defined as the percentage change in an input ratio due to a percentage change in the marginal rate of technical substitution, reflects the ease with which a firm can substitute among inputs in the production process. If a proportional increase in all variable inputs raises output (less than, more than) proportionately, then the firm is operating under constant (decreasing, increasing) returns to scale.
- A firm minimizes its cost of production by using inputs up to the point at which the marginal rate of technical substitution equals the input price ratio. A firm's total cost function is the minimum cost necessary to produce a given amount of output. A firm's minimum efficient scale is that level of output corresponding to the minimum point on a firm's average cost curve. At this point, the firm is operating under constant returns to scale.
- Knowing a firm's cost function provides information on the firm's underlying production technology. The inverse of the elasticity of total cost with respect to output measures a firm's economies of scale. By Shephard's lemma, the elasticity of total cost with respect to input price is the conditional optimal share of the input's expenditures in total costs. The long-run total cost function also provides information on the elasticity of substitution among inputs.
- In addition to economies of scale, transportation firms also experience economies of traffic density, economies of capital utilization, and economies of network size.
- Empirically, there exist several cost function models to characterize transportation activities. The most restrictive is the Leontif cost function model, which assumes constant returns to scale and no substitutability among inputs. The Cobb–Douglas cost function model allows for nonconstant returns to scale and input substitutability, but the elasticity of substitution is constrained to equal one. The least restrictive cost function model is the translog cost function, which allows for nonconstant returns to scale and places no restrictions on substitutability among inputs.
- The motor carrier industry comprises two basic sectors, the truckload or specialized commodity carrier and the less-than-truckload or general freight carrier sector. By having to consolidate and break-bulk shipments, the less-than-truckload sector has a different production technology than the truckload sector.
- Economic regulation of the motor carrier industry began with the Motor Carrier Act of 1935, which regulated firm entry, rates, routes, and goods carried. Many of these regulations were significantly relaxed in the Motor Carrier Act of 1980.
- A case study of the truckload sector of the motor carrier industry under economic regulation found that truckload firms operated under increasing returns to scale, which is inconsistent with the competitive nature of this sector but consistent with regulatory-based economies of network size. This sector was less labor intensive

and relied more on purchased transportation. Input demands for labor, capital, and fuel in this sector were inelastic. But the demand for purchased transportation was elastic. The elasticities of substitution indicated that all inputs were substitutes. The greatest opportunities for input substitution occurred with purchased transportation.

- A case study of the less-than-truckload sector under regulation confirms that differences in production technology exist between this sector and the truckload sector. Less-than-truckload firms operated under constant returns to scale, holding network size constant. However, there was also evidence of generalized returns to scale in this sector, which indicated that a proportional increase in output and network size increased costs less than proportionately. This sector was more labor intensive than the truckload sector and relied much less on purchased transportation. Firms' costs in this sector were sensitive to shipment size, length of haul, and value of commodity shipped. Factor demands, including purchased transportation, were inelastic. Similar to the truckload sector, all inputs were substitutes. However, in contrast to the truckload sector, there were greater substitution possibilities among fuel, capital, and labor inputs, but fewer opportunities for substitution between each of these inputs and purchased transportation.
- Economic regulation of the US airline industry began with the Civil Aeronautics Acts of 1938, which controlled firm entry and exit, route operating authority, and fares. Economic regulation continued until passage of the Airline Deregulation Act in 1978.
- A case study of trunk and local airline costs during the 1970s indicated that air carriers operated under economies of density. Further, during this period, air carriers operated under general constant returns to scale; that is, a proportional increase in output and network size, all else constant, increased costs proportionately. Air carrier operations were relatively capital intensive, with 48% of total costs expended on capital. In the form of lower costs, air carriers benefited from high average loads and longer stage lengths. Factor inputs were price inelastic, and relatively few possibilities appeared to exist for input substitution between capital and labor or capital and fuel. Labor and fuel were complements in production
- A comparison of trunk and local air carriers during the transition to deregulation indicated that local carriers experienced unit costs that were more than 40% higher than those of trunk carriers. This can be attributed to significant differences in traffic density between the two sectors, as well as to the longer stage length of the trunk carriers.

Review questions

1. Assume that the production of less-than-truckload (LTL) motor carrier services depends upon three inputs: capital, labor, and fuel. The production function for LTL ton–miles is $TM = f(L,K,F;\gamma)$, where γ is the state of technology.

(a) Holding fuel and capital constant, graph the total, marginal, and average productivity curves for labor. Graphically depict the expected effect on the total product of labor if the LTL firm invests in more capital.
(b) In general, what is the cost constraint that an LTL firm faces? Graph the isocost equation under the assumption that capital is held fixed at $\overline{K}$.
(c) Holding capital constant at $\overline{K}$, use isoquant and isocost curves to predict the impact that an increase in fuel price will have upon an LTL's optimal use of fuel and labor. Also depict the expected effect upon the consumption of fuel and labor if the per unit price of capital increases.

2. Suppose that the production function for owner–operators in the truckload sector of the motor carrier industry required that capital and labor be used in fixed proportions: one driver with each truck.
(a) Identify the production function for owner–operator services and graphically depict the set of isoquants for this production function.
(b) Define the elasticity of substitution and discuss the extent to which capital and labor are substitutable for this production technology.
(c) Graphically identify the optimal use of capital and labor for a given set of labor and capital input prices, w and r, respectively. What effect on the optimal capital : labor ratio will occur if the relative labor wages increase by 10%, all else held constant?
(d) When truckload services are produced with this technology, what will be the impact on output if capital and labor increase by 15%?

3. Suppose that a transport firm's cost of producing carrier services is solely a function of labor, which is given by the following production function:

$$T = 5L$$

(a) What is the labor input requirement per unit of output produced?
(b) What is the optimal amount of labor used, and what is the cost function for this transportation firm? What is the firm's marginal cost and average cost of production?
(c) Using the cost function obtained in (b), demonstrate that this firm produces output under constant returns to scale.

4. Suppose that an airline company's long-run production depends only upon labor according to the following function: Passenger–Miles $(PM) = AL^{\alpha}$.
(a) What is the air carrier's optimal use of labor in the short run?
(b) What is the long-run total cost function for this air carrier? What is the average cost of production?
(c) It can be shown that the marginal cost of production for this technology equals

$$MC = \frac{1}{\alpha}\kappa(PM)^{(1-\alpha)/\alpha}$$

Using this expression for marginal cost and the expression for average cost derived in (b), what are the returns to scale for this production technology? For what values of α will this firm operate under constant, increasing, and decreasing returns to scale?

5. Over the years, there have been several studies of input substitutability in the public transit industry. Among the studies' results, the elasticity of substitution between labor and fuel has averaged around 0.43, while the elasticity of substitution between capital and fuel has been estimated as 0.35.

(a) Define the elasticity of substitution between fuel and labor. Given the above information, what effect will a 10% increase in the relative price of labor have upon the fuel : labor ratio?

(b) Are fuel and capital substitutes or complements in the production of public transit services?

(c) As manager of a local public transit district, you are concerned about rising energy prices, which raise the cost of fuel to the district. In order to conserve fuel for those bus routes with the highest passenger loads, you schedule your services so that your bus fleet, on average, stays idle for a longer period of time. Is this response consistent with an elasticity of substitution between fuel and capital that lies in the 0.3 range?

6. Consider the following production function for a railroad, which is hypothesized to depend upon four inputs – capital (K), labor (L), fuel (F), and network size (N):

$$\text{Ton–miles} = f(K,L,F,N;\gamma)$$

Based upon this production technology, distinguish between the following returns to scale concepts:

- economies of capital utilization
- economies of traffic density
- economies of network size
- generalized economies of scale

In your answer, be sure to identify which inputs are held fixed and which inputs are not held fixed. Also identify whether the economies of scale measure is a short- or long-run concept.

7. Callan and Thomas (1992) estimated a long-run translog cost function for the household goods sector of the motor carrier industry. The dependent variable was total long-run costs and the independent variables included:

- the quantity of ton–miles produced
- the average length of haul, in miles
- the average load, in tons
- the percentage of household goods shipped, defined as a percentage of the total operating revenues generated by the shipment of personal effects and household goods
- the input prices for labor, fuel, capital, and materials

Table 5.13 First-order coefficients at the sample mean[a]

Regressor	Coefficient Estimate (*t*-statistic)
Constant term	15.78 (488.5)
Output	1.004 (39.1)
Price of Labor	0.310 (45.6)
Price of Capital	0.501 (54.5)
Price of Fuel	0.023 (19.2)
Average Load Per Vehicle	−0.228 (−3.4)
Average Length of Haul	−0.264 (−3.7)
Percentage of Household Goods Shipped	−1.547 (−7.0)

$R^2 = 0.90$
Number of observations = 356

[a] The estimated translog cost function has the following form:

$$\ln C(T;p,o) = \alpha_0 + \alpha_1(\ln T - \ln \bar{T}) + \sum_{i=2}^{5}\alpha_i(\ln p_i - \ln \bar{p}_i) + \sum_{i=6}^{8}\alpha_i(\ln o_i - \ln \bar{o}_i)$$

$$+ \text{“second-order and interaction terms”} + \varepsilon$$

Source: Reprinted from Callan, S. and Thomas, J. 1992: Constant returns to scale in the post-deregulatory period: the case of specialized motor carriers. *Logistics and Transportation Review*, 25, 271–88, with permission from Elsevier Science

(a) For each of the explanatory variables, discuss the effect that you expect this variable to have upon long-run total costs.

(b) Data for the analysis was based upon Class I (revenues greater than \$5 million) and Class II (revenues between \$1 million and \$5 million) interstate household goods carriers operating in 1984. Table 5.13 gives the "first-order" coefficients and associated *t*-statistics for this model. Interpret the coefficient estimates. At the sample mean, are the results in the table consistent with the expected effects that you identified in (a)?

(c) Based upon the estimated value, at the sample mean, do household goods carriers operate under constant, increasing, or decreasing returns to scale? Test the null hypothesis that the coefficient is significantly different from one. What is the total operating cost of the average household goods carrier?

(d) What impact on total cost would you expect if household goods carriers increased their percentage of nonhousehold carriage (for example, business shipments) by 15%. What effect is this likely to have upon the costs of the "typical" carrier? Suppose that the typical household goods firm desired to increase its market area by lengthening its average length of haul by 10%. In doing so, however, it experiences a 5% increase in its labor costs. What will be the net effect on total costs of the typical firm?

8. In 1968, Keeler (1971) identified the per seat–mile costs (shown in table 5.14) associated with four major intercity modes of travel: rail, air, automobile, and intercity bus.

Table 5.14 Intercity modal costs, 1968

Mode	Cost Per Seat–Mile (cents)
Intercity Bus (200-mile trip)	1.44
Air (Lockheed 1,011, 256-seat configuration, 250-mile trip)	3.00
Automobile (two occupants)	4.5
Rail (three-car train seating 240 passengers)	1.5

Source: Reprinted from Keeler (1971), table 7, p. 160, with the permission of The University of Chicago Press.

(a) What does this table tell us about the cost competitiveness of rail in comparison with the other three intercity modes?
(b) Consider the following sets of statistics for 1990:

Intercity modal costs

Mode	Per-Mile Cost	Average Length of Trip
Certificated Air Carrier	13.02	803
Rail	12.85	274
Intercity Bus	11.55	141
Automobile	13.33[a]	115[a]

[a] Per-mile costs of operating a vehicle per vehicle occupant: assumes 1.62 occupants per vehicle in 1990. Average Length of Trip for automobile is based upon intercity vacation trips.

Based upon this information, can you conclude that rail trips are competitive with air trips? How about intercity bus or automobile trips? Use the concept of economies of distance to argue that rail trips *will be more competitive* with shorter-haul air trips, but *will be less competitive* with longer-haul intercity bus and auto trips.

9. Barbera et al. (1987) used a translog cost function to analyze the cost structure for all Class I railroads (revenues over $253.7 million annually, 1993 dollars) for the period 1979–83. The dependent variable was long-run total costs and the explanatory variables included:

- the level of output, measured as net freight ton–miles
- the operating characteristic, measured as net freight tons
- the network size, measured as miles of track operated
- the prices of inputs for labor, capital, fuel, and materials

Table 5.15 below reports the first-order coefficients and associated *t*-statistics for this model. In this paper, the authors interpret net freight tons, net freight ton–miles, and miles of track as firm size measures.

Table 5.15 First-order coefficients at the sample mean[a]

Regressor	Coefficient Estimate (*t*-statistic)
Constant term	−0.364 (−6.4)
Net Freight Tons	0.224 (3.3)
Price of Fuel	0.072 (46.2)
Price of Materials	0.431 (76.6)
Price of Capital	0.177 (23.4)
Price of Labor	0.320 (46.1)
Net Freight Ton–Miles	0.416 (5.4)
Miles of Track	0.390 (5.2)
$R^2 = 0.96$	

[a] The estimated translog cost function has the following form:

$$\ln C(T;p,o) = \alpha_0 + \alpha_1(\ln T - \ln \bar{T}) + \sum_{i=2}^{5}\alpha_i(\ln p_i - \ln \bar{p}_i) + \sum_{i=6}^{7}\alpha_i(\ln o_i - \ln \bar{o}_i)$$

$$+ \text{"second-order and interaction terms"} + \varepsilon$$

Source: Barbera et al. (1987), table 2, p. 240

(a) What proportion of total costs are due to labor, capital, fuel, and equipment? What would be the expected effect of a 5% increase in fuel prices on the total costs of a typical Class I railroad?

(b) For this analysis, the authors define the following relationships:

coefficient of Net Freight Tons = α_{NFT}

coefficient of Net Freight Ton–Miles = α_{NTM}

coefficient of Miles of Track = α_{MT}

economies of length of haul = $\varepsilon_{\text{LH}} = \dfrac{1}{\alpha_{\text{NTM}}}$

economies of density = $\varepsilon_{\text{d}} = \dfrac{1}{\alpha_{\text{NFT}} + \alpha_{\text{NTM}}}$

economies of scale = $\varepsilon_0 = \dfrac{1}{\alpha_{\text{NFT}} + \alpha_{\text{NTM}} + \alpha_{\text{MT}}}$

Explain the intuition behind each of these concepts. From the results, what are the estimated economies of traffic density and economies of scale? The authors also report that the standard error for the estimated economies of traffic density is 0.3348, and that the standard error associated with the estimated economies of scale is 0.936. Use these standard errors to test the null hypothesis of constant economies of traffic density and constant returns to scale. For the purposes of the test, assume 11 degrees of freedom.

(c) Given the model's specification, why is it appropriate to interpret the coefficient of Net Ton–Miles as reflecting length of haul economies? What do the empirical results tell us about length of haul scale economies? Suppose that you had two rail companies, one operating in the southern portion of the East Coast and a second company operating in the northern portion of the East Coast. Could the length of haul results support an "end-to-end" merger of the two rail lines?

(d) Based upon the returns to scale, traffic density, and length of haul results, what policies should rail firms follow in order to reduce their unit cost of production?

10. Pozdena and Merewitz (1978) analyzed 11 rapid rail transit properties operating in North America between 1960 and 1970. From their analysis, they obtained the following long-run total cost function:

$$LRTC = 7.42w^{0.98}p_e^{0.48}Q^{0.76}$$

where w is the wage rate ($ per hour), p_e is the price of energy ($ per kilowatt–hour), and Q is output (million vehicle–miles).

(a) According to this study, do rapid rail transit systems operate under increasing, decreasing or constant returns to scale? (Hint: take the logarithm of the equation and interpret the coefficient estimates.)

(b) In the early 1970s, there was a significant increase in oil prices. What effect would a 20% increase in kilowatt–hour prices have upon long-run rapid rail transit costs?

(c) From the *LRTC* equation, the authors also calculated the long-run marginal cost of rapid rail transit systems to be

$$LRMC = 5.66w^{0.98}p_e^{0.48}Q^{-0.24}$$

What effect on *LRMC* will there be from a 10% increase in output? Is the impact on *LRMC* consistent with your answer in (a)?

(d) At the time of this study, San Francisco's Bay Area Rapid Transit (BART) was not included. In 1975, BART had the following characteristics:

w = $7.48 per hour (base wage of train attendants)

p_e = $0.019 per kilowatt–hour

Q = 22.7 million vehicle–miles

Based upon *LRTC* and *LRMC* identified in (a) and (c), forecast BART's long-run total and marginal costs of operation. Also, calculate BART's long-run average cost per vehicle–mile. Is the average cost per vehicle–mile greater or less than the marginal cost per vehicle–mile, and is this consistent with the results previously obtained?

11. Case and Lave (1970) analyzed inland waterway costs in the United States. In their paper, they identified two trends associated with inland waterway transport during the preceding three decades: a relatively constant cost per ton–mile and a trend for a small number of firms to garner a large share of the market, either through growth or merger. In order examine these issues, the authors estimated the following Cobb–Douglas long-run average cost (*LRAC*) function:

$$LRAC = \alpha_0 (EBM)^{\alpha_1} (SZ)^{\alpha_2} T^{\alpha_3}$$

where *EBM* is "equivalent barge–miles", a measure of output, *SZ* is size of firm, measured by the number of towboats, and *T* is a time trend. α_i ($i = 1, \ldots, 4$) are parameters. Data for this study was based upon quarterly observations for five major inland water carriers between 1962 and 1966. The results of the analysis are shown in table 5.16.

Table 5.16 Inland waterway regression results[a]

Regressor	Coefficient Estimate (*t*-statistic)
Constant term	−0.200
Equivalent Barge Miles (EBM)	−0.615 (−11.0)
Number of Towboats	−0.074 (−1.3)
Time Trend	0.030 (0.88)
$R^2 = 0.865$	
Number of observations = 83	

[a] The estimated model also included three seasonal variables for the first, second, and third quarters, as well as four dummy variables for firms 1, 2, 3, and 4. The constant term reflects the fourth quarter and firm 5. A *t*-statistic was not reported for the constant term.
Source: Case and Lave (1970), table III, p. 188

(a) Based upon the reported results, do inland waterway companies operate under increasing, decreasing, or constant returns to scale?

(b) The authors argue that the measure of firm size, Number of Towboats, should have a negative effect upon long-run average costs. What's the economic intuition behind this hypothesis, and do the reported results support this?

APPENDIX: COST FUNCTION ESTIMATION

The purpose of this appendix is to demonstrate how the empirical cost functions that are commonly used in transportation policy analysis are derived. In order to do this, we make limited use of differential calculus, and so students with some calculus background will find this material a bit easier. However, neither knowledge of calculus nor the material in this appendix are necessary for understanding the material in the chapter. This appendix is primarily intended to give students a more complete understanding of why the empirical cost functions currently in use are so popular.

Taylor series expansion around the mean

Suppose that we have an arbitrary cost function of the form

$$C = C(q) \tag{5.A1}$$

where q is output. Although we don't know the exact empirical specification of the cost function, we do know from economic theory that the slope of this function, which is given by the first derivative, represents marginal cost:

$$C' = \frac{\mathrm{d}C}{\mathrm{d}q} = MC$$

and that the second derivative gives us information on how marginal cost changes when output increases by a small amount. That is,

$$C'' = \frac{\mathrm{d}^2C}{\mathrm{d}q^2} = \frac{\mathrm{d}(MC)}{\mathrm{d}q}$$

If $C'' > 0$, then marginal cost increases with increasing output; alternatively, if $C'' < 0$ then marginal cost decreases with increasing output.

Consider figure 5.A.1, where $C(q)$ depicts a typical total cost function that increases at a decreasing rate from zero to q_1 and increases at an increasing rate after q_1. For the moment, ignore the other information in the graph. For this cost function, marginal cost C' is everywhere positive. C'', on the other

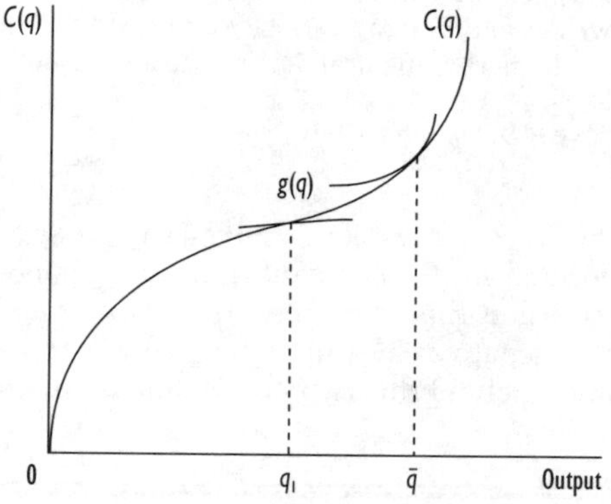

Figure 5.A.1 True and estimated cost curves. $C(q)$ = true total cost curve; $g(q)$ = estimated total cost curve around the mean $\bar{q}$.

hand, is negative up to output q_1 and positive after output q_1; that is, marginal cost decreases with output up to q_1 and thereafter increases with output.

Cost functions of the form in equation (5.A1) are useful for identifying the underlying determinants of cost, the relationship between marginal cost and output supply, and the qualitative effects of alternative policies on costs and firm behavior. However, these cost functions are inadequate if we are interested in *numerical* estimates of marginal cost, economies of scale, input price elasticities, and elasticities of substitution. The objective in this appendix is to derive two popular forms of an empirical cost function that have been successfully used in policy analyses to characterize the underlying cost structure and production technology of transportation firms.

Suppose that $\bar{q}$ is the firm's average rate of production and we want to *empirically estimate* the total cost function in (5.A1) around the mean production level $\bar{q}$. A general method for doing this is to *approximate* the unknown cost function $C(q)$ with a polynomial function of degree 2; that is, a *quadratic* function $g(q)$ such that

$$C(q) \approx g(q) = \alpha_0 + \alpha_1(q - \bar{q}) + \frac{\beta_1}{2}(q - \bar{q})^2 \tag{5.A2}$$

where the symbol "≈" means "is approximately equal to." α_0 and α_1 are referred to as "first-order coefficients," whereas β_1, which is a coefficient associated with the squared term, is a "second-order coefficient." If $g(q)$ is to be a *good* approximation of cost around $\bar{q}$, what values would we give α_0, α_1, and β_1? Intuitively, the following criteria would seem to be reasonable:

$$C(\bar{q}) = g(\bar{q}) \qquad \text{the two functions are equal at } \bar{q} \tag{5.A3}$$

$$\frac{dC(\bar{q})}{dq} = \frac{dg(\bar{q})}{dq} \qquad \text{marginal costs are equal at } \bar{q} \text{ for each function} \tag{5.A4}$$

$$\frac{d^2C(\bar{q})}{dq^2} = \frac{d^2g(\bar{q})}{dq^2} \qquad \text{the behavior of marginal costs is equal at } \bar{q} \text{ for each function} \tag{5.A5}$$

Notice in figure 5.A.1 that these criteria are each met at the mean level of output $\bar{q}$. The curve $g(q)$ in the figure is our polynomial approximation. This curve is a good approximation of $C(q)$ around the mean. Since $g(q)$ is tangent to $C(q)$ at the mean rate of production, we know that $g(\bar{q}) = C(\bar{q})$ and that the first derivatives are equal. Moreover, in the immediate vicinity of $\bar{q}$, the curvature of $g(q)$ is very similar to that of $C(q)$, which suggests that the behavior of marginal cost with output is the same for $g(\bar{q})$ and $C(\bar{q})$.

But why does $g(q)$ motivate an empirical specification of the unknown cost function? To see this, consider from equation (5.A2) the first and second derivatives of $g(q)$:

$$\frac{dg(q)}{dq} = \alpha_1 + \beta_1(q - \bar{q})$$

$$\frac{d^2g(q)}{dq^2} = \beta_1$$

These derivatives, combined with equations (5.A3)–(5.A5), enable us to solve for α_i $(i = 0, 1)$ and β_1 *when q is equal to $\bar{q}$*. In particular, if $q = \bar{q}$, then

$$C(\bar{q}) = g(\bar{q}) \Rightarrow C(\bar{q}) = \alpha_0 \tag{5.A6}$$

$$\frac{dC(\bar{q})}{dq} = \frac{dg(\bar{q})}{dq} \Rightarrow \frac{dC(\bar{q})}{dq} = \alpha_1 \tag{5.A7}$$

$$\frac{d^2C(\bar{q})}{dq^2} = \frac{d^2g(\bar{q})}{dq^2} \Rightarrow \frac{d^2C(\bar{q})}{dq^2} = \beta_1 \qquad (5.A8)$$

Equation (5.A6) says that the parameter α_0 is simply the total cost of producing the mean level of output; equation (5.A7) tells us that the parameter α_1 is marginal cost at mean production, and equation (5.A8) says that the parameter β_1 gives us the extent to which marginal cost increases with an increase in q.

In general, approximating any function around its mean value by a polynomial series is referred to as a *Taylor series expansion* around the mean. Since the polynomial approximation is of degree 2, the expansion is referred to as a *second-order* expansion.

It is important to understand what the Taylor series approximation does and what it does not do. The approximation is *not intended* to characterize the entire cost structure at all output levels. In figure 5.A.1, as we move further away from $\bar{q}$, $g(q)$ diverges more and more from $C(q)$. Rather, it *is intended* to be a good approximation of a firm's cost structure around the mean production level.

Econometric analysis of total costs

For any given firm, suppose we add a *remainder term* ε to our polynomial approximation given in equation (5.A2). This has the effect of converting the approximation into an equality. That is,

$$C(q) = g(q) + \varepsilon = \alpha_0 + \alpha_1(q - \bar{q}) + \frac{\beta_1}{2}(q - \bar{q})^2 + \varepsilon \qquad (5.A10)$$

Suppose that we have a sample of T observations. For example, we could observe total costs $C(q)$ and output q for a single firm over T time periods, or we might have a sample of T firms in a given time period. In either case, we have a sample of T observations, each of which has the cost structure given as

$$C_t = \alpha_0 + \alpha_1(q_t - \bar{q}) + \frac{\beta_1}{2}(q_t - \bar{q})^2 + \varepsilon_t, \qquad t = 1, \ldots, T \qquad (5.A11)$$

where C_t is the total cost for firm t, q_t is the output for firm t, and $\bar{q}$ is the mean output for the sample of T observations. Equation (5.A11) becomes a *linear-in-parameters* regression equation, which is estimable using the standard least-squares techniques that we developed in chapter 2. In addition, if we assume, for this sample of T observations, that the remainder term ε_t is normally distributed, then this allows the analyst to make statistical inferences on the unknown parameters α_i $(i = 0, 1)$ and β_1.

For our purposes, the "first-order coefficients" α_0 and α_1 contain the most useful economic information. As we saw above, in equations (5.A6) and (5.A7), α_0 gives the estimated total cost of production at the sample mean and α_1 estimates the marginal cost of production at the sample mean.

Long-run costs revisited

The above example defined total costs as a simple function of output, whereas on page 156 we identified the long-run cost function for a two-input firm as

$$C = C(Q; w, r, \gamma) \qquad (5.A12)$$

where Q is output, w is the wage rate, r is the rental price of capital, and γ represents the state of technology.

Suppose, for the sake of simplicity, that we ignore the technological parameter by assuming that each firm uses identical technology. In addition, assume that each a firm produces Q with only one input, labor. Then the long-run cost function is

$$C = C(Q; w) \qquad (5.A13)$$

Through exactly the same procedure as in the previous section, we could define a second-order Taylor series expansion about the mean values $\bar{Q}$ and $\bar{w}$, respectively. This expression is given by

$$C(Q,w) = C(\bar{Q},\bar{w}) + \left(\frac{\partial C(\bar{Q},\bar{w})}{\partial Q}\right)(Q - \bar{Q}) + \left(\frac{\partial C(\bar{Q},\bar{w})}{\partial w}\right)(w - \bar{w})$$

$$+ \frac{1}{2}\left[\left(\frac{\partial^2 C(\bar{Q},\bar{w})}{\partial Q^2}\right)(Q - \bar{Q})^2 + \left(\frac{\partial^2 C(\bar{Q},\bar{w})}{\partial Q^2}\right)(w - \bar{w})^2\right.$$

$$\left. + 2\left(\frac{\partial^2 C(\bar{Q},\bar{w})}{\partial Q \partial w}\right)(Q - \bar{Q})(w - \bar{w})\right] + \text{remainder} \tag{5.A14}$$

$$= \alpha_0 + \alpha_1(Q - \bar{Q}) + \alpha_2(w - \bar{w}) + \beta_1(Q - \bar{Q})^2 + \beta_2(w - \bar{w})^2$$

$$+ \phi_1(Q - \bar{Q})(w - \bar{w}) + \varepsilon \tag{5.A15}$$

where the α_i ($i = 0, 1, 2$) are "first-order coefficients", β_i ($i = 1, 2$) are "second-order" coefficients, ϕ_1 is an "interaction coefficient," and ε is a normally distributed error term. Again, for interpretative purposes, the "first-order coefficients" are most revealing. By comparing the respective coefficients in (5.A14) and (5.A15) we see that

$$\alpha_0 = C(\bar{Q},\bar{w}) = \text{total cost at } \bar{Q} \text{ and } \bar{w}$$

$$\alpha_1 = \left(\frac{\partial C(Q,\bar{w})}{\partial Q}\right) = \text{marginal cost of output evaluated at } \bar{Q} \text{ and } \bar{w}$$

$$\alpha_2 = \frac{\partial C(\bar{Q},w)}{\partial w} = \text{optimal use of labor evaluated at } \bar{Q} \text{ and } \bar{w}$$

As in the previous section, α_0 and α_1 represent total production costs and marginal production costs, respectively, at the mean. What about α_2? From the last equation, the coefficient for $w - \bar{w}$ in (5.A15) is the optimal level of the input labor, evaluated at the mean values of $\bar{Q}$ and $\bar{w}$. This is simply the empirical counterpart of Shephard's lemma that we met on page 159, and tells us that the optimal quantity of an input is given by the change in the cost function resulting from a unit change in the price of the input.

Finally, if we again have a sample of T observations, equation (5.A15) becomes a regression equation, where ε is assumed to be a normally distributed error term. Least-squares techniques are then utilized to obtain estimates for each of the "first-order coefficients" α_i ($i = 0, 1, 2$) and "second-order coefficients" β_i ($i = 1, 2, 3$).

A general pattern

From the above example, we can identify a general pattern for second-order Taylor series expansions. Suppose that we have a function of n terms, $f(x_1, \ldots, x_n)$ and we want to expand this function around the n mean values $\bar{x}_1, \ldots, \bar{x}_n$ respectively. Form the n differences $(x - \bar{x}_1), \ldots, (x_n - \bar{x}_n)$. To form an empirical model based upon a second-order Taylor series approximation of $f(x_1, \ldots, x_n)$, we would include the following terms:

- the function evaluated at $\bar{x}_1, \ldots, \bar{x}_n$
- each of the differences, $(x_i - \bar{x}_i)$, $i = 1, \ldots, n$
- $\frac{1}{2}$ times the square of each difference
- the cross-products of the differences
- and a remainder term

Thus, one could immediately write down the appropriate expression as

$$f(x_1, \ldots, x_n) = \alpha_0 + \sum_{i=1}^{n} \alpha_i(x_i - \bar{x}_i) + \sum_{i=1}^{n} \frac{\beta_i}{2}(x_i - \bar{x}_i)^2 + \sum_{\substack{i,j=1 \\ i \neq j}}^{n} \phi_{ij}(x_i - \bar{x}_i)(x_j - \bar{x}_j) + \varepsilon$$

The α_is ($i = 1, \ldots, n$) are "first-order coefficients," while the β_is ($i = 1, \ldots, n$) and ϕ_{ij}s ($i = 1, \ldots, n; j > i$) are "second-order and interaction coefficients," respectively. The "first-order coefficients" are again most easily interpretable:

$\alpha_0 = f(\bar{x}_1, \ldots, \bar{x}_n)$ = value of the function at the mean levels of $\bar{x}_1, \ldots, \bar{x}_n$

$\alpha_i = \dfrac{\partial f(\bar{x}_1, \ldots, x_i, \ldots, \bar{x}_n)}{\partial x_i}$ = change in the function at the mean values of $\bar{x}_1, \ldots, \bar{x}_n$ due to a unit increase in x_i ($i = 1, \ldots, n$)

Long-run costs – visitation II

This section returns to the long-run cost function identified on page 204 and repeated above in equation (5.A12):

$$C = C(Q;w,r,\gamma)$$

Based upon a second-order Taylor series expansion around the mean values $\bar{Q}$, $\bar{w}$, $\bar{r}$, and $\bar{\gamma}$, and using the methodology in the previous section, a regression equation for this "*quadratic*" cost function can be easily expressed as:

$$\begin{aligned} C(Q;w,r,\gamma) = {} & \alpha_0 + \alpha_1(Q - \bar{Q}) + \alpha_2(w - \bar{w}) + \alpha_3(r - \bar{r}) + \alpha_4(\gamma - \bar{\gamma}) \\ & + \tfrac{1}{2}[\beta_1(Q - \bar{Q})^2 + \beta_2(w - \bar{w})^2 + \beta_3(r - \bar{r})^2 + \beta_4(\gamma - \bar{\gamma})^2] \\ & + \phi_{12}(Q - \bar{Q})(w - \bar{w}) + \phi_{13}(Q - \bar{Q})(r - \bar{r}) + \phi_{14}(\gamma - \bar{\gamma})(Q - \bar{Q}) \\ & + \phi_{23}(r - \bar{r})(w - \bar{w}) + \phi_{24}(\gamma - \bar{\gamma})(w - \bar{w}) + \phi_{34}(\gamma - \bar{\gamma})(r - \bar{r}) + \varepsilon \end{aligned} \quad (5.A16)$$

As in previous examples, the "first-order coefficients" have straightforward economic interpretations, which table 5.A.1 summarizes.

Table 5.A.1 Quadratic cost function regression model: interpretation of first-order coefficients

Regressor	Coefficient	Interpretation
Constant term	α_0	Total cost at the sample mean
$Q - \bar{Q}$	α_1	Marginal cost of Q at the sample mean
$w - \bar{w}$	α_2	Labor demanded at the sample mean
$r - \bar{r}$	α_3	Capital demanded at the sample mean
$\gamma - \bar{\gamma}$	α_4	Average change in total cost over time from improving technology, evaluated at the sample mean

Long-run costs – visitation III

Consider once again the long-run cost function for a firm producing output Q with two inputs, capital and labor:

$$C = C(Q;w,r,\gamma)$$

Suppose that, prior to taking a second-order Taylor series approximation of the cost function, we first take a *logarithmic transformation* of each variable and follow exactly the same procedure to derive our Taylor series approximation. This leads to the following regression equation:

$$\begin{aligned}\ln C(Q;w,r,\gamma) &= \alpha_0 + \alpha_1(\ln Q - \ln \bar{Q}) + \alpha_2(\ln w - \ln \bar{w}) + \alpha_3(\ln r - \ln \bar{r}) \\ &+ \alpha_4(\ln \gamma - \ln \bar{\gamma}) + \tfrac{1}{2}[\beta_1(\ln Q - \ln \bar{Q})^2 + \beta_2(\ln w - \ln \bar{w})^2 \\ &+ \beta_3(\ln r - \ln \bar{r})^2 + \beta_4(\gamma - \bar{\gamma})^2] + \phi_{12}(\ln Q - \ln \bar{Q})(\ln w - \ln \bar{w}) \\ &+ \phi_{13}(\ln Q - \ln \bar{Q})(\ln r - \ln \bar{r}) + \phi_{12}(\ln \gamma - \ln \bar{\gamma})(\ln Q - \ln \bar{Q}) \\ &+ \phi_{23}(\ln r - \ln \bar{r})(\ln w - \ln \bar{w}) + \phi_{24}(\ln \gamma - \ln \bar{\gamma})(\ln w - \ln \bar{w}) \\ &+ \phi_{34}(\ln \gamma - \ln \bar{\gamma})(\ln r - \ln \bar{r}) + \varepsilon \qquad (5.A17)\end{aligned}$$

The regression equation in (5.A17) is referred to as a "*translog*" (*trans*cendental *log*arithmic) cost function. Although the equation *looks* formidable, it actually isn't. Comparing equation (5.A17) with the "quadratic" cost function in equation (5.A16) reveals that the only difference between the two specifications is that each variable in (5.A17) is the logarithm of the corresponding variable in equation (5.A16). Examine both equations carefully to verify this.

What interpretations, at the logarithms of mean values $\ln \bar{Q}$, $\ln \bar{w}$, $\ln \bar{r}$, and $\ln \bar{\gamma}$, can we give the "first-order coefficients" $\alpha_i\,(i = 0, 1, 2, 3, 4)$? Consider α_0. If all variables are at their mean values, then α_0 is simply equal to the logarithm of total costs at the mean; that is, $\alpha_0 = \ln C(\bar{Q},\bar{w},\bar{r},\bar{\gamma})$. This also implies that an estimate of total costs at the mean can be obtained by taking the exponential of α_0; that is, $C(\bar{Q},\bar{w},\bar{r},\bar{\gamma}) = \exp(\alpha_0)$.

What about α_1? We know that at the mean values $\ln \bar{Q}$, $\ln \bar{w}$, $\ln \bar{r}$, and $\ln \bar{\gamma}$, α_1 gives the change in $(\ln C(\bar{Q},\bar{w},\bar{r},\bar{\gamma}))$ due to a unit increase in $(\ln Q - \ln \bar{Q})$, which is simply the first derivative:

$$\alpha_1 = \frac{\partial \ln C(Q,\bar{w},\bar{r},\bar{\gamma})}{\partial \ln Q} = \frac{\partial C(Q,\bar{w},\bar{r},\bar{\gamma})}{\partial Q}\frac{Q}{C(Q,\bar{w},\bar{r},\bar{\gamma})}$$

= elasticity of long-run total costs with respect to output evaluated at the mean values

We have seen that the elasticity of long-run total cost with respect to output is a measure of economies of scale at the mean. If $\alpha_1 = 1$, the firm is operating under constant returns to scale; for $\alpha_1 > 1$, the firm is operating under decreasing returns to scale; and for $\alpha_1 < 1$, the firm is operating under increasing returns to scale.

The coefficients for the input prices, on the other hand, represent the optimal *cost shares* of each input. To see this, consider the coefficient α_2, which equals

$$\alpha_2 = \frac{\partial \ln C(\bar{Q},w,\bar{r},\bar{\gamma})}{\partial \ln w} = \frac{\partial C(\bar{Q},w,\bar{r},\bar{\gamma})}{\partial w}\frac{w}{C(\bar{Q},w,\bar{r},\bar{\gamma})} = \frac{Lw}{C(\bar{Q},w,\bar{r},\bar{\gamma})}$$

= share of labor costs at the mean

This result follows since, by Shephard's lemma, the change in total costs from a unit increase in the wage rate, $\partial C(\bar{Q},w,\bar{r},\bar{\gamma})/\partial w$, equals the optimal amount of labor demanded. Similarly,

Table 5.A.2 Translog cost function regression model: interpretation of first-order coefficients

Regressor	Coefficient	Interpretation
Constant term	α_0	Logarithm of total cost at the sample mean
$\ln Q - \ln \bar{Q}$	α_1	Elasticity of total cost with respect to output Q at the sample mean
$\ln w - \ln \bar{w}$	α_2	Share of labor in total costs, evaluated at the sample mean
$\ln r - \ln \bar{r}$	α_3	Share of capital in total costs, evaluated at the sample mean
$\ln \gamma - \ln \bar{\gamma}$	α_4	Percentage change in total cost from a 1% change in technology, evaluated at the sample mean

$$\alpha_3 = \frac{Kr}{C(\bar{Q},\bar{w},r,\bar{\gamma})} = \text{share of labor costs at the mean}$$

Finally, α_4 gives the effect of technological changes on long-run costs at the mean values $\ln \bar{Q}$, $\ln \bar{w}$, $\ln \bar{r}$, and $\ln \bar{\gamma}$:

$$\alpha_4 = \frac{\partial \ln C(\bar{Q},\bar{w},\bar{r},\gamma)}{\partial \ln \gamma} = \frac{\partial C(\bar{Q},\bar{w},\bar{r},\gamma)}{\partial \gamma}\frac{\gamma}{C(\bar{Q},\bar{w},\bar{r},\gamma)}$$

$$= \text{\% change in long-run costs due to a 1\% change in technology, evaluated at the mean}$$

Table 5.A.2 summarizes the interpretation of the "first-order coefficients" in the translog regression model.

As a last point, since our primary interest centers upon the "main effects" given by the first-order coefficients, we will adopt a *shorthand* or *simplified* version for expressing flexible cost functions by suppressing all of the second-order and interaction effects. Equation (5.A17), for example, can be more simply expressed as

$$\ln C(Q;w,r,\gamma) = \alpha_0 + \alpha_1(\ln Q - \ln \bar{Q}) + \alpha_2(\ln w - \ln \bar{w}) + \alpha_3(\ln r - \ln \bar{r}) + \alpha_4(\ln \gamma - \ln \bar{\gamma})$$
$$+ \text{"second-order and interaction terms"} + \varepsilon \qquad (5.A17')$$

which lets the reader know that the model includes second-order and interaction effects, but focuses one's attention on the model's main effects.

Final comments

Some of the most important advances in empirical transportation policy analysis relate to the estimation of so-called "flexible" cost functions, from which information on a firm's costs and underlying production technology are forthcoming. The two most popular forms of flexible cost specifications, both based upon second-order Taylor series approximations around the mean, are the "quadratic" and "translog" cost models, whose first-order coefficients are summarized in tables 5A.1 and 5A.2. For the most important transportation industries – motor carrier, air, railroad, urban transit, automobile production and highway infrastructure – empirical cost functions have been estimated and used to obtain important insights on transportation policy questions.

NOTES

1 Alternatively, at input level L_1 the total product of labor is said to have an "inflection point" which reflects a change in concavity. Up to L_1, the TP_L is concave upward and after L_1 it is concave downward. Still another way of saying the same thing is that output is increasing at an increasing rate up to L_1; after L_1, output is increasing at a decreasing rate.

2 The slope of a ray through the origin to a point on a curve is given by the "rise over the run"; that is, the value on the y-axis divided by the value on the x-axis. In the case of the total product of labor curve, this slope is T/L, the average product of labor. The point on the total product curve at which the slope of the ray through the origin is highest corresponds to the point at which the AP_L is highest. This will be the point at which the ray through the origin is just *tangent* to the total product curve.

3 A ton–mile is the shipment of 1 ton for 1 mile.

4 The limiting cases are L-shaped isoquants which imply no substitutability between K and L, and downward-sloping straight-line isoquants which imply that K and L are perfect substitutes.

5 This is true for homogeneous production functions. A function $f(x,y)$ is homogeneous of degree s if multiplying x and y by k multiplies the function by k^s. That is, $f(kx,ky) = k^s f(x,y)$. Equation (5.5) holds if the production function is homogeneous of degree s. This is not an overly restrictive assumption, since most production functions studied in economics satisfy this condition.

6 A further implication of equation (5.5) is the "exhaustion of the product" property. Suppose that inputs are paid an amount equal to their marginal products. Each unit of labor receives MP_L and each unit of capital receives MP_K. Equation (5.5) tells us that output Q is *just*-exhausted if the firm is operating under constant returns to scale; output is *over*-exhausted if the firm operates under increasing returns to scale; and output is *under*-exhausted if the firm operates under decreasing returns to scale.

7 Equation (5.7) holds for both homogeneous and nonhomogeneous functions that do not meet the conditions described in note 5. For nonhomogeneous functions, s may depend on the amount of inputs used.

8 Note that the cost equation for the firm if formally similar to a budget line for a consumer. If we rewrite the cost equation in slope–intercept form, we obtain

$$K = -(w/r) + C/r$$

where w/r is the slope, in absolute value, of the cost line. C/r is the y-intercept and represents the purchasing power of a firm's budget if it were all spent on capital. Similarly, the x-axis intercept is C/w and is the purchasing power of a budget that is entirely spent on labor.

9 More accurately, the optimal demands defined in equation (5.9) are *conditional* input demands, since they are obtained by minimizing costs subject to a given output level. As such, they do not depend upon output price. However, if one were to solve for the unconditional input demands, which correspond to input levels that are associated with maximum profits, these would be functions of output price.

10 With constant input prices, as assumed here, returns to scale are also called "scale economies," because they reflect how firm costs vary with its scale of operations.

11 For a theoretical derivation of substitution elasticities, see Chung (1994).

12 For the purpose of this section, when examining these alternative cost elasticity measures, we are also assuming that the prices of all inputs and the state of technology are held constant.

13 We have assumed throughout that a firm produces one product or service (for example, freight ton–miles or passenger–miles). In some cases, firms may produce multiple products (for example, some airlines carry passengers and freight). These firms not only experience returns to scale but also *returns to scope*. A firm that produces multiple products experiences (dis)economies of scope if firm costs (increase) decrease under joint production.

14 Varian (1987) illustrates how one derives the cost function from Cobb–Douglas technology.

15 The time variable is specified as a *time trend* or as *time dummy variables*, where each dummy variable corresponds to a particular year (or time period). Obviously, the time variable is included only if the underlying data set includes observations over a time period. If the data are a cross-section of firms, then only operating characteristics are included to capture technological differences.

16 For an expanded discussion of these changes, see Coyle et al. (1994).

17 Moore (1975) identifies the primary economic costs of regulation to include the inefficient supply of transport services (reflecting restrictions on backhauls, routes, and commodities carried), mode-shifting effects (since the relative prices paid by shippers do not reflect the relative marginal costs of the alternative modes), the general absence of marginal cost pricing, dislocation effects in other sectors of the economy, and significant dynamic effects upon incentives to innovate. Similar efficiency arguments were made for the other major transport modes, some of which will be discussed in the following sections. Chapter 8 summarizes the effects of deregulation in the transport industries. Studies documenting the effects of regulation on the motor carrier industry include Moore (1975, 1978), Friedlaender and Spady (1981), Frew (1981), Kim (1984), Rose (1985), Winston (1985), McMullen (1987), McMullen and Stanley (1988), Ying (1990a,b), and Winston et al. (1990).

18 Contract carriers also fell under ICC jurisdiction, but they were a small proportion of the regulated carriers.

19 See Friedlaender and Spady (1981) and Coyle et al. (1994) for a more detailed discussion of general freight and specialized carriers and the role of owner–operators.

20 The price of purchased transportation represents total expenditures for rented vehicles (with and without driver) per rented vehicle–mile.

21 In the regulated environment, ease of entry was not easy in the sense of obtaining operating certificates. However, as previously discussed, owner–operators subcontract their equipment and services to firms that held operating licenses. In this sense, entry/exit in this segment is relatively unrestricted.

22 Recall from chapter 2 that the *t*-statistic equals the coefficient estimate divided by the standard error of the estimate. To get the standard error of α_1 from table 5.5, divide the coefficient estimate (0.721) by the *t*-statistic (4.6), which gives 0.1567. The calculated *t*-statistic for constant returns to scale is $((0.721 - 1)/0.1567) = -1.78$. The critical value for a one-sided test with 36 degrees of freedom is approximately 1.69.

23 This would occur if the regulations were characterized by an increasing number of gateway requirements per distance traveled. A 200 mile trip, for example, could have one gateway restriction, whereas a 400 mile trip could have three gateway restrictions.

24 For the sample, the mean value for Average Length of Haul was 320 miles. However, McMullen and Stanley (1988) did not report the sample standard deviation for Average Length of Haul.

25 If we relate these results to firm isoquants, the values presented in table 5.6 give isoquants between purchased transportation and each other input that are flatter (representing more substitution possibilities) than isoquants for labor–capital, labor–fuel, and capital–fuel inputs.

26 In a related study, McMullen (1987) argues that brokering activities may have generated the finding of scale economies during regulation. During regulation, fleet operators performed these functions, so that the scale economies associated with brokering produced overall scale economies for the firm. However, with deregulation, these activities were shifted to specialized broker firms in order to accommodate the needs of a large number of small firms entering the industry, thereby eliminating a source of scale economies to fleet operators. McMullen provides evidence consistent with this hypothesis.

27 Class I and Class II common carriers were defined during this period as carriers with annual revenues greater than $5 million and between $1 million and $5 million, respectively.

28 Also, it is not possible to reject the null hypothesis of constant returns to scale against an alternative hypothesis of increasing returns to scale. See note 16 and the surrounding text for a fuller discussion of the test.

29 Much of this material is based upon a number of excellent works in the area, including Douglas and Miller (1974), Bailey, Graham, and Kaplan (1985), Meyer and Oster (1984), and Pickrell (1991).

30 Intrastate airlines, such as Pacific Southwest Airlines in California, were also not subject to CAB economic regulations.

31 For example, Caves (1962), Douglas and Miller (1974), and Keeler (1978) estimated that trunk carriers operated under constant returns to scale. Keeler (1978) also provided evidence that smaller carriers operate under increasing returns to scale.

32 Data which include a cross-section of firms over a period of time, as in this case, are referred to as a *panel data*. An advantage of panel data is that we can include dummy variables for each of the firms, in order to control for interfirm differences that are not due to the included variables. This reduces the problem of possible biases in the parameter estimates due to excluded variables. In addition to including firm dummy variables, the authors also include time dummy variables in order to capture systematic changes in output over time that are not due to the included variables.

33 A "translog transformation" of the variable Output, for example, is (ln Output – ln $\overline{\text{Output}}$) where $\overline{\text{Output}}$ is mean output.

34 Although we cannot calculate $s_{(\hat{\varepsilon}_{od}+\hat{\varepsilon}_{or})}$ from the information provided, Caves et al. (1984, p. 478) reported the standard error to be 0.05.

35 $s_{\hat{\varepsilon}_0} = 0.034$ is obtained by dividing the *t*-statistic for Revenue Output–Miles, 23.6, into its coefficient, 0.804.

REFERENCES AND RELATED READINGS

General references on production and cost

Chung, J. W. 1994: *Utility and Production Functions.* Cambridge, Mass.: Blackwell.

Colander, D. C. 1995: *Economics*, 2nd edn. Chicago: Richard D. Irwin.

Intriligator, M. 1978: *Econometric Models, Techniques, and Applications.* Englewood Cliffs, New Jersey: Prentice-Hall.

Nicholson, W. 1998: *Microeconomic Theory*, 7th edn. Fort Worth, Texas: The Dryden Press.

McCloskey, D. N. 1985: *The Applied Theory of Price*, 2nd edn. New York: Macmillan.

Stiglitz, J. E. 1997: *Principles of Microeconomics*, 2nd edn. New York: W. W. Norton.

Varian, H. R. 1987: *Intermediate Microeconomics: A Modern Approach.* New York: W. W. Norton.

General references on transportation

Berechman, J. 1993: *Public Transit Economics and Deregulation Policy*, vol. 23. Studies in Regional Science and Urban Economics, L. Anselin et al. (ed.). Amsterdam: Elsevier Science.

Boyer, K. D. 1998: *Principles of Transportation Economics.* Reading, Mass.: Addison-Wesley.

Button, K. J. 1993: *Transport Economics*, 2nd edn. Brookfield, Vermont: Edward Elgar.

Coyle, J. J., Bardi, E. J., and Novack, R. A. 1994: *Transportation.* St. Paul/Minneapolis: West.

ENO Transportation Foundation, Inc. 1992: *Transportation in America* 11th edn.

MacAvoy, P. W. and Snow, J. W. (eds.) 1977: *Railroad Revitalization and Regulatory Reform.* Washington DC: American Enterprise Institute for Public Policy Research.

Oum, T. H., Dodgson, J. S., Hensher, D. A., Morrison, S. A., Nash, C. A., Small, K. A., and Waters, W. G. II (eds.) 1995: *Transport Economics: Selected Readings.* Seoul, Korea: The Korea Research Foundation for the 21st Century.

Sampson, R. J., Farris, M. T., and Schrock, D. L. 1990: *Domestic Transportation: Practice, Theory, and Policy*, 6th edn. Boston: Houghton Mifflin.

Stubbs, P. C., Tyson, W. J., and Dalvi, M. Q. 1980: *Transport Economics.* London: George Allen and Unwin.

Winston, C. 1985: Conceptual developments in the economics of transportation: an interpretive survey. *Journal of Economic Literature*, XXIII, 57–94.

Specific cost-related studies by mode

Airlines

Bailey, E. E., Graham, D. R., and Kaplan, D. P. 1985: *Deregulating the Airlines*, vol. 10. Regulation of Economic Activity, R. Schmalensee (ed.). Cambridge, Mass.: The MIT Press.

Caves, R. E. 1962: *Air Transport and Its Regulators: An Industry Study*. Cambridge, Mass.: Harvard University Press.

Caves, D. W., Christiansen, L. R., and Tretheway, M. W. 1984: Economies of density versus economies of scale: why trunk and local service airline costs differ. *Rand Journal of Economics*, 15, 470–89.

Douglas, G. W. and Miller, J. C. III 1974: *Economic Regulation of Domestic Air Transport: Theory and Policy*. Washington DC: The Brookings Institution.

McShan, S. and Windle, R. 1989: The implications of hub-and-spoke routing for airline costs and competitiveness. *Logistics and Transportation Review*, 25, 209–30.

Meyer, J. R. and Oster, C. V. Jr. 1984: *Deregulation and the New Airline Entrepreneurs*. Cambridge, Mass.: The MIT Press.

Pickrell, D. 1991: The regulation and deregulation of US airlines. In K. Button (ed.), *Airline Deregulation: International Experiences*. New York: New York University Press, pp. 5–47.

Motor carriers

Allen, W. B. and Dong, L. 1995: Service quality and motor carrier costs: an empirical analysis. *Review of Economics and Statistics*, LXXVII, 499–510.

Callan, S. J. and Thomas, J. M. 1992: Cost differentials among household goods carriers. *Journal of Transport Economics and Policy*, XXVI, 19–34.

Emerson, C. J. et al. 1993: The advantage of size in the US trucking industry: an application of the survivor technique. *Journal of the Transportation Research Forum*, 32, 369–78.

Frew, J. 1981: The existence of monopoly profits in the motor carrier industry. *Journal of Law and Economics*, XXIV, 289–315.

Friedlaender, A. F. and Spady, R. H. 1981: *Freight Transport Regulation*. Cambridge, Mass.: The MIT Press.

Harmatuck, D. J. 1990: Motor carrier cost function comparisons. *Transportation Journal*, 30, 32–46.

Kim, M. 1984: The beneficiaries of trucking regulation, revisited. *The Journal of Law and Economics*, XXVII, 227–41.

Liu, D. 1993: Service quality and industry structure: concentration in the LTL motor carrier industry. *Journal of Transport Economics and Policy*, XXVII, 305–15.

McMullen, B. S. 1987: The impact of regulatory reform on US motor carrier costs. *Journal of Transport Economics and Policy*, XXI, 307–19.

McMullen, S. and Stanley, L. R. 1988: The impact of deregulation on the production structure of the motor carrier industry. *Economic Inquiry*, XXVI, 299–316.

Moore, T. G. 1975: Deregulating surface freight transportation. In A. Phillips (ed.), *Promoting Competition in Regulated Markets*. Washington DC: The Brookings Institution, pp. 55–98.

Moore, T. G. 1978: The beneficiaries of trucking regulation. *Journal of Law and Economics*, 21, 327–43.

Rose, N. L. 1985: The incidence of regulatory rents in the motor carrier industry. *Rand Journal of Economics*, 16, 299–318.

Winston, C., Corsi, T. M., Grinum, C. M., and Evans, C. A. 1990: *The Economic Effects of Surface Freight Deregulation*. Washington DC: The Brookings Institution.

Ying, J. S. 1990a: The inefficiency of regulating a competitive industry: productivity gains in trucking following reform. *The Review of Economics and Statistics*, LXXII, 191–201.

Ying, J. S. 1990b: Regulatory reform and technical change: new evidence of scale economies in trucking. *Southern Economic Journal*, 56, 996–1009.

Public transit

Berechman, J. 1983: Costs, economics of scale and factor demand in bus transport. *Journal of Transport Economics and Policy*, XVII, 7–24.

Berechman, J. and Giuliano, G. 1984: Analysis of the cost structure of an urban bus transit property. *Transportation Research B*, 18, 273–87.

Martin, W. 1979: Firm size and operating costs in urban bus transportation. *The Journal of Industrial Economics*, XXVIII, 209–18.

Obeng, K. 1984: The economics of bus transit operation. *The Logistics and Transportation Review*, 20, 45–65.

Obeng, K. 1985: Bus transit cost, productivity and factor substitution. *Journal of Transport Economics and Policy*, XIX, 183–203.

Pozdena, R. J. and Merewitz, L. 1978: Estimating cost functions for rail rapid transit properties. *Transportation Research B*, 12, 73–8.

Viton, P. A. 1981: A translog cost function for urban bus transit. *The Journal of Industrial Economics*, XXIX, 287–304.

Railroads

Braeutigam, R. R., Daughety, A. F., and Turnquist, M. A. 1984: A firm specific analysis of economies of density in the US railroad industry. *The Journal of Industrial Economics*, XXXIII, 3–19.

Caves, D. W., Christensen, L. R., and Swanson, J. A. 1981: Productivity growth, scale economies, and capacity utilization in US railroads, 1955–74. *American Economic Review*, 71, 994–1002.

Barbera, A. et al. 1987: Railroad cost structure – revisited. *Journal of the Transportation Research Forum*, XXVIII, 237–352.

Keeler, T. E. 1971: The economics of passenger trains. *Journal of Business*, 44, 148–74.

Keeler, T. E. 1978: Railroad costs, returns to scale, and excess capacity. *Review of Economics and Statistics*, LX, 201–8.

Bus and water modes

Case, L. S. and Lave, L. B. 1970: Cost functions for inland waterways transport in the United States. *Journal of Transport Economics and Policy*, IV, 181–91.

Davies, J. E. 1983: An analysis of cost and supply conditions in the linear shipping industry. *The Journal of Industrial Economics*, XXXI, 417–35.

Tauchen, H., Fravel, F. D., and Gilbert, G. 1983: Cost structure of the intercity bus industry. *Journal of Transport Economics and Policy*, XVII, 25–47.

Williams, M. and Hall, C. 1981: Returns to scale in the United States intercity bus industry. *Regional Science and Urban Economics*, 11, 573–84.

6

Firm Production and Cost in Transportation – The Short Run

INTRODUCTION

Chapter 5 developed a firm's long-run production and cost characteristics and examined a number of empirical studies that have estimated scale economies, input substitution, and factor demand characteristics of various transportation firms. In this chapter, we no longer assume that all inputs are variable to the firm, but assume instead that at least one input, typically capital, is held fixed at some level. In the first part of the chapter, we analyze the implications that fixed factors of production have for a firm's cost and supply functions, and develop the explicit relationship between a firm's short-run and long-run cost structures. To illustrate these concepts, we summarize empirical studies of airline profitability and short-run costs in the railroad and urban bus sectors of the transportation industry.

SHORT RUN – LEVEL OF CAPITAL FIXED

In long-run analyses, all costs are assumed to be variable. There are no fixed factors of production, the costs of which had to be met regardless of whether the firm produced. In the long run, all factors of production are variable and all costs are escapable. The short run, by contrast, is a period during which at least one factor of production is fixed. In this analysis, we assume that capital is fixed at some level $\overline{K}$. With the level of capital fixed, the only way a firm can affect its level of output is through changes in the use of labor, which implies that the short-run production function is

$$T = f(\overline{K}, L; \gamma) \tag{6.1}$$

Recalling our discussion of productivity curves when some input is held fixed, equation (6.1) can be viewed as a total product curve for labor, from which one could derive average and marginal productivity curves.

In the short run, a discussion of returns to scale is no longer relevant, since all inputs cannot change in the same proportion. With a fixed factor of production, inputs are used in variable proportions. Increases in output occur with the firm using an increasing amount of labor relative to the fixed input. Although marginal productivity of labor initially rises at an increasing rate, after some point, adding more workers to a fixed amount of capital reduces the marginal productivity of labor, an empirical characteristic of short-run production functions which is commonly referred to as the *law of diminishing returns*.[1]

SHORT-RUN COST CURVES

Since capital is fixed, a firm's input decision relates to labor and the firm hires up to the point at which the wage rate equals the value of the marginal product. A firm's input demands for capital and labor, therefore, are expressed as

$$K = \overline{K}$$
$$L = l(T;w,r,\gamma,\overline{K}) \qquad (6.2)$$

Substituting these into a firm's cost equation gives short-run total cost (STC):

$$\begin{aligned} STC &= wl(T;w,r,\gamma,\overline{K}) + r\overline{K} \\ &= STVC(T;w,r,\gamma,\overline{K}) + STFC \\ &= STC(T;w,r,\gamma,\overline{K}) \end{aligned} \qquad (6.3)$$

where $STVC(T;w,r,\gamma,\overline{K})$ is short-run total variable cost and $STFC$ is the short-run total fixed cost.[2] Each of these curves is depicted in figure 6.1. Since, with constant input prices, the marginal product of labor initially rises, reaches its point of diminishing marginal returns and thereafter falls, $STVC$ increases first at a decreasing rate and then rises at an increasing rate. Also, STC is parallel to $STVC$, but shifted up by an amount equal to fixed costs. Similar to

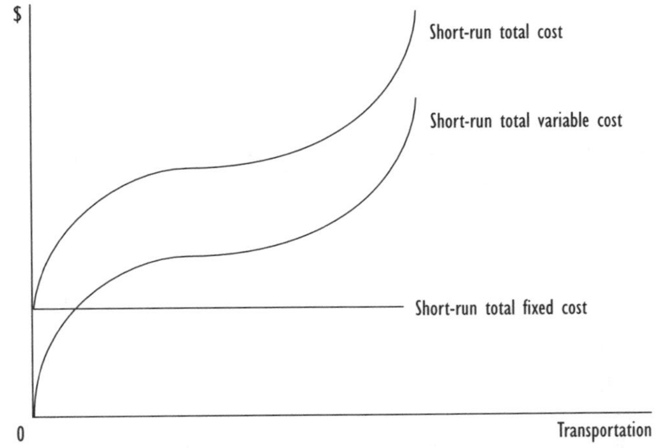

Figure 6.1 Short-run total cost curves.

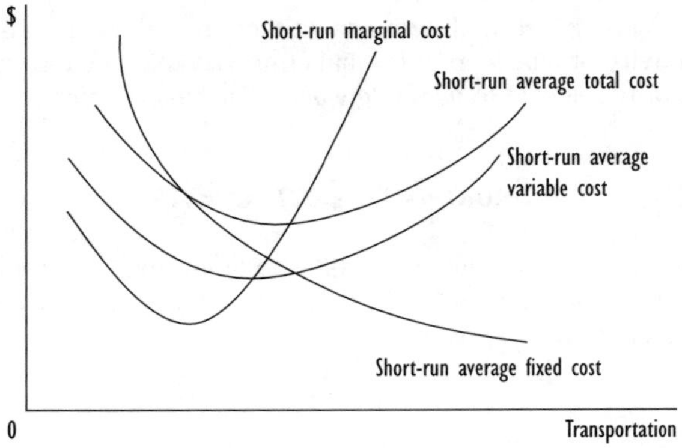

Figure 6.2 Short-run cost average and marginal cost curves.

the long-run cost structures, we can obtain average and marginal cost curves, including short-run average total cost, short-run average variable cost, and short-run marginal cost. Figure 6.2 depicts the short-run average and marginal cost curves derived from the total cost curves in figure 6.1.

THE SHORT-RUN MARKET SUPPLY FUNCTION

As in chapter 5, we assume here that transport firms are operating in a perfectly competitive environment. The explicit objective of a firm is profit maximization; that is, the carrier desires to maximize the difference between total revenues and total costs. From equation (6.3), a firm's short-run total cost function

$$STC(T;w,r,\gamma,\overline{K}) = STVC(T;w,r,\gamma,\overline{K}) + STFC$$

is the sum of its short-run total variable cost plus short-run total fixed cost. Thus, for the short-run period, a firm's profit function can be expressed as

$$\begin{aligned}\pi_S &= pT - STC(T;w,r,\gamma,\overline{K})\\ &= pT - STVC(T;w,r,\gamma,\overline{K}) - STFC \qquad (6.4)\end{aligned}$$

where p is the price of the output T. Since all firms are small in comparison with the size of the market, the price of T is not set by the firm but is determined by the interaction of market demand and supply.

Similar to our long-run analysis, we can ask whether there is a price below which the firm will not operate; that is, will not produce any T. Yes. From equation (6.1), if output equals zero, the firm incurs a cost identically equal to its short-run total fixed costs, *STFC*. In other words, even if the firm produces no output, in the short run it must still pay for its fixed factors of production. At worst, the firm produces no output and its total profit will be a loss equal to its short-run fixed costs, $\pi_S = -STFC$. Alternatively, by subtracting *STFC* from both sides of equation (6.4), we see that a firm produces in the short run as long as its revenues cover its short-run total variable costs (*SAVC*); that is,

$$\pi_S - STFC = pT - STVC(T;w,r,\gamma,\bar{K}) \geqslant 0 \tag{6.5}$$

Dividing all terms on the right-hand side of the equals sign in (6.5) by *T* gives us the lowest price below which a firm, in the short run, will not be found operating. In particular,

$$p \geqslant \frac{STVC(T;w,r,\gamma,\bar{K})}{T} = SAVC(T;w,r,\gamma,\bar{K}) \tag{6.6}$$

As long as output price is at least as great as short-run average variable cost, the firm will produce in the short run.

Also, how will the sale of one more unit of *T* affect short-run profits? Since short-run total fixed costs do not depend upon market output, the cost to the firm of producing an additional *T*, the firm's *short-run marginal cost*, is simply the change in total variable cost from producing one more unit, all else held constant. The sale of an additional *T* also increases a firm's revenues, and since a firm's output decision cannot affect the price of *T*, its *marginal revenue* from the sale of an additional unit increases by *p*, the price of *T*.

Thus, the total effect upon short-run profits from selling one more unit of *T* is

$$\begin{aligned} \frac{\Delta\pi_S}{\Delta T} &= p - \frac{\Delta STVC(T;w,r,\gamma,\bar{K})}{\Delta T} - \frac{\Delta STFC}{\Delta T} \\ &= p - \frac{\Delta STVC(T;w,r,\gamma,\bar{K})}{\Delta T} - 0 = p - SMC(T;w,r,\gamma,\bar{K}) \end{aligned} \tag{6.7}$$

where $SMC(T;w,r,\gamma,\bar{K})$ is the firm's short-run marginal cost of production. Will it be economically worthwhile for the firm to sell an extra unit of *T*? – yes, as long as the sale of the unit adds to its short-run profits; that is, as long as $\Delta\pi_S/\Delta T > 0$; or, equivalently, as long as marginal revenue from selling an additional unit is greater than the marginal cost of producing an additional unit.

At what point will the firm refuse to sell another unit? In figure 6.2, the short-run marginal cost curve intersects "from below" the short-run average variable cost curve at its minimum point. This implies that for those output levels at which a firm finds it economically feasible to produce – that is, where marginal revenue is greater than or equal to minimum average variable cost – short-run marginal cost is *increasing*. A firm will continue to sell output up to the point at which *p* just equals $SMC(T;w,r,\gamma)$. At any level of output beyond this, short-run marginal cost is greater than price, and the sale of an additional unit lowers rather than raises profits. Thus, for any given price of *T*, the *short-run profit maximization condition* for the firm is

$$p = SMC(T;w,r,\gamma,\bar{K}) \tag{6.8}$$

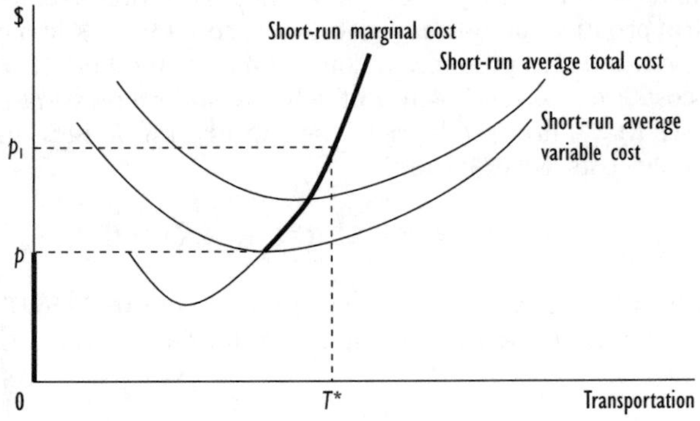

Figure 6.3 The short-run firm supply curve. ——, Short-run supply curve; p, the price below which firm output falls to zero.

which, if we solve for T in terms of price and call the result $T^*(p)$, yields a transport firm's *short-run supply function*:

$$\begin{aligned} T^{sr}(p;w,r,\gamma,\overline{K}) &= T^*(p), \qquad p \geqslant SAVC(T;w,r,\gamma,\overline{K}) \\ &= 0, \qquad p < SAVC(T;w,r,\gamma,\overline{K}) \end{aligned} \tag{6.9}$$

Thus, holding input prices, technology, and capital constant, a firm's short-run supply curve is coincident with its short-run marginal cost curve as long as the price of T is greater than or equal to the short-run average variable cost.

Figure 6.3 depicts a firm's short-run supply curve (darker line) and its profit-maximizing output at price p_1.

The short-run market supply function is simply the horizontal summation of individual supply functions. If there are F firms producing T in the short run, the *short-run market supply function*, S_T^{sr}, is defined as

$$S_T^{sr}(p;w,r,\gamma,\overline{K}) = \sum_{i=1}^{F} T_i^{sr}(p;w,r,\gamma,\overline{K}) \tag{6.10}$$

where T_i^{sr} is the short-run supply function of firm i. Holding input prices, technology, and the fixed factor of production constant yields the short-run supply curve, $S_T^{sr}(p)$. Since an increase in the price of T increases the output of each individual firm, it follows that the short-run market supply curve is also upward-sloping; $\Delta S_T^{sr}/\Delta T > 0$.

Similar to the long-run market supply curve, changes in the short-run market supply curve depends upon the number of firms in the industry, the economic environment as summarized by input prices, taxes, subsidies, and the state of technology.

In the short run, changes in the level of the fixed factor of production also affect the location of the short-run market supply curve. For example, there have been recent concerns over the deterioration of highways in general and the interstate system in particular. If one considers the highway network as a fixed factor of production in the provision of motor carrier transportation, then deteriorating roads effectively reduce the level of the fixed factor of production, leading to a rise in the opportunity cost of providing motor vehicle transportation. But this is equivalent to a leftward (or upward) shift in the short-run aggregate supply curve of highway transportation shipments.

CASE STUDY – SHORT-RUN VARIABLE COSTS IN THE RAILROAD INDUSTRY UNDER REGULATION

We have seen that the origins of economic regulation in the transportation industry occurred in 1887 with passage of the Act to Regulate Commerce (ARC). This was the culmination of years of general disenchantment, primarily due to discriminatory rate practices, that shippers experienced with the railroads. Because the ARC's objective was to restrain abusive pricing practices, its provisions focused upon railroad rate-setting and the creation of a body to oversee these activities (Coyle et al., 1994).

Rate-setting

Among its provisions, the ARC required railroads to charge "just and reasonable" rates and specifically banned a variety of pricing practices. It banned personal discrimination whereby carriers charged different shippers different prices for similar services. Rail carriers could not give "undue or unreasonable" preference to any shipper, commodity shipped, or location. In transporting goods or persons, carriers could not charge different prices for short hauls than they did for longer hauls that traveled in the same direction and over the same line. The ARC outlawed pooling arrangements among the railroads. And all rates and fares charged had to be filed with the Interstate Commerce Commission, and would be publicly available.

Interstate Commerce Commission

In order to administer its provisions, the bill created a five-member commission, the Interstate Commerce Commission (ICC), which was given the authority to inspect a carrier's financial statements, require annual reports, and develop a framework for handling shipper complaints.

Notwithstanding the significance of the legislation, the ICC's power to regulate commerce was circumscribed for two reasons. First, the ICC did not possess enforcement powers. Although the ICC could identify and order a rail company to alter its illegal pricing practices, enforcement of these orders was the responsibility of the courts. Second, the ICC used its authority to set actual or maximum rates. However, in a series of cases in the late 1890s, the Supreme Court ruled that the ICC did not have rate-setting authority.

The Hepburn Act, passed in 1906, strengthened the ICC's authority in a number of ways. This Act extended ICC jurisdiction, increased the size of the commission to ten members, established that ICC orders would be binding on the carriers, and gave the ICC broader range over personal discrimination. But the most important provision of the Hepburn Act was in giving the ICC the power to set maximum rates, which the Supreme Court had outlawed near the turn of the century.

The period between 1906 and 1920 saw passage of relatively minor Acts that generally strengthened the ICC's ability to oversee the rail industry.[3] But, in 1920, Congress passed a major piece of legislation affecting rail carriers, the Transportation Act. A primary feature of this bill was a directive to the ICC to consider not only the welfare of shippers in setting rates but also that of rail carriers. In the preceding decade, the effect of ICC regulatory practices that inadequately compensated rail carriers with rate increases to adjust for rising costs was to lower carrier earnings and cause many carriers to become financially distressed. The Transportation Act of 1920 was intended to rectify this situation by granting the ICC additional authority to set minimum rates in order to prevent cutthroat competition that would be ruinous to the industry. The Act also gave the ICC authority to sanction rail abandonment and joint arrangements if this was believed to be in the public interest. And, importantly, the Act established the "rule of rate-making." Since carriers as well as shippers have a right to a fair return on investment, the rule of rate-making specified that, in setting rates, the ICC was to explicitly consider the impact upon the financial condition of the carriers.

The Transportation Act of 1920 was followed in 1925 by the Hoch–Smith Resolution, which contained two basic provisions. First, in setting minimum rates, the ICC must not only consider the impact upon rail carriers, as stipulated in the 1920 Act, but also the impact upon the industries shipping the freight. The effect of this was to validate *value-of-service* pricing, where prices are set according to what the market will bear. In general, this means that those willing to pay higher prices for transport, such as shippers of higher-valued manufactured goods, are charged more in comparison with shippers of lower-valued bulk commodities, who in turn are less willing to pay higher prices. A second feature of the resolution was to charge the lowest possible rates for agricultural products, a policy that had important financial implications for rail carriers, as they were losing higher-valued manufactured shipments to the growing motor carrier industry.

Two other changes related to the rule of rate-making were passed between 1925 and 1940. In 1933, the Emergency Transportation Act directed the ICC to consider the effect of its rate-setting activities on the movement of traffic, and the Transportation Act of 1940 limited this to movement of traffic to the carriers for which the rates were prescribed. Consistent with a statement of national policy contained in the 1940 Act, this change was intended to exploit the inherent advantages of each mode, rather than set rates on one mode with an objective of protecting traffic on other modes. Subsequent rulings, however, indicated that the ICC continued to take a protective stance in respect to its rate-making. In the Transportation Act of 1958, Congress again amended the rule to explicitly state that rates on one mode are not to be "held up" in order to protect the traffic of any other transport mode. Consistent with this intent, the Supreme Court later ruled that traffic diversion from competitive modes was not sufficient to outlaw rate changes.

The primary goal of the 1958 Transportation Act was to address the worsening financial plight of the railroads. The growth of the motor carrier industry, combined with value-of-service pricing contained in the 1920 legislation, had led to below normal earnings and returns on investment. The legislation hoped to alleviate the financial strain on the industry by providing loan guarantees to the industry, granting the ICC authority over the passenger rail service, and specifically empowering the Commission to authorize discontinued passenger services, as well as its amendment to the rule of rate-making.

The financial problems of the industry continued on into the 1960s and led to the passage of three bills in the 1970s. First, the Rail Passenger Act of 1970 established Amtrak as a "for profit" national rail passenger service, that began operations in 1971. Second, in response to the bankruptcies of seven major railroads in the northeastern United States, the Regional Rail Reorganization Act (the 3-R Act) of 1973 established Conrail, the Consolidated Rail Corporation, which began service in 1976. Third, Congress passed the Rail Revitalization and Regulatory Reform Act (the 4-R Act) in 1976. Although primarily a response to the financial straits of the industry, its provisions constituted a move toward industry deregulation by establishing rational price-setting policies that are characteristic of competitive markets. Except for instances of market dominance, no rate was too high to be judged unreasonable. The act re-emphasized that rates should not be set to protect traffic on other modes. Also, in contrast to past ICC practice that used average total cost as a measure for setting rates, the 4-R Act changed to variable cost of production as the appropriate yardstick for rate-setting, a position long advocated by the railroads. As long as a carrier's rates covered opportunity or variable costs of production, the ICC could not declare the rates unreasonably low. Further, in the two years following its passage, the 4-R Act permitted railroads to adjust their rates, up or down, by as much as 7% without prior ICC approval.

Continuing the trend set by the 1976 4-R Act, the Staggers Rail Act of 1980 significantly relaxed economic regulation in the rail industry. Among its provisions, the Staggers Act gave the railroads greater freedom to raise and lower rates. Minimum rates were defined by variable cost of production. The burden of proof for setting maximum rates now fell on the shipper rather than the carrier, and the Act gave the railroads considerable freedom to negotiate long-term contracts with shippers. The Staggers Act also enabled carriers to abandon unprofitable lines more easily, as well as facilitating mergers with other lines.

As we have seen, much of the railroad legislation over the years has focused in one way or another upon the financial problems of railroads. Although railroads were facing stiff competition from motor carriers, a major difference between railroad transport and other forms of intercity transport, with the exception of pipelines, is that railroads own, operate, and maintain their rights of way and terminals (which include freight yards, sidings, and passenger stations). Airline companies and motor carriers have relatively low fixed costs, because they are not responsible for investment in nor maintenance of the infrastructures that they use. Airlines must pay for the use of airports and airways, but they neither build nor maintain these facilities. Similarly, motor carriers are not responsible for building and operating interstate highways, arterials, and local roads. Water carriers similarly experience high variable and relative low fixed costs, since waterways are generally nature's gift, and their development and maintenance fall to the federal government. Pipeline companies, on the other hand, either own or lease their rights of way, but must construct and maintain the pipelines and pumping stations used for transporting gas and oil. As a result, they also have a high proportion of fixed to variable costs of production.

The presence of large fixed costs leads to an important question regarding a railroads' optimal strategy for competing with other intercity modes for freight traffic. Is the railroad industry characterized by short-run increasing returns to density and, if so, can railroads significantly reduce their average variable costs by more efficiently utilizing fixed factors of production; that is, by moving down their short-run average cost curve? A related question is the effect upon short-run variable costs when the scale of operations is increased. If an increase in fixed factors leads to a significant reduction in variable costs, then the investment in expanded capacity would be worthwhile. Braeutigam et al. (1984) explored these and some other questions in a study on the short-run cost structure for a large Class I railroad during a 35-month period from January 1976 through November 1978.

Econometric specification of railroad short-run variable costs

Equation (6.3) tells us that short-run total variable costs depend upon output, input prices, the fixed factor of production, and technology. In their analysis of rail costs, Braeutigam et al. (1984) specified the following translog empirical total variable cost model:

$$\ln STVC(T;p,o,k) - \ln \overline{STVC}(T;p,o,k)$$
$$= \alpha_1(\ln T - \ln \bar{T}) + \alpha_2(\ln p_l - \ln \bar{p}_l)$$
$$+ \alpha_3(\ln p_f - \ln \bar{p}_f) + \alpha_4(\ln p_e - \ln \bar{p}_e)$$
$$+ \alpha_5(\ln o_{spd} - \ln \bar{o}_{spd}) + \alpha_6(\ln \text{track} - \ln \overline{\text{track}})$$
$$+ \text{"second-order and interaction terms"}$$
$$+ \varepsilon \qquad (6.11)$$

where *STVC* refers to short-run total variable costs, which depend upon output *T*, the prices of inputs *p*, operating characteristics *o*, and the fixed factor of production *k*. The bar (¯) is used to denote the "average sample value" of a variable. Notice in equation (6.11) that the dependent variable is $\ln STVC(T;p,o,k) - \ln \overline{STVC}(T;p,o,k)$ rather than $\ln STVC(T;p,o,k)$. This specification eliminates the constant term from the empirical cost function, but has *no effect* on the interpretation of the first-order coefficients.

The definition of each variable included in the empirical cost model is given below:

- Output – this is measured as the Number of Carloads of freight that the rail carrier moved each month.
- Input prices – in the short run, the variable factors of production are fuel (f), labor (l), and equipment (e). A price for each variable factor is entered in the empirical cost function.
- Operating characteristics – the only operating characteristic included in this model is Average Speed of service (o_{spd}), measured in miles per day for loaded cars and defined as total loaded car–miles per month divided by total loaded car–days-on-line per month. In contrast to other cost models, where operating characteristics reflect differences in the underlying technology across firms, average speed is a quality-of-service variable. Since this analysis is based upon the rail operations of *one* firm over a relatively short 35-month period, it is reasonable to assume that there is little change in technology. Quality of service, however, is a relevant consideration and included in the model as average speed of service.
- Fixed factor of production – among the various factors of production – including track, switches, land, and buildings – that are fixed in rail operations, miles of track is the largest component and is used in this study to measure the diverse fixed factors that the rail company uses. Although during the 35-month sample period, actual miles of track varied little, the rail company was investing in track, which suggests that it was improving the quality of existing track. To measure fixed factors of production, therefore, "Effective Miles of Track" was used. A change in Effective Miles of Track from one month to the next is measured as the difference between gross track investment and track depreciation for the month.[4]

Hypotheses

Similar to our analysis of motor carrier and airline cost structures, the rail cost model in equation (6.11) permits several hypotheses on rail operations to be examined:

HYPOTHESIS 1 Holding all else constant, including effective miles of track (that is, the fixed factor of production), rail firm technology is expected to exhibit increasing returns to capital stock utilization, $\varepsilon_{o|k} > 1$.[5] By more efficient utilization of capital investment, a railroad can reduce its unit cost of production. Thus, a 1% increase in output is expected to increase costs by less than 1%, which is equivalent to the hypothesis that $\alpha_1 = 1/\varepsilon_{o|k}$ is positive and less than one.

HYPOTHESIS 2 Since increases in speed, all else constant, reduce the time of travel, Average Speed reflects a railroad's quality of service, and increases in Average Speed are expected to reduce the cost of the rail service. In general, railroads optimally set speeds so that, at the margin, the marginal cost of a 1 mile per hour increase in speed equals the marginal revenue from a 1 mile per hour increase. For each of the

35 months in the sample period, Braeutigam et al. (1984) calculated the marginal revenue of speed and discovered that this was negative for 65% of the time. Since an optimal rail speed implies a positive rather than negative marginal revenue, the authors concluded that, at least in the short run, the average speed for this rail line is determined exogenously by competitive forces. If this firm is to successfully compete with other rail lines and motor carriers, it must offer a speed of service comparable to that of its competitors. This implies that when input prices, the Number of Carloads, and Effective Miles of Track are held constant, an exogenous increase in Average Speed will decrease total variable costs. α_5, therefore, is expected to be negative.

HYPOTHESIS 3 As we have previously seen, cost-minimization implies that the coefficients on input prices reflect the share of each input in total variable costs. We expect, therefore, that $0 < \alpha_i < 1$ $(i = 2, 3, 4)$ and $\alpha_2 + \alpha_3 + \alpha_4 = 1$.

HYPOTHESIS 4 How will an increase in Effective Miles of Track affect the rail company's short-run total variable costs? Suppose that you're operating the railroad on substandard track and you incur variable costs equal to $5 million per month. The variable costs include maintenance expenditures to assure that the track provide a certain level of serviceability. If, during the next month, you suddenly find that track quality has improved then, with no other changes, your operating costs will likely be less than $5 million. The reason is that your maintenance expenditures are less, since the costs of providing a given level of serviceability are less on higher-quality track.[6] Thus, an increase in Effective Miles of Track, the fixed factor of production, is expected to reduce total variable costs, which implies that α_6 will have a negative sign.

Estimation results

Table 6.1 reports the first-order coefficients for the translog empirical cost model of a Class I railroad. Are the results consistent with expectations? Generally, yes. With the exception of Average Speed, all of the first-order coefficients have their expected signs as well as *t*-statistics above 3.0 in absolute value, which indicates that we can reject the null hypothesis that each coefficient equals zero (based upon a one- or two-tail test). Although, as expected, the negative sign on Average Speed tells us that an increase in quality of service reduces total variable cost at the sample mean (and all else held constant), its *t*-statistic is less than one. For this variable, we cannot reject the null hypothesis that Average Speed is not an important determinant of variable cost at the sample mean.

What do the results tells us quantitatively? First, a 1% increase in the price of labor, equipment, and fuel, respectively, increases the short-run total variable cost by 0.52%, 0.28%, and 0.19%. In addition, from Shephard's lemma, we see that, at 52.5% of the total, labor makes up the bulk of the short-run variable costs for this rail carrier. Also, as expected, the sum of the input price coefficients is one.

The coefficient on the Number of Carloads, our measure of rail output, is 0.3984. This is significantly below unity and says that, at the sample mean, a 1% increase in the Number of Carloads, all else held constant, will increase the short-run total variable costs by 0.398%. If we relate this result to the cost curves in figures 6.1 and 6.2, this rail company is operating to the left of its minimum point on the short-run average variable cost curve and the firm could lower variable costs by increasing its current use of the fixed factor of production. At the sample mean, the rail firm is operating under increasing returns to capital stock utilization. We also see from table 6.1 that the coefficient on Effective Track Miles is negative, as expected, and implies that a 1% increase in the quality of its roadbed reduces short-run total variable costs by 0.277%.

Table 6.1 The translog cost function regression model for a Class I rail company: first-order coefficients at the sample mean[a]

Regressor	Coefficient Estimate (t-statistic)	Interpretation
Number of Carloads	0.3984 (5.7)	Elasticity of short-run total cost with respect to output T at the sample mean
Price of Labor	0.5253 (9.6)	Share of labor in short-run total costs, evaluated at the sample mean
Price of Equipment	0.2845 (11.5)	Share of equipment in short-run total costs, evaluated at the sample mean
Price of Fuel	0.1902 (3.2)	Share of fuel in short-run total costs, evaluated at the sample mean
Average Speed	−0.0659 (−0.88)	Elasticity of short-run total costs with respect to average speed, evaluated at the sample mean
Effective Track Miles	−0.2771 (−3.12)	Elasticity of short-run total cost with respect to effective track miles, at the sample mean

[a] The authors did not report the R^2 for this study. The estimated translog cost function has the following form:

$$\ln STVC(T;p,o) - \ln \overline{STVC}(T;p,o,k) = \alpha_1(\ln T - \ln \bar{T}) + \sum_{i=2}^{4}\alpha_i(\ln p_i - \ln \bar{p}_i)$$
$$+ \alpha_5(\ln o_i - \ln \bar{o}_i) + \alpha_6(\ln track_i - \ln \overline{track}_i)$$
$$+ \text{“second-order and interaction terms”} + \varepsilon$$

Source: Braeutigam et al. (1984), table 1, p. 13

Short-run factor demand elasticities and elasticities of substitution

Short-run own-price and input substitution elasticities are summarized in table 6.2. The factor price elasticities are all below unity, which indicates that labor, fuel, and equipment are relatively *inelastic* at the sample mean. And, holding all else constant, the positive sign on each of the input pairs tells us that each input is a substitute for the other input at the sample mean. Thus, a 10% increase in the relative price of labor, all else constant, increases the equipment : labor ratio by 7.5% and the fuel : labor ratio by 5.1% at the sample mean.

Comments

The translog empirical cost function identified in equation (6.9) and presented in table 6.2 does not include a constant term. If we set all variables to their sample means and the error term

Table 6.2 Short-run own factor demand elasticities and elasticities of substitution at the sample mean: Class I rail carrier, January 1976–November 1978

	Labor	Equipment	Fuel
Own-Price Elasticity	−0.31	−0.53	−0.48
Elasticity of Substitution[a]			
Labor	–	0.75	0.51
Equipment	0.75	–	0.75
Fuel	0.51	0.75	–

[a] Note that the estimated elasticities of substitution are symmetric. The elasticity of substitution of labor for capital, for example, is the same as that of capital for labor.
Source: Braeutigam et al. (1984)

at its assumed zero mean, then the right-hand side of equation (6.9) is zero. Without a constant term, we maintain the equality if we also define the dependent variable as $\ln STVC - \ln \overline{STVC}$ and evaluate *STVC* at its mean, $\overline{STVC}$. Alternatively, if we have a constant term α_0 on the right-hand side of equation (6.9), then evaluating all variables on the right-hand side at their mean values causes all terms to become zero, except for the constant α_0. In this case, it is appropriate to define the dependent variable as ln *STVC* since, as we have previously seen, $\exp(\alpha_0)$ provides an estimate of *STVC* at the sample mean.

Second, the model presented in this section provides insights into the short-run costs and production technology of a large rail carrier, but is silent on the long-run considerations, including long-run economies of scale.

In additional work, Braeutigam et al. found two important characteristics of this carrier's long-run cost structure. First, at the sample mean, the carrier was found to operate under long-run economies of scale, locating the carrier on the downward portion of its *long-run* average cost curve. Second, at least for the rail carrier under study, Effective Track Miles would have to be tripled before exhausting these long-run utilization economies. If, similar to this carrier, all Class I rail carriers are operating with increasing returns to capital utilization over wide ranges in output, a competitive strategy based upon exploiting increasing returns to utilization would not seem to be feasible, since it would require significant investment in the roadbed infrastructure.

CASE STUDY – PROFIT MARGINS IN THE AIRLINE INDUSTRY

In the short run, the standard of economic performance is whether a firm makes an economic profit.[7] If per period revenues exceed short-run total costs, economic profits are positive and the firm makes more than a normal return on investment. Conversely, if a firm's short-run costs exceed revenues, the firm experiences an economic loss and the firm makes a less than normal return on investment. What determines a firm's short-run profitability? From equation (6.4), the firm's short-run economic profits, given some level of output *T*, depend upon the price of the output, the prices of inputs, fixed factors of production (which primarily reflects capital), and the state of technology (reflected by a firm's operating environment). Complementing these factors is a firm's management, an oftentimes intangible but important input that differentiates one firm's financial success from that of another.

Econometric specification of firm profitability

In their work on the US airline industry, Morrison and Winston (1995) developed and estimated an empirical model of airline carrier short-run profitability, measured by annual rate of return, for the period 1970–88. Their empirical model is given as follows:

$$\begin{aligned}&\text{Annual Rate of Return} = \alpha_1 + \alpha_2\text{Average Fare} + \alpha_3\text{Average Compensation}\\&+ \alpha_4\text{Fuel Price} + \alpha_5\text{Maintenance Expense} + \alpha_6(\text{\% Hub Enplanements})\\&+ \alpha_7(\text{1978–83 CRS Dummy}) + \alpha_8(\text{1984–88 CRS Dummy}) + \alpha_9\text{Average Length of Haul}\\&+ \alpha_{10}\text{Average Load Factor} + \alpha_{11}\text{Route Density} + \alpha_{12}\text{President's Carrier Experience}\\&+ \alpha_{13}\text{President's Previous Airline Experience} + \alpha_{14}\text{President's Education Dummy}\\&+ \alpha_{15}\text{Vice-President's Carrier Experience} + \alpha_{16}\text{Vice-President's Education Dummy} + \varepsilon\end{aligned} \quad (6.12)$$

where ε is an error term.

Hypotheses

Based upon our analysis of short-run economic profits and the underlying determinants of profits, we can specify the following hypotheses associated with the empirical profitability model in equation (6.12):[8]

HYPOTHESIS 1 The first two lines in equation (6.9) identify an air carrier's output price, Average Fare, and the prices of three inputs – labor, fuel, and maintenance. Holding all else constant, an increase in output price increases firm profitability, whereas an increase in inputs costs reduces profitability. Thus, it is expected that $\alpha_2 > 0$, $\alpha_3 < 0$, $\alpha_4 < 0$, and $\alpha_5 < 0$.

HYPOTHESIS 2 An airline's technology is reflected in the empirical model by two sets of variables related to the carrier's network and operating characteristics. The "% Hub Enplanements" is the proportion of total enplanements at a carrier's hub airport, and reflects the size of a carrier's operations at hub airports. Large carriers with extensive networks are more likely to have developed a computer reservation system (CRS), in order to exploit the economies associated with large-scale operations. All else constant, it is expected that more hub enplanements and development of a CRS will increase an air carrier's profitability. In addition, in order to test the hypothesis that a CRS may not impact profitability immediately, but will do so over time as airlines use the systems to expand their networks, the CRS dummy variable is divided into two separate variables, one corresponding to the time period 1978–83 and the other to the time period 1984–8. It is expected, therefore, that $\alpha_6 > 0$, $\alpha_7 > 0$, $\alpha_8 > 0$, and $\alpha_7 < \alpha_8$.

As we saw in the last chapter, Average Length of Haul, Average Load Factor, and Route Density are technology-related operating characteristics that are expected to increase the efficiency with which airlines deliver transportation services to their customers. All else constant, an increase in airline efficiency is expected to increase profits, so that we expect $\alpha_9 > 0$, $\alpha_{10} > 0$, and $\alpha_{11} > 0$.

HYPOTHESIS 3 The last set of variables in equation (6.9) reflects the characteristics of an air carrier's top management. These variables test whether a firm's profitability is related to the carrier experience of the President and Vice-President, the industry experience of the carrier's

President, and the educational background of the President and Vice-President. Holding all else constant, the coefficients on each of these variables are expected to be positive.

Estimation results

Table 6.3 reports the regression estimation results on airline profitability, where we see that the included variables explain 62% of the variation in firm profitability. Moreover, the estimation results are generally consistent with our stated hypotheses. As expected, an increase in the price of air travel increases profitability, whereas an increase in input costs lowers profitability, all else constant. The fare results, for example, indicate that a 1 cent per mile increase in the average fare increases a carrier's annual rate of return by 6%. Further, the results on costs indicate, as you might expect, that fuel price increases can significantly impact a carrier's profitability. We see in table 6.3 that $1 per gallon increase in the price of fuel reduces a carrier's profitability by 26.6%. This can be contrasted with a 5.5% decrease in the rate of return from a $1 million dollar increase in maintenance expenditures per aircraft.

Consistent with hypothesis 2, we also see that a carrier's route network, as well as its operating characteristics, have their expected impacts. A 1% increase in enplanements at the carrier's hub airport raises the carrier's rate of return by a modest 0.13%. On the other hand, if a carrier developed and managed a computer reservation system, it had little initial effect, as seen by the

Table 6.3 A regression model for an airline carrier's short-run annual rates of return, 1978–88

Regressor	Coefficient Estimate (*t*-statistic)
Constant term	−1.679 (−3.0)[a]
Average Fare (cents per mile)	0.0637 (3.5)[a]
Average Compensation (thousand $ per employee)	−0.0070 (−2.2)[b]
Fuel Price ($ per gallon)	−0.2661 (−2.5)[a]
Maintenance Expense (million $ per aircraft)	−0.0550 (−1.8)[b]
% Hub Enplanements (%)	0.0013 (0.43)
1978–83 CRS Dummy	0.0140 (0.38)
1984–8 CRS Dummy	0.0700 (2.0)[b]
Average Length of Haul ('000 miles)	0.3119 (2.1)[b]
Average Load Factor (%)	0.0147 (3.1)[a]
Route Density (passenger-miles divided by route miles)	0.0037 (1.4)
President's Carrier Experience (years)	0.0043 (2.7)[a]
President's Previous Airline Experience (years)	0.0063 (1.9)[b]
President's Education Dummy (1 if MBA, 0 otherwise)	0.0408 (1.7)[b]
Vice-President's Carrier Experience (years)	0.0017 (1.9)[b]
Vice-President's Education Dummy (1 if MBA or law degree, 0 otherwise)	0.0372 (1.5)
$R^2 = 0.62$	
Number of observations = 159	

[a] Significant at 0.05 level, two-tail test.
[b] Significant at 0.01 level, one-tail test.
Source: Adapted from Morrison and Winston (1995), table 5-1, p. 99

insignificance of "1978–83 CRS Dummy", but it did have a much larger effect over time. The coefficient for "1984–88 CRS Dummy" is positive and significant, which indicates that a carrier's CRS system raises its annual rate of return by 7%.

The positive sign on each of the three carrier operating characteristics indicates that carriers experience economies of distance, economies of capacity utilization, and economies of density. A 200-mile increase in Average Length of Haul, for example, would raise a carrier's annual rate of return by 6%, and a 10% increase in the Average Load Factor would raise profitability by 14.7%. The weakest of the effects in terms of its estimated effect and statistical significance is route density. A unit increase in the number of passengers served per route mile has an expected 0.3% effect on a carrier's annual rate of return.

We also see in table 6.3 that management experience and training are important to a firm's profitability, consistent with hypothesis 3. A President's carrier and industry experience are both important to firm profitability, although the magnitude of the effect is relatively small. However, human capital investment in the form of an MBA degree has a much larger impact on annual rate of return. From the results in table 6.3, carriers whose President has an MBA degree earn a 4% higher annual rate of return in comparison with carriers whose President does not have an MBA. We see a similar result, although somewhat weaker statistically, for Vice-President education. The estimated effect of a postgraduate degree for the Vice-President (in the form of an MBA or law degree) is a 3.7% boost in the annual rate of return.

Comments

The results from table 6.3 indicate that a carrier's network, rather than its size, is more important to financial success. In addition to "% Hub Enplanements," Morrison and Winston included other size-related variables, including number of cities served and total departures, but these were found to have no effect on profitability. The one exception to this is a computer reservation system. Only carriers with large-scale operations can afford the high developmental costs of these systems, but they do reap benefits in the form of higher annual rates of return, all else constant. On the other hand, both large and small carriers can exploit the network economies associated with length of haul, route density, and load factors in order to boost profitability.

Morrison and Winston used their results to evaluate whether management matters much in a carrier's profitability. Indeed, it does. The top three performers were USAir, Delta, and American, while the bottom three were Continental, Eastern, and Pan American. Assuming that Continental, Eastern, and Pan American had the same President and Vice-President characteristics as USAir, Delta, and American, the authors found that the annual rates of return for the low performers would have risen significantly. For example, under Delta's management, Continental, Eastern, and Pan American's annual rate of return would have risen by 56.5%, 163.0%, and 75.0% respectively.

THE RELATIONSHIP BETWEEN SHORT-RUN AND LONG-RUN COSTS

The difference between the long-run and short-run costs is that short-run costs are conditioned on a fixed factor of production whereas, in the long run, cost minimization implies that all inputs are used optimally. Suppose, for example, that a firm determines that the minimum cost of producing T_1 units of output requires a level of capital equal to $K_1 = k(T_1;w,r,\gamma)$. Its long-run costs will be

$$C = wl(T_1;w,r,\gamma) + rk(T_1;w,r,\gamma)$$
$$= C(T_1;w,r,\gamma) \quad (6.13)$$

Having purchased K_1 units of capital, the firm is now in the short run and faces a cost function given by

$$STC = wl(T_1;w,r,\gamma,K_1) + rK_1$$
$$= STC(T_1;w,r,\gamma,K_1) \quad (6.14)$$

As long as the firm continues to produce T_1 output, it long-run costs C will equal its short-run costs STC. That is, if the level of capital held fixed in the short run *equals* the optimal amount of capital required to produce a specified output level, short-run and long-run costs are identical.

Suppose, on the other hand, that, responding to an increase in demand, the firm in the short run increases its rate of output from T_1 to T_2. Short-run costs are no longer equal to long-run costs since, in the short run, capital is still fixed at K_1, so that the only way to increase output is by employing more labor. In the long run, however, the firm increases its use of labor but also optimally raises its capital investment from K_1 to K_2. Thus,

$$STC(T_2;w,r,\gamma,K_1) > C(T_2;w,r,\gamma) = wl(T_2;w,r,\gamma) + rk(T_2;w,r,\gamma) \quad (6.15)$$

where long-run costs $C(T_2;w,r,\gamma)$ are associated with level of capital K_2. Every point on a long-run cost curve corresponds to an optimal level of capital and represents the minimum possible cost of producing each level of output. Each short-run cost curve, on the other hand, is conditioned on a fixed amount of capital. Thus, the short-run cost curve is *tangent* to the long-run cost curve only at that level of output at which the fixed amount of capital coincides with the optimal level of capital. At all other output levels, short-run cost is greater than long-run cost. For three different capital levels, figure 6.4 illustrates this relationship between long-run and

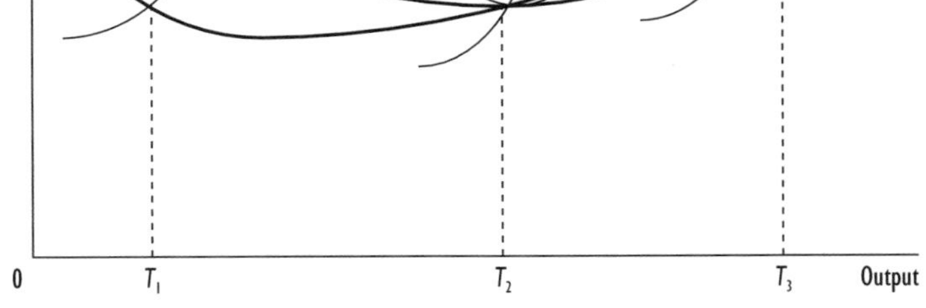

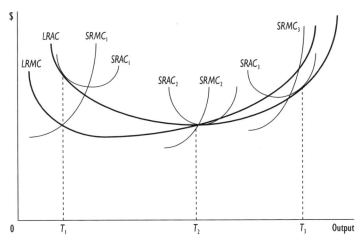

Figure 6.4 Cost curve tangencies and lowest cost outputs. T_i (i = 1, 2, 3), lowest-cost output in the short run and long run when scale of plant is K_i.

short-run average and marginal cost curves. Note that each short-run average cost curve is tangent at one point, representing optimal use of all inputs, to the long-run cost curve. Also, since capital is optimally employed at the tangency point, it is also true that, for small changes in output, short-run and long-run marginal cost are equal. This is seen in figure 6.4 by noting that, at the tangency point, long-run and short-run marginal cost curves intersect. In the following section, we illustrate this relationship between short-run and long-run costs with an analysis of urban bus transportation costs.

CASE STUDY – URBAN BUS TRANSPORTATION COST AND PRODUCTION

An often-stated economic argument for the justification of a single bus system, a market structure that characterizes most urban mass transit markets in the United States, is the presence of large economies of scale.[9] There are a variety of reasons why urban bus systems might experience increasing returns to scale. The simplest argument is to imagine multiple bus systems operating nonoverlapping routes in a city and serving an equal share of the total market. Since each system has its own administrative staff, merging the systems produces a single metropolitan transit authority, whose output is total market demand but whose administrative staff does not increase proportionately. Thus, the single authority exploits the savings in overhead to provide bus services at a lower average cost of production.

But this will not be the only source of scale economies for bus systems. We have seen in the motor carrier, airline, and railroad sectors that firms can exploit economies of capital stock utilization, traffic density, and generalized economies of scale. Bus systems can respond in any number of different ways to increasing demands for their services. They can add capacity in the form of additional rolling stock (that is, buses), they can alter their existing route structure, service frequency, and bus stop locations to better accommodate the increased demand, and they can expand their network of services beyond existing boundaries. Or they can implement any combination of these actions. In general, bus systems can be very flexible in their responses to changes in the demand for their services. In one of the first studies on this issue, Viton (1981) analyzed the cost and production structure of bus systems operating in the United States and Canada in 1975.

Short-run total variable costs of urban bus systems

Viton specified a translog empirical cost model in which short-run total variable cost was assumed to depend upon a bus system's produced output, defined as vehicle–miles (millions), input prices for labor (p_l) and fuel (p_f) and a fixed factor of production (buses), which is defined as the number of buses in the bus system. Specifically, the empirical cost model is

$$\begin{aligned}\ln STVC(T;p,k) &= \alpha_0 + \alpha_1(\ln T - \ln \bar{T}) + \alpha_2(\ln p_l - \ln \bar{p}_l) \\ &\quad + \alpha_3(\ln p_f - \ln \bar{p}_f) + \alpha_4(\ln \text{buses} - \ln \overline{\text{buses}}) \\ &\quad + \text{"second-order and interaction terms"} \\ &\quad + \varepsilon \qquad (6.16)\end{aligned}$$

Data for this analysis was based upon 54 urban transit systems operating in the United States and Canada in 1975, and the sample included both large and small bus properties. The largest system was Chicago, Illinois, which produced 88.5 million vehicle–miles, and the smallest system was Greenfield, Massachusetts, which produced 168,000 vehicle–miles.

Hypotheses

Since the underlying hypotheses for output and factor prices are similar to those for the short-run total variable cost function that we identified for the rail carrier, we summarize them briefly. First, we shall examine the hypothesis that urban bus transit systems operate under increasing returns to capital stock utilization, $\varepsilon_{o|k} > 1$.[10] From the empirical cost model specified in equation (6.16), increasing returns is equivalent to an output cost elasticity that is less than one. Since $E_{\text{Cost},T} = 1/\varepsilon_{o|k}$, then $1/E_{\text{Cost},T} = 1/\alpha_1$. Second, assuming cost-minimizing behavior on the part of bus systems, at the sample mean, we expect $\alpha_2 > 0$, $\alpha_3 > 0$, and $\alpha_2 + \alpha_3 = 1$ (by Shephard's lemma).

Third, what is the effect of an increase in the fixed factor of production on short-run total variable costs. A unit increase in a fixed factor of production has two effects. First, it increases the fixed cost of production by the unit cost of capital. Second, it lowers short-run total variable costs. Thus, a firm continues to expand its capital base as long as the savings on operating costs more than offset the increase in fixed costs. At the point at which the variable cost savings just equals the unit price of the fixed factor, the firm is employing an optimal amount of capital and we have tangency between short-run and long-run cost curves.[11] That is,

savings on variable costs = opportunity cost of capital

$$\Rightarrow \quad -\frac{\Delta STVC}{\Delta K} = r$$

where the negative sign converts the savings on variable costs to a positive number. Thus, holding all else constant, we expect an increase in a bus system's rolling stock to decrease short-run total variable costs; $\alpha_4 < 0$.

Estimation results

Table 6.4 summarizes the translog estimation results for urban bus systems. The high R^2 indicates that the empirical cost function explains over 99% of the variation in short-run total variable costs. Are the results consistent with our hypotheses?

At the sample mean, the coefficient for vehicle–miles, our output variable, is 0.56. Holding all else constant, a 1% increase in vehicle miles leads to a 0.56% increase in short-run total variable costs, which suggests strong economies of capital stock utilization. Although significantly different from zero, is the coefficient for vehicle miles significantly different from one? Yes. Calculating the ratio $(\hat{\alpha}_1 - 1)/s_{\hat{\alpha}_1}$ to test this hypothesis yields a t-statistic equal to −2.8, which rejects the null hypothesis that $\alpha_1 = 1$ at the 0.01 level for a two-tail test.

Also, as expected, the coefficients for the share of labor and fuel are positive and sum to one. Not surprisingly, at just over 80%, labor comprises the lion's share of short-run total variable costs at the sample mean.

Our third hypothesis was that an increase in rolling stock, all else constant, leads to a decrease in short-run total variable cost. For the sample mean, the results from table 6.4 *do not* confirm this hypothesis. From the table, we see that a

Table 6.4 The translog cost function regression model for urban bus systems, 1975: first-order coefficients at the sample mean[a]

Regressor	Coefficient Estimate (*t*-statistic)	Interpretation
Constant term	2.63 (9.8)	Logarithm of short-run total variable cost, at the sample mean
Vehicle–Miles (millions)	0.561 (3.6)	Elasticity of short-run total cost with respect to output *T* at the sample mean
Price of Labor	0.777 (18.4)	Share of labor in short-run total costs, evaluated at the sample mean
Price of Fuel	0.223 (18.4)	Share of fuel in short-run total costs, evaluated at the sample mean
Number of Buses	0.566 (3.7)	Elasticity of short-run total cost with respect to buses, at the sample mean
$R^2 = 0.992$		

[a] The estimated translog cost function has the following form:

$$\ln STVC(T;p,k) = \alpha_0 + \alpha_1(\ln T - \ln \bar{T}) + \sum_{i=2}^{3}\alpha_i(\ln p_i - \ln \bar{p}_i) + \alpha_5(\ln buses_i - \ln \overline{buses})$$

$$+ \text{“second-order and interaction terms”} + \varepsilon$$

Source: Viton (1981), table I, p. 294

1% increase in rolling stock *increases* short-run total variable costs by 0.57%. As discussed below, an explanation for the unexpected positive sign is that bus systems are operating with considerable excess capacity.

Utilization economies and short-run costs for specific systems

For various bus systems in his analysis, Viton calculated economies of capital stock utilization and short-run costs in order to examine whether these varied by size of operation. Table 6.5 identifies five bus systems that vary in size from 200,000 vehicle–miles per year up to 88.5 million vehicle–miles. Regardless of size, each bus system experiences strong economies of utilization. For each of the five systems, the null hypothesis of constant returns to capital stock utilization returns is rejected at the 0.05 level. And, consistent with short-run economies of utilization, each of the five systems is operating on the downward portion of its short-run average cost curve. Since short-run marginal cost is less than short-run average variable cost in this

Table 6.5 Short run economies of capital stock utilization and costs

Location	1975 Output[a]	Economies of Capital Stock Utilization[b]	Short-Run Average Variable Cost ($)[c]	Short-Run Marginal Cost ($)[d]
Chicago, Illinois	88.5	1.96 (1.6)	2.18	1.11 (1.7)
Ottawa, Ontario	20.0	1.67 (1.9)	1.26	0.76 (3.0)
Albany, New York	5.5	1.78 (3.1)	1.1	0.62 (5.3)
Huntington, West Virginia	0.9	1.67 (3.5)	0.91	0.54 (5.1)
Greenfield, Massachusetts	0.2	1.96 (1.8)	0.94	0.48 (1.9)

[a] Output is defined in million vehicle–miles.
[b] Economies of utilization ($\varepsilon_{o|k}$) can be estimated in either of two ways: (1) by taking the ratio of short-run average variable cost in column 3 and the short-run marginal cost in column 4; (2) the inverse of the cost elasticity with respect to output, which equals the reciprocal of the output coefficient reported in table 6.4. The measures reported here use the first method where the *t*-statistic in parentheses tests the null hypothesis that there are no economies of capital stock utilization. Using the alternative approach, capital stock utilization at the sample mean is 1/0.561 = 1.78.
[c] Short-run average variable cost (*SRAVC*) gives the cost per vehicle–mile and is based on actual data.
[d] Short-run marginal cost gives the cost per vehicle–mile and is defined as $((1/\varepsilon_{o|k}))SRAVC$. The *t*-statistic in parentheses tests the null hypothesis that the short-run marginal cost is zero.
Source: Adapted from Viton (1981), table II, p. 296

range, increases in output lead to decreases in the short-run unit cost of production.

It is important to understand what the information in table 6.4 is giving. Although we do see that both short-run marginal cost and short-run average cost are increasing with output, this is *not* giving us points on a particular short-run cost curve. Rather, the different output levels are associated with *different levels of capital*. Thus, the short-run marginal and average variable cost figures reported in table 6.4 reflect points on different short-run cost curves.

Optimal fleet sizes and long-run costs

Are bus systems optimally capitalized, or do they exhibit over- or undercapitalization? To answer this question, Viton calculated the optimal bus fleet size for each of the five bus operations identified in table 6.4. Optimal bus fleet size is obtained from the equilibrium condition, $-\Delta STVC/\Delta K = r$, which says that a firm continues adding rolling stock as long as the savings in variable costs from one more bus exceed the unit bus price. The estimated empirical cost function was used to calculate savings in variable costs, and Viton estimated the cost of renovating an existing bus to be $3,000 (in 1975 prices).[12] Assuming that bus renovation lengthens a bus's useful life by 5 years and given a 6.75% rate of interest, this implies an annual capital cost of $727.[13] The results are reported in table 6.6.

Each of the bus properties in table 6.4 is *overcapitalized*. The optimal fleet ranges between 42% and 66% of the existing fleet, where the higher proportions are generally associated with the smaller bus companies. Although this doesn't imply that the bus properties should immediately downsize their fleets, it does have implications for replacement. The bus companies may want to move to the optimal scale of operations through attrition. As buses are retired from service, bus companies could more efficiently

Table 6.6 Optimal bus fleet size

Location	Observed Fleet	Optimal Fleet[a]
Chicago, Illinois	2,777	1,181
Ottawa, Ontario	629	333
Albany, New York	205	111
Huntington, West Virginia	36	23
Greenfield, Massachusetts	9	6

[a] Based upon $3,000 renovation costs, 6.75% rate of interest, and a five-year extended bus life.
Source: Viton (1981), table IV, p. 299

Table 6.7 Long-run economies of scale and costs[a]

Location	Economies of Scale[b]	Long-Run Average Cost ($)	Long-Run Marginal Cost ($)
Chicago, Illinois	0.87	1.48	1.70
Ottawa, Ontario	0.92	1.17	1.26
Albany, New York	0.98	0.87	0.89
Huntington, West Virginia	1.06	0.90	0.85
Greenfield, Massachusetts	1.15	0.92	0.80

[a] Based upon optimal fleet size in table 6.6 and a replacement cost of $3,000.
[b] Economies of scale are given by the reciprocal of the cost elasticity with respect to output, $1/(E_{\text{Cost},T})$, which equals long-run average cost (*LRAC*) divided by long-run marginal cost (*LRMC*). The ratio of *LRAC* in column 2 and *LRMC* in column 3 is the economies of scale measure reported in column 2.
Source: Viton (1981), table V, p. 300

utilize the remaining buses rather than purchase new capital.

Based upon the optimal fleet sizes identified in table 6.4, Viton estimated long-run scale economies and long-run average and marginal costs for each of the properties. The results of these calculations are reported in table 6.5. In contrast to the short run, where each bus system operated under short-run economies of capital stock utilization, we see in table 6.5 that smaller companies operated under long-run increasing returns to scale, reflected by a cost elasticity less than 1.0, whereas the larger companies operated under long-run diseconomies of scale. Equivalently, we see that long-run marginal cost is less than the long-run average cost for those companies operating under long-run economies of scale, whereas the long-run marginal cost is greater than the long-run average cost for those companies operating under long-run diseconomies of scale. These relationships should not be surprising, since long-run economies of scale are defined as the inverse of the cost elasticity of output:

$$s = \frac{1}{(\Delta \ln C)/(\Delta \ln Y)} = \frac{LRAC}{LRMC}$$

From table 6.5, for example, long-run economies of scale for Chicago are calculated as 0.87 = 1/1.15 = 1.48/1.70.

Comments

The above results are informative for a number of reasons. First, they indicate that in the short run bus companies will have trouble covering their variable costs of service. Regardless of size, each of the bus systems operated with increasing returns to capital utilization, such that short-run marginal costs were less than short-run average variable costs. If bus companies priced at marginal cost, operating losses would occur and subsidies would be required. Second, we also found that bus systems in general appear to be overcapitalized. For a subset of systems included in the study, optimal bus fleets were smaller than existing fleets, which implies that downsizing fleets, possibly through attrition, would yield cost savings to the companies. A third result was that, even with optimal fleets, smaller bus systems may require subsidies. Larger bus systems operated under decreasing returns to scale, which implies that bus fares set at long-run marginal cost would be sufficient to cover costs. For smaller companies, however, pricing at long-run marginal cost will not cover costs, since these systems were found to be operating under increasing returns to scale.

Figure 6.5 depicts the relationships between short-run utilization economies, short-run costs, long-run costs, and long-run economies of scale for urban bus systems. This graph is consistent with the reported results, and can be viewed as depicting two of the bus systems in Viton's study. The subscript refers to a particular scale of operation and the asterisk (*) refers to an optimal fleet. Thus, subscript 1 refers to a system such as Greenfield with 200,000 vehicle–miles. This system initially operated on SAC_1 and experienced short-run utilization economies; its optimal fleet was smaller than its existing fleet. Optimally, it would move to point A on SAC_1^*, where it would continue to operate with economies of capital stock utilization but also operate under long-run economies of scale. In addition, by moving leftward along the long-run average cost curve, it would operate with fewer buses. Similarly, SAC_2 reflects a large system such as Chicago's transit system, which provided 88.5 million vehicle–miles. This system was initially operating to the left of the minimum point on SAC_2, which indicates that it is operating under short-run utilization economies; its existing fleet was larger than its optimal fleet. Producing T_2^* optimally entails a move to point B on the long-run average cost curve and a leftward move on to the short-run average cost curve SAC_2^*. At

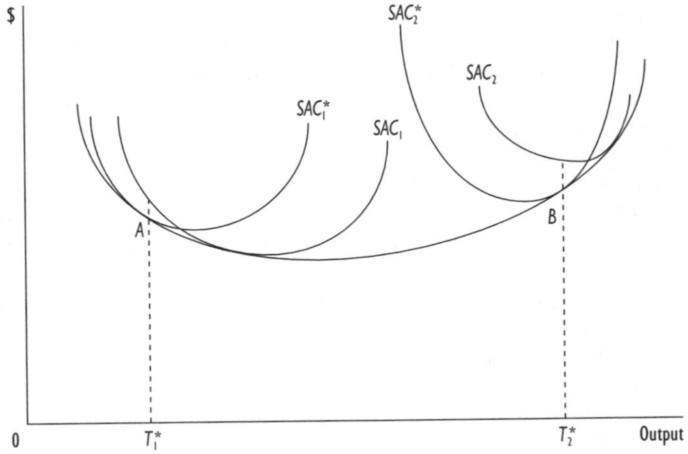

Figure 6.5 A cost and output structure consistent with Viton's study.

point B, the system would operate under short-run diseconomies of utilization, as well as long-run diseconomies of scale.

Fourth, can we identify reasons why bus systems appear to be overcapitalized? One explanation is capital subsidies for buses. The federal government provides generous capital subsidies to bus systems. The Urban Mass Transportation Act (UMTA) of 1964 initiated capital grants to transit systems. By effectively reducing the cost of purchasing buses, these capital subsidies provide economic incentives for overcapitalization, as transit systems substitute the relatively less expensive buses for other inputs in the production of transit services.[14] A second possible explanation is that the results on optimal fleet size focus explicitly upon the costs that a bus system incurs in providing transit. Although this is relevant from the system's perspective, these costs are not the correct measure of the cost of transit provision to society. The production of bus trips not only requires resource inputs provided by the bus system (labor, capital, fuel, and so forth) but also time inputs provided by bus riders. Mohring (1976) has demonstrated that when the time costs of bus users are considered, all bus companies operate under increasing returns to scale, where the long-run marginal cost is less than the long-run average cost. Increased fleet size not only adds to the costs of production, but it also reduces users' time costs. In this case, a bus system would continue to expand its fleet as long as the savings in short-run variable costs – production cost plus bus riders' time costs – are less than or equal to the unit cost of a bus. This suggests that optimal fleet size will be larger when user time costs, as well as transit property costs, are used to define the cost of service.

CHAPTER HIGHLIGHTS

- In contrast to the long run, when all inputs are variable, the short run defines a period during which at least one factor of production is held fixed. In general, inputs are not used optimally in the short run, which implies that the cost of producing a given level of output is higher in the short run than in the long run. A given short-run total and average cost curve lies everywhere above the long-run total and average cost curve, respectively, except at that level of output where short-run and long-run input use is the same;
- Firms in the short run will continue to operate as long as output price is greater than or equal to the minimum point on the average variable cost curve. For all such prices, a firm's short-run supply curve is coincident with its marginal cost curve. And the short-run market supply curve is the horizontal summation of individual firm supply curves.
- With the passage of the Act to Regulate Commerce in 1887 came the economic regulation of transportation in general, and of railroads in particular. The Act curtailed rate-setting activities of railroads and established the Interstate Commerce Commission to oversee rail pricing and market activities. The provisions of the Act were later strengthened in the Hepburn Act of 1906. Concerns about rail as well as shipper welfare were addressed in the 1920 Transportation Act. An important feature of the Hoch–Smith Resolution in 1925 was value-of-service pricing, which allowed the ICC to set transportation rates according to what the market will bear – high rates charged to shippers of high-valued commodities and low rates charged to shippers of low-valued goods.

- Four measures aimed at solving the financial crisis of the rail industry were the Rail Passenger Act of 1970, the Regional Rail Reorganization Act of 1973, the Rail Revitalization and Regulatory Act of 1976, and the Staggers Act of 1980.
- An empirical analysis of a large US rail firm's short-run variable costs found the presence of strong economies of capital utilization. Also, and consistent with economic theory, increases in the fixed factor of production decreased short-run total variable costs. Although the study also found long-run economies of scale, significant increases in roadbed infrastructure would have to occur in order to exploit these economies.
- In the short run, firm profitability depends upon output price, input price, and technology as summarized by its operating environment. An empirical analysis of short-run airline profitability confirmed these relationships. In particular, economies associated with distance, capacity utilization, and density improve an airline's financial status. Also, route network rather than firm size plays a more important role in short-run profitability, and a carrier's management was found to be an important determinant of financial success.
- An empirical analysis of urban transit in the USA revealed significant economies of capital stock utilization, regardless of the transit system's size of operations. An analysis of long-run costs found smaller systems to be operating under short-run utilization economies but long-run economies of scale; large systems were found to be operating under short-run utilization economies but long-run diseconomies of scale.

Review questions

1. Fuel costs are important inputs to any transportation activity. Suppose that real energy prices fall. Graphically depict the impact that this would have upon a firm's total short-run and long-run cost structure. Would you expect a firm's long-run response to a fall in energy prices to be greater, less, or equal to its short-run response to a fall in energy prices? What does this suggest about the firm's short-run input price elasticity of fuel relative to its long-run input price elasticity of fuel?

2. Critically evaluate the following statement: "All constraints on behavior are costly, which explains why the short-run total cost curve lies above the long-run total cost curve."

3. Assume that, in the long run, a motor carrier firm produces transportation using labor, fuel, and capital (in the form of trucks). The firm is currently producing 100,000 ton–miles.
   (a) If the short-run cost of producing 100,000 ton–miles equals the long-run cost of producing this output, is the motor carrier firm currently using its inputs efficiently? If so, why; and if not, why not?

(b) Explain why the motor carrier's long-run cost of producing output T depends upon the price of labor, the price of fuel, and the rental price of trucks, whereas the firm's short-run cost of producing T depends upon the price of labor, the price of fuel, and the *level* of trucks available to the firm.

4. (a) Define short-run average total cost, short-run average variable cost, short-run average fixed cost, and short-run marginal cost. Explain why short-run marginal cost intersects short-run average variable cost at its minimum point.
(b) What is the short-run supply curve of the firm? Why is a firm willing to offer more output when the price of the good increases?

5. According to the *Wall Street Journal* (November 1, 1995), net income for World Airways in the third quarter of 1995 was \$3.359 million, or 33 cents per share. This is a significant rebound from its 1994 third-quarter performance, in which World Airways' net income was –\$7.491 million, reflecting a loss. Around his period, the per share price of World Airways stock was around \$12.
(a) Use short-run average cost curves to explain why World Airways did not shut its operations down in the third quarter of 1994.
(b) From the information provided, can you tell whether World Airways made an economic loss, an economic profit, or a normal return on investment in the third quarter of 1995?

6. Suppose that you are given the following information on All Around Airlines:
   - The average variable cost of producing airline trips varies between 11.5 cents a mile when 50,000 trips per year are produced and 16.7 cents per mile when 500,000 trips per year are produced. Its lowest value is 11.5 cents a mile when 250,000 trips are produced.
   - The average total cost of producing trips varies between 15.3 cents per mile when 250,000 trips are produced and 17.3 cents per mile when 500,000 trips are produced. The minimum short-run average total cost is 13.0 cents when 300,000 trips are produced.

(a) Approximately, how many trips will be produced in the short run if the fare is 15.4 cents per mile?
(b) Will any trips be produced if the fare is 12.1 cents per mile? If so, why; and if not, why not?
(c) Will any trips be produced if the fare is 10 cents per mile? If so, why; and if not, why not?

7. Viton's 1981 study of urban transit costs found that urban transit firms operating in small cities (where fewer than 1 million vehicle–miles are produced annually) operate under increasing returns to scale, in medium-sized cities (which produce between 1 million and 5.5 million vehicle–miles annually) they operate under constant returns to scale, and in large cities (with over 5.5 million vehicle–miles annually) they operate under decreasing returns to scale.
(a) Assuming that fares are set at marginal cost, what do these results imply about the possibility of small-scale profitable entry in small, medium, and large cities?

(b) Based upon Viton's results, are there any benefits to decentralizing urban transit systems in the largest cities?

8. (a) Assume that, in the production of rail services, labor is the only variable input. Graphically depict a labor productivity curve. Identify the point at which diminishing returns to the fixed factor of production occurs.

(b) Over time, there will be technological progress. Identify graphically the effect of technological progress on the labor productivity curve. Holding all else constant, suppose that the level of fixed capital increases. How will this affect the labor productivity curve? Is capital investment the same as technological progress?

(c) Suppose that you are analyzing total costs for a railroad between 1950 and 1970 using a translog cost function framework. You collect information on the costs of production, input prices for labor, fuel, materials, capital, and route structure, and operating characteristics (such as average length of haul and average load). How would you account for technological progress in this study? Can you be sure that you're identifying the effect of technological progress? Why, or why not?

9. The July 7, 1993 *Wall Street Journal* provides the following information: "Northwest Airlines averted – at least for now – a threatened federal bankruptcy-law filing after its pilots' union agreed to a last-minute pact to save the carrier \$365 million over three years." Using Northwest's short-run cost curves, depict where Northwest was operating before and after the agreement with the pilots' union.

10. (a) Consider an airline that produces passenger trips with capital K and labor L. Use isocost curves and isoquants to explain why this airline's long-run cost function will depend upon its output, the passenger–miles served, the prices of K and L, and the state of technology.

(b) Now suppose that capital is held fixed at $\bar{K}$. Again use isocosts and isoquants to explain why the airline's short-run total cost will depend upon the passenger–miles served, the price of labor, the fixed level of capital, and the state of technology.

(c) Suppose that the airline is currently operating with capital held fixed at $\bar{K}$, but that it is contemplating increasing its capital investment. What condition must the airline satisfy in order to achieve an optimal level of capital given its current short-run position? Discuss the economic intuition behind this condition.

11. In a paper on public transit costs, Obeng (1985) reported the following:

< 50 buses	50–149 buses	150–557 buses
Operate under diseconomies of traffic density	Operate under economies of traffic density	Operate under economies of traffic density

(a) Are these results consistent with the findings of Viton? Where would each type of firm be operating on its respective short-run average total cost curve?

(b) In an attempt to explain these short-run results on traffic density, Obeng reported the following regression results:

$$\text{Short Run Economies of Traffic Density} = \underset{(1.45)}{0.1585} - \underset{(3.80)}{0.022}\,(\text{\% of Capacity Utilized})$$

$$R^2 = 0.39$$

where "% of Capacity Utilized" is defined as [(passenger miles)/(capacity miles)] * 100 and the *t*-statistics are in parentheses.

(i) How well does capacity utilization explain short-run economies of traffic density?

(ii) What is the relationship between short-run average total cost and short-run economies of traffic density?

(iii) Interpret the sign and magnitude of the coefficient on capacity utilization. What impact would a 10% increase in capacity utilitization have upon the short-run economies of traffic density?

12. On page 227, we reported the results of an analysis by Morrison and Winston (1995) on airline rates of return. In a previous study, Morrison and Winston (1986) undertook a similar analysis, with the results shown in table 6.8, where the cost of capital is a weighted average of debt and equity costs.

(a) Compare and contrast these findings with those in table 6.3.

Table 6.8 A regression model for an airline carrier's short-run annual rates of return, 1981–3

Dependent variable – Annual rate of return

Regressor	Coefficient Estimate (*t*-statistic)
Constant term	0.0805 (0.31)
Average Fare (dollars)	0.0017 (1.9)[a]
Average Compensation (thousand $ per year)	−0.0064 (−2.4)[b]
Fuel Price ($ per gallon)	−0.5665 (−2.4)[b]
Cost of Capital (%)	−0.0111 (−1.8)[a]
Average Length of Haul ('000 miles)	0.3877 (5.3)[b]
Average Load Factor (%)	0.9733 (3.7)[b]
Total Departures (millions)	0.1755 (2.7)[b]

$R^2 = 0.58$
Number of observations = 63

[a] Significant at 0.01 level, one-tail test.
[b] Significant at 0.05 level, two-tail test.
Source: Adapted from Morrison and Winston (1986), table 3-14, p. 38

(b) What do these results suggest regarding the impact of route network versus size on a firm's financial success?

(c) What impact does a 1% increase in the cost of capital have upon a firm's short-run success?

13. Mohring (1976) reported the following estimated relationship between oil throughput, T, horsepower, and inside diameter of pipe (due to Cookenboo, 1955):

$$T^{2.735} = \frac{HD^{4.135}}{0.01046}$$

(a) Horsepower and inside diameter are two factors of production that determine throughput. Suppose that the oil company wants to increase throughput, given that D is a fixed factor of production. What is the elasticity of throughput with respect to horsepower?

(b) For a given D and a constant unit cost of horsepower, what is the shape of the short-run average cost curve?

(c) Does the oil company experience economies of throughput with respect to inside diameter of pipe? What impact on throughput will occur from a 10% increase in the inside diameter of the pipe? Does this necessarily imply that there are economies of firm size?

NOTES

1 Recall that the point at which the marginal product begins to fall is referred to as the point of diminishing marginal returns.

2 For simplicity, this formulation assumes that all fixed costs are captured in fixed capital. In reality, there may be a variety of noncapital fixed costs, such as annual insurance payments and license fees, that firms also face.

3 Among these were the Mann–Elkins Act in 1910, the Panama Canal Act in 1912, and the Valuation Act in 1913. The Mann–Elkins Act empowered the ICC to suspend proposed rate changes and established a commerce court to facilitate the adjudication of cases. The Panama Canal Act outlawed rail carriers from having an interest in or control of any water common carrier without the approval of the ICC. The Valuation Act enabled the ICC to evaluate railroad properties as part of its rate-making capacity.

4 Let k_t define effective miles of track in period t. Then the change in k_t from one month to the next was defined as $\Delta k_t = I_t - (trk_t - trk_{t-1}) - \delta trk_{t-1}$, where I_t is gross track investment in time period t, trk_t is actual track in time period t, and δ is the monthly rate of track depreciation.

5 Keeler (1974) argues that when short-run costs are a function of output and trackage, we can distinguish between economies of traffic density and network size economies. There is some ambiguity here, since rail trackage can be viewed as fixed capital as well as a measure of route structure. Braeutigam et al. (1984) include effective trackage as capital in the short-run cost function and interpret the result as a measure of economies of traffic density. Since the authors argue that absolute trackage changed little over the 35-month sample period, it is also possible to interpret effective trackage as fixed capital, and interpret the result as a measure of capital utilization rather than traffic density. The latter interpretation is adopted in this analysis.

6 We will analyze firm capital investment more formally in chapter 9.

7 In chapter 7, we will discuss at length economic profit in the short run and long run.

8 The rate of return in their analysis is defined as the ratio of (airline revenues – operating expenses – aircraft depreciation – depreciation of nonflight equipment) to the market value of assets. In excluding the opportunity cost of capital from their definition of cost, Morrison and Winston's measure of profitability only approximates an economic rate of return on investment.

9 Chapter 9 examines the implications that economies of scale have for government policy.

10 Viton called these measures economies of density, which he defined as the returns to a given fleet size. But, as we have previously seen, these are more appropriately returns to capital stock utilization.

11 Recall that if firms are combining all inputs, including its capital stock, in an optimal fashion, then capital is used optimally in the short and long run. In figure 6.4, the short-run average cost curve would be tangent to the long-run average cost curve.

12 For each of the bus properties listed in table 6.5, the first- and second-order, and interaction term coefficients from the regression model are used to calculate the savings, $\Delta STVC/\Delta K$, in short-run total variable costs.

13 In addition to renovating buses, Viton also estimated optimal fleets based upon purchasing new buses at a cost of $70,000 per bus (1975 prices). This gives an annualized cost, assuming a 15-year bus life, equal to $7,567. These results were very similar to those reported in table 6.5.

14 In the early 1960s, prior to the passage of UMTA, 2,200 new buses were purchased and the average bus age was 9.6 years. In the 1970s, 3,400 new buses were purchased per year and the average age fell to 8.3 years (Meyer and Gomez-Ibanez, 1981). Consistent with these numbers, Frankena (1987) found that capital subsidies reduced the expected life of urban buses by increasing the likelihood that a bus will be scrapped.

REFERENCES AND RELATED READINGS

General references on short-run production and cost

Chung, J. 1994: W. *Utility and Production Functions*. Cambridge, Mass.: Blackwell.
Colander, D. C. 1995: *Economics*, 2nd edn. Chicago: Richard D. Irwin.
McCloskey, D. N. 1985: *The Applied Theory of Price*, 2nd edn. New York: Macmillan.
Nicholson, W. 1998: *Microeconomic Theory*, 7th edn. Fort Worth, Texas: The Dryden Press.
Stiglitz, J. E. 1997: *Principles of Microeconomics*, 2nd edn. New York: W. W. Norton.
Varian, H. R. 1987: *Intermediate Microeconomics: A Modern Approach*. New York: W. W. Norton.

General references on transportation

Berechman, J. 1993: *Public Transit Economics and Deregulation Policy*, vol. 23. Studies in Regional Science and Urban Economics, L. Anselin et al. (ed.). Amsterdam: Elsevier Science.
Coyle, J. J., Bardi, E. J., and Novack, R. A. 1994: *Transportation*. St. Paul/Minneapolis: West.
Meyer, J. R. and Gomez-Ibanez, J. A. 1981: *Autos, Transit, and Cities*. Cambridge, Mass.: Harvard University Press.
Mohring, H. 1976: *Transportation Economics*. Cambridge, Mass.: Ballinger.
Sampson, R. J., Farris, M. T., and Schrock, D. L. 1990: *Domestic Transportation: Practice, Theory, and Policy*, 6th edn. Boston: Houghton Mifflin.
Winston, C. 1985: Conceptual developments in the economics of transportation: an interpretive survey. *Journal of Economic Literature*, XXIII, 57–94.

Specific short-run cost studies by mode

Many of the references included in chapter 5 also estimate short-run cost functions or include discussions of short-run versus long-run costs.

Airlines

Morrison, S. and Winston, C. 1986: *The Economic Effects of Airline Deregulation*. Washington DC: The Brookings Institution.

Morrison, S. A. and Winston, C. 1995: *The Evolution of the Airline Industry*. Washington DC: The Brookings Institution.

Railroads

Braeutigam, R. R., Daughety, A. F., and Turnquist, M. A. 1984: A firm specific analysis of economies of density in the US railroad industry. *The Journal of Industrial Economics*, XXXIII, 3–19.

Keeler, T. E. 1974: Railroad costs, returns to scale, and excess capacity. *Review of Economics and Statistics*, LVI, 201–8.

Public transit

Frankena, M. W. 1987: Capital-based subsidies, bureaucratic monitoring, and bus scrapping. *Journal of Urban Economics*, 21, 180–93.

Obeng, K. 1985: Bus transit cost, productivity and factor substitution. *Journal of Transport Economics and Policy*, XIX, 183–203.

Viton, P. 1980: On the economics of rapid transit operations. *Transportation Research*, 14A, 247–53.

Viton, P. A. 1981: A translog cost function for urban bus transit. *The Journal of Industrial Economics*, XXIX, 287–304.

Highways

Keeler, T. E. 1986: Economic issues in US infrastructure investment: public policy and investment in the trucking industry: some evidence on the effects of highway investments, deregulation, and the 55 mph speed limit. *AEA Papers and Proceedings*, 76, 153–8.

Pipelines

Cookenboo, L. Jr. 1955: *Crude Oil Pipelines and Competition in the Oil Industry*. Cambridge, Mass.: Harvard University Press.

7

Competition, Concentration, and Market Power in Transportation

INTRODUCTION

In the previous two chapters, we developed the basic theory of a firm's production and cost: we saw that a theory of production is essentially a theory of cost. As a result, estimating a cost function turned out to be very useful, since it embodied all economically relevant information on a firm's underlying production technology. To fix these ideas, we examined a number of examples in various transportation sectors.

We also examined airline profitability in chapter 6, recognizing that the rate of return not only depends upon the costs incurred to produce the output but also upon the revenue that a firm receives from selling its output. Although we now have a good understanding of the factors that determine a firm's production cost, we have not answered a critical question: What determines the level at which a transport firm *actually* does produce? Do revenue ton–miles vary arbitrarily from year to year, or is there some reason why motor carrier firms produce a large amount in one year and considerably less in another year? Is there any rationale to an airline producing a lot of passenger–miles or just a few? Presumably, a surge in the demand for trips between Los Angeles and Atlanta would increase both the price and the number of passenger–miles flown between the city-pair, all else constant. Correspondingly, we would expect to see a fall in air fare and in the number of passenger–miles between Chicago and New York if there were a sudden drop in the demand for flights between these cities. In each of these cases, the airline is responding to a change in demand by altering the quantity of services provided. But what factors determine the extent to which passenger–miles increase or decrease when faced with a change in demand? The answer to this question depends, at least partly, on whether the firm operates in a perfectly or imperfectly competitive market structure.

This chapter has three objectives. First, we will combine aggregate supply with aggregate demand, in order to characterize market equilibrium price and quantity in perfectly competitive markets. At equilibrium, market demand equals market supply and there is no economic incentive for price or quantity to change. However, just as there are short- and long-run market supply curves, we will see that a competitive market's short-run optimal response to changing conditions generally differs from its long-run optimal response.

The second objective in the chapter is to move away from the perfectly competitive model and consider alternative market structures. We will examine the implication that alternative market structures have for the efficient allocation of resources, as well as for a firm's pricing and output decisions. Our interest will primarily focus on two related but distinct market structures that have played, and continue to play, an important role in transportation: monopolies and oligopolies.

Consistent with the underlying theme throughout the text, the third objective is to illustrate the underlying concepts empirically. In this chapter, we will examine transportation as a derived demand and interregional flows, market concentration in the trucking and airline industries, market contestability, monopoly rents in the motor carrier industry, and market power in the shipping industry. Continuing with our empirical focus on imperfect competition, chapter 8 examines strategic responses to airline deregulation, the effect of mergers on market concentration, intermodal competition, and concludes with an overall assessment of deregulatory actions in the transportation industry.

PERFECTLY COMPETITIVE MARKET STRUCTURE

Under perfect competition, there are assumed to be a large number of firms that produce virtually identical or homogeneous products. Resources are perfectly mobile, relevant information for consumption and production decisions is readily available, there is freedom of entry and exit, and in all markets – whether for consumption, intermediate, or investment goods – market participants incur the social costs of their production decisions and purchasers reap the full benefits of their consumption decisions. Further, there are assumed to be no interdependencies in production or consumption. As a consumer, my consumption decisions do not depend upon the consumption of others. Similarly, as a producer, my production decisions are not dependent upon those of my competitors.

In chapters 5 and 6, we derived the long-run and short market supply functions for a perfectly competitive industry. We will now combine market supply with market demand in order to characterize equilibrium price and quantity in competitive markets. We first characterize market equilibrium price and quantity in the short run when capital is fixed at some level. We then turn to the long-run, where all inputs are variable. While economic profits (or losses) are consistent with equilibrium in the short run, we will see that long-run equilibrium implies zero economic profits.

SHORT-RUN MARKET EQUILIBRIUM

Consider a perfectly competitive market for transportation T with aggregate demand D_T and short-run aggregate supply S_T^{sr}. Setting market demand for T equal to short-run market supply gives

$$D_T(p,\bar{p}_x,\bar{Y}^a;\phi_1,\ldots,\phi_N) = S_T^{sr}(p;\bar{w},\bar{r},\gamma,\bar{K}) \tag{7.1a}$$

$$\Rightarrow \quad D_T(p) = S_T(p) \tag{7.1b}$$

where equation (7.1b) assumes that all influences upon market demand and short-run market supply other than price p_T are held constant. Figure 7.1 characterizes short-run equilibrium for the market as a whole, as well as for a representative firm in the market. The interaction between market demand and supply yields an equilibrium price p^* and an equilibrium market

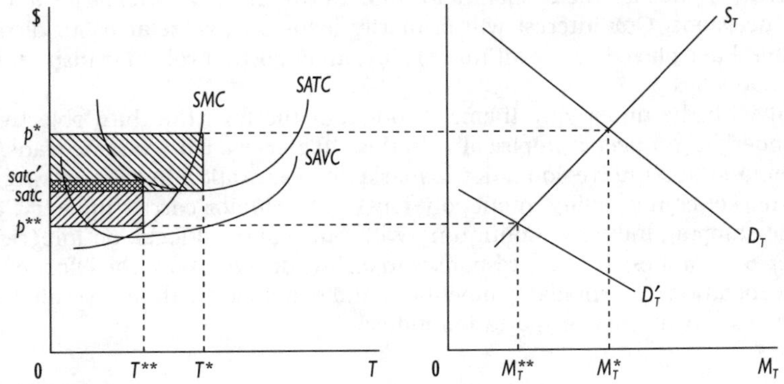

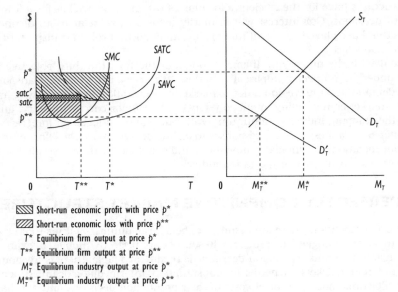

Short-run economic profit with price p^*
Short-run economic loss with price p^{**}
T^* Equilibrium firm output at price p^*
T^{**} Equilibrium firm output at price p^{**}
M_T^* Equilibrium industry output at price p^*
M_T^{**} Equilibrium industry output at price p^{**}

Figure 7.1 Short-run firm and market equilibria.

quantity M_T^*. And, given the market determined price, a profit-maximizing firm produces up to the point at which p^* just equals short-run marginal cost. In the graph, a representative firm provides T^* units of transportation, at which level the firm is more than covering its costs of production. The difference between p^* and short-run average variable cost is the firm's per unit *operating profit*. In the short run, the existence of a positive operating profit ensures that the firm will continue to produce. The difference between p^* and short-run average total cost, $p^* - satc$, is the firm's per unit *economic profit*. The shaded area given by $(p^* - satc)T^*$ is total economic profit and represents a pure profit to the firm after all inputs, including that of the entrepreneur, have received their opportunity costs.

Figure 7.1 also illustrates the effect of a decrease in demand from D_T to D'_T. Equilibrium market quantity and price fall to M_T^{**} and p^{**}, respectively, and representative firm output falls from T^* to T^{**}. In this case, the firm is not covering its total costs of production and makes an *economic loss*. This is seen from the fact that the new price p^{**} is less than the short-run average total cost at the new profit-maximizing output T^{**}. The total amount of the loss is the area $T^{**}(satc' - p^{**})$. However, since p^{**} is greater than the short-run average variable cost at T^{**}, the firm continues to make an operating profit. That is, it is still covering its variable costs of production (and contributing to at least part of its fixed costs) and, as long as it does so, the firm will not shut down in the short run.

LONG-RUN MARKET EQUILIBRIUM

In a perfectly competitive economy, markets have open access, so that firms are free to enter and exit the market at will. At any point in time, we can identify producing firms and a pool of

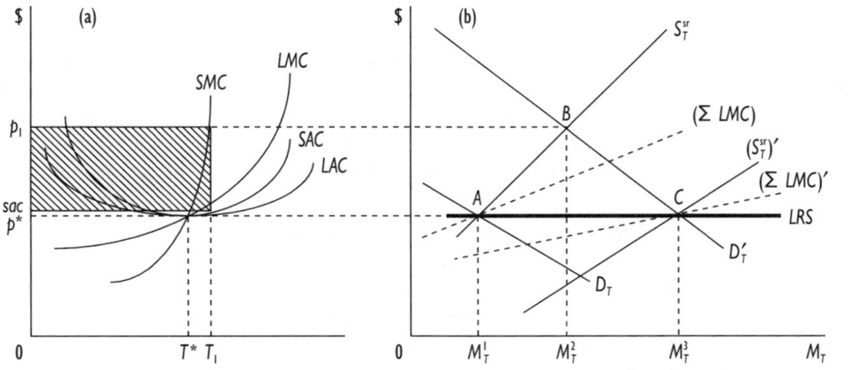

Figure 7.2 Firm costs with a constant industry long-run supply curve. (a) Representative firm; (b) market demand and supply.

potential firms. Producing firms are those firms currently supplying T to the market. Potential firms, on the other hand, are not currently producing but are sitting "on the sidelines" assessing the situation. Whether producing or potential, each of these firms faces the same input prices and has the same set of technological options. In the event that existing firms make pure economic profits, some potential firms will go active and enter the market with an objective of sharing in these profits. Conversely, if existing firms are making pure economic losses at existing prices, there is an incentive to exit the industry, and some of the incumbent firms will move into the pool of potential firms. If existing firms are neither making pure economic profits nor pure economic losses – that is, they are making *zero economic profits or normal accounting profits* – there is no incentive for potential firms to enter, nor for existing firms to exit the market.

Because firms are free to enter or exit the industry, the market's long-run equilibrium occurs where price equals long-run marginal cost. Freedom of entry and exit combined with profit-maximizing behavior ensures that the equilibrium *long-run market supply curve* is a horizontal line. To see this, consider figures 7.2(a) and 7.2(b). Figure 7.2(a) depicts the firm's average cost and marginal cost curves for the short run and the long run. Figure 7.2(b) gives market demand and supply curves for T. Assume that there are currently F firms producing T and that the market for T is initially in equilibrium, depicted as point A in figure 7.2(b). Market demand D_T equals short-run market supply S_T^{sr}. Equilibrium price and quantity are p^* and M_T^1, respectively. In figure 7.2(a), a representative firm in the industry takes p^* as given and, accordingly, produces T^* units of output, which is consistent with short-run and long-run profit maximization. Specifically, we see that when the firm produces T^*,

$$p^* = SMC = SAC = LMC = LAC$$

so that firms are in short-run and long-run equilibrium. All inputs are optimally employed. Moreover, since price just equals long-run average cost, zero economic profits are made, so that no firm has an economic incentive to enter or exit the industry. Further, since each of the F firms has an identical cost function, the horizontal summation of long-run marginal costs at price p^* gives market output M_T^1. That is, the long-run supply curve for the F firms, depicted by the dashed line ($\sum LMC$) in figure 7.2(b), also intersects market demand at point A, giving equilibrium price p^*.

Suppose that market demand suddenly increases from D_T to D_T'. The market equilibrium price initially rises to above p_1 in figure 7.2(b). In figure 7.2(a), each representative firm responds to the higher price of T by riding up its short-run marginal cost curve and increasing output from T^* to T_1. The cumulative effect of these short-run supply responses by the F firms is to increase the quantity of T supplied on the market from point A and M_T^1 to point B and M_T^2 in figure 7.2(b).

Although point B is a short-run equilibrium, it is not a long-run equilibrium. The reason is that at a price of p_1, the representative firm is making a pure economic profit, given by the hatched area and equal to $(p_1 - sac)(T_1)$ in figure 7.2(a). Induced by the prospect of sharing in these profits, some members of the pool of potential entrants decide to enter the industry, which shifts both the short-run and the long-run supply curves rightward. As long as economic profits exist, new firms continue to enter the industry and market supplies continue to expand. The market will ultimately settle back down to an equilibrium when the increased supply from new entrants sufficiently lowers market price to dissipate all of the economic profits. As depicted, point C is a new long-run market equilibrium, where the new short-run market supply is $(S_T^{sr})'$, the new long-run market supply for the incumbent firms is $(\sum LMC)'$, and the long-run equilibrium price is again p^*. At point C, no firm is making economic profits, and each of the larger number of firms is again producing T^* units of T at a price of p^*.

Finally, if we connect A and C, the initial and final long-run equilibrium points, respectively, we obtain a long-run *industry* supply curve that is horizontal. Although the short-run market supply curves are upward-sloping, as market output expands firm entry produces a long-run market response that keeps the representative firm at the minimum point on the long-run average cost curve. And by so doing, long-run increases in industry output move along the price line p^*. An alternative way of looking at this result is to recognize that the long-run supply curve is the horizontal summation of all *potential* firm supply curves.

Do we obtain a similar result if demand falls rather than increases? Yes. Indeed, a useful exercise to insure your understanding of the relationship between short-run and long-run behavior is to trace through these steps when there is an initial decrease in market demand.

LONG-RUN SUPPLY AND EXTERNAL EFFECTS OF SCALE

In our derivation of a horizontal long-run industry supply curve, we have implicitly assumed that factor prices and technology are *independent* of industry scale. In other words, as industry output increases from M_T^1 to M_T^2 there are no changes in per unit factor prices, and production is equally efficient at all levels of industry output.

If factor prices or technology are not independent of industry scale, the long-run supply curve will not be horizontal. Consider, for example, an increase in the demand for air travel. In response to the higher demand, airline companies increase their supply of air travel along their short-run marginal cost curves. As the industry expands, there is an increase in demand for pilots and other airline personnel, which raises the per hour wages of these employees. The increase in employee wages shifts the entire cost structure of the airline upward, the effect of which will be to dampen the industry's long-run response to the higher demand.

Alternatively, assume that factor prices are independent of industry scale, but there are negative technological effects. Continuing with the airline example, suppose that the growth

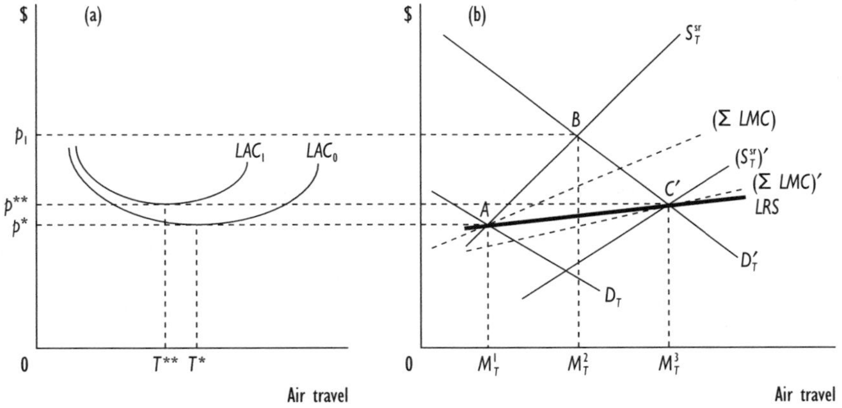

Figure 7.3 Firm costs with a rising long-run industry supply curve.

in air traffic has no effect on factor prices but significantly increases congestion at the nation's airports. The increased congestion raises the travel time and cost to business travelers and these airport congestion effects reduce business traveler productivity, a technological effect.[1]

What impact do the above external diseconomies (that is, negative scale effects) have upon the industry's long-run supply curve? Consider figures 7.3(a) and 7.3(b), which depict long-run firm average cost curves and the demand and supply of air travel, respectively. In order to simplify the firm's cost structure, marginal cost curves and short-run average costs curves have not been drawn. Initially, the market is in long-run and short-run equilibrium at point *A*, and each representative firm, facing long-run average cost LAC_0, is making zero economic profits at the equilibrium price p^*. With an increase in air travel demands from D_T to D_T' existing firms move along their short-run marginal cost curves and industry output increases to M_T^2. The market is in short-run equilibrium at point *B* and existing firms are making pure economic profits. The economic profits induce other firms into the industry, shifting the market supply curve rightward. However, as the market continues to expand, the external diseconomy (factor price increase or a negative technological effect) raises a firm's *entire* cost structure, which is depicted by LAC_1 in figure 7.3(a). In figure 7.3(b), $S_{T'}^{sr}$ and $\sum LMC$ are the summed short-run and long-run marginal cost curves of the incumbent firms, respectively, associated with the initial cost structure. $(S_{T'}^{sr})'$ and $(\sum LMC)'$, on the other hand, are the summed (over a larger number of firms) short-run and long-run marginal cost curves, respectively, associated with the higher cost structure.

The higher cost structure dampens the long-run supply response to the increase in air travel demands. As we see in figure 7.3(b), market supply shifts rightward until the price falls to p^{**}, which is greater than p^*. At p^{**} existing firms are making zero economic profits and producing T^{**} units of output. The new long-run market equilibrium occurs at point C'. And if we connect points *A* and C' we obtain the long-run supply curve of the industry, which is now an upward-sloping curve. When an industry faces rising factor prices or a technological diseconomy, the long-run supply curve of the industry is upward-sloping.

What does the long-run supply curve of the industry look like if factor prices fall or there are positive technological effects; that is, if we have factor price or technological external economies of scale? As industry output increases, these positive external effects shift a firm's cost structure downward. This reinforces industry's response to a demand increase, so that the long-run supply curve of the industry is downward-sloping.

EFFICIENCY AND PERFECT COMPETITION

An important result in economics is that perfectly competitive markets lead to an optimal or efficient allocation of resources whereby: (i) all resource inputs are optimally employed; (ii) all produced goods are distributed efficiently among consumers; and (iii) society produces the right output mix. Let's briefly examine why perfectly competitive markets yield these optimality results.

1 Efficient use of inputs – recall that profit-maximizing firms use inputs up to the point at which the marginal rate of technical substitution equals the input price ratio. Since all firms face the same input price ratio, it follows that in equilibrium the $MRTS_{K,L}$ will be equal across firms. If there are F firms in society, then

$$MRTS^i_{K,L} = \frac{w}{r} = MRTS^j_{K,L}, \qquad i, j = 1, \ldots, F; \; i \neq j \tag{7.2}$$

where w is the wage rate and r is the opportunity cost of capital. But since the marginal rate of technical substitution is the ratio of marginal products, equation (7.2) tells us that in perfectly competitive markets the relative productivity of labor in all firms equals the relative price of labor.

2 Efficient distribution of goods – this is demonstrated along the same lines as efficient input use. In equilibrium, utility-maximizing individuals consume quantities of each good up to the point at which the marginal rate of commodity substitution equals the price ratio. But in perfect competition, each consumer faces the same set of output prices. Thus, if there are n consumers, then

$$MRCS^i_{T,X} = \frac{p_T}{p_X} = MRCS^j_{T,X}, \qquad i, j = 1, \ldots, n; \; i \neq j \tag{7.3}$$

where p_T is the price of transportation and p_X is the price of all other goods. But the marginal rate of commodity substitution gives the relative consumption benefit of T, so that in perfect competition, the relative benefit of T equals the relative cost of T for all consumers.

3 Optimal mix of goods – if society is producing the right mix of goods, then the opportunity cost of increasing any good will equal its relative benefit; that is, the relative cost of producing the good equals the relative benefit of consuming the good. In equilibrium, a profit-maximizing firm produces up to the point at which marginal revenue equals marginal cost. But in perfect competition, marginal revenue equals price. Thus, for each of the goods produced,

$$p_s = MC_s, \qquad s = T, X$$

But this implies that the opportunity cost of producing an additional unit of T, defined as MC_T/MC_X and referred to as the "marginal rate of product transformation" ($MRPT_{T,X}$), is[2]

$$\frac{p_T}{p_X} = \frac{MC_T}{MC_X} = MRPT_{T,X}$$

And since the market dictates the same price ratios to all firms and consumers in perfect competition, the opportunity cost of T equals its relative benefit for all consumers:

$$MRPT_{T,X} = MRCS^i_{T,X}, \qquad i = 1, \ldots, n \tag{7.4}$$

When this condition holds, society is producing an efficient combination of goods.

From equations (7.2)–(7.4), a perfectly competitive market structure results in the efficient (also called Pareto optimal) allocation of resources such that *any* reallocation could not be accomplished without making some firm or consumer worse off.

There are a number of implications and caveats regarding this result that deserve emphasis. First, an efficient allocation of resources implies a *marginal cost pricing* rule; that is, produce up to the point at which the additional revenue from selling one more unit equals its opportunity cost. Second, the efficiency results assume a perfectly competitive market structure. There are a large number of buyers and sellers, none of whose actions are large enough to affect market prices. The perfectly competitive model rules out monopolies, unions, and other institutional arrangements characterized by restricted access, or by groups of producers or consumers that strategically behave in concert and whose actions do affect market prices. Third, each decision-maker's actions are assumed to be independent of any other decision-maker. For example, your travel decisions are assumed to have no effect upon my travel decisions. Or, if one airline adds additional flights to a particular city, this is assumed to have no effect on the schedules of any other airlines flying to that city. If any of the assumptions underlying the perfectly competitive model are violated, there will be a "market failure"; that is, one or more of the efficiency conditions identified above will be violated, which leads to a nonoptimal output mix.

TRANSPORTATION AS A DERIVED DEMAND

Up to this point, our primary focus has been upon the consumer who demands transportation as a final product, or upon the carrier that provides the transportation required by consumers and shippers alike. Although we did examine shipper modal demands at the end of chapter 4, our motivation was not an explicit focus upon shippers as much as it was a recognition of the fact that shipper modal demands can be theoretically and empirically analyzed using the same indirect utility framework as consumption demands for discrete transportation alternatives.

If a producer's goods are not consumed at the site of production, then, similar to labor and capital, transportation is an input in a producer's production function. A producer's demand for any input – labor, land, capital, or transportation – is a *derived demand*, which means that the value of the input to the producer is derived from the value that consumers place upon the final product that the input is employed to produce.

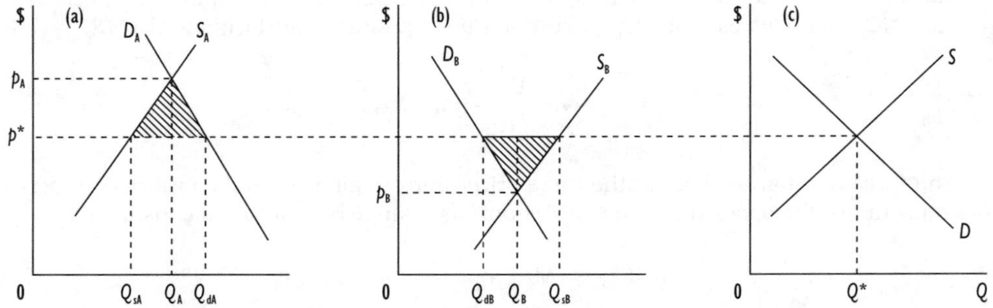

Figure 7.4 Interregional trade flows with zero transportation costs. (a) Region A; (b) region B; (c) total market.

If we wanted to characterize a shipper's production technology and cost characteristics, all of our previous results would apply. The only difference is that a shipper's production and cost functions would include an additional input, transportation. For example, the short-run cost function for a firm that produces its output Q at a location that is spatially separated from the point of consumption is

$$C = C(Q;w,r,p_t,\overline{K},\gamma) \tag{7.5}$$

where w is the wage rate, r is the opportunity cost of capital, p_t is the transport rate, and γ is the state of technology. Capital is held constant at $\overline{K}$. Assuming that the firm minimizes costs, then Shephard's lemma gives us the firm's optimal short-run demand for transportation, holding all else constant:

$$\frac{\Delta C(Q;w,r,p_t,\overline{K},\gamma)}{\Delta p_t} = T(Q;w,r,p_t,\overline{K},\gamma) \tag{7.6}$$

If we horizontally sum individual shipper demands for transportation, we obtain a market demand function for transportation, $D_T(Q;w,r,p_t,\overline{K},\gamma)$. Holding output and nontransportation input prices constant gives us a market demand curve for transportation, $D_T(p_t)$.[3]

Rather than explicitly deriving the market demand for transportation, an alternative approach that highlights the "derived demand" characteristic of transportation focuses upon the market for Q in different locales and the trade that occurs between areas. Suppose that Q is produced and consumed in two regions of the country, region A and region B. Also assume that both regions are initially self-sufficient. Region A consumes what it produces and region B consumes what it produces. Figures 7.4(a) and 7.4(b) depict regions A and B, where the equilibrium prices in each market are p_A and p_B, respectively.

The difference in equilibrium prices in the two markets is $p_A - p_B$. At market A's equilibrium price, market B would have an excess supply, while at market B's equilibrium price, market A would have an excess demand for Q. Thus, there is an economic incentive for specialization and trade which, *in the absence of transportation costs*, would lead to an equilibrium market price of p^* and a market quantity of Q^*, seen in figure 7.4(c). At this price, market A's excess demand just equals market B's excess supply. Total market demand equals market supply, and the excess supply of goods produced in region A are exported to region B.

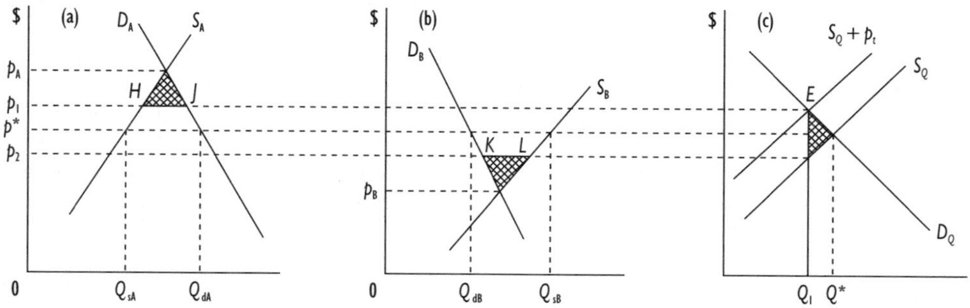

Figure 7.5 Interregional trade flows with positive transportation costs. (a) Region A; (b) region B; (c) total market.

The difference in self-sufficient prices leads to specialization and trade. Relative to self-sufficient prices, region B shifts more of its resources *into* the production of Q, while region A shifts some of its resources *out of* the production of Q and into the production of other goods and services. Why should this be the case? It is because, at the self-sufficient prices, p_A and p_B, region B has a *comparative advantage* in the production of Q.[4] In other words, at the self-sufficient price margin, the opportunity cost of producing an additional unit of Q in region B is less than the opportunity cost of producing an additional unit of Q in region A. It makes economic sense, then, for B to shift resources into Q and A to shift resources out of Q. This will continue until opportunity costs are equalized in both regions, which occurs at the market equilibrium price, p^*. In both region A and region B, p^* is the opportunity cost of producing one more unit of Q. At this price, region A no longer has a comparative advantage over region B in the production of Q.

The gains to society when goods are shipped from region B to region A are depicted in figures 7.4(a) and 7.4(b) by the hatched areas. Both regions gain. Region A experiences a net resource savings by reducing its production of Q from Q_A to Q_{sA} and receives a net benefit by increasing its consumption from Q_A to Q_{dA}. On the other hand, region B experiences a net revenue benefit by increasing its production of Q from Q_B to Q_{sB}. Region B also saves by scaling its consumption back to Q_{dB}, since the marginal benefit that region B would receive from consuming $Q_B - Q_{dB}$ additional units, represented by the area under the demand curve, is less than its opportunity cost, which is the revenue that region B would receive if it exported these units to region A.

What happens to the demand for transportation in the presence of *positive* transportation costs? There will still be an economic incentive to ship goods from region A to region B, as long as the initial price difference $p_A - p_B$ is at least as large as the transportation charge p_t; that is, if $p_A - p_B \geqslant p_t$. Region B will export Q to region A up to the point at which the delivered price of Q to region A just equals the production cost in region B plus the transportation charge. However, if $p_A - p_B < p_t$, there will be no shipments of Q from region B to region A. Figure 7.5 reproduces figure 7.4, except that there is a positive per unit transportation cost, p_t, for goods shipped from region B to region A. It is assumed that $p_t < p_A - p_B$.

There are a number of interesting insights that we can obtain from figure 7.5. First, relative to the absence of any transportation charges, a positive transportation charge implies that a smaller total amount of Q will be traded. In figure 7.5(c), the market supply curve shifts upward by the amount of the freight charge, which implies a market equilibrium at a higher price and a reduced quantity.

Second, the quantity of transportation demanded is inversely related to its price. Here, transportation demands are given by the amount of goods imported by region A from region B. In figures 7.5(a) and 7.5(b), these amounts are depicted by the solid lines *HJ* and *KL*, respectively. The presence of a positive transportation charge has reduced the excess supply in region A and the corresponding excess demand in region B. The reason is seen in figure 7.5(c), which shows that a transportation charge drives a wedge between the price paid by consumers in region A, p_1, and the price received by producers in region B, p_2. The new market equilibrium at point *E* implies a buyer's price in region A that equals region B's price plus a transportation charge, $p_2 + p_t$. As expected, region B exports to region A up to the point at which the price in region A just equals region B's price plus a freight charge.

A further implication of the transportation charge is the presence of a *welfare loss* equal to the hatched triangle in figure 7.5(c). The area under the market demand curve between Q_1 and Q^* represents the marginal benefit of increasing Q, whereas the area under the original supply curve, S_O, represents the marginal production cost of increasing Q from Q_1 to Q^*. The difference is the welfare loss associated with the positive transportation cost. We can't move to Q^* because of the presence of transportation costs. However, it is important to realize that this is not an argument against shipping goods to region A. Rather, the existence of transportation costs limits the extent of gains that are achievable. If there are no transportation costs, complete gains from trade will occur, as depicted in figures 7.4(a) and 7.4(b). These gains will be lessened by the presence of transport costs but, as long as the transport charge is less than the difference in self-sufficient prices, net gains will accrue and there will be a positive demand for transportation.

As a final point, and one which has implications for empirical analysis, we can identify conditions under which we would expect to see a greater flow of goods from region B to region A. One determinant, as we have seen, is transportation cost. All else constant, a decrease in the cost of shipping goods from region B to region A increases the amount of goods shipped and the quantity of transportation demanded. Second, a decrease in the production cost of Q in region B (or an increase in production cost in region A) would have the same effect as a fall in the transportation cost. All else constant, B's supply curve shifts down (or A's supply curve shifts up), which widens the gap between region A's and region B's self-sufficient prices, p_A and p_B, respectively, and provides a greater economic incentive for trade. A third factor that would increase the demand for transportation is an increase in region A's income (or a fall in region B's income). Assuming that Q is a normal good, an increase in region A's income increases its demand for Q and widens the gap between p_A and p_B. All else constant, this leads to stronger incentives for trade, which results in region B expanding its shipments and region A correspondingly expanding its imports. A similar result occurs for a decrease in region B's income.

PASSENGER TRADE FLOWS

A similar framework applies to nonwork passenger travel between cities and regions. Consider, for example, leisure travel. Different parts of the country have a comparative advantage in providing leisure activities: Southern California and Florida for their theme parks, beaches, and sunny climates; Utah and Colorado for skiing; the northwest for a variety of outdoor activities; New York for its museums and theaters; and Washington DC as the seat of government, with its various cultural, musical, and government attractions. The demand that travelers at origin O have for activities at destination D, which are produced at destination D and must be locally consumed, generate a demand for passenger trips between O and D. With its sunny climate, beaches, and theme parks, Florida will have a comparative advantage in producing leisure activities in comparison with a midwestern state such as Indiana. As a result, if the total market for leisure activities is made up of Florida and Indiana, at the equilibrium price there will be an excess demand for trips to Florida from Indiana, which generates passenger flows from Indiana to Florida.[5]

CASE STUDY – AN EMPIRICAL MODEL OF INTERREGIONAL FREIGHT FLOWS

In an analysis of interregional trade flows for manufactured goods, Friedlaender and Spady (1981) hypothesized the following general relationship between commodity flows and economic variables:

$$Q_K^{OD} = f(P_K^{OD}, \tilde{P}_K^{OD}, I^D, D_m) \tag{7.7}$$

where Q_K^{OD} is the quantity of commodity K produced in region O and shipped to region D; P_K^{OD} is region D's *delivered* price (production cost plus transport charge) of commodity K produced in O; $\tilde{P}_K^{OD}$ is region D's delivered price of commodity K if purchased from any region *other than O*; I^D is region D's income; and D_m $(m = 1, \ldots, M)$ represents a series of dummy variables that reflect unmeasured characteristics of the production or consumption areas. Consistent with our discussion in the previous section, the underlying hypothesis is that interregional commodity flows are responsive to *supply side* factors – production costs at the origin and transportation costs from origin O to destination D – and *demand side* factors – income at destination D and the price of substitutes which, in this case, is the price at which K could be obtained from competing regions. All else constant, an increase in the delivered price P_K^{OD} is expected to decrease interregional flows from origin O to destination D; an increase in the substitute price $\tilde{P}_K^{OD}$ is expected to increase interregional flows from O to D; and an increase in destination income I^D is expected to increase interregional flows from O to D. The importance of this model is twofold. First, we want to determine whether the estimation results are consistent with our theoretical expectations. Second, we are interested in the magnitude of the effects. Do increased transportation costs lead to small or large decreases in trade flows? And how responsive are trade flows to changes in regional income? The answers to these and other questions on the quantifiable effects of the explanatory variables are important for their regional development implications and their implications for the volume of traffic and market shares of transportation companies.

Interregional shipment data for the analysis was developed from the *Commodity Transportation Survey*, collected by the Bureau of the Census in 1967 and 1972. The production cost for manufactured goods was derived from information provided in the Census of Manufacturers. The analysis was based upon interregional flows among five US regions: the Official Region (which includes the New England, Mid-Atlantic, and East-Central states), the Southern Region, the South-Western Region, the Western Trunk Line Region, and the Mountain-Pacific Region.[6]

Friedlaender and Spady analyzed interregional shipments of manufactured goods in nine broadly defined categories: food and kindred products; lumber and wood; furniture and fixtures; pulp, paper, and allied products; chemicals and allied products; clay, concrete, glass, and stone; primary metal; fabricated metal; and machinery. For each of the nine groups there were 50 observations, which corresponded to a time series (1967, 1972) of 25 cross-sections (interregional

Table 7.1 Regression results for interregional flows – selected manufactured goods
Dependent variable – Q_K^{OD}, flow (millions of tons) of good K from origin O to destination D

	Industry		
Explanatory Variable[a]	Food and Kindred	Lumber and Wood	Chemicals and Allied
Constant term	–	−49.29 (−0.56)	–
Delivered Price	−0.3289 (−5.4)	−0.35 (−437.5)	−0.1367 (−3.5)
Destination Region 2 Income	0.092 (7.7)	0.0187 (2.1)	0.0292 (2.9)
Destination Region 3 Income	0.0224 (1.9)	0.019 (2.4)	0.0332 (3.4)
Destination Region 4 Income	0.0388 (3.7)	0.018 (3.0)	–
Intraregional Flow Dummy Variable	350.0 (12.7)	–	247.6 (10.0)
Region 5 Origin Dummy Variable	–	–	−102.35 (4.1)
Region 1 Destination Dummy Variable	43.43 (1.6)	–	–
Flow Within Region 5 Dummy Variable	–	310.5 (11.0)	–
R^2	0.82	0.79	0.77

[a] The regions are defined as follows: Region 1, Official Region; Region 2, Southern Region; Region 3, South-Western Region; Region 4, Western Trunk Line Region; Region 5, Mountain-Pacific Region. *t*-statistics are in parentheses. The general form of the estimating equation was

$$Q_K^{OD} = \alpha_0 + \alpha_1 P_K^{OD} + \alpha_2 \tilde{P}_K^{OD} + \alpha_3 I^D + \sum_m \alpha_m D_m + \varepsilon$$

where the variables are defined in the text and ε is an error term.
Source: Friedlaender and Spady (1981), table D.1, p. 298

flows between the five regions for each of the two years).

Table 7.1 reports the interregional flow regression results for three typical manufactured commodity groups: Food; Lumber and Wood; and Chemicals. The R^2 for each equation indicates that 82%, 79%, and 77% of the variation in Food, Lumber and Wood, and Chemical commodity flows, respectively, is due to the included explanatory variables. What do the results presented in table 7.1 tell us?

1 The equations for Food and Chemicals do not include constant terms, whereas the equation for Lumber does. The results presented in table 7.1 represent "best fit" models in the sense that the R^2 and *t*-statistics are high and the signs of the economically relevant variables are consistent with economic theory. In comparison with a model that included a constant term, the results for Food and Chemicals commodities led to lower standard errors and higher *t*-statistics. Similarly, although the constant term in the Lumber and Wood equation is not statistically significant, its inclusion produced a better fit than a model that excluded the constant term.
2 For each origin–destination pair, the production cost was estimated by dividing total tonnage shipped into total value shipped.

Adding a transportation cost index to production cost and dividing by the wholesale price index (to account for the different years in the sample) gave a measure of real delivered price between origin O and destination D. From table 7.1, we see, as expected, that delivered price has a negative sign and is significantly different from zero. Thus, for the food industry, a unit increase in the delivered price index from origin O to destination D reduces interregional food flows by 0.328 million or 328,000 tons, holding all else constant. A similar increase in the delivered price index reduces lumber and chemicals trade flows by 350,000 tons and 136,000 tons respectively. Since the price variable is delivered price, the unit price increase could occur through an increase in production costs, an increase in transport costs, or some combination of the two.

3 For this study, real regional income is measured by per capita regional disposable income, deflated by the national consumer price index. From table 7.1, the effect of income is estimated separately for destinations 2, 3, and 4, and we see that, as expected, an increase in real income has a positive impact upon interregional flows. In particular, a $100 dollar increase in per capita income in the Southern, South-Western, and Western Trunk Line regions raises interregional Food and Kindred flows, and the demand for transportation, by 92,000, 22,400, and 38,800 tons respectively. A similar increase has a positive but smaller effect on Lumber and Wood shipments, raising these demands in each destination region by about 18,000 tons. Last, a $100 increase in per capita income for the Southern and South-Western regions has a 29,200 and 33,200 ton impact on the demand for Chemicals transportation, respectively.

4 In contrast to economic theory, which says that the prices of close substitutes are important determinants of interregional flows, substitute prices were not found to have significant effects upon commodity flows. As a result, these variables were excluded from the model reported in table 7.1. An implication of this empirical finding is not that substitute prices are economically unimportant but, rather, that for this sample, substitute prices exhibited little regional variation. This is consistent with the observation that, at the large level of regional aggregation in this study, manufacturing activities are relatively uniformly dispersed among the regions.

5 The final four dummy variables in the model are included to capture unmeasured attributes and economic activities that influence interregional flows. It is not surprising, given the large geographic size of each region, that flows will be intraregional as well as interregional. In table 7.1, the coefficient for the dummy variable, Intraregional Flow Dummy Variable, indicates that intraregional activities add 350 million tons of food and 247 million tons of chemicals to total commodity flows. Similar interpretations are associated with the other dummy variables. Chemical shipments originating in the Mountain-Pacific region (region 5), all else constant, were 247 million tons smaller than those originating in other regions. Food shipments heading for region 1, on the other hand, are 43 million tons greater than shipments destined for other regions, all else constant. Also, and not surprisingly, lumber shipments that occur within the Mountain-Pacific area are 310 million tons greater than for other origin–destination pairs, all else held constant.

For the nine commodity groups included in this study, table 7.2 reports the price, income, and transport freight elasticities. For each of the commodity groups, interregional flows are income elastic, ranging from a high of 3.61 for Primary Metal to a low of 1.04 for Machinery. On the other hand, with the exception of Food and Kindred, regional flows are inelastic with respect to delivered prices. A 1% increase in the delivered price index leads to an approximate 0.75% decrease in the commodity flows of lumber, chemicals, and clay and concrete; an approximate 0.45% decrease in the metals and machinery flows; and an approximate 0.30% decrease in interregional flows of furnishings and

Table 7.2 Interregional commodity flow elasticities

	Elasticity with Respect to		
Industry	Price	Income	Freight Rates
Food and Kindred	−1.5	1.66	−0.051
Lumber and Wood	−0.72	1.96	−0.022
Furniture and Fixtures	−0.34	1.13	−0.002
Pulp, Paper, and Allied	−0.26	1.88	−0.065
Chemicals and Allied	−0.75	1.21	−0.038
Clay, Concrete, Glass, and Stone	−0.74	1.60	−0.075
Primary Metal	–	3.61	–
Fabricated Metal	−0.44	2.32	−0.006
Machinery	−0.49	1.04	−0.003

Source: Friedlaender and Spady (1981), table D.3, p. 299

pulp products. Interregional flows of food, on the other hand, are price elastic, falling by 1.5% for each 1% increase in the delivered price index.

Are transport costs significant deterrents to interregional trade flows? – not generally. We see in the table that the elasticity of trade flows with respect to a 1% increase in freight costs, all else constant, are highly inelastic, ranging between −0.003 and −0.05.

The implication from these elasticity results is that relatively large changes in delivered prices must occur if there is to be a significant impact upon regional flows. Moreover, the small freight rate elasticities imply that interregional trade flows are typically insensitive to transportation costs, although it is important to remember that the more competitive the market, the more elastic will be the elasticity of trade flows with respect to freight costs. Income, however, plays a much larger role, which suggests that significant regional economic development will generate large effects on interregional trade flows.

THE SPECTRUM OF MARKET STRUCTURES

In real-world markets, many if not most of the perfectly competitive assumptions are at most only weakly satisfied. Firms produce heterogeneous rather than homogeneous products, and they often spend large (advertising) resources to differentiate their product and convince consumers that their products are superior. Resources are mobile, but not perfectly. Moving one's family to another city generally entails large transactions costs that must be weighed against the expected benefits from the move. Frequently, the net benefit is negative and the household stays put. And although we are daily inundated with information, we frequently don't have all relevant information. If I'm booking a flight from Chicago to Washington DC, I will spend some time searching for the best fare, but only up to the point at which the expected gain (in the form of obtaining a lower fare) from further search equals the expected cost (given by the highest-valued alternative use of my time). Like all other goods, information is scarce and has an increasing opportunity cost. Also, some market structures have so few producers that individual firm production decisions are not independent but will depend upon the production activities of competing firms. Notwithstanding that the assumptions of the perfectly competitive model are never fully satisfied, the perfectly competitive market structure plays an important

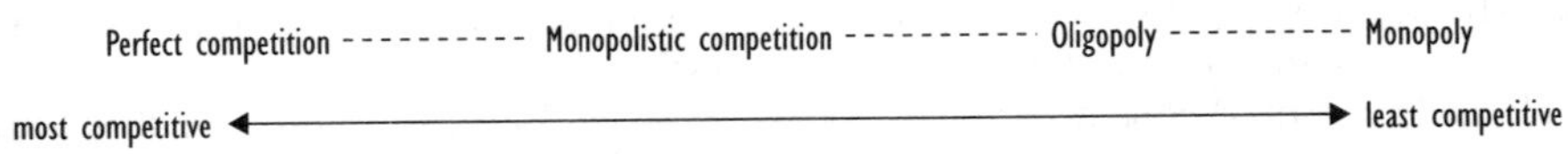

Figure 7.6 Spectra of market structures.

role by providing a context or frame of reference that is used to assess resource allocation in alternative market structures that are less competitive.

In general, there are four basic market structures – perfect competition, monopolistic competition, oligopoly, and monopoly. Figure 7.6 depicts the spectrum of market structures which, as we move from left to right, reflects decreasing levels of competition.

For purposes of contrasting alternative market structures, the assumption of a large number of producers in perfect competition has two important implications. First, when combined with the assumption that each firm produces an identical product, we obtain the result that a perfectly competitive firm faces a horizontal (that is, perfectly elastic) demand curve. Because there are many producers, any one producer's share of the market is so small that, regardless of how much it produces and sells, its production has a negligible impact upon market price. In other words, the perfectly competitive firm is a *price-taker*, a result that we have previously seen.

Second, the presence of a large number of producers precludes strategic behavior as an economically viable option for the firm. In the context used here, a firm strategically behaves when (1) the price and output decisions of one's competitors affect its own price and output decisions, or (2) a firm makes price and output decisions based upon the expected reactions of its competitors. In either case, each firm's pricing and output decisions are *interdependent* with those of its competitors. Since, in perfectly competitive markets, each seller is a price-taker, once the forces of market demand and supply establish an equilibrium price, the perfectly competitive firm takes the price as given. Hence there is no gain to any firm from strategic behavior. One might argue that this result could be upset if many competitive firms colluded, banding together into a *cartel*, and made price and output decisions that maximized joint profits.[7] However, in perfectly competitive markets, this can't occur because, by assumption, there are a large number of sellers. To be a successful cartel, the colluding firms must organize, agree upon a collusive strategy to maximize and distribute joint profits, monitor each of its members behavior to ensure that no one is cheating on the arrangement, enforce the cartel arrangement if some member is cheating, and coordinate responses in the face of changing economic circumstances. This is no little task, even for a small number of firms, and involves significant transactions costs. With a large number of firms, the transactions costs associated with cartelization can be so staggering as to completely dwarf the expected benefits from collusion. Moreover, with freedom of entry, any excess profits initially generated by the cartel would be competed away in the long run.

Similar to perfect competition, *monopolistic competition* is a market structure with many producers. But in contrast to perfect competition, monopolistically competitive firms do not produce identical products, but market-differentiated products. Although the presence of a large number of competitors in monopolistically competitive markets precludes net gains from strategic behavior, the fact that a monopolistically competitive firm differentiates its product from that of its competitors implies that the firm's demand curve is not perfectly elastic but downward-sloping. Whereas a perfectly competitive firm can sell all of its output at the going price, a monopolistically competitive firm must lower its price, to some degree, in order to increase the number of units sold. Alternatively, if a monopolistically competitive firm raises it price, it will lose some, but not all, of its market share.

An *oligopoly* is a market structure with very few sellers.[8] Firms in an oligopolistic market have few actual competitors with whom to compete, which reflects reduced competition and greater potential for setting price and output. But the distinguishing implication of an oligopoly's "smallness" is the introduction of strategic considerations. In sharp contrast to perfectly competitive and monopolistically competitive firms, each oligopolistic firm has a considerable share of the total market. As a result, it is no longer tenable to assume that one firm's actions have such a small impact on the overall market that these effects can be ignored. An oligopolist's pricing and output decisions will appreciably affect the overall market and, accordingly, will appreciably impact one's own profits as well as those of its competitors. Recognizing this, an oligopolist's competitors will always respond, or react to, the pricing and output behavior of its competitors. Thus, an oligopolist will *strategically pursue* profit maximization by evaluating the possible effects that alternative strategies have on its competitors. Similarly, when its competitors embark on new profit-maximizing strategies, an oligopolist will not sit by idly, but will strategically respond to the altered environment.

Last, and the least competitive market structure, is a *monopoly*, a market in which there is only one seller.[9] Being the only seller, a monopolist faces the total (downward-sloping) market demand for the good. As we will see in the next section, this has important implications for resource allocation and for the pricing and output decisions of profit-maximizing monopolists.

Monopolistically competitive markets, oligopolies, and monopolies are imperfect market structures that face downward-sloping demand curves, which implies that each of these market structures has (to varying degrees) market power; that is, an ability to raise price above marginal cost without losing all of its market share.[10] The more elastic the demand for its goods, the less is a firm's ability to raise price and the smaller will be its market power. Perfectly competitive firms have no market power, because they face perfectly elastic (that is, horizontal) demand curves. A firm will lose all of its sales if it raises price above the equilibrium level. Conversely, a perfectly competitive firm will capture the entire market (but incur an economic loss) if it lowers price below the equilibrium level. Monopolies, on the other hand, have the greatest potential for market power, since they are completely sheltered from competition.

Since all imperfectly competitive firms enjoy some degree of market power, the basic principles developed for monopoly markets apply to the other imperfectly competitive market structures. Thus, we will concentrate the bulk of our theoretical discussion on monopolistic market structures, identifying, where appropriate, differences between monopoly and the other imperfectly competitive market structures.

MONOPOLY MARKETS

Even though monopolists face downward-sloping market demand curves, they are no different from perfectly competitive firms in their pursuit of profits. Monopolists are profit maximizers. However, the fact that a monopolist supplies the entire market for the good induces the firm to produce a *smaller* level of output at a *higher* price relative to a perfectly competitive market structure. To see this, first note that a monopolist's short-run profits can be expressed as

$$\pi = pT - STVC(T;w,r,\gamma,\bar{K}) + STFC \qquad (7.8)$$

where p is the price of the good, T is output, *STVC* is short-run total variable cost, and *STFC* is short-run total fixed cost. As we have previously seen, short-run total (economic) profit is simply the difference between short-run total revenues and total costs. Similar to our definition of profit for competitive firms in chapter 5, we see in equation (7.8) that the level of short-run total variable cost depends upon the amount of T produced, per unit wages w, per unit opportunity cost of capital r, the existing state of technology as summarized by γ, and the fixed level of capital $\overline{K}$.

EQUILIBRIUM OUTPUT FOR A MONOPOLIST

Also similar to a perfect competitor, a monopolist will produce up to the point at which marginal cost equals marginal revenue for an additional unit of the good. Marginal revenue is the change in total revenue resulting from a one unit increase in output and can generally be expressed as:

$$MR = \frac{\Delta(pT)}{\Delta T} = p + T\frac{\Delta p}{\Delta T} = p\left(1 + \frac{1}{E_{T,p}}\right) \tag{7.9}$$

where MR is marginal revenue and $E_{T,p}$ is the price elasticity of demand. Since p and T are inversely related by the law of demand, the price elasticity of demand is negative, that is, $0 > E_{T,p} > -\infty$. We see from equation (7.9) the distinction between perfectly competitive firms and a monopolist. In perfect competition, there are so many firms producing the good that no firm's production can affect the market price of the good. In other words, a perfectly competitive firm faces a perfectly elastic demand curve, which is equivalent to saying that $E_{T,p} \to -\infty$. From equation (7.9), this implies that $(1/E_{T,p}) \to 0$, so that marginal revenue simply equals price. However, since a monopolist faces the market demand curve, which is not perfectly elastic, marginal revenue for a monopolist is

$$MR = p\left(1 + \frac{1}{E_{T,p}}\right) < p \tag{7.10}$$

In other words, in monopoly markets, marginal revenue is less than price. An alternative way to see this is by comparing the monopolist's and perfectly competitive firm's behavior when each wants to sell one more unit. Since the perfectly competitive firm produces such a small amount of the good relative to the market as a whole (this is the meaning of its facing a horizontal demand curve), it can sell one more unit without having to decrease its price on any of the previous units. On the other hand, in facing the entire market demand, a monopolist can sell one more unit only by lowering the price. But it can't just lower the price for the last unit – it must lower the price for *all* units.[11] To illustrate the relationship between price and marginal revenue for a monopolist, consider figure 7.7 and assume that a monopolist can sell ten units of T at a price of \$10 per unit. If the monopolist wants to increase sales by one and sell 11 units, he must reduce the price *for each unit* to \$9. To calculate marginal revenue for the 11th unit, we subtract from \$9 (the price of the 11th unit), the \$1 lost on the previous ten units (since the price for selling ten units was \$10 per unit). Thus, the monopolist's marginal revenue actually *decreases* by \$1, which is considerably less than the \$9 price.

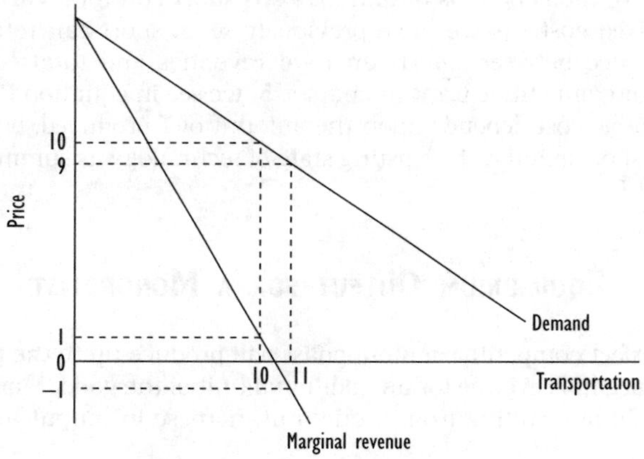

Figure 7.7 Monopolist demand and marginal revenue curves.

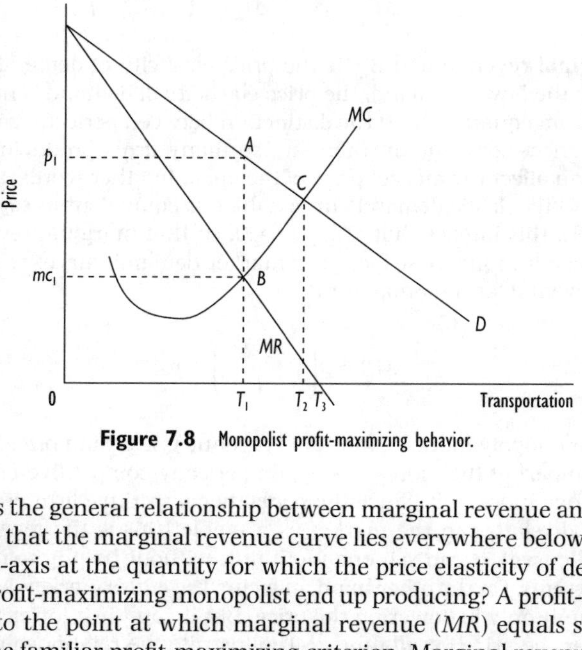

Figure 7.8 Monopolist profit-maximizing behavior.

Figure 7.8 depicts the general relationship between marginal revenue and price for a monopolist; it can be seen that the marginal revenue curve lies everywhere below the demand curve and intersects the x-axis at the quantity for which the price elasticity of demand is -1.[12]

Where will our profit-maximizing monopolist end up producing? A profit-maximizing monopolist produces up to the point at which marginal revenue (MR) equals short-run marginal cost (MC). This is the familiar profit-maximizing criterion. Marginal revenue is given in equation (7.11) and marginal cost is the increase in total variable costs from a one-unit increase in output T. The profit-maximizing condition for a monopolist is

$$MR = MC$$

$$\Rightarrow \quad p\left(1+\frac{1}{E_{T,p}}\right)=\frac{\Delta STVC(T;w,r,\gamma,\overline{K})}{\Delta T} \tag{7.11}$$

In addition to demand and marginal revenue, figure 7.8 also depicts the monopolist's marginal cost curve, where it is assumed that the monopolist faces a rising opportunity cost of production. In the figure, we see that profits are maximized at point B and the monopolist produces T_1 units of output. However, although point B characterizes profit maximization, the monopolist *prices its output according to the market demand curve,* not the marginal revenue curve. The profit-maximizing monopolist in figure 7.8 charges p_1 for each of the T_1 units of transportation sold.

PRICE ELASTICITY OF DEMAND AND TOTAL REVENUE

As monopoly sales increase, we find that total revenues first increase, reach a maximum, and then decrease. This pattern reflects the sensitivity of market demand to price changes, as summarized in the price elasticity of demand. Recall that total firm revenues are simply the product of price and quantity, $TR = pT$. The effect of a small increase in price, Δp, upon total revenue is

$$\frac{\Delta(pT)}{\Delta p} = T + p\frac{\Delta T}{\Delta p} = T(1 + E_{T,p}) \qquad (7.12)$$

If market demand is of *unit elasticity,* the price elasticity of demand equals −1 and a change in price has no effect upon total revenues or expenditures (since $T(1 + (-1)) = 0$ in equation (7.12)). Alternatively, if demand for T is *price inelastic* (that is, $-1 < E_{T,p} < 0$) then $T(1 + E_{T,p})$ is positive and an increase in price raises revenues, while a price decrease lowers revenues. Finally, when T is *price elastic,* $T(1 + E_{T,p})$ is negative. Price changes and total expenditures move in opposite directions.

Related to this, we also see from equation (7.10) that marginal revenue is negative or zero when $(1/E_{T,p})$ is less than or equal to −1, respectively. This occurs when market demand is price inelastic or of unit elasticity, $0 > E_{T,p} \geqslant -1$, and implies that a profit-maximizing monopolist will never be operating on the inelastic portion of the market demand curve.[13] In figure 7.8, as sales increase up to T_3, demand is price elastic, marginal revenue is positive, and total revenues are rising. At T_3, demand is of unitary elasticity, marginal revenue is zero, and small changes in price have no impact on revenues. As sales increase beyond T_3, demand is price inelastic, marginal revenue is negative, and total revenues are falling.

RESOURCE ALLOCATION EFFECTS OF MONOPOLY

To examine the effect of a monopoly structure upon the allocation of resources, let's consider the implication of a monopolist's pricing and output decision in figure 7.8. At its profit-maximizing point, the monopolist charges a price p_1 for each unit sold. Yet the opportunity cost of the T_1st unit of transportation is mc_1. Because a monopolist faces a downward-sloping demand curve, price diverges from marginal revenue at monopoly equilibrium and, therefore, from marginal cost. In other words, the marginal benefit of consuming an additional unit of T, reflected by p_1, is greater then the marginal cost of producing an additional unit, mc_1.

The result that the monopoly equilibrium price exceeds marginal cost has two important implications. First, the monopolist does not follow a marginal cost pricing rule, which implies that society is producing the wrong combination of goods. In particular, too few resources are devoted to the production of transportation at T_1 and too many resources are employed producing all other goods. How many additional resources should be transferred from the production of other goods to transportation? – as many as are necessary to increase transportation output to T_2. At T_2, we see in figure 7.8 that the marginal benefit of the last unit consumed just equals the marginal resource cost, so that any further resource allocation to transportation would be inefficient.

The second, and related, implication when monopoly price exceeds marginal cost is that society suffers a *welfare or efficiency loss*. In figure 7.8, this loss is the area ABC. The additional benefit to society from consuming $T_2 - T_1$ more output is the area AT_1T_2C, while society's resource cost of producing $T_2 - T_1$ more transportation is BT_1T_2C. The difference is the net benefit to society, and represents efficiency gains that are not exploited due to the monopolistic market structure in this market.

MARKET POWER

A monopolist enjoys market power because the equilibrium price lies above marginal production cost. What determines the extent of a monopolist's market power? Consider the monopolist's profit-maximizing condition, which we have expressed in equation (7.11) as

$$p\left(1+\frac{1}{E_{T,p}}\right)=\frac{\Delta STVC(T;w,r,\gamma,\bar{K})}{\Delta T}$$

$$\Rightarrow \quad p+\frac{p}{E_{T,p}}=MC(T;w,r,\gamma,\bar{K})$$

$$\Rightarrow \quad \frac{p-MC(T;w,r,\gamma,\bar{K})}{p}=-\frac{1}{E_{T,p}} \qquad (7.13)$$

The left-hand side of equation (7.13) is the increase in price over marginal cost as a proportion of the price charged and reflects a monopolist's market power. The greater the discrepancy, the more market power a monopolist enjoys. From equation (7.13), we see that market power depends explicitly upon the price elasticity of demand. The more price inelastic market demand is, the smaller is the denominator on the right-hand side of the equal sign in equation (7.13) and the larger is a monopolist's market power. Thus, factors which determine a market's price elasticity of demand also determine market power. Two primary factors are relevant to a market's price elasticity of demand, the *number of close substitutes* and the *market shares* of existing firms. In general, the larger the number of substitutes for a firm's output and the smaller the market shares of existing firms are, the higher is the price elasticity of demand. Applying these criteria to perfect competition, we obtain the expected result of perfectly elastic demands, since each perfectly competitive firm has a negligible share of the total market and produces an identical product. At the other extreme, the market share of a monopolist is one so that its price elasticity of demand depends upon how well its product is differentiated from possible substitutes. When there are very few substitutes, the price elasticity will be close to zero.

Between these two extremes, monopolistically competitive firms are large in number and, although the products are differentiated, they are nevertheless similar. Both of these factors imply larger price elasticities of demand in comparison with a monopolist, but product differentiation leads to smaller price elasticities (in absolute value) relative to perfectly competitive firms.[14] In oligopolistic markets, the fact that few firms produce a large portion of the total market implies that incumbent firms face lower price elasticities of demand relative to competitive or monopolistically competitive structures, but somewhat higher elasticities than a pure monopoly market, all else constant. And, similar to monopolistic market structures, the prevailing price elasticities in oligopolistic markets will depend upon the number of close substitutes that are available.

MONOPOLY RENTS

A further difference between perfectly competitive and monopolistic market structures is the potential for long-run economic profits. Figure 7.7 reproduces figure 7.6, with the addition of the monopolist's short-run average total cost curve. At the monopolist's equilibrium, the equilibrium price not only exceeds marginal cost but also lies above the monopolist's average total cost, atc_1. The monopolist makes a per period pure economic profit, or *monopoly rent*, equal to $(p_1 - atc_1)T_1$, depicted by the shaded area in figure 7.9. Alternatively, if we divide monopoly rent by the amount of invested capital, we obtain $(p_1 - atc_1)T_1/(\text{invested capital})$, which gives the *excess rate of return on investment*.[15] In contrast to a perfectly competitive market structure, these profits are not bid away since, by definition, there are no other competitors. The monopolist is the sole supplier of the good. And as long as price lies above average total cost, the monopolist enjoys a continuing stream of pure economic profits and above-normal rates of return.[16,17]

Although the absence of competitors means that a monopolist can earn long-run economic profits, there are four reasons why these profits may dissipate, to some extent, over time.

Rent-seeking Suppose, as is often the case, that the monopoly position occurs because of some governmental policy that restricts access to the market. The Motor Carrier Act of 1935 virtually regulated all economic aspects, including entry, of motor carriage. If, as a result of this

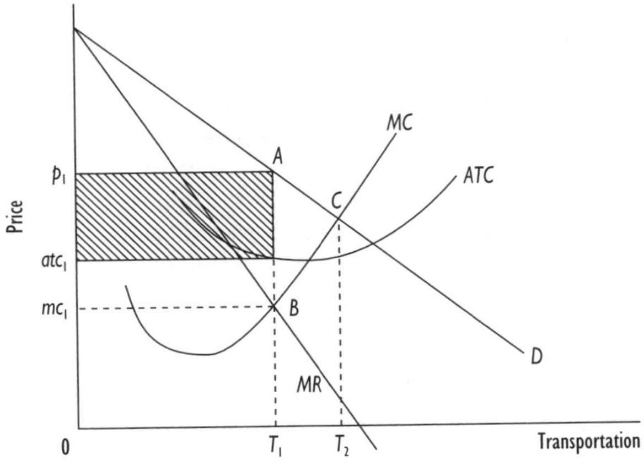

Figure 7.9 Monopoly rents.

policy, the beneficiary receives pure economic rents, denoted by the shaded area in figure 7.9, the beneficiary has an incentive to spend resources per period, *up to the amount of pure economic profit earned*, in order to ensure that these rents continue in the long run.

To illustrate the principle of rent-seeking, suppose in figure 7.9 that $p_1 = \$10$, $atc_1 = \$7$, and $T_1 = 100{,}000$ ton–miles. This produces an annual monopoly rent equal to $300,000. Since the $300,000 monopoly rent is not required for the monopolist to produce T_1 ton–miles of transportation, the monopolist can spend up to $300,000 per year on wining and dining government representatives, lobbyists, information gathering, and other "rent-seeking" activities in order to secure the long-run receipt of these pure economic profits. By not affecting the marginal cost of production, these rent-seeking costs will not alter the monopolist's optimal price–output combination. However, rent-seeking costs do raise the monopolist's average cost curve, which leads to lower economic profits.

Rent-sharing A second way that pure economic monopoly profits may dissipate is through "rent-sharing" activities. Consider figure 7.9 once again and assume that the monopolist is maximizing profits at point B, producing T_1 amount of transportation and charging a price of p_1 per unit. Economic profits are again the shaded area. As we know from earlier chapters, underlying a firm's marginal cost of production is its demand for factors of production, including labor. Suppose that the monopolist does not face a perfectly elastic supply of labor but must negotiate with organized labor through unions, which is the norm for transportation industries.

Recognizing that the monopolist is earning monopoly rents, the union negotiates a more favorable contract, which pays its members a higher wage and better fringe benefits than would be the case in the absence of such rents. The higher-wage contract has two direct effects. First, higher wages raise a monopolist's marginal and average cost of production which, all else constant, leads to higher prices and reduced output. And, second, the higher wages redistribute some of the monopoly rents to labor. In effect, labor becomes a sharing partner in the rents earned by the monopolist.

Capitalization A third reason for the dissipation of long-run monopoly rents occurs if the right to the monopoly rent is transferable. In the motor carrier industry, for example, firms must obtain operating certificates in order to transport goods between an origin and a destination. And prior to motor carrier deregulation in 1980, these operating certificates were not easily obtained. If the economic regulations in the motor carrier industry conferred any monopoly rents to the holders of certificates, and if these certificates could be sold, then the certificate's selling price would measure the value of the stream of economic profits. For the certificate buyer, this is a variation of rent-seeking activity previously discussed. Consider the example above, where pure economic profits were $300,000 per year. Suppose that $6 million is maximum price that a buyer would be willing to pay for the operating license and the right to the annual profit stream of $300,000. At this price, the buyer earns no economic profits.[18] If the buyer pays the full $6 million for the operating authority, the purchase price becomes a cost to the buyer so that, after purchase, the new certificate holder simply earns a normal rate of return on investment. In this case, all of the economic profits have been dissipated.[19] On the other hand, if the purchase price is less than $6 million, holding all else constant, the new holder will still earn a monopoly rent, but the new stream of economic profits will be less than the original $300,000.

X-inefficiency and reduced incentives to innovate A final reason to expect dissipation of monopoly rents is that the absence of competition reduces a monopolist's incentives for efficient production (X-inefficiency) and innovation. Not having to worry about losing market share, a monopolist experiences weaker incentives to produce as efficiently as possible. In addition, there is less incentive to stay on top of recent developments, introduce new technology, or create new products or processes. Both of these effects lead to a rise in marginal and average production costs, higher prices, reduced quantity coming to the market, and lower monopoly rents.

Monopoly rents and price discrimination

In the above analysis, the intersection of the monopolist's marginal cost and marginal revenue curves determine optimal quantity, and from the associated market demand curve we obtain the monopolist's optimal price. The monopolist in this setting is often referred to as a *single price setting* monopolist, because the model assumes that each consumer pays the same price for T. Suppose, on the other hand, that the monopolist has the option to "price discriminate"; that is, to sell its output to different groups of consumers at different prices. Although the monopolist can charge different prices for the good, we will assume that any difference in prices is *not* based upon differences in the cost of production. Can a monopolist increase its profits by price discriminating?

To consider this question, let's take a concrete example. Suppose that an airline has a monopoly in providing passenger air trips on a given route, and it charges one price to business travelers and a lower price to vacation travelers. According to this strategy, the airline "price discriminates" on the basis of trip purpose. The airline reasons that since vacation travelers have more substitutes available, in the form of alternative times of travel, alternative modes of travel, and alternative travel destinations, they will be more sensitive to price than business travelers who have fewer substitutes available (for example, a businessman must oftentimes be at a given destination at a specific time). Will the firm maximize its profits by charging business travelers higher prices than leisure travelers? What is the firm's profit-maximizing strategy?

In general, the airline wants to produce an extra trip for the businessman as long as the marginal revenue generated from the trip is no less than the trip's marginal cost. Similarly, the airline will supply additional trips for the pleasure traveler up to the point at which the trip's marginal revenue equals its marginal cost. The profit-maximizing criteria for the monopolist are:

$$MR_{\mathrm{b}} = p_{\mathrm{b}}\left(1 + \frac{1}{E^{\mathrm{b}}_{T,p}}\right), \qquad MR_{\mathrm{v}} = p_{\mathrm{v}}\left(1 + \frac{1}{E^{\mathrm{v}}_{T,p}}\right) \tag{7.14}$$

where "b" and "v" refer to the "business" and "vacation" traveler, respectively. Notice that the price elasticity is distinguished by type of traveler, in order to reflect the fact that the demand for business trips is not identical to the demand for pleasure trips. Given that the marginal cost of producing an additional business trip is assumed to equal the marginal cost of producing one more pleasure trip, it must be true that a profit-maximizing monopolist equates the marginal revenues associated with the business and pleasure travelers. That is, profits are maximized when

$$p_b\left(1+\frac{1}{E_{T,p}^{b}}\right)=p_v\left(1+\frac{1}{E_{T,p}^{v}}\right) \tag{7.15}$$

We assumed that the airline's pricing strategy charges businessmen higher prices than pleasure travelers, $p_b > p_v$. In order to maintain the equality in equation (7.15), it must then be true that

$$\left(1+\frac{1}{E_{T,p}^{b}}\right)<\left(1+\frac{1}{E_{T,p}^{v}}\right)$$
$$\Rightarrow \left(\frac{1}{E_{T,p}^{b}}\right)<\left(\frac{1}{E_{T,p}^{v}}\right)$$
$$\Rightarrow E_{T,p}^{b} > E_{T,p}^{v} \tag{7.16}$$

Recalling that $0 > E_{T,p} > -\infty$, equation (7.16) says that the monopolist sets a *higher price* in that market which has the *more inelastic* demand; that is, in the market which is less sensitive to changes in price. Alternatively, the more price sensitive the market is, the less will be the divergence between marginal cost and price. Thus, the adopted pricing strategy of charging a higher price to business travelers is rational for our profit-maximizing monopolist. Figure 7.10 depicts this strategy; we have assumed that the marginal trip production cost is constant and equal for business and leisure trips. We see in the graph that the slope of the vacation traveler's demand curve is flatter than that of the business traveler. All else constant, the vacation traveler is more sensitive to price and, accordingly, less willing to bear prices that deviate much from marginal cost. Exhibiting less sensitivity to price, the business traveler is willing to bear a higher fare for the same trip.

Implicit in figure 7.10 and the above results are two necessary conditions for price discrimination. First, the price elasticity of demand must differ in each market. If, in the above example, business and pleasure travelers were equally sensitive to changes in price, $E_{T,p}^{b} = E_{T,p}^{v}$, the price in each market would be identical. Price discrimination would not add profits. Second, it is

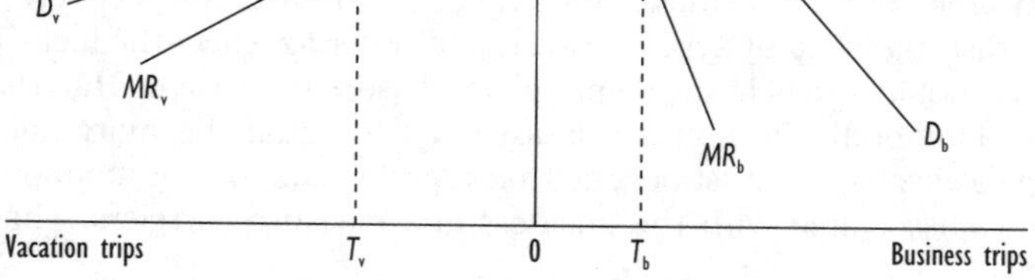

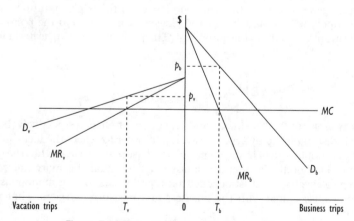

Figure 7.10 Price discrimination with uniform marginal cost.

necessary that the two markets are separate; that is, it is not possible for an individual in the higher-priced market to purchase the good in the lower-priced market.[20] Since, in general, an airline cannot distinguish business from pleasure travelers, a business traveler could claim to be a pleasure traveler and pay a lower price. If this occurs, the airline's price discrimination policy breaks down. One way to get around this problem and ensure that the two markets are separate is to impose restrictions upon length of stay. Many super-saver fares require a minimum 7 day stay. Since most business trips are for shorter periods, this restriction effectively prevents the businessman from entering the lower-priced market. Another strategy is advance reservations. Many airlines require that travelers make their reservations at least 14 days in advance, with heavy penalties for changing reservations, in order to qualify for the lower fare. Since business travelers often fly with little prior notice, but vacationers typically plan well in advance, this also has the effect of separating the market into two distinct submarkets.

The equilibrium condition for profit-maximization in equation (7.15) implies that profits would be lower had the monopolist set a single price and ignored the differences in demand elasticities. And the previous example illustrated the positive effect on profits under uniform marginal cost but different prices. Suppose, alternatively, that a monopolist faces different marginal costs of production. Can the monopolist increase profits by setting a *uniform* price? Yes! Suppose that the marginal cost of providing an airline seat to a business traveler is greater than that for a vacation traveler.[21] In this case, equation (7.15) becomes

$$p\left(1+\frac{1}{E^{\mathrm{b}}_{T,p}}\right)=mc_{\mathrm{b}}>mc_{\mathrm{b}}=p\left(1+\frac{1}{E^{\mathrm{v}}_{T,p}}\right) \tag{7.17}$$

where the price p has not been subscripted since we are assuming that the monopolist charges the same price in both markets. Rewriting equation (7.14) gives the condition

$$\begin{aligned}&\left(1+\frac{1}{E^{\mathrm{b}}_{T,p}}\right)>\left(1+\frac{1}{E^{\mathrm{v}}_{T,p}}\right)\\ \Rightarrow\quad &E^{\mathrm{b}}_{T,p}>E^{\mathrm{v}}_{T,p}\end{aligned} \tag{7.18}$$

which is the same condition as given in equation (7.16). Thus, one must be careful not to equate uniform prices with the absence of price discrimination. When marginal costs differ, charging a uniform price is tantamount to profit enhancing price discrimination, since the difference between price and marginal cost in the more elastic market is less than the difference in the more inelastic market.[22]

In general, then, in comparison with a single price setting strategy, a monopolist can enhance profits by exploiting differences in the price elasticity of demand among markets in such a way that the difference between price and marginal cost is inversely related to the submarket's price elasticity of demand.[23]

Monopoly rents and barriers to entry

Notwithstanding that rent-seeking and rent-sharing activities dissipate some monopoly rents in the long run, a basic conclusion from our analysis of monopoly (and oligopoly) market structures is the continuing existence of long-run economic profits. Although the presence of pure economic profits induces others to enter the industry and compete away these rents, as is the case in competitive and monopolistically competitive markets, for long-run monopoly rents to persist there must exist barriers to entry that preclude competitors from eroding economic rents. In transportation markets, we can identify three primary sources that have traditionally acted as market entry barriers: government policy, control over a critical input, and technological scale economies.

Government policy In chapter 5, we identified various pieces of significant legislation in the United States which either initiated or tightened economic regulation in the transportation sectors. For the rail, motor carrier, and airline industries, the 1887 Act to Regulate Commerce, the Motor Carrier Act of 1935, and the Civil Aeronautics Act of 1938, respectively, contained provisions that controlled entry and exit from the industry. The 1935 Motor Carrier Act also regulated intercity passenger bus service. And the 1940 Transportation Act brought domestic water carriage under the control of the Interstate Commerce Commission. As with the other modes of travel during the period of regulation, firms wishing to transport goods by domestic water carriage were required to satisfy a "fit, willing, and able" criterion, as well as to demonstrate that their services would serve the public convenience. The Hepburn Act of 1906 vested the ICC with control over the other major mode of transport, pipelines. Although the Act regulated rates, the pipeline industry was not subject to entry controls. For pipeline carriage, entry was not believed to be a serious problem because of the high capital investment required for operation.

With the exception of pipelines, existing carriers in each of these transport sectors were "grandfathered in"; that is, a carrier that was operating when the legislation was passed received operating certificates under the new law. Combined with tight entry controls, the effect of these legislative actions was to confer a monopoly status on the existing carriers. It might be noted that, at the time each piece of legislation was enacted, the law may have conferred little or no monopoly power on to existing carriers, in the sense that rates may not have exceeded marginal production costs by very much. However, over time, significant increases in the demand for transportation by all modes, with little entry of new carriers into each sector, imply that existing carriers enjoyed increasingly larger monopoly power and society experienced increasingly greater efficiency losses.

Control over critical inputs A second factor that produces a market entry barrier is monopoly control over a needed input in the production of the product. Although not typically a significant determinant of market power, there are exceptions. Consider airport slots, which are the numbers of take-off and landing rights. In order to provide service to any given city, an airline company must have the rights to one or more slots for arriving or departing passengers. Thus, to the extent that airlines have rights over many of an airport's slots, the airline controls a significant input in providing air travel services to its customers. In the extreme, if one airline controlled all of an airport's slots, the company would face the market demand for air travel from this airport, and we would expect to see the company exercise its monopoly power by raising fares on flights that originate from the city.

Scale economies Economies of scale describe the effect on output when all inputs change in a given proportion. In addition, we demonstrated that, when facing constant input prices, firms operating under increasing (decreasing) returns to scale are on the downward (upward) portion of their long-run average cost curve. At the minimum point on the long-run average cost curve, which we have identified as the minimum efficient scale, firms operate under constant returns to scale.

Although associated with changes in all inputs, economies of scale are generally identified with capital investment and scale of plant, because capital is long-lasting and, once built, puts the firm in the short run. For most firms, economies of scale are exhausted at relatively low levels of output – low in the sense that a firm's minimum efficient scale occurs at a level of output that is small in comparison with the total amount of the good coming on to the market. In addition, since each point on the long-run average cost curve corresponds to a larger scale of plant, when the minimum efficient scale occurs at a low output level, economies of scale are exhausted with relatively little capital investment. In other words, the absence of large economies of scale in the production of a good implies that capital will not be a barrier to market entry. In the motor carrier industry, for example, owner–operators are small one-driver, one-truck firms that subcontract their services to other firms. The required capital for the owner–operator is simply a tractor–trailer, an investment that is quite small. For these firms, economies of scale are quickly exhausted and scale of plant does not constitute a market barrier.

Conversely, if we consider a railroad or a pipeline, economies of scale are exhausted only with very large capital investments. For rail, this would include such items as track, switching equipment, locomotives, rolling stock, roundhouses, and rights of way. For the pipeline industry, capital investment includes rights of way, storage facilities, operating equipment, and the pipes for carrying the oil, natural gas, or other commodity. Because firms have an incentive to make large capital investments in order to reduce long-run average costs, entering firms will not be competitive with existing firms unless comparable amounts of capital investment are forthcoming. In these sectors, the large amount of capital that is required in order to exploit the substantial economies of scale and be competitive do form a market barrier to entry.

Natural monopoly

Whereas monopoly power that originates from restricted entry to a market or restricted access to an input constitutes an artificial barrier to entry, the rise of a monopolistic market structure due to economies of scale occurs as a natural outgrowth of competitive forces. Suppose, for example, that five competing bus companies, A, B, C, D, and E, initially service a city. The resource cost of providing public transit in the city is relatively high, since each company is a separate operation with its own capital and overhead. In addition, some of the routes overlap, as more than one company serves the same customers. If company A convinced company B to merge, the combined company would operate more efficiently. By coordinating routing systems over the two areas, duplicate routes would be eliminated, so that the same total area could be served with fewer buses. Moreover, the merger would significantly reduce administrative costs (since the administrative personnel of company B would be superfluous). In general, the larger scale of operations reduces the average production cost of bus trips below the cost at which each company could separately supply the trips. By a similar argument, it would be advantageous for only one bus company to supply the public transit needs of the city. Thus, the existence of significant returns to scale transforms an ostensibly competitive industry into a monopolistic industry. The resulting monopoly is referred to as a *natural monopoly*, since the structure occurs as a result of firms' continuing pursuits to lower production costs by

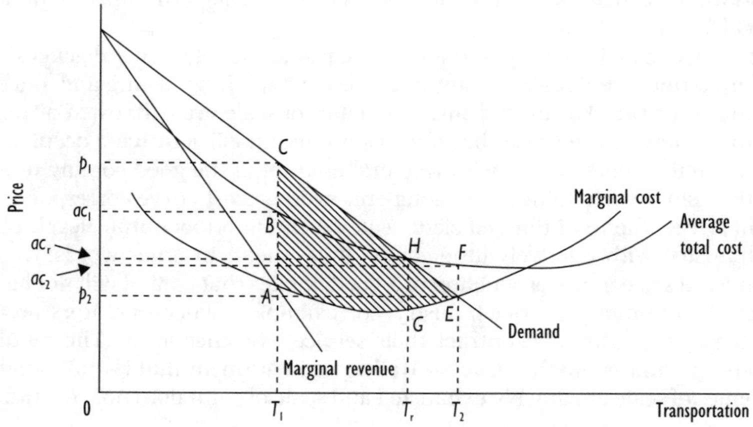

Figure 7.11 The efficiency loss of a monopoly pricing natural monopolist.

exploiting scale economies. In this case, the minimum efficient scale of the monopolistic firm is not reached before market demand is exhausted.

Figure 7.11 depicts the demand and cost structures associated with a natural monopoly. In contrast to the usual monopoly model, the natural monopolist's average cost of production is downward-sloping when demand is exhausted. We see here that the firm satisfies market demand, given by *D* in the figure, *before* all economies of scale are exhausted. Does the presence of large economies of scale affect the monopolist's optimal behavior? No. The profit-maximizing condition for the natural monopolist is no different from that considered above. The monopolist goes to point A, where marginal revenue equals marginal cost, produces output level T_1, and charges a price p_1. Monopoly profits are given by the area p_1CBac_1 and society suffers efficiency losses depicted by the shaded area *AEC*. In effect, economies of large scale imply that the optimal number of firms in the industry is one. And the remaining firm will behave as any other profit-maximizing monopolist, producing up to the point at which marginal revenue equals marginal cost.

Government Responses to Monopoly Behavior

In the transportation industry, government behavior toward monopolistic structures has depended upon the source of the monopoly power. Strict economic regulation of interstate carriage, beginning with the 1887 Act to Regulate Commerce and enduring until the mid-1970s and early 1980s, when the federal government enacted several laws to deregulate the transportation sector, maintained a continued focus on market stability and intermodal equity. Rates were regulated to ensure reasonable returns on investment in particular sectors, as well as to provide equal treatment across modes. As such, the federal government was neither concerned with an efficient allocation of resources nor with their associated efficiency losses due to the severe market entry/exit restrictions. In this case, the monopoly power and attendant welfare losses in the industry could be viewed as necessary by-products of a national policy to provide a coordinated system of intermodal transportation networks in order to meet our nation's burgeoning passenger and freight transportation needs. Indeed, the fact that market entry was so stringently restricted, and that the burden of proof was upon the entering rather than the incumbent firm throughout the regulated era, testifies to the fact that the regulators believed that too much entry would lead to disruptions and destabilize the industry rather than produce a more efficient allocation of resources and welfare gains.

However, when monopoly power results from economies of scale, government's response is substantially different. The government recognizes that, if left to their own profit-maximizing incentives, natural monopolists behave as any other monopolist, producing at the point at which marginal revenue equals marginal cost, but charging a price according to market demand and in excess of marginal cost. The monopolist earns monopoly rents and welfare losses accrue to society.

Ideally, the government wants the monopolist to produce where marginal cost equals marginal benefit. But if the government imposes this requirement, the monopolist would soon exit the industry, because revenues would not be sufficient to cover total production costs. This is seen at point E in figure 7.11, where marginal benefit equals marginal cost. Relative to the monopolist's profit-maximizing equilibrium, point E benefits consumers from an expanded output T_2 and lower price p_2. However, at T_2 average total cost of production is ac_2, which exceeds p_2. Thus, requiring the monopolist to produce at E leads to a per period economic loss equal to $(FE)T_2$, which is the area $(FE)(ac_2 - p_2)$ in figure 7.11.

In order to avoid driving the firm out of business, the government has generally used three alternative policies to regulate natural monopolies:

Marginal cost pricing with subsidy Under this regime, the government requires the monopolist to set a price equal to the marginal cost of production and uses government revenues to subsidize any capital losses. This ensures an efficient allocation of resources in the industry and provides the firm with a normal rate of return on its investment. For example, the Rail Passenger Act of 1970 established Amtrak as a profit-maximizing national passenger rail service. As initially formulated, Amtrak revenues were expected to cover operating or marginal production costs with federal subsidies covering the remaining deficits (Hilton, 1980).

Also, prior to the 1970s, publicly owned and operated urban transit agencies were expected to develop an urban public transportation network that generated operating revenues at least sufficient to cover operating costs. Public subsidies provided for all or part of unrecoverable capital costs (Jones, 1985).

Rate-of-return regulation This is a form of average cost pricing and is the most common method for regulating natural monopolies. Under rate-of-return regulation, the government allows the natural monopolist to set a price equal to long-run average cost, which enables the firm to cover its variable and fixed costs of production. In figure 7.11, the monopolist goes to point H, charges a price ac_r and produces output T_r. Since price exceeds marginal cost at this output level, there still exist some welfare losses, equal to the area HGE. However, relative to the monopolistic equilibrium at point A, price is lower, output is greater, and efficiency losses are less. In addition, economic profits are zero. The monopolist earns no monopoly rents and receives a normal return on investment.[24]

A variation on rate-of-return regulation is rate-setting based on a firm's *operating ratio*, defined as the ratio of operating costs to operating revenues. The ICC argued that this basis for rate-setting was more appropriate in the motor carrier industry, since capital investment in this sector was relatively small in comparison with total operating costs. Graphically, this implies that the average total and average variable cost curves are very close together, and leads to the possibility that a firm's ability to cover its operating costs would be uncomfortably sensitive to small errors in revenue and cost calculations under rate-of-return regulation. In general, the ICC defined 93% to be an appropriate or equitable operating ratio for the motor carrier industry – which, interestingly, implied a rate of return in the 20–40% range (Wilson, 1980)!

Government operation A third solution to the natural monopoly problem is to have the government directly operate the monopoly. Public ownership is a common form of production, for example, in the public transportation industry. Theoretically, this case is identical to private ownership with marginal cost pricing plus subsidy. The marginal cost pricing rule ensures that an efficient number of public transit trips is taken and the resulting deficit is made up through subsidization from public revenues. Practically, however, public ownership and operation may lead to production inefficiencies that are not present, or are less prevalent, under private ownership. Under public ownership and operation, there are substantially lower incentives to maximize profits, since the benefits of these activities go into the public coffers rather than to those who generated the increased wealth. As a result, marginal and average production costs tend to be higher and output lower under public ownership. In comparison with private ownership and operation, the inefficiencies of public ownership are revealed in the form of higher consumer prices and larger deficits.

The belief that private ownership and operation will lead to more efficient production of transportation has fueled a growing movement in the recent past to privatize government-run activities in a number of transportation areas. In the urban transit sector, privately owned and unsubsidized limousine services to and from airports operate in most large cities. In New York and Miami, minibus and van services – private, but oftentimes unlicensed – have appeared. There are ongoing experiments with privately owned toll roads in California and Virginia, and some privatized firms either own airports or contract with private firms to manage publicly owned airports. There have also been proposals to privately develop and operate fixed rail high-speed feeder and connector lines in Boston, Washington DC, and Orlando.[25]

MEASURING MARKET CONCENTRATION

Imperfectly competitive market structures give existing firms market power and, in general, the closer a market structure is to a pure monopoly, the greater will be a firm's ability to exercise its market power, all else held constant. But how concentrated is an industry? This raises the question of how we empirically measure the extent to which an industry is concentrated. In practice, two alternative measures are frequently employed for determining an industry's concentration and inferring whether there exists substantial market power. The first measure focuses upon the market share of the leading four (or eight) firms, and is appropriately called the four-firm (eight-firm) concentration ratio. The four-firm concentration ratio CR_4 gives the market share of the largest four firms in the industry, and is defined as

$$CR_4 = \sum_{i=1}^{4}(MS_i \times 100)$$

where MS_i is the market share of firm i ($i = 1, \ldots, 4$). The eight-firm concentration ratio is similarly defined. By only looking at the top four firms in the industry, the concentration ratio ignores both the total number of firms in the industry as well as distribution of market shares among the firms. For example, suppose that each of the top four firms in industry A has a 15% market share. In contrast, the top four firms in industry B have market shares equal to 5%, 5%, 5%, and 45%, respectively. Although the four-firm concentration ratio is 60 in both industries, industry A characterizes a traditional oligopolistic market, in which each of a few suppliers has a large market share. Industry B, on the other hand, appears to characterize a dominant firm market structure, in which one firm has a substantial share of the market and no close rivals.

A second empirical measure of industry concentration is the Hirschman–Herfindahl Index (*HHI*). For an industry with n firms, the *HHI* is defined as

$$HHI = \sum_{i=1}^{n} (MS_i \times 100)^2 \tag{7.19}$$

The *HHI* differs from the four- (or eight-) firm concentration ratio in two ways. First, the market share of each firm in the index is squared, which gives more weight to firms with larger market shares. Second, the index includes all firms in the industry rather than a small subset. In a perfectly competitive industry where firms produce an identical amount of the good, each firm's market share would be $1/n$ and the *HHI* would be

$$\sum_{i=1}^{n} \left(\frac{1}{n} \times 100\right)^2 = \left(\frac{10{,}000}{n}\right)$$

For example, if there were 100 firms in an industry, the *HHI* would equal 100, whereas in an industry with 10,000 firms the *HHI* would equal one. At the other extreme, in the pure monopoly case, the *HHI* is $(1 \times 100)^2 = 10{,}000$.

CASE STUDY – CONCENTRATION IN THE LTL MOTOR CARRIER SECTOR

To illustrate these ideas, table 7.3 presents concentration measures for the less-than-truckload (LTL) segment of motor carrier industry in 1990. Because the LTL sector requires an extensive distribution network for its transportation activities, LTL firms have an incentive to expand, either through growth or merger, in order to exploit economies of scale associated with network size. This line of reasoning argues that the LTL market will evolve in such a way that only one or a very few large LTL firms will remain to serve all shippers; that is, the optimal market structure is a natural monopoly or small oligopoly. This would give LTLs considerable market power which, if not checked by the government, would lead to an increase in prices.[26] Relative to 10–15 years ago, there are fewer LTLs and the revenues of the largest LTLs have increased. Has this led to undue concentration in the industry and increased shipping rates? At present, the answer appears to be no.

We see from table 7.3 that there is concentration, but the extent of concentration in the LTL sector is not excessive. Whether measured by intercity LTL freight revenue or by total operating revenues, the largest four (eight)

Table 7.3 Concentration ratios in the LTL motor carrier industry, 1990

Revenue Measure	Four-Firm Ratio (%)	Eight-Firm Ratio (%)	*HHI*
Intercity LTL Freight Revenue	52	66	842.7
Total Operating Revenues	49	63	759.8

Source: The US motor carrier industry long after deregulation. Report, Office of Economics, ICC. Interstate Commerce Commission 1992: Data are based on 107 Class I common carrier firms that derive at least 75% of their revenue from intercity transport of general freight

firms in the industry represent about 50% (65%) of the market. Some have argued that a four-firm concentration ratio greater than 60% constitutes a *tight* oligopoly in which the ability to fix prices is strong, whereas a four-firm concentration ratio below 40% is a *loose* oligopoly with little ability to fix prices (Shepherd, 1990). We see in table 7.3 that the LTL sector lies in between, which suggests that the larger LTL firms may have some price-setting potential.

What does the *HHI* tell us? Although we know that larger values of *HHI* reflect greater concentration, how high is high? As a guide, we use the Department of Justice's criterion for evaluating the antitrust implications of company mergers. If the post-merger *HHI* is below 1,000, the market is assumed to be unconcentrated and the merger is not challenged, all other relevant factors held constant. Using the Department of Justice's *HHI* criterion, and based upon either firm size measure, we see in table 7.3 that the *HHI* is less than 1,000, which indicates that the LTL sector of the motor carrier industry is presently not so concentrated as to pose a serious price threat to shippers.

Despite the increasing size of the larger LTL firms, the evidence presented in table 7.3 paints a picture of an industrial sector that is moderately concentrated and may bear watching. However, consistent with the *HHI* values, the tell-tale signs of exploited market power in the form of higher transportation rates and economic profits are not present in the sector. The LTL sector is currently competitive because shippers today face alternatives that were not available in the past (Winston et al., 1990). LTL firms are full service providers in that they perform pick-up, break-bulking, line-haul, and delivery services. In today's environment, however, LTL firms face increased competition from freight forwarders and brokers, who may perform pick-up, break-bulking, and delivery services while subcontracting with a truckload motor carrier for the line-haul portion of the trip. In addition, other modes – including package express services, rail, ocean, and air express – play a larger competing role today for LTL traffic than a decade ago. And the impact of these transport alternatives to freight shippers is to limit, if not completely eliminate, the tendencies of the larger LTL firms to set prices.

CASE STUDY – CONCENTRATION IN THE US AIRLINE INDUSTRY

As another example of concentration ratios, consider the airline industry and the effect on concentration in the industry from economic deregulation in 1978. We have seen that, by enabling airline companies to freely set prices and eliminating route restrictions, the 1978 Airline Deregulation Act provided airline companies with an incentive to rationalize its operations through the development of hub-and-spoke passenger distribution networks. For present purposes, we can ask whether airline hubbing has led to greater or less concentration in the industry. As is often the case, the answer depends upon how we look at the industry.

Table 7.4 Concentration ratios in the domestic passenger airline industry, 1977–90

Year	Four-Firm Ratio (%)	Eight-Firm Ratio (%)	*HHI*
1977	56.2	81.1	1,060
1982	54.2	80.4	930
1987	64.8	86.5	1,230
1990	61.5	90.5	1,210

Source: Adapted from Borenstein (1992), table 1, p. 47

Table 7.5 Average city-pair Hirschman–Herfindahl indices in the domestic passenger airline industry, 1984–90

	Market Distance (miles)					
Year	0–200	201–500	501–1,000	1,000–1,500	> 1,500	All
Direct flights only						
1984	601	598	601	581	536	590
1987	691	648	612	587	532	620
1990	612	641	672	625	536	632
All flights						
1984	600	588	537	479	415	531
1987	689	616	498	444	363	512
1990	618	614	518	424	357	506

Source: Adapted from Borenstein (1992), table 2, p. 49

Table 7.4 reports the four-firm and eight-firm concentration ratios and the *HHI* for the entire industry over the period 1977–90. Between 1977 and 1982, concentration in the industry initially fell, which is consistent with firm entry in the years immediately after economic deregulation. However, from 1982 to 1990, each measure denotes increased concentration in the industry. There was a 13.5%, 12.5%, and 30.1% increase in the four-firm, eight-firm, and *HHI* respectively. As in the LTL sector, the airline industry market structure lies somewhere between a loose oligopoly and tight oligopoly.

In order to see further into the industry's market structure and the extent of competition, consider table 7.5, which reports average *HHIs* for city-pairs for all trips and separately for direct flights. The indices are also reported by distance between cities. There are a number of interesting features in table 7.5. First, in comparison with the *HHIs* reported in table 7.4, the indices in table 7.5 are considerably lower. Regardless of length of trip, city-pair markets are more competitive than is suggested by the national *HHIs* given in table 7.4, which stands to reason, since the actual competition among firms occurs at the route level.

Second, what is the effect of hubbing on direct flights that do not involve a change of plane? For an airline company, a hub plays the same role as break-bulking centers for LTL motor carriers. Passengers traveling from origin A to destination C will be routed through hub H. At H, the airline will "break-bulk" passengers, distributing them to other flights, sometimes on their own airplanes and sometimes on competitors' flights, for "distribution" to destination C. By having more passengers pass through its hub, the airline increases its load factors and the frequency of direct flights between the hub and other cities. Combined with the fact that most airports have the physical capacity to accommodate one or at most two hubs, this suggests that hubbing has increased market concentration for direct flights into and out of the hub. The *HHIs* in table 7.5 are consistent with this interpretation. For direct flights, the *HHIs* in the last column increased between 1984 and 1990. The increasing concentration is also prevalent regardless of trip length, with the exception of the longest flights. From the table, the greatest impact on concentration occurs in the medium-length trips ranging from 200 to 1,500 miles.

Third, what effect has hubbing had on concentration if we consider flights on which passengers must change planes? As mentioned above, hubs enable airlines to funnel more passengers through its hub for distribution to other flights, which oftentimes involves a change of plane. The benefit is that the airline is now able to service many more city-pairs. The down side for the airline, however, is that hubbing also enables other airline companies to service many cities, so that a passenger changing planes will have more choices available. In that most long-distance flights involve a change of plane, this implies that we will see decreased concentration on long-distance flights and increased concentration on short-distance flights. Again, the *HHIs* for All Flights reported in column 6 of table 7.5 are consistent with this. For flights up to 500 miles in length, the *HHI* increased, which points to reduced competition. For flights in excess of 500 miles, however, we see a consistent fall in the *HHI*, which indicates that these market segments became less concentrated and more competitive between 1984 and 1990.

The *HHIs* reported in table 7.5 and the above analysis suggest that there is not marked concentration in these markets, although increased concentration has occurred in the short- to medium-distance markets. But the relevant policy question is whether hubbing effects have resulted in signficant fare increases for the passengers. Generally consistent with table 7.5, Morrison and Winston (1995) analyzed fare premiums at 15 hub airports and found that the highest premia, at 10%, occurred during the 1988–90 period. Subsequently, these premia have fallen by 4–7%, and in 1993 they were estimated at 5.2%.[27]

CASE STUDY – CONTESTABLE MARKET THEORY: ACTUAL VERSUS POTENTIAL COMPETITION

In perfectly competitive markets, the actions of any one firm's *actual* competitors disciplines the behavior of a given firm. If a competitive firm prices above marginal cost, for example, its competitors in the market will undercut their prices and capture all of its customers. Thus, a perfectly competitive firm has an incentive to price at marginal cost for fear that it will lose all of its market share to competitors. In contrast to perfect competition, contestable markets focus upon the total market. Similar to natural monopolies or oligopolies, contestable markets have one or at most very few producers. However, unlike natural monopolies or oligopolies, contestable markets are primarily concerned with competition *for the market*, not with competition among incumbent producers. It is the markets that are contested and, as a result, *potential* competitors rather than actual competitors play prominent roles in disciplining the behavior of incumbent firms.[28]

Consider the problem of providing air service between two small cities that are 150 miles apart. The route is currently serviced by one airline company. Assume that there is freedom of entry into and exit from the market. Further, assume that new entrants in the market face the same production technology and input prices, and therefore identical production costs, as the incumbent. The output of any producing firm is perceived by the traveling public to be a perfect substitute. Finally, assume that fixed costs are not sunk, in the sense that if a new entrant subsequently decides to exit the market, its capital assets can be readily sold off with no loss (other than capital depreciation). Thus, this market for flights between the two cities has neither effective barriers to entry nor barriers to exit.

Let's suppose that average daily demand for air travel is 15 persons, which is less than the capacity of one plane making one flight per day. Although there is freedom of entry into and exit from the market, the small number of daily passengers implies that the optimal number of airline firms in the market is one. Further, with such a small number of daily travelers, demand is not sufficiently large to exhaust economies of scale, so that the demand curve intersects the average cost curve on its downward-sloping portion, and the firm is operating under increasing returns to scale. We know that if this firm prices at marginal cost, it would not be able to cover its fixed costs of production and would exit the market. Alternatively, if the firm exploits its market power and prices at the point at which marginal revenue equaled marginal cost, price would exceed average cost of production, pure economic profits would accrue to the monopolist, and society would incur welfare losses.[29]

Given that the one firm servicing the route is a monopolist, we can ask three related questions. First, does the incumbent monopolist have an incentive to produce where marginal cost equals marginal revenue? Second, is this price *sustainable*; that is, at this price will the firm make at least zero economic profits and not induce entry by other firms? And, third, if the answer to the second question is no, then what price is sustainable? To consider these questions, let's analyze our small-town market in greater detail.

Suppose that Ever Present Airlines company is the incumbent firm and currently offers service between the two cities at a one-way fare of $100, the monopolistic profit-maximizing price at which marginal revenue equals marginal cost. Its average total cost per trip is $70, so that the airline is making a $30 economic profit per person flown or a total daily economic profit of $450.00. Since the firm is a monopolist, the answer to the first question, as we have previously seen, is easy. Ever Present Airlines is a profit-maximizer and certainly has an incentive to price at the point at which its marginal production cost equals its marginal revenue.

Although all of Ever Present's competitors realize that only one company is economically viable in this market, Ever Present's one-way fare provides an incentive for currently nonproducing competitors to enter and compete for the entire market in order to capture the pure economic profits. In other words, the $100 price set by Ever Present Airlines is *not sustainable*. In response to the $100 fare, assume that Hit and Run Airways decides to offer a one flight per day service between the cities, but charges a lower $90 one-way fare. With the same production costs as Ever Present Airlines, Hit and Run Airways will take all of Ever Present's customers and make an economic profit of $20 per ticketed fare or $300 per day. Of course, this is not the end of the story. Ever Present Airlines will respond to this competition by reducing its fare below $90, Hit and Run will similarly respond, and the process continues until the one-way fare falls to $70, which is the average total cost of production. Assuming that Ever Present Airlines remains the incumbent firm, the $70 one-way fare is just sufficient to cover its economic costs. Further, the $70 fare is a sustainable price because Ever Present is making zero economic profits, and there is no longer any incentive on the part of Hit and Run Airways or any other potential competitor to enter the market.[30]

Thus, in a contestable market, pricing where $MC = MR$ is not sustainable, whereas pricing at average total cost is sustainable. Why is this result different from the standard monopoly case that we previously examined? The key to the difference is the assumption made in contestable markets that there are no barriers to entry or exit from the market. It is important to understand what this assumption means. In the standard natural monopoly model, we identified scale economies as a potential barrier to entry. A firm entering the market would have to incur capital investment costs just to get production going. If these capital costs are large, they act as an effective barrier to entry. And the presence of these entry barriers enable the natural monopolist in the typical case to maximize profits where $MC = MR$ with no fear of entry from competitors.

In contestable markets, however, we assumed that there were no entry or exit barriers. For contestable markets, it is not the size of capital investment that constitutes an entry barrier but, rather, the prospect of losing one's investment upon exit that creates a barrier. If, for example, the invested capital either has little value outside of its current use, or there would be significant delays in disposing of the capital, then investment is effectively sunk and this creates a barrier to entry. In this circumstance, our monopolist would behave exactly as the typical monopolist by setting price where $MC = MR$. However, if an entrant can incur the capital cost, however large, but can also easily recoup this investment upon exit from the market, then the market is contestable. Because entry and exit is costless, the *threat of entry* now disciplines the incumbent to set prices at a sustainable level which yields zero economic profit and produces no incentive for entry by potential competitors.

As we saw in our example, if Ever Present Airlines makes pure economic profits, then, with costless entry and exit, Hit and Run Airways enters the market, undercuts the price, and makes a quick profit. If Ever Present Airlines retaliates and sets price at average total cost, Hit and Run costlessly exits the market, selling off its invested capital without loss (other than physical depreciation). In this contestable market, it is the *threat of entry* by Hit and Run Airways and other potential competitors that induces Ever Present Airlines to price at average total cost.[31]

To sum up, we can identify two general factors that are important to contestable markets. First, there must be freedom of entry and exit which, as we have seen, implies that capital costs, although fixed and possibly quite large, are not sunk. Second, there must be a pool of potential entrants "poised for entry," since it is their presence that induces the producing firm to set sustainable prices.

Competition and contestability in the US airline industry

For contestable markets, potential rather than actual competition plays a dominant role in disciplining the market. In the extreme, if a market were perfectly contestable, then the only check on a monopolist's exercise of market power would be the number of potential competitors ready to enter the market if pure profits were available. In reality, contestable markets are not likely to be perfectly contestable. Nevertheless, one of the important insights from contestability theory is the disciplining role of potential competitors.

Figure 7.12 depicts the pattern of nominal fares (in cents per passenger mile) between 1979 and 1989. We see in the figure that fares were relatively volatile, rising by 46% between 1979 and 1981, flattening out between 1981 and 1984, falling by 18% from 1984 through 1986, and rising through 1989. Notice that the nominal fare was in fact lower in 1986 and 1987 relative to 1980.

The rise in air fares in the latter part of the 1980s prompted governmental concern, among other issues, over whether hubbing had contributed to the nominal price rise. This raises a basic question of the roles that actual and potential competition play in price behavior over time. From a sample of 18,573 routes between the fourth quarter of 1978 and the fourth quarter of 1988, Morrison and Winston (1990) investigated the importance of actual competitors versus potential competitors in determining nominal airline prices. In their analysis, Morrison and Winston assume that airline fares depend upon five basic determinants:

- the distance (in miles) between the airports on a route

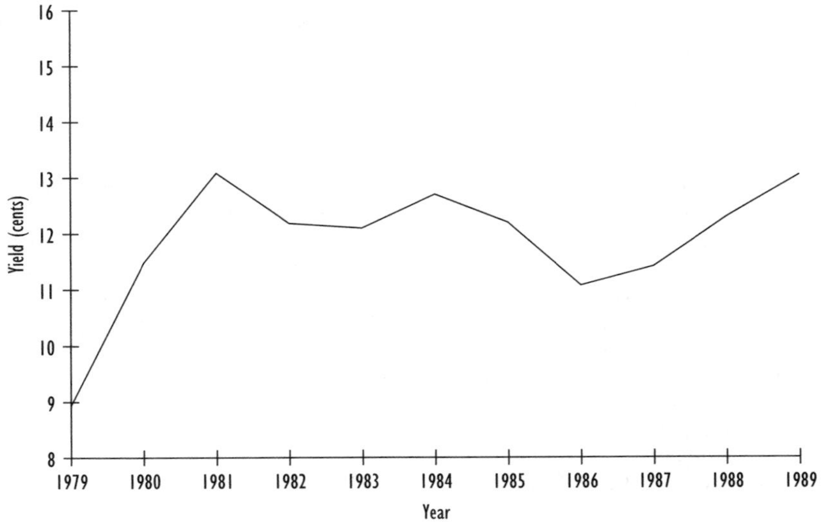

Figure 7.12 Nominal airline revenues, 1979–89.

- the number of effective competitors on routes at fixed-slot airports
- the number of effective competitors on routes at nonfixed-slot airports
- the minimum number of effective competitors at a route's endpoints
- the number of potential carriers

There are a number of points regarding these explanatory variables. First, how do we measure the number of "effective" competitors on a given route? Recall our previous discussion of the Hirschman–Herfindahl Index (*HHI*), which is based upon the market shares of all firms actually in the market. Suppose that we calculate the *HHI* to be 1,000. If we invert the *HHI* (and multiply by 10,000), we obtain $(0.0001) * 10{,}000 = 10$. In other words, a market structure that produces an *HHI* of 1,000 is equivalent to a market structure with ten firms, each of which has a 10% share of the market. To see this, use equation (7.12) to calculate the associated *HHI* for a market with ten firms, each with an equal share. You will get 1,000. Thus, inverting the *HHI* (and multiplying by 10,000) gives the number of "effective" competitors in a market, where each effective competitor has an equal market share. To take one more example, suppose that the *HHI* is 1,430. Then there are $(1/1{,}430) * 10{,}000 = 7$ effective competitors, each with 14.3% of the market.

Second, why do Morrison and Winston distinguish between routes at airports with a fixed number of slots – that is, take-off and landing rights – from routes at airports without a fixed number of slots? New York, Washington DC, and Chicago airports have a fixed number of available slots. For example, Chicago's O'Hare Airport has maintained 1,670 slots since 1969. This imposes a constraint on the total aircraft operations, which implies that the effect of competition at these slot-controlled airports will likely differ from that at slot-uncontrolled airports; that is, airports whose slots increase over time.

Third, Morrison and Winston include the minimum number of effective competitors at a route's endpoint in order to capture possible hubbing effects. If hubbing at a route's endpoint is significant, one would expect greater concentration at the endpoint and potentially a greater ability to raise fares.

Last, the number of potential competitors is defined as the number of carriers operating in the origin city, the endpoint city, or both cities, *but not* flying the route between the two cities. Since these carriers already operate in either or both cities, a decision to fly the route would entail relatively little cost, consistent with the assumptions of contestable market theory.

Associated with these explanatory variables, we can identify four hypotheses:

HYPOTHESIS 1 Since the cost of producing trips between two cities is positively related to distance, the greater the distance is between the two cities, the higher the fare, all else held constant. However, because there are fixed costs associated with take-offs and landings, fares are not expected to increase proportionately with distance. Thus, we expect the coefficient of Distance to be positive.

HYPOTHESIS 2 An increase in the actual number of competitors, all else held constant, will reduce airline fares. This is the standard competitive result. The larger the number of competitors producing the service is, the further to the right is the market supply curve and the lower the price. Since "Number of effective competitors on routes at fixed-slot airports," "Number of effective competitors on routes at nonfixed-slot airports," and "Minimum number of effective competitors at a route's endpoints" are all measures of actual competition, the coefficient on each of these variables is expected to be negative.

HYPOTHESIS 3 The sample covers an 11-year period immediately after passage of the Airline Deregulation Act in 1978, which enabled the authors to examine short-run and long-run effects of actual competition on prices. It is expected that the effects of actual competition on prices will be greater in the long run than in the short run, since it takes time to fully adjust to new economic environments. We can use the fact that entry in the industry was not completely free until 1982 to test this hypothesis. Define two dummy variables, one for the short run (limited entry) period 1978–81, and another for the long-run (unlimited entry) period 1982–8. By interacting each dummy variable with each of the actual competition variables, we can test the hypothesis that short-run effects will be smaller than long-run effects.

HYPOTHESIS 4 If the market for airline routes is contestable, then an increase in the number of potential carriers is expected to reduce air fares, all else held constant. As with actual competition, we use two dummy variables to test whether the short-run effect of potential competition differs from a long-run effect, although in this case there are no prior expectations on whether the short-run effect will be greater or less than the long-run effect.

The estimated model, in double-log form, is reported in table 7.6. The high R^2 indicates a strong model fit and the results are generally consistent with the specified hypotheses. All else held constant, longer routes are associated with higher fares, but not proportionately. A 10% increase in route distance leads to a 5% increase in airfares. Consistent with hypothesis 2, all actual competition variables are negative, with one exception, and significantly different from zero. Notice also that the short-run effect of increasing actual competition is smaller than the associated long-run effect, which is consistent with hypothesis 3. A 10% increase in the "Number of competitors on routes at fixed-slot airports" lowered fares by 0.37% in the short run, but produced a 1.19% fall in the long run. We see a similar pattern at airports without a fixed number of slots, where a 10% rise in competitors produced no short-run effect on price, but a 0.35% price fall in the longer run. An interesting question here is as follows: Why would an increase in actual competition on routes serving fixed-slot airports have a smaller effect on airfares than on routes serving nonfixed-slot airports? With increasing traffic at slot-controlled airports, the opportunity cost of each slot rises, which is simply saying that the value of take-offs and landings at these airports increases. Thus, airfares at slot-restricted airports can be

Table 7.6 Nominal airline fare regression – double-log model

Dependent variable – ln (Airfare, cents per passenger mile)

Explanatory Variables	Coefficient Estimate (*t*-statistic)
ln (Distance, in miles)	0.501 (167.0)
ln (Number of effective competitors on routes at fixed slot airports)	
1978–81	−0.037 (−3.70)
1982–8	−0.119 (−19.8)
ln (Number of effective competitors on routes at non-fixed slot airports)	
1978–81	0.006 (0.46)
1982–8	−0.035 (−4.38)
ln (Minimum number of effective competitors at a route's endpoints)	
1978–81	−0.015 (−1.67)
1982–8	−0.201 (−40.2)
ln (Potential carriers)	
1978–81	−0.0055 (−9.12)
1982–8	−0.0014 (−3.50)
$R^2 = 0.99$	

Source: Morrison and Winston (1990), table 1, p. 390. The estimated model also included time dummy variables for each year but were not reported

expected to reflect, at least partially, the increased value of the airport's slots. And this suggests that increased competition at slot-restricted airports will have a smaller price effect than at slot-unrestricted airports.

Also as expected, we see in table 7.6 that an increase in the minimum number of competitors at the route's endpoint reduces fares. In both time periods, the effect is negative and significant. But the magnitude of the effect differs greatly. The short-run effect of a 10% increase in competition reduced prices by 0.15%, but had a 2.0% effect on fares in the long run. These results are also consistent with the notion that hubbing tends to increase concentration and reduce competition.

Are the results consistent with contestable markets? Yes and no. If markets were perfectly contestable, then only potential competition would matter and we would not find any significant effects due to actual competition. The finding that actual competition induces price reductions implies that airline routes are not perfectly contestable. But the results do indicate that these markets are *imperfectly contestable*. As expected, an increase in the number of potential carriers on a route leads to price reductions, and these effects are statistically significant. The magnitude of these price effects, however, is relatively small, at least in comparison with actual competition, and the effect has decreased over time. In the short- and longer-run periods, a 10% increase in potential competition produces a 0.05% and 0.014% reduction in price, all else held constant.

The implication of these findings is that competition – both actual and potential – is important. Although the finding that markets are at most imperfectly contestable suggests that airline city-pair markets fail to satisfy a fundamental assumption in contestability – namely, the absence of sunk costs – market contestability has been used to support airline mergers in the mid-1980s (Morrison and Winston, 1995).

MONOPOLY RENTS IN THE MOTOR CARRIER INDUSTRY

CASE STUDY – MOTOR CARRIER FIRM RENTS

Our analysis of imperfect competition argued that, among other effects, monopoly power leads to economic profits or monopoly rents that will not be completely dissipated in the long run. We also cited the economic regulation in the motor carrier industry as an example of government policy that, to some degree, conferred monopoly power on firms in the industry. In this section, we want to quantify the extent to which economic regulation, beginning with the 1935 Motor Carrier Act, created monopoly rents, as well as examining what factors most contributed to these rents.

In a paper on the effects of economic regulation in the motor carrier industry, Moore (1978) considered the question of how restrictions on market entry conferred monopoly rents on firms that possessed operating certificates. When the 1935 Motor Carrier Act was passed, the ICC received 89,000 applications to obtain operating certificates based upon a "grandfather" status. Of these, about 27,000 applications, or 30% of the total, were approved. In addition, the firms that received operating rights were limited to the specific commodities and routes that they served prior to the law. In other words, the ICC did not expand firm operating rights beyond a firm's previous transportation activities. Over time, the ICC approved very few applications from new carriers; mergers and bankruptcies reduced the number of firms to 14,648 by 1974; and intercity tons shipped by regulated firms substantially increased from 25.5 million in 1938 to 698.1 million in 1974. Combined, these factors suggest that, by 1974, existing firms in the industry did possess market power and would be expected to have earned some monopoly rents. Can we empirically quantify these economic rents? Yes.

We have seen that one method used to extract long-run monopoly rents is capitalization.[32] A firm wishing to purchase an operating certificate pays the seller the expected value of the operating certificate. Thus, the purchase price of the certificate reveals the value of the monopoly rent that the buyer expects to earn from owning the certificate. For the years 1975 and 1976, Moore obtained information on 23 cases where only operating rights were purchased. For each of these sales, information on estimated revenues and purchase price was available. Moore estimated a regression model in order to analyze the effect of annual revenues on purchase price. The dependent variable was the purchase price of the certificate and the one explanatory variable was expected annual revenues. Moore's results are presented in equation (7.20) below:[33]

$$\text{Purchase Price} = \hat{\alpha}_0 + \underset{(9.5)}{0.152}(\text{Annual Revenues}),$$

$$R^2 = 0.91 \qquad (7.20)$$

where the number in parentheses is the t-statistic. From the R^2 statistic, annual revenues explained 91% of the variation in purchase price. Holding all else constant, economic theory predicts that an increase in expected annual revenues will increase the value of the operating certificate. The positive sign for the coefficient on Annual Revenues is consistent with this prediction, and the 0.152 coefficient value implies that certificate purchasers were paying about 15% of annual revenues for the operating rights. In other words, for every $1 increase in expected annual revenues, 15 cents goes toward purchase of the operating certificate.

What do these results imply for the industry as a whole? A 90% confidence interval for the estimated coefficient in equation (7.20) is (12.5, 17.9).[34] In 1972, total annual operating revenue for Class I and Class II motor carriers was $16.8 billion. Based upon our 90% confidence interval, this implies that the estimated value of existing operating certificates at the time ranged between $2.1 (12.5 × 16.8) and $3 (17.9 × 16.8) billion.

Using a similar procedure, Moore also investigated the rate of return that the operating rights generated by regressing projected before-tax profits on the purchase price. Equation (7.21) reports these results (with the *t*-statistic in parentheses):[35]

$$\text{Before-Tax Profits} = \hat{\alpha}_1 + \underset{(7.1)}{0.568}(\text{Purchase Price}),$$

$$R^2 = 0.70 \qquad (7.21)$$

Based upon 23 observations, a $1 increase in a certificate's purchase price increased expected before-tax profits by 56.8 cents. That is, a $1 increase in purchase price produces a 56.8% rate of return on investment with a 90% confidence interval equal to (43.0, 70.6).

We have just seen that the expected annual income from owning an operating certificate in the motor carrier industry was a significant determinant of the certificate's value. An alternative approach to analyzing a certificate's value focuses upon the determinants of firm profits. Since monopoly rents per period are simply per-period economic profits, factors that lead to higher firm profits would also increase the value of operating certificates, all else held constant. If T is the amount of transportation supplied, p_T is the price of transportation, and ac_T is the average cost of supplied transportation, then profit per period is $(p_T - ac_T)T$. Since firms had to supply all transportation demanded at the ICC regulated rates, this suggests that the values of operating certificates depend upon two basic factors: (1) shipper demands for transportation, T; and (2) a firm's per unit profit on transportation supplied, $(p_T - ac_T)$. By relating shipper demands and per unit profits to firm operating characteristics, it is then possible to analyze how firm operating characteristics contribute to certificate values and monopoly rents.

Frew (1981) adopted this approach and used regression analysis to identify the most important determinants of certificate values for regular route less-than-truckload general commodity carriers. Similar to Moore, the dependent variable in Frew's analysis is the certificate value, and the independent variables include demand-related and per unit profit operating characteristics.[36] Since this analysis is an extension of Moore's original study, we shall not report Frew's regression results but summarize his major findings.

Demand determinants Frew found that, in the area served, *population* and *retail sales* (a measure of disposable income) had significant positive effects upon the certificate value of a general commodity carrier.[37] In addition, the number of competing truck carriers, representing relevant substitutes, was an important determinant of certificate value. As predicted by economic theory, an increase in the number of competing carriers reduced the certificate's value, all else held constant. Two other demand-related operating characteristics are line-haul length and route network. Assuming that the demand for a carrier's services is greater the further goods are carried, then an increase in route length would be expected to increase certificate value, all else held constant. In his analysis, Frew found this to be the case.

An expansive route network was expected to increase the demand for a carrier's services, and thus raise a certificate's value, because a larger network reduces the need for interlining, transfers, and break-bulking activities. Because Frew did not have a direct measure for a carrier's route network, he used as a proxy expected annual income (the same variable that Moore used in his analysis), reasoning that larger expected annual revenues reflect a greater effect of the new certificate on the carrier's network.[38] As expected, and qualitatively consistent with Moore's results, Frew found that annual revenues increased a certificate's value.[39]

Thus, from the above results, an increase in the population served, retail sales, route network, and line-haul length, by increasing the demand for transportation, increases the value of operating certificates, holding all else constant. Alternatively, an increase in the number of competing carriers shifts a particular firm's demand curve for transportation leftward and, all else held constant, reduces the value of an operating certificate.

Per unit profit determinants In addition to demand determinants, Frew argued that certificate values would also reflect the difference between rates charged and the opportunity cost of providing transport services. Frew identified two factors that would influence per unit profit of general carriers in comparison with private carriers: line-haul distance and size of shipment. In his empirical analysis, however, he only included line-haul distance, since data on shipment size was unavailable.

We saw above that route length was an important demand determinant, longer routes leading to higher demands. In addition, general commodity carriers making short-distance trips are expected to have a smaller cost advantage over private carriers. The reason is that private carriers have lower labor costs and, for short trips, loading and unloading comprises a larger fraction of total trip time. Thus, a longer haul not only reflects increased demand for the carrier's services but is also expected to give the carrier a relative cost advantage over alternative private carriage, because break-bulking activities absorb a smaller fraction of total time.[40] Both of these effects have the same predicted effect of increasing certificate values, all else held constant. The coefficient for route length was positive and statistically significant at a 0.05 level of significance, supporting Frew's hypothesis. However, it is not possible to disentangle how much of the effect is demand-related and how much is cost-related.

An important contribution of Frew's analysis was to identify underlying demand and cost factors that influence the value of a motor carrier's operating certificate. The larger a carrier's population base and route network are, the greater is the effect of market entry restrictions and the more valuable are a firm's operating certificates. Conversely, more competition from other common carriers and from private carriage reduce the effect of market entry restrictions and lower the value of operating certificates, all else held constant.

CASE STUDY – MONOPOLY RENT-SHARING IN THE MOTOR CARRIER INDUSTRY

Market entry restrictions combined with increasing demands lead to increasing monopoly rents. However, as discussed in the last chapter, not all of these rents accrue to the protected industry, as some portion dissipates due to rent-sharing activities. For the motor carrier industry, Rose (1987) examined the extent to which labor shared in motor carrier monopoly rents.

The International Brotherhood of Teamsters (IBT) represents virtually all unionized drivers in the regulated motor carrier industry. Since the union leadership negotiates wage contracts with transport carriers, the union effectively represents a monopoly that faces the market demand for unionized motor carrier drivers. This gives the union some market power of its own that it can use to extract a portion of the economic rents earned by the carriers. Several factors contributed to union strength. First, as a general yardstick for normal profitability, the ICC used a 93% operating (expense to revenue) ratio. Carriers operating below this level would be more inclined to use additional labor or less reluctant to pay higher labor costs. Second, the stringent market entry restrictions on the industry implied that the threat of new firms using nonunion labor was not important. And, third, carrier rates were regulated, which limited the extent to which nonunion carriers could compete with union carriers on price.

Conversely, if market entry requirements are significantly loosened in the motor carrier industry, as they were under the 1980 Motor Carrier Act, one would expect a drop in wages paid to unionized truckers, as well as a reduction in the difference between union and non-union truck driver wages.

In her analysis, Rose argued that truck driver wages depended upon several sets of factors, including an employee's characteristics and union status, firm characteristics, occupation- and industry-specific effects, and geographic wage levels. In her empirical analysis, Rose defined the following wage model:

$$\begin{aligned}&\ln(\text{Driver Wage})\\&= \beta_0 + \beta_{1a}\text{Union-Reg} + \beta_{1b}\text{Union-Dereg}\\&\quad + \beta_2\text{Education} + \beta_3\text{Experience}\\&\quad + \beta_4(\text{Experience})^2 + \beta_5\text{Nonwhite}\\&\quad + \beta_6\text{Single} + \beta_7\text{Northeast} + \beta_8\text{South}\\&\quad + \beta_9\text{West} + \text{error term} \qquad (7.22)\end{aligned}$$

Union-Reg is a dummy variable that equals one for the regulated years 1973–8 and zero otherwise. Union-Dereg is a dummy variable that equals one for the deregulated years 1979–85 and zero otherwise.[41] Education is the number of years of schooling and Experience is the number of years of work experience. Nonwhite and Single are dummy variables that equal one if the driver is nonwhite and single, respectively, and zero otherwise. Each of these variables reflects a wage-earner's characteristics. Northeast, South, and West are dummy variables that equal one for the driver location, respectively, and zero otherwise. These three variables represent geographic differences in wage levels where the North Central region is the normalizing geographic area. Rose accounts for industry- and occupation-specific effects by limiting her analysis to full-time truck drivers employed in the for-hire trucking industry. Although Rose hypothesized that firm-specific characteristics also influence wage levels, her data source for this analysis, the Census Bureau's Current Population Survey, did not include information on an employee's firm.

The empirical model defined in equation (7.22) is a log–linear model. The dependent variable is the natural logarithm of hourly wages, which implies that the coefficients of the continuous variables give the percentage impact upon hourly wages due to a unit increase in the variable. For example, a one year increase in Education will have a β_2 percent effect upon hourly wages, holding all else constant. This is not the case, however, for a dummy variable. Consider, for example, the effect of Union-Reg on wages. Holding all else constant, for a union driver in the regulated period, equation (7.22) gives

$$\begin{aligned}&\ln(\text{Driver Wage})\\&= \beta_0 + \beta_{1a}(1) + \text{all other terms}\\ \Rightarrow\ &\text{Driver Wage(Union Driver)}\\&= \exp(\beta_0 + \beta_{1a}(1) + \text{all other terms})\end{aligned}$$

and for a nonunion driver in the regulated period, we have

$$\begin{aligned}&\ln(\text{Driver Wage})\\&= \beta_0 + \beta_{1a}(0) + \text{all other terms}\\ \Rightarrow\ &\text{Driver Wage(Nonunion Driver)}\\&= \exp(\beta_0 + \text{all other terms})\end{aligned}$$

The percentage wage premium due to unionization is given by the ratio

$$\begin{aligned}&\text{Percentage Wage Premium}\\&= \frac{\text{Driver Wage(Union Driver)} - \text{Driver Wage(Nonunion Driver)}}{\text{Driver Wage(Union Driver)}}\\&= \frac{\exp(\beta_0 + \beta_{1a} + \text{all other terms}) - \exp(\beta_0 + \text{all other terms})}{\exp(\beta_0 + \text{all other terms})}\\&= e^{\beta_{1a}} - 1 \qquad (7.23)\end{aligned}$$

Thus, to obtain the percentage wage effect of a dummy variable, we take the exponential of the dummy variable's coefficient and subtract one. Using this procedure, the percentage wage effect of unionization in the deregulated period is $e^{\beta_{1b}} - 1$.

Hypotheses

HYPOTHESIS 1 Membership in a union increases wage levels, all else held constant. To the extent that unions in general and the IBT in particular have monopoly power by virtue of facing a downward-sloping demand for their membership, unions will exert this monopoly power by negotiating higher wage contracts for its members. All else constant, β_{1a} and β_{1b} are each expected to be positive.

HYPOTHESIS 2 Less restrictive market entry requirements reduce union wages and union premia, all else held constant. Open access to markets means that entering motor carrier firms will compete with existing firms by using lower-cost nonunion labor. This reduces a union's monopoly power, which puts downward pressure on wages. In equation (7.22), Union-Reg reflects a period of economic regulation in the motor carrier industry and, for this study, corresponds to the years 1973–8. Union-Dereg, on the other hand, reflects the deregulated period when the ICC significantly relaxed requirements for entering the motor carrier interstate transport market. In Rose's study, this corresponds to the years 1979–85. The hypothesized effect of relaxed entry requirements on rent-sharing implies that $\beta_{1a} > \beta_{1b}$. Equivalently, the union wage premium is expected to fall from $e^{\beta_{1a}} - 1$ in the regulated environment to $e^{\beta_{1b}} - 1$ in the deregulated environment.

HYPOTHESIS 3 Holding all else constant, Education and Experience are expected to increase one's earning power. For education, this implies that $\beta_2 > 0$. As seen in equation (7.22), Experience enters the empirical model linearly and as a quadratic term. One can show that the effect of an increase in Experience on the dependent variable is[42]

$$\frac{\Delta \ln(\text{Driver Wage})}{\Delta \text{Experience}} = \beta_3 + 2\beta_4(\text{Experience}) > 0$$

$$\text{if Experience} > -\frac{\beta_3}{2\beta_4} \qquad (7.24)$$

From equation (7.24), as long as Experience is greater than $-\beta_3/2\beta_4$, this variable will have a positive effect upon one's wages.

A priori, there are no hypotheses regarding the effect of one's location, marital status, or race on wages.

Estimation results

Table 7.7 summarizes Rose's estimation results. Overall, the model fits the data relatively well, as denoted by the R^2 statistic. The explanatory variables explain 43% of the variation in the dependent variable. In addition, with the exception of Single, each of the included variables is statistically significant. Are the results consistent with the underlying hypotheses?

First, we see that the coefficients for Union-Reg and Union-Dereg are both positive, and that the coefficient for Union-Reg is almost twice as large as the coefficient for Union-Dereg. These results are consistent with hypotheses 1 and 2. The coefficient for Union-Reg tells us that, during the regulated period, union membership produced a 50% [exp(0.404) – 1] premium in wages relative to nonunionized truck drivers. This conforms to our basic hypothesis that unionized labor in the motor carrier industry participated in rent-sharing activities during the regulated era.

We also see from the coefficient on Union-Dereg that the extent of rent-sharing decreased in the deregulatory period. Although rent-sharing continued after deregulation, the relaxed requirements on market entry led to a smaller wage premium, 26%, for unionized drivers in comparison with nonunion drivers, all else held constant.

Hypothesis 3 is also confirmed by the results reported in table 7.7. A one-year increase in Education increases hourly wages by 0.018%, and

Table 7.7 Wage equations, 1973–85

Dependent variable – natural logarithm of hourly wage rates for drivers

Explanatory Variable	Coefficient Estimate (*t*-statistic)
Intercept[a]	1.78 (–)
Union-Reg	0.404 (21.3)
Union-Dereg	0.235 (7.83)
Education	0.018 (4.50)
Experience	0.006 (6.00)
Experience Squared	−0.0003 (−3.00)
Single	−0.023 (−1.04)
Nonwhite	−0.117 (−4.33)
Northeast	−0.061 (−2.77)
South	−0.068 (−3.40)
West	0.060 (2.73)
$R^2 = 0.43$	

[a] Rose included time dummies for each of the years. The intercept reported here is the mean of the estimated time effects. Rose did not report the coefficient estimates for the separate time dummy variables.

Source: Reprinted from Rose (1987), table 3, p. 1165, with the permission of The University of Chicago Press.

this is statistically significant at the 0.01 level. Experience has a positive coefficient, whereas the coefficient for (Experience)^2 is negative. From equation (7.5), Experience will have a positive effect on wages if Experience > $(-\beta_3/2\beta_4)$. Substituting 0.006 for β_3 and (−0.0003) for β_4 gives $(-\beta_3/2\beta_4) = 10$, which implies that one's truck-driving experience gives positive returns after ten years of experience.

In addition to these results, nonwhite truck drivers receive an hourly wage that is 11% less than white drivers, all else held constant. And truck drivers in the Northeast, South, and West regions of the country receive hourly wages that are less by 6.3%, 6.6%, and 5.8%, respectively, than those received by truck drivers in the North Central region.

Comments

In her analysis, Rose also investigated whether other labor sectors in the economy shared in motor carrier monopoly rents. Focusing upon nonunion truck drivers within the motor carrier industry and private carriage truck drivers outside the trucking industry, she found no evidence of significant rent spillovers due to economic regulation in the motor carrier industry. She also investigated whether economy-wide factors, and specifically price inflation and unemployment, could explain the 50% drop in union premia between 1973–8 and 1979–85. She found no evidence that these factors caused the precipitous drop in union premia. Last, she investigated whether national trends in union premia during the periods of interest could explain the difference. Again, the answer was no. Average union premia in private blue-collar industries remained fairly stable between 1973 and 1985. And of interest here is that, in the deregulatory period, the 50% drop in union premia for unionized truck drivers brought the premia for these workers into line with the average premia of blue-collar workers. These results provide additional support for the rent-sharing hypothesis that union truck-driver labor in the motor carrier industry actively participated in the monopoly rents created by the strict market entry restrictions under regulation.

How much rent did labor enjoy? Rose estimated that in 1983, and based upon a conservative 35% drop in union wage premia from deregulation, labor lost about $900 million dollars, which constitutes a bit more than 10% of an estimated $8.2 billion total compensation paid to union employees.[43] In all, Rose estimated that labor captured between 65% and 75% of total monopoly rents in the industry, a rather sizable sum!

Two additional comments are relevant here. First, because of data limitations, Rose could not include information on firm characteristics that may tend to overstate the union wage premium. Assume, for example, that smaller firms pay lower wages because nonunion workers are more likely to work for smaller firms. If firm size were included as an additional explanatory variable in the empirical model, we would expect the variable to have a positive coefficient. All else held constant, an increase in firm size increases wages. By not controlling for firm size, however, at least part of this effect gets absorbed in the union coefficients, which gives an upward bias to these coefficients. Similarly, not knowing whether a truck driver works in the less-than-truckload or truckload sector may alter the results. Since the TL sector of the industry was generally more competitive than the LTL sector, one might expect economic regulation to have a larger impact – that is, generated larger monopoly rents – in the LTL sector. By excluding this variable from the model, the positive effect of the LTL sector on wages will be reflected in the union variable coefficient.

Second, Rose's analysis focuses upon money wages and the effect of union membership on monetary earnings. However, unions negotiate for fringe benefits as well as money wages, and studies indicate that benefit packages in the unionized sector are more generous than those in the nonunion sector. Although the absence of these data prevented Rose from considering the effects of fringe benefits, one might expect that excluding this information would alter Rose's quantitative findings, but that it would not significantly affect her basic conclusion that labor shared significantly in the rents generated by economic regulation in the motor carrier industry.

MARKET POWER, SHIPPING CARTELS, AND THE SHIPPING ACT OF 1984[44]

Typical oligopolistic markets include a small number of firms that supply the entire market. By having a relatively large market share, each oligopolist faces a downward-sloping demand curve which provides it with market power and the potential for earning economic rents. We have also seen that oligopoly firms behave strategically. Implicit in this analysis is the assumption that oligopoly firms are *non-cooperatively* behaving, not an unreasonable assumption, since US laws generally prohibit explicit or implicit collusion. However, there are exceptions, and one notable exception in the transportation industry is *shipping conferences*.[45] A shipping conference is a cartel; that is, an organization of carriers that formally meets in order to set prices, apportion traffic, revenues, earnings and losses among its members, and otherwise conduct business for the purpose of maximizing the joint profits of the cartel. In effect, a cartel is made up of *cooperating* oligopolists.

In the late 19th century, concerns about excess capacity provided the impetus for the creation of shipping conferences. By limiting capacity along any given trade route, conferences could ensure that incumbent carriers would make a return on their investments. However, once created, conferences started to engage in various anticompetitive practices, including deferred rebates and the use of "fighting ships." *Deferred rebates*, by which carriers rebated part of the freight charge in return for receiving a shipper's business, was a price-cutting strategy intended to increase the cartel's market share. A *fighting ship* was a conference ship used to specifically undercut nonconference shipping rates on a route, and to continue to do so until the nonconference carrier gave up the route. The losses incurred by the fighting ship would then be shared by all conference members and prices would be subsequently raised.

US regulation of shipping conferences began with passage of the Shipping Act of 1916. Because shipping conferences were prevalent and accepted throughout the world, and recognizing that it could only influence domestic maritime policy, Congress granted limited antitrust immunity to the conferences. However, with the objective of limiting market power abuses, Congress also imposed various restrictions on conferences engaged in US trade. Carriers were required to file their rates with the newly created Federal Maritime Commission (originally called the US Shipping Board), which granted operating authorities, licensed freight forwarders, and approved (or rejected) all conference rate agreements. In addition, all conferences engaging in trade with the USA must be open; that is, must accept any carrier willing to abide by the rules of the conference and not preclude any conference member from leaving the conference. Fighting ships were banned, as were deferred rebates.

Policy toward maritime shipping changed little until recently, when threats to the industry developed in the 1970s and 1980s from three different sources: first, significant subsidies that the former Soviet Union provided its commercial maritime fleet; second, a United Nations policy, addressing concerns from Third World countries, that each country involved in bilateral trade have equal rights to the shipping traffic and that traffic carried by third country shippers (so-called cross traders) be limited; and, third, the existing structure was not equipped to deal with the developing intermodalism in the transportation sector.

The US response to these concerns was to pass the Shipping Act of 1984. In this legislation, Congress traded-off two opposing forces: one, that liner conferences were accepted world-wide and only in the US were there serious concerns about the market power implications of cartel arrangements; and, second, that during the late 1970s and early 1980s, there was considerable interest in Congress to infuse the transportation industry with a strong rush of competitive air. The Shipping Act of 1984 balanced these two forces by facilitating the formation of conferences and strengthening antitrust protection but, at the same time, ensuring strong competitive price pressures on the conferences. The Shipping Act granted antitrust immunity to carrier conferences, ports, and marine terminal operators. Whereas, prior to the Act, the FMC often took years to approve a conference agreement, under the 1984 Shipping Act, conference agreements took effect in 45 days or less. Although this change enhanced a conference's potential for market power, it also provided conferences with the flexibility to quickly respond to changes in the market environment. If new trading routes emerged, the added flexibility enabled conferences to more easily and efficiently adapt to the altered shipping environment.

In order to provide a more competitive environment, the Shipping Act of 1984 continued to require that all conferences serving the US be open, and it outlawed noncompetitive practices. However, the 1984 Act included two additional competitive features. First, the Act gave conference members the right of *independent action* (IA) on services and rates. Intended to increase rate flexibility and responses to new economic environments, IA allows any conference carrier, without permission of other conference members, to file a rate that is lower than the conference-wide rate for the commodity shipped. The only requirements are that the carrier provide a ten-day notice and charge all shippers of the commodity the same rate. The second novel feature is that the Act enabled conference and nonconference carriers to negotiate *service contracts*, whereby a shipper agrees to ship a certain volume of goods over some period of time in exchange for lower rates or improved service.[46]

CASE STUDY – THE ECONOMIC EFFECT OF THE SHIPPING ACT OF 1984

The 1984 legislation increased the potential for market power while simultaneously increasing the support for a competitive environment. Although, theoretically, one cannot unambiguously claim that the law's net effect enhanced competition, the requirement that conferences be open, combined with the right of independent action, suggests that the net effect will be more beneficial than harmful. The effect of the legislation on competition can be seen in figure 7.13. Since members in the cartel carry a significant portion of total traffic, the cartel faces a downward-sloping demand curve. Prior to the legislation, the cartel in figure 7.13 faces demand curve D, marginal revenue curve MR, and marginal cost curve MC. Wanting to maximize joint profits, the cartel produces at the point where $MR = MC$, carries C tons of cargo, and charges shippers a per-ton rate equal to p. Assuming that the legislation enhances competition, the effect of the law will be to flatten the demand curve that the conference faces, which reduces the cartel's market power. In other words, a more competitive environment makes shippers more price sensitive, so that cartel demand becomes the dashed line D', with an associated marginal revenue curve MR'. Setting $MR' = MC$ defines the new joint profit-maximizing point, which implies a fall in the cartel price from p to p' and an increase in tons shipped to C'. In this case, the effect of the legislation leads to lower prices and expanded output. Conversely, if the law has a net effect of restricting competition, then the demand curve facing the cartel would steepen, signifying that demand has become more price inelastic and that the cartel enjoys greater market power. The net result would be a higher cartel price and fewer tons of cargo shipped.

From figure 7.13 we see that the equilibrium price occurs at the intersection of the marginal revenue and the marginal cost curves. But recall that a cartel's demand curve is a relationship between price and quantity, *holding other demand determining factors constant*. From our discussion of interregional trade flows earlier in the chapter, we know that market demand depends upon the delivered price per ton p, income I^D at the destination, and the price of obtaining the

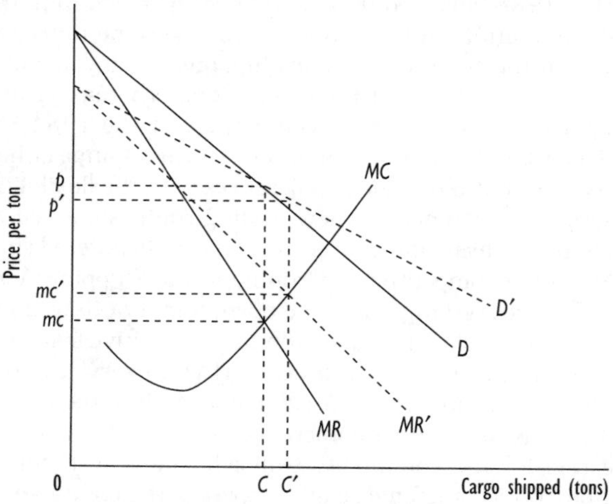

Figure 7.13 The economic effect of the Shipping Act of 1984.

same good from some other source, p^S. Since the 1984 Shipping Act is expected to alter the shape of the demand curve, becoming more or less elastic as the Act enhanced or restricted competition, respectively, we can express a cartel's general demand relationship as

$$T = T(p,p^S,I^D,\theta)$$

where θ represents the passage of the 1984 Shipping Act.

On the cost side, a cartel's marginal cost curve is a relationship between opportunity cost and quantity, *holding other cost determining factors constant*. From the last chapter, we know that opportunity cost depends upon the prices of inputs, w and r, the state of technology, γ, and the fixed factor of production, $\overline{K}$; that is, $MC = MC(r,w;\gamma,\overline{K})$.

Thus, setting marginal cost equal to marginal revenue gives the profit-maximizing condition for the cartel:[47]

$$MR = MC$$

$$\Rightarrow p + T - \frac{\Delta p}{\Delta T}(p,p^S,I^D,\theta) = MC(r,w;\gamma,\overline{K}) \qquad (7.25)$$

The left-hand side of (7.25) depends upon price per ton p, the price of substitutes p^S, income at the destination I^D, and the Shipping Act θ. The right-hand side of (7.25) depends upon input prices w and r, technology γ, and the fixed factor of production $\overline{K}$. Thus, from equation (7.25), it possible to express a cartel's profit-maximizing equilibrium price p^* as a function of these demand and supply factor influences:

$$p^* = p^*(p^S,I^D,\theta,r,w,\gamma,\overline{K}) \qquad (7.26)$$

How would each of these factors affect the cartel's equilibrium price? All else constant, an increase in the price of the substitute good and an increase in income at the destination would be expected to shift the demand curve to the right and raise the equilibrium price. Alternatively, a fall in input prices, advancing technology, or an increase in capacity, all else constant, will shift the marginal cost curve downward, leading to a decrease in the equilibrium price. Finally, if the Shipping Act of 1984 enhanced the competitive environment, a cartel's demand would become more price elastic and lower the equilibrium price. Conversely, if the law on balance increased a conference's market power, its market demand would become more price inelastic, raising equilibrium prices.[48]

An empirical model of equilibrium prices

Wilson and Casavant (1991) examined the economic impact of the 1984 Shipping Act on market equilibrium prices for westbound traffic from the West Coast of the United States to the Pacific Rim. In addition to nonconference carriers, there is the Trans-Pacific Westbound Rate Agreement (TWRA), a liner conference for this transportation market that sets conference-wide rates and allocates traffic among its members. Based upon time series data spanning the fourth quarter of 1978 through the second quarter of 1987, Wilson and Casavant analyzed shipments from the West Coast to Japan for four groups of commodities: fries, hay, onions, and lumber. For each of these commodities, the study estimated the following double-log empirical model of equilibrium price in this market:

$$\begin{aligned} \ln(\text{Price}) = \alpha &+ \beta_1 \ln(\text{Exchange Rate}) \\ &+ \beta_2 \ln(\text{Fuel Price}) \\ &+ \beta_3 \ln(\text{Capacity}) \\ &+ \beta_4(\text{1984 Shipping Act}) \\ &+ \varepsilon \end{aligned}$$

where Price is the shipping rate per 40-foot container equivalent, Exchange Rate is the number of yen per US dollar, Fuel Price is the producer price index (in 1967 dollars) for residual fuels, Capacity is the total sailings from the West Coast in 1,000 20-foot container equivalent units and represents tonnage capacity on westbound trade routes, and "1984 Shipping Act" is a dummy variable that equals zero for each quarter prior to 1984 and one for each quarter in 1984 and thereafter.[49] α and β_i ($i = 1, \ldots, 4$) are parameters to be estimated. From this model, we have the following hypotheses:

HYPOTHESIS 1 All else constant, if one US dollar exchanges for a larger number of yen, then the US dollar is said to be appreciating. In practice, the implication of an appreciating dollar is that it raises the price of US exports and lowers the price of US imports. For example, suppose that \$1 = 100 yen, so that the exchange rate is 100/1 = 100. If the US imports an automobile from Japan that costs 1.5 million yen, then at existing exchange rates, the US consumer pays \$15,000 for the automobile (1,500,000/100). At the same time, a Japanese consumer importing a pound of beef at \$5.00 per pound spends 500 yen (5 · 100). Thus, the 1.5 million yen price of an automobile is equivalent to \$15,000 and the 500 yen price of meat is equivalent to \$5.00.

Now let's assume that the dollar appreciates. Instead of 100 yen per dollar, a dollar now exchanges for 150 yen. What happens to the import and export prices? The 1.5 million yen price of a Japanese automobile now costs the US consumer \$10,000 (1,500,000/150), whereas the pound of beef costs the Japanese consumer 750 yen (5 · 150). An appreciating dollar has decreased the cost of Japanese imports and raised the cost (to Japan) of US exports. Conversely, if the dollar depreciates, then one dollar exchanges for fewer yen, so that the cost of Japanese imports to US consumers rises and the cost of US exports to Japanese consumers falls.

Because of its effect on the price of US exports, the primary impact of an increase in the exchange rate is to reduce the demand for westbound shipments to the Pacific Rim. Holding all else constant, this leads to a fall in the equilibrium price of carrier rates. Thus, we expect $\beta_1 < 0$.

HYPOTHESIS 2 Fuel Price and Capacity affect the opportunity costs faced by carriers. All else constant, an increase in fuel prices raises the opportunity cost of transporting goods and increases equilibrium price. Conversely, the more capacity available on the westbound trade routes, the lower is the opportunity cost of hauling commodities. With very little capacity, carriers seek to fill their ships with high-valued goods, implying, therefore, that hauling lower-valued commodities has a relatively high opportunity cost in terms of high-value goods not carried. But as shipping capacity increases, the opportunity cost falls as carriers search for lower-valued goods to carry. Thus, we expect $\beta_2 > 0$ and $\beta_3 < 0$.

HYPOTHESIS 3 The Shipping Act of 1984 expanded or constrained competitive forces. However, as noted previously, freedom of entry into and exit from conferences, along with the right of independent actions, suggests that the net effect of Act effect will be to reduce equilibrium prices in this market, implying that $\beta_4 < 0$.

Empirical results

Table 7.8 reports the estimation results of the equilibrium price model. Overall, the R^2 for the estimated models ranges between 0.69 and 0.89, which indicates a reasonable fit of the data. Also, an examination of the coefficients and t-statistics for Exchange Rate, Capacity, and Fuel Price are generally consistent with our hypotheses. For each of the commodity groups, we see in the table that an appreciation of the US dollar reduces the equilibrium price, holding all else constant. Also, since the estimated model is a double-log specification, the estimated coefficient is an elasticity which gives the percentage impact upon market transportation rates from a 1% increase in an explanatory variable. Through its effect upon demand, a 1% appreciation in the yen/dollar rate reduces the transport rate of fries, hay, and onions by 1.18%, 1.64%, and 2.56% respectively. Only for lumber is the transport rate inelastic with respect to exchange rate

Table 7.8 Equilibrium Price on westbound Pacific trade routes

Dependent variable – ln (Price)

	Commodity[a]			
Independent Variable	Fries	Hay	Onions	Lumber
Constant	11.81 (8.09)	15.90 (3.70)	28.05 (13.56)	7.47 (9.83)
ln (Exchange Rate)	−1.18 (−5.51)	−1.64 (−3.58)	−2.56 (−10.47)	−0.58 (−7.22)
ln (Fuel Price)	0.08 (0.69)	0.68 (3.19)	0.99 (4.43)	0.012 (0.22)
ln (Capacity)	−0.46 (−2.84)	−1.01 (−2.48)	−2.06 (−7.75)	−0.32 (−3.18)
Shipping Act of 1984	−0.20 (−2.34)	−0.29 (−1.39)	−0.17 (−1.40)	0.11 (3.89)
R^2	0.69	0.74	0.89	0.75

[a] *t*-statistics are in parentheses.

Source: Adapted from Wilson and Casavant (1991), table 1, p. 433

fluctuations. Each 1% rise in the exchange rate reduces market transport rates by just over 0.5%.

We also see in the table that increasing capacity along these trade routes leads to a significant fall in transport rates, consistent with hypothesis 2, but the magnitude of the effect varies by commodity. Transport rates for onions are elastic, those for fries and lumber inelastic, and for hay, rates have a unitary elasticity with respect to expanded capacity. A similar pattern is evident for fuel prices. Although, as expected, an increase in the fuel price increases transport rates, the magnitude of the effect is much larger for hay and onions than for fries and lumber. Indeed, for fries and lumber, we cannot reject the null hypothesis that the effect of increasing fuel prices is zero.

The primary variable of interest in this study is the Shipping Act of 1984. We hypothesized that the net effect of the Act was to enhance the competitive environment, which would lead to a reduction in transport rates. We see from table 7.8 that the results are mixed. For fries, hay, and onions, we obtain the expected negative sign. For fries, the coefficient is statistically significant at the 0.01 level, whereas for hay and onions the coefficient is significant at the 0.10% level (on a one-tail test).[50] The quantitative effect of the Act was to reduce rates for fries, hay, and onions by 0.2%, 0.29%, and 0.17%, respectively. On the other hand, for lumber we see that the effect of the Act produced a significant and positive effect, increasing rates by 0.11%. Thus, the results reported in table 7.8 are consistent with a fall in market power for fries, hay, and onions, but with an increase in market power for lumber. Why is there this difference for lumber?

A possible explanation may be the exempt status of certain commodities, including bulk cargo, forest products, scrap metal, and waste paper shipments. For these items, there are no tariff filing requirements, and under the 1984 Shipping Act members do not have the mandatory right of independent action. Thus, the ability of conference members to reduce rates on lumber shipments below the conference-wide rate and *without conference approval* is not an option. This removes one of the new features of the 1984 legislation that was intended to counteract those provisions in the Act that gave conferences greater market power. Without IAs, the net effect of the Act on lumber shipments would be tipped toward increased market power, and the results in table 7.8 are consistent with this.[51]

Comments

A further interesting feature of the model is the distinction between fronthaul shipments and backhaul shipments. The fronthaul shipment is typically the primary shipment, and carriers seek to find some good for their backhaul trips. Bulk commodities, for example, are oftentimes transported on backhaul trips. In general, the demand for fronthaul shipments lies to the right of the demand for backhaul carriage, which implies that fronthaul shipments may face capacity constraints, whereas backhaul shipments may likely have excess capacity. Thus, pricing for fronthaul shipments is more likely to be based upon value of service, whereas backhaul shipments will be moved as long as marginal costs are met; that is, backhaul shipments are based upon cost of service. An implication of this is that fuel price increases will raise the transport rate for backhaul shipments but have no effect on transport rates for fronthaul shipments (which are already priced well above the opportunity cost of service).

Shipments of fries require refrigerated containers and are typically fronthaul shipments, whereas carriers transport hay and onions, which are bulk commodities, on the backhaul. The above discussion implies that fuel price increases will have no effect on fries, but will have a positive and significant effect on the movement of hay and onions. The results reported in table 7.8 are consistent with this interpretation. Although the fuel price coefficients are positive for each of these commodities, only for hay and onions is the coefficient statistically different from zero.

As a final point, recall at the beginning of this section that the equilibrium price was hypothesized to depend upon demand-related factors and cost-related factors. Absent from the estimated model are two demand factors that may be important determinants of equilibrium prices, the delivered price of the same commodity from an alternative source and the income at the destination. Ideally, one would want to include these factors in order to better isolate the affect of the 1984 Shipping Act on transport rates. However, it might also be noted that, to some degree, the price of substitutes may be captured by the exchange rate variable. Holding all else constant, including the yen exchange rate with other countries, an appreciating dollar will have a similar effect on demand as a fall in the delivered price of the commodity from an alternative source. Conversely, a depreciating dollar is comparable to an increase in the substitute price, all else held constant.

CHAPTER HIGHLIGHTS

- In a perfectly competitive market structure, buyers and sellers are price-takers; firms produce a homogeneous product; there is freedom of entry and exit; and all relevant information is available to market participants. Whereas positive, zero, and negative economic profits are consistent with short-run equilibrium, only zero economic profits or a normal return on investment is consistent with long-run equilibrium. In perfectly competitive markets, inputs are optimally employed, goods are optimally distributed, and society is producing the socially efficient output mix.

- The demand for transportation is derived from the demand for goods and services that are produced in locations separate from their points of consumption. Interregional passenger and freight flows reflect differences in the opportunity costs of producing goods and services at various locations. In an empirical model of interregional goods' flows, the demand for transportation generally depends upon the delivered price, income at the destination, and the price of substitutes.
- A monopolistically competitive market structure is similar to a perfectly competitive market structure, except that firms produce a heterogeneous product, so that its demand curve is slightly downward-sloping. Although these firms have some monopoly power, in the long run monopolistically competitive firms make zero economic profits. An oligopoly has few competitors, and the distinguishing characteristic of this market structure is that each competitor will behave strategically, making own decisions in light of competitors' expected responses.
- In a monopolistic market structure, one firm faces the full downward-sloping market demand curve which gives the monopolist market power; that is, the ability to price above marginal cost of production. In long-run equilibrium, monopolists make pure economic profits – that is, economic rents – and society suffers an efficiency loss from too few goods coming on to the market. Over time, rent-seeking behavior, rent-sharing, capitalization, and reduced incentives to innovate cause monopoly rents to dissipate.
- Price discrimination occurs when a monopolist charges different prices in different markets for goods that cost the same to produce, or charges a uniform price for goods that have different costs of production. In each case, a profit-maximizing monopolist will set a price for the good that is inversely related to the good's price elasticity of demand.
- When production of a good is subject to economies of scale so large that the optimal number of firms in the industry is one, the resulting market structure is a natural monopoly. Actions taken by the government to deal with natural monopolies are marginal cost pricing combined with subsidizing the firm's losses, rate of return regulation, and government operation.
- The four-firm concentration ratio, the eight-firm concentration ratio, and the Hirschman–Herfindahl index are three commonly used measures to evaluate the extent to which a market is concentrated. Although by these measures, the less-than-truckload motor carrier industry is moderately concentrated, competition from freight forwarders and brokers prevents these firms from exploiting their market power.
- The passage of the 1978 Airline Deregulation Act led to a hub-and-spoke passenger distribution network. Empirical evidence presented suggests that an effect of the Act was to decrease concentration at the hub airports for all flights. However, increased concentration was observed for direct flights in comparison with flights that involve a change of plane.
- Under perfect competition, the level of actual competition disciplines competitors' pricing behavior. Under perfect contestability, the threat of entry disciplines incumbents' pricing behavior. Empirical evidence suggests that contestability in the airline

market is imperfect. Although potential competitors play a positive role disciplining the pricing behavior of incumbents, the effect of actual competitors on a firm's pricing behavior is stronger.

- Under regulation, motor carriers in general and the less-than-truckload sector in particular characterized a monopoly market structure with positive economic profits. Empirical studies indicate that operating certificates had a positive value, consistent with making economic profits, and that the value of these certificates depended upon the level of demand, and on cost-related operating characteristics. Consistent with economic theory, motor carrier economic profits were partially dissipated through rent-sharing with labor.
- The equilibrium price in imperfect competition depends upon demand- and cost-related factors and the regulatory environment. To reduce market power and lower prices, it is important to introduce changes in the regulatory environment that have net pro-competitive effects on the industry. This is borne out in an empirical model of shipping conferences, where a regulatory change included competitive provisions and anticompetitive provisions. The equilibrium price fell (rose) when the regulatory change resulted in a more (less) competitive environment.

Review questions

1. (a) In perfectly competitive markets, identify and briefly discuss the three conditions for economic efficiency.
(b) Based upon your current knowledge of intercity rail, bus, and airline passenger modes, in which sector do you believe resources are more efficiently allocated today? Would your answer change if the same question were asked for the year 1975?

2. In table 7.1, interpret the regression results for Chemicals and Allied products. Is intraregional trade important in these commodities? How sensitive are these commodities to changes in prices, incomes, and transportation rates? What will have the greater effect upon flows of these commodities, a 10% increase in transport rates or a 2% increase in price?

3. Because the Pacific Northwest has a comparative advantage in the production of lumber and the Midwest has a comparative advantage in the production of foodstuffs, there will rise a demand for transporting foodstuffs from the Midwest to the Pacific Northwest and for transporting lumber from the Pacific Northwest to the Midwest.
(a) Suppose that a natural disaster, such as flooding, occurs in the Midwest, which raises the cost of supplying wheat. What effect will this have upon the demand for transporting wheat from the Midwest to the Pacific Northwest?

(b) Suppose that wheat is an inferior commodity. Then what will be the effect upon the demand for wheat transportation from a rise in per capita incomes in the Pacific Northwest?
(c) Assume that, nation-wide, there is a general fall in labor productivity. Can we predict the effect that this would have upon the interregional flows between the Pacific Northwest and the Midwest?

4. As of 1982, there were 227,000 miles of pipeline in the USA, over which 537 billion ton–miles of natural gas, crude oil, petroleum products, coal slurry, and chemicals were shipped. Overall, in 1982, pipeline traffic represented 24% of the total ton–miles shipped. The shipment of each of these commodities through the pipeline network illustrates the nonuniform distribution of such products among different regions in the USA.
(a) Assume that there are two regions of the country: the oil-rich Southwest and the not-so-oil-rich rest of the country. Also, there are two goods: oil and "all other goods." Assuming that each region has a similar demand for oil, use demand and supply curves to characterize the self-sufficient equilibrium for oil in each of these regions. In which region is the price of oil highest? Which region has a comparative advantage in oil?
(b) Are there gains to be made from specialization and trade of oil between the Southwest and rest of the country? Assuming no transportation costs, what is the maximum gain from trade possible? Identify the effect that positive transportation costs will have upon gains from trade. What condition must be satisfied for trade and specialization to occur?
(c) Between 1950 and 1990, there were significant expansions in pipeline infrastructure. Would you expect the larger pipeline network to raise, lower, or have no effect upon the nation's economic welfare – and why?
(d) If there are gains to specialization and trade, this also applies to trade in "all other goods." For these commodities, what condition must be satisfied for trade to occur? Does everyone gain from specialization and trade in oil and "all other goods"? If so, why; and if not, why not?

5. Owner–operators in the truckload segment of the motor carrier industry could be viewed as monopolistic competitors, since quality differences in their services enable them to offer similar but differentiated products.
(a) Do firms in this sector have market power?
(b) Will a typical firm in this industry make positive, negative, or zero economic profits? Graphically depict a typical owner–operator's long-run equilibrium.

6. (a) In general, explain why freedom of entry and exit are necessary for an efficient allocation of resources in a perfectly competitive market.
(b) During the period of airline regulation, the government set airline fares and regulated an air carrier's entry into and exit from particular markets. Assuming that the incumbent airlines made economic profits while they were regulated, what impact, if any, did the government's regulation of routes have upon air carrier's ability to make profits?

7. The price elasticity of demand for Amtrak, the nation's rail passenger service, among vacation travelers has been estimated as –1.20. Given that Amtrak faces the market demand for rail passenger trips, what effect will a 15% increase in fares have upon market demand? What effect will the fare increase have upon revenues? (Hint: convert the formula for the effect of a price increase on total revenues to an elasticity.)

8. Suppose that a transport carrier is accused of price discriminating in two separate markets. The carrier replies that he can't be price discriminating, since he is charging the same price in each of the markets. Do you agree or disagree with the carrier's response?

9. Business travelers have more inelastic demands for air services in comparison with vacation travelers. If an airline charges business and vacations travelers the same route fare between Chicago and Los Angeles, does this necessarily imply that the airline is not price discriminating? Under what conditions would this be consistent with price discrimination?

10. In recent work on airline fares, Morrison and Winston (1995) reported the following regression model results for the third quarter of 1993. The sample included carriers providing direct or on-line connecting services for the 1,000 most heavily traveled routes in the USA. The *t*-statistics are given in parentheses:

$$\ln(\text{average fare}) = \underset{(2.1)}{-0.027} \ln(\text{route competitors}) - \underset{(12.0)}{0.120} \ln(\text{airport competitors}) + \underset{(47.9)}{0.383} \ln(\text{distance}) - \underset{(9.6)}{0.048} \ln(\text{route passengers})$$

$R^2 = 0.48$

\# observations = 5,513

(a) From these results, does actual competition discipline the market? How about potential competition?
(b) Are the results consistent with a model of pure contestability?
(c) Why would you expect an increase in flight distance not to have a proportional effect upon airfares? Do the results in the above regression bear this out? What impact does a 10% increase in flight distance have upon airfares in 1993?
(d) From the reported results, what effect does route density have upon airfares? Is it possible to explain the result on route density in terms of an airline's load factors?

11. The truckload sector of the motor carrier industry has been described as highly competitive. For this segment of the industry, identify a typical firm's short-run profit-maximizing problem and explain the condition that must be satisfied for its marginal cost curve to be interpreted as a short-run supply curve. Holding all else constant, identify how each of the following changes affect the firm's supply of transportation services:

(a) an increase in the price of fuel;
(b) a decrease in ton–miles shipped;
(c) an increase in excise taxes on truck tires;
(d) a profits tax, equal to one-third of any economic profits that the firm earns;
(e) an increase in transportation rates;
(f) an increase in the price of a truck tractor;
(g) improved truck design, which raises fuel efficiency.

12. The US interstate system was started in 1950 and completed in 1973.
(a) Use market demand and supply curves to characterize the effect that the completed interstate system had on the market for intercity motor vehicle passenger trips. Similarly, illustrate with market demand and supply curves how the completed system affected shippers' transportation rates.
(b) What effect, if any, would you expect the interstate system to have upon rail rates?

13. What distinguishes a constant-cost industry from an increasing-cost industry? In which case would you expect an increase in market demand to have the greatest long-run effect on price and output: a constant-cost or increasing-cost industry?

14. The July 20, 1993 *Wall Street Journal* reported that Union Pacific expects to lose as much as $30 million because of "track damage, higher operating expenses and lost freight traffic resulting from the Midwestern flood." Drew Lewis, Union Pacific chairman, said that he expected this to reduce net income per share by 10–12 cents. Prior to the floods, some analysts expected Union Pacific to earn $4 per share. Assuming a share price of $65, what effect did the floods have on the railroad's short-run cost curves and its return on investment?

15. The June 29, 1993 issue of the *Wall Street Journal* states: "Two decades after the 1970s energy crisis sparked ambitious, costly efforts to move commuters from gas-guzzling cars to subway, trolley, and bus systems, something odd has happened: Americans are less likely than ever to use public transit." Use market demand and supply curves to evaluate this statement. In your discussion, comment on the effects of changing employment patterns, commuting patterns, public transit subsidies, income, and the price elasticity of demand.

16. (a) Briefly explain why the demand for transportation is a derived demand.
(b) In 1991, average freight revenue per ton–mile was 24.8 cents. Assume that this represents both the constant marginal cost of shipping a ton–mile and the equilibrium price for motor carrier freight movements. Also, in 1991, intercity trucks were responsible for 750 billion ton–miles. Graphically depict the equilibrium for intercity freight movements.
(c) Suppose that the demand for transportation is linear and that innovations in the trucking industry reduced the marginal cost of shipping a ton–mile of freight to 20 cents per ton–mile (in 1991 dollars), which resulted in a 10% increase in ton–miles shipped. Graphically depict the effect of the innovation on the market for intercity freight movements and calculate the net benefit to society from the reduced cost of transportation.

NOTES

1 In effect, the production function of a firm producing some good q and whose employees engage in air travel negatively depends upon the total amount of air travel. The congestion effects of industry-wide increases in air travel reduce a firm's output of q, all else held constant. Chapter 11 analyzes the implications of congestion in transportation.

2 To see this more explicitly, we can express the ratio of marginal costs as $MC_T/MC_X = (\Delta TC_T/\Delta T)/(\Delta TC_X/\Delta X) = \Delta X/\Delta T$. In other words, the ratio of marginal costs reflects the amount of X that society foregoes by increasing its output of T by one unit.

3 D_T in figure 7.1 illustrates shippers' market demand curve for transportation.

4 For example, California has a comparative advantage in the production of agricultural goods, the Northwest has a comparative advantage in the production of lumber, and the Midwest has a comparative advantage in the production of wheat and soybeans, while Alaska and parts of the South have a comparative advantage in the production of oil. Also, the United States has a comparative advantage in the production of capital-intensive goods relative to Central America.

5 Graphically, figure 7.5 depicts these flows where the commodity is leisure activities (which must be consumed where produced): region A is Indiana and region B is Florida.

6 The reason for studying these regions lay in their historical importance for setting rates. For the purpose of simplifying rate setting, the ICC placed individual commodities into a limited number of groups, called freight classifications. By the late 1800s, there were three separate rate classifications that corresponded to railroads operating in three regions of the country: the Official, the Southern, and the Western. For each separate classification or region, there was an alphabetical listing of each commodity together with the commodity's rating, which was the class into which a commodity was placed. A commodity's rating was needed in order to quote the freight rate, usually in cents per hundred pounds. Within the same classification, the relationship between rating classes remained the same regardless of the origin and destination points. However, since different classifications generally had different ratings for the same commodities, freight charges would differ across classifications. Over time, the Western region was further subdivided into three rate territories: the Western Trunk Line region, the South-Western region, and the Mountain-Pacific region. See Locklin (1966) for a discussion of rate territories.

7 A cartel is a formal agreement among a group of firms to jointly coordinate activities in order to pursue a common goal. This is a form of *direct collusion*, in contrast to *tacit* or *indirect* collusion, which reflects an informal agreement among firms to pursue jointly beneficial pricing and output decisions. In general, cartels are outlawed in the United States. Shipping conferences, which are allowed under US laws, are an exception. The last section of this chapter examines whether shipping cartels involved in US trade have significant market power.

8 A market with only two sellers is referred to as a *duopoly*.

9 Although a pure monopoly is rare, a related market structure is a *dominant firm*, which has a substantial portion of the market and no serious rivals (Shepherd, 1990).

10 Contrary to price-taking perfectly competitive firms, imperfectly competitive firms are oftentimes referred to as *price-searchers*, because they are searching their downward-sloping demand curves for the price–output combination that maximizes economic profits.

11 This discussion assumes a *single pricing setting strategy* whereby the monopolist seeks to find one price for the entire market that maximizes profits.

12 If we set marginal revenue (*MR*) in equation (7.10) equal to zero and solve for $E_{T,p}$, we obtain $E_{T,p} = -1$.

13 If marginal cost were zero, then the monopolist would produce up to the point at which demand exhibited unitary elasticity. Alternatively, if the objective of a monopolist were to maximize sales rather than profits, then the monopolist would continue to sell until marginal revenue just equaled zero, where market demand is of unit elasticity.

14 Although firms oftentimes differentiate their products by altering a good's physical attributes (for example, size, taste, color, and so forth), another common form of product differentiation is geographic location. Consumers are willing to pay a higher price for the convenience of purchasing a good at a nearby store rather than one located further away.

15 Recall that if a firm covers all of its *economic costs*, then it is earning a zero economic profit; that is, the firm is making a *normal return on its invested capital*. Positive economic rents are synonymous with positive economic profits and a greater than normal rate of return on invested capital. Since the usual practice uses stockholders' equity to measure invested capital, *rate of return on equity* is a standard measure of firm profitability.

16 Theoretically, it is possible for a monopolist to incur economic losses. If average total cost lies everywhere above market demand, then the firm cannot break even and will incur an economic loss. In the long run, one would expect the firm to exit the industry. However, if a firm must first obtain government approval before abandoning a market – which is the norm in many transportation markets – it is possible for a monopolist to incur long-run economic losses.

17 A significant difference between competitive/monopolistically competitive market structures and oligopolistic/monopolistic market structures is freedom of entry. In the former market structures, there are assumed to be no barriers to entry, which implies a long-run equilibrium where the demand curve is just tangent to the long-run average cost (*LAC*) curve. For monopolistically competitive markets, the presence of pure economic profits induces other firms into the industry. This shifts an incumbent firm's demand curve *to the left*, which has the effect of eroding any economic profits. In long-run equilibrium, the demand curve for each incumbent monopolistically competitive firm is just tangent to the *LAC* curve. However, *in contrast to perfect competition*, this occurs *to the left* of the minimum point (the minimum efficient scale) on the *LAC*, which reflects the impact of product differentiation on firm demand. In oligopolistic/monopolistic market structures, there are significant barriers to entry that preclude the long-run erosion of pure economic profits.

18 The maximum price offered represents the "present discounted value" of the $300,000 profit stream. Assuming that the profit stream lasts forever, and that there is a 5% real market rate of interest, the present discounted value would be $6 million dollars. In chapter 9, we examine the concept of present value and its implications for investment.

19 Referring to figure 7.9, the average total cost curve for the new buyer shifts upward to the point at which it is just tangent to the demand curve. At this point, the monopolistic price equals the average total cost, which earns the monopolist no more than a normal return on investment.

20 An alternative way of stating this is to say that the cross-price elasticities are zero. Business and pleasure trips can be viewed as substitutes, in that the larger the price differential is between the two, the greater is the incentive to cross over. Suppose that the price of a trip decreases for a pleasure traveler. If the cross-price elasticity is zero, this has no effect upon a businessman's demand for trips. On the other hand, if the cross-price elasticity is positive, then there will be a decrease in the demand for business trips as some businessmen now take business trips "disguised" as pleasure trips.

21 Since much of airline capacity is purchased in order to accommodate the business traveler, if a greater proportion of the marginal capacity cost is assigned to the business traveler, the marginal cost of supplying a business seat will be higher even though the marginal operating cost is the same for the business and vacation traveler.

22 From equation (7.13), $(p - mc)/p = -1/E_{T,p}$ which, from equation (7.17), implies that $(p_b - mc_b)/p_b > (p_v - mc_v)/p_v$.

23 This pricing strategy is oftentimes referred to as *third-degree price discrimination*. In third-degree price discrimination, a monopolist knows the price elasticity of demand in each submarket, but does not know the values that each customer places upon different units of the goods. In contrast, when there is *perfect, or first-degree, price discrimination*, the monopolist knows each consumer's demand for the product and charges each consumer according to this demand. The effect of this strategy is to extract all consumer surplus (chapter 8) from purchasers. Interestingly, the profit-maximizing

monopoly output from this pricing strategy is identical to that in a competitive market, since the monopolist's marginal revenue curve is now identical to price as the monopolist travels down the market demand curve. In *second-degree price discrimination*, the monopolist doesn't know each consumer's demand curve, but devises various pricing strategies in order to extract some consumer surplus. To illustrate second-degree price discrimination, consider all-or-nothing options. A cruise ship runs the following advertisement: "Take a Caribbean Cruise for Two from Miami: Only $800 per person." The single person ticket price is $1,400. According to your household demand for cruises, you are willing to pay $1,300 for the first ticket and $700 for the second ticket. At the single-person price, you buy zero tickets and no one takes a cruise. Alternatively, if you could buy as many tickets as you wanted at the $800 price, you would purchase one ticket and receive $500 consumer surplus. The second ticket is not purchased because its household value is less than the $800 price. However, given the *all-or-nothing* constraint, you buy both tickets. Why? The total cost of buying both tickets is $1,600, whereas the maximum value that you're willing to pay for both is $2,000. Since the maximum value exceeds the total cost, you purchase the second ticket. In effect, this pricing strategy has extracted some of your consumer surplus from the first ticket in order to purchase the second ticket. Thus, even though the monopolist can't observe your demand curve, the monopolist's strategy effectively redistributed some of your consumer surplus to monopoly profits.

24 In the early part of the century, the ICC identified a 5.5–6% rate of return as fair and equitable for rail carriers. In the more recent past, however, the US Department of Transportation has argued that a 10.8–12% return is more reasonable if rail carriers are to remain economically viable. The Civil Aeronautics Board also used 12% as a reasonable rate of return for scheduled air carriers (Wilson, 1980).

25 For a detailed analysis of these and other examples, and of privatization in general, see Gomez-Ibanez and Meyer (1993).

26 Most of the concern is concentrated on the three largest LTL firms, Yellow Freight, Consolidated Freightways, and Roadway Express.

27 Morrison and Winston's results contrasts sharply with an analysis by the General Accounting Office (GAO/RECD, 1990) which identified a 27% fare premium due to hubs. However, the GAO study failed to control for a number of fare-related factors, including route distance, number of plane changes, traffic mix, carrier identify, and frequent flier tickets. Morrison and Winston estimate that the number of plane changes and distance account for more than half of the difference in their estimates of hub premia from GAO's estimates.

28 For a discussion of contestable markets, see Bailey (1981), Baumol, Panzar, and Willig (1982), Bailey and Baumol (1984), and Train (1991).

29 In this discussion, we are adopting the standard monopoly case and ignoring the possibility that $MC = MR$ implies prices that yield zero or negative economic profits.

30 Note that a similar result would occur if Ever Present Airlines priced at average total cost but produced airline trips inefficiently. Suppose, for example, that Ever Present Airlines faced an average total cost equal to $75 and set one-way fares at $75. Its economic profit would be zero. However, recognizing that Ever Present Airlines is an inefficient producer, Hit and Run Airways enters the market, efficiently produces trips for average total cost equal to $70, and charges a price of $74. It now captures all of Ever Present Airlines' customers and makes a $4 profit per passenger. As you might guess, however, a $74 fare is also not sustainable, and is driven down to $70.

31 A careful reader will see that the price–output solution in contestable markets is not fully efficient since, at price equal to average total cost, the firm does not price at marginal cost. However, given that it is operating under increasing returns to scale, pricing at marginal cost implies that the firm suffers an economic loss and will exit the industry. The solution is efficient given the constraint that total costs must be covered.

32 Chapter 9 considers the relationship between investment, discounting, and present values in greater detail.

33 Moore (1978, p. 341) did not report the constant term for the regression equation.

34 This is based upon a two-tail test and 21 degrees of freedom.

35 Moore also did not report the estimated value for the constant term in this regression.

36 Frew's analysis is based upon certificate transactions between 1971 and 1977. But in contrast to Moore, Frew did not use the purchase price to measure the certificate value, because in many cases the purchase price was paid in installments. From ICC documents, Frew calculated the present value of the purchase price based on the agreed upon rate of interest, installment period, and payments.

37 Frew tried per capita disposable income in preliminary regression models, but these led to inferior fits in comparison with models that used retail sales.

38 In deciding whether to approve a route transfer, the ICC was generally concerned that the purchasing firm had sufficient profits to pay for the operating certificate without jeopardizing its financial health, that its purchase would not introduce so much competition as to significantly harm other competitors, and that the quality of transport services would be improved. Frew found that certificate purchasers adjusted first year projected revenues upward and adjusted subsequent year projected revenues downward in order to conform to ICC considerations and increase the chances of ICC approval.

39 Recall that the coefficient for expected income in Moore's results was 0.152. Since Moore did not control for other factors that would affect certificate value, one would expect Moore's coefficient to be upward-biased. This was indeed the case. Frew's estimated coefficient for expected annual income was 0.087, almost half the value estimated by Moore.

40 In addition, during this period private carriers were not authorized to carry other firms' freight, so that there was a greater likelihood that private carriers would return empty. A 1977 ICC study supports this, finding that 18% of interstate carrier trucks were empty when passing survey check points, compared with 30% for private carrier trucks.

41 Although the Motor Carrier Act was passed in 1980, the ICC began to administratively loosen requirements for market entry in 1979.

42 For students familiar with differential calculus, differentiating equation (7.24) with respect to Experience gives $\beta_3 + 2\beta_4$ (Experience).

43 These figures only correspond to Class I motor carriers; that is, firms with annual gross revenues equal to or greater than $5 million.

44 For a fuller discussion of international shipping, see Stephenson and Frederick (1987).

45 The maritime shipping industry is generally divided into liner and tramp service. Liners are common carriers that have a regular schedule, which specifies frequency of service, ports of call, and routes traveled. As common carriers, liners typically haul manufactured and packaged goods. Tramp ships, on the other hand, "tramp around" the seas searching for cargo shipments. Rather than scheduled service, they generally enter into service contracts with shippers to haul bulk commodities, and can be likened to the truckload sector of the motor carrier industry.

46 Although allowing conference members to negotiate service contracts, the law did not give conference members independent action over service contracts. The conference has the right to approve or reject any service contract negotiated by one of its members.

47 The demand for tons shipped, $T = T(p, p^S, I^D, \theta)$, gives a relationship between price p, quantity shipped T, and other factors. It also implies an "inverse demand function," $p = p(T, p^S, I^D, \theta)$. Just as $\Delta T/\Delta p$ depends upon p, p^S, I^D, and θ, $\Delta p/\Delta T$ depends upon T, p^S, I^D, and θ. However, since $T = T(p, p^S, I^D, \theta)$, then $\Delta p/\Delta T$ is a function of p, p^S, I^D, and θ; that is, $\Delta p/\Delta T$ will depend upon price p as well as other factors.

48 The model summarized in equation (7.26) characterizes a body of work commonly referred to as the New Empirical Industrial Organization (Bresnahan, 1989) whereby an empirical model identifies the impact that changes in market determinants have upon price and, accordingly, upon market power.

49 Because shipping rates are reported in a number of different units (for example, millions of board-feet), each rate was converted to a 40-foot container equivalent.

50 For a two-tail test, the coefficient would be significant at a 0.20% level.

51 Also consistent with this, Davies (1987) reports that in the years immediately following passage of the 1984 Shipping Act, there were 19,000 IA filings, implying that carriers were activity availing themselves of the rate flexibility feature in the law.

REFERENCES AND RELATED READINGS

General references

Bailey, E. E. and Baumol, W. J. 1984: Deregulation and the theory of contestable markets. *Yale Journal of Regulation*, 1, 111–37.

Baumol, W. J., Panzar, J. C., and Willig, R. D. 1982: *Contestable Markets and the Theory of Industry Structure*. San Diego, Calif.: Harcourt Brace Jovanovich.

Bresnahan, T. F. 1989: Empirical studies of industries with market power. In R. Schmalensee and R. D. Willig (eds.), *Handbook of Industrial Organization*. Amsterdam: North-Holland.

Oum, T. H., Dodgson, J. S., Hensher, D. A., Morrison, S. A., Nash, C. A., Small, K. A., and Waters, W. G. II 1995: *Transport Economics*. Seoul, Korea: The Korea Research Foundation for the 21st Century.

Shepherd, W. G. 1993: *The Economics of Industrial Organization*, 3rd edn. London: Prentice-Hall International.

Train, K. 1991: *Optimal Regulation: The Economic Theory of Natural Monopoly*. Cambridge, Mass.: The MIT Press.

Wilson, G. W. 1980: *Economic Analysis of Intercity Freight Transportation*. Bloomington, Indiana: Indiana University Press.

Viscusi, W. K., Vernon, J. M., and Harrington, J. E. Jr. 1992: *Economics of Regulation and Antitrust*. Lexington, Mass.: D.C. Heath.

General transportation references

Bailey, E. E. 1981: Contestability and the design of regulatory and antitrust policy. *AER Papers and Proceedings*, 71, 178–83.

Button, K. J. and Pearman, A. D. 1985: *Applied Transport Economics*. New York: Gordon and Breach.

Farris, M. T. 1983: Evolution of the transportation regulatory structure of the US. *International Journal of Transport Economics*, XVII, 173–93.

Gomez-Ibanez, J. A. and Meyer, J. R. 1993: *Going Private*. Washington DC: The Brookings Institution.

Hilton, G. 1980: *Amtrak: The National Railroad Passenger Corporation*. Washington DC: American Enterprise Institute.

Jones, D. 1985: *Urban Transit Policy: An Economic and Political History*. Englewood Cliffs, New Jersey: Prentice-Hall.

Locklin, D. P. 1966: *Economics of Transportation*. Homewood, Ill.: Richard D. Irwin.

Stephenson, J. and Frederick, J. 1987: *Transportation USA*. Reading, Mass.: Addison-Wesley.

Specific transportation references by mode

Airlines

Bailey, E. E. 1981: Contestability and the design of regulatory and antitrust policy. *AER Papers and Proceedings*, 71, 178–83.

Bailey, E. E. and Panzar, J. C. 1981: The contestability of airline markets during the transition to deregulation. *Law and Contemporary Problems*, 44, 125–45.

Baker, S. H. and Pratt, J. B. 1989: Experience as a barrier to contestability in airline markets. *Review of Economics and Statistics*, LXXI, 352–6.

Borenstein, S. 1992: The evolution of US airline competition. *Journal of Economic Perspectives*, 6, 45–73.

GAO/RECD 1990: *Airline Competition: Higher Fares and Reduced Competition at Concentrated Airports*. Report 90-102, July.

Keeler, T. E. 1972: Airline regulation and market performance. *The Bell Journal of Economics*, 3, 399–424.
Morrison, S. A. and Winston, C. 1987: Empirical implications and tests of the contestability hypothesis. *Journal of Law and Economics*, XXX, 53–66.
Morrison, S. A. and Winston, C. 1990: The dynamics of airline pricing and competition. *American Economic Review Papers and Proceedings*, 80, 383–93.
Morrison, S. A. and Winston, C. 1995: *The Evolution of the Airline Industry*. Washington DC: The Brookings Institution.
Slovin, M. B., Sushka, M. E., and Hudson, C. D. 1991: Deregulation, contestability, and airline acquisitions. *Journal of Financial Economics*, 30, 231–51.

Motor carriers

Allen, W. B. 1993: The impact of collective ratemaking on motor carrier rates: a test. *International Journal of Transport Economics*, X, 281–309.
Frew, J. 1981: The existence of monopoly profits in the motor carrier industry. *Journal of Law and Economics*, XXIV, 289–315.
Kim, M. 1984: The beneficiaries of trucking regulation, revisited. *Journal of Law and Economics*, XXVII, 227–41.
Friedlaender, A. F. and Spady, R. H. 1981: *Freight Transport Regulation: Equity, Efficiency, and Competition in the Rail and Tracking Industries*. Cambridge, Mass.: The MIT Press.
Moore, T. G. 1975: Deregulating surface freight transportation. In A. Phillips (ed.), *Promoting Competition in Regulated Markets*. Washington DC: The Brookings Institution, pp. 55–98.
Moore, T. G. 1978: The beneficiaries of trucking regulation. *Journal of Law and Economics*, 21, 327–43.
Rose, N. L. 1985: The incidence of regulatory rents in the motor carrier industry. *Rand Journal of Economics*, 16, 299–318.
Rose, N. 1987: Labor rent sharing and regulation: evidence from the trucking industry. *Journal of Political Economy*, 95, 1146–78.
Winston, C., Corsi, T. M., Grinum, C. M., and Evans, C. A. 1990: *The Economic Effects of Surface Freight Deregulation*. Washington DC: The Brookings Institution.

Bus and water carriers

Davies, J. 1987: Ship Act may face an early review. *Journal of Commerce*, 371.
Dodgson, J. S. and Katsoulacos, Y. 1991: Competition, contestability and predation: the economics of competition in deregulated bus markets. *Transportation Planning and Technology*, 15, 263–75.
Fox, N. R. 1992: An empirical analysis of ocean liner shipping. *International Journal of Transport Economics*, XIX, 205–25.
Teece, D. J. 1986: Assessing the competition faced by oil pipelines. *Contemporary Policy Issues*, IV, 65–78.
Wilson, W. W. and Casavant, K. L. 1991: Some market power implications of the Shipping Act of 1984: a case study of the US to Pacific Rim transportation markets. *Western Journal of Agricultural Economics*, 16, 427–34.

8

Regulation, Deregulation, and Efficiency in Transportation

INTRODUCTION

This chapter continues the empirical focus on the implications of imperfectly competitive transportation markets. In the last chapter, we analyzed interregional trade flows, developed measures of firm concentration, and explored how these have been used to evaluate a firm's potential for market power and the ability to price above marginal cost. In addition, we analyzed market power in the motor carrier and shipping industries.

In this chapter, we direct our attention to oligopoly, mergers, and efficiency losses in imperfectly competitive market structures. We examine how airline firms, seeking to maintain economic rents generated under regulation, strategically responded to the federal government's deregulatory actions. We analyze the relationship between transportation markets; specifically, how pricing output behavior in the trucking and rail markets are interrelated. And we explore notions of competition and examine the costs and benefits of horizontal mergers with an empirical example from the airline industry. The chapter concludes with a summary discussion of the economic effects of deregulation in the major transportation sectors.

CASE STUDY – DEREGULATION AND STRATEGIC BEHAVIOR IN THE AIRLINE INDUSTRY

In perfect competition, zero long-run economic rents accrue to market participants; in monopolistic markets, positive economic rents are the norm. And in each of these market structures, strategic behavior is absent because there are either so many (perfect competition) or so few (monopoly) firms in the industry that strategic behavior is of little value.

We have also seen, however, that market structures with few firms – oligopolies – also generate economic rents. But, unlike perfectly competitive and monopolistic market structures, strategic actions are inherent in oligopolistic markets. In order to survive in a market with few firms, an oligopolist must always be attentive to its competitors' pricing and output decisions. Why? – because its economic rents are not as certain as those of a monopolist. Since a pure monopoly has no close substitutes, any economic rents received are "safe" from competitive threats. This is not so with an oligopolist. An oligopolist must, on the one hand, continuously search for ways to maintain and increase its own economic rents; at the same time, it must be vigilant to the competitive threats of its competitors.

What strategies do oligopolists pursue to maintain economic rents? Ultimately, that depends upon the source of its rents. Suppose that entry into the market requires large investments, so that the scale of operations is the source of an oligopolist's economic rents. In this case, an optimal strategy would focus upon policies that strengthen these scale-based rents. On the other hand, if government policy creates entry barriers that generate economic rents for producing firms, the oligopolist will implement strategies designed to maintain the government-sponsored entry barriers. Alternatively, economic rents may derive from an ability to produce at lower cost, in which case the oligopolist will enact strategies to maintain its favorable cost position. In essence, then, in order to insure a continuing stream of economic rents, oligopolists must first recognize how these rents are generated and then identify and implement the most effective strategies for strengthening and building upon its source of rents.

Bailey and Williams (1988) examined the oligopolistic market structure in the airline industry, created during the period of regulation, and analyzed how, in hopes of maintaining or expanding rents, existing and entering firms strategically reacted to economic deregulation in 1978. During the period of economic regulation, the Civil Aeronautics Board (CAB) created a two-tier system for providing air service. Initially, it allocated transcontinental (east–west) routes to three trunk or long-distance carriers: American Airlines received operating authority in the southern tier, TWA in the central tier, and United Airlines in the northern tier. In addition, United Airlines received north–south operating authority on the West Coast and Eastern Airlines received similar authority on the East Coast. Over time, the CAB granted operating authority to other trunk carriers, including Delta, Western, Pan American, Continental, and Northwest. Complementing the trunk-line carriers, the CAB granted operating authority to a number of regional or local carriers that provided subsidized service to smaller cities and feeder service to the trunk carriers. Since the CAB granted local carriers operating authority in geographically distinct areas, the regional carrier markets were local monopolies. In addition to trunk and regional carriers, intrastate airline services not subject to CAB regulation operated in two large states, California and Texas.

Thus, the market structure in the airline industry prior to deregulation was a mixed oligopolistic/monopolistic market. The trunk carriers that provided long-distance services typified an oligopolistic market, in which few firms comprised a large share of the market. These firms were large-scale producers, each carrier having national operating authority and serving the major population centers in its respective geographic area. In addition, by its operating authorities, each trunk carrier enjoyed a greater relative presence in its own region. Regional carriers constituted local monopolies in their respective markets. Thus, an important implication from the prevailing market structure immediately preceding deregulation is that larger trunk carriers previously earned *scale-based* economic rents – that is, rents associated with the size of their operations – while the regional carriers received *location-based* rents reflecting their geographic monopolies.

Economic deregulation in 1978 completely altered the competitive environment in the airline industry, enabling the trunk carriers and the smaller regional carriers to add or delete routes, allowing intrastate carriers to offer interstate service, relaxing entry requirements, and, importantly, providing rate flexibility. During economic regulation, airlines could not compete on price. All carriers offering point-to-point service from city A to city B charged the same fare. As a result, airlines competed on quality of service through the introduction of newer aircraft more quickly than would occur with price competition, enhanced frequency of service, and more in-flight amenities. From a regulated environment of relative security, airline deregulation removed virtually all financial safety nets, thereby forcing firms to compete head-on with one another. But how do firms respond to the much more competitive environment? Should the trunk carriers compete in all national markets? Should they "downlink" their activities by establishing their own feeder services in regional markets? Similarly, how should the regional carriers respond? Should they expand into other regional markets or try to "uplink" by moving into some of the larger trunk markets? And where do new entrants fit in? Do they go after niche markets, or try to compete in the larger trunk markets or the smaller regional markets? Do they have competitive advantages in comparison with existing carriers? Additionally, with rate flexibility, should carriers compete by providing a "no-frills" service at the lowest possible price, or charging higher prices but offering more differentiated products? The questions can go on forever, and the answer to each will depend upon many factors, including the expected (re)actions of a carrier's competitors.

On the basis of Bailey and Williams' study, we can identify three general hypotheses regarding a firm's reaction to the newly created competitive forces from airline deregulation:

HYPOTHESIS 1 Not all firms in the airline industry belong to the same strategic cluster. We have seen above that, historically, the CAB differentiated trunk carriers from regional carriers. In their competitive responses to deregulation, this suggests that regional carriers will be more concerned about competition from other regional carriers than from larger trunk carriers. Conversely, larger trunk carriers identify their strategic competitors to be other trunk carriers rather than regional carriers.

HYPOTHESIS 2 Existing firms in each strategic cluster will pursue strategies aimed at maintaining or enhancing their sources of economic rents. Since trunk airlines have large-scale operations, this implies that the trunk-line carriers will seek to expand the scale or volume of their operations. At the same time, the regulated routes of trunks generally provided them with a greater relative presence in certain regions of the country. United Airlines, as we have seen, was more prevalent in the northern and western United States. Since a greater presence has the potential for generating local-based economic rents, United's route provided the carrier with an incentive to further concentrate its operations at airports in these regions in hopes of capturing additional rents.

Local carriers, on the other hand, whose economic rents derive specifically from location monopolies, are not expected to engage in scale-enhancing activities but, rather, to focus their resources on increasing regional concentrations.

HYPOTHESIS 3 Competitive firms in a multiproduct industry can balance cost differences associated with alternative levels of product differentiation in such way that, regardless of strategy, all firms make normal profits. In this environment, there will be many price–cost combinations, each of which generates a normal return on investment for the firm. If, on the other hand, these multiproduct firms are imperfectly competitive, then choice of strategy will enable them to make above- or below-normal returns on investment.

Under regulation, existing carriers were allowed little flexibility for competing on the price margin. Under deregulation, therefore, we would expect to see greater price competition. Some firms may want to compete with lower prices, while others will differentiate their products by offer higher-quality services at higher prices. The end result will be greater variation in price offerings.

On the cost side, there are two reasons why new entrants might experience cost advantages. First, during regulation, existing firms were insulated from strong competitive pressures. All else constant, this lessens the incentive to innovate and control costs, and generally increases the likelihood of inefficiently providing air services. Second, firms operating during regulation faced less competitive labor markets than existed in the post-regulation environment. As a result, incumbents entered the era of deregulation with significantly higher labor costs than entering firms that could hire labor at much lower wages.

Strategic clusters

Table 8.1 reports 1978 passenger–miles and average trip lengths in the airline industry at the onset of deregulation. Separate data are given for the long-distance trunk carriers, the regional carriers, and the major entrants into the industry upon deregulation. In 1978, as expected, trunk carriers produced at a much large scale, eight times the number of domestic passenger–miles as the regional carriers. And, consistent with this, trip length for the average passenger on a trunk carrier was more than double that of the local carriers. Do the data support the notion that the local and trunk-line carriers form a strategically distinct group,

Table 8.1 Airline operating characteristics, 1978

	Domestic Passenger–Miles (millions)	Average Passenger Trip Length (Miles)
Trunk carriers		
United	39,399	994
American	25,200	1,043
Delta	22,401	652
Eastern	20,750	666
TWA	20,521	1,400
Western	9,446	939
Pan Am	8,833	1,911
Continental	8,411	771
Northwest	4,902	1,087
Average	17,763	1,051
Local carriers		
Republic	5,533	347
USAir	4,083	327
Frontier	2,378	430
Ozark	1,488	346
Piedmont	1,434	318
Alaska	783	566
Average	2,617	389
Major interstate entrants		
PSA	2,831	325
People Ex	404	325
Southwest	545	219

Source: Adapted from Bailey and Williams (1988), table 1, p. 177.

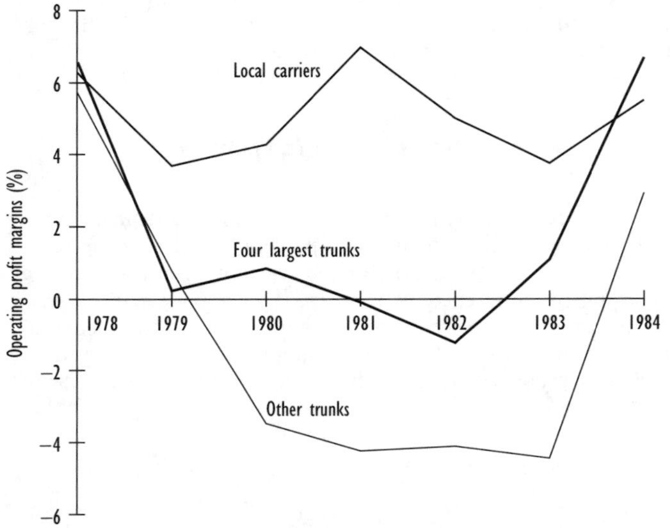

Figure 8.1 Average operating profit margins, 1978–84.

where members of a strategic group are more homogeneous relative to carriers outside the cluster? The answer would appear to be yes. The scale of operations is significantly higher for the trunk carriers. In addition, to the extent that a group of firms in a strategic cluster are more homogeneous, one would expect that a group member's competitive threat to primarily come from other members in the group. Figure 8.1 graphs the average operating profit margins from 1978 through 1983 for three strategic groups: Local Carriers; the four Largest Trunk Carriers; and Other Trunk Carriers. Between 1979 and 1983, the four largest carriers generally had fewer losses than other carriers in the trunk segment. Clearly, the local carriers outperformed the trunk carriers. But we also observe in figure 8.1 that the four largest trunks performed considerably better than the smaller trunks. Although the pattern of profit margins is similar between the two trunk carrier groups, the level of returns for the smaller trunks is consistently more negative.[1]

The data reported in table 8.1 and operating profit margins in figure 8.1 support hypothesis 1, that the airline industry is not an oligopoly of homogeneous firms but, rather, constitutes a set of strategic clusters, each of which – with few exceptions – is relatively homogeneous in its scales of operations and operating profit margins. As a cluster, local carriers may want to solidify their local-based monopolies, and large trunks may want to solidify their scale-based economic rents. For the regional carriers, the primary strategic concern is not from "downlinking" activities by full-service trunk carriers but, rather, from other regional carriers. Similarly, the data reported suggest that the dominant competitive concerns of trunk carriers would be other large trunks rather than smaller trunks. If regional carriers and large trunks successfully pursue their respective rent-maintaining/enhancing strategies, the smaller trunks are squeezed, which places them at much greater competitive risk.

Enhancing sources of economic rents

Location-based rents

Subsequent to deregulation, did the regional carriers seek to broaden their services geographically or intensify their service offerings regionally? Consistent with hypothesis 2, the regional carriers generally sought to strengthen their location-based monopoly rents by concentrating their expansion efforts in their own regional markets. Two factors provided local carriers with the incentive for this competitive response to deregulation. First, as we have seen, during the regulated era, the CAB provided local monopolies to the regional carriers so that, upon entering deregulation, existing carriers had an edge over competitors not currently operating in their markets. Second, because of route and fare restrictions during regulation, trunks typically competed on quality of service, one aspect of which is size of aircraft. Larger aircraft are more comfortable and generally provide more amenities. By entering the deregulated environment with too many long-distance aircraft and too few short-haul aircraft, trunk carriers were not competitive in the regional markets that required smaller short-haul aircraft. Regional carriers found themselves in the enviable position of entering deregulation with few existing competitors and a reduced threat of competition from the trunkline carriers. These factors induced them to strengthen their holds on their local airport hubs through hub-and-spoke operations.

Table 8.2 illustrates the effect of deregulation on regional hub operations between 1978 and 1983. For the five regional carriers, there was an average 163% increase in the percentage of domestic departures between 1978 and 1983. Excluding the very large increase in Piedmont's share at Charlotte, there was still a 97% increase in the percentage of departures from the hub airports. Thus, for Republic, USAir, Frontier, and Ozark, the competitive strategy was to strengthen operations at the airline's existing hub. As noted above, Piedmont's operations at Charlotte increased dramatically in the six-year period following deregulation. This reflects the fact that, during the regulated period, Charlotte was not a hub for Piedmont. Subsequent to deregulation, however, Piedmont established hubs on certain north–south routes that were found to be inadequately served. This explains the 15.9% share rise in operations at Charlotte in table 8.2.[2] Regional carriers not only searched for economic rents by expanding their presence at their existing regional hubs, but also by establishing new hubs in underserved regional markets.

Similar to the regional carriers, trunk carriers also received some location-based economic

Table 8.2 Hub operations – local carriers

		Percentage of Total Domestic Departures Flown from Hub	
Local Carrier	Hub	1978 (Second Quarter)	1984 (Second Quarter)
Republic	Minneapolis	3.4	7.7
USAir	Pittsburgh	16.0	23.2
Frontier	Denver	18.0	33.8
Ozark	St. Louis	15.5	35.6
Piedmont	Charlotte	3.7	19.6

Source: Adapted from Brenner et al. (1985), table 36, p. 81. Data was not available for Alaska Airlines

Table 8.3 Hub operations – trunk carriers

		Percentage of Total Domestic Departures Flown from Hub	
Trunk Carrier	Hub	1978 (Second Quarter)	1983 (Second Quarter)
United	Chicago	13.8	18.9
American	Dallas	11.2	28.6
Delta	Atlanta	18.3	21.4
Eastern	Atlanta	18.3	21.0
TWA	St. Louis	11.9	33.0
Western	Salt Lake City	10.3	16.9
Pan Am	New York	12.3	24.0
Continental	Houston	12.8	22.9
Northwest	Minneapolis	16.1	20.7

Source: Adapted from Brenner et al. (1985), table 36, p. 81

rents during regulation from the parallel route structures carved out by the CAB. On east–west routes, United dominated the north, TWA the central, and American the southern parts of the country. Similarly, on the north–south routes, United had a presence on the West Coast and Eastern Airlines on the East Coast. Thus, it is not surprising that each of these airlines, recognizing that its competitive advantage geographically lay where its presence was greatest during regulation, would seek to strengthen the hubs in these areas. For the major trunks operating in 1978, table 8.3 gives percentage change in operations at their hub airports between 1978 and 1983. Over this period, there was an average 74.2% increase in the proportion of departures at the hub airports. The largest percentage changes in departures at hub facilities were achieved by TWA, American, and Pan Am.

Trunk carriers also looked for expansion markets in order to increase their presence and economic rents. American Airlines, for example, established north–south hubs in Nashville, Tennessee and Raleigh, North Carolina. At the same time, and again consistent with our theoretical expectations, American Airlines dropped virtually all of its short-haul service from New York City. Between August 1978 and August 1984, the number of daily nonstop flights between New York City and seven short-haul markets fell from 47 to 1.[3]

Scale-based rents

Complementing these location-based rents, large trunk-line carriers have a scale advantage over the smaller trunk carriers and the regionals. Because of this, we would expect to see these carriers initiate strategies that would enhance the scale of their operations. Traditionally, the scale of a firm's operations forms an effective barrier to entry, and strategies aimed at expanding the size and scope of operations enable a firm to better solidify its position against competitors.

In the deregulated environment, we can identify three actions undertaken by the large trunk carriers that are consistent with a greater focus on their scale of operations. First, they expanded the frequency of their flights and increased the amount of resources devoted to optimizing fares in the various markets served. Between 1978 and 1984, for example, the number of weekly departures at large and medium hub airports increased by 35.5% and 38.5% respectively. At small hubs and nonhub airports, weekly departures rose by 19.1% and 9.1% respectively. Similarly, the number of airplane seats between 1978 and 1984 increased by 38.3% and 36.1% at large and medium hubs, rose by 7.9% at small hubs, and fell by 9.7% at nonhub airports. These statistics indicate that the scale of flight operations at large and medium hubs, which are the facilities used by trunk carriers, disproportionately rose in comparison with the smaller regional hubs.

In addition, Bailey and Williams report, that during this same period, Delta's tariff department, which is responsible for setting Delta fares and keeping track of its competitors' fares, grew from 27 employees to 147 employees who, in 1984, monitored 70,000 fares offered by Delta and its competitors and sought to optimize 5,000 price changes per day. As an airline's operation network expands and becomes more complex – that is, as its scale increases – the advantages of investing resources to better utilize its assets and optimize its complex price structure also increase. But the increased scale also strengthens entry barriers to its competitors – the smaller trunk airlines, for example – preventing them from competing away its market share.

A second strategy used by the large trunk airlines to strengthen scale-based economic rents was to initiate programs intended to increase customer loyalty and reduce switching between airline carriers. Economic regulation prevented airlines from competing on price and induced them to compete on margins of quality. At the same time, in the post Second World War era, there were major advances in the quality of aircraft, with the introduction of jet engines, long-distance aircraft, and wide-body planes. These advances in airplane capital were easily identified by the traveling public, and enabled carriers to compete for customers by adding airplanes with the most recent innovations to their fleets. More recently, however, quality enhancements have been in the area of fuel efficiency, the effects of which are much less recognized by travelers.

A major innovation in marketing a carrier's product was the introduction of *frequent-flyer programs* (FFP), initially started by American Airlines in 1981. A frequent flyer program gives passengers traveling on its airlines mileage points that the traveler can then redeem for free trips.[4] For example, suppose that an airline awards one mileage point for each mile flown and requires 25,000 mileage points for a free trip in the continental United States. Then the traveler must accumulate 25,000 miles of travel in order to redeem his or her mileage points for a free trip. In addition to increasing customer loyalty, FFPs exploit the scale of large trunk carriers for two reasons. First, holding all else constant, the larger the network of the awarding carrier, the easier it is for the traveler to accumulate miles on the airline. If a carrier only

Table 8.4 The presence of computer reservation systems, 1983

CRS	Number of Locations	%	Domestic Revenues (millions)	%
SABRE (American)	5,692	27	6,376	43
APOLLO (United)	3,865	18	4,041	27
PARS (TWA)	2,159	10	1,561	10
SODA (Eastern)	1,057	5	605	4
DATAS II (Delta)	688	3	259	2
MARS (Tymshare)	344	2	282	2
Unautomated	7,546	35	1,823	12

Source: Adapted from Brenner et al. (1985), table 27, p. 66. Presently, United is the primary owner of APOLLO but USAir and some foreign carriers share in its ownership. APOLLO and SABRE account for 75% of the activity. Also, Delta, TWA, and Northwest Airlines currently share a system, Worldspan, and Continental is a distant third with its SystemOne CRS (Borenstein, 1992)

operates in one part of the country, it becomes more difficult for travelers to generate enough travel to take advantage of the free trips. In addition, the more extensive the network is, the larger is the potential set of destinations to which the awardee could travel. Thus, FFPs enable the larger trunks to strengthen their scale-based economic rents, consistent with hypothesis 2. Also consistent with this hypothesis is the prediction that the larger trunks, having more to gain from FFPs, would be the first to adopt such programs. And, indeed, this was the case. The regional carriers implemented FFPs after they were instituted by the large carriers.

A third strategy for fortifying large-scale economic rents was the development of a computer reservation system (CRS) for travel agents, as well as a carrier's own sales personnel. CRSs enable sales agents to call up a screen on a computer to display departure and arriving schedules, fares, and seat availability on different air carriers. Once a traveler decides upon a specific flight and reserves a seat, the agent transmits the booking information to the central computer, which forwards the data to the specific air carrier's computer system. Having made and received confirmation for the booking, the sales agent issues the ticket and boarding pass for the trip. By eliminating the necessity for the travel agent to telephonically speak with the air carrier, the CRS significantly reduces the cost of booking and altering reservations.[5]

Although early attempts to develop CRSs occurred in the mid-1960s, it was not until the mid-1970s that these systems were successfully implemented. In 1976, United Airlines was first to implement its APOLLO system, followed by American's SABRE, TWA's PARS, and smaller systems by Eastern and Delta. In addition to these carrier-owned systems, the American Society of Travel Agents developed and implemented its own system, MARS.

What impact do these systems have on ticketing activities? Table 8.3 gives the proportion of computer reservations used in the fiscal year 1983. In that year, 65% of all travel agencies used one of the available CRSs, representing 88% of domestic revenues. The most prevalent system was American's SABRE, which was used by nearly 5,700 travel agencies, representing 27% of all agencies. More importantly, SABRE accounted for 43% of domestic revenues. United's APOLLO system was the other major CRS, used by 18% of travel agencies and representing 27% of revenues. The combined impact of the smaller carrier-owned CRS systems was an 18% share of travel agencies and 16% of revenues. Moreover, if we simply focus on the travel agencies that use some CRS, then we see that 69% (45/65) of CRS-based travel agencies used American's SABRE and United's APOLLO, representing 80% (70/88) of domestic revenues.

If one of the smaller trunk carriers or a new entrant hopes to compete with the larger trunk-line carriers, it must either develop its own CRS or gain access to an existing system. The development and implementation costs of having one's own system are formidable. But using an existing system entails its own costs. If carrier A uses carrier B's CRS for booking flights, it must pay carrier A for the use of its system. Carrier A could set the booking costs sufficiently high to deter significant entry into the market. Indeed, consistent with this conjecture, a 1988 DOT study found that booking charges to other airlines were well above marginal opportunity costs (US Department of Transportation, 1988). A further cost of using carrier A's CRS is that carrier A obtains valuable information on the flights and fares of carrier B, which it could use to its own advantage. Thus, having a sophisticated CRS provides the carrier with an asset that creates an entry barrier to other carriers that want to enter the long-distance trunk-line market.

A fourth strategy to counter the potential wealth-reducing effects of economic deregulation is merger. The pursuit of economic rents after deregulation may have placed the smaller trunk-line carriers at risk. The primary incentive for regional carriers is to build upon their existing local-based rents by developing extensive hub-and-spoke networks around regional hubs. At the same, the larger trunk carriers have an incentive to build upon their scale-based economic rents. This puts intense pressure upon the smaller trunk-line carriers, leaving them very little room for maneuver. One possibility is for a smaller trunk-line carrier to merge with a regional carrier, a strategy that would appear to serve the interests of both carriers. The regional airline gains access to more extensive routes without sacrificing its existing location-based rents, while the smaller trunk gains size, enabling it to better exploit scale-based economies.

The 1986 Northwest and Republic Airline merger discussed in the next section is an example. Measured by domestic passenger–miles, we saw from table 8.1 that in 1978 Northwest was the smallest of the trunks, while Republic was the largest of the regionals. Moreover, since both carriers had a hub at Minneapolis, the merger would be expected to significantly increase local-based rents at the Minneapolis hub. Consistent with this, Borenstein (1990) estimates that, between 1985 and 1987, the year prior to and the year after the merger, average ticket prices at the airport increased 9.5% faster than the national average. And for routes on which Northwest and Republic had been the only competitors, the price increase was 22.5% faster than the national average.

Similar incentives existed for the 1986 merger between TWA, a mid-size trunk carrier, and Ozark Airlines, a mid-size regional carrier. Both carriers operated hubs at St. Louis so that local-based rents were reinforced while simultaneously pursuing greater scale-based rents. In this case, however, there was a less dramatic effect on prices. Ticket prices at the St. Louis hub increased by an average of 8% but, in this instance, the price increase was driven largely by a few high-volume routes. And along some routes where TWA and Ozark were the only competitors prior to the merger, prices increased at the national average (Borenstein, 1992).[6]

Competition and entry in an oligopoly market

In addition to strengthening the sources of a firm's economic rents, oligopolistic firms also seek to offer a price/cost combinations that maximize economic rents, identified above in hypothesis 3. We have seen that oligopolistic firms, in contrast to perfectly competitive firms, are not price-takers but rather price-searchers, seeking that price that maximizes profits. In addition, in most if not all transportation markets, multiproduct outputs are differentiated by frequency of service, special care and handling, types of equipment used, and so forth. This diversity in product offerings enables firms to choose any number of price/cost combinations, a choice that ultimately depends upon how it affects economic rents. All else held constant, the price/cost combination that a firm believes will contribute most to economic rents will be offered. Moreover, since oligopolistic firms are not generally identical in all respects, this further implies that a profit-maximizing price/cost offering by one firm may not be profit-maximizing for another firm. Thus, an oligopolistic market structure could simultaneously accommodate different price/cost combinations, each one of which is a profit-maximizing choice for one of the incumbent firms.

In the airline industry, product differentiation is reflected in a carrier's departure frequency, the number of stopovers, changes of plane, sizes of aircraft, and types of services offered (first class, business class, coach, and economy). As we have seen, during the regulated period, the CAB set carrier routes and airfares. However, the prices that the CAB allowed regional carriers to charge were 30% higher than trunk carriers. Combined with the effective location monopolies that the CAB granted to regional carriers, we would expect these carriers to be high-cost, high-price suppliers of regional air-trips. Conversely, we would expect trunk carriers to be low-cost, low-price carriers. Bailey and Williams provided evidence of this two-tier price/quality structure. In 1978, yields (revenues per passenger mile) for Ozark, Piedmont, Republic, and USAir were in the 12–13 cent range, with costs per available seat mile (ASM) in the 7.4–8.3 cent range. For the trunk carriers, however, yields were considerably lower, in the 7–9 cent range, as were costs, which ranged between 4.8

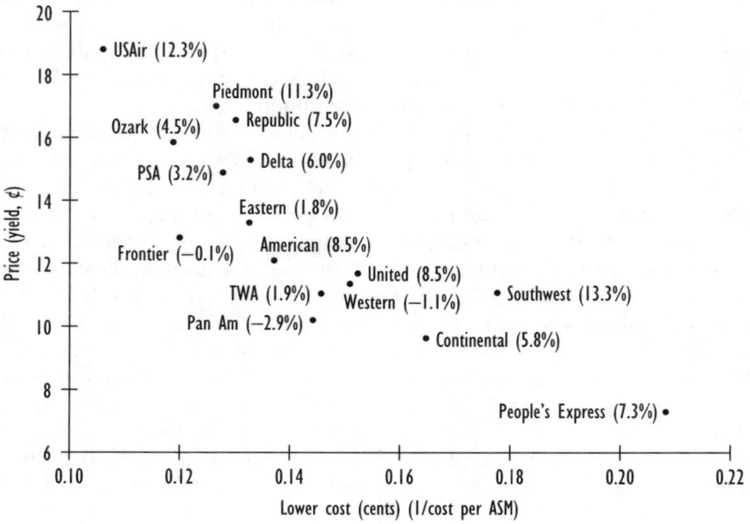

Figure 8.2 The 1984 US airline industry (profit margin, %, in parentheses).

and 5.7 cents per ASM. Also, in the regulated era, the price variations that did exist for trunk carriers reflected differences in average trip distances rather than competitive forces.

In comparison with the regulated period, how would we expect deregulation to affect the price/cost dimension? As noted in hypothesis 3, we can expect greater price/cost variation as multiproduct oligopolistic firms attempt to increase economic rents. Figure 8.2 depicts the relationship between price (yield, in cents) and lower cost (1/(cost per ASM), in cents), where we see considerable variation in offerings. Whereas in 1978 economic regulation-induced regional carriers to cluster in the high-price, high-cost region and the trunks to cluster in the low-price, low-cost region, we see in figure 8.2 a more varied offering of price/cost combinations. Among the regional carriers, only USAir and Piedmont have been able to maintain high prices and higher-cost services. And virtually all of the trunk carriers have moved toward the center, offering higher-price, higher-cost services.[7]

An important result depicted in figure 8.2 is obtained by considering those carriers that are making similar profits. USAir, Piedmont, and Southwest Airlines each have operating profits above 10%. Yet they are offering widely differing price/cost combinations. Similarly, Frontier, Western, and Pan American Airlines have negative profit margins, but again with different price/cost offerings. Between these two groups are the remaining airlines, all of which are making positive operating profits at various price/cost combinations. These findings are consistent with the conjecture that oligopolistic market structures can accommodate a variety of price/cost offerings, each of which may be profit-maximizing to some firm in the market.

To reinforce the result that oligopolistic firms strategically search for price/cost combinations that increase economic rents, table 8.1 identified three major interstate entrants subsequent to deregulation, Pacific Southwest Airlines (PSA), Southwest, and People's Express. PSA and Southwest Airlines had previously operated as intrastate airlines in California and Texas respectively. Each entrant in 1984 operated profitably but differed in their price/cost offerings. PSA had moderate costs and prices, whereas Southwest and People's Express had significantly lower costs. Both Southwest and People's Express strategically exploited lower labor costs that characterized the deregulated environment, consistent with hypothesis 3.[8]

Comments

The above analysis examined the airline industry between 1978 and 1984, identifying strategies that the regional carriers and the trunk-line carriers pursued in response to economic deregulation. In the ensuing years, these air carriers continued to meet the competitive challenges and search for economic rents, some successfully and some unsuccessfully. For the airlines reported in table 8.1, we have seen that TWA acquired Ozark Airlines and Northwest acquired Republic in 1986. Continental merged with Eastern Airlines in 1986. Also, in 1985, Frontier merged with People's Express. Bailey and Williams argue that Frontier's financial problems resulted from the fact that it gave up a variety of monopoly routes in the hopes of competing with two trunk-line carriers, United and Continental, at Denver. But the competition at Denver meant that there were few locational rents to be gained at the hub, and the merger did little to expand scale. In short, the merger was doomed to fail and this materialized two years later when, in 1987, the combined carrier merged with Continental. Also in 1987, Western Airlines merged with Delta and in 1988, PSA merged with USAir, followed in 1989 by USAir's acquisition of Piedmont.

Although we can't be sure which carriers will continue to exist, or what types of price/quality combinations will be offered in the future, we can be sure that the air carriers will continue to search for market niches, price/quality combinations, underserved areas, and size-related and other sources of market power that they can successfully exploit to maximize their economic rents.

MERGERS IN TRANSPORTATION

Why do firms merge? Although there may exist a variety of tax-related, financial, or geographic reasons for mergers, in this section we will focus upon the economic implications when two firms competing in the same market merge, which is referred to as an horizontal merger.[9] Horizontal mergers generally have two economic effects: lower unit costs of production; and increased market power (Williamson, 1968).

We have seen that, in an industry characterized by strong scale economies, incumbent firms have an incentive to produce large quantities of the good by exploiting their economies of large-scale production. One way to do this is for incumbent firms to merge. The unit cost of production for one firm serving the entire market is lower than the unit cost of many firms serving the market. A second effect is an increase in market share for the merged firm, with an associated increase in market power. And, as we have seen, market power enables a firm to price above marginal cost and earn economic profits.

Figure 8.3 depicts the impact on welfare from the trade-off between lower production costs and increased market power from a proposed horizontal merger between two airlines. Prior to the merger, the average cost of production is AC_0, the trip price is P_0, and the output is T_0. In the graph, we assume that there is sufficient competition in the market to drive price down to the unit cost of production. After the merger, two things happen. First, economies of large-scale production associated with the merged firm drive unit costs down to AC_1. However, the greater market power of the merged firm results in a higher price and lower number of trips coming to the market. In the post-merger environment, there is a reduction in net benefits to

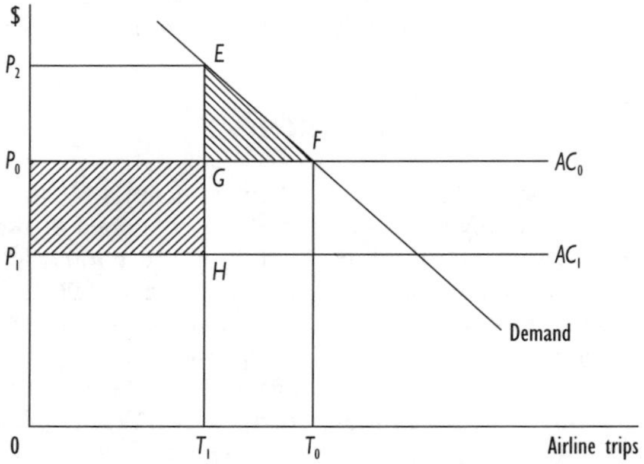

Figure 8.3 The welfare trade-off from mergers.

consumers, an efficiency loss denoted by *EFG*, as trip price rises to P_2 and number of trips falls to T_1. At the same time, T_1 trips are produced with fewer resources, an efficiency gain, and producer profits increase by the shaded rectangle, P_0P_1HG. The net effect on welfare is the difference between these two areas. As shown, there is a net gain. And if the criterion for approving a proposed merger was its impact on social welfare, the proposed merger would be approved.

But some would question this approach. The less price elastic is demand, the more likely will gains in production more than offset efficiency losses to consumers. Suppose, for example, that we take an extreme example and assume that the demand for trips is perfectly price inelastic. The demand curve in figure 8.3 would be a vertical line. And any increase in price associated with greater market power from the merger would simply result in a transfer of income from consumers to producers. Because there is no change in quantity demanded, the net effect on social welfare from this transfer is zero. Thus, as long as the merging firms could demonstrate that the merger would exploit scale economies and lower unit costs, even if all of these resource savings accrued to the merged firm, net welfare would increase and the government should approve the merger. Although net welfare would increase, none of the gain would go to consumers. This extreme example produces the interesting result that merger approval is independent of consumer losses (since they are simply transfers), and that approval simply requires the merging firms to demonstrate that a merged firm will reap some production efficiency gains, however small.

CASE STUDY – ESTIMATING THE BENEFITS FROM MERGERS: REPUBLIC AIRLINES

In the above analysis, the benefit derived from a proposed merger was the resource saving associated with enhanced economies of scale. As long as the reduction in production costs savings more than offsets the loss of consumer net benefits from greater market power, the above analysis indicates that net welfare will increase. Recognizing that part of the full cost of producing a trip includes the time resources that tripmakers expend, Williamson's welfare trade-off can be generalized to include both production cost savings from larger economies of scale and resource savings to travelers making the trip. Thus, it is possible that the primary resource saving from merging accrues to travelers in the form of lower travel times, more convenient scheduling, less time spent at a terminal or walking in the terminal to catch one's next flight, and less time waiting for one's baggage.

Shortly after airline deregulation in 1978, a series of merger applications occurred as existing firms struggled to adapt to the more open economic environment created by deregulation. Carlton, Landes, and Posner (1980) examined the benefits and costs of an approved merger between two smaller airlines, North Central Airlines and Southern Airways, into a new airline called Republic Airlines. The authors identify the primary benefit of the merger to be "product development," in that the merger afforded Republic Airlines to offer single-carrier (as well as more single-plane) services to more than 1,400 city-pairs that had previously been serviced by North Central Airlines and Southern Airways. Improved product development occurs if single-carrier service leads to lower time expenditures and more convenient travel for Republic's customers.

In order to test whether single-carrier service provided benefits to the traveling public, Carlton et al. specified the following indirect utility for single carrier and multicarrier service in city-pair j:

$$
\begin{aligned}
U^1_{sc} &= \alpha_0 + \alpha_1 T^j_{sc} + \alpha_2(F^j_{sc} - F^j_{sc,sp}) + \alpha_3 F^j_{sc,sp} + \varepsilon^j_{sc} \\
&= V^j_{sc} + \varepsilon^j_{sc} \\
U^1_{mc} &= \alpha_1 T^j_{mc} + \alpha_2 F^j_{mc} + \varepsilon^j_{mc} \\
&= V^j_{mc} + \varepsilon^j_{mc} \qquad (8.1)
\end{aligned}
$$

where U^j_i is the indirect utility for single (i = sc) and multicarrier (i = mc) service for city-pair j; V^j_i is the observed portion of indirect utility for single (i = sc) and multicarrier (i = mc) service for city-pair j; T^j_{sc} is the average scheduled travel time, in minutes, of a single carrier for city-pair j; T^j_{mc} is the average scheduled travel time, in minutes, of a multicarrier for city-pair j; F^j_{sc} is the number of single-carrier and single-plane flights per week for city-pair j; F^j_{mc} is the number of multicarrier flights per week for city-pair j; $F^j_{sc,sp}$ is the number of single-plane flights of a single-carrier per week for city-pair j; and ε^j_i is an error term associated with single-carrier (i = sc) and multicarrier (i = mc) for city-pair j. The benefit that a traveler receives from multicarrier service reflects the travel time and flight frequency associated with the trip. Travel time and flight frequency also determine the economic welfare from single-carrier flights. However, notice that the utility for a single-carrier flight distinguishes single-carrier, multiplane flights, $F_{sc} - F_{sc,sp}$, from single-carrier, single-plane flights, $F_{sc,sp}$. As discussed below, it is expected that consumers prefer single-carrier flights which involve no change of plane over single-carrier flights that do involve a change of plane.

It should also be noted from equation (8.1) that indirect utility is not hypothesized to depend upon fare levels. Although, in general, as we have previously seen, airline transportation choices do depend upon fares, in this case fares are irrelevant, because we are analyzing consumers' choices of service type between a given city-pair. Whether one uses single- or multicarrier services, the fare for a particular city-pair will be the same and, therefore, will not affect one's carrier type choice.[10]

In equation (8.1), travelers have two options, single- or multicarrier service which, as we know from chapter 4, generates a probabilistic choice model. Define MS^j as the market share of single-carrier service for city-pair j. Then the probability of single-carrier service for city-pair j can be expressed as

$$MS^j = \Pr(U^j_{sc} > U^j_{mc}) = \Pr(U^j_{sc} + \varepsilon^j_{sc} > U^j_{mc} + \varepsilon^j_{mc}) \qquad (8.2)$$

and the probability of multicarrier service is $1 - MS^j$. Assuming a logistic distribution function, this leads to the following binary logit model of single- and multicarrier choice:

$$MS^j = \frac{e^{V^j_{sc}}}{e^{V^j_{sc}} + e^{V^j_{mc}}}$$

$$1 - MS^j = \frac{e^{V^j_{mc}}}{e^{V^j_{sc}} + e^{V^j_{mc}}} \qquad (8.3)$$

Since MS^j and $1 - MS^j$ are market shares, the odds of choosing single- over multicarrier service are

$$\frac{MS^j}{1 - MS^j} = \exp(V^j_{sc} - V^j_{mc}) \qquad (8.4)$$

Taking the logarithms of both sides and substituting for V^j_i $(i = \text{sc, mc})$ from equation (8.4) yields the following empirical regression model:

$$\ln\left(\frac{MS^j}{1 - MS^j}\right) = V^j_{sc} - V^j_{mc}$$
$$= \alpha_0 + \alpha_1(T^j_{sc} - T^j_{mc}) + \alpha_2(F^j_{sc} - F^j_{mc} - F^j_{sc,sp}) + \alpha_3 F^j_{sc,sp} \qquad (8.5)$$

Equation (8.5) is a log–linear model, and the interpretation of a slope coefficient is the percentage change in the odds of single-carrier service from a unit increase in the associated explanatory variable. This model has two basic hypotheses:

HYPOTHESIS 1 The market share of single-carrier service is sensitive to schedule travel times. In particular, an increase (decrease) in scheduled travel time on single-carrier service decreases (increases) the market share of single-carrier service, all else constant. Conversely, worsening travel times on multicarrier service is expected to increase the market share of single-carrier service. Thus, it is expected that $\alpha_1 < 0$.

HYPOTHESIS 2 Increasing differences in the flight frequencies between single-carrier, multiplane versus multicarrier service will increase the relative market share of single-carrier service. Further, an increase in the frequency of single-carrier, single-plane service is expected to have a larger impact upon single-carrier service than an increase in single-carrier, multiplane service. This implies that $\alpha_2 < 0$ and that $\alpha_3 > \alpha_2$.

Carlton et al. used data on 28 city-pairs in 1977 to estimate the empirical model specified in equation (8.5). For these city-pairs, single carriers had an average market share equal to 75%. Assuming that single- and multicarriers provided identical services, each carrier type would be expected to have a 50% share of the market. So the 75% observed average share suggests that, relative to multicarriers, single carriers were providing additional benefits to travelers. Carlton et al.'s results are presented below:

$$\ln\left(\frac{MS^j}{1 - MS^j}\right) = \underset{(4.26)}{0.863} + \underset{(3.78)}{0.013}(T^j_{sc} - T^j_{mc})$$
$$+ \underset{(5.13)}{0.008}(F^j_{sc} - F^j_{mc} - F^j_{sc,sp})$$
$$+ \underset{(3.33)}{0.021}F^j_{sc,sp}$$
$$R^2 = 0.71 \qquad (8.6)$$

where the t-statistics are in parentheses. Overall, scheduled travel time and flight frequency explains 71% of the variations in the log-odds. Each of the estimated coefficients has its expected sign and is significant at a 0.01 level.[11] We can reject the null hypothesis that $\alpha_i = 0$ $(i = 1, 2, 3)$.

To interpret the results, we need simply remember that the empirical model is a log–linear specification. A one minute increase in scheduled travel time on a single carrier, all else constant, reduces the odds of taking a single carrier by 0.013%. On the other hand, increasing the flight frequency of single-carrier service by one more flight per week raises the odds of taking single-carrier service by 0.008%. Notice that we also obtain the expected result that consumers value single-carrier, single-plane service more than they value single-carrier, multiplane service. The coefficient for $F_{sc,sp}$ is larger than the coefficient for $(F_{sc} - F_{sc,sp}) - F_{mc}$. A unit increase in single-carrier, single-plane service raises the odds of using single-carrier services by 0.021%, almost three times the effect of single-carrier, multiplane service.

What is the predicted market share of single-carrier service if both single and multicarriers offer identical times ($T_{sc} = T_{mc}$), identical frequency ($F_{sc} - F_{sc,sp} = F_{mc}$) and no single-carrier, single-plane service? Under these conditions, we would have $\ln(MS^j/(1 - MS^j)) = 0.863$, which implies that $(MS^j/(1 - MS^j)) = \exp(0.863) = 2.37$. Solving for MS^j gives a single-carrier market share equal to 70% $((2.37/3.37) = 0.70)$.

How do consumers benefit from the introduction of single-carrier services? Consider the pre-merger environment in which each of the city-pairs included in the analysis only offered multicarrier service. In this case, a traveler receives a pre-merger benefit that we can identify as $B^{\text{pre-merger}}$. Alternatively, after the merger, a traveler has the option of taking either single or multicarrier service. Consistent with an expanded set of travel opportunities will be a post-merger benefit given as $B^{\text{post-merger}}$. Thus, the benefit that travelers place upon the introduction of single-carrier service and, in this case upon the merger, is simply the difference between the post- and pre-merger benefits $(B^{\text{post-merger}} - B^{\text{pre-merger}})$. How do we measure these benefits? It turns out that the logit model yields a simple formula for calculating the expected maximum utility associated with a particular choice situation:

$$\text{Expected Maximum Utility} = EMU = \ln\left(\sum_i e^{V_i}\right) \tag{8.7}$$

where V_i is the observed indirect utility associated with alternative i. Since the pre-merger environment included only one alternative (multicarrier service), the expected utility or pre-merger benefit is simply $\ln(e^{V_{mc}^{\text{pre-merger}}}) = V_{mc}^{\text{pre-merge}}$. In the post-merger environment, consumers have two choices, single carrier and multi-carrier, so that the expected maximum benefit or indirect utility after the merger is $\ln(e^{V_{sc}^{\text{post-merger}}} + e^{V_{mc}^{\text{post-merger}}})$.[12]

In their benefit calculations, Carlton et al. made two assumptions: (1) the merger would have no effect upon scheduled travel times; and (2) the total frequency of flights would not change and would be evenly distributed between single- and multicarrier providers. Thus, the increase in benefit associated with the merger is

$$\begin{aligned}(B^{\text{post-merger}} - B^{\text{pre-merger}}) &= EMU_{\text{post-merger}} - EMU_{\text{pre-merger}} \\ &= \ln(e^{V_{sc}^{\text{post-merger}}} + e^{V_{mc}^{\text{post-merger}}}) - V_{mc}^{\text{pre-merger}}\end{aligned}$$

Column 3 in table 8.5 reports the estimated utility benefits that travelers derived from the merger between Northern Central Airlines and Southern Airways, for three different levels of

Table 8.5 The estimated value of utility benefits from the Central Airlines and Southern Airways merger

Estimated Market Share (%)	Flight Frequency (per week)	Increase in Expected Maximum Utility	Equivalent Change in Travel Time[a] (minute decrease)	$ Value of Increase in Maximum Utility[b]
70	30	1.09	84	21.52
70	60	0.97	75	19.21
70	100	0.81	62	15.88

[a] To illustrate the calculation, consider the first row, where expected maximum utility increases 1.09. With no change in frequency of service, our expression for a change in utility is $\Delta U = 0.013\ \Delta\text{Time}$. If $\Delta U = 1.09$, this implies that $\Delta T = (1.09/0.013) = 83.8$ minutes.

[b] Based upon a $15.37 per hour value of time, 1977 dollars. See table 4.10 of chapter 4.

Source: Adapted from Carlton et al. (1980), table 2, p. 73

weekly flight frequency. In order to calculate the dollar value of these benefits, reported in the last column, Carlton et al. calculated by how much travel time must fall to generate an equivalent change in utility. Then multiplying the change in time by an appropriate value of time provides an estimate of the value that travelers placed upon the introduction of single-carrier service after the two airlines merged. From the table, we see that the per traveler value that customers of Republic Airlines placed upon single-carrier service ranged between $15 and $21. As a result of the merger, 270,000 travelers had access to single-carrier service on Republic's routes, which translates into a minimum total annual benefit ranging between $4.29 and $5.81 million (1977 dollars).

CASE STUDY – MERGERS AND CONSUMER PRICES

The example of Republic Airlines illustrates the potential benefits that may accrue to consumers from merger activities. We have also seen that horizontal mergers increase the market share of the merged firm, and to the extent that this gives the firm more market power, the merged firm has an incentive to raise prices above marginal cost. This leads to welfare losses, depicted in figure 8.3 by the triangle *EFG*.

The merger between North Central Airlines and Southern Airways gave rise to the merged firm Republic Airlines. This occurred in 1979. In 1985, Republic Airlines and Northwest Airlines initiated discussions for merging, requested DOT permission to merge in early 1986, and were granted approval in late 1986. This merger was controversial because the Minneapolis/St. Paul airport served both airlines as a major hub for their operations. The merger would presumably give the merged firm considerable market power in the Minneapolis/St. Paul market. This raises two questions. First, did the merged firm experience an increase in market power? And, if so, did the increase in market power lead to a rise in consumer prices?

Borenstein (1990) considered these questions. To determine whether the merger gave the combined firm more market power, Borenstein calculated the average price on routes from the Minneapolis/St. Paul hub relative to the industry average price for routes of a similar distance. In addition, he calculated these relative prices for four different market structures that reflected the competitive environment, and depending upon whether: (1) Republic Airlines and Northwest Airlines competed for a route jointly or separately prior to the merger; and (2) other airlines competed for the route. Table 8.6 presents Borenstein's results for the 1985 pre-merger period, the merger year 1986, and the post-merger environment in 1987. Prior to the merger that occurred in late 1986, the relative price premium in markets where Northwest, Republic, and other airlines competed was small, amounting to 3.1% and 0.2% in 1985 and 1986 respectively. After the merger, however, the relative price premium increased to 10.1%. On the other hand, when either Northwest or Republic, but not both, competed with another airline for the route, the relative price premium was higher in the pre-merger period, 14.3% versus 3.1%, and substantially increased in the merger and post-merger environments. The highest premium, however, occurs on those routes where Northwest or Republic had a monopoly, row 4 in table 8.6. Here we see that in the pre-merger period, the premium was 27%, which increased to 39.4% in the post-merger period. These premia were somewhat lower – 15.2%, 32.1%, and 37.8% in the pre-merger, merger, and post-merger periods, respectively – when Northwest and Republic competed head to head for routes in the pre-merger period, with no other competitors.

The relative price premia in the four markets are consistent with an increase in market power in those markets with the least competition both before and after the merger. We also see evidence of this in the last column, which gives the average change in relative price between the third quarter of 1985 and the third quarter of 1987. The average change is considerably less

Table 8.6 Republic/Northwest price premia and changes

	Did Other Firms Compete?	Number of Markets (routes)	Relative Price[a]			Average Change[a]
			1985	1986	1987	
NW and RC competed for route	Yes	16	3.1	0.2	10.1	6.7
NW or RC competed for route	Yes	41	14.3	21.2	19.9	6.0
NW and RC competed for route	No	11	15.2	32.1	37.8	22.5
NW or RC competed for route	No	16	27.0	36.6	39.4	12.0
Total		84	14.7	21.5	24.1	9.5

[a] Relative price is the price in the particular market divided by the average price in the industry for routes of a similar distance. Average change is the change in the relative price between the third quarter of 1987 and the third quarter of 1985.
Source: Adapted from Borenstein (1990), table 2, p. 401

in those markets with other competitors, averaging a bit higher than 6%. In markets with no competitors, however, the average increase is around 17%. For all Northwest/Republic markets in the Minneapolis/St. Paul hub, the average premium was 9.5% between 1985 and 1987.

Although Borenstein's analysis is consistent with the expected effect that horizontal mergers have on market share, market power, and prices, his study was based upon a three-year period, one year before the merger through one year after the merger. Morrison (1996) re-examined the Northwest/Republic merger from a longer perspective and found less support for monopoly pricing. Morrison's basic argument is that a short-run analysis may reflect market aberrations that could distort the effects of a merger and lead to incorrect conclusions. Suppose, for example, that Northwest and Republic Airlines set fares unusually low in 1985. Comparing these prices with 1987 prices in the post-merger environment would lead one to incorrectly conclude that the merger had a significant effect on market power and prices.

On the basis of quarterly data from the fourth quarter of 1978 through the third quarter of 1995, Morrison analyzed 35 routes that were served by both Northwest and Republic: 21 of these routes originated or departed from the Minneapolis/St. Paul hub. Morrison's analysis of the Northwest/Republic merger yielded the following results:

- At the start of deregulation, Northwest/Republic fares were similar to the fares of other airlines with comparable route characteristics. This is not surprising, since fare structures under regulation were set by distance-based formulas.
- From about 1980 through 1985, pre-merger fares on these routes were about 10% higher than fares on other routes with similar characteristics.
- Between 1986 and early 1989, there was little difference between the fares on Northwest/Republic routes and fares on similar routes.
- Fares rose in the latter part of 1989 and on into 1995, at which time Northwest/Republic fares were 21% higher than on similar routes.
- An analysis of short-run fare changes from one year before the merger to one year after the merger produced a −1.8% change. To take a longer-run perspective, the change in the average relative fare in a pre-merger period (from the first quarter of 1983 through one year before the merger) to a post-merger period (from one year after the merger through the third quarter of 1995) was 2.5%.

- Regarding route competition, Morrison found that, at the beginning of deregulation, competition on routes involved in the merger was essentially the same as that on other routes with comparable characteristics. Just prior to the Northwest/Republic merger, competition was 45% more on these routes than on comparable routes. As expected, competition dropped after the merger. Since 1988, competition on these routes has not been substantially different than on other routes with comparable characteristics.

In addition to the Northwest/Republic merger, Morrison also examined the TWA/Ozark Air Lines merger that occurred in 1986 and the USAir/Piedmont Aviation merger in 1987. Both the Northwest/Republic and the TWA/Ozark Air Lines were controversial, because each involved a merger of two airlines operating a hub at the same airport, Minneapolis/St. Paul for Northwest/Republic and St. Louis for TWA/Ozark. Morrison's longer-run analysis for Northwest/Republic suggests that the resulting impact on prices, and therefore market power, was less than indicated by short-run studies (table 8.6). On the other hand, there was little controversy over the USAir/Piedmont Aviation merger. Yet, in this case, Morrison estimates that the long-run fare increase averaged 22.8%, in comparison with an estimated 4.4% short-run fare increase.

EFFICIENCY LOSSES FROM MARKET PRICE CONTROLS

We have seen that a marginal cost pricing rule produces an optimal mix of outputs. Even if inputs are optimally used and outputs are optimally distributed, failure to satisfy the marginal cost pricing rule produces efficiency losses. Consider figure 8.4, which depicts standard market demand and supply curves for transportation. Assume that we have a competitive market characterized by marginal cost pricing. As denoted in the figure, market demand intersects market supply at the price–quantity combination (p^*,T^*). Up to T^*, the area under the market demand curve reflects the *total benefit* from consuming T^* units of transportation. On the other hand, the area under the supply or opportunity cost curve up to T^* represents the *total variable cost* or *total opportunity cost* of supplying T^* units of transportation. At the point of intersection, the *net benefit* from consuming T^* is maximized. Graphically, the net benefit is depicted by the hatched triangular area *ABC*.

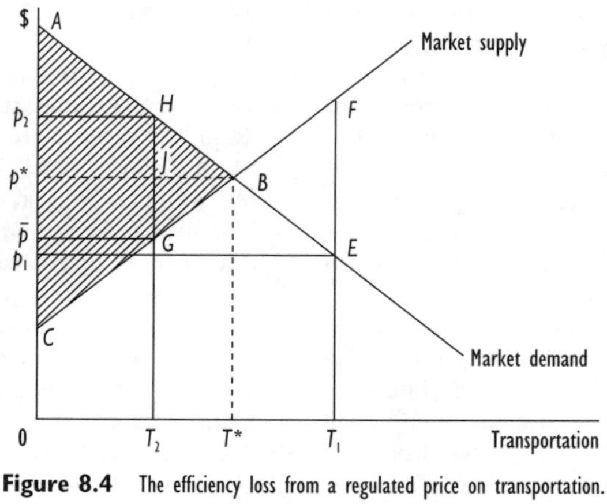

Figure 8.4 The efficiency loss from a regulated price on transportation.

If we look at the net benefit a bit more closely, we can identify the recipients of these benefits. First, since the market clears at price p^*, consumers spend p^*T^* dollars to consume T^* units of transportation. But given that consumers receive a total benefit equal to the area under the demand curve (up to T^*), the triangle p^*AB is that portion of the net benefit that goes to consumers, and is commonly referred to as *consumer surplus*. In general, consumer surplus represents the difference between the amount that consumers are *willing to spend* on a good and the amount that they *actually spend*.[13]

Second, the moneys spent by consumers on T^* are revenues, so that the firms receive p^*T^* for producing and selling T^* units. But the opportunity cost of providing T^* units is the area under the supply curve. Thus, the triangle p^*BC is an amount of money *over and above* what is necessary to bring forth T^* units of transportation to the market. The area p^*BC is that portion of societal net benefits that accrues to producers, and is commonly referred to as *producer surplus*.

The intersection of market demand and market supply maximizes net benefits to society, which is to say that it maximizes the sum of consumer and producer surpluses. Now suppose that we have a regulated price p_1 at which carriers must accommodate all shipper demands. At a price of p_1 shippers demand T_1, so that the total benefit of increasing transport from T^* to T_1 is the area T^*BET_1. What is the opportunity cost to suppliers of providing the $T_1 - T^*$ more transportation? This is the area T^*BFT_1. Pricing at p_1 and producing $T_1 - T^*$ more transportation entails a net cost equal to the triangular area BFE. In comparison with the net benefits from competitive equilibrium at point B, the net benefits to society from the price–quantity combination (p_1, T_1) are reduced by BFE; that is, the area BFE is an efficiency loss.

Alternatively, suppose that the regulated price is p_2, at which price shippers demand amount T_2 of transportation. At this price–output combination, society receives net benefits equal to the trapezoidal area $CAHG$, which is less than the net benefits at the competitive equilibrium by the triangular area GHB. Again, the area GHB represents an efficiency loss, but in this case the loss occurs because we are foregoing potential net benefits by not expanding transportation to T^*.

As a final point, efficiency losses represent net losses in the sense that they do not reflect income transfers between individuals. For example, in figure 8.4 consider point H, at which the price is p_2 and the quantity of transportation demanded is T_2. At this price–output combination, consumer surplus is the area AHp_2 and producer surplus is $p_2HGC\bar{p}$. If we move to the competitive equilibrium at point B, consumer and producer surpluses change in the following ways:

Range	Change in Consumer Surplus	Change in Producer Surplus	Net Effect
From 0 to T_2	$+ (p_2HJp^*)$	$- (p_2HJp^*)$	0
From T_2 to T^*	$+ HJB$	$+ JBG$	$HJB + JBG$

For the additional output $(T^* - T_2)$, there are net gains to consumers and producers equal to $HJB + JBG$, which equals GHB. However, for the original output level, T_2, the reduction in price from p_1 to p^* transfers income from producers to consumers in the amount of p_2HJp^*. Since producers' losses are consumers' gains, these transfers cancel, so that the net effect is the area GHB.[14]

TRUCK–RAIL EQUILIBRIUM IN REGULATED AND COMPETITIVE MARKETS

The short-run market supply function is the horizontal summation of individual-firm marginal costs functions, given that output price is at least equal to the minimum of short-run average variable costs. Similarly, for a given number of firms, the long-run supply function is the horizontal summation of individual-firm long-run marginal cost functions as long as output price is no smaller than the minimum of long-run average costs. Combining market supplies of transportation with shipper demands for freight transportation, it is then possible to identify market equilibrium and explore the effect on equilibrium when the economic environment changes.

In an important contribution to our understanding of modern surface transportation, Friedlaender and Spady (1981) empirically analyzed market behavior for the railroad and motor carrier sectors during regulation and the expected effects on these markets under economic deregulation. For our purposes, the primary concern of Friedlaender and Spady's analysis is whether railroads and motor carriers acted efficiently in a price-controlled environment, where by "efficiently" we mean *marginal cost pricing*, and by *price-controlled environment* we mean a setting in which the government sets the prices that rails and trucks are allowed to charge. We have seen that profit-maximizing firms produce up to the point at which price equals marginal cost. Prices significantly higher or lower than marginal cost signal an inefficient allocation of resources. If the existing price is greater than marginal cost, a firm can add to its profits by selling additional units. Similarly, an existing price below marginal cost implies that a firm can increase profits by reducing its rate of output.

In the event that railroad and motor carrier transport markets are not behaving efficiently under government price controls, a related question is how these transport sectors would respond in the absence of price controls. In other words, relative to the existing equilibrium that characterizes price–output decisions in a price-controlled environment, how would equilibrium price and quantity change if the railroads and motor carriers practiced marginal cost pricing?

PARTIAL AND GENERAL EQUILIBRIUM ANALYSIS

In answering these questions, we cannot lose sight of the fact that railroads and motor carriers are close substitutes in transportation. This implies that changes in the motor carrier market will have a sufficiently large effect on the railroad market that these secondary effects cannot be ignored. In other words, we must take a general equilibrium approach to analyzing the surface transportation market, rather than a more limited *partial equilibrium* approach.

To illustrate the difference between partial and general equilibrium analysis, suppose that we want to consider the effect on the transportation market of a decrease in wages paid in the motor carrier industry. We know that the decrease in labor costs will shift the market supply for motor carrier shipments rightward. This has the *partial equilibrium effect* of decreasing equilibrium price and increasing equilibrium quantity. However, since railroad transport is a close substitute for motor carriers, the decrease in equilibrium motor carrier freight rates decreases the demand for railroad shipments, leading to a decrease in equilibrium rail freight rates. The lower rail rates have a feedback effect upon the motor carrier market by shifting,

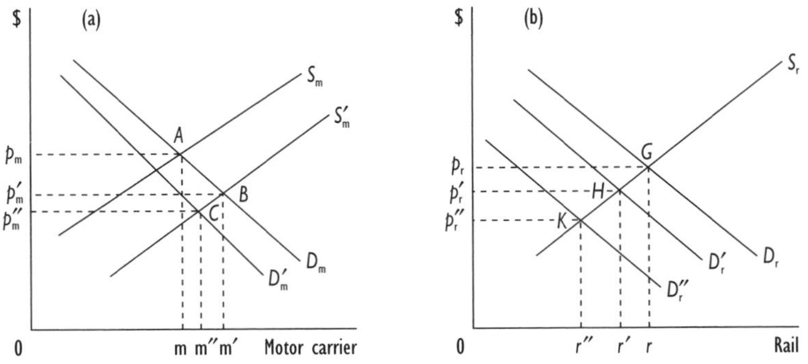

Figure 8.5 The effect of reduced labor costs on an intermodal market. (a) Motor carrier market; (b) rail market.

to some extent, the demand for motor carrier transport leftward. When all of these secondary effects have occurred, the markets for motor carrier *and* rail settle down to new price–quantity combinations that reflect a *general equilibrium* result.

Figure 8.5 depicts these effects. Initially, the motor carrier and rail markets are in equilibrium at A and G. The reduced labor costs in the motor carrier industry shift the supply curve rightward from S_m to S'_m, which reduces the equilibrium price to p_1 and raises the equilibrium quantity to m_1. The price–quantity combination (p'_m, m') is the partial equilibrium effect. The reduced price in the motor carrier market shifts the market demand for rail *leftward* from D_r to D'_r, lowering rail's price to p'_r and reducing quantity to r'. The lower price in the rail market reduces the demand for motor carrier transport (from D_m to D'_m), the price effects of which again affect the demand for rail. After all of these effects have occurred, the market finds a new general equilibrium. In figure 8.5, this is given by demand–supply curves S'_m, D'_m for the motor carrier market and S'_r, D''_r for the rail market. The general equilibrium price–quantity combinations are given by *C* and *K* respectively. In the motor carrier market, the reduction in labor costs leads to a larger price decrease and a smaller quantity increase relative to the partial equilibrium result at B. Also, rather than ignoring the rail market, as in partial equilibrium analysis, we see that the rail market experiences a net decrease in equilibrium price and quantity.

CASE STUDY – MARKET EQUILIBRIUM DURING PRICE-CONTROLLED REGULATION

Friedlaender and Spady's analysis of surface freight transportation assumed two modes, rail and specialized motor carrier; two commodities, bulk and manufactured goods; and two regions, the Official Region and the South-West Region. The Official Region is the same as that identified in the previous chapter on shipper demands, and comprises the older industrialized areas in the Northeast, Mid-Atlantic, and East-Central United States. The South-West Region makes up the rest of the contiguous USA.[15] In contrast to the South-West Region, railroads in the Official Region expended a higher proportion of their resources on pick-up and delivery, switching, and consolidation. Friedlaender and Spady estimated that rail costs in this region were 50% higher than in the rest of the USA, where railroads spent a higher proportion of resources on line-haul activities.

For each of the two regions, separate industry supply and market demand functions were estimated for each of four modal-commodity groupings:

- rail – manufactured goods (rm)
- rail – bulk goods (rb)
- specialized truck – manufactured goods (tm)
- specialized truck – bulk goods (tb)

Market demand functions for each mode and commodity were assumed to primarily depend upon modal shipping prices and modal shipment attributes. For example, the market demand function for bulk commodities shipped by rail depended upon the rail shipping rate for bulk goods, the truck shipping rate for bulk goods, the bulk shipping characteristics for each mode, and nontransportation variables.[16]

As we know, industry supply curves are obtained by a horizontal summation of individual-firm marginal cost curves. In Friedlaender and Spady's analysis, translog cost functions for rail and trucking, similar to those analyzed in chapter 5, formed the basis of their industry supply curves. In particular, from an estimated translog cost function for each sector, it is possible to obtain the marginal cost function for each firm which, when summed over all firms in the sector, yields the industry supply function. However, rather than summing the estimated marginal cost function over all firms to derive the industry supply function, Friedlaender and Spady used the translog cost function to derive the marginal cost for a "representative" firm, defined as a firm that faces factor prices and operating characteristics equal to the sample average, which was then scaled up (by the number of firms) to reflect the actual size of the market. The industry supply curve is then obtained by varying the level of output, holding all else constant. In effect, Friedlaender and Spady's market supply curve in the rail and trucking sector, respectively, assumes that the sector is composed of identical firms, each of which faces the same factor prices and operating characteristics, and each of which produces the representative firm's level of output.[17]

For our purposes, an advantage of generating a market supply curve from the supply curve of a representative firm is that we have a model that effectively mirrors our analysis of cost structures in chapter 5. Moreover, when combined with market demand, we obtain a transportation market that embodies the assumptions underlying a competitive market. Thus, while not a completely accurate description of the rail and trucking markets during the regulated period, this formulation will still provide useful insights into the pricing, output, and resource allocation activities of the industry.[18]

How did the market reach an equilibrium under government price controls? The transportation sector under regulated prices had two basic characteristics:

1 Transportation rates were not set by market demand and supply, but by the ICC.
2 As a common carrier, motor carriers and railroads *had to accept* all traffic offered at prevailing rates.

To understand the implications of these two features, consider a motor carrier operating in a price-controlled environment. The ICC sets the freight rate at which rate shippers reveal their demand for motor carrier services. At the prevailing ICC rate set, the carrier must accept all traffic demanded. This is equivalent to saying that equilibrium output is demand determined which weakens, if not completely breaking, the determination of equilibrium output by the interaction of market demand and supply. As a result, it is likely that at the ICC-determined rate, some carriers will make economic profits while others will incur economic losses. No carrier is likely to operate efficiently.

Initial and competitive equilibrium in the Official Region

The price-controlled and competitive equilibria in the Official Region for railroad and specialized motor carrier modes are given in figures 8.6 and 8.7. In these graphs, the curves S_0 and D_0 depict the market supply and market demand curves that the rail and trucking industry, respectively, faced during regulation for the shipment of manufactured and bulk commodities. For the moment, ignore lines D_1 and S_1. The ICC-specified rate, the price control, is denoted in each graph by the solid horizontal line (for example, in figure 8.6(a), the ICC rate is 2.41 cents) and represents the rate at which the carrier must satisfy all shippers' demands. At the regulated rate, point *A* in each graph is the quantity of ton–miles demanded that the carrier must satisfy. The corresponding marginal or opportunity cost of ton–miles at the controlled rate is point *B* in each graph. Thus, points *A* and *B* illustrate where the industry was actually operating in the price-controlled environment.

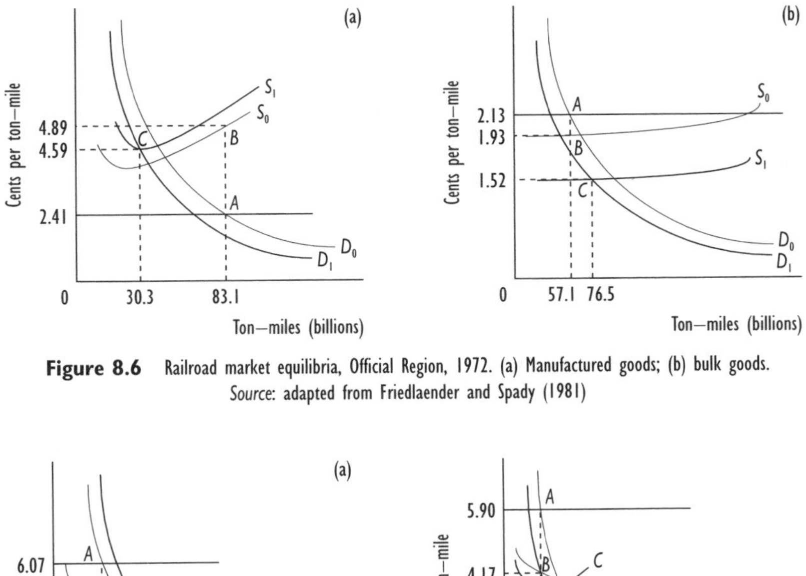

Figure 8.6 Railroad market equilibria, Official Region, 1972. (a) Manufactured goods; (b) bulk goods. *Source*: adapted from Friedlaender and Spady (1981)

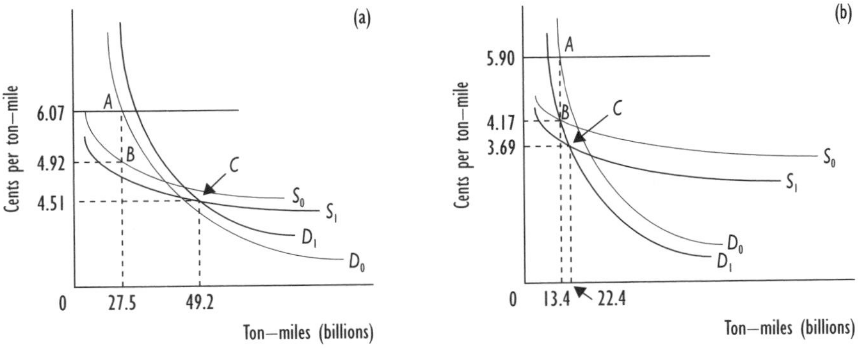

Figure 8.7 Specialized motor carrier market equilibria, Official Region, 1972. (a) Manufactured goods; (b) bulk goods. *Source*: adapted from Friedlaender and Spady (1981)

From these graphs, we can draw several conclusions on railroad and motor carrier activities with respect to price controls, marginal cost pricing, and the efficient allocation of resources in transporting manufactured and bulk commodities.

Railroad transportation during regulation

The rail transport market in figures 8.6(a) and 8.6(b) is based upon the *existing rail infrastructure*, and thus the market supply curves reflect *short-run* marginal costs and equilibria. For the railroad industry, we see in figure 8.6(a) that at the regulated rate of 2.41 cents per ton–mile, railroads in the Official Region transported 83.1 billion ton–miles of manufactured goods in 1972. That is, at this controlled price the quantity of transportation services demanded by shippers equaled 83.1 billion ton–miles. But note also in figure 8.6(a) that, at this high level of output, the rail industry in this region incurred a marginal cost per ton–mile of 4.89 cents, denoted by point *B*. In other words, at the ICC-regulated rate, railway carriers in the Official Region were not operating at a competitive equilibrium where price equals marginal cost, but were operating well beyond this point. For the last ton–mile transported, railroads suffered an estimated 2.48 cent per ton–mile loss.

What about bulk commodities? Figure 8.6(b) depicts this information, where we again see the absence of marginal cost pricing. At the ICC-controlled rate of 2.13 cents per ton–mile, bulk commodity shippers demanded transportation for 57.1 ton–miles. But the marginal cost of providing the last ton–mile was 1.93 cents. Since marginal cost per ton–mile is less than revenue per ton–mile at this rate of output, railroads are not maximizing profits. However, in contrast to the market for transporting manufactured goods, where the last ton–mile shipped incurs a loss, railroads are making a profit on the last ton–mile of bulk goods shipped.

Efficiency implications in the market for rail transportation

The fact that railroads are not producing where price equals marginal costs implies that resources in the rail industry were inefficiently allocated. In particular, too many resources in the rail industry were devoted to transporting higher-valued manufactured goods, whereas too few resources were devoted to transporting lower-valued bulk commodities. At the regulated rates and output levels denoted by points *A* and *B* in figures 8.6(a) and 8.6(b), railroads are losing money on the last ton–mile of the higher-valued manufactured goods while making money on the last ton–mile of the lower-valued bulk commodities. Economic efficiency requires an increase in rail rates for manufactured goods, a decrease in rates for transporting bulk goods, and a reallocation of rail resources away from manufactured traffic and toward bulk traffic.

Specialized motor carrier transportation during regulation

In contrast to the rail market, the marginal cost of specialized motor carrier services is not based upon fixed factors of production, so that the supply curves in figure 8.7 represent long-run supply curves and the resulting equilibria, therefore, give long-run rather than short-run market equilibria. Further, the long-run supply curves for specialized motor carrier services, S_0 in figures 8.7(a) and 8.7(b), are downward-sloping, which suggests the presence of a positive external scale effects. Since, by construction of the supply curve in figure 8.7, factor prices are fixed, the scale effect is expected to be technologically related. Friedlaender and Spady found that the truckload sector of the motor carrier industry exhibited increasing returns to scale, a result that we also found in chapter 5.[19] Since the relatively small capital investment for a typical truckload firm is consistent with constant returns to scale, Friedlaender and Spady looked elsewhere for an explanation and argued that the estimated increasing returns to scale were *regulatory-based economies of scale*. During regulation, a firm's operating certificate generally placed restrictions upon route, backhaul carriage, and commodity transported. Although this produced significant cost inefficiencies for a firm with one or two operating certificates, if a firm possessed many operating certificates, it could improve the efficiency of its operations by increasing its average load, reducing the number of empty backhauls, and raising the average length of haul. Thus, as the specialized truckload market expanded, specialized truckload carriers had an economic incentive to increase the size of their operations in order to exploit the regulatory-based economies of scale. This may be viewed as a positive technological scale effect, but one that would be expected to disappear when the regulatory constraints are removed.

Combined with S_0, D_0 in figures 8.7(a) and 8.7(b) gives market supply and market demand curves for specialized motor carriers in the Official Region during regulation. At a price-controlled rate of 6.07 cents per ton–mile, shippers of manufactured goods demanded 27.5 billion ton–miles of transportation, at which level specialized carriers make a 1.15 cent economic profit on the last ton–mile carried. The regulated rate is also greater than the cost of transporting the last ton–mile for bulk goods. In figure 8.7(b), the regulated rate for shipping bulk commodities is 5.90 cents per ton–mile, while the marginal cost of the last ton–mile is 4.17 cents, giving an economic profit of 1.73 cents. At the regulated rate, 13.4 billion ton–miles were demanded.

Efficiency implications for specialized motor carrier transportation

Similar to the rail industry, specialized motor carrier transportation of manufactured and bulk commodities is not consistent with marginal cost pricing and an efficient allocation of resources. Since, in the price-controlled environment, the mandated rate is greater than the opportunity cost of transportation, we would want to devote more specialized motor carrier resources in transporting manufactured and bulk commodities. This implies a reduction in motor carrier freight rates in transporting both of these goods.

General competitive equilibrium in rail and trucking

In figures 8.6 and 8.7, moving to the intersection between S_0 and D_0, although consistent with marginal cost pricing, is a *partial equilibrium* solution that ignores the effect that changes in rates in one market have upon the markets for close substitutes. The market demand and supply curves in figures 8.6 and 8.7, denoted by D_1 and S_1, denote the estimated general equilibrium demand and supply curves for rail and trucking in the Official Region, respectively. The general equilibrium price–quantity combination occurs at the intersections of these two curves, denoted by point *C* in each graph. These curves account for the effects that changes in the rail market have upon the specialized motor carrier market and vice versa. A decrease in rail rates, for example, will decrease the demand for motor carrier services. Also, the supply curves will shift, since the marginal cost of production depends upon the amounts of each good carried; that is, upon the mix of traffic carried. From figure 8.6, we see that a move from point *A* to point *C* requires the rails to transport fewer manufactured goods and more bulk commodities. The traffic mix shifts toward bulk commodities and this leads to a rise in the cost of transporting manufactured goods, from S_0 to S_1 in figure 8.6(a), and a fall in the cost of transporting bulk goods, from S_0 to S_1 in figure 8.6(b).

In each of the four graphs, the general equilibrium competitive solution is given by point C, the intersection between S_1 and D_1. A move to point C represents marginal cost pricing in the rail and motor carrier sectors, and leads to an efficient allocation of resources devoted to transporting manufactured and bulk goods. In particular, rail loses a significant amount of unprofitable manufactured goods, reducing ton–miles from 83.1 billion to 30.3 billion. At the same time, it is now transporting nearly 20 billion additional ton–miles of profitable bulk commodities. Also, as expected, specialized motor carriers increase the quantities of manufactured and bulk goods transported by 21.7 and 9 billion ton–miles respectively.

It is also worth noting that the competitive equilibrium is not simply reallocating a given amount of traffic. In the regulated environment, rail and motor carriers transport a total of 110.6 billion ton–miles of manufactured goods and 70.5 billion ton–miles of bulk commodities. In the competitive environment, the carriers transport 79.5 billion ton–miles of manufactured goods and 98.9 billion ton–miles of bulk commodities, a net decrease of 2.7 billion ton–miles. Pricing at marginal cost has caused manufactured and bulk commodity shippers to move up or down their respective demand curves.

Table 8.7 summarizes the initial and competitive equilibria for rail and motor carriers in the Official Region. In the initial equilibrium, the high cost of transporting manufactured goods in comparison with the price-controlled rate results in a $251 million loss in 1972. Specialized

Table 8.7 Initial and competitive equilibria, Official Region, 1972

	Price (¢/ton–mile)	Marginal Cost (¢/ton–mile)	Output (billion ton–miles)	Profits ($billion)	Efficiency Loss ($million)
Initial equilibrium					
Railroad					
Manufactured	2.41	4.89	83.1	–	683.8
Bulk	2.13	1.93	57.1	–	62.2
Total	–	–	140.2	–0.251	746.0
Truck					
Manufactured	6.07	4.92	27.5	–	141.2
Bulk	5.90	4.17	13.4	–	95.1
Total	–	–	40.9	0.110	236.3
Competitive equilibrium					
Railroad					
Manufactured	4.59	4.59	30.3	–	–
Bulk	1.52	1.52	76.5	–	–
Total	–	–	106.8	1.20	–
Truck					
Manufactured	4.51	4.51	49.2	–	–
Bulk	3.69	3.69	22.4	–	–
Total	–	–	71.6	–0.609	–

Source: Adapted from Friedlaender and Spady (1981), table 3.1, p. 85, with the permission of the MIT Press.

motor carriers profit, on the other hand, by $110 million, a relatively small amount in view of the fact that regulated rates were 23% and 41% higher than marginal cost for the last ton–mile of manufactured and bulk goods shipped, respectively. The reason for the relatively small profit is the downward-sloping supply curves in figures 8.7(a) and 8.7(b). Since these supply curves are "enlarged" representative firm marginal cost curves, a downward-sloping marginal cost of production lies below the average cost of production, so that a high price-marginal cost ratio is consistent with a *lower* total revenue : total cost ratio and lower profits.[20]

The bottom half of table 8.7 characterizes the competitive equilibrium; it can be seen that marginal cost pricing gives railroads a short-run profit of $1.2 billion. However, given an existing (in 1972) capital stock of $17.9 billion, this represents a 3.4% rate of return, well below the 9% opportunity cost of capital at the time. In other words, if railroads move to their short-run competitive equilibrium, they will not be making a normal return on their investment. Railroad revenues will be sufficient to cover variable costs, but only a portion of fixed costs. If the railroads want to maintain their existing (1972) infrastructure at acceptable operational and safety levels, subsidies will be required. In the long run, this implies reducing capital stock to the point at which existing revenues are consistent with a normal return on investment.

In competitive equilibrium, specialized motor carriers experience a "loss" of $609 million. Ostensibly, this reflects regulatory-based economies of scale, where motor carriers are operating on the declining portion of the marginal cost and, accordingly, the average cost curves. As we discussed above, moving to a competitive environment that placed few operating restrictions on commodities carried and routes traveled would be expected to eliminate the regulatory induced scale economies. In this environment, each specialized motor carrier would operate at the minimum point on its long-run average cost curve, under constant returns to scale, and make a normal return on its investment.

Table 8.7 also reports the efficiency losses from nonmarginal cost pricing. For the rail industry, these losses total $746 million, 91% of which is due to the rail carriers having to accommodate shipper demands for transporting manufactured goods. In the motor carrier industry, efficiency losses amount to $236.3 million and are more evenly divided between manufactured and bulk commodities. Also, note that the efficiency losses associated with rail bulk movements, motor carrier bulk movements, and motor carrier manufactured movements reflect foregone net gains, whereas the losses accruing to rail-manufactured movements reflect actual net losses.

Last, who gains and who loses in moving to a competitive equilibrium? Rail shippers of manufactured goods lose, while rail carriers of these commodities gain. On the other hand, rail shippers of bulk goods and motor carrier shippers of bulk and manufactured goods all gain at the expense of the respective carriers.

Initial and competitive equilibrium in the South-West Region

For the South-West Region, table 8.8 summarizes the rail and specialized motor carrier markets in price-controlled and competitive environments. A comparative analysis of tables 8.7 and 8.8 reveals a number of points:

1 *Modal shares* – In the more densely populated eastern states, rail is responsible for 77% of a total 181.1 billion delivered ton–miles in 1972. In the more sparsely populated central and western regions of the country, however, total output is significantly higher, at 356.9 billion ton–miles, and the share carried by railroads rises to 85%.

2 *Railroad carriers under regulation* – For railroad carriers of manufactured and bulk commodities, the price-controlled rate structure in the South-West Region is similar to that in the Official Region, but the price : marginal cost ratio is significantly *greater* in the South-West Region. The price : marginal cost ratios for manufactured and bulk goods in the Official Region are 0.49 and 1.1

Table 8.8 Initial and competitive equilibria, South-West Region, 1972

	Price (¢/ton–mile)	Marginal Cost (¢/ton–mile)	Output (billion ton–miles)	Profits ($billion)	Efficiency Loss ($million)
Initial equilibrium					
Railroad					
Manufactured	2.79	2.93	168.8	–	21.8
Bulk	1.66	0.98	134.1	–	356.4
Total	–	–	302.9	2.12	377.2
Truck					
Manufactured	5.45	4.60	31.8	–	44.3
Bulk	3.96	3.97	22.2	–	0.6
Total	–	–	54.0	0.145	44.9
Competitive equilibrium					
Railroad					
Manufactured	2.98	2.98	148.9	–	–
Bulk	1.04	1.04	237.2	–	–
Total	–	–	386.1	1.63	–
Truck					
Manufactured	4.61	4.61	42.1	–	–
Bulk	3.98	3.98	16.0	–	–
Total	–	–	58.1	−0.134	–

Source: Adapted from Friedlaender and Spady (1981), table 3.2, p. 89, with the permission of the MIT Press. Copyright © 1981 Massachusetts Institute of Technology

respectively. These same ratios in the South-West Region are 0.95 and 1.69, which indicates that manufactured goods are nearly transported at marginal cost and bulk commodities are transported at rates well above marginal cost. In the initial equilibrium, therefore, one would expect South-West rail carriers to be making a profit over variable costs – and indeed they are. Profits in the regulated environment amounted to $2.1 billion, which is just under an 8% rate of return. As seen in tables 8.7 and 8.8, the difference in profitability between the Official and South-West carriers is not a difference in rates but a difference in marginal costs. Whereas significant resources in the Official Region were devoted to pick-up and delivery, switching, and consolidation, most of the costs in the South-West Region represent line-haul costs.

3 *Specialized motor carriers under regulation* – A comparison of specialized motor carrier services in the South-West and Official Regions also reveals differences between the two geographic areas. Regulated rates are similar in the two regions, but the price : marginal cost ratios in the Official Region, at 1.23 and 1.41 for manufactured and bulk commodities respectively, are considerably larger than those in the South-West Region. In the South-West Region, bulk commodities are virtually shipped at marginal cost, whereas manufactured goods move at a price : marginal cost ratio equal to 1.18. One would expect that specialized motor carriers in the South-West Region would be earning fewer profits than their counterparts in the east. But a glance at table 8.8 indicates that South-West carriers earned $145 million, 32% *more* than in the Official Region. The reason for this

is that motor carriers in the South-West Region operated on the *rising* portion of their marginal cost curves, which implies that average costs lay below marginal costs.[21]

4 *Efficiency and competitive equilibrium* – The absence of marginal cost pricing in the South-West Region implies that equilibrium in the price-controlled environment is inefficient, and that a move to marginal cost pricing benefits some and harms others. The efficiency losses for the South-West Region are given in the lower half of table 8.8. For the railroads, the primary reason for efficiency losses is the foregone net benefits associated with shipping bulk commodities. These losses amount to $356 million and constitute 95% of total efficiency losses. On the other hand, efficiency losses in the motor carrier sector are relatively small at $44.9 million. Given that motor carrier bulk commodities effectively move at marginal cost, the efficiency losses here are negligible.

Who gains and who loses? From the price : marginal cost ratios in the top half of table 8.8, we would expect to see rail shippers of manufactured goods lose, rail bulk shippers gain, motor carrier manufactured goods shippers gain, and motor carrier bulk shippers neither gain nor lose. This is borne out in the bottom half of the table. At the competitive equilibrium, rates increase to rail shippers of manufactured goods, substantially decrease for rail bulk shippers, fall for motor carrier manufactured goods shippers, and remain the same for motor carrier bulk shippers.[22] Profits also move in the expected direction, decreasing in both the rail and motor carrier sectors. The fall in profits for the railroads also implies a reduction in return on investment to 5.3%. Thus, similar to the plight of railroads in the Official Region, short-run equilibrium in the South-West rail market will not produce a normal return on investment.

Comments

Having characterized the rail and motor carrier markets at a competitive equilibrium, Friedlaender and Spady examined whether the equilibrium was sensitive to changes in underlying determinants of market demand and supply. In particular, they evaluated the impact upon competitive equilibrium from a 10% increase in fuel prices, a 10% increase in the average load carried by trucks, and a 10% increase in shipper demands.

Depending upon the specific change, the results indicated that rail and motor carrier markets were sensitive to increases in each of these factors. However, they also found that the results were relatively small when contrasted with the effects that a move to competitive equilibria had upon the markets. In general, rate changes due to fuel price or demand increases were within the 1–3% range. Increasing average loads had a greater net effect on truck rates, lowering them by as much as 13%.

The effect of a move to general competitive equilibrium, reflecting marginal cost pricing, had significantly greater effects upon rates, output levels, and modal shares. With the exception of motor carrier bulk movements (0.2% change) and rail manufactured goods shipments (6% change), the estimated competitive equilibrium led to rate changes ranging from 15% to 90% and output changes ranging between 11% and 79%. With respect to modal shares, the biggest shift was a 49% decrease in rail's share of manufactures carriage in the Official Region. Its bulk transport share in the Official Region fell by 5%, and its manufactures transport share in the South-West fell by 7%. Rail's modal share of bulk movements in the South-West, however, increased by 9%.

As a final comment, Friedlaender and Spady's model of intermodal competition provides insights into the economic inefficiencies that exist when industries are subject to government price controls. Although, in reality, the rail and trucking sectors were less competitive than Friedlaender and Spady's framework suggests, for the purposes of quantifying the markets' status quo, the economic effects of a move to a competitive equilibrium, and the equilibrium effects of alternative transportation policies, their model provided a reasonable approximation to reality. We have not, however, commented on whether Friedlaender and Spady's predictions were borne out when the motor carrier and rail industries were deregulated in the late 1970s and the early 1980s. In the final section, we provide an overview of deregulatory legislation in the transportation industry, summarize the expected economic effects upon prices, outputs, profits, and economic welfare, and analyze the extent to which these expectations were subsequently met.

Value-of-service pricing

An example of price discrimination is the long-standing "value-of-service," or "what the market will bear," pricing. Although maintaining the ban on personal and geographic price discrimination among shippers, the Hoch–Smith Resolution in 1925 affirmed commodity price discrimination. Shippers of low-value bulk goods paid a lower price than shippers of high-value manufactured goods who shipped at the same time, over the same route, and between the same origin–destination pair. The reason for the rate difference is that shippers of low-value bulk commodities have a more elastic demand than shippers of high-value manufactured goods and are thus less willing to bear higher shipping charges.

In markets for a single good, value-of-service pricing is consistent with profit-maximizing price discrimination. However, in the rail and truck markets, intermodal competition has led to two lines of arguments regarding the economic effects of value-of-service pricing:

Traditional argument Meyer et al. (1959) argued that, with the exception of short-haul trips and shipments of very high value, rail carriers have a comparative cost advantage over motor carriers in transporting carload shipments. However, by increasing the price of transporting higher-valued manufactured goods on rail, value-of-service pricing led shippers to substitute their transport demands away from rail and toward the relatively more expensive – but more flexible and service-oriented – motor carrier, resulting in an inefficient allocation of resources in transporting goods.

IMPLICATION If true, this argument implies that abandoning value-of-service pricing will lead to a fall in rail rates on manufactured goods and a corresponding increase in rail shipments of these goods.

Revisionist argument Alternatively, Boyer (1977) argued that value-of-service pricing may have led to smaller economic efficiency distortions than originally believed. Rail carriers do not compete with motor carriers in general, but specifically with *specialized truckload* carriers. And in contrast to less-than-truckload carriers that have relatively high costs due to consolidation and break-bulking activities, the preponderance of truckload carrier costs are line-haul and therefore less. Second, arguing that existing rates failed to cover costs, rail carriers were continually seeking rate increases on manufactured goods from the ICC. It seems odd that rail carriers would consistently make this argument if there were not at least some truth in it.

IMPLICATION If the revisionist argument is true, and existing rates were not sufficient to cover rail costs for transporting manufactured goods, then we would expect to see a rise in manufactured rates in the absence of regulated pricing.

Which hypothesis is likely to be true? Table 8.9 summarizes the price-controlled prices for trucking and rail in the Official and South-West Regions from tables 8.7 and 8.8. These results provide interesting insights on the economic inefficiencies associated with value-of-service pricing. Focusing upon the initial equilibrium that

Table 8.9 Price/marginal cost ratios in the price-controlled environment

	Price/(Marginal Cost)	
	Rail	Truck
Official Region		
Manufactured	0.49	1.23
Bulk	1.10	1.41
South-West Region		
Manufactured	0.95	1.18
Bulk	1.69	0.99

Source: Friedlaender and Spady (1981)

represents the price-controlled environment, the price : marginal cost ratios confirm the revisionist argument and reject the traditional argument. Under value-of-service pricing, the price : marginal cost ratio should be greater for manufactured goods than for bulk commodities. Yet in both the Official and South-West Regions, price : marginal cost ratios for rail are greater for *bulk* than for manufactured commodities. Moreover, in neither region is price greater than marginal cost.

For specialized motor carriers, we see that the price : marginal cost ratio for manufactured goods is also less than that for bulk goods in the Official Region, which is consistent with the revisionist argument. However, motor carrier activity in the South-West Region is consistent with value-of-service pricing. In that area, we find that the price : marginal cost ratios are 1.18 and 0.99 for manufactured and bulk goods respectively.

In three out of the four cases, the transportation market did not characterize value-of-service pricing, and moving to a competitive equilibrium would not generally be expected to produce a reduction in rail rates on manufactured goods. As we have previously seen, moving to competitive equilibrium was expected to increase rail rates on manufactured goods in both regions, consistent with the revisionist theory that rail carriers experienced high marginal costs of transport.

CASE STUDY – AN OVERVIEW OF ECONOMIC DEREGULATION IN TRANSPORTATION

Economic regulation of transportation in the United States was pervasive until the early to mid-1970s when, for a variety of reasons, increasing pressure developed to deregulate the industry. In the case of motor carriers and airlines, evidence of efficiency losses was mounting, and there appeared to be no offsetting rationale to justify continued economic regulation at its current level. Although economies-of-scale arguments are a more appropriate justification for railroads, many analysts cited economic regulation as the reason for the mode's long-lasting poor financial performance.

In this as well as previous chapters, we have studied aspects of transport regulation and deregulation in a particular sector in order to suit a specific objective. In chapter 5 we examined the cost structure of motor carrier and airline firms in a regulated environment; in chapter 7, we analyzed the source of monopoly profits in the motor carrier industry and how these were partially dissipated through rent-sharing with labor; in this chapter, we considered the strategic responses that airlines followed after deregulation in an attempt to preserve monopoly rents generated under regulation; and we considered the likely effect upon prices, outputs, and profits if motor carriers and rails competed in a competitive environment. Although each of these "case studies" provided a glimpse into the effect of economic deregulation in transportation, the separate studies do not present an overall picture. The purpose of this section is to answer three related questions: (1) What was the environment under economic regulation? (2) How did economic deregulation affect this environment? (3) Who were the winners and losers from economic deregulation and, on balance, was economic deregulation in the transportation industry welfare-increasing or welfare-decreasing?

Although there were deregulatory actions that affected pipeline transportation and intercity bus transportation, we will focus here on airlines, motor carriers, and rails, since economic deregulation had the greatest impact on these sectors.

Economic environment under regulation

Table 8.10 summarizes the environment during the period of economic regulation. From the table we see that economic regulation in each of these sectors had two essential characteristics. First, individual firms were not allowed to freely set or alter prices. The CAB set airline fares and the ICC set rail rates and had oversight authority over rates set by rate bureaus in the motor carrier industry. In general, the rates allowed in each of these sectors were inefficient, in that these rates did not satisfy the marginal cost pricing criterion. In the motor carrier and rail sectors, rates were generally above the marginal cost of production, whereas in the airline sector, rates in the long-distance travel market were above the opportunity cost of production in

Table 8.10 Characteristics of the regulated environments for the airline, motor carrier, and railroad sectors

Transportation Sector	Environment under Regulation
Airlines	Generally inefficient fares set by the Civil Aeronautics Board (CAB) which involved cross-subsidization from long-distance travelers to short-distance travelers Route structures determined by the CAB Restrictions on equipment and on entry and exit from the sector
Motor carriers	Rates regulated by the Interstate Commerce Commission (ICC); rates were generally inefficient, particularly for the less-than-truckload sector Gateway restrictions which specified particular routes for carriage Restrictions upon commodities that could and could not be transported
Railroads	Rates regulated by the ICC for commodities carried; rates were generally inefficient Restrictions upon network changes and exit from unprofitable markets Labor input restrictions that prevented rails from using an efficient amount of labor

Source: Adapted from Winston (1993), table 2, p. 1269

order to subsidize the short-distance travel market, where rates were set below the marginal cost of production.

The second important feature of the economic environment under regulation was the restriction upon entry and exit into the industry. Market entry was a major constraint in the airline and motor carrier markets, whereas market exit was more important in the rail sector. The high fixed costs of production in railroads in the form of track and structures was an effective barrier to entry. On the other hand, the ICC prevented rails from exiting unprofitable markets, which led to financial losses and lower than normal rates of return on investment.

Entry and exit restrictions do not simply refer to the number of firms in an industry but also take the form of route or network restrictions. Under regulation, incumbent airlines could not service any route that they expected to be profitable, but could only operate in CAB-approved markets. A similar constraint existed for motor carriers, whose operating certificates would specify which commodities could be carried and which routes could be used.

In addition to these restrictions, we also see in table 8.10 that the regulatory agencies regulated the types of equipment that the airlines could use and rails' abilities to substitute labor for capital in their production of transportation.

Economic environment under deregulation

Table 8.11 identifies the major pieces of legislation – the Airline Deregulation Act of 1978 for airlines, the Motor Carrier Act of 1980 for motor carriers, and the Staggers Rail Act of 1980 for railroads – that deregulated the transportation industry with the aim of transforming these markets into more competitive economic environments. Based upon the mode's expected market structure, the legislation includes price and market access provisions. Because airlines and motor carriers are thought to comprise a highly competitive market structure, the legislative provisions included significant rate flexibility and virtually open access to the market. In the airline sector, for example, fare regulations were eliminated in 1983, and all "fit, willing,

Table 8.11 Characteristics of the deregulated environments for the airline, motor carrier, and railroad sectors

Transportation Sector	Deregulation Legislation (Year)	Environment under Deregulation
Airlines	Airline Deregulation Act (1978)	Relaxed fare regulation until 1983 when all fare regulations eliminated Significantly eased entry restrictions Allowed development of more efficient route structures
Motor carriers	Motor Carrier Act (1980)	Allowed independent rate-setting Significantly relaxed entry restrictions Allowed private and contract carriers to compete with common carriers
Railroads	Staggers Rail Act (1980)	Free to set rates for many commodities Allowed contract rates Eased restrictions on market exit

Source: Adapted from Winston (1993), table 1, p. 1265

and able" providers of airline services had access to the market. Similarly, there is much greater rate flexibility in the motor carrier industry (although not as much as in airlines), and the burden of proof for denying access to new entrants rests with the incumbent rather than the entering firm.

In contrast to the airline and motor carrier sectors, railroads were not expected to evolve into a highly competitive market structure, due to their high fixed costs. However, this is not to say that there were not possibilities for introducing greater competition in the market. Similar to airline and motor carrier companies, rails were given greater freedom to set and alter prices in most markets, the primary exception being markets in which the railroad is the dominant provider. In addition, railroads were allowed to enter into long-term contracts with shippers, and were given greater freedom to exit unprofitable markets.

Combined, price regulation and restrictions on market access produced both consumption and production inefficiencies. On the consumption side, the absence of marginal cost pricing meant that resources were nonoptimally allocated in the production of air, rail, and motor carrier transportation. For example, the cross-subsidization between long-distance and short-distance airline trips was inefficient because it produced too few long-distance trips (priced above marginal production cost) and too many short-distance trips (priced below marginal production cost). And, as we saw in the last section, motor carrier and rail rates generated an inefficiently large number of rail shipments and too few truck shipments of manufactured goods in the northeast. In the South-West Region, on the other hand, rail shipments of bulk goods and truck shipments of manufactured goods was less than optimal.

Restrictions on market access, whether in the form of limiting new entrants, not allowing market exit, or restrictions on permitted routes and commodities, all had the effect of constraining firms to produce transportation at an inefficiently high cost. In general, constraints are costly, and by not allowing firms to use optimal input ratios in their production of transportation, government regulations forced firms to use more resources to produce a given level of transportation volume and quality than was necessary. The finding of labor rent-sharing in the motor carrier industry implies that labor was receiving more than its opportunity cost. And the almost immediate shift to the hub-and-spoke distribution network when the airline industry was deregulated is explicit testimony to the inefficient operating environment that airlines increasingly faced under regulation.

The effect on user welfare

For the airline, motor carrier, and railroad sectors, table 8.12 identifies the predicted and actual effects of economic deregulation. Under deregulation the airline and motor carrier sectors were expected to be highly competitive, whereas the rail sector was expected to characterize an imperfectly competitive market structure. The third column identifies welfare and other effects that analysts expected under deregulation, which are to be contrasted with column (4) that presents the estimated actual welfare effects. Theoretically, consumers were expected to receive welfare gains, because transportation prices would better reflect marginal cost pricing under deregulation than under regulation. From column (3) of the table we see that, in general, these expectations were on target. In the airline sector, consumers were predicted to gain on the order of \$2.7–6.6 billion, compared with an assessed gain equal to \$6.5 billion. Similarly, in the motor carrier sector of the industry, expected welfare gains accruing to shippers through lower prices amounted to \$9.8 billion, compared with a \$7.8 billion actual gain. The welfare gains from reductions in common carrier rates were complemented with an additional \$6.0 billion welfare gain from reductions in private carrier rates.

Table 8.12 Predicted and estimated actual effects of deregulation on price, service, profits, and labor (billions of 1990 dollars, unless otherwise indicated)

Transportation Sector (1)	Expected Industry Structure (2)	Predicted Welfare Effect (3)	Estimated Actual Welfare Effect (4)
Airline	Highly competitive		
Price and service			
Fares		(2.7, 6.6)	(4.3, 6.5)
Service frequency		(−0.60, 0.57)	8.5
Travel time		Not predicted	(−1.0, 1.8)
Travel restrictions		Not predicted	−3.0
Profits		Small change	4.9
Labor			
Wages		Small ambiguous change	Small decline
Employment		Small ambiguous change	6% increase
Motor Carrier	Highly competitive		
Price and service			
Common carrier rates		9.8	7.8
Private carrier rates		(0.43, 4.3)	6.0
Common carrier service time and reliability		Not predicted	1.6
Profits		(−5.8, −4.3)	−4.8
Labor			
Wages		(−3.7, −2.3)	(−1.9, −1.1)
Employment		Decline	Decline
Railroads	Imperfectly competitive		
Price and service			
Rates		(2.5, 6.0)	(0.73, 1.6)
Service time and reliability		Not predicted	9.3
Profits		(2.9, 8.6)	3.2
Labor			
Wages		No change	20% decline
Employment		Ambiguous	No effect

Source: Adapted from Winston (1993), table 3, pp. 1274–5

Only in the rail sector did actual welfare gains from price adjustments fall short of expectations. Recall that a motivation for relaxing economic restrictions on rails was to improve the sector's financial health. This also implies that prices would be rationally set to cover costs of operation. Rail prices in general rose from deregulation, thereby reducing shipper welfare. However, under deregulation rails could also enter into long-run contracts, which enable shippers to exploit rate savings by adjusting their shipment sizes and lengths of haul. The estimated benefits to rail shippers reported in table 8.12 reflect shippers' operational adjustments to the new environment.

The effect on quality of service

The largest discrepancy in table 8.12 relates to service frequency and quality-of-service effects associated with economic deregulation. In the airline industry, service frequency was expected to have minor welfare effects from a negative $600 million to a positive $570 million. The actual effect was positive and quite large, at $8.5 billion. This primarily reflects the fact that analysts did not anticipate airlines' technological responses to a deregulated environment, which included a move away from point-to-point operations and toward hub-and-spoke systems, the development of computerized fare management systems, and more efficient matching of equipment with size of market. This significantly benefited consumers. But it also imposed some costs in the form of increased travel time and travel restrictions that oftentimes accompany hub-and-spoke networks and lower fares, respectively. In the table, travel restrictions are seen to reduce consumer welfare on the order of $3 billion dollars annually.

The inability to predict operational changes to a deregulated environment also shows up in the motor carrier and rail sectors. Shippers in these sectors received welfare gains from enhanced service quality, gains that were generally not expected. Indeed, we see for the railroads that the $9.3 billion gains in reduced time and improved reliability are greater than the net gains to air passengers.

As a group, demanders of transportation services, whether they be airline passengers or freight shippers, reaped welfare gains from the more competitive environment and lower prices under deregulation. What about firms? Did transportation producers also benefit from deregulation?

The effect on profits

On the profit side, we see in table 8.12 that the overall effect on producers was positive, but there were winners and losers from deregulation. For the airline sector, profits were expected to show little change, yet received economic gains to the tune of $4.9 billion. Again, this reflects the underpredicted operational changes in the sector that enabled airlines to produce trips at lower production costs. And lower production costs mean higher profits. Alternatively, in the motor carrier industry, deregulation was expected to lower profits, and this is exactly what happened. In comparison with a predicted profit fall ranging between −$5.8 and −$4.3 billion, assessed profits fell by $4.8 billion. Recall that, under regulation, the less-than-truckload sector looked very much like a monopoly that earned monopoly profits. The introduction of significant competition in this industry had the expected effect of lowering prices and, accordingly, profits. As was the case with price predictions, in the absence of technological responses, analysts' predictions were pretty much on the mark.

This was also true in the rail sector, but for different reasons. Under deregulation, rails were better able to rationalize prices (that is, set prices more in accordance with marginal cost pricing), make long-term contracts, and shed unprofitable markets. The combination of more efficient pricing with lower production costs had the expected positive effect on profits. A gain of $2.9–8.6 billion was predicted; an estimated gain of $3.2 was realized.

The effect on labor

We also see in table 8.12 the predicted and assessed effects of deregulation on labor. To the extent that markets earn monopoly rents under regulation, economic theory predicts that a move toward a more competitive environment will lower consumer prices and reduce rents to firms and labor. In other words, a more competitive environment will redistribute wealth toward consumers and away from producers and labor. And as labor becomes less valuable, there will be employment losses to this group. This prediction was borne out for the motor carrier industry. In table 8.12, the predicted loss of income to labor is in the $3 billion range, which is somewhat more than the estimated effect in the $1.5 billion range. Also, as expected, employment declined. In the rail sector, there was little employment effect but wages suffered, declining by an estimated 20%, as labor in this sector faced a more competitive environment.

In the airline sector, wages declined a little, but employment increased by 6%. Although lower output prices reduce the value of labor, the disemployment effect from deregulation was offset by the increased demand for trips induced by the fall in airline fares.

In sum, predictions that economic deregulation would generate net benefits to society were correct. Looking at column (4) of table 8.12, we see that the positive effects far outweigh the negative effects. Also as expected, economic deregulation was not uniformly beneficial to all groups. There were winners and losers. In general, those making monopoly rents under regulation lose, as they face a more competitive environment under deregulation. Similarly, consumers and shippers paying monopoly-based prices under regulation gain under deregulation. But the above analysis also indicates that there were significant aspects of deregulation that analysts either did not predict well or simply did not predict at all. Most analysts did not anticipate the speed or the extent to which transport firms responded technologically and operationally to the deregulated environment. And it has been said that this is one of the hidden costs of regulation. Because we can not predict how firms under a regulatory umbrella will adjust in a more competitive environment, it is very difficult to assess the true opportunity costs of regulation.

CHAPTER HIGHLIGHTS

- There are many sources of economic rents. In an empirical study of the airline industry, monopoly rents were found to be location-based and scale-based. An airline's response to economic deregulation depended upon the source of its monopoly profits.
- Williamson's welfare trade-off argues that horizontal mergers raise social welfare in the form of lower production costs or improved products, but reduce welfare through price increases as a result of enhanced market power. Evidence on price increases is mixed. Empirical results from the Northwest/Republic merger indicate increased hub dominance and higher prices in the short run. In the long run, however, price increases appear to be more modest.
- Partial equilibrium analysis focuses upon a single market, whereas general equilibrium analysis focuses upon the interactions between related markets.
- Consumer surplus is the difference between what consumers are willing to pay to purchase some level of the good versus what they have to pay. Producer surplus is the difference between the revenues that firms receive to produce a given quantity of the good and the opportunity cost of producing that quantity. Efficient markets maximize the sum of consumer and producer surplus.
- Effective market price controls lead to an inefficient allocation of the good and lower economic welfare, as defined by the sum of producer and consumer surplus.

- In an empirical study of rail and motor carrier markets, there was a general absence of marginal cost pricing, which produced net efficiency losses. A move to a competitive equilibrium was expected to produce significant economic welfare benefits.
- Assessed effects of economic deregulation in the transport sector validated the expectations of many that society would reap net economic gains from a more competitive environment. Many analysts predicted the impact of deregulation on prices and profits, but few foresaw the significant technological and operational changes that economic deregulation induced.

Review questions

1. Similar to oligopolies, monopolies and monopolistically competitive market structures are imperfectly competitive. Yet strategic behavior is only relevant for oligopolistic market structures. Why?

2. (a) Graphically depict and explain Williamson's welfare trade-off from an horizontal merger.
   (b) If demand is perfectly price inelastic, according to Williamson, what determines whether a merger is socially beneficial? Will consumers be better off or worse off?
   (c) Suppose that an horizontal merger has virtually no effect on market power and price but leads to an improved product. Is the merger socially desirable?

3. Mergers are one way in which oligopolistic firms can behave strategically to increase their market power. Prior to the fall of 1986, TWA competed with Ozark airlines at its St. Louis hub and Northwest competed with Republic at its Minneapolis hub. In the fall of 1986, TWA purchased Ozark Airlines and Northwest merged with Republic. In each case, the merged airlines' shares of traffic at their respective hubs was over 75%. Consider the following information on the average difference in route share changes by point of origin. The period 1985–6 represents a pre-merger period and 1986–7 represents a post-merger period. Thus, for example, in the pre-merger period, 1985–6, TWA/Ozark served 48 markets from the St. Louis hub and experienced a 0.8% increase in the share of flights originating in St. Louis relative to flights originating at the other endpoint of these routes. In the post-merger market, TWA/Ozark experienced a 5% increase in the share of flights originating at the St. Louis hub relative to those originating at the other end of the route.
   (a) Interpret the remaining numbers in table 8.13.
   (b) From the evidence presented in the table, discuss whether the mergers significantly increased the market power of TWA/Ozark at its St. Louis hub and Northwest/Republic at its Minneapolis/St. Paul hub.

Table 8.13 Markets served and share of flights

	All Routes			Direct Routes		
	Number of Markets	1985–6	1986–7	Number of Markets	1985–6	1986–7
TWA/Ozark at St. Louis	48	0.8	5.0	16	−3.4	6.6
Northwest/Republic at Minneapolis – St. Paul	57	0.8	1.7	7	0.1	4.5

Source: Borenstein (1990), table 3, p. 403

4. Morrison (1996) estimated the following route competition model for the second quarter of 1995. The dependent variable is ln(Route Competition) and the results are presented in table 8.14.

(a) What impact does a 10% increase in distance have upon route competition? Are there distance-related economies of scale for route competition?

(b) The results displayed in the table are post-merger for Northwest/Republic, TWA/Ozark, and USAir/Piedmont. Evaluate whether the dummy variables, variables (2)–(7), are consistent with the hypothesis that horizontal mergers reduce competition.

Table 8.14 Route competition model

Variable	Coefficient Estimate (*t*-statistic)
(1) Constant	1.45 (1.03)
(2) Northwest and Republic Route Dummy	−0.116 (−1.82)
(3) TWA and Ozark Route Dummy	0.241 (3.23)
(4) USAir and Piedmont Route Dummy	−0.076 (−0.92)
(5) Northwest or Republic Route Dummy	0.065 (1.86)
(6) TWA or Ozark Route Dummy	0.161 (4.28)
(7) USAir or Piedmont Route Dummy	−0.057 (−1.86)
(8) Ln (Distance)	0.353 (17.6)
(9) Ln ($Population_{origin} \cdot Population_{destination}$)	0.005 (0.45)
(10) Ln ($Income_{origin} \cdot Income_{destination}$)	−0.163 (−2.2)
(11) Tourism Dummy Variable	0.082 (3.09)
(12) Washington National Airport Dummy	0.149 (2.75)
(13) Kennedy Airport Dummy	−0.184 (−1.89)
(14) La Guardia Airport Dummy	0.035 (0.61)
(15) Chicago Airport Dummy	0.078 (1.71)

$R^2 = 0.37$
Number of observations = 995

Source: Adapted from Morrison (1996), table 2, p. 242

(c) Higher income is expected to affect route density. Interpret the coefficient on the income variable, variable (10). Is the sign on this variable expected? If so, why; and if not, why not?
(d) The tourism dummy variable reflects markets in Arizona, California, Nevada, and Florida. What impact does tourism have on route competition? Is this what economic theory would predict?
(e) The last four variables, (12)–(15), are "slot-controlled" airports; that is, airports with a FAA limit imposed on the number of take-offs and landings during each hour of the day. Holding all else constant, how much is route competition affected at Chicago?

5. Why are economic profits called economic rents? Explain the distinction between location-based economic rents and scale-based economic rents. Explain why these different sources of rents caused difficulty for the smaller trunk airlines in adjusting to economic deregulation.

6. For a particular air carrier that operates nationally, one could define the carrier's market in three alternative ways: (1) as the nation as a whole; (2) as a particular city-pair; or (3) for a particular geographic region.
(a) On the basis of these definitions, how concentrated do you think the national market, the individual city-pair market, and regional market would be using a four-firm concentration ratio?
(b) If two air carriers merged, would this affect the concentration ratio of the national, regional, or individual city-pair market the most?
(c) In the light of the fact that the government passed legislation to deregulate airlines, do you think that the government uses the individual city-pair market as its definition of an air carrier's market?
(d) There has been a lot of discussion about an air carrier's activities at its "hub" airport. Is the definition of hub operations most consistent with a national, regional, or city-pair market definition?

7. Table 8.15 summarizes operating expense and fare information prior to and subsequent to economic deregulation in the airline industry.

Table 8.15 Operating expenses and revenues, pre- and post-deregulation

Year	Expense per Seat–Mile	Average Fare per Passenger–Mile
1967	3.10	5.49
1977	4.79	8.42
1987	7.53	11.10
Percentage change		
1967–77		
1977–87		

Source: D. H. Pickrell, The demand for short-haul air service. In Meyer and Oster (1984), table 3.A.1, p. 46

(a) Fill in the table for the percentage change between 1967–77 and 1977–87.
(b) In the decade prior to deregulation, evaluate the Civil Aeronautics Board fares policy.
(c) What can you say about airlines' fares policies in the decade after deregulation? Can you determine what fares might have been in the absence of deregulation?

8. Consider table 8.16, which provides information on failures among all business and trucking companies respectively, during the periods 1980, the year of motor carrier deregulation, and 1986. Fill in the table for the percentage changes. Are these results consistent with the increased competition brought about by economic deregulation?

Table 8.16 Business and trucking failures, various years

Year	All Business Failures (% Change)	Trucking Failures (% Change)
1980	11,742 (–)	382 (–)
1981	16,794 (+0.43)	610 (+0.59)
1982	24,908 (+0.48)	960 (+0.57)
1983	31,334 (+0.25)	1,228 (+0.27)
1984	52,078 (+0.66)	1,410 (+0.14)
1985	57,253 (+0.09)	1,539 (+0.09)
1986	61,616 (+0.07)	1,564 (+0.01)

Source: Dun & Bradstreet Failure Data, 1980–90. Copyright © 1986 The Dun & Bradstreet Corporation

9. (a) What is the difference between partial equilibrium analysis and general equilibrium analysis?
(b) In general, when the government imposes a price ceiling – that is, a maximum price that lies below the equilibrium price – the result is that too few resources are allocated to the production of this good. Yet, we have seen in the transportation industry that when the ICC set railroad rates for manufactured goods in the Official Region, *too many* resources were allocated to the carriage of rail freight. Why? Graphically identify the welfare losses associated with such a policy.
(c) We see in table 8.7 that the total output in the initial equilibrium for the Official Region is 181.1 billion ton–miles, whereas in the competitive equilibrium it falls to 178.4. How can a fall in total goods shipped be more economically efficient?

10. Suppose that a shipper has the option of shipping his or her wheat by either rail or water carriage. Graphically depict the partial and general equilibrium effects of a technological innovation in water carriage.

11. The August 30, 1993 *Wall Street Journal* reported that Delta Airlines earned a net income of $7.1 million in the fiscal fourth quarter (April–June), compared with a loss of $180.2 million in the year-ago period. According to the article, Delta's earning performance reflects two industry trends: cost cutting and higher ticket prices. Use firm cost curves and market demand and supply curves to analyze Delta's improvement.

12. (a) What is the difference between a cooperative group of oligopolists and a non-cooperative group of oligopolists? In general, are either of these oligopolistic market structures illegal in the USA? Are there exceptions?
(b) Explain why a cooperative oligopoly essentially acts like a monopolist. What incentives exist that might cause a cooperative oligopoly to ultimately break apart?

13. (a) Consider a price ceiling that mandates that a transport firm can charge no more than a certain rate for transporting goods. Under what condition will the price ceiling have an impact on market equilibrium and price? What are the efficiency effects of an "effective" price ceiling; that is, a price ceiling which constrains the market?
(b) Suppose that the government mandates an effective price ceiling, but also requires that all demand must be met at this rate. Are there efficiency effects from such a policy? If so, how do these differ from a price ceiling with no requirement to meet all demand at the regulated price?

14. (a) What is value-of-service pricing?
(b) During the regulated period, there was an absence of marginal cost pricing in the motor carrier and rail sectors of the transportation industry. How useful was value-of-service pricing as an explanation of the observed difference in marginal cost : price ratios for various commodities?

NOTES

1 Bailey and Williams found the operating profit margin differences between the four largest and the five smaller trunks to be statistically significant.

2 Piedmont also identified a north–south niche in the Midwest and established a hub in Dayton, Ohio to serve this market.

3 The short-haul markets included Boston, Buffalo, Cincinnati, Cleveland, Rochester (New York), Syracuse, and Washington DC: see Brenner et al. (1985), p. 80.

4 Since their introduction, FFPs have become quite complicated by linking mileage points to rental car agencies, hotels, credit cards, other airlines whose routes are not flown by the awarding airline, double and triple bonus points for traveling at certain times or under certain conditions, and different expiration dates for the mileage points earned.

5 Supplementing CRSs are data processing packages that are used to perform necessary information processing and accounting tasks. Without such packages, there would be no way to keep track of the sales transactions.

6 In an earlier study, Borenstein (1990) suggests that an overall decrease in the demand to and from the St. Louis hub may explain the absence of significant price increases despite increased concentration at the hub.

7 Although there is expected to be greater product differentiation, and therefore more variation in price/cost combinations under deregulation, Bailey and Williams recognize that high-price, high-cost combinations may not only reflect product differentiation (for example, higher quality of service) but may also reflect a carrier's monopoly power.

8 Bailey and Williams report that USAir's average pay and benefit package in 1984 was $47,896, in comparison with $17,139 for People's Express. Continental significantly lowered its per-employee labor costs from $36,875 to $23,433 between the first and fourth quarters of 1984, when it emerged from bankruptcy proceedings.

9 A merger of two competitor firms operating in the same market (for example, General Motors merges with Ford) is an *horizontal* merger, in contrast to a *vertical* merger that occurs between two firms in the production–distribution chain for a given product (for example, General Motors purchases a firm that produces windshields for its vehicles).

10 We could include fare in each of the equations in (8.1). However, since consumer choice depends upon differences in attributes, fare would drop out, having no impact upon choice. Carlton et al. did find minor differences in fares for some city-pairs, but re-estimating the model with fare included led to virtually identical results.

11 With 28 observations and four estimated coefficients, there are 24 degrees of freedom. Because our hypotheses identify the direction of the effect, we need to test the null hypothesis using a one-tail test. The critical t-value with 24 degrees of freedom is 2.49.

12 In their analysis, Carlton et al. (1980) use an equivalent approach based upon conditional expected utilities. Details of this can be found in an appendix to their paper.

13 Alternatively, consumer surplus is the difference between value-in-use and value-in-exchange.

14 Technically, for these income transfers to cancel each other, the marginal value of an additional dollar to producers must be identical to the marginal value of an additional dollar to consumers. For this to occur, we must have an optimal distribution of income.

15 The South-West Region includes the Southern Region, the South-Western Region, the Western Trunk Line Region, and the Mountain-Pacific Region. For a brief discussion of these areas, see note 5 in chapter 7.

16 Among the nontransportation variables were dummy variables for region of the country and type of bulk commodity shipped. Market demand functions for other commodity–mode combinations were similarly specified.

17 Generating the market supply curve by "blowing up" the supply curve of a representative firm avoided practical problems that would be encountered when horizontally summing individual firm supply curves. For example, using firm supply functions, the supply curves of individual firms exhibited minimum points which, when horizontally summed, would produce discontinuities in the market supply curve.

18 One of the difficulties with this type of analysis is that the estimated cost functions characterize the behavior of firms during regulation. Cost functions that characterize firm activities after deregulation would likely differ, since they would reflect firms' production responses to the altered environment. Of course, the problem is that "deregulated" data were not available during the "regulated" era and researchers were forced to use whatever data were available.

19 Friedlaender and Spady's results for specialized motor carriers were consistent with those of McMullen and Stanley (1988), which we examined in chapter 5.

20 The following chapter analyzes in some detail the market structure implications when firms face falling marginal cost curves.

21 In fact, the estimated marginal cost curve for specialized motor carriers of bulk and manufactured goods was rising but nearly horizontal, which indicates that South-West carriers were operating near constant returns to scale with slight diseconomies.

22 Friedlaender and Spady estimated that motor carrier bulk prices would increase by two-hundredths of a cent.

REFERENCES AND RELATED READINGS

General references

Shepherd, W. G. 1993: *The Economics of Industrial Organization*, 3rd edn. London: Prentice-Hall International.

Tye, W. B. 1985: On the application of the "Williamsonian Welfare Tradeoff" to rail mergers. *Logistics and Transportation Review*, 21, 239–48.

Viscusi, W. K., Vernon, J. M., and Harrington, J. E. Jr. 1992: *Economics of Regulation and Antitrust*. Lexington, Mass.: D. C. Heath.

Williamson, O. E. 1968: Economics as an antitrust defense: the welfare tradeoffs. *American Economic Review*, 58, 18–36.

General transportation references

Meyer, J. R., Merton, J. P., Stenason, J., and Zwick, C. 1959: *The Economics of Competition in the Transportation Industries*. Cambridge, Mass.: Harvard University Press.

Oum, T. H., Dodgson, J. S., Hensher, D. A., Morrison, S. A., Nash, C. A., Small, K. A., and Waters, W. G. II 1995: *Transport Economics*. Seoul, Korea: The Korea Research Foundation for the 21st Century.

Winston, C. 1985: Conceptual developments in the economics of transportation: an interpretive survey. *Journal of Economic Literature*, XXIII, 57–94.

Winston, C. 1993: Economic deregulation: days of reckoning for microeconomists. *Journal of Economic Literature*, XXXI, 1263–89.

Weiss, L. W. and Klass, M. W. (eds.) 1986: *Regulatory Reform: What Actually Happened*. Boston: Little, Brown.

Transportation regulation/deregulation by mode

Airlines

Bailey, E. E. 1985: Airline deregulation in the United States: the benefits provided and the lessons learned. *International Journal of Transport Economics*, 12, 119–44.

Bailey, E. E. and Williams, J. R. 1988: Sources of economic rent in the deregulated airline industry. *Journal of Law and Economics*, XXXI, 173–202.

Bailey, E. E., Graham, D. R., and Kaplan, D. P. 1985: *Deregulating the Airlines*. Cambridge, Mass.: The MIT Press.

Beneish, M. D. 1991: The effect of regulatory changes in the airline industry on shareholders' wealth. *Journal of Law and Economics*, XXXIV, 395–430.

Berry, S. T. 1990: Airport presence as product differentiation. *AEA Papers and Proceedings*, 80, 394–9.

Borenstein, S. 1990: Airline mergers, airport dominance, and market power. *AEA Papers and Proceedings*, 80, 400–4.

Borenstein, S. 1992: The evolution of US airline competition. *Journal of Economic Perspectives*, 6, 45–73.

Borenstein, S. and Rose, N. L. 1994: Competition and price dispersion in the US airline industry. *Journal of Political Economy*, 102, 653–83.

Brenner, M., Leet, J. O., and Schott, E. 1985: *Airline Deregulation*. Westport, Conn.: ENO Foundation for Transportation.

Button, K. (ed.) 1991: *Regulation and Deregulation: International Experiences*. New York: New York University Press.

Douglas, G. W. and Miller, J. C. III 1974: *Economic Regulation of Domestic Air Transport: Theory and Policy*. Washington DC: The Brookings Institution.

Evans, W. N. and Kessides, I. 1992–3: Structure, conduct, and performance in the deregulated airline industry. *Southern Economic Journal*, 59, 450–67.
Graham, D. R., Kaplan, D. P., and Sibley, D. S. 1983: Efficiency and competition in the airline industry. *The Bell Journal of Economics*, 14, 118–38.
Kahn, A. E. 1988: Surprises of airline deregulation. *AEA Papers and Proceedings*, 78, 316–22.
Kahn, A. E. 1993: The competitive consequences of hub dominance: a case study. *Review of Industrial Organization*, 8, 381–405.
Keeler, T. E. and Abrahams, M. 1981: Market structure, pricing, and service quality in the airline industry under deregulation. In W. Sichel and T. G. Gies (eds.), *Applications of Economic Principles in Public Utility Industries*. Ann Arbor: University of Michigan Press, pp. 103–19.
Levine, M. E. 1987: Airline competition in deregulated markets: theory, firm strategy, and public policy. *Yale Journal of Regulation*, 4, 393–494.
Meyer, J. R. and Oster, C. V. Jr. 1984: *Deregulation and the New Airline Entrepreneurs*. Cambridge, Mass.: The MIT Press.
Meyer, J. R. and Oster, C. V. Jr. 1987: *Deregulation and the Future of Intercity Passenger Travel*. Cambridge, Mass.: The MIT Press.
Meyer, J. R. and Strong, J. R. 1992: From closed set to open set deregulation: an assessment of the US airline industry. *Logistics and Transportation Review*, 28, 1–21.
Moore, T. G. 1986: US airline deregulation: its effect on passengers, capital, and labor. *Journal of Law and Economics*, XXIX, 1–28.
Pickrell, D. 1991: The regulation and deregulation of US airlines. In K. Button (ed.), *Airline Deregulation: International Experiences*. New York: New York University Press, pp. 5–47.
US Department of Transportation 1988: *Study of Airline Computer Reservation Systems*, Washington DC: US Government Printing Office.

Motor carriers

Beilock, R. and Freeman, J. 1987: The effect on rate levels and structures of removing entry and rate controls on motor carriers. *Journal of Transport Economics and Policy*, XXI, 167–188.
Blair, R. D., Kaserman, D. L., and McClave, J. T. 1986: Motor carrier deregulation: the Florida experiment. *Review of Economics and Statistics*, LXVIII, 159–64.
Corsi, T. M., Grinum, C. M., Smith, K. G., and Smith, R. D. 1992: The effects of LTI motor carrier size on strategy and performance. *Logistics and Transportation Review*, 28, 129–45.
Friedlaender, A. F. and Spady, R. H. 1981: *Freight Transport Regulation*. Cambridge, Mass.: The MIT Press.
Mabley, R. E. and Strack, W. D. 1982: Deregulation – a green light for trucking efficiency. *Regulation*, 6, 36–56.
McMullen, S. and Stanley, L. R. 1988: The impact of deregulation on the production structure of the motor carrier industry. *Economic Inquiry*, XXVI, 299–316.
Nelson, J. C. 1983: The emerging effects of deregulation of surface freight transport in the United States. *International Journal of Transport Economics*, X, 219–36.

Railroads

Barnekov, C. C. and Kleit, A. N. 1990: The efficiency effects of railroad deregulation in the United States. *International Journal of Transport Economics*, XVII, 21–36.
Boyer, K. D. 1977: Minimum rate regulation, modal split sensitivities, and the railroad problem. *Journal of Political Economy*, 85, 493–512.
Boyer, K. D. 1987: The costs of price regulation: lessons from railroad deregulation. *Rand Journal of Economics*, 18, 408–16.
Braeutigam, R. R. 1992–3: Consequences of regulatory reform in the American railroad industry. *Southern Economic Journal*, 59, 468–80.

Burton, M. L. 1993: Railroad deregulation, carrier behavior, and shipper response: a disaggregate analysis. *Journal of Regulatory Economics*, 5, 417–34.

Friedlaender, A. F., Berndt, E. R., Chiang, J. S.-E. W., Showalter, M., and Vellturo, C. A. 1993: Rail costs and capital adjustments in a quasi-regulated environment. *Journal of Transport Economics and Policy*, XXVII, 131–52.

Keeler, T. E. 1983: *Railroads, Freight, and Public Policy*. Washington DC: The Brookings Institution.

Levin, R. C. 1981: Railroad rates, profitability, and welfare under deregulation. *The Bell Journal of Economics*, 12, 1–25.

MacDonald, J. M. 1989: Railroad deregulation, innovation, competition: effects of the Staggers Act on grain transportation. *Journal of Law and Economics*, XXXII, 63–96.

Bus transport

Berechman, J. 1993: *Public Transit Economics and Deregulation Policy*, vol. 23. Studies in Regional Science and Urban Economics, L. Anselin, M. Fujita, P. Nijkamp, and J. Thisse (ed.). Amsterdam: Elsevier Science.

Button, K. J. 1987: The effects of regulatory reform on the US Inter-city Bus Industry. *Transport Reviews*, 7, 145–66.

Gwilliam, K. M. 1989: Setting the market free: deregulation of the bus industry. *Journal of Transport Economics and Policy*, XXIII, 29–43.

Mergers in transportation

Boisjoly, R. P. and Corsi, T. M. 1980: The economic implications of less-than-truckload motor carrier mergers. *Journal of Economics and Business*, 33, 13–20.

Carlton, D. W., Landes, W. M., and Posner, R. A. 1980: Benefits and costs of airline mergers: a case study. *The Bell Journal of Economics*, 11, 65–83.

Kim, E. H. and Singal, V. 1993: Mergers and market power: evidence from the airline industry. *The American Economic Journal*, 83, 549–69.

MacDonald, J. M. 1987: Competition and rail rates for the shipment of corn, soybeans, and wheat. *Rand Journal of Economics*, 18, 151–62.

Morrison, S. A. 1996: Airline mergers: a longer view. *Journal of Transport Economics and Policy*, XXX, 237–50.

Werden, G. J. and Froeb, L. M. 1994: The effects of mergers in differentiated products industries: logit demand and merger policy. *Journal of Law, Economics, and Organization*, 10, 407–26.

Werden, G. J., Joskow, A. S., and Johnson, R. L. 1991: The effects of mergers on price and output: two case studies from the airline industry. *Managerial and Decision Economics*, 12, 341–52.

9

Transportation Investment

INTRODUCTION

When developing our theory of cost, we distinguished between short-run and long-run costs, the former assuming that at least one input is fixed, while the latter assumes that all inputs are variable. In the simplest case when there are only two inputs, capital and labor, a firm's optimal combination of inputs is characterized by the condition that the marginal product per dollar spent on labor just equals the marginal product per dollar spent on capital. In the long run, firms substitute capital for labor as long as the relative productivity of capital exceeds capital's relative cost.[1] Transportation companies routinely invest in capital equipment and infrastructure. Airlines purchase airplanes and build maintenance facilities, urban transit companies buy buses and develop fixed-rail transit systems, railroads invest in rolling stock and trackage, federal and state governments build bridges and highways of varying capacity and quality, and shipping companies purchase and maintain their floating stocks of liners and tramp steamers. Once a firm makes the capital investment, the firm is in the short run and the associated capital costs become the firm's fixed costs of production.

Up to this point, however, our discussion of a firm's capital purchases has focused upon implications for a firm's cost structure and generally ignored one important aspect of capital investment that distinguishes capital from labor, the fact that capital goods are durable. Non-durable inputs in the production process are goods purchased and labor that are used in the same period. Capital goods are longer-lived inputs that a firm acquires in one period but productively uses over long periods of time. In this chapter, we introduce the concept of discounted present value, examine its importance to a firm's capital investment decisions, and empirically illustrate its use in valuing motor carrier operating certificates and taxicab medallions. We also examine how discounted present value concepts are used to develop a perfectly competitive firm's optimal pricing and investment strategy. With empirical examples from the urban bus and rail sectors of the transportation industry, we illustrate how these efficiency criteria are used to obtain resource allocation implications if regulated transportation markets were to follow optimal pricing and investment criteria.

FIRM INVESTMENT BEHAVIOR

THE USER COST OF CAPITAL

If perfectly competitive markets prevail, we know that the resulting allocation of resources is Pareto optimal; that is, it is not possible to reallocate resources without making someone else worse off. Consider figure 9.1, which depicts the cost structure for a perfectly competitive firm that is in long-run equilibrium at *E*. Price equals long-run marginal and long-run average cost (as well as short-run marginal cost), and the equilibrium quantity is T_1. Assume that the short-run average total and average variable cost curves are conditioned on a fixed level of capital equal to K_1.

Since short-run average total cost equals long-run average cost, K_1 coincides with the optimal level of capital necessary to produce T_1 units of output. Moreover, since the price line is just tangent to the short- and long-run average cost curves, the firm is making zero economic profit. All opportunity costs are covered. But what is the opportunity cost of capital? Previously, we simply identified r as the per unit rental price of capital, without comment. At this point, however, it will be useful to consider the components of r in some detail.

In general, when a firm purchases a new piece of capital, for example, a new truck, switching equipment, bus, and so forth, for which it pays a price p_K, the firm faces three types of *annual* costs: an interest opportunity cost of capital, a depreciation cost, and an obsolescence cost.

Opportunity cost of capital This represents the foregone interest associated with the use of the funds used to purchase the capital good. For example, suppose that a trucking firm expends $50,000 to purchase a new truck with a useful life of ten years. If the prevailing annual interest rate is 8%, the firm foregoes interest income of $4,000 per year. Regardless of whether the firm borrows the money or finances the truck's purchase out of its own funds, its opportunity cost is $4,000.[2]

Depreciation cost A second cost of capital is a depreciation charge. With continued use of capital over time, the capital good experiences wear and tear until it has no service value left.

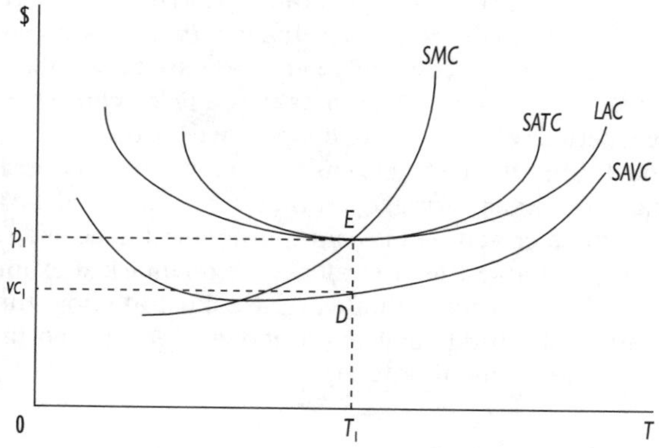

Figure 9.1 A perfectly competitive firm in long-run equilibrium.

If our \$50,000 truck depreciates at an annual rate of 10%, then the firm incurs a \$5,000 depreciation cost in each of the ten years during which the truck is operated. However, capital equipment is not simply purchased and then allowed to depreciate with no interventions. Firms annually incur costs to maintain their capital equipment. In general, there is an inverse relationship between maintenance expenditures and depreciation. Firms that expend higher annual amounts on capital maintenance have lower depreciation rates, while firms that have smaller maintenance budgets experience higher depreciation rates. It is important to note, however, that maintenance costs are generally output-related and, as such, are included in a firm's variable cost of production.[3]

Obsolescence cost This reflects decreases in the price of capital resulting from technological advances. For example, hydraulic lifts on trucks reduced the value, independent of depreciation, of trucks that did not have them. The introduction of jet aircraft in the early 1960s lowered the value of existing propeller aircraft. Another example is the interstate highway system, which was begun in 1950 and completed in 1973. As segments of the interstate system were completed, travelers substituted interstate routes for previously used noninterstate roads, thereby lowering the value of trips along these slower routes.[4]

Do technological advances eliminate the value of capital that embodies the older technologies? No! But the inferior older capital is transferred to lower-valued uses. Trucks without hydraulic lifts are no longer used for interstate shipments, but for the movement of local goods. Propeller aircraft are used for lower-valued commuter and shorter-haul regional trips, or sold to underdeveloped countries for servicing their lower-valued trips – trips for which speed is of lesser importance. And trips along slower noninterstate roads are also of lower value – local visiting and shopping trips, sightseeing and leisure trips, and generally trips where trip time is less valuable.

From the above discussion, the annual rental price of capital r, often referred to as the *user cost of capital*, is defined as

$$r = ip_K + \delta p_K + \dot{p}_K p_K = (i + \delta + \dot{p}_K)p_K \tag{9.1}$$

where i is the annual interest rate, δ is the annual rate of depreciation, p_K is the price of capital, and $\dot{p}_K$ is the annual rate of change in the price of existing capital (reflecting obsolescence costs). Also, by multiplying the rental price of capital by the amount of capital employed, we obtain the *total annual cost of capital, rK*.

QUASI-RENTS

Returning to figure 9.1, if output price is p_1, the firm is covering its variable costs of production, $vc_1 \cdot T_1$, and fixed production costs, given by the area $(p_1 - vc_1)T_1$. What this says is that, anticipating an expected output price of p_1 and given its long-run cost structure, the firm calculated K_1 to be its optimal capital investment. It then invests in K_1, which thrusts the firm into the short run. If, as depicted, expectations are realized and the actual price is p_1, then revenues generated cover all economic costs. In particular, variable costs are sufficient to pay the firm's variable factors of production; producer surplus, which is also referred to as a firm's *quasi-rent*, is the difference between firm revenues and its variable costs.[5] We see in figure 9.1

that quasi-rents, equal to area $(p_1 - vc_1)T_1$, are sufficient to pay the firm's capital costs, which now equal its short-run total fixed costs.

A number of comments can be made regarding the graph. First, the fixed costs represented in figure 9.1 reflect interest opportunity, depreciation, and *anticipated* obsolescence costs. In perfectly competitive markets, capital-producing firms keep their clients informed of existing technologies as well as the development and availability of new technologies. This implies that the "given state of technology" includes those new technologies that "are likely" to be available in the near future. If firms correctly anticipate the new technologies, then the value of *existing* capital will have already fallen, and the quasi-rents depicted in figure 9.2 reflect these obsolescence charges.[6]

Second, the firm's quasi-rent in figure 9.1 is not a total return to capital but, rather, the expected return to capital *per period*. Suppose, for example, that the cost curves in figure 9.1 correspond to the annual production costs which, along with demand conditions, are expected to prevail in the foreseeable future.[7] If capital is expected to last 20 years, then the *SAVC* curve will be relevant for the 20-year period and the earned producer surplus corresponds to an annual return to capital. When capital wears out in 20 years, the firm is again on its long-run cost curve.

Third, at output price p_1, the firm is making a normal return on its investment. To see the implications of this, assume that a normal return on investment is 6% ($i = 0.06$), capital fully depreciates at the end of the first period ($\delta = 1$) so that there is no obsolescence ($\dot{p}_K = 0$), and the firm employs K units of capital at the beginning of the period. Revenues are received at the end of the period. Since capital fully depreciates in the first year, $\delta = 1$, the user cost of capital is $(i + \delta)p_K K = (0.06 + 1)p_K K$, the sum of depreciation costs $1 \cdot p_K K$, and the foregone interest on the moneys tied up in capital $0.06 \cdot p_K K$. At the end of the period, quasi-rents equal $(p_1 - vc_1)T_1$ which, if equal to $(1 + 0.06)p_K K$, is sufficient to cover depreciation and interest opportunity costs. In this example, the *gross rate of return on investment* equals $1.0 + 0.06 = 1.06$. The *net (of depreciation and obsolescence, which equals zero) return on investment*, on the other hand, is 0.06, the gross rate of return minus the sum of depreciation and obsolescence rates. If output price is greater than p_1, then quasi-rents more than cover capital depreciation and interest costs, the firm makes an economic profit, and net return on investment exceeds 6%. Equivalently, if quasi-rents exceed the fixed costs of production, the firm has an incentive to increase its capital investment. Conversely, if output price is less than p_1 but greater than the minimum *SAVC*, then quasi-rents are insufficient to cover ownership costs, the firm incurs an economic loss, net return on investment is less than 6%, and the firm has an economic incentive to dis-invest; that is, reduce its capital investment.

Finally, since capital is a durable good that provides services over a period of time and generates producer surpluses over time, we can gain a better understanding of firm capital investment decisions by examining in greater detail the relationship between present and future values, and the process by which future costs and revenues are converted into present values.

Discounted Present Value – Constant Stream of Net Returns

Suppose that you have a choice between \$100 to be received today or \$100 to be received a year from today. In either case, at the end of 1 year you will have \$100 available to spend. However, you would not be indifferent between the two alternatives. If you receive the \$100 today, you have the ability to do whatever you want with the money. You could buy two pairs of pants and a new shirt. Or you might go to Chicago for the weekend. Alternatively, you could simply put the money in a bank. Regardless of how you use the money, you are better off if you receive the money today rather than 1 year from now, because of its earlier availability.

To pose this question another way, suppose that I ask you the maximum you would be willing to pay today to receive \$100 today. In all likelihood, it would be \$100. Would you also be willing to pay a maximum of \$100 for \$100 to be received a year from now? Clearly not. The most you would pay would be something less than \$100, because you would be forego-ing its use for a 1 year period. If the current interest rate on savings accounts is 10%, then you would be willing to pay no more than \$90.90 for the right to \$100 a year from now. The reason is that, at a 10% rate of interest, \$90.90 will grow to \$100 in 1 year. Thus, you would be indifferent between \$90.90 to be received today or \$100 to be received 1 year from today.

Let PV be the present amount invested, i the rate of interest, $1 + i$ the compound factor, and FV the future amount to be received at the end of 1 year. Then the relationship between present and future values is described by the expression

$$FV = (1 + i)PV \tag{9.2}$$

If i is 10% and PV is \$90.90, the future value of the sum invested is \$100. If, on the other hand, the amount invested is not to be received for 2 years, then interest is also paid on the return after 1 year, $(1 + i)PV$, and the future value becomes

$$\begin{aligned} FV &= (1 + i)[(1 + i)PV] \\ &= (1 + i)^2 PV \end{aligned}$$

After t years, the future value of PV invested today is

$$FV = (1 + i)^t PV \tag{9.3}$$

Thus, \$90.90 invested today grows to \$109.98 after two years and to \$611.53 after 20 years $[(1.10)^{20}(90.90)]$.

Knowing the rate of interest and the number of years, equation (9.3) tells us the future value that a specified present investment of \$$PV$ will become. Suppose, on the other hand, that we know the future amount but would like to determine what amount of present investment is necessary to achieve that future value. To answer this, we simply solve equation (9.3) for PV:

$$PV = \frac{FV}{(1 + i)^t} \tag{9.4}$$

Here, PV represents the *discounted present value* of the specified future value and $(1/(1 + i))$ is the discount factor. To re-examine our previous example, suppose that we ask what present value will give us \$100 a year from now. Given a 10% rate of interest, the present value is

$$PV = \frac{100}{(1.1)^1} = 90.90$$

Similarly, the present value of $100 to be received 20 years from now is

$$PV = \frac{100}{(1.1)^{20}} = 14.86$$

That is, $14.86 will grow to $100 at the end of 20 years.

We can extend the problem to consider future values that are received during many future periods. Assume that FV is a future value to be received at the end of the first, second, third, and on out to the tth year. When the future values are identical, then the series is referred to as an *ordinary annuity*. Given an interest rate i, the discounted present value of the annuity is

$$PV = \frac{FV}{(1+i)} + \frac{FV}{(1+i)^2} + \frac{FV}{(1+i)^3} + \ldots + \frac{FV}{(1+i)^t} \tag{9.5}$$

which can be shown to equal

$$PV = \sum_{s=1}^{t} \frac{FV}{(1+i)^s} = \frac{FV}{i}\left[1 - \frac{1}{(1+i)^t}\right] = FV\left[\frac{(1+i)^t - 1}{i(1+i)^t}\right] \tag{9.6}$$

A special case of an ordinary annuity is a *perpetuity*, in which the series of future values goes on forever. Equation (9.6) collapses to an especially simple formula in this instance. Letting t go to infinity, $(1/(1+i)^t)$ goes to zero and the present value formula becomes

$$PV = \frac{FV}{i} \tag{9.7}$$

For example, given an annual interest rate of 10%, the present value of $100 received annually for ten years is, from equation (9.6), $614.46; if the returns last for 20 years, the present value is $851.35; and if the returns last forever, the present value, from equation (9.7), is $1,000.00 (100/0.1).

As a final point, it is important to recognize the effects on discounted present values due to changes in the future value (FV), the interest rate (i), and the time horizon (t). All else held constant, if the value to be received in the future increases, the present value also increases. It takes a larger amount invested today to grow to a larger specified amount in the future. Alternatively, an increase in the rate of interest reduces the present value, given the time horizon, because a smaller sum today is needed to grow into a specified future value (or, equivalentlty, future values are discounted more heavily – that is, *valued less* – at higher interest rates). Finally, holding the future value and the rate of interest constant, increasing the time horizon also reduces the present value. This reflects the fact that the longer the time span is over which an amount invested today has to grow to some specified future value, the smaller the initial amount invested needs to be. To illustrate, suppose that I want to have $100 in the future and the current rate of interest is 10%. If I define the future to be 2 years, then I need to invest $82.64 today. If I define the future to be 8 years, then I need only invest $46.65 today. The present value has decreased as the time horizon extends further into the future.

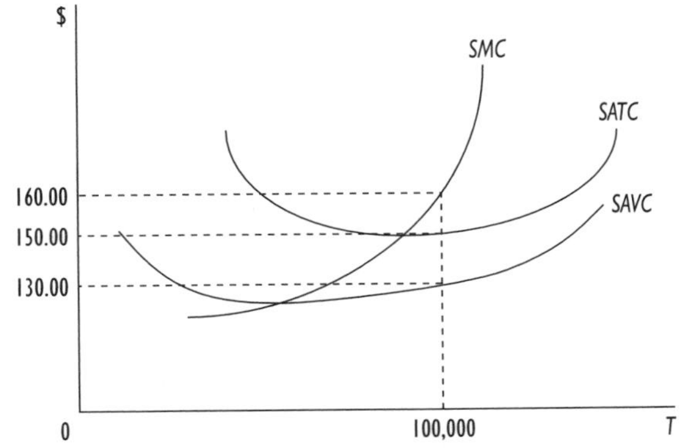

Figure 9.2 The short-run cost structure for an air carrier.

EXAMPLE I

Suppose that an airplane company experiences an increase in the demand for its flights. However, because the company is not sure whether the increase in demand is permanent or temporary, the company forgoes the option of a purchasing a new plane. Rather, it considers leasing a plane for 2 years, at the end of which period the company will re-evaluate its decision.[8] In leasing the plane for 2 years, the firm faces the short-run variable cost curves depicted in figure 9.2. Demand projections indicate that the plane will attract 100,000 passengers per year at a proposed per trip fare of \$160.00. The annual market rate of interest is 10%. The leasing cost of the plane is \$3,471,074. Should the company lease the plane?

The relevant piece of information to the firm is its expected producer's surplus if the firm leases the plane. At a trip price of \$160.00, the firm has expected revenues of \$16 million at the end of the first year and \$16 million at the end of the second year. From figure 9.2, we see that the firm's average variable cost for each of the 100,000 passengers carried is \$130.00 per trip. Thus, at the end of each year, the firm's expected gross return on capital investment – that is, its quasi-rent (producer surplus) – is \$30.00 per trip or \$3 million per year. But since the \$3 million is received at the end of each year, each year's income must be discounted to present value terms. Given a 10% rate of interest, the present value of the firm's 2 year stream of quasi-rents is

$$
\begin{aligned}
PV &= \frac{\$3{,}000{,}000}{(1.1)} + \frac{\$3{,}000{,}000}{(1.1)^2} \\
&= \$2{,}727{,}727 + \$2{,}479{,}339 \\
&= \$5{,}207{,}166
\end{aligned}
$$

To determine whether the plane's purchase is an economically sound investment, the firm compares the discounted present value of its expected quasi-rents with the present value lease cost of the plane. Since the 2 year lease has a present value cost of $3,471,074, the firm will purchase the plane. In present-value terms, the firm receives an economic profit equal to $5,207,166 – $3,471,074 = $1,736,092.

Notice that the total lease cost of the plane was given to the firm as $3,471,074. But figure 9.2 represents the lease cost of the plane as a stream of fixed costs over a 2 year period ($2,000,000 each period). This reflects the fact that any present value can be converted into an *equivalent* series of equal future values; that is, an annuity. Recall equation (9.6), which defines the present value in terms of a series of identical future values:

$$PV = FV\left[\frac{(1+i)^t - 1}{i(1+i)^t}\right]$$

Solving this equation for FV, our present-value formulation is equivalent to a series of equal future values, given as[9]

$$FV = PV\left[\frac{i(1+i)^t}{(1+i)^t - 1}\right] \tag{9.8}$$

where the bracketed term is referred to as the "capital recovery factor." Faced with a 2 year lease cost of $3,471,074, the firm could use equation (9.8) to define two annual fixed cost payments of

$$\begin{aligned} FV &= 3{,}471{,}074\,\frac{0.1(1.1)^2}{(1.1)^2 - 1} \\ &= 3{,}471{,}074\ (0.5762) \\ &= \$2{,}000{,}000 \end{aligned} \tag{9.9}$$

At a 10% rate of interest, two equal payments of $2 million paid at the end of the first and second years, respectively, "recover" the 2 year lease cost of the plane plus foregone interest. In each of the two years, one-half of the capital cost, $1,735,537, is recovered plus an annual interest cost equal to $264,463.

We have seen that the firm's investment in the aircraft yields a gross annual return of $3 million, which is equivalent to the present value of the firm's expected quasi-rents, $5,207,166. Of this amount, $3,471,074 is allocated to recover the cost of the plane, leaving a pure profit of $1,736,092. For the 2 year life of the investment project, this implies a *benefit : cost* ratio, given by the ratio ($5,207,166/$3,471,074), equal to 1.5. A benefit : cost ratio greater than one is an alternative way of stating that the initial investment project is worthwhile, since it implies that the firm is making a return on its investment that exceeds the 10% return available on highest-valued alternative investments. If the benefit : cost ratio were less than one, revenues generated by the project would not be sufficient to pay the project's costs plus providing a normal return on investment.

When the benefit : cost ratio equals one, the investment generates sufficient revenues to give the firm a normal return on its investment. For example, suppose that the minimum point on the average total cost curve corresponds to a price of \$145 per trip and 80,000 trips. Also assume that average variable cost at this level of output is \$120. In this case, quasi-rent in each period is \$2,000,000 which, from (9.9), gives a present value identical to the aircraft's capital cost. The project's benefit : cost ratio is one and the firm is just making a normal return on investment.

DISCOUNTED PRESENT VALUE – VARIABLE STREAM OF NET BENEFITS

In the above calculations, our discounting process assumed a constant value for the future value over the life of the investment good. In general, the flow of quasi-rents or net benefits reflects a capital good's underlying benefits and costs, which are not necessarily equal from period to period. Moreover, it is possible that the capital will have some nonzero scrap value. A more general specification of discounted present value is net present value, *NPV*. Let B_0 be firm revenues at the beginning of the first period, C_0 be the cost of capital at the beginning of the first period, B_i be annual firm revenues at the end of period i ($i = 1, \ldots, t$), C_i be annual operating expenditures at the end of period i ($i = 1, \ldots, t$), and S the salvage value of capital at the end of capital's useful life t. The firm's net present value is

$$NPV = B_0 - C_0 + \frac{(B_1 - C_1)}{(1+i)} + \frac{(B_2 - C_2)}{(1+i)^2} + \ldots + \frac{(B_t - C_t)}{(1+i)^t} + \frac{S}{(1+i)^t} \tag{9.10}$$

Notice that this formulation accounts for each of the components of the user cost of capital: (1) the discount rate used in the process accounts for the interest opportunity cost of capital; (2) including the initial cost of capital C_0 and capital's salvage value S at the end of its useful life implicitly accounts for capital depreciation; and (3) changes in the stream of operating profits B_i ($i = 1, \ldots, t$) implicitly account for capital obsolescence or capital appreciation. Also, recall that capital maintenance expenditures are included in the stream of operating costs C_i since they are output-related.

EXAMPLE 2

Table 9.1 summarizes the expected stream of costs and revenues associated with the purchase of a new piece of capital with an expected life span of 5 years. The expected costs represent a capital initial outlay at the beginning of period 1 plus annual production and output-related maintenance costs over the five years. The expected benefits are the revenues generated each year from the firm's productive activity. The initial cost of capital is \$75,000 and the rate of interest is 12%. It is assumed that no revenues are received at the beginning of the first period.

On the basis of the data presented, purchasing the machine is worthwhile. The series of quasi-rents plus the scrap value are sufficient to cover all costs of the capital good. And the \$5,176 net present value figure is the economic (or pure) profit received by the owner; that is, the amount by which the owner's wealth is increased in present-value terms.

Table 9.1 Annual costs and benefits

Year	Benefit[a]	Cost[a]	Scrap Value[b]
Beginning of Year 1	$0.00	–$75,000.00	$0.00
End of Year 1	$50,000.00	$5,000.00	$0.00
End of Year 2	$40,000.00	$8,000.00	$0.00
End of Year 3	$25,000.00	$13,000.00	$0.00
End of Year 4	$19,000.00	$15,000.00	$0.00
End of Year 5	$17,000.00	$16,000.00	$5,000.00

$$NPV = -75{,}000 + \frac{45{,}000}{1.12} + \frac{32{,}000}{(1.12)^2} + \frac{12{,}000}{(1.12)^3} + \frac{4{,}000}{(1.12)^4} + \frac{1{,}000}{(1.12)^5} + \frac{5{,}000}{(1.12)^5}$$
$$= -75{,}000 + 40{,}179 + 25{,}510 + 8{,}541 + 2{,}542 + 567 + 2{,}837$$
$$= \$5{,}176$$

[a] Benefit equals firm revenues. At the beginning of the first period, there are no revenues, but there is a capital cost outlay equal to $75,000. Included in operating costs are maintenance expenditures. Implicit in reduced costs from Year 1 to Year 5 is capital obsolescence.
[b] Implicit in the difference between the initial capital cost and the discounted scrap value is capital depreciation.

CAPITAL PROJECT CHOICE

Suppose that a firm has one capital expenditure under consideration. Then its decision to go ahead with the investment will depend, as seen above, upon its net present value calculation. There are three possibilities:

Net Present Value Criterion	$NPV > 0$	$\Rightarrow$	undertake investment
	$NPV = 0$	$\Rightarrow$	indifference
	$NPV < 0$	$\Rightarrow$	reject investment

Since all revenues and economic costs have been incorporated into the net present value calculation, positive net present value indicates that, in addition to covering all relevant costs, the firm enjoys a pure economic profit. The firm earns a return greater than that available elsewhere. On the other hand, the firm is indifferent to undertaking the investment if the net present value is zero, since it will be earning a return on its investment that just matches its next best alternative. Finally, in the event that the net present value is negative, the firm rejects the project, since it would be earning a return that is lower than that available on its next best alternative.

The problem is a little more complicated when there are multiple capital projects under consideration. Suppose that a firm is considering four capital projects that are *not* mutually exclusive; that is, undertaking one capital expenditure does not preclude any of the other projects. The costs of projects 1, 2, 3, and 4 are $35,000, $20,000, $50,000, and $35,000, respectively. In this case, net present values are calculated for each of the projects and ranked in order. Assume that the net present values of the four projects are as follows:

Table 9.2 Wealth effects of alternative investment projects

(a) Project	(b) Initial Wealth	(c) Project(s) Cost	(d) Project(s) Benefit	(e) Net Benefit (d) – (c)	(f) Remaining Cash (b) – (c)	(g) Final Wealth (d) + (f)
None	\$60,000	\$0	\$0	\$0	\$60,000	\$60,000
1	\$60,000	\$35,000	\$47,500	\$12,500	\$25,000	\$72,500
2	\$60,000	\$20,000	\$26,200	\$6,200	\$40,000	\$66,200
3	\$60,000	\$50,000	\$65,000	\$15,000	\$10,000	\$75,000
4	\$60,000	\$35,000	\$36,025	\$1,025	\$25,000	\$61,025
1&2	\$60,000	\$55,000	\$73,700	\$18,700	\$5,000	\$78,700
2&4	\$60,000	\$55,000	\$62,225	\$7,225	\$5,000	\$67,225

$$NPV_3 = \$15{,}000.00$$
$$NPV_1 = \$12{,}500.00$$
$$NPV_2 = \$6{,}200.00$$
$$NPV_4 = \$1{,}025.00$$

Ideally, the firm would like to pursue all of these projects, since each has a positive net present value. However, if a firm does not have sufficient resources, \$140,000 in this case, to pursue all projects with a positive net present value, then it is forced to *ration its capital*. Suppose that the firm only has \$60,000 available for capital expenditures. It could undertake project 3, since this yields the highest net present value. But this is not profit-maximizing. Although project 3 yields a \$15,000 pure profit, the firm would be sacrificing a pure profit of \$18,700. This is because the firm could afford to fund projects 1 and 2 (whose total cost is \$55,000). Thus, if a firm is considering multiple projects which are not mutually exclusive, it should invest in those projects that yield the *highest total* net present value. Table 9.2 illustrates this principle. On the other hand, suppose that a firm considers projects some of which *are* mutually exclusive. Undertaking one project precludes investment in one or more other projects. In this case, we select that project or group of projects that is not mutually exclusive with the other projects and that yields the highest total net present value. Using the example in table 9.2, if project 1 is mutually exclusive from all other projects, then the firm's choices, given its limited funds, are to invest in: (1) project 1, 2, 3, or 4 separately; or (2) projects 2 and 4 at a combined cost of \$55,000. The net present values of these five options are \$12,500, \$6,200, \$15,000, \$1,025, and \$7,225, respectively. In this case, the firm funds project 3.

THE EFFECTS OF INFLATION ON NET PRESENT VALUES

Our discussion on net present values has implicitly assumed a stable price level; that is, inflation has been absent from our analysis. In the real world, however, the general price level does rise. What effect does inflation (or deflation) have upon a firm's investment decision? To see this, we need to distinguish between nominal prices and real prices. Recall that *nominal*

Table 9.3 Per-mile costs of owning and operating an automobile: 1950–91 (cents per mile)

Year	(a) Nominal Price	(b) Real Price (1990 $)
1950	6.6	35.8
1960	9.8	43.3
1970	11.9	40.1
1975	18.3	44.2
1980	27.9	44.2
1982	32.3	43.7
1984	31.3	39.4
1986	29.6	35.3
1988	33.4	36.9
1990	41.0	41.0
1991	43.6	41.8

Source: *Statistical Abstract of the United States*, various years. Nominal prices converted to real prices using the consumer price index, 1990 = 100

prices are prices of goods quoted in current dollars. These are "list" prices for commodities that are prevalent during each time period. *Real* prices, on the other hand, are nominal prices adjusted for price level changes (inflation or deflation), and can be expressed as

$$p_r = \frac{p_n}{(1 + \dot{p})}$$

$$\Rightarrow \quad p_n = p_r(1 + \dot{p})$$

where p_n is the nominal (current) price, p_r is the real (constant dollar) price, and $\dot{p}$ is the rate of inflation (that is, the percentage change in prices). Thus, the real price of a good is simply its nominal price deflated by one plus the price rise; alternatively, the nominal price is the real price adjusted for the change in prices. As an example, the average price of an airline ticket from New York to Washington DC in 1991 was $56. Suppose that the average price in 1992 rose to $60.00. If the rate of inflation between 1991 and 1992 were 7%, then the fare would increase in 1992 to 56(1 + 0.07) = $59.92. In this example, although the nominal price has risen, there is virtually no change in the constant dollar (real) price (since 56 = 59.92/1.07) of the ticket.[10]

Table 9.3 provides another example of the difference between real and nominal prices. Column (a) gives nominal costs of owning and operating an automobile from 1950 through 1991. In 1950, the per mile cost of owning and operating a vehicle was 6.6 cents. In 1975, on the other hand, the cost was 18.3 cents per mile. Column (b) reports the same costs adjusted for the overall change in prices between 1975 and 1991. These costs are given in 1990 dollars. Thus, in terms of 1990 purchasing power, it would have cost 35.8 cents per mile to own and operate a vehicle in 1950. Comparing columns (a) and (b), nominal costs steadily increased from 6.6 cents to 32.3 cents per mile in 1982, fell between 1982 and 1986, and then rose from 29.6 to 43.6 from 1986 through 1991. The real cost of owning and operating one's vehicle, however, showed much less fluctuation. It remained reasonably constant between 1960 and 1982, a remarkable finding given the significant oil price increases during the early and mid-1970s. The real price peaked in 1982 and has since fallen. Moreover, relative to 1960, the real cost of owning and operating one's vehicle in 1991 was actually *less*!

Similar to other prices, interest rates can be stated in nominal or real terms. Recall the compound factor $1 + i$, which reflects the income received next year on a dollar invested today at interest rate i. If i_n and i_r is the nominal and real rate of interest, respectively, then the compound factor, expressed in nominal terms, is

$$(1 + i_n) = (1 + i_r)(1 + \dot{p}) \tag{9.11}$$

which is the compound factor in real terms, $(1 + i_r)$, adjusted for the change in prices. If we expand the right-hand side of equation (9.11), we obtain $(1 + i_r + \dot{p} + i_r\dot{p}) \approx (1 + i_r + \dot{p})$, assuming that the product $i_r\dot{p}$ is negligibly small. This implies that the nominal rate of interest is approximately equal to the real rate of interest plus the inflation rate. If, for example, the real rate of interest is 3% and inflation is expected to be 3%, then the nominal rate of interest – that is, the interest rate you see quoted in newspapers – would be approximately 6%.

To determine whether inflation affects net present value results, let B_s and C_s ($s = 0, \ldots, t$) be real net revenues and nonoutput-related maintenance costs, which are assumed to be constant over the life of the capital project. In addition, assume that the real rate of interest is used to convert future to present values. Then the net present value is

$$NPV = B_0 - C_0 + \sum_s \frac{(B - C)}{(1 + i_r)^s} \tag{9.12}$$

where, for simplicity, revenues and costs do not have subscripts since they are assumed to be equal for each period. Alternatively, suppose that we express revenues, costs, and interest rates in nominal terms and assume a constant annual rate of inflation equal to $\dot{p}$. Then

$$\begin{aligned} NPV &= B_0 - C_0 + \sum_s \frac{(B - C)(1 + \dot{p})^s}{(1 + i_n)^s} \\ &= B_0 - C_0 + \sum_s \frac{(B - C)(1 + \dot{p})^s}{(1 + i_r)^s(1 + \dot{p})^s} \\ &= B_0 - C_0 + \sum_t \frac{(B - C)}{(1 + i_r)^s} \end{aligned} \tag{9.13}$$

Since the inflation rate equally affects revenues, costs, and interest rates in each period, it does not affect the discounting process in periods 1 through t. Also, since B_0 and C_0 occur at the beginning of the first period, $\dot{p}$ is zero. To summarize, the inflation does not affect a firm's investment decisions as long as:

1. Revenues, costs, and the interest are expressed consistently. If net revenues are expressed in nominal terms, then interest must be expressed in nominal terms. Similarly, if net revenues are expressed in real terms, interest must be expressed in real terms.
2. Inflation affects each of the components *identically*. In reality, this is not likely to occur. In times of inflation, it is generally the case that some prices will be affected more than others.

Assume, for example, that the initial cost of a capital project is $4,000 and quasi-rents, in real terms, are constant over the 4 year life of the project, at $3,000 per year. If there is no inflation and the real interest rate is 5%, net present value is

$$NPV = -4{,}000 + \frac{3{,}000}{1.05} + \frac{3{,}000}{(1.05)^2} + \frac{3{,}000}{(1.05)^3} + \frac{3{,}000}{(1.05)^4}$$

$$= \$6{,}931$$

If there were an 8% inflation which affected quasi-rents and interest rates *equally* then, by equation (9.13), net present value would also be $6,931. Suppose, however, that producer surpluses rise at 8% per year, whereas nominal interest rates rise 4% per year. Then, net present value is

$$NPV = -4{,}000 + \frac{3{,}000(1.08)}{1.05(1.04)} + \frac{3{,}000(1.08)^2}{(1.05)^2(1.04)^2} + \frac{3{,}000(1.08)^3}{(1.05)^3(1.04)^3} + \frac{3{,}000(1.08)^4}{(1.05)^4(1.04)^4}$$

$$= \$7{,}674$$

Since inflation affects interest rates half as much as producer surpluses, the net present value has increased (by 11% in this case). Thus, in inflationary periods, one must be careful to consider inflation's separate effects on the proposed project's revenues, costs, and interest rate.

CASE STUDY – THE VALUE OF MOTOR CARRIER OPERATING CERTIFICATES UNDER REGULATION

If market entry restrictions are effective constraints on market supply, incumbent firms in the restricted industry will reap the benefits in the form of economic profits. We have already seen this in the motor carrier industry (chapter 7), where we found that demand determinants (for example, population and retail sales) and per unit profit determinants (for example, network size) affected the value of an operating certificate. Based upon typical demand and per unit profit characteristics, Frew (1981) estimated the value of an operating certificate for a regular route general commodity carrier as $50,334 in 1972 dollars.[11] For an irregular route general commodity carrier, a typical certificate was valued at $42,838. The operating certificate for a specialized carrier, on the other hand, was valued considerably less at $12,490. In each of these instances, the certificate value reflects the discounted present value of economic profits expected to be earned in the market.

Data for these estimates were obtained over a period of years between 1971 and 1977. An interesting question is whether certificate buyers expected motor carrier deregulation to pass and whether deregulation would fully dissipate these rents. The likely answer to the first question is yes, since market participants have a vested interest in keeping abreast of industry changes. And let's assume that the answer to the second question is also yes. What does this imply regarding per period monopoly rents associated with these operating certificates? Assuming a 5% interest rate and an expected 6 year time horizon, the annual economic profit expected from a regular route general commodity operating certificate, from equation (9.8), is $9,917 (1972 dollars).[12] Based upon similar assumptions, the annual economic rent associated with an irregular route general commodity carrier and a specialized carrier, respectively, is $8,440 and $2,461. In other words, if potential buyers of operating certificates in the early 1970s correctly anticipated economic deregulation, then, knowing that the stream of economic profits would disappear with deregulation, their willingness to pay for an operating certificate would be considerably less (for example, $9,917 versus $42,838 for an irregular route general commodity carrier certificate) than if they expected those rents to continue forever.

CASE STUDY – THE VALUE OF TAXI MEDALLIONS

Most cities regulate market entry for taxicab services and these restrictions tend to be more restrictive the larger the city. In an analysis of taxicab markets in the USA, Frankena and Pautler (1984) report that the number of fully licensed cabs in New York City actually declined from 13,566 in 1937 to 11,800 in 1982. The number of licensed taxis in Chicago modestly rose from 4,108 in 1934 to 4,600 in 1982. And Detroit had no change in the 1,310 taxis operating in the city between 1946 and 1983. To the extent that they generate monopoly profits, these restraints endow the owners of taxi operating certificates, called "medallions," with value.

Table 9.4 reports the 1980 population, the number of licenses per capita, and the value of taxi medallions for various cities in the USA. The highest price for a medallion is in the $50,000–$60,000 range in New York City, which reflects the high demand for taxis, particularly in Manhattan. Similarly, although at 2.9, the number of licenses per 1,000 population is highest in Boston, the medallion price is also reasonably high at $32,000, again reflecting a large demand for taxis in the city. These high medallion prices reflect the extent to which restrictions on market entry confer monopoly rents to the incumbent firms. Multiplying the number of licenses by the price per medallion, the restriction on market access generated a total monopoly rent for New York City at least equal to $590 million. A comparable calculation for Boston puts the minimum monopoly rent at $48.8 million.

At the other end of the spectrum, we see that New Orleans had a high number of taxi licenses per 1,000 population and a relatively low medallion price at $3,000. The low medallion price

Table 9.4 Value of taxi medallions, various years[a]

City	Year	1980 Population	Licenses per 1,000 Population	Medallion Price
Boston	1983	563,000	2.7	$32,000–33,000
Chicago	1970	3,005,000	1.5	$15,000 or more
Dallas	1976	904,000	1.0	$3,000
Houston	1983	1,595,000	1.1	$10,000–12,000
Indianapolis	1980	701,000	0.5	$400–500
Miami (Dade)	1979	1,626,000	0.9	$18,000
Minneapolis	1983	371,000	0.7	$8,000–12,000
New Orleans	1976	558,000	2.9	$3,000
New York City	1983	7,072,000	1.7	$50,000–60,000
Portland, Oregon	1979	366,000	0.7	$3,000–9,000
San Diego	1979	876,000	0.8	$8,000–15,000
San Diego	1983	876,000	1.0	$1,000–2,000
San Francisco	1983	679,000	1.0	$15,000–20,000

[a] In some cases, a range was presented. The numbers reported give the lower end of the range.
Source: Frankena and Pautler (1984), table 5, pp. 106–7

implies that the restrictions on market entry in New Orleans are less constraining and, accordingly, confer fewer economic benefits on incumbents. Total monopoly rent from entry restrictions in 1976 was only \$4.8 million.

San Diego provides an interesting case. In 1979 the number of licenses per 1,000 population increased from 0.8 to 1.0.[13] The increase in market entry had the expected effect upon the price of a taxi medallion, decreasing the medallion price from \$8,000 or more to \$2,000 or less. This resulted in a minimum loss of economic profits to the industry equal to \$3.8 million (\$5.6 – \$1.8).

One also sees that the least price paid for a medallion is in Indianapolis. Although Indianapolis had the fewest number of licenses per 1,000 population, the low medallion price indicates that entry restrictions have virtually no effect upon economic profits. In total, maximum monopoly rents earned from the 326 licenses was \$163,000.

EFFICIENT PRICING AND INVESTMENT

Consider a competitive firm that spends $P_K K$ on capital in the current period, where P_K is the asset cost per unit of capital. In addition, the firm receives producer surpluses equal to $(p_s - AVC_s)T_s$ in period s. If the firm operates for t periods, then its discounted net present value, which gives the present value of its profits over the t periods, is given by the expression

$$NPV = \sum_{s=1}^{t}\left(\frac{(p_s - AVC_s)T_s}{(1+i)^s}\right) - P_K K \tag{9.14}$$

where the first term reflects the discounted present value of operating profits and the second term is the firm's expenditures upon capital. Assuming that it wants to maximize discounted present value profits, the firm must satisfy two optimality conditions which characterize *first-best pricing and investment* behavior:

Optimality Condition 1: $$\frac{p_s}{(1+i)^s} = \frac{AVC_s + T_s(\Delta AVC_s/\Delta T_s)}{(1+i)^s}, \qquad s = 1, \ldots, t$$

$$\Rightarrow p_s = AVC_s + T_s\frac{\Delta AVC_s}{\Delta T_s}, \qquad s = 1, \ldots, t \tag{9.15}$$

Optimality Condition 2: $$P_K = -\sum_{s=1}^{t}\frac{T_s(\Delta AVC_s/\Delta T_s)}{(1+i)^s}$$

$$\Rightarrow r = \text{“}crf\text{”}\ P_K = \text{annualized cost of capital} \tag{9.16}$$

Equation (9.15) is a *marginal cost pricing* rule. In each period s, the firm sets price equal to marginal cost, where the right-hand side of the equation is another way of writing the marginal cost of production.[14] According to equation (9.15), maximum net present value is obtained if the firm produces in each period in which price equals marginal cost of production, which is simply our profit-maximizing pricing rule that we met previously.[15]

Equation (9.16) is an efficiency rule for capital investment, and says that a firm optimally invests in capital when the marginal cost of an additional unit of capital P_K equals the marginal benefit of capital. Capital investment benefits the firm by lowering the firm's average variable cost of production in each period s; that is, $\Delta AVC_s/\Delta K < 0$. Thus, in any given time period s, the firm's benefit is the total reduction in production costs, defined as $T_s(\Delta AVC_s/\Delta K)$ and equal to $(\Delta STVC_s/\Delta K)$.[16] Discounting the benefits in each of these periods and summing over the entire time horizon gives the marginal return to the firm from its capital investment. Also, since capital investment reduces total production costs, the negative sign in front of the discounted costs converts the cost savings from a negative number to a positive number.

Recalling that any present value can be converted into a series of equivalent payments, Optimality Condition 2 can be equivalently expressed in terms of the user cost of capital, where r is the rental price of capital and "*crf*," the inverse of the bracketed term, is the capital recovery factor defined in equation (9.8).[17] Thus, Optimality Condition 2 implies that profit-maximizing competitive firms invest in capital up to the point at which the per period cost of capital just equals the per period revenues generated by the capital increment.[18]

EMPIRICAL IMPLEMENTATION OF OPTIMALITY RULES

From equation (9.14), a firm seeks to maximize discounted present value profits, defined as the difference between its discounted present value quasi-rents and current capital costs. But how do we determine whether firms in a given industry at a given point in time behave efficiently? After all, at any point in time firms have already invested in a depreciating and obsolescing stock of capital, and are continually evaluating whether to invest in additional capital projects or to disinvest in their existing stock. If the firm invests, does it also face a capital rationing problem and can it postpone some investment activities with additional maintenance expenditures? It takes little effort to recognize the vast complexities associated with trying to empirically identify relevant producer surplus streams generated from past, present, and expected future capital expenditure programs that firms actually undertake.

To apply our optimality rules empirically, we use two previously derived results. First, we know that any discounted present value is equivalent to a fixed value annuity. This implies that we can analyze a firm's efficiency by focusing upon *annualized* costs and revenues. Therefore, per period long-run and short-run cost structures, similar to those depicted in figure 9.2, are appropriate models for characterizing firm behavior. Second, the user cost of capital provides a reasonable approximation to the annual cost of long-lived capital. From equation (9.16), $r = (crf)P_K$ approximates the annual user cost of capital and so approximates the annual operating cost savings that an additional unit of capital has upon a firm's variable cost of production; that is,

$$-T_s\frac{\Delta AVC}{\Delta K} = -\frac{\Delta STVC}{\Delta K} = r \qquad (9.17)$$

If we divide both sides of this equation by the asset price of capital, P_K, we obtain

$$-\frac{(\Delta STVC/\Delta K)}{P_K} = \frac{r}{P_K} = i_{\text{gross}} = (i_{\text{net}} + \delta + \dot{p}) \qquad (9.18)$$

where i_{gross} and i_{net} are the gross and net returns on investment, respectively. A firm continues to invest up to the point at which marginal benefit equals marginal cost; that is, a firm invests as long as the gross saving in operating costs divided by capital's price exceeds the gross rate of return on investment, i_{gross}. Alternatively, since $r/P_K = rK/P_K K$, i_{gross} also has the interpretation of a return on invested capital. Subtracting the rates of depreciation and obsolescence from both sides of equation (9.18) implies that investment continues up to the point at which net operating cost savings as a proportion of invested capital equals the net return on investment.

Thus, equation (9.17) or (9.18) can be used to obtain an optimal level of capital where estimated cost functions are used to measure the effect on annual operating costs from increased capital investment (the left-hand side of equation (9.17) or (9.18)). Alternatively, available information on the interest opportunity cost of capital and depreciation can be used with the asset price of capital to calculate a gross return on investment.[19]

In empirical studies, capital investments are analyzed to answer any or all of the following questions. First, given existing output and capital investment decisions, would firms obtain a normal return on investment under marginal cost pricing? This focuses upon the pricing rule to the exclusion of efficient capital investment considerations. Second, given existing pricing and output decisions, what is the optimal level of capital? By seeking a point on the long-run cost curve at the existing level of output, this question focuses on the investment decision to the exclusion of the pricing rule. Third, what is the optimal level of capital if firms also price at long-run marginal cost? A corollary to each of the latter two questions is determining whether the firm makes a normal return on its investment when it optimally invests in capital. If the net return on investment is less than the prevalent opportunity cost of capital, the firm is overcapitalized and capital downsizing is called for. Conversely, if i_{net} is greater than the opportunity cost of capital, the firm is undercapitalized and capital investment is appropriate. Last, if i_{net} is approximately the same as the opportunity cost of capital, the firm's current level of capital is optimal.

For competitive markets, Optimality Conditions 1 and 2 represent a firm's first best pricing and investment behavior. Based upon annualized costs and revenues, setting price equal to short-run marginal cost using equation (9.15) and calculating an optimal level of capital from equation (9.17) (or (9.18)) satisfies optimal pricing and investment rules and leads to an efficient allocation of resources.

In the sections that follow, we examine how these efficiency rules have been used to analyze resource allocation in two markets, urban bus transit and railroads. It is important to recognize that each of these transportation markets is not competitive, but is a government-regulated market. Because government regulatory actions oftentimes have objectives other than economic efficiency, government policies may result in significant misallocations of our nation's resources. Thus, the objective in applying Optimality Conditions 1 and 2 to these transportation markets is to evaluate the extent to which past regulatory policies have succeeded or failed in allocating resources efficiently.

CASE STUDY – OPTIMAL PRICING AND INVESTMENT IN URBAN BUS TRANSIT SYSTEMS

In chapter 5 we examined the relationship between short-run and long-run cost curves for US urban transit systems. In order to relate some of the findings in chapter 5 to the concepts developed in this chapter, a brief re-examination of those results is useful. For the purposes of this discussion, three empirical findings reported in chapter 5 are of particular interest.

1 At existing output and capital levels prevalent in 1975, each of the representative bus systems identified in table 5.16 (in chapter 5) operated under economies of density, where the short-run average variable cost exceeded the short-run marginal cost.
2 From the short-run cost estimation results presented in table 5.15 (in chapter 5), a 1% increase in buses (capital rolling stock) increased short-run total variable costs by 0.57% at the sample mean.
3 At the level of output prevailing in 1975, large bus systems such as that of Chicago, Illinois operated under long-run diseconomies of scale and smaller systems – for example, in Greenfield, Massachusetts – operated under long-run economies of scale. These economies of scale were based upon a system's optimal fleet size; that is, a policy of efficient capital investment. Using the estimated cost function (table 6.4 in chapter 6) to calculate operating cost savings from an additional bus and calculating the user cost of capital for an additonal bus as $727, a system's optimal fleet size was estimated using equation (9.17).[20]

These factors provide a number of interesting insights into urban transit pricing and investment decisions. First, from empirical finding 1, marginal cost pricing, conditioned upon existing levels of output and capital investment, not only requires capital subsidies but also operating subsidies. That is, short-run marginal cost pricing is not sufficient to cover all variable costs of production. Or equivalently, marginal cost pricing leads to negative producer surpluses. Second, empirical finding 2 provides corroboration of urban transit financing problems under short-run marginal cost pricing. From equation (9.18), empirical finding 2 implies that

$$-\frac{(\Delta STVC/\Delta K)}{P_K} = i_{\text{gross}} = (i_{\text{net}} + \delta) < 0$$

where we have assumed that $\dot{p}_K = 0$. The *positive* effect of an increase in rolling stock on short-run total variable costs implies that the gross return on capital is negative, assuming that the user cost of capital is a reasonable approximation of annual capital cost.[21] Moreover, given a positive depreciation rate, a negative gross rate of return also implies a negative net rate of return on investment at the sample mean. Thus, urban transit systems at existing operating levels in 1975 appear to be making a return on investment well below the 6.75% interest opportunity cost of capital prevalent at the time.

Last, and consistent with the negative net return on existing investment, chapter 6 presented evidence that urban transit systems were overcapitalized by as much as 57% in comparison with optimal capital investment. Empirical finding 3 tells us that when firms optimally invest to produce existing levels of output, smaller urban transit properties operate under increasing returns to scale, whereas larger properties operate under decreasing returns to scale. In other words, under optimal pricing and investment behavior, smaller urban transit properties are expected to yield returns on investment that are below normal, since $LRMC < LRAC$, whereas the larger properties will produce above-normal rates of return on investment, where $LRMC > LRAC$.

However, it must also be remembered that Viton's analysis focuses upon public transit production costs to the exclusion of user time costs. Mohring's (1976) result that transit companies that seek to minimize production costs plus user time costs operate under increasing returns to scale alters the above results. Savings in variable costs from expanded capacity accrue both to the transit authority in the form of lower production costs as well as to bus riders in the form of lower time costs. This implies that optimal pricing will lead to larger optimal fleets (as pointed out in chapter 6) and higher rates of return in comparision to those suggested by Viton's analysis.[22]

CASE STUDY – OPTIMAL PRICING AND INVESTMENT IN RAIL TRANSPORT

In chapter 6, we examined the regulated rail industry and implications for the industry if marginal cost pricing was adopted. In that section, we posed the following question. If the rail industry adopted marginal cost pricing in transporting manufactured and bulk commodities, how would price and output change relative to that observed in the regulated environment? This led to a number of interesting and some unexpected findings regarding resource allocation in rail transport. To summarize, we saw in tables 6.3 and 6.4 of chapter 6 that marginal cost pricing implied increased rail rates on manufactured goods in both the Official and the South-West Regions, and a decrease in bulk rates in each of these regions. In addition, in the absence of marginal cost pricing, the resulting misallocation of resources produced a $746 and $377 million deadweight loss in the Official and South-West Regions respectively.

A further result was the improved profitability of railroads if marginal cost pricing was adopted. Whereas railroads lost an estimated $251 million in 1972 under regulation, they were predicted to earn $1.2 billion under marginal cost pricing. Given a capital stock estimated at $17.98 billion, this represents a gross rate of return equal to ($1.2/$17.89)(100) = 6.6%. Friedlaender and Spady (1981) estimated that railroad capital depreciates by 2% per year and pays 1.2% of its value in property taxes per year. Deducting these from the gross rate of return yields a 3.4% net rate of return.[23] In 1972, the opportunity cost of capital was estimated to be in the 9% range, which implies that the 3.4% return on capital investment was insufficient to give the industry a normal return on investment.

The effect of capital investment on short-run total costs

The results thus far present only a part of the profitability picture for railroads. The move from a regulated to a competitive environment was a move to a *short-run* competitive equilibrium. That is, we examined the allocative effects of marginal cost pricing, holding capital constant at its present (1972) level. This suggests a number of additional questions that are specifically related to capital investment. In this section, we begin by examining the effect of increased capital spending upon short-run total variable costs and rate of return on investment.

We once again draw upon Friedlaender and Spady's (1981) estimation results. Most relevant to our present purpose are their results related to capital investment decisions. Since Friedlaender and Spady estimated a short-run translog cost function, capital investment is included as one of the explanatory variables, which implies that we can identify the effect on short-run total costs, at the sample mean, from an increase in capital investment. Table 9.5 gives the first-order coefficient for capital, the cost elasticity of capital, and factor demand elasticities with respect to capital investment.

The results presented in table 9.5 correspond to the regulated environment in which railroads operated in the early 1970s. In the top half of the table, we see that a $1 increase in capital produces a cost savings to the railroad of 10.9 cents, which corresponds to a 13.08% gross rate of return on investment.[24] Alternatively, a 1% increase in capital expenditures reduces short-run total variable costs by 0.426%. As expected, there is an inverse relationship between total variable costs and capital investment. Increased railroad capital in the form of ways and structures produces lower operating costs of rail transport. Further, deducting 2% depreciation and 1.2% property tax from the gross rate of return yields a 9.9% return on investment, at the sample mean. This tells us that a railroad operating

Table 9.5 Capital expenditures in the rail industry

(a) Cost effects of increased capital expenditures[a]

Marginal Cost Savings from $1 of Invested Capital ($)	Elasticity of Cost
−0.109	−0.426

(b) Factor demand effects of increased capital expenditures[a]

Capital Equipment	General Labor	Yard and Switching Labor	On-Train Labor	Fuel and Materials
−1.065	−0.306	−0.289	−0.194	−0.058

[a] Evaluated at the sample mean.
Source: Adapted from Friedlaender and Spady (1981), table 4.1, p. 124, with the permission of the MIT Press. Copyright © 1981 Massachusetts Institute of Technology

near the sample mean was receiving a normal return on its investment.

However, the fact that a railroad operating at the sample mean receives a normal return on investment does not imply that resources were efficiently allocated during regulation, for two reasons. First, as we have previously seen, railroads were not following a marginal cost pricing rule. Second, a normal return on investment at the sample mean does not imply that each railroad carrier is making a normal return on investment. Among the 19 railroad firms included in their study, Friedlaender and Spady found that only four firms were optimally invested. Nine companies were overinvested and making below-normal rates of return, while six companies were underinvested and received above-normal rates of return.

The lower part of the table identifies the factor demand elasticities associated with a 1% increase in capital investment and provides information on how operational cost savings are achieved. Suppose, for example, that a railroad increases capital investment by 10%. The cost elasticity tells us that this will produce a 4.3% savings on operational costs. Where do the savings occur? We see in the lower part of table 9.5 that a 10% increase in capital expenditures leads to a 10.65% reduction in the demand for equipment and a 0.58% fall in the demand for fuel. Increased capital spending also reduces the demand for labor. There is a 3.06%, 2.89%, and 1.94% fall in the demand for general labor, yard and switching labor, and on-train labor respectively.

Thus, the information in table 9.5 suggests that the primary source of operational cost savings from increased capital spending derives from equipment use, with some additional savings in the use of labor.

The effect of increased capital investment in a regulated environment

We considered above the effect that a 10% increase in capital investment would have upon a firm's operating costs, when evaluated at the sample mean. Although this provides insights into a firm's response to increasing capital expansion, it provides less insight into the effect that such an increase would have on the industry as a whole. In this section, we examine two related questions. First, how would a marginal increase in capital spending affect the operating

Table 9.6 Capital investment and profitability in the rail industry

	Revenues[a] ($billion)		Total Variable Costs ($billion)	Operating Profits ($billion)	Net Rate of Return on Investment[b] (%)
	Manufactured	Bulk			
Official Region					
Initial Equilibrium	1.993	1.214	4.543	−0.251	−4.6
10% Increase in Capital	1.993	1.214	4.350	−0.061	7.4
Competitive Equilibrium	1.390	1.164	2.449	1.194	3.44
10% Increase in Capital	1.416	1.173	2.447	1.222	−1.64
South-West Region					
Initial Equilibrium	4.711	2.230	6.099	2.123	7.97
10% Increase in Capital	4.711	2.230	5.936	2.287	5.43
Competitive Equilibrium	4.437	2.475	6.546	1.627	5.36
10% Increase in Capital	4.462	2.483	6.564	1.663	−1.31

[a] Total revenues include $1.082 and $1.282 billion for coal, agricultural, and passenger traffic in the Official and South-West Regions respectively.
[b] The net rate of return assumes 2% depreciation and 1.2% property tax rates. Stock of capital in the Official and South-West Regions equals $17.98 and $19.00 billion respectively. Also, for the initial equilibrium and competitive equilibrium, the net return on investment corresponds to the return on invested capital. For the 10% increase in capital, the net rate of return reflects the return on the capital increment. For example, in the Official Region and at the initial equilibrium, rails lost $251 million on 17.98 invested capital, representing a −1.4% return. Subtracting 1.2% for property taxes and 2% for depreciation, this produces a net return on invested capital equal to −1.4 − 1.2 − 2.0 = −4.6%. At the competitive equilibrium and with 10% increase in ways and structures, there was a reduction in operating losses equal to $190 million, which represents a 0.19/1.798 = 10.6% gross return or a 10.6 − 1.2 − 2.0 = 7.4% net return on the increased capital investment.
Source: Friedlaender and Spady (1981), tables 3.1, 4.5, 4.8, with the permission of the MIT Press.

profits of the industry, assuming that the industry continues to operate at the regulated equilibrium? Second, how would the same increase in capital investment affect industry behavior and profitability if the industry were in short-run competitive equilibrium?

Table 9.6 reports the results from each of these experiments for the two regions that we considered in chapter 6, the Official Region (the Northeast, Mid-Atlantic, and East-Central States) and the South-West Region (which represents the remaining contiguous states). The capital stock in the Official and South-West Regions was valued at $17.98 billion and $19.00 billion (1972 dollars) respectively. The opportunity cost of capital was 9%.

First, we want to consider the effect on operating profits due to a 10% increase in capital expenditures, assuming that the rails continue to operate at their regulated equilibria. The 10% capital investment amounts to a $1.798 billion investment in the Official Region and a $1.90 billion investment in the South-West Region. We see in table 9.6 that, prior to any investment, carriers in the Official Region incurred a negative net rate of return on investment. Given a $251 million dollar loss on $17.98 billion capital investment, and adjusting for 2% and 1.2%

depreciation and property tax rates, yields a net rate of return equal to

$$i_{\text{net}} = \left(\frac{0.251}{17.98} - 0.02 - 0.012\right)(100) = -4.60\%$$

Holding all else constant, a 10% increase in capital expenditures reduces total transport costs in the Official Region by \$193 (\$4.543 billion – \$4.350 billion) million. Based upon a \$1.798 capital investment, this represents a 7.4% net rate of return on incremental investment. It may seem odd that the Official Region experienced a negative rate of return on investment yet, if capital expenditures are further increased, the investment nearly returns the 9% opportunity cost of capital. However, it is important to remember that all else was held constant. In other words, we are examining the effect of increased capital expenditures in a *partial equilibrium* framework whereby rail rates, output, and therefore revenues remain unchanged. In this environment, as long as capital expenditures lead to reduced operating costs, there will be a positive net rate of return on investment.

Suppose that we move to a short-run competitive equilibrium which satisfies the marginal cost pricing rule. Relative to the regulated equilibrium, carriers in the Official Region operating at a competitive equilibrium would receive a 3.44% net rate of return on total current investment. Recall from chapter 6 (table 6.3) that these profits are the result of a shift of resources in the Official Region away from manufactured goods carriage and toward bulk carriage. Although less than the 9% opportunity cost of capital, the move to a competitive equilibrium is an improvement over the negative return received in the regulated environment.

Assuming now that carriers in the Official Region are at their short-run competitive equilibrium, how will increased capital spending affect profitability? From table 9.6, we see that operating profits increase by \$28 million, which reflects a 1.5% gross rate of return (0.28/1.798 = 0.015) and a net rate of return equal to −1.64%. Why do we have the negative rate of return? It is because, in this case, we are not holding output and price constant but, rather, allowing them to change as we move to a new competitive equilibrium. Because increased capital spending reduces operating costs, we expect that the net effect of increased capital spending in the Official Region is to reduce equilibrium rail prices and increase equilibrium ton–miles carried. Depending upon the quantitative changes in price and quantity, total revenues will either rise or fall. From table 9.6, total revenues on manufactured goods rose by 1.87% and total revenues on bulk goods rose by less than 1%. Further, on the cost side, we see that total costs fell but only slightly. The net effect on profits, therefore, provides a positive gross return. However, this is not sufficient to provide a positive, let alone normal, net return on the investment.

The case is similar in the South-West Region. At the regulated equilibrium, the South-West Region earns a 7.97% return on investment due to the high profit margins on bulk carriage (see table 6.4 in chapter 6). Holding transport rates and output constant, a 10% increase in capital expenditures raises profits by \$164 million, which translates into a 5.43% net rate of return on investment. Moving to a competitive equilibrium and marginal cost pricing, South-West carriers no longer earn high profits on bulk carriage, and this reduces the rate of return from 7.97% to 5.36%.

Similar to the Official Region, we see in the lower half of table 9.6 that the effect of a 10% increase in capital expenditures from a competitive equilibrium leads to a modest \$36 million increase in operating profits. The reason is twofold. First, manufactured and bulk goods revenues increased only slightly, by 0.56% and 0.32% respectively. In addition, the net effect of increased capital spending on total variable costs was positive, rising from \$6.546 billion to \$6.564 billion. The combined effect, then, was a negative net rate of return on investment of −1.31%.

Two comments are in order here. First, it is important to keep in mind the distinction between partial and general equilibrium analysis. At the initial equilibrium, the effect of capital spending on profitability assumed that all else was held constant, including prices charged and ton–miles shipped. Since capital investment reduces operating costs, we obtain the partial equilibrium result that the investment yields a positive gross rate of return.

At the competitive equilibrium, however, the effect of the capital increase takes a general equilibrium approach. Capital spending in rail transport reduces the cost of providing rail services and shifts market supply rightward. The resulting decrease in rail prices reduces the demand for truck carriage which, as we saw in chapter 6, has feedback effects in the rail market. Although we expect the final outcome in the rail market to be lower equilibrium prices and higher quantities, revenues as well as costs are now affected by the increased capital investment, so that the impact on profits ultimately depends upon the price elasticities of demand and supply. The differences in the net rates of return from capital investment in the initial and competitive cases reflects a difference between partial and general equilibrium analysis.

Second, in none of the cases examined in table 9.6 did capital investment yield a normal return on investment. Would the industry obtain a normal rate of return if it were in long-run equilibrium? The cases previously examined were each based upon the *existing level of capital* in the industry. How would these results change if the rail industry satisfied both marginal cost and investment optimality rules?

Efficient pricing and investment in the rail industry

Table 9.7 summarizes pricing, output, and profitability characteristics for the Official and South-West Regions of the rail industry under short-run and long-run competitive equilibrium

Table 9.7 Short- and long-run competitive equilibria in the rail industry

	Short Run	Long Run
(a) Official Region		
Manufactured output (billion ton–miles)	30.284	18.302
Bulk output (billion ton–miles)	76.469	63.243
Manufactured rate (cents/ton–mile)	4.59	6.385
Bulk rate (cents/ton–mile)	1.521	1.747
Total revenue ($billion)	3.634	3.354
Total variable costs ($billion)	2.440	2.355
Operating profits ($billion)	1.194	0.999
Capital ($billion)	17.98	8.962
Net rate of return on investment (%)	3.43	7.95
Subsidy required to achieve 9% return to capital ($billion)	1.001	0.094
(b) South-West Region		
Manufactured output (billion ton–miles)	148.932	139.193
Bulk output (billion ton–miles)	237.234	226.241
Manufactured rate (cents/ton–mile)	2.979	3.143
Bulk rate (cents/ton–mile)	1.043	1.085
Total revenue ($billion)	8.194	8.117
Total variable costs ($billion)	6.567	6.575
Operating profits ($billion)	1.627	1.542
Capital ($billion)	19.00	15.136
Net rate of return on investment (%)	5.36	6.99
Subsidy required to achieve 9% return to capital ($billion)	0.691	0.305

Source: Adapted from Friedlaender and Spady (1981), table 4.19, p. 161, with the permission of the MIT Press. Copyright © 1981 Massachusetts Institute of Technology

when carriers price at marginal cost and optimally invest in capital. In other words, the industry achieves long-run equilibrium. Prices equal marginal cost and the rental price of capital, by satisfying equation (9.17), equals the savings on operating expenditures.

From chapter 6, we saw that, with no change in capital investment, a move from the regulated equilibrium to the short-run competitive equilibrium implied an output reduction in the Official Region and an increase in ton–miles in the South-West Region. As a working hypothesis, this suggests that the Official Region is overcapitalized in the short run relative to the long-run equilibrium, and that the South-West Region is undercapitalized relative to its long-run position. In table 9.7, however, we see that both regions are overcapitalized.

There is a significant drop in long-run equilibrium capital in the Official Region, from $17.98 billion to $8.96 billion, with an accompanying reduction of 39% in manufactured and 17% in bulk goods traffic. Consistent with overcapitalization, long-run marginal costs in this region are greater than short-run marginal costs: 6.385 cents/ton–mile versus 4.59 cents/ton–mile for manufactured goods; and 1.747 cents/ton–mile versus 1.521 cents/ton–mile for bulk goods. The loss in total revenues more than offsets the reduction in total costs, causing profits to fall from $1.19 billion to $999 million.

In contrast to our working hypothesis, the results in table 9.7 also indicate that the South-West Region is overcapitalized, but not by as much as in the Official Region. Relative to short-run equilibrium, capital falls 20% from $19.00 billion to $15.136 billion. This leads to a reduction in total ton–miles carried and smaller increases in rates on both manufactured and bulk goods. Also, the fall in total costs is not sufficient to offset the loss of revenues, leading to a $85 million fall in profits.

Despite lower operating profits, moving to a long-run equilibrium and an optimal use of capital is beneficial. According to the last two rows in tables 9.7(a) and 9.7(b), the move to a competitive long-run equilibrium leads to a 7.95% rate of return on investment in the Official Region and a 6.99% rate of return in the South-West Region. Although these rates of return still require subsidization to make them comparable to alternative investments, the level of subsidy required, as noted by the last row in each table, is considerably lower.

CHAPTER HIGHLIGHTS

- The user cost of capital is the rental price of capital per period and includes interest, depreciation, and obsolescence costs.
- Quasi-rents are returns to fixed capital that are not necessary for continued production in the short run but are necessary in the long run to cover capital costs.
- Discounted present values reflect the fact that a dollar received today is valued more highly than a dollar to be received in some future time period. In the simplest case, the discounted present value of a perpetuity is $PV = FV/i$, where FV is an amount received in the each future period and i is the discount rate.
- Any discounted present value can be expressed as an annuity; that is, as a series of equal future payments.
- The wealth value of licenses reflects the discounted present value of future profits and depends upon demand factors, cost factors, and market access.
- In a perfectly competitive environment, first best pricing and investment requires that output is priced at marginal cost and that the marginal cost of capital, defined

as its asset price, equals the marginal benefit of capital, defined as the discounted present value of average variable cost savings from an additional unit of capital.

- In an empirical analysis of the urban bus industry, urban transit does not generally price at marginal cost, nor optimally invest. This was also true of the rail industry during regulation. An empirical analysis of this industry found that rail firms did not pursue optimal pricing and investment rules. Although a normal return on investment was not achieved under marginal cost pricing and optimal investment in the long run, the required level of subsidy was much less.

Review questions

1. What is the user cost of capital and what cost components does it include? How does the user cost of capital differ from the asset price of capital?
2. Suppose that you are interested in operating a taxi and you are considering purchasing a taxi medallion (that is, an operating certificate) from an existing operator. You estimate that the current operator makes annual excess profits equal to $1,500. At a 5% rate of interest, what is the maximum price you are willing to pay for this license? Would you be willing to pay this same price if the interest rate were 10%?
3. Suppose that 20 firms operate barges on the Mississippi River. All of the firms have identical cost structures and currently each firm is making a normal return on investment.
   (a) If you were considering purchasing the operating license from one of the existing firms, what would be the maximum price you would pay?
   (b) Suppose that one of the barge operators discovers a way to reduce his costs of production which he estimates will increase his net revenues by $10,000, $25,000, $15,000, and $4,000 over the next 4 years. After that, he anticipates that his competitors will also exploit the innovation. Assuming an 7% rate of interest, what effect will this innovation have on the barge operator's wealth?
4. You are deciding whether to purchase an operating certificate to operate a limousine shuttle service to the airport for the next 4 years. At the end of each year, you expect to receive net revenues equal to $100,000, $125,000, $150,000, and $175,000. You have an initial cost outlay equal to $350,000, and in each of the four years you could work for another limousine company for $40,000 per year.
   (a) If the interest rate is expected to be 8% over the 4 year period, what is the maximum amount of money that you would be willing to pay for the operating certificate? Would you enter this business?
   (b) If the initial cost outlay fell to $300,000, would this alter your decision?

5. (a) What are quasi-rents? Is this a short-run or long-run concept?
(b) If you know that a firm is making economic losses in the short run, do you have enough information to determine whether the firm is making enough quasi-rents to cover its fixed costs of production?

6. (a) Briefly discuss the optimality rules that firms must satisfy if they are wealth maximizers over time.
(b) Discuss the economic intuition behind the following equilibrium condition for capital use:

$$-\frac{\Delta STVC}{\Delta K} = r$$

7. Consider table 9.8.
(a) The CPI data is in constant 1982–4 dollars. The rail, aviation, and gasoline data are in nominal dollars. Use the CPI data to convert the fuel data to constant 1980 dollars.
(b) On the basis of your results in (a), what has happened to the real price of rail, aviation, and gasoline fuels over the 13 year period? Which fuel has exhibited the largest change in real price?

Table 9.8 Fuel cost data

Year	Consumer Price Index (CPI) (1982–4 = 100)	Railroad Fuel (Diesel)	Aviation Gasoline	Unleaded Regular Gasoline
1980	82.4	83.0	108.4	124.5
1985	107.6	78.3	120.1	120.2
1990	130.7	69.2	112.0	116.4
1991	136.2	67.2	104.7	114.0
1992	140.3	63.2	102.7	112.7
1993	144.5	63.1	99.0	110.8

8. (a) Suppose that the market for taxi services in the city of Mobile is completely open. Anyone who wants to provide taxi services can do so.
(i) For this market, graph a typical market demand and market supply curve, and identify the equilibrium price and quantity.
(ii) For this open market, assume that the current number of firms offering services is 100. What is the maximum price that an incumbent firm is willing to pay for the right to operate a taxi service? Are any incumbent firms making an economic profit?
(b) (i) Draw a separate graph with number of firms on the x-axis and certificate price on the y-axis. This is the market for operating licenses. Identify on this graph the point that corresponds to an open market equilibrium.

(ii) Suppose that regulators now restrict the number of licenses to 75. In the market for taxi services, graphically depict the effect of this market entry restriction. What happens to equilibrium price and quantity? Are incumbent firms making an economic profit? Graphically depict in the market for licenses the impact of the market restriction. What happens to equilibrium price and quantity in this market?

(c) In general, what does your analysis in (a) and (b) imply regarding market restrictions and the value of operating licenses?

9. A bus company has a fleet of buses that require periodic maintenance. Suppose that the capital cost of a typical bus is $320,000. The current rate of interest is 7.5% and the bus is expected to depreciate at a constant rate over the expected life of the bus, 8 years, assuming normal maintenance activities.

(a) What is the annual interest cost of using the bus? What is the annual depreciation cost? If there are no obsolescence costs, what is the annual user cost of the bus?

(b) What happens to the user cost of capital if the bus company foregoes normal maintenance on the bus?

10. Suppose that you purchase a tractor–trailer truck for your trucking business at a cost of $150,000. The current rate of interest is 5% and you expect the truck to last for 10 years.

(a) Given the information provided, what is the "capital recovery factor"? What is the annual cost of capital to the owner?

(b) How would your answer to (a) change if you expected the truck to last 12 years rather than 10 years? If the interest rate were 8% rather than 5%, what would the annual cost of capital now be?

11. For the Official Region in table 9.6, we found the following:

"At the regulated equilibrium, the net return on investment is negative but positive for an increase in capital investment."

"At the short-run competitive equilibrium, the net return on investment is positive but is negative for an increase in capital investment."

Explain why these findings are not necessarily inconsistent. In your answer, be sure to indicate what is and what is not being held constant.

12. (a) Looking at table 9.7, we see that the net rate of return on investment is higher in the long-run equilibrium than in the short-run equilibrium. Why?

(b) We have argued that market restrictions on entry and exit will generally lead to an inefficient allocation of resources. Comment on the effect that restrictions on rail exit from unprofitable markets would have upon their rates of return on investment. Are the capital changes between short-run and long-run equilibria in table 9.7 consistent with this interpretation?

APPENDIX

To obtain additional insight into Optimality Condition 2, consider the following simplifying assumptions:

- capital and labor are the only inputs in the production of T
- capital is a fixed factor of production and labor is a variable factor of production
- the price of labor and the price of T are constant over time
- capital is equally productive in each time period – that is, the marginal product of capital (MP_K) is equal in each time period s

Given these assumptions, the total variable cost of production at time s is wL_s and the average variable cost of production is wL_s/T_s, where T_s is the amount of T produced in period s. For any given level of output, equation (9.16) tells us that increased capital investment reduces per period average variable production (and output related maintenance) costs. With constant wages per period, this must imply a reduction in the use of labor. That is,

$$\begin{aligned}\frac{\Delta AVC_s}{\Delta K} &= -\frac{\Delta(wL_s/T_s)}{\Delta K}\\ &= -\frac{w}{T_s}\frac{\Delta L_s}{\Delta K}, \qquad \text{where } \Delta L_s < 0\\ &= -\frac{w}{MP_L^s}\frac{1}{T_s}MP_K, \qquad s = 1, \ldots, t \end{aligned} \tag{9.A1}$$

where MP_L^s is the marginal product of labor in time period s and the negative sign converts the savings in operating costs to a positive number. Using the result that the marginal cost of producing one more unit of T is the additional amount of input required to produce an additional T multiplied by the input's price (equation (5.13′) in chapter 5), equation (9.A1) can be expressed as

$$\frac{\Delta AVC_s}{\Delta K} = -\frac{MC_s}{T_s}MP_K \tag{9.A2}$$

which when substituted into equation (9.16) gives

$$\begin{aligned} P_K &= -\sum_{s=1}^{t} T_s\left(-\frac{MC_s}{T_s}MP_K\right)/(1+i)^s\\ &= -\sum_{s=1}^{t}\frac{(-MC_s \cdot MP_K)}{(1+i)^s} \end{aligned} \tag{9.A3}$$

Continuing to assume competitive markets and given the assumption of a constant output price per period, the marginal cost pricing rule ($p = MC_s$) in equilibrium implies that we can express equation (9.A3) as

$$P_K = \sum_{s=1}^{t} \frac{(p \cdot MP_K)}{(1+i)^s}$$

$$\Rightarrow P_K = p \cdot MP_K \sum_{s=1}^{t} \frac{1}{(1+i)^s}$$

$$= p \cdot MP_K \left[\frac{(1+i)^t - 1}{i(1+i)^t} \right] \qquad \text{(from equation (9.6))}$$

$$\Rightarrow r = \text{“}crf\text{”}\ P_K = \text{annualized cost} = p \cdot MP_K \qquad (9.A4)$$

If we assume the absence of capital depreciation and obsolescence, the left-hand side of equation (9.A4) is the user cost of capital and the right-hand side is the value of the marginal product of capital. But note that this is not an overly restrictive assumption. Suppose that we define P_K in equation (9.14) to be net of any salvage value. Then implicit in the stream of operating cost savings is capital obsolescence, the discount rate reflects the interest cost of capital, and the (net) price of capital reflects its salvage value. Output-related maintenance costs are included in the operating costs. These changes will not affect the marginal cost pricing rule, but the user cost of capital in equation (9.A4) will now reflect depreciation, interest, and obsolescence costs.

NOTES

1 As we saw in chapter 5, the optimal use of inputs requires that the marginal rate of technical substitution equals the input price ratio; that is, $r/w = MP_K/MP_L$, where w is the wage rate, r is the rental price of capital, and MP_i is the marginal product of input i ($i = L, K$). That is, the relative productivity of capital equals the relative cost of capital. Also, rearranging this condition gives the equivalent equilibrium condition that the marginal product per dollar spent on all inputs is equal.

2 This assumes perfect capital markets in which the lending interest rate equals the borrowing interest rate.

3 Although there may be some maintenance expenditures that are not related to the amount of output produced, these are small in comparison with maintenance costs directly related to a firm's level of production.

4 It is possible for obsolescence cost to be negative; that is, the capital value increases over time. As economic development occurs, for example, the value of railroad real estate, particularly those parcels associated with infrequent or abandoned service, is more valuable if used for urban development than in its current rail uses.

5 Producer surplus is a rent in the sense that these returns are not necessary to bring forth production in the short run. However, in the long run the firm needs to generate a sufficient amount of rents to cover its fixed costs of production. It is in this sense that the rents are temporary or "quasi-rents."

6 Unanticipated technological advances imply a fall in the equilibrium price and an unexpected loss in the value of existing capital. New technological advances which were not available to the firm depicted in figure 9.1 would be adopted by some firms, enabling them to produce at lower the cost. This shifts market supply to the right which, given demand, lowers the equilibrium price. Producer surplus for the firm in figure 9.1 falls; that is, the capital used by the firm experiences a loss in value. This does not imply, however, that the firm would abandon its use of existing capital. As long as the firm covers its variable costs with the lower-valued capital good, the obsolete capital is still useful to the firm.

7 This means that input prices are not expected to change, demand conditions are not expected to change, and there are no anticipated technological improvements that would make current capital obsolete.

8 To simplify the analysis, we assume that there is no depreciation during the 2 year period during which the plane is used.

9 This is simply a generalization of the inverse relation between *PV* and *FV* reported in equation (9.7).

10 A frequently used measures of inflation is the consumer's price index, which is an aggregate measure of price changes for a bundle of goods that is typically purchased by urban households.

11 Based upon the consumer price index, Frew's original values, reported in 1967 dollars, were updated to 1972 dollars to correspond with the time period of his sample.

12 Using equation (9.8), the cost recovery factor is $[(0.05(1.05)^6)/((1.05)^6 - 1)] = 0.197$. Multiplying by \$50,334 gives \$9,917.

13 In 1983 there were 900 licenses. Given a 128% increase between 1979 and 1983, this implies 703 licenses in 1979.

14 To understand why the right-hand side of (9.15) represents a marginal cost, consider the following example. A firm currently produces 100 units of *T* at an average variable cost of \$5 per unit. Assume that the firm is operating on the rising portion of its average variable cost curve, so that a unit increase in *Q* raises *AVC* by 1 cent, \$0.01. What's the marginal cost to the firm of the 101st unit? It is equal to the present *AVC* plus the *additional* cost that the firm must incur to produce the original 100 units. The additional cost of producing the original 100 units when the firm decides to produce 101 units is 0.01(100) = \$1. Thus, the marginal cost of producing the 101st unit is \$6; that is, $MC = \$5 + \$0.01(100) = \$5 + \$1 = \$6$.

15 Although we have assumed perfectly competitive markets, we would obtain a similar pricing rule for imperfectly competitive markets. In a monopoly, for example, marginal revenue (*MR*) replaces *p* in equation (9.15). In this case, the optimal pricing rule is to produce where marginal revenue equals marginal cost, which is identical to the pricing rule that we obtained for monopolies in chapter 7.

16 Since $T_s(\Delta AVC_s) = \Delta STVC$, $T_s(\Delta AVC_s/\Delta K) = \Delta STVC/\Delta K$.

17 The appendix to this chapter derives this results and illustrates that, under certain conditions, the annualized cost figure also reflects the value of capital's marginal product.

18 Although for simplicity we have assumed perfectly competitive markets, the result generalizes to imperfectly competitive market structures. A monopolist, for example, would pursue investments up to the point at which the user cost of capital equaled the additional revenues generated from capital. Assuming constant marginal revenues (*MR*) over the time horizon, the revenue generated per period *s* is $MR \cdot MP_K$.

19 In addition to obsolescence, changes in the value of capital over time occur from an increase in the general price level; that is, inflation. As we have seen, as long as producer surpluses and interest rates are consistently measured, both in real terms or both in nominal terms, there is no effect on the results. When using real rather than nominal surpluses and interest rates, inflation effects on the value of capital net out, in which case $\dot{p}_K$ represents unanticipated changes in value. If unanticipated, these changes cannot be estimated. As a result, most empirical analyses ignore obsolescence when defining the user cost of capital.

20 In calculating a \$727 user cost of bus capital, Viton assumed that renovation costs per bus were \$3,000 (1975 prices), that renovation extended a bus's life by five years, and that the opportunity cost of capital was 6.75%. Substituting $PV = 3{,}000$, $i = 0.06$, and $n = 5$ into equation (9.8) gives $FV = 727$.

21 For purposes of comparison, the user cost of capital, based upon 20% depreciation per year and a 6.75% opportunity cost of capital, would be (0.2674)(\$3,000) = \$802.

22 In an analysis of bus costs and optimized service, Mohring (1976, pp. 145–57) estimated that marginal costs were 70% and 90% of average costs when demand was nine and 150 passengers per mile per hour, respectively. Also, depending upon the specific demand, cost, and bus stop spacing assumptions, the subsidy : operating cost ratio ranged between 21% and 72%.

23 Like depreciation, property taxes are a cost of capital that must be subtracted from the gross rate of return in order to obtain a net rate of return. In order to present the ideas as clearly and simply as possible, we have not included taxes in our discussion of user costs.

24 In the sample, way and structures were measured in December 1971 prices, but the underlying sample was for the period 1968–70. Friedlaender and Spady used a weighted mean of asset prices for the sample to convert the marginal cost effect (−0.109) to a rate of return for the sample.

REFERENCES AND RELATED READINGS

General references

Jorgenson, D. W. 1963: Capital theory and investment behavior. *American Economic Association Papers and Proceedings*, LIII, 247–59.

McCloskey, D. N. 1985: *The Applied Theory of Price*, 2nd edn. New York: Macmillan.

Munnell, A. H. 1991: *Is There a Shortfall in Public Capital Investment?* Boston: Federal Reserve Bank of Boston.

Nicholson, W. 1998: *Microeconomic Theory*, 7th edn. Fort Worth, Texas: The Dryden Press.

Palm, T. and Qayum, A. 1985: *Private and Public Investment Analysis*. Cincinnati, Ohio: South-Western.

Transportation references

Armour, R. F. 1980: An economic analysis of transit bus replacement. *Transit Journal*, 6, 41–54.

Berechman, J. 1993: *Public Transit Economics and Deregulation Policy*, vol. 23. Studies in Regional Science and Urban Economics, L. Anselin et al. (ed.). Amsterdam: Elsevier Science.

Bittlingmayer, G. 1988: Property rights, progress, and the Aircraft Patent Agreement. *Journal of Law and Economics*, XXXI, 227–49.

Button, K. J. 1993: *Transport Economics*, 2nd edn. Brookfield, Vermont: Edward Elgar.

Button, K. J. and Pearman, A. D. (eds.) 1983: *The Practice of Transport Investment Appraisal*. Aldershot, Hants, UK: Gower.

Button, K. J. and Pearman, A. D. 1985: *Applied Transport Economics*. New York: Gordon and Breach.

Frankena, M. W. and Pautler, P. A. 1984: An economic analysis of taxicab regulation. Federal Trade Commission, May.

Frew, J. 1981: The existence of monopoly profits in the motor carrier industry. *Journal of Law and Economics*, XXIV, 289–315.

Friedlaender, A. F. and Spady, R. H. 1981: *Freight Transport Regulation*. Cambridge, Mass.: The MIT Press.

Mohring, H. 1976: *Transportation Economics*. Cambridge, Mass.: Ballinger.

Oum, T. H., Dodgson, J. S., Hensher, D. A., Morrison, S. A., Nash, C. A., Small, K. A., and Waters, W. G. II 1995: *Transport Economics*. Seoul, Korea: The Korea Research Foundation for the 21st Century.

Polak, J. and Heertje, A. (eds.) 1993: *European Transport Economics*. Oxford: Blackwell.

Starkie, D. 1994: Developments in transport policy: The US market in airport slots. *Journal of Transport Economics and Policy*, XXVIII, 325–9.

Viton, P. A. 1981: A translog cost function for urban bus transit. *Journal of Industrial Economics*, XXIX, 287–304.

10

Welfare Effects of Public-Sector Pricing and Investment

INTRODUCTION

In chapter 9, we saw that a perfectly competitive firm invests in capital goods in order to reduce its variable costs of production. Because these operating cost benefits accrue over many time periods, profit-maximizing firms seek to maximize discounted present value profits. An important result from this analysis is the first-best pricing and investment rule. Firms produce up to the point at which the opportunity cost of producing one more unit of a good equals the additional revenue from selling one more unit; and firms invest up to the point at which the present value of operating cost savings equals the marginal cost of capital. We then went on to examine the resource allocation implications for the urban bus and rail sectors if these sectors followed first-best pricing and investment strategies.

Although identifying how resources are allocated in a first-best world, our analysis ignored the financing implications of first-best pricing and investment. In perfectly competitive markets, financing is not of concern, in that all costs are covered and the firm makes a normal return on investment when in long-run equilibrium. But if a firm operates under increasing returns to scale, financing becomes an issue. Consider, for example, a metropolitan transportation system (MTS), which is the sole provider of public transportation in a metropolitan area, and assume that the MTS operates under increasing returns to scale and produces at the profit-maximizing price at which marginal revenue equals marginal cost. This leads to an inefficient allocation of resources since, as we have already seen in chapter 7, the profit-maximizing price exceeds the marginal cost, which violates the marginal cost pricing rule. However, since a typical transit authority's objective is not to maximize profits anyway, but to provide an efficient level of public transportation, the government could require the MTS to produce at the point at which price equals marginal cost. This satisfies the marginal cost pricing rule, but we now have another problem. With increasing returns to scale, marginal cost pricing will not produce sufficient revenues to cover the total cost of production. Since producing public transit trips is not financially viable, does this also imply that the activity is not economically efficient and should be shut down? Or do we want to subsidize the MTS and, if so, what's the least costly way of doing so?

In this chapter, our main focus centers on the welfare and financing effects of public-sector pricing and investment in transportation sectors under alternative assumptions on returns to scale. Initially, we analyze short-run pricing problems for alternative demand conditions when transportation capacity is fixed. We then proceed to the more general problem of pricing and capacity investment, first developing economically efficient criteria when the transportation authority operates under constant returns to scale. Next, we examine a transportation authority that operates under increasing returns to scale. We will see why it is efficient for the public sector to undertake some investments that the private sector rationally shuns, and explore the pricing implications when a transport authority must satisfy a financial constraint. Throughout, we illustrate many of these principles with empirical examples in the highway, airport, rail, and urban transit sectors.

FIRST-BEST PRICING WITH FIXED CAPACITY[1]

Our analysis of public-sector pricing and investment begins with a simple problem. Suppose that a local transportation department has constructed a bridge from Here to There and now wants to set a price for bridge crossings that is economically efficient. Assume that the total cost of the bridge is *TC* which, if converted into an annuity with equal per period payments, gives a per-period fixed cost equal to *F* over the life of the bridge.[2] We also assume, for simplicity, that bridge crossings are uncongested up to the point of capacity, after which the marginal cost of a crossing becomes infinite. Figure 10.1 depicts the market for bridge trips, where we see that each driver traveling over the bridge causes a small amount of wear and tear *oc*, which represents the opportunity cost of a bridge crossing. As depicted, the opportunity cost for each bridge crossing, up to the bridge's capacity T_c, is constant, which also implies a constant average variable cost per bridge crossing.

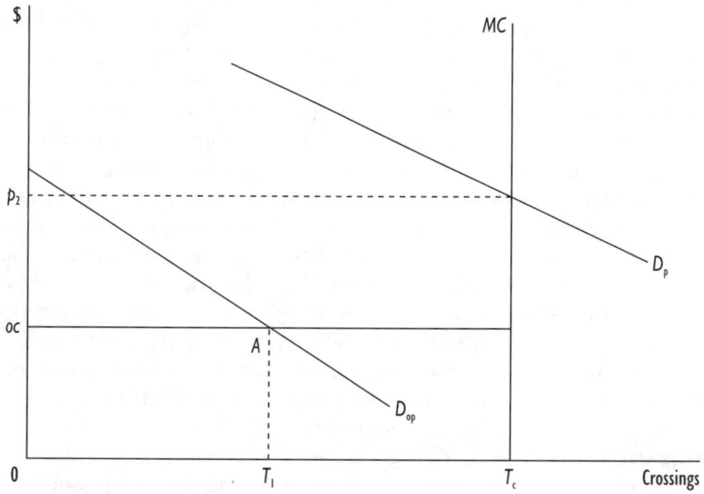

Figure 10.1 Optimal allocation of bridge crossing with fixed capacity.

CONSTANT DEMAND PER PERIOD

Let curve D_{op} in figure 10.1 represent the initial per period demand for bridge crossings. For the moment, ignore curve D_p. We see in the figure that D_{op} intersects the marginal cost line at point A, where the opportunity cost of an additional crossing just equals the marginal benefit of an additional crossing. Point A is an efficient allocation of resources to bridge crossings, and equilibrium price p_1 represents marginal cost pricing for bridge crossings, given the existing and fixed capacity of the bridge. The marginal cost price is the *first-best price*.

Do the revenues collected from the bridge crossings cover the per-period cost of the bridge? No. Since marginal cost and average variable cost are constant, the revenues collected, $(p_1 T_1)$, will cover total variable costs, $(oc)T_1$, but will not add anything to per-period fixed costs, F. Per-period fixed costs are sunk, and since the bridge is already built, fixed costs are incurred regardless of how the bridge is used. Thus, our only concern is to use the existing capacity as efficiently as possible, and this requires that we price bridge crossings at marginal cost. Note also that, although the bridge is efficiently used under marginal cost pricing, there is excess capacity. At the equilibrium price, the available capacity is T_c, whereas the demanded capacity is T_1, giving $T_c - T_1$ excess capacity.

Suppose that per-period demand for bridge crossings suddenly increases to D_p. Since, by assumption, each bridge crossing entails an opportunity cost of oc, do we still want to charge price p_1 for each crossing? No. At a price of p_1, there is excess demand for the bridge's capacity, so we want to raise the price until the quantity of bridge capacity demanded just equals the available capacity. As you see in the figure, excess demand for capacity exists as long as the price per crossing is below p_2. At p_2, quantity demanded just equals quantity supplied, and at any price above p_2 there is an excess supply of bridge capacity.

Given bridge capacity and per-period demand D_p, the first-best price is p_2. Since at capacity T_c the marginal cost of an additional trip is virtually infinite, reflected by the vertical segment associated with the marginal cost curve, the first-best price at capacity is a form of marginal cost pricing. However, in this case, we want to raise the price until all existing capacity is allocated. Any price below this will lead to excess demand, and any price above this will result in excess capacity. Only at p_2 is all capacity used.

Do revenues cover fixed costs in this case? – possibly, but not necessarily. We see in figure 10.1 that total revenues $(p_2 T_c)$ exceed total opportunity costs $(oc)T_c$ by the amount $(p_2 - oc)T_c$, which represents the contribution to fixed costs. If $(p_2 - oc)T_c$ is greater than or equal to F, the bridge is self-financing. If, on the other hand, $(p_2 - oc)T_c$ is less than F, revenues fall short of per-period bridge costs.

In general, when the demand for transportation capacity lies below existing capacity, the first-best pricing rule is to set price equal to the opportunity cost. However, when pricing at opportunity cost leads to an excess demand for the fixed capacity, the first-best pricing rule is to raise the per-unit price until the excess demand is eliminated.

PUBLIC-SECTOR OBJECTIVES – PROFITS VERSUS SOCIAL SURPLUS MAXIMIZATION

Notice the market structure in this example. Since the transport authority faces the entire market demand for bridge crossings, we have a monopoly market structure. However, unlike

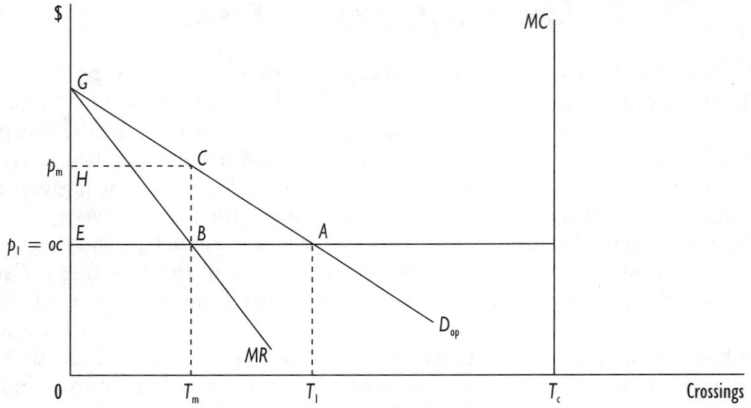

Figure 10.2 Monopoly allocation of capacity to bridge crossings.

a typical profit-maximizing monopolist, the transport authority does not seek to maximize profits but, rather, *desires to maximize social surplus*; that is, the sum of consumer plus producer surplus, the net benefits to society. To fully see this difference, consider figure 10.2, which redraws the opportunity cost and demand structure D_{op} from figure 10.1. If the transport authority behaved as a typical monopolist, profit maximization would occur at point *B*, where the marginal revenue curve intersects the marginal cost curve. The monopolist would then set the price at p_m, which accommodates T_m bridge crossings. At this price and output combination, the monopolist would receive the maximum amount of profits possible, rectangle *EHCB* minus fixed costs *F*.

What is the social surplus in this case? It includes the surplus that consumers receive from level of consumption T_m, area *HGC* in figure 10.2, plus the amount of producer surplus; that is, the quasi-rents, received by the monopolist, *EHCB*.[3] The social surplus under monopolistic pricing is then the area *EGCB*. Is this the maximum possible social surplus? No. Monopolistic pricing involves an efficiency loss which, in figure 10.2, is the triangular area *ABC*. The presence of an efficiency loss is another way of saying that we have not maximized social surplus.

If the transport authority is interested in maximizing the sum of producer and consumer surpluses rather than profits, the authority will want to be at point *A*, which reflects marginal cost pricing and entails no efficiency loss. Social surplus now equals the large triangular area *AEG*, which exceeds the social surplus associated with monopoly pricing by the area *ABC*.

There are three important points about this result. First, relative to the monopolistic equilibrium, marginal cost pricing maximizes social surplus rather than firm profits. Stopping short of point *A*, as in the monopoly case, reduces total social surplus, because not all gains from exchange have been exploited. Conversely, if we were to move past point *A*, the marginal benefit of further bridge crossings would be less than the marginal cost and social surplus would again fall. Second, although point *A* characterizes the maximum possible social surplus, we also see that there has been a redistribution of income from producers to consumers.

At the monopoly equilibrium, the monopolist receives producer surplus equal to *EHCB* while consumers receive consumer surplus *HGC*. At point *A*, however, the producer receives no surplus and total social surplus is consumer surplus. By setting a marginal cost price, all of the monopoly surpluses have been transferred to consumers in the form of consumer surplus. But income transfers matter little *from society's perspective*, since the welfare gain to consumers offsets the loss to the producer which gives a zero net effect upon economic welfare.[4] And, third, the fact that there are no quasi-rents at point *A* is not a general outcome from marginal cost pricing, but reflects our assumption that marginal cost is constant. In the more typical case where the marginal cost increases with output, total social surplus would include both producer and consumer surpluses.

VARYING DEMANDS PER PERIOD: PEAK AND OFF-PEAK TRAVEL

We now want to relax our assumption that per-period demand is constant. In many transportation markets, demand varies throughout the period. The demand for urban road space, for example, exhibits a regular pattern throughout the day. Demand is quite high during the morning and evening work-trip commutes, but remains much lower throughout the remainder of the day. How do varying demands through a given period alter our first-best pricing rule for existing capacity? To explore this, return to figure 10.1 and now assume that we have two demands per period, off-peak demand given by D_{op} and peak demands given by the higher demand curve D_p. Suppose also that the figure refers to daily bridge crossings, so that D_{op} represents the number of daily bridge crossings during off-peak hours of the day and D_p is the number of daily bridge crossings during peak hours of the day.

What are the first-best prices? They will be exactly the same prices that we identified previously. Since off-peak demand is less than bridge capacity, we charge a price equal to the opportunity cost. And since peak demands more than exhaust capacity at the opportunity cost of a bridge crossing, we raise the price sufficiently to choke off all excess demand. Thus, our first-best prices remain p_1 and p_2 for off-peak and peak demands respectively.

What are the daily (that is, per period) revenues from charging first-best prices? This depends upon the portion of the day that peak and off-peak demands are relevant. Suppose that peak period demands last for 12 hours and off-peak demands for 12 hours. Total daily demand for bridge capacity is $T_1 + T_c$. Price p_1 per bridge crossing will be collected for one half of the period (the off-peak) and p_2 per bridge crossing will be collected for the other half of the period (the peak). Total revenues collected will be $\frac{1}{2}p_1T_1 + \frac{1}{2}p_2T_c$. Alternatively, if the peak occurred during 6 hours of the day and the off-peak lasted for an 18 hour period, then total revenues collected would be $\frac{3}{4}p_1T_1 + \frac{1}{4}p_2T_c$. And more generally, if the off-peak operates for α% of the day and the peak for $(1 - \alpha)$%, then daily revenues will be $\alpha p_1T_1 + (1 - \alpha)p_2T_c$.

Also, since the off-peak is priced optimally at marginal cost, bridge users during the off-peak make no contribution to fixed costs, whereas bridge crossers during the peak do make a contribution to fixed costs. But, in contrast to the constant demand case, if the peak only lasts for a $1 - \alpha$ portion of the day, the contribution to fixed costs is $(1 - \alpha)(p_2 - oc)T_c$, which are the revenues collected over and above opportunity costs. The bridge is self-financing if $(1 - \alpha)(p_2 - oc)T_c$ equals or exceeds the daily fixed costs, F; if these peak hour revenues are less than the daily fixed costs, subsidies are required.

FIRST-BEST PRICING AND INVESTMENT – CONSTANT-COST ENVIRONMENT

Instead of assuming that a local transportation department wants to efficiently price existing capacity, we now assume the transport authority is considering building a bridge. Since the bridge doesn't currently exist, the question is: What size or capacity of bridge should the transport authority build, and at what price should bridge users pay to cross over from Here to There? We know that, for any given bridge capacity, there will be a total cost *TC*, which can be converted into a stream of constant per period payments over the life of the bridge, *F*. Dividing *F* by the bridge's capacity gives the *per-unit* cost of bridge capacity per period. In general, if *cc* represents the constant per-period cost for each unit of bridge capacity, then we can interpret this in either of two ways. First, if the local transportation department wants to build a bridge with a capacity of T_c crossings, the per-crossing capacity cost is *cc* per period. Alternatively, if the authority wants to increase existing capacity by one to $T_c + 1$ crossings, bridge capacity cost per period increases by *cc* dollars.

OPTIMAL PRICING AND INVESTMENT WITH CONSTANT DEMAND PER PERIOD

What policy must the local transportation authority pursue to insure that its bridge investment decision is economically efficient? The transportation authority wants to increase capacity up to the point at which the marginal benefit from increased capacity equals the marginal cost of increased capacity. Consider figure 10.3, which depicts the constant per-period demand

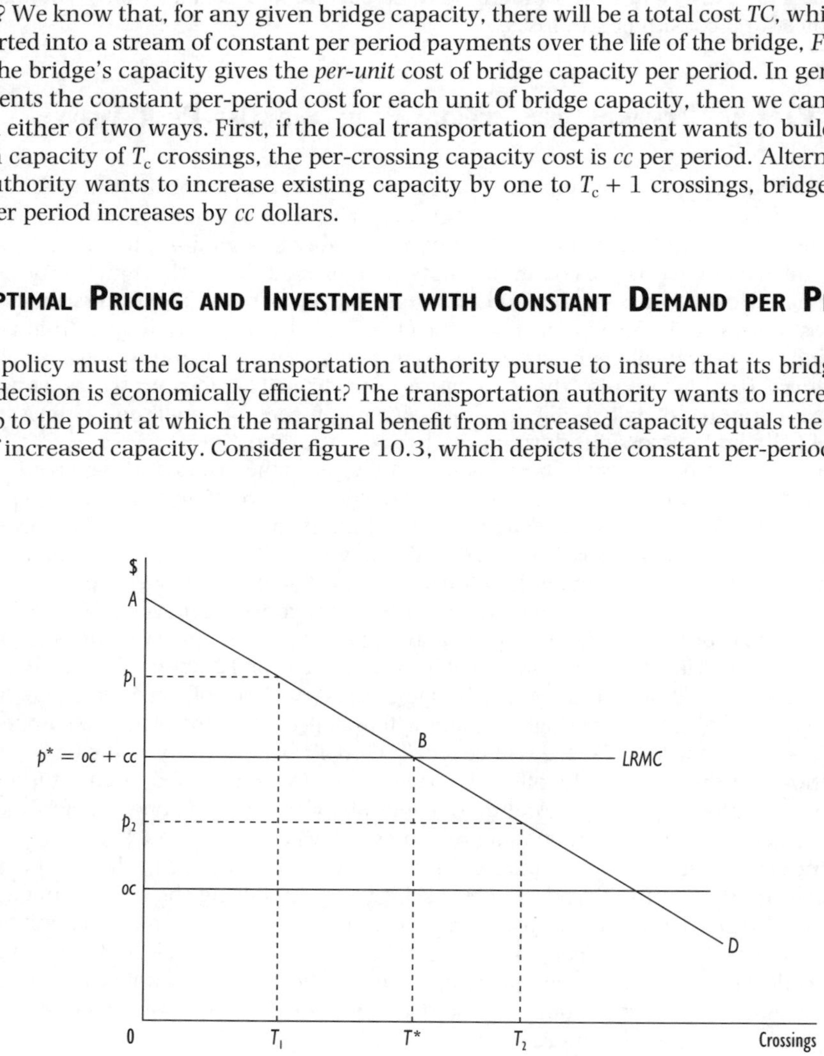

Figure 10.3 Optimal bridge capacity with constant demand per period.

along with the per-unit opportunity cost and capacity cost curves. The long-run marginal cost (*LRMC*) is the sum of per-trip opportunity cost plus capacity cost. Combined with the assumption of constant opportunity cost of a bridge crossing, our assumption of constant per-period bridge capacity costs implies that the *LRMC* curve and the long-run average cost (*LRAC*) curve are constant at $oc + cc$ dollars per crossing.

Suppose that a bridge of capacity T_1 is built. At this capacity, marginal cost pricing implies that the demand price for the marginal trip – that is, the T_1st crossing – is p_1, which is sufficient to cover the opportunity cost of the trip oc, and to contribute the amount $p_1 - oc$ toward recovery of the T_1st unit of capacity, cc. But we see in the figure that $p_1 - oc > cc$, which implies that the marginal benefit of the last unit of capacity demanded exceeds the marginal cost of the last unit supplied. Therefore, too few resources are allocated to bridge capacity and capacity should be increased.

Alternatively, suppose that the local transportation department builds a bridge with capacity T_2. In this case, marginal cost pricing gives an equilibrium price of p_2 which, for the marginal bridge crossing, covers the opportunity cost of the trip and contributes $p_2 - oc$ toward the last unit of capacity supplied. But in this case, $p_1 - oc < cc$, which implies that too many resources are expended on bridge capacity, and a smaller bridge is appropriate.

For all levels of capacity lower and higher than T^*, we can make arguments analogous to those above. Now consider a bridge of size T^*. At this level of output, the demand price p^* covers the opportunity cost oc plus an amount $p^* - oc$ that goes toward the cost of the last unit of supplied capacity. But since $p^* - oc = cc$ at T^*, the marginal benefit of the last unit of capacity consumed equals the marginal cost of supplying the extra unit and T^* is the optimal bridge capacity. In addition, given that a bridge of size T^* is built, the first-best price per bridge crossing is p^*.

What revenues are forthcoming from first-best pricing and optimal investment? From figure 10.3, p^*T^* revenues are collected per period, and these revenues are sufficient to pay the opportunity costs of T^* bridge crossings, which equal $(oc)T^*$, plus all fixed costs, $(p^* - oc)T^*$. Thus, faced with constant long-run marginal costs, and therefore constant long-run average costs, bridge revenues are just sufficient to cover all operating and capital costs of production. In addition, long-run marginal cost pricing ensures that bridge capacity T^* maximizes net welfare to society, which is given in figure 10.3 by the triangular area p^*AB.

CASE STUDY – EFFICIENT PRICING AND INVESTMENT IN HIGHWAY INFRASTRUCTURE

Over the years, the United States, at the federal, state, and local levels, has invested significant amounts of resources toward constructing, expanding, and maintaining a highway infrastructure valued in 1987 at $500 billion (Small et al., 1989). Throughout the 1970s and early 1980s, the highway infrastructure generally deteriorated, as an insufficient level of real resources was expended upon maintaining the road system. Table 10.1 illustrates this point by giving the percentage of rural interstates and other arterials in need of immediate or near-term repair during the period 1975 through 1987. We see in the table that roads in need of immediate repair stayed pretty constant from the mid-1970s through the mid-1980s, although there is evidence of concern for interstate highways in the early 1980s. About 25% of all rural interstate roads and a bit less than 50% of arterials were in need of repair. In addition, the trend for both was increasing until the mid-1980s, when there was an infusion of additional revenues

Table 10.1 The percentage of mileage on rural arterial roads in need of repair, 1975–87

	Needs Immediate Repair[a]		Needs Repair Soon[a]	
Year	Interstates	Other Arterials	Interstates	Other Arterials
1975	10	11	18	45
1978	10	10	24	49
1981	10	11	23	43
1983	13	11	26	44
1985	11	8	24	39
1987	12	6	27	38

[a] Based upon a common used measure of road damage, the Pavement Serviceability Index (*PSI*). For interstates, a *PSI* below 2.5 signals immediate repair and 3.0 indicates that the road needs repair soon. For arterials, a value less than 2.0 signals immediate repair.
Source: Transportation Research Board, National Research Council (1990), table 2.1, p. 23

Table 10.2 Vehicle–miles (billions) traveled on rural interstates, 1981–8

Year	Combination Trucks	All Motor Vehicles
1981	22	139
1982	23	142
1983	23	145
1984	25	149
1985	26	154
1986	27	160
1987	27	170
1988	28	181

Source: Transportation Research Board, National Research Council (1990), table 2.2, p. 24

after passage of the 1982 Surface Transportation Assistance Act. Although the percentage of interstates in need of immediate repair dropped between 1983 and 1985, the trend picked up again in 1987.

There are several reasons for the relatively small improvement in infrastructure quality. First, as a proportion of total expenditures, the percentage going to maintenance has been falling. In 1983, for example, 30.8% of the highway budget went for maintenance. By 1989, the proportion spent on maintenance fell to 27.1%. Second, the volume of traffic has steadily increased. Table 10.2 provides information on vehicle–miles traveled between 1981 and 1988. Throughout the period, there has been a steady increase in total vehicle–miles traveled and combination truck vehicle–miles traveled. The latter group is of particular relevance, since heavy trucks impose the most damage on highway infrastructure. If automobiles and motorcycles were the only users of our nation's 33,000 miles of rural interstate highways, the roads would not wear out.[5] Damage to these systems comes from the heavy trucks that utilize the roads. The increased amount of combination truck traffic in table 10.2 implies greater loads and increased pavement wear on the nation's highways. Not only are combination trucks driving more miles, but their pavement-wearing impact is increasing. This is the third reason for the infrastructure problems that we are currently facing. All newly constructed roads are built to withstand the stresses or loads exerted by motor vehicle traffic. For any motor vehicle, the load exerted is the wear on the road from the weight that each axle carries. Since there are many different types of motor vehicles that have anywhere from two to nine axles, a standard axle weight and configuration is a single axle of 18,000 pounds. Other weights and configurations are then converted into single-axle equivalents, or what are commonly referred to as *esals* (equivalent single-axle loadings). As trucks become larger and heavier, the loads carried on each axle increase, which causes greater wear and tear on the pavement. The average daily pavement wear on rural interstate highways in 1978 due to combination trucks with five or more axles was 3,330 esals. Between 1978 and 1988, the pavement wear from these vehicles increased 55% to 5,100 esals, which reflects the increased number and size of combination trucks on these roads.

The load per axle is an important determinant of pavement wear. Related to this is the fact that pavement wear rises very steeply with the loads carried, approximately to the third power.[6] We can see the implication of this by considering the effect of two vehicles, an automobile weighing 3,000 pounds and a 12 ton two-axle truck. Assume that the rear axle of the automobile has a 1,500 pound load, whereas the rear axle of the 12 ton truck has a 12,000 pound load. Although each truck axle has eight times the load of the automobile, the damage caused to the highway is not eight times as much, but 8^3 = 514 times as much. This is the third-power approximation. Consider, as another example, a 55,000 pound two-axle cement truck. Relative to a 3,000 pound automobile, this vehicle causes more than 6,000 times the structural damage.

In two related studies, Small and Winston (1988) and Small et al. (1989) analyzed our nation's pricing and investment policies in highway infrastructure, in order to evaluate whether existing practices have led to efficient resource allocation and, if not, how we might make better use of our resources to meet our nation's highway needs.

Marginal Maintenance Costs of Increased Pavement Wear

Small et al. identify periodic road resurfacing as the primary maintenance activity on roads as road quality deteriorates to a threshold level. We saw in table 10.1, for example, that rural interstate roads with a Pavement Serviceability Index (PSI) less than 2.5 receive immediate attention, as do arterial roads with PSIs below 2.0. Normally, not all lanes in a road deteriorate at the same rate. In a multilane unidirectional highway, slower traffic, including trucks, travels in the right hand or "slow" lane. Given that the slower trucks move in the slower lanes and are responsible for the bulk of the structural damage to a road, the right-hand lane is expected to deteriorate faster and be the first lane to hit the threshold PSI level. Once a lane requires resurfacing, the transportation agencies generally resurface all lanes.

With this in mind, assume that we have a unidirectional road of width W. Let $N(D)$ be the cumulative number of esals in the right-hand lane before resurfacing is required, and assume that $N(D)$ depends upon the road's durability D, which is defined as pavement thickness. Let λ be the proportion of esals that travel in the right-hand lane. Then the right-hand lane will require resurfacing when the total number of esals on the road reaches $N(D)/\lambda$.

For example, thick pavements typically accommodate 6–10 million esal passages before resurfacing. Suppose that a four-lane highway accommodates 8 million esal passages and that 90% of the traffic loadings occur in the right-hand lane. Then the highway will require resurfacing after (8,000,000/0.9) = 8,888,888.9 esal passages.

Let $C(W)$ be the total cost of resurfacing, which depends upon the number of lanes W. Then the average maintenance cost per axle crossing AC_m is

$$AC_{\mathrm{m}} = \frac{C(W)}{N(D)/\lambda} = \lambda\frac{C(W)}{N(D)} \qquad (10.1)$$

Assuming that the average cost per axle crossing is constant, and thus equal to the marginal cost per crossing, equation (10.1) provides an *initial* estimate of the marginal cost of maintenance. However, if we expect to have an efficient pricing and investment policy, equation (10.1) actually *overestimates* the marginal cost of maintenance. The reason is that the resurfacing cost occurs at some time R in the future. The present value of $C(W)$ dollars expended R periods in the future is less than $C(W)$ dollars spent today, so that the marginal maintenance cost MC_{m} is some fraction α ($0 < \alpha < 1$) of the cost identified in equation (10.1). That is,

$$MC_{\mathrm{m}} = \alpha\frac{\lambda C(W)}{N(D)} \qquad (10.2)$$

Since equation (10.2) reflects a discounting process, α can be shown to depend upon the rate of interest, a result which will be more apparent in the following section.

EFFICIENT PRICING AND DURABILITY

Small and Winston (1988) analyze the pricing and investment decisions of a highway department by converting the present discounted values of expected maintenance and capital expenditures into an equivalent series of annual payments. Let

$$m = iM(Q,W,D)$$
$$k = iK(W,D) \qquad (10.3)$$

be the annualized expenditures upon maintenance and capital, respectively: i is the rate of interest, which reflects the opportunity cost of funds; M is the present discounted value of expected maintenance expenditures; K is the construction cost of the road; W is the number of lanes on the road; D is pavement thickness; and Q is the annual traffic loadings on the road.

A rise in annual traffic loadings Q implies that the threshold level of loadings that triggers resurfacing occurs sooner. Because expenditures that occur sooner are less heavily discounted, the present discounted value of such expenditures rises. Thus, an increase in traffic loadings Q is expected to raise annual expected maintenance expenditures. An increase in pavement thickness D, on the other hand, is expected to reduce maintenance expenditures, because it delays the need to resurface. Moving resurfacing expenditures to the more distant future discounts these expenditures more heavily, which lowers the present discounted value of maintenance expenditures. Finally, an increase in the number of lanes W increases maintenance expenditures.

With respect to annualized construction costs, increasing the number of lanes W and the pavement thickness D is expected to raise the capital costs of construction. Also, since annualized capital costs do not depend upon traffic loadings, these costs represent an annual stream of fixed costs.

What is the present discounted value of maintenance expenditures? For any given road width, annual traffic loadings, and pavement thickness, suppose that, beginning with year R, the highway authority decides to resurface the road every R years, for the next tR years. The cost of resurfacing is $C(W)$. Then the discounted present value of resurfacing expenditures is

$$\begin{aligned} M(Q,W,D) &= C(W)\left[\frac{1}{(1+i)^{R(D)}} + \frac{1}{(1+i)^{2R(D)}} + \frac{1}{(1+i)^{3R(D)}} + \ldots + \frac{1}{(1+i)^{tR(D)}}\right] \\ &= \frac{C(W)}{(1+i)^{R(D)} - 1}\left[1 - \frac{1}{(1+i)^{tR(D)}}\right] \qquad (10.4) \end{aligned}$$

If the resurfacing is expected to continue forever, n goes to infinity and equation (10.4) collapses to

$$M(Q,W,D) = \frac{C(W)}{(1+i)^{R(D)} - 1} \qquad (10.5)$$

Notice in equations (10.4) and (10.5) that the time to resurface, $R(D)$, depends upon pavement thickness, which reflects the relationship between esal passages and the need to resurface. Increasing pavement thickness enables a road to accommodate a higher number of esals before resurfacing. Thus, for a given road width and annual traffic loadings, increasing D lengthens the time R between resurfacing; that is, $\Delta R/\Delta D > 0$.

Can we give an expression for R? Yes. Recall that $N(D)/\lambda$ is the total number of loadings in the right-hand lane before the road needs resurfacing. Dividing this by Q, traffic loadings per year, gives $N(D)/\lambda Q$, the number of years before resurfacing. Thus, $R = N(D)/\lambda Q$, where increasing thickness D, through its positive effect upon $N(D)$, increases R, all else constant.

Is there a need to convert capital costs K to present discounted values? No. Since capital costs are incurred at the beginning of the period, these costs are already in present-value dollars. Thus, multiplying capital costs by the rate of interest gives annualized capital costs, k.

The short-run marginal maintenance cost is the change in total annualized costs resulting from a unit increase in traffic loadings Q. From equations (10.3) and (10.5), this implies that

$$\begin{aligned} MC_m &= \text{short-run marginal maintenance cost} \\ &= i\left[\frac{\Delta M(Q,W,D)}{\Delta Q} + \frac{\Delta K(W,D)}{\Delta Q}\right] \\ &= i\left[\frac{\Delta M(Q,W,D)}{\Delta Q}\right] \\ &= \alpha(i)\frac{\lambda C(W)}{N(D)} \qquad (10.6) \end{aligned}$$

where the second equation results from the fact that annualized capital costs do not vary with traffic loadings Q and the third equation, consistent with equation (10.2) in the previous section, tells us that short-run marginal maintenance costs are proportional to the average cost per loading. The proportionality factor, $\alpha(i)$, lies between zero and one, because it reflects the discounting process associated with resurfacing the road R periods from the present.[7] Thus, as seen in equation (10.3) and from the term after the first equals sign in equation (10.6), short-run marginal maintenance cost depends upon the rate of interest i.

Recall that a given level of thickness accommodates a cumulative loading on the road before resurfacing occurs. Also recall that maintenance expenditures reflect road resurfacing that occurs at some future date. With these two facts in mind, the sense behind equation (10.6) is that an increase in traffic loadings *shortens* the time before resurfacing occurs. But a shorter time horizon means that resurfacing costs occur sooner, which implies that these maintenance costs are not discounted as heavily. Thus, an increase in traffic loadings increases the present discounted value of maintenance expenditures which, when multiplied by the interest rate, gives the marginal maintenance cost of increased loadings.

In order to optimally invest in durability, we want to minimize the annualized present value of maintenance and capital costs; that is, we want to minimize

$$iM(Q,W,D) + iK(W,D) \qquad (10.7)$$

where $M(Q,W,D)$ is defined in (10.5) and $K(W,D)$ is defined as

$$K(W,D) = k_0 + k_1 W + k_2 WD \qquad (10.8)$$

Equation (10.8) implies that

$$\frac{\Delta K(W,D)}{\Delta W} = k_1 + k_2 D$$

$\Rightarrow$ the effect on capital costs from an increase in the number of lanes varies linearly with pavement thickness

$$\frac{\Delta K(W,D)}{\Delta D} = k_2 W$$

⇒ the effect of an increase in pavement thickness on capital costs is proportional to the number of lanes

If we substitute equations (10.5) and (10.8) into equation (10.7), we obtain

$$i[M(Q,W,D) + K(W,D)]$$

$$= i\left[\frac{C(W)}{(1+i)^{R(D)} - 1} + k_0 + k_1 W + k_2 WD\right]$$

Dividing through by road width W, in order to obtain annualized total cost per lane (ATC_L), gives

$$ATC_L(Q,D) = i\left[\frac{C(W)/W}{(1+i)^{R(D)} - 1} + \frac{k_0}{W} + k_1 + k_2 D\right]$$

Since we want to minimize per-lane total cost with respect to pavement thickness D, we can ignore those terms that are unrelated to D. Thus, minimizing the annualized long-run total costs of durability is equivalent to minimizing

$$ATC_L(Q,D) = i\frac{C(W)/W}{(1+i)^{R(D)} - 1} + ik_2 D \quad (10.9)$$

Note the interpretation of the two terms given in equation (10.9). ik_2 is the annualized per-lane marginal capital cost of increased durability. Adding an additional inch of pavement thickness raises annualized capital costs by ik_2 dollars. Also, because the time to resurface R depends upon pavement thickness D, the first term reflects annualized savings on maintenance expenditures from increased investment in per-lane durability. By lengthening the time before resurfacing occurs, increased durability discounts more heavily future resurfacing costs, which lowers the present discounted value of maintenance expenditures, $M(Q,W,D)$ and, accordingly, the annualized value of maintenance expenditures. All else constant, then, increased durability shifts the short-run marginal maintenance curve, MC_m, downward. And at optimum thickness, the savings in maintenance expenditures equals the marginal cost of durability:

$$-i\frac{\Delta MC_m}{\Delta D} = ik_2 \quad (10.10)$$

To sum up, if we are to efficiently price and invest in capital, we must once again satisfy our two optimality conditions: (1) marginal cost pricing; and (2) investment up to the point at which the marginal cost of capital equals the marginal savings from capital investment. For investments in highway infrastructure, these conditions are given by equations (10.6) and (10.10).

In the following section, we will use these equilibrium conditions to evaluate past investments in highway durability, existing taxes on heavy vehicle users, and implications for future investment and pricing policy.

THE INEFFICIENCY OF EXISTING HIGHWAY INVESTMENTS

To illustrate the relationship between optimal pricing and investment, consider a six-lane rural interstate highway, with three lanes moving in each direction. In general, interstate highways are a subset of highways referred to as "rigid pavements," which includes all roads made of Portland cement concrete. Since rigid roads with thicker concrete slabs are also stronger and more durable, road thickness is a common measure of pavement strength for this class of road. Assuming that the rural interstate road has a 10 inch pavement thickness, which is consistent with current road-building practice, what can we say about optimal pricing and investment? – not very much until we identify some other features of the road. Let's make the following assumptions:[8]

- annual traffic loadings, Q, equal 1,000,000, the median traffic load
- the per-lane–mile capital cost, k_2, is \$12,800 per inch (1984 dollars)

Table 10.3 Marginal maintenance costs and annualized capital costs existing and optimal values for a rural interstate: traffic loading = 1,000,000

	Thickness, D (inches)	Short Run Marginal Maintenance Cost, MC_m (cents per esal)	Annualized Total Cost per Lane, ATC_L (\$)
Current behavior	10	2.4	16,284
Optimal behavior	11.6	0.9	14,529

Source: Small and Winston (1988) and author's calculations

- the per-lane–mile resurfacing cost, $C(W)/W$, is \$113,400 (1984 dollars)
- the opportunity cost of funds, i, is 9%
- 70% of truck traffic occurs in the right-hand lane $\Rightarrow \lambda = 0.7$

In their analysis, Small and Winston estimated that a concrete road 10 inches thick would support 9.3 million cumulative esal loadings before resurfacing. Based upon this information, we can calculate existing and optimal short-run marginal maintenance costs per esal, and annualized capital costs. For our 10 inch interstate highway, these costs are summarized in the first row of table 10.3. In the table, the 2.4 cents per esal loading associated with current practice is obtained by inserting the cost and esal loading assumptions into equation (10.6). Specifically,

$$MC_{\mathrm{m}} = 0.937\frac{\lambda C(W)}{N(D)}$$

$$= 0.937\frac{0.7(340{,}200)}{9{,}300{,}000} = 2.4$$

where $0.937 = \alpha(i)$ is calculated from the expression given in note 7. Similarly, we use equation (10.9) to calculate the annualized total per-lane cost. This gives

$$ATC_{\mathrm{L}} = i\frac{C(W)/W}{(1+i)^{R(D)}-1} + ik_2D$$

$$= 0.09\left[\frac{113{,}400}{(1.09)^{13.28}-1} + 12{,}800(10)\right]$$

$$= 16,284$$

where 13.28 is the number of years between resurfacing, and is calculated from the relationship that $R(D) = N(D)/\lambda Q(9.3/0.7(1))$.

Short-run marginal maintenance cost and annualized total per-lane cost for an optimal pricing and investment strategy are obtained in a similar fashion. The only difference here is the greater durability under optimality. Whereas current road-building practices call for a 10 inch thick slab of concrete for an interstate that carries 1,000,000 esals annually, Small and Winston found that 10 inch slabs were sub-optimal. If we solve equation (10.9) for the value of D that minimizes the annualized total per-lane cost, we obtain an optimal durability equal to 11.6 inches. As seen in table 10.3, this produces two beneficial effects. First, marginal maintenance cost per esal crossing falls from 2.4 cents to less than 1 cent. Second, annualized total costs decrease from \$16.2 to \$14.5 thousand dollars. The reason for this latter result is the much longer pavement life. Whereas the 10 inch slab led to a 9.3 million esal pavement life, an 11.6 inch slab produced a pavement life equal to 17.8 million esals. With a constant 1,000,000 annual loading, this increases the time between resurfacing to 26.4 (17.8/0.7) years and reduces the discounted present value of total costs, which correspondingly reduces the annualized total costs.

In addition to examining interstate highways in rural areas, Small et al. evaluated the effect that optimal investment would have on other principal arterials, as well as on major and minor collectors located in urban and rural areas. Similar to the results identified in table 10.3, there has generally been too little investment in durability, leading to excessively high marginal maintenance costs. Under optimal investment in infrastructure, Small et al. found that marginal maintenance costs for all road types in rural and urban locations would fall significantly.

TRUCK TAXES AND MARGINAL MAINTENANCE COSTS

In the previous section, we saw that past highway investments in infrastructure have led to sub-optimal durability and marginal maintenance costs. Recognizing that heavy trucks are a major source of highway deterioration, a related question is whether trucks are paying their "fair share" in taxes for highway use. Economically, "fair share" goes to the question of whether trucks are paying for the deterioration to roads caused by their heavy loads.

In general, the taxes that truckers currently pay fall into three categories: distance-based, including fuel and ton–mile taxes; weight-based, which includes heavy vehicle registration taxes; and special excise taxes, such as those on tires. For urban and intercity truck traffic, table 10.4 gives the amounts of current taxes paid by different truck types and truck weights. The single-unit two-axle truck is the dominant truck type for urban and intercity travel respectively. In 1982, for example, the single-unit two-axle truck accounted for 91% of urban truck traffic, 91% of urban highway loadings, and 89% of urban vehicle–miles traveled. The single-unit three-axle truck comprised 6% of urban truck vehicles, 2% of esal loadings, and 5% of urban vehicle–miles traveled. In intercity travel, two- and three-axle single-unit trucks made up 76% of all vehicles, 49% of esal loadings, and 48% of vehicle–miles traveled.

Conventional five-axle tractor–trailers accounted for 17% of intercity trucks, 40% of esal loadings, and 39% of vehicle–miles traveled. For interstate travel, an 80,000 pound five-axle tractor–semitrailer is the dominant truck type. Currently, double trailers with six or more axles make up a tiny portion of urban and intercity trucking.

Table 10.4 illustrates an interesting pattern of taxes among alternative truck types. For any given truck type, as we move across the table, per-mile taxes increase with weight. Since heavier trucks of any given type damage a road more than lighter trucks of the same type, the

Table 10.4 Current truck taxes (1982 cents per vehicle–mile)

	Gross Vehicle Weight ('000 pounds)				
Truck Type	26	33	35	80	105
Urban trucks					
Single-unit, two-axle truck	2.52	3.01	4.22	–	–
Single-unit, three-axle truck	3.88	4.38	5.61	7.43	–
Conventional five-axle tractor–semitrailer	–	4.07	5.34	7.19	8.28
Double-trailer, six or more axle truck	–	–	6.06	7.90	9.01
Intercity trucks					
Single-unit, two-axle truck	1.95	2.24	2.91	–	–
Single-unit, three-axle truck	3.25	3.55	4.23	5.31	–
Conventional five-axle tractor–semitrailer	–	3.16	3.86	4.96	5.56
Double-trailer, six or more axle truck	–	–	4.46	5.56	6.17

Source: Adapted from Small et al. (1989), tables 3-4, 3-5; pp. 45–6

positive relationship between taxes and vehicle weight is consistent with economic theory. Vehicle types using more of society's scarce resources should pay a higher use tax.

An alternative way of looking at table 10.4 is to move down the table for a given weight class of vehicle. Here again we see a positive relationship between taxes paid and truck size. But this pattern *does not* accord with economic theory. Why? Recall that damage to a road occurs through the loadings on a truck's axles. The more weight a given axle carries, the more damage is caused to a road from a truck passing. In table 10.4, as we move down a particular weight category, the given load is distributed over more axles. This *lessens* the load on each axle, which *reduces* damage to the road. In other words, if truck taxes are to bear any relationship to marginal maintenance costs, per-vehicle–mile taxes for a given weight category should fall, not rise, with the number of truck axles.

How would the table change if the trucking industry faced marginal maintenance taxes? The answer here depends upon society's highway investment decisions. Assume first that we impose taxes on truckers for the damage caused to the existing roads which, as we saw in the previous section, are sub-optimally built. Table 10.5 gives these taxes. There are two features in table 10.5 that are immediately clear. First, in comparison with table 10.4, taxes would increase significantly as weight classifications increased for any given truck type. Consider, for example, a 35,000 pound single-unit two-axle truck. If these highway users were assessed taxes based upon the damage to the road, their taxes would skyrocket from 4.2 cents to 183.38 cents per vehicle–mile. Conversely, we now see in table 10.5 that marginal maintenance taxes are rational as we move down a given weight classification. As the size of truck increases, taxes per vehicle–mile fall, reflecting the smaller amount of highway damage from trucks with more axles. Moreover, notice that some trucking types actually gain from economically based taxes. In the intercity environment, five-axle tractor–semitrailers with a 35,000 pound gross vehicle weight (GVW) currently pay 3.86 cents per vehicle mile. With efficient pricing, this falls to 3.23 cents per vehicle–mile. Double trailers in the same weight category experience an even greater benefit from efficient pricing, a reduction from 4.46 to 2.18 cents per vehicle–mile.

A feature of table 10.5 is the sub-optimal investment in highway infrastructure. How would truck taxes change if we were to invest optimally

Table 10.5 Efficient truck taxes with current (sub-optimal) infrastructure investment (1982 cents per vehicle–mile)

	Gross Vehicle Weight ('000 pounds)				
Truck Type	26	33	35	80	105
Urban trucks					
Single-unit, two-axle truck	9.16	23.77	183.38	–	–
Single-unit, three-axle truck	2.07	5.37	41.43	125.43	–
Conventional five-axle tractor–semitrailer	–	1.20	9.22	41.26	122.44
Double-trailer, six or more axle truck	–	0.81	6.22	27.83	82.58
Intercity trucks					
Single-unit, two-axle truck	3.21	8.33	64.26	–	–
Single-unit, three-axle truck	0.73	1.88	14.52	64.98	–
Conventional five-axle tractor–semitrailer	–	0.42	3.23	14.46	42.91
Double-trailer, six or more axle truck	–	0.28	2.18	9.75	28.94

Source: Adapted from Small et al. (1989), tables 3-4, 3-5; pp. 45–6

Table 10.6 Efficient truck taxes with optimal infrastructure investment (1982 cents per vehicle–mile)

	Gross Vehicle Weight ('000 pounds)				
Truck Type	26	33	35	80	105
Urban trucks					
Single-unit, two-axle truck	3.59	9.32	71.89	–	–
Single-unit, three-axle truck	0.81	2.11	16.24	72.69	–
Conventional five-axle tractor–semitrailer	–	0.47	3.61	16.17	48.00
Double-trailer, six or more axle truck	–	0.32	2.44	10.91	32.37
Intercity trucks					
Single-unit, two-axle truck	0.69	1.78	13.74	–	–
Single-unit, three-axle truck	0.16	0.40	3.10	13.89	–
Conventional five-axle tractor–semitrailer	–	0.09	0.69	3.09	9.17
Double-trailer, six or more axle truck	–	–	0.47	2.08	6.19

Source: Adapted from Small et al. (1989), tables 3-4, 3-5; pp. 45–6

in highway infrastructure? You should be able to anticipate the answer at this point. We have seen that the effect of increased capital investment is to lower current operating costs. Since we have found that past highway investments have been inefficiently small, a move to an efficient level of highway investment – that is, greater durability – should reduce marginal maintenance costs. This is precisely what we observe in table 10.6. Although taxes continue to increase sharply across weight categories, the increase is much less than that given in table 10.5. In comparison with existing taxes, a single-unit two-axle truck with a 35,000 pound gross vehicle weight would still pay a significantly higher tax with optimal investment, but the tax is less than half that with existing infrastructure investments.

With efficient pricing and optimal investment in infrastructure, we see in table 10.6 that many truck categories gain. In the urban environment, three-axle single-unit trucks, conventional tractor–semitrailers, and double-trailer trucks with six or more axles, each with a GVW of 33,000 pounds or less, gain with a move to efficient pricing and investment. Correspondingly, heavier truck categories lose under this strategy, for all axle configurations.

For the rural environment, the gains are broader. For GVW of 33,000 pounds or less, two-axle single-unit trucks gain at the expense of heavier trucks with the same configuration. Three-axle single-unit trucks also gain in the 35,000 GVW category. For the larger trucks, we see in table 10.6 that conventional tractor–semitrailers gain in all but the heaviest (105,000) weight category. And double trailer trucks with six or more axles likewise gain in the 35,000 and 80,000 GVW group. In the 105,000 GVW category, there is little difference between existing taxes and efficient taxes with optimal investment.

POLICY IMPLICATIONS

The trucking industry oftentimes argues that its members are paying more than their fair share, because existing roads are not optimally built. Do the results presented in tables 10.4–10.6 support this claim? Yes and no. The answer is yes, in the sense that if roads were built optimally, marginal maintenance taxes imposed upon the trucking industry would be less than

Table 10.7 The percentage distribution of selected truck types under current and efficient pricing and investment

	Urban		Intercity	
Truck Type	Current	Optimal	Current	Optimal
Single-unit, two-axle truck	91.22	84.58	69.36	65.72
Single-unit, three-axle truck	6.34	9.43	6.31	7.07
Conventional five-axle tractor–semitrailer	0.78	1.13	17.15	18.24
Double-trailer, six or more axle truck	0.01	0.07	0.02	0.02

Source: Adapted from Small et al. (1989), table 3-9, p. 56

marginal maintenance taxes *based upon existing investment in infrastructure*. This compares per-vehicle–mile taxes in tables 10.5 and 10.6. But the answer is generally no if we compare marginal maintenance taxes with *current* taxes; that is, taxes in table 10.4 with those for table 10.5 or table 10.6.

The basic result is that per-vehicle–mile taxes which increase with the number of axles are economically inefficient, because they induce trucking firms to use trucks with fewer axles. But, all else constant (including GVW), trucks with fewer axles have more deteriorating effects upon roads. In other words, the existing structure of taxes provides firms with an economic incentive in the form of lower vehicle use taxes to ship goods with trucks that have greater damaging effects upon highways.

If firms face the true opportunity costs of using the highway network, the operating costs of trucks with fewer axles would generally rise relative to the operating costs of trucks with more axles. All else constant, this implies that firms would substitute in their truck type choices away from the lower-axle and toward higher-axle trucks.

As a final question, what would happen to the existing distribution of truck types if current use taxes were replaced with economically efficient marginal maintenance taxes, and roads were built optimally? Table 10.7 gives these percentages for the truck types identified in tables 10.4–10.6, based on a demand model for truck types estimated by Small et al. Not surprisingly, the largest changes in the distribution of truck types occur in the urban environment, where the existing incentives are the most perverse. The proportion of single-unit two-axle trucks would fall by 7.3%, from over 90% to just under 85%. Single-unit three-axle trucks would enjoy a significant 49% increase. Although larger trucks make up a small portion of urban travel, their presence would increase under efficient pricing and investment. Conventional tractor–semitrailers would rise to 1.13% from their current 0.78% and double trailers would rise dramatically, at least in a relative sense, from 0.01% to 0.07%.

The distribution of these vehicle types in rural environments changes in the same direction as in the urban environment, but the changes are less spectacular. The use of single-unit two-axle trucks would fall by 5% and that of single-unit three-axle trucks would rise by 12%. Conventional five-axle tractor–semitrailers would rise by 6%, whereas double trailers would experience no change.

CASE STUDY – WELFARE EFFECTS OF FIRST-BEST PRICING AND INVESTMENT IN HIGHWAY CAPACITY

We have seen that the current thickness or durability of roads is less than optimal and, correspondingly, existing marginal maintenance costs are higher than optimal. Since first-best

Table 10.8 Welfare effects of first-best pricing and investment on our nation's roads: savings in billions of 1982 dollars

Affected Group	Efficient Pricing and Investment (1)	Efficient Pricing with Current Investment (2)	Efficient Investment with Current Pricing (3)
Investment costs			
Maintenance savings	9.428	6.441	8.536
Annualized capital savings	−1.276	–	−2.236
Total savings	8.152	6.441	6.300
Trucking firms' and shippers' welfare	0.134	−5.586	–
Government revenues	−0.574	3.884	–
Modal shifting			
Modal surplus	0.029	0.204	–
Rail profits	0.011	0.411	–
Total welfare	7.752	5.334	6.300
Percentage change in standard loadings	−38.12	−48.38	0.0

Source: Adapted from Winston (1991), table 1, p. 118. Trucker and shipper welfare changes reflect the reduction in road wear taxes and the modal surplus figures reflect the benefits to shippers who either move to or from rail in response to the altered truck taxes

pricing and investment maximizes society's net welfare, society will experience a net welfare gain if first-best pricing and investment replaced current highway pricing and investment polices. But to what extent would society gain? Has existing policy significantly lowered social welfare?

Small et al. (1989) examined this question and estimated the annual welfare effects if roads, produced under constant returns to scale, were optimally supplied and priced.[9] Using current pricing and investment as a base, table 10.8 summarizes the welfare effects under three alternative investment practices: current pricing and efficient investment; optimal pricing with current investment; and first-best pricing and investment.

We see in table 10.8 that, regardless of policy, there are clear welfare gains in comparison with present practices. From column (2), if the nation were to continue its present investment practices but change to an efficient pricing policy, society's annual welfare would increase by $5.3 billion.

Alternatively, if society maintained its existing pricing policy but moved to an efficient investment policy, annual welfare would rise by $6.3 billion. On the basis of these figures, society is better off with an optimal investment policy and a sub-optimal pricing policy, rather than an optimal pricing policy and a sub-optimal investment policy. Not only are the welfare effects higher but one would also expect that this would be more politically acceptable. Consider the distribution effects of the two policies. From column (3), the economic effects of an efficient investment policy with current pricing are limited to highway maintenance costs and capital expenditures. Under this policy, there is an annual $2.23 billion increase in capital expenditures in order to make our highways more durable. But the increased durability directly produces annual savings amounting to $8.53 billion, yielding the reported $6.3 billion annual net benefit.

On the other hand, the effect on investment costs from a strategy of efficient pricing with current investment yields an annual saving of

$6.44 billion, somewhat higher than under a policy of optimal investment with current pricing. However, because efficient prices alter the prices that shippers pay and carriers receive, there will be additional welfare effects. Moreover, if roads are not optimally built, the marginal maintenance costs will be higher than optimal, which imposes an unnecessarily large burden on trucker and shipper welfare. This cost is clearly seen in column (2) of table 10.8, where annual welfare for the group falls $5.58 billion. Although the $3.88 increase in annual tax revenues offsets this decrease in welfare to some degree, the primary loser of the policy is the motor carrier transport sector, which would argue against the policy on equity grounds. And, as we have seen, this is not a completely empty argument, since efficient road taxes with *current* investment would be substantially higher than efficient road taxes with *efficient* investment.

Column (1) of table 10.8 demonstrates the positive welfare effects of first-best pricing and investment. As with the two partial policies in columns (2) and (3), first-best pricing and investment increase net welfare in comparison with current pricing and investment practices. But also, as expected from our previous discussion, net welfare is significantly higher than the other two policies, which are not fully efficient. Relative to columns (2) and (3), respectively, first-best pricing and investment raise social welfare by 40% and 23% respectively. In addition, column (1) does not exhibit the negative distribution effects associated with column (2)'s policy. In particular, with the exception of government revenues, all significant groups gain from an efficient pricing and investment policy. Welfare in the motor carrier transport sector receives an annual gain of $134 million, modal shifting effects are small but positive, and total annual investment costs fall by $8.15 billion.

We have also seen that if motor carriers faced marginal maintenance costs of road usage, these efficient prices would induce firms to alter the composition of their truck fleets and shift to truck types with a larger number of axles. The shift to trucks with more axles reduces the number of equivalent single-axle loadings (esal) and lowers their taxes. In column (1) of table 10.8, first-best pricing and investment generates a 38.1% fall in esals.[10] Not only does the firm benefit through lower taxes, but society gains by less wear and tear on the roads and lower maintenance costs.

Thus, under existing investment policy, the marginal benefit, in the form of annual maintenance savings, exceeds the marginal (annualized) capital cost of additional investments in road durability. Optimal investment implies an increase in road durability, generating net benefits from more durable capacity and lower maintenance costs. And under existing pricing policy, the marginal benefit of using existing roads, reflected by taxes paid, is less than the marginal costs of maintaining these roads. Optimal pricing implies higher road charges and lower esals, generating net savings in maintenance costs on the existing capacity. By extending road life and reducing maintenance expenses, each policy efficiently allocates scarce highway resources and maximizes net social surplus.

As a final point, what are the revenue consequences of optimal pricing and investment? In the constant-cost case, we know that capacity investment would be self-financing, whereas subsidies are required if production characterizes increasing returns to scale. Since Small et al. (1989) found that investment in durability occurs under increasing returns to scale, optimal pricing combined with optimal investment in highway durability would generate revenues that fall short of production costs. This implies that the beneficial effects reported in table 10.8 would be reduced by tax-induced welfare losses elsewhere in the economy.[11]

OPTIMAL INVESTMENT WITH VARYING DEMANDS PER PERIOD

To consider varying demands per period, let's return to our bridge example. Instead of constant demand per period, assume as we did in the fixed capacity case that we have an off-peak

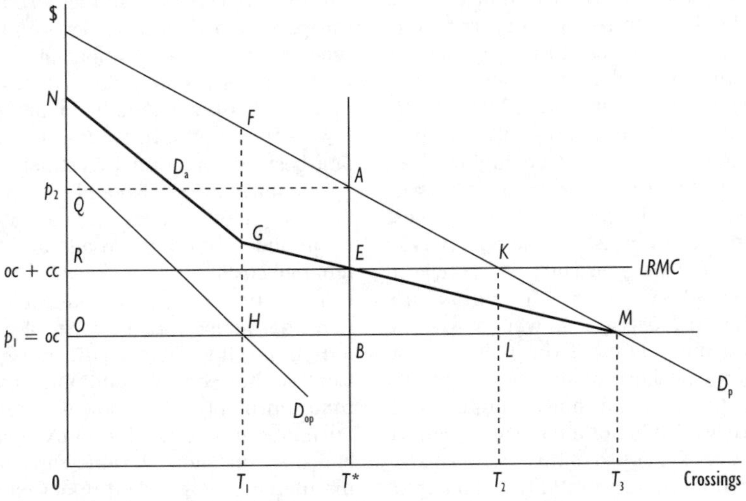

Figure 10.4 Optimal bridge capacity with varying demand per period.

demand, D_{op}, and a peak demand, D_p, for bridge crossings. The off-peak demand lasts for α% of the day, while the peak occurs for $(1 - \alpha)$% of the day. In order to analyze this situation, we must consider the price that peak users of the bridge are willing to pay for the extra capacity and the price that off-peak users are willing to pay for extra capacity. Assume that the cost of an additional unit of capacity, whether the capacity is added during the peak period or the off-peak period, is *cc*. Thus, the total cost of additional capacity *per day*, which includes peak and off-peak times, is 2(*cc*). Also, for simplicity, assume that α is $\frac{1}{2}$, so that half of the day accommodates peak bridge crossings and the other half of the day accommodates off-peak crossings. Figure 10.4 depicts peak, off-peak, and average daily demands, D_a, for bridge crossings. In the figure, the bold line D_a is the simple average of peak and off-peak demands. Since we assume that peak and off-peak trips each occur for half of the total period, D_a is $\frac{1}{2}D_{op} + \frac{1}{2}D_p$. Let's look more closely at how this curve is obtained.

Consider capacity level T_1 where off-peak demand intersects the opportunity cost curve *oc* at point *H* and peak demand lies well above the opportunity cost curve (point *F*). This implies that the T_1st off-peak bridge user is willing to pay the opportunity cost of crossing the bridge, but is not willing to pay for any bridge capacity. The marginal peak user, on the other hand, is willing to pay an amount equal to *FH* for a marginal unit of bridge capacity. However, since peak usage occurs for only half of the day, the contribution to the *daily* capacity cost of 2(*cc*) is $\frac{1}{2}FH = GH$. Up to capacity level T_1, therefore, both off-peak and peak bridge users contribute to bridge capacity costs, and the darkened line segment *NG* represents the average revenue that these users are willing to pay for an additional unit of bridge capacity.

Alternatively, consider bridge capacity T_2. Since T_2 is greater than T_1, off-peak users contribute nothing to bridge capacity costs, whereas peak users are willing to contribute the amount *KL*. But, again, this represents a $\frac{1}{2}KL$ contribution to daily bridge capacity costs, since peak usage is relevant for 50% of the total period. Thus, for all bridge capacities beyond T_1 and up to T_3, off-peak users are not willing to pay anything for bridge capacity costs, while peak users are willing to contribute the difference between the constant opportunity cost curve *oc* and the peak demand curve D_p. Similar to segment *NG*, the dark-line segment *GM* in figure 10.4 represents the average revenue that peak and nonpeak users are willing to pay for bridge capacity. However, since off-peak users pay nothing for capacity along this segment, the total contribution to daily capacity cost is simply half the contribution that peak users are willing to make.

Finally, for a capacity level greater than T_3, neither peak nor off-peak users are willing to pay for capacity costs. Both peak and off-peak demand curves lie below the opportunity cost curve *oc*.

Having derived average per period demand for capacity, D_a, what is the optimal level of capacity and what prices do we charge peak and off-peak users for this capacity? To answer these questions, we can now rely on the principles developed previously. First, optimal capacity is that level for which the marginal benefit of an additional unit of capacity equals the marginal cost of an extra unit of capacity. And this occurs where D_a, the average daily demand curve, intersects the long-run marginal cost curve. In figure 10.4, this occurs at point *E*. At capacity levels below T^*, marginal benefit of additional capacity exceeds marginal cost and more capacity is warranted. Conversely, at capacity levels greater than T^*, the marginal cost of a unit of capacity exceeds the willingness of users to pay for the extra capacity, implying a reduction in capacity. Only at point *E* will the average revenue generated from bridge users, reflecting the marginal benefit of added capacity, equal the additional cost of added capacity.

Once capacity level T^* is built, what are the first-best prices? We see in figure 10.4 that off-peak bridge demand intersects the opportunity cost curve to the left of T^*. Marginal cost pricing with fixed capacity at T^* gives the first-best price, so that off-peak users pay $p_1 = oc$ for each bridge crossing. The peak users, however, exhibit an excess demand for T^* capacity at the opportunity cost *oc*. In order to efficiently allocate demand, price is raised to a level that eliminates the excess demand which, in figure 10.4, occurs when we set the price at p_2.

Do revenues cover costs at these first-best prices? As in the constant-demand case, the answer is yes. However, when there is varying demand, the *distribution* of capacity costs depends upon the levels of peak and off-peak demands. For the curves drawn in figure 10.4 and the associated first-best prices, we know that off-peak users pay nothing for capacity. Peak users are charged a price p_2, which implies that their total contribution to bridge capacity is $(p_2 - oc)T^*$.

Recall our assumption that the capacity cost for each 12-hour peak and off-peak period, respectively, was *cc*, which implies a total daily capacity cost equal to $2(cc)$. In figure 10.4, this corresponds to twice the rectangular area *OREB*. Off-peak users pay nothing for capacity, but peak users pay a total of p_2T^* for bridge crossings, $oc(T^*)$ of which pays for the opportunity cost of crossings. The difference, given by the area *OQAB*, is the contribution to capacity costs. From our assumption that peak and off-peak crossings are equally divided over the period, the distance *AE* equals the distance *EB* at bridge capacity T^*, which implies that the area *OQAB* equals twice the area *OREB*. In other words, total capacity costs per period are completely financed by peak users.

This leads to two conclusions. First, assuming constant long-run marginal costs and investing in capacity at the point at which the average demand curve intersects the long-run marginal cost curve, the bridge capacity costs are self-financing. Neither subsidies nor surpluses are generated. Second, the distribution of payments toward capacity costs depends upon the levels of peak and off-peak demands. As we discovered above, in our particular example, peak-hour bridge users pay all of the capacity costs and off-peak users contribute nothing to capacity costs.

CASE STUDY – WELFARE EFFECTS OF FIRST-BEST PRICING IN AIRPORT INFRASTRUCTURE

A second example of first-best pricing and investment in a constant returns to scale environment occurs in the area of airport pricing. Similar to highways, airports have capacity and

Table 10.9 The structure of landing fees by aircraft size (1978 dollars)

	Aircraft (maximum landing weight, thousands)				
Airport	DC9-30 (110)	B727-200 (154.5)	B707-320C (247)	L1011-200C (368)	B747-200C (564)
Albuquerque	16	22	36	–	–
Dallas – Fort Worth	91	128	205	305	468
Los Angeles	44	62	99	147	226
LaGuardia	182	286	–	716	–
Seattle	143	201	321	478	733

Source: Adapted from Morrison (1982), table 3, p. 155; Morrison (1983), table 2, p. 119

capacity users. Although airport capacity comprises a system of terminals, landing strips, parking garages, service facilities, and so forth, the component of capacity that is of most interest for our purposes is the set of landing strips or runways that an airport offers. One can think of runways as airport capacity in the context of figure 10.1, where the existing number of runways will accommodate a maximum number (T_c in figure 10.1) of take-offs or landings (TOLs) per hour. The airport users are the planes that use the runways for take-offs or landings. If demand is constant per period and given by D_{op} in figure 10.1, then first-best pricing implies that TOLs be priced at the opportunity cost of $oc = p_1$ of an additional TOL.

Alternatively, if the constant per-period demand for TOLs were D_p, then first-best pricing would imply that each TOL should be charged a price p_2 in order to ration the limited capacity. As we have seen, capacity should be reduced in the long run with demand D_{op}, whereas capacity should be expanded when demand is D_p. In the more typical case, there are peak and off-peak demands, so that we would adapt figure 10.4 appropriately to reflect optimal pricing and investment of airport capacity. Assuming that the x-axis reflects TOLs, optimal airport capacity would allow for T^* TOLs, off-peak users would pay an opportunity cost of $oc = p_1$, and peak users would pay p_2 for each TOL during the peak period. Notice again that off-peak users simply pay the opportunity cost of an additional TOL, contributing nothing to capacity, whereas peak users pay for the full amount of available capacity.[12]

How are runway usage fees assessed in today's airport markets? In the majority of airports, the basis for assessing TOL fees is size of aircraft. Larger planes are assessed higher TOL fees than are smaller planes. Table 10.9 reports typical landing fees for different-sized aircraft in various airports in various US cities in 1978. Consistent with rising weight-based fees, we see in the table, for example, that landing fees at Dallas – Fort Worth Airport increased fivefold from \$91 for a smaller 110,000 pound DC-9 to \$468 for a 546,000 pound Boeing 747. Are these fees efficient, and what determines optimal airport capacity?

In evaluating whether existing airport capacity is optimal, we need to consider the cost that an airplane's take-off or landing causes. The primary effect of an additional TOL is the delay that it causes other passengers. Think of the times that you have flown from school to your home or on some vacation trip. Once you have boarded, the plane leaves the gate and taxis to the runway. But normally you won't take off immediately. Rather, you wait in a queue for arriving planes to land and other outward-bound planes to depart. Similarly, when you are flying into your destination airport, the airplane oftentimes does not land immediately but, rather, is "stacked up"; that is, the airport traffic control center places the aircraft into a queue,

Table 10.10 Welfare effects of first-best pricing and investment on airport capacity: savings in billions of 1988 dollars

Affected Group	Efficient Pricing and Investment (1)	Efficient Pricing with Current Investment (2)
Consumer surplus change from TOL fees	1.10	−12.53
Reduced traveler delays	7.91	3.62
Carriers' operating cost savings	2.77	1.23
Airport revenues less costs	−0.77	11.50
Total welfare	11.01	3.82

Source: Adapted from Winston (1991), table 2, p. 124

where your plane waits its turn for the limited runway capacity.

But why is the present schedule of landing fees nonoptimal? If you think about this for a moment, you will realize that the delay costs that an aircraft imposes upon other travelers are virtually independent of the aircraft's size. Suppose, for example, that you are flying a small four-person aircraft out of a major airport, such as Chicago's O'Hare or Los Angeles International Airport, during the peak period. You're waiting your turn to take off and behind you is a large 747 Jumbo Jet. Although you're in a very small plane by comparison, you're causing the *same delays* to the travelers on the 747 as if you were in a Jumbo Jet yourself, waiting for take-off. The size of your plane has little to do with the delays that you impose on other travelers. Thus, from an efficiency standpoint, basing landing fees on the weight of the plane misses the point and leads to an inefficient allocation of resources. Suppose, to carry the example a little further, that you value a peak-period take-off at $50 and an off-peak period take-off at $5. Also assume that the landing fee is $25 in both the peak period and the off-peak period. Since your net benefit from flying during the peak period, $25 ($50 – $25), exceeds your net benefit from flying during the off-peak period, −$20 ($5 – $25), you will take off during the peak period. However, if you are causing delays to other travelers that amount to $150, then your use of the scarce airport runway during the peak period is inefficient. The marginal cost of your peak trip exceeds the marginal benefit that you receive. If prices were optimally set, the landing fee during the peak would be $150 and the $0 during the off-peak (reflecting no delays to any other travelers). If you faced these prices, you would then decide to take off during the off-peak period, since your net benefit in the off-peak period, $5 ($5 – $0) would exceed your peak-period net benefit of −$100 ($50 – $150).

Our analysis implies that travelers during the off-peak period, when there is very little delay imposed on other travelers, should pay small landing fees that approximate the negligible opportunity cost of the TOL. Peak travelers, on the other hand, should pay a much higher price for the limited runway capacity, since these travelers are imposing significant delays on other travelers. In addition, an efficient strategy or airport investment is to increase runway capacity up to the point at which the marginal cost of additional capacity equals the marginal benefit of reduced time delays.

Thus, if all airports were to efficiently invest in capacity and charge efficient usage prices, society would reap net welfare benefits and reduce its costs on scarce airport capacity. How large would the welfare effects be if we were to efficiently invest in and price airport capacity? Table 10.10 reports the findings of a study by Morrison and Winston (1989), which summarizes the expected annual benefits to society from a first-best pricing and investment policy. Relative to current pricing and investment practices, table 10.10 analyzes the welfare effects from efficient pricing under optimal and current investment. We see in the table that a move to efficient pricing and investment will affect consumers, air carriers, and airport operations. Further, consumers are affected by price changes in two ways. First, by altering the structure of landing fees, optimal pricing affects fare prices that consumers pay and thus generates changes in consumer surplus. In general, travelers on large aircraft are expected to reap net benefits through a reduction in fares, while travelers in the smaller general aviation aircraft would be expected to suffer net losses. Given the proportion of travelers on large commercial airlines, it's expected that consumers as a whole would experience a net gain. Second, since efficient landing fees are explicitly based upon traveler delay costs, optimal prices should produce consumer benefits in the form of reduced delays. The reduced delays experienced by travelers are also expected to produce benefits to carriers in the form of lower operating costs (for example, less time sitting on a runway or in a holding pattern, burning fuel). Finally, to the extent that airports have nonoptimal capacity, a move to optimal pricing and investment will not only alter airport net revenues by changing the structure of landing fees but also through its effect on annualized capital expenditures.

As we found with highway infrastructure investment, we see in table 10.10 that a move away from current practices and toward efficient pricing produces significant annual benefits to society. With no change in investment policies, column (2) in the table reports a net welfare increase that amounts to $3.82 billion dollars annually. This significantly rises to an annual saving of $11.01 billion if we invest our resources optimally in airport capacity. But notice the distribution effects. A partial move to efficiency based upon optimal pricing and current investment produces a large $12.5 billion annual decrease in consumer surplus. This directly reflects the fact that, under current sub-optimal investment in runway capacity, landing fees will rise in order to ration existing capacity. Despite the fact that the higher prices reduce traveler delays, valued at $3.62 billion, the large negative effect on consumer surplus implies that commercial, as well as general aviation, travelers lose from this policy. Another reflection of this is the significant rise in net revenues for the airport. In an earlier study, Morrison (1983) found that airport capacity is produced under constant returns to scale. The $11.50 billion annual increase, then, must be attributed to an inefficiently low level of current investment in runway capacity, which can only be rationed by high landing fees.

From column (1), we see a very different story. First, in comparison with efficient pricing and current investment, first-best pricing and investment produces large net benefits to society, increasing from $3.82 billion per year to $11.01 billion per year. Second, we see in column (1) that all affected groups, with the exception of airport operations, gain. Not only do consumers experience reductions in traveler delays, valued at $7.91 billion, but also consumer surplus rises, with a net gain amounting to $1.10 billion per year. The reduced traveler delays resulting from optimal pricing and expanded investment in runway facilities more than double the savings in operating costs that carriers experience. Last, airport net revenues fall, which reflects an estimated $1.5 billion increase in annualized capital expenditures and decreased revenues from lower landing fees. However, since airport capacity is produced under constant returns to scale, expanding capacity will be self-financing, so that the gains identified in table 10.10 will not be lessened by deficit financing tax increases elsewhere in the economy.

The lesson to be learned from this example, as we saw earlier, is that considerable gains to society are possible if we move away from inefficient current pricing and investment strategies and toward first-best pricing strategies, particularly when infrastructure expansion occurs under constant returns to scale. This has a particularly important implication for how airport capacity is expanded. One alternative is to build additional airports; another is to efficiently invest in and price existing facilities. Both strategies increase capacity and, depending upon the relative costs, generate different decisions. Building a new airport, such as the recently opened Denver International Airport at a final price tag over $5 billion, *may* have been an efficient decision. But one wonders if this decision would still have been made if the existing facilities at Denver's Stapleton Airport had followed first-best pricing and investment rules. Among the arguments in favor of Denver's new airport was an FAA estimate that existing delays at Denver's Stapleton Airport would fall between 35% and 50%. But Morrison and Winston's (1989) results suggest that first-best pricing policies at Stapleton would have produced at least part of these reductions in delay, and that these reductions would have been achieved at a lower cost.

With continuing increases in air traffic, there is little doubt that society will need to build additional landing capacity. But an important policy question is when. It is very difficult, if not impossible, to determine whether a new airport is really necessary unless we first allocate existing resources rationally.

FIRST-BEST PRICING AND INVESTMENT – DECREASING-COST ENVIRONMENT

In the last section, we assumed that increases in bridge capacity could be obtained at a constant cost of *cc* dollars per unit of capacity. Suppose, however, that a larger bridge increases the volume of traffic in greater proportion than it increases the cost of production. For example, assume that our transport authority desires to build a bridge that accommodates 500,000 annual crossings and costs $10,000,000 to build. If the bridge lasts for 20 years and the interest rate is 5%, then our present value formula implies a constant annual cost equal to $802,425, which is equivalent to $1.60 per crossing.[13] If twice the capacity is desired, the local authority finds that costs increase by 50% to $15,000,000. In this instance, the constant annual cost per period is $1,203,638, or $1.20 per crossing.

Because the larger bridge accommodates more traffic in greater proportion than the increase in cost, the larger bridge has reduced the capital cost of a crossing per period. In other words, the transport authority faces increasing returns to bridge capacity, which implies that the long-run average cost (*LRAC*) curve is downward-sloping. In addition, from chapter 7, we noted that the presence of increasing returns to scale leads to a natural monopoly and constitutes one of the traditional reasons for government intervention. In this section, we explore why some form of government intervention is necessary when there are increasing returns to scale.

Figure 10.5 depicts the market for bridge crossings where we assume that the local transport authority faces a constant per-period demand for crossings, depicted as *D*. On the cost side, we continue to assume that the opportunity cost of a bridge crossing is constant at *oc*, but we now assume that bridge capacity is produced under increasing returns to scale. Adding the constant opportunity cost of a bridge crossing, *oc*, to the *declining* capital cost of bridge capacity per crossing gives the downward-sloping *LRAC* curve shown in figure 10.5. Figure 10.5 also depicts the long-run marginal cost curve, *LRMC*, which is seen to lie everywhere below the *LRAC* curve.[14]

Given this cost and demand structure, what is the transport authority's first-best pricing and investment behavior? The objective for the local transport authority is to maximize social surplus, and we have previously shown that this occurs at the point at which marginal capacity cost equals marginal capacity benefit. For bridge capacities less than T_1, the market demand for bridge crossings lies above the *LRMC*, implying greater capacity with a larger social surplus. Conversely, for bridge capacities greater than T_1, *LRMC* lies above the demand curve, which implies that less capacity is required, which again would increase social surplus.

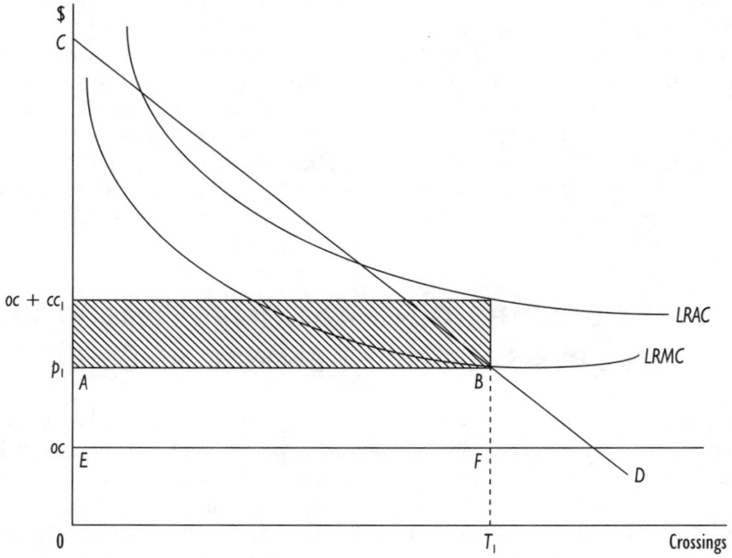

Figure 10.5 Optimal bridge capacity under increasing returns to scale.

Optimal capacity is T_1, where society's willingness to pay for an extra unit of capacity equals society's cost of supplying an extra unit of capacity. At this level of capacity, social surplus, area *ABC*, is maximized.

For this optimal level of investment, what is the first-best price? Our first-best pricing rule calls for marginal cost pricing, so once the local authority builds a bridge with capacity T_1, it sets a first-best price at p_1. These pricing and investment principles are completely analogous to the constant-cost case that we considered earlier. But in the decreasing-cost environment we have a problem. We see in figure 10.5 that the *LRAC* for supplying bridge capacity T_1 is $oc + cc_1$, the opportunity cost of a bridge crossing plus the appropriate capital cost of a bridge crossing. The total cost of supplying T_1 capacity is then $T_1(oc + cc_1)$. On the other hand, the revenues collected from first-best pricing, p_1T_1, fall short of total costs and lead to economic losses, depicted in the graph by the shaded area. First best pricing covers the opportunity costs of bridge crossings and contributes to the capital cost, but is not fully self-financing. This finding is a direct result of our assumption that bridge capacity is produced under increasing returns to scale.

Will the bridge be built? After all, when applying our principles for optimal investment and pricing, we concluded that the bridge is not financially viable. Is this a sufficient reason for the local transport authority to forego the bridge and use its scarce economic resources elsewhere? As you might have already guessed, the answer is no.

Remember that the local transport authority is not interested in maximizing profits but rather social surplus, the sum of producer and consumer surpluses. If society were to build the bridge and price each crossing at marginal cost, we would be at point *B*. But, from society's perspective, the per period benefits achieved from building the bridge are not simply the consumption expenditures of the trip-makers (area $0T_1BA$), but rather the total value (in money terms) of T_1 crossings (area $0T_1BC$). As seen in figure 10.5, the total value of T_1 crossings per period is much greater than its opportunity cost, which implies that society is better off with than without the bridge. Thus, although the bridge is not self-financing, and would not rationally be undertaken by the private sector, the government, acting in the interests of society, will build the bridge. As long as the total per period value of T_1 crossings, net of opportunity cost expenditures $T_1(oc)$, exceeds per period capital costs, it is rational for the transport authority to build the bridge.

Another way of looking at this problem is to recall from chapter 9 the investment criterion of profit-maximizing firms that the expected stream of revenues over the life of the project must exceed expected costs. Net present value was defined to be

$$NPV = B_0 - C_0 + \frac{B_1 - C_1}{(1+i)} + \frac{B_2 - C_2}{(1+i)^2} + \ldots + \frac{B_t - C_t}{(1+i)^t} + \frac{S}{(1+i)^t} \qquad (10.11)$$

where B_i and C_i ($i = 0, \ldots, t$) are the real revenues and opportunity costs of the project, S is the salvage value, and i is the discount rate. In general, the project is undertaken if its net present value is zero or positive.

Similar to the investment decisions of a firm, equation (10.11) summarizes society's investment criterion. The difference lies in how costs and benefits are measured. Although it may be true that society's opportunity costs of production are identical to those faced by a profit-maximizing firm, we have seen above that the benefits accruing to society are not identical to those received by a firm. The firm only counts consumer expenditures as benefits, whereas society looks to the total value that consumers place upon consumption as the relevant measure of benefit. Thus, when producing under increasing returns to scale, and assuming first-best pricing and investment, projects whose net present value is negative when consumer spending is the measure of benefit may have a positive net present value when the total value of consumption is used to measure benefit. In the former (private-sector) case, the project is not funded. In the latter (public-sector) case, the project is funded when $NPV > 0$. Thus, even under increasing returns to scale, society is pursuing a first-best pricing and investment strategy as long as it undertakes projects for which total benefits exceed total costs and then prices per unit consumption at marginal cost.

Notwithstanding this desirable result, we have conveniently ignored the financing implications of first-best pricing and investment policy in the decreasing-cost environment. Marginal cost pricing does not produce sufficient revenues to cover the total cost of production and the economic losses that accrue must somehow be covered.[15] Even though our local transport authority has followed an efficient pricing and investment rule, it must come to grips with the resulting deficits.

Chapter 7 identified three approaches that are often used to resolve a natural monopolist's insolvency problem: (1) price at marginal cost and subsidize the industry from general tax revenues; (2) price at average cost; and (3) and nationalize production. In the example that follows, we examine the case of Amtrak, the US passenger rail service run by the quasi-public National Railroad Passenger Corporation. Amtrak reflects two of the three responses to the financial problems of a natural monopolist: subsidize deficits from general tax funds and nationalization. In the next section, we examine the welfare implications of average cost pricing.

CASE STUDY – ARE AMTRAK BENEFITS WORTH THE COSTS?

Amtrak, an acronym for "American Travel by Track," came into existence in 1970, when the US Congress passed the Rail Passenger Service Act. Passage of this act culminated a long slow decline in the demand for passenger rail services, following the industry's peak demand in 1920. Table 10.11 summarizes passenger rail travel from 1890 through 1970, when the provision of passenger rail travel was federally reorganized. By the late 1800s, railroads had developed into a major mode of intercity travel and their presence continued to grow on into the 20th century. We see in table 10.11 that the number of passengers carried, passenger–miles traveled, and the number of cars in service expanded significantly in the first two decades and peaked in 1920.

The growth of commercial buses and private automobiles in the 1920s, combined with the recession of 1921–2, began to dampen the attraction of travelers for rails. Then came the Depression. Although by 1930 the number of passenger cars in service was not much below that in 1920, passengers carried and passenger–miles experienced 44% and 43% reductions respectively. At the height of the Depression in 1933, the number of passengers carried accounted for only 34% of peak demand in 1920. Rail travel grew in the latter part of the 1930s as the economy came out of the Depression, and the excess capacity in rail passenger cars that characterized the industry in the early 1930s was trimmed by 1940. During the ten-year period from 1930 through 1940, passenger rail cars in service fell by 28%. A brief resurgence in demand occurred during the Second World War, as US troop movements, and restrictions on commercial air and automobile travel, increased the demand for rail services. With slightly fewer rail cars than in 1940, the number of passengers in 1944 equaled 75% of the industry's peak demand in 1920. Moreover, in 1944, rail travel accounted for more than double the passenger–miles in 1920.

Not surprisingly, a return to peacetime also meant a return to the continued decline in rail services. During the latter part of the 1940s and on into the 1950s, pent-up demands for automobile travel from a period of sacrifice during the Second World War, the effect of rising per capita incomes on automobile demands, the start of the interstate highway network, and aircraft technology transfer from wartime uses to peacetime commercial aviation each contributed to the decline in passenger rail demand. Passengers and passenger–miles dramatically fell between 1944 and 1950, and continued to decline in the ensuing two decades. And, accommodating the

Table 10.11 Rail passenger travel, 1890–1970

Year	Passengers Carried (millions)	Passenger–Miles (billions)	Passenger Cars in Service (units)
1890	492	11.8	26,820
1900	577	16.0	34,713
1910	972	32.3	47,179
1920	1,270	47.4	56,102
1930	708	26.9	53,484
1933	435	16.4	50,598
1940	456	16.4	38,308
1944	916	95.7	38,217
1950	488	31.8	37,359
1960	327	21.3	25,746
1970	289	10.8	11,378

Source: *Historical Statistics of the United States*, vol. 2 (Washington DC, 1975), p. 729

loss of customers, the industry continued to reduce its rolling stock capacity. Between 1944 and 1970, the number of cars in service fell by 69%.

The declining demand for passenger rail services had significant financial implications for the railroad companies, which suffered continual losses on their passenger operations in the period after the Second World War. Hilton (1980) reports, for example, that deficits on passenger rail services, as a percentage of freight net revenues, fluctuated from a low of 19.5% in 1966 to a high of 44.0% in 1957. In 1970, passenger rail deficits constituted 26.2% of freight net revenues. There was little doubt that the underlying structure of intercity travel had changed in the first half of the 20th century and, given the strong economic pressures faced by the rail companies for abandoning passenger services, Congress was faced with the alternative of allowing rail companies to significantly downsize their rail operations or provide some form of subsidized support. In passing the Rail Passenger Service Act in 1970, Congress chose to nationalize the industry, but attempted to organize the resulting "firm" as a for-profit industry.

Table 10.12 summarizes rail passenger operations in the ten years since the creation of Amtrak. The financial data reported in this table indicate that the government's decision not to forsake rail passenger service may well have been unwarranted. Starting from a 50% revenue : cost ratio in 1971, the financial picture steadily worsened in the following decade, so that at the beginning of 1980, operating revenues covered only 34% of operating costs. Contrary to government expectations, nationalizing passenger rail travel and running the industry as a for-profit entity did not stem the decreasing demand or the bleak financial picture for passenger rail services in the USA.

Did the US Congress make a mistake when it decided to insure the continued existence of passenger rail services? – maybe, but not necessarily. Recall that if a firm in the private sector does not receive sufficient revenues to cover its variable (or operating) costs of production, the profit-maximizing strategy is to abandon production of the good. Why add to fixed cost losses by continuing to produce at an operating loss? The decision to quit producing is an economic decision for the firm. But is this an economic decision for society?

Economic theory tells us that the decision to nationalize passenger rail services is an economic decision for society as long as the total benefits of rail production exceed the total costs of rail production. Although other studies (Meyer et al., 1959; Keeler, 1971) documented the relative cost disadvantages of rail in comparison with other modes of intercity travel, which was consistent with the desires of private rail firms to eliminate or severely reduce their offerings of passenger rail services, there was little work done to evaluate whether continuing passenger rail services were economic for the nation as a whole. Morrison (1990) considered this question and estimated Amtrak's net benefits to the USA for the year 1977.

Table 10.12 Amtrak's operating revenues and costs, 1970–90

Year	Operating Revenues (thousands)	Operating Costs (thousands)	Revenue as a Percentage of Costs
1971	22,645	45,301	50.0
1972	152,709	306,179	49.9
1973	177,303	319,151	55.6
1974	240,071	437,932	54.8
1975	246,549	559,807	44.0
1976	268,038	674,307	39.8
1978	313,002	856,598	36.5
1980	368,240	1,081,239	34.0

Source: Hilton (1980) and US DOT, *National Transportation Statistics* (1993)

Consumer surplus, economic welfare, and discrete choice models

In the standard model of consumer behavior, we know that the area under the demand curve measures the total benefit of consumption. For example, in figure 10.5 the area $OCBT_1$ is the total benefit associated with consuming T_1 transportation. If we are pricing at marginal cost, consumers are spending p_1T_1 dollars to consume T_1 units and consumer surplus is the triangular area ABC, the difference between the amount of money that consumers are willing to pay to consume T_1 and the amount that they have to pay. More importantly, consumer surplus is a measure of how much better off we are with transportation T_1 at price p_1 than without transportation T_1.

To see this explicit relationship between economic welfare and consumer surplus, assume that T in figure 10.5 represents Amtrak trips. Suppose that Amtrak is not available, which simply says that the current price for trips on Amtrak is above OC. If Amtrak becomes available at a price of p_1 per trip, the nation consumes T_1 trips. But recall from our discussion of consumer equilibrium in chapter 3 that a decrease in price, all else held constant, increases one's economic welfare. That is, at a lower price, we are able to reach a higher indifference curve. What this implies for figure 10.5 is that society's welfare at the high price OC for Amtrak trips is *lower* than society's welfare at the lower price p_1. All else constant, economic welfare rises when price falls. But this leads to an interesting question. What is the maximum amount of money that society would pay to have Amtrak available at p_1 price per trip rather than not have Amtrak available at all? Society would be willing to pay no more than an amount of money that would give society the same level of welfare that it would receive if Amtrak were not available. This amount is the area under the demand curve, $OCBT_1$. From a welfare standpoint, society is indifferent between not having Amtrak available and paying $OCBT_1$ for T_1 trips. But since society only has to pay p_1T_1 for these trips, its welfare has increased by the amount ABC. Consumer surplus, then, measures the increase in society's welfare from the availability of Amtrak.

In this example, we have assumed that the demand for Amtrak is a demand for the number of trips. But suppose that we characterize demand in a discrete choice framework. Individual travelers can take one of many alternative modes in their intercity trips. We have seen in chapter 4 that our demand model for discrete goods is a probability model for each of the available alternatives. And the market demand for each alternative is simply the probability that an individual, drawn at random, will take each alternative. Do we have a measure of consumer surplus in a discrete choice model? Yes.

Consider a discrete choice model for four intercity travel modes: (1) automobile, (2) bus, (3) air, and (4) rail. Assuming that our demand model is a multinomial logit model, we can express the choice probabilities as

$$P_i = \frac{\exp(V_i)}{\sum_j \exp(V_j)}, \qquad i, j = 1, 2, 3, 4; i \neq j \tag{10.12}$$

Although the derivation is beyond the scope of this book, Small and Rosen (1981) have shown that a measure of consumer surplus for discrete choice models is given by the simple expression

$$CS = -\frac{1}{\lambda}\log\left(\sum_j \exp(V_j)\right) \tag{10.13}$$

where $\log(\sum_j \exp(V_j))$ is the logarithm of the denominator in equation (10.12) and measures the "expected maximum utility" of intercity mode choice. λ is the marginal utility of income.[16]

Since V_j $(j = 1, \ldots, 4)$ is expressed in terms of utility, $\log(\sum_j \exp(V_j))$ is also in utility terms, and minus the inverse of λ $(-1/\lambda)$ converts this utility measure into a monetary measure of welfare gain. Further, notice that the necessary information for deriving consumer surplus in discrete choice models is readily available. Once we have estimated the model, we first calculate the denominator and then take the logarithm. This produces an expected maximum utility associated with the choice context. Second, an appropriate measure for the marginal utility of income turns out to be minus the coefficient of the price variable.[17]

How do we use this consumer surplus measure to evaluate whether society is better or worse off with Amtrak? The answer is to calculate consumer surplus with and without Amtrak. The difference between these two numbers reflects the welfare change to society from having Amtrak available. We have already seen that if all four intercity modes are available, then consumer surplus is

$$CS_{\text{Amtrak}} = -\frac{1}{\lambda}\log\left(\sum_{j=1}^{4}\exp(V_j)\right)$$

Alternatively, if Amtrak is not available, then intercity travelers can make their trips either by automobile, bus, or air. In this case, the price of Amtrak is effectively infinite, which causes Amtrak's indirect utility, V_4, to approach minus infinity. As V_4 approaches $-\infty$, $\exp(V_4)$ approaches $\exp(-\infty)$, which equals zero. In other words, this term drops out of the consumer surplus expression so that, without Amtrak, consumer surplus is

$$CS_{\text{No Amtrak}} = -\frac{1}{\lambda}\log\left(\sum_{j=1}^{3}\exp(V_j)\right)$$

Therefore, our measure of society's benefit from having Amtrak is

$$\begin{aligned} WG_{\text{Amtrak}} &= \text{Welfare Gain from Amtrak} \\ &= CS_{\text{Amtrak}} - CS_{\text{No Amtrak}} \\ &= -\frac{1}{\lambda}\left[\log\sum_{j=1}^{4}\exp(V_j) - \log\sum_{j=1}^{3}V_j\right] \end{aligned} \quad (10.14)$$

Beneficiaries of Amtrak service

In chapter 4, we reported and analyzed the estimation results of a study by Morrison and Winston (1985) that used 1977 trip information on intercity travelers in order to examine the important factors underlying a vacation traveler's demand for intercity travel modes. These results were part of a larger study of intercity travel, which included business as well as vacation travelers. Among the study's findings, some of which were discussed in chapter 4, was information on travel cost and travel time elasticities of demand, as well as value-of-time estimates.

Table 10.13 summarizes these estimates for vacation and business trips. Since there are fewer opportunities for rescheduling times and destinations for business travel, we would expect that the business demand for intercity travel would be less elastic than the pleasure demand for intercity travel. Table 10.13 confirms this; for each mode of travel, the cost elasticity is a smaller number (in absolute value). Business travel is less sensitive to cost changes, all else constant. With few exceptions, we also see that business travelers are more sensitive to time than vacation travelers. This is especially true for automobile travel time and departure frequency for bus and rail modes.[18]

The value-of-time estimates given in the bottom half of table 10.13 also conform to expectations. Recognizing that decisions for business travel are firm decisions, the values of time for business travelers reflect the values that firms attach to one's business travel rather than the values attached by the travelers themselves. For example, we see that rail vacation travelers value their time travel time at \$4.37 and \$8.80 dollars per hour, depending upon the vacation traveler's income status (low-income, less than \$20,000, household; high-income, greater than or equal to \$20,000, household). The value of travel time for a business traveler is \$12.20, which says that firms value their employees' travel times on rail at \$12.20 per hour, which

Table 10.13 Elasticity estimates and values of time for vacation and business intercity travelers

	Elasticity With Respect to					
	Cost		Travel Time		Departure Frequency	
Mode	Vacation Trips	Business Trips	Vacation Trips	Business Trips	Vacation Trips	Business Trips
Auto	−0.96	−0.70	−0.39	−2.15	–	–
Bus	−0.69	−0.32	−2.11	−1.50	−1.23	−3.37
Rail	−1.20	−0.57	−1.58	−1.67	−1.27	−4.02
Air	−0.38	−0.18	−0.43	−0.16	−0.05	−0.21

	Value of Time ($ per hour)					
	Value of Travel Time			Value of Time Between Departures		
	Vacation Trips			Vacation Trips		
Mode	Low-Income	High-Income	Business Trips	Low-Income	High-Income	Business Trips
Auto	0.63	0.63	12.20	–	–	–
Bus	4.33	14.03	12.20	21.67	33.87	131.54
Rail	4.37	8.80	12.20	5.98	5.98	30.29
Air	15.37	15.37	12.20	2.32	2.32	20.67

Source: Morrison (1990), table 1, p. 365. Copyright © 1990 by The University of Chicago.

is not unreasonable given that this amounts to 85% of the average wage rate. The value of time associated with departure frequency is even higher for business travelers. Departure frequency reflects both schedule delays, when actual departure times are different from a traveler's optimal departure time, and stochastic delays, which occur when one has to wait for another departure because of capacity constraints. In general, the higher values of time associated with departure frequency likely reflect productivity losses when firms and employees must rearrange travel plans to accommodate public carrier schedules. For rail and air, frequency delays are valued at somewhat more than double travel time. For the bus mode, however, there is a ten-fold increase in the value of time, which seems quite high but may not be completely unreasonable. Generally, there is no reserved seating on buses, so that bus travelers purchase a ticket and then queue up to board the bus. In the event that there is excess demand, some travelers experience stochastic delay, as they have to wait at the terminal for the availability of an additional bus and driver. That is, stochastic delays for buses are more likely to involve spending time at relatively unattractive and uncomfortable terminals with few amenities, and this imposes higher costs on bus travelers. As seen in table 10.13, this explanation holds for both business and vacation travelers, as each group places considerably higher values on the time between bus departures than the time between departures by the other common carriers.

Morrison (1990) used the empirical results on vacation and business travelers to estimate the net social value of Amtrak in 1977. To do this, Morrison took the following steps:

1 For 1977, 11 Amtrak routes corresponding to trips of different length and trips in different parts of the country were selected. In addition to the origin and destination cities for each route, Morrison included several intermediate cities along the route. In all, Morrison's study included a sample of 188 nondirectional city-pairs. As an example, one route selected was a north–south route from Chicago (Illinois) to New Orleans (Louisiana). Included along this route were the intermediate cities of Champaign (Illinois), Carbondale (Illinois), Memphis (Tennessee), and Jackson (Mississippi). For the six points along this route there are $6(6-1)/2 = 15$ nondirectional city-pairs.[19] For all 11 routes, there are a total of 63 cities and 188 city-pairs.

2 For each of the 188 city-pairs, Morrison obtained information on the important determinants of vacation and business travel, respectively, and calculated the indirect utility for each of the four modes, $\hat{V}_i^c$ ($i = 1, 2, 3, 4$; $c = 1, \ldots, 188$).[20] Also, in order to compare the benefits per city-pair with those of the overall route, Morrison calculated the indirect utility for each of the 11 routes, $\hat{V}_i^r$ ($i = 1, 2, 3, 4$; $r = 1, \ldots, 11$).

3 For each city-pair c ($c = 1, \ldots, 188$) and route r ($r = 1, \ldots, 11$) Morrison calculated the welfare gain per traveler using equation (10.14):

$$\begin{aligned} WG^c_{\text{Amtrak}} &= \text{Welfare Gain from Amtrak for city-pair } c, \quad c = 1, \ldots, 188 \\ &= CS^c_{\text{Amtrak}} - CS^c_{\text{No Amtrak}} \\ &= -\frac{1}{\lambda}\left[\log \sum_{j=1}^{4} \exp(\hat{V}_j^c) - \log \sum_{j=1}^{3} \hat{V}_j^c\right] \end{aligned}$$

and

$$\begin{aligned} WG^r_{\text{Amtrak}} &= \text{Welfare Gain from Amtrak for route } r, \quad r = 1, \ldots, 11 \\ &= CS^r_{\text{Amtrak}} - CS^r_{\text{No Amtrak}} \\ &= -\frac{1}{\lambda}\left[\log \sum_{j=1}^{4} \exp(\hat{V}_j^r) - \log \sum_{j=1}^{3} \hat{V}_j^r\right] \end{aligned}$$

Also, by multiplying the welfare gain per traveler by the number of travelers for each of the 188 city-pairs, we obtain the total annual benefit for that city-pair.

4 In 1977, Amtrak served 399 towns and metropolitan areas, which corresponded to 6,235 nondirectional city-pairs. In order to calculate system-wide benefits, Morrison estimated a total benefit regression model on the 188 city-pairs. He then used the coefficients from this regression equation to predict the total benefits for each of the 6,235 city-pairs. Summing the welfare benefits over the entire Amtrak network then gives the 1977 system-wide benefits from Amtrak's operation.

5 Recall that total or system-wide benefits reflect a difference between the amount that consumers are willing to pay versus what consumers actually pay for Amtrak. In other words, it does not take into account any deficits that Amtrak may incur in its operations. Thus, to obtain the net welfare gain to society from Amtrak's operation, it is necessary to subtract annual deficits from the estimated consumer surplus.

For the 11 selected routes, table 10.14 reports the per traveler benefits for vacation travelers, by income category, and for business travelers. From these benefits, we obtain an interesting picture regarding the beneficiaries of Amtrak service. First, columns (1) and (2) identify benefits going to vacation travelers; for each of the 11 routes, low-income households receive higher benefits than higher-income households. For example, low-income vacation travelers valued the Boston–Washington route most, at $11.29 per traveler, followed by New York – Albany, at $9.95 per traveler, and then Los Angeles – San Diego, at $8.30 per traveler. By comparison, high-income vacation travelers for these same routes received per traveler benefits of $6.63, $5.00, and $5.68 respectively. These findings are consistent with our economic intuition, since lower-income households are expected to have lower values of time than higher-income households. As a result, we would expect lower-income households to value time-intensive modes

Table 10.14 Welfare gain per traveler (1977 dollars)

	Welfare Benefit Per Traveler (dollars)		
	Vacation Travelers		
Route	Low-Income (1)	High-Income (2)	Business Travelers (3)
Boston–Providence – New York – Philadelphia–Baltimore–Washington	11.29	6.63	31.39
New York–Albany–Syracuse–Rochester–Buffalo	9.95	5.00	12.61
Philadelphia–Harrisburg–Pittsburgh	2.56	1.24	0.91
Los Angeles – Phoenix–Tucson – El Paso – San Antonio – Houston – New Orleans	3.58	1.25	0.11
Oakland–Sacramento–Reno–Elko–Ogden–Cheyenne–Denver–Lincoln–Omaha–Galesburg–Chicago	3.18	0.97	0.15
Seattle–Portland–Sacramento–Oakland – Los Angeles	3.97	1.69	2.63
Seattle–Spokane–Havre–Fargo–Minneapolis–Milwaukee–Chicago	6.14	2.51	3.07
Chicago–Lafayette–Louisville–Nashville–Birmingham–Montgomery–Jacksonville–Orlando–Tampa	2.99	0.94	0.99
Minneapolis–Duluth	2.37	1.51	0.13
Chicago–Champaign–Carbondale–Memphis–Jackson – New Orleans	3.98	1.60	1.50
Los Angeles – San Diego	8.30	5.68	13.13

Source: Morrison (1990), table 3, p. 367.

such as passenger rail service more highly than do higher-income households, all else constant.

Second, comparing columns (1) and (3), we find that, for all but three routes, low-income households value Amtrak more than business travelers. The three exceptions are the Boston–Washington, New York – Buffalo, and Los Angeles – San Diego routes, which yield per business traveler benefits of \$31.39, \$12.61, and \$13.13 respectively. Why would business travelers on any rail route value Amtrak more highly than low-income pleasure travelers? From table 10.13 we have seen that business travelers value their travel and delay time more highly than vacation travelers, which reflects their preference for faster modes. Yet they are receiving large benefits on these three routes. The answer is that these are short-distance routes in densely populated areas, that justify frequent departures. Each of these factors works to the advantage of passenger rail for many work-related trips. Business travelers who value their time highly will choose rail over alternative modes, including air, because the short distance and frequent departures on these routes enable rail to dominate air travel's time and cost expenditures. However, on the other eight routes in table 10.14, distances are longer and departures less frequent, which causes rail to have a comparative disadvantage relative to air for those travelers who value their time highly.

For the same set of routes identified in table 10.14, table 10.15 reports the annual benefits from Amtrak's continued operation, annual losses on Amtrak's annual operating and capital costs, and net social benefits. In the table, we find that 8 out of the 11 routes yielded benefits that were insufficient to offset the losses incurred on the route. In other words, for these routes in 1977, the annual subsidy out of general tax funds was not offset by the benefits society received from Amtrak's availability. On the Boston–Washington, New York – Buffalo, and Los Angeles – San Diego routes, however, benefits did offset annual losses.[21] Note that these are the same routes that provided business travelers with large benefits. Combining the results from tables 10.14 and 10.15 leads to the conclusion that short-distance routes with frequent service, and located in populous areas, are socially worthwhile, since the annual benefits from Amtrak exceeded the losses incurred.

Amtrak's net value to society

We have seen that Amtrak service is not equally beneficial to all regions or all routes in the nation. Long-distance routes are not likely to pass a social cost–social benefit test, whereas short-distance routes in populated areas are likely to pass such a test. The Northeast Corridor on the East Coast and Southern California on the West Coast clearly justify continued rail passenger operations. Many routes in the Northwest, Southwest, Midwest, and Southeast, however, lack sufficient patronage to justify continued operations.

A related question is whether the short-distance, densely populated routes generate sufficient benefits to justify *system-wide* availability of Amtrak. That is, are the net benefits on these routes large enough to offset the deficits on other routes for the Amtrak system as a whole. Morrison considered this by assuming that the total benefit for a given city-pair c ($c = 1, \ldots, 188$) is *inversely* related to distance between the city-pairs and *positively* related to the population in each city of the pair. Specifically, Morrison adopted the following relationship:

$$\text{Total Benefit in City-Pair } c$$

$$= TB^c = \frac{K(\text{Pop}_{1c} \cdot \text{Pop}_{2c})^{\beta}}{(D_c)^{\gamma}} \qquad (10.15)$$

where Pop_{ic} ($i = 1, 2$) is the population in city i of the city-pair, D_c is the distance between the two cities, and β and γ are parameters.[22] If we take the logarithm of both sides and add an error term, we obtain the following empirical model:

$$\log TB_c = \alpha + \beta \log(\text{Pop}_{1c} \cdot \text{Pop}_{2c}) + \gamma \log D_c + u_c \qquad (10.16)$$

Table 10.15 Total benefits and costs per route (1977 dollars)

Route	Total Benefits (millions)	Amtrak Loss (millions)	Net Benefits (millions)
Boston–Providence – New York – Philadelphia–Baltimore–Washington	247.8	92.8	155.0
New York–Albany–Syracuse–Rochester–Buffalo	33.3	13.4	19.9
Philadelphia–Harrisburg–Pittsburgh	1.8	–	–
Los Angeles – Phoenix–Tucson – El Paso – San Antonio – Houston – New Orleans	4.5	9.9	–5.4
Oakland–Sacramento–Reno–Elko–Ogden–Cheyenne–Denver–Lincoln–Omaha–Galesburg–Chicago	4.0	27.4	–23.4
Seattle–Portland–Sacramento–Oakland – Los Angeles	11.7	20.0	–8.3
Seattle–Spokane–Havre–Fargo–Minneapolis–Milwaukee–Chicago	9.4	27.3	–6.5
Chicago–Lafayette–Louisville–Nashville–Birmingham–Montgomery–Jacksonville–Orlando–Tampa	3.3	15.9	–12.6
Minneapolis–Duluth	0.1	0.5	–0.4
Chicago–Champaign–Carbondale–Memphis–Jackson – New Orleans	2.1	6.3	–4.2
Los Angeles – San Diego	8.0	4.3	3.7

Source: Morrison (1990), table 5, p. 370.

where $\alpha = \exp(K)$ and $\gamma < 0$. Morrison estimated this "double-log" empirical model on the sample of 188 city-pairs. His estimated regression equation (with t-statistics in parentheses below the coefficient estimates) is as follows:

$$\log TB_c = \underset{(6.48)}{-15.75} + \underset{(17.4)}{1.215} \log(\text{Pop}_{1c} \cdot \text{Pop}_{2c}) - \underset{(5.29)}{0.9933} \log D_c$$
$$R^2 = 0.664 \qquad (10.17)$$

Overall, in double-log form, the product of city populations and distance between the cities explains 66% of the variation in total benefits. If we look at the coefficients, we see that increases in distance between cities lead to a proportional decrease in traveler benefits. A 1% increase in distance between cities reduces total benefits from Amtrak's availability 1%. On the other hand, increases in the attraction of the city-pair produce more than a proportional effect. A 1% increase in a city-pair's attraction increases total benefits by 1.21%, which reinforces our earlier finding that the benefits of Amtrak increase in more densely populated areas.

Based upon the coefficient estimates in equation (10.17), Morrison calculated the total benefits for each of the 6,235 nondirectional city-pairs serviced by Amtrak in 1977. Summing up the benefits per city-pair yielded a system-wide benefit from Amtrak's availability that totaled $970 million in 1977. The total deficit in 1977 was $521.6 million. Taking the difference, we reach the conclusion that in 1977 Amtrak's presence generated net positive benefits of $448.4 million. These positive net benefits provide an economic efficiency argument for subsidization.

Discussion

What can we conclude from this study? First, because the benefits to society outweigh resource costs, subsidizing Amtrak is an economically efficient outcome for society. However, even though system-wide benefits more than offset the subsidies, and justify its existence, Amtrak's benefits are skewed in favor of short-distance routes located in densely populated areas. Because these markets can effectively compete with air travel, intercity travelers receive significant benefits from Amtrak's existence. Long-distance routes in thinly populated areas, on the other hand, generate too few benefits to make Amtrak's provision economically efficient. Thus, whether one determines that Amtrak as a whole is economically provided depends upon one's interpretation. If we only look at the aggregate totals, Amtrak is viable. But if we consider a route-by-route evaluation, Morrison's analysis suggests that social welfare would rise if we eliminated all but the densest parts of the system.

A further point is that Morrison's study analyzed the net gains from Amtrak for 1977, which just preceded the onset of airline deregulation. As we have seen, airline deregulation wrought significant changes in the airline market structure, which could have consequences for the provision of rail passenger services. Based upon a comparison of Amtrak's 1977 benefits with its 1987 losses, deflated to 1977 dollars, Morrison's conclusions did not change. Overall, system-wide benefits exceed system-wide costs, but this is because the large surpluses on the densely populated short-haul routes continued to offset the systematic deficits on its longer-haul sparsely populated routes.

PRICING, INVESTMENT, AND A ZERO-PROFIT CONSTRAINT

When our transport authority operates under increasing returns to scale, a tug-of-war occurs between social surplus maximization and financial viability. First-best prices are efficient, but not sufficient to cover total fixed costs.

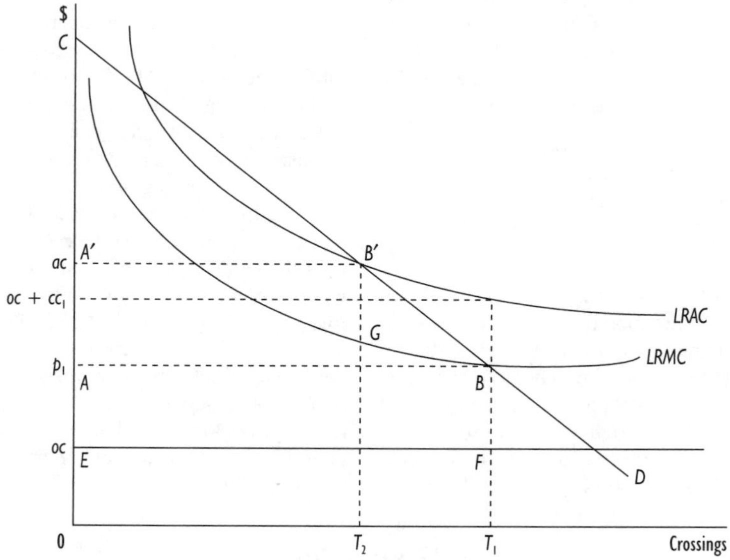

Figure 10.6 Second-best allocation of bridge crossing – average cost pricing.

Average cost pricing is perhaps the simplest of the solutions for eliminating the deficit generated by increasing returns to scale. Consider figure 10.6, which reproduces figure 10.5. Pricing at *LRMC* is efficient, yields *ABC* social surplus to society, and produces economic losses. Pricing at *LRAC*, *ac*, eliminates the deficit, reduces bridge capacity from T_1 to T_2, reduces consumer surplus from *ABC* to *A′B′C*, and reduces social surplus. In order to cover the deficit there is a transfer of income from consumers to the transport authority. In addition, the loss of social surplus is depicted in figure 10.6 by the area *BB′G*, which is the amount by which the additional benefit exceeds the additional cost of increasing capacity from T_2 to T_1. This is the inefficiency of average cost pricing.

The average cost price *ac* charged to bridge crossers in the decreasing cost case is referred to as a *second-best price*. Because average cost pricing does not price at marginal cost, *ac* is not a first best price. However, *relative to any other price that satisfies a zero profit constraint, ac* maximizes social surplus. If the price falls below *ac*, social surplus increases but economic losses occur. And for prices above *ac*, costs are covered but social surplus decreases further. Thus, *ac* is a second-best price, because society attains the highest possible social surplus given that costs must be covered.

Average cost pricing appears to be a reasonable method for covering the cost of a bridge that produces trips under increasing returns to scale. However, we have made an implicit assumption that the local transport authority only produces one good, bridge crossings. Let's complicate the problem a bit and assume that the local transport authority is not only responsible for bridge crossings but also for local highway trips. Further, let's assume that highways are produced under constant returns to scale, whereas bridges are produced under increasing returns to scale. Assuming that we follow our first-best pricing and investment principles, road construction is self-financing, but bridge construction runs a deficit. Although, for one good, average cost pricing is second best, when the transport authority produces two (or more)

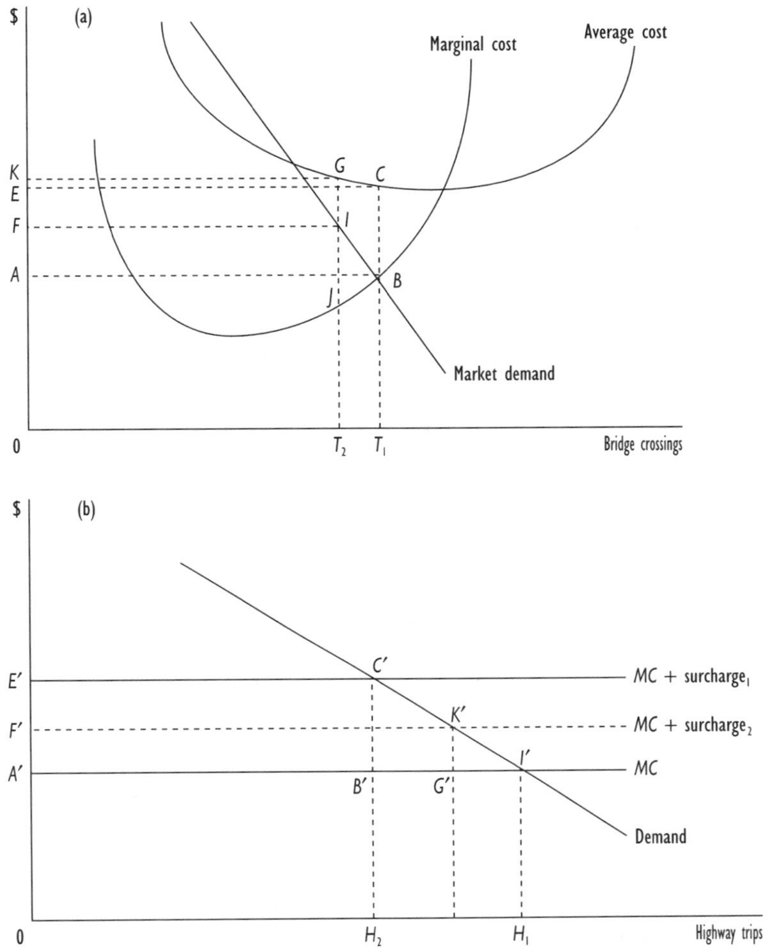

Figure 10.7 Markets for (a) bridge crossings and (b) highway trips – second-best prices.

goods, there is a problem. If we are to impose a zero-profit constraint on the local transport authority, we need to identify a set of prices for bridge crossings and highway use that produces sufficient revenues to pay for bridge and highway construction. But the question is: What set of prices are appropriate; that is, what set of prices maximize social surplus given that costs must be covered? After all, we could set a high price for bridge crossings and a low price for highway use; or we could set a low price for bridge crossings and a high price for highway use; or we could set any other combination of prices as long as we pay our fixed capacity costs.

To analyze this, consider figures 10.7(a) and 10.7(b), which graph the equilibrium for each of the local authority's activities. Since bridge construction incurs a deficit, suppose that the local authority raises the price of highway trips H to highway users in order to obtain enough revenue over costs to equal the deficit in the bridge sector. Thus, area $ABCE$ (the deficit) in the bridge sector equals area $A'B'C'E'$ (net revenues collected) in the highway sector. Notice that marginal cost pricing is prevalent in the bridge sector but not present in the highway sector. Raising the price above opportunity costs in the highway sector drives a wedge between price and marginal cost, which produces a "deadweight" or efficiency loss. This loss, given by the triangular area $C'B'I'$ in figure 10.7(b), represents the net gains to society that are not achieved because of the highway surcharge to users.[23]

Given that we cannot have marginal cost pricing (first-best pricing) in each sector, the question that arises is whether we want marginal cost pricing at all. That is, suppose we eliminate marginal cost pricing in the bridge sector. Would it then be possible to define a set of prices – second-best prices – for bridge crossings and highway trips, which yields zero profits to the transport authority but *reduces* the total deadweight loss to society? To examine this, return to figures 10.7(a) and 10.7(b), and assume we charge a price of $0F$ in the bridge sector and $0F'$ in the highway sector. Thus, marginal cost pricing has been abandoned in both sectors. What are the economic effects of this pricing scheme?

In the bridge sector, there still exists a deficit, amounting to the area $FIGK$ in figure 10.7(a), but the deficit is smaller than before. In addition, pricing above marginal cost has driven $T_1 - T_2$ bridge users out of the market, which results in a deadweight loss to society equal to the area IJB. Thus, the overall effect of the new pricing policy in the bridge market is a reduction of deficits and the creation of efficiency losses.

What about the highway market? In figure 10.7(b), we see that the highway surcharge falls from $A'E'$ to $A'F'$ which reduces the price of highway trips from $0E'$ to $0F'$. Total net revenues fall from $A'B'C'E'$ to $A'G'K'F'$ which, by construction, equals the lower deficits ($FIGK$ in figure 10.7(a)). Moreover, since the highway surcharge is lower, so too is the welfare loss. The "deadweight" loss decreases from $C'B'I'$ to $K'G'I'$. Thus, the overall effect in the highway market is lower net revenues (brought about by a lower surcharge) and a smaller welfare loss.

The fundamental question is whether society is better off with the new pricing scheme. To answer this, we need to compare society's efficiency losses under both pricing schemes. Under the first pricing regime, there were no efficiency losses in the bridge sector, but there were losses equal to area $C'B'I'$ in the highway sector. Under the second pricing regime, there were some losses in both markets, equaling IJB and $K'G'I'$ in the bridge and highway sectors, respectively. Under both regimes, bridge and highway costs are covered and the transport authority earns zero economic profits. Society will be better off if the total losses under the second pricing strategy are less than those associated with the first. And this is indeed the case. Since the efficiency loss in the bridge sector, area IJB in figure 10.7(a), is less than the efficiency gain in the highway sector, area $C'B'G'K'$ in figure 10.7(b), society is better off abandoning its marginal cost pricing rule in the bridge sector. Basically, this result tells us that if we raise prices to cover the deficit, then we want to set prices that have the least effect on economic welfare.

Raising prices above marginal costs has two effects. First, as seen above, they create efficiency or welfare losses. On the other hand, they produce needed revenues. Thus, when marginal cost pricing on all goods is not possible, setting prices such that *the marginal welfare loss per dollar of revenue generated is equal for all goods* minimizes the efficiency losses. In other words, satisfying this condition produces an optimal set of prices.

Consider the market for highway trips in figure 10.8. Highway trips are priced above marginal cost by the amount s $(= p_H - c_H)$. This produces an efficiency loss equal to $G'I'L'$ and net revenues equal to $A'G'L'E'$. What effect will a further \$1 increase in the surcharge on the price of highway trips have upon welfare and net revenues. For a small increase in the surcharge, the efficiency loss can be approximated by[24]

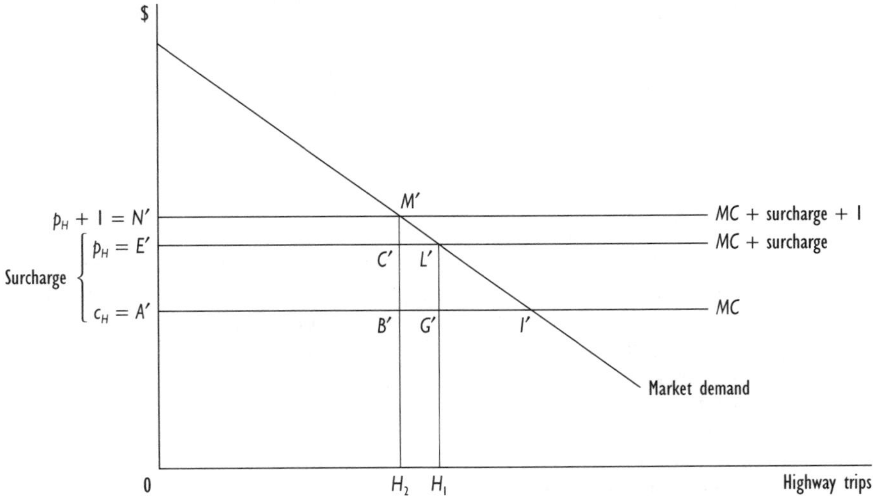

Figure 10.8 Efficiency losses in the highway sector.

$$\begin{aligned}\text{change in efficiency loss} &= (p_H - c_H)\frac{\Delta H}{\Delta p_H}\\ &= \text{area } B'G'L'C' \end{aligned} \tag{10.18}$$

The increase in net revenues, on the other hand, can be approximated by

$$\begin{aligned}\text{change in tax revenues} &= \frac{\Delta H}{\Delta s}H_2 + (p_H - c_H)\frac{\Delta H}{\Delta p_H}\\ &= H_2 + (p_H - c_H)\frac{\Delta H}{\Delta p_H} \qquad \left(\text{since } \frac{\Delta H}{\Delta s} = 1\right)\\ &= \text{area } C'M'N'E' - \text{area } B'G'L'C' \end{aligned} \tag{10.19}$$

which represents the increase in revenues associated with consumption H_2 minus the lost revenues associated with consumption $H_1 - H_2$. Thus, the efficiency loss per dollar revenue generated by the price rise is

$$\text{efficiency loss/dollar collected} = \frac{(p_H - c_H)\Delta H/\Delta p_H}{H + (p_H - c_H)\Delta H/\Delta p_H} \tag{10.20}$$

and an optimal set of prices requires that the efficiency loss per dollar collected be equal in each sector. Returning to our transport authority example, an optimal set of prices requires that the marginal efficiency loss per dollar collected in the highway sector be equal to the marginal efficiency loss per *dollar reduction* in the bridge sector's deficit. That is,

$$\frac{(p_H - c_H)\Delta H/\Delta p_H}{H + (p_H - c_H)\Delta H/\Delta p_H} = \frac{(p_T - c_T)\Delta T/\Delta p_T}{T + (p_T - c_T)\Delta T/\Delta p_T} \tag{10.21}$$

It is demonstrated in the appendix to this chapter that equation (10.21) implies the following relationship between the price elasticity of demand and distortions from marginal cost pricing:

$$\frac{(p_H - c_H)/p_H}{(p_T - c_T)/p_T} = \frac{E_{Tp}}{E_{Hp}} \tag{10.22}$$

where $(p_i - c_i)/p_i$ $(i = H,T)$ is the extent to which price is set above marginal cost (or the rate of distortion from marginal cost pricing) and E_{ip} is the price elasticity of demand for good i $(i = H,T)$. The prices p_i $(i = T,H)$ that maximize social surplus subject to a zero-profit constraint are second-best or *Ramsey prices*, named after the economist who first addressed this problem in the 1920s (see Ramsey, 1927).

According to equation (10.22), the extent to which prices diverge from marginal cost is inversely related to the good's price elasticity of demand. This is the *inverse elasticity rule* that we met in chapter 7 when discussing price discrimination.[25] The relationship between surcharges and the price elasticity of demand makes intuitive sense. If a good is price inelastic, it will take a larger per-unit increase in the surcharge to produce a given welfare loss, since an increase in price has a relatively small effect upon quantity demanded. On the other hand, if demand is price elastic, a small increase in price will produce a relatively large decrease in quantity demanded. Thus, only a small increase in the per-unit surcharge is required to obtain a given loss in welfare.

To gain further insights into the meaning of the inverse elasticity rule, rearrange equation (10.22):

$$\frac{(p_H - c_H)E_{Hp}}{p_H} = \frac{(p_T - c_T)E_{Tp}}{p_T}$$

$$\Rightarrow \quad \frac{(p_H - c_H)}{p_H}\frac{\Delta H}{\Delta p_H}\frac{p_H}{H} = \frac{(p_T - c_T)}{p_T}\frac{\Delta T p_T}{\Delta p_T T}$$

$$\Rightarrow \quad \frac{(p_H - c_H)(\Delta H/\Delta p_H)}{H} = \frac{(p_T - c_T)(\Delta T/\Delta p_T)}{T} \tag{10.22'}$$

If demand is linear, the numerator on each side of this equation is the slope of the demand curve, $\Delta i/\Delta p_i$ $(i = T,H)$ multiplied by the change in price $p_i - c_i$, which is simply the change in quantity demanded from raising price above marginal cost. Thus, if market demands are linear and prices are set according to the inverse elasticity rule, we can rewrite (10.22′) as[26]

$$\frac{\Delta H}{H} = \frac{\Delta T}{T} \Rightarrow \frac{\Delta H}{\Delta T} = \frac{H}{T} \tag{10.23}$$

Second-best prices that satisfy a zero-profit constraint are set in such a way that the quantity of bridge crossings and highway trips demanded decrease proportionately. Again, this makes intuitive sense. Under first-best pricing, there will be some optimal ratio of outputs in each sector, H/T. If first-best pricing fails to cover all costs of production, then second-best pricing aims to maintain the same output ratio as first-best prices. That is, the local authority would want to proportionately decrease output in each sector until prices sufficiently rose to cover all costs of production.[27]

Marginal Cost Pricing Plus Subsidy – A Comment

In prior sections, we first examined the welfare effects of pricing at marginal cost and covering the deficit from the general tax fund. And our examples supported the theoretical prediction that welfare would increase under first-best pricing and investment. However, our discussion of second-best prices implies that first-best prices in a decreasing-cost industry when the deficit is financed from the general revenue fund may not maximize society's social surplus. Suppose, in the bridge and highway example, that we set the price for bridge crossings at marginal cost, but now we raise the price of some other *nontransportation* commodity above marginal cost in order to obtain the needed revenues to cover the deficit. This leads to exactly the same type of second-best problem that we considered above. The only difference between subsidizing from the general fund and the zero-profit policy considered above is the good whose price gets distorted. Under the zero-profit constraint, the local transportation authority is required to meet all costs, in which case second-best prices are applied to bridge crossings and highway trips. Under a subsidy scheme in which subsidies come from the general tax fund, the local authority continues to set first-best prices for highway trips. However, in order to cover the bridge deficit, second-best prices are now applied to bridge crossings and commodity X. In this case, no distortions occur in the market for highway trips, but distortions are present in the market for bridge crossings and the market for X. One way or the other, the deficit must be covered, and each pricing alternative involves welfare losses. The important question is: Which pricing strategy leads to the smallest losses? And the analysis on second-best prices indicates that setting prices which lead to equi-proportional decreases in outputs produces the least distorting effect on social surplus.

Case Study – Pricing Urban Transit Under a Zero-Profit Constraint

The primary result from our theoretical analysis of second-best, or Ramsey, pricing is that deficits can be covered and welfare losses to society minimized when we set prices in such a way that the output of each good is reduced proportionately. In a study associated with the initial development of rapid transit in the San Francisco Bay Area, Train (1977, 1991) calculated second-best prices for bus and rapid transit services.

Train considered two public transit services on the East Bay of the San Francisco Bay Area, bus services provided by Alameda – Contra Costa Transit (ACT) and rapid transit services provided by Bay Area Rapid Transit (BART). Since, by law, BART was required to generate enough revenues to cover operating (but not capital) costs, Train assumed that BART prices should be set to cover average operating costs. On the other hand, he assumed ACT would have to generate revenues to cover all costs of operation, which implies that the second-best bus price would cover average total costs of production. Thus, the zero-profit budget constraint faced by the combined bus–BART transit authority is as follows:

Table 10.16 Ramsey prices in urban transit

Transit Mode	Average Variable Cost[a]	Average Total Cost[a]	Short-Run Marginal Cost[a,b]	Long-Run Marginal Cost[a,c]
Alameda–Contra Costa Transit	–	2.0	0.0	2.0
BART	1.74	–	0.0	0.88

[a] Cost are in cents (1972 dollars) per passenger–mile.
[b] Short-run marginal cost assumes that an additional passenger–mile requires no additional capacity.
[c] Long-run marginal cost assumes that an additional passenger–mile requires additional capacity.
Source: Train (1977)

$$(p_{\text{BART}} - AVC_{\text{BART}})Q_{\text{BART}} + (p_{\text{ACT}} - ATC_{\text{ACT}})Q_{\text{ACT}} = 0 \quad (10.24)$$

where AVC_{BART} is BART's average variable cost and ATC_{ACT} is the average total cost for Alameda – Contra Costa Transit.

Table 10.16 reports the estimated average and marginal costs of bus and rapid transit trips (in 1972 dollars) that were used for this study. Previous research on the Alameda – Contra Costa bus system found that bus trips were produced under constant returns to scale. This is the reason why Average Total Cost in table 10.16 equals Long-Run Marginal Cost. On the other hand, for the BART system we see that Long-Run Marginal Cost is less than Average Variable Cost which, irrespective of capital costs, implies that BART runs at a deficit. Within this framework, Train set out to estimate the second best prices. That is: What per passenger–mile price for ACT bus trips and per passenger–mile price for BART trips would generate sufficient revenues to cover the total operating costs of BART and the total costs of ACT?

Our inverse elasticity rule specifies that second-best prices must satisfy the following equation:

$$\frac{(p_i - c_i)E_{i,p}}{p_i} = \frac{(p_j - c_j)E_{j,p}}{p_j}, \qquad i \neq j$$

where $E_{k,p}$ is the price elasticity of demand for transit mode k. However, this equation assumes that the cross-price elasticity of demand is equal to zero. In other words, changes in bus prices have no effect upon the demand for BART, and changes in BART prices have no effect on the demand for bus. Although for some second-best problems (one of which we will examine in the next section), this may be a reasonable assumption, in the transit case considered here, the assumption is not appropriate. In general, bus trips and BART trips are substitutes.[28] Although not proven here, it is possible to derive a more general formulation of the inverse elasticity rule which takes into account the cross-price elasticity between bus and BART (Train, 1977, p. 186). This is given in equation (10.25) below:

$$\left(\frac{p_{\text{BART}} - MC_{\text{BART}}}{p_{\text{BART}}}\right)(E_{\text{BART},p} - E_{\text{BART,ACT}}) = \left(\frac{p_{\text{ACT}} - MC_{\text{ACT}}}{p_{\text{ACT}}}\right)(E_{\text{ACT},p} - E_{\text{BART,ACT}}) \quad (10.25)$$

where $E_{i,p}$ (i = BART,ACT) is the own-price elasticity of demand and $E_{\text{BART,ACT}}$ is the cross-price elasticity of demand. The only difference between equation (10.25) and the inverse elasticity rule given earlier is that the percentage increase of price over marginal cost is weighted by the "net" own-price elasticity of demand, which is defined as the own-price elasticity of demand minus the cross-price elasticity of demand.[29]

On the basis of the set of average and marginal prices in table 10.16, Train solved for the second-best set of prices, p_{BART} and p_{ACT}, that

Table 10.17 Second-best prices for bus and rapid transit trips with a zero profit constraint

Transit Mode	Average Variable Cost[a] (1)	Average Total Cost[a] (2)	Marginal Cost[a,b] (3)	Optimal Price[a,c] (4)
Short run				
Alameda–Contra Costa Transit	–	2.0	0.0	1.95
BART	1.74	–	0.0	1.78
Long run				
Alameda–Contra Costa Transit	–	2.0	2.0	2.42
BART	1.74	–	0.88	1.28

[a] Cost are in cents (1972 dollars) per passenger–mile.
[b] Short-run marginal cost assumes that an additional passenger–mile requires no additional capacity.
[c] Long-run marginal cost assumes that an additional passenger–mile requires additional capacity.
Source: Train (1977)

satisfy the budget constraint expressed in equation (10.24) and the generalized inverse elasticity rule given by equation (10.25).

Since from table 10.16 we have short-run and long-run marginal costs of a passenger–mile, and the generalized inverse elasticity rule depends upon the marginal cost of production, we will have two sets of second-best prices, one associated with short-run marginal costs and the other associated with long-run marginal costs. These optimal prices are reported in table 10.17. Assuming that an additional passenger–mile requires no additional capacity, then second-best prices are virtually identical to average cost pricing. From column (4), the optimal price for ACT is 1.95 cents per passenger–mile, in comparison with its 2.0 cent average total cost. Also, the optimal price for BART is 1.78 per passenger–mile in comparison with its 1.74 cent average operating cost.

The story, however, is drastically different if we assume that an additional passenger–mile requires additional capacity. Here we see that the bus price is nearly 25% above its average total cost, whereas BART's optimal price is 26% below its average variable cost. Whereas under short-run marginal costs, there was no cross-subsidization between modes, under long-run marginal costs there is cross-subsidization from bus travelers to BART travelers.

The optimal prices in the lower half of table 10.17 make clear the potentially inequitable effects associated with second-best prices. On the East Bay of San Francisco, many BART users are high-income earners who live in well-to-do suburban areas and ride BART in their daily work trips to downtown San Francisco. Although many of these individuals own automobiles which they could use in their work trips, the generalized cost (that is, time, operating, and parking cost) of BART is less than the generalized cost of using private transportation. Many users of Alameda – Contra Costa Transit, on the other hand, come from lower-income inner cities on the East Bay and use the bus for relatively short trips. Moreover, because many of these households have lower incomes, fewer households own automobiles. What this means is that BART users will generally have more options available for their trips to work. If the price of BART becomes too high, users will simply switch to private means of travel, either driving themselves to work or forming a carpool with others. The lower-income households that use ACT do not have as many options. If the household does not own a vehicle, rising bus fares are simply endured. The options for many of these households, walking for example, will still have a higher generalized price than bus, so that no switching occurs.

The result is that bus riders, who on average have lower incomes, subsidize the higher-income BART riders. From an efficiency standpoint, this is exactly what we want, because second-best prices penalize more those users who have more inelastic demands. And since lower-income households have fewer alternatives for their trip-making, their demands are less elastic than those of the higher-income households. But from an equity perspective, second-best prices redistribute money from lower-income households to higher-income households, which leads to a more unequal distribution of income. Thus, although second-best prices maximize social surplus, subject to a budgetary constraint, these prices are silent on who wins and who loses. This implies that implementation of second-best prices must be accompanied by complementary policies to insure that there are no significant income transfers from the poor to the rich.

CASE STUDY – SETTING AIRPLANE LANDING FEES UNDER A ZERO-PROFIT CONSTRAINT

In earlier sections of this chapter, we considered the problem of pricing and investment for airport infrastructure, and analyzed the welfare implications of moving from the current level of airport investment and structure of landing fees to efficient investment and pricing. In this section, we consider the related but different problem of setting appropriate landing fees at uncongested or overcapitalized airports. Suppose, in particular, that we have an airport that can accommodate more landings and take-offs than are currently demanded. If the opportunity cost of an additional landing is relatively small, then marginal cost pricing is efficient but will not generate sufficient revenues to pay for the facility. In order to cover the resulting deficit, the airport facility will implement average cost pricing but, as we have seen, this leads to welfare losses.

An interesting aspect of this short-run uncongested airport problem is that airport costs are not solely related to aircraft take-offs and landings. Airports also provide parking facilities and terminals. Analogously, airports generate revenues from landing fees as well as from nonlanding-fee sources, including parking facilities, and rents from gift shops, restaurants, and other retail outlets at the terminal. We have previously seen that landing fees are based upon the aircraft's landing weight, and in table 10.9 we illustrated this pattern of landing fees for various cities, increasing with size and weight of aircraft. Moreover, airports oftentimes set their landing fees to insure that the airport's total costs will be covered. In other words, if the revenues from nonlanding activities are insufficient to cover an airport's total cost of operation, the airport will set landing fees in order to balance its budget. Thus, one could argue that airport authorities engage in some form of average cost pricing when setting landing fees. But this raises the question of whether the existing landing fees, based upon aircraft weight, are efficient. That is, is there another set of landing fees that would also cover the airport's budget but lead to fewer welfare losses?

Morrison (1982) considered this problem by calculating the second-best landing fees at uncongested airports for different sizes of aircraft such that the revenues generated from the landing fees plus the revenues from nonlanding-fee sources equal total costs. By comparing the second-best prices with actual landing fees, Morrison was able to determine whether the current structure of landing fees was efficient.

Applying our inverse elasticity rule to aircraft landings gives us

$$\frac{(\text{Fee}_i - MC_i)}{\text{Fee}_i} E_{i,\text{Fee}} = \frac{(\text{Fee}_j - MC_j)}{\text{Fee}_j} E_{j,\text{Fee}}, \quad i \neq j$$

where Fee_i is the landing fee for aircraft of size i, MC_i is the marginal cost to the airport authority when aircraft of size i lands, and $E_{i,\text{Fee}}$ is elasticity of the demand for landings with respect to landing fees. If, for example, $E_{i,\text{Fee}} = -0.25$ a 1%

increase in the landing fee reduces by 0.25% the quantity of landings demanded by an aircraft of size i. The above expression also assumes that the demand for landings by an aircraft of size i does not depend upon the landing fee on other sized aircraft. That is, the cross-price elasticity of the demand for landings is zero. This is not an overly restrictive assumption, since an airline's decision to use a particular type of aircraft generally depends upon load factors, departure frequency, and distance.

Although we don't know the demand elasticities with respect to landing fees, we can obtain this information from the price elasticity of demand for flights. Suppose that we define an airline flight as one flight of distance d miles on aircraft of size i plus a landing. We denote this flight by F_d^i. If we further assume that flights are produced by a fixed proportions production function, then we can express F_d^i as[30]

$$F_d^i = \min\left(\frac{\text{Aircraft}_d^i}{a}, \frac{\text{Landing}^i}{b}\right)$$

where Aircraft_d^i is an Aircraft of size i traveling d miles, Landing^i is a landing by an aircraft of size i, and a and b are the input requirements of Aircraft and Landings per unit of output, Flight. Since one Aircraft plus one Landing produces one Flight, $a = b = 1$ and our Flight production function can be more simply expressed as

$$F_d^i = \min(\text{Aircraft}_d^i, \text{Landing}^i)$$

and the price a consumer pays to fly d miles on aircraft size i, P_d^i, is simply the sum of the flight's cost, C_d^i, plus the landing fee, Fee_i. That is,

$$P_d^i = C_d^i + \text{Fee}_i$$

$$\Rightarrow \frac{\Delta P_d^i}{P_d^i} = \frac{C_d^i}{C_d^i + \text{Fee}_i}\frac{\Delta C_d^i}{C_d^i} + \frac{\text{Fee}_i}{C_d^i + \text{Fee}_i}\frac{\Delta \text{Fee}_i}{\text{Fee}_i} \tag{10.26}$$

where C_d^i is the cost of producing a flight of d miles on aircraft of size i.[31]

Suppose that the cost of the flight doesn't change, but that there is an increase in landing fees. Then, from equation (10.26), $\Delta C_d^i/C_d^i = 0$, and we obtain the result that a proportional increase in landing fees will be reflected by a proportional increase in price. Moreover, the rise in price will reduce the quantity of flights demanded. If $E_{F_d^i,P_d^i}$ is the price elasticity of the demand for flights of d miles on aircraft of size i, then

$$E_{F_d^i,P_d^i} = \frac{\Delta F_d^i}{\Delta P_d^i}\frac{P_d^i}{F_d^i}$$

$$\Rightarrow \frac{\Delta F_d^i}{F_d^i} = E_{F_d^i,P_d^i}\frac{\Delta P_d^i}{P_d^i} \tag{10.27}$$

The percentage fall in the quantity of flights demanded equals the percentage rise in the price of the flight weighted by the price elasticity of demand. But since the production of flights is in fixed proportions, the decrease in the quantity of flights demanded leads to a proportional fall in use of both inputs, Aircraft_d^i and Landing^i. We can thus express equation (10.27) as

$$\frac{\Delta \text{Landing}^i}{\text{Landing}^i} = E_{F_d^i,P_d^i}\frac{\Delta P_d^i}{P_d^i}$$

$$\Rightarrow \frac{\Delta P_d^i}{P_d^i} = \frac{1}{E_{F_d^i,P_d^i}}\frac{\Delta \text{Landing}^i}{\text{Landing}^i} \tag{10.28}$$

If we now use equation (10.28) to substitute for $\Delta P_d^i/P_d^i$ in equation (10.26), recalling that the $\Delta C_d^i/C_d^i = 0$, we obtain

$$\frac{1}{E_{F_d^i,P_d^i}}\frac{\Delta \text{Landing}^i}{\text{Landing}^i} = \frac{\text{Fee}_i}{C_d^i + \text{Fee}_i}\frac{\Delta \text{Fee}_i}{\text{Fee}_i}$$

$$\Rightarrow E_{i,\text{Fee}} = \frac{\Delta \text{Landing}^i}{\Delta \text{Fee}_i}\frac{\text{Fee}_i}{\text{Landing}^i}$$

$$= \frac{\text{Fee}_i}{C_d^i + \text{Fee}_i}E_{F_d^i,P_d^i} \tag{10.29}$$

From equation (10.29), we see that there is a relationship between the landing demand elasticity with respect to landing fees, $E_{i,\text{Fee}}$, and the price elasticity of the demand for flights. A moment's thought will suggest the intuition behind this result. Since an aircraft landing is an input in the production of flights, the landing is a derived demand, derived from the demand for flights. Thus, if consumers' flight demands are very sensitive to the price of flights, a change in the price of landings, which shows up as a higher price for flights, will lead to a large change in the quantity of flights – and therefore landings – demanded. Thus, the higher the price elasticity of the demand for flights is, the higher is the landing elasticity with respect to landing fees, all else held constant. We also see in (10.29) that $E_{i,\text{Fee}}$ depends upon the proportion of total costs that landing fees comprise. This too makes intuitive sense. If landing fees are a small proportion of the total cost of production, then we would expect consumers to be less sensitive to fee changes than if landing fees made up a large proportion of total production cost. All else constant, the higher the share of an input in the cost of production is, the greater is the input's elasticity of demand.

Substituting $E_{i,\text{Fee}}$ from equation (10.29) into our inverse elasticity rule, we obtain

$$\frac{(\text{Fee}_i - MC_i)}{\text{Fee}_i}\frac{\text{Fee}_i}{C_d^i + \text{Fee}_i}E_{F_d^i,P_d^i} = \frac{(\text{Fee}_j - MC_j)}{\text{Fee}_j}\frac{\text{Fee}_j}{C_d^j + \text{Fee}_j}E_{F_d^j,P_d^j}, \qquad i \neq j$$

$$\Rightarrow \frac{(\text{Fee}_i - MC_i)}{P_d^i}E_{F_d^i,P_d^i} = \frac{(\text{Fee}_j - MC_j)}{P_d^j}E_{F_d^j,P_d^j}, \qquad i \neq j \qquad (10.30)$$

Equation (10.30) tells us that the optimal landing fees will depend upon three pieces of information: the marginal cost of the landing to the airport authority, the price of the trip, and the price elasticity of the demand for flights.

For different-sized aircraft and for flight distances ranging from 500 miles to 2,500 miles, Morrison obtained information on flight costs per block hour.[32] Combined with data on the price elasticities of demand for flights and the marginal cost of a landing to an airport, table 10.18 reports Morrison's second-best estimates of landing fees for different-sized aircraft. These landing fees maximize social surplus subject to the constraint that the airport's revenues equal its costs.[33]

Similar to existing landing fees, we see in table 10.18 that, for a given distance, the optimal landing fee increases with aircraft size. This follows directly from equation (10.30) where the relative fee structure can be expressed as

$$\frac{(\text{Fee}_i - MC_i)}{(\text{Fee}_j - MC_j)} = \frac{P_d^i\, E_{F_d^j,P_d^j}}{P_d^j\, E_{F_d^i,P_d^i}}, \qquad i \neq j$$

Given the price elasticities of demand, landing fees are directly related to the cost that the airport incurs from a landing. Since heavier aircraft impose higher costs for any given distance, the optimal landing fee for the larger aircraft will be higher.

We also see in table 10.18 that, for a given aircraft type, the optimal landing fee rises with flight distance. From the inverse elasticity rule, this implies that the demand for landings is less elastic for longer flights than for shorter flights. Although the passenger demand for longer flights is more elastic than that for shorter flights, the cost of producing a longer flight is higher. And as long as the cost rises faster than the price elasticity of demand, the demand for landings will be more price inelastic. We can see this explicitly from equation (10.29):

$$E_{i,\text{Fee}} = \frac{\text{Fee}_i}{C_d^i + \text{Fee}_i}E_{F_d^i,P_d^i}$$

As long as the increase in C_d^i for longer flights increases the denominator in greater proportion than the rise in $E_{F_d^i,P_d^i}$, the demand for landings will be less elastic on longer flights.

How do the optimal landing fees reported in table 10.18 compare with existing landing fees? To make this comparison, Morrison initially converted optimal and current landing fees per aircraft to an equivalent fee per 1,000 pounds of landing weight. Since current landing fees are typically levied in proportion to aircraft weight, we can assume that under the current system the landing fee per 1,000 pounds of landing

Table 10.18 Structure of landing fees (1979 dollars)

	Aircraft Type (weight, '000 pounds)				
Distance (miles)	DC9-30 (110)	B727-200 (154.5)	DC8-61 (240)	DC10-10 (363.5)	B747 (564)
500	102	132	202	261	321
1,000	147	195	283	370	458
1,500	191	258	365	481	597
2,000	236	321	449	592	738
2,500	281	385	532	705	879

Source: Morrison (1982), table 4, p. 157

Table 10.19 Normalized ratio of second-best to current landing fees

	Aircraft (maximum landing weight, '000 pounds)				
Distance (miles)	DC9-30 (110)	B727-200 (154.5)	DC8-61 (240)	DC10-10 (363.5)	B747 (564)
500	1.00	0.92	0.91	0.77	0.61
1,000	1.44	1.36	1.27	1.09	0.87
1,500	1.87	1.80	1.64	1.42	1.14
2,000	2.31	2.24	2.01	1.75	1.41
2,500	2.75	2.68	2.39	2.09	1.68

Source: Adapted from Morrison (1982), table 5, p. 157

weight is constant. If we use the DC9-30 for a 500-mile trip as a basis of comparison, we can then derive the ratio of optimal to current fee for the different-sized aircraft and flight distances. These ratios are reported in table 10.19.

To understand this table, let's start with the optimal landing fee from table 10.18 for a DC9-30 on a 500-mile trip. From table 10.18, this fee is $102, or $0.927 per 1,000 pounds (102/110 = 0.927) of landing weight. Assume that the existing landing fee for this aircraft and distance is also $0.927 per 1,000 pounds. Then the ratio of the two landing fees is simply 1.0, which is the entry in the first row and first column of table 10.19. Consider next the 0.92 ratio in table 10.19 for a B727-200 aircraft on a 500-mile flight. The optimal landing fee for this aircraft is $132, or $0.854 per 1,000 pounds. Since, under the current system, we have assumed that landing fees are constant per 1,000 pounds of landing weight, the current landing fee is again $0.927 per 1,000 pounds. The ratio 0.854/0.927 = 0.92, the entry in the first row and second column of table 10.19. As a final example, consider a 1,000-mile trip on a B727-200 aircraft. Morrison estimated an optimal landing fee of $195 (from table 10.19) or $1.26 per 1,000 pounds. Dividing $1.26 by $0.927 gives the ratio 1.36, which is the entry in the second row and second column of the table.

Now that we understand the numerical values in table 10.19, let's interpret the results. For any given distance, we see that the normalized ratios decrease with increasing size of plane. This implies that the current landing fees rise more quickly with size of plane than the optimal second-best prices. On the other hand, for any give size of aircraft, the ratios increase with flight distance, which implies that the optimal prices rise more quickly than current weight-based landing fees.[34] This result should not be surprising, since existing landing fees are only related to aircraft size, whereas the second-best prices are determined by both aircraft size and flight distance.

If the airport's overall budget is satisfied with the existing set of landing fees, changing to second-best prices would reduce the social welfare losses from the current structure of weight-based fees while continuing to satisfy the budget constraint. Moreover, table 10.19 tells us that implementing an optimal set of prices would mean higher landing fees for smaller planes making longer trips and lower landing fees for larger planes making shorter trips. This further implies a redistribution of income from passengers making long-distance trips on smaller aircraft to those making short-distance trips on larger aircraft.

CHAPTER HIGHLIGHTS

- With fixed capacity and noncapacity market demand, first-best pricing efficiently allocates resources, prices at marginal cost, and generates no revenues to cover fixed capital costs. With fixed capacity and capacity market demand, first-best pricing sets a price that rations the fixed capacity to the highest-valued uses and generates revenues above variable costs that offset at least part of the fixed capital costs.
- In the presence of fixed capacity and varying demands per period, first-best pricing requires peak-period users to make a contribution to the capital production costs. Off-peak users only pay the opportunity costs of consumption.
- Average costs that are constant as industry output expands characterize constant-cost industries; average costs that decline (rise) as industry output expands characterize decreasing- (increasing-) cost industries.
- First-best pricing and investment in a constant-cost industry requires capital investment at a level at which the market demand curve intersects the long-run marginal cost curve. In the constant-cost case, revenues are sufficient to pay for all variable and fixed costs of production.
- First-best investment in highways implies that agencies invest in highway durability up to the point at which an additional unit of thickness just equals the savings in maintenance expenditures. And first-best pricing implies that the price a user pays equals the marginal maintenance expenditures from the increased loading.
- In an empirical example of highway pricing, current investment in highway durability was found to be sub-optimal, which implies a short-run marginal maintenance cost that is higher than optimal. Current road taxes based upon the number of axles increase with size of truck for a given weight, producing an inefficient allocation of resources. Efficient taxes would be based upon weights per axle load, which would increase substantially as weight increases for a given size of truck but, for a given weight, decrease with number of axles. Optimal pricing and investment of highways implies reducing the esal loadings, increasing the proportion of large trucks on our highways, and producing large welfare gains to society.

- In an empirical study of airports, first-best pricing and investment generate significant welfare gains to society. Except for a decline in airport net revenues, all other groups gain. Efficient pricing with current investment, however, generates high revenues for airports and large welfare losses for travelers. Similar to the highway case, there are significant distribution differences between efficient pricing/current investment and efficient pricing/optimal investment.
- In a decreasing-cost environment, first-best pricing and investment leads to an efficient allocation of resources, but also produces deficits that must somehow be covered. One way of covering deficits is subsidization. In an empirical model of Amtrak, sufficiently high benefits accrue to the Northeast Corridor and the Los Angeles – San Diego corridor to warrant Amtrak's continuation. Further, on a route-by-route basis, only in these corridors do the benefits outweigh the costs.
- A second-best price is a price that maximizes social surplus given the constraint that costs must be covered; that is, a zero-profit constraint. For a single good, a second-best price implies average cost pricing. For multiple goods, second-best (Ramsey) prices imply an inverse elasticity rule where the price : marginal cost margin is negatively related to the price elasticity of demand. At these prices, the marginal welfare loss per revenue gain is equal for all goods.
- In an empirical model of second-best pricing of urban transit, bus trips were less elastic than rapid transit trips, which implied that lower-income bus travelers subsidized higher-income rapid transit travelers. Although efficient in a second-best sense, this outcome illustrates potential distribution problems with second-best pricing.
- In an empirical model of airplane landing fees at uncongested airports, current landing fees increase with size and weight of aircraft. Optimal fees increase with size of aircraft for a given trip distance, reflecting the higher cost to the airport when a larger plane lands; optimal fees also increase with trip distance for given size of aircraft, which reflects the lower elasticity of demand for landings on longer flights.

Review questions

1. There currently exists a causeway that connects two cities. The cost of building the causeway was \$1,000,000 and the marginal cost per causing crossing is \$0.25. At peak use, the causeway can accommodate 1,500 hourly crossings.
   (a) If there are 750 crossings per hour and each causeway crossing costs \$1.00, is this a first-best price? If so, why; and if not, what is the first-best price?
   (b) At the first-best price for each crossing, how much of the revenue is generated per hour to offset the capital cost of the causeway?
   (c) As a result of an increase in population, the hourly demand for causeway crossings is now 2,000. Suppose that a per crossing charge of \$1.25 equates hourly demand for crossings with supply. How much revenue daily revenue is generated to offset the cost of the causeway?

2. Assuming a constant-cost industry, graphically depict and briefly discuss a firm's first-best pricing and investment decisions. Will the efficient price generate sufficient revenues to pay for the cost of capital?

3. Assume that the per-lane–mile cost of resurfacing a road is $130,000 and that the interest rate is 8%.

(a) If the road must be resurfaced today, what is the present value cost of resurfacing?

(b) If the road must be resurfaced in ten years, what is the present value cost of resurfacing? What is the present value cost if resurfacing occurs 12 years from today? Use this information to discuss why an increase in highway durability will lower marginal maintenance taxes upon users.

4. In our empirical study of highway pricing and investment, the short-run marginal maintenance cost from an increase in traffic loadings was given as

$$MC_m = \alpha(i)\frac{\lambda C(W)}{N(D)}$$

Assuming, as was done in the text, that $\alpha(i) = 0.937$, answer the following questions.

(a) Calculate the marginal maintenance cost for a two-lane road under the following conditions:

$$\lambda = 0.70$$
$$C(W)/W = \$120{,}000$$
$$D = 10 \Rightarrow N(D) = 9.3 \text{ million esals}$$

(b) How would the marginal maintenance cost change if the highway agency wanted to build a four-lane highway?

(c) Suppose that the proportion of truck traffic in the right-hand lane increases to 80%. How will this affect the marginal maintenance cost calculated in (a)?

(d) Suppose that the annual traffic loading on the two-lane highway in (a) is 1.2 million. What is the number of years between resurfacing, and what is the annualized total per-lane cost?

4. Conventionally, an 18,000 pound single axle is 1.00 esal (equivalent single axle load). Thus, a 9,000 pound single axle is 0.50 esal. In the recent past, there has been discussion of a Turner proposal, named after a former FHA commissioner, that would increase the gross weight of trucks but reduce the allowable weight per axle. For example, a standard five-axle tractor–semitrailer with a gross weight of 80,000 would have a 4.09 esal. On the other hand, a 101,000 pound double trailer with seven axles would have a 3.56 esal.

(a) Based upon the definition of an esal, verify that a five-axle tractor trailer has a 4.09 esal.

(b) Based upon these two truck types, how would introduction of a seven axle double affect the marginal maintenance cost?

(c) A 122,000 pound truck with nine axles has a 4.43 esal. Will the damage per trip with this truck be greater or less than the damage per trip of a five-axle tractor–semitrailer? What impact do you think introduction of these trucks would have upon the total number of trips and, therefore, the total loadings on a road network?

5. Why might the American Trucking Association be in favor of marginal maintenance taxation if combined with optimal investment, but vehemently against marginal maintenance taxation if combined with current investment? Under which regime is society's welfare likely to be higher?

6. City planners build a new bridge with the following characteristics:

- there are two demand cycles – demand cycle 1 for the bridge occurs for 75% of the day, and demand cycle 2 occurs for 25% of the day
- the bridge will be optimally built, meaning that the bridge's capacity will occur at the point at which the daily demand for the bridge intersects the (constant) *LRMC* curve – the optimal capacity will be 3,000 trips per day
- α is the opportunity cost per bridge crossing in each period (peak and off-peak), which is constant up the point of capacity
- β is the *daily* cost of capacity per bridge crossing

(a) If, at a price of α, off-peak demand exceeds 3,000 trips, will cycle 1 demanders contribute anything to daily fixed costs?
(b) If, at a price of α, off-peak demand just equals 3,000, will cycle 1 trip-makers contribute anything to capacity costs?
(c) Briefly describe how you would derive the daily demand curve from the information given above.

7. In 1995, Oregon recommended a new set of mileage tax tables for heavy trucks, part of which is given in table 10.20. Comment on whether these tax rates are consistent with the efficient pricing principles developed in this chapter.

Table 10.20 Tax rates (cents per mile)

	Number of Axles				
Weight Group	5	6	7	8	≥9
80,001–82,000	14.1	12.9	12.05	11.45	10.8
82,001–84,000	14.55	13.10	12.25	11.60	10.95
84,001–86,000	15.00	13.40	12.45	11.75	11.10
86,001–88,000	15.50	13.70	12.65	11.95	11.25
88,001–90,000	16.10	14.05	12.85	12.15	11.45
90,001–92,000	16.80	14.45	13.05	12.35	11.65
92,001–94,000	17.55	14.85	13.25	12.55	11.80

8. Critique the following statement: "We currently do not have sufficient airport capacity to meet the continuing growth in airline traffic. In order to avert 'gridlock' at our nation's airports, we need to build additional airports."

9. Suppose that the city of Redville decides to build a rapid transit system. Its cost studies indicate that rapid transit trips are produced under increasing returns to scale and that demand is currently not sufficient to exhaust these scale economies.
   (a) Graphically depict the market for rapid transit trips in Redville. What is Redville's first-best pricing and investment strategy?
   (b) What financial implications exist for Redville if it follows its first-best pricing and investment strategy?
   (c) What is Redville's second-best policy for pricing rapid transit trips? Identify the welfare implications of this policy. In what sense is this a second-best policy?

10. There have been recent discussions in the USA about the development of high-speed ground rail systems, similar to the high-speed trains in Japan and Europe. What implications does the analysis of Amtrak have upon the economic viability of high-speed ground systems in the USA? Can you identify city-pair market areas that would most likely benefit from a high-speed ground rail system?

11. Although subsidizing capital costs in a decreasing-cost industry can be justified on economic grounds, subsidizing operating costs in a decreasing-cost industry cannot be justified on economic grounds. Do you agree or disagree? Justify your answer.

12. Why is it in table 10.15 that, for the Minneapolis–Duluth route, the welfare gain per traveler is highest for the low-income vacation traveler and lowest for the business traveler, whereas for the Los Angeles – San Diego route the welfare gain per traveler is highest for the business traveler and lowest for the high-income vacation traveler.

13. The city of Indianapolis offers demand response public transit services as well as traditional mass transit bus services.
   (a) Assuming that demand responsive systems are produced under constant returns to scale but mass transit is produced under increasing returns to scale, why might a welfare-maximizing strategy mean that neither service is priced at marginal cost?
   (b) If the demand for bus trips is more price inelastic than that for demand-responsive trips, what does this imply regarding the "second-best" tax rate on bus and demand-responsive trips?
   (c) Suppose that the marginal cost of producing a demand-responsive trip is twice the marginal cost of producing a bus trip, but that the city charges the same price for each trip. What does this imply regarding the tax rates on each trip type in a second-best world?

14. Assume that an airport produces two types of trips, large-aircraft trips and small-aircraft trips. A second-best price for airline trips would require that the proportion of large plane trips taken to small plane trips taken is the same as would occur under first-best pricing. Do you agree or disagree? Explain your answer.

APPENDIX

This appendix demonstrates the inverse elasticity rule if the marginal welfare loss per dollar revenue collected is equal for all goods. Recall equation (10.8):

$$\frac{(p_H - c_H)\Delta H/\Delta p_H}{H + (p_H - c_H)\Delta H/\Delta p_H} = \frac{(p_T - c_T)\Delta T/\Delta p_T}{T + (p_T - c_T)\Delta T/\Delta p_T}$$

$$\Rightarrow \frac{(p_H - c_H)\Delta H/\Delta p_H}{H + (p_H - c_H)\Delta H/\Delta p_H} = \frac{(p_T - c_T)\Delta T/\Delta p_T}{T + (p_T - c_T)\Delta T/\Delta p_T}$$

$$\Rightarrow \frac{H + (p_H - c_H)\Delta H/\Delta p_H}{(p_H - c_H)\Delta H/\Delta p_H} = \frac{T + (p_T - c_T)\Delta T/\Delta p_T}{(p_T - c_T)\Delta T/\Delta p_T}$$

$$\Rightarrow 1 + \frac{H}{(p_H - c_H)}\frac{\Delta p_H}{\Delta H}\frac{p_H}{p_H} = 1 + \frac{T}{(p_T - c_T)}\frac{\Delta p_T}{\Delta T}\frac{p_T}{p_T}$$

$$\Rightarrow \frac{p_H}{(p_H - c_H)}\frac{\Delta p_H}{\Delta H}\frac{H}{p_H} = \frac{p_T}{(p_T - c_T)}\frac{\Delta p_T}{\Delta T}\frac{T}{p_T}$$

$$\Rightarrow \frac{p_H}{(p_H - c_H)}\frac{1}{E_{H,p}} = \frac{p_T}{(p_T - c_T)}\frac{1}{E_{T,p}}$$

$$\Rightarrow \frac{p_H/(p_H - c_H)}{p_T/(p_T - c_T)} = \frac{E_{T,p}}{E_{H,p}}$$

NOTES

1 This material has benefited from Train's (1991) study of regulation and regulatory pricing.

2 Recall the present-value formula, $FV = PV(i(1 + i)^t/((1 + i)^t - 1))$, where PV is the present value (the total bridge cost here) and FV is the constant annualized payment. In the text, F refers to total cost per period of time, which is analogous to FV in the present-value formulation. To illustrate, assume that the present cost of a building the bridge is \$1,000,000, the bridge will last 20 years, and the interest rate is 5%. Using the above formula, this implies a constant per-period cost of $(1{,}000{,}000)(0.05(1.05)^{20})/((1.05)^{20} - 1) = \$80{,}242$.

3 Recall from chapter 8 that quasi-rents are the difference between total revenues and total variable costs. Since marginal cost, *oc*, is assumed to be constant, marginal cost equals average variable cost. Total variable cost is the area $0EBT_m$ which, when subtracted from total revenues, $0P_mCT_m$, gives quasi-rents (area *EHCB*).

4 Although the gains and losses matter little to society, we cannot say the same for the affected parties. In this case, consumers gain from the lower price and increased consumer surplus, whereas the monopolist, if seeking to maximize profits, would lose from the transfer.

5 For interstate roads, studies indicate that there is no significant deterioration due to weathering (Small and Winston, 1988).

6 Based upon experimental test data conducted between 1958 and 1960, AASHTO estimated that esals rose to the fourth power. Re-estimating this data using state-of-the-art econometric techniques, Small et al. (1989) found that esals rising to the third power provided a better fit.

7 For the discrete time period case considered here, $\alpha(i) = (1 + i)^{R(D)}[(1 + i)^{R(D)}]^{-2}R^2(i)\ln(1 + i)$. See Small and Winston (1988) and Small et al. (1989) for details.

8 Values for each of these parameters are identical to those assumed in Small and Winston (1988).

9 Since highways produce two products, durability and capacity, the appropriate measure for evaluating returns to scale is multiproduct economies of scale for highway production, defined as $C(Y)/\Sigma Y_i(MC_i)$, where $C(Y)$ is total cost, Y_i is output i, and MC_i is the marginal cost of producing output i. Small et al. (1989) concluded that the joint production of durability and capacity was generally characterized by constant returns to scale.

10 From table 10.8, optimal pricing with current investment leads to a larger 48.4% reduction in esals than under first-best pricing and investment. This is another reflection of the higher than optimal maintenance costs when investments in road durability remain at their sub-optimal current levels.

11 Taxes would be levied elsewhere in the economy to cover the deficit, and the resulting welfare losses would reduce the benefits observed in table 10.8. However, if optimal investment is combined with congestion pricing (chapter 11), constant returns prevail and capacity investment is self-financing (Small et al., 1989).

12 The discussion here assumes that the opportunity cost of additional TOLs is constant until capacity is reached. This is not strictly true for airport capacity, as we will see in chapter 11, where the opportunity cost of TOLs begins to rise as we near capacity. However, since our primary concern in this section is the welfare effects of first-best pricing and investment, we shall postpone a full discussion of these "congestion" effects to chapter 11.

13 From note 2, the relevant present-value formula is $FV = PV(i(1 + i)^t/((1 + i)^t - 1))$.

14 Recall from chapters 5 and 7 that the marginal cost curve intersects the average cost curve from below at its minimum point. This implies that the marginal cost curve lies below the average cost curve when average cost is declining, and that it lies above the average cost curve when average cost is rising.

15 If there are no indivisibilities for the capital projects under consideration (for example, buses of any size, highways of any width, and so on) then marginal cost pricing causes no problem. As we have previously seen, optimal levels of capital imply that long-run marginal costs equal long-run average costs. It is the presence of indivisibilities that lead to a decreasing-cost industry where long-run marginal cost is below long-run average cost and deficits occur.

16 Recall our analysis of vehicle ownership in chapter 4. "Average Utility from Vehicle Type Choice" was an explanatory variable that affected a household's demand for automobile ownership and reflected expected maximum utility of vehicle type choice. This variable was empirically measured by the logarithm of the denominator in multinomial logit model of a vehicle type choice (see note 13 in that chapter).

17 Although this is not immediately intuitive, it does follow straightforwardly from economic theory. From chapter 4, our indirect utility function was $\hat{U}(p_{Ta},p_{Tb},p_x,Y;\phi)$. Suppose that we hold utility, the price of bus transportation, the price of all other goods, and preferences constant. Then a change in utility can only come about through a change in the price of an automobile trip or income. Since we are assuming that utility is held constant, we have $\Delta\hat{U} = (\Delta\hat{U}/p_{aT})\Delta p_{aT} + (\Delta\hat{U}/\Delta Y)\Delta Y = 0$. We also know from our budget constraint that, holding all else constant, if an individual takes an automobile ($T_a = 1$), then the additional income required to offset an increase in the price of an automobile trip is simply the change in price, Δp_{aT}; that is, $\Delta Y = T_a\Delta p_{aT} = \Delta p_{aT}$. Substituting ΔY in the expression for $\Delta\hat{U}$ gives $\Delta\hat{U} = (\Delta\hat{U}/p_{aT})\Delta p_{aT} + (\Delta\hat{U}/\Delta Y)T_a\Delta Y p_{aT} = 0$, which implies that $T_a = -(\Delta\hat{U}/p_{aT})/(\Delta\hat{U}/\Delta Y)$, a result known as Roy's Identity. But since $T_a = 1$ in the discrete choice case, we can rearrange this expression to solve for the marginal utility of income, $\Delta\hat{U}/\Delta Y = -\Delta\hat{U}/\Delta p_{aT}$ which, for our linear in parameters empirical model, is minus the coefficient of the price variable.

18 The low-elasticity measures for business air travelers reflect the large air share of the business traveler market rather than low sensitivities. Recall that in a discrete choice model, the percentage change in the probability P_i of choosing mode i from a 1% increase in x_i is $(1 - P_i)\alpha x_i$, where α is the coefficient of x_i. Thus, the larger the market share, all else constant, the lower will be the elasticity. In the limit, if mode i captured the entire market share, the elasticity would be zero!

19 In general, if there are n points along a route then there are $n(n - 1)/2$ nondirectional pairs of points.

20 For vacation travel, we examined these determinants in table 4.8 of chapter 4. For business travel, Morrison and Winston (1985) found travel time, travel cost, departure frequency, and the number of travelers to be important determinants of mode choice. The empirical results of the business traveler model are reported in Morrison and Winston (1985).

21 For the Boston–Washington route, more than half of the total benefits were due to travel between two city-pairs, Boston – New York and New York – Washington.

22 A model of this form where the "interaction" between two areas is assumed to be inversely related to the distance or "impedance" between the two areas and positively related to the population or "attraction" of each of the areas is referred to as a *gravity model*. Gravity models and related spatial interaction models, extensively used in transportation and urban planning, have their origins in Newton's law of universal gravitation that the gravitational pull between two bodies is proportional to the masses of each body and inversely related to the square of the distance between the two bodies. For an example of the use of gravity models in transportation, see Wilson (1967).

23 In the absence of any "surcharge" on highway trips, H_1 would be produced at a price (which equals marginal cost) of $0A'$. After the surcharge, H_2 is produced at a price (which exceeds marginal cost) of $0E'$. The total cost to society of increasing output from H_2 to H_1 is the area $H_2B'I'H_1$. The total benefits received by society is the area under the demand curve between H_2 and H_1; that is, $H_2C'I'H_1$. This exceeds total cost by the amount $B'C'I'$.

24 For small changes in price, we can ignore the triangular area $C'L'M'$ in our computations.

25 The validity of the inverse elasticity rule as stated in equation (10.22) assumes that there are no cross-effects. An increase in the price of bridge crossings (highway trips) will have no effect on the consumption of highway trips (bridge crossings). T and H are independent (Corlett and Hague, 1953). In an example below, we identify a more complicated relationship between price elasticity of demand and tax rates in the presence of cross-effects.

26 For linear demands, $p_i - c_i = \Delta p_i$, so that $(p_i - c_i)(\Delta Q_i/\Delta p_i) = \Delta Q_i$.

27 As noted, this result assumes that the market demand curves are linear. If we alternatively assume that market demand curves are nonlinear, the equality in equation (10.23) would be replaced with an approximation; that is, $\Delta H/H \approx \Delta T/T$.

28 This is not entirely true, since bus may be an access mode for a longer-distance BART trip. In these cases, bus and BART are complements rather than substitutes in consumption.

29 If the cross-price elasticities are zero, then equation (10.25) collapses to equation (10.22).

30 For a review of fixed proportions production functions, see chapter 5.

31 In general, if y is the sum of n variables, the percentage change in y is the weighted sum of the percentage change in each of the n variables, with the weight equaling the share of each variable in the sum (McCloskey, 1985, p. 143).

32 A block hour represents the amount of time an aircraft is under its own power and, accordingly, includes actual flight time plus the time arriving/leaving the gate and taxiing to/from the runway.

33 Based upon work by DeVany (1974), Morrison estimated the price elasticity of the demand for flights to rise with distance traveled. For example, the price elasticities of demand for a 500- and 2,500-mile flight, respectively, were −1.04 and −1.16. Also, he estimated the marginal cost of a landing to be $30 in 1979 dollars.

34 Note that this result is consistent with our discussion of the welfare effects of first-best pricing and investment in airport capacity.

REFERENCES AND RELATED READINGS

General references

Corlett, W. J. and Hague, D. C. 1953: Complementarity and the excess burden of taxation. *Review of Economic Studies*, 21, 21–30.

McCloskey, D. N. 1985: *The Applied Theory of Price*, 2nd edn. New York: Macmillan.

Ramsey, F. 1927: A contribution to the theory of taxation. *Economic Journal*, 37, 47–61.

Small, K. A. and Rosen, H. S. 1981: Applied welfare economics with discrete choice models. *Econometrica*, 49, 105–30.

Train, K. 1991: *Optimal Regulation: The Economic Theory of Natural Monopoly*. Cambridge, Mass.: The MIT Press.

Wilson, A. G. 1967: A statistical theory of spatial distribution models. *Transportation Research*, 1, 253–69.

General references on transportation infrastructure

Aschauer, D. A. 1989: Is public expenditure productive? *Journal of Monetary Economics*, 23, 177–200.

Aschauer, D. A. 1993: Genuine economic returns to infrastructure investment. *Policy Studies Journal*, 21, 380–390.

Boyer, K. D. 1998: *Principles of Transportation Economics*. Reading, Mass.: Addison-Wesley.

Button, K. J. 1993: *Transport Economics*, 2nd edn. Brookfield, Vermont: Edward Elgar.

Button, K. J. and Pearman, A. D. 1985: *Applied Transport Economics*. New York: Gordon and Breach.

Button, K. J. and Pearman, A. D. (eds.) 1983: *The Practice of Transport Investment Appraisal*. Aldershot, Hants, UK: Gower.

Lewis, D. 1991: Primer on transportation, productivity, and economic development. National Cooperative Highway Research Program. Transportation Research Board, National Research Council, Report 342, September.

Meyer, J. R., Merton, J. P., Stenason, J., and Zwick, C. 1959: *The Economics of Competition in the Transportation Industries*. Cambridge, Mass.: Harvard University Press.

Mohring, H. 1976: *Transportation Economics*. Cambridge, Mass.: Ballinger.

Morrison, S. A. and Winston, C. 1985: An econometric analysis of the demand for intercity passenger transportation. In T. E. Keeler (ed.), *Research in Transportation*, vol. 2, Greenwith, Conn.: JAI Press, pp. 213–37.

Mushkin, S. J. 1972: *Public Prices for Public Products*. Washington DC: The Brookings Institution.

Oum, T. H., Dodgson, J. S., Hensher, D. A., Morrison, S. A., Nash, C. A., Small, K. A., and Waters, W. G. II 1995: *Transport Economics*. Seoul, Korea: The Korea Research Foundation for the 21st Century.

Polak, J. and Heertje, A. (eds.) 1993: *European Transport Economics*. Oxford: Blackwell.

Transportation Research Board, National Research Council 1990: *New Trucks for Greater Productivity and Less Road Wear*. Special Report 227. Washington DC.

Winston, C. 1991: Efficient transportation infrastructure policy. *Journal of Economic Perspectives*, 5, 113–27.

Specific transportation references by mode

Airports

DeVany, A. 1974: The revealed value of time in air travel. *Review of Economics and Statistics*, 56, 77–82.

Morrison, S. A. 1982: The structure of landing fees at uncongested airports. *Journal of Transport Economics and Policy*, XVI, 151–9.

Morrison, S. A. 1983: Estimation of long-run prices and investment levels for airport runways. In T. E. Keeler (ed.), *Research In Transportation Economics*, vol. 1. Greenwich, Conn.: JAI Press, pp. 103–30.

Morrison, S. A. 1987: The equity and efficiency of runway pricing. *Journal of Public Economics*, 34, 45–60.

Morrison, S. A. and Winston, C. 1989: Enhancing the performance of the deregulated air transportation system. In M. N. Bailey and C. Winston (eds.), *Brookings Papers on Economic Activity*. Washington DC: The Brookings Institution, pp. 61–112.

Vickrey, W. S. 1972: Economic efficiency and pricing. In S. J. Mushkin (ed.), *Public Prices for Public Products*. Washington DC: The Urban Institute, pp. 53–72.

Walters, A. A. 1973: Investment in airports and the economist's role. John F. Kennedy International Airport: an example and some comparisons. In J. N. Wolfe (ed.), *Cost Benefit and Cost Effectiveness: Studies and Analysis*. London: George Allen and Unwin, pp. 140–54.

Walters, A. A. 1978: Airports – an economic survey. *Journal of Transport Economics and Policy*, XII, 125–60.

Highways

Enis, C. R. and Morash, E. A. 1993: Infrastructure taxes, investment policy, and intermodal competition for the transportation industries. *Journal of Economics and Business*, 45, 69–89.

Holtz-Eakin, D. and Schwartz, A. E. 1995: Spatial productivity spillovers from public infrastructure: evidence from state highways. *International Tax and Finance*, 2, 459–68.

Keeler, T. E. 1986: Public policy and investment in the trucking industry: some evidence on the effects of highway investments, deregulation, and the 55 mph speed limit. *American Economic Review Papers and Proceedings*, 76, 153–8.

Keeler, T. E. and Ying, J. S. 1988: Measuring the benefits of a large public investment. *Journal of Public Economics*, 36, 69–85.

Mohring, H. 1965: Urban highway investments. In R. Dorfman (ed.), *Measuring Benefits of Government Investments*. Washington, DC: The Brookings Institution, pp. 231–91.

Small, K. A. and Winston, C. 1986: Efficient pricing and investment solutions to highway infrastructure needs. *AEA Paper and Proceedings*, 76, 165–9.

Small, K. A. and Winston, C. 1988: Optimal highway durability. *American Economic Review*, 78, 560–9.

Small, K. A., Winston, C., and Evans, C. 1989: *Road Work: A New Highway Pricing and Investment Policy*. Washington DC: The Brookings Institution.

Public transit

Berechman, J. 1993: *Public Transit Economics and Deregulation Policy*, vol. 23. Studies in Regional Science and Urban Economics, L. Anselin et al. (eds.), Amsterdam: Elsevier Science.

Cervero, R. 1984: Cost and performance impacts of transit subsidy programs. *Transportation Research A*, 18, 407–13.

Cromwell, B. A. 1989: Capital subsidies and the infrastructure crisis: evidence from the local mass-transit industry. *Economic Review*. Federal Reserve Bank of Cleveland, Quarter 2, 11–21.

Frankena, M. W. 1987: Capital-based subsidies, bureaucratic monitoring, and bus scrapping. *Journal of Urban Economics*, 21, 180–93.

Jones, D. 1985: *Urban Transit Policy: An Economic and Political History*. Englewood Cliffs, New Jersey: Prentice-Hall.

Pucher, J. 1995: Urban passenger transport in the united states and europe: a comparative analysis of public policies – part 2: public transport, overall comparisons and recommendations. *Transport Reviews*, 15, 211–27.

Pucher, J. and Markstedt, A. 1983: Consequences of public ownership and subsidies for mass transit: evidence from case studies and regression analysis. *Transportation*, 11, 323–45.

Train, K. 1977: Optimal transit prices under increasing returns to scale and a loss constraint. *Journal of Transport Economics and Policy*, XI, 184–94.

Turvey, R. and Mohring, H. 1975: Optimal bus fares. *Journal of Transport Economics and Policy*, XXII, 280–6.

Viton, P. A. 1980: Equilibrium short-run-marginal-cost pricing of a transport facility. *Journal of Transport Economics and Policy*, 14, 185–203.

Railroads

Kain, J. F. 1992: The use of straw men in the economic evaluation of rail transport projects. *Transportation Economics*, 82, 487–93.

Hilton, G. 1980: *Amtrak: The National Railroad Passenger Corporation*. Washington DC: American Enterprise Institute.

Keeler, T. E. 1971: The economics of passenger trains. *Journal of Business*, 44, 148–74.

Martin, A. 1992: *Railroads Triumphant*. New York: Oxford University Press.

Morrison, S. A. 1990: The value of Amtrak. *Journal of Law and Economics*, XXXIII, 361–82.

Tye, W. B. and Leonard, H. B. 1983: On the problems of applying Ramsey pricing to the railroad industry with uncertain demand elasticities. *Transportation Research A*, 17, 439–50.

11

Congestion Pricing

INTRODUCTION

In chapter 10, we analyzed the welfare effects of first-best pricing and investment for the public sector. If the transport authority operates under constant or decreasing returns to scale, first-best prices maximize social surplus and are efficient. However, if the authority operates under increasing returns to scale and is required to cover its production costs, then pricing at average cost maximizes social surplus. Although we considered varying demands in chapter 10, for the purposes of that chapter we initially assumed that all trips were uncongested up to the level of capacity, and that the opportunity cost of travel was constant up to the level of capacity, at which point it became infinite. In this chapter, we adopt the more realistic assumption that congestion occurs prior to reaching capacity, which leads to rising average variable and marginal cost of trip-making. In general, congestion occurs when the travel decisions of one trip-maker have a direct impact upon the opportunity costs incurred by other trip-makers. When this "external" congestion effect upon others is ignored by trip-makers, the opportunity cost of the marginal trip exceeds the benefit that accrues to the marginal trip-maker. This implies that travelers allocate an inefficiently large number of resources to the production of trips, which further deteriorates a transportation system's ability to efficiently move people and freight.

Introducing congestion into the analysis raises a number of interesting questions, which we explore in this chapter. For example, from an economic standpoint, do we want to eliminate congestion, or is there an optimal level of congestion on transportation networks? And if there is an optimal level, how do we induce individuals and firms to allocate their resources efficiently in the production of trips? Also, since there is a relationship between congestion and transportation capacity, we could reduce the level of congestion by expanding existing capacity. Is this an economically efficient response to the problem, or do we want to maintain existing capacity and allocate road space by some other means? And do the same financing conditions hold for congested systems that we found for uncongested systems?

CONGESTION WITH FIXED CAPACITY

A distinguishing feature of most transportation activities is that buyers of transportation combine seller-supplied inputs with user-supplied inputs to provide the service. An airline passenger combines the airline's inputs, including airplane, pilot, stewards, and food, with her own time to produce a trip. Automobile drivers employ the services of the road space with their automobiles and time to produce automobile trips. Cargo ships combine the loading/unloading facilities of a port with freighter, line-haul, queuing, and port service time to yield freight cargo trips. Bus riders add their own time to the inputs of the bus company to produce bus trips. In each of these instances, the cost of transportation is not simply the direct cost associated with using the transport service but also includes the costs of the inputs that the user provides.

THE GENERALIZED COST OF A TRIP

To investigate the role of user inputs in transportation decision-making, let's reconsider our bridge problem. In chapter 10, we made two simplifying assumptions in order to focus our attention on the welfare and financing implications of first-best pricing and investment. First, we assumed that individuals crossing the bridge incurred a constant opportunity cost *oc*, which reflected the marginal wear and tear on the bridge for each crossing. We ignored the users' money and time costs for each bridge crossing. Second, we assumed that all bridge crossings were uncongested trips up to the point of capacity.

Depending upon the mode of travel, bridge crossers incur out-of-pocket money costs as well as time costs. Automobile travelers, for example, incur gasoline and oil expenses per crossing in addition to the time costs of each trip. Those choosing to walk or bicycle across the bridge, on the other hand, only incur time costs per crossing. Focusing upon automobile trips, if we include bridge crossers' out-of-pocket money costs and the time costs for each bridge crossing, but continue to assume that all crossings are uncongested trips up to the point of capacity, then the "generalized" opportunity cost per bridge crossing, *goc*, is the sum of the marginal bridge wear and tear, *oc*, plus out-of-pocket money expenses plus the time cost per bridge crossing. Figure 11.1 depicts the equilibrium bridge crossings during the off-peak and peak periods, respectively. Notice the similarity of this graph to figure 10.1 of chapter 10. A bridge crosser makes a trip as long as the marginal benefit of the trip equals or exceeds the cost of the crossing.

When the only cost of a bridge crossing is the marginal wear and tear on the bridge, we obtain the same off-peak equilibrium as in chapter 10. T_1 trips would be taken at a price of p_1 per trip. However, when we make the more realistic assumption that bridge crossings include both bridge and user inputs, then each bridge crosser is expected to make a trip as long as the marginal benefit is greater than or equal to the "generalized" opportunity cost of a trip, *goc*. Since *goc* is greater than *oc*, we see in figure 11.1 that there are T_2 optimal bridge crossings, reflecting the higher "generalized" opportunity cost per crossing, p_1'. In the peak period, we obtain the same solution as in chapter 10. Since peak period demand is so high, the bridge is used at capacity, T_c, and price of p_2 is charged in order to ration the scarce capacity.

Will revenues collected pay for the per-period fixed cost of the bridge, *FC*? The results here are again analogous to those in chapter 10. If per period demand is D_{op}, then only the opportunity cost of bridge wear and tear, $T_2(oc)$, is collected and no contribution to fixed costs is made. If, alternatively, per period demand is D_p, a bridge toll of p_2 is charged and the contribution to fixed costs is $(p_2 - oc)T_c$, the difference between bridge revenues and the opportunity costs of bridge wear and tear. Per-period fixed costs are covered as long as $(p_2 - oc)T_c$ is greater than or equal to *FC*.

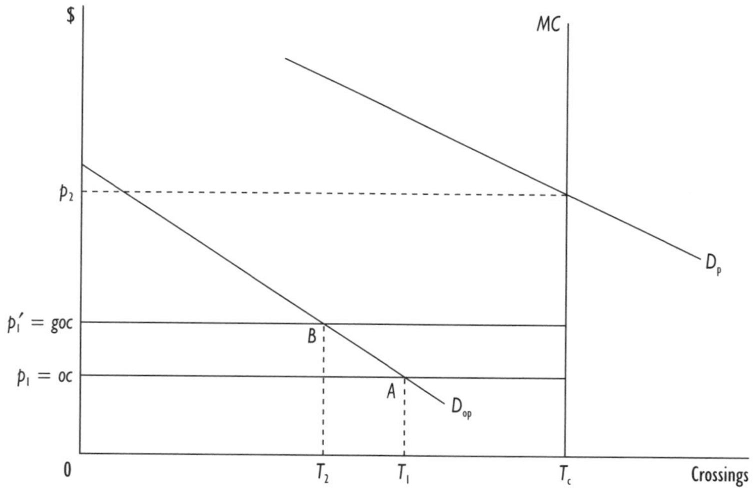

Figure 11.1 Optimal bridge crossings with fixed capacity and generalized costs.

AVERAGE VARIABLE COST VERSUS MARGINAL COST OF A TRIP

We assumed above that bridge crossings were always uncongested up to the point of capacity, at which time the system suddenly locked and the marginal cost of an additional trip was essentially infinite. We now want to replace this assumption with the more realistic assumption that the generalized cost to bridge crossers rises, at some point, as the bridge is used more heavily. This reflects the capacity constraints of the transport facility, which are manifested through increased congestion. In general, congestion occurs whenever *user supplied* inputs depend upon the rate at which the transport facility is used.

Figure 11.2 reproduces the market for bridge crossings but now allows for congestion as the volume of traffic over the bridge increases. Up to traffic level T_g, the generalized cost of a bridge crossing is constant at *goc*, so that the average variable cost (AVC) of a bridge crossing is identical to the marginal cost of a bridge crossing. If per-period demand is given by off-peak demand D_{op}, equilibrium occurs at point B, where the off-peak demand intersects the constant opportunity cost curve. The optimal number of off-peak bridge crossings is T_2.

At T_g, congestion sets in. For levels of bridge traffic greater than T_g, the average variable cost of a bridge crossing rises. Why? Recall that the generalized cost of a bridge crossing includes three components: the marginal wear and tear on the bridge per crossing; the out-of-pocket money expenses to the trip-maker; and the trip-maker's time costs. In order to focus upon the role of congestion costs in allocating resources, let's assume that the marginal wear and tear per crossing and the marginal out-of-pocket money costs are constant for all levels of traffic. As the level of bridge traffic increases above T_g, the trip-maker faces rising costs per trip, which reflect the increased travel time that the trip-maker faces as congestion rises with increasing traffic volumes. It is important to recognize that an individual continues to cross the bridge as long as the marginal benefit per crossing equals or exceeds the trip's cost. But in

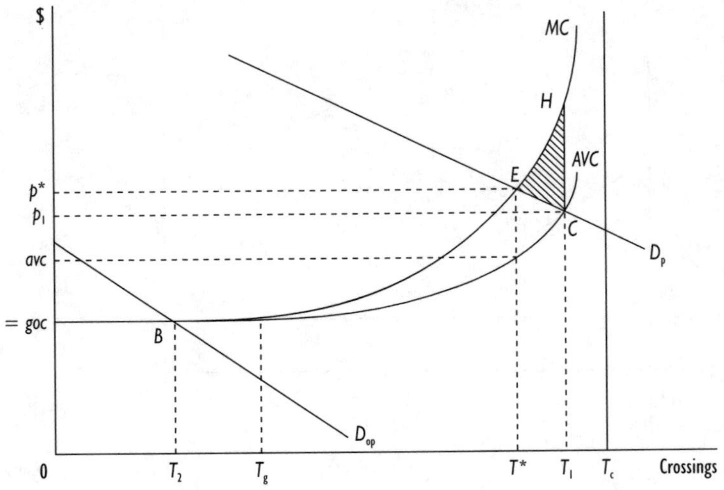

Figure 11.2 Nonoptimal bridge crossings with congestion.

the presence of congestion, an individual's trip costs increase, because the time that it takes to make the trip is higher when there is more congestion. Not surprisingly, because congestion raises trip costs to an individual traveler, fewer trips would be made during congested periods in comparison with uncongested periods, all else held constant. To see this, assume that per period demand is given by peak period demand D_p. From figure 11.1, which assumes no congestion up to capacity, the optimal number of trips is simply the bridge's capacity, T_c, where the peak period demand intersects the (vertical) marginal cost curve at capacity. In figure 11.2, however, because congestion raises the per-crossing cost to individual travelers at bridge volumes greater than T_g, market equilibrium occurs where the demand curve intersects the upward-sloping average variable cost curve. This implies an equilibrium number of trips equal to T_1, which is just short of bridge capacity. At this market equilibrium, the marginal benefit of a bridge crossing to the last traveler just equals the additional cost that the *trip-maker* incurs. The presence of congestion has reduced the number of trips from T_c to T_1.

However, it is important to recognize that although point C in figure 11.2 is a market equilibrium, this does *not reflect* an optimal allocation of resources to bridge crossings. Rather, when T_1 peak period trips are made, too many resources are devoted to bridge crossings than is economically optimal. Why? Consider an individual's decision to cross the bridge during the off-peak period, and assume that he faces 10 cents in marginal bridge wear and tear costs, 25 cents in out-of-pocket money costs, and 50 cents in time costs. This same trip during the peak period costs 10 cents in marginal bridge wear and tear costs, 25 cents in out-of-pocket money costs, and $1.50 in time costs. The added $1 in time costs reflects the impact of peak period congestion on the trip-maker's time costs. Thus, during the peak period, the total cost of the trip is $1.85, and as long as this is less than or equal to the benefit the traveler expects from crossing the bridge, the bridge crossing will occur. Notice, however, that the only costs that the individual considers are those costs specific to himself. Although he includes in his decision calculus the effect of congestion on his own time costs, he *does not* consider the *additional* time costs that his trip imposes upon all other trip-makers who are currently crossing the bridge. If these additional time costs are added to the individual's trip cost, we obtain the marginal cost curve in figure 11.2, which lies above the average variable cost curve once congestion sets in at T_g. Thus, in the market for bridge crossings during the peak period, the average variable cost curve reflects the monetary and time costs that the individual trip-maker explicitly incurs when making the trip. During congested periods, however, the average variable cost curve does not reflect the additional resource costs that a trip-maker's decisions have upon other travelers. When these "external" costs are added to average variable costs, we obtain the marginal cost of the trip.

If we want to efficiently allocate resources to bridge crossings during peak periods, we go to the point at which the marginal benefit of the last bridge crossing just equals the marginal resource cost of the last bridge crossing; that is, we go to the point at which the demand curve intersects the marginal cost curve. This is point *E* in figure 11.2, at which point the optimal number of bridge crossings during the peak period is T^*.

We can draw a number of important conclusions from this analysis:

- During off-peak periods, where there is an absence of congestion, market equilibrium leads to an efficient allocation of resources. Given the fixed capacity, this is our standard first-best pricing outcome.
- During peak travel periods where congestion is present, market equilibrium does not lead to an efficient allocation of resources, because individual trip-makers ignore the congestion effects that their travel decisions impose upon others. We do not get a first-best pricing outcome because, at the margin, the resource cost of the last bridge crossing exceeds the marginal benefit. The efficiency loss associated with market equilibrium is depicted in figure 11.2 by the hatched area *EHC*. The total resource cost of $T_1 - T^*$ trips, given by the area under the *MC* curve, is greater than the total benefit of these trips, which is the area under the peak period demand curve. The difference between these areas, *EHC*, is the efficiency or deadweight loss associated with a nonoptimal number of bridge crossings.
- The fact that the market by itself will not generate the optimal number of trips when congestion is present provides an argument for government intervention. From figure 11.2, T^* is the optimal number of bridge crossings during the peak period. At this level of bridge crossings, the marginal resource cost of the last crossing is p^*. Part of this cost, *avc*, reflects the monetary and time costs incurred by the individual trip-maker. The remaining part of the marginal trip cost, $p^* - avc$, reflects the congestion costs imposed on other trip-makers. If the government imposed a *congestion tax* on each bridge crossing equal to $p^* - avc$, it would induce the optimal number of bridge crossing trips.
- It is important to note that the objective of government intervention is *not* to eliminate congestion but, rather, to induce the optimal level of congestion. In figure 11.2, the optimal number of bridge crossings during the peak is T^*. This level of bridge traffic still entails some congestion, as seen by the rising average variable cost curve. Eliminating peak period congestion by reducing bridge crossings to T_g is highly inefficient, since the foregone benefits from $T^* - T_g$ additional bridge crossings are significantly greater than the resource costs of providing these additional trips.

CONGESTION ON A STRETCH OF ROAD – AN ILLUSTRATIVE EXAMPLE

To focus the ideas presented above, consider a simple example of traveling along a mile stretch of road. Let N be the number of cars per hour on the road, and let the capacity of the road be 4,000 cars per hour. Suppose that the travel time along this stretch can be expressed as

$$T = 5.0 - 3.0(1 - N/4{,}000)^{1/2} \tag{11.1}$$

where $N/4{,}000$ is the volume : capacity ratio.[1] For various traffic levels, we obtain different values for the time needed to undertake the trip. Table 11.1 provides this information, and we can see that the average trip time increases as the traffic flow rises. This is a perfectly sensible result. The more traffic there is on the road, the slower your trip time is and the longer it takes you to reach your destination. Now look at what is happening to marginal trip time. Whereas average trip time is total trip time divided by the number of vehicles, marginal trip time is the additional time cost of an additional trip. Why is marginal trip time increasing at an increasing rate? In order to calculate marginal trip time, we must take into account not only the trip time for the last vehicle entering the road, but we must add to this the additional time that this last vehicle *adds* to the trip times of vehicles already on the road. Thus, although the 3,751st driver estimates his trip time to be 4.25 minutes, which is the average trip time for the first 3,750 drivers *and which includes the congestion that he expects to experience*, it actually takes 9.875 minutes, where the 5.625 minute difference (9.875 – 4.25) is the *additional congestion costs* that his trip imposed on the existing 3,750 drivers.[2] As stated above, congestion exists whenever user supplied inputs depend upon a facility's utilization rate. Let $avc(x)$ be the per user transportation cost of using a facility. Since $avc(x)$ depends upon the number of users x, the total variable cost incurred by all facility users is

$$tvc = avc(x)x \tag{11.2}$$

which is the product of the average variable trip cost and x, the number of users. This implies that the average variable and marginal cost of use are

Table 11.1 Congestion on a stretch of road

Traffic Flow (Vehicles per hour)	Volume : Capacity Ratio	Average Travel Time (minutes)	Marginal Travel Time (minutes)
500	0.1250	2.194	2.394
1,000	0.2500	2.402	2.835
1,500	0.3750	2.628	3.340
2,000	0.5000	2.879	3.939
2,500	0.6250	3.163	4.694
3,000	0.7500	3.500	5.750
3,500	0.8750	3.939	7.652
3,750	0.9375	4.250	9.875
3,950	0.9875	4.665	17.913

$$avc(x) = \frac{tvc}{x}$$

$$mc(x) = \text{marginal cost} = \frac{\Delta tvc}{\Delta x} = avc(x) + \frac{\Delta avc(x)}{\Delta x}x$$

$$= avc(x)\left(1 + \frac{\Delta avc(x)}{\Delta x}\frac{x}{avc(x)}\right) = avc(x)(1 + E_{avc,x}) \qquad (11.3)$$

where $E_{avc,x}$ is the elasticity of average variable cost with respect to traffic flow. As given in equation (11.3), marginal cost is composed of two components: average variable trip cost, $avc(x)$, plus the additional cost imposed on current users of the facility, $avc(x)E_{avc,x}$. Note also from equation (11.3) that if the cost elasticity with respect to traffic volume is zero, average variable cost equals marginal costs. In other words, when an additional trip imposes no additional time costs on current users, average variable costs and marginal trip costs are identical and we obtain the off-peak efficient solution.

Returning to figure 11.2, up to T_g trips, additional travelers impose no additional costs upon current drivers (that is, $E_{avc,x} = 0$). After T_g, additional users impose congestion costs on current users such that the marginal cost of a trip diverges from average variable cost. Moreover, once the facility's capacity is reached at T_c trips, the cost elasticity goes to infinity, as does the marginal cost of a trip. This is the case of "gridlock," when traffic is virtually at a standstill.

Using the information in table 11.1, table 11.2 calculates average variable and marginal costs of a trip on a ten-mile stretch of road. In the table, it is assumed that travelers value their time at $4.50 per hour and that vehicle operating costs are constant at 25 cents per mile, or $2.50 per ten miles. This information is depicted in figure 11.3, where it is seen that marginal costs become much larger than average variable costs as the volume of traffic rises. This again reflects the congestion costs imposed on other drivers as traffic flow increases. Consider, for example, the costs associated with a traffic flow of 3,000 vehicles per hour along this stretch of

Table 11.2 Trip costs on a ten-mile stretch of road

Volume : Capacity Ratio	Average Time (minutes)	Average Variable Cost[a] ($)	Marginal Time (minutes)	Marginal Cost[a] ($)
0.1250	21.94	4.15	23.94	4.30
0.2500	24.02	4.30	28.35	4.63
0.3750	26.28	4.47	33.40	5.00
0.5000	28.79	4.66	39.39	5.45
0.6250	31.63	4.87	46.94	6.02
0.7500	35.00	5.12	57.50	6.81
0.8750	39.39	5.47	76.52	8.24
0.9375	42.50	5.69	98.75	9.91
0.9875	46.65	6.00	179.13	15.93

[a] The average cost of a trip equals the hourly value of travel time ($4.50) times the number of hours traveled (average time/60) plus vehicle operating costs ($2.50). Thus, for a 0.125 volume : capacity ratio, average time value is 21.94 and average variable cost = (21.94/60) * 4.5 + 2.5 = 4.15. Marginal trip costs are calculated in a similar manner.

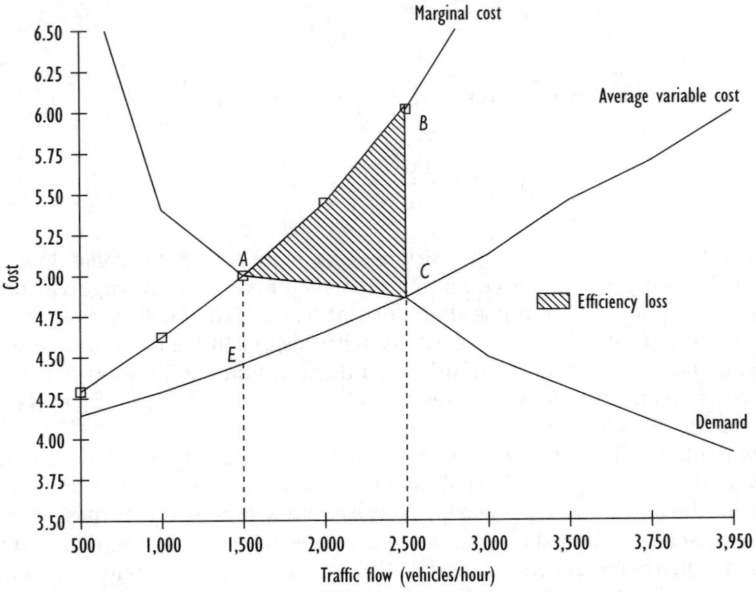

Figure 11.3 The efficiency loss from a congestion externality.

road (which represents a 0.75 volume : capacity ratio). At this level of traffic flow, the average variable cost of a trip is $5.12. The marginal cost of a trip is $6.81, which represents the direct cost of the trip to the marginal trip-maker, $5.12, plus indirect costs of $1.69 which is the value of the time lost to current drivers who must now drive somewhat slower.

We can also illustrate in figure 11.3 an important distinction between average variable and marginal costs of a trip. In both table 11.2 and figure 11.3, average variable trip cost is a resource cost, in terms of money and time, expended by an individual traveler on the trip. Recall that individuals take into account average congestion to themselves when making the trip. For this reason, the average variable cost is oftentimes referred to as the marginal *private* cost of a trip, private in the sense that the *individual* traveler only takes into account the direct costs to herself and ignores any congestion costs that her trip may impose upon other travelers. When these additional costs are included, the cost incurred in making an additional trip is the marginal cost of the trip, oftentimes referred to as the *marginal social cost*, since this represents the amount of *society's* resources expended to produce another trip, not simply the individual trip-maker's resource expenditure.[3]

Optimal Congestion Prices

Also drawn in figure 11.3 is a demand curve that reflects the marginal benefit of trips at alternative traffic flows along this stretch of road. We have seen that resources are efficiently allocated when the marginal cost of production equals the marginal benefit of consumption.

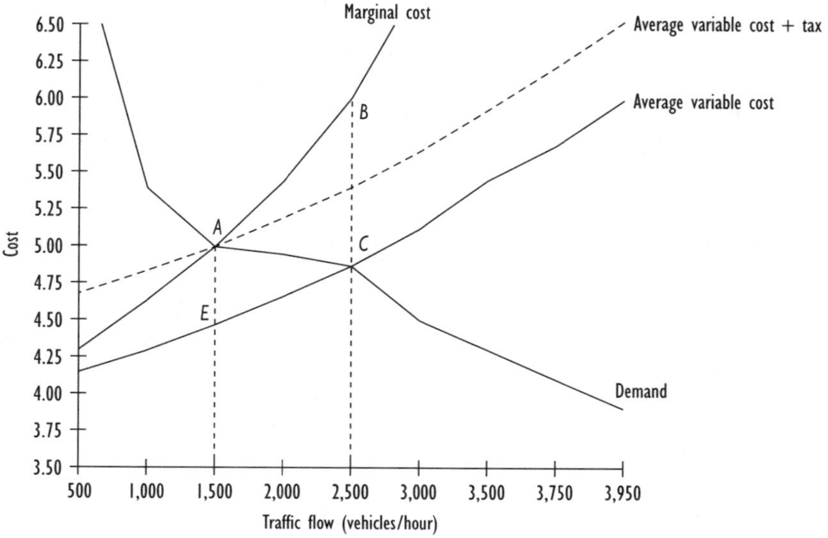

Figure 11.4 Optimal congestion pricing.

This occurs at point *A* in the graph. At a traffic flow below (above) 1,500 vehicles per hour, marginal cost is less (greater) than marginal benefit, which indicates that additional (fewer) resources should be devoted to trip-making. However, we know that society will in fact go to point *C*, since travelers ignore the time costs that their trips impose on other travelers. At point *C*, traffic flow is 2,500 vehicles per hour, and you will make the trip as long as you minimally value the trip at $4.87. But this is less than the $6.02 marginal cost (which equals the marginal social cost) of the trip. An efficient allocation of resources requires a less congested traffic flow, 1,500 vehicles per hour (point *A*), at which marginal cost equals marginal benefit.[4] To see this result in another way, we can examine the effect of reducing traffic flow from 2,500 to 1,500 vehicles per hour. Since many trips are made when traffic flow is 2,500, society loses benefits equaling the area under the demand curve between 1,500 and 2,500 traffic flows. At the same time, society reduces its resource costs by the area under the *marginal* cost curve. Since the savings in resource costs are greater than the loss of benefits, there is a net benefit, or a welfare gain, to society in reallocating resources away from the production of trips towards other uses. The net benefit is given by the area *ABC* in figure 11.3.

Given that resources are inefficiently allocated when individuals do not take into account the effect which their behavior has on others, how can society insure an efficient distribution of resources? Consider figure 11.4, which reproduces figure 11.3. Note that at the optimal level of traffic flow, the difference between marginal cost and average variable cost is the distance *AE*. Suppose that society were to impose a tax, equal to *AE* and appropriately called a *congestion price or congestion tax*, for all trips on this road. The effect of the tax would be to shift up the average variable cost of travel by the amount of the tax. At the optimum point A, both (Average variable cost + tax) and (Marginal cost) represent an individual's average variable cost of a trip. Hence, since trips are undertaken up to the point at which marginal cost equals marginal benefit, the optimum traffic flow is now 1,500. Notice what the congestion tax does and does not do. It does not cause an individual to face the marginal cost of her trip for all trips. At all levels of traffic flow greater than or less than 1,500 vehicles per hour, resources are inefficiently allocated if an individual equalizes marginal benefit with (Average variable cost + tax). What the optimal congestion tax does, however, is to raise the average variable cost of a trip by *exactly* the amount needed to equalize marginal costs and marginal benefits at the socially optimum level of traffic flow.

First-Best Pricing with Nonoptimal Capacity and Congestion[5]

To insure the efficient use of an existing congested transportation facility, a congestion tax is required. By equating marginal cost with marginal benefit, an optimal congestion tax is equivalent to a first-best pricing rule. Moreover, in addition to inducing an efficient use of the transport infrastructure, a congestion tax generates revenues that can be used to pay for the infrastructure. Figure 11.5 depicts the demand and short-run cost curves for an existing facility that is subject to congestion. In addition to short-run average variable and marginal cost curves, figure 11.5 depicts the short-run average total cost curve. The difference between short-run average total cost and short-run average variable cost is short-run average fixed cost. And the difference between the price and short-run average variable cost is the per unit quasi-rent. Other than the fact that some of the inputs in the production of trips are supplied by the user, the analysis is identical to that developed in chapter 10.

The intersection between market demand and the marginal cost curve defines the optimum, which corresponds to T^* trips. p^* is the first-best price. At this level of trips, the short-run average variable cost, which includes the cost of user inputs, is *savc**, which implies that the

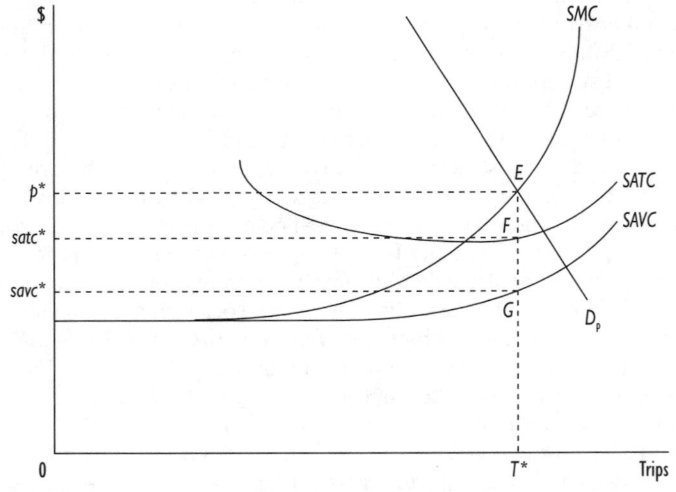

Figure 11.5 Short-run congestion pricing.

average fixed cost is $safc^* = (satc^* - savc^*)$. Because the rise in the short-run average variable cost reflects increasing congestion, a congestion tax equal to the difference between p^* and $savc^*$ is necessary in order to obtain an efficient level of trip-making. From figure 11.5, the revenues generated from the congestion tax, $(p^* - savc^*)T^*$ are more than sufficient to cover the fixed costs of existing capacity, $(satc^* - savc^*)T^*$. In other words, at the optimum number of trips, quasi-rents on existing capital are equivalent to the proceeds of the congestion tax, $(p^* - savc^*)T^*$. And we see in figure 11.5 that these proceeds are greater than the per-period fixed costs of capital, which implies that a short-run economic profit is made on the production of trips.

In general, if existing capacity is fixed, the revenues from a congestion tax may exceed or fall short of capacity costs. This is precisely the result that we obtained in an uncongested environment.[6] In an uncongested environment, pricing excess demand for capacity at short-run marginal costs leads to an efficient allocation of resources to trip-making and produces revenues that contribute to the fixed costs of capacity. Whether these revenues are sufficient to offset the fixed costs ultimately depends upon the demand and cost characteristics. In a congested environment, we have the same pricing strategy, with the following twist. First-best pricing at short-run marginal cost in a congested environment *is equivalent* to setting an optimal congestion price that just equals the difference between price and short-run average variable cost.

CONGESTION WITH OPTIMAL CAPACITY

In figure 11.5, given the demand and cost curves, the government authority would reap an economic profit, equal to $(p^* - satc^*)T^*$, if it optimally priced its congested facility; that is, if the government set an optimal congestion price equal to the difference between price and short-run average variable cost at T^*. Equivalently, the presence of economic profits implies that the facility's quasi-rents are more than sufficient to cover the fixed costs of production. But we have already seen in chapters 8 and 9 that quasi-rents in excess of fixed costs provide an economic incentive to expand capital investment. Thus, although the transport infrastructure depicted in figure 11.5 is efficiently used at point E, the government has nonoptimally invested in too little capital.

OPTIMAL PRICING AND INVESTMENT UNDER CONSTANT RETURNS TO SCALE

Figure 11.6 depicts efficient pricing and investment of a congested facility that produces under constant returns to scale. Initially, assume that demand is D_p and that the transport facility, which corresponds to K_1 units of capital, is in long-run equilibrium at point *E*. T^* optimal trips are produced at an equilibrium price of p^*. Optimal pricing requires a per-trip congestion toll equal to $p^* - savc^*$, which generates $(p^* - savc^*)T^*$ congestion revenues. Quasi-rents accruing to the existing K_1 units of capital are $(satc^* - savc^*)T^*$, which just equal congestion toll revenues since $p^* = satc^*$. And since short-run average total cost equals long-run average total cost at this price, the market is in long-run equilibrium. Given these demand and cost structures, there is no incentive for the government to expand or contract the transport system size.

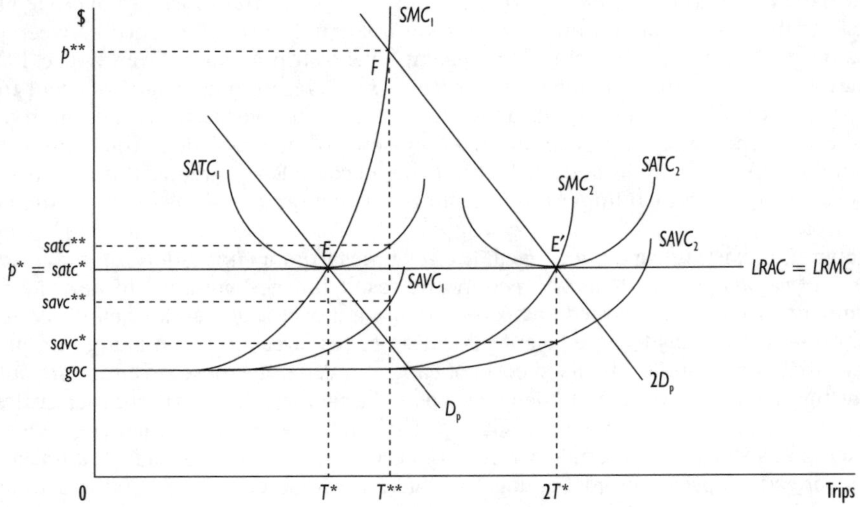

Figure 11.6 Optimal congestion pricing under constant returns to scale.

Now assume that the demand for trips doubles from D_p to $2D_p$. At the existing capacity, the new market demand curve cuts the original short-run marginal cost curve at point F. Given the existing transportation infrastructure, equilibrium output increases to T^{**} and the new equilibrium price is p^{**}. Optimal short-run pricing requires a significant increase in the congestion toll, from $p^* - savc^*$ to $p^{**} - savc^{**}$, which raises quasi-rents on existing capital to a level that more than covers the fixed costs of production. The government is now making an economic profit, $(p^{**} - satc^{**})T^{**}$, on its transport infrastructure, which induces it to increase capital investment. Since we have assumed that production occurs under constant returns to scale, the government increases its transport capacity from K_1 to K_2 units of capital. In figure 11.6, this corresponds to short-run average total, average variable, and marginal cost curves depicted as $SATC_2$, $SAVC_2$, and SMC_2 respectively. The end result is that capital investment in transport infrastructure doubles from K_1 to K_2 $(= 2K_1)$ in order to accommodate the 100% increase in trip demand. With the higher capacity, the optimal pricing rule again takes us back to an equilibrium price of p^*, which corresponds to an optimal congestion price of $p^* - savc^*$. Congestion revenues have doubled to $2(p^* - savc^*)T^*$, which are just sufficient to cover the doubled fixed costs of production, $2(satc^* - savc)T^*$. Quasi-rents on existing capital are again just sufficient to cover the fixed costs of production.

One last point: similar to the standard theory of the firm that we discussed in chapters 5 and 8, the government has an incentive to increase its investment in transport infrastructure so long as the marginal benefit of an additional dollar's investment in capital is greater than or equal to the savings in short-run total variable costs. But in the case of congested facilities, the savings in short-run total variable costs reflect the time savings that accrue to facility users when capacity expands. This implies that our two optimality rules for pricing and investment derived in chapter 8 also apply to pricing and investment decisions of congested facilities. In particular, for time period s, optimal pricing and investment in a perfectly competitive environment, and assuming constant output prices, imply the following:

Optimal Pricing Rule: $$p = AVC_s + Q_s \frac{\Delta AVC_s}{\Delta Q_s}, \qquad s = 1, \ldots, t$$

Optimal Investment Rule: $$P_K = -\sum_{s=1}^{t} \frac{Q_s(\Delta AVC_s/\Delta K)}{(1+i)^s} = \frac{p \cdot MP_K}{crf}$$

where *crf* is the capital recovery factor. The optimal pricing rule is identical to our pricing rule for congested facilities, that we derived in equation (11.3). In this case, $Q_s(\Delta AVC_s/\Delta Q_s)$ is the optimal congestion toll. Further, the optimal investment rule implies that the user cost of capital *r*, which reflects the per-period savings on total variable costs, is

$$\begin{aligned} r = crf\, P_K K &= \left[\frac{i(1+i)^t}{(1+i)^t - 1}\right] \times \text{expenditures upon capital} \\ &= \rho(K) \end{aligned} \tag{11.4}$$

where $\rho(K)$ is general notation that indicates that the user cost of capital is a function of the amount of capital K.

Using this framework, we can again demonstrate that roads produced under constant returns to scale will generate sufficient per-period congestion charges to pay for per-period capital costs. From our optimal investment rule, the reduction in per-period variable costs must equal the cost of an additional unit of capital:

$$-Q_s(\Delta AVC_s/\Delta K) = \text{per-period cost of additional capital}$$

Congestion revenues are $Q_s(Q_s\Delta AVC_s/\Delta Q_s) = (p - AVC_s)Q_s$. But if a proportional increase in both demand and capacity have no effect on average variable costs, then it must be true that the increase in total variable costs from increased demand is just offset by the decrease in total variable costs due to increased capacity.[7] In other words,

$$\frac{\Delta AVC_s}{\Delta Q_s/Q_s} = -\frac{\Delta AVC_s}{\Delta K/K}$$

$$\Rightarrow Q_s \frac{\Delta AVC_s}{\Delta Q_s} = -K\frac{\Delta AVC_s}{\Delta K}, \qquad s = 1, \ldots, t$$

Multiplying both sides by Q_s gives

$$Q_s\left(Q_s \frac{\Delta AVC_s}{\Delta Q_s}\right) = -\left(Q_s \frac{\Delta AVC_s}{\Delta K}\right)K = \text{total of cost additional capital} \tag{11.5}$$

The left-hand side of equation (11.5) gives congestion toll revenues, $(p - AVC_s)Q_s$, and the right-hand side is total expenditures on capital. Thus, using our optimal pricing and investment rules, and assuming that roads are produced under constant returns to scale, we obtain our expected result that congestion revenues equal expenditures on capital.

Graphically, we see this result in figure 11.6. The increased capacity shifts the average variable cost down to its opportunity cost level *goc*. Not until the number of trips has doubled to $2T^*$ is there sufficient congestion on the new facility to raise short-run average variable cost to its original level. Since quasi-rents just cover the fixed costs of the doubled capacity, the government has no further incentive to increase capital investment beyond K_2. Or, equivalently, a marginal increase in capital investment above K_2 will not reduce average variable (time) costs, and therefore not increase quasi-rents, sufficiently to pay for the increased capital investment. E' is the new long-run equilibrium.

Optimal Pricing and Investment under Increasing Returns to Scale

Given the result that optimal pricing and investment under constant returns to scale generates sufficient congestion revenues to pay for the facility's fixed costs, one might expect that optimal pricing and investment under increasing returns to scale would generate insufficient congestion revenues to cover the fixed costs of production. This is indeed correct, as seen in figure 11.7. In the figure, the *LRAC* curve is downward-sloping with the *LRMC* lying below it, consistent with increasing returns to scale. Our first-best pricing rule stipulates producing where the demand curve intersects the short-run marginal cost curve. This occurs at point *E* in the graph, where there are T^* optimum trips and a first-best equilibrium price of p^*. Consistent with the results in previous sections, at the optimum, the short-run average variable cost curve is rising, so that facility users are experiencing some congestion delays in their trip-making. Also consistent with prior findings, our first-best pricing policy implies that a congestion tax be levied, equal to the difference between price and short-run average variable cost at the optimum, $p^* - savc^*$. However, because the production of trips occurs under increasing returns to scale, congestion revenues, which equal the quasi-rents to existing capital, are

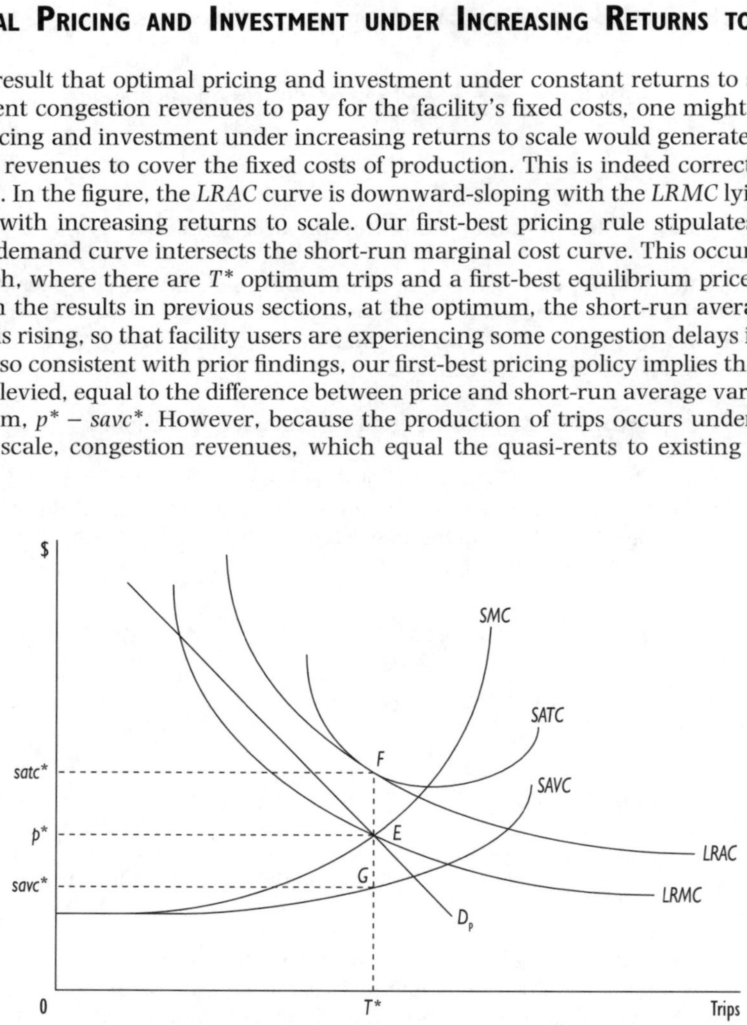

Figure 11.7 Optimal congestion pricing under increasing returns to scale.

insufficient to cover the fixed costs of production. Fixed costs of production, $(satc^* - savc^*)T^*$, are greater than the congestion revenues collected, $(p^* - savc^*)T^*$, leading to a budgetary shortfall of $(satc^* - p^*)T^*$.

Again, we can demonstrate this result from our optimal pricing and investment rules. In equilibrium, if a proportional increase in both demand and capacity leads to a fall in the short-run average total cost curve, then it must be the case that the impact of increased trip demands upon short-run total variable costs is less than the impact of increased capacity upon costs. Thus,

$$\frac{\Delta AVC_s}{\Delta Q_s/Q_s} < -\frac{\Delta AVC_s}{\Delta K/K}$$

$$\Rightarrow Q_s\frac{\Delta AVC_s}{\Delta Q_s} < -K\frac{\Delta AVC_s}{\Delta K}, \qquad s = 1, \ldots, t$$

Multiplying both sides by Q_s gives

$$Q_t\left(Q_s\frac{\Delta AVC_s}{\Delta Q_s}\right) < -\left(Q_s\frac{\Delta AVC_s}{\Delta K}\right)K = \text{total of cost additional capital} \qquad (11.6)$$

which tells us that toll revenues, the left-hand side of equation (11.6), are less than the cost of additional capital.

CASE STUDY – THE INCIDENCE OF TRAFFIC CONGESTION IN US CITIES

In general, vehicle congestion is not uniform but varies spatially, temporally, and by vehicle type. Most rural communities, for example, experience very little congestion, while virtually all urban communities experience some level of congestion throughout the day. Even within a given community, congestion spatially varies. Downtown urban centers or suburban subcenters are typically more congested than suburban residential areas.

Just as traffic congestion varies by location, so too congestion is not uniform throughout the day. Average speeds on a city's roads are much higher at 3:00 am than 9:00 am. Travelers may move at a snail's pace at 4:30 pm in large urban centers but enjoy 35–40 mph speeds at 8:30 pm. Urban communities generally experience significant congestion problems twice a day, once during the morning peak or rush hour as commuters are traveling to work and again in the evening rush hour as these same commuters return home. Depending upon a host of factors, including population, concentration of employment, road mileage, the availability of public transit, parking availability, and so forth, daily rush hours may last anywhere from half an hour to 3–4 hours.

Traffic congestion also varies by vehicle type and the distribution of vehicle types on the roads. Motorcycles, for example, cause much less delay to other travelers than tractor–trailer trucks. Similarly, large buses create greater delays than subcompact vehicles, although if automobile travel is the alternative mode for bus riders, then the net effect of the bus reduces overall congestion. With higher proportions of truck traffic, major highways for intracity vehicle movements, such as principal arterials and freeway networks, experience more severe congestion problems. Further, the effect on travel time and traveler delays from tractor–trailer (or other large vehicle) highway accidents, in comparison with automobile accidents, is significantly higher, since truck accidents are more likely to close multiple lanes.

How extensive is road congestion in the United States? This is a difficult question to answer, because there are many ways of measuring traffic congestion. Population density, vehicles per capita, vehicles per mile of road, the length of the peak period, travel time increases during the peak, and urban concentration each provides some insight into traffic congestion. Recently, Hanks and Lomax (1990) developed a measure of traffic congestion, called the Road Congestion Index (*RCI*). This measure focuses upon the extent to which a transportation system's main thoroughfares are utilized. The Road Congestion Index is defined as

$$RCI = \frac{\left(\frac{\text{Freeway}}{\text{VMT/lane–mile}} \times \frac{\text{Freeway}}{\text{VMT}}\right) + \left(\frac{\text{Principal Arterial}}{\text{VMT/lane–mile}} \times \frac{\text{Principal Arterial}}{\text{VMT}}\right)}{\left(13{,}000 \times \frac{\text{Freeway}}{\text{VMT}}\right) + \left(5{,}000 \times \frac{\text{Principal Arterial}}{\text{VMT}}\right)} \tag{11.7}$$

where VMT is "vehicle–miles traveled."

From previous work, Hanks and Lomax (1990) concluded that at 13,000 freeway VMT per lane–mile, traffic is approaching congestion conditions, defined by speeds falling to between 35 and 40 mph. For principle arterials, congestion conditions arise when VMT per lane–mile reaches 5,000. From equation (11.7), suppose that both freeways and arterials just reach their congested conditions, 13,000 and 5,000 miles per lane–mile respectively. In this case, the RCI is identically 1.0; that is,

$$RCI = \frac{\left(13{,}000 \times \frac{\text{Freeway}}{\text{VMT}}\right) + \left(5{,}000 \times \frac{\text{Principal Arterial}}{\text{VMT}}\right)}{\left(13{,}000 \times \frac{\text{Freeway}}{\text{VMT}}\right) + \left(5{,}000 \times \frac{\text{Principal Arterial}}{\text{VMT}}\right)} = 1$$

This suggest that an *RCI* of 1.0 is natural base from which to evaluate whether congestion is a serious problem in metropolitan areas. To the extent that freeway VMT per lane–mile exceeds 13,000, or principal arterial VMT per lane–mile exceeds 5,000, the *RCI* index will rise above 1.0. Obviously, the higher these lane–mile numbers are, the more severe is traffic congestion. In addition, we see from the definition in equation (11.7) that there can be trade-offs between congested conditions on each type of road. Heavily congested freeway systems may more than offset by lightly traveled arterial roads, leading to an overall index less than 1.0.

On the basis of the road congestion index, how extensive is congestion is our cities? For 16 metropolitan US areas in 1988, table 11.3 reports Hanks and Lomax's road congestion index along with an area's population, daily VMT, congestion costs, and "equivalent." capital costs.[8] Column (5) in the table reports the *RCI* for each of these cities, where we see that serious congestion characterizes all but two reported cities. Not unexpectedly, at 1.52, Los Angeles has the highest congestion measure, followed in decreasing order by San Francisco – Oakland and Washington DC. Miami and Chicago tie for fourth, with an *RCI* of 1.18. Among the reported cities, Baltimore and Corpus Christi are "uncongested." With a relatively low *RCI* of 0.70, Corpus Christi forms a basis for comparison with the other urban areas.

Has congestion worsened in the recent past? Column (6) reports the percentage change in the *RCI* between 1982 and 1988 for the selected cities. Here we see that, with four exceptions, all cities experienced double-digit growth in the *RCI*. New York and Philadelphia experienced modest increases in congestion during the period, while Detroit and Houston actually experienced some

Table 11.3 Congestion indexes for highly congested urbanized areas (Hanks and Lomax, 1990)

(1) Urbanized Area	(2) 1988 Population	(3) 1988 Total Daily VMT ('000s)	(4) Percentage Freeway and Principal Arterial	(5) RCI	(6) RCI Percentage Change 1982–8	(7a) Total Cost per Vehicle ($)	(7b) Delay/Fuel Cost per vehicle ($)	(8) Capital Cost for RCI = 1 (million $)
Washington DC	3,040	61,480	69	1.32	23.0	1,050	920	1,220
Boston	2,910	49,260	72	1.12	24.0	830	760	490
New York	16,320	221,430	57	1.10	9.0	1,030	730	1,370
Los Angeles	11,140	234,410	77	1.52	25.0	880	670	8,040
SF – Oakland	3,630	74,790	72	1.33	32.0	780	670	1,650
Seattle–Everett	1,630	39,030	67	1.17	23.0	680	630	460
Houston	2,840	69,160	54	1.15	−2.0	660	520	620
Dallas	1,950	49,500	61	1.02	21.0	600	500	70
Miami	1,810	33,540	65	1.18	12.0	770	450	390
Atlanta	1,780	57,210	57	1.10	24.0	480	420	370
Detroit	3,900	76,620	57	1.09	−4.0	520	360	440
Baltimore	1,910	33,330	69	0.92	10.0	520	330	n/a
Chicago	7,340	113,010	51	1.18	16.0	470	330	1,060
San Diego	2,180	47,480	72	1.13	45.0	410	330	480
Philadelphia	4,130	64,250	60	1.07	7.0	570	280	310
Mean of heavily congested areas	4,433	81,634	64	1	18	683	345	n/a
Corpus Christi	280	6,260	47	0.70	4.0	60	30	n/a

Source: Adapted from Kain (1994), table 7, p. 529

congestion relief. The complex nature of traffic congestion is also apparent from the table, in that it recognizes that serious congestion is not perfectly correlated with population (column (2)) or daily VMT (column (3)). Although larger cities tend to have higher *RCIs*, there are exceptions. San Francisco – Oakland, for example, has the second worst congestion by the *RCI*, but is only sixth largest in population and fifth largest in daily vehicle–miles traveled. Alternatively, New York is ranked first and second in terms of population and daily vehicle–miles, respectively, but is tenth in terms of traffic congestion. Nor is there a strong relationship between *RCI* rank and the proportion of roads that are freeways and principal arterials. With the exception of Los Angeles and San Francisco – Oakland which are one and two, respectively, on each of these measures, the *RCI* rankings are loosely correlated with the share of these roads. Chicago ranks fifth in traffic congestion, but only 51% of its roads are freeways and principal arteries, placing it next to last on this criterion. Conversely, Baltimore ranks 15th on the congestion index, yet nearly 70% of its road space is made up of freeways and principal arterials.

If we look at columns (7a) and (7b), we see that the *RCI* index is more closely related to congestion costs. With respect to Delay and Fuel Costs per Vehicle, for example, Houston and Dallas rank sixth and seventh, respectively, on both measures. Atlanta and Detroit are 11th and 12th on the congestion index and 10th and 11th on the congestion cost measure. But again there are noted exceptions. New York imposes the third largest delay and fuel cost on vehicles whereas it ranks tenth on the congestion index.

One response to congested conditions is to increase freeway and principal arterial capacity until the congested conditions disappear; that is, until the *RCI* falls to one. Column (8) in table 11.3 reports the expected capital cost associated with this strategy. According to the table, Los Angeles would have to spend $8.04 billion to reduce its *RCI* to 1.0. Although much less than Los Angeles, Washington DC, New York, San Francisco – Oakland, and Chicago's capacity costs exceed $1 billion. Of course, this assumes that the sole objective of capital expenditure is to relieve congestion which, as we have seen earlier, may be uneconomic. From an economic standpoint, our goal is an optimal level of congestion, not the elimination of congestion.

THE RELATIONSHIP BETWEEN TRAVEL SPEED, TRAFFIC FLOW, AND USER COSTS

Motor vehicle congestion on a city's road network exists whenever the trip decisions of one traveler reduce travel speeds, and therefore increase the travel times, of other travelers. We also know that the presence of traffic congestion is equivalent to a rising average variable cost curve. And, for a given traffic level, the difference between the marginal and average variable cost curves represents time costs imposed on others; that is, the congestion externality. When analyzing traffic congestion, we can graphically demonstrate how the average variable cost curve arises from a more fundamental speed–flow curve. Consider figure 11.8. Figure 11.8(a) depicts a speed–density curve, which relates speed in miles per hour on the y-axis and density in vehicles per lane–mile on the x-axis. As traffic density increases to D_0, speed remains constant. There are not enough vehicles on the highway to significantly lower speed. After D_0, however, further increases in traffic density steadily reduce speeds. The product of speed and density, which is a rectangular area in figure 11.8(a), gives traffic flow, defined as vehicles per lane–hour (that is, the number of vehicles per lane per hour). Thus, traffic flows in figure 11.8(b) reflect rectangular areas in figure 11.8(a). For example, traffic flow F_1 in figure 11.8(b) is equal to the area ABD_00 in figure 11.8(a). Similarly, the rectangular area outlined by $0S^mCD^m$ in figure 11.8(a) gives the maximum traffic flow F^{max} in figure 11.8(b). We see from the top half of the curve in figure 11.8(b) that traffic flow initially increases with little impact

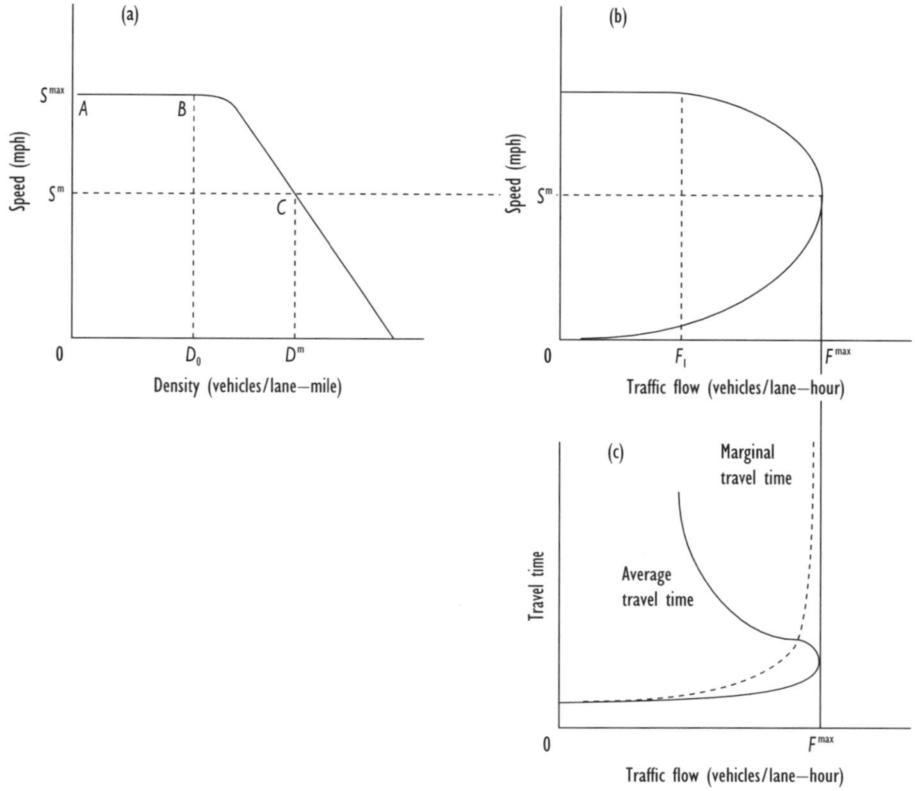

Figure 11.8 The relationship between speed, density, traffic flow, and travel time.

upon maximum speed. However, as traffic flow continues to rise, speeds fall. At S^m, traffic flow is at a maximum, and as more vehicles attempt to enter the system, there are reductions both in travel speed and traffic flow. The effect of additional traffic leads to a decline in traffic flow, which is the lower half of the speed–flow curve depicted in figure 11.8(b).[9]

Since travel time is simply the reciprocal of travel speed, we redraw figure 11.8(b) as an average travel time curve in figure 11.8(c). Associated with average travel time will be a marginal travel time, which is denoted in figure 11.8(c) by the dashed line. Finally, multiplying the average and marginal travel time curves by an appropriate value of time measure and adding in road maintenance and user operating costs gives us our average variable cost and marginal cost curves previously depicted in figure 11.2.

CASE STUDY – A SPEED–FLOW CURVE FOR THE SAN FRANCISCO BAY AREA

Keeler and Small (1977) estimated speed–flow relationships for three freeways in the San Francisco Bay Area.[10] The form of the empirical model was as follows:

$$V/C = \alpha + \beta\text{Speed} + \gamma\text{Speed}^2 + \varepsilon$$

where V/C is the volume : capacity ratio over different stretches of freeway and Speed is the average speed on these stretches. Notice that the empirical model specifies a quadratic relationship between the volume : capacity ratio and Speed, which is intended to capture the backward-bending portion of the speed–flow curve depicted in figure 11.8(b).[11] Consider one of the freeway systems examined, the Eastshore Freeway. For this system, the authors estimated the following model:

$$V/C = \underset{(-3.99)}{-3.153} + \underset{(5.65)}{0.1757}\text{Speed} - \underset{(-6.35)}{0.001923}\text{Speed}^2,$$
$$R^2 = 0.76 \qquad (11.8)$$

where we see that the two speed variables explain 76% of the variation in traffic flow, and that each variable is statistically significant at a 0.05 level. Figure 11.9 graphs the speed–flow curve from the estimated empirical model in equation (11.8). In the figure, the estimated speed–flow curve depicts the "reverse-C" shape that we theoretically identified in figure 11.8(b). Starting on the upper portion of the curve, average speeds steadily decline as more traffic enters the freeway and the V/C ratio approaches its maximum. After this point, which appears to be at around 0.85 on the graph, we are on the lower portion of the curve, and further increases in traffic have a clogging effect upon the V/C ratio, so that both speed and traffic flow fall.

Can we determine the maximum V/C ratio? Yes. Equation (11.8) can be shown to be equivalent to the following expression:[12]

$$V/C = 0.8603 - 0.001923(\text{Speed} - 45.68)^2 \qquad (11.9)$$

For a maximum V/C ratio, the second term must go to zero, which occurs when Speed equals 45.68 mph, at which the maximum V/C ratio is 0.86, quite close to our initial "guess" of 0.85. Relating these numbers back to figure 11.8(b) and reinterpreting F as the volume : capacity ratio, $S^m = 45.68$ and $F^{max} = 0.8603$.

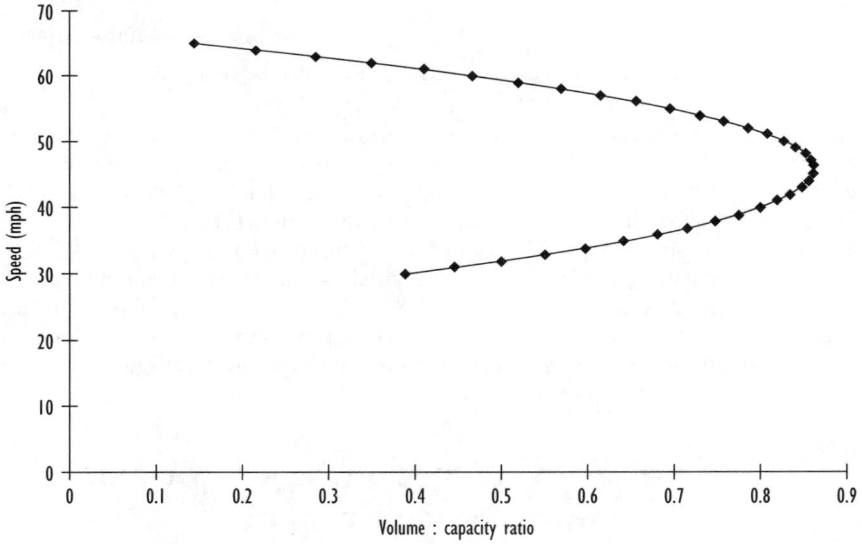

Figure 11.9 The speed–flow curve for the Eastshore Freeway.

Table 11.4 Marginal effect of average speed increases

Average Speed (mph)	Marginal Effect of a 1 mph Increase in Speed on V/C
30	0.06032
35	0.04109
40	0.02186
45	0.00263
50	−0.0166
55	−0.03583
60	−0.05506

On the basis of equation (11.9), table 11.4 reports the effect of an increase in average speed on the volume : capacity ratio. At an average speed of 30 mph, we are on the lower portion of the speed–flow curve, so that a 1 mph increase leads to an improved flow of 0.06. The increased V/C ratio reflects improved traffic flow and a reduction in congestion. This would occur, for example, toward the end of the peak period, when fewer vehicles enter the traffic stream. This leads to a freer flow of traffic and a corresponding increase in travel speed. Alternatively, at an initial speed of 60 mph, a 1 mph increase in average speed is associated with a 0.05 decrease in the V/C ratio. This occurs because we are now on the upper portion of the speed flow curve. Fewer vehicles on the road imply a lower V/C ratio and less interaction allows for higher speeds.

Finally, we can convert our speed–flow curve into an average travel time curve by solving equation (11.9) for Speed and taking the reciprocal. Rewriting equation (11.9) as a quadratic equation gives

$$-0.001923\text{Speed}^2 + 0.1757\text{Speed} - (V/C + 3.153) = 0$$

For the upper portion of the speed–flow curve, the solution to this quadratic equation is[13]

$$S = 46 + \sqrt{2{,}111 - 520.1(3.153 + V/C)}$$

which implies that average travel time per vehicle, the reciprocal of speed, is

$$\text{Time} = \frac{1}{S} = \frac{1}{46 + \sqrt{2{,}111 - 520.1(3.153 + V/C)}} \qquad (11.10)$$

This expression tells us, for example, that at a volume : capacity ratio of 0.50, it would take just under 1 minute to travel a mile (≈ 60 mph). At a maximum 0.85 volume : capacity ratio, travel time per mile increases by 25% to 1.25 minutes. Note also that multiplying travel time by the value of time, *VOT*, gives the average variable cost of travel.

CASE STUDY – OPTIMAL CONGESTION CHARGES IN THE SAN FRANCISCO BAY AREA

In an important paper on long-run peak period prices, Keeler and Small (1977) empirically implemented optimal pricing and investment rules in order to derive optimal congestion charges for the travel day. The focus of their study was the San Francisco Bay Area, which we identified in table 11.3 as one of the more heavily congested metropolitan areas.

Assume that travel per day is divided into five periods according to the level of traffic peaking. Society's objective is to minimize the total annual cost per mile of trip-making,

$$TC = \sum_{p=1}^{5} TUC_p + \rho(w)$$
$$= \sum_{p=1}^{5} VOT(n_p X_p)\,(\text{Per Mile Travel Time})_p + \rho(w) \qquad (11.11)$$

where TC is the total annual cost per mile, TUC_p is the annual user cost per mile in period p ($p = 1, \ldots, 5$) and VOT is the value of time per vehicle–hour.[14] $\rho(w)$ is the annualized capital cost per lane–mile, which is assumed to depend upon the width of the road, w. In the second line of equation (11.11), X_p ($p = 1, \ldots, 5$) is the hourly volume of traffic per mile in period p, and n_p is the number of hours annually associated with traffic level X_p. We then have the following relationships:

$n_p X_p$ = the annual volume (vehicles/lane–mile) of traffic in period p

$n_p X_p$ (Travel Time Per Mile)$_p$ = annual travel time (vehicle hours) per mile in period p

$VOT(n_p X_p)$(Travel Time Per Mile)$_p$ = annual time costs per mile in period p

In the following sections, we estimate $\rho(w)$ and TUC_p ($t = 1, \ldots, 5$) in order to derive optimal capacities and optimal congestion prices in each travel period.

Annualized capital costs

Let $KLM(w)$ and $ALM(w)$ be per-lane–mile highway construction costs and land costs, respectively. Assuming that roads have an estimated lifetime of 25 years, land has an infinite lifetime, and the rate of interest is 6%, annualized construction and land costs per lane–mile (using equations (11.6) and (11.7) in chapter 8) are[15]

(a)

$$\text{Annualized } KLM(w) = KLM(w)i\left[\frac{(1+i)^{25} - 1}{(1+i)^{25}}\right]$$

(b) $$\text{Annualized } ALM(w) = ALM(w)i \qquad (11.12)$$

If we include capacity-related annual maintenance costs per lane–mile, $MLM(w)$, then total annual capital costs per lane–mile are

$$\rho(w) = \text{Annualized } KLM(w) + \text{Annualized } ALM(w) + MLM(w)$$
$$= KLM(w)i\left[\frac{(1+i)^{25} - 1}{(1+i)^{25}}\right] + ALM(w)i + MLM(w) \qquad (11.13)$$

Empirically estimating capital costs

In order to obtain an estimate for annualized construction costs using equation (11.12a), it is first necessary to obtain an estimate of total highway construction costs per lane–mile. To do this, Keeler and Small specified a double-log regression model between total highway construction costs per lane–mile and the number of lanes, w:

$$\ln KLM(w) = a_1 CRS + a_2 CUC + a_3 FR + a_4 FSU + a_5 FC + a_6 \ln(w) + \varepsilon \qquad (11.14)$$

where $KLM(w)$ is the construction cost per lane–mile in 1972 dollars. In this specification, CRS

is the fraction of the road that is made up of arterial streets outside city limits; *CUC* is the fraction of the road that is made up of arterial streets within city limits; *FR* is the fraction of the road that is a rural freeway; *FSU* is the fraction of the road that is an urban or suburban freeway; and *FC* is the fraction of the road that is a freeway within city limits. Recognizing that various technical features, such as signaling, interchanges, overpasses, and tunneling, can significantly affect the cost of adding an additional lane of capacity, Keeler and Small included these road type variables in order to separate the effect of urbanization from the effect of scale economies on construction costs. We see from equation (11.14) that, holding all else constant, a_6 is the elasticity of per-lane–mile construction cost with respect to the number of lanes. In other words, the coefficient of $\ln(w)$ provides information on economies of scale in highway construction after controlling for the effect of urbanization. Thus, depending upon whether a_6 is less than, equal to, or greater than zero, highway capacity is produced under increasing, decreasing, or constant returns to lane width, respectively.

Data for the analysis came from a sample of 57 state-maintained roads in the nine-county San Francisco Bay Area in 1972. The estimated regression equation for this empirical model of highway construction costs in the nine-county San Francisco Bay Area was

$$\begin{aligned}\ln(KLM) = {} & \underset{(2.07)}{11.609CRS} + \underset{(-0.07)}{12.767CUC} \\ & + \underset{(32.3)}{12.993FR} + \underset{(21.4)}{13.255FSU} \\ & + \underset{(17.8)}{1.115FC} - \underset{(17.2)}{0.0305\ln(w)} \\ R^2 = 0.518 & \qquad (11.15)\end{aligned}$$

The R^2 for the estimated model indicates that land width and the urbanization variables explained just under 52% of the variation in construction costs per lane–mile. There are two major conclusions from these estimation results. First, from the *t*-statistics for the urbanization variables, we can reject the null hypothesis that each coefficient equals zero, indicating that there are significant differences in highway constructions costs across road types. Second, all else held constant, highways are produced under constant returns to width. From the low *t*-statistic for $\ln(w)$, we cannot reject the null hypothesis that this coefficient equals zero.

What do the estimation results in equation (11.15) tell us about the total cost of construction? Taking the exponential of both sides of equation (11.15) gives us an estimate of total construction cost per lane–mile:

$$\begin{aligned}KLM = \exp(& 11.609CRS + 12.767CUC \\ & + 12.993FR + 13.255FSU \\ & + 1.115FC)w^{-0.0305}\end{aligned}$$

Assuming that the mean value for lane width was 6, Keeler and Small used this equation to calculate per-lane–mile construction costs for three types of roads:

Urban – Central City Freeway:
$KLM = \exp(13.255 + 1.115)(6^{-0.0305})$
$= \$1{,}741{,}051.8(0.9468) = \$1{,}648{,}427$

Urban–Suburban Freeway:
$KLM = \exp(13.255)(6^{-0.0305})$
$= \$570{,}917.5(0.9468) = \$540{,}545$

Rural Freeway: $KLM = \exp(13.255)(6^{-0.0305})$
$= \$439{,}327.3(0.9468) = \$415{,}955$

There needs to be one other adjustment to these construction costs before we can use them to derive annualized costs. Keeler and Small's analysis was primarily concerned with optimal price and investment for automobile travel. But, as we saw in chapter 7, roads are not only wide but thick. And to accommodate the truck traffic, roads are generally built to a greater thickness than would be the case for roads built solely for automobile traffic, which obviously raises highway construction costs. The US Bureau of Public Roads provided Keeler and Smaller with information that roads built only for automobiles would incur approximately 77% of the cost that a general purpose – that is, truck-accommodating – road cost. In order to focus specifically upon highway construction costs attributed to automobile travel, the above construction costs were multiplied by 0.77.

Table 11.5 Freeway capital costs (1972 dollars)

Capital Cost Category (per lane–mile)	Urban – Central City Freeway	Urban–Suburban Freeway	Rural Freeway
(1) Adjusted construction cost[a]	1,269,289	416,219	320,285
(2) Annualized capital cost[b]	86,767	28,456	21,898
(3) Land acquisition cost[c]	465,829	134,439	124,787
(4) Annualized land cost[b]	27,950	8,066	7,487
(5) Annual capacity-related maintenance costs	2,917	2,917	2,917
(6) Total annualized rental price per lane–mile of capital, $\rho(w)$	117,634	39,439	32,302

[a] The figures in this row equal 0.77 *KLM*, where *KLM* is given on the previous page.
[b] See equation (11.12) for the relevant formula. The figures assume a 6% rate of interest.
[c] For Urban – Central City Freeway, Urban–Suburban Freeway, and Rural Freeway, land acquisition was estimated to be 36.7%, 32.3%, and 38.96% of construction costs respectively.
Source: Adapted from Keeler and Small (1977), table 2, p. 8, with the permission of The University of Chicago Press.

In table 11.5, rows (1) and (2) report the adjusted per lane–mile construction costs and the annualized construction costs, assuming a 6% rate of interest, for an Urban – Central City Freeway, an Urban–Suburban Freeway, and a Rural Freeway. Although detailed information was not available for estimating a land acquisition cost model similar to the above construction cost model, the authors were able to use county-wide data on highway projects for each of the nine counties during the 1968–72 period to determine that, on average, land acquisition costs for an Urban – Central City Freeway, an Urban–Suburban Freeway, and a Rural Freeway accounted for 36.7%, 33.3%, and 38.9% of highway construction costs, respectively. Per lane–mile land acquisition costs and annualized land acquisition costs, again based upon a 6% interest rate, are reported in rows (3) and (4).

Table 11.5 also gives expected annual maintenance costs that are capacity-related; that is, maintenance costs that do not depend upon traffic flow. Given in row (5), these are estimated as $2,917 per lane–mile.[16] The last row in table 11.5 gives the estimate for the rental price of highway capital per lane–mile, $\rho(w)$ in equation (11.13). Not surprisingly, annualized costs for centrally located urban freeways are highest at $117,634 per lane–mile in 1972 dollars. This is nearly triple the cost of urban-oriented freeways outside the central city and rural freeways. The high cost of land in the central city, combined with the greater need for overpasses and interchanges, primarily explains the differences in costs.

Annualized user time costs

When analyzing peaking characteristics of daily travel, Keeler and Small distinguished two characteristics of travel: (1) time of day during which travel occurs, and (2) the direction of travel. Consider the morning peak hour. In Keeler and Small's analysis, the time of day for these trips is 7:00 am to 8:00 am. In addition to time of day, we would expect traffic density to depend upon the direction of travel. For those traveling from suburban residences to downtown centers – which is the direction of travel for most worktrip commuters – we would expect much denser

Table 11.6 Daily traffic flows and peaking characteristics

Period	Description of Travel (1)	Peaking Ratio, $X_p/\overline{X}$ (2)	Peaking Ratio as Fraction of Highest Peaking Ratio, X_p/X_1 (3)
1	Major direction during peak period	3.0	1.00
2	Major direction during near peak period	2.1	0.70
3	Major direction during daytime travel, excluding peak and near peak periods	1.5	0.50
4	Minor direction during daytime travel	1.15	0.383
5	Major and minor directions during night travel	0.40	0.133

Peak, Near Peak, Day, and Night travel times definitions in their analysis are as follows:

Peak Period Travel	7:00 am–8:00 am 5:00 pm–6:00 pm
Near Peak Period Travel	6:00 am–7:00 am, 8:00 pm–9:00 pm 3:00 pm–4:00 pm, 6:00 pm–7:00 pm
Day	9:00 am–4:00 pm
Night	7:00 pm–6:00 am

Source: Adapted from Keeler and Small (1977), table 4, p. 15, with the permission of The University of Chicago Press.

traffic, and more congestion, than "reverse commuting" during the same hour; that is, traveling from a central city residence to a suburban job. Travel from suburban housing to central jobs is the Major Direction. Travel during the same morning hour from central housing to suburban jobs is the Minor Direction. Based upon California Department of Public Works data, the authors identified the daily distribution for the major and minor directional traffic flows. From their analysis of traffic distribution flows, Keeler and Small defined the previously discussed five periods during the day to distinguish different peaking characteristics. If $\overline{X}$ is the average hourly traffic over the entire day, then the ratio of hourly traffic in period p ($p = 1, \ldots, 5$) to total average hourly traffic is $X_p/\overline{X}$, which Keeler and Small define as the "peaking ratio" for period p.

Table 11.6 describes the five daily travel periods employed in Keeler and Small's analysis. We see in the table that there is a 7.5 difference between the highest and lowest peaking ratios. Near-peak traffic is 70% of peak traffic flows, and even during daytime hours traffic density stays relatively high, at 50% of peak period flows. As one would expect, minor directional flows are relatively free of congestion problems, accounting for 38% of peak traffic flows. On the basis of the peaking ratios in table 11.6, we would expect to see optimal congestion tolls in Period 1 to be much greater than those in Periods 4 and 5.

Empirically estimating user time costs

Total user costs per mile in period p are $(VOT)(n_pX_p)$(Per Mile Travel Time). Keeler and Small analyzed the speed–flow relationship for a typical urban freeway, the Eastshore Freeway in the Bay Area, which is depicted in figure 11.9. The estimated speed–flow relationship for travel time given in equation (11.10) is used here to obtain total user costs. In particular, total annual user costs per lane–mile, *TUC*, over the five travel periods are defined as

$$TUC = \sum_{p=1}^{5} VOT(n_p X_p) \text{ (Per Mile Travel Time)}_p$$

$$= \sum_{p=1}^{5} \frac{VOTn_p X_p}{46 + \sqrt{2{,}111 - 520.1(3.153 + V/C)}}$$

$$= \sum_{p=1}^{5} \frac{VOTn_p X_p}{46 + \sqrt{2{,}111 - 520.1(3.153 + X_p(2{,}000w))}}$$

$$= \sum_{p=1}^{5} \frac{VOTn_p X_p}{46 + \sqrt{471 - 0.26(X_p/w)}} \qquad (11.16)$$

where X_p is the hourly traffic volume per mile and $C = 2{,}000w$ is the hourly road capacity per mile. *w* is the number of lanes.

Computing optimal capacity and congestion prices

Combining total user cost with highway capital costs leads to the following annual total cost per lane–mile of highways:

$$TC = \sum_{p=1}^{5} \frac{VOTn_p X_p}{46 + \sqrt{471 - 0.26(X_p/w)}} + \rho(w)$$

Recall the finding that highways are produced under constant returns to scale. Under these circumstances, we can then write $\rho(w)$ as Aw, where *A* is a constant that reflects the annualized cost per lane–mile of highway capital.[17] Thus, society's objective is to solve for the optimal capacity utilizations, X_t ($t = 1, \ldots, 5$), that minimize annual highway costs, *TC*:

$$TC = \sum_{p=1}^{5} \frac{VOTn_p X_p}{46 + \sqrt{471 - 0.26(X_p/w)}} + Aw \qquad (11.17)$$

Finally, Keeler and Small demonstrate that minimizing *TC* is equivalent to minimizing the total costs per peak period vehicle–mile, which depends upon the value of time (*VOT*), annualized capital costs (*A*), and peak period traffic per lane–hour (X_1/w).[18] That is,

$$\frac{\text{Annual Total Costs}}{\text{Peak Period Vehicle–Mile}} = f\left(\frac{X_1}{w}, VOT, A\right) \qquad (11.18)$$

Given *VOT* and *A*, we want to find that value of peak period capacity utilization X_1/w that minimizes the annual total costs per peak-period vehicle–mile. The advantage of minimizing the annual total costs per peak-period vehicle–mile is that the minimization problem now only depends upon one variable, X_1/w. But, from column (3) in table 11.6, once we know X_1/w, we can solve for each of the other per-lane–hour traffic flows, X_p/w ($p \neq 1$). For example, we know that X_2/X_1 is 0.70, which implies that $X_2/w = 0.70(X_1/w)$. Thus, *optimal highway capacity utilization*, in terms of vehicle flow per lane–mile, for each of the five travel periods is as follows:

X_1 – solved by minimizing annual total costs per peak period vehicle–mile

$X_2 = 0.70X_1$

$X_3 = 0.50X_1$

$X_4 = 0.383X_1$

$X_5 = 0.133X_1$

As seen above, total costs per peak-period vehicle–mile are conditioned upon two parameters, the value of travel time, *VOT*, and annualized capital costs, *A*. Based upon various travel demand studies, Keeler and Small used \$4.25 (in 1972 dollars) as the value of time. From table 11.5, *A* is the annualized capital cost per lane–mile, which are \$117,634, \$39,439, and \$32,302 for an Urban – Central City, Urban–Suburban, and Rural Freeway, respectively.

Given optimal traffic flows, we can then solve for the optimal congestion price per vehicle–mile in each period *p*, using the expression

$$\text{Toll} = \text{Optimal Congestion Price}$$
$$= X_p \frac{\Delta \text{Average Variable Cost}}{\Delta X_p}$$

where average variable cost is *VOT* (Time), the value of time multiplied by average travel time. For Urban – Central City, Urban–Suburban, and Rural Freeway systems, we calculate optimal congestion prices in each period, which are reported in table 11.7 along with optimal traffic flows and the associated travel speed.

The estimated optimal flows, tolls, and speed are consistent with expectations. Peak-period optimal capacity utilization is highest, and speed lowest, for urban – central city freeways, followed in order by urban–suburban and rural freeways. Also, for a given freeway system, we see that speeds steadily increase as we move from Period 1, the highest-peaking ratio, to Period 5, the lowest-peaking ratio.

Optimal congestion prices denote significant differences across freeway systems and time periods. For centrally located freeways, the optimal toll during the morning and evening peak is 15 cents per vehicle–mile. For a typical 20-mile round-trip work commute, this implies a per-trip congestion price of $3.00 (1972 dollars). On the other hand, trips made on urban–suburban and rural freeways during the peak require much lower congestion charges, amounting to 3.3 cents and 2.7 cents per vehicle–mile respectively.

Once we leave the peak period, congestion tolls on urban – central city freeways drop sharply. In the near-peak period, Period 2 in table 11.7, the optimal congestion toll is 1.8 cents per vehicle mile, almost nine times less than during the peak period. Although we also observe decreases in tolls in Period 2 relative to Period 1 on urban–suburban and rural freeway systems, the percentage reduction is much less, about half in each case. During the remaining three peaking periods, congestion tolls are required, but their magnitudes are relatively small, ranging from a high of 0.9 cents per vehicle–mile on urban – central city systems during Period 3 to a low of 0.1 cent per vehicle mile on urban–suburban and rural freeways respectively.

The results in table 11.7 assumed a value of time equal to $4.50 (1972 dollars) and an interest rate equal to 6%. How sensitive are the results to these parameters? Keeler and Small calculated optimal tolls using a lower value of time, $2.25, and a higher interest rate, 12%. As expected, an increase in interest rates, by raising the cost of highway capital and reducing the amount of highway capital provided, leads to an increase in traffic flows per lane–mile, a reduction in speeds, and an increase in congestion tolls. For example, depending upon the value of time, a 12% interest rate led to peak-period congestion tolls of from 5–6 cents per vehicle–mile for rural freeways up to 27–38 cents per vehicle–mile for urban – central city freeways.

Because travelers with lower values of time have lower opportunity costs of travel, congestion costs, and therefore congestion prices, are expected to be less. Consistent with this hypothesis, Keeler and Small found that lower time values led to higher traffic flows, lower speeds, and lower congestion prices in all off-peak periods; that is, Periods 2–4. However, during the peak period, the lower time values were generally associated with *higher* optimal congestion tolls. Why might this occur? Since travelers with lower values of time do not place a premium on travel time, an optimally sized road will be one with fewer lanes, which implies higher traffic flow and more congestion per lane–mile, given the demand for road space. If the resulting increase in congestion during the peak period is sufficiently large, congestion tolls will increase despite the lower value of time.

Table 11.7 Optimal capacity utilization and pricing

	Freeway Type		
	Urban – Central City	Urban–Suburban	Rural
Period 1[a]			
Flow	1,777	1,512	1,427
Speed	49.0	54.8	56.0
Toll	15.0	3.3	2.7
Period 2			
Flow	1,244	1,058	998
Speed	58.2	60.0	60.5
Toll	1.8	1.2	1.1
Period 3			
Flow	888	756	713
Speed	61.5	62.6	62.9
Toll	0.9	0.7	0.6
Period 4			
Flow	681	579	547
Speed	63.1	63.9	64.1
Toll	0.6	0.5	0.4
Period 5			
Flow	236	201	190
Speed	66.2	66.5	66.5
Toll	0.2	0.1	0.1

Assumptions: value of time is $4.50 per vehicle–mile. Annualized capital cost for Urban – Central City, Urban–Suburban, and Rural Freeway is $117,634, $39,439, and $32,302, respectively, based upon a 6% interest rate. X_1 = Flow in period 1 and is calculated from the minimization problem. X_p ($p = 2, \ldots, 4$) equals 0.70, 0.50, 0.383, 0.133 times X_1 respectively. Speed $= 46 + \sqrt{2{,}111 - 520.1(3.153 + X_t/2{,}000)}$.

[a] Flow is vehicles/lane–mile per hour; Speed is miles per hour; and Toll is cents per mile.

Source: Adapted from Keeler and Small (1977), table 5, p. 18, with the permission of The University of Chicago Press.

Optimal versus current use of road space

Even though the results from table 11.7 indicate that optimal investment and pricing of freeway systems in the San Francisco Bay Area require congestion tolls, the results do not tell us by themselves whether existing capacity is under- or overutilized. There are two reasons for this. First, in order to answer this question, we need to compare total costs of travel under optimality with the actual costs of travel. Second, the optimal prices in table 11.7 only reflect capacity-related congestion charges. To arrive at the full societal costs of automobile travel, we need to include the costs of police, highway administration services, other local government

Table 11.8 Full and actual cost of automobile travel (1972 cents per vehicle–mile)

	Freeway Type		
	Urban – Central City	Urban–Suburban	Rural
Full cost			
Period 1	16.3	4.4	3.8
Period 2	2.9	2.3	2.2
Period 3	2.0	1.8	1.7
Period 4	1.7	1.6	1.5
Period 5	1.3	1.2	1.2
Actual price	1.15	1.15	1.15

Assumptions: value of time = $4.50 per vehicle–mile, interest rate = 6%.
Source: Keeler and Small (1977), p. 18

services (for example, the fire and legal systems) and environmental impacts (noise and air pollution) attributed to automobile use. Estimating these additional costs as 1.1 cents per vehicle–mile (Keeler and Small, 1977), table 11.8 reports, for each of the three freeway systems, the optimum toll inclusive of congestion, local government, and environmental costs of automobile travel.[19]

Road users pay vehicle registration fees and a variety of taxes for the use of road space. At the time of Keeler and Small's study, these revenues amounted to 1.15 cents per automobile mile, which is the last line in table 11.8. Comparing the full cost of automobile travel with the actual prices, we see that actual prices paid are everywhere lower than optimal prices.

In order to determine whether existing capacity is under- or overutilized, it is necessary to compare the total costs of travel under optimal price and investment with the total costs of travel under current pricing and current investment. Since optimal and actual prices are similar during the nonpeak travel periods, capacity utilization is likely to change little if we move to optimal pricing and investment during these periods. Since implementation of optimal tolls during the peak period will likely have a significant impact upon capacity utilization, we can focus upon the peak period and ask the following question: Is peak-period capacity overutilized?

One's immediate response to this question may be yes, since peak-period traffic is three times the average daily flow and optimal prices are significantly greater than current prices. However, the answer depends upon a comparison between the current total price of automobile travel and the optimal total price. Suppose that highway capacity is fixed, so that we are in the short run. In order to efficiently use existing capacity during peak periods, we need to levy an optimal toll. This toll raises a traveler's out-of-pocket trip costs and reduces the quantity of trips demanded to its efficient level. In other words, total trip cost under optimal pricing and current investment is higher than current total trip cost, implying that too many resources are currently devoted to the production of trips, and that current capacity is initially overutilized.

Conversely, if optimal tolls reduce out-of-pocket trip costs, there is an increase in the quantity of trips demanded to its efficient level. In this case, capacity is underutilized and too few resources are devoted to the production of trips.

Does this result also hold in the long run? – not necessarily. Whereas capacity is fixed in the short run, it is variable in the long run. Although charging optimal prices could raise out-of-pocket trip costs to travelers, in the long run there is also an improvement in the quality of travel as capacity is adjusted and time costs are reduced. And if the reduction in time costs more than offsets the increase in out-of-pocket costs, total trip costs fall. But a fall in total trip costs implies an increase in the quantity of automobile travel demanded. That is, too few resources are devoted to automobile trip-making and there is too little automobile use! Alternatively, if the reduction in time costs is not sufficient to offset the increase in out-of-pocket trip costs, then we obtain the short-run result. Total trip costs increase, which decreases the quantity of auto trips demanded, implying that there is too much automobile travel and that too many automobile trips are currently taken.

In their analysis, Keeler and Small compared optimal peak-period total trip costs to actual total trip costs for the Eastshore Freeway, using different combinations of values of time and interest rates. Although their results were not conclusive for all values of time and interest rates, they generally found that total trip costs under optimal pricing and investment were greater than total trip costs under current pricing and investment, implying that there is too much automobile use and that the existing capacity is overutilized.

THE EFFECTS OF CONGESTION CHARGES ON METROPOLITAN TRAVEL DECISIONS

Starting from a theoretical base of optimal pricing and investment, we have seen how these rules are empirically implemented in order to determine the extent to which resources are (in)efficiently allocated to trip-making in congested environments. Since automobiles are the primary source of congestion in road traffic, the focus has been upon automobile travel. But implementing congestion pricing significantly alters the travel environment that travelers face. All else constant, congestion pricing raises the price of automobile travel. But, as we saw in chapter 4, this has implications for consumers' modal choices. An increase in the relative price of automobile trips reduces the quantity of automobile trips demanded and raises the demand for trips on substitute modes, particularly public transit. However, even for the automobile, one can identify differential effects. Work-trip commutes are not homogeneous in which all trips, for example, are single-occupant trips in fuel-efficient vehicles. Some automobile trips are single-occupancy, while others are two-, three-, and four-person carpools. Some individuals travel to work in fuel-efficient vehicles, and others in fuel-inefficient vehicles. By raising the cost of automobile trips, congestion pricing also increases the relative price of single-occupancy vehicle (SOV) trips. At the margin, we would expect to see an increase in the demand for carpooling and, in the long run, a greater demand for fuel-efficient vehicles.

Further, these effects are complicated by the fact that the average variable cost of trip production depends upon a traveler's value of time. Individuals with high values of time place a premium upon higher speeds and less travel time. As a result, we might well expect that congestion pricing would induce fewer of these individuals to switch from automobile to public transit (or carpool). Conversely, a greater proportion of individuals with lower values of time would be expected to make the switch.

In the event that a significant number of automobile users respond to congestion pricing by increasing their demands for public transit, this has important implications for the ability of public transit to accommodate the increased demands. Since public transit use is a small proportion of total travel, a small percentage decrease in the quantity of automobile travel demanded could translate into a large percentage increase in the demand for public transit. Thus, any implementation of widespread congestion pricing will have important supply side implications for public transit.

CASE STUDY – THE EFFECT OF CONGESTION PRICING ON GENERALIZED COSTS

In an analysis of the implications of congestion pricing for mode choice and public transit supply, Kain (1994) calculated generalized costs (that is, out-of-pocket and time cost) for a hy-pothetical ten-mile trip in a heavily congested major metropolitan area, typical of those identified in table 11.3. In deriving these costs, Kain adopted several assumptions to characterize the pre-congestion pricing environment:

- SOV, carpool, and express bus modes travel at 20 mph
- the local bus travels at 12 mph
- bus trips are differentiated by 15 minute and 7.5 minute headways
- carpool trips have an additional "circuitry" time cost equal to 8 minutes, 10 minutes, and 12 minutes for two-, three-, and four-person trips, respectively
- each trip includes 5 minutes of out-of-vehicle (walking and waiting) travel time
- parking costs are either \$0 or \$4.00
- there are three types of consumers with different values of time (*VOT*) – rich, whose *VOT* is \$10.00 per hour, poor, whose *VOT* is \$2.50 per hour, and average, whose *VOT* is \$5.00 per hour

In the post-congestion pricing environment, the travel speed for SOV, carpool, and express bus trips increases to 30 mph, the travel speed on local buses increases to 18 mph, and automobile users pay a 15 cent per mile congestion tax.[20]

Table 11.9 presents Kain's generalized costs prior to and after implementation of congestion pricing. We see in the table that the effect of congestion pricing depends upon the distribution of income in the metropolitan area. For the rich, those with high values of time, congestion pricing reduces the generalized cost of travel. This is true for SOV, carpools of any size, and local or express bus travel. Although identical qualitative effects occur for carpool and bus riders with average values of time, SOV travelers suffer an increase in their generalized costs. For the poor, whose value of time is \$2.50, we see mixed results. SOV users experience an increase in generalized costs regardless of whether parking is free. Two- and three-person carpools also incur higher costs under congestion pricing, whereas four-person carpools have a slight (0.04) reduction in costs. With congestion pricing, the cost of local bus service falls significantly, from \$4.14 with no congestion pricing to \$3.44 under congestion pricing. The express bus with a 15 minute headway also gains from congestion pricing, but the gain is not as great as for the local bus service. The results for local and express bus service under congestion pricing *unambiguously* increase the demand for public transit services. One response to accommodate the higher demands is to provide services with shorter headways. In table 11.10, we examine whether this is a viable alternative.

Modal and welfare effects of congestion pricing

Free parking

This section focuses upon whether congestion pricing is likely to induce drivers to switch from SOV to an alternative mode. Assuming that parking is free, the entries in table 11.10 reflect the difference between the congestion price (*CP*) generalized cost of alternative mode *i* (*i* = carpool, local bus, express) and *CP* generalized cost of an SOV given in table 11.9. For example, in the first line of table 11.10, "Carpool minus SOV," consider the row labeled "2 persons." For an

Table 11.9 Total generalized cost per trip with and without congestion pricing (CP)

	Generalized Cost Per Trip					
	Average ($5/hour)		Rich ($10/hour)		Poor ($2.5/hour)	
Mode	With CP	Without CP	With CP	Without CP	With CP	Without CP
Single Occupant Vehicle (SOV)						
Free Parking	5.05	4.38	7.76	7.92	3.69	2.61
$4.00 per day	7.05	6.38	9.76	9.92	5.69	4.61
Carpool: Free Parking						
2 Persons	4.59	4.67	7.96	8.88	2.90	2.57
3 Persons	4.38	4.71	7.92	9.09	2.61	2.52
4 Persons	4.36	4.81	8.06	9.36	2.50	2.54
Carpool: $4 per day						
2 Persons	5.59	5.67	8.96	9.88	3.90	3.57
3 Persons	5.04	5.38	8.59	9.75	3.27	3.19
4 Persons	4.86	5.31	8.56	9.86	3.00	3.04
Local Bus						
Headway: 15 minutes	6.13	7.52	11.51	14.29	3.44	4.14
Headway: 7.5 minutes	5.35	n/a	9.95	n/a	3.05	n/a
Express Bus						
Headway: 15 minutes	5.27	6.10	9.54	11.21	3.14	3.55
Headway: 7.5 minutes	4.49	n/a	7.98	n/a	2.74	n/a

Assumptions: congestion tax of $0.15 per mile which would increase peak-period speeds for SOVs and carpools from 20 mph to 30 mph; operating speeds of local buses = 0.6 of automobile speeds; express buses assumed to travel at same speed as automobiles and carpools; all workers travel the same hypothetical distance (10 miles) to work; all workers have access to frequent and direct (i.e., no transfer) bus service; users of all modes incur 5 minutes of mode access time; two-, three-, and four-person carpools incur 8, 10, and 12 additional minutes of travel time, respectively.
Source: Adapted from Kain (1994), table 1, p. 510

individual with Average ($5/hours) value of time, the entry −0.46 is the difference between the *CP* generalized cost for Carpool with 2 Persons in table 11.9 (4.59) minus the *CP* generalized cost for SOV (5.05).

In order to analyze the implications of congestion pricing on mode choice, consider the top half of table 11.10. We can directly compare the numbers in a given column, since the basis of comparison is always SOV. The largest negative number represents the assumed mode chosen under congestion pricing. Alternatively, if all numbers in a column are positive, then SOV is the chosen mode. To illustrate, we see in column 1 that the largest negative number is –0.69 for a Carpool with 4 Persons. This says that, relative to SOV, the generalized cost of a Carpool with 4 Persons was 69 cents less. In contrast, a local bus with a 15 minute headway is $1.08 more expensive under congestion pricing.

Table 11.10 Generalized cost differences under congestion pricing and free parking

	Average ($5/hour)	Rich ($10/hour)	Poor ($2.5/hour)
Congestion pricing impact on mode choice			
Carpool minus SOV			
2 Persons	−0.46	0.21	−0.79
3 Persons	−0.67	0.16	−1.09
4 Persons	−0.69	0.31	−1.19
Local Bus minus SOV			
Headway: 15 minutes	1.08	3.76	−0.25
Headway: 7.5 minutes	0.30	2.19	−0.64
Express Bus minus SOV			
Headway: 15 minutes	0.22	1.79	−0.56
Headway: 7.5 minutes	−0.56	0.22	−0.95
Before-and-after comparison			
SOV with CP minus SOV without CP	0.13	−0.71	0.54
Carpool with CP minus SOV without CP			
2 Persons	−0.33	−0.50	−0.25
3 Persons	−0.54	−0.54	−0.54
4 Persons	−0.57	−0.40	−0.65
Local Bus with CP minus SOV without CP			
Headway: 15 minutes	1.21	3.05	0.29
Headway: 7.5 minutes	0.43	1.49	−0.10
Express Bus with CP minus SOV without CP			
Headway: 15 minutes	0.35	1.08	−0.02
Headway: 7.5 minutes	−0.43	−0.48	−0.41

Assumptions: congestion tax of $0.15 per mile which would increase peak-period speeds for SOVs and carpools from 20 mph to 30 mph; operating speeds of local buses = 0.6 of automobile speeds; express buses assumed to travel at same speed as automobiles and carpools; all workers travel the same hypothetical distance (10 miles) to work; all workers have access to frequent and direct (i.e., no transfer) bus service; users of all modes incur 5 minutes of mode access time; two-, three-, and four-person carpools incur 8, 10, and 12 additional minutes of travel time, respectively.
Source: Adapted from Kain (1994), table 2, p. 512

In the top half of the table, travelers with average values of time have an incentive to form carpools under congestion pricing. Each carpool mode has a lower generalized cost in comparison with SOV, although a Carpool with 4 Persons yields the largest difference. Local bus and express bus with 15 minute headways do not fare well relative to SOV. If, however, public transit agencies introduce a more frequent service with 7.5 minute headways, then Express Bus has lower generalized costs in comparison with an SOV.

In general, similar results hold for individuals with lower values of time. However, in this case the value of time is sufficiently low that under congestion pricing SOV has a higher generalized cost relative to all private and public alternative modes, since each of the entries in column 3 is negative. As with "Average" value of time travelers, the largest cost difference is a Carpool with 4 Persons. In comparison with SOV, the generalized cost for this mode is $1.19 less than SOV with the onset of congestion pricing.

Last, we obtain the expected result that higher-income individuals – that is, those with values of time equal to $10 – continue to use SOVs. None of the entries in the top half in column 2 are negative, which indicates that SOV provides the least generalized cost mode of travel under congestion pricing.

The lower half of table 11.10 evaluates the effect of *revenue-neutral* congestion pricing upon SOV users. "Revenue-neutral" means that the government neither gains nor loses revenues from congestion pricing. All collected revenues are returned to the traveling population. On the basis of a congestion study for Los Angeles (discussed below), Small (1992) estimated that the government would net $3 billion in congestion price revenues. Using this figure in his analysis, Kain estimated that a revenue-neutral policy would imply an annual rebate of $269 per capita. For SOV users, and assuming 500 trips per year, the $269 annual rebate translates into 54 cents per peak-period trip.

Since a 54 cent rebate is a gain to travelers under congestion pricing, the entries in the lower half of table 11.10 enable us to determine whether SOV users are better or worse off under congestion pricing relative to alternative modes of travel. For example, consider the first row and first column under "Before and After Comparison," labeled "SOV with *CP* minus SOV without *CP*," assuming an average value of time. From table 11.9, the generalized costs for these two alternatives are 5.05 and 4.38, respectively. Their difference is 0.67, from which the 54 cent rebate is subtracted, leaving a net figure of 0.13. In other words, SOV with "revenue-neutral" congestion pricing increases the individual's generalized cost by 13 cents compared to SOV without congestion pricing. In this instance, the SOV user is worse off under congestion pricing.

An examination of generalized cost differences in a "revenue-neutral" congestion pricing environment (and free parking) reveals that, for travelers with average values of time, each of the carpool modes has a lower generalized cost with *CP* than the generalized cost of SOV without congestion pricing. In other words, an individual is better off using a carpool in a "revenue-neutral" congestion pricing environment relative to an SOV choice with no congestion pricing. Alternatively, the generalized cost of an SOV user with no congestion pricing is less than the generlized cost of all public transit alternatives, with the exception of Express Bus Service with a 7.5 minute headway, in a "revenue-neutral" congestion pricing environment. Thus, in comparing generalized costs in a pre-*CP* environment with those in a "revenue-neutral" *CP* environment, SOV users experience a gain, in this generalized cost sense, by switching to carpool and express bus service with low headways. But these same users would experience a loss if they switched from SOV to local bus modes or express bus service with high headways. Further, comparing the cost differences indicates that Carpool with 4 Persons provides the greatest advantage.

Not surprisingly, for lower value of time travelers, we obtain similar results. Now, however, all express bus service and local bus service with low headways have lower generalized costs in comparison with SOV without congestion pricing. Again, Carpool with 4 Persons provides the largest gain.

There are two primary differences in the results for SOV users with high values of time. First, there is a cost saving for SOV users relative to an environment without congestion pricing, which provides an incentive to continue using a single-occupant vehicle. Second, the local bus service and the express service (with high headways) are at a strong cost disadvantage. We see in the table that generalized costs are from $1.08 to $3.05 greater for these modes relative to SOV without pricing. Moreover, relative to SOV without pricing, the largest decrease in generalized cost is SOV. Even with "revenue-neutral" congestion pricing, SOV dominates for high value of time travelers.

Parking at $4 per day

All of the results in table 11.10 assume that parking is free. Table 11.11 reproduces the analysis underlying table 11.10, but now assumes that parking costs $4 per day. Here we see that parking policies can significantly affect modal outcomes. Whereas, in table 11.10, all non-SOV modes with congestion pricing had lower costs than SOV with congestion pricing for individuals with lower time values, in table 11.11 this is true for both lower and average time value persons. And the cost differences are relatively large, generally between $1 and $3 per trip. Further, in table 11.10, SOV dominates all other modes for persons with higher values

Table 11.11 Generalized cost differences under congestion pricing and $4 per day parking

	Average ($5/hour)	Rich ($10/hour)	Poor ($2.5/hour)
Congestion pricing impact on mode choice			
Carpool minus SOV			
2 Persons	−1.46	−0.79	−1.79
3 Persons	−2.00	−1.17	−2.42
4 Persons	−2.19	−1.19	−2.69
Local Bus minus SOV			
Headway: 15 minutes	−0.92	1.76	−2.25
Headway: 7.5 minutes	−1.70	0.19	−2.64
Express Bus minus SOV			
Headway: 15 minutes	−1.78	0.19	−2.64
Headway: 7.5 minutes	−2.56	−1.78	−2.95
Before and after comparison			
SOV with CP minus SOV without CP	0.13	−0.71	0.54
Carpool with CP minus SOV without CP			
2 Persons	−1.33	−1.50	−1.25
3 Persons	−1.88	−1.88	−1.88
4 Persons	−2.07	−1.90	−2.15
Local Bus with CP minus SOV without CP			
Headway: 15 minutes	−0.79	1.05	−1.71
Headway: 7.5 minutes	−1.57	−0.51	−2.10
Express Bus with CP minus SOV without CP			
Headway: 15 minutes	−1.65	−0.92	−2.02
Headway: 7.5 minutes	−2.43	−2.48	−2.41

Assumptions: congestion tax of $0.15 per mile which would increase peak-period speeds for SOVs and carpools from 20 mph to 30 mph; operating speeds of local buses = 0.6 of automobile speeds; express buses assumed to travel at same speed as automobiles and carpools; all workers travel the same hypothetical distance (10 miles) to work; all workers have access to frequent and direct (i.e., no transfer) bus service; users of all modes incur 5 minutes of mode access time; two-, three-, and four-person carpools incur 8, 10, and 12 additional minutes of travel time, respectively.
Source: Adapted from Kain (1994), table 3, p. 513

of time. In contrast, when there is a $4 per day parking charge, all carpool modes and an express buses with 7.5 minute headways dominate SOVs.

Turning to the lower half of table 11.11, an examination of generalized cost differences in a "revenue-neutral" congestion pricing environment for travelers with average values of time reveals mode choices in a "revenue-neutral" *CP* environment. A comparison of the cost differences indicates that the mode with the greatest advantage is an express bus with a 7.5 minute headway. Not surprisingly, for lower value of time travelers, we obtain precisely the same results, except that the net gain to travelers of non-SOV modes is generally larger. The express bus service with a 7.5 minute headway again gives the largest gain. For those with high values of time, we see that in all but one case, the generalized cost of the non-SOV under "revenue-neutral" *CP* is less than the generalized cost of the SOV mode without *CP*. Under "revenue-neutral" *CP*, carpools, express buses, and local buses with 7.5 minute headways have lower generalized costs than SOV prior to congestion pricing. The exception is a local bus with a 15 minute headway, where we see a $1.05 increase in generalized cost relative to SOV without pricing. Although SOV with "revenue-neutral" *CP* reduces generalized costs $.71 for those with high values of time, at $2.48, express bus service again gives the largest cost reduction.

Discussion

These results are important for a number of reasons:

- Much of the work on congestion pricing tends to focus upon the policy's direct target, the single-occupant vehicle, to the general exclusion of the policy's impact upon other travel modes. Kain's analysis provides insights on these other modal effects.
- We see the importance that one's assumptions on the value of time plays in the policy's effects. Congestion pricing is least successful for individuals who are willing to pay high prices in order to save a minute of travel time. And since higher values of time are correlated with higher incomes, we would expect less modal shifting under congestion pricing among the affluent.
- We also see the importance of parking policies. Many firms either provide free parking or heavily subsidize the parking costs of their employees. The results from tables 11.10 and 11.11 demonstrate the impact that this has upon one's modal choices. To the extent that the responsibility for parking costs is transferred to the commuter, we would expect to see greater shifts toward carpooling and express bus services.

We must also remember, however, that Kain's analysis provides insights on modal shifting and welfare for a hypothetical ten-mile trip in a stereotypical heavily congested metropolitan area. Modal choices are assumed to depend only upon generalized costs; that is, out-of-pocket money and time costs. But we have seen in chapter 4 that one's work-trip modal choice generally depends upon other factors, including a mode's comfort, safety, and privacy characteristics. Since SOV trips generally score high on these criteria, the mode-shifting effects of congestion pricing will be attenuated. Further, this analysis has implicitly assumed that alternatives to SOV trips are readily available. This is not in general true. Although Carpool with 4 Persons may have lower generalized costs, the success of making such arrangements depends upon the distribution of employment destinations and work schedules among one's residential neighbors. In addition, we have assumed that public transit agencies can readily accommodate increasing demands by additional and new services.

Supply responses to congestion pricing

Pricing of a metropolitan area's congested roads will increase travel speeds, decrease travel times, and, by increasing the relative price of single-occupancy vehicle trips, provide a subset of SOV trip-makers with incentives to carpool and use public transit. In the existing non-priced environment, few formalized mechanisms exist for carpooling. Existing options may include forming carpools with fellow employees who reside nearby, or with one's neighbors who have similar work locations. But one can envision that broad-based congestion pricing would create incentives for developing more formal, and hence less costly, mechanisms for arranging carpools. For example, one could imagine a "pick-up" point at which commuting residents congregate to make temporary or permanent carpooling arrangements. And just as there is a demand for "freight-forwarder" services to match shippers with suppliers, so too "people-forwarders" could match times and destinations among commuters in carpooling arrangements.

Similarly, we would expect to see public transit make supply side responses. Kain (1994) identifies a number of options that public transit agencies could use to meet the increased demand for public transit. These include the following:

- Public transit firms could increase frequencies and lower headways on those routes not characterized by excess capacity. Recall from chapter 4 that travelers find waiting time more onerous than in-vehicle travel time. By reducing headways, increased bus frequencies lead to further increases in the quantity of bus trips demanded. In the previous section, local and express bus service with 7.5 minute headways was an assumed response to congestion pricing. And based upon generalized costs, it compared favorably with SOV trips.
- Public transit firms could expand their services by developing new routes in their existing geographic coverage or extending their breadth of coverage. In addition, they could offer new types of services, such as limited or nonstop travel between specific origin-destination pairs, or providing more direct service, on routes by eliminating the need for transfers.
- Complementing broader coverage and specialized services, public transit firms could provide improved service through their bus fleets. As demand for public transit increased, firms would increase fleet sizes, adding newer buses that were more comfortable and less noisy than those in their existing fleet.

In addition to its implications for public transit supply, congestion pricing may improve the financial health of the public transit industry if load factors for the bus system improve. Combined with lower operating costs from reduced congestion, improved load factors reduce operating deficits, all else held constant.

As a last point, fixed rail transit may not enjoy the same increase in demand as the above analysis suggests would occur for bus. Relative to SOV, fixed rail systems generally have comparable line-haul times, but are at a comparative disadvantage with respect to out-of-vehicle travel time, because fixed rail transit stations are relatively far apart. Reaching a station from one's origin or destination may require walking some distance and often requires using feeder modes (automobile or local bus). Relative to local bus services in existing environments, the combined use of feeder and fixed rail services may be acceptable. However, if congestion pricing increases travel speeds sufficiently, local bus service may improve to such an extent that the generalized cost of fixed rail trips increases relative to local bus service. In other words, rather than increasing the demand, congestion pricing may actually reduce the demand for fixed-rail transit trips, all else constant.

CASE STUDY – TOWARD A FEASIBLE POLICY OF ROAD PRICING: LOS ANGELES

The previous section identified the expected effects of congestion pricing on the modal choices of travelers residing in a typical congested metropolitan area. These hypothesized effects were based upon changes in travelers' generalized costs prior to and after congestion pricing. Further, by assuming that congestion pricing was revenue-neutral, we identified, in a generalized cost sense, whether individual welfare rose or fell with congestion pricing.

Although providing insights into modal choice changes that would occur under congestion pricing, the analysis was silent on perhaps one of the most important questions surrounding congestion pricing – its political feasibility. As we know, the theory behind congestion pricing is straightforward. From figure 11.5, the optimal number of trips occurs at the point at which the demand curve intersects the marginal cost curve. And the optimal congestion charge is the difference between a trip's marginal cost and average variable cost at the optimal number of trips. Assuming that all congestion revenues collected are returned back to the traveling population – that is, road pricing is revenue-neutral – the welfare effects of the fees collected will just equal the welfare effect of the fees returned. Moreover, those travelers whose trip benefits fall short of trip costs (including the congestion charge) are priced off the road and are worse off from the policy. Those remaining on the road, however, gain from the reduced level of congestion. Thus, as Small (1992) notes, there are four direct effects from a policy of congestion pricing:

1 The congestion revenues collected from those using congested roads during the peak period.
2 Additional costs, in the form of less preferred routes, travel times, and so forth, to those travelers priced off the congested road.
3 Reduced congestion experienced by those traveling during the congested period.
4 Benefits to the population from spending the collected congestion revenues.

If congestion pricing is revenue-neutral, then items 1 and 4 are offsetting in a welfare sense, and the difference between items 2 and 3 reflects the net benefit, or efficiency gain, from congestion pricing. But the difficulty is that implementing any explicit pricing policy is a radical change for road users who are used to viewing highways as a "nonpriced" free good. Further, the efficiency gains from road pricing are aggregate gains, which ignore the numerous groups that have vested interests in the metropolitan travel environment, including individual travelers, the trucking industry, state and local highway departments, public transit agencies, taxicab and private transport service providers, environmentalists, business firms, and taxpayers as a whole. For a feasible congestion pricing policy, it is imperative that, on balance, each interest group perceives a net benefit from the policy.

Using Los Angeles as a case study, Small (1992) devised a metropolitan area wide congestion pricing plan with an explicit objective that most individuals in each of the diverse interest groups could identify benefits that would offset to some degree the negative effects of congestion pricing. In order keep the plan simple and to explicitly link the plan to the transportation sector, Small proposed that one-third of the congestion revenues be used as monetary payments to reimburse road users for their higher costs, a second third of the revenues be used to replace existing taxes currently earmarked for highway use, and the last third be used to provide new transportation services.

There are two necessary conditions for Small's plan to work. First, in order to obtain the support of the various interest groups, specific revenue allocation programs must be devised and targeted to each group. Within the above general framework, Small identified seven specific spending programs that could be implemented:

1 Monetary reimbursement to each commuting employee, regardless of the commuter's time of travel or mode of travel. Even with

this reimbursement, however, commuters during the peak face a higher price of travel, and will still have an incentive to reduce peak-period trips.

2 Reduction of existing highway-related taxes, such as the gasoline tax and vehicle registration fees.
3 Reduction or elimination of sales tax surcharges earmarked for transportation.
4 Reduction of the portion of local property taxes that funds highway construction and maintenance activities.
5 Construction of new highway capacity and elimination of high occupancy vehicle (HOV) lanes that are currently in use.
6 Provision of additional or upgrading of existing public transit services.
7 Provision of new or improvement of existing transportation-related infrastructure and services surrounding business centers. This would include such features as bicycle paths, bus shelters, street lighting, and so on.

A second necessary condition for the plan's success is that there must be sufficient revenues to feasibly implement the revenue allocation schemes. On this score, existing research indicates that efficient congestion charges will generate revenues that are more than sufficient to cover local government contributions to highway networks.[21]

Table 11.12 summarizes expected revenues, collection costs, and revenue disbursements from a congestion pricing policy in metropolitan Los Angeles.[22] Gross revenues are based upon a congestion charge of 15 cents per vehicle–mile, an average peak-period trip length of ten miles, and a 26% reduction in peak-period vehicle–miles traveled.[23] Peak-period VMT is expected to fall from 28 to 20.8 billion. Multiplying 20.8 billion by 15 cents provides congestion revenues of $3.12 billion. As seen in table 11.12, $137 million of these gross revenues are disbursed for collection costs, $1.044 billion for reimbursing travelers, $990 million to offset reduced taxes, and $949 million for transportation-related service improvements. Roughly, one-third of the net revenues is allocated to each of the main beneficiary groups. As designed, the effect of these programs is to divvy up the large cache of

Table 11.12 Congestion pricing revenue allocation program

	Annual Amount ($million)
Monetary reimbursement to travelers	
Employee commuting allowance ($10/month)	696
Fuel tax reduction (5 cents/gallon)	348
Reduced general taxes	
Sales tax reduction ($\frac{1}{2}$ of transportation surcharge)	525
Property tax rebate (eliminate local highway subsidy)	465
New transportation services	
Highway improvements	315
Public transit improvements	312
Transportation-related improvements in business centers	322
Net revenue	2,983
Collection costs	137
Gross revenue	3,120

Source: Reprinted from Small (1992), with permission from Elsevier Science

congestion revenues among the diverse interest groups, so that each group benefits in some way. Individual travelers and general taxpayers benefit from reimbursement and tax reduction schemes. Highways and public transit agencies gain through new and improved services. Business centers gain, on average by $11.8 million per year, through various transportation-related infrastructural and service improvements.[24] It might also be noted that congestion pricing may receive some support from environmental groups, to the extent that the policy reduces VMTs and lessens motor vehicle impacts on air quality.

How would the proposed congestion tax plus revenue redistribution affect a typical commuter in the Los Angeles area? For a typical SOV, carpool, and public transit user, table 11.13 reports the net benefits from the comprehensive congestion pricing policy. Based upon the assumptions reported at the bottom of table 11.13, we see that SOV commuters are expected to pay $750 per year in congestion charges for their peak period trips. For this $750 expenditure, commuters who continue to use the road network during the peak hour receive a 20 minute per day saving in travel time. For an average-income commuter, whose time is valued at $6.05 per hour, this yields an annual time saving of $504. Higher- and lower-income commuters experience annual time savings valued at $686 and $393 respectively. Those switching from a private automobile to a carpool receive the least time saving benefits, $98, because of the added inconvenience of carpooling, while nonswitching carpoolers receive the highest annual time saving, at $756. Time savings to transit users are valued at $197. Notice that, with the exception of carpoolers, no other commuter experiences a time saving that would offset the annual congestion charge imposed, a result that is generally consistent with the findings in the previous section. Based only upon congestion fees and time savings, only those who carpooled prior to congestion pricing would favor a congestion pricing policy.

Rows (7)–(10) in table 11.13 report additional monetary benefits from compensation and tax rebates associated with a comprehensive congestion pricing program. With the exception of transit users who receive no direct savings from reduced fuel taxes or property taxes (Small assumed that transit users live in rental housing), highway users receive additional monetary benefits. As you might expect, we see in row (11) that high-income households receive the greatest benefit from these rebates, since they are likely to spend more on gasoline, housing, and consumption. Adding rows (6) and (11), the net time and money benefits from congestion charges, time savings, reimbursements, and tax rebates provide a net benefit to all but two groups, low-income single-occupant auto users and commuters who switch from auto to carpool. In each of these cases, the low values that these commuters place upon their time do not produce sufficient time savings, even when combined with reimbursements and tax rebates, to offset the high congestion charges during the peak period.

Through increased transportation services for highways, transit, and business centers, rows (12)–(14) provide a final set of benefits that Small's plan would generate. For each group of commuters, the combined effect has an estimated dollar value on the order of $130 (a bit higher for transit), an amount that is sufficient to provide a positive net benefit to each of the identified groups.[25] Note that among the single-occupant vehicle users, high-income households gain the most. The expected benefit for this group is $409, in comparison to benefits of $166 and $19 for the average and low-income households, respectively. Does this imply that the tax is regressive? – not necessarily. The reason is that the net benefits accruing to higher-income households reflect their higher values of travel time. Because higher-income households have higher values of time, they are also less likely to shift out of the peak and more likely to pay the most in congestion charges. Conversely, to the extent that households can shift to other modes, times of day, and so forth, they will be able to avoid some, if not all congestion charges, while reaping the time saving benefits that accrue from lower congestion and improved transportation services.

To sum up, the importance of table 11.13 is that a congestion policy based solely upon the

Table 11.13 The effects of congestion pricing (*CP*) revenue redistribution on a typical commuter

	Continuing Auto Driver					
	Average Income	High Income	Low Income	Switch to Carpool	Continuing Carpool	Continuing Transit
Travel mode						
(1) Before *CP*	Solo	Solo	Solo	Solo	Carpool	Transit
(2) After *CP*	Solo	Solo	Solo	Carpool	Carpool	Transit
Costs						
(3) Congestion Costs ($/year)	750	750	750	375	562.5	0
Time savings						
(4) Amount (minutes/day)	20	20	20	20	30	10
(5) Carpool Inconvenience				−15		
(6) Value ($/year)	504	686	393	98	756	197
Monetary benefits						
(7) Travel allowance	120	120	120	120	120	120
(8) Fuel tax	20	24	1	13	16	0
(9) Sales tax	86	103	73	73	86	73
(10) Property tax	57	97	37	37	57	0
(11) Total	283	344	246	243	279	193
Net time and money benefits	37	279	−111	−34	472	389
Other benefits ($/year)						
(12) Improved highways	64	64	64	64	64	0
(13) Transit service	32	32	32	32	32	127
(14) Business centers	33	33	33	33	33	33
Total net benefits ($)	166	409	19	95	602	550

Assumptions:

	Continuing Auto Driver					
	Average Income	High Income	Low Income	Switch to Carpool	Continuing Carpool	Continuing Transit
Value of Time	6.05	8.23	4.72	4.72	6.05	4.72
One way road distance (miles)	10	10	10	10	15	10
Average Speed (mph)						
Before Congestion Pricing	20	20	20	20	20	20
After Congestion Pricing	30	30	30	30	30	30
Fuel Consumed (gallons/year)	400	480	320	256	320	0
Sales tax surcharge (relative to average household)	1.0	1.2	0.85	0.85	1.0	0.85
Property tax (relative to average household)	1.0	1.7	0.65	0.65	1.0	0

Source: Reprinted from Small (1992), with permission from Elsevier Science

collection of congestion fees and imputed time savings will likely fall on deaf ears. Only for carpoolers will the time savings offset, and just so, the congestion charges. All other groups suffer relatively large losses. When combined with a comprehensive scheme for redistributing congestion revenues, however, we find that all groups may benefit. Moreover, a further advantage of multiple redistribution plans is that most, if not all, interest groups receive some benefits that make the policy politically more acceptable.

CASE STUDY – OPTIMAL CONGESTION CHARGES FOR RUNWAY SPACE

This chapter has focused upon the most important congestion problem in the USA, that associated with highway use. However, similar principles apply when other transport modes suffer congestion. In chapter 10, we examined the welfare effects of optimal pricing and investment of airport capacity. We saw in that chapter that the existing structure of take-off and landing (TOL) fees is based upon the size of aircraft. The heavier the aircraft, the greater is the TOL fee. We also argued that this is inefficient, since the time delays imposed upon passengers of other aircraft are generally independent of size of plane. A large Jumbo Jet filled to capacity will experience the same time delays regardless of whether it is awaiting the departure of a small general aviation aircraft or a larger commercial aircraft. Just as an individual motorist entering a congested network imposes time delays upon others using the road system, so too an additional aircraft using a congested airport facility will impose time delays upon other aircrafts' passengers who are utilizing the facility.

Analyzing the efficient use of airport infrastructure is formally identical to our analysis of highway infrastructure. In each case, users of the facility bear part of costs necessary to generate the supply of trips. In the case of airports, there are runway capacity costs, airport use costs, and user costs. Airport use costs reflect maintenance, operations, and administrative costs. User costs reflect flight costs, average delay costs, and "external" congestion costs. In general, each departing aircraft during congested periods imposes congestion costs upon other departing aircraft, as well as upon arriving planes that have queued in a "holding pattern" waiting to land. Similarly, each landing aircraft imposes congestion costs upon other departing and arriving aircraft wanting to use runway capacity.

On the basis of optimal pricing and investment criteria, Morrison and Winston (1989) solved for long-run efficient prices and runway capacity. In their analysis, the authors defined six classes of aircraft – international, cargo, majors and nationals, commuter, regionals, and general aviation – and 24 time periods, one corresponding to each hour of the day. The optimal toll for a departure (arrival) in each classification is the difference between the marginal cost of the departure (arrival) and its average variable cost (which equals passengers' flight costs, passengers' delay costs, and marginal runway maintenance, operation, and administrative costs). Thus, assuming marginal cost pricing, congestion tolls are set where the marginal benefit of a take-off or landing just equals the additional costs that this activity imposes on other runway users and on the airport authority. For optimal capacity, the marginal benefit of an additional runway must equal its marginal cost. The marginal benefit of an additional runway is the total time savings – that is, the time savings over all aircraft classifications and all time periods – afforded by the increased capacity. The marginal cost of an additional runway includes land, construction, and maintenance costs.[26]

For five airports, table 11.14 reports landing fees, delays, and runway capacity under three scenarios: existing pricing and investment, optimal pricing and existing capacity, and optimal pricing and capacity. For current operating conditions, we see in table 11.14 that landing fees vary from a low of 50 cents per passenger at

Table 11.14 Airport congestion, optimal pricing, and investment

	Washington (National)	Denver (Stapleton)	New York (La Guardia)	Chicago (O'Hare)	San Antonio (International)
Landing fees per passenger ($)					
Current pricing and investment	0.75	0.92	3.22	1.20	0.50
Optimal pricing, current investment	9.81	9.26	32.05	10.89	2.52
Optimal pricing, optimal investment	1.32	1.29	1.15	1.12	1.52
Average delay (minutes)					
Current pricing and investment	9.3	7.3	27.9	8.4	3.0
Optimal pricing, current investment	5.5	5.4	12.8	6.0	2.5
Optimal pricing, optimal investment	1.8	1.8	1.8	1.7	2.5
Number of runways					
Current pricing and investment	3.0	5.0	2.0	7.0	3.0
Optimal pricing, optimal investment	12	17	17.7	29.2	4.4

Source: Adapted from Morrison and Winston (1989), table 12, p. 94

San Antonio International Airport to a high of $3.22 at New York's La Guardia Airport. Similarly, average delays are lowest at San Antonio (3 minutes) and highest at New York (just shy of half an hour). To understand the large differences in delays, look at the number of runways. La Guardia Airport has the fewest runways among the five cities. San Antonio's International Airport serves a much smaller market, with one *additional* runway than New York's La Guardia Airport. Relative to New York La Guardia, the effect of Chicago O'Hare's five additional runways is a 20 minute reduction in average delays.

Assuming current investment in capacity but implementing congestion – that is, optimal – pricing, we see the dramatic effect that limited runway space has on landing fees and average delays. San Antonio's International Airport experiences a five-fold increase in landing fees per passenger, while landing fees at Washington DC National Airport rise 13-fold. The other three airports in table 11.14 experience about a ten-fold increase. The dramatic rise in landing fees has obvious implications for travel delays. Imposing congestion prices on existing facilities necessarily implies a reduction in traffic and congestion externalities. Aircraft passengers who value delay savings less than the congestion toll will be "tolled off" the facility. They will either forego the flight altogether, fly at a different time, or fly out of a different airport. Those continuing to use the airport experience reduced congestion and travel delays. We see in the table that, with congestion pricing, travel delays are less than the delays under current operations. Airline passengers at New York's La Guardia Airport receive the largest absolute and percentage reduction in average delay, falling by over 50%.

In an environment of optimal pricing *and* investment, table 11.14 illustrates the effect that optimal investment has upon optimal landing fees and travel delays. For three of the five airports, optimal landing fees rise, and for two others – La Guardia and O'Hare – fees actually fall. San Antonio experiences the largest percentage rise, because its optimal capacity increases the least. Optimal capacity at La Guardia increases by 16 runways and at O'Hare by 23. The results of this analysis strongly imply that current investment in airport capacity at the nation's most congested airports is much too low.

What would happen to average delay if we efficiently priced and invested our resources? At this point, the results are to be expected. Travel delays fall to about two minutes, considerably less than those experienced under current conditions. As with optimal landing fees, the significant reductions in average travel delay are due to the large reductions in congestion brought about by increased capacity investments.

For Washington National, Chicago O'Hare, and San Antonio International airports, table 11.15 examines the distributional effects of congestion pricing with and without optimal investment. Column 1 provides the combined effect on carriers' operating costs and passenger delays, while column 2 gives the impact on

Table 11.15 Net benefit changes per passenger from optimal pricing and investment (1988 dollars)[a]

Airport and Activity	Carrier Operating Cost Plus Delay Costs Per Passenger		Per Passenger Landing Fees		Per Passenger Net Benefit	
	(1) (a) Optimal Pricing	(b) Optimal Pricing and Investment	(2) (a) Optimal Pricing	(b) Optimal Pricing and Investment	(3) (a) Optimal Pricing	(b) Optimal Pricing and Investment
Washington (National)						
Commercial Carriers	3.62	7.3	−7.66	−0.31	−4.04	6.99
Commuters	3.39	7.45	−21.94	−1.82	−18.55	5.63
General Aviation	3.81	9.05	−111.26	−13.09	−107.45	−4.04
Chicago (O'Hare)						
Cargo	0.08	0.67	0.50	1.03	0.58	1.70
International	2.48	6.88	−5.07	0.64	−2.59	7.52
Commercial Carriers	2.18	6.46	−9.63	0.12	−7.45	6.58
Commuters	2.29	7.06	−19.42	−0.67	−17.13	6.39
General Aviation	2.89	9.08	−141.71	−14.68	−138.82	−5.60
San Antonio (International)						
Cargo	0.07	0.28	−1.80	−0.97	−1.73	−0.69
International	0.44	1.15	−0.88	−0.32	−0.44	0.83
Commercial Carriers	0.33	0.87	−1.01	−0.42	−0.68	0.45
Commuters	0.35	0.95	−4.43	−2.17	−4.08	−1.22
General Aviation	0.49	1.28	−22.02	−12.04	−21.53	−10.76

[a] In each column, positive numbers reflect gains and negative numbers reflect losses.
Source: Adapted from Morrison and Winston (1989), table 13, p. 95

landing fees. Summing columns 1 and 2 gives column 3, the net benefit to airport users. Consistent with table 11.4, we see in table 11.15 that, under optimal pricing with current investment, the large increase in landing fees produces a welfare loss for each aviation category. All entries in column 2(a) (excepting Cargo at O'Hare) are negative. Moreover, the biggest loser is General Aviation, which suffers a loss that is an order of magnitude larger than for any other aviation category. This should not be surprising. General Aviation typically comprises small aircraft with few passengers, but causes congestion delays – and requires congestion tolls – that are comparable to those for much larger aircraft. Allocating large increases in landing fees on a per passenger basis produces large per passenger losses in table 11.15. On the other hand, optimal pricing increases benefits by lowering both carrier costs and traveler delays.[27] On balance, when congestion pricing is not associated with optimal investment strategies, we see in column 3 that all aviation categories, with the exception of Cargo at Chicago's O'Hare Airport, are net losers. The size of loss depends upon the airport. At relatively uncongested airports, typified by San Antonio, net benefits fall anywhere from \$0.44 for Cargo to \$21.53 for General Aviation. At more congested airports, such as Chicago O'Hare, on the other hand, net benefits decrease by a whopping \$138.82 per passenger for General Aviation activities. If we combine optimal investment with optimal pricing, we no longer see large net benefit reductions across categories. The reason is that optimal investment requires increasing capacity, which in itself alleviates congestion. Although there is still a need to impose congestion tolls, the optimal tolls are much less. In table 11.15, this translates into smaller reductions and, in some cases, increases in net benefit. Combined with reductions in traveler delays and carriers' costs, the net effect in column 3(b) is that virtually all categories, excepting General Aviation, gain. At the more congested airports, only General Aviation loses while at less congested airports, Cargo and Commuters experience a loss as well. In the latter case, existing capacity is not much less than optimal capacity, so that the welfare effect from savings on carriers' costs and travelers delays are not sufficient to offset the effect from higher landing fees.

There are two conclusions that we can reach from this analysis. First, to reiterate a finding in chapter 10, our nation's existing airport infrastructure is neither efficiently priced nor adequately capitalized. The existing structure of landing fees based upon size of aircraft provides an incentive for General Aviation to overuse congested airport facilities. Pricing the use of runways based upon marginal congestion costs would lead to an efficient use of this scarce resource. Second, efficient investment requires that additional runways be constructed, particularly for the nation's busiest airports. If efficient pricing is imposed at existing capacities, there will be large distribution effects. This is evident from table 11.15, where General Aviation experiences large welfare losses from optimal pricing at current capacity levels. Because the distribution effects are much less with optimal investment, congestion pricing policies are more likely to be politically feasible.

CHAPTER HIGHLIGHTS

- Congestion occurs when user supplied inputs depend upon the rate at which a transportation facility is used. The more congested a facility is, the more user supplied inputs are expended.
- During free flow conditions, one individual's use of a transportation facility has no impact upon another's use of the facility. There is no congestion and, given existing

investment, the first-best price occurs where market demand intersects the average variable cost (marginal private cost) curve.

- During congested conditions, the marginal cost of an additional trip rises above the average variable cost, as the marginal user imposes time costs upon existing users but does not consider these costs in the trip decision. This is a congestion externality and implies that too many resources are allocated to trip-making. The first-best price occurs where market demand intersects the marginal (social) cost curve. To reach this point, an optimal congestion tax or congestion price is required.
- If a transportation capital (for example, highways, airports, ports, and so on) is produced under constant returns to scale, then optimal pricing and investment requires an optimal congestion tax. The revenues from the congestion tax are sufficient to pay the capital costs of the facility. If the facility is produced under decreasing returns to scale, congestion revenues are not sufficient to pay the capital cost. Under increasing returns to scale, congestion revenues generate more than enough revenues to pay for invested capital.
- Similar to the optimality criterion for private firms, optimal investment in transportation infrastructure continues up to the point at which the marginal capital cost equals the savings in average variable costs. Many of these savings will be user time cost savings.
- Most of our major cities experience a relatively high degree of traffic congestion. Increasing capacity to eliminate or substantially reduce congestion is not only very costly but also likely to be uneconomic. An efficient use of our scarce resources requires that we efficiently price and invest in transportation capacity.
- One early empirical study of congestion in San Francisco estimated optimal congestion prices that ranged from 0.1 cents for rural freeways in an off-peak period to 15 cents (1972 dollars) on a urban central freeway during the peak period. A more recent study for Los Angeles calls for a 15 cent per mile congestion charge during peak periods. Because the estimated 15 cent congestion tax for Los Angeles is in 1992 dollars, the more recent estimate for Los Angeles is a lower congestion charge in real terms than the estimate for San Francisco.
- An empirical study of the effect of congestion pricing on modal choice, assuming free parking, indicates that only lower-income travelers (with low values of time) will have an incentive to shift from single-occupant travel to carpools or mass transit. Travelers with average values of time have an incentive to carpool but not take mass transit. And high-income travelers have no incentive to shift out of their single-occupant vehicles. If parking is no longer free of charge, the high-income traveler also has an incentive to shift into a carpool. However, the high value of time continues to preclude a high-income traveler from shifting to local bus service.
- A case study of the distribution effects of congestion pricing in Los Angeles suggests that a successful policy can be implemented if congestion revenues are returned through reductions in other taxes that travelers pay, through reduced general taxes, and through city-wide improvements in transportation and related facilities.

- Assuming current investment, airport landing fees based upon congestion externalities are much higher than landing fees when airports pursue optimal investment in runways. Further, there will be more general support for congestion-based landing fees if airports invest optimally. Virtually all airport users lose under optimal pricing and current investment. Under optimal pricing and investment, general aviation is the primary loser.

Review questions

1. Consider the following table, which gives the estimated price elasticity of demand for bus fares associated with fare discounts during peak and off-peak periods:

Fare Change	Estimated Fare Elasticity
Off-peak discount	−0.667
Peak surcharge	−0.268

(a) What impact upon off-peak bus travel will occur from a 10% decrease in off-peak fares? Will bus revenues increase or decrease from such a fare change?
(b) What impact upon peak demand will occur from a 10% increase in peak fares? Will revenues increase or decrease from such a fare change?
(c) In absolute value, the fare elasticity for off-peak travel is larger than the fare elasticity for peak period travel. Economically, what explains the greater value for off-peak period travel?

2. The following table lists volume : capacity (V/C) ratios and the average travel time (minutes) per mile. The marginal travel time for this table is $1 + 5(V/C)^4$.

Table 11.16 Time and speed measures

V/C	Average Time	Marginal Time	Speed (mph)
0.1	1.0001		
0.2	1.0016		
0.3	1.0081		
0.4	1.0256		
0.5	1.0625		
0.6	1.1296		
0.7	1.2401		
0.8	1.4096		
0.9	1.6561		
1.0	2.000		

(a) Fill in the values for marginal time and speed. Graph average time and marginal time with the volume : capacity ratio on the x-axis and minutes per mile on the y-axis.
(b) In the graph, draw in a market demand curve such that the marginal traveler is traveling at 57.5 mph. What volume : capacity ratio does the marginal traveler face? If this an economically efficient solution? If so, why; and if not, why not?
(c) At a volume capacity ratio of 0.8, what is the extent of the congestion externality?
(d) Suppose that the V/C is at 1.0. If additional traffic continues to enter the road, what do you think will happen to the average travel and marginal travel time curves?

3. Critically evaluate the following statement: "For all levels of traffic, an optimal congestion tax leads to an efficient allocation of resources."

4. In the graph below, the distance $0a$ reflects road maintenance costs, the distance ab reflects vehicle operating costs, and the distance bc reflects time costs.
(a) In the graph, which costs vary with traffic flow and which costs do not vary with traffic flow?
(b) In general, which costs are borne privately by the motorist on this road?
(c) In the absence of any government intervention, where will the market equilibrium occur? Demonstrate that this is an inefficient allocation of resources and identify the welfare losses associated with the equilibrium.
(d) What is an efficient allocation of resources? Are all travelers better off from this efficient outcome?

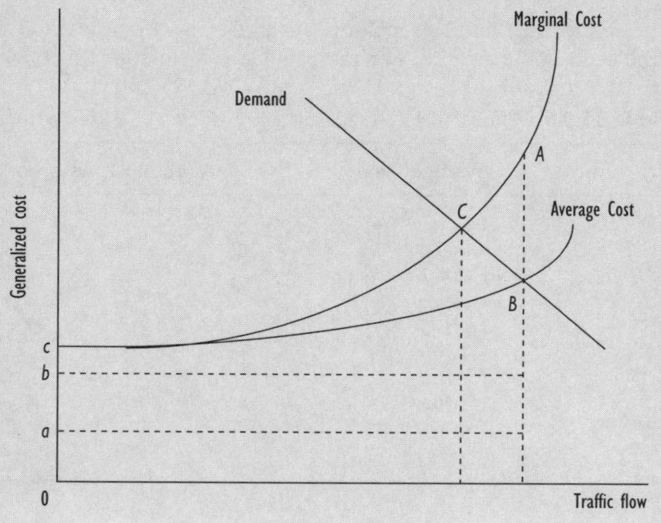

5. The city is currently grappling with how to best use its local airport. In its deliberations, the city council is deciding upon the best landing fee to charge. There is one runway, which is most often used early in the morning and in late afternoon as businessmen travel to and from the city. At present, passengers incur few delays in their flights into and out of the airport. You are an economic adviser to the city council.
   (a) Assume that the marginal damage to the runway per landing is constant. If the city council is interested in using the airport to maximize economic welfare, what landing fee would you advise the council to adopt? How much of this landing fee would be used to cover the airport's capital costs?
   (b) Suppose that a boom in the city significantly increases the demand for early morning and late evening trips from the airport. During these peak periods, the demand for runway capacity exceeds the available supply. Demand for airport capacity throughout the day remains the same. Would you alter your recommendations to the city council on the appropriate landing fee to charge? If so, how? In this case, would the revenues collected contribute to the capital cost of the airport?

6. Some would argue that the goal of public policy is not to reduce congestion but, rather, to eliminate congestion. In the graph below, we see that congestion sets in at traffic flow T_1. Existing demand equals D_1. The market attains an equilibrium at T_3. Suppose that a road tax were levied on travelers that reduced traffic flow to its uncongested level T_1.
   (a) What would be the loss in consumer benefits from such a tax?
   (b) What would be the resource savings from this tax?
   (c) What congestion revenues would be collected from such a tax?
   (d) Assuming that all congestion revenues were returned to a city's residents, what would the net welfare effects of this policy?
   (e) In general, if too many resources are currently allocated to trip-making because of congestion policies, how much congestion should be eliminated if we want an efficient allocation of resources to trip-making?

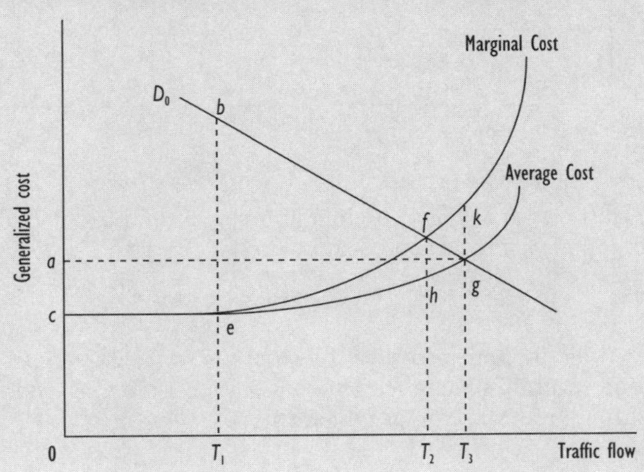

7. In what sense do peak-period prices reflect marginal cost pricing, and in what sense are these prices rationing capacity to the most highly valued uses?

8. Suppose that the cost of a new bridge is \$1,000,000. The rate of interest is 6.5% and the bridge is expected to last for 30 years.
   (a) Identify and interpret the optimality condition for investment.
   (b) Given the information on the capital cost, interest rate, and lifetime of the bridge, by how much must annual variable costs fall for this to be a worthwhile investment?

9. Consider two possible modes of travel, single-vehicle automobile and bus trips. Consider two interrelated markets, the market for bus trips and the market for automobile trips. Assume that a congestion price is levied upon all automobile trips during the peak period. Bus riders do not have to pay any congestion tax.
   (a) In the graphs below, identify the effect that an optimal congestion tax will have upon the number of automobile trips taken and the number of bus trips taken.
   (b) Are these predictions consistent with the predicted impact on mode choice identified in table 11.10? If not, why not?

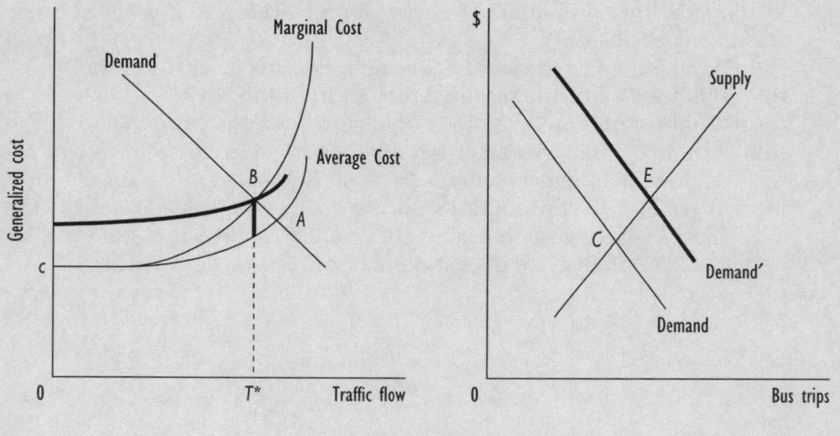

10. Port authorities desire to optimally invest in and use port capacity. Let the cost function for a port be expressed as

$$C = sht(s/k) + p_k k$$

where h is the hourly cost of the ship; t is the average port time (hours), which includes waiting time in a queue and service time at the port – average port time is a function of the rate at which the port is used (s/k); s is the number of ships serviced at the port; and k is the port capacity, which equals the total number of ships that a port can service at one time.

(a) Interpret the right-hand side of the cost function. Does this cost function represent a private or social cost function?

(b) Given that the two inputs to port costs are capacity k and the number of ships serviced s, does the port experience increasing, decreasing, or constant returns to scale?

(c) From this cost equation, the additional cost to the port from servicing another ship can be shown to be

$$\frac{\Delta C}{\Delta s} = ht + sh\,\frac{\Delta(\text{average port time})}{\Delta s}$$

Interpret the right-hand side of the equation.

(d) If the port wishes to have that level of capacity k that minimizes its costs, the appropriate marginal condition for cost minimization can be shown to be

$$p_k = sh\,\frac{\Delta(\text{average port time})}{\Delta k}$$

Interpret this equation.

(e) From these two marginal conditions, demonstrate that marginal cost pricing will generate sufficient revenues to pay for port capacity, $p_k k$.

11. Suppose that there is a road from A to B. The demand for trips from A to B is given by the function

$$\text{value} = 20 - 0.001N$$

where N is the number of trips. However, the more trips that are taken, the slower each trip is, since one person's extra journey imposes costs on the other drivers. The relation of time taken to trips made (which is the average cost of a trip) is given by

$$\text{cost} = 2 + 0.001N$$

(which implies a per-trip social cost of $(2 + 0.002)$.

(a) What is the market equilibrium number of trips?

(b) If society wants to allocate trip-making resources efficiently, what congestion tax per trip should be levied on trip-makers?

12. In the late 1960s, there was talk about the possibility of extending the Kennedy International Airport on Jamaica Bay. The reason for this was the air traffic congestion that was building up on this and the other two airports in the area, namely, La Guardia and Newark, New Jersey. The landing fees prevalent during the time led to three observations (Walters, 1973): (1) landing fees fixed by weight of the aircraft; (2) among the three airports, there was a progression of landing fees that was negatively related to the degree of air traffic congestion; and (3) landing fees appeared to be low relative to the cost of expanding capacity.

(a) What is "value-of-service" pricing, and how is this principle related to a structure of landing fees based upon aircraft weight? Is the setting of landing fees based upon value-of-service pricing more or less appropriate for capacity-constrained airports?

(b) By setting low landing fees, what signal is this giving for future investment?

13. In an effort to reduce midday congestion due to nonwork (that is, shopping, recreational, and so on) automobile trips, a transportation economist proposes a 15% increase in the gasoline tax. She estimates a discrete choice model, the results of which are reported in table 11.17.

(a) What do these results tell you about the effect of travel time and travel cost on nonwork mode choice?

(b) According to these results, are higher-income households more or less likely to take the bus for their nonwork trips?

(c) Will the proposed increase in the gasoline tax have any effect on nonwork trips? Assume that 95% of the population currently use an automobile in their nonwork trips, and that the average cost of an automobile trip is $1. What is the elasticity of nonwork trip auto with respect to automobile costs? What does this imply about nonwork trip auto use if the gasoline tax raises per-trip auto costs by 15%? (Hint: for the elasticity, refer to chapter 4.)

(d) Given your answer to (c), will the economist's proposal meet her objective?

Table 11.17 Mode choice model

Variable	Coefficient Estimate	*t*-statistic
Constant (auto)	−4.23	−2.10
Travel Cost (bus,auto)	−0.04	−2.65
Travel Time (bus,auto)	−0.001	−0.05
Total Waiting Time (bus)	−0.529	−2.62
# Cars in Household (auto)	1.52	2.51
Family Income (auto)	0.00006	1.67

14. "Gridlock" is a term that characterizes a transportation network on which all traffic has stopped. No one is going anywhere. Although most urban systems experience gridlock at times, the more common phenomenon is slow-moving, although heavily congested, traffic.

(a) Why do economists believe that traffic congestion produces an inefficient allocation of resources?

(b) "The objective of congestion pricing is to smooth out peak period demand so that the level of congestion during the peak period is no higher than during the off-peak period." Critically evaluate this statement.

15. Table 11.18 provides estimates (Lee, 1982) of efficient user charges (cents/VMT) for vehicles under alternative operating conditions.

(a) In comparing efficient with existing fees in 1982, what are the resource allocation implications for trip-making?

(b) What congestion pricing implications does the table have for automobile and truck trips?

(c) It is seen in the table that a major portion of the efficient charge for trucks relates to the damage that a truck inflicts upon the road, particularly for urban highways. Are these results consistent with those discussed in chapter 10?

(d) The pavement charges are based upon 10 inch thick highways, but we have seen that optimal durability considerations require highways that are an inch or so thicker. If highways were optimally built, what implications would this have upon the pavement repair costs reported in the table?

Table 11.18 Efficient user charges

Vehicle Type	Location	Pavement Repair	User Cost	Excess Delay	Air Pollution	Other	Total Efficient User Fee	Existing Average User Fee
Automobile	Rural	0	0	0.3	0	0.3	0.6	1.3
Automobile	Urban	0	0	11.2	1.5	0.8	13.5	1.7
Three-Axle Truck	Small Urban	25.6	7.5	2.2	0.2	0.7	36.2	4.8
Truck Combination	Rural Interstate	8.0	5.9	0.4	0	0.3	14.6	9.0
Truck Combination	Urban Interstate	24.0	16.3	1.4	3.0	4.3	49.0	9.0

Source: Adapted from Lee (1982), table 12, pp. 49–50

NOTES

1 A relationship similar to this was found by Coleman (1961) for city traffic.

2 The average time cost of the 3,751st trip is 4.25 minutes. Given 3,750 current users, this implies that the 3,751st trip imposes 0.0015 minutes (9/100 of a second) on the trip time of existing drivers. Although this is minuscule for each traveler, it constitutes a nontrivial cost for the total number of travelers on the road.

3 Although the different terminology for the same concept may cause some confusion, it is not surprising to understand how the terms arose. The effect of congestion is an example of an external diseconomy. External (dis)economies exist if an expansion of industry output leads to technological (in)efficiencies for individual firms in the industry. In the present case, expansion of traffic leads to road congestion, which raises the cost of producing trips. Those focusing upon congestion as an externality distinguish between marginal private versus marginal social cost, whereas those analyzing congestion in the context of standard firm behavior distinguish between average variable cost and marginal cost. As long as one recognizes that marginal private cost is synonymous with average variable cost, and that marginal social cost is synonymous with marginal cost, there should be no confusion.

4 The fundamental problem here is that road space is a scarce good, the access to which is not being priced. Anyone who wants to use the road can do so with a zero access fee. This is true for any scarce good that is not allocated by price.

5 This section has significantly benefited from Hau's (1992) research on road pricing.

6 Recall that in an uncongested (off-peak) environment, only opportunity costs are covered. However, assuming peak demands but uncongested trips up to the point of capacity, the function of equilibrium price was to ration scarce capacity. With peak period demand, pricing at opportunity cost resulted in excess demand for capacity.

7 For those familiar with differential calculus, this says that the cost function is homogeneous of degree zero. Let $C(q,k)$ be a homogenous of degree zero cost function, where q is output and k is capital. According to Euler's theorem, if $f(x,y)$ is homogeneous of degree r, then $(\partial f/\partial x)x + (\partial f/\partial y)y = r$. Applying Euler's Theorem to the cost function gives $(\partial C/\partial q)q + (\partial C/\partial k)k = 0$, which implies that $-(\partial C/\partial q)q = (\partial C/\partial k)k$.

8 This information is based upon Kain (1994).

9 Haight (1963) referred to the speed–flow curve as the "fundamental diagram of road traffic."

10 The three freeway systems studied were the Eastshore Freeway, Bayshore Freeway, and Nimitz Freeway.

11 Traffic flow in figure 11.8 is defined by vehicles per lane–hour. Dividing by per-lane capacity gives traffic flow as a volume : capacity ratio.

12 Suppose that I write equation (11.8) as: $V/C = a + b(\text{Speed} - c)^2 = a + b\text{Speed}^2 - 2cb\text{Speed} + bc^2$. This implies that $b = -0.001923$. Then $-2cb = 2(0.001923)c = 0.1757$, which means that $c = 45.684$. Finally, $-3.153 = a + bc^2$, which implies that $a = -3.153 - bc^2 = -3.153 + (0.001923)(45.684)^2 = 0.8603$.

13 Given the quadratic equation $ax^2 + bx + c = 0$, the solution for x is: $x = (-b \pm \sqrt{b^2 - 4ac})/2a$. For the speed–flow curve, $a = -0.001923$, $b = 0.1757$, and $c = -(V/C + 3.153)$. A word of caution for the assiduous student who works through all the details: applying the quadratic formula to solve for T leads to two small discrepancies relative to that reported in equation (11.8). Instead of $(2{,}111 - 520.1(3.153 + V/C))$ under the radical, you will get $(2{,}087 - 520.02(3.153 + V/C))$. This occurs because the authors' calculations used 0.1767 instead of 0.1757 for the coefficient of Speed.

14 Recall from the previous section that $VOT(T)$ is the average variable cost of travel.

15 Annualized land costs have a formulation similar to annualized capital costs in equation (11.12a). However, since land is assumed to last forever, its time horizon is infinity, which implies that the term in brackets goes to 1.

16 Based upon 66 stretches of road in the Bay Area in 1972, the expected capacity-related maintenance costs were obtained from the following regression: $MCLM = \alpha + \beta V/L + \varepsilon$, where $MCLM$ is maintenance costs per lane–mile, V/L is average annual traffic per lane, and ε is the error term. The estimated results were $MCLM = \$2{,}917 + \$0.00045V/L$, where the estimated coefficients of both variables were highly significant. Assume that V/L is zero; that is, there is no traffic on the road. Then $MCLM$ will be \$2,917, which is the expected capacity-related (that is, nontraffic-related) maintenance costs.

17 In general, if $y = f(x)$ is homogeneous of degree one, then it can be shown that $y = Ax$, where A is a constant.

18 The derivation of this result is beyond the scope of our analysis. For details, see Keeler and Small (1977).

19 In chapter 13, we explicitly look at pollution costs generated from motor vehicle travel.

20 The 15 cent value was based upon a simulation study for the Los Angeles area by Harvey, and reported in Cameron (1991). Harvey concluded that a 15 cent average peak period congestion toll would generate service level improvements to allow 35–40 mph movements on the most congested roads.

21 As an example, Small calculates that, based upon an optimum congestion charge of 18.2 cents per vehicle–mile for expressways and principal arterials in Atlanta, congestion revenues in 1989 would

be $760 million, which is $402 million *more* than the direct highway subsidy from local property taxes and general revenues.

22 Estimated collection costs are in the range of 4.0–12.0 cents per trip. Small used 6.6 cents per trip in his analysis.

23 Out of a total 97 billion VMT in fiscal year 1990–1, 28 billion occurred during congested periods. The congestion charge was estimated to reduce total VMT by 5%, or 4.8 billion VMT, by tolling off some travelers and modal shifts. An additional 2.4 billion reduction is expected from shifting travel times to uncongested periods. This produces an overall reduction of 7.2 billion VMT, or 26% of peak-period VMT.

24 Giuliano and Small (1991) identified 32 employment centers in the Los Angeles area. Dividing $322 by 32 gives $11.8 million per center.

25 Based upon 4.9 million households in the area, Small assumed that each auto-using household received benefits from highway improvements equal to the household's average expenditure ($315 in table 11.12 divided by 4.9) and transit benefits equal to half the average expenditure ((0.5) $312 in table 11.12 divided by 4.9). Transit users are assumed to receive no benefits from highway improvements, but the average benefit from transit improvements ($312 divided by 4.9). Last, the benefit from business center improvements equal the average expenditure per household on such improvements ($322 from table 11.12 divided by 4.9).

26 In their analysis, Morrison and Winston assumed that the opportunity cost of land was zero, which reduces the marginal cost of additional investment and may lead to more expansion than would otherwise be justified.

27 Although not reported in the table, the separate figures for carriers' operating cost and passenger delay costs are positive for all aviation groups.

REFERENCES AND RELATED READINGS

General references

Haight, F. 1963: *Mathematical Theories of Traffic Flow.* New York: Academic Press.

Train, K. 1991: *Optimal Regulation: The Economic Theory of Natural Monopoly.* Cambridge, Mass.: The MIT Press.

General references on congestion and investment

Boyer, K. D. 1998: *Principles of Transportation Economics.* Reading, Mass.: Addison-Wesley.

Button, K. J. 1993: *Transport Economics*, 2nd edn. Brookfield, Vermont: Edward Elgar.

Button, K. J. and Pearman, A. D. 1985: *Applied Transport Economics.* New York: Gordon and Breach.

Downs, A. 1992: *Stuck in Traffic.* Washington, DC: The Brookings Institution/The Lincoln Institute of Land Policy.

Hau, T. D. 1992: Economic fundamentals of road pricing. The World Bank, December.

Johansson, B. and Lars-Goran, M. 1995: *Road Pricing: Theory, Empirical Assessment and Policy.* Boston: Kluwer Academic.

Mohring, H. 1976: *Transportation Economics.* Cambridge, Mass.: Ballinger.

Mohring, H. 1985: Profit maximization, cost minimization, and pricing for congestion-prone facilities. *Logistics and Transportation Review*, 21, 27–36.

Polak, J. and Heertje, A. (eds.) 1993: *European Transport Economics.* Oxford: Blackwell.

Transportation Research Board 1994a: *Curbing Gridlock: Peak-Period Fees to Relieve Traffic Congestion*, vol. 1. National Research Council, Committee on Study for Urban Transportation Congestion Pricing.

Transportation Research Board 1994b: *Curbing Gridlock: Peak-Period Fees to Relieve Traffic Congestion*, vol. 2. National Research Council, Committee on Study for Urban Transportation Congestion Pricing.

Vickrey, W. S. 1969: Congestion theory and transport investment. *American Economic Review*, LXIX, 251–60.

Winston, C. 1985: Conceptual developments in the economics of transportation: an interpretive survey. *Journal of Economic Literature*, XXIII, 57–94.

Specific references on congestion pricing by mode

Air

Bishop, M. and Thompson, D. 1992: Peak-load pricing in aviation. *Journal of Transport Economics and Policy*, XXVI, 71–82.

Morrison, S. A. and Winston, C. 1989: Enhancing the performance of the deregulated air transportation system. In M. N. Bailey and C. Winston (eds.), *Brookings Papers on Economic Activity: Microeconomics 1989*. Washington DC: The Brookings Institution, pp. 61–112.

Morrison, S. A. and Winston, C. 1995: *The Evolution of the Airline Industry*. Washington DC: The Brookings Institution.

Nelson, J. P. 1980: Airports and property values. *Journal of Transport Economics and Policy*, XIV, 37–52.

Walters, A. A. 1973: Investment in airports and the economist's role. John F. Kennedy International Airport: an example and some comparisons. In J. N. Wolfe (ed.), *Cost Benefits and Cost Effectiveness: Studies and Analysis*. London: George Allen and Unwin, pp. 140–54.

Highways

Beesley, M. E. and Hensher, D. A. 1990: Private tollroads in urban areas. *Transportation*, 16, 329–41.

Cameron, M. 1991: Transportation efficiency: tackling Southern California's air pollution and congestion. Regional Institute of Southern California, Environmental Defense Fund, Oakland, California.

Coleman, R. R. 1961: A study of urban travel times in Pennsylvania cities. *Highway Research Board Bulletin*, 306, 39–63.

Elliot, W. 1986: Fumbling toward the edge of history: California's quest for a road-pricing experiment. *Transportation Research*, 20, 151–6.

Giuliano, G. and Small, K. A. 1991: Subcenters in the Los Angeles Region. *Regional Science and Urban Economics*, 21, 163–82.

Hanks, J. W., Jr. and Lomax, T. J. 1990: *1989 Roadway Congesting Estimates and Trends*. Report FHWA/TX-90/113–4. Texas Transportation Institute. Texas A&M University, College Station, Texas.

Hau, T. D. 1990: Electronic road pricing: developments in Hong Kong 1983–1989. *Journal of Transport Economics and Policy*, XXIV, 203–14.

Hau, T. D. 1992: Congestion charging mechanisms for roads: an evaluation of current practice. The World Bank, December.

Kain, J. F. 1994: Impacts of congestion pricing on transit and carpool demand and supply. In Transportation Research Board, National Research Council, *Curbing Gridlock: Peak-Period Fees to Relieve Traffic Congestion*. Special Report 242, pp. 502–53.

Keeler, T. E. and Small, K. A. 1977: Optimal peak-load pricing, investment, and service levels on urban expressways. *Journal of Political Economy*, 85, 1–25.

Lee, D. B. 1982: Efficient highway user charges. In *Final Report on the Federal Highway Cost Allocation Study*. US Department of Transportation, Transportation Systems Center, May, Appendix E.

Morrison, S. A. 1986: A survey of road pricing. *Transportation Research A*, 20, 87–97.

Nelson, J. P. 1982: Highway noise and property values. *Journal of Transport Economics and Policy*, XVI, 117–38.

Newbery, D. M. 1989: Cost recovery from optimally designed roads. *Economica*, 56, 165–85.

Newbery, D. M. 1990: Pricing and congestion. *Oxford Review of Economic Policy*, 6, 22–38.

Richardson, H. W. 1974: A note on the distributional effects of road pricing. *Journal of Transport Economics and Policy*, VIII, 82–5.

Small, K. A. 1992: Using the revenues from congestion pricing. *Transportation*, 19, 359–81.

Verhoef, E. 1994: External effects and social costs of road transport. *Transportation Research B*, 28, 173–287.

Walters, A. A. 1961: The theory and measurement of private and social cost of highway congestion. *Econometrica*, 29, 676–99.

Wilson, R. W. 1992: Estimating the travel and parking demand effects of employer-paid parking. *Regional Science and Urban Economics*, 22, 133–45.

Water

Bennathan, E. and Walters, A. A. 1979: *Port Pricing and Investment Policy for Developing Countries*. New York: Oxford University Press.

Glaister, S. 1976: Peak load Pricing and the Channel Tunnel. *Journal of Transport Economics and Policy*, X, 99–112.

12

Transportation and Land Use in Urban Areas

INTRODUCTION

This chapter examines the role that transportation plays in the spatial development of urban areas. In previous chapters, we developed the basic principles underlying a utility-maximizing individual's optimal consumption of divisible and discrete goods, respectively. In those chapters, we identified the equilibrium conditions for optimal consumption, and investigated the effect that changes in consumer preferences or in one's economic environment would have upon consumption behavior. Similarly, in chapter 5 we characterized a cost-minimizing firm's optimal use of inputs, derived a firm's cost function, and showed how firms combine information on their costs with output price to produce profit-maximizing levels of output.

In this chapter, however, our attention turns away from the question of how much to consume or produce and toward the question of where consumption or production occurs. And, specifically, we shall be concerned with land-use activities in urban areas; that is, spatial areas characterized by relatively high population densities. There are various reasons for examining land-use allocations in urban areas. First, according to the 1990 census, 63% of the nation's population resided in urbanized areas.[1] Since the majority of our nation's population lives and works in urban areas, understanding the role of transportation in residential and employment location decisions is important. Second, a characteristic of most urban areas is residential and employment decentralization. What factors have contributed to this trend and, specifically, what is the relationship between transportation and decentralized growth in urban areas? Third, many of the nation's most pressing transportation problems – traffic congestion, air and noise pollution, energy use, and infrastructure decay – are urban problems.

In order to examine these issues, we shall develop a monocentric theory of residential and employment location. As we shall see below, a monocentric framework assumes that the Central Business District (CBD) is the center of the urban area in which all employment activities occur. Households reside in the area surrounding the CBD. Although most large metropolitan areas are not monocentric but multicentric – that is, have a number of subcenters spread throughout the urban area – we shall see that a monocentric model provides important insights into the location activities of households and firms, and identifies the effect that changes in the economic environment have upon these decisions.

FIRM LOCATION DECISIONS

In order to simplify the analysis, let's assume that the only business activity in the urban area is the production of commodity q. Also assume that each firm faces the following production and market environments:

1 Using constant returns to scale technology, each firm annually produces q tons of output with land (L) and nonland (Z) inputs.
2 Each firm in the city is a price-taker in the output market for q and all input markets. In addition, there is no spatial variation in the output price or in the prices of the nonland inputs.
3 The market for q is perfectly competitive so that, in long-run equilibrium, zero economic profits are made.
4 Regardless of where it locates in the city, each firm transports its output of q to a regional transportation node located in the center of the Central Business District (CBD) for shipment to areas outside the city. The firm incurs an annual per ton–mile cost of t_q to transport q to the CBD.

In this city, a typical firm's profit function is

$$\pi = pq - p_z Z(u) - R(u)L(u) - t_q uq$$

$$= q(p - t_q u) - p_z Z(u) - R(u)L(u) \qquad (12.1a)$$

$$= p_{\text{net}}(u)q - (p_z Z(u) + R(u)L(u)) \qquad (12.1b)$$

where p is the per unit price of q; p_{net} is the price received by the firm net of transportation costs; p_z is the per unit price of nonland inputs; $Z(u)$ is the quantity of nonland inputs employed, which varies by distance u from the export node; $R(u)$ is the annual rent per acre of land, which depends upon distance from the export node; and $L(u)$ is the acreage for the production facility, which also depends upon distance from the export node. $t_q uq$ is the annual cost of transporting q tons of output u miles from the plant's location to the CBD. Equation (12.1a) identifies firm profits as the difference between total revenues and expenditures upon nonland inputs, land, and shipping to the central export node. Equivalently, equation (12.1b) gives firm profits as the difference between net (of transportation costs) revenues and expenditures upon nonland and land inputs.

For any given distance from the export node, profit-maximizing firms will optimally use land and nonland inputs. Recall from chapter 5 (equation (5.13)) that a firm's optimal use of inputs requires that the marginal rate of technical substitution equals the ratio of input prices. Adapting this criterion to the present case, and noting that the marginal rate of technical substitution equals the ratio of marginal products, we have the following profit-maximizing condition that a firm must satisfy *at all locations*:

$$MRTS_{L(u),Z(u)} = \frac{MP_{L(u)}}{MP_{Z(u)}} = \frac{R(u)}{p_z}$$

$$\Rightarrow \quad \frac{MP_{L(u)}}{R(u)} = \frac{MP_{Z(u)}}{p_z} \qquad (12.2)$$

where the second expression characterizes optimal input use by equating the marginal product per dollar spent on land to the marginal product per dollar expenditure on nonland inputs. Also, since the market for q is competitive and firms are price-takers, we know that firms produce up to the point at which price equals marginal cost of production. But the marginal cost of production for firms in equilibrium can be expressed as

$$MC_q = \frac{R(u)}{MP_{L(u)}} = \frac{p_z}{MP_{Z(u)}}$$

so that marginal cost pricing implies

$$p_{\text{net}} = p - t_q u = \frac{R(u)}{MP_{L(u)}} = \frac{p_z}{MP_{Z(u)}}$$

$$\Rightarrow \begin{cases} p_{\text{net}} MP_{L(u)} = R(u) \\ p_{\text{net}} MP_{Z(u)} = p_z \end{cases} \tag{12.3}$$

where $p_{\text{net}} MP_i$ ($i = L(u)$, $Z(u)$) is input i's value of the marginal product, which represents the net revenues to the firm from employing one more unit of input i at location u. In equilibrium, profit-maximizing firms use each input up to the point at which the additional revenues generated by employing one more unit just equal the additional cost of the input.

If a firm moves closer to the center or a little further from the center, a further implication from profit-maximizing behavior is that the firm will optimally adjust its land and nonland inputs in order to insure that equations (12.2) and (12.3) are satisfied.

FIRM BID-RENT CURVES

Although the rental price of land and the consumption of land and nonland inputs depend upon distance from the downtown node, profits do not depend upon distance. The reason for this is our assumption that output markets are perfectly competitive, in which case all firms make normal accounting profits; that is, zero economic profits. Assuming competitive output markets is important, because it enables us to derive the annual rent per acre of land at distance u from the central node by simply setting $\pi = 0$ in equation (12.1) and solving for $R(u)$:

$$R(u) = \frac{(p - t_q u)q - nN(u)}{L(u)} \tag{12.4}$$

Equation (12.4) is referred to as a firm's *bid-rent* function per acre of land. Multiplying $R(u)$ by $L(u)$ gives the maximum amount that a firm is willing to pay for $L(u)$ acres u miles from the downtown node. The assumption of zero economic profits implies that all revenues over nonland costs are used to bid for land, so that $R(u)$ represents the maximum per acre rental price that a firm is willing to pay for land u miles from the city center.

It is important to note the role that distance from the central point plays in equation (12.4). Firms that locate further from downtown have higher transport costs to the downtown node. All else constant, this raises the firm's nonland input expenditures and reduces its "pre-rent"

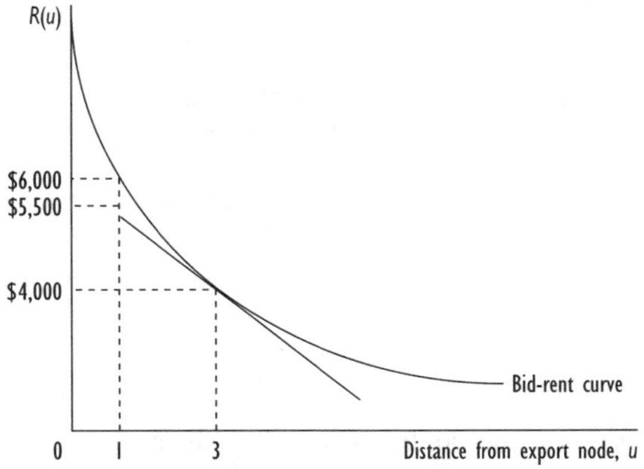

Figure 12.1 The firm bid-rent curve.

profits; that is, the firm's profits *excluding* land costs. Because of the higher shipment costs and lower pre-rent profits, the firm's bid rent per acre will be less. In effect, a firm is indifferent to where it locates its manufacturing facility. Accessibility is important to firms only because of lower shipment costs. However, since this is true for all firms, locations nearer the center will be in high demand, which raises the per acre price of land. Similarly, sites further from the center are less desirable because of higher shipment costs. This lowers the demand for these sites and correspondingly the sites' per acre rental prices. In equilibrium, firms locate at various distances from the downtown node, and the per-acre price of land appropriately adjusts to firms' location demands, so that no firm is making an economic profit.

How does a firm's bid rent vary with distance from downtown? Assuming that a firm employs its land and nonland inputs optimally to satisfy profit-maximizing behavior, a firm's equilibrium location condition can be shown to equal[2]

$$-L(u)\frac{\Delta R(u)}{\Delta u} = qt_q \tag{12.5}$$

$$\Rightarrow \frac{\Delta R(u)}{\Delta u} = -\frac{qt_q}{L(u)} \tag{12.5$'$}$$

The left-hand side of equation (12.5) is the savings in land costs as a firm moves further from downtown. The right-hand side represents the additional costs of shipping q when the firm locates at greater distances from downtown. Thus, a profit-maximizing firm is in *location equilibrium* when the marginal savings on land expenditures from an increase in distance just equals the marginal cost of shipping its output the additional distance.

Figure 12.1 a bid-rent curve for a typical firm in the city. There are two features of the bid-rent curve that are worth noting. First, the curve is downward-sloping. At a distance of 1 mile from the city center, land rents for $6,000 per acre. Moving out to 3 miles from the center reduces land rents to $4,000. As expressed in equation (12.5), this reflects the trade-off that a firm faces between transportation costs and land rents. In the monocentric city, the only way to lower transportation costs is to incur higher land costs. Conversely, the only opportunity for a firm to lower its land costs is by moving further from the center and incurring higher transportation costs.

The second feature of a firm's bid-rent curve is that the curve is convex to the origin. As a firm moves closer to the CBD, land prices not only increase but they increase disproportionately. To see why this is so, assume that, regardless of where a firm locates in the city, it builds an identical production facility and uses the same amounts of land and nonland inputs to produce q.[3] In this case, $L(u)$ in equation (12.5′) is held fixed at $\bar{L}$ and the firm's equilibrium condition becomes

$$\frac{\Delta R(u)}{\Delta u} = -\frac{qt_q}{\bar{L}} \tag{12.6}$$

Since the production of q is fixed and, by assumption, the same amount of land is employed at all locations, we see in equation (12.6) that the effect of an increase in distance from the export node is to increase land rent by a constant amount. If a firm decides to move 1 mile closer to the export node, its shipping costs per acre decrease by $qt_q/\bar{L}$. In order to maintain zero economic profits, this means that land rent per acre must increase by just this amount. Assuming that the amount of land (and therefore nonland) inputs used for production do not change with location, land rent is simply a linear function of distance from the export node. In reality, however, whenever a firm experiences an increase in the price of an input, it alters its production process by decreasing its use of the more expensive input and increasing its use of the relatively cheaper input. As we saw in chapter 5, firms substitute one input for another when relative input prices change. Thus, in figure 12.1, if a firm moves from 3 miles to 1 mile from the export node *but does not alter its consumption of land and nonland inputs*, land rents would increase from \$4,000 to \$5,500, an increase of \$750 per mile. However, as it moves closer to the center, the firm reacts to the higher land prices by substituting away from land and toward nonland inputs in production. From equation (12.5′), this means that the denominator is smaller the closer a firm moves to the center, $L(3) > L(1)$. All else constant, a smaller denominator in equation (12.5′) increases per-acre land rents. For anyone who has traveled through urban areas, this is an intuitive result. As one nears a city's downtown area, the height of buildings rises and the tallest buildings are generally in the center of downtown. This is nothing more than a three-dimensional illustration of firms' substitution of land for other inputs, specifically capital. As a firm locates nearer the center, the per-acre land rent rises and firms respond to this by substituting capital, a relatively cheaper input, for land. And the increased capital literally shows up as tall buildings. Similarly, the further a firm locates from the center, the cheaper are land rents. In order to exploit the relatively cheap land prices far from the center, the firm substitutes land for capital in its production process. Hence, in the outer regions of an urban area, we typically see manufacturing plants that are sprawling one-story buildings.

Finally, what determines the steepness of a firm's bid-rent curve? The steepness of the curve will depend upon three factors:

- *Per-mile transportation costs.* The larger the savings that a firm experiences when moving closer to the CBD, the more land rent a firm is able to offer and still earn zero economic profits. Thus, by affecting per-mile transport costs, improvements in transportation technology affect bid rents.

- *The amount of q that the city produces.* All else constant, the more q a firm produces and sells, the higher are its pre-rent profits and the steeper is the bid-rent curve. As a general principle, then, a city's economic growth can be expected to steepen its bid-rent curve.
- *The substitutability of inputs.* With no input substitutability, a firm's bid rent is a linear function of distance. But the more that a firm can substitute nonland inputs for land as it moves closer to the center, the greater will be the firm's reduction in production costs and, accordingly, the greater will be its pre-rent profits. These increased pre-rent profits will be used to bid for land nearer the CBD, thereby raising land rents even more. In equilibrium, the ratio of nonland to land inputs at each distance u will be consistent with a bid-rent curve $R(u)$ that just enables the firm to earn zero economic profits.

As a final point, the discussion so far has assumed that the city only produces one good, q. In reality, a city is made up of commercial firms, light manufacturing firms, heavy manufacturing enterprises, the service sector, and so forth. For each of these business ventures, there will be a separate bid-rent curve characterized by equation (12.4) and whose slope is given by equation (12.5′). And the steepness of each of these bid-rent curves will depend upon the per-mile transportation cost, firm output, and input substitutability.

HOUSEHOLD LOCATION DECISIONS

Having characterized firm location decisions, we can next identify the conditions that must be satisfied for equilibrium in the housing sector. To focus our attention on the primary determinants of residential location decisions, we make the following simplifying assumptions:

1 All households have identical incomes and identical preferences for housing H and all other goods x.
2 There are no location preferences.
3 All employment occurs in the CBD and each household has one full-time worker commuting to the CBD.
4 Cross-town travel and nonwork-related trips are negligible.
5 Geographic amenities are uniformly distributed throughout the urban area, as are tax rates and public services.
6 The opportunity cost of time is zero.

Similar to the standard theory of consumer behavior, a household's objective is to maximize its economic welfare subject to a budget constraint. An important implication of assumptions 1 and 2, however, is that a household's utility depends only upon two commodities, housing $H(u)$ and all other goods $x(u)$, both of which depend upon distance from the CBD. Note that a household's location – that is, distance from the CBD – has *no direct effect* upon its economic welfare.[4] The only role that distance plays in this simplified framework is making the CBD more or less accessible to the household for its daily work-trip commute. And the CBD's accessibility has obvious implications for the household's cost of commuting.

Since residential location, as opposed to housing consumption, has no direct effect upon household utility, we can characterize a household's equilibrium location condition by considering the impact that a 1 mile move further from the CBD would have upon its housing and

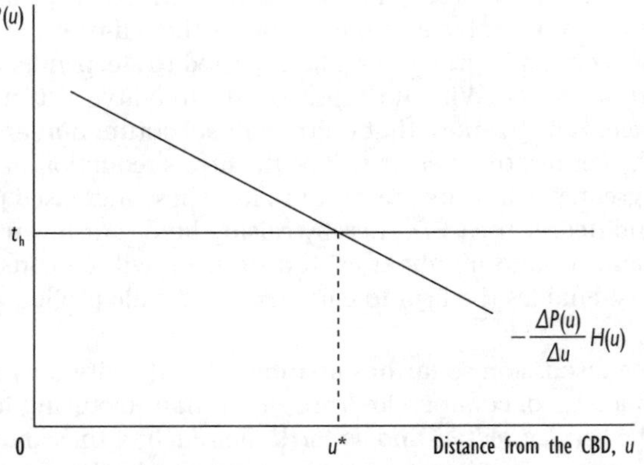

Figure 12.2 Household equilibrium location.

commuting costs. If t_h is the annual cost of traveling 1 mile, then the household's commuting costs will increase by t_h. At the same time, since the household has no location preference, the per unit price of housing must be lower at more distant locations in order to compensate for the increased commuting costs. Let $\Delta P(u)/\Delta u$ be the change in the price of housing due to a unit increase in distance from the CBD. Then the decrease in housing costs from moving a mile further from the CBD is $[\Delta P(u)/\Delta u]H(u)$. If the increase in transportation costs is less than the decrease in housing costs, the household is better off and will make the move. Alternatively, if the increase in commutation costs exceeds the fall in housing expenditures, the household is worse off and will not make the move. In other words, the household is in location equilibrium at that distance from the CBD at which marginal transportation costs equal marginal housing expenditures; that is, where

$$t_h = -\frac{\Delta P(u)}{\Delta u}H(u) \tag{12.7}$$

Since per unit housing prices fall with distance from the CBD, $\Delta P(u)/\Delta u < 0$ and the right-hand side represents savings on housing expenditures. Figure 12.2 depicts a household's location equilibrium. In the figure, at distances less than u^*, savings on housing expenditures from a move further out exceed marginal transportation costs, so that moving out is in the household's economic interest. Similarly, at distances greater than u^*, household welfare falls, since marginal transportation costs exceed savings on housing expenditures. At u^*, the household is in equilibrium, since the marginal benefit from a small move outward just equals the marginal cost of making the move. Why is it that some household cannot improve its economic welfare over other households by moving closer to the CBD? The answer is that all households are in competition for the scarce land. Since all households recognize the cost advantage of a location that is more accessible to the CBD, the demand for housing nearer the CBD is bid up while the demand for housing further away is bid down. Demands at various locations will continue to fluctuate until an equilibrium housing price function develops such

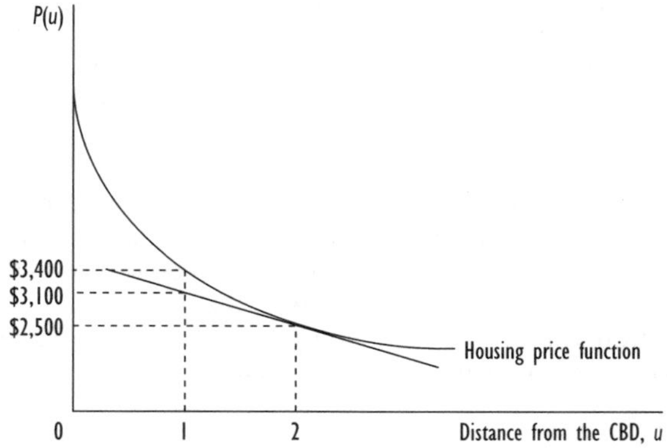

Figure 12.3 The household bid-rent curve.

that all households are in equilibrium and no household has an economic incentive to change its location.

To obtain additional insight into the residential equilibrium condition, divide both sides of equation (12.7) by $H(u)$:

$$\frac{\Delta P(u)}{\Delta u} = -\frac{t_{\mathrm{h}}}{H(u)} < 0 \tag{12.8}$$

$\Delta P(u)/\Delta u$ gives the slope of the housing price function. Since marginal transportation costs and housing consumption are both positive, from the right-hand side of equation (12.8), we obtain the expected result that the slope of the housing price function is negative. A move further from the CBD decreases the per-unit price of housing. In addition, the housing price function is steeper the larger are per-mile transportation costs and the smaller is the consumption of housing. Figure 12.3 plots a housing price function for this city, which is seen to be downward-sloping and convex to the origin. The shape of housing price function in the residential sector occurs for precisely the same reason that a firm's bid-rent curve is convex and downward-sloping. The negative slope reflects the trade-off between accessibility costs and housing expenditures at distances further from the CBD. To examine why the equilibrium housing price is convex to the origin, consider again the household's equilibrium condition

$$\frac{\Delta P(u)}{\Delta u} = -\frac{t_{\mathrm{h}}}{\overline{H}} \tag{12.9}$$

where we have now assumed that the household consumes the same amount of housing $\overline{H}$ at all locations. Since the right-hand side of equation (12.9) does not depend upon distance u, the slope of the housing price function is constant at all locations. In other words, if households consume the same amount of housing at all locations, the per-unit price of housing rises by the same amount for each 1 mile decrease in distance. This is depicted in figure 12.3 by the straight line. A household residing 2 miles from the CBD is paying a per-unit price of housing equal to \$2,500. At a distance of 1 mile, the per-unit price of housing increases to \$3,100, a \$600 dollar per mile change in the per-unit price.

But do households consume the same amount of housing at all distances? No. As the per-unit price of housing rises with accessibility to the CBD, the law of demand tells us that households reduce the quantity of housing demanded. That is, $H(u)$ is inversely related to distance from the CBD. At locations nearer the CBD, households substitute the good whose price has not changed, nonhousing, for the good whose price has increased, housing, in their consumption bundles. $H(u)$ falls which, from equation (12.9), means that the per-unit price of housing rises more than linearly. In figure 12.3, when households respond to higher housing prices by consuming less housing and more of everything else, the per-unit price of housing rises more than \$600. At 1 mile from the CBD, the per-unit price of housing is \$3,400, \$300 more than the price rise in the constant housing consumption case.

Residential Bid-Rent Curves

What is the relationship between housing price functions in the residential sector and housing producers' underlying bid rent for land? To analyze this, consider firms in the city whose output is housing. Since the output of these firms is "on-site," housing producers have no transportation costs and their profit function is

$$\pi = P(u)q_{\text{h}} - p_z Z(u) - R(u)L(u) \tag{12.10}$$

where $P(u)$ is the price of housing at distance u from the CBD and q_{h} is the quantity of housing produced. Assuming that housing producers maximize profits at all locations, the slope of their bid-rent function can be expressed as[5]

$$\frac{\Delta R(u)}{\Delta u} = -\frac{\Delta P(u)}{\Delta u}\frac{q_{\text{h}}}{L(u)} \tag{12.11}$$

which is seen to depend upon the slope of the housing price function and the amount of land used in the production of housing. The steeper the housing price function, the steeper is the land rent function. And the more that a housing producer can substitute nonland inputs for land, the steeper will be the residential bid-rent curve.[6] Notice, however, that if the housing producer could not substitute nonland for land inputs when the price of land increased – that is, $L(u)$ was held fixed at $\bar{L}$ – the residential bid-rent function would still be convex to the origin as long as households substituted nonhousing for housing in their consumption activities as the price of housing rose. This result directly reflects the fact that the residential bid rents for land depend upon the housing price function. If the housing price function is convex to the origin, as it is when consumers substitute between housing and nonhousing consumption when relative prices change, then the land-rent function will be convex to the origin, even though housing producers may not substitute between land and nonland inputs when the relative price of inputs change. The fact that both housing consumers and housing producers, in reality, do alter the ratio of housing to nonhousing and land to nonland inputs with changes in relative prices simply makes the housing land-rent function more convex than otherwise.

LAND-USE ALLOCATION IN A MONOCENTRIC CITY

Having derived bid-rent functions for the firm and residential sectors, we can now analyze what determines land-use allocation in a monocentric city. For this, we need one additional assumption, that land will be allocated to the highest bidder. As long as land goes to the highest bidder, we can identify land uses by simply comparing bid rents from the residential and business sectors at various distances from the CBD. Land will be allocated from city center outward according to who values center city accessibility the most. And the valuation of accessibility is in large part dependent upon per mile transportation costs. The sector with the higher per mile transportation costs will have the steepest bid-rent curves, and will successfully bid for land close to the city center.[7] Conversely, the sector with the lower transportation cost will have a flatter bid-rent curve and successfully bid for land that is further from the city center. We see this in figure 12.4, which depicts the bid-rent functions for high transport cost firms and low transport cost households. From the center of the city to a distance of $\bar{u}$, the bid-rent curve for the business sector is higher than that of the residential sector. Given that land goes to the highest bidder, the business sector occupies all land surrounding the city within a distance of $\bar{u}$ from the center. The business and residential bid-rent curves intersect at $\bar{u}$, so that for all distances greater than $\bar{u}$ the residential bid-rent curve is higher than the business sector bid-rent curve. All land surrounding the city at a distance greater than $\bar{u}$ will be allocated to the housing sector. Where does the city end? We also see in the graph a horizontal line that represents an amount of rent equal to r_a. This is the rent per acre that agricultural land commands and represents the opportunity cost of urban land. In figure 12.4, u_b is the boundary of the city, since at distances greater than u_b land rent for farming exceeds bid rents from both the business and housing sectors.

If in figure 12.4 we connect that portion of the firm's bid rent that lies above the housing sector's bid rent, segment *AB*, with that portion of the housing sector's bid rent that lies above the firm's bid-rent curve, segment *BC*, we obtain the bold "scalloped" line, *ABC*. This line represents the city's equilibrium land-rent curve. If land is allocated according to bid-rent

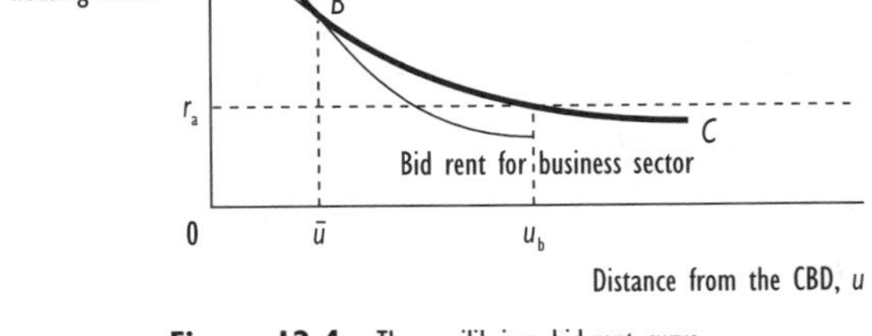

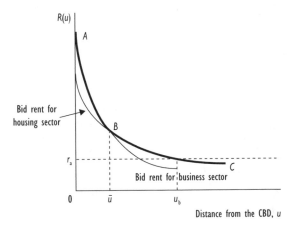

Figure 12.4 The equilibrium bid-rent curve.

curve *ABC*, then no household or firm has an incentive to alter its location. All decision-makers are in location equilibrium. Each firm in the city makes zero economic profits (that is, normal accounting profits) and each household receives the same level of economic welfare.

POPULATION AND EMPLOYMENT DENSITY IN A MONOCENTRIC CITY

How does population density, defined as the number of persons per square mile, change in a monocentric framework as distance from the CBD increases? Casual observation suggests that population densities decrease with distance from the city center, and this observation is consistent with the general model developed above. We have already seen that residential bid rents decrease with distance from the CBD in order to compensate households for the higher commuting costs. But consumers respond to the lower housing prices by increasing the consumption of housing, and housing producers accommodate these increased demands by building houses on larger lots. All else constant, then, population density falls with distance from the CBD because fewer households reside on a given acre of land. Alternatively, near the downtown area, housing is capital-intensive as housing producers substitute capital for the relatively more expensive land. As a result, we observe multi-story apartments and condominiums. If a typical condominium is constructed on an acre of land, accommodates 10 families, and the average family size is three persons, the population density is 30 persons per acre or 19,200 persons per square mile.[8] If, on the other hand, two households of average size reside on an acre of land 4 miles from downtown, the population density falls to 3,840 per square mile (6 persons per acre).

Similarly, we have seen that firm bid rents increase as accessibility to the CBD rises. The rise in bid rents causes firms to substitute nonland inputs for land inputs in the production process as distance to the CBD decreases. But this implies that the employment density – that is, the number of employees per square mile – decreases with distance from the CBD.

CASE STUDY – POPULATION AND EMPLOYMENT DENSITIES IN THE BOSTON AREA

In general, researchers use a negative exponential function to empirically model density functions:

$$\text{Density} = D_0 e^{\beta(\text{Distance})}$$

where Distance is distance from the CBD, D_0 is the density at the center of the city, and β is a parameter to be estimated. Taking logarithms and adding an error term ε, we obtain

$$\begin{aligned}\ln(\text{Density}) &= \ln(D_0) + \beta(\text{Distance}) + \varepsilon \\ &= \alpha + \beta(\text{Distance}) + \varepsilon \end{aligned} \quad (12.12)$$

which is a semi-log regression model, and where it is seen that β gives the percentage change in density from a 1 mile increase in distance from the CBD. Since D_0 represents density at the CBD, we expect D_0 to be positive. In addition, we have argued above that consumer (firm) substitution of land for nonland consumption (inputs) at distances further from the CBD will cause population (employment) densities to fall with distance from the CBD. Thus, for both the population and employment density function, we expect $\beta < 0$.

Based upon 146 towns and communities in the greater Boston area, DiPisquale and Wheaton

Table 12.1 Population and employment density functions

(a) Dependent variable – ln (Population Density)

Variable	1970 Coefficient (*t*-statistic)	1990 Coefficient (*t*-statistic)
Distance	−0.11 (−14.1)	−0.09 (−12.7)
Constant	9.03 (11.1)	8.80 (11.7)
R^2	0.58	0.53

(b) Dependent variable – ln (Employment Density)

Variable	1967 Coefficient (*t*-statistic)	1990 Coefficient (*t*-statistic)
Distance	−0.126 (−11.3)	−0.10 (−11.1)
Constant	7.75 (6.6)	8.05 (8.1)
R^2	0.47	0.46

Source: Adapted from DiPasquale and Wheaton (1996), table 4.1, p. 63; pp. 93–4

(1996) used the empirical model in equation (12.12) to estimate population and employment density functions. Table 12.1 reports their estimation results. Consistent with expectations, we see in table 12.1(a) that the constant term is positive and the coefficient of Distance is negative. From the *t*-statistics, we can reject the null hypothesis that the associated coefficient is zero. Further, despite the fact that the Boston area (similar to all modern metropolitan areas) is not strictly monocentric, we see from the R^2 statistics that distance from downtown Boston explains 58% of the variation in population density in 1970 and 53% in 1990.

Because of the large number of towns with small population densities in the Boston area, DiPasquale and Wheaton found that the model does a good job of predicting population densities at distances of eight or more miles from downtown Boston, but underpredicts densities at closer distances. For example, consider downtown Boston. From the empirical model for 1990, the constant term is 8.80. This implies that population density in downtown Boston is predicted to be $e^{8.8} = 6{,}634$ persons per square mile, which underpredicts the actual density (11,860 persons per square mile) by 79%.

How does population density decrease with distance from the downtown? In 1990, the coefficient for distance was −0.09, which implies that for each mile increase from downtown Boston, population density decreases by 9%. Thus, at 10 miles from downtown Boston, the population density is predicted to be $(6{,}634)e^{-0.09(10)} = 2{,}697$ persons per square mile. At 11 miles from downtown, the population density is $(6{,}634)e^{-0.09(11)} = 2{,}465$, an 8.6% decrease.

We also see in table 12.1(a) that during the 20-year period between 1970 and 1990, there has been greater suburbanization of population in the Boston area. The empirical results for 1970 are qualitatively similar to those for 1990, but the constant term is larger and the coefficient for Distance is smaller. This tells us that population density in downtown Boston was greater in 1970 and decreased faster, at 11%, for each mile increase from the central city. And, within a monocentric framework, this implies a redistribution of population away from the central area and toward the outlying or suburban regions between 1970 and 1990.

Turning to the employment density, the results in table 12.1(b) are qualitatively similar to the behavior of population densities. The constant terms and slope coefficients have their expected signs and are statistically significant. And, overall, the models explain about 46% of the variation in employment densities. As with population density, DiPasquale and Wheaton found that the model underpredicts employment density at distances closer to downtown Boston, but yields good predictions at further distances (5 miles or more in this case).[9] We also see in table 12.1(b) that employment density in 1990 falls by 10% for each mile increase in distance from the downtown area. Analogous to a suburbanizing population, the density function for employment has become flatter over time. The estimated coefficient of Distance in 1967 indicates that employment density fell by 12.6% for each mile increase from the downtown area, in comparison with a slower 10% decrease in 1990.

Income differences and urban location

When analyzing land rents for the residential sector, we assumed that all households had identical incomes. What is the effect upon residential bid rents and land allocation if households have different incomes? Assume that there are two types of workers in the city, high-income earners and low-income earners. In equilibrium, each household's location satisfies the condition

$$t_h = -\frac{\Delta P(u)}{\Delta u} H(u)$$

where marginal transportation costs equal marginal savings on housing expenditures. But will high-income households be interspersed among the low-income households, or will high-income households be spatially segregated from low-income households? To see that the two household types will be segregated, consider the location equilibrium condition for a low-income household:

$$t_h = -\frac{\Delta P(u)}{\Delta u} H_{low}(u) \qquad (12.13)$$

where $H_{low}(u)$ is the consumption of housing for the low-income household. Now suppose that the low-income earner becomes a high-income earner. Will equation (12.13) continue to describe this household's equilibrium? No. The reason is that housing is a normal good. An increase in income increases the demand for housing so that $H(u)$ for a high-income household will be greater than $H(u)$ for a low-income household. Thus, the new equilibrium condition for the high-income household is

$$t_h = -\frac{\Delta P(u)}{\Delta u} H_{High}(u) \qquad (12.14)$$

But since marginal transportation cost is constant, this implies that the equilibrium location for the high-income household is further from the CBD than for the low-income household. All else constant, in the monocentric model, low-income households occupy land closer to the city center and high-income households occupy land further away. Figure 12.5 depicts the location equilibria for the two household types. The higher consumption of housing for higher-income households shifts the marginal housing savings curve rightward, which implies an equilibrium distance, u_{High}, that is to the right of the low household income equilibrium location, u_{Low}.

Dividing equations (12.12) and (12.13), respectively, by $H_{Low}(u)$ and $H_{High}(u)$ gives the slope of the housing price curves for low- and high-income households. As we would expect, at distances nearer to the CBD the slope of the housing price (and land rent) curve for high-income households is less (in absolute value) than that

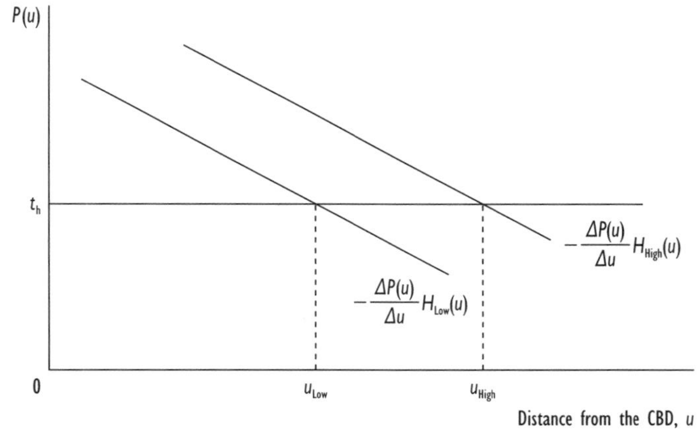

Figure 12.5 Equilibrium location when income affects housing consumption only.

for the low-income household because the consumption of housing is greater. As long as land is allocated to the highest bidder, this implies that lower- (higher-) income households will outbid higher- (lower-) income households for land close to (further from) the CBD.

The effect of time costs on land use

From our demand studies of transportation mode choice in the journey to work, we know that individual commuters value the time spent traveling to work. But the monocentric model assumed that the only work-trip costs were out-of-pocket expenses. If we adopt the more realistic assumption that a commuter's work-trip cost includes both monetary and time costs, what we have previously called "generalized" costs, will this affect any of our previous results? The introduction of time costs will have two primary effects. First, adding time costs to the monetary costs of travel increases the per-mile cost of moving further from the CBD. This steepens the housing price and land bid-rent curves for the residential sector which, all else constant, reduces the size of the city. In general, any factor that raises the marginal cost of transportation steepens the bid-rent curve and reduces the size of the city.

A second effect of including time costs in the transportation cost function is that income increases now have an ambiguous effect on equilibrium location. The reason is that empirical studies generally find that a traveler's value of time is related to the wage rate. Recent studies, for example, have estimated the value of work-trip travel time to be approximately 50% of the gross wage rate (Small, 1992). Generalizing the results in the previous section, an increase in income will not only increase the demand for housing but also increase marginal transportation costs by raising the value of travel time. Because, *a priori*, we don't know whether income's effect on travel time is greater or less than its effect on the consumption of housing, we cannot predict its effect upon equilibrium location. Figure 12.6 illustrates the case in which an increase in income has offsetting effects upon marginal transportation costs and housing demand. Initially, the increase in income raises the demand for housing from $H_1(u)$ to $H_2(u)$. This shifts the marginal savings curve rightward, which implies an equilibrium distance from the CBD, *assuming no change in marginal transportation costs*. However, by raising the value of time, the

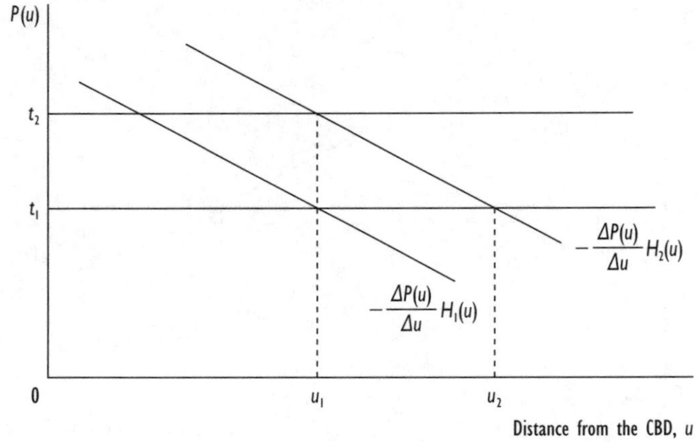

Figure 12.6 Equilibrium location when income affects housing and transportation costs.

rise in income also raises marginal transportation costs from t_1 to t_2. Since the two effects just offset one another, the net result is no change in equilibrium location. The household continues to live u_1 miles from the CBD.[10] To the extent that income increases have comparable effects upon marginal transportation costs and housing demands, one must look elsewhere for an explanation to the observed pattern of land use that allocates land further from the CBD to wealthier households.[11]

Other considerations

In addition to constant income and the absence of time costs, we also assumed that only one member of a household is a wage earner, that geographic amenities (and disamenities), public services, and tax rates were uniformly distributed throughout the urban area, and that the primary focus of trips was the CBD. Allowing for each of these factors will influence the shape of the housing price and land-rent functions in the residential sector. In general, to the extent that some feature of the urban landscape increases the value of accessibility to the CBD, the land-rent function steepens and households reside closer to the downtown area. For example, if a household has two wage earners making trips to downtown, then the time cost of travel is twice that of a household that has only one wage earner. The increased per-mile transportation cost increases the slope of the land-rent function, which implies that multiple wage earner families live closer to the CBD, all else held constant. Similarly, to the extent that the downtown area offers a variety of cultural activities that are not found in suburban locales, households with preferences for cultural offerings have a greater demand for housing closer to the CBD than households without such preferences. The model predicts, for example, that museum-minded households will reside closer to the CBD, all else constant.

If downtown areas have disamenities or suburban locales have desirable features, this lowers the demand for housing close to the CBD and increases the demand for housing at more distant locations. In many cities, for example, manufacturing and industrial activities in the CBD create severe pollution in downtown areas relative to more suburban sites. All else constant, this flattens the housing price function by increasing the demand for suburban relative to more centrally located housing. Similar predictions are forthcoming if, as is oftentimes the case, downtown areas have higher crime rates, higher property tax rates, and fewer recreational facilities than suburban locales. Alternatively, suburban sites with proximity to lakes or forested areas weaken the attraction of downtown accessibility and increase the relative demands for suburban sites.

Even if a relatively large portion of a household's annual travel, noncommuting trips will not significantly upset the predictions of the monocentric model and may reinforce the results. When noncommuting travel is uniformly distributed around a household's location, the primary focus of one's trips, and therefore location decision, continues to be the CBD. The reason is that the lower travel costs from moving closer to one nonemployment destination are offset by the higher travel costs to other nonemployment destinations. Although households locate so as to balance these noncommuting cost effects, the CBD remains the dominant force in a household's location decision. Moreover, if the noncommuting destination is the CBD itself, then accessibility to the CBD becomes more important and we get the expected result that the land-rent function steepens. All else held constant, households with CBD oriented noncommuting destinations live closer to the CBD.

CASE STUDY – TESTING THE EQUILIBRIUM LOCATION CONDITION

Within a monocentric model of urban location, assume the annual cost of traveling to the CBD is $TC(u,y)$, which depends upon distance u from the CBD as well as household income y. Holding all else constant, the general form of the equilibrium condition for residential location is

$$\frac{\Delta TC(u,y)}{\Delta u} = -H\frac{\Delta P(u)}{\Delta u}$$

where marginal transportation costs include time as well as monetary costs. An implication of this equilibrium condition is that equilibrium distance is inversely related to changes in marginal transportation costs. An increase (decrease) in the marginal cost of traveling to the CBD leads to an equilibrium distance that is closer to (further from) the CBD. Equivalently, since the equilibrium location condition must be satisfied after the increase (decrease) in marginal transportation cost, at the new equilibrium distance the slope of the rent function must be higher (lower). That is, the equilibrium location condition implies the comparative static result that increases (decreases) in marginal transportation costs lead to increases (decreases) in the slope of the rent function.

On the basis of data for six metropolitan areas (Atlanta, Detroit, Houston, Los Angeles, Minneapolis – St. Paul, and San Diego) from 1974 through 1979, Coulson and Engle (1987) test this equilibrium relationship between marginal transportation costs and the slope of the rent function. Suppose that equilibrium distance to the CBD increases from u_1 to u_2. We know that, holding all else constant, *including the consumption of housing*, the savings in housing expenditures equal the decrease in annual rent, $-\Delta R$, associated with a location that is further from the CBD. But this fall in annual rents between distances u_1 and u_2 is an annuity whose present value, given an annual interest rate of r and assuming that land lasts forever, is $PV = -\Delta R/r$. In other words, if V_1 is the value of a standard house at u_1 miles from the CBD and the equilibrium distance increases from u_1 to u_2, then the value of the same standard house at u_2 miles is $V_2 = V_1 - \Delta R/r$, so that the location-induced decrease in the value of the house is $-\Delta V = V_2 - V_1 = -\Delta R/r$.

Since both u_1 and u_2 are equilibrium distances, our location equilibrium condition tells us that $\Delta TC = -\Delta R$, which says that the increased transportation costs in moving from u_1 to u_2 equal the decrease in annual rents. But this implies that the change in the value of a standardized house between u_1 and u_2 equals the present value of the change in transportation costs between the two locations. In other words, $-\Delta V = \Delta TC/r$.

In Coulson and Engle's analysis, ΔTC is the increase in the annual cost of travel to the more distant location from the CBD. Because an increase in distance also implies an increase in travel time to the CBD, Coulson and Engle defined the increase in travel cost at the more distant location as

$$\begin{aligned}\Delta TC &= \text{value of time costs} + \text{gasoline costs} \\ &\quad + \text{nongasoline costs} \\ &= (VOT)N\Delta(\text{Time}) + (P_{\text{gas}}/MPG)N\Delta u \\ &\quad + NO_{\text{Cost}}\Delta u \qquad (12.15)\end{aligned}$$

where VOT is the value of travel time ($ per minute), N is the number of one-way trips to the CBD per year, P_{gas} is the price per gallon of gasoline ($ per gallon), MPG is automobile mileage (miles per gallon), O_{Cost} represents other monetary costs ($ per mile), $\Delta(\text{Time})$ is the change in travel time (minutes), and Δu, which equals $u_2 - u_1$, is the change in distance from the CBD (miles).[12] Using this definition of cost, the equilibrium location condition can be expressed as

$$\begin{aligned}-\Delta V &= \frac{(VOT)N\Delta(\text{Time}) + (P_{\text{gas}}/MPG)N\Delta u + NO_{\text{Cost}}\Delta u}{r} \\ &= \frac{N}{r}(VOT)\Delta(\text{Time}) + \frac{N}{r}(P_{\text{gas}}/MPG)\Delta u \\ &\quad + \frac{N}{r}O_{\text{Cost}}\Delta u) \\ &= \beta_1(VOT)\Delta(\text{Time}) + \beta_2(P_{\text{gas}}/MPG)\Delta u \\ &\quad + \beta_3 O_{\text{Cost}}\Delta u \\ &= \beta_1(\Delta\text{Time Costs}) + \beta_2(\Delta\text{Gasoline Costs}) \\ &\quad + \beta_3(\Delta\text{Nongasoline Costs}) \qquad (12.16)\end{aligned}$$

Equation (12.16) is the foundation for an empirical regression model of the equilibrium condition. The dependent variable, $-\Delta V$, is the change in the price of a standardized house at two different locations, and the three independent variables correspond to travel time costs, gasoline costs, and nongasoline monetary costs.

A couple of comments are in order. First, in equation (12.16), we assume that we have information on the value of time, $\Delta(\text{Time})$, P_{gas}, MPG, O_{Cost}, and Δu. On the other hand, information on the number of trips per year, N, and the discount rate, r, is assumed to be unavailable, and thus the ratio, N/r, is inferred from the parameter estimates. If, alternatively, we knew the number of one-day trips that each household made per year, we could define three new explanatory variables, z_i (i = 1, 2, 3), as $z_1 = N(\Delta\text{Time Costs})$, $z_2 = N(\Delta\text{Gasoline Costs})$, and $z_3 = N(\Delta\text{Nongasoline Costs})$, so that equation (12.16) becomes $-\Delta V = \gamma_1 z_1 + \gamma_2 z_2 + \gamma_3 z_3$, where $\gamma_i = 1/r$.

Second, the above formulation implies that the discount rate r is the same for each of the cost components. If a given increase in gasoline or nongasoline costs was perfectly capitalized in the value of housing, there would be no reason to expect the discount rate for gasoline costs to differ from the discount rate for nongasoline costs. However, the discount rate depends upon expectations. Suppose, for example, that an increase in gasoline costs is expected to increase marginal transport costs by 10%. In the absence of any expectations of future increases in the price of gasoline, the 10% increase in marginal transport costs will be capitalized in the value of housing. For a standardized house, expenditures will fall by 10%. However, if households expect further increases in the price of gasoline, then marginal transportation costs will increase by more than 10% and expenditures for a standardized house will fall by more than 10%.

In equation (12.16), β_i estimates the number of trips per year divided by the discount rate. For a given number of trips, if households have identical expectations with respect to future increases in the components of transportation costs, we would expect that $\beta_i = \beta_j$ ($i, j = 1, 2, 3$; $i \neq j$). Conversely, if households have different expectations on the future increases in monetary and time costs, there is no reason to expect the betas for each transportation cost component to be equal.

Coulson and Engle estimated the following regression model:

$$\begin{aligned}-\Delta V = \beta_0 &+ \beta_1(\Delta\text{Time Costs}) \\ &+ \beta_2(\Delta\text{Gasoline Costs}) \\ &+ \beta_3(\Delta\text{Nongasoline Costs}) \\ &+ \beta_4\text{Income} + \beta_5\text{Atlanta} + \beta_6\text{Detroit} \\ &+ \beta_7\text{Houston} + \beta_8\text{Minneapolis–St. Paul} \\ &+ \beta_9\text{Los Angeles} + \varepsilon \qquad (12.17)\end{aligned}$$

where ε is an error term. From housing information in the Annual Survey of Housing, Coulson and Engle estimated the price of a standardized house within the central city of a metropolitan area, P_{CC}, and a standardized house outside of the metropolitan area, P_{OC}.[13] The dependent variable in equation (12.17) is the difference between these two prices, $-\Delta V = P_{CC} - P_{OC}$. In addition to housing information, the Annual Survey of Housing contained information on the average distance and average commuting time for centrally and noncentrally located housing. Differences in the average location distances and commuting times between the two locales provide estimates of Δu and (ΔTime) in equation (12.16) which, when combined with information on automobile mileage, the price of gasoline, and nongasoline expenses, give the estimated difference in gasoline and nongasoline costs between central-city and noncentral-city locations, (ΔGasoline Costs) and (ΔNongasoline Costs), respectively. The difference in time costs between the two locations, Δ(Time Costs), is simply Δu multiplied by the value of time, which the authors estimated using a commuter's average wage rate.

Hypotheses

HYPOTHESIS 1 The basic hypothesis to be tested is that increases in marginal transportation costs increase the slope of the rent gradient, holding all else constant. From equation (12.17), we expect that an increase in each component of the marginal transportation cost will increase the price of centrally located housing relative to noncentrally located housing, which implies that β_i $(i = 1, 2, 3) > 0$. Also, if there is perfect capitalization and stable price and commuter time expectations, the coefficient for each marginal transport cost component will be equal to some $\bar{\beta} = N/r$ $(i, j = 1, 2, 3)$, where r is the rate of capitalization and N is the number of one-way trips per year. This implies a constant rate of capitalization for given N. Alternatively, in the presence of unstable expectations, the β_is $(i = 1, 2, 3)$ are not equal and this implies unequal rates of capitalization r_i for a given N.

HYPOTHESIS 2 We have previously seen that within a metropolitan area, differences in income may affect a household's location in two ways. First, since housing is a normal good, an increase in household income raises the demand for housing, which induces a household to live further from the CBD. At the same time, higher incomes increase one's value of time, which increases the time costs of commuting and induces a household to live closer to the CBD. The net effect on location is ambiguous. However, in our empirical model we have already included the effect that time costs have upon location, so that including household income as an additional explanatory variable isolates the differential demand effect that income has upon housing. And since an increase in income induces households to move further out, higher incomes will decrease the demand for central-city relative to suburban housing. That is, β_4 is expected to be negative.

HYPOTHESIS 3 In addition to differences in transportation costs and household incomes, metropolitan areas differ in numerous other dimensions, including public safety, air pollution, property taxes, climates, topography, and so forth. Recall that the data for this analysis is based upon six cities (Atlanta, Detroit, Houston, Los Angeles, Minneapolis – St. Paul, and San Diego) and six time periods (1974–9). In order to capture the net effect of differences across metropolitan areas, Coulson and Engle included in their empirical model a set of city dummy variables. In equation (12.17), for example, Atlanta = 1 if the observation is Atlanta = 0 if the observation comes from one of the other cities. Similarly, if the observation is (is not) Los Angeles, then the variable Los Angeles = 1 (0).[14] Notice that only five of the six cities are explicitly included in the empirical model. The regression model for San Diego, the missing city, is

$$\begin{aligned} -\Delta V = \beta_0 &+ \beta_1(\Delta \text{Time Costs}) \\ &+ \beta_2(\Delta \text{Gasoline Costs}) \\ &+ \beta_3(\Delta \text{Nongasoline Costs}) + \beta_4 \text{Income} \end{aligned}$$

where all other city dummy variables are zero and the intercept is β_0. Alternatively, if the observation comes from Atlanta, then the model is

$$\begin{aligned} -\Delta V &= \beta_0 + \beta_1(\Delta \text{Time Costs}) \\ &\quad + \beta_2(\Delta \text{Gasoline Costs}) \\ &\quad + \beta_3(\Delta \text{Nongasoline Costs}) \\ &\quad + \beta_4 \text{Income} + \beta_5 \\ &= (\beta_0 + \beta_5) + \beta_1(\Delta \text{Time Costs}) \\ &\quad + \beta_2(\Delta \text{Gasoline Costs}) \\ &\quad + \beta_3(\Delta \text{Nongasoline Costs}) + \beta_4 \text{Incomem} \end{aligned}$$

and the intercept is $\beta_0 + \beta_5$. Thus, except for the intercept term and city dummy variables, the empirical model for each city is the same. In this model, differences between cities due to factors other than transportation costs or income are captured by differences in the intercept term. In general, we have no expectations as to the signs of β_i ($i = 5, \ldots, 9$).

Estimation results

Table 12.2 summarizes Coulson and Engle's estimation results. Overall, the model fits the data well, explaining 90% of the variation in central-city versus noncentral-city prices for a standardized house.

Are the results consistent with our stated hypotheses? In general, yes. First, we see that the three cost coefficients and income have their expected signs. Holding all else constant, an increase in each of the cost coefficients raises the price of central-city housing relative to its suburban counterpart, which is consistent with our residential location equilibrium condition. An increase in marginal transportation costs increases the slope of the rent function. Second, Coulson and Engle also obtain the expected result that increases in income, all else held constant, decrease the relative price of central-city housing.

Although the results in table 12.2 are qualitatively consistent with underlying theory, what are the quantitative implications? In particular, we see from table that the separate cost coefficients are not equal. The cost coefficient for ΔTime Costs ($/minute) is ten times the coefficient of (ΔNongasoline Costs) and more than three times the coefficient of (ΔGasoline Costs). An implication of unequal cost coefficients is that the associated capitalization rates are unequal. Consider, for example, the coefficient of (ΔNongasoline Costs), which equals 25,424. From our theoretical discussion, this coefficient approximates N/r. If we assume that a typical household makes 500 one-way trips per year (ten one-way trips per week for 50 weeks), then the capitalization rate estimate implied by this coefficient is 1.97% ($r = 500/\beta_3 = 500/25{,}424 = 0.0197$). Coulson and Engle report that this value is similar to other evidence on capitalization rates in the housing market and conclude, accordingly, that the coefficient on (ΔNongasoline Costs) reflects a housing market with perfect capitalization and stable expectations.

Consider, alternatively, the estimated coefficient on (ΔGasoline Costs), which equals 70,392. Assuming 500 trips per year and following the same procedure as above, the estimated

Table 12.2 Estimation results for household location equilibrium

Dependent Variable – variation in the price of a central-city standardized house relative to a noncentral-city standardized house

Independent Variable	Coefficient Estimate (*t*-statistic)
ΔTime Costs ($/minute)	226,293 (3.91)
ΔGasoline Costs ($/trip)	70,392 (1.92)
ΔNongasoline Costs	25,424 (1.79)
Income ($/minute)	−4.07 (−3.73)
Atlanta Dummy	−21,239 (−3.61)
Detroit Dummy	58,566 (3.18)
Houston Dummy	32,874 (4.00)
Los Angeles Dummy	38,677 (4.18)
Minneapolis–St. Paul	−15,463 (−3.66)
Dummy constant term	−59,164 (−3.11)
$R^2 = 0.90$	

Source: Adapted from Coulson and Engle (1987), table 4, p. 294

capitalization rate is 0.71%, an unreasonably low rate, which implies that gasoline price increases are overcapitalized in housing prices. A possible explanation for this result is that during this period households expected growing rather than stable gasoline prices. During the 1970s there were two oil price shocks, one in the early part of the decade and a second shock in the latter part of the decade. Suppose that households experience a one-shot increase in the gasoline costs of a trip. In an environment of stable price expectations, this cost increase would be capitalized into the price of housing and, consistent with the nongasoline cost results, produce a capitalization rate around 2%. However, if households responded to the one-shot increase by assuming that gasoline prices would continue to rise, then both the initial price rise and the expected price rise would be capitalized in the price of housing. And, as we saw earlier, rising gasoline prices imply a lower capitalization rate. Thus, the estimated coefficient of (ΔGasoline Costs) in table 12.2 is consistent with household expectations of rising gasoline prices and overcapitalization.

Finally, what can be said about the estimated 226,293 coefficient of (ΔTime Costs)? Similar to our comments on (ΔGasoline Costs), the very high coefficient on (ΔTime Costs) implies an unreasonably low 0.22% capitalization rate (assuming 500 one-way trips per year). One possible reason for this result was the authors' assumption that commuters' value of time equaled the wage rate. However, as we have seen in chapter 4, values of time may lie above or below the wage rate. To obtain some insight on this, suppose that we rewrite the change in time costs as

$$\frac{N}{r}(VOT)\Delta(\text{Time}) = \frac{N}{r}\left(\frac{VOT}{\text{Wage}}\right)\text{Wage}(\Delta(\text{Time}))$$
$$= \frac{N}{r}(\phi)\text{Wage}(\Delta(\text{Time}))$$

Previously, the value of time (*VOT*) was assumed to equal the wage rate, which implies that ϕ in the above equation equals one. However, assuming that we have perfect capitalization at 2% and 500 one-way trips per year, the estimated coefficient on (ΔTime Costs) in table 12.2 provides an estimate of ϕ. Specifically, $\beta_1 = (N/r)(\phi) = (500/0.02)\phi$. This implies that $\phi = 226{,}293r/N = 226{,}293(0.00004) = 9.05$. That is, the results in table 12.2 imply that households value their travel time at nine times their wage rate. Just as a 0.22% capitalization rate is too low, commute times valued at nine times the wage rate are inconsistent with existing studies on travel time valuation. Another possible explanation for a low capitalization rate is that an expectation of growing congestion produces higher travel time costs, which would lead to overcapitalization, or there may be some combination of unstable expectations and higher than normal values of time that have produced this high coefficient on ΔTime Costs.[15]

TRANSPORTATION AND LAND-USE ALLOCATION IN A MONOCENTRIC CITY

Marginal transportation costs in the monocentric model play a key role in determining the steepness of bid-rent curves and, therefore, in determining land-use allocation among alternative bidders. By analyzing the effect that alternative transportation developments and policies have on marginal transportation costs, we can predict their impacts upon land use in a monocentric setting.

DECREASE IN FIRM MARGINAL SHIPPING COSTS

In order to focus upon the effect of firm-related transport improvements on land use and urban development, suppose that a new form of intracity shipping is developed that greatly lowers a firm's transportation costs.[16] What effect would innovation in goods' shipping have upon land-use allocation in the city? Figure 12.7 depicts current firm and residential bid-rent curves. In the existing setting, manufacturing occupies land up to u_1 miles from the center and housing occupies land between u_1 and u_b, the boundary of the city. After the innovation in shipping and the corresponding reduction in transport costs, the firm bid-rent curve pivots

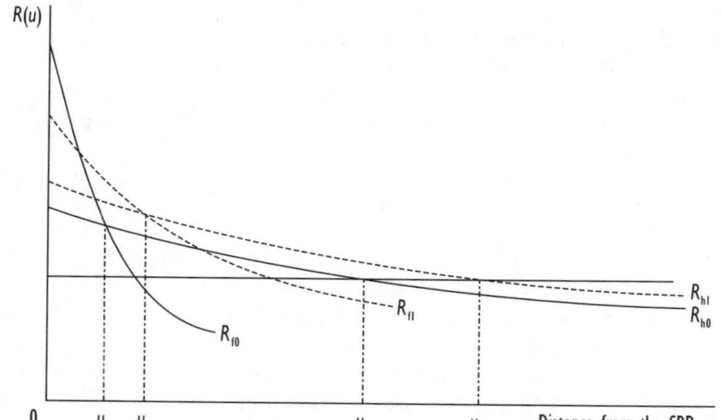

Figure 12.7 The impact of decreased shipping costs on urban locations. u_1 = initial CBD boundary, u_2 = final CBD boundary, u_b = initial city boundary, $u_{b'}$ = final city boundary; R_{f0} = initial bid-rent curve for firm sector, R_{f1} = final bid-rent curve for firm sector, R_{h0} = initial bid-rent curve for housing sector, R_{h1} = final bid-rent curve for housing sector.

on the y-intercept, rotating upward. By lowering intracity transport costs, the innovation increases pre-rent profits and firm bid rents and raises employment densities as firms substitute labor (nonland) for land inputs in the production process. In addition, manufacturing now outbids the residential sector between u_1 and u_2 miles from the CBD. But there are secondary effects. The higher labor to land ratios (that is, higher employment densities) in production, combined with a larger physical area used for manufacturing, increases the demand for labor, which raises wage rates. The increase in wages has two effects: (1) higher wages attract workers from other cities which have not introduced the new shipping innovation. This raises the city's population and increases the demand for housing, which shifts residential bid rents upward; and (2) higher wages reduce firm pre-rent profits, which shifts firm bid rents down. We graphically see the net results of these effects in figure 12.7. The initial bid rents for the firm and residential sectors are R_{f0} and R_{h0} respectively. By flattening out the firm's bid-rent curve, the innovation induces firms to expand further from the CBD, which increases the demand for labor, raises equilibrium wages, and shifts firm bid rents down. The final firm bid-rent curve, R_{f1}, is flatter and has a lower intercept than the original bid-rent curve.

In the housing sector, increased wages attract new workers to the city, which increases the demand for housing, shifting the residential bid rent upward to R_{h1}. In the final equilibrium, the CBD expands as firms move out to $u_{2'}$, the edge of the city increases to $u_{b'}$, population increases, and employment density increases.[17]

DECREASE IN HOUSEHOLD MARGINAL COMMUTING COSTS

Rather than a decrease in intracity marginal shipping costs, suppose instead that we have an innovation in transporting commuters from their suburban residences to the downtown employment center. Figure 12.8 depicts the initial and final bid-rent curves from the innovation. The improved capability of transporting workers to the CBD lowers per-mile transportation

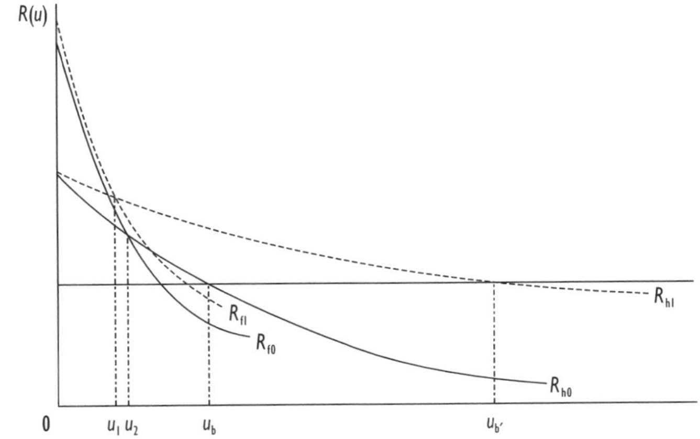

Figure 12.8 The impact of decreased commuting costs on urban locations. u_1 = initial CBD boundary, u_2 = final CBD boundary, u_b = initial city boundary, $u_{b'}$ = final city boundary; R_{f0} = initial bid-rent curve for firm sector, R_{f1} = final bid-rent curve for firm sector, R_{h0} = initial bid-rent curve for housing sector, R_{h1} = final bid-rent curve for housing sector.

costs, which increases residential bid rents by rotating the residential bid-rent curve upward. The initial effect is to contract the CBD and geographically expand the city as the boundary increases outward to $u_{b'}$. Reduced transportation costs increase household net incomes, which raise household economic welfare above that of residents in cities without the innovation in commuter transport. This induces a population increase in the innovating city, which increases the demand for housing, raises residential bid rents, and increases labor supplies. Moreover, the rise in residential bid rents raises population density as households substitute nonhousing for housing in their consumption bundles. The final residential bid-rent curve, R_{h1}, is flatter and has a lower intercept than the original bid-rent curve. On the firm side, the increased labor supply reduces equilibrium wages, increases pre-rent profits, and shifts firm bid rents upward from R_{f0} to R_{f1}. This expands the CBD and causes employment densities to rise as increased bid rents induce firms to increase their nonland to land input ratios in production. In the final equilibrium, the city is geographically larger with more people, the CBD is smaller with higher employment densities, and the residential sector is larger and more densely populated.[18]

THE MULTICENTRIC PATTERN OF URBAN DEVELOPMENT

In the traditional monocentric city, a radial transportation network developed around the CBD, causing business and residential sectors to locate around this area. Because firms value the regional transportation center downtown, one can easily understand why manufacturers value accessibility to the CBD. For exactly the same reason, importing firms – that is, firms that buy goods from producers located elsewhere – also value CBD accessibility. It is less clear, however, why commercial firms, office firms, and retailers in the traditional monocentric city value CBD accessibility. The explanation is *agglomeration economies*. Agglomeration economies refer to reduced production costs, higher productivity, or more opportunities for creativity and innovation when firms cluster together in a geographic area. The proximity of firms engaged in similar activities provides cost-reducing opportunities.

Consider a commercial bank that is evaluating whether to locate in the CBD or in some suburban site. The firm receives two benefits from locating in the suburbs. First, land rents will be less. Second, the firm can draw its labor force from the surrounding suburban areas, which enables it to pay lower wages. The reason for the lower wages is the reduced transportation costs that commuters incur if their jobs are located in the suburbs – that is, closer to home – than in the CBD. Suppose, for example, that you are earning $1,500 per month working downtown and incur $100 in transportation costs. Your net-of-transportation earnings are $1,400. You now take a job near your home at a monthly salary of $1,425, but your monthly transportation costs fall to $25. Although your suburban job pays less, your net earnings remain the same because of the reduction in commuting costs. You are no worse off with the suburban job but the firm's labor costs have fallen, which induces the firm to decentralize and relocate to the suburbs.

On the other hand, if the commercial bank locates in the suburbs, its costs of production increase since all of its large customers are downtown. When located in the city, the bank can easily meet with customers to transact business. If located in the suburbs, however, the cost of transacting central-city business rises. To be competitive with centrally located banks, the decentralized bank must now send its loan officers and other representatives downtown to meet with customers. This raises its production costs, which induces the firm to locate closer to the CBD.

If the commercial bank is the only decentralized firm in the area, the savings in wages and land rents would not be sufficient to offset its higher production costs and it would locate in the CBD. However, if the bank is motivated to relocate in the suburbs because there already exists a cluster of firms at the decentralized site, the clustering of firms provides cost-reducing agglomeration economies to the bank. The bank no longer needs to send its representatives downtown to conduct business if the customer base is an existing cluster of local firms.

O'Sullivan (1996) identifies four sources of agglomeration economies:

- *Scale economies in the production of intermediate inputs.* These will lead to a clustering of customers around the supplier if the input demand of any single customer is not sufficient to exhaust the scale economies, and if transportation costs between the supplier and the customer are high. Transportation costs will be high when input suppliers work closely with their clients to customize the product for the client's needs. Because constant and oftentimes face-to-face communication between supplier and customer are so important, transportation costs are lowered when customers locate near the supplier.[19]
- *More efficient labor market.* When firms cluster together, they generally share a common labor market pool. The close proximity of firms lowers job search costs as well as reducing the cost of moving when a job change occurs.
- *Information gathering.* In a cluster of firms, information on new developments, processes, technology, suppliers, and so forth is more readily available, and generally works to lower firm production costs and improve productivity. Further, enhanced opportunities to exchange information provide a more fertile environment for creative endeavors and innovation.
- *Urbanization economies.* These reflect the benefits of clustering associated with the overall growth of the urban economy. Whereas agglomeration economies due to intermediate-scale economies, labor pool efficiencies, and information diffusion are generally specific to a particular industry, urbanization economies are not specific to any one industry or set of industries. Rather, urbanization economies reflect productivity gains and cost reductions that accrue to all urban firms as the urban economy grows.

CASE STUDY – SUBCENTERS AND COMMUTER FLOWS IN THE LOS ANGELES METROPOLITAN AREA (LAMA)

Giuliano and Small (1991) analyzed data on 1,146 traffic analysis zones for the metropolitan area of Los Angeles, which comprises 3,536 square miles and includes the urban parts of five counties – Los Angeles, Orange, Ventura, Riverside, and San Bernadino. In 1980, there were 10.7 million residents and 4.65 million jobs within this geographic area. Giuliano and Small used employment densities and the total employment of contiguous zones to define three sets of urban centers in LAMA. Each of the contiguous zones in a center must have an employment density at least equal to ten employees per acre, and the total employment of the contiguous zones must be at least 10,000. Based upon these criteria, the authors identified 28 *subcenters* plus the *main center* which encompasses the area around downtown Los Angeles. In addition, three *outer centers* were identified, two of which correspond to counties east of Los Angeles (Riverside and San Bernadino) and one county north of Los Angeles (Ventura).[20] The authors also define the

Table 12.3 The characteristics of the top ten centers in Los Angeles

Center	Employment ('000s)	Employment Density (#/acre)	Area ('000 acres)	Employment : Population Ratio	Distance from CBD (miles)
Downtown Los Angeles	469.0	36.0	13.0	1.47	0.1
West Los Angeles	176.2	25.5	6.9	1.37	15.8
Santa Monica	65.1	16.9	3.8	1.11	16.7
Hollywood	64.2	21.4	3.0	0.73	7.3
Los Angeles Airport	59.1	16.7	3.5	4.32	18.8
Orange County Airport	47.7	16.1	3.0	1,589.87	40.7
Glendale	43.0	15.5	2.8	1.07	12.3
Commerce	41.9	17.0	2.5	4.05	9.8
Vernon/Huntington Park	39.2	33.2	1.2	2.42	4.9
San Pedro	37.6	15.7	2.4	2.74	23.3
Total centers (32)	1,490.9	21.0	71.0	1.55	n/a
Total subcenters (28)	922.2	17.7	56.2	1.58	n/a

Source: Reprinted from Giuliano and Small (1991), with permission from Elsevier Science

Wilshire Corridor as the *core*. The core comprises downtown Los Angeles plus the next three largest subcenters (West Los Angeles, Santa Monica, and Hollywood) and a smaller subcenter (East Los Angeles) that map out a regional arc starting just east of downtown Los Angeles and moving westward to the coastal areas.

On the basis of total employment, table 12.3 identifies employment and distance characteristics for the top ten centers in Los Angeles. An important finding in this table is the significant role that downtown Los Angeles plays in the metropolitan area.[21] In contrast to popular thinking that LAMA exemplifies the worst of urban sprawl with uniform densities throughout the area, we see in table 12.3 that the geographically large LAMA appears to mimic a major characteristic of the monocentric model; namely, high employment densities at the center that decline as distance from the center increases. With less than 1% of LAMA's total area, Downtown Los Angeles is responsible for 10% of its jobs and 31% of all jobs within the region's 32 centers. Giuliano and Small also found a significant inverse relationship between distance from Downtown Los Angeles and employment density. In other words, as distance from Downtown Los Angeles increases, there is a drop in employment density, which is consistent with a negatively sloped land rent function.

On the other hand, the data are also consistent with the formation of centers and the resulting benefits from agglomeration economies. Spatially, the 32 centers in LAMA comprise 3% of the region's area but are responsible for nearly one-third of the region's employment (1.49/4.65).[22] Notwithstanding this, however, the majority of employment in LAMA is outside the centers. Although agglomeration economies are important, dispersed employment extending outward from the core area, rather than a clustering of activities, explains the majority of employment locations in the metropolitan area.

Another interesting finding in table 12.3, and inconsistent with a monocentric framework, is the relatively low values for the employment : population ratios. According to the monocentric model, employment occurs in the CBD and the population resides in the surrounding areas. There is very little overlap between employment and residential activities. Thus, according to the monocentric model, employment : population ratios in the center will be quite high. In table

Table 12.4 Mean commuting distance and time by job location

	Distance (miles)	Time (minutes)
Within centers		
Main center	13.9	29.5
Other core centers	11.2	24.8
Other LA County centers	13.2	27.2
LA County total	13.0	27.4
Orange County	11.3	23.8
Outer counties	8.3	17.2
Total in centers	12.7	26.8
Not within centers		
LA County	10.8	22.8
Orange County	9.9	21.0
Outer counties	8.8	18.2
Total not in centers	10.3	21.8
All Zones		
LA County	11.7	24.6
Orange County	10.1	21.5
Outer counties	8.8	18.1
Region total	11.1	23.4

Source: Reprinted from Giuliano and Small (1991), with permission from Elsevier Science

12.3, however, we see that the mean employment : population ratio for all centers is only 1.55, which indicates that population and employment are significantly interspersed within areas. As you might expect, exceptions to the low employment : population ratios are the region's airport centers. For example, the employment : population ratios for Long Beach Airport, Orange County Airport, and Burbank Airport are 3,684, 1,589, and 10.86, respectively.

For locations within and outside of the centers in LAMA, table 12.4 reports the average distances and travel times in the work-trip commute. From the table we can draw three general conclusions:

- Employment within centers requires longer commutes on average than employment outside of centers. We see in table 12.4 that the average commute for each category within centers is larger than the corresponding commute outside of centers. The average commute, for example, is 13.0 miles to locations within centers in LA County, but only 10.8 miles to LA County locations not in centers. A similar relationship is true for locations within and outside centers in Orange County and the Outer Counties. Complementing this is the finding that the Main Center (downtown Los Angeles) has the longest average commute at 13.9 miles. These data are broadly consistent with our theory of urban structure, that urban centers are concentrations of employment that must draw their workers from larger geographic areas surrounding the center.
- Employment in larger and more dense locations requires longer commutes on average

than employment in smaller and more dispersed areas. In terms of total employment and employment densities, centers in Orange County and the Outer Counties are significantly smaller than centers in Los Angeles County. The total employment and employment density within centers in Los Angeles County are 1.32 million and 59.8 persons per 1,000 acres. In contrast, within-center total employment in Orange County and the Outer Counties is 136,000 and 298,000 respectively, with an associated employment density equal to 14.4 and 15.7 persons per 1,000 acres. We see in table 12.4 that the average commute to LA County jobs within centers is 13.0 miles, which is 1.7 and 4.7 miles longer than the average commute to jobs within Orange County and the Outer Counties centers. Notice also that this pattern holds for locations outside of the centers. Just as LA County has more total employment and higher employment densities within centers relative to Orange County and the Outer Counties, this is also true for locations outside of the centers. And we again see in table 12.4 that the mean commute for locations outside the centers in LA County is longer (10.8 miles) than for locations outside the Orange County (9.9 miles) and the Outer Counties (8.8 miles) centers.

- There is interspersing of employment and population. We have seen that employment : population ratios are relatively low in LAMA, which signifies the integration of job and residential activities in the urban areas. A reflection of this is also seen in table 12.4 by the 11.2 mile average commute for locations within the Other Core Centers, which is 2.7 miles less than the average commute to the main center, 2 miles less than the average commute to Other LA County Centers, and only 0.4 miles longer than the average commute to LA County jobs outside of centers. Although the Outer Core is a large and dense employment corridor, it is nevertheless amenable to mixed employment and residential activities. The employment : population ratio for the Outer Core is 1.14, which is substantially below that in the Main Center (1.47) and Other LA County Centers (1.80) but higher than the ratio for LA County employment not within centers (0.32).

LAND RENTS IN A MULTICENTRIC METROPOLITAN AREA

Suppose, for some reason, that a subcenter develops u_2 miles from the CBD. What effect will this have upon the city's land-rent function? As we have seen above, firms experience lower production costs from lower land rents and, because their workforces are drawn locally, from lower wages. With lower transportation costs from shorter commutes, households working in the subcenter are willing to accept a lower wage. In addition, a city's land-rent function will no longer be a continuously downward-sloping curve but, as seen in figure 12.9, will be "scalloped." The land-rent function falls from the CBD out to a distance of u_1 miles from the center, then rises to a local peak at u_2, and thereafter falls.

In order to fix these ideas, assume that all households living within u_1 miles from the CBD work in the CBD, whereas all households living u_1 or more miles from the CBD work in the subcenter. The falling rents up to u_1 miles reflect the increased transportation costs that are necessary to access centrally located employment. After u_1 miles, however, we now see that the land-rent function increases. Just as accessibility to the downtown area determines the shape of the land-rent function in the monocentric framework, in a multicentric setting, similar economic forces are at work. Access to the subcenter is valuable and, as a result, the closer a subcenter employee lives to the subcenter, the lower are transportation costs. Thus, individuals working in the subcenter are willing to pay higher per-unit land prices at locations that are closer to the subcenter. From u_1 to u_2 miles from the CBD, land rents increase, and we have a "minor" peak at u_2 miles where the subcenter is located. Similarly, at distances further

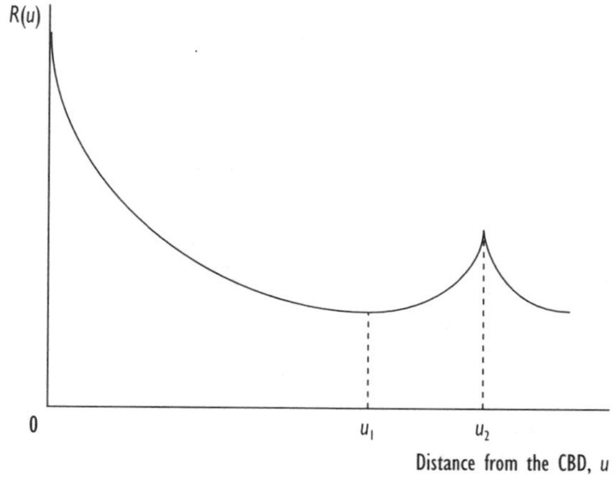

Figure 12.9 Land rents in a multicentric urban area.

than u_2, accessibility to the subcenter falls, transportation costs rise, and, accordingly, land rents decline.

But we have also seen that wages to individuals working in the subcenter will be less because their commutes are shorter. The savings in transportation costs to the subcenter, relative to the CBD, allow employers to offer lower wages in the subcenter, and enable households to accept lower wages because their net incomes remain the same. An important result in multicentric urban structures is that differences in wage rates across different subcenters in a metropolitan environment compensate workers for differences in "boundary" commuting distances to alternative places of employment (DiPasquale and Wheaton, 1996).

To explain this, let's go back to figure 12.9. Distance u_1 is the subcenter boundary; that is, the distance at which land rents begin to rise because of greater accessibility to the subcenter. Assume that Tim lives at the boundary, so that he has a choice of working either in the CBD or in the subcenter. Also assume for the moment that wages are equal at the CBD and at the subcenter. Regardless of where Tim works, he pays a land rent equal to R_1. If Tim decides to work in the CBD, we know that the land-rent function between the CBD and u_1 reflects the trade-off between transportation costs and accessibility to the CBD, so that no one working in the CBD is any better or worse off than anyone else. Similarly, if Tim works in the subcenter, the land-rent function between u_1 and u_2 reflects the trade-off between transportation costs and accessibility *to the subcenter* so that, regardless of location, all subcenter employees are equally well off. However, we have assumed that Tim receives the same wage in the CBD as in the subcenter. Clearly, since Tim's commute to the subcenter is shorter than his commute to the CBD, he will be better off working in the subcenter. But Tim is not unique and other households would see that they could improve their economic welfare by relocating and working in the subcenter. This increases (decreases) the supply of labor to the subcenter (center) which decreases wages in the subcenter relative to wages in the center. How much will the wage fall? It will fall by just enough to make Tim indifferent between working in the subcenter and working in the CBD. Specifically, the difference in wages will equal the difference at u_1 between Tim's transportation cost to the CBD and his transportation cost to the subcenter. In other words, it is the difference in commuting costs from the boundary u_1 to the CBD and to the subcenter that determines the equilibrium difference in wages in a multicentric urban environment.

In general, then, metropolitan areas with a CBD and several subcenters will have a scalloped land-rent function with local land rent peaks reflecting subcenter developments. From each subcenter, land rents fall in order to compensate the subcenter's employees for higher transportation costs. In addition, there will be a wage structure throughout the metropolitan area, where the differences in wages among the subcenters reflect differences in commuting costs from subcenter boundaries to the respective centers. An equilibrium wage structure ensures that all households receive the same net income and are equally well off.

CASE STUDY – INTRAURBAN WAGE FUNCTIONS IN CHICAGO

An implication of the above analysis is that if the CBD competes with a subcenter for workers, we will observe higher wages paid by CBD employers in order to compensate workers for the longer commute to the CBD. Do we observe such wage variations as distance from the CBD increases? Eberts (1981) considered this question for public-sector workers in Chicago. From the Cook County Bureau of Administration, Eberts obtained 1974 wage, employment, and residential location data on five categories of non-educational municipal workers in over 100 municipalities in the Chicago metropolitan area. In his study, Eberts set up the following basic empirical model:

$$\begin{aligned} w_{im} = \alpha &+ \beta_1(\text{Per Capita Municipal Expenditures})_{im} \\ &+ \beta_2(\text{Length of Workweek})_{im} \\ &+ \beta_3(\text{Population})_m \\ &+ \gamma(\text{CBD Distance})_m \\ &+ \varepsilon_{im} \end{aligned} \qquad (12.18)$$

where w_{im} is the wage rate for labor category i and municipality m, Per Capita Municipal Expenditures reflects the size of a municipality's budget relative to the population, Length of Workweek is the number of hours that a typical employee in municipality m works per week, Population is the community's population in 1970, and CBD Distance is the straight-line distance from municipality m to Chicago's central business district (the Loop). Each of the non-distance variables, discussed in greater detail below, was included in the empirical model in order to control for differences in the organizational structure of the municipalities. α, β_i (i = 1, 2, 3), and γ are parameters.

Hypotheses

HYPOTHESIS 1 Consistent with work in public-sector economics, Eberts argued that public-sector managers remain in their positions longer the more successfully they respond to the needs of their constituents and employees. Responding to the needs of constituents requires providing a range of high-quality services to the community's residents, whereas responding to the needs of employees generally means higher incomes, more fringe benefits, and improved working conditions. Since larger municipal budgets provide administrators with more resources for meeting constituent and employee demands, we expect the coefficient on Per Capita Municipal Expenditures to be positive.

Related to this, the size of the community has implications for the average skill level of its workers. Smaller communities generally have fewer requirements and smaller resources for employing highly skilled workers to meet community needs. Since, all else constant, more populous communities are expected to have a workforce with higher average skills, the coefficient on Population is expected to be positive.

HYPOTHESIS 2 In general, increased labor productivity implies increased wages. Since information on worker productivity was unavailable, Eberts used Length of Workweek to capture the effect of productivity on the wage function. To the extent that more productive workers in municipal governments are also those who work longer hours, Length of Workweek captures the productivity effect on wages and we would expect the coefficient of this variable to be positive.

HYPOTHESIS 3 CBD Distance is the variable of interest in Eberts' analysis. According to the empirical model, after controlling for the size of the municipality and worker productivity, we expect an increase in distance from Chicago's CBD to reduce wages. However, Eberts also recognized that the extent to which wages fall with distance depends upon exogenous market demand and supply factors. In particular, if a community experiences an excess supply of labor, this reduces the wage rate, lessens the attractive pull of the community in competing for workers further out, and lowers the wage–distance function. Conversely, an increase in the excess demand for labor increases the wage rate and strengthens the community's ability to compete for workers further out. Eberts incorporated these market influences on the wage function by expressing γ, the coefficient for distance, as

$$\gamma = \beta_4 + \beta_5(\text{Population Change}) + \beta_6(\text{Employment Concentration}) + \beta_7(\text{Per Unit Housing Cost}) \quad (12.19)$$

An excess supply of workers to the municipality lowers the wage function. Although Eberts did not have information on recent changes in the excess supply of labor, he argued that jobs generally move less quickly than people, so that a recent surge in population would reflect – although likely overstate – excess supply conditions. All else constant, increases in Population Change are expected to reduce the wage function, so that β_5 is expected to be negative. Employment Concentration, defined for each labor group as the ratio of employment to the number of workers that reside in the community, reflects an excess demand for labor. Since increases in excess demand raise the wage–distance function, β_6 is expected to be positive.

The third variable, Per Unit Housing Cost, is also expected to increase the wage–distance function. To the extent that municipalities cannot substitute other inputs for low-skilled labor (that is, the elasticity of substitution between low-skilled workers and other inputs is low), municipalities with high housing costs may have to offer higher wages to offset the higher living costs at nearby locations or higher commuting costs, because these workers must live at locations further away. All else constant, then, β_7 is expected to be positive.

Substituting equation (12.19) into equation (12.18) gives an expanded empirical model

$$\begin{aligned} w_{im} = {} & \alpha + \beta_1(\text{Per Capita Municipal Expenditures})_{im} + \beta_2(\text{Length of Workweek})_{im} + \beta_3(\text{Population})_m \\ & + \beta_4(\text{CBD Distance})_m + \beta_5(\text{Population Change})_m(\text{CBD Distance})_m \\ & + \beta_6(\text{Employment Concentration})_{im}(\text{CBD Distance})_m + \beta_7(\text{Per Unit Housing Cost})_m(\text{CBD Distance})_m \\ & + \varepsilon_{im} \end{aligned} \quad (12.20)$$

where we see that the market demand and supply effects enter the empirical model as *interaction terms*; that is, as variables that are interacted or multiplied by CBD Distance. Eberts estimated equation (12.20) in double-log form, the results of which are presented in table 12.5. Given that we have a cross-section database with relatively few variables, the data fit the model reasonably well. Overall, the model explains from 21% to 30% of the variation in the dependent variable.[23]

In the table, we see that the results are mixed with respect to the first hypothesis. Contrary to expectations, increases in Per Capita Municipal Expenditures decrease wages for each of the labor groups and the coefficient is statistically significant at the 0.1 level for all but clerical labor. Similarly, Length of Workweek has a consistently negative sign, although the coefficient is only significant for administrative employees. These results are contrary to our hypotheses, suggesting that Per Capita Municipal Expenditures and Length of Workweek, respectively, are

Table 12.5 Estimation results for intraurban wage function double-log model[a]

Dependent variable – ln(Average Wages) of selected labor groups

Explanatory Variable[b]	Administration	Clerical	Fire	Police	Public Works
CBD Distance	−0.379 (−2.14)	−0.324 (−4.18)	−0.088 (−1.54)	−0.209 (−3.79)	−0.217 (−2.08)
Per Capita Municipal Expenditures	−0.183 (−1.83)	−0.032 (−0.64)	−0.129 (−3.65)	−0.058 (−1.69)	−0.088 (−1.35)
Length of Workweek	−0.397 (−1.83)	−2.95 (−1.03)	−0.089 (−1.05)	−0.669 (−0.72)	−0.987 (−1.02)
Population	0.084 (1.19)	−0.025 (−0.74)	−0.001 (−0.05)	−0.014 (−0.59)	−0.002 (−0.04)
(Population Change) (CBD Distance)	−0.009 (−0.39)	−0.017 (−1.60)	−0.019 (−2.40)	−0.012 (−1.52)	0.043 (2.29)
(Employment Concentration) (CBD Distance)	−0.054 (−1.41)	0.002 (0.11)	0.050 (3.05)	0.018 (1.12)	0.028 (1.47)
(Per Unit Housing Cost) (CBD Distance)	0.470 (2.58)	0.400 (4.69)	0.036 (0.54)	0.192 (2.94)	0.078 (0.65)
R^2	0.24	0.30	0.35	0.29	0.21

[a] Flow is vehicles/lane–mile per hour; Speed is miles per hour; and Toll is cents per mile. Eberts did not report a constant term.
[b] All explanatory variables are in logarithmic form.
Source: Adapted from Eberts (1981), table 4, p. 58

poor proxies for constituent needs and labor productivity.[24] Population, on the other hand, is expected to be positively related to wages and has a positive sign in three of the five regressions. However, the variable is not statistically significant in any of the models.

The strongest results in table 12.5 relate to distance. The coefficient for distance is negative and statistically significant in four out of the five cases. Only for firemen is the coefficient not statistically significant. Looking at the coefficients of the interaction variables which reflect market demand and supply factors, we obtain some consistency in the results, but also a fair amount of variation. We argued above that the expected sign on Employment Concentration and Population Change interaction variables, respectively, is positive and negative. From the regression results, we obtain the expected sign in four out of the five models. However, at the 0.05 level of significance, seven of these coefficients are not statistically significant. And one of the three that is significant (Population Change in the Public Works equation) has an unexpected positive sign.

Last, each of the coefficients on the Per Unit Cost of Housing interaction variable is positive and statistically significant for Administration,

Table 12.6 Wage–distance relationships for different labor groups[a]

Labor Group	$E_{w,\text{distance}} = \dfrac{\Delta w}{\Delta u}\dfrac{u}{w}$	$\dfrac{\Delta w}{\Delta u} = E_{w,\text{distance}} \cdot \dfrac{w}{u}(\$)$	$\dfrac{\Delta w/w}{\Delta u} = E_{w,\text{distance}} \cdot \dfrac{1}{u}$
Administration	−0.379	−26	−0.017
Clerical	−0.324	−10	−0.015
Fire[b]	–	–	–
Police	−0.209	−11	−0.009
Public Works	−0.217	−9.40	−0.010

[a] These estimates are based upon the direct effect of CBD distance on wages from table 12.5. Eberts did not report the total effect of CBD Distance, which would include the CBD's direct and interactive effects. Mean monthly income in 1974 for the respective groups was: Administration, $1,510; Clerical, $682; Fire, $1,188; Police, $1,176; and Public Works, $951. The mean distance from the CBD is 22 miles.
[b] The estimated CBD Distance coefficient for this labor group was not significantly different from zero.
Source: Adapted from Eberts (1981), table 5, p. 58

Clerical, and Police labor groups, suggesting that high housing costs in municipalities lead to increased wages for these workers.

What implications can we draw from these results? Focusing upon the direct effect of CBD Distance on wages (that is, ignoring CBD's interactive effects that reflect organizational structure and market supply/demand conditions), the coefficient of CBD Distance provides an estimate of the elasticity of wages with respect to distance from downtown Chicago, $E_{w,\text{distance}}$. On the basis of mean wages for each of the labor groups and mean distance from the CBD, table 12.6 reports the elasticities as well as information on the absolute and percentage fall in wages with a 1 mile increase from Chicago's CBD. With the exception of the Fire labor group, the elasticity of wages with respect to distance from the CBD ranges between −0.20 and −0.37. The third column in table 12.6 provides more insight by giving the estimated decrease in the monthly wage with a 1 mile increase in distance from Chicago's CBD. The per-mile drop in monthly wages for Clerical, Police, and Public Works hover around $10. For administrative personnel, however, the estimated per-mile decrease in wages is considerably higher at $26. This suggests, for example, that a typical manager working for a municipality 10 miles from downtown Chicago will receive $260 less than if she worked in downtown Chicago. The last column in table 12.6 converts the monetary figures in column three to percentages. Here we see that wages fall by between 0.9% and 1.7% for each mile further from Chicago's CBD.

Discussion

If firms locate outside of the CBD, they can experience savings not only in land costs but also in wages paid, since their workers will not have as long a commute in their work trips. Eberts' results provide evidence that are generally consistent with this theory. With the exception of the Fire labor group, Eberts found a strong negative relationship between distance from downtown Chicago and wages. At the same time, his results were inconsistent and generally weak with respect to the effect of organizational structure and the impact that market demand and supply factors have upon the wage–distance relationship, which suggests the need for improvements in model specification and variable measurement. A possible reason for some of these weaker findings is that Eberts examined the attractive forces of municipalities in the Chicago metropolitan area. But there is no reason to believe that each of the municipalities constitute a subcenter with relatively strong agglomeration economies. Similar to Giuliano and Small's work, it is more likely that a smaller number of contiguous areas would more accurately characterize subcenter agglomeration forces present in the Chicago metropolitan area.

One might also wonder whether an analysis of workers in private firms would lead to similar results. Eberts argues that the answer to this question is likely to be yes. He provides evidence that wages and salaries in Chicago's metropolitan area is similar for private- and public-sector employees in comparable jobs. Although an analysis of private firm workers' wages may lead to different quantitative estimates of the wage–distance function, there is no reason to expect that such a study would provide different qualitative insights. That is, one would expect to find a negative and significant relationship between private-sector wages and distance from the CBD.

CASE STUDY – CONGESTION AND METROPOLITAN DEVELOPMENT

In the last chapter we demonstrated that existing markets for automobile trips in congested environments lead to an overallocation of resources to trip-making. Because trip-makers do not consider the time costs their trips have upon other travelers, the marginal cost of the last trip taken exceeds the trip's marginal benefit. In the past, a typical solution to the congestion problem was to build more highway capacity. Although, given existing traffic levels, additional capacity increases average speed, decreases travel times, and increases traffic flows, the additional capacity also generates additional traffic. In the final analysis, demand for the expanded road network increases, so that the level of congestion changes little, if at all. We have also seen that charging a congestion price, equal to the difference between marginal and average variable trip costs at the optimum, induces an efficient level of trip-making and an efficient level of congestion. Although area-wide congestion taxes reduce congestion and insure an efficient allocation of resources to the highway system, no city in the United States has adopted area-wide congestion pricing, and it is unlikely that such a plan will be adopted in the near future.

In a multicentric metropolitan environment where the expansion of highway capacity is much less a viable option than in the past, and in the absence of congestion pricing, an alternative behavioral response to unpriced congestion is suburbanization. Return to figure 12.9 and consider an individual who works in the CBD and lives at the boundary u_1 between the CBD and a subcenter. Assume further that the boundary u_1 is equidistant from the CBD and the subcenter. If markets are in equilibrium, this individual is indifferent between working in the CBD or working in the subcenter. In addition, even though distance to the CBD and the sub-center are equal, speeds are higher and travel times lower to the subcenter because there is less congestion.

Now suppose that additional congestion in trips to the CBD increases the individual's travel time and raises his trip cost to work. Holding all else constant, the individual's level of economic welfare is now higher if he relocates his job from the CBD to the subcenter. Although he is still equidistant from the two centers, since he has not moved his residence, his marginal trip cost falls due to the faster flow of traffic to the subcenter. If he chose to relocate both his job and his residence, then his suburbanizing decision would lead to a fall in both travel time and travel distance in his trip to work. Since all individuals in the city would see similar opportunities, there would continue to be a reallocation of jobs and residences toward the subcenters until all households were again in location equilibrium, at which point no household could improve its welfare by changing jobs or residences. The point of this example is that increasing congestion, by

Table 12.7 Mean trip time (minutes) and distance (miles) for nonstop trips in private vehicles within central cities

Population			AM Peak[a]		PM Peak[b]		Off-Peak[c]	
			Work	Other	Work	Other	Work	Other
Below 250,000	Time	1983	15.2	15.7	17.2	12.2	13.6	16.0
		1990	15.0	11.5	16.8	13.6	13.0	14.3
	Distance	1983	6.7	7.6	7.6	5.0	6.2	7.8
		1990	7.8	6.4	9.6	7.3	7.0	8.3
250,000–499,999	Time	1983	15.1	13.9	15.2	11.7	15.7	13.3
		1990	14.8	10.1	15.7	11.8	14.2	14.8
	Distance	1983	6.1	6.0	7.7	5.0	7.5	5.6
		1990	7.6	3.7	7.7	5.6	7.8	8.8
500,000–999,999	Time	1983	17.3	17.9	20.8	12.3	14.9	17.2
		1990	17.9	12.5	17.9	14.1	16.1	14.8
	Distance	1983	8.5	8.5	9.3	5.0	6.9	9.0
		1990	10.2	5.7	9.2	7.5	9.2	8.0
1,000,000–3,000,000	Time	1983	18.3	16.4	20.8	14.0	17.9	15.1
		1990	19.5	12.4	21.3	14.1	17.8	14.8
	Distance	1983	8.7	–	8.3	5.5	8.7	6.8
		1990	10.4	6.1	11.1	7.1	9.7	8.0
Over 3,000,000	Time	1983	28.8	15.1	29.4	17.8	23.0	17.3
		1990	22.9	15.7	24.6	14.7	21.7	16.1
	Distance	1983	12.7	5.3	12.3	6.7	10.4	7.4
		1990	11.7	7.4	11.8	6.9	12.1	8.5

[a] The AM Peak is defined as 6:00 am – 9:00 am.
[b] The PM Peak is defined as 4:00 pm – 7:00 pm.
[c] The Off-Peak corresponds to all hours exclusive of the AM and PM Peaks.
Source: Adapted from Gordon and Richardson (1994), table 4, p. 9

raising the time costs of travel, provides firms and households with incentives to suburbanize their production and housing consumption activities in order to conserve on congestion expenditures.

Gordon and Richardson (1994) argue that household and job suburbanization have been important disciplining forces in reducing the effects of traffic congestion in urban areas. Using data from the 1983 and 1990 Nationwide Personal Transportation Surveys (NPTS), tables 12.7 and 12.8 report mean trip travel times and distances for private vehicle trips within and outside of central cities, respectively. The lightly shaded areas in the tables indicate that mean travel time for the associated category decreased between 1983 and 1990. The darker shaded areas denote a decrease in average distance between the two time periods. For example, the box that corresponds to the AM Peak Work trip

Table 12.8 Mean trip time (minutes) and distance (miles) for nonstop trips in private vehicles outside central cities

			AM Peak		PM Peak		Off-Peak	
Population			Work	Other	Work	Other	Work	Other
Below 250,000	Time	1983	18.4	9.8	20.2	12.9	16.6	13.3
		1990	19.1	19.5	20.0	17.5	20.4	17.5
	Distance	1983	9.9	4.3	9.9	6.6	8.8	6.9
		1990	11.7	12.3	12.2	11.1	13.2	11.4
250,000–499,999	Time	1983	19.2	18.2	19.7	14.9	16.9	14.1
		1990	19.3	13.1	21.9	12.5	19.4	17.2
	Distance	1983	10.6	12.4	9.9	7.9	8.8	7.6
		1990	12.0	6.9	13.6	6.5	12.5	10.2
500,000–999,999	Time	1983	22.5	17.9	25.5	13.5	21.7	15.8
		1990	21.1	16.9	23.0	13.3	20.8	15.9
	Distance	1983	12.1	10.4	13.2	6.5	11.1	8.6
		1990	13.1	10.3	13.9	7.5	13.2	9.8
1,000,000–3,000,000	Time	1983	22.1	14.9	23.2	17.7	19.5	16.1
		1990	21.5	13.2	22.8	15.1	21.0	16.6
	Distance	1983	11.2	7.4	11.2	9.3	10.7	8.8
		1990	12.5	7.2	12.1	8.1	12.9	10.5
Over 3,000,000	Time	1983	22.3	15.9	25.5	14.1	18.3	17.3
		1990	24.3	13.2	26.4	14.3	21.7	15.9
	Distance	1983	11.2	7.6	11.5	6.9	9.3	9.0
		1990	13.5	6.8	14.0	7.1	12.9	9.0

Source: Adapted from Gordon and Richardson (1994), table 5, p. 10

in cities with a population less than 250,000 gives a mean 1990 travel time of 15.0 minutes. The light shading in this box indicates that the 1990 mean travel time is less the 1983 mean travel time (15.2).

Tables 12.7 and 12.8 provide mixed evidence on the changes in mean travel times and distances. Within central cities, we see in table 12.7 that work trip travel times in the morning peak improved in cities with populations below 500,000 and in the largest cities. Evening peak work trips also improved in the smallest and largest cities as well as in some medium-sized cities (500,000–999,999). Most nonwork trips during the morning peak and off-peak hours experienced a general improvement in mean travel times between 1983 and 1990. With the exception of the largest cities, mean travel times for nonwork trips during the evening peak rose. Mean distances, on the other hand, were generally higher in all categories except for nonwork morning peak period trips in cities with populations less than 1 million and peak period trips in cities over 3 million.

Mean travel times during the morning and evening peak periods rose in three of the five

Table 12.9 Sectoral employment trends in 12 major CMSAs, 1982–7

	Sector			
	Manufacturing	Retail	Wholesale	Services
Central city				
1982 share	0.302	0.281	0.377	0.416
1987 share	0.258	0.258	0.319	0.261
Annual growth rate, 1982–7	−0.0388	0.0215	−0.0029	0.0397
Ring I				
1982 share	0.349	0.368	0.336	0.300
1987 share	0.377	0.379	0.360	0.327
Annual growth rate, 1982–7	0.0075	0.0454	0.0445	0.0885
Ring II				
1982 share	0.349	0.351	0.287	0.284
1987 share	0.365	0.364	0.321	0.313
Annual growth rate, 1982–7	0.0021	0.0468	0.0535	0.0904

Source: Adapted from Gordon and Richardson (1994), Table 16, p. 27

city size groupings. Average work-trip distances increased for all city size groupings for the peak and off-peak periods, whereas morning (evening) peak period distances fell in four (two) of the city size classifications.

These results are broadly consistent with a general trend of residential suburbanization. From the tables, there was a general pattern for mean travel times to fall within central cities but to rise outside central cities. Distances in both areas typically rose. Both within each area and between central-city and outside areas, the data are consistent with residential reallocation away from the more heavily congested locales and toward less congested areas. As the population disperses, congestion in the denser areas eases, leading to smaller increases or reductions in mean travel time, while the less congested growth areas experience some additional congestion. Although population dispersion may lead to longer trip distances, if these distances are combined with higher speeds, there may well be little net impact on travel times. Corroborating evidence on household suburbanization comes from two additional pieces of information. First, Gordon and Richardson calculated average trip speeds for each of the categories in tables 12.7 and 12.8 and found that, in all but three cases, average speeds were significantly higher in 1990. Second, using the same NPTS information, Hu and Young (1992) found that average commute trip lengths increased 7% between 1983 and 1990 but mean trip times fell 3% during the same period.[25]

Complementing household suburbanizing activities is greater suburbanization of jobs. Table 12.9 reports the average growth rates for 12 Consolidated Metropolitan Statistical Areas (CMSAs).[26] Growth rates in the outer rings exceeded those in the central city, which implies that jobs are dispersing outward. For manufacturing and wholesale activities, average annual growth in the central city was negative between 1982 and 1987, while retail and services experienced positive growth. In outer rings I and II, however, there was positive growth in each of the four job sectors and, with the exception of manufacturing, the growth rates in more distant suburban locations (Ring II) were higher than in less distant suburban locations (Ring I).

In summary, although the 50% increase in urban vehicle–miles traveled during the 1980s was tempered with a 21% increase in urban mileage, the average commuter experienced a minor 40 second increase in the work trip. By further demonstrating that mean travel time differences between 1977 and 1990 are not a result of peak spreading or differences in work-trip departures, Gordon and Richardson conclude that spatial accommodation by households and businesses has resulted in relatively minor increases, and some decreases, in mean travel time during the 1980s.

EMPIRICAL MODELS OF FIRM AND HOUSEHOLD LOCATION

CASE STUDY – FIRM DECISIONS TO RELOCATE IN METROPOLITAN AREAS

In a multicentric metropolitan environment, firms' location decisions depend upon the trade-off between land prices and transportation costs, as well as the pull of attractive forces from agglomeration economies. In order to examine the extent to which agglomeration economies, transportation, and land prices influence a firm's metropolitan location, Erickson and Wasylenko (1980) developed an empirical model that attempts to explain the demand for suburban land by firms that are initially located in the central city.

For certain types of industrial activities such as construction, manufacturing, transportation, and wholesale trade, relocating will have at most a small effect upon sales and revenues. The desire to maximize profits is then equivalent to minimizing its costs of production. For these industry types, Erickson and Wasylenko assume that a firm in industrial sector i has production function

$$Q_i = f(N_i, L_i, K_i, AG_i, G_i)$$

where Q_i is output for industrial sector i, N_i is labor, L_i is land, K_i is capital, AG_i reflects agglomeration economies due to the concentration of firms at a given location, and G_i is the amount of public services provided. In producing Q_i, firms in sector i face the following cost function:

$$C_i = (P_N)_i N_i + (P'_K)_i(1 + t_i/r)K_i + (P_L)_i L_i$$

where C_i is the cost of production, P_{si} (s = N,L) is the price of input s in sector i, and P'_{Ki} is the net price of capital, which is assumed to be equal for all suburban locations. However, property tax rates differ across different suburban communities and these tax rates are capitalized into the price of capital. Thus, the gross price of capital, P_{Ki} equals P'_{Ki} $(1 + t_i/r)$, which is the net price of capital plus the present value of taxes for tax rate t_i and rate of interest r.[27] Solving this cost minimization problem, subject to the production function, yields the following demand function for land by industrial sector i, L_i,

$$L_i = g(Q_i, P_{Li}, P_{Ni}, AG_i, t_i, G_i)$$

which is seen to depend upon the level of output, the prices of land and labor, agglomeration economies, the property tax rate, and public-sector expenditures.[28]

Although the theoretical development is straightforward, empirically testing the relationship between the demand for land and its determinants turns out to be a difficult measurement problem, because one does not normally observe the demand for land, nor its price.[29] To get around this problem, Erickson and Wasylenko used data on 380 firms in Milwaukee City that relocated to one of Milwaukee's 56 municipalities outside of the central city between 1964 and 1974. Erickson and Wasylenko argued that a firm's relocation from the central city to suburban municipality j is a proxy for the firm's demand for land at location j.[30] Summing over all relocating firms in sector i and dividing by the total number of relocating firms in the sector gives the proportion of firms in sector i that relocated to one of Milwaukee's 56 suburban municipalities j, $S_i(j)$ $(j = 1, \ldots, 56)$.

If $S_i(j)$ is the probability of relocating to community j, then $1 - S_i(j)$ is the probability of relocating to one of the other suburban municipalities. Also, let $NEB_i(j)$ be the net economic benefit to sector i of locating in municipality j, which is assumed to reflect the factors that influence the demand for land and site choice. Erickson and Wasylenko define the following binary logit model for relocating firms in sector i:

$$S_i(j) = \frac{e^{(NEB_i(j)+\varepsilon)}}{1 + e^{(NEB_i(j)+\varepsilon)}}$$

$$\Rightarrow 1 - S_i(j) = \frac{1}{1 + e^{(NEB_i(j)+\varepsilon)}}$$

where ε is an error term. Since $S_i(j)$ is a proportion that lies between zero and one, we can divide $S_i(j)$ by $1 - S_i(j)$ to obtain the odds of a sector i firm relocating in municipality j:

$$\frac{S_i(j)}{1 - S_i(j)} = e^{NEB_i(j)+\varepsilon}$$

Taking logarithms yields

$$\ln\left(\frac{S_i(j)}{1 - S_i(j)}\right) = NEB_i(j) + \varepsilon, \quad j = 1, \ldots, 56$$

where the dependent variable is defined as the logarithm of the odds of locating in municipality j.[31] Defining $NEB_i(j)$ as a linear function of those factors that influence the demand for land and site choice leads to the following linear regression model:

$$\ln\left(\frac{S_i(j)}{1 - S_i(j)}\right) = \beta_0 + \beta_1 P_{Li} + \beta_2 P_{Ni} + \beta_3 AG_i + \beta_4 t_i + \beta_6 G_i + \varepsilon \qquad (12.21)$$

In their empirical analysis, Erickson and Wasylenko did not have information on price of land or the wage rate in each of the municipalities. As a proxy for the price of land, they used four variables: CBD Distance, defined as the distance from the suburban community to Milwaukee's CBD; a dummy variable that equals one if there is access to an interstate highway in the municipality and zero if not; the proportion of vacant land in the municipality; and the proportion of land used for industrial purposes.

Our theory of urban land use tells us that firms have an incentive to decentralize if they can save on wage costs, since workers commute smaller distances. This suggests that municipalities with a large workforce will be more attractive, since firms will be more likely to draw workers locally and avoid having to pay a wage premium to compensate for the higher transportation costs associated with drawing workers from further locations. Hence, the larger a municipality's workforce in industry i, the more likely firms in industry i will save wage costs by relocating to that municipality. To capture this workforce size effect, Erickson and Wasylenko included the variable Residential Employees, defined as the number of employees in industrial sector i living within a 7 mile radius of municipality j.[32]

To measure the attractive force of a municipality in drawing firms from an industrial sector, Erickson and Wasylenko used the proportion of the industrial sector's noncentral city employment that works in municipality j.

Substituting these empirical measures of the theoretical constructs into equation (12.21) gives the following empirical regression model:

$$\begin{aligned}
\ln\left(\frac{S_i(j)}{1 - S_i(j)}\right)
&= \beta_0 + \beta_1(1/\text{CBD Distance } (j)) \\
&\quad + \beta_2\text{Interstate Access } (j) \\
&\quad + \beta_3(\%\text{ Industrial Land } (j)) \\
&\quad + \beta_4(\%\text{ Vacant Land } (j)) \\
&\quad + \beta_5(\text{Residential Employment in } i\ (j)) \\
&\quad + \beta_6(\%\text{ Industrial Employment in } i\ (j)) \\
&\quad + \beta_7\text{Safety Expenditures } (j) \\
&\quad + \beta_8\text{Service Expenditures } (j) \\
&\quad + \beta_9\text{Tax Rate } (j) + \varepsilon(j) \qquad (12.22)
\end{aligned}$$

Hypotheses

HYPOTHESIS 1 *Variables related to land price.* Equation (12.22) contains four variables that are intended to capture the influence of land prices on a firm's site selection. First, CBD Distance is specified as a reciprocal in order to capture the nonlinear relationship between accessibility and site selection. Since declining accessibility of a more distant municipality to the CBD is expected to lower the price of land, then, all else held constant, it is expected to increase the odds of a suburban location. This will occur if the coefficient of (1/CBD Distance), β_1, is negative.

Second, accessibility to an interstate highway may have a positive or negative effect upon site selection. Holding all else constant, if the benefits of interstate accessibility more than offset the higher land prices associated with a more accessible site, then β_2 will be positive. Conversely, if higher land prices more than offset the benefits of interstate accessibility, β_2 will be negative.

The coefficient for %Vacant Land, β_3, is expected to be positive. An increased supply of vacant land lowers land prices, which would be expected to increase the demand for the site, all else held constant. However, an increase in %Industrial Land has an uncertain effect on the likelihood of relocating to a particular municipality. Higher concentrations of land in industrial use attract firms if these concentrations signal the greater availability of industrial rental space, which would lower land prices. Alternatively, increased concentrations may indicate high industrial demands or may signal municipal constraints on further industrial development, which would raise land prices. All else constant, then, we have no expectation for the sign of β_4.

HYPOTHESIS 2 *Wage-related variable.* In the empirical model, (Residential Employment in *i*) reflects the size of the workforce in industrial sector *i* that lives within 7 miles of the municipality. The larger the available workforce, the more attractive the municipality will be, since the firm will not have to pay a wage premium in order to draw workers from a more distant location. All else constant, we expect β_5 to be positive.

HYPOTHESIS 3 *Agglomeration economies.* For each industrial sector *i*, Erickson and Wasylenko's measure of a municipality's agglomeration economies is the proportion of the metropolitan area's noncentral area workforce in the sector that works in municipality *i*. The greater this proportion, the larger is the attractive pull of the municipality. Holding all else constant, the coefficient of (% Industrial Employment in *i*), β_6, is expected to be positive;

HYPOTHESIS 4 *Public services.* Erickson and Wasylenko's empirical model includes three variables related to a municipality's activities, per capita expenditures on public safety (that is, police and fire), per capita expenditures on streets and sanitation, and the property tax rate. We would expect that increases in expenditures on public services would enhance a municipality's site selection, whereas increases in its property tax rate would reduce its selection. This implies that $\beta_7 > 0$, $\beta_8 > 0$, and $\beta_9 < 0$.

Estimation results

Table 12.10 summarizes the Erickson and Wasylenko's estimation results. For the Construction, Manufacturing, Transportation, and Wholesale Trade sectors, respectively, the model explains 67%, 50%, 42%, and 78% of the variation in the dependent variable. For each of the industrial sectors, the results are consistent with agglomeration economies and work force availability. Consistent with hypothesis 3, the greater the proportion of noncentral employment in a municipality, the greater is that municipality's ability to attract relocating firms from the center. Also, we see that the coefficient for "% Residential Employment in *i*" is positive and significant

Table 12.10 Estimation results for site relocation[a]

Dependent variable – $\ln\left(\frac{S_i(j)}{1 - S_i(j)}\right)$

Independent Variables	Construction	Manufacturing	Transportation	Wholesale Trade
1/CBD Distance	−8.45 (−3.85)	−0.05 (−0.01)	−2.34 (−1.49)	−6.73 (−2.71)
Interstate Access	0.06 (0.49)	0.31 (1.59)	0.02 (0.36)	−0.14 (−1.11)
% Industrial Land	−2.55 (−1.65)	−10.06 (−3.56)	−1.23 (−1.31)	−1.48 (−0.95)
% Vacant Land	0.12 (0.30)	1.27 (2.00)	0.14 (0.61)	−0.92 (−2.27)
Residential Employment in *i*	0.21 (5.35)	0.02 (1.77)	0.04 (2.29)	0.22 (6.28)
% Industrial Employment in *i*	13.05 (3.11)	19.50 (4.50)	6.38 (3.45)	12.93 (4.37)
Safety Expenditures	0.0003 (0.07)	0.004 (0.65)	0.00001 (0.004)	−0.01 (−2.34)
Service Expenditures	0.001 (0.87)	−0.002 (−0.62)	0.0003 (0.32)	−0.0005 (−0.26)
Tax Rate	21.73 (1.54)	20.76 (0.82)	1.85 (0.23)	−16.65 (−1.08)
R^2	0.67	0.50	0.42	0.78
Number of observations	56	56	56	56

[a] *j* indexes municipality and *i* indexes industrial sector. *t*-statistics in parentheses.
Source: Adapted from Erickson and Wasylenko (1980), table 3, p. 80

at the 0.05 level in all cases, which is consistent with hypothesis 2, that a local supply of labor precludes firms from paying wage premia.

In general, the results are inconsistent with hypothesis 4. Public-sector variables play little role in relocation decisions. Per capita expenditures upon public safety only have an effect upon the relocation of wholesale trade firms, but in this case the effect is unexpected. An increase in public safety expenditures decreases the probability of relocating to a municipality. Similarly, per capita expenditures upon streets and sanitation as well as the property tax rate have little effect upon firm relocation decisions.

With respect to hypothesis 1, we see mixed results. Interstate Access is not important in firms' relocation decisions, with the possible exception of the manufacturing sector, where the coefficient is positive and significant at the 0.10 level. Similarly, increasing availability of vacant land has no effect upon site selection of construction, manufacturing, and transportation firms. For wholesale trade firms, however, the effect is negative and statistically significant. Although signaling lower land prices, more vacant space may also indicate lower demands for land in the area. The results suggest that these two effects are offsetting in the construction, manufacturing, and transportation sectors, whereas in the wholesale trade sector, the demand effect is dominant.

On the other hand, an increasing percentage of land used for industrial purposes in a municipality significantly decreases the likelihood of construction and manufacturing firms relocating there. This suggests that the positive effect on land prices from larger demands more than offsets the negative effect on land prices from the greater availability of industrial land.

Last, the coefficient of the distance variable, (1/CBD Distance), has a negative sign which is statistically significant at the 0.05 level in three of the four industrial sectors. This is consistent with the hypothesis that lower land prices at distances further from the CBD induce firms in the construction, transportation, and wholesale trade sectors to relocate.

Discussion

For each of the industrial sectors except manufacturing, the results in table 12.10 are consistent with the hypothesis that, holding all else constant, increasing distance from the CBD reflects decreasing land prices, which influence firms' relocation decisions. In the manufacturing sector, however, the coefficient on distance was not statistically significant. Since municipalities further from the CBD are more residential, stringent zoning laws may prevent manufacturing firms from locating in certain areas. At the same time, the results in table 12.10 tell us that manufacturing firms avoid locations in which there is a high percentage of industrial use and look for locations with vacant land. The coefficient on "% Industrial Land" for the manufacturing sector is much larger (in absolute value) than that for the other sectors. And only for the manufacturing sector is the coefficient for "% Vacant Land" statistically significant.

We also saw in table 12.10 that the property tax rate has no impact upon relocation decisions for any industrial sector. Erickson and Wasylenko report that the property tax rate in the central city is 4.4% and averages 3% in the 56 suburban municipalities (with a standard deviation of 0.003). This suggests that the property tax rate is an important factor in moving from the central city to the suburbs. However, the analysis reported in table 12.10 only examines firms that have relocated to the suburban areas. Erickson and Wasylenko do not examine a firm's central city–suburban choice, but only a firm's decision to locate in the suburb. And the fact that there is very little variation in the property tax rate among the suburban municipalities may explain why this variable was not found to be an important determinant of relocation choice.

CASE STUDY – TRANSPORTATION POLICY, HOUSEHOLD DECISIONS, AND URBAN DEVELOPMENT

A primary finding from our examination of urban environments was that the cost of accessibility is an important determinant of metropolitan development. By significantly reducing the cost of travel, advances in passenger and freight transportation during the past 60 or so years have produced strong decentralizing trends in our nation's metropolitan areas. Whether it be to an export node, the CBD, or a subcenter, accessibility plays a vital role in the development of our urban centers. But this raises an interesting question. Can transportation policy play a central role in shaping a metropolitan area's spatial development? We know that transportation planners can alter households' modal choices in the commute to work through pricing and service policies. Reducing public transit fares, increasing network size, and providing more frequent service will lead to increased ridership. Yet this result ignores the potential impact that these pricing and service changes may have upon other household decisions, such as automobile ownership and residential location decisions. In general, households' location and transportation choices are related. Although we tend to think of a household's location decision determining its transportation decision, in the long run, when a household has yet to make its location decision, the availability of transportation will influence its final choice of location. And to the extent that transportation policy affects the quantity and quality of transportation available in a metropolitan area, it will have some impact upon the spatial development of the area. The question that we want to examine here is whether urban transportation policy is likely to play an important role in a metropolitan area's spatial development.

In one of the few analyses that examines this question, Lerman (1979) developed a multinomial logit model of a household's joint transportation and residential location decisions. The transportation decisions included in the model are a household's choice of mode in the trip to work and the number of automobiles to own. The residential location decision encompasses a household's choice of neighborhood and housing type. Lerman's analysis can be viewed as a long-run demand model in which a household simultaneously decides where to reside in the metropolitan area, whether to purchase or rent its housing (and if it rents, does it rent a single or multifamily dwelling), how many automobiles to own (which could be zero), and whether to take public transit or use an own automobile in the trip to work.[33]

Lerman identified six groups of attributes which affect a household's choice of neighborhood, housing, automobile ownership, and mode choices. These included:

1 Transportation level of service in the trip to work (for example, travel time and travel cost).
2 Automobile ownership attributes (for example, annual maintenance, registration and other legalities, and expenditures upon automobile ownership).
3 Location attributes (for example, property taxes, community services, neighborhood quality, and local insurance rates).
4 Housing attributes (for example, age and quality of structure, type of structure, and so on).
5 Spatial opportunities (for example, accessibility to shopping, schools, and recreational facilities).
6 Socioeconomic characteristics (for example, number of licensed drivers in the household, household size, marital status, and race).

On the basis of a 1968 sample of 177 single-worker households residing in the Washington DC area, Lerman's estimation results fit the data well and are consistent with expectations. Increases in a given mode's travel time to work reduce the likelihood of using that mode, and higher automobile costs lowers the level of automobile ownership. An increase in property taxes lowers the demand for particular locations, and raising the cost of accessing alternative spatial opportunities lowers the demand for these nonwork destinations.

Lerman used this model to examine the impact that alternative transportation policies would have upon household location and transportation decisions. To do this, he defined a hypothetical city, depicted in figure 12.10, that has two main corridors emanating from the CBD. In this hypothetical city, there are 11 zones. The CBD is the central zone (Zone 1) that accommodates both residential and employment activities. Zones 2–11 (five zones in each corridor) are symmetric zones that ring the CBD at distances ranging from 2 to 25 miles. The central zone has a

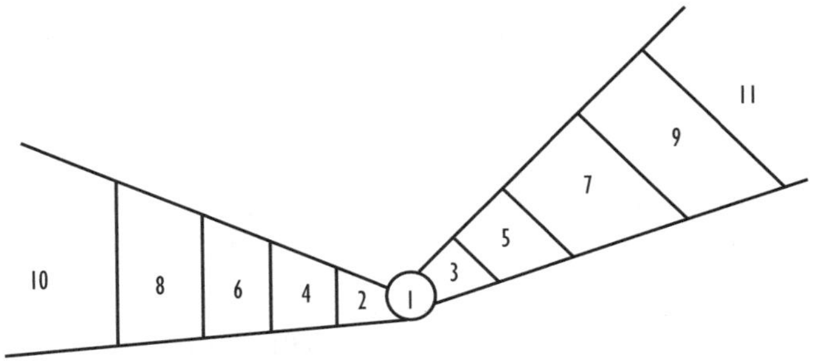

Figure 12.10 A hypothetical city. Zone 1, 2 miles; Zones 2 and 3, 4 miles; Zones 4 and 5, 7 miles; Zones 6 and 7, 12 miles; Zones 8 and 9, 15 miles; Zones 10 and 11, 25 miles.

Table 12.11 Housing and transportation base case

Income	Race	Work-Trip Distance	Own, Single Family	Rent, Single Family	Rent, Multifamily	Expected Auto Ownership	Transit Choice Probability	Expected Total VMT
Low	White	6.42	0	0.094	0.907	1.02	0.409	8.37
Medium	White	12.10	0.299	0.398	0.304	1.50	0.181	21.00
High	White	16.83	0.676	0.240	0.085	1.69	0.084	31.74
Low	Black	4.56	0	0.061	0.949	0.972	0.451	5.17
Medium	Black	7.16	0.138	0.151	0.712	1.17	0.296	11.48
High	Black	16.77	0.692	0.130	0.178	1.59	0.086	32.45

Source: Adapted from Lerman (1979), table 5, p. 105

high population density with only multi-family dwellings. Average income is relatively low and the residential population is 75% black. The two contiguous zones to the CBD reflect urban ghettos whose residents have very low incomes and, as a result, no single-family housing. One zone is 98% black while the other is 90% white. The population density in these zones is lower than in the CBD. As distance from the CBD increases, average household incomes increase, population density falls, more single-family housing is available, and the proportion of blacks decreases. Transportation in this hypothetical city is by automobile or bus. The cost of bus public transportation rises with distance from the CBD, but public transportation is assumed to be unavailable in the more distant zones.

Lerman applied his estimated model to this hypothetical city in order to generate predicted choice probabilities for a prototypical household, defined as a household with one CBD worker, a spouse, and two small children. From these predictions, he calculated five summary measures that he used to evaluate the impact of alternative transportation policies:

- one-way distance to the CBD
- housing type distribution
- expected automobile ownership
- transit usage
- daily VMT for automobile users

Table 12.11 reports the base case, which summarizes the household location and transportation characteristics by income and race in the hypothetical city.[34] For both blacks and whites, expected auto ownership increases with income, although the ownership levels for whites are uniformly higher. Further, single-family house ownership for blacks and whites increases with both income and distance from CBD as households substitute land for nonland inputs in their housing consumption. Black households' locations nearer the CBD also explain why lower- and middle-income blacks have a higher probability of taking public transit in their work trips, a lower probability of living in single-family housing, and fewer expected VMTs per day. Higher-income blacks, however, exhibit housing and transportation characteristics that are similar to higher-income whites.

Automobile disincentive policies

Tables 12.12 and 12.13 indicate the effects upon transport and housing decisions from transportation policies that induce households away from automobile use. Table 12.12 reflects a moderate disincentive plan that encompasses a $1.00 parking charge downtown, an increased fuel tax

Table 12.12 Policy 1 – moderate auto use disincentives

Income	Race	Work-Trip Distance	Own, Single Family	Rent, Single Family	Rent, Multifamily	Expected Auto Ownership	Transit Choice Probability	Expected Total VMT
Low	White	6.01	0	0.083	0.916	0.965	0.597	0.547
Medium	White	11.54	0.245	0.421	0.334	1.46	0.231	18.98
High	White	16.77	0.672	0.243	0.086	1.69	0.095	31.36
Low	Black	4.42	0	0.051	0.950	0.947	0.621	3.42
Medium	Black	6.63	0.103	0.155	0.743	1.13	0.356	9.83
High	Black	16.69	0.687	0.132	0.181	1.58	0.098	32.13

Source: Adapted from Lerman (1979), table 6, p. 109

Table 12.13 Policy 2 – strong auto use disincentives

Income	Race	Work-Trip Distance	Own, Single Family	Rent, Single Family	Rent, Multifamily	Expected Auto Ownership	Transit Choice Probability	Expected Total VMT
Low	White	5.62	0	0.081	0.919	0.892	0.687	3.82
Medium	White	10.76	0.172	0.443	0.379	1.40	0.270	16.80
High	White	16.31	0.647	0.260	0.093	1.68	0.111	30.08
Low	Black	4.31	0	0.048	0.952	0.908	0.691	2.62
Medium	Black	5.96	0.065	0.154	0.782	1.09	0.387	8.20
High	Black	16.01	0.651	0.142	0.208	1.54	0.117	30.51

Source: Adapted from Lerman (1979), table 7, p. 110

that raises automobile operating costs 50%, and parking regulations that raise per trip out-of-vehicle travel time by 5 minutes. Comparing the impact of this policy with the base case, we see that these moderate disincentives have the greatest impact upon lower-income households' work-trip modal choices, but *relatively little impact* upon their automobile ownership and housing decisions. For lower- and middle-income white households, the probability of using public transit in the work-trip increases from 0.409 and 0.181, respectively, to 0.597 and 0.231. The predicted effect for black lower- and middle-income households is an increase from 0.451 and 0.296, respectively, to 0.621 and 0.356. The larger effect on black household transit choices reflects their housing location in zones nearer the CBD where public transit is more available. Expected automobile ownership decreases for all categories, but not by very much. Similarly, as you might expect, the higher cost of CBD accessibility has a compacting effect upon the city, as reflected by the lower average work-trip distances and the smaller demand for single-family housing. But these effects are relatively small.

In table 12.13, we see the impact on housing and transportation if, in addition to the moderate automobile disincentives, we add a 25% automobile ownership tax and induce a 25% increase in in-vehicle travel times by restricting downtown traffic in some areas. As expected, this policy reinforces the modal shift toward public transportation identified in table 12.12. For lower-income households, transit probabilities rise to 0.687 for white households and 0.691 for black households. There is a further decline in the demand for automobile ownership and single-family housing among middle-income households. Despite the significant increase in automobile ownership costs, there is little effect upon the demand for automobiles and single-family housing among higher-income households. Although the relative cost of automobile travel increases, public transportation is not available in the outer suburbs where higher-income households locate, and the increases are not sufficient to induce these households to locate closer to the CBD. The average work-trip distance for higher-income white and black households decreases modestly from 16.83 and 16.77, respectively, to 16.31 and 16.01.

To sum up, despite the impact upon work-trip modal split, automobile disincentives have relatively little effect upon the form of the urban structure. However, the combined effect of increased public transit use with relatively little change in work-trip distance leads to a significant reduction in daily VMT for lower- and middle-income households and a smaller change for higher-income households.

Public transit incentive policies

Rather than automobile disincentives, tables 12.14 and 12.15 summarize the effect on urban form from transportation policies that provide incentives to use public transportation. Table 12.14 reflects a moderate transit improvement which combines a 50% reduction in fares with improved scheduling and routing that lowers in-vehicle and out-of-vehicle travel times by 20% and 50% respectively. The primary effect of these changes is upon modal choice, but the magnitude of the effect is smaller than either of the auto disincentive schemes. We also see that improving the public transit supply increases the average work-trip distance for lower-income households. The improved accessibility to the CBD allows these households to occupy zones a bit further from the CBD than in the base case. But this policy has virtually no impact upon automobile ownership and urban form.

Table 12.15 reflects a major improvement in the public transportation, a rapid transit network that serves the entire urban area and offers speeds comparable to the automobile in non-CBD zones, and two minutes faster than auto travel in the CBD. Relative to the base case, wait times are halved (with a 15 minute maximum) and fares are halved, with no fare higher than $0.25. Public transit travel times and costs for nonwork shopping trips are similarly improved. From table 12.15, the effect of an area-wide rapid transit system on household transportation and housing choices is significant. For middle-

Table 12.14 Policy 3 – moderate transit improvements

Income	Race	Work-Trip Distance	Own, Single Family	Rent, Single Family	Rent, Multifamily	Expected Auto Ownership	Transit Choice Probability	Expected Total VMT
Low	White	7.06	0	0.119	0.880	1.00	0.501	7.06
Medium	White	11.94	0.291	0.403	0.306	1.49	0.246	19.32
High	White	16.62	0.664	0.248	0.088	1.69	0.122	30.42
Low	Black	4.58	0	0.068	0.932	0.965	0.524	4.49
Medium	Black	7.01	0.130	0.152	0.718	0.965	0.524	10.58
High	Black	16.53	0.678	0.135	0.188	1.57	0.110	31.61

Source: Adapted from Lerman (1979), table 8, p. 111

Table 12.15 Policy 4 – major transit improvements

Income	Race	Work-Trip Distance	Own, Single Family	Rent, Single Family	Rent, Multifamily	Expected Auto Ownership	Transit Choice Probability	Expected Total VMT
Low	White	5.72	0	0.137	0.863	0.925	0.562	4.76
Medium	White	7.90	0.128	0.307	0.566	1.01	0.425	8.98
High	White	11.90	0.442	0.333	0.226	0.972	0.400	14.09
Low	Black	4.43	0	0.070	0.931	0.951	0.544	3.96
Medium	Black	5.13	0.035	0.147	0.819	1.05	0.426	5.88
High	Black	9.10	0.181	0.276	0.544	1.03	0.406	9.10

Source: Adapted from Lerman (1979), table 9, p. 112

and higher-income households, average work-trip distances fall by 31% and 37% respectively, which reflects a much more compact city. As the city constricts, there is a corresponding fall in the demand for single-family housing. For example, the probability that a higher-income white household owns a single family house falls from 0.676 to 0.442. The drop for black households is even larger, from 0.692 to 0.181. Automobile ownership for middle- and higher-income households decreases by at least 30%, with corresponding reductions in daily VMT. And in contrast to the auto disincentive and moderate public transit policies, building a rapid transit system has a dramatic effect upon modal split for all income categories.

Discussion

Notwithstanding the fact that Lerman's analysis is based upon data from 1968, his findings are still relevant today and provide important insights into the interactions that exist between residential location and transportation decisions of households. Importantly, his analysis suggests that transportation policies can influence a household's residential choices by altering a neighborhood's desirable attributes. Improving a neighborhood's accessibility to public transit, for example, is beneficial and increases the neighborhood's attractiveness relative to those with poorer public transit service. However, Lerman also found that the extent to which transportation policy can significantly alter location choices is limited. Only when there is a significant change in transportation services, such as major investments in rapid rail systems, will household locations choices be substantially altered. This finding is consistent with a more recent study by Gomez-Ibanez (1985), who concluded that transportation policies may be important in enhancing our understanding of the interplay between transportation and land use, but will not be a major determining factor in a metropolitan area's development.

CASE STUDY – INFORMATION TECHNOLOGY AND URBAN DEVELOPMENT

Throughout this chapter, we have seen that accessibility plays a key role in determining metropolitan development. In a monocentric world, the introduction of automobile travel significantly lowers household transportation costs and, combined with increasing standards of living, provides strong decentralizing tendencies for households. Further, strong agglomeration economies and their cost-reducing or revenue-generating effects provide incentives for firms to locate near other firms in the centralized area. However, as the population decentralizes, this creates economic incentives for firms to decentralize as well. As the city expands, the centralizing effect of positive agglomeration economies weakens, as firms must also pay higher wages to compensate workers for higher transportation costs. At some point, the increase in wages more than offset the agglomeration economies that a firm experiences, and the firm decentralizes. This effect is further complemented by other firms – for example, service and retail outlets – following their customers to the suburbs.

In contrast to the marginal effect of public-sector transportation policy on metropolitan development, recent advances in electronic communications provide a technological innovation that has the potential to significantly alter the future shape of our cities. Fax machines, videoconferencing, and intra- and interfirm computer networks facilitate information exchanges between humans and between machines (that is, data transfers). In a very general sense, these developments, like the automobile in the early part of the century, significantly reduce transportation costs for activities that are information intensive. Further, Baumol (1986) argues that the widening use of smaller but more powerful personal computers is conducive to more competitive market structures in which there are a large number of smaller and less concentrated firms. These advances in computer technology and electronic communication not only strengthen a firm's existing incentives to decentralize, but the ability to electronically communicate opens up a much broader set of location opportunities for the decentralizing firms.

Kumar (1990) examines whether information technologies have led to a more dispersed distribution of firms. Kumar argues that the introduction of advanced information technologies does not have the same impact on all occupations. Workers involved in the production, processing, or distribution of information are more affected by the innovating technologies, whereas those whose jobs are more "site specific" are less affected, at least in the sense that there are fewer opportunities for the worker to telecommute or for the firm to exploit "information" economies by dispersing some of its activities to decentralized locations.[35]

To test this hypothesis, Kumar estimated a regression model on data obtained from the 1983–4 Nationwide Personal Transportation Study (NPTS), a household survey conducted by the Department of Transportation. For Kumar's purposes, these data provide two important pieces of information: a worker's distance from home to work and a worker's occupation. In his regression model, workers were grouped into one of eight mutually exclusive occupations: computer analyst, manager, sales, administrator, professional, engineer, technician, and blue collar. Of these eight categories, Kumar hypothesized that the first five occupations were more involved in information production and distribution, which implied that firms associated with these occupations have greater location flexibility. Holding all else constant, working as a computer analyst, manager, sales person, administrator, or professional is expected to decrease the commute distance, whereas engineers, technicians, and blue-collar workers are expected to have longer commute distances.

Table 12.16 reports Kumar's regression results on a sample of 8,314 workers. The dependent variable for the analysis is the worker's work-trip distance, and the independent variables include socioeconomic characteristics and occupation categories. The regression model in table 12.16 reflects a number of hypotheses on the spatial distribution of households and firms.

1 As we have seen, increases in income have two opposing effects on household location decisions. Assuming that housing is a normal good, higher incomes induce individuals to move further from a central

Table 12.16 Regression equation on worktrip commuting distance, 1983

Dependent variable – Worktrip Distance (miles)

Independent Variable	Coefficient Estimate (*t*-statistic)
Personal attributes	
Household Income ('000s)	0.0002 (1.02)
# Persons in Household	0.50 (2.05)[a]
Married	1.62 (2.22)[b]
Resides Outside Central City	0.42 (1.95)[c]
Occupation-specific attributes	
Computer Analyst	−3.02 (−2.91)[a]
Manager	−1.07 (−1.68)[c]
Sales	−3.08 (−3.89)[a]
Administrator	−0.93 (−1.99)[a]
Professional	−1.38 (−2.84)[a]
Engineer	0.37 (1.84)[c]
Technician	0.84 (2.05)[a]
Constant term	7.47 (7.60)[b]
$\bar{R}^2 = 0.58$	

[a] Significant at 0.05 level, one-tail test.
[b] Significant at 0.01 level, two-tail test.
[c] Significant at 0.05 level, one-tail test.
Source: Adapted from Kumar (1990), table 5, p. 143, with the permission of Taylor & Francis Ltd, PO Box 25, Abingdon, Oxfordshire OX14 3UE, UK (http://www.tandf.co.uk/journals)

area. At the same time, higher incomes increase a worker's value of time, which raises one's transportation costs. The net effect of Household Income on work-trip distance is ambiguous.

2 Household size is expected to increase work-trip distance from a central area. With more members in the household, the demand for housing will be larger, which increases the savings on housing expenditures as one moves further from an urban center. All else constant, an increase in Persons is expected to increase work-trip distance.

3 In his analysis, Kumar controls for whether a worker resides outside the central city. In general, persons residing within central cities are expected to have smaller commute distances, which primarily reflects the smaller geographic size of an urban area's central city relative to its surrounding areas. All else constant, the variable "Resides Outside Central City" is expected to increase a person's work-trip distance. Kumar also includes Marital Status, to control for possible differences in location preferences between single and married households. *A priori*, the effect on work-trip distance is ambiguous.

4 Each of the occupation categories, Computer Analyst, Manager, Sales, Administrator, Professional, Engineer, and Technician, is a dummy variable that equals one if the individual is in that occupation and equals zero if the individual is not in that occupation. Blue Collar is the omitted category, so that

> the interpretation of each of the included occupation variables is relative to the Blue Collar category. If the data are consistent with the hypothesis of greater firm location flexibility for information-intensive occupations, then we expect the coefficients on Computer Analyst, Manager, Sales, Administrator, and Professional to be negative and the coefficients on Engineer and Technician to be larger than the coefficients on the information-related occupations.

From table 12.16, the model explains nearly 60% of the variation in work-trip distances. In addition, the coefficients of the variables are generally consistent with our hypotheses. Although an increase in income increases distance from the CBD, we cannot reject the null hypothesis that the coefficient is in fact zero. This suggests that the decentralizing effect of higher incomes due to greater housing demands is offset by the centralizing effect of higher incomes on transportation costs, a result which is consistent with Wheaton's (1977) work on the location effects of income.

Also consistent with expectations, we see in the table that an increase in the number of persons per household and residing outside of the central city leads to longer commutes. Specifically, a one-person increase in household size increases the average commute distance by half a mile, and households residing outside the central city have a 0.42 mile longer commute in the daily work trip. Although we had no prior expectations of the effect that marital status would have upon commute length, we see in table 12.16 that married households – all else constant, including household size – commute an additional 1.62 miles to work. This is consistent with married households consuming more housing than the unmarried household, thereby providing married households with larger housing expenditure savings at further distances.

Are the results consistent with Kumar's hypothesis that firms in information-intensive activities have more flexible location opportunities that translate into greater dispersal and lower commute distances? From the findings reported in table 12.16, the answer is yes. Consistent with hypothesis 4, we see in the table that, relative to Blue Collar workers, Computer Analysts, Managers, Sales, Professionals, and Administrators have shorter worktrip commutes. And each of these effects is significant at the 0.05 level. Looking at the respective coefficients, the results suggest that Computer Analyst and Sales occupations benefit most from information-induced location flexibility. Relative to Blue Collar workers, computer analysts and those in sales commute on average 3 miles less. Professionals commute 1.3 miles less than Blue Collar workers whereas Managers and Administrators have commutes that are about 1 mile less than those of blue-collar workers.

Also consistent with expectations, the other occupations hypothesized to be "site specific" (in addition to blue-collar workers) that enjoy fewer location opportunities have positive signs and the coefficients are statistically significant. Relative to blue-collar workers, engineers and technicians travel 0.37 and 0.84 miles further (which also implies that these workers travel further than those in the information-intensive occupations).

Discussion

If Kumar's hypothesis is true, one would also expect that work-related trips – that is, those trips that originate and end at the work site – should decrease for those persons engaged in information-intensive activities. Average trip distances for work-related trips in 1983 for computer analysts, managers, sales, administrators, and professionals were 5.4, 8.5, 7.3, 6.0, and 7.2 miles respectively. On the other hand, engineers, technicians, and blue-collar workers had work-related trips that averaged 10.1, 10.4, and 10.0 miles respectively. Moreover, these effects were generally stable for small as well as large metropolitan areas.

One must, however, be careful not to overemphasize the importance of these findings. The results suggest that there is a systematic relationship between information-intensive occupations and commute distance which, if true, may have important implications for the development and shaping of future metropolitan areas. However, modern metropolitan areas are typically large multicentric entities that reflect complex interactions among their multitude of actors, interactions that are summarized by simple statistics such as average trip length and frequency. Moreover, recall that a basic assumption of this analysis is that commuter travel patterns provide information on the spatial distribution of employment locations. In a multicentric environment, there are a variety of other factors – including employment wage structures, transportation infrastructure, and the extent of agglomeration and localization economies – that influence average work-trip distances. If these are important influences on commute distances, ignoring them may overstate the importance of information innovations on commute distances and metropolitan development.

CHAPTER HIGHLIGHTS

- In a monocentric model of urban land use, the transportation cost to the central business district is an important determinant of land rents at various distances from the CBD. For the firm, all pre-rent revenues are capitalized in the value of the land as firms bid with one another for alternative land parcels. The slope of a firm's bid-rent curve depends upon per mile transportation costs, the amount a firm produces, and its ability to substitute land for nonland inputs in the production process.
- In the monocentric model, bid rents for land in the household sector are based upon residential demand for housing. The slope of the bid-rent function depends upon the amount of housing consumed, the ability of housing producers to substitute land for nonland in housing construction, and the ability of housing consumers to substitute land for nonland in housing consumption.
- In an empirical study of employment and population density, densities were lower at locations further from the CBD, consistent with the monocentric model. However, estimating the spatial pattern of densities from the CBD is complicated by the fact that few cities today are truly monocentric.
- In an empirical study of a household's equilibrium location, an increase in transportation costs, all else constant, was found to increase the price of a centrally located house of standard quality relative to a standard quality noncentrally located house. However, rates of capitalization differed depending upon the source of the cost increase.
- Although virtually all urban centers today are multicentric, the economic forces identified in the monocentric model continue to be relevant in a multicentric environment. This was seen in an empirical study of the Los Angeles Metropolitan Area, an urban environment that is unquestionably polycentric. Those working within centers, for example, have longer commutes than those outside centers, which is consistent with a monocentric model.

- Multicentric areas typically have a "scalloped" land-rent function that reflects local peaks outside the CBD. In equilibrium, urban wages adjust to CBD and subcenter accessibility such that wage differences among centers reflect differences in commuting costs from the centers' boundaries to other centers. An empirical study of wage structures in Chicago was consistent with a lower wage structure with increasing distance, finding that wages fell around by 1% per mile from the CBD.
- In a monocentric environment, urban growth leads to population suburbanization but longer commute distances and travel times as the urban boundary lengthens. This need not be the case in a multicentric setting, as firms decentralize to accommodate decentralizing households or to exploit developing suburban agglomeration economies. Large increases in urban vehicle–miles traveled between 1983 and 1990 produced small changes in trip times and distances, which is consistent with decentralizing firms and a decentralizing population.
- In an empirical study of firm location from central-city to suburban municipalities, the likelihood of a move increased as distance from the CBD increased, which is consistent with predictions from urban models that land prices fall with reduced accessibility.
- An empirical study of the role that transportation policy plays in an urban area's spatial development found that the effect is generally small. Only if the policy has a significant impact upon relevant costs, such as the construction of a fixed-rail rapid transit system, will the policy appreciably affect the pattern of urban development.
- The net effect of recent advances in telecommunications on suburbanization is unclear. To the extent that low-cost, high-quality communications occur without the need for face-to-face meetings, these advances reduce the importance of accessibility to CBDs and subcenters. On the other hand, these advances are likely to generate additional demands for interactions, some of which will take the form of face-to-face meetings and will enhance the desirability of a location accessible to a (sub)center. A recent empirical analysis indicates that individuals in information-intensive occupations have shorter commutes, suggesting that recent advances have a net suburbanizing effect for information-intensive industries.

Review questions

1. One would expect that the demand for automobile ownership in metropolitan areas would be influenced by population density. Holding all else constant, the more dense the area is, the more public transit will be provided. Also, the denser the area is, the more traffic congestion will be present.
   (a) Assuming that the public transit fare remains constant, explain why an increased supply of public transit in denser areas reduces the opportunity cost of public transit.
   (b) Assuming no change in the per mile monetary cost of automobile travel, explain why increased congestion increases the opportunity cost of automobile travel.

(c) On the basis of 65 large US central cities in 1970, Kain (1983) assumed that the demand for automobiles depended upon median household income and population density. He obtained the following linear regression results:

$$\text{Auto per Household} = \underset{(6.1)}{0.224} + \underset{(6.1)}{0.069}\text{Median Income}$$

$$- \underset{(-13.9)}{0.013}\text{Population Density}$$

$$R^2 = 0.77$$

where Median Income is thousands of dollars and Population Density is thousands of persons per square mile. The t-statistics are in parentheses.

(i) Are these results consistent with expectations?

(ii) What effect will a $1,000 increase in median family income have upon automobile ownership? From these results, what difference in automobile ownership would you expect to see between a household earning $50,000 per year and one earning $20,000 per year?

(iii) According to Kain's model, how many automobiles will a typical household own if it resides in a low-density area characterized by 50 persons per square mile? Compare this with a high-density city that has 8,000 persons per square mile.

(iv) Throughout this century, we have seen population movements away from rural areas and into urban areas. At the same time, household median income has steadily risen. Using Kain's empirical model, what can you say about the net effect of these changes on automobile ownership?

2. What direct effect will the following changes have upon land-use allocation in a monocentric model?

(a) A decrease in the cost of transporting manufacturing output to the CBD for shipment to other areas.

(b) An increase in household per capita income.

(c) An innovation in public transit that reduces the per-mile cost of workers.

(d) A city-wide increase in the cost of nonland inputs.

3. How will the following factors likely affect a household's equilibrium location and urban development in a monocentric urban area?

(a) An increase in nonwage income.

(b) An increase in wage income.

(c) Significant improvements in motor vehicle gas mileage.

(d) An increase in the number of household workers.

(e) The development of significant air pollution near the CBD.

4. Mills (1972) reported the following empirical land-rent function:

$$\log R(u) = \underset{(27.6)}{10.6} - \underset{(-7.2)}{0.492}u, \qquad R^2 = 0.88$$

where $R(u)$ is the daily rent ($) per square mile, u is the distance (miles) from the CBD, and the t-statistics are in parentheses.

(a) For values of u that vary from 1 to 9, graph the land-rent function. Is the shape of the land-rent function consistent with a monocentric urban model?

(b) What is the daily rent per acre at the center of the CBD?

(c) Suppose that the distance from the CBD increases by 2 miles. What percentage change will this have upon land rents?

5. Suppose that an individual's transportation cost to the CBD increases by $200 per year if she moves 1 mile further from the CBD.

(a) According to the monocentric model, and holding all else constant, by how much must the annual cost of housing change at the further distance?

(b) If the rate at which changes in transportation costs get capitalized into land values is 8%, what impact does the $200 increase in transport cost have upon land values at the further distance? What would happen if the capitalization rate were 10%?

6. What are agglomeration economies and how do urbanization economies differ from labor market economies? "The stronger are agglomeration economies, the steeper is the urban area's land rent function." Do you agree or disagree, and why?

7. Mills (1972) assumed an exponential density function of the form,

$$\text{Density} = De^{-\gamma u}$$

which implies a log-linear empirical model:

$$\log(\text{Density}) = \log(\text{D}) - \gamma u + \varepsilon$$

where D is the density (persons per square mile) at the center, u is the distance (miles) from the center, and ε is an error term. Mills reported the following empirical population density functions for Baltimore in 1920, 1940, and 1963:

1920 $\log(\text{Density}) = 4.84 - 0.70u$
1940 $\log(\text{Density}) = 4.81 - 0.60u$
1963 $\log(\text{Density}) = 4.53 - 0.33u$

(a) Fill in the following table and graph the results:

	Population Density		
Distance (miles)	1920	1940	1963
1			
2			
3			
4			
5			
6			
7			

(b) What was population density at the center in 1920? How about 1963?
(c) What percentage impact did a 1 mile increase in distance from the center have upon population density in 1920, 1940, and 1963 respectively?
(d) It is commonly thought that cities began to suburbanize after the Second World War. Do the data on Baltimore bear this out?
(e) What are some likely reasons for the pattern of development observed in Baltimore over the 43-year period?

8. Below are manufacturing and service employment density functions for Albuquerque between 1954 and 1963. The density functions are of the same functional form as given in question 5 and the estimation results are as follows (Mills, 1972):

Manufacturing sector
1954 $\log(\text{Density}) = 2.17 - 0.32u$
1958 $\log(\text{Density}) = 2.40 - 0.49u$
1963 $\log(\text{Density}) = 2.68 - 0.61u$

Service sector
1954 $\log(\text{Density}) = 2.87 - 1.20u$
1958 $\log(\text{Density}) = 2.79 - 0.93u$
1963 $\log(\text{Density}) = 2.73 - 0.80u$

(a) Discuss the spatial development of each of these employment sectors over the 9 year period.
(b) For each sector, identify how the sector's bid-rent curve likely changed, and what implication this would have upon land-use allocation between the two sectors.

9. Shown in table 12.17 is part of the estimation results that McDonald and McMillen (1990) report for residential land value (cents per square foot) functions in Chicago.
(a) Are the reported results for 1961 and 1981 consistent with a monocentric pattern of urban development?
(b) If your house was adjacent to a commuter rail line in 1961, what impact did this have upon the value of your land? What impact did it have in 1981? What might explain the difference?
(c) During this 20-year period, O'Hare Airport became a major subcenter in the Chicago area. What impact did this development have upon land values, and why?
(d) Often one hears that accessibility to transportation is good as long as it's not "too close." Are the results above consistent with this notion?
(e) Suppose that in 1981 you lived 3 miles from downtown Chicago. If you moved 2 miles further out, holding all else constant, what impact would this have upon your land value?

10. In a multicentric framework, explain why one would expect to see a fall in average wages as distance from the CBD increases. Is this also true in a monocentric setting? If so, why; and if not, why not?

Table 12.17 Residential land value functions (cents per square foot)

Dependent variable – log (single family housing land value)

Variable	1961 Coefficient Estimate (*t*-statistic)	1981 Coefficient Estimate (*t*-statistic)
Constant	5.86 (33.3)	6.80 (28.2)
Commuter Rail Line		
Adjacent to residence = 1, 0 otherwise	0.410 (2.9)	−0.257 (−0.48)
Near residence = 1, 0 otherwise	0.193 (3.5)	−0.026 (−0.15)
Freight Rail Line		
Adjacent to residence = 1, 0 otherwise	0.060 (0.43)	−0.423 (−0.98)
Near residence = 1, 0 otherwise	−0.060 (−0.84)	−0.360 (−1.9)
Interstate Highway		
Near residence = 1, 0 otherwise	−0.052 (0.40)	−0.136 (−0.61)
Distance (miles) to:		
Downtown Chicago	−0.060 (−6.3)	−0.036 (−1.8)
Nearest village hall	−0.083 (−1.3)	−0.170 (−2.4)
O'Hare Airport	0.033 (2.2)	−0.045 (−2.2)
Interstate highway interchange	−0.048 (−1.6)	−0.016 (−0.50)
Village hall near commuter rail station = 1, 0 otherwise	0.045 (0.73)	0.202 (1.2)

Source: Reprinted from McDonald and McMillen (1990), table 4, p. 1572, with the permission of Pion Limited, London

NOTES

1 As defined by the census, an urbanized area is an area of 50,000 people or more that includes at least one large central city and a minimum population density in the surrounding area equal to 1,000 persons per square mile.

2 Using calculus, totally differentiate the profit function in equation (12.1b) and set the result to zero. This gives

$$\begin{aligned} \mathrm{d}\pi &= q\mathrm{d}p_{\mathrm{net}} + p_{\mathrm{net}}\mathrm{d}q - p_z\mathrm{d}Z(u) - Z(u)\mathrm{d}p_z - R(u)\mathrm{d}L(u) - L(u)\mathrm{d}R(u) = 0 \\ &= [q\mathrm{d}p_{\mathrm{net}} - Z(u)\mathrm{d}p_z - L(u)\mathrm{d}R(u)] + [p_{\mathrm{net}}\mathrm{d}q - p_z\mathrm{d}Z(u) - R(u)\mathrm{d}L(u)] = 0 \end{aligned}$$

Assuming constant returns to scale in the production of q and perfectly competitive markets implies that the expression in the second set of brackets is zero (refer to equation (5.5) in chapter 5 and equation (12.4) in this chapter). We can then write the total change in profits as $\mathrm{d}\pi = q\mathrm{d}p_{\mathrm{net}} - Z(u)\mathrm{d}p_z - L(u)\mathrm{d}R(u) = 0$ or $\mathrm{d}R(u)L(u) = q\mathrm{d}p_{\mathrm{net}} - Z(u)\mathrm{d}p_z$. Assuming that nonland costs do not vary spatially in the city, $\mathrm{d}p_z = 0$, we obtain

$$-L(u)\frac{\mathrm{d}R(u)}{\mathrm{d}u}\mathrm{d}u = q\frac{\mathrm{d}p_{\mathrm{net}}}{\mathrm{d}u}\mathrm{d}u \;\Rightarrow\; -L(u)\frac{\mathrm{d}R(u)}{\mathrm{d}u} = qt_q$$

3 This is equivalent to assuming a fixed proportions production function at all locations in the city.

4 If households exhibited location preferences, then household utility would be expressed as $U(H(u), x(u), u)$, where we see that distance from the CBD directly affects welfare. With no location preferences, utility is expressed as $U(H(u), x(u))$. Here, distance effects welfare, but only through its effect upon housing and nonhousing consumption.

5 Assuming profit-maximizing behavior and spatially constant per unit costs of nonland inputs, then, from note 3, the total differential of profits is $d\pi = q_h dp_{net} - L(u)dR(u) = 0$. Since housing producers incur no transportation costs, a comparable expression for these producers is $d\pi = q_h dP(u) - L(u)dR(u) = 0$ or $dR(u)L(u) = q_h dP(u)$. But this implies that

$$-L(u)\frac{dR(u)}{du}du = q_h\frac{dP(u)}{du}du \Rightarrow \frac{dR(u)}{du} = -\frac{dP(u)}{du}\frac{q_h}{L(u)}$$

The first expression says that savings in housing expenditures from a unit move out are entirely reflected in reduced land costs. The second equation is equation (12.11) in derivative form.

6 Dividing both sides of equation (12.11) by $R(u)$ and multiplying the right-hand side by one, defined as $P(u)/P(u)$, gives

$$\frac{dR(u)/du}{R(u)} = \frac{dP(u)/du}{P(u)}\frac{P(u)q}{R(u)L(u)} = \frac{dP(u)/du}{P(u)}\frac{1}{s_L}$$

where s_L is the share of land in the cost of producing housing. This expression says that the percentage change in land rents with a unit increase in distance from the CBD is proportionately related to the percentage change in housing prices with a unit increase in distance, with the factor of proportion defined as the inverse share of land in the cost of producing housing. If, for example, a unit increase in distance reduces housing prices by 2% and land costs are 10% of the total cost of housing, then land rents will decrease by $(0.02/0.1) = 0.2$ or 20%. To accommodate the 2% drop in housing prices, land prices must fall by 20%. The reason for the large decrease is our assumption that nonland input prices do not vary spatially. If they did, then part of the decrease in housing prices would be reflected in the prices of the nonland inputs.

7 Comparing the savings in land expenditures for the business and residential sectors for a unit of good q ($q = 1$) and a unit of housing produced and consumed ($q_h = H(u) = 1$), respectively, we have

business sector: $-L(u)\frac{\Delta R(u)}{\Delta u} = qt_q = t_q$, for $q = 1$

residential sector: $-L(u)\frac{\Delta R(u)}{\Delta u} = -\frac{\Delta P(u)}{\Delta u}q_h = t_h$, for $q_h = H(u) = 1$

If the per-mile shipping cost for a firm's commodity is greater than the per-mile shipping cost of a household's commuter, that is $t_q > t_h$, then the marginal savings on land costs will be greater for the business sector which, for comparable amounts of $L(u)$, implies that the slope of the bid-rent curve for the business sector is greater than that of the residential sector. However, these expressions also illustrate the fact that the steepness of a bid-rent function depends upon the ease with which commodity and housing producers can substitute nonland for land inputs.

8 There are 640 acres to a square mile.

9 Predicted employment density at the center is $e^{8.05} = 3{,}134$ jobs per square mile, which compares with an actual employment density equal to 11,104.

10 In general, the effect of an increase in household income on equilibrium location depends upon the relative magnitude of the income elasticity of housing versus the income elasticity of transportation costs. In particular, all else constant, $(\Delta P(u)/\Delta u)H(u)E_{H,Y} = tE_{t,Y}$, where $E_{H,Y}$ and $E_{t,Y}$ are the elasticities of housing and transportation cost, respectively, with respect to income Y.

11 Alternative explanations for the observed segmentation include: new housing construction typically occurs in the suburbs; households move to the suburbs to escape disamenities (for example, crime, pollution, traffic, higher property tax rates, and so on) found in the central areas; and zoning policies. For a more extensive discussion, see O'Sullivan (1996).

12 Dividing the price of gasoline by miles per gallon gives the per-mile gasoline cost of travel. Multiplying this number by the increase in distance gives the per-trip increase in cost. The annual increase in gasoline costs is simply the per-trip cost multiplied by the number of one-way trips per year, N.

13 Housing is an heterogeneous good that is made up of many different attributes, including square footage, the number of bedrooms, the number of bathrooms, the presence of a fireplace or pool, attached garage, type of neighborhood, and so forth. In order to identify the effect of a particular housing attribute on the house's price, researchers oftentimes regress price on housing attributes, which is referred to as an *hedonic regression model*. The estimated coefficient of a housing attribute reflects the impact that a unit increase in this attribute will have upon the house's price. In their work, Coulson and Engle (1987) estimated an hedonic regression model with price as the dependent variable and various housing attributes, including location, as independent variables. The coefficients from this equation were then used along with standardized unit housing characteristics to estimate the price of a standardized house located within and outside the central city.

14 The authors also included a set of time dummy variables to capture any differences across time. These time effects, however, were statistically insignificant and were excluded from the reported model.

15 Coulson and Engle also offer a statistical explanation for the observed result, the correlation between (ΔTime Costs) and Income in the model. In regression models, if two explanatory variables are highly correlated, the model has difficulty distinguishing the separate effects of the correlated variables. This condition, known as multicollinearity, may lead to unexpected coefficient estimates and may explain the unexpectedly high coefficient on (ΔTime Costs) in table 12.2.

16 Motorized trucks, for example, significantly reduced the per-mile cost of intracity shipping in the early 1900s.

17 Although figure 12.7 depicts an expansion of the CBD, this result is theoretically ambiguous. The initial innovation in intracity shipping leads to an expansion in the CBD, whereas the subsequent increase in wages causes the CBD to contract. Assuming that the direct effect is greater leads to a net expansion in the CBD, as depicted in the figure.

18 In general, the net effect on the size of the CBD is ambiguous, since the initial effect of improved commuter transportation reduces CBD size, whereas the secondary effect from raised firm bid rents increases CBD size. Assuming that the direct effect is dominant implies that CBD size will fall, as depicted in figure 12.8, which further reinforces the increase in employment densities due to input substitution.

19 In contrast, if the customer requires only standardized inputs, there is neither a need for face-to-face communication nor for the customer to locate near the input supplier.

20 For these smaller counties, the total employment criterion was 7,000.

21 This finding is not contradicted by the total employment and employment density patterns of the 22 smaller centers not listed in table 12.3.

22 In total, the 32 centers comprise 110 square miles. Also, the employment in the 32 centers is 1.49 million, compared with a total employment of 4.65 million.

23 The reported R^2s are adjusted for degrees of freedom.

24 Implicitly, Eberts' definition of productivity is equivalent to a labor theory of value whereby the amount of time spent working is positively correlated to productively. Interestingly, if one alternatively assumes that more productive workers achieve the same output as less productive workers but in less time, then Eberts' results are consistent with the hypothesis that increased productivity increases wages.

25 Also consistent with these findings, Gordon et al. (1991), using data from a 1985 American Housing Survey and 1980 Census, found that in 15 of the largest 20 Primary Metropolitan Statistical Areas, average automobile commuting time was significantly lower (at the 0.05 level) in 1985.

26 The 12 areas include New York, Los Angeles, Chicago, Philadelphia, San Francisco, Detroit, Houston, Miami, Cleveland, Milwaukee, Cincinnati, and Seattle.

27 This formulation makes the restrictive but simplifying assumption that capital lasts forever.

28 Recall from chapter 5 that solving the cost minimization problem also gives the demand for the other two inputs, labor and capital. We ignore these here, since the primary focus of the analysis is on the demand for land.

29 One might be able to obtain data on the prices that firms paid for structures at various locations. However, unless the transaction was for vacant property, the price paid combines the demand for land with the demand for the structures on the land.

30 The number of firms relocating to a municipality is a better proxy for the demand for land if the relocating firms are of similar size and have the same demands for land. To at least a first approximation, the firms included in Erickson and Wasylenko's study satisfy this condition since, based upon employment data, they are relatively small.

31 It may be the case, as is true for Erickson and Wasylenko's data, that for some sectors no firms moved to a particular municipality during the 10 year period. In this case, $S_i(j) = 0$, which implies that $\ln(S_i(j))$ is undefined. To account for these cases, the probability of moving to municipality j is redefined as $P_i(j) + 1/[2N_i(j)]$, where $N_i(j)$ is the total number of firms in industrial sector i moving to municipality j (Cox, 1970).

32 Erickson and Wasylenko used 7 miles because this is the median commuting distance for all residents in all industries in the Milwaukee metropolitan area.

33 In Lerman's model, a household work location was fixed.

34 The calculations reported in tables 12.11–12.15 assume that all adults in the household drive. Lerman also simulated the location and transportation decisions of households with no drivers. Not surprisingly, these households are captive to transit and have shorter work-trip distances.

35 "Telecommuting," first used by Nilles et al. (1976), is a term to describe individuals working on their personal computers at home while staying in touch with their employers and customers electronically through fax machines, e-mail, voice-mail, pagers, and so on.

REFERENCES AND RELATED READINGS

General references

Cox, D. R. 1970: *The Analysis of Binary Data*. London: Methuen.

DiPasquale, D. and Wheaton, W. C. 1996: *Urban Economics and Real Estate Markets*. Englewood Cliffs, New Jersey: Prentice-Hall.

Mills, E. S. 1972: *Studies in the Structure of the Urban Economy*. Baltimore, Maryland: The Johns Hopkins Press.

O'Sullivan, A. 1996: *Urban Economics*, 3rd edn. Homewood, Ill.: Richard D. Irwin.

Segal, D. (ed.). 1979: *The Economics of the Neighborhood*. New York: Academic Press.

Small, K. A. 1992: *Urban Transportation Economics*. Chur, Switzerland: Harwood.

Urban location decisions

Lerman, S. R. 1979: Neighborhood choice and transportation services. In D. Segal (ed.), *The Economics of the Neighborhood*. New York: Academic Press, pp. 83–118.

McDonald, J. F. 1987: The identification of urban employment subcenters. *Journal of Urban Economics*, 21, 242–58.

Wheaton, W. 1977: Income and urban residence: an analysis of consumer demand for location. *American Economic Review*, 67, 620–31.

Zax, J. S. and Kain, J. F. 1991: Commutes, quits, and moves. *Journal of Urban Economics*, 29, 153–65.

Rent, density, and wage gradients

Coulson, N. E. and Engle, R. F. 1987: Transportation costs and rent gradient. *Journal of Urban Economics*, 21, 287–97.

Eberts, R. W. 1981: An empirical investigation of intraurban wage gradients. *Journal of Urban Economics*, 10, 50–60.

Erickson, R. A. and Wasylenko, M. 1980: Firm relocation and site selection in suburban municipalities. *Journal of Urban Economics*, 8, 69–85.

Ihlanfeldt, K. R. 1992: Intraurban wage gradients: evidence by race, gender, occupational class, and sector. *Journal of Urban Economics*, 32, 70–91.

Madden, J. F. 1985: Urban wage gradients: empirical evidence. *Journal of Urban Economics*, 18, 291–301.

Transportation and multicentric urban structure

Baumol, W. 1986: Information, computers, and the structure of industry. Economic research. Report No. 86–29. C. V. Starr Center for Applied Economics, New York University.

Cervero, R. 1984: Light rail transit and urban development. *Journal of the American Planning Association*, 49, 133–47.

Giuliano, G. and Small, K. A. 1991: Subcenters in Los Angeles Region. *Regional Science and Urban Economics*, 21, 163–82.

Goldstein, G. S. and Moses, L. N. 1975: Transportation controls and the spatial structure of urban areas. *American Economic Association Papers and Proceedings*, 65, 289–94.

Goldstein, G. S. and Moses, L. N. 1975: Transport controls. Travel costs, and urban spatial structure. *Public Policy*, 23, 355–80.

Gomez-Ibanez, J. 1985: Transportation policy as a tool for shaping metropolitan development. In T. E. Keeler (ed.), *Research in Transportation Economics*, vol. 2. Greenwich, Conn.: JAI Press, pp. 55–81.

Gordon, P. and Richardson, H. W. 1994: Congestion trends in metropolitan areas. In Transportation Research Board, National Research Council, *Curbing Gridlock: Peak-Period Fees to Relieve Traffic Congestion*, vol. 2, pp. 1–31.

Gordon, P., Richardson, H. W., and Jun, M. J. 1991: L. A. The commuting paradox: evidence from the Top Twenty. *Journal of the American Planning Association*, 416, 461–520.

Gordon, P., Richardson, H. W., and Wong, H. L. 1986: The distribution of population and employment in a polycentric city: the case of Los Angeles. *Environment and Planning*, 18, 161–73.

Hu, P. and Young, J. 1992: Summary of travel trends: 1990 nationwide personal transportation survey. Report Number FHWA-PL-92-027, Federal Highway Administration, Department of Transportation.

Humphrey, T. F. 1990: Suburban congestion: recommendations for transportation and land use responses. *Transportation*, 16, 221–40.

Kain, J. F. 1983: Impacts of higher petroleum prices on transportation patterns and urban development. *Research in Transportation Economics*, 1, 1–26.

Kumar, A. 1990: Impact of technological developments on urban form and travel behaviour. *Regional Studies*, 24, 137–48.

McDonald, J. F. and McMillen, D. P. 1990: Employment subcenters and land values in polycentric urban area: the case of Chicago. *Environment and Planning*, 22, 1561–74.

Mills, E. S. 1992: The measurement and determinants of suburbanization. *Journal of Urban Economics*, 32, 377–87.

Nilles, J. M., Carlson, F. R., Gray, P., and Hanneman, G. J. 1976: *The Telecommunications–Transportation Trade Off: Options for Tomorrow*. New York: John Wiley.

13

Public Health Effects of Transportation

INTRODUCTION

Transportation combines infrastructure, labor, and equipment inputs in order to move freight and passengers from an origin to a destination. But this movement does not occur in a self-contained and completely risk-free environment. One or more of the inputs required to produce a trip may fail and cause an accident that results in damaged freight, injury, or loss of life. Air-traffic control systems that unexpectedly shut down, worn rail track, potholes on our nation's roads, and the absence of appropriate signaling devices are examples of where infrastructure lapses increase the risk of travel and the probability of an accident. Lack of sleep, speeding, inattention, and driving while under the influence of drugs and alcohol are examples of poor driver decisions that oftentimes result in accidents. Unexpected equipment failures lead to accidents. And even when all inputs are functioning properly, abrupt weather changes or other acts of God occasionally occur, that not only disrupt the normal flow of freight and passenger traffic but also increase accident risks. Accidents do happen and are a by-product of our consumption and travel activities.

In addition, casual observation tells us that governments regulate many aspects of transportation safety for all modes of travel. Whereas recent trends in transportation reflect less government regulation of economic activities, the trend has been for greater regulation of transportation safety. Have safety regulations in transportation produced an unambiguously safer environment or have the effects been less than expected? More generally, when might we expect increased safety regulation to have little effect?

In chapter 11, we discussed the problem of congestion, and saw that as traffic flow increases there will come a point after which further increases in traffic cause marginal cost to deviate from a user's average variable cost. Additional users not only incur congestion costs in their trip-making, but they also impose additional time or congestion costs on existing users of the facility. This difference between marginal cost and a user's average variable cost reflects a negative externality which, if not internalized, leads to an inefficient allocation of transportation resources.

Although congestion is oftentimes the most prevalent externality associated with many transportation systems, the movement of people and goods from an origin to a destination generates additional external effects, including air and water pollution, noise pollution, visual intrusion, and accidents. Motor vehicles emit hydrocarbons, sulfur oxides, and particulate matter that not only discolor the air we breathe but, more importantly, have serious health implications for travelers and nontravelers alike. Offshore spills from tankers transporting oil despoil our waterways and oceans, and the sound waves generated by airplane operations in and around airports physically damage buildings in the surrounding area and invade the quiet serenity of nearby residents.

In some instances, insurance markets internalize these external public health effects. For example, I can purchase liability insurance to cover the contingency that I cause an accident which injures a passenger or some other person. To the extent that insurance markets cover all accident costs, accident externalities are internalized. In reality, however, there are some accident costs that are not insurable. Suppose that a truck accident on an eight-lane expressway during rush hour traffic causes gridlock for over 2 hours. Part of the accident cost is the time cost of those stuck on the expressway until the accident is cleared and traffic can again flow. Although these time costs are part of the social cost of the accident, they are not insurable and thus constitute a negative eternality from the accident.

In short, all transportation activities have some negative environmental and public health effects that are not fully internalized in existing transportation markets which, as we have seen, implies an inefficient allocation of resources.

In the following sections, we summarize the extent to which individual travelers are at risk when traveling by various modes, and develop simple models for the individual and the firm that incorporate risk in one's transportation decisions. These models enable us to analyze the impact that government regulations and other safety-related factors have upon transportation safety. We then present a number of empirical models to illustrate these concepts. In particular, we will examine various aspects of accident risks in two of the more important sectors of the industry, highway and airlines. We will also consider the public health effects of motor vehicle emissions.

TRANSPORT SAFETY IN THE UNITED STATES

For the major transport modes in the USA, column (a) in table 13.1 summarizes the number of persons annually killed over the past 30 years. We see in the table that, with the exception of motor vehicle travel, fatal accidents are a relatively rare occurrence. In 1995, for example, 168 individuals died in crashes on US Air Carriers and only nine fatalities occurred on Commuter Air Carriers. More than four times as many persons died in General Aviation, however, than on US Air Carriers. The number of deaths in recreational boating is somewhat higher than that in general aviation, at 836 in 1995. Railroads accounted for over 1,000 deaths in 1995, with over half of these associated with rail/highway crossings. In addition to those reported in table 13.1, there were 46 and 15 deaths associated with nonrecreational water transport and gas pipelines, respectively, in the mid-1990s.

By far, however, motor vehicle travel accounts for the largest number of persons killed in the transportation industry. In 1960, 36,399 persons were killed in motor vehicle accidents. This increased significantly during the 1960s, peaking at over 54,000 in 1970, but has since declined. In 1995, highways accounted for 41,798 deaths, the bulk of which were related to automobile or light truck travel. We also see in the table that between 1975 and 1985, the number of persons killed in accidents involving large trucks hovered around 1,000,

Table 13.1 Fatalities and fatality rates: various modes, various years

Year	US Air Carrier[a] (a) Fatalities	(b) Per Million Miles	Commuter Air Carrier[a] (a) Fatalities	(b) Per Million Miles	General Aviation (a) Fatalities	(b) Per 100,000 Hours	Motor Vehicles[a] (a) Fatalities	(b) Per 100 Million VMT
1960	499	0.442	–	–	787	59.985	36,399	5.062
1965	261	0.148	–	–	1,029	61.506	47,089	5.303
1970	146	0.054	100	–	1,310	50.327	54,180	4.881
1975	122	0.052	28	–	1,252	43.472	44,525	3.353
1980	1	0.000	37	0.193	1,239	34.038	51,091	3.346
1985	526	0.145	37	0.123	955	33.722	43,825	2.470
1990	39	0.008	6	0.013	766	26.868	44,599	2.080
1991	50	0.010	77	0.202	781	28.682	41,508	1.911
1992	33	0.006	21	0.048	862	36.234	39,250	1.747
1995	168	0.030	9	0.014	732	36.600	41,798	1.725

Year	Large Trucks[a] (a) Fatalities	(b) Per 100 Million VMT	Railroad[a] (a) Fatalities	(b) Per Million Train–Miles	Rail/Highway Grade Crossing[a] (a) Fatalities	(b) Per Million Train–Miles	Recreational Boating[a] (a) Fatalities	(b) Per Million Boats
1960	–	–	924	–	–	–	819	327.60
1965	–	–	923	–	–	–	1,360	212.50
1970	–	–	785	0.936	–	–	1,418	191.62
1975	961	1.2	575	0.762	966	1.279	1,466	200.82
1980	1,262	1.2	584	0.814	833	1.161	1,360	158.14
1985	977	0.8	454	0.795	582	1.019	1,116	116.25
1990	705	0.5	599	0.984	698	1.147	865	78.64
1991	661	0.4	586	1.016	608	1.054	924	83.24
1992	585	0.4	591	0.995	579	0.975	816	73.51
1995	644	0.4	567	0.847	579	0.864	836	71.45

[a] Air Carrier data does not include fatalities from air-taxis. Exposure for US Air Carriers and Commuter Air Carriers is in aircraft–miles. Exposure for motor vehicles and large trucks is vehicle–miles traveled (VMT). Exposure for railroads is in train–miles. Railroad fatalities include train accidents, train incidents, and nontrain accidents.

Source: US Department of Transportation, Bureau of Transportation Statistics, *National Transportation Statistics 1997* (various tables)

but this number has fallen in the past ten years. Large truck accidents claimed 644 lives in 1995.

In addition to the absolute number of persons killed by mode, column (b) in table 13.1 reports fatality rates. This is a more relevant measure of safety performance, since it accounts for exposure to risk. Although exposure is not uniform across modes, it is possible to compare the safety performance of a subset of modes as well as to comment on each mode's safety record over a period of time.

The general trend in the transport industry characterizes improved safety. Notwithstanding the impact that one crash may have upon the statistics in the airline sector, US Air Carrier fatalities per million miles have decreased from 0.442 in 1960 to 0.03 in 1995. Commuter Carriers have also experienced improvements, with fatality rates falling from 0.193 in 1980 to 0.014 in 1995. And despite the fact that a similar number of General Aviation fatalities occurred 1995 as in 1960, the number of fatalities per 100,000 hours of exposure has fallen by 39%. A similar decreasing trend in fatality rates has occurred in the rail industry although the improvement has not been as dramatic as for public air carriers. Nonhighway-grade crossing fatalities per million train–miles, the majority of which are trespassers beyond the control of the rails, fell by 9.5% between 1970 and 1995; grade crossing fatalities per million train–miles fell by 49.6% during the same period. And between 1960 and 1995, recreational boating fatalities per million boats decreased from 327.6 to 71.4, a 78.2% improvement.

When normalized by exposure, motor vehicle travel has also become safer. In 1960, 5.06 persons were killed per 100 million VMT. This fell to 1.72 fatalities per hundred million VMT in 1995, representing a 65.9% reduction. Over a shorter time span, 1975–95, trucks have experienced a similar 67% improvement in the fatality rate.

How do highways fare with US Air Carriers? Converting the highway fatality rate to a rate per million VMT, we see that in 1960 and 1995, there were 0.051 and 0.017 fatalities per million VMT, respectively. In comparison with motor vehicle travel, travel on air carriers has become relatively safer. And in recent years, airline travel tends to be absolutely safer, although this depends upon the specific year. In 1992, for example, US carriers were almost three times more safe than motor vehicle travel; in 1995, however, motor vehicle travel was almost twice as safe as US carriers.

As a final point, US Air Carriers, Commuter Air Carriers, and Railroads are common carriers. In addition, large trucks are predominantly common carriers. General Aviation, the bulk of Motor Vehicles, and Recreational Boating, on the other hand, are used for private use. In general, fatality rates for the common carriers are lower than for private use vehicles. This should not be surprising, since there is greater government oversight for common carriers to insure safe operation and operating environments for the shipment of goods and, more importantly, the transportation of the general public.

THE MARKETS FOR SAFETY-DIFFERENTIATED TRIPS

Suppose that self-interested buyers have perfect information on the risks associated with goods and services available to them. For example, you can take either of two airlines from Washington DC to New York City. If the probability of a crash is higher for Airline 1 than for Airline 2, then you would be willing to pay a higher fare for your trip to New York City on Airline 1. More generally, if all consumers are equally well informed about the safety of the

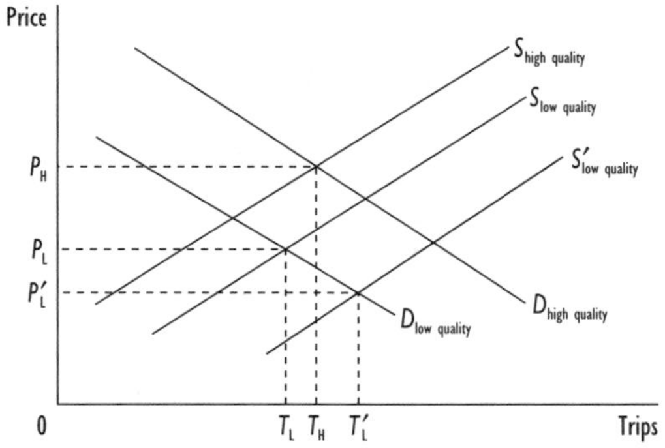

Figure 13.1 Market equilibria for low- and high-quality trips.

two airlines, then the market demand curve for Airline 1 flights will lie everywhere to the right of the market demand curve for Airline 2 flights.

Why, if Airline 1 is more safe, will anyone fly on Airline 2? Since market demand for Airline 1 lies to the right of market demand for Airline 2, some consumers will trade-off a lower price on Airline 2 for an increased *risk* – not certainty, but risk – of a crash on Airline 2. As table 13.1 indicates, airline travel is a very safe mode of transportation. Even if the fatality rate increased by 50% from its 1995 level, the probability of a fatality per million miles would still be less than 0.05; that is, fewer than five persons killed per million aircraft miles flown. Thus, if I make the trip on Airline 2, I'm consuming a lower-quality good but I'm also paying a lower price. The market demands for Airlines 1 and 2 reflect the systematic relationship between price and quality. Consumers place greater (less) value on higher- (lower-) quality goods.

Similarly, in their production activities, firms produce goods and services that span the spectrum from lower to higher quality. Firms producing goods of the highest quality incur higher opportunity costs of production. Conversely, firms that use inferior materials, have less quality control in their production processes, and provide little training to their workforces enjoy lower opportunity costs of production but also supply a lower quality and potentially less safe good or service. Holding all else constant, the market supply of higher-quality, safer transportation lies to the left of the market supply for lower-quality, less safe transportation. Although one cannot predict whether the equilibrium quantity of higher-quality, safer transportation is greater or less than the quantity of lower-quality, less safe transportation, one can unambiguously predict that the equilibrium price of higher-quality, safer transportation is greater than that of lower-quality, less safe transportation. Figure 13.1 depicts the market demand and supply curves for higher and lower quality (that is, safer and less safe) trips. In the graph, as expected, equilibrium price for safer trips is higher and, as drawn, there are more safe trips taken, $T_H > T_L$. However, by shifting $S_{\text{low quality}}$ to the right, for example to $S'_{\text{low quality}}$, we see that the equilibrium price of higher-quality trips continues to exceed that of lower-quality trips, but the number of lower-quality trips now exceeds the quantity of higher-quality trips. Thus, although economic theory unambiguously predicts a higher price for the higher-quality good, we need to know the characteristics of market demand and supply before we can determine which of the providers gets the larger share of the market.

CASE STUDY – SEAT BELT USE AND THE DEMAND FOR SAFER TRIPS

To illustrate the demand for safety-differentiated trips, consider an individual who decides to take a trip by automobile. In making this trip, she can either fasten her seat belt or drive with the seat belt unfastened. In the context of our previous discussion, you could view the "buckled" trip as a safer or higher-quality trip and the "unbuckled" trip as the less safe or lower-quality trip.

Individuals making trips exhibit a demand for safety, and one way in which trip-makers reveal this demand is by using their seat belts. If seat belt use reflects the demand for a safer trip, we can ask what factors are important in determining this demand for safety. Winston and Associates (1987) developed and estimated a simple binary logit model of seat belt use based upon a 1984 random sample of drivers in Washington DC and State College, Pennsylvania. According to their empirical model, a driver's decision to use a seat belt depends upon factors related to the cost of using a seat belt, accident experience, driving exposure, and perceived seat belt effectiveness. In particular, we have the following hypotheses:

HYPOTHESIS 1 Holding all else constant, an increase in the cost of using a seat belt reduces the probability that a driver buckles up. In the study, two variables measure the cost imposed upon a driver from using a seat belt. "Time to Fasten Belts" measures the number of seconds that a driver spends buckling and unbuckling her belt. A second cost related variable is "Comfort Indicator," which is a 0–1 variable that indicates whether a driver reported that the seat belt was comfortable to wear. If the seat belt was not uncomfortable, "Comfort Indicator" = 1; if it was uncomfortable, "Comfort Indicator" = 0. Since we expect that an increase in cost reduces the likelihood of using the system, we expect the coefficient of "Time to Fasten Belts" to be negative and the coefficient of "Comfort Indicator" to be positive.

HYPOTHESIS 2 A trip-maker's driving experience is expected to influence one's decision to wear a seat belt. The study includes two driving-related variables: "Annual Miles Traveled" and "No Serious Accident." All else constant, the more risk one faces, the higher the likelihood of using a seat belt. "Annual Miles Traveled" captures the extent to which a trip-maker is exposed to a risky driving environment and its coefficient is expected to be positive, all else constant. In addition, a driver's previous accident experience is relevant to her decision to buckle up. In this study, "No Serious Accident" is a 0–1 variable that indicates whether the driver had been in a serious accident within the past three years. If not, "No Serious Accident" takes on a value of one; on the other hand, if recently involved in a serious accident, "No Serious Accident" equals zero. Because recent involvement in an accident is expected to increase the expected benefits from wearing a seat belt, the coefficient for this variable is expected to be negative.

HYPOTHESIS 3 In addition to cost and driving experience, a vehicle's inherent safety and the safety of the driving environment are also important. To capture a vehicle's inherent safety, the study included the variable "Vehicle Weight." Since larger and heavier vehicles provide more protection to a vehicle's occupants, it is expected that this variable will *reduce* the likelihood of using a seat belt. The weight of the vehicle basically reduces the expected marginal benefit from wearing a seat belt, all else constant. In addition to Vehicle Weight, the study included a variable, "Annual Probability of Auto-Related Injury," which is an objective measure of the accident risk faced by an automobile trip-maker. Holding all else constant, an increase in the risk of an injury accident is expected to increase the likelihood of wearing a seat belt.

HYPOTHESIS 4 A driver's decision to wear a seat belt also depends upon a driver's preferences for risk, as well as her belief that seat belts are indeed effective in reducing injuries and fatalities.

Table 13.2 The seat belt use model

Variable	Dependent variable – the probability of regularly wearing a seat belt Coefficient Estimate (*t*-statistic)
Constant	11.08 (1.64)
Time to Fasten Belts (seconds)	−2.78 (−5.13)
Comfort Indicator	0.782 (1.47)
No Serious Accident	−1.84 (−3.30)
Annual Vehicle–Miles Traveled (miles)	0.00038 (1.81)
Vehicle Weight (pounds)	−0.0060 (−2.61)
Annual Probability of Auto-Related Injury (for households with incomes < $35,000)	1.198 (3.52)
Seat Belt Effectiveness Belief	3.305 (1.16)
Age of Driver	0.079 (2.08)
Number of observations = 310	

Source: Adapted from Winston and Associates (1987), table 5-2, p. 75

The variable "Age of Driver" was included to reflect a driver's preferences for risk. Assuming that older persons take fewer risks, an increase in a driver's age is expected to increase the probability of using a seat belt, all else constant. Also, to the extent that a driver believes a seat belt is effective, she is more likely to use a restraint system. Thus, the coefficient on "Age of Driver" is expected to be positive and the coefficient on "Seat Belt Effectiveness Belief" is expected to be positive.[1]

Table 13.2 gives the estimation results for the seat belt use model. The dependent variable is the probability that a driver uses a seat belt in his or her trips. In general, the signs and statistical significance of the variables are consistent with the four hypotheses above. Although a driver only spends a few seconds buckling and unbuckling the seat belt, these seconds are sufficient to deter him or her from buckling up. "Time to Fasten Belts" has a negative sign as expected and is significant. Complementing this result, the extent to which wearing a seat belt imposes a "comfort cost" on a driver also reduces the likelihood of seat belt usage. "Comfort Indicator" is positive, although it is only significant at a 0.10 level, based upon a one-tail test.

Driving experience is important to the seat belt use decision, as is driver involvement in a serious accident within the past three years. Apparently, all else constant, drivers with no recent serious accidents feel less need to wear a seat belt, possibly because this gives them a false sense of security. "Annual Vehicle Miles Traveled" has its expected positive sign and is significant, which indicates that the more miles driven annually the more likely it is that the driver will use a seat belt.

Operational conditions, denoted by the weight of a driver's vehicle and by the probability of an auto-related injury, are also important factors in the demand for a safer trip. Here we see that an increase in vehicle weight reduces the likelihood of wearing a seat belt, consistent with hypothesis 3, that heavier vehicles provide more occupant protection. In addition, drivers – at least those with household incomes less than $35,000 – are sensitive to the fact that accidents do happen. An increase in the probability of an auto-related injury increases the likelihood of seat belt usage, all else constant. Interestingly, the study did not find this effect for households with incomes equal to or greater than $35,000. A possible explanation is that higher-income households own more expensive vehicles that offer high levels of safety. And the increased safety of these vehicles lessens the importance of the risky traveling environment in a driver's seat belt decision.

Last, we see in table 13.2 that "Age of Driver" is positive and significant, consistent with hypothesis 4, that younger drivers have stronger preferences for risk. We also see that the more a driver believes that seat belts are effective in reducing injuries, the higher is the probability that he or she will use a seat belt. "Seat Belt Effectiveness Belief" is positive. However, given a *t*-statistic equal to 1.16, at standard levels of significance, we cannot reject the null hypothesis that the coefficient is zero.

Discussion

In this example, we have assumed that the higher-quality auto trip occurs when the driver buckles up and the lower-quality trip is an unbuckled trip. And any factor which increases the probability of a driver using his or her seat belt increases the demand for the higher-quality trip. From table 13.2, this implies that reductions in the cost of using a seat belt, involvement in a serious accident in the past three years, driving a lighter vehicle, increased risk exposure, an increase in the probability of an automobile accident, and an increase in driver age will each increase the demand for higher-quality trips.[2]

Among these factors, which factor has the greatest impact upon seat belt use? The elasticity of seat belt use with respect to the more important determinants in table 13.2 is given below:

Seat belt use elasticity with respect to	
Time to Fasten Belts	−5.64
No Serious Accident	−1.00
Annual Vehicle Miles Traveled	3.60
Vehicle Weight	−11.42
Probability of an Auto-Related Injury	0.97
Age of Driver	1.88

Here we see that drivers are most sensitive to vehicle weight and least sensitive to the probability of an auto-related injury. A 1% decrease in a vehicle's weight increases the probability of using a seat belt by 11.4%. But drivers are also sensitive to the cost of using a seat belt and risk exposure. All else constant, a 1% reduction in the time that it takes to buckle/unbuckle leads to a 5.4% increase in the probability of wearing a seat belt; a 1% increase in annual vehicle miles traveled leads to a 3.6% increase in seat belt usage; and a 1% increase in driver age increases seat belt use 1.8%, reflecting the assumed reduction in risk preferences as people age.

As a final point, 33% of the drivers in this analysis regularly used a seat belt. Consistent with the law of demand, an increase in the cost of using a seat belt significantly reduces the probability of use, all else constant. If policymakers want to protect vehicle occupants in the event of an accident, one policy is to make the cost of using a seat belt as low as possible, namely zero. In the mid-1980s, the government began to advocate the use of "passive" restraints and airbags for front-seat occupants, both of which have a zero fastening cost. Airbags have the added feature of greater comfort. All new vehicles sold today have driver-side airbags, and many have passenger-side airbags in the front. Back-seat passengers must still use seat belts.[3] These changes are expected to increase safety, all else constant but, as we will see in a later section, there may be unintended offsetting effects.

SAFETY REGULATION IN TRANSPORTATION

Implicit in the above analysis is the assumption that the market demand and supply curves represent the social benefits and costs of safety-differentiated trips. At the margin, marginal benefit equals marginal cost and we have an efficient allocation of resources to each type of trip. Is it reasonable to expect that unregulated markets will lead to an efficient allocation of resources?

Since freight and passenger travel are inherently risky, there is some positive probability that, with sufficient exposure, transportation carriers will experience crashes. For some modes, such as automobiles, crashes are frequent occurrences, whereas for other modes, including air, rail, and ocean carriers, crashes are generally more spectacular but much less frequent. But in all cases, accidents produce economic costs. When crashes occur, persons involved may be killed or suffer serious bodily injuries; there will be pain and suffering; property is damaged; police, fire, and medical resources are expended. Further resources are used up in litigation as victims seek compensation for losses suffered. Assuming negligible contracting costs and perfectly informed agents, individual firms supplying transport services could separately contract with shippers and passengers for the damages to be paid in the event of an accident. In this case, resources would be efficiently allocated to safety-differentiated transportation services in unregulated markets since, at the margin, the additional benefit of safety-reducing actions would just equal the opportunity cost of implementing such behaviors. If, at the margin, transport shippers and travel passengers valued more safety than currently provided, transportation carriers would have an economic incentive to incorporate higher levels of safety in their carrier services. And competition among carriers would insure that safer carrier services would be forthcoming. Conversely, if the marginal benefit of additional safety fell short of the marginal cost of providing more safety, firms would have an incentive to reduce their levels of safety.

Although in reality the costs of contracting are not negligible, insurance markets enable individuals to transfer some or all accident risks to others for a premium. Essentially, those purchasing insurance are trading off a certain but lower income (lower by the amount of the insurance premium) for a higher but uncertain income. With perfectly informed agents and efficient insurance markets, in the sense that insurance premia equal the expected losses in the event of an accident, there would be no need to regulate safety in the transportation sector, since the operation of private markets would bring forth an efficient level of safety. Once again, at the margin, the marginal benefit of an additional unit of safety would just equal the marginal cost of producing a bit more safety.

However, there are at least three reasons why one might expect a *market failure* in the provision of safety in the transportation sector:

- *Moral hazard.* This typically refers to a situation in which one decision-maker in an exchange has an incentive to behave in ways that affect a second decision-maker's valuation of the exchange, but the second decision-maker is unable to monitor the person's actions. Consider the case of a trucking firm that insures its trucks against losses in the event of an accident. If the trucking company is 100% insured, the insurance company will reimburse the company for all property damage and medical costs if one of its trucks is involved in an accident. Recognizing this, the carrier has an incentive to provide less safety than would be the case if the company were faced with the full amount of accident costs. Thus, the firm may reduce scheduled maintenance of its trucks, provide less training or hire lower quality drivers, push drivers to maintain tight schedules, and so forth. In this case, the trucking company and insurance company are the two parties to the transaction – the firm's purchase of insurance. Also note that the essential problem here is informational. The insurance company agrees to provide accident insurance to the trucking firm but is not able to monitor the firm's behavior. If the insurance company were able to perfectly monitor the trucking firm's behavior, the insurance company would set a premium that would appropriately account for the firm's maintenance activities, quality of drivers, and so on. Alternatively, in order to reduce its insurance costs, with perfect monitoring, the firm would have to maintain its fleet better and improve the quality of its driver pool. Because insuring firms cannot perfectly monitor the actions of their clients, moral hazard is a common phenomenon in insurance markets. Among the implications for transport carriers, moral hazard problems imply that firms are more likely to invest in less than an optimal level of safety.

- *Adverse selection.* Similar to moral hazard, adverse selection is an informational problem and reflects a situation in which one party to a transaction has relevant information that is not available to the other party. Consider, for example, a rail company that is negotiating with shippers. The company knows a lot more about its personnel, operations, quality of equipment, on-time performance, and safety record than do the shippers. Asymmetry in the availability of relevant information presents the rail company with an advantage. In such instances, shippers "adversely select" a rail carrier on the basis of incomplete information. As another example, the Federal Aviation Authority (FAA) has responsibility for the safety of airlines. Its investigators undertake numerous safety checks and require considerable documentation from airlines to insure that the carriers are complying with existing safety standards. However, after a crash occurs, *ex post* analysis of a carrier's safety and maintenance actions may indicate that the carrier was negligent and not fully compliant with regulations. In these cases, the airline company has more complete information on the safety of its fleet than does the traveling public. Without relevant information on all aspects of a carrier's safety activities, the traveling public "adversely selects" the unsafe carrier with, oftentimes, disastrous consequences.
- *External effects.* In the context of congestion, we have previously discussed the notion of externalities and their effects on the efficient allocation of resources. There also exist negative external effects associated with transportation accidents. Shippers and passengers contract with transport carriers for transport services. Yet when accidents occur, the effects of these accidents are generally not limited to the contractual parties. An overturned tractor–trailer on an interstate highway, for example, may impose significant time, property, and personal losses on other road (and possibly nonroad) users. A plane that crashes in a residential neighborhood causes serious damages to innocent bystanders. In each of these cases, there are external accident effects from the movement of goods or people. And if these external effects are ignored, we get a nonoptimal allocation of resources to this activity; that is, the marginal benefit of an additional trip is likely to be less than the marginal cost, implying that too many resources are expended on this activity.

The presence of imperfect information, as revealed in moral hazard and adverse selection problems, and accident externalities suggests that unregulated markets will not produce an optimal level of safety. The market failure in transportation safety justifies government regulatory actions to insure that transport carriers incorporate in their operations appropriate levels of safety. For most transport modes, safety regulations fall into one of two groups, regulations aimed at reducing accidents and those aimed at reducing losses in the event of an accident.

HIGHWAY SAFETY BEHAVIOR AND REGULATION

The presence of externalities in the market for safety will likely produce a market failure and justify government intervention in the form of mandating safety standards. In this section, we develop a simple model of individual behavior in order to determine the relationship between optimal level of safety, expected losses, and regulation. In contrast to our earlier models of consumer behavior, which assumed that individuals knew with certainty all relevant information, here we assume that individuals don't know all relevant information. In particular, rather than knowing that an accident will or will not occur, individuals face an environment in which there is some positive probability of an accident.

EXPECTED INCOME MAXIMIZATION

In the standard theory of consumer behavior, consumers face known prices and income. And given the known economic environment, they seek to consume quantities of goods and services that maximize utility. In this world, accidents don't happen. Admitting the possibility of accidents introduces uncertainty into a consumer's problem. In the simplest of cases, suppose that we analyze a particular driver, Connie, and assume that her income depends upon whether she experiences an accident. Since Connie's income is uncertain, it is useful to talk about her *expected income (EI)*. Define P_A to be the probability that she suffers an accident, which implies that the probability of not being involved in an accident is $1 - P_A$. Also assume that Connie will undertake various safety actions e, and that the cost per unit of safety is mc. If not involved in an accident, Connie's income is $M - mc \cdot e$; alternatively, if involved in an accident, Connie's income is $M - L - mc \cdot e$, where L is the monetary loss that she suffers from the accident. Thus, prior to knowing whether she actually gets into an accident, Connie's expected income EI can be expressed as

$$EI = \{P_A(M - L - mc \cdot e) + (1 - P_A)(M - mc \cdot e\} = M - P_AL - mc \cdot e$$

On the left-hand side of the equation, Connie's expected income is the weighted average of her income in each of the two possible states, where the weight is the associated probability of being in that state. Alternatively, by canceling common terms, we can write her expected income more simply as $M - P_AL - mc \cdot e$.

To explore the relationship between transportation safety and regulation, assume that the probability of Connie getting into an accident, P_A, depends upon four factors:

- x, the traveling environment
- r, the regulatory environment
- e, safety-related actions
- γ, the risk preferences

In addition, the extent of loss L associated with an accident depends upon x, r, and e. As with any activity, the additional effort expended to obtain more safety is costly. Given a constant opportunity cost of additional safety effort, Connie's expected income EI is

$$\text{Expected Income} = EI = M - P_A(e;x,r,\gamma)L(e;x,r) - mc \cdot e \qquad (13.1)$$

where she incurs opportunity cost $mc \cdot e$ regardless of whether she experiences an accident.

Assuming that Connie desires to maximize her expected income, what amount of safety effort achieves this goal? From an economic standpoint, Connie continues to increase safety-related behaviors up to the point at which the marginal benefit of additional safety effort is just equal to the marginal cost of that effort. Can we identify the components of marginal benefit and marginal cost? Yes. It can be shown that the equilibrium condition of expected income maximization from equation (13.1) is

$$-\frac{\Delta P_e}{\Delta e}L(e;x,r,\gamma) - \frac{\Delta L_e}{\Delta e}P_{\mathrm{A}}(e;x,r) = mc$$

$$\Rightarrow MB(e;x,r,\gamma) = mc \tag{13.2}$$

The left-hand side of equation (13.2) is the expected marginal benefit from an additional unit of safety effort and the right-hand side of equation (13.2) is the marginal cost of additional safety effort. Connie devotes an optimal amount of effort to safety when the expected marginal benefit is just equal to the marginal cost of an additional unit of effort. Since safety behaviors are expected to reduce the probability of an accident and the losses suffered in an accident, $\Delta P_{\mathrm{A}}/\Delta e < 0$ and $\Delta L/\Delta e < 0$, which implies that $MB(e;x,r,\gamma) > 0$.

There are three points that we can make regarding the equilibrium condition in equation (13.2):

- The first component of marginal benefit on the left-hand side of the equals sign reflects lower expected losses due to the beneficial effect that Connie's efforts have on the probability of getting into an accident, and the second component reflects the impact on expected losses resulting from a decrease in losses suffered when an accident occurs. For example, if Connie is a defensive driver and wears a seat belt, she reduces the probability of getting into an accident but, if an accident does occur, she is also likely to suffer a smaller loss.
- Because the probability of an accident, P_{A}, and the loss from an accident depend upon the traveling environment (x), safety regulations (r), and risk preferences, so too does Connie's optimal effort. In addition, her optimal effort depends upon the marginal cost mc of additional effort. Therefore, Connie's optimal effort e^* can be expressed as

$$e^* = e^*(x,r,mc;\gamma) \tag{13.3}$$

To see that changes in the traveling environment, safety regulations, or the cost of safety alters Connie's optimal level of effort, consider figure 13.2, which depicts the marginal benefit (negative expected losses = $-EL$) and marginal cost (mc) of additional safety effort. In the figure, we see that the optimal level of safety effort is e^*. However, if the marginal cost of safety decreases to mc_1, then optimal effort increases to e_1. Alternatively, suppose that Connie consumes an optimal level of safety at e^* but suddenly faces an exogenous change in the level of expected benefits. For example, she is traveling on the interstate highway when a thunderstorm suddenly arises. How will she respond? She now finds that the marginal benefit from an additional unit of safety at e^* exceeds the marginal cost. Given a constant marginal opportunity cost of safety at mc, she has an incentive to increase the amount of effort devoted to safety, that is, she starts driving more defensively, decreases her speed, and so forth. Graphically, this is seen as a shift in the curve MB to MB_1, which

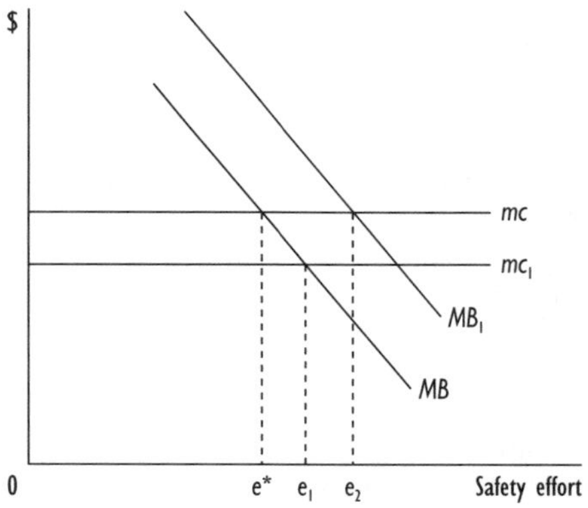

Figure 13.2 Optimal safety effort.

produces a new and higher optimal level of safety equal to e_2. Similarly, if Connie experiences a sudden decrease in her preferences for risk, then the marginal benefit of additional safety behavior rises, which induces her to increase her level of safety effort (moving for example from e^* to e_2 in figure 13.2 if a reduced preference for risk shifts her marginal benefit curve from MB to MB_1).

- In equation (13.2), the probability of an accident, P_A, and the loss in the event of an accident, L, depend upon individual behaviors (e) as well as factors exogenous to the individual (x,r). In addition, from equation (13.3), we know that optimal safety effort depends upon the traveling environment, the regulatory environment, risk preferences, and the marginal cost of safety effort. This implies that an optimal accident probability, P_A^*, and optimal accident losses L^* can be expressed as

$$P_A^* = P_A^*(e^*(x,r,mc,\gamma);x,r,\gamma)$$
$$L^* = L^*(e^*(x,r,mc,\gamma);x,r) \qquad (13.4)$$

where the product $P_A^*L^*$ gives expected losses EL^* at the optimum. P_A^* and L^* each depend upon e^*, x, and r. But the optimal level of safety e^* itself depends upon x, r, γ, and mc. Thus, optimal expected losses EL^* ultimately depend upon the marginal cost of safety effort, mc, the traveling environment x, and the regulatory environment r. That is,

$$EL^* = EL^*(e^*(x,r,\gamma,mc);x,r) = EL^*(x,r,mc,\gamma) \qquad (13.5)$$

From equation (13.5), changes in the traveling environment (for example, weather conditions, type of road, quality of road, and so forth), the regulatory environment (speed limits, automobile safety requirements, drinking under the influence of alcohol laws, and so forth), and cost per unit of safety will each have an impact on expected losses. In general, factors that reduce the likelihood of an accident or the severity of injury given that an accident occurs reduce one's expected losses from an accident. Alternatively, reductions in safety effort increase the probability and/or severity of an accident, while an increase in the per unit cost of safety, by reducing the amount of safety demanded, increases the losses from an accident.

CASE STUDY – THE EFFECTS OF CAFE ON HIGHWAY SAFETY

In chapter 3, we examined the effects upon the gasoline market during the oil crisis in the early 1970s, when OPEC sharply reduced the supply of oil on the world market. In response to the crisis, the federal government took a number of actions. There were price controls on gasoline in the United States, the allocative effects of which were analyzed in chapter 3. In addition, Congress passed various pieces of legislation with the aim reducing our nation's consumption of oil. An important law enacted in 1975 was the Energy Policy and Conservation Act which, among its provisions, set a 27.5 mile per gallon Corporate Average Fuel Economy (CAFE) standard for US automobile manufacturers. For all vehicles sold, the average fuel economy must meet the standard. Given that average fuel economy in 1975 was 15.8 mpg, meeting a 27.5 mpg standard in the following year was impossible. Recognizing this, law-makers gradually phased in more restrictive fuel economy standards between 1975 and 1985. In particular, the government set a 22 mpg standard in 1981, a 26 mpg one in 1983, and the 27.5 mpg standard in 1985. Further, to the extent that manufacturers failed to meet the standard, they would pay a penalty of $50 per car produced for each mile per gallon that the average fell below the standard. For example, if General Motors produced 5 million cars and the actual fleet fuel economy fell 1 mpg short of the required fuel economy, then General Motors would have to pay the government a $250,000,000 fine. This penalty provided manufacturers with a strong incentive to meet the CAFE standard.

Meeting the standards required that vehicle manufacturers go back to the drawing board (literally) and redesign their vehicles with the explicit intent of boosting fuel economy. However, whether one looks at a vehicle's transmission, body, interior, engine, tires, and so on, the bulk of fuel economy savings require that manufacturers produce a lighter car. Large increases in fuel economy will be the result of substituting lighter for heavier materials and reducing the overall size of the vehicle. This is exactly what occurred. Between 1975 and 1985, the average curb weight of new passenger cars fell by 25%, from 4,058 to 3,094 pounds; and engine displacement fell from 288 to 177 cubic inches (Crandall and Graham, 1989).

From an energy perspective, the policy appeared to be successful. Technological advances and significant reductions in vehicle weights enabled manufacturers to meet the CAFE standard in 1985. An interesting question, however, is whether the policy imposed any significant externality costs on society in the form of an increase in the number of people killed on our nation's highways. Lighter vehicles generally provide less protection to a vehicle's occupants so that, in the event of an accident, there are likely to be a larger number of serious injuries and fatalities.

Crandall and Graham (1989) examined this issue and analyzed the extent to which the mandated CAFE standard compromised highway safety, as well as whether the standard was on balance beneficial or detrimental to society.

In their analysis, Crandall and Graham considered the following problem. Assuming that domestic model year car sales average 11.2 million vehicles, what monetary value can we place upon accident externalities resulting from the CAFE standard, and are these sufficient to offset the monetary value of energy savings? In order to estimate the effect of the CAFE standard on accident externalities, one needs to know two pieces of information: (1) the effect of the fuel economy standard on the average weight of vehicles produced; and (2) the effect that changes in vehicle weight have upon highway safety. Noting that it takes four years to bring a car from conception to production, the authors estimated that a car designed in 1985 and coming to the market in 1989 would, as a result of the CAFE restraints, weigh on average 500 pounds less than in 1985.

What implications does a 500 pound reduction in the average weight of a new car have for highway safety? To consider this, the authors estimated a regression model in which the dependent variable was the fatality rate, defined as the number of passenger car occupant fatalities per 100 million vehicle–miles, on a number of factors thought to be important determinants of highway safety. Annual time series data for the period 1947–81 were used to estimate the empirical model.

Hypotheses

HYPOTHESIS 1 Increased vehicle safety decreases the fatality rate. Holding all else constant, an increase in the proportion of vehicles on the road that provide more safety in the form of occupant protection and accident prevention will decrease the fatality rate. In their regression equation, Crandall and Graham included two variables to reflect vehicle safety. SAFETY is an index of average crashworthiness of the average car, that takes into account a series of passenger protection and accident avoidance standards contained in the National Traffic and Motor Vehicle Safety Act of 1966. Crandall and Graham define the index such that high numbers are associated with *lower* levels of safety. The second safety variable, and the variable of most interest for this discussion, is WEIGHT, defined as the average weight of vehicles on the road. As discussed earlier, heavier vehicles afford their occupants greater protection in the event of an accident. It is expected, therefore, that the coefficient for WEIGHT will be negative and the coefficient for SAFETY will be positive (since higher numbers for SAFETY reflect *lower* safety).

HYPOTHESIS 2 Economic factors are important determinants of highway safety. Two economic variables are included in the model, COST and INCOME. Defined as an index that reflects the cost of medical and automobile repair services, COST is expected to have a negative sign. All else constant, by increasing the opportunity cost of services required in the event of an accident, an increase in cost is expected to enhance highway safety.

INCOME is real per capita income (1977 dollars) and captures two influences upon a driver's safety efforts. First, if safety is a normal good, an increase in income increases the demand for safety, which has the effect of reducing the fatality rate. Second, an increase in income also increases the value that drivers place upon their time. In an effort to economize on a resource that has now become more valuable, drivers will take more risks on the road (for example, drive less defensively), which raises the fatality rate. The net effect, therefore, is theoretically ambiguous.

HYPOTHESIS 3 The travel environment is also expected to influence highway safety. In the empirical model, the authors include TRUCKS, defined as the proportion of total vehicle–miles accounted for by trucks, LIMITED ACCESS, which gives the proportion of total vehicle–miles traveled on limited access highways, and SPEED, the average speed of vehicles on noninterstate rural roads during off-peak conditions. Since the dependent variable is the fatality rate for passenger car occupants, size differences between trucks and automobiles imply that automobile passengers will fare worse than truck occupants in an accident. Accordingly, TRUCKS is expected to have a positive sign. LIMITED ACCESS, on the other hand, is expected to have a negative sign. The absence of intersections that require vehicles to "stop and start," the limited opportunity for vehicles to disrupt existing traffic through entry and exit, and the high level of road quality to accommodate higher speeds produces a more uniform traffic flow. An increase in the proportion of such roads, then, is expected to lower the fatality rate. Because of the impact that higher speeds have on the extent of injury in the event of an accident, SPEED is expected to increase the fatality rate, all else constant.

HYPOTHESIS 4 The authors also hypothesized that the consumption of alcohol and the age distribution of drivers would be important determinants of highway safety. These variables may be interpreted as indicators of the population's preferences for risk. To capture the effects of alcohol, the authors included the variable ALCOHOL that represents the per capita consumption of alcohol. Increases in alcohol consumption are expected to increase the fatality rate. Additionally, an increase in the proportion of youthful drivers is expected to increase the fatality rate since younger drivers, as previously discussed, have less driving experience and are prone to take more risks when driving. Defined as the proportion of 15–25-year-old drivers in the driving population, YOUTH is expected to have a positive sign.

Estimation results

Table 13.3 reports Crandall and Graham's regression results for their highway safety model. All explanatory variables in their model are in logarithms, so that the estimated coefficients are estimates of the elasticity of the fatality rate with respect to each variable. With some exceptions, the results are consistent with expectations. First, vehicle safety is an important determinant of highway safety. A 1% decrease in the safety index (recall that an decrease in this index reflects an *increase* in safety) leads to a 2.1% decrease in the fatality rate. Similarly, a 1% increase in the average weight of a vehicle produces a 2.3% reduction in the fatality rate. INCOME is positive and significant, which indicates that a 1% increase in real per capita income increases the fatality rate by 0.84%. The positive sign on this variable implies that income's effect on values of time more than offset its effect on demands for safety.

Each of the travel environment variables has the expected effect on highway safety. Increasing the proportion of trucks on the roads is detrimental to safety, whereas increasing the

Table 13.3 A regression model of highway safety, 1947–81

Dependent variable – ln (passenger car occupant fatalities per 100 million passenger car–miles traveled)

Explanatory Variable	Coefficient Estimate (*t*-statistic)
ln (SAFETY)	2.10 (9.78)
ln (WEIGHT)	−2.30 (3.74)
ln (INCOME)	0.848 (3.39)
ln (YOUTH)	−0.170 (0.77)
ln (ALCOHOL)	−0.190 (0.61)
ln (TRUCKS)	0.678 (5.15)
ln (SPEED)	0.463 (1.21)
ln (COST)	0.849 (1.50)
ln (LIMITED ACCESS)	−0.109 (6.54)
CONSTANT	17.7 (3.21)

$R^2 = 0.991$

Source: Adapted from Crandall and Graham (1999), table 5, p. 114.

proportion of limited access roads enhances safety. And although an increase in average speed is consistent with our hypothesis that accidents which occur at higher speeds will produce more fatalities, this is a relatively weak result, since we can only reject the null hypothesis at a 0.10 level (one-tail test).

For this model, YOUTH and ALCOHOL do not appear to be important determinants of highway safety and COST has an unexpected positive sign. A possible reason for these results will be discussed below.

For the purposes of evaluating the effects of an increase in vehicle weight on highway safety, Crandall and Graham focus upon the estimated coefficient for WEIGHT. Since the fatality rate is elastic with respect to this variable, can we determine how many additional accidents would occur as manufacturers reduced vehicle weights in response to the CAFE standard? Yes. Crandall and Graham estimated that CAFE reduced the average weight of a vehicle produced in 1989 by 500 pounds. Given an average 3,100 pound weight of a vehicle in 1989 under the CAFE standard, this implies that the average vehicle would have weighed 3,600 pounds in the absence of CAFE. Thus, the CAFE standard was responsible for a 14% reduction in the average vehicle weight in 1989.

Recall from table 13.3 that the coefficient for WEIGHT represents an elasticity. A 1% increase in WEIGHT produces a 2.30% reduction in the occupant fatality rate. This implies that a 14% decrease in WEIGHT produces a 32.2% increase in the fatality rate.

Based on the number of fatalities and the number of vehicles in 1985, there were 1.9 fatalities per 10,000 cars. Assuming that the 11.2 million vehicles last for ten years, that the 1.9 fatalities per 10,000 cars applies to the 11.2 million model vehicles over the ten-year period, and that 4% of the produced vehicles are scrapped each year, table 13.4 summarizes the annual fatalities associated with the model year's production over the ten-year period. Column (a) gives the number of vehicles remaining per year and column (b) estimates the number of occupant fatalities associated with this model year's production.[4] We see that, in total, the number of fatalities for these vehicles under

Table 13.4 Expected annual fatalities over a ten-year period

Year	Vehicles (million) (a)	CAFE Occupant Fatalities $((a) \div 10{,}000) \cdot 1.9 \cdot 10^6$ (b)	No CAFE Occupant Fatalities $((b) \div 1.322)$ (c)	Discounted Present Value (billion \$) $(((b) - (c)) \cdot 1) \div 1.05^{\text{Year}}) \cdot 10^{-3}$ (d)
1	11.20	2,128.0	1,609.7	0.49
2	10.75	2,042.5	1,545.0	0.45
3	10.32	1,960.8	1,483.2	0.41
4	9.91	1,882.9	1,424.3	0.38
5	9.51	1,806.9	1,366.8	0.34
6	9.13	1,734.7	1,312.2	0.32
7	8.77	1,666.3	1,260.4	0.29
8	8.42	1,599.8	1,210.1	0.26
9	8.08	1,535.2	1,161.3	0.24
10	7.76	1,474.4	1,115.3	0.22
Total		17,831.5	13,488.3	3.41

Assumptions: 11.2 million cars produced; 1.9 fatalities per 10,000 cars; 4% scrappage per year; 10 year life-span.
Source: Author's calculations

the CAFE standard and for the ten-year period is 17,831. But we have also seen that the CAFE standard decreased average vehicle weight by 14%, which implied a 32.2% increase in the fatality rate. If we assume that a 32.2% increase in the fatality rate per 100 million vehicle–miles traveled will also show up as a 32.2% increase in occupant fatalities per 10,000 vehicles, then, in the absence of CAFE, the number of fatalities per 10,000 vehicles would have been 1.9/1.322 = 1.437. This rate generates the predicted fatalities in column (c), where we see that over the ten-year period, the total number of fatalities is 13,488, a 24% reduction in fatalities.[5]

Ignoring the impact of the smaller vehicle weights on serious injuries, assuming a $1 million estimate for the value of a life, and a 5% discount rate, column (d) gives the discounted present value of the increase in fatalities due to CAFE. Over the ten-year period, the estimated accident cost impact from the CAFE standard is $3.41 billion dollars. How does this compare with the energy savings? Assuming a 5% discount rate, a $1 per gallon real price of gasoline, and 500 gallons of gasoline per vehicle per year, the estimated discounted present value of energy savings is on the order of $2.4–2.8 billion dollars. From these figures, the CAFE standard produced a net loss to society.

Discussion

Crandall and Graham also reported the results from a second specification in which the estimated elasticity for WEIGHT was −1.22. Using this figure, the discounted present value of fatality costs for the ten-year period due to CAFE is $2.1 billion, less than the estimated energy savings. However, it must also be remembered that these estimates do not include: (1) costs associated with increased serious injuries from CAFE; (2) the potentially large costs that manufacturers incurred developing and implementing new fuel efficient technologies which would not have been developed in the absence of CAFE; and (3) welfare loss from the nonoptimal change in the mix of vehicles produced as a result of the CAFE standard. Even with lower elasticity estimates for WEIGHT, it is likely that the federal government's regulation of fuel efficiency has produced a net loss for society.

As a final point, recall that the estimation results for YOUTH, ALCOHOL, and COST in table 13.3 were unexpected. The first two variables were not found to be important determinants of highway safety and COST had an unexpected positive sign. A likely explanation for these findings is that some of the explanatory variables in the model are highly correlated; that is, their behavior over time is similar. When two important variables move together over time, this has three effects. First, the model produces a high goodness-of-fit statistic, since there is a strong relationship between the explanatory variables and the dependent variable. Second, the empirical model is not able to distinguish the separate effects of each independent variable, which means that a variable's *t*-statistic will be quite low. Third, the model can be sensitive to minor specification changes (for example, adding or subtracting variables) or to changes in the sample size (dropping or adding observations) in that signs and significance of variables may change from one specification to another.

CASE STUDY – HIGHWAY SPEEDS AND SPEED VARIANCE

In addition to requiring vehicle manufacturers to satisfy the CAFE standard, the Energy Policy and Conservation Act also mandated a national maximum speed limit (NMSL) equal to 55 mph. The thrust of the mandate was to lower speed limits on US interstate highways. Furthermore, to insure compliance, the federal government threatened states with the loss of highway funds if states could not demonstrate that its drivers were traveling at speeds consistent with a 55 mph limit. The primary objective of setting a lower speed limit was to reduce the consumption of energy. However, it turned out that the nation received an unexpected bonus in the form of reductions in fatalities and serious injuries. One national study (National Research Council, Transportation Research Board, 1984) estimated that the 55 mph speed limit law annually saved between 2,000 and 4,000 lives.

Over time, there were many complaints, particularly in the Western states, that the lower speed limit was imposing significant costs upon individual and business highway users. It was estimated, for example, that in 1983 an additional 852 million person–hours were spent in travel time as a result of the lower speed limit. Ultimately, in 1987 Congress passed the Surface Transportation and Uniform Relocation Act which, among its provisions, permitted states to increase the speed limit to 65 mph on rural interstate highways. The reason that higher speed limits were confined to rural interstate highways is that these highways have traditionally been the safest roads. In 1995 the number of fatalities per 100 million vehicle–miles traveled was 1.20 on rural interstate roads, in comparison with 2.69 on arterial roads, 3.13 on rural collector roads, and 3.82 on local rural roads. This is also true in urban areas where the 1995 fatality rate was 0.63, 1.32, 1.12, and 1.69 on urban interstates, urban arterials, urban collectors, and local urban roads, respectively. Within two years after passage of the law, 40 states had increased speed limits on rural interstate highways within their boundaries.[6]

There have been numerous studies of the impact that relaxed speed limits on rural interstate highways have had upon highway safety. And the results have been mixed. There is not a consensus on the highway safety effects of higher rural interstate speed limits. Among the issues involved in this debate is whether "speed kills." In the last section, SPEED was an explanatory variable in Crandall and Graham's model and we hypothesized that accidents at higher speeds would result in more severe injuries, including fatalities. Thus, we expected a positive sign. However, although the estimated sign was positive, we could not reject the null hypothesis at normal levels of significance that the coefficient equaled zero.

Although average speeds increase with increased speed limits, does this necessarily imply more accidents, more injuries, and more fatalities? In an interesting but controversial paper, Lave (1985) considered this question. He hypothesized that once one controls for the variation of speeds on a road, increasing speeds will have little impact upon highway safety. One can imagine, for example, a single road in which all traffic is moving at exactly the same speed. Speed variance is zero on this road and, regardless of whether traffic is uniformly traveling at 30 mph or 50 mph, there will be no accidents. Of course, in reality vehicles enter and exit the stream of traffic, there are different types of vehicles using the road, as well as a distribution of drivers by age, sex, driving abilities and so forth. All of these factors produce a distribution of speeds which, according to Lave, generates accidents.[7]

In order to test this hypothesis, Lave estimated the following empirical model of highway safety:

$$\begin{aligned}&\text{Fatality rate for road type } i\\&= \alpha + \beta_1(\text{Speed Variance}) + \beta_2(\text{Average Speed})\\&\quad + \beta_3(\text{Citations per Driver})\\&\quad + \beta_4(\text{Hospital Access}) + \varepsilon \qquad (13.6)\end{aligned}$$

where Fatality Rate is the number of fatalities on road type i per 100 million vehicle–miles traveled on road type i, Speed Variance is a measure of speed variation on road type i, Average Speed is a measure of average speed on road type i, Citations per Driver is the speeding citations on all highways per 100 drivers, and Hospital Access = (hospitals per square mile)(% population living in nonmetropolitan areas). Citations per Driver controls for traffic enforcement and is expected to have a negative sign – increased enforcement reduces the fatality rate. Hospital Access is also expected to reduce the fatality rate. The further one is from medical facilities, the greater is the likelihood that a serious injury will turn into a fatality. According to Lave's hypothesis, after controlling for Speed Variance, the coefficient on Average Speed will not be significant; however, after controlling for Average Speed, the coefficient on Speed Variance is expected to be positive and significant.

Data for the analysis is a cross-section of states for 1982, excluding Hawaii and Alaska, and excluding any observation for which there were five or fewer fatalities. Table 13.5 reports Lave's findings for six road types.

The results produce mixed evidence on the separate effects of Average Speed and Speed Variance. For all functional road types, we cannot reject the null hypothesis that Average Speed has no effect on the fatality rate. However, for three road types, Rural Collector, Urban Freeway, and Urban Interstate, Speed Variance is also insignificant. The poor results for these road types is also apparent from the R^2 values, which generally lie below 0.20. The only significant variable in these equations is Citations per Driver, which carries an unexpected positive sign. Lave argues that Citations per Driver actually reflects two types of behaviors: aggressive driving on the part of travelers and enforcement on the part of traffic police. The estimated positive sign suggests that this variable is a better index of driver behavior than enforcement activities. Hospital Access is seen as an important determinant in only two equations, that for Rural Interstate and Urban Arterial. In both cases, the variable has the expected negative sign.

Lave's findings reported in table 13.5 are strongest for Rural Interstate highways. Despite the limited number of explanatory variables, we see that the included variables explain over 50% of the variation in rural interstate fatality rates. A 1 mph increase in Speed Variance on rural interstate highways increases the number of fatalities per 100 million vehicle–miles traveled by 0.019. The rural interstate results are consistent with Lave's underlying hypothesis that Speed Variance rather than Average Speed is the relevant safety measure, and provide some evidence that policy-makers and traffic enforcement personnel focus their efforts on those drivers that contribute to higher variations in speed rather than higher speeds. However, the reported results don't support this as a general policy across all road types.

Subsequent work on speed limit effects, partly in response to Lave's findings and partly independent of his work, suggest that both average speed and speed variance are important determinants of highway safety.[8] However, the extent to which each contributes to the fatality rate remains a point of debate and awaits further studies.

HIGHWAY SAFETY AND RISK COMPENSATION

We have seen that negative externalities and informational asymmetries are likely to produce inefficient levels of transportation safety in unregulated markets. Suppose that the government intervenes in the market and mandates a higher level of safety than the private unregulated market currently provides. For example, the government mandates that all new cars must have anti-lock braking systems (which is accident-reducing) as well as driver- and passenger-side airbags (which are injury-reducing in the event of an accident). The theory is that, by lowering the incidence of accidents and the severity of injuries when an accident occurs, these regulations will lead to an overall improvement in highway safety? This is probably true, but not necessarily. Arguing that such government mandates necessarily imply higher levels of safety ignores one important aspect of the regulations, the impact that such regulations have upon individual behavior. We can identify many instances of individual responses to one's altered driving conditions. Drivers may travel at 70 mph on an interstate highway during good weather. However, during heavy snowstorms it would be surprising if drivers continued to travel at 70 mph. Recognizing the more dangerous conditions during a snowstorm, drivers lower their speeds, increase headways, and make fewer risky maneuvers during

Table 13.5 Average speed, speed variance results, 1982[a]

	Dependent variable – fatalities per 100 million vehicle–miles					
Explanatory Variable	Rural Interstate	Rural Arterial	Rural Collector	Urban Freeway	Urban Interstate	Urban Arterial
Speed Variance	0.190 (2.6)	0.375 (2.0)	0.011 (0.046)	0.281 (0.7)	−0.011 (−0.2)	0.304 (1.9)
Average Speed	nr (−0.4)	nr (−0.5)	nr (−1.2)	nr (−0.5)	nr (0.3)	nr (−1.0)
Citations per Driver	0.0071 (2.8)	0.0116 (1.7)	0.0139 (2.4)	0.0410 (2.5)	0.0106 (2.8)	−0.0068 (−1.2)
Hospital Access	−5.29 (−3.7)	−0.424 (−0.1)	−0.83 (0.2)	−2.86 (−0.5)	−0.168 (−0.1)	−5.72 (−2.2)
R^2	0.532	0.101	0.089	0.193	0.167	0.168
Number of observations	44	47	41	18	27	21

[a] Numbers in parentheses are *t*-statistics. Coefficients of Average Speed not reported (nr). Regression constant term not reported. Reported R^2 adjusted for degrees of freedom.

Source: Adapted from Lave (1985), table 4, p. 1162

the trip. This accords with one's common sense. Conversely, if driving conditions suddenly improve, drivers respond to the safer conditions by increasing speed, reducing headways, and driving a bit less carefully.

This suggests that government regulations which lead to improved driving conditions will have some impact upon drivers' actions: specifically, these mandates will cause drivers to drive less safely. The hypothesis that government-mandated safety may lead to offsetting behavior was first put forward by Peltzman (1975) and is referred to as the *risk compensation* hypothesis.

From equation (13.4), we saw that an individual's decision to optimally expend effort on safety produces an optimal accident probability P_A^* and optimal accident losses L^* for the individual. In this section, we want to focus upon accident probability and ask the following question: What is the impact of an increase in the marginal cost of safety effort on the probability of an accident? From equation (13.4), this effect will be

$$\frac{\Delta P_A^*}{\Delta mc} = \frac{\Delta P_A^*}{\Delta e^*}\frac{\Delta e^*}{\Delta mc} > 0 \qquad (13.7)$$

Holding all else constant, an increase in the opportunity cost of safety effort reduces the amount of safety effort. In addition, any increase in safety effort reduces the probability of an accident, all else constant. Since each term on the right-hand side of the equals sign in equation (13.7) is positive, an increase in the opportunity cost of safety effort increases the probability of experiencing an accident, all else constant.

In figure 13.2, we analyzed the effect on optimal safety if Connie suddenly experiences a thunderstorm as she drives on the interstate highway. In the figure, we saw that, by increasing the marginal benefit from additional safety effort, inclement weather increases the optimal level of safety effort. What will be the effect of inclement weather on the probability of Connie's experiencing an accident? Assume that driving in more inclement weather is denoted by an increase in x. Then, from equation (13.4), the effect of inclement weather is

$$\begin{aligned}\frac{\Delta P_A^*}{\Delta x} &= \frac{\Delta P_A^*}{\Delta e^*}\frac{\Delta e^*}{\Delta x} + \left(\frac{\Delta P_A^*}{\Delta x}\right)_{\text{given } e} > 0 \\ &= \text{compensating effect} + \text{direct effect} \qquad (13.8)\end{aligned}$$

Here we see that the effect of adverse weather conditions impacts the probability of an accident in two ways. The second term on the right-hand side of the equals sign in equation (13.8) gives the direct effect of the thunderstorm, which will have a positive sign, since driving in thunderstorms is inherently more risky. But this direct effect assumes that Connie exerts the same level of safety effort. The first term on the right-hand side of the equals sign gives the "indirect effect" of the worsening weather on Connie's safety effort. As we saw in figure 13.2, the presence of a thunderstorm raises the expected benefit of safety effort, which induces Connie to increase her safety behaviors; that is, $\Delta e^*/\Delta x > 0$. Combined with a negative sign on $\Delta P_A^*/\Delta e^*$, the combined effect $(\Delta P_A^*/\Delta e^*)(\Delta e^*/\Delta x) < 0$. In other words, the presence of a thunderstorm will cause Connie to exhibit some "compensating" behavior. Moreover, if this compensating behavior is large enough, the indirect effect, $(\Delta P_A^*/\Delta e^*)(\Delta e^*/\Delta x)$, will more than offset the direct effect, $(\Delta P_A^*/\Delta x)_{\text{given } e}$, so that the net effect is *negative*. Connie becomes so careful when driving in a thunderstorm that the probability of her involvement in an accident actually falls.

The important point is that individuals are not passive to exogenous changes in the perceived safety of one's surrounding environment, but respond to altered environments in order to maintain an optimal level of safety effort.

All of this seems pretty reasonable and is not likely to produce much, if any, controversy. Drawing upon your own driving experiences, you can undoubtedly identify particular weather conditions, road conditions, or some other environmental feature that has caused you to alter your driving in some way.

However, these effects have caused considerable controversy when, instead of analyzing the effects of inclement weather, we analyze the effect of federal safety regulations. We have seen that market failure in markets for safety provides a justification for government intervention. In theory, by mandating safety standards, the government regulations increase the level of safety, which produces a safer environment. This is possibly true, even probably, but not necessarily.

Let's continue with Connie's interstate trip and assume that an increase in r reflects an increase in government-mandated vehicle safety regulations. Cars are now equipped with an anti-lock braking system that is intended to reduce the likelihood of Connie experiencing an accident. Rewriting equation (13.8) gives

$$\frac{\Delta P_{\mathrm{A}}^{*}}{\Delta r} = \frac{\Delta P_{\mathrm{A}}^{*}}{\Delta e^{*}}\frac{\Delta e^{*}}{\Delta r} + \left(\frac{\Delta P_{\mathrm{A}}^{*}}{\Delta r}\right)_{\text{given } e^{*}} \tag{13.9}$$

Holding all else constant, including the level of safety effort, the direct effect of these mandates, $(\Delta P_{\mathrm{A}}^{*}/\Delta r)_{\text{given } e^{*}}$, is unambiguously positive. However, by reducing the probability of an accident, these mandates provide a safer environment for Connie's trip and reduce the expected benefits from an additional unit of safety effort. That is, the indirect effect of the government mandates is a reduction in safety effort which, all else constant, increases the probability of an accident, $(\Delta P_{\mathrm{A}}^{*}/\Delta e^{*})(\Delta e^{*}/\Delta r) > 0$. This implies that the net effect of government safety legislation is not unambiguously positive, but is ambiguous. Moreover, if the "offsetting" indirect effect is large enough, the probability of experiencing an accident increases since the indirect effect more than offsets the direct beneficial effect of the regulation. It is this result that has caused considerable controversy among safety researchers.

Figure 13.3 illustrates these effects. Points A and A'' represent Connie's initial equilibrium, where her optimal level of safety is e_1. Prior to anti-lock braking systems, in figure 13.3(b), safety effort e_1 implies an accident probability equal to $P_{\mathrm{A}1}$. The government now mandates anti-lock braking systems and predicts that these systems will reduce the accident probability from $P_{\mathrm{A}1}$ to $P_{\mathrm{A}2}$ for a typical driver such as Connie. In figure 13.3(b), the regulation shifts the probability curve downward and reduces Connie's accident probability from $P_{\mathrm{A}1}$ to $P_{\mathrm{A}2}$, *given Connie's current level of safety effort*, e_1. But Connie is not passive to the government-mandated increase in safety. In figure 13.3(a), the marginal benefit from safety effort falls from MB_1 to MB_2, which reduces Connie's optimal effort from e_1 to e_2. This is the offsetting behavior which, in figure 13.3(b), moves Connie from point A'' to point B'. As depicted in figure 13.3, points B and B' represent Connie's final equilibrium. She has e_2 level of safety effort with an associated accident probability equal to $P_{\mathrm{A}3}$. Notice that the mandated system has led to a safer environment, $P_{\mathrm{A}3} < P_{\mathrm{A}1}$. But the environment is not as safe as government regulators predicted. Connie's response to the safety regulation reduced her optimal safety effort to e_2, leading to a partially offsetting increase in accident probability, $P_{\mathrm{A}3} > P_{\mathrm{A}2}$.

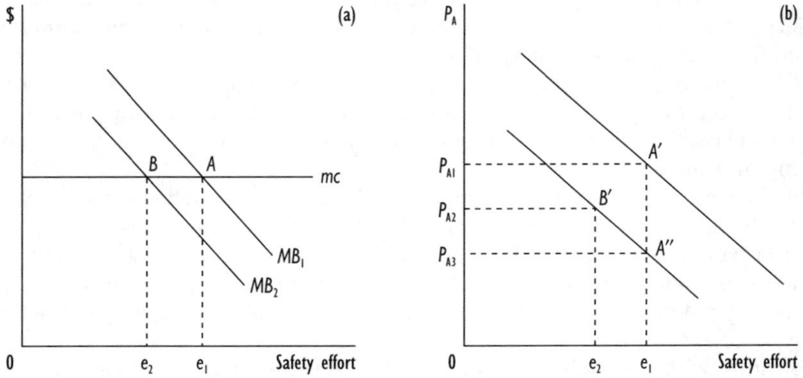

Figure 13.3 Direct and indirect effects of safety improvement on safety effort.

Thus, in the presence of offsetting behavior, government regulators should not be surprised that their safety-mandated regulations oftentimes fall short of their predicted effects. There are three additional points that we can make here:

- If the offsetting behavior is sufficiently strong, not only will the actual effect of the safety regulation fall short of the predicted effect, but it may dominate the predicted effect and lead to a decrease in safety.
- In the above example, the offsetting effect for Connie was not sufficient to dominate the direct effect of anti-locking brakes. And suppose that for all vehicle occupants the improved occupant safety from the vehicle standards more than offsets any increase in aggressive behavior on the part of drivers. This implies fewer occupant deaths, but could produce more *nonoccupant* deaths. This was exactly the point that Peltzman (1975) made. Although government-mandated vehicle safety regulations improved occupant safety, Peltzman presented evidence consistent with the hypothesis more aggressive driver behavior increased pedestrian and cyclist fatalities.
- In the above discussion, we have focused upon Connie's offsetting behavior. It may be the case, however, that Connie's compensating behavior will be *negative*; that is, Connie will undertake actions that reinforce rather than offset the mandated safety regulations. For example, aware that proper application of anti-lock brakes is to depress the brakes gently rather than harshly, Connie becomes a more defensive driver in order to avoid situations which would require harsh braking. In this instance, Connie's response to the introduction of anti-lock brakes reinforces the direct effect of the brake and further reduces the probability of her experiencing an accident.

CASE STUDY – AIRBAGS

In a recent paper, Peterson et al. (1995) investigated whether new cars equipped with airbags produce more aggressive driver behavior consistent with Peltzman's hypothesis. By increasing driver safety, airbags effectively reduce the risk price of driving and drivers respond to a lower risk price by increasing the amount of risk taken. Thus, relative to a pre-airbag environment, the compensating hypothesis implies an increase in the likelihood of an accident in the post-airbag environment.

To test this hypothesis, Peterson et al. obtained data on the personal injury claims for every non-station-wagon make–model in 1989.[9] For these same make–models, personal injury claims data were also collected for the years 1990, 1991, 1992, and 1993. From these data, a relative personal injury claim (RPIC) index was defined, the value of which equaled 100 for all vehicles of a given year. Thus, if a Volvo had a relative personal injury claim index equal to 65, the average frequency of personal injury claims filed against Volvo was 65% of the average for all vehicles. Similarly, a RPIC value equal to 150 for a particular vehicle says that this make–model has 50% more claims filed against it than the average vehicle.

If a particular make–model equipped with an airbag produces more aggressive driver behavior, then one would expect this make–model to be involved in more accidents, all else constant, and a higher accident incidence would increase the number of claims filed against the make–model. Thus, if the compensating hypothesis holds, a vehicle newly equipped with an airbag is expected to have a higher relative personal injury claim in that year than the make–model experienced in the previous year.

Peterson et al.'s empirical model to test the risk compensation hypothesis is as follows:

$$\Delta RPIC_i = \alpha + \beta_1(\text{Air Bag})_i + \beta_2\text{Resize}_i + \varepsilon_i \qquad (13.10)$$

where $\Delta RPIC_i$ is the change in the relative personal injury claim for make–model i from one year to the next; $(\text{Air Bag})_i$ is a dummy variable that equals one if the make–model i was equipped with an airbag from one year to the next, zero if not; Resize_i is a dummy variable that equals one if make–model i was made larger from one year to the next, zero if not resized; α, β_1, and β_2 are parameters to be estimated; and ε is the error term. According to the risk compensation hypothesis, $\beta_1 > 0$; that is, a make–model equipped with an airbag is expected to experience an increase in the relative personal injury claim from one year to the next. However, we know from our discussion of CAFE standards that vehicle weight is an important determinant of injury severity and therefore to the incidence of personal injury claims. In order to account for any changes in claims due to a change in the size of the make–model, the authors also included in the regression model the variable Resize_i. Table 13.6 reports Peterson et al.'s estimation results.

The authors estimated the model for all included years, 1989–93, as well as for each separate pair of years. In column (a), we see that the results are consistent with Peltzman's compensation hypothesis. The coefficient for Air Bag Dummy is positive and significant at the 0.05 level (one-tail test). All else constant, equipping a vehicle with an airbag increases the relative

Table 13.6 Changes in relative personal injury claims: newly equipped versus nonairbag make–models

Explanatory Variable	All Years (a)	1989–90 (b)	1990–1 (c)	1991–2 (d)	1992–3 (e)
Constant	0.754 (1.03)	1.20 (0.89)	−1.34 (−0.97)	2.55 (1.93)	−0.36 (−0.30)
Airbag Dummy	3.22 (1.79)	6.76 (2.29)	−4.16 (−0.83)	7.78 (2.19)	−0.24 (−0.08)
Resize Dummy	−4.94 (−2.34)	4.50 (1.03)	−3.16 (−0.82)	−10.9 (−2.81)	−11.1 (2.67)

Source: Adapted from Peterson et al. (1995), table 1, p. 257. R^2 and number of observations for each regression not reported

personal injury claims against that make–model. We also see that, consistent with larger cars being safer cars, if a make–model was made larger from one year to the next, personal injury claims fell relative to the average of all vehicles. Looking at the separate years, the results are mixed. For 1989–90 and 1991–2, introducing airbags increased claim frequency, supporting risk compensation; in 1990–1 and 1992–3, there was no effect from the introduction of airbags.

Discussion

In Peterson et al.'s empirical specification of the model, there are no economic variables or other determinants of highway safety. The reason for this is twofold. First, the relative personal injury claims data have already adjusted for the driver's age group. Second, the data are relative personal injury claims, where the base is defined as "all vehicles." Therefore, although it is expected that an increase in real per capita income, for example, will affect highway safety, there is no reason to believe that changes in this variable will affect the relative injury claims of one make–model any differently than another make–model. This is a maintained hypothesis in the authors' empirical model. However, if, for some reason, changes in a determinant of highway safety affected the claims of some make–models differently than others, the empirical model in equation (13.10) would be misspecified and the parameters biased.

It could be the case that, rather than risk compensation, the results reported in table 13.6 reflect a "sorting hypothesis" whereby drivers who are at most risk would be the first to purchase vehicles equipped with airbags. According to this hypothesis, more aggressive drivers would be the first to purchase airbag-equipped vehicles and the increase in claim frequency would reflect this. However, the sorting hypothesis also implies that, over time, as nonaggressive drivers purchased airbags, there would be no impact on relative personal injury claims. The estimation results are inconsistent with the hypothesis. Rather than observing a declining effect of Air Bag Dummy from 1989–90 through 1992–3, we see that the impact of the variable is strong in 1989–90, absent in 1990–1, strong in 1991–2, and again absent in 1992–3. The absence of a continual reduction in the effect of the Air Bag Dummy contradicts the sorting hypothesis.

FIRM PROFITABILITY AND SAFETY

We have seen that individual drivers, faced with uncertain outcomes, choose their safety behaviors in order to maximize expected income. Further, individuals optimize their level of safety when the marginal benefit from additional safety equals the marginal resource cost of increased safety. It should not be surprising to learn that firms follow a similar optimizing rule. In general, a firm will invest in safety up to the point at which marginal benefit equals marginal cost. Marginal benefit to the firm reflects the additional revenues generated by safer operations or reduced operational costs (due at least in part to a lower accident probability) as a result of a firm's providing safer operations. These additional revenues will be balanced against the marginal cost of providing more safety. As long as the marginal cost of additional safety is less than the additional revenues, firms will continue to invest in safety.

A firm's optimal level of safety s^* will generally depend upon the economic environment that the firm faces (that is, output price and nonsafety-related input prices), summarized by p and the marginal cost of safety, mc), the level of technology γ, the regulatory environment r, and a firm's operating attributes x (reflecting the traveling environment) which can be summarized as

$$s^* = s^*(p;x,r,mc,\gamma) \tag{13.11}$$

In general, changes in the economic and operating environment affect a firm's profitability, and a topic of some interest in transportation safety is the extent to which changes in a firm's profitability induce firms to alter their levels of safety. In particular, are firms in financial difficulties more likely to invest in less safety than firms that are financially more healthy? Golbe (1983) examined this question for railroads and found that an increase in profitability either had no effect upon safety or had a weak beneficial effect upon safety when the railroad was financially healthy. For unprofitable railroads, however, Golbe found an inverse relationship between profitability and accidents. Lower profits led to more accidents.

CASE STUDY – AIRLINE SAFETY AND PROFITABILITY

In a study of the airline industry, Rose (1989) analyzed the impact that an airline's financial attributes had upon its accident rate. Rose argued that airlines have an incentive to invest in more safety for three reasons:

- In order to appropriately set insurance premiums for liability, insurance companies need to evaluate an airline's exposure to risk. Airline companies that do not invest much in safety will be higher-risk companies and, accordingly, will pay higher insurance premiums. Thus, when the reduction in insurance costs is greater than the cost of increased safety, an airline company has an economic incentive to invest in more safety.
- Much of an airline company's reputation is built upon the firm's ability to offer reliable and safe travel. These reputations are valuable and give airline companies strong incentives to invest in safety in order to maintain their reputations. The recent crashes of TWA Flight 800 and ValuJet Flight 592 in 1996 indicate how quickly a company's reputation for safety can be jeopardized. Indeed, after the ValuJet crash, the company changed its name to Airtran Airlines, possibly recognizing that only at a very high cost, if at all, would it be possible to win back its market share under the old name. Thus, a company's desire to maintain a strong customer base provides airline companies with an incentive to invest in safety.
- The lives of many employees in airline companies, particularly cabin attendants and pilots, critically depend upon the company's ability and interest in aircraft maintenance and implementing safe operational procedures. The personal safety interests of these employees provide strong incentives to resist company decisions that are seen to reduce the level of airline safety, although these incentives will be weakened if an airline company compensates its attendants and pilots for the additional risk through higher wages.

For the period 1957–86, Rose collected information on 26 scheduled air passenger carriers certificated by the CAB. This sample of airlines includes 12 trunk carriers, six local service carriers, five Alaskan and intra-Hawaiian carriers, and three territorial carriers. Due to the lack of data or the lack of comparable data, commuter airlines, air-taxis, intrastate air carriers, charter services, and new jet carrier entrants were not included in the analysis. The focus on passenger services also eliminated air cargo companies from her analysis.[10]

After controlling for an airline's operational characteristics, Rose examined whether there was a relationship between firm profitability and safety investment where increased safety investment is revealed through lower accident rates. Rose specified the following log–linear empirical model:

$$\ln\left(\frac{\text{Total Accidents}}{\text{Departures}}\right)_{it} = \beta_0 + \beta_1\text{Time}_t + \beta_2(\text{Average Length})_{it} + \beta_3\text{Experience}_{it} + \beta_4(\text{Operating Margin})_{i,t-1} + \beta_5\text{International}_{it} + \beta_6\text{Alaska}_{it} + \varepsilon_{it} \quad (13.12)$$

where the index *it* reflects company *i* in time period *t*, and ε_{it} is a normally distributed error term. Rose's measure of airline safety is accident probability, defined as the total number of accidents per 1,000 departures (Total Accidents/Departures)$_{it}$ that air carrier *i* experiences in time period *t*.

Hypotheses

HYPOTHESIS 1 Technological improvements in aircraft, operating procedures, and air-traffic control systems over time have made airline travel safer. In order to capture the effects of these technological advances, Rose included a variable for the passage of time, Time$_t$. It is expected that the coefficient of Time$_t$ will be negative.

HYPOTHESIS 2 Airline operating characteristics affect accident probability. Rose included two operating attributes in her equation. (Average Length)$_{it}$ is the average length of flight, defined as miles per departure and measured in units of 1,000 miles. Since longer flights imply higher risk exposure, it is expected that, all else constant, an increase in stage length will increase a carrier's accident probability. Also, cumulative operating experience (million miles flown), Experience$_{it}$, was included in the model to capture learning effects that airline operations have on safety levels. Since, holding all else constant, more experienced airlines are expected to have better safety records than less experienced carriers, the expected sign on Experience$_{it}$ is negative.

HYPOTHESIS 3 Increased profitability reduces accident rates. To reflect financial performance, Rose included an air carrier's operating margin, defined as 1 – (operating expenses)/(operating revenues) in the last period.

Because accidents that occur in period *t* affect a firm's operating margin in the same period, including current period operating margin as a variable will not reflect the role that firm profits have in firm decisions to provide safe trips. To better isolate the effect that firm financial performance has upon accident rates, Rose included operating margin in the last period, Operating Margin$_{i,t-1}$, as an explanatory variable. Thus, Rose's main hypothesis is that an increase in firm profitability in period $t-1$ will reduce accident rates in period *t*. All else constant, (Operating Margin)$_{i,t-1}$ is expected to have a negative sign.

As seen in equation (13.12), Rose also included in her empirical model two dummy variables (0,1), Alaska$_{it}$ and International$_{it}$ in order to capture any impact upon air safety from operations in Alaska or outside the United States.[11]

Table 13.7 reports Rose's estimation results. Consistent with the long-term safety trends, the coefficient on Time$_t$ is negative and highly significant. For the entire set of carriers, technological and other safety-related changes in the industry have resulted in a 2.9% annual decrease in the accident rate. Also as expected, an increase in the average length of flight, by increasing exposure, increases the accident probability. A 200-mile increase in average stage length, for example, leads to a 10.8% increase in accident probability. And the more experience the airline has, the lower its accident probability is, all else constant. A million mile increase in cumulative experience reduces the accident probability by 1.41%.

International flights are not seen in table 13.7 to affect airline safety (very low *t*-statistic) but flying in Alaska does. Alaskan carriers experience a 75% increase in accident probability in comparison with their non-Alaskan counterparts.

Consistent with Rose's hypothesis that financial problems increase accident probabilities, we see in table 13.7 that the coefficient for (Last

Table 13.7 A regression model of airline safety, 1957–86[a]

Dependent variable – ln(accidents/departures)

Explanatory Variables	Coefficient Estimate (*t*-statistic)
Time	−0.029 (−9.67)
Average Length (thousand miles per departure)	0.540 (4.32)
Experience (million miles)	−0.141 (5.22)
Last Period Operating Margin (%)	−0.922 (−3.16)
International	−0.010 (−0.17)
Alaska	0.758 (7.15)
Constant	4.01 (66.8)
Number of observations = 663	

[a] R^2 was not reported, but the sum of squared residuals was reported as 211.26. Not all data were available for each air carrier over the entire period.
Source: Adapted from Rose (1989), table 8.6, p. 108

Period Operating Margin) is negative. A one percentage point increase in a carrier's operating margin last period reduces its accident probability by 0.99% this period. Increasing air carrier profitability is conducive to improving safety. Conversely, the results imply that public concerns about air safety among carriers experiencing financial distress are not displaced.

CASE STUDY – NEW ENTRANTS AND AIRLINE SAFETY

The 1978 Airline Deregulation Act (ADA) had a significant effect upon the economic activities and market structure of the airline industry. In addition to pricing and route flexibility, a major component of the legislation was open entry into the market. Prior restrictions on access were effectively eliminated, so that airline markets were accessible to new entrants. Between 1978 and 1985, there were nine new airline carriers in a sector that had a total of 25 or so carriers. Although the ADA had no direct implications for safety, an important question is whether passenger safety would be compromised because more passengers would be using carriers with relatively little experience in the industry. Further, we saw in the last section that firm profitability does have an impact upon airline safety. If, in an effort to keep costs down, new entrants provide less training to their pilots or use less experienced pilots, perform maintenance activities at lower standards, or generally have less quality control over their activities, passengers are exposed to greater risks in their travel. Thus, with no change in airline safety standards, the fact that airline safety behaviors cannot be perfectly monitored implies that the altered structure of the airline sector from economic deregulation could, as a by-product, result in a less safe flying environment.

However, new entrants also have an incentive to invest in safety, because they want to develop and keep a loyal customer base. In other words, new entrants are very concerned with establishing a reputation for safety, and the only way to do this is to build up a record of safe travel. It is likely, for example, that an airplane crash will do more damage to the customer base of a new entrant that has yet to establish a reputation for safety than to an established carrier that does have a reputation for safety. This provides a strong inducement for new entrants to establish a reputation for safety as quickly as possible.

Kanafani and Keeler (1989) considered whether safety actions by new air carrier entrants behaved any differently from established incumbents. To test this hypothesis, they obtained maintenance expenditures for 22 airlines that operated during the period 1971–85. Thus, the sample for this study covers the pre-deregulation period (1971–5), the regulation period (1976–8), and seven years of post-deregulation activities (1979–85). For this cross-section–time series sample, they developed a basic empirical model for maintenance expenditures:

$$\begin{aligned}&\%\ \text{Maintenance Expenditures}_{it}\\&= \alpha + \beta_1(\text{New Entrant})_{it} + \beta_2(\text{Flight Hours})_{it}\\&\quad + \beta_2(\text{Braniff/Continental})_t + \varepsilon_{it}\end{aligned}$$

where % Maintenance Expenditures$_{it}$ is the proportion of total costs spent on maintenance for air carrier i in time period t, (New Entrant)$_{it}$ is a dummy variable that equals one (zero) if air carrier i was (was not) a new entrant in time period t, (Flight Hours)$_{it}$ is the cumulative flight hours for carrier i in time period t, α and β_i (i = 1, 2, 3) are parameters to be estimated, and ε_{it} is a normally distributed random error term. A separate dummy variable for two air carriers, Braniff and Continental, is also included to reflect bankruptcy proceedings that Continental and Braniff underwent in 1983 and 1984 respectively, which may have affected the carriers' maintenance activities relative to financially healthier air carriers. In addition to these variables, the authors also included a time variable for each of the years 1972–85. All else held constant, the time dummy variables capture any change in maintenance activities, relative to 1971, due to factors not explicitly included in the model. The empirical model embodies two fundamental hypotheses:

HYPOTHESIS 1 A primary determinant of maintenance expenditures is aircraft use. It is expected that an increase in the number of flight hours will increase an air carrier's maintenance expenditures, all else constant. Thus, we expect $\beta_2 > 0$.

HYPOTHESIS 2 The primary focus in this model is the hypothesis that the maintenance expenditures of new entrants are no different from those of established carriers. If the null hypothesis is true then the variable New Entrant has no effect on maintenance expenditures. That is, under the null hypothesis, we expect $\beta_1 = 0$.

Table 13.8 summarizes Kanafani and Keeler's findings. Since expenditures on some types of maintenance may be more closely related to safety than other types, we see in the table that the authors used three alternative maintenance expenditure measures: total maintenance expenditures, a general measure; maintenance expenditures related to flight equipment, a measure more closely identified with safety; and direct aircraft maintenance expenditures, a measure specific to aircraft.

From the R^2 statistic, we see in column (a) that the first model has very little explanatory power. Consistent with this, no explanatory variable is related to PCMAINT. This tells us two things. First, there is no difference between incumbents and new entrants with respect to the percentage of total costs spent on maintenance. Second, maintenance expenditures are too broadly defined to capture a relationship between flight hours and maintenance, which suggests that the PCMAINT is not a particularly good measure for safety.

In contrast, the results in columns (b) and (c) provide a much improved explanation of maintenance expenditures. Whether we measure the share of maintenance by expenditures on flight-related equipment or by direct expenditures on aircraft, the included variables explain 55% of the variation in the dependent variable. Also, as expected, Flight Hours is an important determinant of these expenditure shares indicating, for example, that a million mile increase in flight hours increases the share of costs spent on flight connected and direct aircraft maintenance, respectively, by 3.1% and 2.3%. We also see in the table that the bankruptcy proceedings of Braniff and Continental had no differential impact on maintenance, regardless of how maintenance is defined. The coefficient of this variable is quite small and statistically insignificant.

Table 13.8 Maintenance expenditures[a]

Dependent variables – PCMAINT = % of costs on all maintenance
PCFLT = % of costs on maintenance related to flight equipment
PCDIR = % of costs on aircraft maintenance

	Dependent Variable		
Variable	PCMAINT (a) Coefficient Estimate (*t*-statistic)	PCFLT (b) Coefficient Estimate (*t*-statistic)	PCDIR (c) Coefficient Estimate (*t*-statistic)
Constant	0.154 (25.7)	0.098 (19.6)	0.101 (20.2)
New Entrant	0.0039 (0.78)	0.0180 (4.61)	0.014 (3.59)
Braniff/Continental	−0.008 (−0.89)	0.0007 (0.1)	0.0002 (0.03)
Flight Hours (million)	0.002 (0.33)	0.031 (6.60)	0.023 (4.90)
R^2	0.065	0.556	0.553
Number of observations	208	208	208

[a] Year dummy variables included in the model were not reported.
Source: Adapted from Kanafani and Keeler (1989), table 9.2, p. 120

Do new entrants pose a safety threat to passengers, at least in terms of a reduced cost share going to maintenance? The answer appears to no. As we have seen above, if we use the share of all maintenance expenditures as the dependent variable, the results in column (a) indicate that new entrants spend the same proportion as incumbents. However, in columns (b) and (c) we see the opposite effect. Rather than devoting a smaller share of their costs to maintenance, whether flight connected or directly on aircraft, new entrants devoted a larger share to maintenance. In particular, the share of costs devoted to flight connected maintenance was 1.8% higher than incumbents; and the share devoted to aircraft maintenance was 1.4% higher. Both coefficients are statistically significant.

Kanafani and Keeler offer two possible reasons for the increased share that new entrants spend on maintenance. First, new entrants may not have the resources to undertake their own maintenance and therefore contract these services out to established airlines. Relative to established carriers that provide their own maintenance, this raises the cost and the share of expenditures incurred by new entrants. Second, new entrants may have older fleets in comparison with established carriers. All else constant, maintenance on an older fleet of planes will be more costly.

Although the finding that new entrants pay more for expenditures than established carriers may not indicate that new entrants are investing in greater safety, the results do suggest that new entrants are not skimping on safety relative to established carriers.

Discussion

In addition to maintenance expenditures, Kanafani and Keeler also considered whether new entrants had more accidents or mid-air collisions in comparison with incumbent carriers. The findings were consistent with those above. Although economic deregulation of the airline industry did not change existing safety regulations, there were concerns that access to the market by new carriers would compromise passenger safety. Kanafani and Keeler's analysis did not find support for this.

In a related study on airline safety subsequent to deregulation, Oster and Zorn (1989) found that accident rates due to equipment problems were significantly lower in the post-deregulation period. Further, under deregulation, all carriers, new and incumbent, adapted their networks and operations to the new competitive environment. Would these changes affect safety? They found no evidence of this. The substitution of commuter airlines for trunk and local service carriers in small towns did not compromise safety; in the post-deregulation period, the rate of traffic control related accidents was lower despite the increased pressure upon traffic controllers at hub airports as carriers shifted to a hub-and-spoke system; and they found small differences in the accidents rates between established airlines, new entrants, and the former intrastate carriers.

CASE STUDY – UNINTENDED SAFETY EFFECTS FROM ECONOMIC DEREGULATION

In chapter 8 we explored the competitive relationship between motor carriers and railroads in the transport of freight during the regulated period. We further saw in the latter part of that chapter that, on balance, the estimated welfare effect for motor carrier shippers was considerably larger than for rail shippers. The larger benefits accruing to motor carrier shippers primarily reflected an increase in the relative cost of shipping freight by rail. As the relative price of motor carrier freight fell, the market demand for rail shifted leftward, which implies a reallocation of freight traffic away from rail and toward motor carriers.

In the previous section, we commented on the finding that economic deregulation in the airline industry caused a reallocation of air traffic in small towns away from jetliners and local service providers and toward commuter airlines. In other words, commuter airlines are a substitute for jet and local service providers. We also reported Oster and Zorn's (1989) finding that this reallocation had little affect on overall air safety because the fatality rates of the competing services, particularly the commuters and jet airlines, were similar.

The fact that motor carrier and rail services are substitutes for a shipper raises the same question. If economic deregulation in these sectors shifted traffic away from the rails and toward the motor carriers, what impact would this have upon overall safety? From table 13.1, motor carrier safety appears to be safer than railroads. In 1995, for example, there were 0.4 fatalities per 100 million vehicle–miles for large trucks. Rails suffered 84.6 fatalities per 100 million train–miles. However, this is not an appropriate comparison for at least two reasons. First, the number of rail fatalities includes rail passenger fatalities, which should be excluded if we are interested in shifts of freight traffic between rails and motor carriers. This is a minor correction, since there are few passenger fatalities per year. Second, and more importantly, the relevant basis for comparison is not a vehicle–mile but a ton–mile. For Class I railroads and large trucks, table 13.9 presents ton–miles shipped and the associated number of fatalities per billion ton–miles. Here we see that the fatality rate for rail is uniformly lower than for the motor carriers. But even here the rate for rails paints a bleaker picture than is actually the case. The rail fatality rates reported in table 13.9 include train and nontrain rail accidents, which includes fatalities associated with maintaining the infrastructure and the rolling capital. If, similar to motor carriers, fatalities only included data based upon equipment operation, the difference in the safety records of motor carriers and rails would be even greater.

Thus, by shifting traffic from rails to motor carriers, economic deregulation in the motor carrier and rail sectors of the industry shifted freight from a safer to a less safe mode. And,

Table 13.9 Motor carrier and rail fatality rates

Year	Large Trucks (a) Ton–Miles (billion)	Large Trucks (b) Fatalities per Billion Ton–Miles	Railroad (a) Ton–Miles (billion)	Railroad (b) Fatalities per Billion Ton–Miles
1975	555.0	3.372	919.0	0.762
1980	610.0	3.515	877.0	0.636
1985	735.0	2.371	1,034.0	0.518
1990	758.0	1.191	1,038.9	0.579
1991	815.0	0.959	106.7	0.554
1995	921.0	0.876	1,305.7	0.434

Source: US Department of Transportation, Bureau of Transportation Statistics, *National Transportation Statistics 1997*

holding all else constant, including existing safety regulations, we would expect economic deregulation to produce an unintended net reduction in transportation safety. In one of the few studies examining this problem, Boyer (1989) estimated the impact upon transportation safety due to shifts in the shares of rail and motor carrier traffic shipments induced by economic deregulation. Based on a low and high estimated shift of 7.7 and 49.0 billion ton–miles, respectively, from rail to motor carriers due to deregulation, Boyer estimated the number of additional fatalities to range from a low of 29 to a high of 236. Assuming that this range captures the full external safety effects associated with deregulation of the motor carrier and rail sectors, the value of these lives are a cost to society that must be subtracted from the welfare benefits generated by deregulation.

PUBLIC HEALTH EFFECTS OF MOTOR VEHICLE EMISSIONS

Motor vehicle travel is directly responsible for four types of air pollution emissions: hydrocarbons, carbon monoxide, nitrogen oxides, and sulfur oxides. In addition, motor vehicles, particularly those using diesel fuel, directly emit particulate matter into the atmosphere. Hydrocarbons combine with nitrogen oxides to produce lower-atmosphere ozone, which can produce a variety of health effects such as coughing and eye irritation.[12] Carbon monoxide in large doses can have serious health consequences, but at the low dosages typically observed in the atmosphere it has little effect on human health. Nitrogen oxide and sulfur oxide emissions contribute to the production of irritants, particulates, and acid rain. Inhalable particulates, those less than 10 microns in diameter, are particularly dangerous, because they are associated with increased mortality.

Table 13.10 summarizes the extent to which transportation, which primarily reflects motor vehicle activities, is responsible for each of these polluting emittants. For the USA as a whole, transportation accounts for 66% of carbon monoxide emissions and just under 50% for hydrocarbons and nitrogen oxides. Air pollution depends on a variety of factors, including the mix of gasoline- and diesel-fueled vehicles, and atmospheric and topographic conditions,

Table 13.10 The proportion of emittants due to transportation

Pollutant	USA (%)	Los Angeles (%)
Carbon monoxide	66	98
Hydrocarbons	48	75
Nitrogen oxides	43	83
Sulfur oxides	n/a	68

Source: Adapted from Small and Kazimi (1995), table 1, p. 9

Table 13.11 Federal exhaust emission standards for new gasoline-fueled light duty vehicles[a] (grams/mile)

Model Year	Carbon Monoxide	Hydrocarbons	Nitrogen Oxides
Average pre-control car	84.0	10.6	4.1
1968–9	51.0	6.30	–[b]
1970	34.0	4.10	–
1971	34.0	4.10	–
1972	28.0	3.00	–
1973	28.0	3.00	3.0
1974	28.0	3.00	3.0
1975–6	15.0	1.50	3.1
1977–9	15.0	1.50	2.0
1980	7.0	0.41	2.0
1981–2	3.4	0.41	1.0
1983–92	3.4	0.41	1.0
1993	3.4	0.41	1.0

[a] Beginning in 1984, diesel vehicles in California must also meet particulate matter standards; for the rest of the country particulate standards were set beginning in 1986.
[b] Uncontrolled nitrogen oxides increased when the carbon monoxide and hydrocarbon standards reduced emissions.
Source: Adapted from Small and Kazimi (1995), table 2, p. 10

as well as the presence of other chemicals in the air. In Los Angeles, whose topography, atmospheric conditions, and vehicle use are much different than other regions in the USA, we see that transportation accounts for a much different proportion of each pollutant. In particular, transportation activities are responsible for nearly all carbon monoxide emissions, three-quarters of hydrocarbon emissions, and over 80% of the nitrogen oxides. In addition, transportation is responsible for 68% of sulfur oxide emissions in Los Angeles.

In 1963, the US Congress began to regulate motor vehicle emissions with passage of the Clean Air Act. In addition to setting ambient air standards, the Act set vehicle emission standards for carbon monoxide, hydrocarbons, and nitrogen oxides. Table 13.11 identifies these standards: we see that the permitted emissions have significantly fallen during the past 20 years. In 1972, for example, federal emission controls on carbon monoxide and hydrocarbons led to 33% and 28% reductions, respectively, relative to the average emissions in the absence of any standards. Mandated federal standards by 1980 constituted 8%, 3.8%, and

48.7% of the average emissions in the pre-standard era. Further tightening reduced allowable emissions in 1993 to 3.4, 0.41, and 1.0 grams per mile for each of these emittants. Although not shown in the table, California has separately legislated emission standards that typically equal or exceed those set at the federal level. In 1993, for example, allowable emissions of carbon monoxide, hydrocarbons, and nitrogen oxides in California were set at 3.4, 0.25, and 0.4 grams per mile, respectively.

In order to evaluate the external health effects associated with motor vehicle emissions, it is necessary to (1) identify the mechanism through which vehicle-produced pollutants interact with each other and other chemicals in the air to reduce air quality; (2) assess the impact that air quality reductions have upon human health; and (3) determine the value that society places upon these effects. Because the health effects of ambient air pollution depend upon conditions in the atmosphere, topography of the land, the presence of other chemicals in the air, the mix of vehicles, as well as the extent to which individuals are exposed to the harmful pollutants, assessing the health effects is extremely difficult. Extending earlier work by Small (1977), Small and Kazimi (1995) estimated the average per-mile external cost associated with motor vehicle emissions for the Los Angeles area. The specific costs included in their analysis are mortality from particulates, morbidity (that is, nonfatal health effects) from particulates, and morbidity from ozone. Table 13.12 summarizes Small and Kazimi's findings for gasoline-powered automobiles and heavy duty diesel trucks.

For the gasoline car, we see that the total per-mile external cost equals 3.28 cents, nearly 75% of which is due to pollution's mortality effects. The morbidity effects of pollution account for 0.85 cents per mile and for these the health effects from ozone are most important. Also note that 35% (1.17 cents per mile) of the mortality cost is due to nitrogen oxides, which reflects this pollutant's role in secondary particulate formation.[13]

Whereas the estimated average external cost for vehicles in the Los Angeles fleet is relatively small, we see in the lower half of table 13.12 that this is not the case for heavy duty diesel trucks. The total estimated per mile cost from diesel truck pollution is 52.7 cents per mile. In

Table 13.12 1992 Fleet average air pollution costs in the Los Angeles region (cents/vehicle–mile)

	Hydrocarbons	Nitrogen Oxides	Sulfur Oxides	Particulates	Total
Gasoline car					
Mortality from particulates[a]	0.70	1.17	0.44	0.12	2.43
Morbidity from particulates	0.03	0.06	0.02	0.01	0.12
Morbidity from ozone[b]	0.48	0.25	0.0	0.0	0.73
Total	1.21	1.48	0.46	0.13	3.28
Heavy duty diesel truck					
Mortality from particulates[a]	0.44	14.60	6.65	25.27	46.97
Morbidity from particulates	0.02	0.72	0.33	1.24	2.31
Morbidity from ozone[b]	0.30	3.13	0.0	0.0	3.43
Total	0.76	18.45	6.98	26.51	52.70

[a] The mortality estimates are based upon a $4.87 million value of life.
[b] Attributes $\frac{1}{2}$ ozone production to nitrogen oxides and $\frac{1}{2}$ to hydrocarbons.
Source: Adapted from Small and Kazimi (1995), table 6, p. 23

this case, nearly 90% of the external cost is from the estimated mortality effects. We also see that, although important, secondary particulate formation from nitrogen oxides has a smaller effect than primary particulate emissions, 14.6 cents per mile versus 25.27 cents per mile, which reflects the fact that diesel-powered vehicles have much higher particulate emissions than gasoline-powered vehicles. And although comprising only 10% of the total cost, it is interesting that total morbidity costs of the average truck, equal to 5.74 cents per mile, exceed the 3.28 total external cost estimated for the average gasoline vehicle in the Los Angeles area.

DISCUSSION

From the results in tables 13.11 and 13.12, the absolute levels of motor vehicle emissions are not only significant but impose external costs on society that, for some vehicle types, may be quite large. The estimated costs reported in table 13.12 provide rough estimates of the pollution externality associated with motor vehicle travel in the Los Angeles area. However, we must keep in mind a number of points:

- The per-mile cost estimates for the Los Angeles area are likely to be high because of its topographic and climatic features, which are favorable to the production and retention of air pollution. The pollution external costs of other large metropolitan areas whose physical characteristics are less "pollution friendly" will be less than those estimated for Los Angeles.
- The estimated pollution costs in table 13.12 are generally dominated by costs associated with mortality from particulates. But these costs depend upon estimates of the mortality effect of pollutants as well as assumptions on the value of life. In a sensitivity analysis, Small and Kazimi calculate that the mortality cost of particulates decreases by 1.89 cents (from 2.43 to 0.54) if one uses a lower mortality effect and a $2.1 million value of life. Conversely, using a higher mortality effect and a $11.3 value of life estimate raises the mortality cost by 8.63 cents per mile (11.06 – 2.43). Similar calculations for a heavy diesel truck imply that mortality costs change by –36.6 and +166.6 cents per mile, respectively. Obviously, if public policy is to be effective in guiding the efficient use of resources, it is important that mortality coefficients and value of life values be estimated as accurately as possible.
- Further tightening of emission standards will cut the pollution cost on new vehicles. For example, the 1992 fleet average cost for a gasoline car is 3.28 cents per mile in table 13.12. New car standards legislated in 1993 call for further reductions of hydrocarbon emissions which Small and Kazimi estimate will cut pollution costs from 3.28 to 1.31 cents per mile. Tighter standards also reduce per-mile pollution costs for heavy trucks, but the fleet average cost is still estimated to be 35 cents per mile in the year 2000. The reason for this is that tightened standards apply to new vehicles. If vehicles are kept for many years, fleet average pollution costs will primarily reflect the polluting characteristics of the existing older fleet.
- Do the results reported in table 13.12 justify public policies intended to reduce motor vehicle use? For gasoline automobiles, the answer may well be no. Consider an automobile fleet that averages 23 miles per gallon and faces a gasoline cost equal to $1.20 per gallon. This implies a per-mile cost of 5.2 cents (1.2/23). Further assuming that Small and Kazimi's pollution cost estimate of 3.28 cents is approximately correct, a 3.28 cents per mile pollution tax amounts to a 63% increase in motor vehicle costs, raising the per-mile cost to 8.42 cents per mile. What effect will this have upon miles traveled? Estimates of the price elasti-

city of demand for motor vehicle travel range between 0.5 and 1.5, which implies that a pollution tax effect on miles driven lies in the −3.15% to −9.45% range. If, on the other hand, the pollution tax varied by type of vehicle, one would expect to see consumers switching to less polluting vehicles. The story is likely to be different for heavy duty trucks, where a 53 cent per-mile pollution tax amounts to a +300% increase in fuel costs. Such a hefty increase in fuel expenses would substantially reduce miles driven for the existing fleet and, presumably, provide very strong incentives to replace the existing polluting fleet of heavy duty trucks with newer vehicles that are more friendly to the environment and its inhabitants.

- The large differences in pollution costs associated with gasoline automobiles and heavy duty diesel trucks suggest different emission policy approaches. For the gasoline automobile, the pollution cost is relatively small, and will become smaller during the next decade as a higher proportion of the fleet meets the tougher emission standards. Restrictions on automobile use in urban areas are likely to have little impact on pollution costs. In contrast, the external pollution costs from heavy duty diesel trucks are sufficiently large that, absent a pollution tax, restrictions on the use of these trucks in urban areas may have identifiable effects on ambient air pollution and a city's health.

How do pollution externalities compare with other estimated congestion and other externalities associated with motor vehicle use? Recent evidence suggests a per-mile congestion toll of 15 cents, in 1992 dollars.[14] Further, estimates of accident and noise externality costs in 1992 dollars are 20.2 and 0.1 cent per mile respectively (Small, 1992). Thus, a measure of the average congestion and environmental cost from noise, pollution, and accidents is on the order of 35 cents per mile, the most important of which are congestion and accident externalities.

CHAPTER HIGHLIGHTS

- Over the past three decades, technological developments and government safety regulations have led to significant improvements in transportation safety across all transportation modes. Notwithstanding these improvements, however, motor vehicle travel is annually responsible for over 40,000 deaths.
- In markets that offer consumers and shippers safety-differentiated transportation services, buyers will trade off a lower transport price for a lower quality; that is, less safe, service. This was illustrated in an empirical example of seat belt use. Reductions in the cost of using a seat belt, vehicle downsizing, and increased risk exposure increase the demand for safer trips, all else constant. In this example, the demand for safer trips was most sensitive to vehicle weight.
- Competitive markets with no government regulation of safety are likely to produce an inefficient level of safety due to moral hazard, adverse selection, and external effects from accidents that affect third parties not directly involved in the exchange.
- How do individuals react to government safety regulation? On the basis of a model of expected income maximization, an individual's optimal level of safety occurs where the marginal benefit of additional safety equals the marginal cost and, in general,

depends upon the operating environment, safety regulations, cost of safety, and risk preferences.

- An empirical model of the effects of CAFE found that the government's mandate that manufacturers meet fuel economy standards produced the expected savings in energy through a reduction in vehicle size. But this also led to an unintended increase in fatalities.
- Government regularly sets speed limits on our nation's highways and roads, and many would argue that "speed kills." Although higher speeds lead to more severe injuries when an accident occurs, there is less certainty whether higher speeds produce more accidents. One empirical study suggests that a more important determinant of accidents is speed variance, particularly on our nation's expressways.
- Will safety regulations always generate their expected safety effects? Assuming all else is held constant, including individual safety efforts, an increase in safety regulation enhances safety. However, individuals are not passive to safety regulation, but alter their safety actions in response to government-mandated increases in safety. This offsets to some degree the original safety effect and, if strong enough, could actually produce a reduction in observed safety. An empirical case study found evidence that new vehicles equipped with airbags experienced higher than expected personal injury claims, which is consistent with an offsetting hypothesis.
- Similar to individuals, firms invest in safety up to the point at which the marginal benefit (increased revenue or decreased nonsafety costs) equals the marginal cost of increased safety. If firms are in financial stress, is it to their benefit to skimp on safety? Empirical studies in the rail and airline transport sectors suggest an inverse relationship between firm profitability and accident probability. The more profitable the firm, the better the accident record is.
- New entrants do not appear to pose a threat to airline safety. Empirical studies indicate that new entrants do not spend proportionately less on maintenance and do not have more accidents or mid-air collisions than incumbents.
- Transportation modes are alternatives for one another and do not generally have identical accident rates. Shifts in traffic, therefore, from one mode to another have implications for transportation safety. There exists some evidence of this in the rail-motor carrier sector of the industry. There was a shift of traffic from the relatively safer rail mode to the relatively less safe motor carriers, which produced a deregulation-induced increase in fatalities.
- Estimating the pollution externality from motor vehicle travel is difficult, because it is necessary to identify the interaction between motor vehicle emissions and other atmospheric chemicals, to estimate the resulting health effects, and then to place a value upon these effects. An empirical study of this issue suggests that the pollution externality for automobiles is relatively small, at least in comparison with congestion externalities. An exception is large diesel trucks for which there is a significant pollution externality associated with the mortality effects from particulate and nitrogen oxide emissions.

Review questions

1. Consider the market for transportation safety in the city of Riskless. The marginal benefit of safety falls with increasing safety and the marginal cost of providing safer trips rises.
   (a) Graphically depict the market for safety.
   (b) In an effort to eliminate all highway transportation accidents, Riskless bans motor vehicle travel. Graphically depict the economic effects of this policy and briefly explain whether Riskless is worse off or better off from this policy.
   (c) What is an optimum amount of safety and what is meant by an "optimum number of fatalities"?

2. (a) What is a negative externality? Identify some of the ways in which airline accidents impose negative externalities upon society.
   (b) In the presence of negative external effects from airline crashes, graphically demonstrate why too many resources are used in making airline trips.
   (c) What is meant by "internalizing the externality"?
      (i) Explain the economic consequences of a government policy that taxes airlines by the amount of the negative externality.
      (ii) What are the economic consequences of a government subsidy aimed at enabling airlines to reduce crashes (and therefore reduce negative externalities) by purchasing more safety equipment.

3. What types of technological improvements in motor vehicle travel over the past 25 years can you identify that have increased accident avoidance and occupant protection?

4. (a) Based upon the information in table 13.1 for 1995, what is the probability of a fatality on a US Air Carrier for a 5,000-mile round trip flight from Here to There?
   (b) How does this compare with the probability of a fatality if you decided to make the trip by car rather than by plane?
   (c) Based upon the probability of a fatality, which mode would you take for your trip? Suppose that the airline added some safety improvements that reduced the probability of a fatality by a third. Would this change your modal decision?
   (d) In general, you will be willing to pay a certain amount of money in order to reduce your risk of a fatality. Consider the following expression:

$$\text{Value of Life} = \frac{\text{Willingness to Pay}}{\text{Reduction in Probability of Fatality}}$$

   Suppose that you are willing to pay \$100 for the reduction in fatality risk from the safety improvements. What implicit value are you placing upon life?

5. For the seat belt use model in table 13.2, we can write the following indirect utility functions associated with "no seat belt" and "seat belt" use:

$V_{\text{no seat belt}} = 0$

$V_{\text{seat belt}} = 11.08 - 2.78$(Time to Fasten) + 0.782(Comfort Indicator) − 1.84(No Serious Accident) + 0.00038(Annual Vehicle Miles Traveled) − 0.006(Vehicle Weight) + 1.198(Probability of Auto-Related Injury for Households with Incomes < $35,000) + 3.305(Seat Belt Effectiveness Belief) + 0.079(Age of Driver)

(a) What impact does a 1,000-mile increase in Annual Vehicle–Miles have upon the indirect utility of seat belt use relative to the indirect utility of no seat belt use? What about a minute increase in Time to Fasten Seat Belts; or a 1% (that is, 0.01) increase in the Probability of an Auto-Related Injury for Households with incomes < $35,000; or a 500-pound increase in Vehicle Weight?

(b) Suppose that an individual driver values her time at $15.00 per hour. If it takes her three seconds to buckle her seat belt, what value does she place upon the time spent buckling? Holding all else constant, assume that she buckles and unbuckles six times a day for, 365 days a year. How much annually would she be willing to pay for an airbag that entails no buckling? Assume that she plans to purchase a new car. In the new car, she has a choice of either seat belts or an airbag, but the airbag-equipped car costs $300 more. If she plans to keep the car for the rest of her life, assuming a 10% rate of interest, will she buy the airbag-equipped car? What if the interest rate falls to 5%?

6. (a) In the standard theory of consumer behavior, we assume that an individual has a given amount of income per period of time. In a world with risks, why does it make sense to talk about expected income per period of time?

(b) Is maximizing expected income with respect to safety behavior the same as minimizing expected losses?

7. (a) In general, what factors determine an individual's optimal level of safety?

(b) Describe and graphically depict an individual driver's optimal speed on an interstate system. Identify some of the components in the opportunity cost of higher speeds.

(c) Due to budget cuts, police officers spend less time catching speeders. Discuss, and graphically depict, the likely impact that this will have upon your optimal speed.

(d) Suppose that your optimal speed on an interstate highway is 68 mph. The speed limit is posted at 65 mph. Are there any the efficiency effects of your traveling at 65 mph?

8. Because smaller vehicles provide less occupant protection, vehicle downsizing leads to a less safe environment. Suppose that you studied the accident rates of minicars and found that, all else constant, the fatality rates for these vehicles were

no worse than the fatality rates for larger cars. How could explain this unexpected result?

9. Explain why individuals are prone to drive more safely if they fully insure themselves rather than purchasing automobile insurance. What role do you think insurance deductibles play in affecting drivers' incentives to drive safely?

10. Use risk-compensating arguments to explain the following:
(a) increasing vehicle size saves fewer lives than expected;
(b) using personal floatation devices when boating reduces injuries less than predicted;
(c) average driving speeds are significantly lower during hailstorms;
(d) improvements in air-traffic control systems did not produce a large reduction in airline safety incidents;
(e) few reductions in safety were seen after safety improvements in general aviation aircraft.

11. Consider the following truck safety model, based upon annual time series data between 1976 and 1989.

Dependent variable – fatalities per 100 million vehicle–miles in accidents involving motor carrier combination trucks
MCA1 – reflects administrative deregulation in the motor carrier industry prior to enactment of the 1980 Motor Carrier Act
MCA2 – reflects enactment of the 1980 Motor Carrier Act
STAA – reflects enactment of the 1982 Surface Transportation Assistance Act, which increased minimum truck lengths and maximum truck widths, mandated states to allow twin trailers, and barred states from reducing truck lengths and widths if these exceeded those in the STAA law
SPD65 – reflects the 1987 federal law that allowed 65 mph speed limits on rural interstate highways

Table 13.13 A regression model of truck safety

Explanatory Variable	Coefficient Estimate (*t*-statistic)
Constant term	425.7 (5.90)
STAA (0 for 1976–82, 1 for 1983–9)	0.095 (0.66)
MCA1 (1 for 1978–9, 0 otherwise)	0.238 (2.04)
MCA2 (0 for 1976–9, 1 for 1980–9)	−0.337 (−1.91)
65 Speed Limit (0 for 1976–86, 1 for 1987–9)	−0.198 (−1.37)
Time Trend	−0.211 (−5.79)
$R^2 = 0.989$	
Number of observations = 14	

Source: Reprinted from McCarthy (1995), with permission from Elsevier Science

(a) Over the period of the analysis, are the results consistent with an overall improvement in motor carrier safety?
(b) As you know, the 1980 Motor Carrier Act significantly relaxed economic regulations of the industry, allowing for price and route flexibility, greater freedom on commodities carried, and freer market entry. What do the results say about the impact of the 1980 Act on truck safety? What implications, if any, might this have on the safety characteristics of new entrants?
(c) The 1982 STAA generally led to an increase in the size and weight of large trucks on the road which might be expected to increase the fatality rate. The Act also led to a more uniform fleet size across the nation, which could be argued as safety-enhancing. From the above results, which of these effects dominated?
(d) All else constant, was the increase in rural interstate speed limits detrimental to truck safety? Could this result be explained in terms of the law's impact on speed variance?

12. Table 13.14 presents results of a binary logit seat belt use analysis based on a survey of 2,035 individuals in 1983. (Note that, at the time of the survey, only

Table 13.14 A seat belt use model

Dependent variable – the probability of wearing a seat belt

Explanatory Variable	Coefficient Estimate (*t*-statistic)
Constant	–1.39 (–5.1)
Vehicle Weight (pounds)	–0.00018 (–4.1)
Annual Vacation Miles (miles)	0.0000932 (3.5)
Speed Limit (1 if driver reports traveling over the 55 mph speed limit in safe conditions, 0 otherwise)	0.4541 (4.4)
Age (years)	0.0105 (2.5)
Some College (1 if person has college experience, 0 otherwise)	0.5483 (5.3)
Population < 500,000 (1 if density < 500k, 0 otherwise)	0.1714 (1.1)
Population < 2 million (1 if density < 2 million, 0 otherwise)	0.3222 (2.3)
Population > 2 million (1 if density > 2 million, 0 otherwise)	0.4007 (2.7)
Distance to Work (miles)	0.00687 (1.0)
Child Restraint Law (1 if person resides in state with child occupant restraint law, 0 otherwise)	0.3215 (3.0)
American (1 if person owns an American vehicle, 0 otherwise)	–0.3122 (–2.3)
New England (1 if person resides in New England state, 0 otherwise)	–3.05 (–3.0)
Mountain (1 if person resides in Mountain state, 0 otherwise)	0.5554 (2.3)
Pacific (1 if person resides in Pacific state, 0 otherwise)	0.5238 (3.2)
Number of observations = 2,035	

Source: Reprinted from McCarthy (1986), table 3, p. 433, with permission from Elsevier Science

36% of the states had passed child restraint laws.) From the results in this table comment on:

(a) the role of vehicle safety on seat belt use;
(b) whether the results are consistent with the notion that, by reducing the per-mile cost of using seat belts, longer trips increase seat usage;
(c) whether increasing congestion leads to greater seat belt use and, if so, why;
(d) how these drivers perceive the relative safety of American versus non-American vehicles;
(e) differing risk preferences among survey respondents;
(f) whether persons with some college experience are more likely to wear seat belts and, if so, why;
(g) whether child restraint laws have external positive effects on "nonchildren";
(h) whether seat belt use across the country is uniform.

13. What are reputation effects, and how might these affect a carrier's decision to invest in safety and more diligently maintain its equipment?

14. In both the airline and motor carrier industries, studies typically find that new entrants do not pose a safety threat to the carrier's users. Briefly describe the economic incentives that new entrants have to offer safe transportation services.

15. Suppose that oil producers have two alternatives for shipping their product, pipeline and rail. Assume further that both markets are initially in equilibrium. If there is an innovation in pipeline technology that reduces the cost of providing safety oil transport, what impact will this have upon the amount of oil shipped by each mode? How would this affect the total number of oil spillage accidents for each mode?

NOTES

1 To measure "Seat Belt Effectiveness Belief," the study first estimated a "beliefs" binary logit model. The dependent variable was one if respondents believed seat belts were effective and zero if not. Independent variables included various socioeconomic characteristics. From this model, an "estimated beliefs probability" was obtained for each respondent, and included in the seat belt model as the variable "Seat Belt Effectiveness Belief." For some variables, the variable name used in the Winston and Associates study has been changed to simplify the exposition.

2 Note that, all else constant, a change in the cost of using seat belts changes the quantity of high-quality trips demanded, whereas a change in the other determinants of seat belt use shifts the location of the high-quality trip demand curve.

3 A recent concern with airbag technology on the passenger side is serious injury and some fatalities among smaller children, due to the force with which airbags inflate. Beginning in 1998, the National Highway Traffic Safety Administration (NHTSA) allows vehicle dealers and repair businesses to install on–off airbag switches in vehicles owned or used by persons whose requests for on–off switches have been approved by NHTSA.

4 On the basis of 25,000 car occupant fatalities and 130 million vehicles in 1985, the number of fatalities per 10,000 vehicles is (25,000/13,000) = 1.92.

5 Assuming that the elasticity of fatalities per mile from a 1% change in weight equals the elasticity of fatalities per vehicle from a 1% change in weight requires that fatalities per mile are proportional to fatalities per vehicle. For example, let y = fatalities per mile, x = fatalities per vehicle, z = vehicle weight, and $y = \alpha x$. Then $E_{y,z}y = (\alpha x)E_{x,z}$. But since $y = \alpha x$, $E_{y,z} = E_{x,z}$.

6 In 1995, the National Highway System Designation Act was passed, which allowed states to freely set speed limits on all roads.

7 David Solomon (1964) was first to find a U-shaped relationship between crash involvement rates and speed variations.

8 See Fowles and Loeb (1989), Graves et al. (1989), and Snyder (1989).

9 The authors' data source was the Highway Loss Data Institute. The data were adjusted for operator age group, and reflected claim experience regardless of whether a driver was at fault.

10 Due to mergers, acquisitions, and industry exits, data for all included carriers are not available over the entire 33-year period.

11 Rose includes one other variable, $Zerodum_{it}$, in the model, to control for air carriers that experienced zero accidents in a given year. With zero accidents, $(\text{Total Accidents/Departures})_{it} = 0$ and the logarithm of zero is undefined. A common empirical procedure to statistically correct for this is to set the dependent variable equal to zero, but to include an additional exogenous variable that equals one if the dependent variable is zero and zero otherwise.

12 Hydrocarbon emissions, unlike carbon monoxide, are not odorless and account for the smell of vehicle exhausts; nitrogen oxides, when reacting with other chemicals in the atmosphere, form nitrogen dioxide, which gives smog its brown color. Although not harmful, these aesthetic effects are also externalities that result from motor vehicle travel.

13 Small and Kazimi (1995) estimated a 7.79 cent per mile pollution cost for a light diesel truck, which has similar characteristics to an automobile. The higher cost is due to the higher particulate emission associated with diesel vehicles.

14 The figure reported in chapter 10 was 15 cents per mile, which is updated to 1992 dollars using the consumer price index.

REFERENCES AND RELATED READINGS

General references

Graham, J. D. (ed.) 1988: *Preventing Automobile Injury*. Dover, Mass.: Auburn House.

Haight, F. A. 1994: Problems in estimating comparative costs of safety and mobility. *Journal of Transport Economics and Policy*, 28, 7–30.

Loeb, P. D., Talley, W. K., and Zlatoper, T. J. 1994: *Causes and Deterrents of Transportation Accidents*. Westport, Conn.: Quorum Books.

Moses, L. N. and Savage, I. (eds.) 1989: *Transportation Safety in an Age of Deregulation*. New York: Oxford University Press.

National Research Council, Transportation Research Board 1984: *Fifty-Five: A Decade of Experience*. Washington DC, February.

Oster, C. V. J., Strong, J. S., and Zorn, C. K. 1992: *Why Airplanes Crash*. New York: Oxford University Press.

Winston, C. and Associates 1987: *Blind Intersection? Policy and the Automobile Industry*. Washington DC: The Brookings Institution.

Specific references by mode

Automobile

Crandall, R. W. and Graham, J. D. 1989: The effect of fuel economy standards on automobile safety. *Journal of Law and Economics*, XXII, 97–118.

Fowles, R. and Loeb, P. D. 1989: Speeding, coordination, and the 55-mph speed limit. *American Economic Review*, 79, 916–21.

Graves, P. E., Lee, D. R. and Sexton, R. L. 1989: Statutes versus enforcement: the case of the optimal speed limit. *American Economic Review*, 79, 932–6.
Lave, C. 1985: Speeding, coordination, and the 55-mph limit. *American Economic Review*, 75, 1159–64.
Lave, C. 1989: Speeding, coordination, and the 55-mph limit: reply. *American Economic Review*, 79, 926–31.
Mannering, F. and Winston, C. 1995: Automobile air bags in the 1990s: market failure or market efficiency. *Journal of Law and Economics*, XXXVIII, 265–79.
McCarthy, P. S. 1986: Seat belt usage rates: a test of Peltzman's hypothesis. *Accident Analysis and Prevention*, 18, 425–38.
Peltzman, S. 1975: The effects of automobile safety regulation. *Journal of Political Economy*, 83, 677–725.
Peterson, S., Hoffer, G., and Millner, E. 1995: Are drivers of air-bag-equipped cars more aggressive? A test of the offsetting behavior hypothesis. *Journal of Law and Economics*, 38, 251–64.
Snyder, D. 1989: Speeding, coordination, and the 55–mph limit: comment. *American Economic Review*, 79, 922–5.

Airlines

Golbe, D. L. 1986: Safety and profits in the airline industry. *The Journal of Industrial Economics*, XXXIV, 305–17.
Kanafani, A. and Keeler, T. E. 1989: New entrants and safety. In L. N. Moses and I. Savage (eds.), *Transportation Safety in an Age of Deregulation*. New York: Oxford University Press, pp. 115–28.
Oster, C. V. Jr. and Zorn, C. K. 1989: Is it still safe to fly? In L. N. Moses and I. Savage (eds.), *Transportation Safety in an Age of Deregulation*. New York: Oxford University Press, pp. 129–52.
Phillips, R. A. and Talley, W. K. 1992: Airline safety investments and operating conditions: determinants of aircraft damage severity. *Southern Economic Journal*, 59, 157–64.
Rose, N. L. 1989: Financial Influences on airline safety. In L. N. Moses and I. Savage (eds.), *Transportation Safety in an Age of Deregulation*. New York: Oxford University Press, pp. 93–114.
Talley, W. K. and Bossert, P. A. Jr. 1990: Determinants of aircraft accidents and policy implications for air safety. *International Journal of Transport Economics*, 17, 115–30.

Motor carriers

Boyer, K. D. 1989: The safety effects of mode shifting following deregulation. In L. N. Moses and I. Savage (eds.), *Transportation Safety in an Age of Deregulation*. New York: Oxford University Press, pp. 258–76.
McCarthy, P. S. 1995: The 1982 Surface Transportation Assistance Act (STAA): implications of relaxed truck weight and size limits for highway safety. *Transportation Policy*, 2, 107–17.
Traynor, T. and McCarthy, P. 1991: The effect of the 1980 Motor Carrier Act on highway safety. *Journal of Regulatory Economics*, 3, 338–48.

Highways

Blomquist, G. 1986: A utility maximization model of driver traffic safety behavior. *Accident Analysis and Prevention*, 18, 371–5.
Blomquist, G. C., Miller, T. R., and Levy, D. T. 1996: Values of risk reduction implied by motorist use of protection equipment. *Journal of Transport Economics and Policy*, XXX, 55–66.
Cameron, M. 1991: Transportation efficiency: tackling Southern California's air pollution and congestion. Regional Institute of Southern California. Environmental Defense Fund, Oakland, California.
Evans, A. W. and Morrison, A. D. 1997: Incorporating accident risk and disruption in economic models of public transport. *Journal of Transport Economics and Policy*, XXXI, 117–46.
Garber, S. and Graham, J. D. 1990: The effects of the new 65 mile-per-hour speed limit on rural highway fatalities: a state-by-state analysis. *Accident Analysis and Prevention*, 22, 137–49.
Godwin, S. R. 1992: Effect of the 65 m.p.h. speed limit on highway safety in the USA (with comments and reply to comments). *Transport Reviews*, 12, 1–14.

Jondrow, J., Bowes, M., and Levy, R. 1983: The optimal speed limit. *Economic Inquiry*, XXI, 325–36.

Kamerud, D. B. 1988: Benefits and costs of the 55-mph speed limit: new estimates and their implications. *Journal of Policy Analysis and Management*, 7, 341–452.

Keeler, T. 1994: Highway safety, economic behavior, and driving environment. *American Economic Review*, 84, 684–93.

Lave, C. and Elias, P. 1997: Resource allocation in public policy: the effects of the 65-mph speed limit. *Economic Inquiry*, XXXV, 614–20.

Leigh, P. and Wilkinson, J. T. 1991: The effect of gasoline taxes on highway fatalities. *Journal of Policy Analysis and Management*, 10, 474–81.

Small, K. A. 1977: Estimating the air pollution costs of transport modes. *Journal of Transport Economics and Policy*, XI, 109–32.

Small, K. A. and Kazimi, C. 1995: On the costs of air pollution from motor vehicles. *Journal of Transport Economics and Policy*, XXIX, 7–32.

Solomon, D. 1964: *Accidents on Main Rural Highways Related to Speed, Driver, and Vehicle*. Federal Highway Administration, US Department of Transportation, July.

Marine and rail carriers

Dennis, S. 1996: Estimating risk costs per unit of exposure for hazardous materials transported by rail. *Logistics and Transportation Review*, 32, 351–75.

Golbe, D. L. 1983: Product safety in a regulated industry: evidence from the railroads. *Economic Inquiry*, 34, 39–52.

Talley, W. K. 1995a: Safety investments and operating conditions: determinants of accident passenger–vessel damage cost. *Southern Economic Journal*, 61, 819–29.

Talley, W. K. 1995b: Vessel damage severity of tanker accidents. *Logistics and Transportation Review*, 31, 191–207.

Talley, W. K. 1996: Linkages between transportation infrastructure investment and economic production. *Logistics and Transportation Review*, 32, 145–54.

Talley, W. K. and Anderson, E. E. 1996: Determinants of tanker accident oil spill risk. *International Journal of Transport Economics*, 23, 3–16.

APPENDIX TRANSPORTATION RESOURCES ON THE INTERNET

With the advent of the information highway, there is now easy computer access to an extensive network of transportation resources on the Internet. These include federal, state, and local transportation agencies, transportation institutes affiliated with universities, nonprofit organizations with a special interest in transportation, and private transportation firms. In addition to current activities, many of these Internet sites include downloadable reports and data, as well as hypertext that provides links to related sites. An excellent source for transport information on the internet is the *Internet Starter Kit: Update 1997*, published by the Department of Transportation, Bureau of Transportation Statistics (1997). The document is provided free of charge. Below are some useful internet sites, many of which are identified in this publication.

FEDERAL AGENCIES

Commerce Department	http://www.census.gov
Bureau of Economic Analysis	http://www.bea.doc.gov/
Bureau of the Census Transportation Activities	http://www.census.gov/ftp/pub/econ/www/servmenu.html
Energy Department	
Oak Ridge National Laboratory (ORNL), Center for Transportation Analysis	http://cta.ed.ornl.gov/
Sandia National Laboratory, Transportation Technology Programs	http://www.sandia.gov/tp/tp.htm
Labor Department	http://stats.bls.gov
National Academy of Sciences	
Transportation Research Board	http://www.nas.edu/trb/
Transportation Department	http://www.dot.gov
Bureau of Transportation Statistics	http://www.bts.gov
Federal Aviation Administration	http://www.faa.gov

Federal Highway Administration	http://www.fhwa.dot.gov/
Federal Railroad Administration	http://www.fra.dot.gov/site/index.htm
Maritime Administration	http://www.marad.dot.gov/
National Highway Traffic Safety Administration	http://www.nhtsa.dot.gov
Environmental Protection Agency	http://www.epa.gov

UNIVERSITIES

Center for Transportation Research, University of Texas at Austin	http://www.utexas.edu/depts/ctr/
Center for Transportation Studies, MIT	http://web.mit.edu/afs/athena.mit.edu/org/c/cts/www/
Center for Urban Transportation Research, University of South Florida	http://www.cutr.eng.usf.edu/CUTR/
Institute of Transportation Studies, University of California at Berkeley	http://www.its.berkeley.edu/
Institute of Transportation Studies, University of California at Davis	http://www.engr.ucdavis.edu/~its/
Institute of Transportation Studies, University of California at Irvine	http://www.its.uci.edu/
Joint Transportation Research Program, Purdue University	http://rebar.ecn.purdue.edu/JTRP/
Pennsylvania Transportation Institute, Pennsylvania State University	http://pti.psu.edu/
Texas Transportation Institute, Texas A&M University	http://tti.tamu.edu/
The Transportation Institute, University of North Carolina	http://w3.ncat.edu/~transins/
Transportation Center, Northwestern University	http://nutcweb.tpc.northwestern.edu/
Transportation Institute, Georgia Institute of Technology	http://www.gati.edu
Transportation Research Center, University of Michigan	http://www.umtri.umich.edu/
Transportation Information and Decision Engineering, Princeton University	http://www.njtide.org

MODE

AVIATION

Air Transport Association	http://www.air-transport.org/
Federal Aviation Administration	http://www.faa.gov
International Air Transport Association	http://www.iata.org/
National Air Traffic Controllers Association	http://www.natca.org/
Office of Airline Information	http://www.bts.gov/oai

HIGHWAY AND SURFACE TRANSPORTATION

American Association of State Highway and Transportation Officials	http://www.aashto.org/main/
American Trucking Association	http://www.trucking.org/
Congestion Pricing Internet Resources	http://www.ecel.uwa.edu.au/~vsapkota/cp-sites.htm
Federal Highway Administration	http://www.fhwa.dot.gov/
Intelligent Transportation Systems	http://www.its.dot.gov/

MARITIME

Maritime Administration	http://www.marad.dot.gov/
United States Coast Guard	http://www.uscg.mil/
Waterborne Commerce Statistics	http://www.wrsc.usace.army-mil/ndc/

RAIL TRANSPORTATION

Association of American Railroads	http://www.aar.org
Federal Railroad Administration	http://www.fra.dot.gov/sike/index.htm
Institute of Railway Studies	http://www.york.ac.uk/inst/irs/
Transport News: Rail	http://www.transportnews.com/rail/

PUBLIC TRANSIT

American Public Transit Association	http://www.apta.com/
Community Transportation Association	http://www.ctaa.org/
Federal Transit Administration	http://www.fta.dot.gov/
International Union of Public Transport	http://www.uitp.com/
National Transit Institute	http://policy.rutgers.edu/nti/

TOPICS OF INTEREST

TRANSPORTATION SAFETY

AAA Foundation for Traffic Safety	http://www.aaafts.org/
Highway Loss Data Institute	http://www.carsafety.org/
Insurance Institute for Highway Safety	http://www.hwysafety.org/
National Highway Traffic Safety Administration	http://nhtsa.dot.gov
National Crash Analysis Center	http://gwuva.gwu.edu/ncac/
National Safety Council	http://www.nsc.org/
National Transportation Safety Board	http://www.ntsb.gov/

Energy and Transportation

Energy Information Agency	http://www.eia.doe.gov
International Energy Agency	http://www.iea.org
Oak Ridge National Laboratory (ORNL), Center for Transportation Analysis	http://www-cta.ed.ornl.gov/

Environment and Transportation

International Environmental Information Network	http://www.envirobiz.com/
Office of Mobile Resources, EPA	http://www.epa.gov/omswww/

Intelligent Transportation Systems

Integrated Transportation Management Center, Texas Transportation Institute	http://tti.tamu.edu/
Intelligent Transportation Systems	http://www.its.dot.gov/
Intelligent Transportation Society	http://www.itsa.org/
Intelligent Transportation Systems, Princeton University	http://www.sor.princeton.edu/~dhb/its.html

International Transportation

European Transport Services	http://www.europages.com/
French National Institute for Transport and Safety Research	http://www.inrets.fr/index.e.html
International Energy Agency	http://www.iea.org
International Trade Administration, Commerce Department	http://www.ita.doc.gov
International Trade Statistics, Census Bureau	http://census/gov/ftp/pub/foreigntrade/www/
Mexican Institute of Transport	http://catlali.imt.mx/English/
Organization for Economic Cooperation and Development, Transportation	http://www.oecd.org/transport/
Statistics Canada	http://www.statcan.ca
Transport Canada	http://www.tc.gc.ca/en/menu.htm
Transport Economics Laboratory	http://www.ish-lyon.cnrs.fr/labollet
United Nations	http://www.un.org/
Waterborne Commerce Statistics	http://www.wrsc.usace.army.mil/ndc/
World Bank	http://www.worldbank.org
World Trade Organization	http://www.wto.org/

INDEX